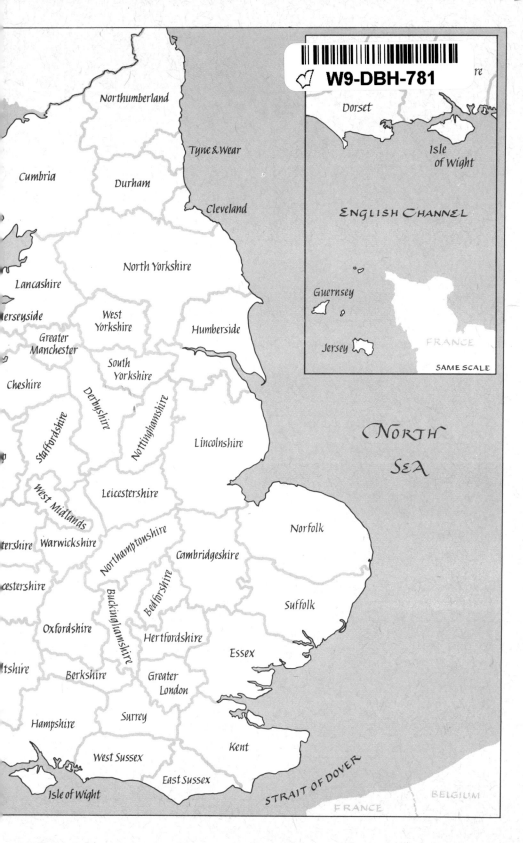

8 00

re

Dorset

Isle of Wight

ENGLISH CHANNEL

Guernsey

Jersey

FRANCE

SAME SCALE

Northumberland

Tyne & Wear

Cumbria

Durham

Cleveland

North Yorkshire

Lancashire

Merseyside

West Yorkshire

Humberside

Greater Manchester

South Yorkshire

Cheshire

Derbyshire

Nottinghamshire

Staffordshire

Lincolnshire

West Midlands

Leicestershire

Warwickshire

Northamptonshire

Cambridgeshire

Norfolk

tershire

cestershire

Buckinghamshire

Bedfordshire

Suffolk

Oxfordshire

Hertfordshire

Essex

tshire

Berkshire

Greater London

Hampshire

Surrey

West Sussex

East Sussex

Kent

Isle of Wight

NORTH SEA

STRAIT OF DOVER

FRANCE

BELGIUM

THE INTELLIGENT TRAVELLER'S GUIDE TO HISTORIC BRITAIN

THE INTELLIGENT TRAVELLER'S GUIDE TO Historic Britain

England, Wales, The Crown Dependencies

PHILIP A. CROWL

FOREWORD BY JOHN JULIUS NORWICH

CONGDON & WEED, INC.
NEW YORK

Library of Congress Cataloging in Publication Data

Crowl, Philip Axtell, 1914–
    The intelligent traveller's guide to historic Britain.

    Bibliography: p.
    Includes index.
    1. Great Britain—Description and travel—1971–   —
Guide-books.   2. Historic sites—Great Britain—Guide-
books.   I. Title.
DA650.C86 1981   914.1′04858   81 19469
ISBN 0–86553–037–8   AACR2
ISBN 0–86553–040–8 (pbk.)
ISBN 0–312–92337–6 (St. Martin's Press)
ISBN 0–312–92338–4 (St. Martin's Press: pbk.)

Published by Congdon & Weed, Inc.
298 Fifth Avenue, New York, N.Y. 10001

Distributed by St. Martin's Press
175 Fifth Avenue, New York, N.Y. 10010

Published simultaneously in Canada by Thomas Nelson & Sons Ltd.
81 Curlew Drive, Don Mills, Ontario M3A 2R1

TO MY WIFE:
MARY ELLEN WOOD CROWL

Acknowledgments

FEW BOOKS are entirely the work of a single mind and hand, and this one is not among them. I hope the following people will accept my sincere thanks for their very real assistance, always cheerfully given: George Woodbridge for his meticulous critique of the manuscript and for rescuing me from numerous errors; Katharine Woodbridge for help on the sections covering Oxford and Cambridge; the late Reverend Lawrence Hunt, O.P., for guidance on ecclesiastical matters; Mollie Phillips for her painstaking review of the text; Thomas Congdon and Patricia Falk Feeley for encouragement when it was most needed; Donald Berwick and Commander David C. W. Elliot OBE, RN, for sundry useful advices from London; the library staffs of the Naval War College, the U.S. Naval Academy, and the Johns Hopkins University for unfailingly courteous assistance; Christine Anderson, Barbara Campbell, and Mary Ann Wysocki for typing the manuscript; John E. Murphy for wise legal counsel; and Jean Monroe for help in preparing the index.

Philip A. Crowl
Annapolis, Maryland

Contents

Foreword

THIS BOOK is a labour of love; the difficulty is to know which is greater, the love or the labour. Mr. Crowl's affection for this country must be deep indeed—he could never otherwise have travelled it as methodically and conscientiously as he obviously has, with such untiring curiosity and such unswerving dedication. Leafing through his gazetteer, one is again and again astonished by his thoroughness; no distance is too great, no journey too arduous, no hamlet too remote. How many Englishmen, one wonders, have visited both Eddisbury Hill Fort in Cheshire ("an unmarked monument difficult to locate") and the National Museum of Labour History in Limehouse ("something more ambitious than this effort might have been undertaken")? How many have made pilgrimages both to the subtropical gardens of Tresco in the Scillies and to the neoclassical railway station at Monkwearmouth, Sunderland?

But Mr. Crowl is not an Englishman; he is an American, and herein lies his strength. First of all, he takes nothing for granted in the way that we natives inevitably do; he comes upon everything—church, castle, or cathedral, stately home or prehistoric barrow—with a fresh and wondering eye, unclouded by familiarity or custom. This is not to say that his spectacles are rose-tinted. On the contrary, some monuments he finds disappointing, and he is never afraid to criticise: St. Pancras station, for example, is "frankly ugly by almost any standard." After all, many of his readers will be travelling considerable distances on his recommendation; they must not be allowed to regret doing so. He remains, however, an enthusiast—and his one overriding aim is to infuse others with some of his own enthusiasm.

If he is to succeed, it is clearly essential that those others should understand what they see. And since they are by definition intelligent—that word was not inserted into the title for nothing—this means that they must be able to relate things to their historical background. Mr. Crowl has therefore provided them, as the first part of his book, with the longest and most comprehensive narrative history that I can ever remember seeing in any work of this kind: the story of these islands from prehistoric times to the present, told primarily in terms of what he calls "the visible and visitable remains" still extant. This was an admirable idea; and it is made more admirable still by the elaborate cross-referencing, which enables any monument mentioned in the historical section to be immediately tracked down in the gazetteer, and vice versa.

Writing as he is primarily for his own countrymen, it may be thought that Mr. Crowl's history is a little too elementary for English readers. Perhaps it is—for some of them. But we all have our *lacunae*, names and dates slip away all too easily ("How," we used to be asked in *1066 And All That*, "can you be so numb and vague about Arabella Stuart?"), and I for one am only grateful to be reminded of things that I know (or knew) already—particularly when at the same time I am learning much that I never knew before. Besides, the author casts his net as wide in the historical section as he does in the geographical. His is no bald recital of events; he throws in for good measure illuminating little essays on Roman military methods, medieval religious beliefs, Palladian architecture, or seventeenth-century gardening. I doubt if there will be any reader, of whatever nationality, who will lay down Part One of this book and not find his store of knowledge increased.

But this is not in essence a book for the library or the study; it is designed as a working guidebook, planned with meticulous care and furnished with maps and mileages, road numbers and grid references, to satisfy even those travellers—if such there be—as tireless, painstaking, and determined as Mr. Crowl himself. To all of them I wish journeys as happy and as rewarding as his have obviously been. To him, I can only convey the gratitude of us all—and my best wishes for a long and well-deserved rest.

John Julius Norwich

Introduction

MOST TRAVELLERS in Britain in search of their cultural past lack the knowledge to detect or comprehend the traces of the past they seek. All those ruined abbeys, those crenellated towers, those massive cathedrals, those stately homes and gardens seem to melt into a sort of undifferentiated blur. Undeniably picturesque it all is, but what does it mean?

The purpose of this book is to help the intelligent traveller in Britain understand the meaning of what he sees, to provide him with a historical perspective against which to view this crowded landscape of ancient relics, and to suggest criteria for his selection of particular places to visit and sights to see. It is part history textbook and part gazetteer, the two parts knit together by a simple system of cross-references. The book is designed to escort the intelligent traveller through time as well as space and to link the visible present with the invisible past.

PART ONE: NARRATIVE HISTORY

Part One is a narrative history of Britain—but with a difference. It is a chronological account of Britain's past, but primarily in terms of the visible and visitable remains of that past. In Part One there are ten chapters, each covering a distinct period of the prehistory and history of England, Wales, and the Crown Dependencies from earliest times to the end of World War II.* Woven into the narrative are the names of a vast number of sites that are open to view. These names appear in **Bold Print** and are followed parenthetically by page references to Part Two.

PART TWO: GAZETTEER

Whereas Part One deals with the sites of southern Britain in chronological order and in their historic context, Part Two (a) organizes the sites by geographical region, (b) evaluates the merits of each as an attraction, and (c) describes it as it appears today.

---

*Scotland will be included in a separate volume yet to be published.

LOCATION

The traveller's first need is to know the general area in which each site is located. Therefore the Gazetteer is divided into three sections: England, Wales, and the Crown Dependencies. The section on England is subdivided into eleven regions, starting with London, followed by southeastern England, and so on through the other identifiable regions of the country, from east to west and from south to north. Each region is further subdivided into counties, also listed from east to west and south to north. County names and boundaries are those prescribed by the Local Government Act of 1972 which redrew many ancient county lines, consolidated old counties, created new ones, and changed the names of a significant number.

Within each county the Gazetteer lists in alphabetical order the names of population centers of two thousand or more in which or near which are situated the sites mentioned in Part One. Under these place-names, the site-names appear in **Bold Print**. Wales receives similar treatment, except that it is divided into only two regions, each in turn subdivided into counties. The Crown Dependencies of Man, Jersey, and Guernsey, being islands separated from the main island of Britain, are treated separately.

Having listed the sites of southern Britain in geographic order, the Gazetteer then proceeds to pinpoint them precisely. For most city sites, street names are given. For sites situated in the country or in small hamlets, the Gazetteer specifies the mileage and compass direction from the nearest population center of two thousand or more and in most cases the numbers of the main and/or secondary roads by which the sites can be reached.

Certain field sites are so remotely situated as to require even further pinpointing. This is especially true of prehistoric and Roman sites, the great majority of which are classified as Ancient Monuments under the care of the Department of the Environment (see below). For these the Gazetteer provides grid references to the appropriate Ordnance Survey (OS) map in the Landranger Series drawn on a scale of 1:50,000. All of Britain, except the Channel Islands, is covered by these maps, of which there are 204 in all. In the Gazetteer, the grid references appear as a number between 85 and 204 (maps 1 to 84 cover Scotland), followed by two capital letters, followed by a six-digit number (e.g., 184 SU 123 422, which is the grid reference for Stonehenge). The first number is that of the map in the 1:50,000 series; the two letters identify the 100-square-kilometer grid of the National Grid System in which the site lies; the six digits represent distances in kilometers and tenths of kilometers measured from the southwest corner of the grid square. In locating a site on a 1:50,000 Ordnance Survey map, start at the lower left (southwest) corner and read right along the bottom edge to the figure indicated by the first two digits. Continue right to the number of tenths of a kilometer indicated by the third digit. From this point north is your longitude line. Starting again at the lower left corner, read up the left edge of the map to the figure indicated by the fourth and fifth digits. Continue up to the number of tenths of a kilometer indicated by the sixth digit. From this point east is your latitude. Where longitude and latitude lines intersect is the precise location of the site you are looking for. It sounds complicated, but is really quite easy.

EVALUATION

Not every prehistoric or historic site is of equal merit as a tourist attraction and one of the functions of this guidebook is to draw qualitative distinctions among the many sites identified throughout the text. The Gazetteer fulfills this function in two ways: (a) by a rating system expressed in asterisks and (b) by indicating which sites are under the care of either of the two great national custodial organizations whose function is to preserve and display only those sites of some significance and distinction.

ASTERISKS

The number of asterisks preceding a site-name (or the absence of an asterisk) is indicative not only of its historic or architectural significance but also of its attractiveness to travellers. Attractiveness is measured both in terms of the intrinsic beauty or interest of the site and its surroundings, and in terms of its convenience to visitors and the amenities provided. Convenience is measured by such factors as accessibility by car or public transportation, the adequacy of roadside signposts, and above all by the frequency and duration of visiting hours. Amenities include car parks (i.e., parking lots), on-site restaurants, toilet facilities, well-informed and hospitable custodial staffs, and an adequate supply of on-site guidebooks or other informational material. Guided tours, incidentally, are not considered an amenity, especially if protracted. Mandatory guided tours are, in most cases, an abomination.

The rating of three asterisks means "outstanding"; two asterisks, "very good"; and one asterisk, "good." Where no asterisks at all precede the site-name in the Gazetteer, it is because the site in question, though of historic interest, is either too difficult of access or insufficiently attractive to warrant the attention of most travellers.

NATIONAL CUSTODIAL ORGANIZATIONS

Following the information on site location in the Gazetteer, the letters *AM* or *NT*, or sometimes both, will frequently appear. *AM* stands for Ancient Monument under the guardianship of the Department of the Environment, which means that the site will be reasonably well tended and, more importantly from the point of view of the visiting traveller, reasonably well signposted. Reading roadside signposts point-ing in the direction of Ancient Monuments is, however, a special art and requires some understanding of the system. Arrows are seldom used. Instead, the free end of the sign (i.e., the end away from the post) angles in the direction you are meant to go. If the post is attached to the middle of the sign, or if there are posts at both ends, go no farther: You are there.

The letters *NT* stand for National Trust. The National Trust is a charita-ble organization, founded in 1895, which is now the largest private land-owner and conservation society in Britain. It owns more than four hundred thousand acres of land and is in possession of a hundred odd gardens and more than two hundred historic buildings, over half of which are large country houses. Acquisition of a property by the National Trust is a guarantee that it will be well maintained, open to the public at announced times (usually), well signposted, intelligently displayed, and well provided with amenities for visitors.

INFORMATION *NOT* INCLUDED

Readers will be quick to note the omission from the Gazetteer of two categories of information of understandable interest to tourists: (a) hours of admission and (b) price of admission. The oversight is intentional for the reasons stated below.

HOURS OF ADMISSION

With one major exception, visiting hours at historic sites in Britain are infuriatingly eccentric. The exception is the host of sites maintained by the Department of the Environment and classified as Ancient Monu-ments *(AM)*. Standard visiting hours for these sites are as follows:

Months	Weekdays	Sundays
March–April	9:30 A.M.—5:30 P.M.	2:00 P.M.—5:30 P.M.
May–September	9:30 A.M.—7:00 P.M.	2:00 P.M.—7:00 P.M.
October	9:30 A.M.—5:30 P.M.	2:00 P.M.—5:30 P.M.
November–February	9:30 A.M.—4:00 P.M.	2:00 P.M.—4:00 P.M.

Readers can be reasonably certain that if a site is marked *AM* in the Gazetteer, it will be open during these hours. There are occasional ex-ceptions, however: A few Ancient Monuments are closed on some week-days, and more are closed for an hour around lunchtime.

As for the great bulk of sites not under the guardianship of the Depart-ment of the Environment, hours of admission are so varied as to defy description. Furthermore they are subject to unpredictable change. Country houses are the chief offenders in this regard, closely followed by museums. To avoid misleading readers, therefore, the Gazetteer omits any mention of hours of admission except for the occasional notation that visiting hours are "restricted" or "very restricted," indicating that even during the summer these places open their doors less frequently than four days a week. (In these cases the number of asterisks is reduced.)

Light on the subject, however, can be gleaned from three publications which are produced annually and are therefore more or less up to date. These are the British Automobile Association's (AA) *Stately Homes, Museums, Castles & Gardens in Britain* and two ABC Historic Publications entitled respectively *Historic Houses, Castles & Gardens* and *Museums and Galleries.* They can be purchased in most bookstores in Britain. In America they can be obtained by mail from The British Travel Bookshop, Ltd., 680 Fifth Avenue, New York, N. Y. 10019. All three publications provide updated information on hours of admission at almost every historic site and/or museum in Britain. Armed with one or more of these publications, the traveller can be reasonably well protected against the frustration of arriving at his destination after a long drive only to find the doors closed. Even so, changes and closures do take place between publication dates, and some disappointments are to be expected.

Another important source of timely information for visitors to Britain is provided by the British Tourist Authority and its allied organizations, the English Tourist Board, the Wales Tourist Board, and the Scottish Tourist Board. The three Tourist Boards together maintain more than 650 Tourist Information Centres throughout Britain and these can be of enormous assistance to travellers who will take the trouble to seek them out. Being well signposted, they are not hard to find. Look for the words Tourist Information accompanied by the small letter *i* in red. In London, the British Tourist Authority maintains a Welcome to Britain Tourist Information Centre at 64 St. James Street, SW 1, a short distance off Piccadilly. It is a mine of useful information and a good first stop for any traveller concerned with getting his bearings.

PRICE OF ADMISSION

The great majority of British historic sites charge an admission fee, ranging from 10 p. up to £ 2.50. No figures are quoted in the Gazetteer, however, because they are constantly being revised upward and because the value of the pound sterling is constantly fluctuating in relation to other currencies. In this connection there are two ways the diligent sightseer in Britain can save money. One is to become a member of the National Trust on the occasion of his first visit to one of its properties. Membership automatically insures admission to all sites under the care of the National Trust free of charge. An even better bargain is an Open to View ticket which guarantees free admission to every Ancient Monument under the guardianship of the Department of the Environment *and* every National Trust Property *and* more than fifty other sites under private or Crown management. These tickets are good only for one month after first use. They can be purchased at the British Tourist Authority's Tourist Information Centre, 64 St. James Street, London, SW 1, or by mail from the British Tourist Authority, 680 Fifth Avenue, New York, N. Y. 10019.

MAPS

In this book are two maps. One is of England and Wales, showing county names and boundaries. The other is of London, indicating the boundaries of postal districts. Readers not already familiar with these basic geographic data are urged to study these maps before they read the text. Since the Gazetteer lists all sites under the names of the counties or London postal districts in which they lie, it is essential for the reader to know in general where these administrative units are located.

No one can hope to visit any significant number of the sites mentioned in this book without proper road maps or better still a road atlas. These are available in many shapes and sizes and are purchasable in all good book stores in Britain and obtainable in America by mail from The British Travel Bookshop, Ltd., 680 Fifth Avenue, New York, N. Y. 10019. The author's preference is *The Hamlyn Road Atlas of Great Britain*, John Bartholomew & Son Ltd., 1979. Atlases are generally preferable to folded roadmaps because they are less cumbersome to use in the narrow confines of a car, and more particularly because they are usually well indexed. Whatever atlas you purchase, be sure that it contains a detailed index of place-names.

Travellers who intend to spend much time visiting prehistoric and Roman field sites should avail themselves of the appropriate 1:50,000 Ordnance Survey maps mentioned above. As already stated, these too can be obtained at almost any large book store in Britain. Or, they can be purchased in advance by writing Cook Hammond and Kell Ltd., The London Map Centre, 22–24 Caxton Street, London SW 1H OQU, the main agency in London for all of the Ordnance Survey's many publications. Readers should be forewarned, however, that the 1:50,000 scale maps run as high as £ 1.50 each and they cover areas of only forty square kilometers.

APPENDIX A: THE BEST OF BRITAIN

Appendix A lists under a number of categories (e.g., ruined abbeys, military museums, etc.) those sites considered to be the most attractive to the intelligent traveller and therefore deserving of three asterisks in the rating system described above. This is meant to help readers in their selection of places to visit, but it should be remembered that the lists reflect the author's own biases and therefore are to be viewed with some skepticism. There is much room for argument over what is the best of Britain.

APPENDIX B: SELECTED READINGS

This is not a complete bibliography of the works used in the preparation of this volume but a selection of those the reader might find useful for further study. They fall into two categories: (1) guidebooks and other types of travel literature; and (2) general histories and scholarly monographs of the sort that can be found in the bibliography of any good textbook on British history.

INDEX

Page references in the Index appear in two types of print. Those in **boldface** refer to Part Two (Gazetteer); all others to Part One (Narrative History).

HOW TO PREPARE AN ITINERARY

Although some people prefer to travel at random and play it by ear, most serious visitors to Britain, as well as native British tourists, will want to plan their trip in some detail before they go. It is to such intelligent travellers that this book is primarily addressed. Here are some suggestions as to how to use it.

1. If you are unfamiliar with the administrative geography of Britain, study the maps at the beginning and end of this book. Unless you know the location of British counties and London postal districts, you will be lost in reading this book and, if you are a stranger, lost when you get to Britain.

2. Read Part One as needed. British readers presumably already know enough of their own nation's history to be able to skim rapidly through this historical narrative; non-British readers should study it more carefully. In either case, the information contained in Part One is a necessary prerequisite to a proper understanding of the historical context in which to place the sites you are about to visit.

3. Decide at the outset whether to concentrate on one or more periods of time or on one or more regions of Britain. For British readers, or non-British with lots of time to spend, the former choice is feasible. For most visitors to Britain the latter alternative is the most practicable.

4. Most visitors to Britain, on any single trip, should confine themselves to no more than two or three regions. As small as the country is, by American or Australian standards at least, you can't see it all on a three-week visit. It should be added that no region of Britain is poor in significant and interesting historical sites. In selecting among them it's hard to go wrong.

Having made the selection, turn to the Gazetteer. Here each region is treated separately, and within each region all recommended sites are arranged in clusters according to the counties in which they lie and the towns or other population centers in which or near which they are situated. This arrangement is designed to help tourists avoid needless driving in circles and backtracking.

5. Both British and foreign travellers should consult the Gazetteer for the precise geographic location of the sites they are seeking. With a good map or atlas, the data contained here should be sufficient to preclude getting lost—at least most of the time.

6. Read the site descriptions in the Gazetteer just prior to visiting the premises. This may save you the cost of an on-site guidebook or a guided tour.

7. Exercise severe self-discipline in keeping the number of sites on your itinerary reasonably low. A good rule of thumb for the motoring tourist is no more than six sites and no more than a hundred miles per day. In selecting places to visit, pay attention to the number of asterisks assigned to each site in the Gazetteer. These ratings are not infallible but they do offer a useful yardstick for measuring the relative merits of the vast number of sites in Britain open to view. Finally, and especially if this is your first trip, consult Appendix A: The Best of Britain. The sites listed here are guaranteed to satisfy even the most discriminating of intelligent travellers.

The best of Britain is, of course, the country as a whole—its people, its landscapes, its general ambience. The truly intelligent traveller will not be so intent upon his serious sightseeing as to fail to notice and enjoy the thousands of simple domestic gardens that adorn the land, the fields of purple heather, the green, green hedgerows, the dappled Constable skies, the thatched cottages, the omnipresent chimneypots, the double-decker busses, the cosy pubs, and above all, the pleasing harmonies of British voices, pronouncing the mother tongue in a hundred dialects, all testifying to Britain's most admirable characteristic: its infinite variety.

PART ONE

NARRATIVE HISTORY

CHAPTER I

PREHISTORIC BRITAIN

To begin at the beginning, the intelligent traveller will want first to visit the **British Museum of Natural History** *(525)* in South Kensington, London, SW 7. Entering the building on the ground floor, he must climb the great central stairway to reach the first floor. (Americans would dub these the first and second floors, respectively, but in this book the English usage will be followed.) On reaching the top of the stairs he should turn right to the exhibition called Man's Place in Evolution. There, in a prominent place, is the skull of Swanscombe Man—or rather a model of the skull whose original is locked up somewhere in the museum's vaults. Actually what we have here is only part of a skull, i.e., the occipital bone forming the posterior part of the skull, and two parietal bones forming its roof. Moreover, it belonged, in all probability, not to a man, but to a young woman who died more than two hundred thousand years ago.

The three pieces of the skull were discovered in gravels of the hundred-foot terraces of the River Thames at Swanscombe in Kent. At the same level were found a number of flint tools, a few of which are also on display at the Museum of Natural History. Prominent among these is a pear-shaped object called an Acheulian hand ax. Exhibited too are a number of skulls labeled Neanderthal. To understand the significance of these skulls and implements requires a brief examination of the first phase of that long period of human prehistory in Britain called the Old Stone or Paleolithic Age. The span of years covered by the prehistory of mankind is immense. Even in Britain, where human habitation is fairly recent, it stretches back more than four hundred thousand years; four hundred millennia of unrecorded time before the Romans brought Britain into history.

To reduce this vastness to more manageable proportions and to highlight the major cultural changes that took place over these aeons of time, prehistory in Britain can be subdivided into five main periods. The dates ascribed to each are approximate only, take no account of cultural overlaps, are not adjusted for regional differences within Britain, and are very much subject to dispute. These periods are

Paleolithic (Old Stone Age) . . . . *circa* 450,000–8,300 B.C.
Mesolithic (Middle Stone Age). . . . . *circa* 8,300–4,000 B.C.
Neolithic (New Stone Age). . . . . *circa* 4,000–2,000 B.C.
Bronze Age. . . . . *circa* 2,000–700 B.C.
Iron Age. . . . . *circa* 700 B.C.–A.D. 43

THE OLD STONE AGE

The Paleolithic period, or Old Stone Age, coincided in both Britain and western Europe with what is popularly known as the Ice Age. Four times, an ice sheet thousands of feet thick spread southward from the Arctic Circle until it covered much of northern Europe, rendering habitation by man or beast impossible in the immediate vicinity and barely possible beyond its southern fringe, where only mosses, lichens, and stunted shrubs could grow on the arctic tundra. As they advanced, the glaciers locked up vast quantities of the earth's water and lowered the sea level by as much as two hundred feet. As a consequence, Britain was not an island, but a western promontory of Europe. At its maximum the ice covered all of Scotland and Wales and most of England south to a line running east from Gloucester through Warwick to Ipswich, passing about thirty miles north of modern London. At its minimum the glacier advanced to a line that exposed some of southern Wales, much of England north to Yorkshire, but none of Scotland.

But the ice did retreat. Three times during the earth's long winter Europe's temperatures grew mild; the ice melted; the sea level rose, possibly high enough to cover the land bridge between England and France. These periods of temperate climate are called interglacials. It was during the second, or Hoxnian, interglacial that man, or at least his immediate ancestor, called *Homo erectus*, first made his appearance in Britain; and it was toward the end of this long respite that the young woman whose skull resides in the Museum of Natural History lived and died in the valley of the Thames. Not long thereafter the weather turned cold again as the third glaciation crept southward, though not so far this time. It was interrupted by a relatively short-lived improvement of the climate called an interstadial. Next came the third and final interglacial of about 55,000 years, commencing about 125,000 years ago. And on its heels arrived the fourth and final glaciation, with at least two more interstadials. Then, about 8,300 B.C. the ice began to melt away altogether, eventually leaving Britain an island with a climate approximating that of today.

As the ice came and went, so also did different varieties of animals. When the glaciers crept south, cold-resistant fauna predominated in northern Europe and Britain—the mammoth, the woolly rhinoceros, the long-haired horse, the bison, and the reindeer. During the long interglacials, as temperatures rose to at least those prevailing in the summertime today, woodland animals flourished—the long-tusked elephant, the red deer, the roe deer, wild oxen, and wild boar. And where the wild animals went, there also went men and women—hunters and food gatherers, nomads moving over long distances in small family groups, camping in open sites along the lakes and rivers in the warmer periods and in the mouths of caves as the days grew colder. Their numbers were small—probably never more than a few hundred at any given time in the habitable parts of Britain. Still, it is amazing that so few of their skeletal remains have been unearthed. For the approximately three hundred millennia of British prehistory before the beginning of the final (Devensian) glaciation about 70,000 B.C., only one bona fide human fossil has yet been discovered: the partial skull of Swanscombe Man.

Earlier in this century it was generally believed that the fragments of a skull and jawbone discovered between 1908 and 1915 in a gravel deposit at Piltdown in Sussex belonged to an extremely primitive type of ape-man—perhaps the "missing link" in Darwin's chain of human evolution. Shortly after World War II, however, newly devised chemical tests were applied to these fossils, with the amazing result that Piltdown Man turned out to be a hoax. The jaw proved to be that of an orangutan and the human skull to be not much more than six hundred years of age. Both had been chemically treated so as to give them a false appearance of antiquity. Later radiocarbon dating of the skull fragments indicated a date of about A.D. 1330 for the human skull fragments of Piltdown Man.

Since its discovery in 1949, the technique of dating prehistoric fossils and other organic remains by measuring their radiocarbon (C14) content has become a common device for establishing prehistoric chronology with some exactitude. The technique, however, has limitations. It is based on the fixed rate of decay of the radiocarbon isotope contained in all living matter and is measured from the moment that life ceased to exist. Therefore it works only for organic substances like animal or human remains, wood, charcoal, nuts, and grain. It cannot be used on stone, pottery, glass, metals, or any other inorganic substance. Moreover, the buildup of radiocarbon in living things has not been constant over the millennia, so that from about 1300 B.C. backwards, the C14 dates diverge significantly from the actual dates; the older the object, the greater the divergence. Finally, since the technique relies on the measurement of residual radioactive carbon, the older the object, the smaller the residue until finally so little remains as to become immeasurable. Although recent refinements may make it possible to correct this deficiency, for the time being at least the radiocarbon method cannot be used to obtain dates older than about 60,000 B.C.

Other prehistoric dating techniques, however, have been recently used to good effect. The potassium-argon method, roughly comparable with radiocarbon dating, measures the rate of decay of radioactive potassium (K40) and argon (A40) in inorganic matter like rocks, giving highly accurate figures for at least the closing years of the final glaciation. Another method involves testing bones for fluorine content. Still another employs X-ray crystallography. Finally, new techniques of thermoluminescence have proved useful in dating pottery as well as organic fossils.

None of the above, however, should be interpreted to mean that prehistoric events can be fixed in time with the same accuracy as those of conventional history. Archaeologists can construct a sequence of events at any given site on the principle that the deeper beneath the surface an object is found the older it is likely to be. Geology and its several subdisciplines, botany and the science of pollen analysis, paleontology, comparative anthropology, macrophotography and microphotography, plus a wide variety of laboratory techniques all help to lend greater precision to the chronology of mankind's ancient past. Prehistory has come a long way since the mid-seventeenth century when Archbishop Ussher of Armagh, Ireland, declared that the earth had been created on 23 October in the year 4004 B.C., citing the Old Testament as his only and sufficient source. Nevertheless, the precise dating of prehistoric events still eludes the science of archaeology, and the further back in time the greater the chances of error. All dates mentioned in this chapter, therefore, are at best approximate.

Given the extremely slow rate of technological change in the Paleolithic period, this lack of chronological precision is no great loss. The history of man in the earliest phase of his existence is largely to be told by the tools he left behind; and for tens of thousands of years these remained remarkably unchanged. Which brings us back to the Museum of Natural History and the implements on display there, called hand axes.

A hand ax is not an ax at all, if by that word is meant a tool with a bladed head mounted on a handle or haft. It is an implement that fits easily into the palm of the hand. Normally about six inches in length, it is shaped somewhat like a flattened pear, the butt bulbous and the business end more or less pointed. In Paleolithic times the instrument was manufactured by chipping away at a lump of stone. For purposes of chipping, or *knapping* as it is called in Britain, the most suitable raw material is siliceous rock, such as flint, chert, obsidian, or chalcedony. These have a microcrystalline, almost glasslike quality and can therefore be readily hammered or punched into a desired size and shape. In Britain the most commonly used material was flint, which is almost pure silica and which lay in great abundance in layers a few inches thick or in scattered nodules in the chalky soil of England as far north as Yorkshire.

The hand ax was no doubt an all-purpose tool which could be used to grub for edible roots or dig for burrowing animals. The pointed variety could be employed to stab or pierce the hide of an animal preliminary to skinning. Hand axes were also good for dressing meat, scraping hides, or smashing bones. In a sense the hand ax is a mere extension of the hand—harder than the fist, stronger than the fingernails, and of course much more durable than either, which accounts for the tool's survival by the tens of thousands all over Africa, the Middle East, Europe, and Britain.

The name attached by archaeologists to this standard tool in its earliest form, wherever located, is Acheulian, after St. Acheul in the Somme

Valley, France, the site where the type was first identified. By archaeological convention, the same name is applied to the entire Lower (i.e., early) Paleolithic culture during which the Acheulian hand ax prevailed. It is a long period of time, perhaps as long as two hundred thousand years, from the second (great) interglacial well into the third glaciation. Not until then did a new type of tool culture, the Levalloisian, begin to replace the Acheulian.

Another flint instrument, contemporaneous with the Acheulian hand ax, though perhaps of even earlier origin, is the Clactonian scraper—also named after its type-site, Clacton-on-Sea in Essex. These may have appeared in Britain with the arrival of the first manlike creatures, *Homo erectus*, early in the second interglacial and before the appearance of *Homo sapiens*. They are representative of what archaeologists call a *flake industry*; that is, tools made from flakes struck from flint nodules called cores. Hand axes, by contrast, belong to the species called *core industry* since they consist of the residual cores of nodules after chipping or flaking has taken place.

Clactonian flake tools are less abundant in Britain than Acheulian hand axes, though together their number must reach into tens of thousands. Observant hikers still occasionally spot them in gravel pits and freshly dug ditches or even on the bare hill slopes of southeastern England or the moors of Devon, Cornwall, and Yorkshire. But of course the most convenient place to observe them, as well as other Stone Age artifacts, is in the museums of history and archaeology of which there are hundreds in Britain. The reader is referred to the end of this section for the names and locations of some of those especially well endowed with prehistoric objects.

The traveller who spends very much of his time gazing at flint implements lodged in museum cases will soon begin to find the experience repetitious and dull. Until well into the Upper (i.e., late) Paleolithic period when technological specialization set in, there is a monotonous sameness to these objects, except for minor differences in size, texture, and color. Nevertheless, it should be remembered how truly crucial these primitive tools were to the gradual evolution of mankind. It is primarily as a toolmaker that man as such can be distinguished from the nonhuman primates that were his ancestors. To manufacture a tool for a specific purpose implies foresight and the mental capacity to conceptualize and to plan. These qualities are not given to the lower forms of animal life, even the most advanced. The chimpanzee can extend his reach by using a stick and can even join two sticks together to make a longer one. But he lives in the present only and his object is the gratification of desires immediately within reach. Only man learned to forego immediate satisfactions for the achievement of future goals—to search for raw materials, collect them, and devise techniques to work them into finished products for specific purposes. No work of Renaissance art or of modern technology can take precedence over the humble hand ax as testimony to the genius of the human species. The hand ax persisted as the basic human tool until well into the third glaciation. Then Acheulian culture gave way to a new technology, called Levalloisian after the French type-site at Levallois. Levalloisian tools were closer to the Clactonian flake products than they were to the core implements of the Acheulian era. The object of the Levalloisian technique was to strike off flakes of a predetermined size and shape from a prepared core that had a humped shape like that of a tortoise. The end result was a large, flat, sharp-edged flake that could then be finished into a variety of forms, especially knives and skin scrapers that no doubt were more appropriate than hand axes to life in cold or wet climates. The all-purpose hand ax was yielding slowly to a more sophisticated technology.

This slow progression continued until about the beginning of the fourth and last glacial period (ca. 70,000 B.C.) when it merged with a new culture, called Mousterian after the French type-site in Moustier. Mousterian tools were also made of flakes, but were struck, not from tortoise cores, as were the Levalloisian, but from disc cores which were flat and circular. Two main tools were thus manufactured: the side-scraper, sometimes D-shaped; and the triangular point, with one or both edges dressed for use as a knife. These were the implements fashioned and used during the final ice age by Neanderthal Man.

This creature, whose skeleton was first excavated in the mid-nineteenth century in the Neander Valley east of Düsseldorf, Germany, is the slope-headed, beetle-browed, slack-jawed, caveman of popular fancy. In fact, however, he had a brain larger in size than the average modern human brain. He lived in caves; hunted bear, rhinoceros, and mammoth; cooked over fires; buried his dead; survived for perhaps thirty thousand years and then vanished from the earth between thirty thousand and forty thousand years ago. Was he human? Was he a direct ancestor of modern man? The answer to the first question is yes; to the second, a probable no. The consensus among archaeologists and anthropologists is that Neanderthal Man was an aberrant sideline of evolution, a sort of retrogressive sport, not in the direct line of succession to modern man.

Skeletal remains ascribed to Neanderthal Man are, however, fairly numerous. They have been discovered in North Africa, Siberia, Russia, France, Italy, and Gibraltar. Plaster casts of Neanderthal skulls from continental sites can be observed in the Museum of Natural History alongside that of Swanscombe Man. No skeletal remains of Neanderthal Man have yet been discovered in Britain proper, though a set of thirteen Neanderthal teeth in a good state of preservation have been recovered in a cave called La Cotte de St. Brelade in Jersey, Channel Islands. In other caves in England and Wales, however, there is ample evidence of occupation by Levalloisian and Mousterian hunters, among them presumably Neanderthalers. The cave showing the longest and oldest record of human habitation is **Kent's Cavern** *(589)*, now to be found not far from the town center of Torquay, Devon. Another cave occupied by Neanderthal Man was The Pinhole, located on a cliffside of the limestone gorge in eastern Derbyshire called **Creswell Crags** *(660)*.

With a suddenness unusual in prehistoric times, the thirtieth millennium B.C. saw the disappearance of Neanderthal Man and his culture and his replacement in western Europe by modern man, *Homo sapiens,* in his final, or at least most recent, stage of evolution. This was Cro-Magnon Man, named after the site in the Dordogne region of southern France where his bones were first discovered. He was tall and well proportioned and had a brain capacity above that of the average modern man and a culture at least as advanced as that of the modern Eskimo or Laplander. The period ushered in by the appearance of Cro-Magnon Man is called Upper Paleolithic and roughly corresponds with the fourth and final glaciation. Its relics include a fair number of human skeletons and a vast number and wide range of specialized tools, weapons, and personal ornaments, not only of flint, but of bone and reindeer antler as well. Upper Paleolithic man lived in caves, which he sometimes decorated; used fire; buried his dead, sometimes with elaborate finery; and hunted horse, reindeer, red deer, giant Irish deer, bison, woolly rhinoceros, cave lion, bear, fox, and wolf wherever and whenever climatic conditions permitted the presence of any or all of these animals.

On the continent the sequence of Upper Paleolithic cultures, stretching out over a period of about thirty thousand years, is Aurignacian, Gravettian, Solutrean, and Magdalenian, named as usual after the French type-sites where each was first identified. All these cultures used flint implements manufactured from blades rather than flakes, the blades being long, flat, and narrow and struck with the aid of a punch rather than by direct percussion. Aurignacian flintwork is characterized by scrapers and burins. The Aurignacians also knew how to work with bone and antler and produced a great variety of polished pins or awls and points with cleft bases for the insertion of a wedge-shaped shaft. The Gravettians are distinguished by their invention of the backed flint blade, very much like a modern pen knife. They also carved jewelry out of bone and ivory and decorated it with geometric patterns. They wore headdresses and necklaces of perforated shells and animal teeth, and, like the Aurignacians before them and the Magdalenians later, decorated their bodies with red ochre and sometimes applied the same treatment to their dead. The Solutreans carried the art of flint chipping to its highest point. They fashioned thin, almost translucent, and often beautiful laurel-leaf and willow-leaf shaped points that may have originally served as spearheads. Finally the Magdalenians are noted for their fine blades and bladelets, and especially for their work in bone and antler. Out of these they made spearheads, barbed points and harpoons, needles with eyes, and various other artifacts including *batons de commandement* which may have served some unknown ritualistic purpose or may have been put to the more practical use of straightening spear shafts softened in water. But most of all the Magdalenians are famous for the elaborate and altogether beautiful murals with which they decorated their caves, found chiefly in southern France and northern Spain (Lascaux and Altamira are the two most famous). Using pigments of black oxide of manganese and red and yellow oxides of iron (ochres) they produced delicately shaded polychrome paintings of horses, bison, and reindeer of an aesthetic quality unequaled by any of their European descendants until the Minoans.

In Britain the Upper Paleolithic period can be divided into only two main cultures, separated by a period of from seven to ten thousand years when the ice had come so far south and the weather had turned so cold that no humans at all occupied the promontory that is now the British Isles. The first of these cultures is called Aurignacian or Proto-Solutrean; the second, which is roughly contemporaneous with the French Magdalenian, is called Creswellian or Cheddarian after the British cave sites which have yielded the richest finds.

Perhaps the most famous of British caves occupied by Aurignacian hunters is the Goat's Hole at Paviland in the Gower Peninsula, Wales, now under the custody of the National Trust. There in 1823, William Buckland, professor of geology at Oxford and an ordained priest in the Church of England, discovered a large cache of bones of wild horses, rhinoceri, mammoths, and other extinct animals along with parts of a human skeleton which had been strongly impregnated with red ochre, i.e., iron oxide, and wore a necklace of ivory amulets. On the basis of Archbishop Ussher's chronology, Buckland reasoned that the animal bones must have been swept into the cave by the Flood; but since no man could possibly have reached western Europe until long after that Biblical catastrophe, the human skeleton must have been a later intrusion. Also he knew that no Englishman, nor even Welshman, could possibly have been buried wearing a necklace. From these premises he deduced that the ochre-reddened bones belonged to a Roman-British woman of perhaps the first century A.D. Thus the fossil, which fell into the possession of Oxford University, became known as the Red Lady of Paviland. Subsequent research indicated that the skeleton in fact was that of a male hunter of about five feet, ten inches in height and about twenty-five years old when he died about 16,500 B.C. Oxford's ochred skeleton then is the second oldest human fossil in Britain. It is on display at the **Oxford University Museum** *(632)*.

Other Aurignacian cave sites, already mentioned as places of earlier habitation, are **Kent's Cavern** *(589)* in Torquay, Devon, and the **Creswell Crags** *(660)* in eastern Derbyshire. In Somerset there are at least two caves once occupied by Upper Paleolithic people of the Aurignacian period. One is called the Hyena Den and is adjacent to the more famous caverns of **Wookey Hole** *(585)* near Wells, a well-lighted and much visited cavern embellished with impressive stalagmites and stalactites. Wookey Hole itself has little prehistoric significance, except for a brief Iron Age occupation, but within its grounds the visitor will pass by the

Hyena Den, whose excavation yielded vast numbers of prehistoric animal bones as well as flint tools of Aurignacian design, some of which are on display in the small site museum.

About six miles northwest of Wookey Hole is the Cheddar Gorge which is pitted with caves that once offered shelter to Upper Paleolithic hunters. Among them is Gough's Cave which was occupied from about 11,000 B.C., when the weather had improved enough for hunters to return to England after their long absence, until about 8,300 B.C., which more or less marks the end of the Old Stone Age. At its mouth today is located the finest museum of Stone Age finds in Britain, the **Cheddar Caves Museum** *(582)*.

THE MIDDLE STONE AGE

In comparison with the almost incomprehensible time span of the Old Stone Age, the years of the Mesolithic period of prehistory are few in number—only about four or five thousand by the usual reckoning. Yet they were years of drastic climatic changes in northern Europe that radically restructured the environment of man and forced him into an entirely new mode of living.

It all began with the great thaw, which commenced as long ago as 14,000 B.C., then reversed itself, then began with dramatic suddenness around 8,300 B.C. Inexorably the climate grew warmer. The sparse tundra disappeared. The arctic mosses and lichens and stunted dryas gave way to birch; then birch to pine; then hazel; and that in turn to oak, lime, alder, elm, ash, beech and the whole range of deciduous trees found today in Britain and western Europe. The spread of forest and the destruction of the grassland drove off the great herds of reindeer, giant Irish deer, bison, and even the wild horse. Into the forest came new species —the red deer, roe deer, elk, wild boar, and aurochs (wild ox)—animals that moved through the woods stealthily and alone, or at most in very small numbers. With them came smaller woodland creatures like the marten and the squirrel. As the ice melted, the sea rose—not in a flood, but slowly—trespassing in tiny steps and making marshes of what had once been dry land. With it came new breeds of waterfowl, also otters and beavers, and of course fish in numbers never before imagined.

Unlike the ice age reindeer which retreated to the north, Man stayed and adapted his life style to meet these new conditions. He learned how to stalk these strange elusive animals through the forest. He killed them with arrows shot from newly invented bows or with light spears tipped with tiny points of flint or bone. He domesticated the dog to be his partner in the hunt. He devised fishhooks and barbs and nets and canoes to catch the bounty of the sea. Finally he fixed hafts or handles to his stone axes to cut down the trees that threatened to overrun the land and to build himself temporary shelters as he roamed, even more broadly than before, from campsite to campsite.

The best known of these sites to have been excavated in Britain is Star Carr, a few miles south of Scarborough in North Yorkshire. The excavators left nothing for today's visitor to see, but the site is the most important relic of Mesolithic civilization yet discovered in Britain. There, about 7,500 B.C., a small band of hunter/fishers made their winter camp and left behind an astonishing number of artifacts—about twenty-five hundred small flints or microliths, including scrapers, burins, bladelets, arrowheads, and barbs; a number of flint axes and adzes; and a host of implements of bone and antler including barbed antler-points, mattock heads, batons, bodkins, fastening pins, and a harpoon head. Also discovered was the fragment of a wooden paddle; the remains of a birch-wood platform on top of which these lakeside hunters presumably camped; two felled birch trees showing unmistakable ax marks; and a number of birch rolls from which resin was probably extracted to glue spearheads and arrowheads to their shafts. And most illuminating of all was the discovery at Star Carr of twenty-one sets of carefully truncated stag antlers, each set attached to a piece of skull for ease of fitting to a human head. Presumably these so-called *frontlets* were worn either as camouflage and decoy for hunters moving through the forest or in ritual dances to celebrate the chase. They can be seen today in the Man Before Metals room of the **British Museum** *(516)*.

How many more of such settlements are now buried underwater is unknown. Some there must be, for during the seventh millennium B.C., the sea began to rise. Imperceptibly at first, but inexorably, the lowlands between Holland and East Anglia turned to marsh; the marsh, to open water. The land bridge between Normandy and Kent disappeared under the waves as the English Channel joined the North Sea to the Atlantic. No more would men and animals traverse the land bridge to the European continent. Britain was finally, and one presumes irreversibly, an island—"this precious stone," in Shakespeare's words, "set in a silver sea."

THE NEW STONE AGE

Of the five ages into which the prehistory of man is conventionally divided, only the New Stone Age is in a sense misnamed. For it was not new implements of stone that chiefly distinguished the Neolithic revolution from what had gone before, but rather a radically new economy, based on settled agriculture and animal husbandry instead of nomadic hunting, fishing, and food gathering.

Some time around ten thousand years ago in the Fertile Crescent, arching north from the mouth of the Nile and then south and east along the valleys of the Tigris and the Euphrates toward the head of the Persian Gulf, men began to raise wheat and barley; domesticate dogs, goats, and sheep; dwell in villages; make pottery; weave cloth; store food; and in general settle down on the land their hunting ancestors had previously roamed. This Neolithic revolution, accomplished within a few millennia, marked a more radical change in human existence than anything that had happened before or would happen after, at least until the Industrial Revolution. Slowly the techniques of mixed farming spread outward. By the beginning of the fourth millennium B.C. they had penetrated most of Europe, and not long after the year 4,000 B.C. farming communities were firmly established in England and in Wales.

Today, almost all that is known about these early farmers is derived from (a) the traces of their so-called causewayed camps, (b) a large number of their communal grave sites, (c) a few field sites thought to be associated with their religious worship, (d) vast quantities of polished stone axes and other stone implements, as well as traces of the mines and quarries from which came the raw material for their production, and (e) equally vast quantities of Neolithic pottery.

THE CAUSEWAYED CAMP

The early British *causewayed camp* consisted of two or more concentric rings of banks and ditches. The ditches were not continuous but were interrupted at intervals by gaps of undisturbed soil which could function as a causeway stretched across a moat. Hence the name that archaeologists have applied to these curious relics; "curious" because no one really knows what they were for. Clearly they were not camps in any military sense. Neolithic peoples were apparently innocent of the arts of war. Possibly they were cattle compounds where herds were rounded up for autumn slaughtering. More likely they served as fairgrounds or tribal gathering points for social or religious purposes. In any case they were not permanent settlements but places of seasonal occupation only.

More than a dozen of these camps are to be found in southern England, crowning low hills in the chalk country from East Sussex to Devon. Fully half of these are overlaid by Iron Age hill forts constructed at least two thousand years later. Of the remainder, time and the plow have pretty well removed all visible signs of Neolithic occupation. Only one is really worth a visit and even it would be a disappointment except for the remembrance of the herdsmen who used this place more than five thousand years ago. This is **Windmill Hill** (574) the type-site after which the earliest Neolithic British culture is named. It lies north of Avebury, Wiltshire, just west of the road to Swindon. The hill is crowned by three roughly concentric and barely visible ditches, and at the very peak are several Bronze Age barrows. There is not much to see—except for a glorious view of the surrounding Wiltshire countryside and the inevitable grazing sheep, which may more closely resemble their Neolithic counterparts than does the much eroded site itself.

COMMUNAL BURIAL SITES

England, Wales, and the Crown Dependencies together cannot boast a Neolithic dwelling place to compare to the famous village of Skara Brae in mainland Orkney. The absence of human habitations surviving from the New Stone Age is, however, compensated for by the ubiquity of communal grave sites. Neolithic man, at least in southern Britain, made better provision for the dead than for the living. Each tomb normally held a sizeable number of bodies, laid out in crouched or fetal position, seldom if ever cremated, and only occasionally accompanied by grave goods such as pots or personal ornaments. Tombs were commonly reopened to receive additional bodies.

BARROWS

As used here the term *barrow* applies only to those large mounds of earth thrown up by people of the Windmill Hill culture to cover their dead. The mounds were sometimes revetted by wooden posts, and often the bodies were laid out beneath a wooden shelter or mortuary house before the earth was piled on. By far the greater number are elongated in form and therefore called long barrows. And, although there are more than two hundred of these tombs surviving in Britain, mostly measuring from one hundred to three hundred feet in length, they are not very interesting to look at, and in most cases not even distinguishable to the unpracticed eye. A few examples should suffice to satisfy the curiosity of even the most ardent traveller. In Dorset there is a fairly heavy concentration of long barrows, of which the most impressive are **Pimperne Long Barrow** *(567)*, 350 feet long and 90 feet wide, northeast of Blandford Forum; **Thickthorn Long Barrows** *(567)*, lying at the south end of the Dorset Cursus (below); and **Wor Barrow** *(567)* near the junction of A 354 and B 3081, where excavators have cleared out the original ditch surrounding the earthworks but mostly leveled the mound within. Another concentration of long barrows occurs in Lincolnshire. The best preserved is **Ash Hill Long Barrow** *(652)* northwest of Louth, measuring about 125 by 50 feet and 7 feet high at the east end. A site northwest of Skegness (near Willoughby) called **Deadman's Graves** *(652)* consists of two barrows, each measuring more than 160 by 50 feet and about 6 feet in height. About a mile to the west are the **Giants Hill Long Barrows** *(652)*, more than 200 feet long and about 5 feet high.

A few large round barrows can also be attributed to Neolithic communal grave builders. One of the most impressive is **Duggleby Howe Round Barrow** *(684)* southeast of Malton, North Yorkshire. Another northern round barrow of Neolithic attribution is **Willy Howe Round Barrow** *(677)* near Burton Fleming, Humberside, northwest of Bridlington. This reaches a height of 24 feet. Much higher still (130 feet) is **Silbury Hill** *(573)*, west of Marlborough in Wiltshire. This enormous mound, visible for miles around, is one of the great archaeological mysteries of Britain, for excavators have as yet found no clue inside as to its possible function. Carbon-14 samples, however, definitely indicate a late-Neolithic construction, which would make it contemporary with the great round barrows of the north which it resembles.

MEGALITHIC TOMBS

The word megalithic derives from the Greek *mega*, meaning "large," and *lithos*, meaning "stone." A megalithic tomb, then, is a communal burial vault built of large upright stone slabs roofed over with large horizontal slabs or capstones. There are over 350 of them in England, Wales, and the Crown Dependencies, mostly situated on remote hillsides accessible only by long and often steep footpaths. Though sometimes hard to locate and difficult to reach, they are nonetheless the most rewarding to the traveller of all Neolithic field sites in Britain. In essence these megalithic monuments are simply the stone counterparts of the wooden mortuary houses of the long barrows which have long since rotted away. In both cases the protective covering built to house the bones of the deceased was overlaid with mounds of earth, chalk, or small stones. Since the stone infrastructure was normally compartmentalized, these burial sites are often referred to as *chambered tombs*. The covering mounds of earth are sometimes called *tumuli*. In Gloucestershire the earthen mounds are occasionally designated *tumps*. In Scotland, and occasionally in Wales, where small stones were used in place of earth to cover the megalithic chambers, they are called *cairns*. Still another nomenclature is used to identify those stone chambers which have been denuded of their covering mounds by erosion, the plow, or the spade. These free-standing megaliths, sometimes but not always capped by horizontal slabs, are usually called *dolmens,* a word of Breton origin. In Wales they are sometimes designated *cromlechs,* and in Cornwall, *quoits*.

Archaeologists generally classify chambered tombs, whether covered with mounds or uncovered, according to the architectural arrangement of the megaliths. Unfortunately there is no universally agreed-upon taxonomy, and the layman can easily get lost in the arcane terminology of the experts. For the novice, the following somewhat oversimplified classification should suffice: (a) *Gallery graves* are megalithic tombs, rectangular or trapezoidal in shape, with no distinct passageway or corridor leading in from the entrance. Gallery graves are sometimes segmented by transverse slabs and sometimes transepted by pairs of adjoining chambers on either side. In southern England and South Wales the majority of gallery graves belong to a subtype known as the Severn-Cotswold group. In western Scotland, the Isle of Man, and western Wales, a second subtype known as the Clyde-Carlingford group are very much in evidence. (b) *Passage graves* consist typically of a circular or rectangular burial chamber at the end of a narrow passageway leading from the entrance. Sometimes side chambers lead off the passageway, and the whole ensemble was originally often covered with a round, rather than an elongated mound as was usually the case with gallery graves. Passage graves are found mostly in North Wales, especially on the island of Anglesey; in the Channel Islands; and in northern Scotland and the Hebrides and Orkney Islands. (c) *Entrance graves* consist usually of a single large chamber entered through a simple stone portal located at the wide end of the mound. They are found chiefly in Cornwall and the Scilly Islands, though the so-called Medway group of entrance graves is located in Kent. (d) *Cists* are simply stone coffins, i.e., burial pits lined with stone slabs and roofed with one or more capstones or a chest-shaped stone container built above ground and then covered with a mound. A longitudinal series of these can be called a *segmented cist*.

These distinctions, however, will be of less interest to the average traveller than the obvious difference to the naked eye between a covered chambered tomb and a naked dolmen, cromlech, or quoit. It is this distinction, therefore, that forms the basis of the classification used in this book. The megalithic structures listed below are divided into (a) those that are still covered with mounds and therefore can be presumed to appear today much as they did to their Neolithic builders and (b) tombs whose covering mounds have disappeared, leaving only the skeletal megalithic ruins (i.e., dolmens). The sites mentioned here are representative of the 350-odd Neolithic tombs scattered throughout England, Wales, and the Crown Dependencies. Each of these regions is considered separately, and the order of the arrangement below is the same as in the Gazetteer, i.e., from east to west and from south to north.

COVERED CHAMBERED TOMBS

ENGLAND

One of the most accessible of England's chambered tombs is also one of the most rewarding to visit, if for no other reason than that it is so spacious inside. This is **West Kennet Chambered Tomb** *(574)* west of Marlborough, Wiltshire. It is a gallery grave of the Severn-Cotswold group used as a communal burial place from about 3500 to 2500 B.C. Its gallery is transepted by two pairs of side chambers with a fifth chamber at the end, and there is standing room under the capstones forming the roof. Another Severn-Cotswold gallery grave is **Stoney Littleton Chambered Tomb** *(581)* near Radstock, Avon. The tomb is dated sometime between 3500 and 2500 B.C. and has been restored. Its 48-foot-long gallery is transepted by three pairs of side chambers and leads to a seventh terminal chamber, and the roofs are corbelled, i.e., so constructed that each course of stone in two parallel walls projects slightly forward of the course just beneath until the walls join at the top to form a vault. Cornwall's best covered Neolithic burial site is **Brane Chambered Tomb** *(596)* near St. Just. Built about 2500 B.C., it is classified as an entrance grave, is covered by a round barrow about 20 feet in diameter and 6½ feet high, and the chamber is roofed with two capstones. **Pennance Chambered Tomb** *(596)*, otherwise known as The Giant's House, lies not far away, near Zennor. It, too, is an entrance grave of about the same date as Brane, is covered with a mound of about 25 feet in diameter and 6 feet in height. St. Mary's Island in the Isles of Scilly boasts three well-preserved covered chambered tombs. They are **Bant's Carn** *(592)*, **Innisidgen** *(592)*, and **Porth Hellick Down** *(592)*, situated, respectively, on the northwest, the northeast, and eastern coasts of the island. All are late Neolithic entrance graves. They are covered by more or less circular mounds, ranging in diameter from 25 to 40 feet, and the chambers are both low and narrow. In southern Oxfordshire, west of Wantage, lies another Severn-Cotswold gallery grave dating from about 2500, called **Wayland's Smithy Chambered Tomb** *(638)*. Underneath a barrow 180 feet in length and located in a lovely hilltop copse is a Neolithic transepted tomb with three burial chambers laid out in cruciform plan under a stone roof with sufficient headroom for a man to stand upright. **Belas Knap Chambered Tomb** *(642)* near Winchcombe, Gloucestershire, on the other hand, can only be observed from the outside. It is a Severn-Cotswold tomb of about 3500 to 2500 B.C., but what appears to be the entrance, approached by a forecourt between two convex dry-wall horns, is in fact a false portal, leading nowhere (presumably to deceive grave-robbers). The four small burial chambers are underneath the sides and at the rear end of this 170-foot-long mound. The visitor who undertakes the long walk to it over footpath and open field will be rewarded by a spectacular view of the Cotswold and Malvern Hills. Also in Gloucestershire, near Stroud, is another long (120 feet) Severn-Cotswold chambered tomb of about 3500–3000 B.C. called **Hetty Pegler's Tump** *(641)*, or Uley Bury Tumulus from the name of the closest village. Here too a horned forecourt leads into the main entrance, but this one opens into a gallery originally transepted by two pairs of smaller chambers and terminating in an end chamber. The two chambers on the right from the entrance are now walled up. Although the tomb can be entered, the key to the heavy wooden door leading into the gallery must be picked up at the nearest roadside cottage, and the gallery is low and dark. Exploring it without a flashlight can be a spooky experience. "The grave's a fine and private place" wrote Andrew Marvell, and here's a place to put his theory to test.

WALES

In the Black Mountains of southeastern Wales, south of Talgarth, Powys, lies a well-known chambered tomb of the Severn-Cotswold group called **Ty-Isaf** *(723)*. Like Belas Knap, it has a false portal behind a horned forecourt. Two burial chambers were inserted on either side of the long mound and at the rear end are two more chambers covered by an oval appendage to it. Even closer in appearance to Hetty Pegler's Tump is **Parc Cwm Chambered Tomb** *(721)* in the Gower Peninsula north of the village of Penmaen west of Swansea, West Glamorgan. A Severn-Cotswold tomb, 75 feet in length, its entrance is guarded by horn works, and the long gallery is transepted by two pairs of chambers. In Gwynedd, east of Betws-y-Coed lies **Capel Garmon Chambered Tomb** *(736)*, 140 feet in length with a false portal behind a horned forecourt and a double burial chamber entered from the side. The Isle of Anglesey in Gwynedd boasts two of Wales's best preserved Neolithic chambered tombs. They are **Bryn Celli Ddu** *(734)* southwest of the northern terminus of the Menai Bridge and **Barclodiad Y Gawres** *(733)* on the west coast of the island northwest of Aberffraw. Both are passage graves dating from about 2500–2000 B.C. In the first a 16-foot passageway leads to a polygonal chamber formed by six uprights with a seventh freestanding stone inside the chamber. There is standing room inside, and on display is the cast of a five-foot stone covered with meandering linear decorations. The interior of the second grave is much the same except that three subsidiary chambers open off the main polygonal chamber at the end of the passageway. This tomb has been restored by the Department of the Environment, and although there is plenty of space inside, entry is barred by an iron grill. On display here also is an example of Neolithic art rare in Britain—stones incised with chevrons, lozenges, and spirals.

JERSEY

Perhaps the most impressive of all Neolithic chambered tombs in Britain is on the Island of Jersey. This is **La Hogue Bie** *(744)*, a gigantic passage grave covered by a 40-foot mound of earth, on top of which sits a medieval chapel. The passage is 32 feet long, terminating in an oval-shaped chamber, 30 feet by 12 feet, and adjoined by three side cells. The tomb is well lighted (electrically) and there is ample standing room.

GUERNSEY

West of St. Peter Port, Guernsey, in the parish of St. Peter-in-the-Wood, is the covered tomb called **Le Creux des Faies** *(746)*. It is a passage grave, about 28 feet in length with two large capstones forming the roof which stands more than 6 feet high. The sea is not far distant and the view of the coast magnificent.

UNCOVERED CHAMBERED TOMBS—DOLMENS

ENGLAND

Kits Coty *(538)*, northeast of Aylesford, Kent, was built about 3,000 B.C. as an elongated entrance grave. All that now survives after centuries of plowing and natural erosion are three upright megaliths and a capstone, the sole remains of what was once a large rectangular burial chamber. A few miles to the west lies **Coldrum Chambered Tomb** *(546)*, originally another entrance grave of the same date, but now a rectangle of standing stones without a roof. In the other corner of southern England, Cornwall has a splendid collection of dolmens, referred to locally as quoits. **Trethevy Stone** *(593)*, near Liskeard, is known as a portal dolmen and was built between 3200 and 2500 B.C. when it was enclosed in a covering mound. Today it appears as six standing stones supporting a huge capstone, with another megalith fallen on its side. **Chun Quoit** *(594)* northwest of Penzance is another portal dolmen of about the same date now consisting of four slabs supporting a thick capstone 12 feet square. The climb from the farmyard carpark to this Neolithic site (and the adjacent Iron Age hill fort, called Chun Castle) is an arduous one, but the view of the Cornish coast alone is worth it. Not far to the east is **Lanyon Quoit** *(594)*, one of the most photographed of all Cornish dolmens, probably because it is more accessible than most, lying as it does on the east side of the road between Penzance and Morvah. It consists of three upright megaliths, 6 feet high, supporting a huge capstone which no doubt formed the burial chamber of a covered tomb of between 3200 and 2500 B.C. It should be noted, however, that it was rebuilt in the nineteenth century after the stones had collapsed. **Zennor Quoit** *(595)*, southwest of St. Ives, is the largest of these Cornish dolmens. Its huge capstone has partially collapsed, but the five large uprights of the chamber it once covered are still standing, as are two others forming the facade of an antechamber. In Oxfordshire, near Chipping Norton, is another portal dolmen called **Whispering Knights** *(627)*. Here are four uprights forming the vertical sides of a Neolithic burial chamber whose capstone, like that of Zennor Quoit, now rests at an angle.

WALES

Even more than Cornwall, Wales is the land of dolmens, mostly referred to locally as cromlechs. Two of the best known are **Tinkinswood** *(718)* and **St. Lythan's** *(718)*, located a short distance from each other southwest of Cardiff, South Glamorgan. Tinkinswood, the larger of the two, now consists of five uprights supporting a huge capstone weighing about forty tons. St. Lythan's is much the same in structure. Both belong to the Severn-Cotswold group of chambered tombs. On the Gower Peninsula west of Swansea, West Glamorgan, is a curious cromlech consisting of a huge glacial boulder underpinned by nine uprights to form two irregular burial compartments. It is called **Maen Ceti** *(721)* or Arthur's Stone after a legend that it was originally a pebble flung by King Arthur (here transformed into a giant) after he had removed it from his shoe. Southwest of Cardigan, Dyfed, lies a cromlech considered to be one of the finest megalithic tombs in Wales. This is **Pentre Ifan** *(724)* with a huge capstone of seventeen tons which appears to be delicately balanced on the tips of four pointed uprights. On the island of Anglesey in Gwynedd are three Neolithic cromlechs of note. The first, though least impressive, is called **Plas Newydd** *(735)* after the estate of the same name on whose grounds it is located, just south of the Menai Bridge. Here are two capstones supported by uprights which once covered adjacent burial chambers. On the island's northeast coast is **Lligwy Burial Chamber** *(735)*, a huge capstone resting on several short uprights, looking very much like a stone table. Finally, on Holy Island south of Holyhead is **Trefignath Burial Chamber** *(734)*, a rare example of a segmented cist with two portal stones still standing 7 feet in height, its length stretching to 45 feet.

THE ISLE OF MAN

This little island set in the Irish Sea boasts two noteworthy ruined chambered tombs dating back to the New Stone Age: **King Orry's Grave** *(742)* and **Cashtal yn Ard** *(742)*, both near the east coast north of Douglas. A modern road slices through the first; on the east side is a forecourt with a portal of two standing stones and on the west another forecourt leading to a burial chamber of two compartments. Cashtal yn Ard is more remotely situated in the Maughold peninsula. It, too, has a semicircular forecourt marked by ten upright megaliths opening onto a portal of two standing stones and five burial chambers built of stone slabs slightly sloping inward.

JERSEY

Jersey's best ruined Neolithic chambered tomb is **Faldouet Dolmen** *(744)*, also called La Pouquelaye, also called Gorey Dolmen because of its proximity to Gorey (Mont Orgueil) Castle on the east coast. Like most other Neolithic burial sites in the Channel Islands, this is a passage grave with two parallel rows of standing stones marking the approach to the burial chamber of uprights capped by large flat stones. The whole ensemble looks vaguely like the outlines of a bottle. On the northeast coast overlooking Rozel Bay is a splendid example of a Neolithic segmented cist, a type rare in southern Britain. It is called **Le Couperon** *(745)* and is locally referred to as an *allee couverte*. The 25-foot *allee* consists of two parallel lines of twenty upright stones, 2 or 3 feet high and 3 feet apart and roofed with seven capstones. This is a quiet and secluded spot with a view of unsurpassed beauty.

North of St. Peter Port in the Parish of Vale is the megalithic tomb called **Le Dehus** *(747)*, a ruined Neolithic passage grave. The monument consists of a main chamber 20 feet long and 11 feet wide approached by an entrance passage 11 feet long and about 3 feet wide. Four smaller side chambers abut the main chamber. Seven capstones roof the tomb and entrance passage. On the underside of the second capstone is a rare example of Neolithic art—an incised human figure consisting of a face, arms, and hands, called locally *le gardien du tombeau.* Le Dehus is the second largest chambered tomb on Guernsey. The largest lies at the western end of L'Ancresse Common and is called **La Varde Dolmen** *(746)*. Bottle shaped like Faldouet Dolmen on Jersey, this passage grave consists of a burial chamber measuring 33 by 12 feet and 7 feet in height, roofed by six capstones resting on short uprights and approached by a short and narrow alley marked by stones on either side. To the southwest near Le Catiorac headland is a small dolmen called **Le Trepied** *(747)*, consisting of a chamber 18 feet long and 6 feet wide, and roofed with three capstones standing about 4 feet above ground. The site overlooks the wild west coast of Guernsey and for a long while had an unsavory reputation as the favorite meeting place of the island's witches.

NEOLITHIC RELIGIOUS SITES

What gods these Neolithic people worshiped, and by what rites, is a complete mystery. Presumably, like other primitive peoples, they deified and sought to propitiate those powerful forces of nature, both friendly and unfriendly, which experience had taught them to respect, though not to understand. But even this is supposition. No ruined temples remain from the New Stone Age in Britain; only a few field sites which, for want of a better explanation, archaeologists assume must have been associated with some kind of religious ceremony. These are the cursus and henge monuments of Wiltshire and Dorset.

A *cursus* consists of two parallel banks with outside ditches which may run for several miles across country. Its original function is unknown, though it probably had some religious or ritualistic significance connected with the burial of the dead. The two best known, and the only two worth visiting, are the **Stonehenge Cursus** *(571)* in Wiltshire and the **Dorset Cursus** *(566)* northeast of Blandford Forum. The former is located about a half mile north of Stonehenge proper and runs in an east-west direction for about three thousand yards, though most of it has been leveled by the plow. The latter runs for more than six miles to the east of and parallel to the A 354 between Blandford Forum, Dorset, and Salisbury, Wiltshire.

The word *henge* is Anglo-Saxon for "hanging stone" and was first employed to describe the massive lintels suspended between pairs of uprights at Stonehenge. Although Stonehenge is unique in this respect, the word has come to be employed as a generic term describing a great variety of Neolithic and Bronze Age sites, whose common characteristics include a circular bank and ditch (usually internal) with one or more entrances that enclose one or more circles of timber posts or stones, either standing or recumbent. Most of the henge monuments belong properly to the Bronze Age and will therefore be described in some detail later. Several, however, date from Neolithic times at least in their original form, and of these, two are worth mention here.

The first is **Stonehenge** *(570)* itself, certainly the most famous prehistoric monument in Britain and perhaps in all of Europe. Lying just west of Amesbury, Wiltshire, only the outer circular ditch, the Heel Stone, and the ring of Aubrey Holes date from Neolithic times. These latter, named after the seventeenth century antiquary John Aubrey, form a circular ring around the present ruined stone monument and predate it by as much as eight centuries. Originally they were fifty-six in number and measured about four feet across and three feet deep. Only those that have been excavated are now observable as chalk-filled discs in the grass. What they were first meant for is unknown, and in later years they were filled in, sometimes with wood ash, sometimes with flint implements, and sometimes with cremated human remains. The Heel Stone, a natural sarsen monolith about fifteen feet high, was later incorporated into the Bronze Age monument and will be further discussed below.

The second Neolithic henge considered to be worth a visit is **Woodhenge** *(571)*, just north of Amesbury. It originally consisted of a series of concentric rings of wooden postholes inside the normal henge arrangement of a ditch inside a circular bank. Possibly these posts supported the roof of a neolithic temple. Today they are marked by small concrete pillars which give the visitor a fair idea of what the base of the original structure may have looked like.

STONE IMPLEMENTS

The first mark of distinction drawn by archaeologists between the Old and New Stone Ages is the manner of shaping ax heads. Specifically, in the Neolithic period chipping or knapping gave way to grinding and polishing, an art that produced sharper and smoother ax heads capable of making deep cuts into standing timber without binding. For the first task facing Neolithic farmers immigrating to Britain was the same as that which faced the first settlers in America, i.e., clearing the forests and constructing wooden shelters for themselves and fences for their domestic livestock. For these purposes, of course, axes had to be hafted; that is, the blade or head had to be affixed at right angles to a handle of wood or antler so that sufficient power could be imparted to the chopping motion. Hafting was accomplished in three ways: (1) by pecking or drilling a vertical hole through the ax head and inserting the handle into it, (2) by drilling or cutting a slit in the handle of wood or antler and inserting the ax head into it at right angles, or (3) by binding the ax head to the handle with thongs. In manufacturing the ax heads themselves, Neolithic farmers seem to have preferred igneous or metamorphic rock to flint; and in the western and northern highlands, there were numerous stone quarries and "ax factories" where rock was mined and shaped into rough ax heads, then shipped all over Britain for later grinding and polishing. The sites of a few of these are known and can be visited, though there is nothing much to see. One of them is **Craig Lwyd Axe Factory** *(739)* on the western slope of Moel Llys mountain just east of Penmaenmawr in Gwynedd. Another is the **Pike of Stickel Axe Factory** *(708)* on the north side of Great Langdale, near Ambleside, Cumbria.

This is not to say that flint fell out of use in Neolithic times. It was still extensively employed in the manufacture not only of ax heads but also of sickle blades for harvesting wheat and barley and of the leaf-shaped arrowheads that Neolithic bowmen used for shooting game. The raw material out of which such implements were fashioned came, as often as not, from underground seams of high quality flint, which Neolithic men learned to mine by sinking shafts deep into the chalk with picks of bone and antler and even carving out radiating galleries, much in the manner of modern coal mines. The best known among Neolithic flint mines is the site called **Grimes Graves** *(610)* northwest of Thetford, Norfolk. Here, in an area of thirty-four acres, more than 360 mine shafts and shallower excavations were dug out, as long ago as 2500 B.C., by Neolithic men wielding picks and shovels made of red-deer antlers and shoulder-blades. The site is maintained by the Department of the Environment and visitors can descend into one of the shafts by means of a ladder. They will probably be surprised to discover that the flint itself is black and glossy, looking more like polished jet than like the common "flints" used in modern cigarette-lighters.

NEOLITHIC POTTERY

Though the manufacture of ax heads was a major industry of the New Stone Age, the most significant technological innovation of the Neolithic period was pottery. No other surviving artifacts more clearly reflect the newly acquired sedentary habits of Neolithic farmers. The salient characteristic of all pottery is its frangibility. It would simply not have been suitable to the nomadic life of Paleolithic or even Mesolithic hunters. Not until people settled down in more or less permanent village communities would they have found it useful to shape and fire earthenware pots for cooking and for storing grain and liquids.

The earliest pots discovered in Britain belong to the Windmill Hill culture of southern England. These are smooth and round bottomed, shaped more or less like leather bags, which may indeed have been the prototypes on which they were modeled. They are gray or buff in color and usually full of grit holes. From a somewhat later period came two other types of secondary Neolithic pottery. The first is called Peterborough and can be classified into three main subtypes: Ebbsfleet, Mortlake, and Fengate. Ebbsfleet is distinguished by primitive linear or pocked designs made with the end of a stick. Mortlake is more heavily decorated with imprints from cord, bird bones, fingernails, or shells. Both types are round bottomed and it must be assumed that they were held upright in racks of some kind. Fengate ware, on the other hand, had narrow flat bases and urn-shaped tops. Also flat bottomed is a later type of secondary Neolithic ware called Rinyo-Clacton. This was apparently a ceramic invention unique to the British Isles and is distinguished by the heavily grooved decoration somewhat resembling wicker basketry.

MUSEUMS

The craze for collecting prehistoric artifacts hit the leisure classes of Britain in the late seventeenth century and only abated in the twentieth when most of the discoverable items had been gathered up. The greater part of this enormous corpus of Stone Age hand axes, stone axes, microliths, as well as weapons and tools from the Bronze and Iron Ages and pottery from all prehistoric periods has found its way into small museums of local history and archaeology, of which there is a superabundance in every part of Britain. Indeed the traveller is faced with an embarrassment of riches, and it is hoped that the foregoing pages will help him move through these endless showcases of artifacts with some degree of informed confidence. It must be said that the art of museumship has made tremendous strides in Britain over the past few decades, and in many of these repositories the exhibits are beautifully arranged, well lighted, and liberally supplied with clearly written placards and other visual aids. In some of the older museums, however, the contents are likely to be crowded into dark showcases with little or no identification. Also, British museums too often display an annoying indifference to the convenience of the public in the matter of visiting hours, and it is not unusual for large collections to be closed for months-on-end for repairs or "rearrangements."

Notwithstanding these hazards, no traveller seriously interested in Britain's prehistoric past can afford *not* to visit at least two or three archaeological museums. More than two or three in the course of a single trip to Britain would, probably, be redundant. A surfeit of hand axes and pottery shards can soon spoil the appetite for archaeology.

Out of the hundreds of museums in Britain that give shelter to Stone

Age artifacts, those mentioned below have been selected because they happen to be the repositories, *inter alia*, of finds from the Paleolithic, Mesolithic, and Neolithic sites described above. First in quality and in accessibility to the average traveller is the Man Before Metals room (Room 36) in the **British Museum** *(516)* on Great Russell Street, London, WC 1. Devoted entirely to artifacts from the Stone Age (including finds from Creswell Crags, Star Carr, and Grimes Graves) this beautifully arranged display should not be missed. As an educational experience, no other archaeological exhibit in Britain quite equals it. A close second is the **National Museum of Wales** *(717)* in Cardiff, South Glamorgan, whose archaeology department includes a large collection of paleoliths from Paviland and other Welsh caves and grave goods from Bryn Celli Ddu and other chambered tombs on Anglesey. (Note: The "Red Lady of Paviland" here is only a copy.) Each of the Crown Dependencies boasts an excellent archaeological museum. Grave goods from Cashtal yn Ard and other megalithic tombs on the Isle of Man, as well as a large collection of Mesolithic microliths are to be found in the **Manx Museum** *(741)* in Douglas. The **Jersey Museum** *(744)* is on the grounds of La Hogue Bie chambered tomb, but it is more than a site museum. Here is a splendid collection of prehistoric artifacts gathered from caves and tombs all over the island. Also on display is a cast of the thirteen teeth of Britain's only surviving Neanderthal fossil, found in the nearby cave of La Cotte de St. Brelade. (The originals are under lock and key in the museum of La Société Jersiase in St. Helier.) Guernsey has nothing quite so rare as this in the way of prehistoric relics, but the recently constructed **Guernsey Museum and Art Gallery** *(745)* in St. Peter Port is a gem of modern museumship. Here are most of the grave goods from the island's several chambered tombs as well as a fine set of visual aids to instruct the visitor in the island's prehistory.

England's two great universities, not surprisingly, are host to noteworthy archaeological collections. The **Oxford University Museum** *(632)*, itself a fascinating monument to Victorian architectural taste, is chiefly devoted to natural history (entomology, geology, mineralogy, and zoology). It does contain, however, one famous prehistoric human fossil —the ochred skeleton of the Red Lady of Paviland. Next door is the **Pitt Rivers Museum** *(633)*, which possesses, among other things, probably the largest collection of Paleolithic hand axes in the country. The displays, however, are overcrowded, and this distinguished collection badly needs culling. A few blocks away is the famous **Ashmolean Museum** *(628)*, the first public museum to be opened in Britain (in 1659 in the building on Broad Street now housing the Museum of the History of Science). The John Evans Room contains a good representative collection of prehistoric artifacts, many of them recovered from the chambered tombs of Oxfordshire. In Cambridge, the **University Museum of Archaeology and Anthropology** *(616)* is also well endowed with prehistoric finds from the surrounding countryside, though the exhibits themselves are a trifle tacky.

There are few towns in England of so little consequence as not to possess a museum of local history and archaeology. One of the best, naturally enough, is the **Museum of London** *(512)*. The section called The Thames in Prehistory is a model of modern museumship, displaying and explaining with well-contrived visual aids a carefully chosen selection of artifacts dredged up from the river or recovered during excavations incident to the construction of city skyscrapers and Heathrow Airport. Conveniently located near St. Paul's Cathedral, this is one of the most educational tourist-attractions in the ancient City.

As indicated above, the provinces offer an embarrassment of riches in the way of archaeological repositories. Mention will be made below of those museums which are particularly distinguished for their Bronze Age, Iron Age, Roman, and Anglo-Saxon collections. Here are listed only those that contain finds from those Stone Age sites mentioned above. Starting in the southeast of England, the **Museum and Art Gallery** *(543)*, in Maidstone, Kent, has on display the grave goods recovered from the nearby Coldrum chambered tomb. In Berkshire, the **Museum and Art Gallery** *(564)*, Reading, contains those from Wayland's Smithy. In the little village of Avebury, Wiltshire, sits one of the best prehistoric museums in England, the **Alexander Keiller Museum** *(573)*, which houses a priceless collection of Neolithic artifacts, including finds from Windmill Hill. Ten miles farther south in the same county, and of equal if not greater merit, is the **Devizes Museum** *(572)*, which has on display the grave goods from West Kennet chambered tomb and from a host of other burial sites in the Wiltshire Downs. In the village of Cheddar, Somerset, at the mouth of the Gorge of the same name is one of the best displays in England of Paleolithic and Mesolithic relics. This is the **Cheddar Caves Museum** *(582)*, situated at the mouth of Gough's Cave and replete with important finds from this and nearby caverns. Here are two *batons de commandement*, made of reindeer antlers, which may have been used for some unknown ceremonial purpose, as the name suggests, but were more probably tools for straightening arrows and spear shafts. Even more interesting are the bones of Cheddar Man, a rare late Neolithic or Mesolithic human fossil. The **City Museum and Art Gallery** *(580)*, in Bristol, Avon, also possesses Paleolithic finds from one of the Cheddar caves (Aveline's Hole) as well as grave goods from Stoney Littleton and other Neolithic burial sites. In Devon, the **Torquay Museum of Natural History** *(590)* is the chief repository of the finds from nearby Kent's Cavern, including the skull of a young woman dating about 14,000 B.C. The **Cornwall County Museum** *(597)* in Truro has a good collection of grave goods from Zennor Quoit and other megalithic tombs, though its best items on display are Bronze Age artifacts. In Suffolk, **Ipswich Museum** *(602)* contains a number of microliths from Grimes Graves, and still more of these Mesolithic artifacts are housed in the **Norwich Castle Museum** *(608)*, including a rare example of a Mesolithic harpoon netted about fifty years ago by fishermen in the North Sea. Those finds from Star Carr not sent to the British Museum in London are mostly deposited in the **Rotunda Museum** *(687)*, Scarborough, North Yorkshire.

The mention of specific objects or of specific sites dating to the Stone Age in the paragraphs immediately above should not be taken to mean that these museums are exclusively, or even predominantly, devoted to the custodianship of Paleolithic, Mesolithic, or Neolithic objects. The great majority of them, as well as others to be mentioned later, are repositories also of relics of the Bronze and Iron Ages. It is to these two final periods of British prehistory, then, that we now must turn.

THE BRONZE AGE

Some time around the year 2,000 B.C., or perhaps even earlier, there began to arrive in Britain from the lowlands across the North Sea a new wave of settlers known to archaeologists as the Beaker Folk. Racially they differed from the indigenous Neolithic population in that they were tall, heavy boned, and round headed. Originating probably in the coastal regions of Spain and Portugal, they had in the last centuries of the third millennium B.C. spread eastward as far as Sicily, northeast into Poland, and north into France, Germany, and the lowlands before crossing the North Sea into Britain. Into all these areas they brought a standard type of highly decorated and well-fired vessels from which they derive their name—the reddish brown beakers which were probably used to contain both food and drink. They also buried their dead in single graves, using inhumation rather than cremation to dispose of the remains.

Because they did not bring with them instruments or weapons of bronze, some archaeologists have assigned the Beaker Folk to the late Neolithic period. But they did use metal—copper and gold—and their customs and lifestyle were sufficiently different from those of the New Stone Age to justify their being considered at least precursors of the Bronze Age, if not squarely within the Bronze Age culture. They seem to have been a warrior race—probably the first to bring the military arts to Britain. Certainly they were skilled in archery, as evidenced by the thousands of tanged and barbed arrowheads of flint they left behind, as well as the hundreds of small stone plaques pierced by one or more holes at either end which served as wristguards against the snap of a returning bowstring.

The Beaker Folk brought with them implements and ornaments of copper, such as daggers, pins, and awls. After tin was discovered in Cornwall, however, copper gradually gave way to bronze, an alloy of about nine parts copper to one part tin. Bronze was more easily cast than either of the pure metals from which it was compounded. Casts or molds in the desired shape of ax or dagger were carved into stone and later formed out of clay; the metal was melted in a crucible, poured into the mold, and allowed to cool; the casting could then be removed and hammered or ground to the proper degree of sharpness.

The most skilled among these early Bronze Age metalworkers belonged to what is called the Wessex culture, which succeeded that of the Beaker Folk and prevailed in the south of England in Hampshire, Dorset, Wiltshire, and Somerset and eventually spread into south Wales, East Anglia, Lincolnshire, and as far north as Yorkshire. In Wessex by about 1600 B.C., a warrior and merchant aristocracy, probably originating in Brittany, had developed a civilization superior in wealth and technology to any yet known in Britain. It was these people who were responsible for engineering the final remodeling of Stonehenge. It was they who established a widespread network of trade, importing amber from the Baltic, gold from Ireland, bronze ornaments from central Europe, faience beads from Egypt, and, from the eastern Mediterranean and Aegean seas a variety of fine ornaments and utensils, or at least the skills to fabricate them.

At about the same time as the Wessex chieftains were flourishing in the south, there developed in northern England a distinct society called the Food Vessel culture after the coarse ornamented pottery they left behind. These people were probably of native stock, or a mixture of Neolithic people with Beaker immigrants, and they appear to have relied more heavily on implements of flint and stone than on bronze. Like their Wessex contemporaries, however, they were traders, and it was they apparently who first imported from Ireland those priceless and beautiful gold ornaments called *lunulae*—crescent-shaped necklaces which were later copied in jade by native artisans.

Some time around 1400 B.C., both the Wessex and Food Vessel cultures disappeared for reasons unknown. They were replaced by the civilization of the Middle Bronze Age about which relatively little is known except that these people universally adopted cremation as a burial rite. This drove them to the manufacture of a new form of ceramic ware to use as cinerary urns—large coarse pots with overhanging rims, evolving into biconical, collared, and cordoned types. That they too were warlike is indicated by their development of a whole new range of bronze weapons: rapiers, spearheads, and especially palstaves, a new type of ax with a flared cutting edge, prominent flanges, and a stop ridge to prevent the ax handle from splitting. Large numbers of these weapons and implements have survived, not as grave goods, but in hoards which apparently belonged to travelling smiths.

Finally, commencing about the beginning of the first millennium B.C., and lasting about three hundred years, material and technological progress in Britain took another leap in what is known as the Late

Bronze Age. This may have come about as a result of new migrations from the continent, commencing perhaps as early as 1200 B.C., of a people known as Deverel-Rimbury from two of their burial sites in Dorset. It was these invaders who probably introduced the ox-drawn plow. They may also be responsible for the first arrival of the domesticated horse, whose presence is known from brass horse-fittings found in numerous museums. They manufactured cauldrons and buckets of sheet bronze. They used unsocketed sickles to harvest their wheat and barley. They produced a variety of new bronze tools—chisels, hammers, and saws. They buried their dead in cemeteries or urnfields, using distinctive globular, barrel- or bucket-shaped pots. They invented a new ax-form with a socket to hold the haft, and they manufactured these implements in larger numbers than ever before. Finally, they gave proof of their warlike proclivities by developing the slashing sword in place of the pointed rapier.

It should not be assumed, however, that warfare was the chief occupation of Bronze Age peoples. Subsistence agriculture was obviously the chief concern of the vast majority of the population, especially after the decline of the Wessex culture when maritime trade seems to have gone into eclipse. Agriculture, of course, implies permanent settlements. Traces of such communities can be found in various parts of southern England. Of these the most noteworthy is **Grimspound** *(587)* near Moretonhampstead, Devon, on the edge of that bleak and forbidding wasteland called Dartmoor. Only the foundations remain, but they reveal a village of twenty-four huts spread over an area of about four acres surrounded by a wall nine feet in thickness and originally about six feet high. The huts are fifteen feet in diameter, each containing a hearth or cooking hole. Some show evidence of having had raised platforms or benches which presumably acted as beds. Cattle pens were built against the inside of the enclosing wall. The village dates from around 1000 to 800 B.C., and was a pastoral community that lived by farming and grazing.

BURIAL SITES

Grimspound is a rarity, however, and one of the frustrations that students of prehistory must face is that inevitably less can be discovered about how these ancient peoples lived than about how they disposed of their dead. As already indicated, one of the striking differences between Neolithic and Bronze Age cultures is in their respective burial rites. In the New Stone Age the dead were buried in collective graves. With the arrival of the Beaker Folk began a new custom of interment in single graves under circular mounds or *round barrows*. This tradition was to last until late in the Bronze Age when it began to give way to the concentration of individual graves leveled flat to the ground in cemeteries or urnfields. For most of the period under consideration, however, the round barrow was the typical form of grave site, and today they constitute the Bronze Age's most noticeable legacy to the British landscape.

Archaeologists have classified the round barrows of southern Britain as bowl, bell, disc, saucer, and pond barrows, according to their present appearance. The first is by far the most numerous and derives its name from the fact that it resembles an inverted bowl. The second is so called because of its bell-like profile which was achieved by leaving a berm or ledge between the foot of the mound and the edge of its surrounding ditch. Disc barrows are flat with only a slight protrusion in the center; saucer barrows look like very low bowl barrows; and in pond barrows the earth is depressed inside a surrounding ditch.

All together there are between thirty thousand and forty thousand surviving round barrows in England and Wales. In all truth, however, they are for the most part no more interesting to look at than the turf-covered golf bunkers which they most closely resemble. It should be sufficient, even for the most ardent sightseer, to restrict his inspection of these Bronze Age relics to a single geographic area.

The best known concentration of round barrows is in Wiltshire, in the neighborhood of Stonehenge. The **Cursus Round Barrows** *(571)* lie about a half mile northwest of that famous monument; the group consists of seven barrows along an east-west axis, some of them measuring more than 150 feet in diameter. About a mile south of Stonehenge, running along the south side of the A 303 is the **Normanton Down Cemetery** *(570)*, consisting of about thirty-five round barrows, including Bush Barrow which once housed the corpse of a powerful Wessex chieftain wearing a magnificent chestpiece of sheet gold now in the British Museum. This is a bowl barrow, and the group includes several others of this type, as well as a number of bell barrows and disc barrows. Still further west, and just north of the juncture of the A 303 with the A 360, lies the **Winterbourne Stoke Round Barrow Group** *(571)*. Here are bell barrows, disc barrows, saucer barrows, and pond barrows, as well as the more common type of bowl barrows. About one and a half miles southwest of Stonehenge is a very compact group called the **Lake Round Barrows** *(570)* consisting of five bell barrows, three disc barrows, and about a dozen bowl barrows.

ARTIFACTS AND MUSEUMS

It is not graves, however, but grave goods that reveal most of what is known about life in Bronze Age Britain three thousand years ago and more. For the past two centuries at least, British parsons, landed gentry, university dons, and professional archaeologists have been rifling the tombs of their remote ancestors to fill the museums of England and Wales with a plethora of Bronze Age artifacts. For the interested traveller there is an embarrassment of riches indeed. Any of the following institutions can be visited with the assurance of plentiful offerings of the material relics of the Bronze Age as well as of the succeeding period of prehistory called the Iron Age:

London: **British Museum** *(516)*, **Museum of London** *(512)*
Dorchester, Dorset: **Dorset County Museum** *(567)*
Salisbury, Wiltshire: **Salisbury and South Wiltshire Museum** *(574)*
Avebury, Wiltshire: **Alexander Keiller Museum** *(573)*
Devizes, Wiltshire: **Devizes Museum** *(572)*
Taunton, Somerset: **Somerset County Museum** *(584)*
Bristol, Avon: **City Museum and Art Gallery** *(580)*
Exeter, Devon: **Rougement House Museum** *(587)*
Truro, Cornwall: **County Museum and Art Gallery** *(597)*
Bury St. Edmunds, Suffolk: **Moyse's Hall Museum** *(601)*
Norwich, Norfolk: **Norwich Castle Museum** *(608)*
Cambridge, Cambridgeshire: **University Museum of Archaeology and Anthropology** *(616)*
Oxford, Oxfordshire: **Ashmolean Museum of Art and Archaeology** *(628)*, **Pitt Rivers Museum** *(633)*
Cheltenham, Gloucestershire: **Art Gallery and Museum** *(639)*
Gloucester, Gloucestershire: **City Museum and Art Gallery,** *(640)*
Lincoln, Lincolnshire: **Lincoln City and County Museum** *(651)*
Leicester, Leicestershire: **Jewry Wall Museum** *(658)*
Sheffield, South Yorkshire: **Sheffield City Museum** *(679)*
Newcastle-upon-Tyne, Tyne and Wear: **University Museum of Antiquities** *(701)*
Cardiff, South Glamorgan: **National Museum of Wales** *(717)*
Douglas, Isle of Man: **Manx Museum** *(741)*
Jersey, Channel Islands: **Jersey (La Hogue Bie) Museum** *(744)*
Guernsey, Channel Islands: **Guernsey Museum and Art Gallery** *(745)*, St. Peter Port

The problem with all museums, of course, is that they tend to be overstuffed. This applies especially to archaeological exhibits, and though the trend in modern museumship is toward more rigorous selectivity in the items chosen for display, the museum goer is still likely to suffer from an excess of observable artifacts. To guide the intelligent traveller through the inevitable maze of showcases, the following information may be helpful:

BRONZE AGE AXES

All improvements in ax design were intended to secure the ax head more firmly to the haft or ax handle. All Bronze Age axes were hafted in carved L-shaped pieces of wood, the short arm at first being split to hold the ax head which was then bound by rope or leather thongs. Beaker ax heads were flat and trapeze-shaped with slightly curved and splayed-out cutting edges. The first significant improvement of the Early Bronze Age was the shaping of a slight stop ridge across the middle of the ax to prevent the haft from being split by the backward pressure of the ax head. Also flanges were hammered up along the side of the ax to prevent lateral slippage. Wessex culture axes had exaggerated curves to the cutting edges and the high flanges were cast, not hammered up. In the Middle Bronze Age came the palstave which was a variation on the flanged axe, produced by fusing the stop ridge with the flanges to form a pocket on each face into which the split end of the haft could be snugly fitted. Finally in the Late Bronze Age, the socketed ax became the standard type. With this development the unsplit haft could be fit into a hole cast in the butt of the ax head. It will be noted that as time passed, the ax head tended to become smaller—almost tack-hammer size. This has led some archaeologists to speculate that the Late Bronze Age axes, and perhaps even those of an earlier date, were manufactured not so much for utilitarian as for ceremonial purposes or perhaps even to serve as a primitive form of currency.

POTTERY

Considering its frangibility, it is remarkable that so much Bronze Age pottery has survived intact, and all of the museums mentioned above, as well as many others, are endowed with an abundance of beakers, funerary urns, and food vessels. It must be admitted, however, that no pre-Roman British pottery is especially attractive to the eye. Lovers of fine ceramics will be disappointed. As indicated above, the Bronze Age starts with beakers—flat bottomed, wide mouthed, S-shaped more or less in the manner of inverted bells, rust colored, and usually incised with geometric designs or horizontal lines imprinted with cords. Next come the food vessels of the north—thick, coarse, gritted, somewhat conical in shape, crudely patterned—and the Wessex urns—sometimes conical or biconical, also coarse and lacking the refinement one would have expected of this otherwise aesthetically advanced culture. Finally come the great urns of the Middle and Late Bronze Age—tall vessels with overhanging rims or collars—followed by a variety of pots shaped like buckets, barrels, or spheres. Of all this collection the most interesting are probably the tiny "pygmy" vessels frequently found in Wessex barrows —Aldbourne or Grape cups whose exact function is unknown but was presumably sacramental in character.

JEWELRY

A wide variety of personal ornaments grace the museum cases of Britain, many of them a pleasure to look at. From the Beaker Folk and their immediate successors comes a scattering of copper and bronze pins and plain and ribbed bracelets. Gold comes on the scene in the Wessex culture in the form of decorated plaques of sheet gold, belt hooks, gold-covered conical buttons, and circular pendants of amber mounted in gold. In the north, and on the edge of the Wessex culture in Cornwall, crescent-shaped gold *lunulae* were imported from Ireland. Beads of shale, bone, and Baltic amber survive in fair abundance. So do crutch- and circle-headed pins of bronze, obviously used as clothing fasteners. From the Middle and Late Bronze Age come gold torques, necklaces, and bracelets made of twisted bands of brass or gold.

WEAPONS

One indication of the martial character of the Beaker Folk is the number of copper and bronze daggers they left behind. These are of two types: (a) tongue-shaped blades with ground edges and projecting tangs for attachment to hilts which were presumably of hollow bone or split wood, and (b) triangular blades attached to wooden hilts with rivets. The Wessex culture produced tanged and socketed spearheads as well as halberds, i.e., daggers mounted sideways on long shafts. The principal innovations of the Middle Bronze Age were improved spears and rapiers. The latter were simply elongated daggers used for thrusting only. Spearheads were normally leaf-shaped and socketed, with loops cast on either side of the socket to secure the bronze head to its wooden shaft. The Late Bronze Age brought the swords with heavy leaf-shaped blades designed for slashing as well as thrusting and a variety of other weapons—dirks, rapiers, and spearheads with pegs instead of loops for securing to the shafts—and round brass shields. It is well to remember that these are *Bronze Age* weapons (though they were presumably also employed in hunting). The Age of Iron was not the first to develop the military arts.

TOOLS AND OTHER UTILITARIAN ARTIFACTS

Other than axes, the chief tools to survive are knobbed sickles from the Middle Bronze Age and, from the Late Bronze Age, socketed sickles, knives of great variety, awls, chisels, and gouges, some tanged and some socketed. An interesting curiosity is the bronze razor, rectangular in shape and tanged. Finally, a fair number of horse fittings have survived —harness rings and tiny bugle-shaped objects thought to have been harness fittings. Curiously, no bronze plowshares are known to have been discovered, though geologists have found plenty of plow marks dating from the period. Undoubtedly the implement employed was the *ard*— a simple wooden plowshare, whose point might or might not have been tipped with metal. This implement could do little more than pierce the surface of the soil; it would not turn the sod—a deficiency which probably required cross-plowing.

HENGES, STONE CIRCLES, AND STANDING STONES

From the viewpoint of the traveller in Britain, certainly the greatest contribution of the Beaker Folk and their successors of the Bronze Age was their construction of stone circles and other arrangements of standing stones. There are over seven hundred of these, large and small, scattered through England and Wales. They fall into three main categories: First are the henges, which are circles or near circles of large stones, enclosed by an earthwork bank and ditch, usually, but not always, with the bank outside the ditch. Most henges have either a single entrance through the bank and across the ditch or two diametrically opposed entrances. At none but Stonehenge do the standing stones support lintels or "hanging stones," which is the literal translation of the Anglo-Saxon word *henge*. In the second category are circles of freestanding or recumbent stones without any enclosing earthworks. Not included are those circles of contiguous small stones which are simply the surviving curbstones that once shored up the bases of round barrows. Third are single freestanding stones, also called menhirs, and alignments of two or more of such stones.

What purpose did these stoneworks serve? As we shall see in dealing specifically with Stonehenge, this question has been the source of unending dispute. The consensus among the majority of modern archaeologists and prehistorians seems to be that most, if not all, of these monuments were open-air temples dedicated to the worship of primitive sky gods, especially the sun and the moon. In recent years a number of astronomers, mathematicians, and engineers, who can be loosely termed "astro-archaeologists" have developed the interesting hypothesis that the primary purpose of these circles and alignments was to enable a Bronze Age caste of astronomer-priests to plot the movements of the planets across the sky, anticipate planetary risings and settings, predict eclipses, and promulgate calendars. Although the case for this proposition has been ingeniously and fervently argued, the verdict, at least for the present, must be: Not Proven. This is not to say, however, that these stone circles served no astronomical function. It is quite clear that the arrangement of stones in many, if not most, of them was oriented to the seasonal movements of the sun and moon, and perhaps to those of other stars and planets. What seems most likely is that powerful magical properties were attributed to these heavenly bodies and that the architecture of the sanctuaries where they were worshiped was designed with reference to the points on the earth's horizon where they predictably appeared and disappeared. All this, however, is guesswork. In the end, one is driven to agree with the verdict of the diarist Samuel Pepys, who wrote three hundred years ago of the megaliths of Stonehenge: "God knows what their use was!" The mystery remains.

Many of these monuments are today so depleted as to be of little interest to any save professional archaeologists. But there are still a fair number that are complete enough and stand high enough above ground to merit inspection by the interested layman. Noteworthy among these are the following:

ENGLAND

Moving from east to west across the southern tier of English counties, the first of the henges the traveller comes across is also the greatest. This, of course, is **Stonehenge** *(570)*, just west of Amesbury in Wiltshire.

Mention has already been made of the fact that late Neolithic people around the year 2,200 B.C. dug the original ditch and the embankment inside it. Inside the 320-foot-wide circle thus created, they also dug a ring of fifty-six holes known as the Aubrey Holes, and just outside the causewayed entrance on the northeast they placed the Heel Stone, a natural sarsen stone some fifteen feet high. This was Phase I of Stonehenge.

About five hundred or six hundred years later (ca. 1700–1600 B.C.) came Phase II: the erection by Beaker Folk of a double circle of eighty bluestones in the center of the circle. These were undressed stones weighing up to four tons apiece, and they could only have come from the Preseli Mountains in Dyfed, Wales, 140 miles from Stonehenge as the crow flies and 240 miles by the shortest water and land routes over which they must have been hauled. This phase of the building was never completed and the double circle was dismantled.

Thereafter, in three stages over a period of about three hundred years, Bronze Age people of the Wessex culture completed the final building of the monument whose ruins are to be seen today. This involved dragging eighty blocks of sarsen stone, weighing between twenty and thirty tons each, from the Marlborough Downs near Avebury more than twenty miles away, dressing them into rectangular shape, raising them into upright position, and then capping them with enormous lintels which were fitted to the uprights by mortise and tenon joints. Without benefit of pulley or block and tackle or any known mechanical devices other than logs used as rollers and levers, this massive engineering feat boggles the mind.

When completed, looking outward from the center, Stonehenge consisted of a large sandstone monolith (now inappropriately called the Altar Stone) inside a horseshoe-shaped line of nineteen slender bluestones (up to eight feet in height) inside another horseshoe of five enormous trilithons (pairs of uprights each capped with a lintel), the tallest being seventeen feet, inside a circle of sixty shorter and stubbier bluestones inside another circle of thirty dressed sarsen stones rising about thirteen feet above ground, this entire outer circle capped with lintels forming a sort of circular colonnade roughly one hundred feet in diameter. To the northeast of the circle, lying 256 feet from its center, was the so-called Heel Stone which had also been part of the Neolithic henge monument.

To be able to visualize the monument as it stood originally, stark and majestic on the Salisbury Plain, the intelligent traveller would be well advised to visit first the **Salisbury and South Wiltshire Museum** *(574)* in Salisbury, Wiltshire, and examine there the models of Stonehenge in all its phases of construction. Otherwise the site itself is likely to appear to be an incoherent litter of massive rocks. For, of the outer sarsen circle of thirty standing stones, six are missing, seven are fallen, and most of the lintels are gone; only ten stones of the bluestone circle remain in place; three of the five trilithons are intact; and only eight of the nineteen bluestones in the inner horseshoe remain standing. Along with the distractions of the adjacent parking lot and souvenir stand, to say nothing of the mobs of tourists during the summer, Stonehenge's ruined state can prove disappointing unless the traveller is prepared to recreate its original glory, at least in his mind's eye.

Why was Stonehenge built, by whom, and what was it used for? Dispute over these questions has raged for more than three hundred years. It will be sufficient here to list the many hypotheses advanced and to comment briefly on each.

1. At the behest of King Arthur's father Uther Pendragon, Merlin, the legendary magician, transported the stones from Ireland to the Salisbury Plain where they were raised as a tomb to a host of British nobles murdered there by the Saxon chief Hengist. Merlin was a powerful magician and might have pulled it off, but the dates are wrong. Stonehenge was completed about eighteen centuries before the dates ascribed to Uther Pendragon.

2. Stonehenge was a Roman temple of the Tuscan order dedicated to the sky god Coelus. This was the theory advanced by Inigo Jones, the great architect of the seventeenth-century classical revival. Again the dates are wrong.

3. Stonehenge was erected as a royal court for the Danish kings who ruled in England in the ninth century A.D. Once more there is the matter of dates.

4. Stonehenge was a temple erected by the Druids, the priestly caste of the Celtic tribes who overran Britain in the fourth century B.C. There they engaged in gruesome heathen rites involving, among other things, human sacrifice on the Altar Stone in the center of the monument. This hypothesis was first given general circulation in the seventeenth century by the antiquaries John Aubrey and William Stukely; was perpetuated in the eighteenth century by John Wood, the architect of Bath; and popularized by the romantic English poets of the nineteenth century. It is still widely believed and, of course, is utterly false. At least a thousand years elapsed between the final building of Stonehenge and the arrival in Britain of the Celts and their Druidical religion.

5. Stonehenge was a scientifically designed observatory and astronomical computer used primarily in the preparation of solar and lunar calendars by Bronze Age astronomer-priests. The builders of the final phase of the monument placed their circles and horseshoes in such a way that,

by looking outward from the center through one of the five central trilithons, an observer could clearly see, through arches of the outer circle, eight distinct risings and settings of the sun and moon (i.e., midsummer sunrise, moonrise, sunset, and moonset; midwinter sunrise, moonrise, sunset, and moonset). The function of the Aubrey Holes was to serve as a calculator for the prediction of eclipses of both sun and moon.

The originator of this hypothesis is a Scottish engineer named Alexander Thom, and it has been further refined and popularized by Professor Gerald Hawkins of Boston University. Most archaeologists and prehistorians, however, remain doubtful of its validity. While acknowledging that the trilithons, outer circle, Heel Stone, and Altar Stone were obviously aligned with points on the horizon where the sun and moon appeared and disappeared at different times of the year, they question whether the precise astronomical measurements postulated by Hawkins and likeminded scientists would have been possible. For one thing the absence of any known science of numbers during the second millennium B.C. renders such mathematical accuracy unlikely. For another, the archways of the outer circle when viewed through the trilithons, enclose too wide an arc of skyline to permit a precise line of sight on any single point on the horizon. Astronomical measurements require much greater precision than this. Whatever it was, Stonehenge was hardly a Bronze Age version of the Mount Wilson Observatory.

6. Stonehenge was (and is) a cosmic power center. From Stonehenge as a center radiated a number of "ley lines" along which were raised all manner of ancient holy monuments. The whole arrangement made up a sort of grid—a cosmic system whereby the energies of the sun were fused with those of the earth into a powerful life force. Supporters of this thesis go so far as to claim that the leys were (and are) used as navigational aids to extraterrestrial visitors cruising the skies in flying saucers or other unidentified flying objects. Anyone who can swallow this one ought not to choke on Merlin; *his* claim at least enjoys the stamp of antiquity.

7. Stonehenge was a Bronze Age temple to the gods of the sky, particularly the sun and moon. This hypothesis seems to enjoy the endorsement of most responsible prehistorians and, to the layman, appears to be the most plausible. There is little doubt of course that the stones were deliberately arranged in alignment with calculated risings and settings of the sun and moon at different times throughout the year. Looking outward from the center the sun can still be seen to rise almost over the top of the Heel Stone on midsummer day, and, looking in the opposite direction on the shortest day of winter it sets between the gap in the largest trilithon. But the purpose of the arrangement was, in all likelihood, religious and not scientific. It takes no great act of imagination to sense the awe that must have been inspired by sacred ceremonies held under the open sky and orchestrated to the visible appearance

and disappearance of the very gods who were being worshiped. What better way could these ancient priests have found to minister to the elemental spiritual needs of their congregations than to harness the very heavens to their sacramental rites?

One final question concerning Stonehenge remains: How could any group of Bronze Age primitives have acquired sufficient knowledge of geometry, or achieved the engineering and organizational sophistication necessary, to complete such a mammoth and complex structure as this? One answer is that, in its final form, Stonehenge was constructed under the leadership of Middle Bronze Age Wessex warrior-merchants who had frequent contacts with Mycenae, the great mercantile center of the eastern Aegean in the mid–second millennium B.C. Through these contacts, it is argued, they could have imported such highly skilled technicians as were responsible for the Lion Gate at Mycenae. The architectural similarities between this well-known engineering wonder and the outer circle at Stonehenge lend some credence to this hypothesis. So too does the imprint of a Mycenaean-type dagger carved into one of the sarsen stones at Stonehenge. Finally, the discovery in a number of contemporary graves in the surrounding Salisbury Plain of eastern Aegean jewelry and metalwork seems to testify to strong Mycenaean influences on Wessex culture in general. Though highly circumstantial, all this evidence together lends weight to the argument that Stonehenge was but a distant echo of that great civilization of ancient Greece which brought about the fall of Troy and supplied the raw material out of which the poet Homer was to fashion his great epics. Nativist Britons, however, loath to admit that one of their greatest monuments might have been the handiwork of foreigners, remain skeptical.

Less than twenty miles north of Stonehenge lies the second greatest henge monument in Britain—and some would say the first. This is **Avebury** (573), probably built by Beaker Folk in the early part of the second millennium B.C. It is the largest of its kind in Europe, covering more than twenty-eight acres and enclosing most of the present village which has given the site its name. Its outer circle consists of the usual ditch and outer bank, pierced here by four entrances where modern roads now run and measuring about fifteen hundred feet in diameter. Immediately inside the ditch were one hundred undressed standing sarsen stones weighing up to forty tons, of which less than thirty still survive. Inside this outer circle were two others each measuring about 330 feet across. These consisted of twenty-seven and twenty-nine standing stones respectively, of which only four remain in what is called the Central Circle, and five in the South Circle. Inside another possible circle to the north, two stones remain of a U-shaped "cove." Leading south from Avebury for about a half mile are two parallel lines of sarsen stones, known as West Kennet (or just Kennet) Avenue which was originally three miles in length, terminating in a now destroyed double circle of standing stones located on Overton Hill, five miles west of Marlborough, Wiltshire, and called the Sanctuary. Avebury should not be missed. It was probably as important a sacred site as Stonehenge and is today much less infested with tourists than the latter. At no other prehistoric site in Britain is the awesome sense of mystery so pervasive as among these towering megaliths.

A few miles south of Bristol, Avon, lies **Stanton Drew** *(587)*, a sacred site built by Beaker Folk, consisting today of the remains of three stone circles, adjoining avenues, and a U-shaped "cove." The largest of the circles had thirty stones, of which twenty-seven are still visible, and three are standing. To the northeast is another of eight stones, half of them still standing. To the southwest lies the third with eleven recumbent stones still visible. Two upright stones and one fallen, lying behind the Druid's Arms Inn, represent what remains of the cove. Two avenues leading to the River Chew can be discerned, one with eight, the other with seven stones still standing. All these lie within an untended cow pasture—which somewhat diminishes their grandeur, though the cattle are admittedly less distracting than tourists, who seldom come here.

Cornwall is rich in stone circles, most of them remotely situated and difficult for today's motorist to reach. North of Liskeard just northeast of the village of Minions lies the **Hurlers** *(593)*, a monument consisting of three circles in a line, the northernmost with thirteen surviving stones, the center one with seventeen, and the southernmost with nine. The name derives from a local myth that these were impious men turned into stone for "hurling the ball" on the Sabbath day. In the peninsula of Land's End the diligent traveller in search of stone circles will be well rewarded, provided he has a good map and stout shoes. Southwest of Penzance lies the **Merry Maidens** *(594)*. This is a circle of nineteen standing stones with a pair of stones called the Pipers about a quarter mile to the northeast and a single megalith known as the Fiddler to the west. Like the Hurlers, the whole ensemble was turned into stone for breaking the Sabbath, in this case dancing to music. West of Penzance is the stone circle known as **Boscawen-un** *(594)*, which is really an elipse of nineteen standing stones with a single inclined stone in the center. Farther north, in the hills lying between St. Just and St. Ives, and very hard to reach, is the **Nine Maidens** *(596)*, also known as Boskednan, with eleven stones left out of an original nineteen, seven still standing and the rest fallen. About five miles to the southwest, just northeast of St. Just, are the **Tregeseal Stone Circles** *(596)*, one with sixteen stones still standing, the other with only two.

In the band of counties from East Anglia west to Hereford and Worcester, stone circles are rare. Oxfordshire has only one: the **Rollright Stones** *(627)* near Chipping Norton. Two separate, but perhaps related, monuments are included under this title. First is the King's Men, an almost complete circle, 105 feet in diameter and now consisting of fifty-three or fifty-four standing stones. Local folklore has it that they cannot be exactly counted. Just across the road, in Warwickshire, lies the second, called the King Stone, a single upright more than eight feet high. A short distance to the east lies the **Whispering Knights** *(627)*, a Neolithic chambered tomb, already described. The pastoral beauty of the surrounding countryside alone would make this once-holy spot well worth a visit.

Proceeding northward, Derbyshire has one of the most interesting and beautifully situated stone circles in England. This is **Arbor Low** *(661)* near Bakewell, sometimes referred to as the Stonehenge of the Midlands. It consists of a circular bank 250 feet in diameter with two entrances surrounding a ditch inside of which lies a circle of fifty recumbent stones surrounding a U-shaped cove of four stones, also recumbent. Presumably all these stones once stood upright. The largest of them measures fourteen feet. The view from here of the Peak District is spectacular. In Salop are two noteworthy circles, both lying about sixteen miles south of Shrewsbury. The southernmost is **Mitchell's Fold** *(671)* with fourteen stones of an original circle 75 feet in diameter, the highest being about six feet. A half mile to the northeast is **Hemford Stone Circle** *(671)* with thirty-seven surviving stones, the tallest only about two and a half feet in height. Both sites recommend themselves chiefly by their magnificent views westward toward the Welsh mountains.

North of the Humber in Old Yorkshire, we find two of England's most interesting menhirs. The first is the **Rudstone** *(677)*, standing in the village churchyard of Rudston, west of Bridlington, Humberside. This is the largest monolith in Britain, measuring more than twenty-five feet in height. The stone was quarried over ten miles away. Its probable date of construction is Bronze Age, and its incorporation into the grounds of a Christian church was in keeping with instructions handed down by Pope Gregory in the early seventh century that pagan temples should not be destroyed but rather aspersed with holy water and converted into Christian monuments. Near Boroughbridge, northeast of Harrogate, North Yorkshire, sits an alignment of three natural stones, measuring from eighteen to twenty-two feet in height and 200 and 370 feet apart. They are called the **Devil's Arrows** *(683)* and were quarried at Knaresborough over six miles away and must have been dragged to their present site.

Finally, Cumbria contains two of England's best preserved Bronze Age stone circles. The first is called **Long Meg and Her Daughters** *(713)* and is located northeast of Penrith. A flattened circle, considered next in importance to Stonehenge, Avebury, and Stanton Drew, it measures 360 feet on its long axis and originally had sixty-five stones, of which twenty-seven are still standing. There are three outlying stones, the tallest of which (Long Meg) measures twelve feet and bears small "cup and ring" markings, a form of Bronze Age artwork found chiefly in northern England and Scotland. Near Keswick stands another flattened circle called the **Carles, Castlerigg** *(712)* with thirty-eight stones and an interior rectangular setting of ten. Only a mile away is Derwent Water on the eastern edge of the Lake District and, as one would expect in this scenic wonderland, the view from the site is magnificent.

WALES

Wales has a large number of Bronze Age stone circles tucked away in its mountain fastnesses, but most of them are badly depleted and almost all are hard to reach. Two of the best, lying in the vicinity of Trecastle west of Brecon, Powys, are **Nant Tarw** *(721)*, consisting of two small circles, each about sixty feet in diameter with fifteen stones surviving out of the original twenty, and **Mynydd-Bach Trecastell Circles** (721), another double circle with twenty surviving stones, none higher than two feet. Nearby, on the west bank of the Tawe near its source, is another circle of stubby stones, twenty in all, called **Cerrig Duon** *(721)*. In North Wales, near Penmaenmawr, Gwynedd, is one of the more impressive of Welsh Bronze Age monuments, called **Druid's Circle** *(740)*, consisting of ten stones up to six feet high inside a low circular bank about seventy-five feet in diameter.

CHANNEL ISLANDS

The island of Guernsey boasts the two most interesting menhirs in Britain. The first is called **La Gran'mere du Chimiquiere** *(746)*, and it forms today one of the gateposts to the churchyard of St. Martin's Church south of St. Peter Port. This is a single standing stone of about five and a half feet in height, whose upper portion is carved to represent a human head and shoulders, probably that of a female wearing a headdress from under which protrudes a row of curls. The second is **Catel Menhir** *(745)* in the churchyard of Catel Parish Church west of St. Peter Port. Formerly buried under the chancel, this six-and-a-half foot standing stone is faintly carved on one side in the representation of the head, shoulders, and breasts of a woman. Both menhirs were probably fertility figures, probably, but not certainly, attributable to the Bronze Age.

THE BRITISH BRONZE AGE IN PERSPECTIVE

In Britain the Bronze Age lasted for roughly thirteen centuries (2000–700 B.C.). It was a period of great cultural and technological advancement as witnessed by Stonehenge III and the grave goods of the Wessex chieftains. Yet Britain was a backwater—at best a mere outpost on the farthest edges of the world. It was known vaguely if at all from the reports of a few adventurous travellers from lands far to the east where infinitely richer and more cultivated civilizations rose and fell and rose again.

In Mesopotamia the Amorites came to power near the beginning of the second millennium B.C., and founded their great capital at Babylon, only to be destroyed by the Assyrians who transferred the seat of their empire to Ninevah, which was in turn destroyed in 612 B.C. In Palestine toward the end of the second millennium B.C., the Hebrews, led by Moses, escaped from Egypt into Sinai and finally toward the Dead Sea and the Jordan River. There, about 1025 B.C., Saul established an independent kingdom to which David and then Solomon succeeded. In Egypt the pharaohs of the New Kingdom reigned in glory. Among them was Amenhotep III (1417–1379 B.C.) who built the great temple gateway at Karnak, near Thebes. Another was Tutankhamen (ca. 1361–1352 B.C.) whose tomb, discovered in 1922, was to reveal so much of the magnificent splendor of the Eighteenth Dynasty. In the Mediterranean soon after 2000 B.C., the first wave of Greek-speaking immigrants from the north, called Minyans, swept over the mainland of Greece. Contemporary with this development was the rapid rise of a non-Greek civilization on Crete which is called Minoan from the name of its legendary ruler Minos. From their splendid palace at Cnossos the Cretans developed an extensive commerce throughout the Mediterranean. They too were overrun, and Cnossos was burned around 1450 B.C. probably by warriors from Mycenae, a fortress city on mainland Greece. It was these pirates turned traders who penetrated as far west as Britain and exchanged objects of gold and amber with the chieftains of the Wessex culture. It was the Mycenaeans too, along with their Achaean Greek allies, who about 1200 B.C. sacked the Anatolian city of Troy in a trade war which Homer would later celebrate in the greatest heroic epic poem of all time. Soon the Achaeans too would give way under the pressure of still another invasion from the north, this time by a Greek-speaking people called Dorians.

It was the Dorians who probably first brought iron to Europe. The secret of forging implements out of this metal had been known to the Hittites at least two hundred years before. In prehistoric times there was no known process for heating iron to a high enough temperature for casting, as in the case of copper and bronze. Objects of wrought iron were manufactured, first by reducing the ore in a smelting furnace, then picking out pieces of metal from the slag, then reheating and fusing it into a solid lump, which in turn was forged by hammering into whatever shape was required. It was a laborious process, unknown to bronzesmiths and therefore an original invention—so original that the Hittites kept it a secret for almost two centuries. But with the fall of the Hittite empire around 1200 B.C., the secret leaked out. The great advantage of iron over copper and bronze was that it was far more plentiful. Iron ore was abundant and widely distributed. Its use for tools and weapons therefore spread fast—from Greece to Italy; then across the Alps to the Urnfield peoples of central Europe, thence to Spain and France; and finally, around 700 B.C., across the Channel to Britain. Here was the beginning of a new, and final, prehistoric age.

THE IRON AGE

In central Europe the earliest phase of Iron Age culture is called Hallstatt after the site in Austria where a significant number of early European wrought iron implements were first found. The Hallstatt phase lasted from the eighth century until about 500 B.C., when it gave way to a somewhat more sophisticated culture called La Tène from the type-site in Switzerland. La Tène culture lasted on the Continent until Julius Caesar's invasion of Gaul in the first century B.C. Wrought iron products of the Hallstatt culture first appeared in Britain around 700 B.C. and about 250 years later immigrants of the La Tène culture began to cross over. Immigration to Britain from the Continent apparently took place not in massive waves, but rather in a steady trickle spread out over several centuries. British archaeologists sometimes divide this period of insular prehistory into Iron Age A and Iron Age B. Although these labels do not exactly correspond to the conventional division into Hallstatt and La Tène cultures, the distinctions are of interest to professional archaeologists only; the ordinary traveller can assume that Hallstatt roughly equals Iron Age A (Early Iron Age) while La Tène equals Iron Age B (Later Iron Age). Still a third period, called Iron Age C, encompasses the Belgic invasions of Britain in the first century B.C. and will be discussed separately below.

Although neither the Hallstatt nor the La Tène cultures left behind any written records (presumably because these people were illiterate), it is safe to assume that both were associated with the Celtic tribes whose homeland was central Europe east of the Rhine and who spread thence westward into Spain, France (Gaul), and eventually Britain, and eastward to Galatia in Asia Minor. The Celts were different from the Late Bronze Age peoples of Europe in a number of ways, such as tribal organization, religion, dress, and military prowess; but their chief distinction was one of language. Theirs was a separate Indo-European tongue which was in turn differentiated into two principal groups, called Q-Celtic and P-Celtic. The former, also referred to by modern linguists as Goidelic, survives in Ireland, the Highlands and Western Isles of Scotland, and on the Isle of Man. The latter, called Brythonic, survives in Brittany and especially in Wales, where Welsh nationalists have assiduously cultivated its revival—to the great confusion of English-speaking travellers.

These are the dialects that the ancient Greeks and Romans designated barbarous. The word was also used to describe the conduct of the Celtic tribes in war, which even by the unsqueamish standards of the ancients was considered excessively ruthless. Classical Greece and Rome had reason to fear these savages. In 390 B.C., having crossed the Alps and plundered northern Italy, they laid waste to Rome itself. In 279 B.C., they sacked the famous sanctuary of Apollo at Delphi. Later, as the Romans commenced their own expansion northward and westward, it was the fierce Celts of Gaul whose defeat and subjugation first opened the gates of power to Julius Caesar. It was of these people that the Roman historian Strabo wrote: "The whole race . . . is madly fond of war, high-spirited and quick to battle . . ."

Tribal warfare was endemic too among the Celts of Britain. No other fact about the Iron Age is better known than this. Today silent testimony to the Celtic obsession with war abounds all over Britain in the form of hill forts, of which there are more than fourteen hundred still in evidence in England and Wales. Though some of these date back to the Late Bronze Age, the great majority fall within the period of Celtic occupation. As has been noted, Celtic immigration did not occur in a single wave, or even in a few massive waves, but rather in small increments stretched out over several centuries of time. But, being Celts, each new group of immigrants was likely to be led by bands of warriors, and against these newcomers, earlier settlers, though Celtic themselves, had to defend themselves. To do so they constructed earthen fortifications, sometimes reinforced by stone and timber, usually more or less circular in shape and enclosing from three to thirty acres (though some few were as large as two hundred acres). The process was repeated again and again, which accounts for the huge number of these defensive enclosures built in a time of comparative light density of population.

Hill forts are classified as either contour or promontory. The former, and by far the more numerous, are situated on hilltops, and their defensive lines more or less follow the contours of the hill. Promontory forts are to be found mostly in southwest England and in Wales where they are situated on coastal peninsulas surrounded on three sides by water or on mountain escarpments where on three sides there is a sheer drop. In either case, nature dictated that only one side of the fort needed manmade protection against an approaching enemy.

Early in the Iron Age the typical hill fort consisted of a single earthen rampart surrounded by a deep ditch out of which the earth for the rampart had been dug. Very soon the practice developed of revetting the outer face of the rampart with stone and timber. In time new ditches were dug and new ramparts thrown up, sometimes revetted on both sides. These are known today as bivallate or multivallate (from the Latin *vallum,* meaning "rampart"). As in later castles and walled towns, the vulnerable point of the fortification was its entrance. Therefore a common practice was to turn the outer ramparts on either side of the entrance inward, thus creating a kind of funnel or horn at the bottom of which gates of massive timber were raised. Another method of protecting the entrance was to build the earthen ramparts so that those on the outside overlapped the entrance gaps of those on the inside, thus creating a kind of maze which would require attacking forces to make one or more 180-degree turns before reaching the main inner gate.

Originally the enclosures served primarily as refuges to which Iron

Age farmers and herdsmen could flee in times of trouble, bringing with them their few possessions, their livestock, and whatever foodstuffs they could carry. In time, permanent settlements might grow up within these protective banks and ditches, and by the time of the Roman invasion it would appear that some of the larger hill forts served as market towns or perhaps even provincial capitals.

How effective they were as citadels must be a matter of conjecture. Certainly the task of an attacking army, equipped only with swords, spears, and perhaps incendiary torches, could not have been easy. The intruders had first to traverse one or more deep ditches, then cross the intervening narrow strip of ground under direct fire from sheer ramparts, and finally storm the gates through an ever-narrowing passageway whose shape hampered maneuver and facilitated the defense. Even the Romans, with their superior discipline and firepower, were hard put to reduce these mighty fortifications. To the less well-armed and less well-ordered Celtic warriors, it must indeed have been a formidable endeavor.

In the intervening twenty centuries, these Iron Age ramparts, once rising perhaps forty feet above the bottom of their adjacent ditches, have mostly collapsed, leaving grass-grown banks seldom even half as high. Most of them are situated in remote areas of the countryside, are badly signposted and hard to find, and are usually to be reached only by arduous climbing up steep and treacherous footpaths. Nevertheless (or perhaps therefore) they are still much favored by ardent hikers, and it must be said that nowhere else will the traveller come upon more breathtaking panoramic views of the British countryside. The following selection of a score of hill forts, out of a possible fourteen hundred, should, however, more than satisfy the requirements of the traveller concerned more with sightseeing than with scenic beauty or physical exercise. They are a representative group and most, as hill forts go, are reasonably accessible.

HILL FORTS

ENGLAND

In West Sussex, north of Worthing, **Cissbury Ring** *(554)* is a univallate hill fort enclosing about sixty acres. It was built on the site of a Neolithic flint-mining community, and there are still a number of observable depressions in the earth where mine shafts were once sunk. The climb from the carpark just south of the village of Findon is long and steep, but the view from the top is sufficiently rewarding. Also in West Sussex is the **Trundle** *(552)* north of Chichester. Here an octagonal single ditch and rampart enclose about twelve acres of a hill fort constructed in the third century B.C. Inside are the less visible remains of a Neolithic causewayed camp which was laid out as early as 3000 B.C.

Dorset boasts the best collection of Iron Age hill forts of any county in England. **Badbury Rings** *(570)* near Wimborne Minster is a conspicuous landmark for miles around by reason of the circular copse of trees that crowns its summit. Here stands a multivallate fort with three ramparts and two ditches and entrances at both east and west ends. **Hod Hill** *(567)* near Blandford Forum is unusual in that its shape is roughly rectangular. Originally built as a strong bivallate fortification enclosing more than fifty acres, it had two inturned entrances. It was probably one of the Celtic forts which the Romans termed *oppida* and which the soon-to-be emperor Vespasian stormed and captured in the early years of the Roman conquest. In the northwest corner of the enclosure are the remains of a Roman fortress built over the Celtic site. A few miles to the north is **Hambledon Hill** *(567)*, a multivallate fort enclosing thirty acres, of which only the southeastern sector survives to any significant height. This and neighboring Hod Hill are good examples of overlapping ramparts where the entrance ways to exterior and interior ramparts are staggered. Easily the most impressive of all Iron Age hill forts in Britain is **Maiden Castle** *(568)* near Dorchester. In the nineteenth century the famous Dorset novelist, Thomas Hardy, likened it to "an enormous many-limbed organism of an antediluvian time . . . lying lifeless, and covered with a thin green cloth, which hides its substance while revealing its contour." Less metaphorically, Maiden Castle is a multivallate fortress enclosing about forty-five acres, first built about 300 B.C. on the site of an earlier Neolithic causewayed camp, then twice enlarged, the last time being around 75 B.C., presumably by Belgic invaders. Even today, with nothing left but turf-covered banks and ditches denuded of all timber or stone reinforcements, the position looks almost impregnable. But it was not. As we shall see in the next chapter, Roman soldiers under Vespasian stormed the fort and overcame it in A.D. 44–45.

Wiltshire, home of so many important prehistoric sites, has two hill forts of note: **Old Sarum** *(575)* and **Figsbury Ring** *(575)*, both near Salisbury. Because of its medieval associations, Old Sarum will be treated in another chapter. Figsbury Ring, nearby, is an area of about fifteen acres enclosed by a bank and two ditches with entrances at both west and east ends. This is a good spot from which to view the city of Salisbury with its splendid cathedral tower.

Cornwall is almost as rich as Wiltshire in visible relics of the Ages of Bronze and Iron. Among its many hill forts is **Carn Brea** *(595)* near Redruth, another Iron Age defensive work built over a Neolithic settlement. The site consists of about thirty-six acres enclosed by a single rampart on the north and a double rampart around the south side of the hill. Both are well preserved. Of particular interest is the western entrance to the inner rampart which is lined with large stone slabs and flanked by guard chambers. Further west is **Chun Castle** *(594)* near St. Just and only a short distance from the above mentioned Neolithic dolmen called Chun Quoit. There is more to see here than at many hill forts because so much of the stonework has survived. The monument consists of two overlapping concentric ramparts of dry stone, the outer one about seven feet in height, the inner somewhat higher. Here it is easy to visualize how offsetting the inner entrance from the outer one would have exposed the right flank and rear of any attackers lucky enough to have breached the outer gate. The site commands a marvelous view of the Cornish coast. Even closer to the coast is **Trevelgue Head** *(593)* near Newquay. A typical promontory fort, it is defended on the landward (eastern) side by three pairs of banks and ditches and on the western seaward side by another triple set of banks and ditches through one of which runs the sea itself.

Returning now to Oxfordshire, near Wantage we come to one of England's most famous hill figures, lying in close proximity to a small Iron Age hill fort with which it was probably associated. **Uffington Castle** *(637)* is an eight-acre fort enclosed by a bank, a ditch, and a counterscarp bank. Just to the northwest, over the brow of the hill, lies the famous **White Horse of Uffington** *(637)*. This is probably the earliest chalk-cut hill figure in Britain and is in all likelihood of Iron Age date. It is the outline figure of a prancing horse, cut through the turf so as to reveal the natural chalk beneath. The horse is 365 feet long from front ear to tail tip and 130 feet high. It is cut at a thirty-degree angle which makes it clearly visible from the road beneath or from neighboring hillsides. Horse figures of this general character were a fairly common Celtic design, and this was probably the tribal emblem of the folk who lived nearby and whose military headquarters was Uffington Castle.

Proceeding west into the Malvern Hills, the county of Hereford and Worcester holds two hill forts of note. The first is **Bredon Hill** *(648)* south of Pershore, a promontory fort covering eleven acres with two lines of ramparts, the outer one of which still stands about eight feet high. Archaeologists have discovered that shortly before the Roman conquest the inner gateway was burned to the ground, carrying with it a number of human skulls which had been fixed there as trophies. At the time of this attack, presumably by Belgic invaders, fifty young warriors were hacked to death defending the gate. When Celt met Celt in combat, the name of the game was slaughter. **Herefordshire Beacon** *(647)* east of Ledbury is a thirty-two-acre hill fort consisting of a bank, ditch, and counterscarp bank pierced by four entranceways of which the westernmost is approachable by footpath. Near the summit of the ridge is an older fortress, dating to the third century B.C., which consists of a single bank and ditch enclosing an area of about eight acres. Inside this enclosure are the remains of a Norman castle motte.

In Salop, a few miles southwest of Telford, are the scanty remains of a hill fort named after the solitary mountain whose summit it crowns— the **Wrekin** *(672)*. Possibly the capital of the Celtic tribe called Cornovii by the Romans, it was built about 200 B.C. and the ramparts, now all but gone, enclosed about ten acres. The two entranceways are known locally as Hellgate and Heavengate. The path to the top is about a mile in length and very steep, but the view from the summit takes in at least four English counties and two in Wales. Another Shropshire (Salop) hill fort is **Old Oswestry** *(670)*, just north of the town of Oswestry. The fort went through many rebuildings and the present remains consist of three ramparts with accompanying ditches, earthen outworks, and a long bank marking the passage into the interior.

WALES

Due south of Old Oswestry, across the border in Wales, lies **Breiddin Hill** *(723)*, northeast of Welshpool, Powys. Touching Offa's Dyke (below), the fort sits on a hill over one thousand feet high and boasts a double line of ramparts with a funneled entrance on the southeastern side. Sheer cliffs protect it on the north and west, making this an especially formidable promontory fort of the inland variety. In North Wales, nearly two thousand feet above sea level and overlooking Caernarvon Bay north of Pwllheli, Gwynedd, sits **Tre'r Ceiri** *(744)*, "the town of the giants," an Iron Age hill fort whose enclosing wall still stands to a height of thirteen feet in places. Inside are the foundations of 150 contemporary round huts. This is a site for mountain climbers only. More accessible to motorists is **Caer y Twr** *(733)* on the Holy Island off Anglesey just west of Holyhead, Gwynedd. Here a dry stone wall, still close to nine feet high in places, ran across the northeastern approaches to the enclosure while the sheer cliffs on the south and west made further man-made defenses unnecessary.

IRON AGE SETTLEMENTS

A short distance south of Caer y Twr lie the remains of a group of about twenty Iron Age huts in a settlement called **Ty Mawr** *(734)*, known locally as Cytiau Gwyddelod (huts of the Irishmen) in the mistaken belief that they belonged to Goidelic-speaking Irish occupants driven out by Brythonic-speaking Celts in the fifth century A.D. The survival of this agricultural village within the shadow of a hill fort is a useful reminder that Iron Age Britons did not spend all their time waging war. They were, like their forebears and descendants unto many generations, primarily farmers and herdsmen with a side interest in fishing and hunting. Unfortunately for the archaeologist, most of their domestic dwellings were built of wood, or perhaps of clay and wattle, and have long since been victims of weather and decay. But here and there in Britain, as already indicated, they built of stone. One such Iron Age settlement is **Chysauster** *(595)* south of St. Ives, Cornwall. This well-excavated site contains the foundations of four pairs of circular houses with inner courtyards set on opposite sides of a street. Not far away are the ruins of a *fougou,* a prehistoric underground chamber peculiar to Cornwall whose original function has never been positively determined. Another famous Cornish *fougou* is in the center of **Carn Euny** *(594),* an Iron Age village southwest of Penzance. Here the stone huts form a series of interlocking circles around the *fougou,* each sharing a wall with its neighbor. As in the case of Chysauster, the site is under the care of the Department of the Environment and is therefore well preserved and well maintained.

Most famous of all Iron Age village sites are the Lake Villages of Meare and Glastonbury in Somerset. Glastonbury, the better known of the two, was a late Iron Age village constructed on top of an artificial island built in a pond or merely created by overflow from the River Brue. The island, measuring more than ten thousand square yards, was constructed of brushwood, stone, and tree trunks topped with wooden platforms and surrounded by a stockade. Inside stood some sixty round huts with wattled sides, clay floors, and thatched roofs. Outside was a boat landing-stage, made of clay held in place by oak planks and topped with stone.

Nothing remains to be seen of either Glastonbury or Meare. But archaeologists have done their work well, and the numerous finds from both sites now on display at the **Somerset County Museum** *(584)* in Taunton and the **Glastonbury Tribunal** *(583),* Glastonbury, Somerset will provide the traveller with a fairly complete picture of domestic life in an Iron Age village. Literally hundreds of objects of iron, bronze, tin, lead, bone, antler, flint, clay, glass, amber, jet, and wood have been dug up out of the peat overlying the Lake Villages. From this feast of artifacts the following are worth special attention: (a) devices for cloth-making, including needles, spindle-whorls, and loom weights and long-handled combs for weaving; (b) personal ornaments including beads, bracelets, brooches, and very modern-looking safety pins; (c) kitchen and table ware including a magnificent brass bowl, a wooden tub, a number of ladles, and a great variety of hand-molded pots and other vessels highly decorated in typical La Tène curvilinear style; (d) milling equipment consisting of saddle querns, in which grain was crushed by moving an upper stone back and forth over a lower stone, and rotary mills in which the upper stone was rotated by means of a wooden handle; (e) horse fittings, including harness ornaments, bits, cheek pieces, and a lathe-turned wheel spoke which may have belonged to a horsecart; (f) miscellaneous tools of bronze and iron, including saws, gouges, adzes, files, sickles, and pruning hooks; (g) iron currency bars, which look like swords but were in fact used as media of exchange; and (h) a far fewer number of iron weapons, including only three spearheads and a single dagger.

IRON AGE ART AND ARTIFACTS

If all these domestic artifacts on display at Glastonbury and Taunton are poignant reminders of the lives of ordinary Iron Age folk, not so most of the contemporary objects housed in other museums of England and Wales, including those listed in the early part of this chapter. There the Iron Age finds come mostly from hill forts or from inhumation burials of great warrior chieftains accompanied by their military accouterments and personal finery. Long iron swords and bronze scabbards, daggers with anthropoid hilts, decorated shields, elaborate horse trappings, and the metal parts of chariots, along with giant fire dogs, great cauldrons, bronze tankards, and lengths of shackled slave chains—all bespeak a warrior aristocracy much given to fierce fighting and high living.

Horse fittings, as well as much of the military equipment and personal ornamentation carried and worn by these warriors and their ladies was of intricately ornamented bronze. Indeed, La Tène culture is known mostly for its highly original art work, essentially curvilinear in style. Probably derived from such classical forms as the tendril and palmette, it departed from the strict representational models of the Greeks and Romans and developed a highly abstract art form typified by asymmetrical yet balanced curving patterns, interlocking scrolls, and flamboyant *triskeles* and *roundels.* Samples of this lovely artistry abound, but the best are three bronze mirror backs: the Birdlip Mirror in the **Gloucester City Museum and Art Gallery** *(640)*; the mirror in the Joseph Mayer collection in the **Merseyside County Museum** *(695)*, Liverpool; and especially the Desborough mirror in the **British Museum** *(516)*.

Also in the British Museum are four of the most elaborate of all relics of Celtic art and craftmanship: the double-horned bronze Waterloo helmet; the oval-shaped embossed bronze Battersea shield with champlevé studs of red glass enamel; the Aylesford bucket, a wooden stave-built vessel bound together with bronze bands of beautiful anthropoid design; and the Snettisham torque, made from eight strands of gold wire with intricately designed golden globules at either end. These were the products of Belgic invaders, the last of the Celtic immigrants, who brought to Britain a still more advanced culture known to archaeologists as Iron Age C.

THE BELGIC IMMIGRATION

The Belgae came from that part of Gaul lying between the Seine, the Marne, and the Rhine Rivers. Of all the tribes of Gaul, said Julius Caesar, they were the bravest *(Horum omnium fortissimi sunt Belgae);* in part because they were constantly at war with their next-door neighbors, the Germans from across the Rhine *(proximique sunt Germanis, qui trans*

Rhenum incolunt, quibuscum continenter bellum gerunt). Caesar's praise would echo throughout the modern Belgian nation in 1914 as it grimly faced the advancing armies of Imperial Germany. But in the first century B.C., or perhaps even earlier, a number of Belgic tribal leaders took a more prudent course than their successors and escaped the Teutonic invaders by fleeing with their families and followers to Britain. Others followed as Caesar himself pushed northward with his unconquerable Roman legions. By mid-century a Belgic aristocracy was in control of most of southeastern Britain from Essex, west through Buckinghamshire, to south Hampshire.

The habits and customs of the Belgae were in several ways distinct from those of their Celtic predecessors. For one thing, they buried their dead not by inhumation, but by cremation. For this they employed delicately turned pedestal urns or bead-rim vessels, often heavily combed. It was they who introduced the potter's wheel to Britain. Contrary to an earlier view entertained by most archaeologists, they did not, however, introduce the coultered plow with moldboard, designed to turn the sod as well as slice the earth. That was not to come until the Roman conquest. Belgic princes were, on the other hand, the first in Britain to issue coins. The earliest of these were made of gold, mostly crude copies of Greek and Roman models. Later Belgic coins were of silver and bronze and bore the name of the royal issuers and sometimes the location of their mints. Large numbers of these survive and can be seen in many British archaeological museums.

In war the Belgae fought like other Celts—in chariots where appropriate with spears and long swords as their major weapons. For fixed defenses they fortified their towns in such places as Wheathampstead in Hertfordshire and Colchester in Essex with enclosing ramparts and ditches. They also greatly reinforced a fair number of earlier Iron Age forts with additional ramparts and more elaborate entrance ways. These the Romans were to call *oppida* and, as we shall see in the next chapter, would expend considerable energy in their reduction.

Of Belgic religious practices little is known in particular, though it can be presumed they were no different from other Gallic tribes who, in the words of Caesar, were much given to religion *(Natio est omnis Gallorum admodum dedita religionibus)* and, like the Romans, worshiped many gods. Their priests were called Druids. Druidism in Gaul was already ancient in Caesar's time, and it may be, as he suggests, that the cult originated in Britain. If so, it left no remains, though a host of mythmakers would have it otherwise. Stonehenge, it will be remembered, was *not* a Druid monument, nor was any other Bronze Age stone circle. The Druids made up a distinctly separate priestly caste whose members were well versed in customary law, as well as religious ritual, astronomy, and the arts of divination. They engaged in human sacrifice, sometimes stabbing their victims in the back, sometimes impaling them or shooting them with arrows, and worst of all, sometimes caging them in great wicker baskets which they then set on fire. The Romans pretended to be much shocked by these practices, though they themselves had given up human sacrifice less than two generations before Caesar invaded Gaul.

In 58 B.C., Caius Julius Caesar became governor of the provinces of Illyricum and of Cisalpine and Transalpine Gaul, the latter located in southern France. Within a year he had subdued the unruly Helvetian tribes on his borders and pushed invading Germans back across the Rhine, had defeated a confederation of Belgic tribes in northwestern Gaul, and had received the surrender of the maritime tribes of Armorica (Brittany and Normandy). When the Armoricans revolted in 56 B.C., he correctly suspected that aid and comfort to the rebels was coming from the Celts of Britain, and he decided to put a stop to it. This would require an amphibious expedition across the Channel—a dangerous enterprise, for the island called *Britannia* was still a land of mystery lying beyond the limits of the *oikoumene,* the known and habitable world.

But danger held no terror for Caesar. On 26 August 55 B.C., he embarked from the neighborhood of modern Boulogne with two legions of infantry, about ten thousand men. A day later he beached his ships on the Kentish shore near Deal. In a single charge he scattered the natives who had gathered to oppose the landings and accepted the surrender of those who had not escaped into the forest. Four days later a storm nearly wrecked his fleet. This catastrophe plus renewed harassment by native troops induced him to reembark his troops and return to Gaul. Whatever his original intentions, the expedition turned into a mere reconnaissance in force.

The following summer (54 B.C.) he returned—this time with five legions of infantry plus about two thousand cavalry. The expedition set sail on 6 July and landed again near Deal, but without opposition. The Britons rallied, however, and near Canterbury put up an unsuccessful fight, after which they retired to the hill fort at Bigbury.

The next day another storm struck the waiting fleet—this one worse than the first. It took ten days to repair the damage, and the delay afforded the Britons a chance to regroup. They chose as their supreme commander one Cassivellaunus, the first Briton to have his name recorded in history. He attacked the invaders with chariots. The Romans drove them off, pressed northward, crossed the Thames, probably in the vicinity of modern London, and stormed and captured their enemy's chief town, which was probably at Wheathampstead, Hertfordshire. Cassivellaunus surrendered, gave hostages, and promised an annual tribute. Caesar then returned his army to their original beachhead, reembarked, and some time in mid-September sailed back to Gaul. He had spent just over two months in Britain. Almost a century was to pass before the Romans would return.

Meanwhile the Belgic tribes spread outward from their bases in the southeast until they either occupied or controlled most of England as far west as the Welsh marches and as far north as North Yorkshire. They either conquered or infiltrated most of the Celtic tribes of the earlier (Iron Age B) culture that had come before them, seizing or savaging their hill forts and occupying their best lands. With the Roman Empire of Augustus and Tiberius they kept their peace, neglecting the promised tribute payments but sending sizeable shipments of wheat, cattle, gold, silver, iron, hides, slaves, and hunting dogs in exchange for bracelets, necklaces, amber, glassware, and especially amphorae of Mediterranean and Gallic wine. This the Celts drank neat—to the great disgust of the Romans who watered theirs. Celtic tribal princes lived luxuriously, made war upon each other, and issued coins of silver and bronze bearing outlandish Celtic names in Latin script. It is from the study of such coins that the little that is known about the political history of Britain in this period has been inferred.

It is clear that in the first centuries B.C. and A.D., as throughout most of British history, wealth and power were centered in the southeast quadrant of England. For control of this rich area two royal houses vied with each other. Their founders were Commius, King of the Atrebates, whose capital was at Calleva, now Silchester, in Hampshire and Cassivel-launus, King of the Catuvellauni defeated by Caesar, whose heirs moved the tribal capital first to Prae Wood near St. Albans in Hertfordshire and then to Camulodunum, now Colchester, in Essex.

King of the Catuvellauni from about A.D. 10 to 43, was Cunobelinus (renamed Cymbeline by Shakespeare) whose rule extended from Essex south to Kent. His death at the beginning of the fifth decade of the first century A.D. apparently touched off another series of tribal wars in southeast England which once again called Rome's attention to Britannia. Shortly before this event, the mad Emperor Gaius (better known to history as Caligula) had organized a cross-channel expedition, but his troops mutinied and the operation was canceled. Now with Britain in apparent disorder, opportunity again beckoned, and the new emperor, Claudius, was quick to seize it. An unsoldierly man himself, he needed a spectacular military victory to secure his uncertain hold on the principate. Britain was thought to be rich in resources needed by the Empire. It was known to be a hotbed of Druidism which all the early Roman emperors were keen to extirpate. And so it was that, in spite of mutinous objections from superstitious soldiers, the Romans once again set sail for England. Again the port of embarkation was Boulogne. Aboard the convoy was an army of four legions with auxiliary troops— in all about forty thousand men. Their commanding general was Aulus Plautius.

CHAPTER II

ROMAN BRITAIN: A.D. 43–410

OCCUPATION AND CONQUEST:
A.D. 43–180

On an unknown date in late summer of A.D. 43 the army of Aulus Plautius, forty thousand strong, disembarked on the coast of Kent some forty miles from their point of departure across the Channel. Their beachhead was at Richborough on the Isle of Thanet near the present town of Sandwich.

Richborough *(545)*, whose Roman name was *Rutupiae*, is an appropriate starting place for the intelligent traveller in his search for the visible remains of Roman Britain. Not that there is much left to remind the visitor of the invasion; even the harbor has long since been silted up. Nevertheless, a few yards remain of the two parallel ditches that marked the boundaries of the first Roman camp constructed after the landing. Of greater visual interest today are the cruciform foundations of the great Tetrapylon set up by the famous general Agricola about A.D. 85, the remnants of a third century fort composed of earthen ramparts and their adjacent ditches, and the substantial remains of the Saxon Shore fort erected shortly thereafter.

Richborough is noteworthy neither for the classical elegance of its ruins, as is the case of Bath, nor for their impressive magnitude, as is Hadrian's Wall. But no other Roman site in Britain better demonstrates the duration of Roman rule. It is easy to forget that Britain was a province of Rome for almost four centuries—a span of years roughly equivalent to that separating the reigns of the two Queen Elizabeths. Like the Eternal City itself, Roman Britain was not built in a day. In viewing these ancient relics, therefore, the intelligent traveller should be alert to chronological distinctions, no less significant in this than in more recent periods of history. Britain at the turn of the fifth century was a different country from what it had been in the first when the Emperor Claudius brought it under Roman dominion.

From the beachhead at Richborough the invading troops spread westward searching for the enemy that had failed to oppose their landing. By this time the anti-Roman elements among the Britons had two leaders: Togodumnus and Caratacus, both sons of the recently deceased King Cunobelinus (Cymbeline). In all likelihood their forces consisted of levies of infantry equipped with long swords and reinforced by javelin throwers riding into battle in light, two-wheeled, open-ended, horse-drawn, wicker-bodied chariots. A reconstructed model of one of these can be seen in the **National Museum of Wales** *(717)* in Cardiff, South Glamorgan. Except for their leaders, these Britons bore no body armor, relying instead on the magical powers of the blue woad with which they painted their almost naked bodies, no doubt in the intricate curvilinear patterns typical of Celtic artistry still much admired today.

Somewhere in the present county of Kent the Romans met and defeated the forces of Caratacus, who promptly escaped, probably to Wales which was to become the center of a major resistance movement led by Druid priests. Meanwhile the bulk of the British forces drew up along the northern bank of the River Medway. There, not far from the present city of Rochester, they were decisively beaten by the advancing Romans and driven back beyond the Thames where their other leader, Togodumnus, was killed.

At this point the Romans paused and awaited the arrival of the Emperor Claudius for the final coup de grace. He came, accompanied by his Praetorian Guard and a complement of elephants; led the advance to the British capital at *Camulodunum*, now Colchester, Essex; accepted the surrender of eleven British tribal "kings"; and, after sixteen days in Britain, returned to Rome to receive from the Senate the most lavish triumph to be awarded any emperor since the great Augustus himself. Nineteen hundred years later a life-sized bronze head of Claudius was dragged out of the River Alde in Suffolk and is now on view at the **British Museum** *(516)*.

The emperor's acceptance of the surrender of these eleven British kings at Camulodunum was symptomatic of the system of imperial defense instituted by Augustus and maintained by all his successors down through Nero. Fundamental to that system was the establishment, on the outer fringes of the empire, of loyal client kingdoms to serve as buffer states against the incursions of hostile barbarians from beyond the Imperial boundaries. The rulers of only three of these British client states are known to history. One was Queen Cartimandua who held uneasy sway over the Brigantes occupying the territory now covered by the counties of Lancashire, Cumbria, West and North Yorkshire, Durham, and Northumberland. The second was Prasutagus, king of the Iceni of Norfolk and husband to Boudicca, of whom more would be heard later. The third was Cogidubnus, whose tribal capital was at Chichester, West Sussex. It was probably he who built the nearby palace of **Fishbourne** *(551)*, which today is certainly one of the most attractive sites dating to the Roman occupation of Britain. The foundations, walls, and mosaics can be viewed from a raised and sheltered catwalk, the formal garden has been replanted, and the site museum offers cogent explanations of the history of the palace.

The imperial government could rely to some extent on client kings, but ultimately Roman authority depended upon the army. Throughout most of the four centuries of occupation, the garrison in Britain amounted to a tenth part of the total armed forces of Rome, which is remarkable considering that in actual square miles Britain represented only a tiny fraction of the entire empire.

At the heart of the army were the legions, of which there were never more than four nor less than three in Britain. Each legion consisted of from five thousand to six thousand men, mostly infantry, all Roman citizens. Legions were divided into ten cohorts, the cohorts into six centuries of eighty men, each century commanded by a centurion. Each legionary was equipped with an armored vest of overlapping metal strips, a broad metal-studded belt from which hung a sporranlike attachment to protect the genitals, a rectangular shield curved to fit the body and made of leather or of plywood edged with metal, and a helmet of iron or bronze which was a plain cap with a projecting guard to cover the nape of the neck, looking more or less like a baseball cap worn backwards. The **Grosvenor Museum** *(673)* in Chester, Cheshire, has an excellent life-sized model of a Roman legionary, fully accoutered. So does the **University Museum of Antiquities** *(701)*, Newcastle-upon-Tyne, Tyne and Wear, and the site museum of **Caerleon** *(716)* near Newport, Gwent. Original helmets in good state of repair are to be seen in the **British Museum** *(516)*, London, and the **Colchester and Essex Museum** *(598)*, Colchester, Essex.

Unfortunately there is nothing in Britain comparable to Trajan's Column in Rome with its hundred-foot spiral bas-reliefs depicting the Roman soldiery in every pose and circumstance imaginable. Only an occasional tombstone remains, carved with the dress and features of a man who once wore the standard uniform of the imperial army. The best preserved of these is that of M. Favonius Facilis in the **Colchester and Essex Museum.** Here is the image of a centurion of the 20th Legion carved in high relief—a lifelike representation of a typically tough, stern, intractable company commander, the backbone of the Roman army. Another tombstone worth noting is that of S. Valerius Genialis in the **Corinium Museum** *(638)*, Cirencester, Gloucestershire. Depicted in low relief in the act of spearing a fallen foe, this is a Thracian trooper attached to an *ala* of Roman auxiliaries.

Roman weapons are widely distributed among many of the museums mentioned in this and the earlier chapter. The basic infantry weapon was the *gladius*, a short heavy sword, double-edged, sharply pointed, and designed more for stabbing than for slashing. With it each soldier carried two *pila*, javelins seven feet in length, each with a hardened iron point connected to the wooden shaft by a shank of untempered metal. These were thrown in volleys from distances of about forty feet and were designed not so much to kill as to penetrate the enemy's shield. Once lodged there, the soft end of the spear's shank bent so that the shield became useless and had to be discarded. Thus disabled, a "barbarian" soldier would have small defense against an attacking Roman infantryman armed with his sturdy *gladius.*

Supplementing the legions, though about equal in number, were the *auxilia.* These were recruited originally from barbarian tribes, and were equipped with a variety of weapons and accouterments. They were cavalry troops, archers, lancers, slingers, and light infantry, organized into cohorts of infantry or *alae* of cavalry or mixed units of both, the normal unit numbering sometimes five hundred and sometimes a thousand. A cavalryman, needing a greater reach, carried a longer sword than the gladius, a lance rather than a javelin, and an oval or circular shield rather than a rectangular one.

Artillery was mostly organic to the legions. It consisted of two types of weapons: the *ballista*, which operated somewhat like a crossbow and could fire a stone missile, arrow, or iron bolt at a killing range of about four hundred yards, and the *onager*, or "wild ass" which was a catapult capable of lobbing a stone ball weighing up to 175 pounds to a distance of two hundred yards. Although both weapons could be employed to break up massed attacks of infantry, their major use was in siege warfare at which the Romans were notoriously expert.

In addition to his combat duties, the Roman soldier had to be an engineer. On the march he carried a saw, an ax, an entrenching tool, stakes for palisades, and a wicker basket for hauling earth. He was, as Josephus, the first century Jewish historian, remarked, "as heavily laden as a mule." The purpose of all this paraphernalia was self-protection. When marching through hostile territory, Roman soldiers built entrenchments each night. It was, said the historian Vegetius, "as though they carried a walled town in their packs." These earthworks are known as marching camps. Traces of them, rectangular in shape with rounded corners, are observable all over Britain, though mostly, it must be admitted, from the air. Larger in size and more elaborate in construction were the semipermanent forts that dotted the countryside in the wake of the advancing Roman armies. In the first century these were made of earthen ramparts topped by wooden palisade fences and sealed by wooden gates. One of them, built about A.D. 60, was **The Lunt** *(665)*, Baginton, just south of Coventry, West Midlands. It has recently been partially reconstructed and is well worth a visit. On view are the earthen ramparts, the main gateway, a tower fighting-platform, and a palisade, stretching away on either side on top of the ramparts of turf. Also there is a reconstructed barracks block large enough to house a century of eighty men and a granary, now employed as a site museum.

Less than two decades before this fort was built, the western Midlands, and all the rest of Britain for that matter, was a wilderness. Into this unknown territory Aulus Plautius, operating out of Colchester, launched his legions and their auxiliaries.

Probably the original plan called for the occupation of no more of Britain than the lowland zone, i.e., southeastern England, east of Devon and Wales and south of the Pennines. In accordance, the Ninth Legion moved northward through East Anglia as far as Lincoln where a legionary fort was established. The Second Legion went west. Its record is the better known since its commanding general was Vespasian who later became emperor and subject of a biography by the historian Suetonius. Vespasian, we are told, fought thirty battles and destroyed two very powerful tribes, occupied the Isle of Wight, and reduced twenty *oppida*, or hill forts. One of these was certainly **Hod Hill** *(567)* near Blandford Forum, Dorset, where a barrage of ballista bullets was later excavated. There, in the northwest corner of the Iron Age hill fort the Romans erected a fort of their own, enclosing almost eleven acres and utilizing the banks and ditches of the original enclosure to form two sides of the newly built square. Like many another fort of the Claudian period, this one appears to have been abandoned after about ten years of occupation.

The key to military control of the southwest, however, was not Hod Hill, but **Maiden Castle** *(568)* near Dorchester, Dorset. Here, in and around the *oppidum* of the Durotriges, a mighty battle took place in A.D. 44. Though the British defenders were adept in the use of the sling and had a stockpile of over fifty thousand beach pebbles for ammunition, they were no match for Roman siege artillery under the able command of Vespasian, that stubborn soldier who would one day invest and capture the far more formidable Jewish stronghold of Jotapata (Jefat). Even today some trace of the carnage of the Maiden Castle remains to be seen. In the **Dorset County Museum** *(567)*, Dorchester, are skulls of some of the fort's defenders bearing the marks of the fatal sword cuts that dispensed them and a segment of human vertebrae with an imbedded Roman *ballista* bolt. When it was all over, the Romans slighted the hill fort and moved on. Within three years they succeeded in securing lowland Britain as far as the Fosse Way, the Roman road that runs diagonally across southern England from the neighborhood of Exeter northeast to Lincoln.

Now the scene of action shifts to Wales, a country ideally suited for guerrilla operations. All the ingredients for a successful resistance movement were there: a mountainous and densely wooded terrain; an intrepid and dedicated leader in the person of Caracatus; a conservative, primitive society stubbornly resistant to alien intrusions; a strong nativist ideology supported by a political infrastructure organized by the Druids in their headquarters on Mona, the Isle of Anglesey. But the mighty Roman army was not to be gainsaid; and on a mountaintop somewhere in Powys, the Britons again suffered a decisive defeat. The wife and daughters of Caratacus were captured, and he himself fled to the court of Cartimandua, Queen of the Brigantes. She betrayed him, bound him in chains, and handed him over to the conquerors, who shipped him off to Rome. There in a speech made famous by the historian Tacitus, he defiantly asked his captors: "For if you would rule the world, does it follow that the world must welcome slavery?" *(Nam si vos omnibus imperitare vultis, sequitur ut omnes servitutem accipiant?)* Surprisingly, the Emperor Claudius forgave this insolence and granted Caratacus, if not freedom, at least an unmolested life in exile.

But Caratacus's removal did not end the troubles in Wales. For another decade rebellion flourished. At last in A.D. 61, a new governor,

C. Suetonius Paulinus, with two legions under his command, penetrated North Wales as far as the Menai Strait which separates the mainland from the Isle of Anglesey, last refuge of the Druids. As the troops pushed across the narrow waters by boat and on horseback, they met a terrifying sight, as described by Tacitus:

> On the beach stood the adverse array, a serried mass of arms and men, with women flitting between the ranks. In the style of Furies, in robes of deathly black and with disheveled hair, they brandished their torches; while a circle of Druids, lifting their hands to heaven, showered imprecations. . . .

The Romans paused, then pushed forward, drove the maddened Britons into the fires their priests had prepared for human sacrifice, and leveled to the ground their sacred groves. Years later during World War II excavators at Llyn Cerrig Bach near Holyhead on Anglesey unearthed a huge votive deposit of all kinds of iron objects (including a set of slave chains) which archaeologists believe to have been offerings to a Druidical shrine concealed there in advance of the Roman attack. The hoard is now on deposit at the **National Museum of Wales** *(717)* in Cardiff.

Anglesey now lay at the conquerors' feet. But before they could move on, messengers from the east brought the terrible news of the rebellion of Boudicca, Queen of the Iceni of Norfolk. The year was now A.D. 61; the reigning emperor, Nero. The greed and cruelty of the provincial Roman government had nourished the seeds of rebellion among an East Anglian nobility, still untamed after almost twenty years of suppression. On the death of the old client King Prasutagus, Roman officials confiscated his estates, enslaved his retainers, raped his daughters, and flogged his widowed queen, Boudicca. The lady retaliated by raising the standard of revolt, and, with the help of her own and neighboring tribesmen, succeeded in sacking the Roman settlements at *Camulodunum* (Colchester) and *Verulamium* (St. Albans) and setting fire to *Londinium* (London), the rising commercial center on the Thames.

All together an estimated seventy thousand Romans and Romanized Britons perished by fire, sword, or rope before the troops of Suetonius Paulinus could beat their way back from Wales and put down the revolt. Boudicca herself took poison. The governor's vengeance was terrible and would have been worse had not Suetonius been recalled by Nero under the persuasion of the newly appointed procurator, the chief fiscal officer of the province who reported directly to the emperor. This was Julius Classicianus whose restored tombstone is prominently and deservedly displayed in the **British Museum** *(516)*.

In the year A.D. 70, following the death of Nero, the last of the Julio-Claudian line of emperors, a new dynasty came into power in Rome and ruled for twenty-six years. These were the Flavians, the first of whom was the Emperor Vespasian, a veteran of the British wars of conquest. These years and those of the succeeding two emperors, Nerva (96–98) and Trajan (98–117) saw the dismantling of the client-state system of imperial rule, a consolidation of direct military control around the Empire's perimeters, and the garrisoning of large numbers of troops in permanent fortifications interconnected by a network of military roads.

In Britain the work of consolidation was carried out chiefly by three successive governors, all distinguished soldiers: Petillius Cerialis (71–74), Julius Frontinus (74–78), and Julius Agricola (78–84). Of these the last is the best known, owing to his good fortune in having as son-in-law the historian Tacitus, whose eulogistic biography of Agricola is a major source for what is known today of the history of first century Britain.

In Brigantia, Queen Cartimandua, Rome's only remaining client-chief, had fallen on evil days after divorcing her husband Venutius and marrying his squire. The aggrieved ex-husband promptly made war on the faithless ex-wife and drove her out of the kingdom into the arms of her protectors, thus in Tacitus's words "leaving the throne to Venutius, the war to us." Then, out of the newly established fortress at York, Cerialis marched his Ninth Legion against Venutius, now ensconced at **Stanwick** *(686)* north of Richmond, North Yorkshire, the largest Iron Age hill fort in Britain. Enlarged by the Brigantian leader to include 750 acres through which ran three widely separated sets of ramparts and ditches, it was fully as formidable a stronghold as Maiden Castle, Dorset. It fell, nevertheless, to Cerialis's legionnaires sometime before A.D. 74, and the Brigantes were thenceforth leaderless. Finds from the battle, including a well-preserved Roman sword and scabbard, are in the **Yorkshire Museum** *(693)*, in York.

Next on the Romans' list was Wales, still unsubdued. Operating out of the new legionary fortress at Chester, Julius Frontinus succeeded in subjecting most of the country to Roman rule, leaving to his successor Agricola the task of finishing the job. This Agricola did in the first year of his governorship by capturing Anglesey. To Agricola can be ascribed the building of the auxiliary fort at **Tomen Y Mur** *(739)* near Ffestiniog, Gwynedd, Wales. Like all Roman forts of the Flavian period, this was a rectangular enclosure bounded by earthen ramparts and a ditch. Nearby are the remains of an amphitheater, the only known example in Britain connected with an auxiliary fort.

Next Agricola turned north toward the land of the Brigantes. On the way he set up a small cavalry fort at **Ribchester** *(Bremetennacum)* (697) near Longridge, Lancashire. The site museum there is worth a visit. The most interesting object found at Ribchester, though, is not there but in the **British Museum** *(516)*. This is the Ribchester helmet. Attached to the headpiece is a face mask of thin beaten bronze with openings for the eyes and features shaped according to classical standards of male beauty, though in fact it probably adorned the barbarian Slavic features of a Sarmatian cavalryman stationed at Ribchester a century or more after Agricola. Helmets of this type were worn by the participants in *hippika* *gymnasia,* cavalry exercises not unlike medieval jousts. Another example can be seen at the **Norwich Castle Museum** *(608)*, Norfolk.

As he pushed northward through the territory of the Brigantes and into the lowlands of present day Scotland, Agricola studded the conquered territory with earthenworks; about sixty forts were established in northern England and another twenty or thirty in Scotland. Deep in the Grampian mountains, at a place called *Mons Graupius,* he at last met up with thirty thousand wild Caledonians under the command of a native chieftain called, by the Romans, Calgacus. Roman discipline prevailed again; ten thousand of the barbarians were slain, the rest routed.

It was a great tactical victory, but strategically of little consequence. Troubles with barbarians along the Danube induced the imperial government to withdraw the Second Legion from Britain. Soon after the battle of *Mons Graupius,* the Roman army in Scotland pulled back to the line of lowland forts stretching across the isthmus between the Clyde and the Forth. Within a few years after that the frontier was pulled back further to the Stanegate, the road that Agricola had laid out across the Tyne-Solway isthmus between the present cities of Newcastle-upon-Tyne and Carlisle. By that time, Agricola himself had been recalled to Rome. Before he left, however, he set up the great Tetrapylon at *Rutupiae* in **Richborough** *(545)* near Sandwich, Kent. This huge four-way triumphal arch, whose cruciform foundation can still be seen, mistakenly proclaimed the final conquest of the island of Britain.

But if Britain was not conquered, most of England at least was at peace. Urbanization and Romanization of the province were proceeding apace, encouraged by the deliberate policy of Agricola and other governors. Of this development, Tacitus cynically remarks that the innocent Britons were seduced by "alluring vices—the porticoes, the baths, the elegant banquets—which they called civilization when it was in fact part of their servitude."

The subject of town growth will be treated in detail in another section of this chapter. Of equal importance to the civilizing mission of Rome was the construction of a vast network of more than five thousand miles of skillfully engineered roads, most of which were completed before the end of the first century A.D. All the chief population centers and most of the major military establishments were joined together by a web of primary roads which had its nodal point at London. The Roman names of these highways are unknown; for the most part they are still called by titles of Anglo-Saxon derivation, with the word "street" attached. Eight major roads converged in London. These were Watling Street, with one branch running southeast through Canterbury to Dover in Kent and another heading northwest to Wroxeter, Salop; two almost parallel roads running south, one to Lewes, the other to Brighton, both in East Sussex; Stane Street leading to Chichester, West Sussex; a southwesterly road to Silchester, Hampshire, and on to Old Sarum in Wiltshire; Ermine Street, which headed north to Lincoln and beyond; and the northeast road to

Colchester, Essex. Besides these, worth special mention are the Fosse Way which ran diagonally northeast from the mouth of the River Axe in Devon, through Bath, Cirencester, and Leicester, to Lincoln; Akeman Street between St. Albans, Hertfordshire, and Bath by way of Cirencester; and Dere Street which ran north into Scotland from Corbridge in Northumberland.

Among the secondary roads in Britain even today, those that follow the ancient Roman lines are noted for their straightness—a phenomenon that still strikes many an Englishman as odd and somehow alien. Actually the Romans did not build their roads entirely straight, though in the lowlands deviations from straightness were rare. Normally Roman surveyors laid out a direct course from one high point of land to the next one visible, and if angles were required they would be laid out on the high ground only. In hilly country Roman roads sometimes zigzagged or even followed natural ridge lines.

For the most part a road was laid upon an earthen embankment dug up from ditches on either side. This was called the *agger*. On it was placed the actual roadway which consisted of a foundation of large stones into which was rammed a thick layer of gravel, chipped flint, or sometimes even iron slag—a process which, when rediscovered in the eighteenth century, was called metaling or macadamizing. On hilly ground curbstones were sometimes set in place to keep the gravel from drifting —along the edges, laterally, or even down the middle. The maximum width of a Roman road was thirty feet; median width about twenty-four.

Unfortunately for the traveller, most have disappeared. Natural erosion and the plow have taken their toll; gravel and foundation stones alike have been carted away; modern roads, highways, and railways following the same lines have obliterated all traces of the original routes. But here and there are a few remnants of the Roman roads. In Dorset, in the vicinity of the hill fort called Badbury Rings near Wimborne Minster, can be seen an eight-mile stretch of *agger* on which was laid a portion of the main road between Old Sarum, north of Salisbury, Wiltshire, and Dorchester. It is called the **Ackling Dyke** *(570)* and the earthwork rises to a height of seven feet and is over forty feet wide. More interesting as a sight is the piece of Roman road at **Blackstone Edge** *(697)* near Littleborough, Lancashire. Here on the high moors lies a section of the old military road from Manchester to Ilkley. It consists of curbed flagstones, sixteen feet in width; and down the center runs a shallow trough which may have served as a slot for brake poles as wagons descended the steep incline. Where the ground flattens out, the trough disappears. Finally, in terrain almost as wild as Blackstone Edge, is the misnamed **Wade's Causeway** *(690)* north of Pickering, North Yorkshire. Running for more than a mile across Wheeldale Moor, it too consists of curbed flagstones about sixteen feet in width. What it was used for in this isolated region is unknown, though no doubt it had some connection with the Cawthorn Roman camps north of Pickering.

Indeed it can safely be assumed that most Roman roads in Britain were initially laid out by army engineers for purposes primarily military. By the end of the first century lowland Britain was largely pacified and civilized. But the highland zone, i.e., Wales and the North, was still, in part at least, a military frontier, and it was in this area that permanent army garrisons continued to flourish. Symptomatic of the permanence was the widespread conversion of the ramparts and buildings of Roman fortifications from earth and timber to stone. This new construction began about the beginning of the second century and continued into the fourth.

Fortress is the name given to the permanent bases of Roman legions, as distinct from fort which applies only to the installations of auxiliary units. By the year A.D. 100, with the completion of the initial conquest of England and Wales, legionary troops were established at three fortresses: *Deva* at Chester, *Eboracum* at York, and *Isca Silurum* at Caerleon-on-Usk, Gwent, Wales. As a glance at the map will indicate, these fortresses were located so as to provide quick access to potential trouble spots where native tribesmen might still prove unruly. Between them, Caerleon and Chester held Wales in a sort of vise, while York was positioned to take care of the north country as far as the Scottish lowlands.

Each of these fortresses contained close to fifty acres within its ramparts and each had the same layout. The military base was laid out in the form of a rectangle with rounded corners between which, on all four sides, gated entrance ways were located. The headquarters building, *principia*, occupied the center behind the main road, *via principia*, which ran laterally across the rectangle and led to each of the side gates. Another road, the *via praetoria*, led from the main gate to form a T-junction with the *via principia* in front of the headquarters building. From the rear of that building ran another road straight to the rear gate. Thus the entire area was divided into four quadrilateral segments with the *principia*, the commandant's quarters, and the hospital in the center, the barracks blocks, stables, granaries, and workshops off to the sides. It should be noted that the defensive works of these fortresses, at least when first converted to stone in the second century, were not terribly impressive. They do not remotely compare, for example, to the great fortified castles of the Middle Ages. The reason is that they were not meant to serve defensive purposes. Theirs was a forward-defense strategy that drove them to seek battle far away from their own bases and from the territories they were supposed to protect.

Of the three legionary fortresses, *Isca Silurum* or **Caerleon** *(716)*, two miles north of Newport, Gwent, is today the least submerged beneath medieval and modern buildings. True, the parish church now stands where the headquarters building of the 2nd Legion once occupied the center of the fort, but the rest is open field, partially excavated. Next to the church is a fine site museum. Down the lane running southwest of the museum are a few fragments of the fortress wall, built in the early second century to reinforce the earthenworks of the original establishment laid out around A.D. 75. In the angle of the fortress formed by the southwest and northwest walls lies Prysg Field, which has been fully excavated. Here can be seen the foundations and lower courses of the barracks block that housed the common soldiers of the 2nd Legion. Here are twenty-four small rooms in pairs of twelve, each pair housing six legionnaires. At the northwest end of the block was a larger accommodation for the centurion. Nearby are the remains of the latrine in which can still be observed the three-sided stone channel through which water was flushed and which was originally surmounted by a row of wooden seats. Sponges would have been supplied to serve as toilet paper. Such conveniences were not to be seen again in Britain until late in the eighteenth century. Also in the same area are traces of six legionary ovens. Across the lane to the south lies Caerleon's chief attraction, the amphitheater—the only completely excavated Roman amphitheater in Britain and certainly the one most worth visiting. It now appears as a massive grass-covered oval earthen ring with eight entrances down which ramps descend to the enclosed arena. Originally this arena was surrounded by a twelve-foot high internal stone wall behind which rose banks of wooden benches to a height of twenty-eight feet. Around the entire structure ran an external wall, thirty-two feet high. What it was mostly used for remains somewhat in doubt. In a provincial city of any size it would have been largely devoted to entertainment: wild animal fights, bear-baiting, even gladiatorial contests. Here it was more likely used as a *ludum* for drills, parades, and an assembly ground for mustering the full legion of six thousand troops. It should be remembered that the heart of Roman military might was troop discipline; and the heart of discipline was training. Significantly the Latin word for army, *exercitus,* was derived from the word for exercise, *exercitando.* Welsh tradition claims the amphitheater at Caerleon as the site of the coronation of the legendary King Arthur, but no known evidence supports the claim, and, for reasons to be explained in the following chapter, the episode is undoubtedly fictitious.

Deva at Chester, Cheshire, was the home of the 20th Legion which moved there from Wroxeter about A.D. 88. Much less is visible today of Roman occupation than at *Caerleon;* on the other hand, the models of the legionary fortress on display at the **Grosvenor Museum** *(673)* are the best of their kind in Britain. Within the city itself, the scanty remains of the legionary fortress are chiefly to be observed along the eastern leg of the city wall, which, though mostly medieval in provenance, still contains portions of Roman construction. Just to the north of Eastgate is a stretch of **Roman Wall** *(673)* fifteen feet high in places. Immediately to the left of Newgate, heading away from the city center, are the foundations of the **Southeast Angle Tower** *(673)* of the Roman fort. A little way beyond Newgate about half of the **Roman Amphitheater** *(673)* still stands. With a seating capacity of eight thousand, it is thought to have been the largest in Roman Britain. To the right of Newgate lie what are now known as the **Roman Gardens** *(674)*. In this charming and well-tended park are the substantial remains of a reconstructed hypocaust and some columns which may have come from the headquarters building.

Eboracum, now the city of York, became the home base of the 9th Legion when it was moved north from Lincoln in A.D. 71. In the early years of the second century it was fitted with stone walls and buildings. In the third and fourth centuries it became the major military and administrative headquarters for the north of Britain and underwent extensive rebuilding. As at Chester, however, most Roman remains were obliterated in medieval and modern times. A good place for the traveller to commence to recreate York's Roman past is at the **Yorkshire Museum** *(693)* in Museum Gardens, which has a rich collection of Roman finds, and in whose garden is located the **Multiangular Tower** *(690)*, a fourth century bastion added to the second century fortress wall. Of about the same date is the **Roman East Bastion** *(690)* located on the city wall southeast of Monk Bar. In the undercroft of **York Minster** *(692)*, the medieval cathedral, are to be seen the remains of the headquarters building which once stood at the center of the fortress. Here also is a superb small museum of Roman and later finds from the city. Finally in a pub on St. Sampson's Square called the Roman Bath Inn, part of the legionary **Roman Bathhouse** *(690)* can be clearly observed underneath the partially glassed floor.

In plan and construction, auxiliary forts were simply miniature versions of the legionary fortresses, reduced by a factor of about ten; that is, large enough to house a single cohort or cavalry *ala.* There are two hundred of them known to have existed in Britain. Like the legionary fortresses, some of these were converted to stone in the early second century and have thus left some fairly impressive remains.

Mediobogdum, now known as **Hardknott Castle** *(708)*, west of Ambleside, Cumbria, was built first around A.D. 100 and reconstructed in recent years using the original stones. Here are the foundations of a Roman fort with an external bathhouse, situated in a wild mountain pass of extraordinary ruggedness and extraordinary beauty as well (that is when not blanketed by fog, which is often). Wales was well covered with auxiliary forts, and a number have survived. **Castell Collon** *(722)* near Llandrindod Wells, Powys, is one of the better preserved. Here are the remains of the ramparts, headquarters building, a commandant's house, granary, and the usual bathhouse. At **Brecon Gaer** *(721)* near Brecon, Powys, are the remains of a five-acre auxiliary cavalry fort established about A.D. 80 and rebuilt in stone in the second century. Still visible are substantial remains of the south and west gates and of the enclosing wall. **Segontium** *(737)* at Caernarvon, Gwynedd, was built first of earth and timber by Agricola in A.D. 78 to guard the Menai Strait overlooking Anglesey. Its walls and internal structures were then converted to stone in the early and mid-second century, rebuilt in the third, and again in the fourth. The remains today are among the best and most instructive of all Roman military sites in Britain. The wall is four feet thick and at one place eleven feet high with traces of a corner turret at the northern angle. Three of the four gateways can be observed, as can the foundations of the head-quarters building, the commandant's house with an adjoining workshop, three large granaries, and barracks blocks. Outside the fort are traces of the bathhouse, substantial walls of a large building of unknown purpose, and the foundations of a second century temple to Mithras, a Near East-ern cult figure very popular in Britain, especially among the military. There is an ancient Welsh tradition that *Segontium* was the birthplace of the Emperor Constantine (A.D. 272–337) who first legalized Christian-ity. Like most such legends this one cannot be authenticated and is almost certainly false. The true history of the fort, so far as it is known, is well explained in the displays at the site museum.

The logical culmination of all this fort building in the early second century was the erection of **Hadrian's Wall** *(701)*, which stretched across the waist of Britain from the mouth of the Tyne on the west to the Solway Firth on the east through the present counties of Northumberland and Cumbria. Hadrian (A.D. 117–138), whose more than life-sized bronze head can be seen at the **British Museum** *(516)* was the first Roman emperor to spend most of his time away from Rome touring the prov-inces, including Britain, which he visited in the year A.D. 122. While there, he ordered the building of the great wall to delineate the outer boundary of the British province. It was not an isolated act. In Germany a trench and palisade barrier had been laid out between the upper reaches of the Rhine and Danube rivers; in the Dobruja (modern Ru-mania) a fortified frontier had been established between the Danube and the Black Sea; and even in Africa, in modern Algeria, a trench-and-wall system (the *Fossatum Africae*) 750 kilometers in length ran along the northern edge of the Sahara Desert. None of these frontier defenses was intended to serve as a barrier against massive attacks or as a Roman version of the Maginot Line. Hadrian's Wall, the most solidly constructed of them all, was only fifteen feet in height and at the most nine feet thick and was not a fighting platform reinforced with heavy artillery emplace-ments. It was part of a system of perimeter defense intended to mark the political boundary of the provinces, to separate the barbarians to the north from the only slightly more civilized tribes to the immediate south, to act as an early warning system against threats of infiltration, and to serve as a base for mobile striking forces against exterior concentrations of native troops.

By the time the first period of construction was over, i.e., about A.D. 130, the system consisted of (a) a stone wall seventy-three miles (eighty Roman miles) in length, (b) sixteen forts for auxiliary units of cavalry or infantry on the wall, (c) two milecastles or fortlets between each fort, each accommodating from twenty to fifty men, (d) two turrets between each milecastle to serve as outlooks and signaling stations, (e) a deep V-shaped ditch in front (north) of the wall, except in those places where the land dropped off so steeply that no further protection was necessary,

(f) a *vallum*, i.e., a wide ditch, flanked on either side by earthworks, running laterally to the rear (south) of the wall, and (g) additional auxiliary forts serving also as supply depots along the road called the Stanegate still farther to the rear. It should be noted that the wall underwent three major phases of rebuilding; the first under the Emperor Severus around A.D. 208, the second by the Emperor Constantius Chlorus about A.D. 300, and the third by Count Theodosius in A.D. 369. It should also be noted that what remains today, though unquestionably impressive, is a very much eroded and diminished version of the original stoneworks. The visitor should not expect to see anything so grand as the Great Wall of China.

The best place to commence an inspection of Hadrian's Wall is at the **University Museum of Antiquities** *(701)*, Newcastle-upon-Tyne, Tyne and Wear, which displays a number of Roman finds and, more importantly, a well-constructed scale model of the entire wall as it presumably appeared when it was in operation.

From Newcastle the traveller should proceed west along the A 69 to the military road (B 6318) which is not a Roman road but was built by General Wade at the time of the Jacobite rising in 1715 mostly out of stones robbed from the wall itself, portions of which are still visible from the road. Where the B 6318 intersects the A 68 (built along the line of the Roman Dere Street), the traveller should cut south to **Corbridge** *(702)* for a visit to nearby *Corstopitium*, an auxiliary fort, supply base, and arsenal on the Stanegate.

The first fort at *Corstopitium* was built of turf by Agricola about A.D. 80, to be evacuated around the year 125 when the wall was built. A second fort came into being about 140 and was drastically remodeled about twenty years later and again during the early years of the third century when the Emperor Septimius Severus (193–211) was campaigning in Scotland. It is to this period that most of the building whose present remains are visible belongs. Most significant are the foundations and walls of two granaries which indicate that this fort was employed as a supply depot. Other interesting remains are those of a stone water tank and fountain, an enormous storehouse possibly converted from the earlier administrative headquarters of a legion stationed here, three temple sites, and two military compounds in one of which can be seen the remains of a chapel with stairs leading down to a sunken strong-room. The site museum is rich in finds, the most important being the Corbridge Lion, a stone statue of a lion devouring a stag.

Returning to the military way (B 6138) and proceeding west, the next important site is **Chesters** *(702)*, Northumbria *(Cilernum)*. This was an auxiliary fort for an *ala* of cavalry built astride the wall shortly after its initial construction. More than half the total area enclosed by the fort projects north of the line of the wall so as to allow space for three gates (facing east, north, and west) through which mounted cavalry could make a quick exit in case of emergency. Remains of these gates, as well as one to the south, are visible, though it is admittedly difficult to visualize them as they originally stood. The most impressive of the structures within the fort is the headquarters building, *principia*, with its great hall behind which lay the chapel of the *ala*, flanked by two pairs of rooms and with a stairway leading down to a subterranean strong-room, where no doubt the soldiers' pay was stored. Also within the enclosure are the remains of the commandant's house with attached bathhouse suite and substantial remains of a hypocaust. Outside the fort can be seen the abutments of the Roman bridge across the Tyne, though, since the river has since changed course, one of them is below water while the other is some distance from the river bank. Downstream from the bridge are the remains of the troop bathhouse, one of the best of its kind in Britain. Of special interest is the series of niches, which were lockers, where bathers deposited their clothes.

Two miles west of Chesters along the military way is a fine stretch of the wall, including a turret much of which is six feet high. South of the road is a clearly visible length of the vallum. About a mile further on, the wall begins to climb the peak of Whin Sill where the views are spectacular and the remains are in their best state of preservation. Still a little farther on is **Carrawburgh** *(702)*, or *Brocolita*, which is interesting only for the remains of the Mithraic temple just south of the fort.

Another four miles west will bring the traveller to **Housesteads** *(Borcovicium)* (702), Northumberland, which is both scenically and archaeologically the site of Hadrian's Wall most worth visiting. *Borcovicium*, unlike the fort at Chesters, was an infantry fort designed to house an eight-hundred-man auxiliary cohort. Also unlike Chesters, it does not project beyond the wall, its north side being flush with the wall itself with only one gate, which was sufficient for the purposes of infantry troops. Otherwise in general plan and layout it conforms to the standard pattern of auxiliary forts. Remains of all four gates are visible, as are those of the commandant's house, the hospital, and granaries. The headquarters building is less well preserved than at Chesters and elsewhere, but the Roman latrine is the best of its kind in Britain. Good stretches of the wall itself can be seen on either side of the fort, and the view is truly spectacular. There is the usual site museum.

Just west of the fort at Housesteads are the remains of a milecastle, one of the best preserved of its kind. A mile south of the wall is the Roman station *Vindolanda* at **Chesterholm** *(702)*, Northumbria. First constructed by Agricola as one of the Stanegate forts in A.D. 80, it was abandoned when the wall was built, then reoccupied and rebuilt in the 160s. The principal remains of the fort are the north and west gates, and the headquarters building. Of great interest too are the remains of the civil settlement (the *vicus*) outside the walls, including those of the bathhouse. Recent excavations here have produced an unusually rich hoard of domestic equipment of all kinds—leather shoes, writing tablets, household altars, etc.—all on view in the excellent site museum. Also for travellers bored with looking at tumbled walls and buildings without sides or roofs, here is a full scale replica in stone of a portion of Hadrian's Wall, including a turret.

Back to the wall at **Cawfields** *(703)* is another well-preserved milecastle as well as a length of the vallum, ten feet deep with the flanking earthworks still visible. Ten miles farther on is the westernmost remaining fort, **Birdsowald** *(Camboglanna) (703)* across the county line in Cumbria. Like Housesteads, this was an infantry station. Large sections of its walls still stand, as do the remains of the south and east gates, the headquarters building, and the commandant's house. West of Birdoswald segments of the wall and remains of its turrets can be seen as far as Walton Village, Cumbria. Beyond that it disappears. In Carlisle, Cumbria, at the **Tullie House Museum and Art Gallery** *(710)* are finds from the western end of the wall and from the long gone signal towers and mileforts that extended the frontier defenses another forty miles down the Cumbrian coast.

The Emperor Hadrian died in A.D. 138. Within two years his successor, Antonius Pius (138–161) initiated a radically new frontier policy in Britain. A new governor, Q. Lollius Urbicus, was ordered to reconquer lowland Scotland. Agricola's old forts north of the wall were rebuilt and regarrisoned. Hadrian's frontier was thrown open. The vallum behind the wall was formally breached by throwing in earth from the two flanking mounds every forty-five yards to form causeways across the ditch. Gates were removed from the milecastles, although the wall forts themselves seem to have been maintained. Finally, some ninety miles to the northwest Lollius Urbicus built a new frontier defensework which was to mark the westernmost extremity of the Roman Empire. This came to be called the Antonine Wall, and it ran for thirty-seven miles across the waist of Scotland from the Firth of Forth to the Firth of Clyde.

This new frontier enjoyed only a brief existence. Sometime after A.D. 154 the Caledonians again rose in revolt and the Romans withdrew to Hadrian's Wall which was restored. Though briefly reoccupied, the Antonine Wall was overrun again early in the reign of the next emperor, Commodus (180–192). This time the Romans gave up and returned to a refortified Hadrian's Wall. Except for a short-lived attempt by the Emperor Septimius Severus early in the third century to reoccupy the Scottish lowlands, the Romans thereafter left the wild Caledonians to their own devices.

DECLINE AND FALL:
A.D. 180–410

In his monumental work on the subject, Gibbon dates the decline and fall of the Roman Empire from the death of the philosopher Emperor Marcus Aurelius in A.D. 180. If the empire's well-being is to be measured only in terms of the stability of its central government, then Gibbon's judgment cannot be faulted. The chief constitutional weakness of the imperial system established by Augustus was that it provided no clear-cut rules of succession to the office of emperor. During most of the first century the principate passed from one member of Augustus's adoptive family, the Claudians, to another, but the dynastic principle was too weak to survive the outrageous behavior of Nero, the fourth of the Claudian emperors. During most of the second century, the Antonine emperors solved the problem by selecting competent soldier/administrators to be their adoptive sons and heirs, thus establishing a pseudo-dynastic principle that assured peaceful succession and continuous good government. Trouble started when Marcus Aurelius left the office to his real son, Commodus, who proved totally unfit for office and was shortly assassinated. Thereafter for most of the third century the empire was in a state of almost constant civil war among contenders for the imperial throne and whatever military forces they could muster from the army or the Praetorian Guard. From the death of Commodus in A.D. 192 until the succession of Diocletian in 284 there were twenty-seven more or less legitimate emperors and an even larger number of usurpers. Few of either suffered natural deaths. Simultaneously and from many directions, barbarian hordes seized the opportunity to assault from without the great imperial state that seemed to be crumbling from within.

In Britain this unhappy near-century of imperial disorder opened appropriately with the departure of the governor, Clodius Albinus, to claim the throne. He took with him as large an army as he could muster, thus stripping the British frontier of the bulk of the forces holding Hadrian's Wall and its adjacent forts. Albinus was defeated by the successful contender to the throne, Septimius Severus, at a great battle near Lyon, Gaul, in A.D. 197, but not before a federation of Caledonians, Brigantians, and a Scottish lowland tribe called the Maeatae had overwhelmed the wall and penetrated deep into northern England.

Severus, the new emperor, succeeded in bribing the Maeatae to withdraw across the border; then, with his two sons, Caracalla and Geta, he himself came to Britain to lead a punitive expedition into the north. This probably started out as an amphibious operation, the port of debarkation being at the mouth of the River Tyne at *Arbeia*, South Shields, Tyne and Wear. Today, in the **Roman Remains Park** *(703)*, can be seen parts of the fort, which was already there when Severus sailed, and the remains of a number of storehouses, probably constructed to supply his expedition.

There is no record of Severus having fought any great battles in Scotland, but by the time he returned to his base at York, the frontier was quiet again and was to remain so for most of the rest of the third century. Meanwhile the damage done to Hadrian's Wall had been rectified, though the nature of the repairs, especially the walling up or the narrowing of the north gates, indicated a new strategy of static defense. Forts north of the wall were restored and new outposts added. Comparable reconstruction took place simultaneously at Chester, Caerleon, Castell Collen, and Brecon. At the same time the civil administration of Britain was reformed with the division of the province into two parts, one, *Britannia Superior*, with its capital at London, the other, *Britannia Inferior* (being farther from Rome), with York as its capital. It was from York that Severus issued his famous decree *constitutio Antoniana* giving Roman citizenship to all free men in the empire, including the provinces. It was also at York that the emperor died.

The throne now passed jointly to the brothers Caracalla and Geta. The former promptly assassinated the latter, only to be shortly assassinated himself and replaced by Elagabalus, a Syrian catamite whose blatant sexual deviancy shocked even the Romans. Then followed that dreary sequence, already mentioned, of murders, usurpations, and civil wars, coupled with battles on all fronts against Persians, Dacians, Sarmatians, Franks, Alamanni, and Goths. Yet Britain during this period was remarkably peaceful and prosperous. This was not the last time in her history that the English Channel served to safeguard the country against dangerous infections from abroad.

At last toward the end of the century, in A.D. 285, there appeared an emperor—Diocletian—with a novel solution to the hitherto insoluble constitutional problem of succession to the imperial throne. This was called the Tetrarchy. The empire was to be divided between two augusti, each with a caesar who was to be his deputy, son-in-law, and heir apparent. For a while the system seemed to promise stability, and before he voluntarily retired in A.D. 305 (an event unique in Roman history), Diocletian and his fellow augustus had greatly strengthened imperial defenses and reorganized imperial administration. This resulted in Britain's being converted into a diocese under the administrative control of a vicar and subdivided into four provinces with capitals at London, Cirencester, Lincoln, and York. Ironically, Diocletian's reign coincided with a renewal of barbarian incursions (the first in nearly a century) and with civil war.

This time the barbarians were Saxons from the north coast of Germany and they came in raiding parties by sea. In A.D. 285, a Belgian named Carausius was appointed to put down this nuisance. He greatly strengthened the Roman fleet *(Classis Britannica)* stationed in the Channel and then crossed to Britain where he declared himself emperor. It was he who was probably responsible for constructing a significant part of the chain of fortifications that lined the east and south coasts of England from Brancaster in Norfolk to Portsmouth Harbor in Hampshire. They are called the Saxon Shore forts, though it is uncertain whether they were built to guard the English coastline against Saxon pirates or Carausius himself against a punitive expedition launched by the legitimate government. In any case, they represented a radical departure in military architecture. Whereas the walls of the earlier legionary and auxiliary forts and fortresses had been built mainly to reinforce the original earthen ramparts and were therefore neither high nor very thick, those of these new forts were both. They were strong points meant to withstand bands of armed marauders. In time they were provided with projecting bastions to serve as artillery platforms from which flanking fire could be delivered at close quarters. Their construction at the end of the third century was clearly symbolic of a new stage of Roman strategy. The empire was at bay and was going on the defensive.

The Saxon Shore forts are among the most impressive of all Roman remains in Britain. Not all have survived, and some are so badly eroded as to be almost unrecognizable, but the remains of a few are substantial enough to attract the intelligent traveller's attention. They are listed here more or less in the order of their construction:

Burgh Castle *(Gariannonum) (606)* near Great Yarmouth, Norfolk, is, with the disappearance of the fort at Brancaster, the northernmost survivor of the chain. It is also one of the most impressive. The walls on the north, east, and south sides are imposing, rising as they do almost to their original height of fifteen feet. The semicircular bastions are probably a fourth century addition. On their tops can still be observed the circular depressions where heavy artillery pieces—*ballistae* in all likelihood—were mounted. **Othana Fort** *(599)* at Bradwell near Maldon, Essex, is only half the size of the original, but at the northwest corner one of its circular bastions still stands, while an internal tower can be seen to the south. Against the south wall is the seventh century chapel of **St. Peter-on-the-Wall** *(599)* founded by St. Cedd. **Richborough** *(Rutupiae) (545)* near Sandwich, Kent, has already been described at the beginning of this chapter. Of all the Roman remains at this important site, the walls of the third century fort are the most distinctive. Those on the south, west, and north are still standing, at places twenty-five feet high. *Dubris* was the Romans' name for Dover on the Kentish coast, whose white cliffs then as now served as a welcoming landmark to anyone approaching England from the Pas de Calais in France. Here on the heights now occupied by the medieval castle they built a great lighthouse, or **Pharos** *(541)*, which still stands sixty-two feet in height, of which the lower two thirds are of Roman construction. Here also was one of the two headquarters of the Channel fleet, the *Classis Britannica.* (The other was at Boulogne.) In the second century, *Dubris* was a thriving naval base whose commander may have occupied the **Roman Painted House** *(541)*. Only recently excavated, this is the most complete relic of a Roman town house now extant in England. Of particular interest are the well-preserved wall paintings, chiefly rectangular panels separated by painted columns above green or red dadoes. Around A.D. 270, no doubt in response to Saxon intrusions, the Roman army laid out a new fort in *Dubris* enclosing more than five acres and cutting through a portion of the Painted House on whose premises a segment of the fort's west wall can now be seen, rising to a height of seven feet. Still later, perhaps at the instance of

Carausius, bastions were added to the walls, and one of these, about twenty feet long and twelve feet wide still survives *in situ*. All of the above is roofed over, and the entire ensemble, along with a well-arranged series of explanatory posters, is maintained as a museum—one of the best of its kind in Britain.

Carausius was also probably responsible for the initial construction of **Portchester Castle** *(561)* on the Hampshire coast near the present city of Portsmouth. Its Roman name was *Portus Adurni*. Today its substantial remains constitute a sort of textbook covering a dozen centuries of English history. The Roman wall, eighteen feet high, encloses a Norman keep, a Romanesque church, and a late medieval palace. The walls are the best preserved of any Roman fort in Europe, with fourteen bastions remaining. About seventy miles eastward along the coast lies the last of the Saxon Shore forts, **Pevensey Castle** *(548)*, near Eastbourne, East Sussex. Called *Anderida* by the Romans who built it in the mid-fourth century, it became in the late eleventh century one of the first stone castles to be built by the conquering Normans. The Roman walls, at places still twenty-eight feet high, are still to be seen surrounding the Norman keep and a thirteenth century gatehouse and inner bailey, both in the southeast corner of the enclosure. At the west end are the ruins of a massive Roman gateway with guard chambers on the inside, while along the original walls, ten large U-shaped bastions survive out of a possible fifteen.

Carausius, for all his abilities as both naval commander and fort builder, lasted no longer than most usurpers. He was murdered by his finance minister Allectus who was in turn defeated in battle and killed. Before legitimate government could be reestablished, however, Allectus had withdrawn so many troops from Hadrian's Wall that it was overrun again, this time by a people whom the Romans called Picts. Thus the fourth century in Britain, like the third, opened on the heels of a massive and destructive barbarian invasion from the north. To repair the damage and punish its perpetrators, the new Emperor Constantius himself came to Britain with his son Constantine. Together they campaigned in Scotland and returned to York where Constantius died and Constantine was declared emperor. Perhaps at this time was carved the colossal stone head of Constantine now in the **Yorkshire Museum** *(693)* in York, which so well captures the strength of character of the only late Roman emperor whom posterity would call the Great. It was he, of course, who established his capital at Byzantium (later called Constantinople) and who legalized the Christian religion. In Britain, Hadrian's Wall was restored, as were a number of forts and fortresses. It was probably about this time that the wall around York was rebuilt in monumental style with bastions installed as artillery emplacements, including the still standing **Multiangular Tower** *(690)*.

For almost a half century Britain enjoyed peace, but civil war broke out again in A.D. 350, this time provoked by a British-born usurper named Magentius, who was soon defeated in battle by the forces of the legitimate emperor, Constantius II. Then came a short period of persecution of Magentius's followers in Britain; then another breathing spell; then in A.D. 367, a fourth massive invasion of England, a concerted action of Franks, Saxons, Irish, and Picts, who again overran the wall. Once more order was restored, this time by Count Theodosius, the emperor's delegate who rebuilt the wall for the fourth time. He also installed a number of stone signal towers north of Flamborough Head on the North Yorkshire coast to coordinate naval action among fleets stationed in the adjacent river mouths. Remains of some of these can still be seen, the best preserved being the **Roman Signal Station** *(687)* at Scarborough, North Yorkshire. At about the same time Theodosius erected a new naval station on Anglesey in Wales as a defense against Irish marauders. This fort, now called **Caer Gybi** *(733)*, is situated in the harbor of Holyhead, Gwynedd. Its walls still stand up to fifteen feet in height with projecting bastions at two corners, inside of which sits the medieval church of St. Gybi.

The visit by Theodosius was the last occasion when the disintegrating imperial government intervened effectively in the affairs of Britain. On the Continent, attacks by Goths, Franks, Vandals, and Saxons increased in fury. In A.D. 383, a British general of Spanish origin sailed off to Gaul to make his bid for the tottering throne. This was Magnus Maximus, later celebrated in Welsh folklore as Macsen Wledig, claimed to be a progenitor of that country's kings. Within five years after his departure he was defeated in battle by the legitimate emperor of the West, but not before he had denuded the wall and the legionary fortresses of their best troops. Once again the Picts attacked. This was the end of the wall as an effective barrier against the barbarians. Chester was evacuated, leaving the way open for tribes from Ireland, Scots and Deisi, to invade and occupy parts of the Welsh coast. This was in A.D. 403 when the Romanized Vandal general, Stilicho, all but stripped the garrison in Britain to fight against the Visigoths who had crossed the Alps into Italy. Still more troops left the next year with Constantine III, a British-born usurper whose bid for the imperial throne was no more successful than those of previous British-based pretenders. Britain was now completely denuded of its regular army.

In August of A.D. 410, Rome itself opened its gates to Alaric the Visigoth who looted the city and then abandoned it. Earlier that year the Emperor Honorius had rejected a plea signed by the magistrates of the cities *(civitates)* of Britain for military aid against the barbarians. They were told to look to their own defenses.

Thus ended Roman rule in Britain—not with a bang but a whimper. There was no declaration of independence, no secession, no act of emancipation. There was simply a vacuum. Rome could no longer defend Britain and the Romanized Britons were on their own.

THE TOWNS

Nowhere in Britain had the process of Romanization been applied more conscientiously or more successfully than in the towns. Aristotle had defined man as "a political animal"—or more literally as "an animal that dwells within a city *(polis)*." The Romans agreed. To them barbarism could be defined as the absence of towns or cities, and civilization as their presence. Warlike as the Romans were, they cherished the amenities of peace which could flourish only in an urban environment. Moreover, the Romans were not fools who valued war for its own sake or for the mere sake of conquest, plunder, and booty. They were imperialists whose objective, for whatever motives, was to establish a widespread *Pax Romana* where Roman customs, law, and language would prevail and where the subject peoples would themselves become Roman in heart and mind. Hence, as a matter of policy, the imperial government encouraged throughout the empire the establishment of towns that were meant to be, and in fact were, small replicas of the Eternal City itself.

In Britain there were four main types of such communities. The first was called a *colonia* and it consisted of a settlement of army veterans to whom were awarded building plots inside town and land grants outside in payment for their services and in expectation of future armed assistance in the event of native uprisings. Three of these were established in the very wake of the early conquest: *Camulodunum* at Colchester, *Glevum* at Gloucester, and *Lindum* at Lincoln. A fourth *colonia* was set up much later on the west side of the River Ouse outside the legionary fortress of *Eboracum* at York.

The second type was termed a *municipium,* a preexisting community which was given a charter endowing its residents with some of the rights of Roman citizenship. There is only one known example in Britain— *Verulamium* at St. Albans, Hertfordshire. *Londinium* (London) also probably enjoyed municipal status since it became the *de facto* capital of the province very soon after the conquest.

The third, and by far the most common type of civic community founded by act of policy, was the *civitas*. The *civitates* were Romanized tribal capitals whose inhabitants enjoyed a great deal of self-government, though most of them without the right of Roman citizenship. Fourteen such cantonal capitals are known. They are, more or less in order of their founding: *Durovernum* (Canterbury), *Calleva* (Silchester, Hampshire), *Caesaromagnus* (Chelmsford, Essex), *Venta Belgarum* (Winchester), *Noviomagus* (Chichester, West Sussex), *Icenorum* (Caistor-by-Norwich, Norfolk), *Corinium* (Cirencester, Gloucestershire), *Durnovaria* (Dorchester), *Isca* (Exeter), *Ratae* (Leicester), *Peturia* (Brough-on-Humber, Humberside), *Isurium* (Aldborough, North Yorkshire), *Venta Silurum*

(Caerwent, Gwynedd), and *Moridunum* (Carmarthen, Dyfed). There may be others, including the Roman settlements at Carlisle in Cumbria and Ilchester in Somerset, though the status of these is uncertain.

The fourth type includes a variety of population centers that appear to have grown up spontaneously: market towns outside forts, roadside posting stations that developed into mercantile communities, industrial centers for the manufacture of pottery or the mining of iron, and spas exploiting the salutary waters of mineral springs.

Whatever their origin or legal status, most towns of any size in Roman Britain had assumed, by the early second century, the same basic characteristics. Each was laid out in a gridiron of straight streets in close rectangular blocks or *insulae*. At the center was the *forum* which was both a civic center and marketplace. On three sides of the open courtyard were colonnades behind which lay the shops. At the far end was the *basilica*, a long, aisled hall which contained the town hall, the law court, offices for the magistrates, and a small room sometimes called the *curia* which may have been the local shrine or official chapel.

The shops were narrow stall-like buildings. The owner often lived in back, or possibly on the second floor, and combined the functions of craftsman and retailer. A great variety of wares was for sale: pottery, glassware, copperware, ironware, tools, jewelry, shoes, clothing, etc. A vast and varied number of these items survive and can be seen today in numerous museums throughout Britain—too vast and varied to warrant precise itemization here. One type of merchandise—perhaps the most ordinary and certainly the most durable—does deserve special mention, i.e., pottery, the most common archaeological material surviving from Roman, as from prehistoric, times.

Museumgoers in Britain cannot avoid being confronted with endless showcases full of glossy red or orange-red earthenware bowls, dishes, cups, pitchers, flagons, jars, etc., identified as Samian ware. The name is misleading since this vast quantity of tableware did not come from the island of Samos, but was mass-produced at potteries in Gaul. Most decorated Samian vessels were made in terra-cotta molds stamped with mythological figures, animals, birds, foliage, etc. Some were decorated more impressionistically by a method called *barbotine* which was accomplished by trailing a thick paste of clay along the surface of the vessel before firing—much in the manner of a pastry cook's icing a cake. Imitation Samian, executed by native British potteries, became fairly common in the third and fourth centuries. By that time war and civil commotion had put most of the Gaulish manufacturers out of business, and the Rhineland had captured much of the British market. Rhenish ware was typically black or bronze in color, decorated *en barbotine* or with white paint, sometimes bearing mottoes such as *Bibe* ("Drink up!"). From the mid-second century onwards British potteries in the Nene Valley were producing cups and dishes, mostly black or bronze in hue with barbotine decoration, called Castor ware. Similar wares were manufactured in

Colchester; and from potteries in Hampshire came a variety of off-white vessels now called New Forest parchment.

Back to the Roman towns themselves, the next item of interest are the private houses—especially those of the upper classes, those Romanized Britons of *decurion* rank who served as magistrates, sat on the governing councils *(curiae)*, and in general dominated the affairs of their communities. They lived in comfortable town houses, usually L-shaped with a separate wing for servants, heated by *hypocausts* (under floor hot air ducts with additional channels to carry the heat up through the walls), but mostly lacking private baths since public bathhouses were so accessible. Interior walls were often decorated, as in the case of the Roman Painted House in Dover, already mentioned. The most remarkable surviving relics of these establishments are, however, the mosaics, usually from the floors of their dining rooms. Mosaics served the same purpose as today's oriental rugs; that is, they covered the floor with attractive designs and proclaimed the wealth and status of the owner. In this case, however, the design was permanently embedded into the floor and was constructed out of tiny fragments of stone, marble, terra-cotta, or glass paste. These fragments were called *tesserae;* hence a mosaic floor is a "tessellated pavement." The designs could be either geometric in nature or representational of flowers, birds, beasts, humans, gods, goddesses, etc. They could be either in black and white or colored. Whether geometric or representational, they were far different from, and mostly not as attractive as, the curvilinear patterns typical of Celtic La Tène art. Unlike the elaborate tessellated works that abounded in Romano-British villas of the fourth century, city mosaics, which are mostly products of the first and second centuries, were predominantly, though not entirely, geometric in design and black and white in hue.

Frequent mention has already been made of Roman bathhouses. Those located in the towns of Britain were essentially similar to those established in, or just outside of, Roman forts, except that they tended to be larger and slightly more elaborate. The public bath was fundamental to the Roman way of life, and no provincial community could possibly have held up its head without one. Normally a bathhouse consisted of a series of rooms in which the temperature, regulated by means of a hypocaust, progressed from cold to tepid to hot. The bather entered in that order and left in the reverse. There was also a dressing room, an exercise room, and a rubbing-down room where the natural oils the body had lost through perspiration could be restored by the application of olive oil which was then scraped off with metal *strigil.* The similarities between this arrangement and a modern Turkish bath are obvious, but the Roman bath was far more of a social club than a health establishment. Normally separate hours were maintained for men and women—a curiously unRoman concession to prudery.

For public entertainment there was the theater or the amphitheater. Known examples of the former are rare in Britain. Greek pantomimes, which were their customary offerings, were perhaps too sophisticated for most provincial audiences. Amphitheaters, usually but not always located just outside the town walls, were much more popular. The typical amphitheater consisted of an oval arena surrounded by earthen banks revetted by walls of either wood or stone. What type of show was commonly staged is uncertain. Gladiators were expensive and expendable commodities, and it is probable that most British audiences had to be content with bearbaiting, cockfighting, and the like. This is not to say that gladiator shows were never given. The mosaics found at **Brading Villa** *(559)*, Isle of Wight, and the two bronze figurines in the **British Museum** *(516)* and the **Museum of London** *(512)* respectively, are proof enough that this manly and lethal art was not entirely unknown in Britain.

The history of Romano-British town walls is much the same as that of forts. With the exception of *Verulamium* (St. Albans, Hertfordshire), *Venta Belgarum* (Winchester), and *Calleva* (Silchester, Hampshire), no towns are known to have been fortified in the first century A.D. In the latter part of the second century most were provided with an encircling earthen rampart surrounded by a ditch. Sometime in the third century, and perhaps contemporaneously with the construction of the Saxon Shore forts, walls of stone were added with one or more ditches dug around them. With a stone wall of four to ten feet thick backed by a solid bank of earth, the total rampart could measure up to forty feet across. Finally, in the fourth century, probably about the time when Count Theodosius was restoring Hadrian's Wall and rebuilding the legionary fortresses, still more defenses were added to the towns' fortifications. As in the former cases these consisted of towers or bastions fixed to the outer faces of existing walls as artillery emplacements. By this measure the towns of Roman Britain became truly formidable bulwarks against hostile invaders. And some of their buildings have survived—even after fourteen centuries of neglect, decay, deliberate destruction, superimposed construction, and urban renewal.

London *(Londinium)*, not surprisingly, is among the least rich of English cities in Roman ruins, although it was, from the first century on, the provincial capital with an eventual population of about thirty thousand and the fifth largest Roman city north of the Alps. *Londinium* received a protective stone wall early—perhaps about A.D. 200. Portions of this **Roman Wall** *(512)* are visible in the following places: (a) at the base of the ruined Wardrobe Tower on the premises of the **Tower of London** *(513)* are a few courses of red Roman bonding-tiles which were part of the wall, (b) off Trinity Square just north of the Tower and behind the City of London Polytechnic School is a short segment, (c) on Cooper's Row on Tower Hill behind Midland House is another segment of medieval wall with Roman lower courses, (d) in St. Alphage Garden near the corner of London Wall and Wood Street, is the choicest stretch of Roman and medieval wall, and (e) in the churchyard of St. Giles, Cripplegate, at the bottom of Fore Street, are some remains of the Cripplegate bastion of the wall with lower courses of Roman provenance. The most interesting Roman ruin in London, however, is not the wall, but the remains of the **Walbrook Mithraeum** *(516)* in front of Temple Court next to Bucklersbury House on Queen Victoria Street. Here are the foundations of a temple to the god Mithras, an Eastern deity very popular among merchants and soldiers. A marble head of the god, as well as many other *objets d'art* and artifacts from Roman London are on display in the beautifully arranged exhibits of the **Museum of London** *(512)*.

London, then as now, was unique. The traveller in search of the relics of Roman Britain's urban development is likely to find greater satisfaction in the provinces. Proceeding from the southeast corner of England toward the west and north, the following urban sites are noteworthy:

Canterbury *(Durovernum)*, Kent: Probably the first of the *civitates*, this was also among the few Roman towns to have been razed by invading Saxons in the fifth century—which accounts for the fact that not much of it remains to be seen aboveground. In a basement in Butchery Lane, a room designated the **Roman Pavement** *(539)* is part of a Roman town house with a hypocaust and a well-preserved mosaic floor of an interesting geometric design. Otherwise most of the Roman remains are to be found in the **Royal Museum** *(539)* on High Street.

Silchester *(565)*, Hampshire near Reading, Berkshire: This was the *civitas* of the Atrebates, one of the first tribes to submit to Roman rule. Founded in the first century, its size was constricted in the second; and in the third it received a polygonal masonry wall which served as a revetment to the earlier earthen rampart. Unlike most town walls it was not reinforced with bastions in the fourth. Still fourteen feet high in places, this is the most complete town wall now standing in Britain. Most of the mile and a half circuit can be walked, although permission to see the two surviving gates must be obtained at Rye House and Manor Farm respectively. The most approachable portions are along Church Lane and Wall Lane. Inside the walls there is nothing but plowed land. Near the rectory is a small site museum. The greater part of the finds, however, are in the nearby **Reading Museum and Art Gallery** *(564)*.

Dorchester *(Durnovaria)*, Dorset: A fort may have been established here shortly after Vespasian's victories at Hod Hill and nearby Maiden Castle. In any case, by the end of the first century this was the *civitas* of the pacified Durotriges. With the exception of a small fragment of the fourth century wall on Albert Road, nothing remains of Roman buildings in the town. On the southern outskirts, however, lies **Maumbury Ring** *(568)*, one of the best remaining amphitheaters in Britain. Because it was built around a Neolithic henge monument, it is round rather than oval, the usual shape for such structures, and has only one entrance. The banks, now grassed over, stand to a height of thirty feet above the arena floor. Finds from here, as well as from numerous other Roman sites in Dorset, are in the **Dorset County Museum** *(567)* in Dorchester.

Bath *(Aquae Sulis)*, Avon: One of the most famous of Roman sites in

Britain, this is also the least typical of urban development, having neither wall, nor forum, nor basilica. The community that flourished at Bath between the first and fourth centuries owed its being to the thermal hot springs that attracted invalids, health faddists, and rest seekers. It was one of two such spas in Roman Britain; the other, now obliterated, was at Buxton, Derbyshire. The great colonnaded **Roman Bath** *(578)*, now open to the sky, measures eighty-three feet by forty feet and is the most "classical" of all Roman architectural remains in Britain. Adjacent to it are smaller baths, part of a hypocaust, and a museum which contains, among other things, sculptured fragments from the temple to the Romano-Celtic goddess Sulis Minerva.

Colchester *(Camulodunum)*, Essex: It was here that the Emperor Claudius received the surrender of the kings of Britain in A.D. 43. Here too, after a *colonia* of army veterans had been established, was erected a temple to the deified Claudius, the foundations of which can still be seen in the basement of the Norman Castle. On the ground floor of the castle is the outstanding **Colchester and Essex Museum** *(598)* with a plenitude of Roman relics including the best collection of town-house mosaics in Britain. Good sections of the **Roman Wall** *(598)* can still be walked, and of special interest is the **Balkerne Gate** *(598)* which can be seen partly concealed under the Hole in the Wall Inn. The visitor should keep an eye out for Roman red bricks in a number of church buildings throughout the town. These would have been pilfered from the town wall and other Roman buildings.

St. Albans *(Verulamium)*, Hertfordshire: The only town in Britain known positively to have enjoyed the status of *municipium*, *Verulamium* was much restored in the first century after having been burned down by Boudicca, rebuilt in the third, and refortified in the fourth. It is the legendary site of the martyrdom in A.D. 304 of St. Alban, a Christian soldier in the Roman army. The **Verulamium Museum** *(621)* contains a number of excellent geometric mosaics and a great variety of other Roman relics as well as a model of the Roman city. In the playing field outside the museum is a bungalow inside of which two rooms of a **Roman House** *(620)* are on display. Here is a full mosaic floor of geometric design and a very well-preserved hypocaust. Just to the south, in the public park, is a good stretch of the **Roman Wall** *(621)*. On the other side of the ring road (A 414) from the museum are the remains of the **Roman Theater** *(620)*, the best example of its kind in Britain.

Cirencester *(Corinium)*, Gloucestershire: Founded in the first century as the *civitas* of the Dobunni, and situated at the hub of three major roads, *Corinium* became one of the most prosperous towns of southern Britain and was probably the capital of *Britannia Prima* under Diocletian. Today all that remains above ground are a short section of the earthen **Roman Wall** *(639)* north of the London Road and the grass-covered form of the **Roman Amphitheater** *(639)* southwest of town. Cirencester's most notable attraction is the **Corinium Museum** *(638)* with its splendid collection of Roman antiquities. Of greatest interest are the mosaics, for Corinium in the fourth century was the center of a thriving "school" of mosaicists whose products were much in demand throughout Gloucestershire and adjacent counties. Among those on display here are an Orpheus from nearby Barton Farm and, from Dyer Street in Cirencester, a hunting scene and a depiction of the story of Actaeon and the Four Seasons. Also to be noted are the Genialis tombstone, the Dannicus tombstone, the Hunting Dogs mosaic, the Christian acrostic, and the imaginative reconstructions of a Roman dining room and kitchen.

Gloucester *(Glevum)*, Gloucestershire: Originally the site of a legionary fortress, *Glevum* became a *colonia* toward the end of the first century. Nothing of the Roman town remains visible today aboveground. In the **Gloucester City Museum and Art Gallery** *(640)* is a fourth century town-house mosaic and a six-foot-high Corinthian column (original height about thirty feet) recently excavated in Westgate Street.

Lincoln *(Lindum)*, Lincolnshire: First established as a legionary fortress, this became a *colonia* toward the end of the first century when the 9th Legion moved on to York. Remains of the Roman Wall and its gates constitute the town's most interesting Roman sights. Of these the best is the **Newport Arch** *(651)* at the top of Bailgate, which was the north gate. Also of interest is the bastion from the north side of the **East Gate** *(650)* located in front of the East Gate Hotel near the Cathedral and the remains of the **West Gate** *(652)* on Orchard Street. Adjoining this last is a substantial segment of the **Roman Wall** *(652)*. Another good section can be seen south of the Bishop's Palace.

Leicester *(Ratae)*, Leicestershire: The *civitas* of the Coritani tribe, *Ratae*'s Romanization probably did not get started until Hadrian's visit to Britain in A.D. 122. Today the most important Roman site is the **Jewry Wall Museum** *(658)*. Outside the museum is a restored column that probably belonged to the forum and, more impressive, a substantial piece of wall called the Jewry Wall Site next to St. Nicholas' Church. This probably belonged to the municipal bathhouse. Inside the museum is an excellent display showing the prehistoric and Roman history of Leicester and a number of brilliantly executed mosaics, the most notable being the Peacock pavement, the Blackfriar's pavement, and the Cyparissus pavement.

Wall *(667)* in Staffordshire near Lichfield: Originally a posting station called *Letocetum* on Watling Street running from London to Wroxeter, the site eventually attracted a large enough population to afford a substantial bathhouse. It is the remains of this structure that constitutes the site's chief attraction today. Outside of Bath itself, whose baths were medicinal and therefore atypical, this is the best preserved public bathhouse in Britain. Better than any other it demonstrates the sequence of rooms through which the bather traveled and returned in this highly ritualized procedure so important to Roman civilization.

Wroxeter *(672) (Virconium)*, Salop near Shrewsbury: Originally a legionary fortress, this became the *civitas* of the Cornovi when the 20th Legion moved to Chester near the close of the first century A.D. The town enjoyed a lavish building boom under Hadrian and was very prosperous. Sometime in the mid-second century an accidental fire destroyed the forum and most of the shops, but the damage was repaired and sometime later a great public bathhouse was constructed. It is this structure that constitutes the most imposing part of the present ruins of the town. Most impressive is the high wall that once separated the *palaestra* ("exercise hall") from the baths proper. Across the road is a length of the forum colonnade. The site museum is outstanding. At **Rowley's House Museum** *(670)* in nearby Shrewsbury are a number of finds from Wroxeter including some interesting legionary tombstones. The town was abandoned in the late fourth or early fifth century and never rebuilt. Therefore it is one of the few town sites of Roman Britain not overlaid by subsequent construction.

Aldborough *(683)* east of Harrogate, North Yorkshire: A small town, known as *Isurium Brigantum*, this was the *civitas* of the Brigantes, probably founded under Hadrian. Not much remains to be seen. Part of the lower courses of the southwest corner of the town wall survive as does a grass-covered length of the eastern rampart. More interesting are two mosaic pavements, one of geometric pattern, the other, of a lion resting under a tree. Also from a Roman house in Aldborough, but now in the **Leeds City Museum** *(681)*, West Yorkshire, is a fascinating mosaic of the famous Roman she-wolf suckling the infants Romulus and Remus, though the provincial artist left out the teats—an unusual departure from Roman realism. The site museum at Aldborough itself contains a representative offering of the usual Roman artifacts.

In Wales, two of the tribal cantonal cities have left traces of their original buildings. The first, and by far the more substantial, is **Caerwent** *(Venta Silurum) (715)* near Chepstow, Gwent. The *civitas* of the Silures was established as such probably in the last quarter of the first century, was walled with earth in the second; with stone in the third, and reinforced with bastions in the fourth. It was smaller and more densely packed than most Romano-British towns, as can be seen today from examining the one *insula* west of the forum that has been excavated. Most impressive are the remains of the town walls and gates. The west and south walls stand as high as seventeen feet and the bastions on the latter, added in the fourth century, are especially notable. Remains of all four gates can be observed, the south gate being in the best state of preservation. There is no site museum, which makes it difficult for the visitor to visualize the layout and appearance of the town. The official Department of the Environment handbook, however, can be purchased in the village and in this case is a necessity. The second surviving urban site in Wales has far less to offer today's tourist. This is *Moridunum* in Carmarthen, Dyfed. The *civitas* of the unruly Demetae, it was probably founded in Hadrian's time when the Roman army's commitment to Wales was drastically reduced in favor of the northern military zone. Although excavations are in progress, little has yet been found except for the remains of a **Roman Amphitheater** *(725)* in the northern part of the present town. At the new **Carmarthen Museum** *(725)* in nearby Abergwili, there is a large display of Roman artifacts.

THE COUNTRYSIDE

Whatever its impact on urbanization, Roman conquest and occupation brought no great revolution in agriculture to Britain. True, some new crops were introduced: chiefly rye, oats, vetch, and flax, as well as turnips and parsnips for winter feeding of livestock. True also, the Romans introduced a great variety of new or improved iron tools, many of them part of the army's standard equipment. There was the iron-tipped spade, the rake, the two-handed scythe, the pickax, the turf cutter, and an improved and properly balanced sickle. Most of all there was the Roman plow. Whether it normally came equipped with a moldboard for turning the sod is arguable. Not arguable is the fact that it usually came equipped with a coulter—a vertical knife to cut the soil in front of the plowshare, which was a vast improvement over the simple Celtic *ard.*

Yet, despite these technological innovations, there was no great change in the method of farming. The standard unit of land was still the squarish tiny Celtic field—misnamed because it harked back at least to Bronze Age times. Yet three important changes in agriculture did take place over time: (1) an enlargement of the total acreage under cultivation, (2) a marked expansion of the domestic market for agricultural products, and (3) the consolidation of agricultural holdings into fewer hands. The first came about partly as result of the government's ditching and draining of marshland, especially the fens of Norfolk and Lincolnshire. The second was the inevitable byproduct of town development, road construction, and above all, the never ending requirement of the army for grain. The third was a function of the villa system.

Strictly speaking, a villa is an isolated country house forming the center of a farm or agricultural estate. Its owner was normally a Romanized Briton, probably a magistrate *(decurion)* from a nearby *civitas* and certainly a member of the local tribal aristocracy. The land holdings of these people were large, at least by comparison to the small plots of earlier Celtic farmers. They were worked by slaves, hired laborers, free tenants, or a combination of all three. In terms of size and luxury, the houses ranged from the simple rectangular farmhouse with stone foundations and timbered superstructure, through the "winged corridor house" of masonry with a long veranda in front and large projecting rooms at either end, to the palatial mansion built around an interior courtyard and entered by a front gateway. In general the first is typical of the first century, the second of the second, and the last of the third and fourth. Throughout the whole period of Roman occupation the trend was toward increased luxury, marked by bath wings, heated rooms, and above all decorative mosaic floors. However, of the thousand or so known villas in Britain only about seventy-five could be considered truly luxurious, the great majority located in the lowlands of southern England. Almost all of these belonged to the fourth century which in Britain was a period of prolonged agricultural prosperity in spite of the turmoil that was wracking the empire as a whole.

If the villa was a status symbol as well as a home for the provincial Romano-British owner, the purest expression of that symbol was the mosaic floor that usually graced the dining room or one of the living rooms or the bath or all of them. By the fourth century there were in Britain several schools of mosaicists, that is, ateliers or workshops of artists working from copybooks and either prefabricating tessellated pavements or constructing them *in situ* at villas in the vicinity. The four schools whose works are most distinctive were located at *Corinium* (Cirencester), *Durnovaria* (Dorchester), *Durobrivae* (Water Newton, Cambridgeshire), and *Petuaria* (Brough-on-Humber, Humberside). The first two, being located in the south, were by far the most prolific. Designs of great complexity included Cupids, maenads, Nereids, nymphs, satyrs, shepherds, tritons, dolphins, fish, scallop shells, mythological figures (Orpheus predominating), gods, goddesses, and Christian and other nonclassical religious imagery. Colors tended to be rich and even gawdy. As with all Roman art, figures were representational—or at least meant to be.

The following villas are the best preserved and therefore the most worth visiting. They are listed in the usual order from east to west and south to north. All are dated to the fourth century.

Lullingstone *(542)* near Eynsford, Kent: There is more to see above ground here than at most villa sites, some of the walls still standing as high as eight feet. There are two outstanding mosaics. One in the dining room showing Jupiter disguised as a white bull kidnapping Europa is inscribed with a couplet based on Virgil's *Aeneid* alluding to Juno's undoubted disapproval of the affair. Another mosaic in the reception room represents the hero Bellerophon on his winged horse Pegasus attacking the monster Chimaera. Not *in situ*, but on display at the **British Museum** *(516)*, London, are two well-preserved marble portrait busts from Lullingstone of bearded Roman citizens who may possibly have been owners of the villa. Also in the British Museum is a reconstructed wall painting from Lullingstone showing six Christian figures in an attitude of prayer.

Bignor *(551)* near Arundel, West Sussex: Here small thatched huts protect the six mosaics which are among the best in Britain. They include representations of the boy Ganymede being flown off to Olympus by Jupiter in the guise of an eagle, Venus with cupids dressed as gladiators, two Medusa heads, and two geometric panels.

Brading *(559)* north of Sandown, Isle of Wight: This has more mosaics *in situ* than any villa site in Britain. They include a well-preserved Orpheus surrounded by exotic animals, a Bacchus with maenads, a pair of gladiators, Perseus with the severed head of Andromeda, Lycurgus attacking the maenad Ambrosia, Ceres bestowing corn and a plowshare on Triptolemus, a satyr pursuing a maenad, the pictured bust of an astronomer, presumably Pythagoras, and, most interesting of all, a set of curious images apparently derived from Gnosticism, a rival cult to Christianity in the late empire.

Rockbourne *(558)* near Fordingbridge, Hampshire: An enormous courtyard villa of more than seventy rooms, the hypocaust is especially well preserved. Untypically for the fourth century the mosaics are mostly of geometric patterns and not very interesting. There is a good site museum.

North Leigh *(638)* north of Witney, Oxfordshire: Here the foundations of two wings of a four-sided second century villa have been excavated. Also on view are the remains of a bathhouse with lovely geometric mosaics in blue and coral.

Chedworth, *(639)* near Northleach, Gloucestershire: Probably the finest villa site in Britain if for no other reason than that more of it has survived than in most. It is a typical fourth century courtyard style villa. In the dining room figures of the four seasons decorate the corners of a large mosaic whose central character was probably Bacchus. There is a large bath suite with a hypocaust. In the site museum are examples of the Chi Rho monogram, looking like the Latin letter *X* superimposed on top of an elongated *P*. These were, of course, the first two Greek letters of the word Christ, indicating probably that one of the late owners of Chedworth was a Christian.

Great Witcombe *(640)* near Gloucester: Another courtyard villa, three of its rooms and the bath suite are presently under roofing. The mosaics in the bath suite have a typically aquatic theme, with lots of dolphins, fish, eels, etc.

Though villas were abundant in the lowland zones of Roman Britain, it cannot be assumed that their owners enjoyed a monopoly of agricultural production. It is more than likely that in Wales and northern England farms and agricultural communities did not change much from their earlier Iron Age patterns. In Anglesey at least, a number of natives are known to have reoccupied some of the ancient hill forts to establish nucleated farm communities. Others built individual homesteads out of stone. One of these has survived at **Din Lligwy** *(735)* near the village of Moelfre about twelve miles north of Menai Bridge. Here stand the substantial foundations of an Iron Age circular house and three rectangular buildings surrounded by a pentagonal stone wall, all dating from the period of Roman occupation.

RELIGION

"The various modes of worship which prevailed in the Roman world," wrote an admiring Gibbon, "were all considered by the people as equally true; by the philosopher as equally false; and by the magistrate as equally useful." Except for Druidism and early Christianity, which were special cases, Gibbon's epigram holds true, as does his statement that "the Greek, the Roman and the Barbarian, as they met before their respective altars, easily persuaded themselves that, under various names and with various ceremonies, they adored the same deities." To the Romans admission to the enormous pantheon of gods and goddesses was unrestricted.

That the Olympian gods received their due in Britain is indicated by the large sampling of sculpted classical deities scattered throughout the country's museums. In the **British Museum** *(516)* there are good bronze statuettes of Jupiter, Mars, Venus, and Mercury, and marble statues of Bacchus and Diana. A life-sized stone statue of Mars, naturally a favorite in the Roman army, is at the **Yorkshire Museum** *(693)* in York, while at the site museum at **Chesters** *(702)* in Hadrian's Wall are two sculptured reliefs of the god of war from the Roman fort at Housesteads. Mercury, another favorite of the soldiers, is represented by a fine head in the **Corinium Museum** *(638)*, Cirencester, Gloucestershire; a large bronze statuette at the **Colchester and Essex Museum** *(598)* and eight stone reliefs at the **University Museum of Antiquities** *(701)*, Newcastle-upon-Tyne. The demigod Hercules is depicted slaying the many-headed Learnean Hydra on a stone slab deposited in the museum at **Corbridge** *(702)*. He appears again carrying a club in the giant hill-figure called the **Cerne Abbas Giant** *(568)* just outside the Dorset village of Cerne Abbas a few miles north of Dorchester.

Of the goddesses, Minerva appears to have been a British favorite, and is honored by a beautiful marble head on display at the **Museum of London** *(512)*. Better known is the hollow-cast, gilded, almost life-sized head of the goddess Sulis Minerva in the museum connected with the **Roman Bath** *(578)*, Bath, Avon, where a temple was raised to this goddess of the local mineral springs. There also is a fragment from the temple pediment with the shield of the goddess displaying the famous so-called Gorgonhead. This is obviously a misnomer since the mythological Gorgons were female and this heavily mustached face is clearly male —very likely meant to represent Sul, a local Celtic river god.

This amalgamation of Roman and Celtic deities was commonplace in Britain. So was the worship of Celtic and other pagan deities in their own right. Sculpted remains, either in the round or in relief, abound throughout the country's museums, and only a few require specific mention here: Epona, goddess of horses, in the **British Museum** *(516)* where there is also a good relief of the Genii Cucullati, hooded spirits of the Celtic underworld. Another set of Genii Cucullati is at the **Corinium Museum** *(638)*, Cirencester, Gloucestershire, as well as a relief of the three mother goddesses and a reclining river god. Others include the stone head of a Celtic god called Antenociticus at the **University Museum of Antiquities** *(701)*, Newcastle-upon-Tyne; an unknown god sprouting ram's horns behind each ear at **Tullie House Museum and Art Gallery** *(710)*, Carlisle, Cumbria; and at the **Dorset County Museum** *(567)* in Dorchester, a bronze relief of a curious grouping of a three-headed bull, two draped female figures, and a human-headed bird, found in the fourth century Romano-Celtic temple at nearby **Maiden Castle** *(568)*.

Temples of this sort were widely scattered throughout Britain. They were small sanctuaries, usually square but sometimes round, with a *cella* or inner shrine surrounded by an outer wall enclosing the sacred precinct. The example at Maiden Castle is typical. So is the ruined temple, 247 feet square, at nearby **Jordan Hill** *(570)*, also in Dorset, overlooking Weymouth Bay.

From the Middle East to Britain came Mithras, originally a Persian god but by the end of the first century very popular in the Roman Empire, especially in military and mercantile circles. He was a god of light, sometimes identified as the unconquered sun, slayer of the forces of darkness, giver of life. His great act of sacrifice, the slaying of a wild bull, was represented pictorially or in sculpture on all the altarpieces of his temples, and the ritual performance of this deed was the climax of the cult service offering redemption to his worshippers. It was an exclusive cult, with graduated ranks, limited to men.

In Britain, relics of Mithraism are found in London and in the northern military zone. The best known is the **Walbrook Mithraeum** *(516)* on Queen Victoria Street, London. From the site came a seventeen-inch-high marble head of the god—a handsome youth with curly hair wearing a Phrygian cap. It is on display in the **Museum of London** *(512)*, along with an artist's impression of a Mithraic service. All the other Mithraic sites are, naturally enough, associated with military forts: one at **Segontium** *(737)*, Caernarvon, Gwynedd; three others along **Hadrian's Wall** *(701)* at Carrawburgh, Chesterholm, and Housesteads. At the **University Museum of Antiquities** *(701)*, Newcastle-upon-Tyne, is a full-sized reconstruction of the Mithraeum at Carrawburgh with a recorded commentary. All the Mithraea show signs of having been deliberately wrecked. The statuary now in the Museum of London was apparently carefully buried for safekeeping. In all probability fourth century Christians succeeded in destroying the cult, which they found especially loathsome—and alarmingly competitive.

Christianity in Britain was probably a slow starter, making little headway until Constantine the Great legalized its worship by the Edict of Milan in A.D. 313 and later established it as the state religion. It is known that three British bishops, a priest, and a deacon were in attendance at the Council of Arles in 314. Archaeological remains of fourth century British Christianity, however, are rare. At **Silchester** *(Calleva) (565)*, Silchester, Hampshire, there was a small church on the site of the present parish church. For the rest, the evidence consists mostly of the Chi Rho monogram cut into the floors of villas or worked into their mosaics.

As already mentioned, wherever these two Greek letters appear superimposed on each other, the handiwork of Christians can be assumed. Two sets of interesting examples are the monogrammed silver spoons from the Water Newton hoard and the Mildenhall hoard, both in the **British Museum** *(516)*. The latter is especially interesting because, in addition to its five spoons carrying Christian inscriptions, it contains a magnificent round dish nearly two feet in diameter covered with figured reliefs of the god Pan with accompanying maenads, nymphs, etc., and, in the center, a mask of what might be the god Neptune but looks very much like the Celtic water deity depicted on Sulis Minerva's shield at Bath.

The juxtaposition of Christian and pagan symbolism in the Mildenhall Treasure is indicative of the theological confusion that beset the Roman Empire in the days of its decline. Soon the confusion would be confounded by the introduction into England of a new pantheon of gods whose home was neither Olympus nor Paradise, but Valhalla. The Romanized Britons who buried their most precious possessions at Water Newton, Cambridgeshire, and Mildenhall, Suffolk, were no doubt trying to guard them from the oncoming Saxons from across the sea. The silverware they saved. They could not save the land itself. Soon barbarism would be in the ascendant. Anarchy would replace the rule of law. Literacy would disappear. Commerce would die and cities soon decay. Not for centuries to come would Britain and the rest of western Europe enjoy again such ordered well-being as had followed in the wake of Rome's conquering legions.

CHAPTER III

THE ANGLO-SAXON PERIOD:
410–1066

In the Galilee Porch, at the west end of **Durham Cathedral** *(699)*, County Durham, lies the tomb of the Venerable Bede, who died at the nearby monastery of Jarrow in 735. No serious investigator into the beginnings of the English nation should fail to pay brief homage to the mortal remains of this Benedictine monk, the first great English historian. His magnum opus, *The Ecclesiastical History of the English Peoples,* is the major source for what is known today of British history from the end of Roman rule in the early fifth century to the author's own death in the eighth. For the early years of this period Bede relied heavily on the writings of a native British monk named Gildas, whose *De Excidio et Conquestu Britanniae* was composed in the mid-sixth century. About a century after Bede's death appeared another chronicle, the *Historia Brittonum,* edited by a Welshman named Nennius. Finally at the end of the ninth century, in the court of King Alfred the Great, scholars undertook the compilation of *The Anglo-Saxon Chronicle* which began with the English conquest of Britain. From these four sources, reinforced by the manuscript remains of royal genealogies, miscellaneous ecclesiastical writings, and a few bardic poems, plus the scanty evidence of archaeology, historians have pieced together a plausible but sparse account of what took place in Britain from the end of Roman rule in 410 to the mid-sixth century when the Anglo-Saxon conquest began in earnest. It is a murky period, the darkest of the Dark Ages. In the absence of sufficient solid evidence, scholars have had to fall back on inference and conjecture. All conclusions are therefore tentative, and the brief narrative account below can only claim to approximate the truth.

SUB-ROMAN BRITAIN:
410–ca. 550

Britain did not cease to be Roman in the year 410. The *civitates* had been advised by the Emperor Honorius to look to their own defenses, but these were by no means negligible. In the time of Count Theodosius city walls had been made stout and they remained in good repair. Nor were the Romanized Britons unfamiliar with the arts of government and warfare. When St. Germanus, bishop of Auxerre, visited the island in 429 to put down heresy within the Christian church, he found at *Verulamium* (St. Albans) a functioning chief magistrate whom he described as *vir tribuniciae potestatis,* a recognized imperial title. He also found an organized British militia which he himself led into battle against barbarian Picts and Saxons, who were reportedly so distracted when the Christian host shouted "Alleluia" three times in unison that they fled the field.

Gradually however the absence of a central government and especially of a disciplined and stable army began to make itself felt. Roads went unrepaired, trade fell off, towns decayed, lawlessness flourished, and the barbarians kept coming. Into this power vacuum stepped a number of so-called kings—native military leaders, perhaps veteran officers of the Roman army—to make war against the barbarians and against each other. One of these was called *Vortigern*, meaning "chief lord" or "overking," who in Wales is thought to be the ancester of the kings of Powys. It is he who is credited with having invited two Germanic tribal leaders, Hengist and Horsa, to bring three shiploads of Saxons to settle in southeastern England to serve as a *cordon sanitaire* against the raiding Picts and Scots.

It was not an unprecedented tactic. Years before the Romans had settled German *feoderati* in the valleys of the Po, the Rhine, and the Danube to keep out Huns and Vandals; and Saxon immigrants are known to have been planted in Roman Britain at least as early as the fourth century. For a while it worked. The Picts were indeed turned back, and not until the seventeenth century did an invading army from Scotland get as far south as the English Midlands. But soon more settlers came—land hungry and warlike. Inevitably they pushed westward, and inevitably they clashed with the Romanized Britons in possession of the lands they coveted. Thus began the Anglo-Saxon conquest.

Who were these immigrants? Bede identifies them as (a) Angles from eastern Schleswig, (b) Saxons from the north German coast between the Elbe and the Weser, and (c) Jutes from Jutland in southern Denmark. He says also that they settled respectively in (a) Suffolk, Norfolk, Cambridgeshire, Humberside, and North Yorkshire; (b) Essex, Sussex, northern Hampshire, and westward up the Thames valley; and (c) Kent, the Isle of Wight, and the adjacent coast of southern Hampshire. Later historians have found Bede's categories too simplistic. Instead of an orderly migration of separate tribal units from specific geographic areas on the continent to others equally specific in Britain, it seems more likely that the Germanic settlers were of mixed origins and were intermingled on arrival. Also it seems likely that there were among them substantial numbers of Frisians from the area east of the Zuyder Zee (the Ijselmeer) in modern Netherlands—a hypothesis supported by the fact that the English language is linguistically closer to the Frisian dialect than to any other Germanic tongue.

In any case "the vile unspeakable Saxons," as Gildas called them, kept coming. And the native Britons kept falling back. Eventually another Welsh chieftain replaced Vortigern as leader of the British. This was Ambrosius Aurelianus. His central headquarters may have been at **Dinas**

Emrys *(736)* near Beddgelert in Gwynedd. Here on a high hill are the remains of a fortified dwelling whose excavation has produced clear evidence of occupation in the fifth century. Emrys is the Welsh name for Ambrosius, and tradition holds that this was the site of his victory over Vortigern in a contest of magic.

Enter King Arthur. He was apparently successor to Ambrosius and took over leadership of the war against the Saxons in the final quarter of the fifth century. Some historians trace his origins to the Anglo-Scottish borders, but it is more likely that he hailed from southwestern England, which in his day was the area chiefly threatened by Anglo-Saxon inundation. He was presumably a Christian, and his name, Artorius, indicates Romano-British origins. He was not a king, even by the loose definition of that word in fifth century Britain. At most he was *dux bellorum,* a military leader, who fought for kings—in twelve separate and victorious battles as far apart as southern Scotland and Somerset, Lincolnshire and Cheshire according to Nennius. His greatest victory occurred around the year 500 at a place called Mount Badon which has been conjecturally located near Bath in Avon, Swindon in Wiltshire, and Wimborne Minster in Dorset. Wherever it was, it was a glorious victory for the British, and for the next forty or fifty years the Anglo-Saxon flood subsided and some of the immigrants even went back to Germany. Arthur himself was killed twenty-one years later in the Battle of Camlann, which may have been the old Roman fort of *Camboglanna* at **Birdoswald** *(703)* in Cumbria. He was the last of the Romans.

From a military point of view, Arthur's victories are fairly easily explained. He was apparently leader of a small mobile army of cavalrymen, fighting in the manner of late Roman cavalry. The Saxons fought on foot. Against helmeted horsemen protected perhaps by chain mail armor, infantrymen with nothing but swords and spears would be at a distinct disadvantage—especially if caught by surprise on the march or in camp or at river crossings where Nennius says many of Arthur's battles took place.

So much for history, or at least a reasonable facsimile thereof. What of the legendary King Arthur—the flower of chivalry, lord of Camelot, master of the Round Table, the Once and Future King? The existence of the legend itself is fact, and though its provenance lies in the Middle Ages, it deserves examination here.

Exaggerated versions of Arthur's prowess no doubt flourished in the folk-memory of generations of Britons whom defeat had driven westward into Wales and Cornwall, northward across the Solway Firth into Scotland, or over the seas to Brittany. The Norman conquerors of England and their successors found the legend useful as a device to enhance their legitimacy and strengthen their rule, especially over the still recalcitrant Welsh. Accordingly, the grandson of King Henry II was given the name of Arthur in 1187, though his untimely death, perhaps at the hands of his uncle King John, prevented his succession to the throne as Arthur II. Henry also arranged for the reconstruction of **Glastonbury Abbey** *(583)* in Somerset, where King Arthur and his queen, Guinivere, were allegedly buried. In the process of rebuilding, two skeletons, purported to be those of the royal couple, were unearthed, along with a tombstone and a lead cross inscribed *Hic iacet sepultus Rex Arthurius in Insula Avalonia,* "Here lies buried King Arthur in the Isle of Avalon." Less than a century later, King Edward I, the conqueror of Wales, had the bones reinterred before the high altar of the abbey church. With the accession of Henry Tudor (Henry VII) to the throne of England in 1485, the Arthurian connection with the royal family was again reasserted. The Tudors were Welsh and therefore in tune with the special Celtic mystique of the Arthurian legend. Henry named his eldest son Arthur, but again the succession to the throne was thwarted by premature death. Prince Arthur's brother, Henry VIII, became king of England instead.

Royal exploitation of the Arthurian legend for political purposes was matched throughout the Middle Ages by a flourishing literary tradition. It was begun by Geoffrey of Monmouth with the publication, about 1135, of the *Historia Regum Brittaniae,* continued about twenty years later with the poem *Roman de Brut* by Robert Wace, and in the third quarter of the twelfth century by the epic poems of Chretien de Troyes. At the very end of the Middle Ages, in 1485, came the publication by the newly established Caxton press of Sir Thomas Malory's *Morte d'Arthur.* Since then the tale has been retold many times: poetically by Alfred Lord Tennyson in *Idylls of the King,* satirically by Mark Twain in *A Connecticut Yankee in King Arthur's Court,* whimsically by T. H. White in *The Once and Future King,* and tunefully by Lerner and Lowe in *Camelot.* Yet for all its archaic language and redundancy, Malory's *Morte d'Arthur* still captures, better than any other version, the glory and the tragedy of the Arthurian legend. It is a truly splendid medieval romance.

Malory has Arthur born at Tintagel Castle on the Cornish coast, the son of King Uther Pendragon and the Duchess of Cornwall. Tutored by Merlin the Magician, the boy Arthur miraculously frees the royal sword of England from the anvil and stone into which it is embedded, thereby establishing his claim to the throne of his father. He is crowned at Caerleon, and from the Lady of the Lake receives the magic sword Excalibur. He marries Guinivere who brings as dowry the Round Table which will seat 150 knights. To this table in King Arthur's court (which Malory places at Winchester and not in Camelot as do the French poets) come knights from many lands to swear fealty to the greatest of kings. And the greatest of these knights is Sir Lancelot who is to compromise himself by falling in love with the queen. Another is Sir Tristram who elopes with Iseult, the betrothed of his patron, King Mark of Cornwall. Together and separately the Knights of the Round Table spend their days in jousts and tourneys and quests, slaying dragons and rescuing damsels in distress, putting wicked tyrants to the sword, and above all worshiping the Christian God. Then one day appears before the king and his assembled knights a vision of the Holy Grail—the chalice from which Our Lord drank at the Last Supper and into which His blood was shed at the Crucifixion—covered in white samite. Whereupon the knights depart from the Round Table to seek the Holy Grail. Only three ever see it—Sir Bors, Sir Percivale, and Sir Galahad, Lancelot's son born out of his brief dalliance with the Lady Elaine. Lancelot himself returns, soon to face the scandal caused by rumors of his affair with Queen Guinivere; Arthur makes war on Sir Lancelot, but is in turn attacked by his own illegitimate son, Sir Mordred, who now covets the throne. The two meet in battle; Mordred is slain and Arthur receives a mortal wound. He commands Sir Bedivere to cast the sword Excalibur into a lake whence it is retrieved by a ghostly arm. He then himself is borne away on a magic barge to the sacred Isle of Avalon. Some men in England say that Arthur is not dead but will come again to win the Holy Cross; while others say he is entombed and on his tomb these words are written: *Hic jacet Arthurus, Rex Quondam, Rexque Futurus,* "Here lies Arthur, Once and Future King."

Of course the story is pure fiction. The scenes and characters it describes belong to the Age of Chivalry not to the Dark Ages and least of all to sub-Roman Britain. There is not a shred of archaeological evidence that unequivocally substantiates the Arthurian romance. No team of excavators has done for Camelot what Heinrich Schliemann did for Homer's Troy. Yet it must be said again: The existence of the legend itself is fact. And those travellers to whom fiction is as real as history will want to visit the sites mentioned below which are associated with the Arthurian legend:

In the Great Hall of **Winchester Castle** *(562)* in the Hampshire town that was once the capital of Wessex, hangs the Round Table, eighteen feet in diameter. It is of course not of Arthurian origin. It was probably constructed in the mid-fourteenth century in the reign of Edward III who contemplated founding a chivalric Order of the Round Table before he in fact established the Order of the Garter. It was decorated with the Tudor rose by Henry VII and repainted in the Tudor colors of green and white on the occasion of a visit to England in 1522 by the Emperor Charles V.

Moving westward into Somerset we come to **South Cadbury** *(586)* near Yeovil. Identified as Camelot by the sixteenth century antiquary John Leland, this Iron Age hill fort has been the most exhaustively excavated of all so-called Arthurian sites. On a steep isolated hill, South Cadbury was first occupied by early Neolithic farmers before 3,000 B.C.; again by Bronze Age settlers in the eighth century B.C.; and still again by Iron Age Celts who fortified it with ramparts and ditches. It was one of the *oppida* stormed and wasted by Vespasian in A.D. 44. Thereafter the fort lay vacant during most of the Roman occupation of Britain, but it was reoccupied and refortified around the turn of the fifth century, thus placing it within the Arthurian period. New ramparts were built of timber and rubble in the Celtic manner, betraying neither Roman nor Saxon influences. Undoubtedly it was the headquarters of some powerful sub-Roman local chief. It could have been Arthur's. Unfortunately for the traveller who makes his way up the steep and stony footpath, there is not much to see except a circle of low-lying, turf-covered earthen ramparts, now used as pastureland for cattle. It is hard to visualize this place as Camelot—where Lancelot made love to Guinivere and Arthur dreamed of justice under law.

Not far away in Somerset lie the scant remains of **Glastonbury Abbey** *(583)*. On land once surrounded by a marshy lake, there was probably an abbey here on the legendary Isle of Avalon as early as the fifth century. It was rebuilt in stone by Saxon abbots between the eighth and tenth centuries and again at the end of the twelfth century in the reign of Henry II. It was during this phase that the tomb containing two skeletons, thought to be Arthur's and Guinivere's, was discovered. The bones which Edward I had reinterred before the high altar of the abbey church were stolen and dispersed during Henry VIII's reign when the abbeys were dissolved. Among the medieval ruins nothing now remains of any Arthurian relic, except perhaps for a thorn tree grown from a cutting from the original Glastonbury Thorn said to have sprung from the staff of Joseph of Arimathea who brought the Holy Grail to England.

In Cornwall near Fowey is another Iron Age hill fort reoccupied in the fifth century. This is **Castle Dore** *(591)* which legend associated with King Mark of Cornwall who is also identified as Cunomorus. At a road crossing two miles south of the fort stands the **Tristan Stone** *(591)*, six feet high, which carries the inscription: *DRUSTANUS HIC JACIT DUNOMORI FILIUS*, "Here lies Tristan, son of Cunomorus." The stone is authentically fifth or sixth century, so there can be little doubt of the existence of a historical Tristan (spelled Tristram by Malory). This is the closest that archaeologists have come to substantiating any part of the Arthurian legend, though it still requires a mighty act of faith to infer from this lone marker the historicity of the tragic story of Tristan and Iseult.

Finally on the rocky west coast of Cornwall sits **Tintagel Castle** *(590)*, the romantic ruin which medieval chroniclers selected as Arthur's birthplace. Actually the castle was built by the earl of Cornwall in the mid-twelfth century and rebuilt in the mid-thirteenth. It is a place of haunting beauty—a magic spot where Merlin's ghostly presence seems almost palpable. Here is it hard *not* to believe in the Arthurian legend, especially on observing the ruined Celtic monastery lying next to the sea below the castle which is correctly dated to the fifth century, though it does not appear in any of the stories about King Arthur.

ANGLO-SAXON CONQUEST AND SETTLEMENT:
ca. 550–871

For about fifty years after Mount Badon, the Anglo-Saxon invaders seemed content with their possessions in the southern and eastern parts of England and ceased molesting the Britons in the west and north. Then in 552, a band of warriors from Wessex, led by one Cynric, struck again, and at **Old Sarum** *(575)* north of Salisbury, Wiltshire, routed the British defenders, and opened up the southwest to further expansion. The site of the battle was an Iron Age hill fort which the British may have used as a strong point, although excavation has revealed no sixth century occupation. Today the Iron Age earthworks enclose a huge Norman motte and the foundations of an eleventh–twelfth century cathedral, the precursor of Salisbury Cathedral.

From Old Sarum, the West Saxons pushed northward, and in 577 at Dyrham, north of Bath, again defeated the Britons decisively. The victor of the battle was a Wessex chieftain named Cealwin. Within a period of twenty-five years the Saxons had pushed their dominion westward from Hampshire to the Bristol Channel, thus separating the British of Cornwall from their compatriots in Wales. It was probably during this time, or shortly thereafter, that the invaders constructed a great linear earthwork now called **Wansdyke** *(573)* that ran for almost fifty miles west from the Kennet Valley to the Bristol Channel, though not in a continuous line. The eastern portion of it can be seen today on either side of the A 361 just four miles northeast of Devizes, Wiltshire. That these were defensive works of some kind is clear, though exactly by whom they were built and against whom is less so. The eastern section, however, is usually attributed to Cealwin and is thought to have been erected to mark the northern frontier of Wessex some time after the battle of Dyrham.

Wessex was not the only kingdom of the Anglo-Saxons. There were seven major kingdoms and several minor ones of which relatively little is known. The former are usually referred to as the Heptarchy, although this is a historical fiction and does not remotely imply any sort of federation among them. Of the seven, besides Wessex—which by the end of the sixth century included Hampshire, Wiltshire, Somerset, Avon, and part of Devon—there were the kingdoms of Kent, more or less coterminous with the modern county of that name; Sussex, including the modern counties of East Sussex, West Sussex, and parts of Surrey; Essex, which encompassed the present county of that name plus parts of Hertfordshire and of modern Greater London; East Anglia, that is, modern Suffolk and Norfolk; Mercia, whose borders at least by the late seventh century included most of the Midland counties between East Anglia and Wales north to the Humber; and Northumbria which eventually embraced all the English counties north of the Humber as well as southeastern Scotland.

Warfare among these petty kingdoms was constant from the end of the sixth century until the invasion of the Danes in the ninth. They fought against the Britons, against each other, and on occasion with the Britons against their fellow Anglo-Saxons. Gradually three kingdoms emerged, if not exactly supreme over all the others, at least more powerful than their neighbors. These were Northumbria in the seventh century, Mercia in the eighth, and finally Wessex in the ninth.

Northumbria was formed out of a fusion of two still smaller enclaves of immigrant Angles: Deira in North Yorkshire and Bernicia in Northumberland. The nucleus of Bernician power was **Bamburgh** *(704)* on the Northumberland coast, where a much renovated Norman castle now overlies the timbered seventh century stronghold of the kings of Bernicia. One of these was named Aethelfrith, who, in the early years of the century, beat the North Britons at a battle near Catterick, North Yorkshire; the Scots at an unidentified place called Degsastan; and the Welsh at Chester, where he is alleged to have killed twelve hundred Christian monks for having prayed against him to their God. Meanwhile he had taken over his southern neighbor, Deira, to form the united kingdom of Northumbria. In revenge, Edwin, scion of the royal house of Deira, captured the throne of Northumbria on Aethelfrith's death; but in a short while the Bernicians returned to the throne in the persons of Aethelfrith's sons, Oswald and Oswiu. These brothers between them succeeded in defeating the Welsh decisively at a battle near Hexham, Northumberland; capturing Edinburgh, thereby opening Lothian to English occupation; and through treaty of marriage acquiring the northwest British kingdom of Rheged whose capital was in Carlisle, Cumbria. Such good fortune, however, was not to last. By the end of the seventh century, Northumbria had reached and passed its zenith. In 674 its army under King Ecgfrith was defeated by the Mercians in the south, and in the north the king was killed at a place called Necthansmere in a battle against the Picts. Nevertheless, by then the native Britons had been split into three parts, each isolated from the other: the Cornwall peninsula, Wales, and southwestern Scotland between the Solway and the Firth of Clyde. Most of England and southeastern Scotland had become Anglicized, though it was not until the eleventh century that the words England and English came into a general usage.

Few architectural remains, however, attest to the thoroughness of the English conquest. Except for some of their churches, they built of wood, not stone; and wood decays. Only the proliferation of still extant place-names offers proof positive of the pervasiveness of Anglo-Saxon culture by the end of the seventh century. The most common are those ending in *ing* or *ings*, meaning "people of" (e.g., Reading, Hastings); *ton*, meaning "settlement" or "village" (e.g., Luton, Taunton); *ham*, meaning the same, only smaller (e.g., Chippenham, Birmingham); *wic* or *wich*, meaning the same (e.g., Ipswich, Norwich); *hurst*, meaning "forest clearing" (e.g., Sandhurst, Sissinghurst); *borough* or *bury*, meaning "fortified place" (e.g., Peterborough, Canterbury); and *caster* or *chester*, a loanword from Latin meaning the same, though usually applied to a former Roman town or fort (e.g., Brancaster, Dorchester).

All these *tons, hams,* etc., scattered profusely over the map of England, were initially small villages, tiny clusters of peasants living together for convenience and protection. The English village is a product of Anglo-Saxon necessities, and there are few existing even today that cannot trace their origin back to the period before the Norman Conquest. Surrounding the villages were open fields of arable land which were used for pasturing cattle, sheep, swine, etc., and for raising oats, wheat, rye, and especially barley. The Old English name for barley was *bere,* whence came the word "beer"—which explains in part the ubiquity of the crop. In most parts of England (Kent was the major exception) the villagers farmed their land under the open field system whereby every man had a number of strips of land scattered throughout the area surrounding the village. What kind of plow they used has long been a matter of scholarly debate, but the consensus now seems to be that the Anglo-Saxon plow was no heavier than, or in any other way significantly different from, the standard Roman plow. It probably did not have a moldboard, but probably did have a movable coulter which eliminated the need for cross-plowing and therefore made possible the cultivation of arable land in long strips rather than the square Celtic fields of prehistoric and Roman times. Unfortunately only one substantial fragment of a plow from this period has yet been discovered in England: a plowshare now on exhibit at the **Norwich Castle Museum** *(608)* in Norfolk. From an examination of this single object one can deduce a capability for some kind of deep plowing, but not much more. In any case it seems probable that the Anglo-Saxons were the first to cultivate much of the damp, heavily forested lowlands of the river valleys into which they penetrated where the Romans before them had not.

At the other end of the social spectrum from the lowly villagers were the tribal and regional kings of the Anglo-Saxons—that interminable procession of Aethelreds, Aethelwufs, Eadberhts, Eadrics, et al., whose names have plagued generations of English schoolboys compelled to memorize them. Their predecessors in the German homelands may have been mere military chieftains, but by the time the settlements in England were well established, these people were royal personages with most of the trappings and some of the reality of true sovereignty. Eligibility to the office was partly hereditary, partly elective. Descent from royal stock (ordinarily traced back to the pagan god Wotan) was essential, but the principle of primogeniture was not. Brothers of deceased kings sometimes succeeded to their thrones, even though sons were available. This was because the principle of election by the leading men of the kingdom still persisted. In addition to being of royal blood, the king had to be a leader of his people—wise, just, and, above all, mighty in battle. His person was sacrosanct, especially after the church began to play a signal role in coronation ceremonies.

The chief attributes of kingship then were sovereignty (derived from birth, election, and divine ordination), material wealth, and military prowess. Elements of all three are apparent in the collection of grave goods from the Sutton Hoo ship burial now on prominent display in the **British Museum** *(516)*. In 1939 at Sutton Hoo near Woodbridge, Suffolk, excavators dug up the remains of a buried wooden ship, some eighty-five feet long by fourteen feet in width. Inside was found no body, but instead a vast and miscellaneous hoard of seventh century artifacts—the richest archaeological find of the Anglo-Saxon period. It was no doubt a cenotaph erected to one of the kings of East Anglia—probably Raedwald who died about 625. All of the objects buried can be construed to be of a symbolic nature. Symbolic of the king's sovereign power is the iron standard and the whetstone which apparently served as a scepter. Symbolic of his wealth is a variety of objects: a great Byzantine silver dish, a large fluted silver bowl, three bronze hanging bowls of Celtic design, a harp, silver mounted drinking horns, nineteen pieces of gold jewelry, including a great gold buckle covered with skillfully interlaced snakes bordered by designs of elongated animals, a purse lid of twisted wire filigree and panels inlaid with garnet and colored glass, and a pair of curved clasps hinged on a gold animal-headed pin, and finally a hoard of gold coins of Merovingian provenance. Symbolic of his military prowess is a sword with jeweled pommel and scabbard, a shield decorated with bird and dragon figures, a helmet with attached facemask, and a number of wrought-iron spears and battle-axes. Raedwald was presumably a powerful military chief, for at the end of his reign in East Anglia he was acknowledged as the overking or *bretwalda* of all the southern English.

That was in the seventh century. By the eighth century, East Anglia was no more than an appendage to the Midlands kingdom of Mercia and so powerless that one of its kings could be executed on the order of a Mercian monarch. Mercian ascendancy began with the accession of Aethelbald to the throne in 716 and lasted for eighty years through the reign of his successor, Offa. Between the two of them they succeeded in eclipsing Northumbria; absorbing the once independent kingdoms of Lindsey (Lincolnshire), East Anglia, and Essex; dominating the external politics of Kent and Sussex; and even exercising strong influence over those of Wessex. Offa was the greatest king that England was to see until the appearance of Alfred the Great. He dealt with Charlemagne on equal terms and even dared to decline the latter's offer of a marriage treaty between their two houses. In 786 at his court at Tamworth, Staffordshire, Offa received legates from the Pope, the first to appear in England since the arrival of Augustine in Canterbury nearly two centuries before. And, most significantly of all, just before his death in 796 he completed the greatest of all Anglo-Saxon public works, known ever since as **Offa's Dyke** *(647,716,723,733)*.

This is an earthwork running from Prestatyn, Clwyd, on the north coast of Wales south to the Severn River below Chepstow, Gwent, a distance of about 120 miles not counting several gaps left in the line. It was about fifteen to twenty feet in height with a six-foot ditch on the western (i.e., Welsh) side, the overall width of bank and ditch coming to about sixty feet. Historians and archaeologists have long been puzzled as to its purpose and how it worked. It is unlikely that it was kept continually manned for its entire length, and no archaeological evidence has come to light of any accommodations for supporting garrisons as in the case of Hadrian's Wall. Certainly it served as a frontier marker between Mercia on the east and the country of the Welsh on the west. Possibly it was also meant to be a lasting monument to the greatness of the king who could organize and command the manpower needed to construct it. Yet it is hard to believe that such an enormous project would have been undertaken in the eighth century except for specific military purposes, i.e., to defend Mercia against Welsh war bands and raiders. Possibly the answer lies in the gaps in the dyke which may have been deliberately left unfilled so as to channel all traffic from the west through fairly narrow defiles and thus intercept it, if hostile, with a minimum expenditure of force.

Today, Offa's Dyke can best be observed in the following places: (a) just west of Bersham, a village about a mile and a half southwest of Wrexham, Clwyd; (b) in the park of Chirk Castle, Clwyd; (c) on the B 4388 between Buttington and Kingswood south of Welshpool, Powys (especially good); (d) just south of Knighton, Powys, west of the B 4355 and on the B 4356 between Presteigne and Whitton, Powys; (e) on the A 438 about seven miles northwest of Hereford in Hereford and Worcester; and (f) near Chepstow, Gwent, just north of Tintern Abbey.

In the year 796 the great King Offa died, and with him the hope that Mercia, with its capital at Tamworth, its cathedral and archbishopric at Lichfield, and its great commercial mart at London, would become the permanent center of political power in England. A new star was soon to rise in the south: the ancient kingdom of Wessex which, though overshadowed by Mercia, had never been completely subject to her rule. In 802 Egbert became king of Wessex and within twenty years, by a brilliant display of generalship, had attacked Cornwall and won its submission; defeated the Mercians in battle and deprived them of their hegemony over Kent, Surrey, Sussex, and Essex; conquered Mercia itself; and finally even led an expedition into Northumbria where he won recognition of his overlordship. In time Mercia regained her independence and Northumbria escaped West Saxon domination. But by the middle of the ninth century the kingdom of Wessex controlled all of southern England from the Downs to Land's End, and its kings were clearly the most powerful in the island. By force of arms they had won their dominion, and by force of arms they kept it.

War, it must be remembered, was the chief preoccupation, if not the *raison d'être,* of the Anglo-Saxon kings and their retainers and chief tenants whose status approached that of the feudal nobility of the Middle Ages. These kingdoms had originated as territorial entities conquered by migrant war bands from Germany and Denmark; and throughout the Anglo-Saxon period, at least until well into the eighth century, they retained much of their martial character. This was the "heroic age" described so dramatically in the great epic poem *Beowulf.* This Nordic saga was written in the Anglian dialect probably about the year 700; a tenth century copy is on exhibit in the **British Museum** *(516)* in London. The virtues it applauds are those of a military aristocracy—honor, valor, physical prowess, skill at arms, absolute loyalty to the king, bountiful generosity from the king, etc. War then was the rule; peace the exception. Wars were fought for land, booty, political power, prestige, self-defense, revenge, or simply for the hell of it.

Not surprisingly then, weapons and other implements of war feature prominently among the Anglo-Saxon grave goods unearthed in recent years by archaeologists. The best single display of weaponry is in the British Museum, but most of the local and county museums mentioned in previous chapters have their own smaller collections, so they are not hard to find. The most common single weapon is the spear. Chiefly a thrusting weapon employed by the infantry, the Anglo-Saxon spear had a leaf-shaped iron head, up to sixteen inches long with a socket for the shaft, which normally was about seven feet in length and made of ash. Related to the spear was the *angon,* a missile weapon not unlike the Roman *pilum* or javelin. The *angon* had a short barbed head, a long slender iron shaft, and a short socket, all in one piece and with an overall length of about two feet. Although angons have been found at royal burial sites, including Sutton Hoo, it was a weapon much more common on the Continent than in Britain. Also rare among Anglo-Saxon grave finds is the bow and arrow. A few arrowheads have been discovered, but they are uncommon and it may be that the bow was not employed as a weapon by the Anglo-Saxons. More common is the curved-edge ax which could be used, of course, for cutting down both trees and people. Related to it was the *francisca,* a throwing ax with a short handle and an upward-curving head, which again was more continental than English. Of more frequent occurrence is the *scramasax,* a vicious looking single-edged long knife, fifteen to twenty inches in length, with an asymmetrical tang, and often decorated on the back. Finally comes the sword, clearly a prestigious weapon, normally employed by the king and his retainers but probably not by the commonality of the army. It was a double-edged weapon about two and a half feet long, pointed at one end and tanged at the other for insertion into the hilt of wood or bone. Some swords were pattern welded, a technique that consisted of twisting iron bands into a sort of rope which was then beaten flat into a thin blade edged with steel.

The sword was carried in a scabbard of leather-covered wood and slung from a baldric or belt fastened by a loop or clasp. Both sword and scabbard could be highly decorated. Among the many very elegant swords found in England, the most noteworthy are the Fetter Lane sword in the **British Museum** *(516)*; the Abingdon sword in the **Ashmolean Museum** *(628)*, Oxford; and the Witham sword in the **Sheffield City Museum** *(679)*, South Yorkshire.

The commonest weapon of defense was the shield, a flat or slightly convex circle of wood covered with leather and ranging in size from twelve to thirty inches in diameter. In the center was a hole into which was inserted a hollow iron boss big enough to allow room for the fist as it gripped the handle attached to the inside of the shield. The location of this central handgrip is significant because it means that in close-in fighting the shield could be used as a club as well as for protection. Metal helmets were probably not used in combat. Only two are known from Anglo-Saxon graves and both are so elaborate as to suggest that their usage was primarily ceremonial. One is the Sutton Hoo helmet in the British Museum, already mentioned. The other is the Benty Grange helmet in the Sheffield City Museum. This latter is an elegant affair of flat iron bands built up in a spherical form with a nose guard decorated with a silver crucifix and at the top a crest in the form of a silver boar with eyes of garnet set in filigree mounts. When found, the Benty Grange helmet was covered with mail. Fragments of mail were also discovered at the Sutton Hoo site, indicating the possibility that chain-mail armor was a common Anglo-Saxon accouterment.

Anglo-Saxon armies fought on foot. Noblemen—members of the king's own retinue or provincial magnates—might ride to battle and then dismount, but there is no evidence to suggest the existence of an Anglo-Saxon cavalry. Tactics were simple. Troops on either side were drawn up in close formation behind a wall of interlocking shields; then, on closing, they stabbed away at each other until one side broke. Battles probably mostly ended in bloody melees and indiscriminate butchery. A king's mercenary household troops might fight alongside provincial levies of landholders owing military duties and/or large bodies of freemen organized into a sort of militia known as the fyrd. Before the late ninth century, however, it does not appear that there were very large numbers of troops on campaign at any one time. The economy would not have allowed it. War was still in large measure the sport of kings and their immediate retinues.

By the standards of the time, these martial leaders were wealthy. They enjoyed luxury and loved to indulge in conspicuous consumption, especially in the matter of personal jewelry. Here they were fortunate in having on hand in England a truly superb body of master metalworkers and lapidaries. Today's travellers are fortunate too in that much of this ancient handiwork has survived and is widely distributed throughout the museums of Britain. It consists of necklaces, earrings, pendants, buckles, bracelets, amulets, and, most of all, brooches.

Brooches, the most common pieces of Anglo-Saxon jewelry, were worn by men and women as dress fastenings, especially to pin together the ends of cloaks or mantles at the right shoulder. There are three main categories: (1) saucer or disc brooches, the latter flat, the former slightly concave; (2) ring brooches, either annular (complete ring) or penannular (broken ring); (3) bow brooches, either square-headed and resembling miniature doorknockers, or cruciform in shape. All, of course, had attached pins, either straight or safety. They were made of gold, silver, or brass and decorated with semiprecious stones (garnet, amethyst, amber), colored glass, or millefiori glass made by fusing glass rods of different colors and then cutting the amalgam into small sections. Three techniques of metalworking were carried out to a degree of perfection seldom if ever equalled by jewelers before or since. The first is called chip-carving—an adaption of a well-known woodcarving technique. It consisted of chiseling a series of tiny pyramidal holes into a metal base (usually bronze) so as to produce a glittering, many-faceted effect. The second is cloisonné work. Here tiny cells or *cloisons* are built up on a metal base plate in a sort of honeycomb fashion; and into these cells are inserted minute garnets, shells, pieces of colored glass, or niello—a black paste made from silver sulphide. The third is filigree, made by twisting fine gold wire into intricate patterns.

These marvelous *objets d'art* are to be seen in any number of museums throughout the land; the best collections are in the following repositories: the **British Museum** *(516)*, London; the **Ashmolean Museum** *(628)*, Oxford; the **Cambridge University Museum of Archaeology and Anthropology** *(616)*; the **Merseyside County Museum** *(695)*, Liverpool; and the **Sheffield City Museum** *(679)*, South Yorkshire. Specific Anglo-Saxon brooches worth special attention are: the Strickland Brooch and the Fuller Brooch in the British Museum, the Monkton Kentish Brooch in the Ashmolean Museum, the Haslingfield Brooch in the Cambridge University Museum, and the Kingston Brooch in the Bryan Faussett Collection of the Merseyside Museum in Liverpool.

In style of design, Anglo-Saxon metalwork was influenced and informed by three great artistic traditions: Celtic, German, and Roman. From the Celts, these craftsmen seem to have inherited their abhorrence of naturalism and their love of the abstract in the form of curvilinear ribbons and scrolls; from the Germans a preference for geometric figures, interlace, and especially an affinity for zoomorphic patterns contrived of distorted animal or bird forms; and from the Romans a return to the naturalistic and representational styles, especially in products of the ninth century Winchester school under the patronage of King Alfred the Great. Two objects in this latter category deserving special mention are both on display in the **Ashmolean Museum** *(628)*, Oxford. These are the Minster Lovell Jewel and the Alfred Jewel, both probably originally designed as the ornamental heads of elegant bookmarkers. The Minster Lovell Jewel carries the design of a round-armed Anglian cross. The Alfred Jewel is still more representational, showing a male figure holding two wands or plants, probably meant to be Alfred himself in his role as the patron of learning. On it are inscribed the words: *ALFRED MEC HEHT TEWRYCAN*, "Alfred ordered me to be made." If the reference is indeed to King Alfred, then the jewel must be the product of the later years of his reign. For during his early years as king of Wessex he was almost totally absorbed in warfare with the Danes and in laying the foundations of the strong monarchy that would be the nucleus around which the first truly united kingdom in Britain was constructed.

ALFRED THE GREAT TO EDWARD THE CONFESSOR:
871–1066

England had long been exposed to the raids of hostile Vikings from Norway and Denmark before Alfred acquired his throne. In the year 789 three strange ships had anchored in Portland Harbor, Dorset, and disembarked their crews. Beorthic, son-in-law to Offa, was king of Wessex then. His reeve, who was in charge of collecting customs, rode down to investigate and was promptly assassinated by the visitors. "These were," says the *Anglo-Saxon Chronicle*, "the first ships of Danish men that sought the land of the English race." Four years later on Holy Island off the coast of Northumberland **Lindisfarne Priory** *(706)* was sacked. This had been the center from which most of Northumbria had been converted to Christianity and the seat of the sainted Bishop Cuthbert who was buried there. The atrocity electrified western Christendom. "Behold the church of St. Cuthbert," wrote the Northumbrian scholar Alcuin from the court of Charlemagne, "spattered with the blood of the priests of God, despoiled of all its ornaments; a place more venerable than all in Britain is given as prey to pagan peoples."

Holy Island can be visited today—by foot or car at low tide. There are ample ruins of a priory there, but it was built late in the eleventh century on the site of St. Cuthbert's church, long since deserted. Under threat of a second Danish onslaught the monks abandoned Lindisfarne, carrying with them the body of St. Cuthbert and his sacred relics. After seven years of wandering they settled at Chester le Street, Durham, but a century later the entire congregation moved again—this time to the shelter of **Durham Cathedral** *(699)*. Here, behind the high altar, the saint's body lies buried still. Here also in the chapter library are his carved wooden coffin and sacred relics, including a beautifully wrought pectoral cross of gold inlaid with garnets and a set of richly embroidered vestments woven in Winchester in the tenth century and presented to St. Cuthbert's shrine by King Aethalstan of Wessex.

The two incidents cited were only the beginnings of a century of Viking incursions into Britain and Ireland. These early marauders were mere forerunners of the great Scandinavian folk-movement that was to carry these fair-haired giants as far east as the Black Sea and as far west as Greenland and probably the coast of North America. Many motives drove them: land hunger, lust for booty, love of adventure, trade, disorders at home. But the principal explanation for this sudden mass irruption is technological. Ahead of any other Europeans, the Scandinavians in the late eighth century had mastered the art of building stout ships with deep keels, driven by sails as well as oars, narrow of beam yet seaworthy, and faster than any other vessels afloat. With these they could safely execute commandolike raids on almost any coastline of Europe; and in time they could land conquering armies as well.

There were two main westward routes for the Vikings. From Norway it was a mere two hundred-odd miles to Shetland and Orkney, and thence an easy run southward to England's east coast or westward to the Hebrides, the Isle of Man, and the eastern coast of Ireland. From Denmark expeditions normally sailed down the Frisian coast, thence into the North Sea or the English Channel, to make landings in either northern France or England. England was doubly attractive because of the great wealth of its monasteries coupled with the weakness of its defenses owing to its internal political divisions. And when, in the autumn of 865, a great Danish army landed in East Anglia, England's vulnerability became apparent. Within five years the invaders had captured York, most of Northumberland, and all of East Anglia. They murdered the East Anglian king —with arrows à la St. Sebastian—and thus provided the English with their first national martyr, St. Edmund the King. Soon they invaded Wessex, where in 871 King Alfred was to inherit from his brother both the throne and the war. He was the sole remaining adult representative of the old Anglo-Saxon dynasties.

It was Alfred who stopped the Danes. In 878 at Edington, on the western edge of the Salisbury Plain, he beat them decisively and then extracted a promise from their leader, Guthrum, to leave Wessex and receive Christian baptism. The two signed a treaty establishing a fixed border between the English and the Danish intruders. From the Thames estuary the frontier line zigzagged in a northwesterly direction almost as far as Worcester. Everything south and west of that line was to be English. Everything north and east as far as the River Tees—about half of England—was Danelaw.

The conquering Danes had destroyed much; they built little of permanence. Like their early Anglo-Saxon predecessors, their most indelible mark on the landscape was a proliferation of Scandinavian place-names. Those ending in *by* (e.g., Derby, Witby) mean "village" or "settlement." Those ending in *thorpe* (e.g., Scunthorpe, Mablethorpe) denote a settlement smaller than a village. The well-known *ridings* of Yorkshire mean "the third parts." As will be mentioned below, the Norse settlers in Cumbria and on the Isle of Man left many material mementos of their presence. Not so those of the Danelaw.

Alfred reigned in Wessex from 871 to 899. He deserves his cognomen, the Great. He codified the law; he commenced the compilation of *The Anglo-Saxon Chronicle,* the first official government archive in England; he founded schools; he directed the translation of a number of Latin texts into English; he built the first English navy; he fortified or refortified a number of English towns. But his greatest achievement was to preserve intact the kingdom which in time would evolve into the English nation. And, unlike most English kings before and many after, he was blessed with worthy successors.

His son, Edward the Elder, reigned in Wessex from 899 to 924. His daughter, Aethelflaed, became ruler of Mercia on the death of her husband. Their combined generalship succeeded in crushing the Danes of Northumbria, East Anglia, and the eastern Midlands and holding in check a new influx of Norsemen from Ireland to the northwest coast of England between Cumbria and the Wirral Peninsula near modern Liverpool. Toward the end of his reign, Edward also succeeded in establishing at least titular lordship over the princes of Wales, the kings of both southwestern and southeastern Scotland, the Norse king of York, and the English ruler of Bamburgh.

These spectacular gains of Edward and his sister can largely be attributed to their establishment throughout England and the Midlands of a system of fortified towns. This development was in fact merely the continuation of a policy initiated by their father, and it is not altogether clear which of these so-called *burhs* were built by Alfred and which by his children. In any case, a document called the *Burghal Hidage,* which dates from Edward's reign, lists thirty fortified strongpoints, all but one on the Thames or south of it, while it is known from other sources that another twenty-seven stretched across the Midlands from Essex in the east to the Mersey in the west. Some of these were simply old Roman towns refurbished; some were sited on Iron Age hill forts; some were strongpoints captured from the Danes; and some were new towns fortified by large, rectangular enclosures surrounded by banks and ditches. Each fortified town or strongpoint was repaired and garrisoned when necessary by the men of the surrounding country; and in Edward's reign it was claimed that no village in the kingdom of Wessex was more than twenty miles from a fortress.

Remains of three of these Anglo-Saxon burhs still survive. At Wareham in Dorset, most of the modern city is still surrounded by the earthen **Town Walls** *(569)* of Anglo-Saxon origin. They date from no later than Alfred's reign. Edward the Elder was probably responsible for the **Anglo-Saxon Ramparts** *(576)* at Cricklade, Wiltshire, and at Wallingford, Oxfordshire *(637)*. An entirely different sort of fortification was the **Eddisbury Hill**

Fort *(674)* in Cheshire east of Chester. Here Alfred's daughter Aethel-flaed built a new set of ramparts on top of the remains of an Iron Age hill fort which had been slighted by the Romans and abandoned. This was probably built in 914 and was meant to guard western Mercia from infiltration by recent Norse immigrants from Ireland into the area now included in the counties of Merseyside, Lancashire, and Cumbria.

It should be noted at this point that most of the medieval towns of England, and therefore most of its modern towns, derived originally from the military necessities brought about by the invasion and settlement of the Danes in the ninth and tenth centuries. There is very little evidence that organized town life in the old Roman urban centers survived for very long after the Anglo-Saxon invasions of the fifth century. Most of the Roman town sites, to be sure, were eventually reoccupied, but this does not indicate their unbroken continuity as communities. In large measure English towns owe their origin to the defensive measures taken by Alfred the Great and his immediate successors or to the Danish invaders themselves. Some of these too disappeared, when not sustained by commercial developments. But many more flourished, at least to the extent that by the time of the Norman Conquest perhaps as much as ten percent of England's population were town-dwellers.

For fifty years after the death of Edward the Elder in 924, succeeding kings of Wessex expanded and consolidated their control over an increasingly unified England. This involved wars against the Cornish, the Welsh, Norse invaders from Dublin, Norse invaders from Norway, Danish settlers in York, Strathclyde Britons of southwestern Scotland, and Scots of the Kingdom of Alban in southeastern Scotland. In the end, and in spite of substantial immigration into northwestern England of Scandinavians from Ireland and the Isle of Man, the English prevailed, and the primacy of the House of Wessex seemed to be assured in 973 at a great ceremony in Chester in honor of King Edgar. There the kings of Alban, Strathclyde, the Isle of Man, Gwynedd in Wales, and at least two other princes acknowledged the English king's supremacy, promised to serve him by sea and by land, and, as a token of their fealty, manned the oars while Edgar steered a small boat around the mouth of the River Dee.

Eight years later disaster struck again—again at the hands of the Danes, led this time by their king, Swegn Forkbeard. These were not the spontaneous, unauthorized Viking raids of old. This was naked imperialism, organized by the king of Denmark for the specific purpose of annexing England to his own kingdom. He succeeded. The English king was Aethelred, nicknamed *unrade*, meaning "of evil counsel" but later parodied as "unready" meaning "incompetent." Either version is apt. The Danes swept all before them, nor were they to be appeased by the payment of protection money ("Danegeld"). Edward escaped to Normandy, returned, won a minor victory over Cnut, Swegn's successor, then died in 1016. His son, Edmund, nicknamed Ironside, carried on for a short while but when he too died, the English accepted the Dane, Cnut, as their king.

To consolidate his position, Cnut accepted Christianity and married Emma, Aethelred's widow. She returned to England gladly enough from her exile in her brother's court in Normandy and in due time produced an heir to the English throne, named Harthacnut. In Normandy she had left behind two sons by her first husband. One of these was Edward, later to be called the Confessor. It was he who was to be recalled to England as the final Anglo-Saxon king after the death of Cnut in 1035 and of Harthacnut in 1042.

Edward was a just and pious man, but his reign was troubled by the rebelliousness of Godwine, elevated to the earldom of Wessex by Cnut, and father of an unruly tribe, half-English and half-Danish, which included Edward's own Queen Edith and her ambitious brother, Earl Harold. The Confessor's greatest deficiency, however, was his childlessness. The English law of succession, always vague, had become even more confused as a result of the Danish usurpation of the throne. The four elements which traditionally established a right to the throne were inheritance, designation by the late king, election or recognition by magnates of the realm, and consecration by the church. In Edward's case, however, there was no direct heir and there had been no unequivocal public declaration of his own preference in the matter. The first two elements listed above, then, were missing. It is not surprising that on his death in January 1066 there should have been several claimants to the throne. Nor, considering the nature of the prize—a united kingdom, large and rich by early medieval standards—is it surprising that some, at least, of the contenders were willing to press their claims by force of arms. They were four in number:

(1) Edgar the Aetheling, grandson of Edmund Ironside and the Confessor's grandnephew, was by modern laws of succession his proper heir. He was, however, only a boy of fourteen without power or supporters. (2) Harold Hardraada, king of Norway, had a tenuous claim to the throne of England based on an alleged earlier promise to his predecessor by Harthacnut. (3) Harold Godwineson, King Edward's brother-in-law, claimed to be his deathbed designate and was in fact the choice of a group of English magnates. (4) William, duke of Normandy, first cousin-once-removed to King Edward on his mother's side, rested his claim chiefly on an alleged promise made personally by Edward and reinforced later by the oath of fealty given by Harold Godwineson, later renounced as having been extracted under duress.

THE CELTIC FRINGE

England on the eve of the Norman Conquest was a unified kingdom, but even so it constituted less than half of the total area of Britain. And though the king of England in 1066 claimed lordship over Scotland, Wales, and the Isle of Man, it cannot be said that he actually ruled those regions. They remained essentially autonomous and mostly Celtic or Norse in language and culture. Still, England was the dominant power on the island and that dominance was the hard-won product of six centuries of war against both native Britons and Scandinavian immigrants.

In the fifth and sixth centuries the British were either exterminated, enslaved, absorbed by intermarriage into the master race, or pushed westward to the Cornish peninsula and Wales or northward into Cumbria and the Scottish lowlands. By that time they had reverted to the tribal organization of their Iron Age forebears, had shed their thin veneer of Roman culture, and were again speaking the Celtish tongue. In Cornwall and Wales the dialect was Brythonic or P-Celtic; in Scotland and the Isle of Man, both heavily infiltrated by the Irish, it was Goidelic or Q-Celtic (i.e., modern Gaelic).

CORNWALL

Caught between West Saxon invaders from the east and Irish marauders from the west, thousands of beleaguered Cornishmen resolved their dilemma by escaping overseas to Amorica in Gaul. The whole peninsula became British and is today called Brittany or Bretagne, where French culture has not entirely extinguished the ancient Cornish customs or the Brythonic language.

Those who did not escape fell under the rule of self-styled native kings. One of these was Cunomorus, the King Mark of the Arthurian legend. His headquarters at **Castle Dore** *(591)* near Fowey has already been described. Another may have been the occupant of **Chun Castle** *(594)* near St. Just. This too was an Iron Age hill fort reoccupied and refortified in the sixth century. About two miles to the northeast, in an open field, stands a single stone six feet in height called **Men Scryfa** *(595)*. Along one face is incised, in letters now all but illegible, the caption *RIALOBRAN CUNOVAL FIL,* meaning "Rialobran, son of Cunoval." In Cornish the names mean "royal raven" and "powerful chief." Since the stone dates from the late fifth or early sixth century, it presumably memorializes local chieftains, father and son, of the early post-Roman period.

The Anglo-Saxon tide, however slow, was inexorable. In 815 King Egbert of Wessex harried Cornwall from one end to the other. The Cornishmen responded by making common cause with an army of Danish marauders against the English, but in 838 Egbert routed their combined forces at Hingston Down, annexed large domains in Cornwall to the royal house of Wessex, and subordinated the Cornish church to the archbishop of Canterbury. Nearly a century later, Alfred the Great's grandson, King Athelstan, completed the process of Cornish pacification. He resettled a number of recalcitrant Britons to the west of the Tamar

River, imposed English law and the English system of local administration on the newly delineated county of Cornwall, and established an auxiliary bishopric at St. Germans. By the mid-tenth century Cornwall was English, though the Cornish tongue continued to be used as late as the eighteenth century.

WALES

Wales derives its name from the Saxon word *wealh*, meaning "foreigner." In their own language the Welsh were *cymri*, meaning "fellow countrymen," from which root also comes the name for Cumbria, another early British enclave.

By any name, Wales is a country of mountain masses dissected by rivers flowing in almost every direction. The mountains have served historically as a protective barrier against the English; the river valleys have attracted isolated settlements shut off from each other by the intervening mountains. Immune from easy conquest, the country proved no easier to unite. The history of Wales until the late Middle Ages is marked by local separatism, internecine war, and the impermanency of any single region's dominion over the others.

Each region was ruled by a king, the four chief kingdoms being Gwynedd, Powys, Deheubarth, and Morgannwg, located respectively in northern, central, southwestern, and southeastern Wales. The kings of Gwynedd laid claim to supreme overlordship by virtue of their descent from King Arthur's contemporary, Maelgwn Gwynedd, who in turn claimed descent from Cunedda, a leader of the British kingdom of Manaw Gododdin in southeastern Scotland whom the Romans had invited into Wales at the end of the fourth century to repel Irish invaders. Judging from the survival of a large number of Irish Ogam inscriptions in western Wales, Cunedda was less successful in accomplishing his assigned mission than in founding a lasting dynasty. However, this early immigration of Britons from the north may be responsible in some measure for the fact that the dominant Welsh language remained Brythonic rather than Goidelic.

Except for the Ogam stones, relics of Wales' sub-Roman past are few. A scattering of hill forts yield evidence of fifth–sixth century occupation. One of these was **Dinas Emrys** *(736)* near Beddgelert, Gwynedd, already mentioned as the possible stronghold of Ambrosius Aurelianus. At **Dinas Powys** *(718)* south of Cardiff in South Glamorgan, are the barely visible remains of a tiny fortified enclosure less than a third of an acre in size that was probably the court of some petty Welsh chief of the sixth century. Of the innumerable Dark Age kings in Wales, identifiable relics of only two survive. One of these is a stone dedicated to Vorteporix, a sixth century prince of Dyfed, now in the **Carmarthen Museum** *(725)* in Abergwili, Dyfed. The other is the Catamanus stone in **Llangadwaldr Church** *(733)* on Anglesey, Gwynedd, memorializing Cadfan, father of the more famous King Cadwallon of Gwynedd who in the seventh century was for a while the scourge of the English of Northumbria.

In alliance with the pagan King Penda of Mercia, Cadwallon defeated and killed King Edwin of Northumbria in 633, only to be killed himself a year later by Edwin's successor. Again in 655 Welsh and Mercians invaded Northumbria, this time to be routed by King Oswiu. It was the last chance the Welsh had to break out of their confinement and join forces with their fellow Britons in the north against the English.

The next Welsh king of any consequence was Rhodri the Great (844–878) who by inheritance and marriage succeeded in uniting Gwynedd, Powys, and all of southwest Wales except Dyfed. His greatest accomplishment was to hold the raiding Danes at bay, so that Wales never suffered a large-scale Viking invasion comparable to England's. Unfortunately for Welsh unity, Rhodri left six sons, among whom his territories were divided. These princes so terrorized the lesser kings of southern Wales that they became vassals of Alfred the Great in return for his protection. Danish incursions along the coast drove other Welsh princes into the arms of the English, and in 927, at a council held at Hereford, King Athelstan of Wessex imposed a tribute on the Welsh princes and fixed the Wye River as the boundary between Wales and England. One of the Welsh leaders who acknowledged the suzerainty of the royal house of Wessex was Hywel Dda, ruler of Deheubarth, the largest kingdom in Wales and first codifier of its laws.

One final bid for Welsh independence was made by Gruffydd ap Llwywelyn, ruler of Gwynedd and Powys (1039–1063) and for a time of Deheubarth and Morgannwg, thus uniting the whole of Wales under his sway. A powerful and ruthless fighter, he launched repeated attacks into England, defeated the English at Welshpool and Leominster, sacked the cathedral city of Hereford, and was finally stopped only by the treachery of his own men. His assassins delivered his severed head to the English earl Harold Godwineson, who in turn brought it in person to King Edward the Confessor. Wales was divided again into a number of petty principalities, their rulers swearing fealty to the English king. Six centuries of war, external and internal, had only served to close the circle.

THE ISLE OF MAN

The Isle of Man in the Irish Sea lies almost equidistant from the coasts of Cumbria on the east, Galloway on the north, and County Down, Ireland, on the west. Some time in the fourth or fifth centuries it was colonized from Ireland, and the Manx language is accordingly a form of Goidelic or Q-Celt. In the ninth century the island became a prime target for Vikings en route to Ireland. Soon after the pirates, came Scandinavian settlers. The first Manx king known to history is Magnus Haroldsson, obviously Norse, who was one of the rulers to pay homage to King Edgar of Wessex at Chester in 973. He was succeeded by his brother Godfrey, a notorious pirate and scourge of the Welsh coast. Near the end of the tenth century, Man came under the control of the earl of Orkney, Sigurd the Great, who was converted to Christianity at the point of a sword and accordingly imposed the new faith on all his dominions. His son was Thorfinn the Mighty who ruled the Northern Isles, the Hebrides, and Man until his death in 1064, after which Man passed to another Scandinavian dynasty.

The Vikings left a more indelible mark on Man than anywhere else in southern Britain. Near St. Johns is a terraced mound which is claimed to be the site of the oldest legislative body in Britain. This is **Tynwald Hill** *(742)* where the Norse conquerors of Man, perhaps as early as the ninth century, held regular assemblies for the passing of laws and the promulgation of justice. The name derives from the Norse words *thing*, meaning "assembly," and *vollr*, meaning "open space." It is the parent body of the House of Keys, the Manx equivalent of the House of Commons. In the **Manx Museum** *(741)* in Douglas is a splendid collection of Norse weapons, silver jewelry, and other such items dating to the ninth and tenth centuries and discovered in various hoards buried on the island. Here also is a large-scale model of a Viking warship. Most interesting of all the museum's displays are its early Christian inscribed and sculpted stones of both Celtic and Scandinavian origin. The Isle of Man is rich in works of lithic art inspired by the Christian faith, and it is in that context that they will be described in some detail.

CHRISTIANITY AND THE CHURCH

Even before the Romans departed, the Christian church in Britain had produced three martyrs, one heretic, and three well-known missionary saints. The martyrs were Aaron and Julius of Caerleon and Alban of *Verulamium*, allegedly a converted Roman soldier beheaded during the Diocletian persecutions of the early fourth century. In his honor King Offa was to found a great Benedictine monastery on the site of which was later raised the magnificent Norman cathedral that today graces the city of St. Albans, Hertfordshire. The heretic was Pelagius who preached a doctrine of free will and salvation through works which ran counter to the doctrine of salvation by the grace of God alone as taught by St. Augustine of Hippo and accepted by the Roman church. The heresy was put down with the help of St. Germanus of Auxerre, though it would crop up again in later years to disturb the peace of the established church. The saints were Iltud, Patrick, and Ninian.

Iltud, a disciple of Germanus, became the head of a great monastery at Llantwit Major in South Glamorgan, Wales, where the writer Gildas was educated, as well perhaps as St. David (Dewi) who was to become the patron saint of Wales. Patrick was a young Romanized Briton who was kidnapped by Irish raiders from his Christian father's villa somewhere near the Irish Sea at a spot variously claimed to be the Bristol

Channel, the Solway Firth near Carlisle, and the Firth of Clyde in Scotland. In any case, he escaped, studied under St. Germanus at Auxerre, and in 432 was consecrated bishop and sent back to convert the northern Irish. The last of the trio, though in fact the first in point of time, was Ninian, who founded the first known monastery in Britain—at Whithorn on the Solway Firth.

Originating in Egypt in the third century, Christian monasticism spread westward through Italy and Gaul, temporarily by-passed pagan England, and in the sixth century took deep root in the Celtic lands to the west and north. The movement spawned both communal houses and solitary hermitages, though the remains of either in Britain are scanty. In an islet in St. Aubin's Bay on the south coast of Jersey is the **Hermitage Rock** *(743)* where St. Helier, after whom the island's capital city is named, is said to have built his cell in the sixth century. The tiny stone building there now (reached by causeway from Elizabeth Castle) is of later construction. At the end of the Cornish promontory on which **Tintagel Castle** *(590)* stands are the sparse remains of an early sixth century monastery overlooking the Atlantic Ocean. Scattered all over the Isle of Man are the vestiges of early Christian oratories called *keeils,* small rectangular structures which served as either chapels or monastic cells or both. There are traces of more than 180 on the island, but the best preserved are the three in the yard of the **Maughold Parish Church** *(742)* and the foundation stones of **St. Patrick's Chapel** *(743)* near Spooyt Vane.

More common in the Celtic regions of southern Britain than early Christian monastic ruins is a variety of funerary stones of the fifth through ninth centuries. These are pillar stones, some bearing incised crosses, some inscribed in Latin letters, some in Ogam, some in both. Ogam is a script consisting of long or short lines, horizontal or diagonal, carved along the edge of a stone. It is of Irish origin and the language is the Goedelic form of Celtic. It was used exclusively for funerary monuments and is usually read from bottom to top, as too are many of the Latin inscriptions of the same period. The largest number of these stones is to be found in Wales and the Isle of Man. The best single collection of Welsh stones is in the **National Museum of Wales** *(717)* in Cardiff, which displays both originals and replicas. Others of interest are to be found in the **Margam Stones Museum** *(720)* southeast of Port Talbot, West Glamorgan; the **Brecknock Museum** *(721)*, Brecon, Powys; and the **Carmarthen Museum** *(725)*, Abergwili, Dyfed. Other Welsh memorial stones may be seen *in situ.* In **St. Brynach's, Nevern** *(725)* southwest of Cardigan, Dyfed, there is a clearly marked Ogam stone in the nave, an early Christian incised crucifixion in the windowsill of the south transept, a stone in both Ogam and Latin in the churchyard, and a high tenth century cross also in the churchyard. In **St. Dogmael's Church** *(725)* about a mile west of Cardigan, next to the ruins of a Benedictine abbey, is the Segranus Stone with incisions in both Ogam and Latin which first provided the key to the Ogam alphabet. In the **Manx Museum** *(741)* in Douglas, Isle of

Man, there are several fifth and sixth century pillar stones with Ogam markings and one, from Knock y Doone, with a Latin inscription on the front repeated in Ogam on the side. But the most interesting early Christian monument in this museum is the famous Calf of Man Crucifixion, an eighth century stone carving in low relief which probably belonged to an altar table.

Celtic Christianity reached its zenith in Britain in the person of St. Columba, a monk of Irish royal stock who emigrated to Scotland in 563 to found a monastery at Iona, a tiny island off the coast of Mull. Iona was to become the cradle of Christianity not only for Scotland, but for much of northern England as well.

St. Columba died in 597, the same year St. Augustine came to Canterbury in Kent. (He is not to be confused with St. Augustine of Hippo, the learned theologian.) Pope Gregory the Great had sent him there to convert the heathen English. The grim gods and goddesses of the North, to whom the English still paid homage, bore names like Tiw and Woden, Thunor and Frig. The days of the English week (Tuesday, Wednesday, Thursday, Friday) still echo these ancient idolatries, as do a number of English place names (e.g., Wednesbury, West Midlands, Thundersley, Essex). Yet these primitive gods proved feeble against the compelling message of the Christian gospel (i.e., *godspell,* Old English for "good news"). "Like the swift flight of a lone sparrow through the banqueting hall," exclaimed one Anglian convert, "man appears on earth for a little while, knowing nothing of what went before this life and what follows. Therefore if this new teaching can reveal any more certain knowledge, it seems only right that we should follow it." Such arguments, coupled with the missionaries' astuteness in concentrating their efforts on kings and nobles, won the day. Although there was some backsliding, within twenty-five years of Augustine's arrival, Kent, Essex, East Anglia, and Northumbria were officially within the Christian fold.

In Canterbury today faint traces of the Church of Saints Peter and Paul, founded by St. Augustine himself before his death in 604, can still be seen embedded in the ruins of **St. Augustine's Abbey** *(539)*, built in Norman times. Just to the east are the ruins of the Chapel of St. Pancras which was part of the missionary saint's original establishment. At **Richborough** *(545)*, Kent, within the ruins of the Roman fortress of *Rutupiae* are the fragmentary remains of St. Augustine's Chapel also dated to the early seventh century. Of about the same date is the tiny ruined chapel of **St. Peter-on-the-Wall**, built by St. Cedd on the site of **Othona** *(599)*, a Saxon Shore fort on the Essex coast at Bradwell-on-Sea near Maldron.

In Northumbria, where King Edwin had been converted by Paulinus, one of Augustine's monks, the course of Christianity took an unexpected turn with the accession of King Oswald in 633. The king's youth had been spent in exile among the Scots. Not surprisingly, he invited Aidan, a monk from Iona, to set up a missionary monastery at Lindisfarne on Holy Island, Northumberland. By this time the Celtic church in Scotland,

Ireland, and Wales had lost touch with Rome and was following a number of archaic practices long since rejected by the Pope, particularly in the matter of clerical tonsure (haircuts) and the proper dating of Easter. The archepiscopal see at Canterbury, created by Pope Gregory, naturally stood with Rome. Matters came to a head in 664 at a synod called by Oswiu, the reigning Northumbrian king, at **Whitby Abbey** *(689)* in North Yorkshire. Today the standing ruins at Whitby are those of a thirteenth century rebuilding of a Norman church, but just to the north lie extensive traces of the seventh century abbey where the great council met in 664.

The king's decision went for Rome, and thereafter the churches in Northumbria adopted the papal practices. Those of southern Ireland had already submitted to Rome; after Whitby, those in Scotland, including Iona, eventually followed suit; but not until 768 was the Easter date altered among the Welsh. Whitby was a turning point in the history of the church in Britain, but too much should not be made of it. The Celtic churches had never been schismatic; there were no major doctrinal differences with Rome; there were no accusations and counteraccusations of heresy; no martyrs were made. But after the council had made its decision, the influence of Iona gradually faded, and the primacy of Canterbury became firmly established.

Whitby was a double monastery, housing both men and women, and, as was the custom, ruled over by an abbess—in this case St. Hild, a relative of the Northumbrian king. There were others of this description in the seventh and eighth centuries, though most monasteries were for men only. They were religious communities where monks lived, worked, and worshiped according to a rule established by the presiding abbot. The Latin word for rule is *regulus;* hence monks are called "regular" clergy as distinct from the "secular" clergy who served the laity in parish churches, or in cathedrals which were the seats of diocesan bishops. The rule most widely followed in the seventh and eighth centuries was that of St. Benedict, introduced into England by Wilfrid, Bishop of York. Within the monasteries themselves stood a variety of private cells and public buildings, including the refectory or communal dining room, dormitories, guest quarters, and above all the church.

Most of the examples of ecclesiastical architecture surviving from the seventh and eighth centuries are from monastic churches. Although there were regional differences in styles of early church architecture between the north and south of England, certain characteristics were common to both. First, all Christian churches were laid out on an east-west axis, the main entrance being at the west end. The main body of the church was rectangular in shape. This is called the nave. It might or might not be flanked by passages called aisles, separated from the nave by pillars or piers usually supporting arches. The room at the east end of the nave, appropriated to the use of those officiating in the services, is called the chancel. In Anglo-Saxon times it was usually square in shape, but sometimes had a rounded or polygonal east end, called the apse. A small room projecting perpendicularly to the main axis of the nave from either side was called a porticus. A pair of these extending north and south of the nave gave the church a cruciform shape, in which case the porticus becomes a transept.

Not much survives from this earliest period of church building in England, but here and there in the Midlands and the north are some interesting relics from the missionary phase of the English church. Considered by many architectural historians to be the most impressive early Saxon building in the country is **All Saints, Brixworth** *(655)* north of Northampton. Here most of the nave, the apsidal chancel, the west porch and tower date from the seventh century when the church was founded for monks to spread the gospel among the heathen of Mercia. Another Mercian church was **St. Wystan's, Repton** *(663)* south of Derby. Here only the crypt is clearly early Anglo-Saxon. It may have served as a mausoleum for the royal house of Mercia after its conversion following the death of King Offa. **Ripon Cathedral** *(686)*, North Yorkshire, dates from the twelfth to the sixteenth century when it served as a church of secular canons, but the site it occupies belonged to an earlier monastic church built for St. Wilfred about 670, and the present grottolike crypt is a survival from this Anglo-Saxon edifice. **Escombe Parish Church** *(698)* near Bishop Auckland, County Durham, tops all other surviving Anglo-Saxon churches in architectural purity. Here almost everything dates from the seventh century—nave, chancel arch, and rectangular chancel. Only the windows are later insertions. **St. Peter's, Monkwearmouth** *(703)* near Sunderland, Tyne and Wear, was one of the twin monasteries built by Benedict Biscop about 675 and was the scene of the Venerable Bede's novitiate. Surviving Anglo-Saxon features include the west wall of the nave and the west porch and tower. In the modern chapter house is an excellent information center with good audio-visual aids explaining the history of the church. Bede spent most of his life and died not far away in the monastery of Sts. Peter and Paul on the south side of the River Tyne near Newcastle-upon-Tyne. Some remains of the seventh century monastic buildings are still to be seen on the grounds of **St. Paul's, Jarrow** *(700)*, the chancel of which dates to the days of Bede's residency. Next door, in Jarrow Hall is the **Bede Monastery Museum** *(700)* which houses finds from the monastic site, but more importantly, provides the visitor with an excellent arrangement of instructional material concerning not only this site but the whole history of early Christianity in Britain. This is an outstanding example of the laudable tendency of modern museums to serve as centers of education. About twenty-five miles to the west of Jarrow is another church with seventh century remnants. This is **St. Andrew's, Hexham** *(707)*, not far from Hadrian's Wall in Northumberland. Here there are reminders of almost every period of English history from the Roman occupation to the Victorian era. Of the original seventh century monastic church built by St. Wilfred, only the crypt remains. In its walls are stones from the nearby fort of *Corstopitium* (Corbridge) with Latin inscriptions.

It would be hard to overestimate the importance of these monastic establishments either at this period or later in British history. In those troubled times when war was endemic and secular society provided little in the way of either security or stability, these isolated religious institutions offered men and women of all ranks sanctuary from the turmoil outside, opportunities for creative thought and labor, a life of the mind and spirit impossible to pursue elsewhere, and, best of all, some measure of peace. Also, it is to these monasteries and their occupants that posterity owes the most significant artistic legacies from what is correctly called the Dark Ages.

Chief among these are the great illuminated manuscripts of which the Lindisfarne Gospels in the **British Museum** *(516)* and the Gospels of St. Chad in the library of **Lichfield Cathedral** *(667)* in Staffordshire are the best examples now on view in Britain. Both are products of an artistic style developed in Northumbria in which Roman, Celtic, and German artistic traditions were superbly mixed. The Lindisfarne Gospels are written in a flowing Irish half-uncial script, decorated with Celtic spirals, with Irish illuminated capitals, and Germanic interlace and animal ornamentation coupled with elements of Mediterranean naturalism.

Closely related in artistic style are the contemporary Anglian Crosses, freestanding crosses of sculptured stone which were either funereal monuments or the focii of outdoor worship or both. The best known in England is the **Bewcastle Cross** *(710)* in Cumbria about eighteen miles northeast of Carlisle almost on the Scottish border. It is actually only the shaft of the original cross. It stands more than fourteen feet high and is carved with "inhabited vine" work of interlaced foliage peopled with birds and animals as well as with a figure of Christ.

A multitude of standing crosses and crosses carved on stone slabs is to be found scattered all over northern England and the Midlands, Wales, and the Isle of Man. Some have been removed to museums or have been copied for display in museums; among them the **British Museum** *(516)* in London; the **National Museum of Wales** *(717)* in Cardiff; the **Margam Stones Museum** *(720)* near Swansea, West Glamorgan; the **Tullie House Museum and Art Gallery** *(710)* in Carlisle; and the Monk's Dormitory museum at **Durham Cathedral** *(699)*, County Durham. A large number still stand *in situ* or inside the parish churches in whose yards they presumably originally stood. Among those in England are the eighth century carved stones in **St. Mary and St. Hardulph, Breedon-on-the-Hill** *(657)*, northeast of Ashby-de-la-Zouche, Leicestershire; the shafts of two Anglo-Saxon crosses in the churchyard of **All Saints, Bakewell** *(661)*, southeast of Buxton, Derbyshire; the **Sandbach Crosses** *(675)* in the marketplace of the Cheshire village of that name, northeast of Crewe; a cast of the fine Easby Cross in **St. Agatha's, Easby** *(686)*, southeast of Richmond, North Yorkshire; the Acca Cross, another tall carved cross-shaft, in the south transept of **St. Andrew's, Hexham** *(707)*, Northumberland; and the shaft worked into the baptismal font at **All Saints, Rothbury** *(707)*, southwest of Alnwick, Northumberland.

Contemporary Welsh crosses include the tenth century cross already mentioned in the churchyard of **St. Brynach's, Nevern** *(725)* in Dyfed; the **Maen Achwynfan Cross** *(730)*, almost eleven feet high, standing on the roadside west of Holywell Clwyd near the village of Whitford; and **Eliseg's Pillar** *(731)*, an eight-foot shaft dating from the ninth century, standing in a field near Valle Crucis Abbey north of Llangollen, Clwyd.

It should be noted that a number of these ninth and tenth century crosses are wheel headed, i.e., with a circle enclosing the crossing of the arms and shaft. These are also called Celtic crosses, though they are not uniquely Celtic in origin. This design for stone crosses was utilitarian as well as aesthetically attractive. The four arcs between the shaft and the arms gave structural support to the latter, without which so many of them might not have survived.

None of the above should be confused, however, with another group of stone crosses, dating from the ninth and tenth centuries which were the products of the Vikings' conversion to Christianity. It was a slow process. The Danish king of East Anglia agreed to be baptized as part of the terms of his treaty with King Alfred in 878, but twenty years later the Pope was still reproaching English bishops for their failure to convert the pagans of the Danelaw. In the north the progress of conversion was even slower. Most of the Scandinavian kings of York were pagan, and not until the mid-tenth century when Northumbria was permanently annexed to the English crown did it become completely Christianized. The Isle of Man presumably became officially Christian at about the same time.

It is in fact on Man that the most interesting relics of Viking Christianity are to be seen. These are the so-called Viking Crosses of sculptured stone, many of them inscribed in the Scandinavian runic alphabet. This was an alphabet of twenty-four letters, made up in almost every case of straight strokes—probably because it was first employed for carving across the grain of wood or on stone. It dates back as early as the late fourth century. The **Manx Museum** *(741)* in Douglas has a fine display of Viking crosses, but all of them are latex copies. To see the originals, the traveller must visit the churchyard of **Maughold Parish Church** *(742)* where a sizeable number are on view under a shed created for their protection; **St. Michael's, Kirkmichael** *(743)*, which houses twelve Celtic and Viking crosses; **Jurby Parish Church** *(743)* with eight cross-incised slabs; and **St. Andreas Church** *(743)* with eleven Viking crosses, slabs, or related carved stone fragments. Stylistically related to the Manx crosses is the famous **Gosforth Cross** *(711)* that stands fourteen and a half feet high in the churchyard at Gosforth, Cumbria, south of Egremont. It is a wheel-head cross of a design usually associated with Celtic crosses, but in this case clearly of Viking design and probably to be attributed to the

Norse-Irish who emigrated from Ireland to northwestern England in the first years of the tenth century.

Eventually, then, the Scandinavian invaders became Christians. But at the beginning of King Alfred's reign (871) the church in England was at its nadir. Between them the Danes and Norse had wrecked most of the country's monasteries, burned their churches, and dispersed their monks and nuns. Of the almost four hundred churches existing today which show some evidence of having been constructed before the Norman Conquest, only fourteen date from the period before 800, i.e., during and before the Viking conquests.

Alfred, of course, was a devout Christian and did what he could to revive the monastic movement. But it was not until the reign of his great-grandson Edgar (959–975) that monasticism in England really enjoyed a rebirth. This was largely the work of three great clerics of the tenth century: Dunstan, Archbishop of Canterbury; Ethelwold, Bishop of Winchester; and Oswald, Bishop of Worcester and Archbishop of York. Inspired in part by the great continental revival of the Benedictine Order emanating from the abbey at Cluny in Burgundy, these men not only rejuvenated monastic life in England by imposing the reformed rule of St. Benedict, but gave new life to the cathedrals by a wholesale replacement of their secular clergy with a more zealous and better-educated breed of monks. One result was a renaissance of monastic art work which found its highest expression in the Winchester school of manuscript illumination. The two finest products of the new style, both in the **British Museum** *(516)* are King Edward's Charter to the New Minster at Winchester and the Benedictional of St. Aethelwold. Though both retain decorative features usually associated with the mixed Celtic and Saxon artistic traditions commonly called Hiberno-Saxon, both also show marked Mediterranean influences in their more or less realistic representations of the human form.

It should not be thought that the religious revival of the tenth and eleventh centuries was confined to monasteries. This was a period of extensive church building, encouraged by King Cnut as well as by the monarchs of the House of Wessex. Of the more than three hundred extant churches or parts of churches dating from the century before the Norman Conquest all but one are built of stone. Those listed below are among the most representative, and in most cases among the most complete, of these survivors. The great majority of Anglo-Saxon churches of course have been subsequently enlarged, restored, restyled, or otherwise modified. Yet they almost all retain some of their original features, which can be recognized from the following characteristics which are typically and for the most part uniquely Anglo-Saxon: (a) double windows in the tower extending through the full thickness of the wall with a mid-wall shaft supporting a slab also running through the wall; (b) doorways or windows with round (semicircular) or triangular heads; (c) pilaster wall strips, i.e., long vertical stone strips extending two or three inches forward from the main face of walls both interior and exterior; (d) long-and-short quoining, i.e., wall corners constructed of large stones laid alternately flat and upright; (e) double-splayed windows in which the aperture is embedded in the middle of the thickness of the wall and the opening in the wall is beveled away from the aperture both inside and out (the general effect from either side of the wall is that of a picture set in a deep frame); (f) tall, narrow doorways, either square headed, triangular headed, or round headed, the openings for doors being usually cut straight through the wall and lined with large "through stones"; (g) string courses, i.e., horizontal strips especially on tower walls, each constructed of a single protruding course of bricks or stones; (h) thin walls, seldom more than three inches thick; (i) square chancels projecting eastward from a rectangular nave, the former being roughly half the size of the latter; and (j) narrow arched openings between chancel and nave and between nave and transepts.

The following churches, whose surviving Anglo-Saxon features are indicated in parentheses, all display one or more of the above characteristics. Starting in southeastern England and moving west and north, they are: **St. Nicholas, Worth** *(553)*, east of Crawley, West Sussex (pilaster strips, long-and-short quoins, double windows on both sides of nave, chancel arch, transeptal arches, and narrow doorways on north and south sides of nave); **St. Mary's, Sompting** *(554)*, northeast of Worthing, West Sussex (west tower with pilaster strips, string courses, double windows, and triangular-headed windows, and parts of the nave walls. The unique Rhenish helm spire is an eighteenth century addition.); **St. Martin's, Wareham** *(569)*, Dorset (nave minus the north aisle, chancel, and chancel arch); **St. Laurence, Bradford-on-Avon** *(571)*, Wiltshire (nave with flanking porches, chancel, chancel arch, double-splayed windows, and pilaster strips); **St. Andrew's, Greensted** *(598)*, west of Chelmsford, Essex (nave walls of split oak logs, the unique survival of a wooden Anglo-Saxon church); **Holy Trinity, Colchester** *(598)*, Essex (west tower faced with Roman brick, with triangular-headed doorway, pilaster strips, string courses and round-headed double splayed windows [blocked], and the west wall of the nave); **North Elmham Cathedral** *(605)*, southeast of Fakenham, Norfolk (entire ruin consisting of lower courses of west tower and turret stair, nave flanked by two small towers, transepts, and a small apsidal chancel); **St. Bene't's, Cambridge** *(617)* (west tower with double windows and long-and-short quoins, and upper parts of the nave walls); **All Saints, Wing** *(624)*, Buckinghamshire (aisled nave, polygonal apse, pilaster strips, and crypt); **St. Mary's, Deerhurst** *(639)*, northwest of Cheltenham, Gloucestershire (west tower with double triangular-headed window and the ninth century font); **All Saints, Earls Barton** *(657)*, Northamptonshire (west tower with pilaster strips, double windows, and triangular-headed windows—probably the best known of Anglo-Saxon church towers in England); **St. John the Baptist, Barnack** *(654)* in Cambridgeshire, near Stamford, Lincolnshire (west tower with long-and-short quoins, pilaster strips, round-headed and triangular windows, and a sun dial over the south window); **St. Peter's, Barton-on-Humber** *(678)*, southwest of Hull, Humberside (west tower with long-and-short quoins, pilaster strips, string courses, and double windows, and the western annex with round-headed, double-splayed windows, and long-and-short quoins); **St. Helen's, Skipwith** *(693)*, southeast of York (lower western tower with double-splayed windows, and the western part of the nave); and **St. Andrew's, Corbridge** *(702)*, Northumberland, seventeen miles west of Newcastle-upon-Tyne (west porch and tower built of Roman stones from *Corstopitium*, and the walls of the nave).

One very fragmentary monastic survival from the very end of the Anglo-Saxon period deserves special mention. This is **Westminster Abbey** *(523)*, London, built on the order of Edward the Confessor, last of the truly English kings of England. He chose Westminster for his burial place and rebuilt an ancient monastery there into a personal mausoleum. Most of what he constructed was torn down in the thirteenth century by King Henry III to be replaced by the splendid Gothic church now visible. About all that remains of the Confessor's great accomplishment is in the Pyx Chamber which is usually kept locked but may be visited on application at the chapter house. All that can be seen, in any case, is a square chamber consisting of two bays of the undercroft of the original eleventh century dormitory of the monks associated with the abbey. Nearly contemporary with this is the Norman cloister which gives access to the Norman undercroft with its museum illustrating the abbey's history. These are meager remnants of the Confessor's great abbey church with its long nave of six double bays, its lantern tower over the crossing, and its two western towers. On 28 December 1065, as King Edward lay dying, his new church was dedicated. Built in the Romanesque style, it was a close copy of a half-dozen Benedictine abbey churches in Normandy. The intrusion into England of Norman fashions of architecture would soon be followed by a more dramatic Norman invasion. Edward the Confessor had built a fitting site for the coronation of his successor, Duke William of Normandy, King William I of England.

CHAPTER IV

THE EARLY MIDDLE AGES

War and Politics:

1066–1307

THE NORMANS

In an obscure and unmarked corner of the **Victoria and Albert Museum** *(526)* in South Kensington, London, sits a curious contraption that merits close inspection by the intelligent traveller as he begins his journey through Britain's medieval past. This is a photocopy of the famous Bayeux Tapestry, reproduced in brilliant color, enclosed in a glass-covered cabinet, and attached at either end to electronically controlled rollers. Here, by merely pushing a button, the viewer can see the stirring events of the Norman Conquest slowly unfold before his eyes.

To view the original tapestry would, of course, require a trip across the Channel to Bayeux in Normandy, where it hangs in the Old Archbishop's Palace across the street from Notre Dame Cathedral. Technically it is not a tapestry at all, but an embroidered strip of linen measuring 230 feet by 20 inches, depicting, in the manner of a modern strip cartoon, the events leading up to the Norman invasion of England and ending in the Battle of Hastings. It is a very busy work of art, featuring 623 people, 762 animals, 37 buildings, and 41 ships and boats—all stitched in brilliant colors, perhaps by Matilda, the Conqueror's queen. Fully half the tapestry is devoted to the Norman version of Harold Godwineson's perfidy in accepting the Crown of England after having previously sworn on holy relics to support the legitimate claim to the English kingdom of the Norman duke, known to his contemporaries as William the Bastard. The rest describes in detail how William launched his invading fleet, landed at Pevensey on the Sussex coast, marched to nearby Hastings, and thence to the battle of 14 October 1066 where the English forces were routed.

It will be remembered that there were four claimants to the throne of the childless King Edward the Confessor who died on 5 January 1066. Edgar the Aetheling was a minor and powerless to enforce his claims. Harold Hardraada, King of Norway, to support *his* claim, launched a fleet of three-hundred ships loaded with Norse warriors against the Yorkshire coast in September of 1066. On the twenty-fifth of that month, however, at Stamford Bridge on the Derwent in Humberside, he was slain and his forces routed by Harold Godwineson who had been elected king by the Anglo-Saxon Witan and crowned at Westminster on the very day of the old king's death. *His* claim was contested by William, duke of Normandy on the grounds of an alleged promise of the throne by his kinsman Edward the Confessor coupled with Harold's oath of fealty sworn in Normandy three years before. (This episode and the events leading up to it constitute the main theme of the first half of the Bayeux Tapestry.)

Two days after Earl Godwineson's victory at Stamford Bridge, Duke William sailed for England from St. Valery-sur-Somme with a fair wind behind, the papal banner flying from his mainmast, and consecrated relics around his neck to demonstrate the holiness of his cause. More importantly (though perhaps not to Pope Alexander II who had blessed the enterprise), his mighty fleet carried an army of six to seven thousand men—Norman knights and foot soldiers plus a horde of land-hungry adventurers from Brittany, Picardy, Poitou, Flanders, and as far away as Sicily. They landed at Pevensey Bay, East Sussex; established temporary quarters on the site of the ruined Roman fort of *Anderida;* then moved on to nearby Hastings where they built a castle of earth and timber. Meanwhile Harold had hastily marched his troops 190 miles south from York to London, and then pushed on impulsively another 50 miles to the neighborhood of Hastings. On 14 October at a place called Senlac in the present town of Battle in East Sussex the two armies confronted one another. Today the ruins of the thirteenth century buildings of **Battle Abbey** *(547)* stand on the site of perhaps the most fateful battle in English history. In the undercroft of what was once the guest lodge is a three-dimensional model of the affair, complete with toy soldiers in Norman and Saxon attire, and at a spot thought to be near the center of the Norman line is a diagram of the battlefield from William's point of view.

The two armies were about equal in size but unequal in firepower and mobility. Harold's fought altogether on foot. His elite troops of housecarls wore armor of chain mail and conical-shaped helmets with protective iron nosepieces. They were armed with swords, javelins, and fearsome two-handed Danish axes. William had a more balanced force of foot soldiers, archers, and cavalry. The infantry were armed with pike and sword and some were protected by mail shirts. The Norman bow was about five feet long and the archers, too, wore chain mail and conical iron helmets. There may have been crossbowmen present, but it is not certain. The pride of the invading army was the cavalry—some two or three thousand mounted and armored knights, carrying swords, lances, and sometimes maces; their heads covered with conical helmets; their bodies protected by kite-shaped shields. All this is clearly depicted on the Bayeux Tapestry.

The battle raged from dawn to late afternoon. At first the English infantry ensconced behind their wall of shields, had the advantage. They lost it when they broke ranks to pursue groups of retreating Normans, thus giving the more mobile cavalrymen the chance to wheel and cut their attackers to pieces. The final turning point came in the late afternoon when William sent his archers uphill on the run, immediately followed by his mounted knights. A hundred yards short of the English line the bowmen halted and loosed their arrows almost vertically in the air. As they fell, the massed cavalry charged, and in the confusion the English broke ranks. It was probably at this point that Harold himself was killed—his eye pierced by an arrow. The rest was carnage. Historical tradition points to the battle, misnamed Hastings, as a notable victory of cavalry over infantry. In fact it was a victory of combined arms, though, not surprisingly, the knights hogged most of the credit.

WILLIAM I: 1066–1087

Victorious in the field, the Conqueror had yet to conquer England. His first strategic objective was London, the principal city of the kingdom, though not yet the seat of its government. William approached it cautiously and circuitously. He first took Dover, then Canterbury and Winchester, set fire to Southwark, crossed the Thames at Wallingford, and circled west of the city. To Berkhamstead in Hertfordshire, the London city fathers rode for twenty-five miles to capitulate and to swear fealty. With them came a significant number of English prelates and great lords as well as Edgar the Aetheling, the only surviving contestant for the throne.

And so it was that on Christmas Day 1066, William, the bastard son of the sixth duke of Normandy by Harleve, daughter of a tanner of Falaise, was crowned King of England at Westminster Abbey, the magnificent new church built by Edward the Confessor as his personal memorial and mausoleum. The contrast between the two princes could not have been more striking: Edward—frail, contemplative, cautious, and pious; William—burly, loud, ardent, and above all martial. The one was destined for sainthood (he was canonized in 1181); the other to found a great cross-Channel empire and a dynasty that still survives.

It took about a decade to complete the conquest of England. Rebellions in Yorkshire and East Anglia were put down ruthlessly. On the Welsh border the new king set up buffer states endowing their marcher lords with semiregal powers: William fitz Osbern (i.e., William *fils de*—son of—Osbern) as earl of Hereford; Roger de Montgomery as earl of Shrewsbury; and Hugh d'Avranches as earl of Chester. All three gradually pushed their power westward beyond the marches (i.e., frontier or borderland) into the Welsh uplands. In the southwest the Conqueror left a native prince, Rhys ap Tewdwr, as ruler of Deheubarth, though establishing at least nominal feudal suzerainty over him.

Scotland, however, was another matter. There King Malcolm Canmore (Malcolm III, Macbeth's slayer) had established a degree of unified control over most of the country, and in 1070 married Margaret, sister of the now exiled Edgar the Aetheling to whom he had given refuge. The Scottish king, however, was no match for the Conqueror of England whose northern counties he was wont to raid. In 1071 William invaded Scotland and at Abernathy compelled King Malcolm to render homage and to expel the Aetheling from his court.

In England itself the first and most revolutionary result of the conquest was the almost total dispossession of the ancient Anglo-Saxon nobility and their replacement by the warriors who had accompanied William across the Channel. By conquest, the king owned the entire country. Large portions of it, however, he doled out to his military leaders (barons) as reward for past services and in expectation of services to come. The barons in turn parceled out portions of their holdings to their knightly followers, again in exchange for past and future services. All these grants of land were conditional, the chief condition being the obligation of military service by the grantee (the vassal) to the grantor (the lord). In time the estates became hereditary. They were called *fiefs* in French, *fees* in English, or *feuda* in Latin—whence comes the term feudal system, a seventeenth century phrase coined to describe the military organization prevalent throughout western Europe in the Middle Ages and the social and political arrangements that derived from it.

Post-Conquest England, then, was a country occupied by a small alien military aristocracy; its native population still unruly and rebellious; its borders always subject to incursion from the still unconquered Welsh and Scots and its shores to amphibious operations mounted in Scandinavia. And though the king had an ever-present need for field armies of mounted knights to lead against his enemies in Britain and Normandy, he had an even greater requirement for fortified strongpoints to govern and control a fractious population. Hence the castle: a truly Norman innovation, of which about eighty-six were built in England before the close of the eleventh century. The castle was at once the product of the Norman Conquest and the means of insuring its permanence; it was the architectural embodiment of the feudal system. By definition, a castle is a fortified residence or a residential fortress, occupied either by the king, his constable, a baron, or a lesser great lord. It is a home, an armory, a military outpost, and a seat of government.

In the Conqueror's time and even later, most castles were built of earth and timber according to a standard plan called motte and bailey. The *motte* was a mound of earth surrounded by a ditch or moat and compressed sufficiently to take the weight of a square tower or keep, usually made of timber and surrounded by a wooden palisade. In it lived the lord and his household. Adjacent to the tower was the *bailey*, an enclosure, also palisaded and often moated, inside of which were laborers' houses, stables, a smithy, etc. A stepped flying-bridge of timber connected the bailey with the motte.

Naturally none of these timbered structures has survived, though there are hundreds of mottes. On many of these, stone keeps were later built to replace the timbered towers and are among some of the most famous castles of Britain. In some cases, however, the original mottes were abandoned and remain now only as grassy mounds. The highest of these extant is **Castle Hill** *(609)* at Thetford, Norfolk, which measures eighty feet high and one thousand in circumference. Other denuded Norman mottes are the **Castle Mounds at Pleshey** *(598)* and **Chipping Ongar** *(599)* in Essex; **Skipsea Castle** *(677)* near Bridlington,

Humberside; and, on the grounds of the eleventh century **Montgomery Castle** *(723)* near the town of the same name in Powys, a motte called Hen Domen, which is Welsh for "the old mound." Occasionally, instead of throwing up an artificial mound, Norman builders would level off a natural hillock. This was done at **Old Sarum** *(575)* north of Salisbury, Wiltshire, where inside an ancient Iron Age hill fort is an impressive Norman motte upon which was later built a stone castle whose scanty remains can still be seen.

Naturally, as the Normans tightened their control over their new island kingdom and speed of construction was no longer the first requisite for security, stone came to replace wood and earth as the prime material for castle construction. Now began a nationwide building program that would last for at least a century. Although the stone castle was eventually to undergo many changes in style and form, the original prototype was the square or rectangular tower keep—a product of the eleventh and twelfth centuries.

This was a thick-walled stone structure, laid out on a quadrilateral ground plan about 40 by 50 feet and normally rising to a height of 100 to 120 feet. On the outside, the four corners were reinforced by flat buttresses, as were the faces of each of the four sides. The base was splayed outward, forming a plinth. The wooden roof had a steep pitch and was hidden from view by a high parapet, sometimes crenellated, i.e., notched with square apertures at regular intervals to form a battlement. The main entrance was by way of a wooden stairway leading to the first floor above the ground floor or undercroft. Later this was often covered by a fore building. Normally there were four stories. The undercroft or cellar stood on the ground floor and was used for storage. On this floor was also sunk the castle well. Visitors should be wary of stories about the undercrofts being used as prisons unless there is corroborative evidence to that effect. Confusion arises from the fact that the modern word *dungeon,* meaning "underground prison" derives from *donjon* which was French for "keep." In fact, not all *donjons* were prisons and none preeminently so. Above the ground floor were usually three stories. The first floor was occupied by servants and armed retainers and had only slit windows. The second contained the great hall which normally had a hearth in the center with no chimney for the smoke. Fireplaces might be set in the outer walls with flues angling out to the exterior face. Windows were narrow and usually round headed, i.e., topped by a semi-circular arch. Wooden shutters kept out the rain and snow. If there was a third floor, it might contain the private rooms of the lord of the castle and his family. Small bedrooms might also be built within the thickness of the walls of the second floor. Within the walls were also found the garderobes (latrines) with stone seats. Vents connected these rooms with the outside walls or with a cesspool below. Between stories ran spiral stone stairways, built that way for reasons of economy and ease of construction and not (romantic movies to the contrary) because they could be more easily defended by a single swordsman.

Though in times of peace castles functioned as royal or baronial residences, law courts, administrative centers, and even jails, their primary purpose and *raison d'être* was military. They served as bases of operations for guaranteeing the submission of the surrounding countryside or for conducting expeditions into hostile territory, especially on the Welsh and the Scottish borders. Against invading armies or armed bands they served as refuge for as many of the neighborhood's population as could be crowded into the keep or within its adjacent palisades or stone curtain walls. Invaders or even raiders dared not bypass a castle for fear of being harassed from the rear or having their lines of communication to their own bases cut off. Early medieval warfare, therefore, whether civil or international, almost always involved the siege of castles. As we shall later see, improvements in siegecraft eventually led to radical changes in castle construction; but in the eleventh and twelfth centuries the rectangular or square stone keep was almost impregnable.

The majority of these are now ruins, but many are substantial enough to offer the visitor a fair idea of what life inside them was like. Gone are the wooden floors and wooden roofs. But stone walls still stand to great heights; stone stairways can still be climbed; garderobes and private chambers still observed. If one can reconstruct in his mind's eye the heavy wooden benches, the rushes on the floor, the woolen tapestries hanging on the cold stone walls, the general darkness broken only by flickering hearths and flaming torches, one can perhaps then visualize the domestic life of the early medieval English nobility. It was garrison existence—cold, bleak, and dangerous. Today, a ruined castle standing in the rain—gray, glistening, stark, forlorn—provides as good an introduction as any to the harsh realities of life in early medieval Britain.

The Conqueror himself was probably the first to build such a fortified dwelling—the three-story White Tower, the oldest medieval building in the complex known as the **Tower of London** *(513)*. It was probably begun in 1078 at about the same time as the even larger two-story **Colchester Castle** *(598)* in Essex which now houses the county museum. **Arundel Castle** *(550)* in the town of the same name in West Sussex owes its initial construction to Roger de Montgomery to whom the Conqueror had entrusted the administration of Normandy in 1066 as he went off to invade England. The early Norman portions of the present building include the lower parts of the south front, the inner gateway, and the oval keep built of Caen stone between 1070 and 1090 on top of the original post-Conquest motte. Most of what the visitor sees here today, however, is the product of an extensive nineteenth century restoration in the Victorian Gothic style by the then duke of Norfolk. At Lincoln, 166 houses had to be cleared to make room for **Lincoln Castle** *(651)* of which the base of the present Observatory Tower is early Norman. To the north, **Durham Castle** *(699)* still contains a few Norman remnants including the small chapel underneath the Durham University Senate

Room, part of the keep and the curtain walling, and Bishop Pudsey's Doorway above the kitchen. At **Richmond Castle** *(685)* in North Yorkshire, the castle wall and the main hall date from early Norman times when it was built by Alan Rufus, first Norman earl of Richmond. **Lancaster Castle** *(696)* in the county town of Lancashire was originally built by Roger of Poitou, a kinsman of the Conqueror. Though much rebuilt and extended over the centuries and converted into the county prison, which it still is, the early Norman castle still survives in part, including the great keep, called Lungess Tower. At Ludlow, Salop, on the Welsh borders, Roger de Lacey, one of the first Norman marcher lords, built **Ludlow Castle** *(670)* about 1086. The Norman keep still stands more than a hundred feet high. Finally in the Welsh county of Gwent stands **Chepstow Castle** *(715)*, built by William fitz Osbern, one of the three great Norman magnates sent by the Conqueror to hold the Welsh frontier. Though most of the present ruins are of a later date, the cellar and two lower stories of the Great Tower belong to the period of original construction. Standing above the River Wye this is one of the most magnificent castle ruins in Britain and serves as an ideal textbook for understanding the evolution of castle construction from the late eleventh to the late thirteenth century, at which latter date the adjacent **Town Walls** *(715)* were also built.

How many of these early castles, royal and baronial, were frequented by the king himself is unknown. What is known is that he, like all medieval kings, was constantly on the go. There was no capital or permanent seat of government. Even when not on campaign, the king moved incessantly from castle to hunting lodge to abbey and back again to castle. There were sound reasons of state for all this restless mobility. It was useful for the king to show himself and to hold court in many different parts of the kingdom. But there was another reason perhaps more compelling: The royal forests were widely scattered, and the royal forests were full of game.

Hunting was a mania with medieval kings and nobles alike. Yet it should not be thought that this was only for recreational purposes. Meat was scarce and the king had to feed a large household of family, friends, councillors, servants, clerks, and armed retainers. Moreover, hunting served as basic training in the martial arts. "The prince should never turn his mind from the study of war," wrote Machiavelli at the very end of the Middle Ages; and "in times of peace he should do much hunting and thus harden his body to strenuous exercise, meanwhile learning to read terrain." William would have agreed. He set aside enormous tracts of land as game preserves subject to a special forest law designed to preserve the red and fallow deer, the roe, the wild boar, and the growing timber and undergrowth that gave them shelter. And harsh were the penalties imposed on those who poached upon the forbidden ground or even tried to cultivate crops within it. His royal successors followed suit, so that by the end of the twelfth century perhaps as much as a third of

England was under forest law. Indeed only three counties (Suffolk, Norfolk, and Kent) remained entirely unaffected.

The most famous of William the Conqueror's afforestations was the **New Forest** *(560)*, which included about 100,000 acres of woods and wasteland in Hampshire. In the process a number of villages had to be evacuated and a number of villagers evicted. Much of the area is still under Crown ownership; and around Lyndhurst the traveller can still feast his eyes on ancient oaks and beeches, perhaps glimpsing among them one or more of the famous New Forest ponies who browse there. In William's day almost all of the county of Essex also lay within the king's forest, and **Epping Forest** *(599)*, visible from the A 11 between the towns of Chingford and Epping, is a tiny remnant of that vast preserve. Finally, just north of Edwinstowe, Nottinghamshire, is a well-wooded section of the ancient **Sherwood Forest** *(660)* with its **Visitors' Centre** *(660)* featuring literature and souvenirs associated with the mythical Robin Hood.

The forests of England were the king's special preserve, but all of England was his realm. Yet much of it was unknown territory to the French-speaking duke who had conquered it. To learn more about it and the better to extract more revenue from it, King William, twenty years after the battle of Hastings, sent his officials into every part of England, except the extreme northern counties, to make a survey of all the estates or manors of the country, the names of their owners, their acreage, the number of peasants attached to each, the number of livestock, and, most importantly, their monetary value. The thoroughness of the inquiry invited a comparison with the Last Day of Judgment; hence, it came to be known as Domesday Book. Two books contain the final results of all these labors. Both are to be seen today on exhibit in the **Public Records Office Museum** *(518)* in Chancery Lane, London. The smaller of the two, Little Domesday Book, contains the returns for Essex, Norfolk, and Suffolk; the larger, called Great Domesday, those for all the rest of England south of the Tees. A third, containing preliminary returns for southwestern England and called the Exon Domesday, is in the library of **Exeter Cathedral** *(587)* in Devon.

The Domesday survey was the supreme administrative achievement of the early Middle Ages. No other contemporary king could have brought it off. Nor could any other feudal king have curbed the centrifugal forces inherent in the feudal system as effectively as William. In August 1086 he held a great council at Old Sarum near Salisbury and there he compelled "all the people occupying land who were of any account all over England, whosoever's vassals they might be" to swear oaths of allegiance to the king and to promise their fealty to him "against all other men." It was a brilliant piece of statesmanship. Though it could not curb forever baronial rebellion against the king of England, the Oath of Salisbury did establish the principle in English law that the fealty which a tenant owed to his immediate lord could not conflict with the fealty which he, as subject, owed the king.

The following year William was dead, mortally injured during an assault on Mantes, a town on the border between France and Normandy. To his oldest son Robert, he willed his Norman duchy; to his favorite and second son William, his English kingdom; to his third son Henry, no land but a large sum of silver money. The settlement was not to last.

WILLIAM II: 1087–1100

Of the reign of William II little need be said. Corpulent, like his father in later life, his ruddy complexion earned him the nickname William Rufus (the Red). His character was universally condemned by all medieval chroniclers who, being churchmen, were scandalized by his cynicism and blatant irreverence, to say nothing of his vanity and foul temper. Even the fact that the king had no paramours and acknowledged no bastards was held against him. It only confirmed the clerics in their dark suspicions that William Rufus was a sexual deviant.

Yet he was not altogether a bad king. He advanced the centralization of power commenced by his father. He built **Westminster Hall** *(524)* which still stands next to the Houses of Parliament in London. This building, which later housed the royal law courts, marked the beginning of the process by which the permanent seat of government became fixed at Westminster. Yet William was more successful in the arts of war than in those of peace. Twice he met and beat the Scottish king in battle, the second time at Alnwick, Northumberland, where Malcolm III was slain. The king spent the last six years of his reign in Normandy making war on his brother Robert, who was at last persuaded to hand over his dukedom in exchange for ten thousand marks of silver.

Then, at the pinnacle of his power, while hunting in the New Forest, King William Rufus was fatally struck down by an arrow. The supposed site of the incident is marked today by the **Rufus Stone** *(560)* off the A 31 north of Lyndhurst. Some kindly peasants threw the unattended body into a cart and hauled it off to Winchester where it was buried in a place unknown. The killing may have been an accident, though Walter Tirel who fired the fatal arrow promptly took ship for Normandy. Suspicion pointed, however, to the king's younger brother Henry as instigator of the deed. Certainly it was he who profited most from it. Riding quickly to Winchester, he seized the royal treasury. Three days later Henry I was crowned King of England at Westminster.

In Hampshire, it is sometimes said that no human hand guided the lethal arrow that August day in the New Forest. It was Divine Justice exacting payment in blood for the Conqueror's great wickedness in seizing the forest from its rightful English owners. It was a curse. If so, the Conqueror's youngest son, the new King Henry, was to prove remarkably exempt from its baleful operation.

HENRY I: 1100–1135

The reign of Henry I started off badly enough. The new king was no better thought of than his brother, although, in view of his eventual accumulation of twenty-one known bastards, no one at least could question his heterosexuality. But he was ruthless and greedy and at the very beginning of his reign a number of his barons rebelled in favor of his brother Robert's claim to the English throne. Robert himself landed at Portsmouth with a large army, but Henry was able to buy him off with an annual subsidy of three thousand marks, while both brothers agreed to renounce their claims to each other's respective domains. Notwithstanding, two years later King Henry turned the tables and invaded Normandy. At the battle of Tinchebrai 28 September 1106, dismounted English knights carried the day. Robert was captured and spent the rest of his life a prisoner in Cardiff learning the Welsh language.

The victorious Henry was now duke of Normandy as well as king of England. More than half of the remaining twenty-nine years of his reign were spent fighting on the Continent. That he was able to be absent from England for so long a time was partly due to the many new castles he left behind, manned by his own troops or by barons loyal to the Crown. The keep of **Norwich Castle** *(608)*, standing on the Conqueror's motte, was one of the finest in the kingdom. Though much restored, it is still an impressive building and contains an excellent local museum. Near King's Lynn, also in Norfolk, lies **Castle Rising** *(607)*, fifty feet high and similar in appearance to Norwich Castle. It dates from about the end of Henry's reign and was built by William d'Albini who later married Henry's widow. The now ruined **Rochester Castle** *(543)* in Kent was built for the king by the Archbishop of Canterbury about 1127–1135 and is perhaps the most representative Norman rectangular keep in England, and certainly the most menacing in appearance. Another, lying close to the southern coast in East Sussex, is **Pevensey Castle** *(548)*, site of the Roman fortress of *Anderida* and of William the Conqueror's first encampment before he moved on to Hastings. The badly ruined keep is Norman, its construction begun by the Conqueror's half brother, Robert of Mortain. Farther west along the coast and again on the site of an ancient Roman fortress *(Portus Aduni)*, King Henry built the keep of **Portchester Castle** *(561)*, Hampshire, whose undercroft and first floor still stand among the later ruins of Portsmouth Harbor's guardian fortress. Westward again, in Dorset, lies **Sherborne Old Castle** *(569)*, built by Roger, Bishop of Sarum (later Salisbury), who often served as regent of England while the king was away in Normandy. Time has dealt cruelly with this ruin, though portions of the bishop's inner ward survive, as well as the twelfth century gatehouse.

Victorious over his own rebellious barons and generally successful in his campaigns in Normandy, Henry I dealt cautiously with Wales. In 1144 he invaded Gwynedd in the north, but when the native Prince Gruffydd ap Cynan agreed to swear an oath of homage, Henry was satisfied and thereafter let North Wales alone. In the south it was different. At Chepstow Castle, Gwent, he installed as lord of Striguil a henchman, Walter fitz Richard of the great family of Clare. At **Ogmore Castle** *(719)* and at **Coity Castle** *(719)*, both close to Bridgend, Mid-Glamorgan, the ruined rectangular keeps can probably be attributed to the reign of Henry I. In Pembrokeshire on the southern coast, the king planted a colony of naturalized Flemish artisans, a stroke of genius that had a more lasting effect on the Anglicization of South Wales than all the Norman castles. By the end of his reign, at any rate, Henry I could be satisfied that southern Wales had been almost converted into an Anglo-Norman province— almost, but not quite, as later events were to show.

In the matter of Scotland, things went even more smoothly for the English king. He was married to Matilda (originally Edith), daughter of King Malcolm III and the sainted Queen Margaret. For a while, out of deference to his pious bride, Henry even gave up his mistresses and led a monogamous life. This marriage made him brother-in-law to three successive Scottish kings, all of whom acknowledged his overlordship and paid him homage. More importantly from King Henry's viewpoint, King David I of Scotland was among the first of the great magnates to take the oath to the Empress Matilda, Henry's daughter, whom he had selected to succeed him to the throne of England.

For in spite of his prodigious virility, Henry had only two legitimate children. Of these, William, his chosen heir, had perished at sea in 1120 when the magnificent new *White Ship* had sunk off Barfleur. The other was Matilda (or Maud), widow of the Holy Roman Emperor and married a second time to Geoffrey, count of Anjou. In the absence of any clear legal sanction for the principle of primogeniture, the king sought to guarantee a quiet succession by exacting oaths of all his barons and other tenants-in-chief to support Matilda's claim. But as Harold Godwineson had shown seventy years before, oaths taken under duress are as scraps of paper. And when the old king died from a meal of lampreys in 1135, his nephew Stephen of Blois promptly had himself crowned at Westminster with the concurrence of all in England who abhorred the thought of a woman as ruler. And so materialized that nightmare of all medieval kings, as of all Roman emperors before them: a disputed succession.

STEPHEN: 1135–1154

For almost nineteen years England was wracked with civil war. Historians refer to the period simply as the Anarchy. In September 1135 Matilda crossed over from France, and the fight was on. The rule for everyone was *sauve qui peut*. Castles sprang up everywhere. Most of these, to be sure, were hastily built of earth and timber, but at least two rectangular stone keeps probably date from this period: **Guildford Castle**

(555) in Surrey and **Clun Castle** *(669)* in Salop. "They filled the land with castles," wrote a monkish chronicler at Peterborough, "and men said openly that 'Christ slept—and His saints.' "

In Wales almost all of Henry I's efforts at Normanization were undone. By the close of the civil war, all of South Wales except for a remnant of the little Flemish colony in Pembrokeshire had broken off from England and acknowledged the lordship of Rhys ap Gruffydd, grandson of Rhys ap Tewdwr. In the north, Owain Gwynedd reigned supreme.

As to the Scots, King David was happy to honor his oath to Matilda as it gave legal color to his own territorial ambitions. In 1138 he raided the northern English counties with a savagery remarkable even in those troubled times; and, though routed at the Battle of the Standard on Cowton Moor near Northallerton, North Yorkshire, he won from the beleaguered Stephen the recognition of his family's right to the earldom of Northumberland and his own claim to dominion over Cumbria and part of Lancashire. Thereafter David retired to Carlisle to preside over his enlarged kingdom. There he built a castle which may have been the structural foundation of the Great Tower in the present **Carlisle Castle** *(709)*. Thereafter he bothered the English no more.

In 1148 Matilda gave up the fight and recrossed the Channel. Meanwhile, her husband, Geoffrey of Anjou, had conquered Normandy and turned it over to their son as rightful heir of Henry I to the duchy. This son was called Henry Plantagenet after the sprig of flowering broom *(plante genet)* which his father had adopted as a family badge. In 1152 he married Eleanor, duchess of Acquitaine, who had divorced King Philip of France. She was ten years Henry's senior, but the defect was more than made up for by the fact that her duchy comprised the greater part of the southwest quarter of modern France.

Next year the young Henry invaded England and carried all before him. At Oxford early in 1154 the barons rendered homage to him as rightful heir to the kingdom. The following October King Stephen died, and Henry II was promptly crowned at Westminster.

HENRY II: 1154–1189

In his own day he was called Henry fitz Empress (i.e., son of the Empress Matilda) or Henry of Anjou (the place of his birth). He was a big man, taller than average, broad shouldered, muscular, ruddy of complexion like his Norman forebears. He was quick to anger, his blue eyes turning bloodshot when the king was in a rage. His most noted characteristic was his restless energy bordering on the frenetic. He was a good soldier, more comfortable in the saddle than out of it. Unlike his grandfather, Henry I, he had little time for dalliance, and though alienated from his wife Eleanor, had only one steady mistress, Rosamund Clifford—"the fair Rosamund." For a king he was well read, though he scorned troubadors and all that modern cult of chivalry made fashionable by Queen Eleanor at her court at Acquitaine. Indeed he had little time to spare from the management of new domain acquired by inheritance, marriage, and conquest—the vast Angevin Empire stretching from Scotland to the Pyrenees.

His first task was to undo the anarchy of Stephen's reign and reestablish royal power in England. He promptly set a time limit for the demolition of all the unlicensed or adulterine castles which the civil war had spawned—more than eleven hundred of them, mostly built of wood and earth. More important, he ordered all his barons to relinquish custody of those castles belonging to the Crown but alienated by his predecessors. Finally, he built new ones and strengthened old ones and gave encouragement to his loyal barons, with his license, and sometimes with financial assistance, to do the same.

Castle construction in the latter half of the twelfth century was becoming more sophisticated. It had to be if these strongholds were to withstand improvements in the art of siege warfare which returning Crusaders were bringing back from the East. There were four main ways of storming a castle: (1) by scaling the walls, using ladders, i.e., escalade; (2) by breaching walls or gates with battering rams or bores; (3) by mining, i.e., digging tunnels or saps under the walls, especially at their corners, inserting wooden props to shore up the tunnels, then setting fire to the props so that the walls above would collapse; and (4) by the use of siege engines such as the *mangonel* or the *trebuchet,* enormous mechanical slings with high trajectories capable of firing huge stones, incendiaries, or even putrid and disease-laden animal carcasses into castle enclosures.

Against these various devices the three most effective measures of defense were: (1) building castle walls to a greater height so as to guard against the scaling ladder and the *trebuchet;* (2) building keeps of round or polygonal shape so as to eliminate corners which were especially vulnerable to mining; and (3) protecting the castle walls and the main entrance through them by: (a) water-filled moats around the castle precincts; (b) defensive outworks, called barbicans, set in front of the main gate; (c) heavy iron-bound wooden gates; (d) projecting galleries, called machicolations, with open spaces in their floors through which missiles could be fired or dropped on the terrain beneath; and (e) projecting towers and turrets pierced with arrow slits (also called loops) so as to allow enfilade fire along the face of the adjoining wall. Some or all of these features are still very much in evidence among British castles—even those that have survived only in a ruined condition.

Those castles built or rebuilt in the reign of Henry II can mostly be categorized into three types according to ground plan: (1) rectangular keeps, (2) round or polygonal keeps, and (3) shell keeps. There is, however, no logical or chronological sequence in this arrangement; it reflects no consistent trend from primitive to complex forms of architecture. The determinant factors, rather, were cost, the nature of the terrain, availability of building materials, previous construction on the site, and the personal preferences of the builders.

RECTANGULAR KEEPS

Henry II was himself responsible for the rectangular tower keeps at his castles of **Scarborough** *(687)*, North Yorkshire; **Peveril** *(661)*, northeast of Buxton, Derbyshire; **Newcastle** *(700)*, Tyne and Wear; and **Dover** *(541)* in Kent. Scarborough is now a magnificent ruin overlooking the North Sea on a site where the Romans had built a signal tower to warn the countryside against the approach of pirates. Peveril is a well-preserved ruin in the Derbyshire Peaks, its walls still standing to their original height. It was the smallest of Henry II's keeps. The restored keep at Newcastle-upon-Tyne, also small, is remarkable chiefly for the thickness of its walls and the large number of mural chambers within them. Also well endowed with mural chambers is the larger rectangular keep at Dover, built by Henry II but later enveloped with elaborate outer defenses put up by Kings John and Henry III. In addition to these four, Henry completed the keeps at **Bamburgh** *(704)*, Northumberland, and **Bowes** *(698)*, County Durham, west of Barnard Castle. The former, magnificently sited on a steep basalt crag overlooking the North Sea, suffered an unfortunate remodeling in the nineteenth century; the latter is today a ruin standing high above the River Greta.

Also in the north of England lie several rectangular keeps built by greater or lesser barons during Henry II's reign—always with a license to crenellate issued by the king himself. Among these are **Middleham** *(683)* near Leyburn, North Yorkshire, raised by Ralph fitz Ranulph about 1170; **Barnard Castle** *(697)*, County Durham, built on a high cliff overlooking the River Tees by the second Bernard de Balliol; **Norham** *(706)* near Berwick-upon-Tweed, put up by Hugh Puiset (Pudsey), Bishop of Durham, on a steep cliff commanding a ford over the River Tweed; **Brougham** *(712)*, just west of Penrith, Cumbria, probably erected by Hugh d'Albini; and **Brough** *(713)*, built by the Clifford family eighteen miles to the east. All these are now in ruins. Deep in the Welsh marches, near Ross-on-Wye, Hereford and Worcester, stands the imposing ruin of **Goodrich Castle** *(648)*, built by the Talbots during Henry II's reign, on a spur of land overlooking the Wye. In Wales itself, east of Pembroke, lies **Manorbier Castle** *(727)*, whose original keep dates from the mid-twelfth century, though much has been added since, including the modern roofing, electric lighting, and costumed dummies purporting to represent the castle's more famous inhabitants.

ROUND AND POLYGONAL KEEPS

Neither cylindrical nor many-sided tower keeps were as popular in Britain as on the Continent, regardless of their defensive advantages against mining. Henry II, however, himself built at **Orford** *(604)* northeast of Woodbridge, Suffolk, a splendid and massive castle which looks circular, but in fact has eighteen sides and is buttressed by three rectangular projecting turrets rising to battlemented tops above the summit of the central tower. It was the king's most favored building project, designed to keep East Anglia under surveillance, and is still today the most impressive and best preserved castle in that region. The king's half-brother Hamelin built **Conisbrough** *(679)* which lies between Doncaster and Rotherham, South Yorkshire. Apparently modeled on Orford, it is equally as impressive, though marred somewhat today by the industrial setting.

Three interesting ruins of cylindrical keeps are to be seen in Wales and the adjacent marches. They are: **Caldicot Castle** *(716)* near Chepstow, Gwent, built probably by Humphrey de Bohun; **Bronllys Castle** *(722)* near Talgarth, Powys; and standing high on an earlier Norman motte, the castle at **Longtown** *(647)* in the adjacent English county of Hereford and Worcester. Wales might have been backward in many respects, but never in matters pertaining to war.

SHELL KEEPS

In its simplest form a shell keep is a circular or polygonal stone wall surrounding a motte. It is therefore shaped like a ring and is sometimes referred to as a ringwork. There is not much doubt that the shell keep originated as a stone substitute for the wooden palisade normally enclosing the motte of the early Norman motte-and-bailey castle. Sometimes the wooden tower atop the motte was also replaced with stone. In other cases living quarters in wood or stone were built along the inside of the ring, thus making a tower keep unnecessary. Normally the palisade around the bailey was also replaced by a stone curtain wall. Sometimes stone turrets were built along the outside of the curtain for greater protection. In these instances one can say that the shell keep was both traditional and innovative: It harked back to the eleventh century motte and bailey, but at the same time anticipated the castle of *enceinte* of the thirteenth and fourteenth centuries.

Two famous stone castles, both originating in Henry II's time, best illustrate how a Norman motte and bailey grew naturally into an Angevin shell keep. The first is **Berkhamstead** *(619)* in Hertfordshire. A motte-and-bailey castle in the Conqueror's time, it was converted into a shell keep probably by Thomas Becket, Henry II's chancellor, later archbishop of Canterbury. The tall earthen motte, forty-five feet high, which no doubt was once surmounted by a timber tower and palisade, now supports the ruins of a shell—a circular ring-shaped keep about sixty feet in diameter. The motte stands in one corner of a great oblong bailey enclosed by what is left of a stone curtain wall. Both motte and bailey are surrounded by ditches, certainly once filled with water. **Windsor Castle** *(565)*, Berkshire, a royal residence since the reign of Henry I, also began life as a motte set between two baileys, now called the Upper and Lower

Wards. On the motte Henry II first built the great stone shell keep, now known as the Round Tower. Though many buildings have been added to the establishment and the tower itself was heightened in the nineteenth century, Henry II's keep, perched high on its Norman motte, still dominates the scene at Windsor.

Farnham Castle *(555)* in Surrey, the property of the bishops of Winchester, has a twelfth century ring of stone built around the base of the motte rather than further up the slope as was usual. Inside, and on top of the motte, was once a rectangular stone keep built during the Anarchy, but torn down probably by order of Henry II. **Lewes Castle** *(550)*, East Sussex, originally owned by the de Warrennes, has two mottes; the one on the southwest still carries the remains of an elliptical shell keep. As at Farnham, the twelfth century part of **Berkeley Castle** *(641)* west of Stroud, Gloucestershire, is a shell keep built around the base of the motte, inside of which were added the great hall and the chapel in the fourteenth century. Near Newport on the Isle of Wight the shell keep of **Carisbrooke Castle** *(558)* still stands on its Norman motte, though somewhat lower in height than when originally built in the twelfth century, probably by Earl Baldwin de Redvers who supported Matilda's claim to the throne and was brought back from exile by her son Henry II. At **Cardiff Castle** *(717)*, South Glamorgan, the Normans threw up a huge motte on the site of an ancient Roman fort; and sometime after 1158, when the wooden castle was stormed by a Welsh chieftain, they built the present polygonal shell keep of stone and dug a ditch around the motte. **Pickering Castle** *(685)* in North Yorkshire, has a badly ruined shell keep standing on an exceptionally high motte with the inner bailey wall running down from it. Finally in southwest England are to be found a handful of the best preserved and most charmingly situated shell keeps in the country. At **Totnes Castle** *(590)*, Devon, the almost perfect crenellated shell keep is a fourteenth century reconstruction of an earlier wall surrounding a Norman motte. At **Launceston Castle** *(593)*, Cornwall, the high ring wall of stone, dating from the late twelfth or early thirteenth century, is six feet thick. Inside it, in the thirteenth century, Earl Richard of Cornwall erected a much higher shell keep. **Restormel Castle** *(593)*, high above the River Fowey near Lostwithiel, Cornwall, has a shell keep twenty-five feet high, built by Robert de Cardinan in the latter part of the twelfth century. The buildings within the shell wall and the staircases are thirteenth century. They are particularly interesting as an example of how living quarters were arranged on the inner side of the protective stone ring after shell keeps replaced the earlier Norman central towers. **Trematon Castle** *(597)* near Saltash, built late in the twelfth century by Reginald de Valletort, is a shell keep attached to a bailey surrounded by a curtain wall.

Castles were expensive to build, to maintain, and to garrison. Henry II himself spent well over twenty thousand pounds in constructing new castles and restoring old ones—an enormous outlay in the twelfth century. Presumably the barons of England spent commensurate sums, if only to protect themselves from the encroachments of royal power. The one enduring theme of the political history of medieval England was the never-ending tension between king and barons, and in the reign of Henry fitz Empress the balance definitely shifted in favor of the Crown. Much of his success was due to his reliance on mercenary infantrymen as the backbone of his military power. The traditional feudal levies of mounted knights were obliged by custom and their oaths of fealty to serve the king without pay, but they were unreliable and could not be held in the field for more than forty days. Anyway, cavalrymen were of minimal use in siege warfare which called for bowmen, sappers, and swordsmen. These too cost money, but by the efficient management of his kingdom, Henry was able to stay solvent.

One new source of revenue was the sale of royal justice. In 1166 Henry instituted the practice of sending out itinerant justices to preside over a host of criminal cases and to collect fines from convicted wrongdoers, which, in the absence of prisons, was the normal penalty exacted for breaches of the King's peace. In time these justices in eyre were also authorized to hear civil cases, especially those involving forcible or arbitrary dispossession in which parties claiming injury could purchase royal writs to bring their claims before the king's judges. Out of these practices was to emerge the famous Common Law of England of which Henry II is justly known as the progenitor. Fines and writs served a double purpose: They enhanced the king's revenues and they strengthened royal authority in local affairs, both at the expense of the barons.

For this and other reasons a number of the great magnates in 1173 joined forces with the king's eldest son, Henry the Younger, in a plot to usurp the throne. Other conspirators were the king's estranged wife, Eleanor of Acquitaine, and King Philip of France. The rebellion was put down, the young prince bought off, the French king placated, Queen Eleanor imprisoned for the rest of King Henry's reign, and some of the barons deprived of their castles. Among these was Roger Bigod, earl of Norfolk. His castle at **Framlingham** *(602)* in Suffolk was destroyed, completely razed to the ground by the king's order. It was rebuilt by the succeeding earl who was responsible for the present curtain wall with its thirteen projecting towers—a very advanced style for its time and one that anticipated the elaborate *enceintes* of the late thirteenth century. From now on castles begin to assume elaborate features more aesthetically appealing than the grim *donjons* and shell keeps of the twelfth century.

Roger Bigod lost his castle, but William the Lion, King of Scotland (1165–1214) almost lost his kingdom as a result of his joining the rebellion of 1173–1174. Invading Northumberland he was captured at Alnwick and brought to King Henry at Falaise, his feet shackled beneath his horse's belly. There he was compelled to do homage to the king of England "for Scotland and all his other lands," to make the Scottish church subject to the Anglican archbishop of York, to require his barons, abbots, and bishops to do homage to Henry, and to surrender into the English king's hands five of his strongest castles, including that of Edinburgh. This was almost tantamount to the complete subjection of Scotland to English rule. It was a short-lived settlement.

With the Welsh princes, King Henry began his reign on a note of extreme discord but ended it in harmony. He invaded North Wales in 1157 and South Wales in 1163, compelling the princes of those regions, Owain of Gwynedd and Rhys ap Gruffydd respectively, to do public homage to the English king. Once more the Welsh rebelled, this time successfully while Henry was off fighting on the Continent. Never again did he bring force against the princes of Wales; indeed he relied on them as counterweights to the Marcher lords and the great English families of Pembrokeshire. During the rebellion of 1173–1174 both Rhys and Owain's son Dafydd of Gwynedd lent the king military support. After it was over they again swore homage to Henry II as overlord and were in turn acknowledged as kings in their respective domains. For the next eighteen years the Welsh and the English were at peace. It was about this time that the Welsh princes began to erect stone castles in imitation of the Anglo-Norman invaders. One of these, the rectangular keep of **Dolwyddelan** *(736)* southwest of Betws-y-Coed in Gwynedd—now a well-preserved ruin with restored battlements—was probably built by Prince Owain himself.

None of King Henry's trials—with the Welsh, the Scots, the English barons, the king of France, the queen, his eldest son—was quite so agonizing as his quarrel with Thomas Becket, Archbishop of Canterbury. Relationships between the medieval church and state were always in a condition of precarious balance, but in England a fairly stable *modus operandi* had been reached by the time Henry came to the throne. The episcopal see (i.e., archbishopric) of Canterbury had been recognized as supreme over the English church in the Conqueror's time, ecclesiastical courts were firmly established, and the king and Archbishop Lanfranc were on friendly terms. William Rufus, to be sure, had quarreled bitterly with Archbishop Anselm, had virtually driven him into exile, and had confiscated the episcopal revenues. But on Henry I's accession Anselm returned, and a working compromise was reached over the question of royal control over the election of bishops and royal claims to church revenues—a compromise which on the whole favored the king. Thus matters stood when Henry II acceded to the throne. Eight years later he was able to get his chancellor and bosom companion, Thomas Becket, elected archbishop, no doubt in the expectation of cementing royal influence over the vastly wealthy and powerful English church. If so, he was wrong. In his new position, Becket seized every occasion to assert his independence and vigorously to oppose the king at every turn: on the question of the trial of criminous clerks (clergymen) in lay courts; on the right of the king to enjoy the revenues of vacant bishoprics and abbacies;

on the right of the clergy to leave the country to carry appeals to the papacy. Forced to yield at a council held by the king at Clarendon in 1164, Becket then took ship for France. Publicly reconciled with the king, he returned to England in 1170, only to rekindle the feud, this time by excommunicating those clergymen who had sided with Henry.

When news of this latest act of defiance reached the king's ears in Normandy he fell into a paroxysm of rage, cursed the archbishop violently, and reportedly demanded: "Will no one rid me of the turbulent priest?" Four knights, overhearing the question, decided to answer it affirmatively. Taking ship for England, they repaired to **Saltwood Castle** *(542)* near Hythe in Kent, and thence to **Canterbury Cathedral** *(538)* where they hacked the archbishop to death while he was at vespers. The spot where he is believed to have fallen is marked by a stone set in the pavement in the cathedral's northwest transept.

All Christendom was horrified. Becket became a martyr overnight and in three years time was canonized. His tomb at Canterbury became the prime national shrine of England and remained so throughout the Middle Ages, as Chaucer's famous *Canterbury Tales* attests. Under threat of excommunication, Henry walked barefoot through the city of Canterbury to the scene of the crime, submitted to a public scourging, and performed an all-night vigil. Among other acts of penance he founded the first Carthusian monastic house in Britain—**Witham Priory** *(583)*, near Frome, Somerset, the lay brothers' church of which is still in use.

Whatever rewards Becket's martyrdom may have won him in heaven, on most of the immediate issues at stake King Henry's views prevailed. True, he made concessions on the matter of criminous clerks and of appeals to Rome, but otherwise royal authority over the church continued to be exercised as before.

In the end, the now aging king was done in not by the church, nor by the barons, but by his own family. Henry the Younger having died of dysentery, Richard, the second son, was now the heir. In league with the king of France and cheered on by Queen Eleanor, he raised rebellion in his father's Continental domains; drove him from the field of battle; and forced him to a humiliating surrender. Two days later at Chinon, the old king died.

RICHARD I: 1189–1199

Of Richard's reign in England little need be said because he spent so little time there. Crowned at Westminster in September 1189, his actual residence in the kingdom was no more than six months out of the ten years of his reign. The rest of the time he was off crusading in the east, languishing in German prisons, or fighting in France. Not surprisingly, he left no architectural monument to his memory in England, although his castle on the Seine, the Château Gaillard, was one of the most famous and superbly built in western Europe.

Concerning his character and personality there is much controversy. That he was a soldier of great skill and prowess there is little doubt. This alone brought him high respect in the Middle Ages when kings were expected above all else to be great military leaders. The church approved of him for his stellar role in the Third Crusade, even though he deserted his kingdom in order to play it. Romantic poets through the ages have depicted him as the flower of chivalry, perhaps because he wrote poetry himself and patronized the troubadors—those literate but landless knights who roamed the courts of Europe, composing lays, jousting in tourneys, and seducing the wives and daughters of their betters. Modern historians, however, have been less kind. They have condemned him as irresponsible, bloodthirsty, and a sodomist to boot, though the evidence for this latter charge is flimsy. In any case, he was the most un-English of the kings of England—which may account for his tarnished reputation among English scholars.

The Third Crusade was the high watermark of Richard's career. It was occasioned by the capture in 1187 of Jerusalem by Saladin, King of Egypt and Syria. This and other cities of the Holy Land had been the property of the so-called Latin states for almost the entire century since Pope Urban II had proclaimed the First Crusade against the Moslem conquerors of Palestine, promising paradise and the remission of sins for all those who took arms against the hated infidel. When another pope renewed the appeal, Richard the Lionheart was no laggard. To finance his Eastern expedition he squeezed his new kingdom dry—not so much by taxation as by auctioneering. He sold charters, offices, lordships, towns, and land. "I would sell London," he is reported to have said, "if I could find a suitable purchaser." In effect he did sell Scotland —by releasing King William the Lion from his oath of homage to Henry II, thereby restoring Scottish independence. The price was ten thousand marks.

Joined for a while by King Philip Augustus of France, the English king recaptured from the Saracens the city of Acre; then, while Philip returned to France to pursue his designs against the Angevin Empire, Richard stayed on to besiege Jerusalem—without success. In 1192 he arranged a treaty with Saladin which guaranteed a Christian foothold along the coast of Palestine and access to the holy places of Jerusalem, then started home. En route he was captured by the archduke of Austria and delivered to the Emperor Henry VI who gladly welcomed the royal prisoner and set his ransom at 150,000 marks of silver.

Vacated thrones invite usurpation, and Prince John, the youngest son of Henry II and Eleanor, was quick to seize the opportunity raised by his elder brother's misfortune. His ambitions struck sympathetic chords among the ever mutinous barons and once more England was ripe for rebellion. Luckily for him, Richard was still his mother's favorite son. Queen Eleanor, with the help of the two justiciars left behind to govern the realm, stood firm in the king's behalf, and John, the heir apparent, had to back down.

It is to this period that legend has assigned the familiar exploits of Robin Hood. Though there are many versions of the story, the one best known today is that of the sturdy outlaw of Sherwood Forest, robbed of his patrimony by the wicked Prince John, persecuted by the equally wicked sheriff of Nottingham, stealing from the rich to feed the poor, and remaining steadfastly loyal to the great King Richard who at last returned to pardon and reinstate this just and innocent man. The tale is pure fiction, and, though many efforts have been made to establish its historicity, the myth has even less basis in fact than that of King Arthur. Travellers who wish to indulge their fancies, however, can visit the **Sherwood Forest Visitors' Centre** *(660)* near Edwinstow, Nottinghamshire, and see the Major Oak, an ancient tree of tremendous girth like that which once gave shelter to Maid Marian, Little John, Will Scarlet, Friar Tuck, and all of Robin's "merrie men" in days of yore.

Also to this period belongs the authentic tragedy of the massacre of the English Jews. In the early Middle Ages, Jews had a virtual monopoly on banking, since canon law forbade Christians to lend money at interest. A colony of Jews had been brought to London by William I, and others had since settled in most of the towns of England where there was sufficient commerce to warrant their presence. They were under the protection of the king, who taxed them heavily and borrowed from them frequently, as did the great nobles, bishops, and abbots. Without the Jews' financial assistance, many a war would have had to go unfought and many a castle, cathedral, and monastery unbuilt. To keep their money well guarded, Jews often built their domestic quarters of stone instead of the usual timber; therefore Jews' houses provide the only examples of urban domestic architecture surviving from the early medieval period. The best preserved are the **Jew's House** *(651)* in Lincoln and **Moyse's Hall** *(601)* in Bury St. Edmunds, Suffolk, now a museum.

Because the Jews were aliens and heretics and because they were moneylenders they were, of course, much hated, both by their debtors and by the general populace. When Jerusalem fell to the Saracens in 1187, Christian indignation reached a peak of frenzy which turned, irrelevantly, against the Jews. On the occasion of Richard's coronation, mobs burned and pillaged the Jewry of London and the hysteria soon spread to other towns, especially York, where 150 Jews were burned to death in the town castle on the site of the present ruin of **Clifford's Tower** *(690)*. However, these people were too useful to the Crown to be allowed to perish altogether. They were compelled to pay a good share of Richard's ransom, and succeeding kings taxed them heavily until, in 1290, King Edward I found he could borrow from Italian banking houses and banished the Jews from England altogether.

Richard returned to his kingdom in March 1194 and in mid-May left for good—this time to wage war against King Philip Augustus of France who was threatening Normandy, Acquitaine, and the Plantagenets' hereditary homeland of Anjou. Fittingly, the Lionheart was struck down by a bolt from a crossbow, a new and deadly weapon which he himself had done much to popularize.

JOHN: 1199–1216

John, the youngest and favorite son of Henry II, arrived on the throne already skilled in the devious arts of dynastic politics. As a young man he had been sent to Ireland to reestablish royal control over the fractious Marcher lords whom King Henry had dispatched there early in his reign. The expedition was a failure, but from it John learned caution. He stayed aloof from his brother Richard's rebellion, though he did desert his father at the last minute when the old king's defeat seemed certain. He plotted against his brother while Richard was languishing in a German prison, but on the king's return, John somehow redeemed himself and suffered no recrimination. On Richard's death, he seized the Angevin treasure at Chinon, promptly had himself declared duke of Normandy at Rouen, and then took ship to England to be crowned king at Westminster. His haste is understandable. Though Richard had declared him heir, there was another claimant. This was Arthur of Brittany, son of John's late older brother Geoffrey. If succession had been governed strictly by the rule of primogeniture, Arthur would have been king. When the nobles of Brittany, egged on by Philip Augustus, rebelled in support of Arthur's claim, John gave them a sound drubbing at the Battle of Mirebeau, and sent two dozen of them off to prison in **Corfe Castle** *(569)*, near Swanage, Dorset, where they were starved to death.

As to Arthur, he too was done in—perhaps by the hand of John himself while in a drunken rage. The story, much garbled, forms the central theme of Shakespeare's *King John*, a play in part responsible for John's bad press among later generations of Englishmen.

The death of Arthur did nothing to stay the drive of Philip Augustus to oust the English king from his cross-Channel possessions. One after another, the great cities of Normandy fell before the French onslaught; Château Gaillard, Richard's great bastion on the Seine, surrendered in March 1204; Rouen, the following June. All that was left to John of the great duchy of Normandy were the little Channel Islands off the northern coast of France. To save this tiny remnant he ordered the construction of two castles, **Gorey Castle** *(744)*, later called Mont Orgueil, on the eastern coast of Jersey, and **Castle Cornet** *(745)*, St. Peter Port, in Guernsey. Both stand today, high on their rocky pinnacles and well preserved, though much enlarged in later times.

Another by-product of the loss of Normandy was the rebirth of the English navy. Unneeded as long as both Channel coasts were under the king of England's control, naval power became an imperative as soon as

Normandy fell to the French. John renewed the charters of the Cinque Ports: Hastings, Romney, Hythe, Dover, and Sandwich, to which were later added Rye and Winchelsea. In return for substantial trading privileges these towns were required to furnish fifty-seven ships for fifteen days service at their own cost. The fleet thus formed was the maritime equivalent of the feudal host, the army formed by the king's vassals and their retainers. John also built at his own expense a fleet of royal galleys to patrol the Channel coast and converted the ancient Roman **Pharos** *(541)* into a medieval lighthouse overlooking the Dover harbor.

Like his father, King John had problems with the church. After failing to get papal approval for his own candidate to the vacant see of Canterbury, he refused to allow the Pope's appointee, Stephen Langton, to enter the kingdom. Then he proceeded to confiscate the revenues of the empty archbishopric. Innocent III retaliated by placing England under an interdict which meant that for six years all ecclesiastical rites were officially suspended, including burials, baptisms, and marriages. The king then ordered the wholesale confiscation of church properties; whereupon he was excommunicated. In the end John wisely submitted, admitted Stephen Langton to Canterbury, agreed to compensate the church for its losses and to an annual tribute of one thousand marks to Rome. He even resigned the kingdoms of England and Ireland to Innocent III to receive them back as the Pope's feudal vassal.

The next episode in this troubled reign was the king's quarrel with the barons of England, or at least some of them. Against high odds, John mounted another expedition against the French king early in 1214. At first successful, the enterprise collapsed when his ally Otto of Brunswick, the Holy Roman Emperor, was decisively beaten by Philip's forces at Bouvines in June. This ended all hope for an Angevin reconquest of Normandy and Brittany. The defeat also brought to a head a mounting resentment among the English nobility occasioned by the king's growing disregard for their customary feudal rights and liberties, especially in the matter of money payments exacted by the Crown. Revolt broke out in the north and spread to the eastern counties. In May 1215 the rebel lords took London, but a month later, thanks to the intervention of Archbishop Stephen Langton, they met the king in conference at Runnymede, a field half way between Windsor and the barons' camp at Staines in Surrey. The supposed site of the conference is marked by the **Magna Carta Memorial** *(556)*, a quasi-classical rotunda enclosing a pillar of English granite installed by the American Bar Association.

Magna Carta (the Great Charter) is the name indiscriminately given to the Articles of the Barons to which King John set his seal at Runnymede on 15 June 1215 and the somewhat amplified charter which was formally drafted later. The former consists of a strip of parchment twenty-three by ten-and-a-half inches in size and is now on display in the Manuscript Saloon of the **British Museum** *(516)* in London. Also at the British Museum is one of the three original copies or exemplifications of the Charter itself. Only two other copies survive: one in the library of **Lincoln Cathedral** *(651)*, the other in **Salisbury Cathedral** *(574)*, both on display.

Magna Carta is a feudal document dealing mostly with the special privileges of the barons. But its guarantee against arbitrary action by the king extended also to the church, to towns and cities, to dwellers in or near the king's forests, and in some small measure to all free men in the realm. "No free man," read Article 39, "shall be seized or imprisoned, or stripped of his rights or possessions, or outlawed or exiled, or deprived of his standing in any other way, nor will we [the king] proceed with force against him, or send others to do so, except by the lawful judgment of his equals or by the law of the land." Small wonder that English lawyers in later ages seized upon this single clause and raised it up to be the foundation stone of English liberty. Small wonder too that rebellious colonists in America were to do the same.

At the time of its issue, however, the charter was of little consequence, because, within ten weeks, the now friendly Pope Innocent III condemned it as base, illegal, and unjust and promptly excommunicated the signatory barons by name. England again tasted civil war. The rebellious barons seized **Rochester Castle** *(543)* which the king invested for seven weeks before the defenders surrendered. In the course of the siege he sank a mine beneath the southeast corner, saturated the timber props with bacon fat from forty pigs, and set the wood afire, thus bringing down an entire section of the great tower. Today's visitor to the castle will note that the southeast corner is round, not right angled like the other three. This represents a later modification when the damage done by John's investment came to be repaired.

From that point on, the rebels made little headway against the king, though they solicited and got the help of Prince Louis of France to whom they offered the Crown of England. John carried all before him; raided the Scottish lowlands to punish King Alexander II who had allied himself to the barons; seized Colchester Castle, and subdued the north and east. In October 1216, still on campaign, the king crossed the estuary of the River Nene where it flows into the Wash and lost his baggage train, including the royal treasure. Already suffering from a severe attack of dysentery he repaired to Newark Castle where, on 18 October, he died. By his own request he was buried at **Worcester Cathedral** *(649)* where his effigy of Purbeck marble can still be seen in the choir.

In contradistinction to his brother Richard, the legendary John suffers by comparison to the actual king of history. Legend notwithstanding, he was no more tyrannical nor violent nor capricious than was to be expected of a king, though perhaps more secretive and suspicious. A small man, he was skillful in arms, energetic, industrious, and clever. Like his father he was restless and always on the move; like his great-grandfather he was promiscuous, though siring only five bastards against the latter's twenty-one. His greatest fault was his consistency in losing—to the Pope, to the barons, and to the king of France. This last was the most serious. As the reign closed, the Dauphin of France was still at large in England. And though, in the final scene of *King John,* Shakespeare could later boast, "This England never did, nor never shall/Lie at the proud foot of a conqueror," the prospects looked otherwise when the nine-year-old Prince Henry was crowned at Gloucester with a circlet donated by his mother.

HENRY III: 1216–1272

A royal minority was almost as dangerous to domestic peace as a disputed succession. England was lucky in 1216 that the great William the Marshal, then in his seventies, was on hand to serve as regent. Here was a man whose rise to wealth and power was one of the great success stories of the Middle Ages. A landless younger son, he won a fortune from the sale of horses and armor and the ransom of prisoners captured in tournaments. In the early thirteenth century tourneys were not the chivalric jousting matches of the later Middle Ages, but bloody melees, realistic war games in which squads of mounted knights charged furiously at each other on open boundless plains. Since by now the conical helmet had given place to the pot helm, a barrel-shaped device covering a man's head and neck, the players were unrecognizable without some identification. Necessity, if not exactly the mother of invention in this case, provided a ready market for the art of heraldry—the employment of distinctive devices on shields, surcoats, lance pennants, and horse trappings, announcing the identity of the bearers. The first known grant of arms occurred in 1127 when Henry I gave his son-in-law Geoffrey Plantagenet a shield painted with golden lions. Richard I was probably the first of the English kings to adopt a coat of arms—three gold leopards (or lions *passant gardant*) on a red field, which have ever since remained the Arms of England. In time the practice spread, not only among barons and knights but to cities and boroughs, merchant and craft guilds, universities, and all manner of corporate organizations. In the later Middle Ages, when tournaments became athletic contests between individual jousters, a new profession developed—of experts in armorial bearings and in the elaborate rules and ceremonies associated with tourneys. These were the heralds, officers in the royal court and in great households, who also served as messengers in war and peace enjoying diplomatic immunity and as judges in disputes over coats of arms and the right to bear them. Still later the profession became bureaucratized when in 1484 King Richard III incorporated its practitioners into the College of Arms which is still in existence. Many of the college's most interesting records, including the colorful paintings of a host of medieval armorial devices, are now on display in the beautifully arranged Heralds' Museum in the **Tower of London** *(513)*. Another good collection is in the Shire Hall of **Lancaster**

Castle *(696)* on the walls of which are hung in dazzling splendor a fine array of the arms of the English sovereigns, constables of the castle, and the high sheriffs of Lancashire.

It was not by tournament winnings alone that William the Marshal made his fortune. In 1189 King Henry II gave him the hand of one of the richest heiresses in the kingdom, Isabel, daughter of the late Richard Strongbow, the largest landholder in South Wales and founder of the first Anglo-Norman settlement in Ireland. Through her inheritance, the Marshal became lord of Striguil in the Wye Valley, earl of Pembroke in southwest Wales, and earl of Leinster in Ireland. In the first of these capacities, he was owner of **Chepstow Castle** *(715)*, Gwent, the first stone keep in Wales. In its present form much of the castle is his work or that of his son—the curtain wall between the middle and lower baileys with its gateway and towers, the remodeled Norman keep of the great tower, the barbican at the western entrance, and the double-towered gatehouse on the east. The Marshal's other great stronghold was **Pembroke Castle** *(727)* in Dyfed, of which the massive circular great keep and the so-called Norman Hall probably date from his tenure.

Under the Marshal's leadership, Prince Louis, the Dauphin, was driven back to France, thus ending the last serious attempted invasion of England until the arrival of the Spanish Armada in 1588. William died in 1219, but not before he had reissued, in the name of the king, the Great Charter signed by King John at Runnymede. This was the first of Henry III's reissues, of which the third (1225) is on display in the **Public Records Office Museum** *(518)* in Chancery Lane, London. Without these confirmations, Magna Carta would no doubt have become a dead letter; in this sense they are more significant as historical documents than the original. William the Marshal was buried in the **Temple Church** *(515)* in London, where his much defaced effigy can still be seen. His place was taken by another great noble, the justiciar, Hubert de Burgh. The seat of his power too was in Wales. On Henry III's accession he already held the famous Three Castles guarding the Monnow valley in upper Gwent—one of the chief passageways between Wales and England. Later he received **Montgomery Castle** *(723)*, whose slight remains can still be seen on the hill above the county town of the same name in Powys, and the castles at Cardigan and Carmarthen in Dyfed, now all but gone. The Three Castles are **White Castle** *(715)*, **Skenfrith** *(715)*, and **Grosmont** *(714)*, all near Abergavenny, Gwent, and all very much worth visiting. The first two especially are excellent examples of an intermediate type of castle that came into being in the early thirteenth century between the phasing-out of the great rectangular and circular keeps and the full development of the elaborate fortress-castles of the reign of Edward I (1272–1307). Castle builders now concentrated upon strengthening the curtain walls surrounding the castle yard so as to make the perimeter of the castle, rather than its center, the main line of defense. This was accomplished by placing huge circular towers at regular intervals along the curtain to protect it with flanking fire. Recognizing that the point of greatest vulnerability was the entrance passage through the wall, this was guarded by a great gatehouse—two projecting mural towers on either side. Behind the wooden gate was installed a portcullis, a massive iron grating fitted into grooves so that it could be raised or lowered as the situation required. Above the gate, and perhaps around the wall as well, machicolations would project outward on supporting corbels between which open spaces in the platform provided a field of fire against the terrain immediately below. In front might be a barbican—a wall or tower or narrow passageway (sometimes Z-shaped) to impede access to the gate. In front of this could be a drawbridge spanning the castle moat. These were castles of *enceinte,* i.e., castles "girdled" with stone fortifications. The Three Castles with their still-standing round mural towers all point in this direction.

Hubert de Burgh's quasi-regal lordship over Wales was short-lived. He was challenged first by Llywelyn the Great, grandson of Owain Gwynedd, and lord of North Wales. Llywelyn had married Joan, the illegitimate daughter of King John of England. He nonetheless had joined the rebellious barons at Runnymede and extracted from the king three clauses in the Great Charter guaranteeing Welsh liberties. By the end of John's reign this prince of Gwynedd had established his lordship over most of Wales, and by the Peace of Worcester signed in 1218 the boy king, Henry III, recognized Llywelyn's mastery in exchange for his oath of homage. So great a prince could not tolerate the pretensions of a mere justiciar, so Llywelyn went on the warpath. Partly as a result of the Welshman's successes, Hubert lost both his position at court and his castles, and Henry and Llywelyn signed a peace which was to last for the remainder of the latter's life. He too was a castle builder. He built **Dolbadarn Castle** *(739),* a circular keep, now in ruins, overlooking the pass of Llanberis in Gwynedd and also possibly **Criccieth Castle** *(740)* on the Lleyn Peninsula, Gwynedd. Llywelyn died in 1240, having almost succeeded in establishing a single overlordship in Wales with only nominal fealty to the English Crown. Within six years of his death, his son and heir David had lost control of everything outside the borders of Gwynedd.

After the dismissal and degradation of Hubert de Burgh, Henry III began to rely more and more on court favorites to the exclusion of members of the older baronage who had traditionally made up the king's council. A new bureaucracy was weakening the personal contact between king and magnates, and the situation was exacerbated when Henry married Eleanor of Provence who brought with her to England a number of greedy relatives and other fellow countrymen from Provence and Savoy. In due time the barons, as was their custom when displeased, rose in revolt, choosing as their leader Simon de Montfort, himself a foreigner from the south of France. De Montfort had secretly married the king's sister and been granted **Kenilworth Castle** *(643)* in Warwickshire. This may well be the best known and most visited castle ruin in England, partly because of its location on one of the main tourist routes through the Shakespeare country and partly because Sir Walter Scott used it for the setting and title of one of his most popular novels. Only a portion of the remains can be attributed to the thirteenth century. To the last year of King John's reign belong the curtain walls and the now drained lake that once surrounded the castle. Simon de Montfort was responsible for the mural towers, now called Lunn's Tower, the Water Tower, and Mortimer's Tower.

Henry III himself was not much of a castle builder, though he did enlarge the **Tower of London** *(513)* and built most of what can now be seen of the Great Hall of **Winchester Castle** *(562)* in Hampshire. More typical of the period are the numerous baronial castles constructed during his reign. **Beeston Castle** *(674)* near Tarporley, Cheshire, was built by the Earl of Chester about 1220 and for a time occupied by Simon de Montfort. Of the original huge fortress, only the ruins of the inner ward with a curtain wall, three mural towers, and a gatehouse remain to be seen on top of a huge sandstone crag. Hubert de Burgh was the builder of **Hadleigh Castle** *(600)* overlooking the Thames estuary not far from Leigh-on-Sea in Essex. All that is left is the curtain wall and two mural towers, the latter rebuilt in the fourteenth century. Hadleigh today is known chiefly as the subject of a famous painting by John Constable. **Tintagel Castle** *(590)* mostly famous for its Arthurian associations and its spectacular views of the rocky Cornish coast, was built by Richard, earl of Cornwall, younger brother of the king. The much tumbled-down remains consist of the outer ward of the castle and a gatehouse. **Helmsley Castle** *(689)*, North Yorkshire, was the property of the baronial family named de Roos. The keep, the curtain walls with mural towers at their corners, and the barbicans were all erected in the thirteenth century. **Tretower Castle** *(722)* in Powys was built early in the thirteenth century by the Anglo-Norman John Picard at the confluence of the Rivers Usk and Rhiangoll. Standing in the same grounds as a fourteenth century ruined manor house, the castle has a high circular keep built in the middle of an earlier shell keep. **Cilgerran Castle** *(724)* overlooks the River Teifi, near Cardigan in Dyfed. Rebuilt probably by William the Marshal's son of the same name, its remaining parts consist mostly of two round towers not unlike the great circular keep at Pembroke.

Finally, the most unusual of the mid-thirteenth century English castles is **Clifford's Tower** *(690)* in the city of York—unusual because of its shape and because it was constructed, by order of King Henry himself, by a French master mason on the model of the keep at Etampes, thirty miles south of Paris. Built on top of a high Norman motte whose wooden tower had been burned down along with 150 of its Jewish occupants during the anti-Jewish riots of 1190, this thirteenth century keep was constructed in the form of a quatrefoil, i.e., four overlapping circles with the junctions between the foils covered by small round turrets supported on corbel stones. The castle walls still stand to most of their original height, though the interior has been much gutted. This was the only castle built in its entirety by Henry III. Perhaps if he had followed his grandfather's example and built more, he would not have had so much trouble with his contentious barons.

The particulars of the king's quarrel with his feudal tenants-in-chief need not detain us. At the heart of the matter lay the barons' determination to dominate the king's council and thereby exercise control of, or at least veto power over, important governmental decisions affecting taxation, the distribution of lands and offices, military expeditions overseas, etc. For seven years (1258–1265) England again was wracked by civil war. Simon de Montfort, now alienated from his brother-in-law, the king, led the baronial faction. In a battle fought north of Lewes, East Sussex, in May 1264, de Montfort overwhelmed the king's army and made prisoners of both Henry and his eldest son, Prince Edward. The following year in August, Prince Edward, who had since escaped, succeeded by a brilliant piece of generalship in trapping de Montfort's army in a bend of the River Avon just north of Evesham, in Hereford and Worcester. This time the royal forces were victorious and Simon himself slain. With de Montfort's death the rebellion broke up, though some of his followers held out in Kenilworth Castle until December of 1266 when starvation forced them to surrender.

Nothing of note can be observed on the sites of the great battles of Lewes and Evesham. Like most English battlefields of historic importance they have fallen into private hands and are either under cultivation or covered with buildings. As to tactics, the cavalry arm was decisive in both battles. Only minor changes in arms and equipment had taken place since the time of William the Conqueror. The mounted knight's chief weapons were still the lance, the long sword, the ax, and the mace, though the last two were going out of style. By the thirteenth century the kite-shaped shield had mostly given way to a shorter convex triangle, curved to fit against the bearer's body, and usually carrying heraldic markings. Helmets, if worn at all, tended to be dome shaped, though the barrel-shaped pot helm might still be worn over a mail coif. Body armor was still of chain mail, though toward the end of the century small pieces of plate or leather were being attached to the mail at vulnerable points such as the elbows and knees. The knight was covered from head to foot. Over his head and shoulders was fitted a mailed hood or coif with an opening only for the face. His *hauberk*, or shirt of mail, enclosed his whole body. It was a sleeved garment extending to mittens over the hands and *chausses* or stockings, to cover the legs and feet. Underneath this suit of mail, to prevent chafing, he wore a quilted undergarment called a *gambeson*. Over the mail he wore a long surcoat, usually made of linen, girded at the waist. Over the surcoat was slung the sword belt resting low on the hips. Spurs were strapped to his ankles. They were an essential part of his equipment as he rode astride his great war horse or *destrier*, whose trappings were normally emblazoned with his coat of arms.

Time and corruption have done away with medieval suits of mail, but a fair number of funereal monuments have preserved the essential features of this knightly costume. These are of two kinds, stone effigies and commemorative brass plates, both to be found inside the churches where the wearers were buried.

The largest single collection of effigies is located at the **Temple Church** *(515)* in London, but they are so badly damaged that their details are barely recognizable. A well-preserved monument is that of William Longespee in **Salisbury Cathedral** *(574)*, Wiltshire. He died in 1226 and was the illegitimate son of Henry II. Purbeck marble effigies of thirteenth century knights can be seen in the parish churches of **Walkern** *(621)*, Hertfordshire, and **Dodford** *(654)*, Northamptonshire. Here the knights' legs are crossed above the knees—a posture once mistakenly believed to indicate their status as former Crusaders. At **Pershore Abbey Church** *(648)*, Hereford and Worcester, lies a knightly effigy in freestone. This was a softer material than Purbeck marble and therefore held paint better. Like the other interior furnishings of medieval churches, funereal effigies were brightly painted. Though the custom no doubt lent verisimilitude to the statues, it must have given these houses of worship something of the looks of a modern wax museum.

A less costly form of commemorative monument was the incised brass plate embedded in the church wall or flagstone floor. As is the case with the stone effigies, people were not represented in lifelike portraits, but as types, so that details of dress and accouterments are more accurately drawn than those of physiognomy. Among the types thus represented are, of course, knights. Though the practice of commemorating the dead with incised brasses did not become popular before the fourteenth century, the earliest of these is dated 1277. It is that of Sir John d'Abernon at **Stoke d'Abernon Church** *(556)* in Surrey and provides an excellent depiction of typical thirteenth century knightly attire: lance, sword, shield, spurs, mail coif, hauberk, and leggings, linen surcoat stretching to below the knees. Another, very similar in appearance, is the brass of Sir Roger de Trumpington (d. 1289) in **Trumpington Church** *(617)*, Cambridgeshire. Of a slightly later date are those of Sir Robert de Bures (d. 1302) at **Acton Church** *(603)*, Suffolk, and Sir Robert de Septvans (d. 1306) at **Chartham Church** *(539)*, Kent. Aside from their intrinsic interest as objects of art and subjects for brass rubbings, these monuments offer the best illustrations available of what a thirteenth century knight in armor really looked like.

Against these mail-suited knights and their powerful horses, the most effective weapon was the crossbow, the medieval equivalent of the antitank gun. The weapon consisted of a bowstring attached crosswise to a stock, which was held horizontally by the bowman while firing. It shot out arrows and bolts at a high velocity and with considerable accuracy. Crossbows were known in Europe in the tenth century. In 1139 Pope Innocent III had tried without success to ban their use as "a deadly art, hated by God." Richard the Lionheart had been killed at Chalus by a crossbow bolt in the neck, but that did not stop his brother John from importing foreign crossbowmen to garrison his castles. The weapon indeed saw its most effective use in the defense of castles, though, in spite of its slow rate of fire, it was employed also by field armies. In the White Tower of the **Tower of London** *(513)* is the Armouries with an outstanding collection of crossbows, though all belong to the sixteenth century or later and have mechanical devices for pulling the bowstring not known to the early Middle Ages.

Simon de Montfort was the greatest burden King Henry had to bear, but not the only one. Once again, in the latter part of his reign, Wales erupted. This time the instigator was Llywelyn the Last, grandson of Llywelyn the Great, and son of Gruffydd who had broken his neck while trying to escape from the Tower of London. By virtue of a series of quick victories over the lesser Welsh princes, he had himself formally declared Prince of Wales in 1258. During the revolt of the barons he gave aid and comfort to Simon de Montfort and indeed married his daughter. Nevertheless King Henry made peace with him in 1267 and acknowledged Llywelyn as supreme prince of Wales in return for tribute. His was the greatest dominion ever to be held by a single prince in Wales—greater even than his grandfather's. Two of his castles survive, though both in ruins: **Ewloe Castle** *(730)* near Hawarden in Clwyd and **Dolforwyn Castle** *(722)* in Abermule, near Newtown, Powys.

With the barons subdued and Wales temporarily quiescent, King Henry could now devote the remaining years of his life to his major preoccupation, the rebuilding of **Westminster Abbey** *(523)*. It was a fitting end to a king whose piety was prodigious even in the thirteenth century. Three times a day he attended mass, kissing the hand of the priest as he elevated the Host. Pilgrimages were his favorite recreation. When the bones of St. Edward the Confessor were translated to their new shrine behind the high altar at Westminster, it was the king's finest hour. He died soon after—in November 1272. Suitably, his own life-sized effigy, cast in bronze, was placed in the Abbey's chapel of St. Edward where it still lies.

Lacking either the martial skill or the strength of character expected of a medieval ruler, Henry III's greatest contribution to both kingship and kingdom was his longevity. He reigned for fifty-six years—longer than any other English ruler before or since, save only King George III and Queen Victoria. Also, he sired a male heir—Prince Edward, who had already reached majority on the king's death. In an age when quarrels over royal succession were a major threat to political stability, these were significant accomplishments.

EDWARD I: 1272–1307

At the high altar of the rebuilt abbey at Westminster the great magnates and prelates of the realm at once swore fealty to the Lord Edward, victor of Evesham and the old king's eldest son. That he had not yet returned from crusading in the East and would be out of the kingdom for another year was no bar to his succession. The principle of primogeniture was by this time firmly fixed in English customary law. Moreover, the new king was known to be skilled in warfare and wise in counsel. Exceptionally tall for the Middle Ages, he was powerfully built and regular of feature except that his left eyelid drooped like his father's. Like many a well-bred Englishman to this day, he had a slight stammer. Unlike most of his Plantagenet ancestors he was an affectionate and faithful husband. Testimony to this unusual trait can still be seen in the remains of the beautiful **Eleanor Crosses** which he put up along the route of the funeral procession of his first wife, Eleanor of Castile, who died in 1290. Out of the original dozen crosses, three remain —at **Geddington** *(655)* and **Hardingstone** *(656)* in Northamptonshire and just west of **Waltham Abbey** *(597, 601)* north of Enfield, Essex. Though different from each other in design, each of the three contains three statues of the queen—not portraits, but idealized figures modeled after conventional sculpted likenesses of the Virgin Mary.

Though conventionally devout, Edward I did not try to compete with his father or uncle, St. Louis of France, in architectural exercises in piety. His only ecclesiastical building was St. Stephen's Chapel, Westminster Palace, where Parliament met until most of the buildings were burned to the ground in 1834. From the mid-sixteenth century until the fire, St. Stephen's was the assembly room of the House of Commons. All that is left today of the original building is the much restored and highly decorated crypt, now known also as the Church of St. Mary Undercroft, located beneath the present **Houses of Parliament** *(521)*.

In Edward's day of course there was no House of Commons as such. Parliaments there were, and the king summoned them often. They were, however, nothing more than meetings of the king's council, expanded to include most of the great lords and prelates of the realm. Their business was essentially judicial—hence the term the High Court of Parliament. But the king in parliament also heard petitions from all sorts of people, imposed new taxes, reissued the old charters of liberties (Magna Carta and the Forest Charter), and proclaimed the many new statutes that were to bring Edward I renown as the English Justinian. Occasionally, like Simon de Montfort before him, the king invited representative knights from the shires and burgesses from the towns to be present at these meetings. Though these lesser members of the community of the realm had no power to legislate, their mere presence established the precedent out of which was to grow the permanent institution of the House of Commons.

Fiscal necessity was, of course, the main reason for the king's frequent summoning of parliaments, and his requirement for higher taxes grew out of the increasingly high cost of war and national defense. The biggest single item in the royal defense budget was still the castle, which in Edward's day reached the apogee of both its functional development and cost. Although strongly influenced by the advanced engineering practices of the Middle East as observed by Crusaders, castle builders in Edward's reign merely carried to their logical conclusion the principles already developed in the early thirteenth century castles of *enceinte*. The main principle was that of multiple peripheral defense: to protect the innermost enclosure by a number of separate curtain walls built either concentrically or longitudinally. In either case the object was the same: to keep inviolate the castle's central core which was its command post and the site of its treasury and domestic buildings, including the residence of the castellan or constable. A peculiarly English characteristic was the massive gatehouse most often at the entrance of the inner ward. It was usually three or four stories high, flanked by towers, reinforced by machicolations, portcullises, and two-leaved doors, their approaches guarded by drawbridges and barbicans. In concentric castles it was customary to raise the walls of the inner ward higher than those of the outer so that archers stationed on the top of the inner curtain could fire over the heads of those manning the outer. Arrow slits (loopholes) abounded, and overheads were often pierced with *meurtrieres* or "murder holes."

A good example of the new style is the **Tower of London** *(513)* which owes its present shape mostly to Edward I, though expansion of the Tower's fortifications began under Richard I who built the Bell Tower. During the reign of Henry III the inner curtain wall with its mural towers was built. To this, Edward added the outer curtain, surrounded by a moat (now dry) thus making the Tower a formidable concentric castle, one of the strongest in his kingdom. He also added two twin-towered gatehouses, namely the Byward Tower and the Middle Tower, and beyond the latter a half-moon barbican later known as the Lion's Tower and now almost vanished. It is by way of these two gates that the visitor now enters the castle. Moreover the old main gate to the west was replaced by what is now called the Beauchamp Tower and a new watergate (Traitor's Gate) was erected on filled land next to the river.

The king was not alone, however, in pushing castle construction. Some of the most powerful strongholds of the period, especially in Wales, were privately built. Among these, pride of place must go to **Caerphilly Castle** *(719)* in Mid-Glamorgan. This is the largest castle in Wales or England, except for Windsor. Begun in the last year of Henry III's reign by Gilbert de Clare, it was completed while Edward I was on the throne and was probably the model for the king's own great castles in northern Wales, of which more will be said below. Caerphilly consists of two concentric rectangles of curtain walls and was originally surrounded by a lake, now partly dry. The eastern and western approaches were protected by barbicans, one, a great stone hornwork, the other a high crenellated wall which also served as a dam to keep the surrounding lake full of water. Caerphilly was impregnable.

Another South Welsh castle of Edwardian date is **Kidwelly Castle (726)**, Dyfed, today a well-preserved ruin. Its ground plan is unusual: a rectangle within a semicircle, the base of which is the straight line formed by the River Gwendraeth. The castle was started on the site of a twelfth century keep by Payn de Chaworth, one of Edward I's crusading companions, from whom it passed to the king's nephew, Henry of Lancaster, who completed most of the construction. The outer ward is surrounded by a semicircular curtain wall interspersed with mural towers and two gatehouses, north and south. The inner ward has large cylindrical towers at each of its four angles.

Two other ruined castles of Edwardian date in Dyfed merit attention. The first is **Carreg Cennen Castle (726)** near Llandeilo, built by John Giffard, perhaps the first among Edward's military captains in Wales. Here the plan is not concentric since two sides of the rectangular inner curtain wall rest against the edges of a steep-sided cliff with an outer curtain wall protecting the other sides. **Llanstephan Castle (725)**, near Carmarthen, achieved its final form in the later thirteenth and early fourteenth centuries. Like Carreg Cennen, the ground plan was not concentric but consisted of an inner ward standing on abrupt headlands overlooking the Tywi estuary and protected on its landward side by an outer curtain wall with mural towers and a great gatehouse.

In North Wales the best of the nonroyal castles of the late thirteenth and early fourteenth centuries is **Denbigh Castle (729)**, Clwyd, built by Henry de Lacey, earl of Lincoln, and Thomas, earl of Lancaster. Its outer walls, parts of which still stand, enclosed the town of Denbigh which has since moved out into the valley below. The inner ward, pentagonal in shape, is entered by way of a gatehouse of twin octagonal towers between which is an archway surmounted by a mutilated statue, perhaps of Edward I. Also in Clwyd is **Chirk Castle (729)**, the only North Welsh castle of Edwardian date still lived in. Built by Roger de Mortimer between 1274 and 1310, it has been occupied by the Myddleton family since late in the sixteenth century and is now exhibited as a stately home. The Edwardian features of the castle can best be viewed from the outside.

Of course, the truly great castles of northern Wales were those designed and constructed by the King Edward himself, or more precisely by his master masons, especially James of St. George. There were nine altogether, of which remains of all but two (Builth and Hope) still stand. All together they cost the king approximately ninety-three thousand pounds. They were built specifically in response to the great Welsh uprisings of 1276–1294 and stood for centuries as symbols of the final English subjection of that proud and stubborn land.

Llywelyn the Last, son of Gruffyd and grandson of Llywelyn the Great, had by 1258 reasserted his family's claim to the title Prince of Wales and received the homage of most of the lesser princes. He soon allied himself with Simon de Montfort and, after the latter's defeat at Evesham, Llywelyn agreed to pay homage and an annual tribute to Henry III in return for English recognition of his princely title. With the accession of Edward I, however, Anglo-Welsh relations turned sour again as Llywelyn refused to attend the new king's coronation, declined to take the expected oath of fealty, and withheld the promised payment of annual tribute. This meant war. In 1277 Edward launched a massive assault against Snowdonia and Anglesey which ended in Llywelyn's capitulation. It was immediately after this operation that the English king commenced the building of the first four of his great Welsh castles: Flint, Rhuddlan, Aberystwyth, and Builth, all of which but the last survive in part.

The most ruined of all Edwardian castles in North Wales is the first to have been built—**Flint Castle** *(730)* on a low rock overlooking the Dee estuary in Clwyd. It was concentric in plan with a strongly built rectangular inner ward inside a roughly D-shaped outer curtain wall extending from the river's edge. Projecting mural drum towers covered three of the four corners of the rectangle; the fourth was guarded by a massive cylindrical keep, with its own moat, separated from walls of the inner ward. Only twelve miles northwest of Edward's main base of operations at Chester, Flint marked the first stage in the penetration of North Wales. The second was the building of **Rhuddlan Castle** *(731)*, commenced at the same time, about fourteen miles farther west. Rhuddlan was designed by Master James of St. George, also on a concentric plan, this time a square inside a pentagon. The outer curtain wall was surrounded on four sides by a moat and on the fifth by the River Clwyd which was diverted and canalized so as to give the castle access to the sea. It is in a better state of preservation than Flint. Contemporaneous with both Flint and Rhuddlan was **Aberystwyth Castle** *(724)*, Dyfed, on the west coast of Wales. This too was concentric. Some of the outer curtain walls remain, as does a large semicylindrical mural tower of the inner ward pierced by a postern gate from which steps descend to a second passage in the outer curtain wall.

The peace settlement between Edward and Llywelyn was of short duration. It was broken in 1282 when the Welsh prince's brother David seized **Hawarden Old Castle** *(730)*, Clwyd, whose ruined keep can still be seen in the park of an eighteenth century residence of the same name overlooking the Dee. From Rhuddlan, Edward launched another great expedition by land and sea. Suddenly all Wales was aflame and turned again to Llywelyn for leadership. Overawed by the English forces in the north, he dashed southward into central Wales. Near Builth Castle his forces met the English under John Giffard at Orewin (Irfon) Bridge and were badly mauled by a combined force of cavalry and bowmen. Llywelyn was absent from the battle, but on his return was killed by a Shropshire squire who failed to recognize his victim. The fact that a commoner should kill a prince, unrecognized, was recorded in the chronicles with near astonishment. Few recognized then what history has since made clear: The Age of Chivalry was entering its final phase. The Welsh rebellion, more than anything else, was bringing about a revolution in warfare.

Recognizing the inappropriateness of massed cavalry against the guerrilla tactics of Welsh mountaineers, Edward I began to rely more heavily on dismounted men-at-arms intermingled with archers, armed with the long bow. This weapon, invented in South Wales in the twelfth century, was a stave of yew or elm measuring between five and six feet, with a range of up to 350 yards, and a rate of fire much higher than that of the traditional crossbow. Its efficacy had been clearly demonstrated at Orewin Bridge, and for the next century and a half the English long bow, when properly employed, was to be the queen of battle. Well in advance of the appearance of the handgun, the preeminence of the mounted and armored knight was being challenged by this simple—and inexpensive —weapon.

Llywelyn lost his head, hacked off and sent to London to be exposed to public view at the Tower. It would soon be joined by that of his brother David, betrayed by men of his own tongue, condemned for treason, and hanged, drawn, and quartered. Thereafter the Welsh revolt collapsed. By the Statute of Wales proclaimed in 1284, Edward annexed the ancient principality, divided it into shires, and subsequently declared his infant son, Edward, born at the new castle at Caernarvon, to be the Prince of Wales.

It was now that three of the four of Edward's greatest castles in northwestern Wales were begun. The first was **Conwy Castle** (737), Gwynedd, built with prodigious speed between 1283 and 1287. It guards the upper end of the Menai Strait which separates the island of Anglesey from the mainland. Designed by Master James of St. George longitudinally on an east-west axis, its oblong outer ward on the west guards the square inner ward on the east, the two being separated by a cross wall with a narrow entrance. Eight great drum towers linked by a tall curtain wall surround this double enclosure, with barbicans covering both the eastern and western approaches. West and northwest of the castle lies the town of Conwy girdled by the best surviving example of a medieval **Town Wall** (738) in Britain. It is fourteen hundred yards in length with an average height of thirty feet and was originally linked to the outer curtain wall of the castle to form an additional protective curtain.

Caernarvon Castle (737), begun at the same time, lies at the south end of the Menai Strait. It too is laid out longitudinally on an east-west axis, the eastern (outer) ward being hexagonal in shape, the western (inner) pentagonal. The two were originally separated by a cross wall, but that and the other interior buildings are now gone, so that all that remains is the exterior shell. Around the walls are seven polygonal towers, each turreted. The largest, the Eagle Tower, has three turrets and the remains of an eagle carved in its face. This unique design is thought to be deliberately reminiscent of the Theodosian wall of Constantinople, in deference to the entirely fictitious Welsh legend that the Emperor Constantine had been born at nearby Segontium. Another spurious legend is that when Prince Edward (later Edward II) was born within Caernarvon's walls, he was presented to the local population as their Welsh-born future king "who could speak no English." Actually Edward of Caernarvon had an older brother still living, and though Edward was to be the first of a long line of heirs-apparent to the English throne to carry the title of Prince of Wales, that honor did not come till later. It was, however, this Edward who completed most of this impressive fortress. As at Conwy, **Caernarvon Town Wall** *(737)* was built out from the castle to encircle the adjacent settlement. It is about a half mile in length and stands twenty-eight feet high with towers about ten feet higher still.

Harlech Castle *(740)*, contemporaneous with Conwy and Caernarvon, is the most splendidly sited of the three, rising as it does on a high rock above what was once the estuary of the River Dwyryd. Though built by Master James on a concentric plan, it is unusual in that the outer curtain walls are so low and so close to the huge inner curtain as to be completely overshadowed. The most notable feature is the massive twin-towered eastern gatehouse into the trapezoidal inner ward. Great drum towers guard the four corners of this ward, and against its interior walls are the remains of the usual domestic buildings.

While all three of these coastal castles were still in the process of being built, the Welsh once again broke out in revolt in 1294—this time led by one Madog ap Llywelyn. Within a few months the rebellion was ruthlessly crushed, and in April 1295 King Edward moved across the Menai Strait to occupy Anglesey. Here he built his final, and in some respects most perfect, castle at **Beaumaris** *(734)* on the island's east coast facing the strait. In plan it is concentric, a square within an octagon. Originally lapped by the sea on one side, the remainder of the low outer curtain walls were belted by a moat, parts of which are still filled with water over which float stately swans. Between the swans, the peaceful setting, and its almost perfect geometrical design, Beaumaris is today the most romantic in appearance of all of Edward I's Welsh castles, with its four great drum towers and two D-shaped towers covering the inner ward, and twelve mural towers, the outer. Though occupied, Beaumaris was never completed according to its original design. There was no urgent need to do so because the Welsh after 1295 were thoroughly subdued. Not so the Scots. Out of the north now came troubles aplenty to hold King Edward's attention for the last twelve years of his reign.

The troubles began on a stormy night in March 1286 when the forty-four-year-old Scottish King Alexander III, hastening to join his new second wife in Kinghorn, Fife, died from a broken neck as his hard-pressed horse stumbled and fell. His only heir was a three-year-old grand-daughter, Margaret, the Maid of Norway. When she too died on her way to Scotland, this daughter of the king of Norway left that most dangerous of medieval legacies—a vacant and contested throne. The magnates of the realm then turned to Edward I to choose among the various claim-ants, thus acknowledging what the last two Scottish kings had denied, i.e., the king of England's suzerainty over Scotland. Edward's choice lay between two competitors, both descendants of King David I, both mem-bers of old Anglo-Norman–Scottish families, both possessors of large es-tates in England as well as Scotland. The first was John Balliol of **Barnard Castle** *(697)*, County Durham. The other was Robert Bruce of Annan-dale and County Durham. King Edward accepted the role of arbitrator and at the same time required the competitors to accept him as superior lord of Scotland. On 17 November 1292 at **Berwick Castle** *(705)*, of which only fragments still stand in Berwick-upon-Tweed, Northumber-land, he declared in favor of John Balliol's claim. Three days later Balliol in turn swore fealty to Edward for the realm of Scotland at **Norham Castle** *(706)*. On 30 November, King John of Scotland was installed in the traditional manner on the Stone of Scone.

Soon Edward revealed his true intentions. To Westminster he sum-moned the new Scottish king to answer an appeal in a petty civil case. At first Balliol refused, was cited for contempt, and for nonappearance was treated like a defaulting debtor. Their king humiliated and deprived of his strongest castles, the Scots turned to France—the natural enemy of their natural enemy. Though almost a century had passed since King John had lost Normandy, the English king was still duke of Acquitaine and therefore lord of much of what is now southwestern France, includ-ing Gascony and its thriving port at Bordeaux. When in 1294 King Philip IV of France declared these lands forfeited to the French crown, King Edward summoned the feudal host for an invasion of France. Included in the summons were King John of Scotland and his leading magnates. Instead of complying, the Scots sent commissioners to France and there concluded a renewal of an ancient pact of mutual defense. In Scotland this is called the Auld Alliance and it was to be a thorn in England's side for a full three hundred years.

Edward promptly invaded Scotland. Offering very little resistance, King John surrendered, resigned his kingdom, and was shipped off to London along with the Stone of Scone which was donated to **Westminster Abbey** *(523)* where it has resided ever since except for a brief time in the 1950s when it was repossessed by a group of nameless Scottish nation-alists. On his return to Berwick, the English king summoned all the Scottish magnates, prelates, and leading men of the shires to do homage. Thoroughly cowed, most of the Scots complied. Two who did not were William Wallace and Andrew of Moray who instead took up arms against the hated Sassenach and became the leaders of a spontaneous nationalist rebellion which in time gave Scotland complete independence from the English Crown.

At a battle fought near Stirling Bridge in September 1297 the Scots won the day, though Moray was fatally wounded. Two years later at Falkirk the tables were turned and Wallace was driven into hiding to wage unremitting guerrilla warfare against the English. Three more times King Edward invaded southern Scotland and at last captured Wallace himself. This greatest of Scottish national heroes was carted off to London, tried in **Westminster Hall** *(524)* for treason (against a king to whom he had never sworn fealty), condemned, dragged behind a horse to Smithfield, hanged, disemboweled, beheaded, and quartered. His severed head was then impaled on London Bridge.

Edward returned no more to Scotland. In his absence rebellion broke out again, this time led by Sir Robert Bruce, grandson of the Bruce whose claim to the throne the English king had rejected. Having slain his chief Scottish rival, Sir John (the Red) Comyn on the high altar of the Greyfriar's church in Dumfries, the outlawed Bruce had himself proclaimed King of Scotland at Scone in March 1306. An English army routed Bruce's forces at Methven and again at Loch Tay. He escaped to Rathlin off the north coast of Ireland, while his friends and family suffered the terrible consequences of the Sassenach's revenge. Once more King Edward girded himself for what he hoped would be the final *coup de grace.* With another large army he marched north as far as **Lanercost Priory** *(710)* in Cumbria whose nave still serves as a parish church. There, too ill to ride farther even on the litter that had carried him this far, he spent the winter of 1306–1307. Infirm as he was, on hearing the news of Bruce's return to Scotland, he pushed on as far as Burgh-on-Sands just north of Carlisle. There on 3 July 1307, in his sixty-eighth year, the Hammer of the Scots expired. Scotland was still unconquered.

CHAPTER V

THE LATER MIDDLE AGES

War, Politics, and Urban Growth:

1307–1485

MILITARY AND POLITICAL AFFAIRS:
1307–1461

For God's sake, let us sit upon the ground
And tell sad stories of the death of kings;
How some have been deposed; some slain in war;
Some haunted by the ghosts they have deposed . . .
All murder'd. . . .

Thus, in the words of King Richard II, does Shakespeare summarize the history of English royalty in the later Middle Ages. The Bard exaggerates —but not much. From the death of Edward I (1307) to the accession of Henry VII (1485), four English monarchs were murdered (Edward II, Richard II, Henry VI, Edward V); one was killed in battle (Richard III); and one died of disease contracted during battle (Henry V). Out of this bloody chronicle came the material for eight of Shakespeare's plays, and out of these plays English-speaking people everywhere have derived an indelible image of the fourteenth and fifteenth centuries as a time of almost unrelieved bloodletting on and off the battlefield. The great duke of Marlborough once referred to this corpus of historical drama as "the only History of England I ever read." Countless others could have said the same before and since. That Shakespeare as a historian is unreliable, that he distorted the truth for dramatic purposes, that his plays were vehicles for Tudor propaganda—is now well known. It is also mostly beside the point. The fact is that much of what is significant about the history of England in the later Middle Ages can best be appreciated as drama or even melodrama. The center stage is peopled mostly with kings and queens, princes and nobles; the plot revolves around their personal ambitions, fears, jealousies, and affections; the denouement, more often than not, is tragic. Shakespeare was right.

EDWARD II: 1307–1327

The first "sad story" is that of King Edward II. Heir to his father's looks, his father's kingdom, and his father's war with Scotland, Edward of Caernarvon had none of the old king's strength of character, his skill at arms, or his good fortune. Twenty-three years of age on achieving the throne, he was tall, blond, and athletic—but not on the jousting field which he mostly scorned. He preferred plebian sports like swimming, rowing, and wrestling; and he preferred the low company of minstrels and other commoners to that of his "natural counsellors," the barons of England.

166

Mostly he preferred the company of a young, handsome, and impoverished Gascon knight, Piers Gaveston, with whom he had fallen in love while still Prince of Wales. Gaveston was banished from England by the old king, but returned under the new, to be showered with affection, the rich duchy of Cornwall, and a profitable marriage to Edward's niece. Edward's new queen—Isabella, daughter of the king of France—was offended. So were the barons, led by Thomas, earl of Lancaster, the king's cousin and first magnate of the realm. To such as Lancaster, King Edward's infatuation for this arrogant young parvenu was not only disgusting but threatening. Royal patronage—in the form of lands, offices, marriage to heiresses in the king's custody, and other emoluments—was an important source of baronial income and power throughout the Middle Ages. If the flow of these benefits was to be diverted to the likes of Piers Gaveston, the established nobility of England would be the losers. Gaveston would have to go.

Go he did, but not for long. Twice banished from the kingdom at the insistence of the more powerful barons, Gaveston was back in England to spend Christmas of 1311 with the king; then given custody of **Scarborough Castle** *(687)* on the North Yorkshire coast. Besieged in this mighty keep, the favorite surrendered on the promise of a safe conduct by Aymer de Valence, earl of Pembroke. The earl was an honorable man; not so his fellow Lords Ordainers (so called after the Ordinance of 1311 which these barons had forced on the king). Gaveston was secreted away from his captor, summarily tried, and beheaded. This was the first of the long series of judicial murders that were to punctuate the history of English politics over the next two centuries.

Two years later, at a place called Bannockburn in Scotland, Edward II suffered an even more humiliating reversal. Here in the valley south of Stirling Castle, twenty thousand English troops led by the king himself were routed by less than half of that number of Scots under Robert Bruce, claimant to the Scottish throne. For Scottish independence, the battle was a decisive victory; for Edward, a disaster. His reputation as a king still further shattered, he yielded at last to Lancaster and the Lords Ordainers. Again, however, he sought refuge in the counsels of court favorites, this time the Hugh Despensers, father and son, themselves powerful barons from Gloucestershire and the Welsh Marches. Again the magnates rebelled, and again the favorites were banished. But by now the king had regained sufficient power in his own hands to strike back. When the constable of **Leeds Castle** *(543)* near Maidstone, Kent, unlawfully refused admission to Queen Isabella, Edward collected a powerful army and laid siege to the stronghold. Though well fortified and surrounded by a lake (as it still is), the castle surrendered. Having collected a force for such a worthy cause, the king now used it in behalf of one that, in his own mind, was even worthier. He proceeded to attack his baronial enemies, captured their leader, Thomas of Lancaster, and outside the latter's own castle of **Pontefract** *(681)*, West Yorkshire, had him executed. At a parliament held in York in 1322, attended by knights and burgesses as well as by the greater magnates, the hated Ordinances were repealed, and the king restored to his full dignity.

Promptly the Despensers returned to court, and again the king affronted baronial sensibilities by his excessive generosity to the favorites. This time the opposition centered around Queen Isabella. From her father's royal court in France, this spirited young woman and her lover, the Marcher lord Roger de Mortimer, organized a coup d'état. In September 1326 Isabella and Mortimer landed on the coast of Suffolk with a small force loaned by the count of Hainault who had betrothed his daughter Philippa to the young heir apparent, Edward, Prince of Wales. London opened its gates to the invaders. The Despensers were hunted down and killed. The king himself was captured and imprisoned at **Kenilworth Castle** *(643)* in Warwickshire. There he was compelled to abdicate in favor of Prince Edward. Shortly removed to **Berkeley Castle** *(641)*, Gloucestershire, Edward II was to suffer the inevitable fate of deposed kings, i.e., assassination. Political necessity virtually compelled usurpers to eliminate their displaced predecessors as potential focal points for counterrevolution. Isabella and Mortimer were usurpers (Edward III was still a minor); and the former king had to die. The manner of his death, however, was appalling, even by medieval standards. Probably on the order of Mortimer, and presumably as a cruel jest on Edward's alleged role as Piers Gaveston's catamite, a red hot iron was inserted anally into his bowels through an inverted horn. Or at least this was the generally accepted explanation for there being no marks on the dead king's body when he was taken to Gloucester Abbey, now **Gloucester Cathedral** *(640)*, for burial.

An object of general contempt while alive, Edward of Caernarvon became a martyr in death. His tomb with its lovely alabaster effigy soon proved to be a popular shrine for pilgrims and a source of great profit to the monks of Gloucester. It is still a sight worth seeing.

EDWARD III: 1327–1377

The fourteen-year-old King Edward III was crowned on 1 February 1327. The kingdom, however, really belonged to his mother, Queen Isabella, and her paramour Roger de Mortimer. Isabella's brazenness and Mortimer's avarice, combined with a widespread revulsion over the manner of the late king's assassination, soon produced a countercoup led by the youthful king himself. On an October night in 1330, Edward III, then only eighteen years of age, secreted a small armed band into **Nottingham Castle** *(659)* through a subterranean passage, seized his mother's lover, and in spite of her pleas to "have pity on gentle Mortimer," hustled him off to London to be hanged, drawn, and quartered. Today's castle bears little resemblance to the original medieval keep. But outside the museum is the entrance to Mortimer's Hole, the long tunnel by which the young Edward III is thought to have made his entry. As to the queen, bereft of her lover, she was spared further recrimination beyond being dispatched to her favorite residence of **Castle Rising** *(607)*, Norfolk, where she lived in state until taking the veil.

Edward III now entered his long period of personal rule. Tall, blond, strong, and handsome like his father, he was in every other way the exact opposite. He was a womanizer, though happily married to Queen Philippa; he was magnanimous in spirit, charming in manner, and above all strong and brave in battle. To his contemporaries he was the new King Arthur, and though his fifty-year reign was to end in disillusionment, he retained his subjects' deep devotion and admiration for most of his life.

The first order of business was Scotland. After Bannockburn, Bruce had carried the war into England, ravaged the northern counties, and in 1318 captured his enemy's main base of operations at Berwick-upon-Tweed, Northumberland. Ten years later at Northampton, the English signed a treaty recognizing Scotland as an independent nation and Robert Bruce as her king. But Bruce died in 1329, leaving as heir his son David, a boy of five. This was a splendid opportunity for a small group of nobles who had lost their Scottish estates, "the disinherited," to back the claim to the throne of Scotland of Edward Balliol, son of the late puppet king. Urged on by Edward III, a rebel army landed in Fife in 1332 and won an unexpected victory at Dupplin Moor not far from Perth. Within six months, however, the Scots recovered, and Balliol was a fugitive. The English king responded by leading an army north to besiege Berwick. Just north of that fortified city, on Halidon's Hill, he met and annihilated a Scottish force intent on raising the siege. The battle is famous for the decisive part played by the English longbowmen—a foretaste of victories soon to come in France.

Berwick, of course, fell to the English. Balliol reoccupied the throne of Scotland, acknowledged Edward as his overlord, and handed over to the English Crown most of southern Scotland as well as the Isle of Man which Bruce had conquered some twenty years previously. Edward now bestowed the island on his old companion-at-arms Sir William de Montacute (Montague) who had been with him on that fateful night in Nottingham Castle. It was he who repaired the damage done by the Scots to **Castle Rushen** *(741)*, Castletown, and restored it to the form it mostly still retains.

Berwick and Man were to remain English. But that was all. The Scots quickly reasserted themselves. Edward led another army into Scotland in 1336 and again in 1337. Thereafter developments in France distracted his attention. David Bruce returned from his French exile and regained his throne by default. The outbreak of the Hundred Years War between the kings of France and England was to assure the permanency of Scottish independence. But forty years of intermittent warfare between Scotland and her southern neighbor was not soon forgotten or erased.

Edward I and his successors were to saddle both countries with the *damnosa hereditas* of three centuries of border raids in both directions —unremitting irregular warfare that was not to end until the seventeenth century when the two kingdoms came under one crown.

Relics of these many years of institutionalized violence still abound in northern England—mostly in Northumberland and Cumbria, but plentiful enough as far south of the border as Yorkshire and Lancashire. These are the *pele* towers of the north. (The word "pele," coming from the Latin *pilium*, refers to the paling or stockaded enclosure and by transference to the tower itself.) They are obviously the lineal descendants of the great tower keeps of the twelfth century and are built more or less along the same lines, though usually less massively. They are normally stone built, rectangular in shape, and three stories high—the ground floor or basement for storage or for housing cattle during times of danger; the two upper floors for residential purposes. Sometimes the top of the building was crenellated, sometimes not. Usually it stood within a walled courtyard, here called a *barmkin* instead of bailey. Mostly these buildings were put up in the thirteenth and fourteenth centuries, though some are earlier and a few later. They were built not to withstand armies or sieges but to protect their owners, their livestock, and perhaps some of their neighbors, against Scottish marauders whose frequent and devastating raids were an inescapable fact of life. On their side of the border the Scots built likewise and for the same reasons, for the English were themselves adept at arson and pillage.

In Northumberland, Cumbria, and adjacent areas to the south there are remains of some two hundred such towers, of which the following are merely representative. In Northumberland, there is a convenient cluster of five, not far from Newcastle and Hexham. Moving from east to west, the first of these is **Belsay Castle** *(707)*, an unusually elaborate tower with two wings in an L-shape and equipped with bartizans or corner turrets at the top. It is well preserved with a modern roof. **Aydon Castle** *(707)*, northeast of Corbridge, is also in good shape. It was crenellated in the first years of the fourteenth century and is surrounded by a stonewalled barmkin. Just to the northwest lies **Halton Tower** *(706)*, a fifteenth century pele with seventeenth century additions. East of Chollerton is **Cocklaw Tower** *(707)*, also fifteenth century. All of the above, except for Belsay, are virtually within the shadow of Hadrian's Wall. Further to the southwest, near Haydon Bridge, lies **Langley Castle** *(707)*, a well-restored tower house of the mid-fourteenth century with four bartizans and a portcullis guarding the single ground floor entrance. Still farther west, near Haltwhistle, is **Featherstone Castle** *(706)* on the banks of the South Tyne, a thirteenth century pele tower refortified in the fourteenth. Well north of Newcastle-upon-Tyne, lies **Edlingham Castle** *(705)* between Alnwick and Rothbury. It dates from about 1350 and consists of a simple walled barmkin with a rectangular tower at one end. Still farther north, near Wooler, is **Chillingham Castle Park** *(708)*. The fourteenth century pele tower here is not open to the public, but within the grounds can be seen the famous herd of pure white wild cattle. They are probably descended from prehistoric wild oxen (aurochs), and Chillingham's owners, the lords Tankerville, have kept them undomesticated for at least seven hundred years. In the Middle Ages and later this would have been a sensible precaution against the herd's being driven across the border by Scottish raiders. So, in a sense, they are today as significant a reminder of the centuries of border war as are the neighboring pele towers. Of these, one final and interesting Northumberland example is **Etal Castle** *(708)* only a few miles from the Scottish border—an unusually massive ruined keep with an equally massive gatehouse.

Cumbria, too, has its share of pele towers, some of them in former Lancashire, which indicates how far south Scottish raiding parties were wont to penetrate. In the Furness peninsula on Morecambe Bay, for example, there are at least two: **Dalton Tower** *(711)*, Dalton-in-Furness, and **Gleaston Tower** *(713)* south of Ulverston. Around Kendall is another important cluster. To the south are **Arnside Tower** *(712)*, a ruined pele built about 1330, and **Levens Hall** *(712)*, an Elizabethan house attached to a fourteenth century pele tower, the grounds now especially famous for their topiary. About two miles to the north of this is **Sizergh Castle** *(712)*, the family seat of the Stricklands. The pele tower here dates from about 1340, though the biggest attraction now is the attached Elizabethan house which, with its garden, is one of the more distinguished stately homes in this part of the country. South of Penrith on a bluff overlooking the Eamont is **Yanwath Hall** *(713)*, considered by some to be the finest pele tower in Cumbria. Modified somewhat in the sixteenth century, it is three stories in height and has four turrets with an original and rare fourteenth century molded octagonal chimney stack.

In a separate category of northern fortified tower houses are those called vicars' peles. These were strongholds built by and for English priests against the perennial raiders from across the border. They are striking testimony to the uncontrovertable fact that Scots on the rampage feared neither God nor man. In Northumberland the best of these is the **Corbridge Vicar's Pele** *(702)*, built in the early fourteenth century in the parish churchyard out of stones from the nearby Roman fort. It has three stories, each of a single room, the basement being vaulted and pierced with arrow slits. On the tower is a defensive parapet with square turrets at the corners and embrazures fitted with shutters. It is a sturdy fortress, constructed no doubt in memory of the monks and schoolboys of Corbridge who had been burnt alive in a Scottish raid in 1296. At Hexham, is the **Hexham Moot Hall** *(707)*, which in the fifteenth century was the tower house of the local bailiff of the archbishop of York. In Cumbria, west of Carlisle sits the **Newton Arlosh Tower** *(710)*, built about 1305 by the monks of nearby Holmculgram Abbey. It has no windows on the ground floor, is equipped with an overhanging turret, and can be entered only through the church to which it is attached.

Raids by the Scots into northern England in the fourteenth and fifteenth centuries were brutal, but they were for the most part short and limited in scope. Certainly the sufferings of the English at the hands of their northern neighbors were trivial in comparison to those which they themselves inflicted on the French during the long series of cross-Channel excursions known to history as the Hundred Years War.

The origins of the war, which in fact lasted 116 years (from 1337 to 1453) were complex. First was the issue of Gascony. This was that prosperous region of southwestern France, including the busy port of Bordeaux, to which the kings of both England and France laid claim. The English claim derived from the legacy of the Duchess Eleanor of Acquitaine who was Henry II's queen; the French from the still more ancient feudal suzerainty of the kings of France over the duchy of Acquitaine (or Guienne). Full-scale war between the two kingdoms late in the thirteenth century had been averted only by the preoccupation of Edward I with Wales, and of the French king, Philip the Fair, with Flanders. Then, after an uneasy truce of about three decades, a new French king, Philip VI, declared Gascony forfeit to the crown of France and dispatched an army to recover it.

The second issue was Scotland. Since 1195 France and Scotland had enjoyed an amicable relationship, which the Scots referred to as the Auld Alliance and which was based mostly on a shared hostility to England. When the boy-king David Bruce escaped to France after the disaster of Halidon's Hill, he was made welcome at the court of Philip VI who reaffirmed the Auld Alliance and stipulated further that no settlement would be made with Edward III on the question of Gascony without a simultaneous recognition of his Scottish protégé as King David II. The prospect of a French puppet on the throne of Scotland was, of course, more than the English could tolerate.

The third issue at stake, and to the medieval mind perhaps the most important, was the question of the right of succession to the throne of France. When King Philip the Fair had died in 1314 he left three sons and one daughter. Each of the three sons in succession wore the crown briefly, and each died without surviving male issue. The daughter was Isabella, widow of the late King Edward II of England. Her claim to the throne was promptly set aside in favor of her cousin, the count of Valois, who was proclaimed King Philip VI of France. Her son, Edward III, considered himself to have been wrongfully and unlawfully disinherited. And when Philip VI proceeded to tighten the screws in both Gascony and Scotland, Edward retaliated in October 1337 by declaring himself King of France. A year later he invaded Flanders, and the century-long war began.

By this time the ancient feudal method of raising an army as an obligation of land tenure was out of date. It had proved unsuitable for protracted foreign wars, since service in the feudal levy was limited to forty days and it was doubtful anyway whether the king could lawfully raise the levy for expeditions overseas. Hence, like his grandfather before him, Edward III gathered his troops of armored knights, light horsemen (hobelars), and archers (mostly mounted) by a system of indenture. Indentures were contracts drawn up between the king and his captains—and between them with their subordinates—stipulating in detail the length of service (usually six months), rates of pay, and the division of the spoils of war, including the ransoms of captured prisoners. And though common soldiers could still be impressed, as in the time of Edward I, the great majority of English troops who fought in France were volunteers. They were a well-paid mercenary army who fought for pelf. From the English point of view, the Hundred Years War was a great bonanza—a mammoth profiteering enterprise on a national scale.

The elite corps of the army still consisted of the heavily armed and armored knights. Though plate armor was beginning to make its appearance, the English man-at-arms was still protected mainly by chain mail of interlinked metal rings. In the early part of the fourteenth century he wore a knee-length shirt or hauberk of mail over a padded tunic laced to a conical visored helmet called a *bascinet,* from the bottom of which loosely hung a *camail* of chain mail to protect the neck. He usually wore a steel breast plate; small steel plates protected his arms and elbows; leggings of mail (like pantyhose) protected his lower legs and feet; and he carried a small flatiron-shaped convex shield normally decorated with his personal heraldic markings. Around his hips he fastened a heavy leather belt or *baldric* from which were suspended on one side a long straight sword and on the other a short dagger, called a *misericord* or mercy-killer used to dispatch the mortally wounded. Over the mail hauberk was draped a loose sleeveless knee-length tunic of linen called a *cyclas.* By the mid-century the *cyclas* had given way to a tight short sleeveless surcoat called a *jupon.* Later the *bascinet* became more pointed and voluted to ward off sword strokes; greaves of plate covered the shins; and as more body plate was added to the basic suit of armor, the shield came to be discarded.

This basic costume, with variations, is repeatedly reproduced in the host of contemporary memorial brasses and funereal effigies that still grace many of the churches of England. Examples from the early fourteenth century, when the long cyclas was still in fashion, can be seen in the brasses of Sir John d'Abernon the younger (d. 1327) at **Stoke d'Abernon Church** *(556)*, Surrey, and Sir John de Northwood (d. 1333) at **Minster Church** *(546)*, Isle of Sheppey, Kent. For the mid-century when the short jupon had replaced the cyclas, the best example is the brass of Sir Hugh Hastyngs (d. 1347) at **Elsing Church** *(605)*, Norfolk, in which the central figure is surrounded by panels depicting King Edward III and five of his great captains. For the latter half of the century, when the bascinet had become more pointed, plate mail distributed more extensively over the body, and the shield discarded, good examples are the brasses of Sir John de Cobham (d. 1354) and his son, another Sir John (d. 1365), at

Cobham Church *(544)*, Kent; Sir Ralph de Knevyngton (d. 1370), **Aveley Church** *(600)*, Essex; and Sir Andrew Luttrell (d. 1390) at **Irnham Church** *(650)*, Lincolnshire.

Three-dimensional knightly effigies of stone, alabaster, or brass are also abundant and provide perhaps an even more accurate perception of what a fourteenth century man-at-arms looked like. In **Westminster Abbey** *(523)*, beside the door into the Chapel of Saints Edmund and Thomas the Martyr, is the beautifully carved alabaster effigy of John of Eltham, earl of Cornwall and second son of King Edward II. He died in 1337, on the eve of the Hundred Years War and is represented here in full armor, carefully carved. In **Tewkesbury Abbey** *(641)*, Gloucestershire, is an excellent armored effigy of Sir Hugh Despenser (d. 1349). Those of lesser-known knights are to be found at **Reepham Church** *(609)*, Norfolk (Sir Roger de Kerdeston), and **Holbeach Church** *(653)*, Lincolnshire. But the finest and best-known of all martial monuments from the fourteenth century is the bronze effigy of the Black Prince which lies in the Trinity Chapel of **Canterbury Cathedral** *(538)*. He was, of course, Edward III's eldest son, the Prince of Wales, and the most famous warrior of his generation. He died in 1376 of dysentery contracted during his last campaign in France. The effigy provides a good example of late fourteenth century armor in transition. Here plate has mostly replaced chain mail in the body armor, but the long camail falling from the bascinet over the prince's neck and shoulders is of mail. Above the tomb hang reproductions of his "achievements," i.e., his scabbard, gauntlets, shield, and surcoat. He was, in the eyes of his contemporaries, the pure embodiment of the poet Chaucer's "verray, parfit, gentil knyght."

For all their glory and renown, however, for all their heavy and expensive armor, their mighty warhorses *(destriers)*, their heraldic trappings and their noble names, it was not the likes of the Black Prince that first won the day for the English in the war in France. It was instead the stout yeomanry of England, the horny-handed archers with their fast shooting longbows. This weapon, though of Welsh origin, had been adopted by the English armies of Edward I in his wars against the Scots. At Halidon's Hill (1333) it had conclusively proved its worth against the conventional cavalry of mounted knights clothed in mail. Archers were usually mounted on the march, but fought on foot. Edward III probably had as many as six thousand of them with him on his first major campaign in France.

This was in the year 1346. Having won command of the Channel at the naval battle off Sluys six years before, the English king set sail from Portchester in July with an army of perhaps fifteen thousand men and landed at La Hogue near Cherbourg. After capturing Caen, he headed north toward Flanders, crossed the Seine and the Somme rivers, and, near the village of Crecy in Ponthieu, was finally intercepted on 26 August by King Philip at the head of an army outnumbering the English three to one. Fifteen times the flower of French chivalry charged the

British lines and fifteen times they were halted mostly by the lethal rain of arrows that greeted them. By nightfall over fifteen hundred French lords and knights were dead—along with perhaps ten thousand common soldiers. Total English losses came to about one hundred. Edward then marched on to Calais, on the French side of the Channel at its narrowest point. In September he commenced his siege of the city, but the defenders held on for eleven months, notwithstanding the English employment for the first time on a large scale of cannons fired by gunpowder. Starvation forced them to surrender in the end. Edward evicted most of them and colonized Calais with English settlers. It was to remain in English hands for over two centuries, a bridgehead on the Continent of enormous military and commercial value.

For the better part of ten years there were no more big battles, and the English contented themselves with plundering raids—called chevauchées—wide-sweeping campaigns of arson and pillage which were to be the curse of France for a full century. On one of these raids, Edward the Black Prince was intercepted in September 1356 near Poitiers by a superior French army under command of the newly crowned King John II. Again the English were victorious, this time capturing the king of France himself who was promptly dispatched to England. There he joined King David II of Scotland, France's loyal ally who had been taken prisoner at the recent battle of Neville's Cross near Durham, where his invading army had been routed. As a result of all these French reverses, the Treaty of Bretigny was signed in 1359, setting King John's ransom at the exorbitant sum of three million crowns (about £170,000) and yielding to Edward III full sovereign rights over a much enlarged Gascony.

It was a short-lived victory. Under a new French king (Charles V) and inspired by the leadership of a great general, Bertrand du Guesclin, the French became adept at a scorched earth strategy combined with guerrilla raids and gradually retook almost everything they had lost. The Black Prince contracted dysentery and came home to England to die. By the close of Edward III's reign, all that was left under English control in France were Calais and a much reduced portion of Gascony.

Much of France had been devastated, but even England did not escape entirely the ravages of war. The offshore Channel Islands, naturally enough, suffered heavily. In the first forty-five years of the war **Castle Cornet** *(745)* on Guernsey changed hands six times between the French and English, and **Gorey Castle** *(744)* on Jersey, twice, both ending up (in 1382) still in possession of the English. More threatening still were the intermittent raids on the coast of England proper. In June 1338 French galleys descended on Portsmouth and burnt it to the ground. Four months later they attacked Southampton, sacking the town and setting it afire. Next year Harwich and Hastings went up in flames, Rye suffered severe damage, and the Isle of Wight was put to fire and sword. In 1342, in spite of the English naval victory off Sluys, the French were back again to sack Plymouth. In 1360 Winchelsea was devastated and Rye and

Hastings destroyed for the second time. The worst year was 1377. Winchelsea, Rye, and Hastings were sacked again; Portsmouth set afire for the second time, and Folkstone, Dartmouth, Plymouth, and Yarmouth on the Isle of Wight were devastated. French soldiers and their Spanish allies even marched inland six miles to burn Lewes and hold a number of its citizens for ransom.

This was small stuff compared to what the French were suffering, but the longstanding English confidence in their island's invulnerability was shattered. One result was the hasty building, or rebuilding, of town walls, a few of which still survive in part. The **Rye Landgate** *(550)*, at the north end of this once great port in East Sussex, is all that remains of its mid-fourteenth century wall. At Canterbury, Kent, the most notable feature of the town's fourteenth century defenses is **West Gate** *(539)*, though on the eastern side of the city, there are fairly well-preserved sections of the **Town Wall** *(539)* with semicircular towers. Southampton, Hampshire, displays the best of all these mural fortifications put up in response to the French threat during the Hundred Years War. Here more than a mile of **Town Wall** *(562)* survives, as well as thirteen towers of the original twenty-nine, and four gates out of seven, the most impressive of which are **Bargate** *(562)* at the head of High Street and **Westgate** *(562)* adjacent to West Quay.

Nor were defensive measures restricted to the towns. Throughout southeastern England, old manor houses were fortified and new castles built in direct response to the French threat. One of these was **Scotney Castle** *(545)* near Lamberhurst, Kent, which was fortified by Roger Ashburnham as a direct consequence of the sackings of 1377. It was a moated stronghold girdled by a curtain wall with four circular towers, of which only one remains today attached to a seventeenth century house. Also in Kent, near Edenbridge, is **Hever Castle** *(544)*, another manor house fortified in 1384, probably with the French threat in mind even though it lies some thirty miles inland. It was much altered in the fifteenth century by Sir Geoffrey Boleyn, Lord Mayor of London and great-grandfather to Anne Boleyn, Henry VIII's second queen. It was even more radically altered in this century by Viscount Astor, so that only the massive three story gatehouse is unmistakably medieval. Hever was first fortified by John, Lord Cobham, a veteran of the French war. It was he too who in 1381 began the building of **Cooling Castle** *(544)* on the barren Kentish peninsula lying between the River Medway and the Thames. This was a new fortification built in direct response to a French raid against nearby Gravesend just two years previously. Most of the mighty defenses raised by Cobham have disappeared, but the elaborate twin-towered and machicolated gatehouse still stands, and on it a copper plate bearing the inscription:

> Knouwyth the beth and schul be
> That I am made in help of the cuntre

In knowyng of whyche thyng
This is chatre and wytnessaying.

In East Sussex, on the Rother River north of Hastings, stands the most imposing of all late fourteenth century fortified residences—**Bodiam Castle** *(549)*. Built in the 1380s when the river was still navigable, it too was a by-product of the recent attacks on Rye and Winchelsea. It is today a ruin, but a well-preserved one, thanks to the efforts of Lord Curzon who restored it in the 1920s. The castle, set in the middle of a lake and approachable over a causeway, is a simple rectangular enclosure surrounded by a high curtain wall which is fortified by still higher cylindrical towers at each corner and square ones in the middle of three walls. The fourth (north) wall is bisected by a powerful twin-towered gatehouse defended by machicolations, arrow loops, and three portcullises (one of which survives). The original approaches over the wide moat were much more complex (and more formidable to a would-be aggressor) than the modern causeway. Three drawbridges and a barbican—all exposed to flanking fire from the north wall—barred the way to the gatehouse. Inside the curtain wall, however, the castle's military aspects gave way to purely residential features. Here is a courtyard house built for the convenience and pleasure of its owners and not for defense. Here, backing against three sides of the curtain wall and facing a spacious courtyard, were the hall, kitchen, living quarters, chapel, and rooms for domestic servants and retainers, all generously endowed with fireplaces and garderobes.

Bodiam was, in short, a well-equipped and costly dwelling place as well as a fortress. In this respect it was typical of most of the great castles built, or rebuilt from earlier foundations, in the late fourteenth and fifteenth centuries. Architectural historians refer to this form of fortified residence as the courtyard castle to distinguish it from the earlier castle of *enceinte* and the still earlier Norman tower keep. Although there are many variations, the typical plan of the late medieval castle is a square or rectangle of curtain wall surrounding a courtyard and surrounded by a moat, with corner towers, a strong gatehouse in the middle of the front face (the facade), and residential buildings inside, either against the curtain or across the middle of the courtyard. The amenities of life were slowly taking precedence over purely military considerations and would continue to do so until the sixteenth century when English builders first produced that triumph of domestic architecture—the country house or stately home—for which Britain is so justly famous.

Bodiam is typical in another sense. Its builder and first occupant was Sir Edward Dalyngrigge, one of Edward III's great military captains, who undoubtedly financed the project out of his share of the spoils of war. As we shall see below he was not alone, for many of the great castles of fourteenth century England were paid for with French gold. For high-ranking soldiers like Dalyngrigge, huge profits could be made from the sale of plunder wrested from fallen towns, castles, churches, and abbeys, and most of all, from the ransom of French prisoners captured in the field. Normally a third of the ransom money went to the king, a third to a half to the company captain, and the rest to the soldier who had actually seized the prisoner alive. The sums involved were enormous, sometimes, in the case of the most blue-blooded Frenchmen, reaching thousands of pounds. A mere handful of such prizes was alone enough to finance the construction of a really ambitious castle.

One such was **Old Wardour Castle** *(575)* in Wiltshire, south of Warminster, which owed its architectural inspiration as well as its economic foundation to the wars in France. Its builder (in the 1390s) was John, the fifth Lord Lovel, who appears to have copied the plan of Concressault Castle near Bourges. It is hexagonal in shape, the front face flanked by two high towers. The great hall occupies the top three floors over the main entrance, while the remainder of the domestic quarters are bunched around the interior hexagonal courtyard. "Modernized" by the insertion of windows in Elizabethan times, the castle today is a well-preserved ruin situated in a romantic setting. Another building, apparently copied in the 1370s from a French prototype, was **Nunney Castle** *(583)* south of Frome in Somerset. Here the builder was Sir John de la Mare, another soldier of fortune, and the model seems to have been the famous Bastille of Paris. Constructed around an inner courtyard, the castle is rectangular in shape with cylindrical towers at each corner, those on the shorter sides almost touching each other. Originally surrounded by a moat, the present ruin rises sheer through four stories, though its north face has collapsed. Also in Somerset near Trowbridge, Wiltshire, is **Farleigh Hungerford Castle** *(577)*, constructed in the 1380s on the site of an earlier manor house by Sir Thomas Hungerford, another veteran of the French wars. Today's ruins consist mostly of the chapel and the two northern corner towers of the inner ward. Another much ruined converted manor house of the late fourteenth century is **Wingfield Castle** *(602)* north of Framlingham in Suffolk, of which only the twin-towered gatehouse and south front survive from the original building. It was put up by Michael de la Pole, earl of Suffolk, who fought under both the Black Prince and his brother John of Gaunt and at one time served as captain of Calais. A much better-preserved ruin is **Bolton Castle** *(685)* southwest of Richmond, North Yorkshire, built in the 1380s by Pole's brother-in-law, Richard le Scrope. Its reputed cost was twelve thousand pounds which certainly derived from military profiteering, for Baron Scrope was actively engaged in almost every one of Edward III's campaigns against both French and Scots. His was a three-story quadrangular building built around an interior courtyard. At each corner of the present ruin is a rectangular tower rising to almost one hundred feet while smaller towers bisect both the north and south sides of the rectangle. Inside were more than seventy rooms, including eight separate suites of accommodations plus the great hall, the chapel, and a plethora of kitchens, pantries, storerooms, etc. This was one of the great castles of the north.

Still farther north, on the Northumberland coast, lies the lonely ruin of **Dunstanburgh Castle** *(704)*, an early fourteenth century stronghold refortified in the 1370s by John of Gaunt (or Ghent, his birthplace), King Edward's third surviving son. Almost as active a campaigner as his older brother the Black Prince, Gaunt fought extensively and presumably profitably, not only in France but also in Spain in pursuit of the throne of Castile which he claimed in the right of his second wife, Constance. His first wife was Blanche through whom he had inherited the rich duchy of Lancaster and a host of estates throughout England, including Dunstanburgh. Most of the present remains date from the original building (by Henry of Lancaster, Gaunt's father-in-law) and consist chiefly of the gatehouse, the south curtain wall with two squat towers, and the east curtain with the turreted Lilburn Tower. Of Gaunt's improvements, which included an inner ward alongside with a new gateway, there are only scant remains today. At **Kenilworth Castle** *(643)* in Warwickshire, on the other hand, the magnificent great hall and its ancillary buildings are very much in evidence. These too were the work of John of Gaunt who inherited this castle also in the right of his first wife. Another of Gaunt's strongholds was **Knaresborough Castle** *(683)* in North Yorkshire whose present remains consist of the fourteenth century ruined rectangular keep which once stood between an outer and inner ward.

In his day, John of Gaunt was the second or third richest man in England. The richest was his father, King Edward III. And none of his sons or barons could approach his munificence in the matter of castle building. On his birthplace, **Windsor Castle** *(565)*, alone he spent over fifty-one thousand pounds—a prodigious sum. The "chief keeper and surveyor" of this and the king's other castles and manor houses was William of Wykeham, later to become bishop of Winchester and chancellor of England. It was he who supervised the new construction at Windsor which included the presently designated State Apartments and Private Apartments surrounding the Upper Ward as well as the misnamed Norman Gate leading into it. The Lower Ward the king converted to serve as the center of the Order of the Garter which he founded in 1348 in honor of St. George and in celebration of his recent victories at Crecy and Calais. Its motto, *Honi soit qui mal y pense*, "Evil to him who evil thinks," allegedly derives from a rebuke administered to several jesting bystanders at a great ball in Calais when the king stooped to bind around his own knee the blue garter dropped by the beautiful countess of Salisbury. This was to be the most honorific of all English chivalric orders, modeled on the legendary Round Table of King Arthur's court, and dedicated to the celebration of all the knightly virtues. To the modern conscience it may seem strange that among the order's charter members were several of the most savage despoilers of France. The irony, however, would have escaped the attention of their contemporaries, and it is no accident that the words "chivalry" and "chevauchée" share the same etymological root.

Windsor was no doubt the king's favorite residence, but the exigencies of government required him to spend much time at the royal palace of Westminster, to which he added the present **Jewel Tower** *(521)* —among the few remains of the ancient royal palace after the great fire of 1834. Westminster had by now become to all intents and purposes the central seat of government—in modern terminology the nation's capital. Though the king's personal staff still travelled with him on his peregrinations, Westminster was the home of the Exchequer and of the central courts, the King's Bench and the Court of Common Pleas. Here too, with increasing frequency, came the assembled parliaments—those meetings of the king's expanded council which both Edward I and Edward II had found increasingly useful to convene. Forty-eight times throughout his reign, their successor Edward III was to summon to parliament his lords spiritual and temporal, together with representatives from the shires, cities, and boroughs. His purpose was taxation. Only by frequent consultation with his subjects could the king obtain the wherewithal to finance his costly campaigns abroad, his castles, the extravagant tourneys to which he was addicted, and his expensive mistresses. Parliaments, then, were called to attend the king in Westminster Palace to consider his requests for "supply." In the reign of Edward III, knights and burgesses (the commons) developed the practice of holding separate meetings, usually in the chapter house of **Westminster Abbey** *(523)* across Old Palace Yard. In time they discovered that by withholding supply until the king agreed to redress their stated grievances, they could in effect legislate. Petitions of the commons, when consented to by the king in parliament, became statutes of the realm. Thus originated what was in later times to be called the House of Commons, the prototype of representative assemblies all over the world.

Edward III's last parliament, which met in 1376 for an unheard of duration of ten weeks, was dubbed by subsequent historians, the Good Parliament. The king could not have thought so. Angered by the long series of reverses in France and the sorry state of the royal finances, the commons presented the longest list of petitions ever sent to a medieval king. They impeached the king's chamberlain, his mistress Alice Perrers, and a group of rich London merchants. Next spring John of Gaunt, acting on his father's behalf, succeeded in quashing the impeachments; but before the end of the summer, the old king was dead. To his ten-year-old grandson and heir, Richard of Bordeaux, only son of the deceased Black Prince, he left a failing war in France, a near-depleted treasury, and a restive and rebellious kingdom.

RICHARD II: 1377–1399

Another legacy from the reign of Edward III, though of course not of the king's making, was the aftermath of the Black Death. This deadly plague, which had spread from Asia all over Europe, reached Dorset in the summer of 1348 and quickly penetrated the entire country. A second visitation followed in 1361–1362, and a third in 1369. It was a deadly pestilence, probably a combination of bubonic plague, spread by flea-infested rats, and pneumonic plague, spread by direct contagion among humans. Before the Black Death had run its course, its English victims numbered between a third and a half of the country's total population. It was the fourteenth century equivalent of a nuclear holocaust.

The effects of the plague on every facet of English life were, of course, far reaching. Among other things it brought on an acute shortage of agricultural labor, a consequent sharp rise in wages, a breakdown of manorial discipline, and the widespread desertion of hamlets and villages by peasants in search of higher remuneration for their labor elsewhere. To protect themselves against desertion and exorbitant wage demands, manorial lords took to reimposing the ancient but disappearing obligations of serfdom which had tied the peasants to the land and forced them to perform labor services on their lord's demesne. The result was rebellion—first local and scattered, then on a larger scale culminating in the so-called Peasant's Revolt of 1381. Though the uprisings of that year were touched off by a heavy and inequitable poll tax initiated by the commons in parliament two years before, the most insistent of the rebels' demands was for the abolition of all vestiges of serfdom.

The main centers of rebellion were in Essex and Kent, though before it spent itself a London mob had beheaded the archbishop of Canterbury and burned to the ground John of Gaunt's great palace of Savoy; rebels in Suffolk had executed the prior of the abbey of Bury St. Edmunds; and the townspeople of Cambridge had sacked Corpus Christi College and burned most of the university's archives. The leader of the Kentish revolt was one Wat Tyler assisted by a vagrant priest, named John Ball, made famous by his sermons based on the text: "When Adam delved and Eve span/Who was then a gentleman?" In mid-June rebel forces from Kent and Essex converged on London, the former establishing their camp at Mile End, the latter at Black Heath. On the fourteenth, Richard II, not yet fifteen, rode out to face the mob at Mile End; the next day he parleyed with Tyler at Black Heath. There, a fracas developed which ended with the mayor of London's killing Wat Tyler and Richard's overawing the rebels by sheer brazenness. It was a dramatic triumph for the young king; and it went to his head. Thereafter, he was to speak and act as a divinely inspired potentate, accountable to none but God. He probably did indeed hold the opinion later attributed to him by Shakespeare (*Richard II*, Act III, scene ii):

> Not all the water in the rough rude sea
> Can wash the balm off from an anointed king;
> The breath of worldly men cannot depose
> The deputy elected by the Lord . . .

For an English king, this was a vain and dangerous doctrine.

If his portrait, which hangs today close to the western entrance of **Westminster Abbey** *(523)* is a true likeness, Richard II was a young man of refined and somewhat effeminate features. Certainly he did not share his father's martial prowess, and, though he led an expedition into Scotland and two into Ireland, he made peace with France and sealed it by taking as his second wife King Charles VI's nine-year-old daughter Isabel. Indeed in taste and manners he was more French than English. He introduced the handkerchief (which his barons considered effete); he was a generous patron of the arts and commissioned the painting of the marvelous Wilton Diptych now on display in the **National Gallery** *(518)* in London; he ordered the installation of the splendid hammer-beam roof that still graces **Westminster Hall** *(524)*; and he gave profitable employment to the poet, Geoffrey Chaucer. None of these accomplishments, however, weighed much against the fact that the king, like Edward II before him, spurned the counsel of the country's leading magnates in favor of his personal friends and courtiers. As was their wont, the barons rebelled. They overcame the king's forces at Radcot Bridge in 1387, and next year appealed (i.e., indicted) a number of his favorites before the Merciless Parliament. Among the antiroyalist Lords Appellant was Thomas Beauchamp, the second earl of Warwick. He was the lord of **Warwick Castle** *(646)*, Warwickshire, and, along with his father, was chiefly responsible for rebuilding this ancient stronghold into its present form. Although later owners dressed up the living apartments and filled them with paintings, sculpture, furniture, and a splendid collection of armor, the outer walls and the two great five-story polygonal towers (Guy's Tower and Caesar's Tower) are the work of the two Thomas Beauchamps.

The Lords Appellant did not stay long in power. The king reasserted himself, had them arrested, and arraigned for treason. Warwick escaped execution by throwing himself on the king's mercy and was sentenced to perpetual imprisonment on the Isle of Man where he was banished for a time but later returned to confinement in that part of the **Tower of London** *(513)* still called Beauchamp's Tower. While on Man he was placed under the harsh custody of William le Scrope, the earl of Wiltshire and a favorite of the king. Scrope had bought the island from William de Montacute, earl of Salisbury, in 1392. There, on St. Patrick's Isle, he completed the construction of **Peel Castle** *(742)* which his predecessor had begun and which no doubt served for a while as Warwick's prison. The portions of this splendid red sandstone ruin overlooking the Irish Sea that were built or rebuilt by Scrope include the turret beside the foot of the steps leading up to the castle entrance, the gatehouse and curtain wall, and the rectangular tower which guards the wall above the present causeway.

Donnington Castle *(564)* near Newbury, Berkshire, was the residence of another of King Richard's intimates expelled by the Lords Appellant. This was Richard de Adderbury, a companion in arms of the Black Prince, so highly esteemed as to be appointed one of three guardians over the prince's young son, Richard. The castle, crenellated in 1386 and after, was mostly destroyed after a long siege in the seventeenth century civil war (see the surviving earthen outworks), but the fine three-story twin-towered gatehouse still survives, though not intact.

King Richard's victory over the Lords Appellant soon proved to be Pyrrhic. In 1397 he saw fit to banish for a term of ten years his cousin Henry of Bolingbroke, eldest son of the aging John of Gaunt. In two years' time Gaunt was dead, his vast estates sequestered by the king, his son Henry banished now for life. This subversion of the laws of inheritance, the foundation stone of any feudal society, proved to be Richard's final undoing. While the king was off on a second expedition to Ireland, Bolingbroke landed at Ravenspur in Humberside with the declared intention of reestablishing his just claim to the duchy of Lancaster and his father's other estates. A growing host gathered around him, including the greatest of the northern lords, Henry Percy, earl of Northumberland, his son Harry Hotspur, and Ralph Neville, earl of Westmoreland. Returned from Ireland, the king was soon deserted by his own troops, and at Conwy in North Wales agreed to restore the Lancastrian inheritance and surrender his most hated councillors for trial on condition he should retain his royal dignity and power. He was then betrayed. Ambushed at nearby Flint, he was delivered up to Bolingbroke, carried off to London, compelled to resign the Crown, and confined to the Tower, a prisoner of Henry IV, the newly acclaimed king of England. It was a clear case of usurpation.

HENRY IV: 1399–1413

"Uneasy lies the head that wears the crown" was Shakespeare's fitting summary of the reign of the first Lancastrian king (*Henry IV, Part II*, Act III, scene i). Having come to the throne unlawfully, Henry IV was never really to enjoy it. His was the proverbial tragedy of premature success. Aged thirty-three when he became king, he was handsome, robust, athletic, renowned for his knightly skill and horsemanship, an accomplished musician, a bibliophile, in all a rare combination of physical and intellectual virtues. He died fourteen years later, broken in health and in spirit. He was the most English of all the kings of England since the Conquest. Born in England, of English parentage on both sides, married at a tender age to an English woman (Mary Bohun), he was the first of England's kings to speak and write the mother tongue as well as Anglo-Norman French which, up to his time had been the preferred language of both court and country aristocracy. It is no surprise that he kept at court that first great master of vernacular literature, Geoffrey Chaucer, who had been patronized as well by the two previous kings. Henry raised his pay, and when the poet died in 1400 he was buried with honor in the east aisle of the south transept of **Westminster Abbey** *(523)*, where his tomb (rebuilt in the sixteenth century) can still be seen in that part of the church called Poets' Corner.

Within four months of his succession, the new king had to face the first of the several revolts that were to plague his reign. This one was aimed at the restoration of King Richard II, still a prisoner of the usurper. Easily quelled, the rebellion accomplished nothing except the death of the deposed monarch in whose favor it had been raised. Richard died at **Pontefract Castle** *(681)* in West Yorkshire, presumably murdered on King Henry's orders. Ironically, it was at the same site where Henry's great-grandfather, Thomas of Lancaster, had been executed by order of King Edward II, great-grandfather to both Richard and Henry. Of the Plantagenets, it could not be said that blood was thicker than water.

The next rebellion was more serious, engineered as it was by the Percys, one of the two great northern families who had assisted Bolingbroke in his ascent to the throne. The Percys were an ancient tribe originating in Yorkshire who had received much favor at the hands of John of Gaunt. In 1376 Henry Percy had been made earl of Northumberland, and his son Henry, nicknamed Harry Hotspur, soon came to share the bounty and power bestowed upon his father. Both had joined Bolingbroke, and the new king was duly and demonstrably grateful. He made Northumberland constable for life, gave him the lordship of the Isle of Man after the execution of William le Scrope, lord treasurer under Richard II, and bestowed on him the wardenship of the West March, one of the two semi-autonomous palatinates set up to guard the Scottish border. At the same time Hotspur became warden of the East March and constable of the royal castles in Chester and northern Wales. A third Percy, Thomas, Northumberland's brother and earl of Worcester, was made the king's lieutenant in southern Wales.

The original seat of the Percys, and the birthplace of Harry Hotspur, was **Spofforth Castle** *(683)*, North Yorkshire, southeast of Harrogate. Here are the remains of a fourteenth century hall with traces of a still older fortified manor. **Wressle Castle** *(688)*, on the east bank of the Derwent, belonged to Thomas Percy. Today an unattended ruin, it is noteworthy chiefly for its unusually white walls of well-dressed stone and its one great protruding oriel window. Not Yorkshire, however, but Northumberland was the real center of Percy strength in the fourteenth and fifteenth centuries, and it is in this border county that the family's major castles lay. **Warkworth Castle** *(705)*, parts of whose remains date to the twelfth and thirteenth centuries, was given to the Percys in 1322.

The first and second earls of Northumberland are responsible for the present keep put up early in the fifteenth century. It is a great three-storied structure, square in shape with polygonal wings projecting from the center of each face. It is a well-preserved ruin, complete except for roof and window glass, and is without equal as a medieval residence. Its exterior was a powerful fortress, its interior a maze of sumptuous living quarters, well lighted from within by a central shaft or lantern running the full height of the building, and from without by ample windows in the upper stories—in marked contrast to the great Norman keeps of the twelfth century. In the bailey below the keep, the most interesting of the many ruined buildings is the fifteenth century Lion Tower, so called from the carved Percy crest on its eastern face, consisting of a lion with a crescent badge around its neck engraved with the word *Esperance*. About eight miles north of Warkworth is **Alnwick Castle** *(704)*, still owned and occupied by the present duke of Northumberland. There had been a Norman castle on the site which the Percys took over in 1309. The towers along the curtain wall date from this period, as does the gatehouse to the inner ward with its original Norman arch. The gatehouse to the outer ward, with its ingenious gate and barbican, was erected in the mid-fifteenth century. The luxurious residential quarters, now on display as a stately home, are the product of two radical renovations in the eighteenth and nineteenth centuries respectively. Another much restored Percy stronghold of the fourteenth century is **Bamburgh Castle** *(704)*, standing high on a basalt rock overlooking the North Sea and enjoying one of the most dramatic views in northern England. This was Harry Hotspur's domain, though little of the present building can be traced to the fourteenth century.

The second great family of the north were the Nevilles, whose power eventually surpassed that of the Percys. They too were protégés of John of Gaunt, and Ralph Neville cemented the alliance by taking as his second wife, Joan Beaufort, Gaunt's youngest daughter by his mistress and third wife, Catherine Swynford. Neville also sided with Bolingbroke in his struggle for the throne and was amply rewarded by King Henry IV with the earldom of Westmoreland, and life tenure as the Marshal of England. In this case the king's munificence paid off, for without the aid of Westmoreland, the first Lancastrian monarch would no doubt have quickly lost his newly acquired crown.

The first seat of the Nevilles was **Raby Castle** *(698)* midway between Bishop Auckland and Barnard Castle in County Durham. Though still occupied, the buildings have been much less altered than either Alnwick or Bamburgh, which makes Raby one of the most completely authentic fourteenth century castles in the north. It consists of a rectangular enclosure (once moated) entered through an outer gatehouse leading to the inner gatehouse beyond which is the courtyard surrounded by the residential and service buildings and the defensive works. The oldest part of the castle is Bulmer's Tower, built in the twelfth century. The largest part is the fourteenth century Clifford's Tower with walls ten feet thick. Another Neville stronghold was **Sheriff Hutton Castle** *(693)*, north of the city of York. Built in 1379 by Lord Neville, the earl of Westmoreland's father, the present ruins are a faint echo only of the splendor of this once great four-towered, double-moated, courtyard castle. Also in North Yorkshire are the ruined **Castles of Middleham** *(683)* **and Richmond** *(685)*, both built originally in the twelfth century. The former was acquired by the Nevilles in the fourteenth century by the gift of a grateful King Henry IV; the latter came to them in the thirteenth by right of marriage.

With Richard II in his grave and the Scottish border sealed by a *cordon sanitaire* guarded by the many-castled Percys and Nevilles, Henry IV might reasonably have expected a well-earned respite. It was not to be. Trouble first cropped up in Wales where a minor land dispute escalated into full-scale rebellion led by one Owain Glyndwr. Joined by a significant number of his countrymen, Glyndwr defied the English, besieged their castles, and commenced negotiations for a grand Celtic alliance of Ireland, Scotland, and Wales. He also formed a family alliance with the Percys by marrying his daughter to Harry Hotspur's brother-in-law. By this time Hotspur and his father, the earl of Northumberland, were beginning to regret having eased the path of Henry of Bolingbroke to the throne. Their annoyance grew acute when the new king refused to allow them the ransom money due from Scottish nobles they had captured during a recent raid. Proud and ungovernable in the manner of the northern lords, young Percy raised the standard of revolt. Hoping to join forces with Glyndwr, he made for Shrewsbury near the Welsh border, where in fact he was joined only by his uncle Thomas, the earl of Worcester. A few miles south of town, on 20 July 1403, in a bloody battle ending with fifteen hundred killed in action, King Henry's superior forces met and defeated the rebels. Hotspur was killed in the fighting; Worcester captured and executed; the seventeen-year-old Prince of Wales (later Henry V) was launched on his career as warrior-king *par excellence.* Four years after the battle, King Henry built a chantry chapel on the site. Now called **Battlefield Church** *(671)*, the chapel's east wall houses a statue of the king looking out toward the scene of the victory to which he owed his life and his throne.

It did not, however, restore peace to his kingdom. Glyndwr was still at large. In May of 1404 he captured the royal castles of **Harlech** *(740)* and **Aberystwyth** *(724)* and convened a Welsh parliament at Machynelleth, Powys. It was probably there, in the stone house called the **Owain Glyndwr Institute** *(722)* that he was proclaimed Prince of Wales. Under that title he made a pact with his son-in-law, Sir Edmund Mortimer, and with the earl of Northumberland for a tripartite division of Henry of Lancaster's kingdom. He then persuaded the king of France to send a force of nearly three thousand soldiers, who landed at Milford Haven in August 1405 and helped Glyndwr capture Cardigan and Carmarthen. This was to be the high watermark of his campaign. An expedition into England turned back at Worcester in the face of a superior English force. In the spring of 1406 the French went home. Two years later, Aberystwyth Castle yielded to Prince Henry's formidable train of siege guns, and in 1409 Harlech too surrendered. Mortimer was killed at Harlech, but Glyndwr escaped by sea and disappeared from history to take his place in the pantheon of legendary Welsh national heroes.

Meanwhile, rebellion in the north had flared up again. Henry Percy, earl of Northumberland, unchastened by the fate of his son and brother at Shrewsbury, conspired to undo the settlement of 1399—this time with his kinsman Richard Scrope, Archbishop of York. Again the king prevailed. Scrope was captured and summarily beheaded, his high episcopal status notwithstanding; Northumberland escaped to Scotland, then to Wales and France in search of allies, and finally invaded England from the north, only to be defeated and killed in 1408 in a skirmish at Branham Moor near Durham. For the time being at least, Percy power in the north went into almost total eclipse. The Isle of Man went to Sir John Stanley and his heirs who are responsible for most of the surviving outerworks of both **Peel Castle** *(742)* and **Castle Rushen** *(741)*. The Percy lands and castles in Yorkshire and Northumberland reverted to the Crown and were distributed mostly among the king's sons and the Nevilles. Not until the next reign would the earl's heirs be reinstated and the wardenship of the East March be returned to Percy hands.

The last four or five years of Henry's reign were to be unmarred by rebellion, but not by other troubles. The king was perennially broke. This meant that his government had to lay frequent demands for extra financial support on the great landholders, which, of course, put a strain on their good will and sapped the security of the Crown. Henry also had to look often to the commons in parliament for grants of taxes and subsidies. And although the reign saw no great constitutional revolution, as historians once believed, there is no doubt that the knights and burgesses whom the king called frequently to parliament succeeded in expanding their corporate influence and winning important concessions from the king especially in the field of public finance.

Even more worrisome to the king than the state of his exchequer was the state of his health. Beginning in 1405 Henry suffered a series of crippling seizures which were thought at the time to be attacks of leprosy brought on by divine wrath over the execution of Archbishop Scrope. What they really were can only be guessed at—perhaps syphilis, perhaps cerebral embolism, perhaps acute anxiety induced by guilt for the prodigal bloodletting of his reign. Then too the king was distressed by his eldest son's apparent impatience to succeed him. Although there is no reason to accept as fact the scene invented by Shakespeare (*Henry IV, Part II*, Act IV, Scene v) where the young prince tries on his dying father's crown, neither is there reason to doubt that the young Henry was ambitious for power or that he became the center of a baronial party increasingly hostile to the king.

The end came on 20 March 1413 with the death of Henry IV in the Jerusalem Chamber of **Westminster Abbey** *(523)*, thereby fulfilling a well-known prophecy that he would die in Jerusalem (presumably on a visit to the Holy Land). He was buried behind the high altar of **Canterbury Cathedral** *(538)*, and the unheroic recumbent statue of a stout, fork-bearded, middle-aged man is probably the first of the royal effigies to bear a real resemblance to its living model.

HENRY V: 1413–1422

With the possible exception of Edward I, no medieval English king succeeded to the throne so well trained for the job as Henry V. Born in Wales, in the now ruined **Monmouth Castle** *(716)*, Gwent, he had spent most of his youth pacifying that unruly country, and much of his young manhood as an active member of the king's council. He was of medium height, wiry, athletic, thought to be handsome, his thick brown hair cut in the then fashionable bowl-like coiffure. Viewers of the splendid 1945 movie production of Shakespeare's *King Henry V* find it hard not to picture him as Laurence Olivier minus sideburns. There is no reason to accept Shakespeare's version of his wasted youth spent in the company of those entirely fictitious scoundrels, Sir John Falstaff, Pistol, Bardolph, et al. There is reason to think, however, that on ascending to the throne he rededicated himself to a life of piety, sobriety, and hard work. It is also easy to believe that he accepted in principle the advice attributed by Shakespeare to the dying king, his father: "Therefore, my Harry, be it thy course to busy giddy minds with foreign quarrels" (*Henry IV, Part II*, Act IV, scene v).

So it was that within eighteen months of coming to the throne, the young king was off for France to renew the Hundred Years War; and there he stayed for most of his reign. His war aims were simple and straightforward: to conquer as much of France as he could and, if possible, to make good his inherited claim to the French crown. It could not have escaped his attention either that war could be a profitable business for himself and for his soldiers.

The king set sail from Southampton in August 1415 with an army of about nine thousand indentured troops, including cannoneers. The archers' dress was no different from what it had been in the fourteenth century, but the men-at-arms were now almost entirely clothed in plate armor. Gone was the chain mail, gone the surcoat. The *camail* hanging from the helmet had been replaced by a *gorget* of plate and a protective chinpiece riveted to the bascinet. Breastplate and backplate were globular in shape, and below them hung a short skirt of metal strips fixed to a leather lining. Good examples of memorial brasses illustrating these features are those of P. Halle (ca. 1430) at **Herne Church** *(539)* just south of Herne Bay, Kent; J. Hadresham (1417) at **Lingfield Church** *(553)*, Surrey, north of East Grinstead, West Sussex; Sir Simon Felbrygge (1416) at **Felbrig Church** *(605)*, Norfolk, just south of Cromer, and Matthew Swetenham (1416) at **Blakesley Church** *(657)*, Northamptonshire, west of Towcester. Even more impressive and more representational than these, is the fine three-dimensional brass effigy of Richard Beauchamp, earl of Warwick (d. 1439) in the Beauchamp Chapel of **St. Mary's, Warwick** *(645)* in Warwickshire. He played a significant part in the French war, especially after the death of Henry V, and this monument is a rare example of a true likeness. The armor is obviously Milanese, indicating high quality and high cost. It is worth close study, as are the lineaments of the haughty and patrician face of the man who burned Joan of Arc.

Disembarking on the north shore of the Seine, the English king laid siege to Harfleur, which capitulated after five weeks of investment and bombardment by twelve-foot long cast iron cannon firing stone balls weighing nearly half a ton. After expelling the inhabitants and resettling the town with English, as his great-grandfather had done at Calais, Henry then set out for that city, 150 miles distant. It was a replay of the Crecy campaign. After crossing the Somme, he came upon a vastly superior French army blocking his way at the tiny village of Agincourt. There on St. Crispin's Day, 25 October 1415, the English, employing their usual combination of longbow archers and dismounted men-at-arms, decimated the French host, killing perhaps as many as seven thousand of the enemy in exchange for a few hundred of their own troops. It was a glorious victory, never to be forgotten by the English, engraved forever in the national consciousness by Shakespeare's incomparable lines attributed to King Henry on the eve of battle:

> This day is call'd the feast of Crispian . . .
> And Crispin Crispian shall ne'er go by,
> From this day to the ending of the world,
> But we in it shall be remembered;
> We few, we happy few, we band of brothers;
> For he today that sheds his blood with me
> Shall be my brother; be he ne'er so vile,
> This day shall gentle his condition:
> And gentlemen in England now a-bed
> Shall think themselves accursed they were not here,
> And hold their manhoods cheap whiles any speaks
> That fought with us upon Saint Crispin's day.
> —*Henry V*, Act IV, scene iii

After Agincourt, the king went home a national hero; and if there had been "giddy minds" still inclined to dispute the Lancastrian succession, their hopes were quashed. In two years time Henry was back in France to conquer Normandy in a series of long hard sieges culminating in the capitulation of Rouen. Internal political strife sapped the energies of the French. Their king, Charles VI, went mad; his heir, the Dauphin, engineered the murder of the duke of Burgundy, which brought the new duke over to the English side; the queen repudiated her son, the Dauphin, and declared him a bastard. The English of course profited from this disarray, and by the Treaty of Troyes, concluded in May 1420, it was agreed by all concerned except the Dauphin that Henry should marry the royal princess Catherine, Charles VI should keep his crown for life, but on his death it should revert to Henry and his heirs forever. After a one-day honeymoon the English king went back to the tedious business of siege warfare. While investing Meaux on the River Marne he contracted dysentery and died in the Bois de Vincennes in August 1422. Charles VI died two months later. That left the infant Prince Henry, born to Queen Catherine less than a year before, heir to the thrones of France and England.

In England the renewal of the wars produced another residential building boom among the rich and powerful, this too mostly financed directly or indirectly from the profits of war. Now, however, there was no need to put up strong fortifications against the threat of seaborne invasion. The French were hard put enough to survive at all, let alone undertake a counterattack, and anyway, until the last years of the war, most of the eastern coast of the Channel was in English hands. Architectural styles in England therefore gradually became demilitarized. True, the quadrangular layout of the fourteenth century courtyard castles persisted and the reflections of more dangerous times could still be seen in the plethora of bartizans and battlements and machicolations with which these fifteenth century buildings were tricked out. Indeed to the untutored modern eye some of these great towers and gatehouses seem formidable enough. But the appearance is mostly illusory. Their walls were thin (especially when made of brick), their exterior windows too numerous and ample, their protective devices too casual to justify their being classified with the great *donjons* of the twelfth century, the *enceintes* of the thirteenth, or the sophisticated fortified residences of the fourteenth. With some exceptions, they were built primarily for luxury and comfort and to proclaim the wealth and status of their owners, many of them made newly rich by royal largesse or by the fortunes of war.

Prominent in the latter category was Sir John Fastolf, a soldier of renown, whose actual character bore no resemblance to the braggart Falstaff of Shakespeare's invention. Offspring of an obscure Norfolk family, he served with distinction in the French war under Henry V, and after his death, under his brother, the duke of Bedford. That he served profitably as well is indicated by the fact that from one noble French prisoner alone, he collected over thirteen thousand pounds in ransom money. Out of his profits he built **Caister Castle** *(606)* north of Great Yarmouth, Norfolk, close by his own far humbler birthplace. Constructed of brick, it may have been modeled after some robber baron's castle on the lower Rhine and cost its builder six thousand pounds. Originally it was a moated courtyard castle, three hundred feet square, with a tower at each corner, protected by a second outer court whose moat was linked with the River Bure by a specially cut canal. In this case, though luxuriously appointed, the castle was meant to be a fortress as well as a residence, and the single surviving tower, more than ninety feet in height, is topped by machicolations and equipped with gunports. In fact, after the estate had passed to the Paston family (whose *Letters* constitute one of the major sources of information about fifteenth century England), the castle held out for five weeks against a siege by the duke of Norfolk and three thousand of his retainers. Today, next to the partly ruined tower stands the great hall, still occupied and, incongruously, housing a vintage car museum.

Like Caister, **Raglan Castle** *(714)* southwest of Abergavenny in Gwent, retained significant military features, which is not surprising considering its location in the Welsh marches where martial traditions were slow in dying. The earliest parts of the surviving building are the moated hexagonal great tower and the south gatehouse, both built from 1430 to 1445 by Sir William ap Thomas who did well in the French wars and had returned home to marry an heiress. This now ruined keep stands high on an ancient motte and was fitted with gunports combined with recessed arrow slits, so there can be no doubt about its intended function as a fortress. The remainder of the extensive buildings were put up later in the fifteenth century by ap Thomas's son, Sir William Herbert, earl of Pembroke, or later still in the sixteenth century by his successors. Even these additions display strong defensive characteristics, including thirty-seven gunports. Not so the splendid fifteenth century tower, called **Tattershall Castle** *(653)*, northeast of Sleaford, Lincolnshire, built by Ralph, Lord Cromwell, a veteran of Agincourt who later became King Henry VI's treasurer and one of the richest men in the kingdom. Here was a building clearly designed for comfort, not defense. Constructed entirely of brick, the rectangular tower has four stories above the basement, and above the roof at each corner rises an octagonal turret, bringing the total height to 120 feet. Restored by Lord Curzon, the interior rooms are spacious and luxurious. And though the exterior is machicolated and crenellated in the medieval manner, the huge windows on each floor and the absence of gunports clearly indicate that Lord Cromwell expected to enjoy his sumptuous quarters in peace. The same could be said for his contemporary, another veteran of Agincourt turned courtier to Henry VI: Sir Roger Fiennes, builder of **Herstmonceux Castle** *(548)* west of Bexhill, East Sussex. Now restored to house the Royal Observatory, this splendid edifice of brick superficially resembles the conventional late medieval courtyard castle with its enclosing moat, its twin-towered gatehouse protected by a portcullis, its octagonal towers projecting at the four corners, its semioctagonal towers at intervals in the curtain walls, its battlements and machicolations and arrow slits. All this is mostly sham, however; the plethora of spacious exterior windows and the internal arrangements of the rooms reveal that Herstmonceux was designed, almost exclusively, for ease and comfort. It is a country house, not a castle. So is **Sudeley Castle** *(642)* near Winchcombe, Gloucestershire, partly built by spoils from the French wars; later the home of Henry VIII's sixth and last queen, Catherine Parr; and in the nineteenth century reconstructed in its present form.

Even more decisively domestic in function and design are the smaller manor houses of the later Middle Ages, though some of these too bear the earmarks of military architecture. A very early and very well-preserved specimen is **Stokesay Castle** *(670)* northwest of Ludlow, Salop. Constructed mostly in the reign of Edward I by a prosperous wool merchant, Lawrence of Ludlow, the establishment consists of the luxurious great hall with high windows, adjacent residential buildings, and, for protection, a crenellated tower at the south end. Not much later **Longthorpe Tower** *(619)* west of Peterborough, Cambridgeshire, was built by one Robert Thorpe, a man of humble origins whose great-grandfather had been a serf. Here too, a crenellated tower was added to an earlier undefended mansion. Longthorpe, however, is chiefly noted for the remarkable series of mural paintings in its great chamber, recently discovered and painstakingly restored. This is the most complete set of medieval wall paintings in England. The subjects include the Nativity, the Apostles, the Allegory of the Three Living and Three Dead, the Wheel of the Five Senses, the Ages of Man, and other biblical and didactic matters. These are paintings on dry plaster, not frescoes, and their survival is almost as miraculous as some of the scenes they depict.

Obviously the owners of Longthorpe were more concerned with elegance than with defense. Their decorated walls are symptomatic of a decided trend toward luxury, comfort, and style at the expense of security. It is a trend, not a straight linear progression from purely military architecture to purely domestic. But the movement in that direction is unmistakable in the last two centuries of the Middle Ages, at least in those parts of England far from the Scottish border.

Clevedon Court *(581)* just east of Clevedon, Avon, on the Bristol Channel is a case in point. Built as a manor house about 1320 by Sir John de Clevedon, the surviving building with its large windows and octagonal chimney shafts is purely residential in character. Another example from the opposite side of southern England is **Ightham Mote** *(546)* east of Sevenoaks in Kent. The present manor house is built around four sides of a courtyard and is surrounded by a moat, but in the early fourteenth century it consisted only of the east wing, comprising the great hall, kitchen, one or two bedrooms, and a solar. The solar is the late medieval equivalent of a sitting room or drawing room. As here, it is usually located on an upper floor and its function was to provide privacy for the owner and his family away from servants and retainers who ate and otherwise occupied themselves in the great hall. Here again there are no surviving military features, except possibly for the moat, and that may have been dug when the other three wings were added in the sixteenth century. The building material is part stone and part half-timbering. This is a form of construction more common in the Tudor period than in the Middle Ages. The exterior walls consist of perpendicular timber struts, interlaced with horizontal or diagonal wooden braces and ties, the spaces between filled with brick or lathing covered with plaster. To the naked eye the contrast of dark timber and light plaster creates patterns of black on white, which accounts for these structures sometimes being called black-and-white houses.

Not far from Ightham, near Tonbridge, Kent, is **Penshurst Place** *(546)*, one of the great show places of England. The poet Ben Jonson, after a visit there in 1616, captured in verse the quintessentially domestic charms of this great sprawling country house.

> Now, Penshurst, they that will proportion thee
> With other edifices, when they see
> Those proud, ambitious heaps, and nothing else,
> May say, *their* lords have built, but *thy* lord dwells.
> —"To Penshurst," in *The Forest*

The original manor house, which today serves as the hub for the entire establishment, is centered in the great hall with an open timber roof, Decorated Gothic windows, and a central hearth—built in the 1340s by Sir John de Pulteney, a rich draper who had served four times as mayor of London. It is the finest surviving fourteenth century hall in Britain. Contemporary with it is the adjacent solar approached by a circular staircase enclosed in an external tower. To the solar was added, in the early fifteenth century, an extension later called Buckingham Hall. The other wings were put up in the sixteenth and early seventeenth centuries by the soldier-poet Sir Philip Sidney's father and brother. The present formal garden was laid out in the nineteenth century, but in the fashion of the seventeenth.

Of equal interest and possibly even greater charm is **Haddon Hall** *(662)*, south of Bakewell, Derbyshire. Nestled among the Derbyshire Peaks here is perhaps the finest example of an English manor house to survive from the Middle Ages. Although parts of the building are as old as the twelfth century, most of its walls and rooms date from the fourteenth and fifteenth centuries when the manor was owned by the Vernon family. In the sixteenth it came into the hands of John Manners, son of the earl of Rutland, whose alleged elopement with Dorothy Vernon provided the plot of a famous romantic novel. Manners was responsible for the construction of the Long Gallery, but the other major rooms—the Banqueting Hall, the Dining Room, and the Great Chamber—are medieval. The terraced garden is modern and gorgeous—a lush display of floral plenitude such as only the English can produce.

Much simpler in construction and appearance is **Lower Brockhampton Hall** *(648)*, east of Bromyard, Hereford and Worcester. Here is a black and white half-timbered hall, all that survives of a moated manor house built in the early fifteenth century. More than a century later, a gatehouse in the same style was set up at the edge of the moat, though the walls that it must have pierced have disappeared. **Lytes Cary** *(585)*, northeast of Ilchester, Somerset, has a great hall of the fifteenth century, though the rest of the manor dates from the sixteenth through the eighteenth. Also at **Bradley Manor** *(588)* on the western edge of Newton Abbot, Devon, most of the surviving east wing, including the great hall and chapel, belongs to the fifteenth century. So does **Great Chalfield Manor** *(577)* northeast of Bradford-on-Avon, Wiltshire. A modest house, built of local stone, it is noteworthy chiefly for its splendid oriel windows. In Wales, the best surviving example of a fifteenth century manor house is **Tretower Court** *(722)*, north of Crickhowell, Powys, today a partially restored ruin adjacent to the thirteenth century castle of the same name. Building on an earlier house, Sir Roger Vaughan put up most of the north and west ranges of his manor sometime after 1450, while his son, Sir Thomas, added the south and east curtain walls and the gatehouse. Even with these defensive features, the establishment lacks any significant military character and stands in interesting contrast to the ruined but formidable great keep of an earlier and more dangerous age only two hundred yards away. On a more magnificent scale, but dating also from the last half of the fifteenth century, is **Oxburgh Hall** *(609)*, southwest of Swaffham, Norfolk. At first glance, the moated twin-towered gatehouse with its battlemented turrets looks formidable enough; but this is a sham castle, built of brick, its machicolations sealed, its front face pierced by spacious windows. It was constructed by Sir Edmund Bedingfield sometime after 1482 and is, remarkably, still owned by his descendants. Opposite the gatehouse the northern range of the original quadrangle has been torn down, so that the courtyard to the rear is open, its two far corners occupied by Gothicized towers put up in the eighteenth and nineteenth centuries.

The last six manor houses mentioned above were all built in the fifteenth century. All are distinguished by the nonmilitary nature of their architecture. Yet these were years marked by the last of England's great baronial struggles, by fierce dynastic conflict, and by civil war between supporters of the White Rose and the Red.

To understand this anomaly one must turn to an examination of the bloody and Byzantine politics of the reign of the last of the Lancastrian kings.

HENRY VI: 1422–1461

Two main events marked and shaped the long reign of King Henry VI: the end of the Hundred Years War and the beginning of the War of the Roses. Still an infant when his father died in the Bois de Vincennes, the heir to the kingdoms of both England and France seemed destined for a glorious future. His uncle, the duke of Bedford, as regent of France sustained the winning streak begun by Henry V. All France north of the Loire was his, as well as Gascony. Only in the south central portions of the country were the forces of the Dauphin still able to maintain a tenuous hold. Then in April of 1429 the tide turned, swayed, miraculously it would seem, by the simple peasant girl from the village of Donremy, known to history as Jeanne d'Arc (Joan of Arc) and to her contemporaries simply as La Pucelle (the Maid). Inspired by the "voices" of the archangel Michael, St. Catherine, and St. Margaret, who, she claimed, had ordered her to deliver the Dauphin and his kingdom from the English, she appeared at the head of an army which was to break the siege of Orleans and enter the city in triumph. At her insistence the Dauphin went to Rheims to be crowned King Charles VII; then a series of French victories drove the English back to Rouen, the capital of Normandy. It was to that city that the Maid was brought in irons after her capture by Burgundian forces who sold her to the English for ten thousand gold crowns. She was tried and condemned for heresy by a French ecclesiastical court of the Burgundian faction. It was English soldiers, however, under orders of the earl of Warwick, who burned her alive. It was an act of statecraft, not wanton cruelty. To refute the new French king's claim to this throne, it was obviously expedient to demonstrate that he had been deluded by a witch whose "voices" were diabolical, not divine. In the event, the gesture was futile. In 1435, at Arras, the duke of Burgundy made his peace with Charles VII, and the English position became untenable. The duke of Bedford died. The French king hired a new master gunner, Jean Bureau, to modernize his artillery, and soon quick firing culverins proved to be the answer to the hitherto unbeatable masses of English longbowmen. By 1450 Normandy was cleared of the invading forces. Three years later they were driven out of Gascony. At Bordeaux, in July of 1453, a lone herald mounted the tallest tower in town, looked seaward, and proclaimed: "*Au secours de ceux d'Angleterre pour ceux de Bordeaux!*" There was no help, and Bordeaux too surrendered. Of all the vast English conquests in France, only Calais remained.

By the time the news reached England, its king had quietly lost his mind. Of all the medieval kings of England, Henry VI was clearly the least competent to rule. Meek, pious, unprepossessing in appearance, physically awkward, and mentally unstable, he was totally unfit to steer the ship of state in these troublous times. The power vacuum created by his ineptitude was largely responsible for the fierce factionalism both in court circles and in the country at large which eventually culminated in civil war. During the king's minority the chief contenders for power in the central government had been his uncle Humphrey, duke of Gloucester, and his great uncle, Henry Beaufort, Bishop of Winchester, and cardinal of England. Duke Humphrey, youngest brother to Henry V, was a rash, ambitious man whom history has treated more kindly than he deserves because of his gift of manuscripts to Oxford University, a collection which was housed in the handsome Divinity School, now part of **Bodleian Library** *(632)*, in a room, however, that is no longer open to the public. Cardinal Beaufort was the second son of John of Gaunt by his mistress and later wife, Catherine Swynford. Gloucester and Beaufort both died in 1447, but by this time the king had come of age, which made matters worse. Power now fell mostly to William de la Pole, duke of Suffolk, who rose to the top in the king's esteem only to receive most of the blame for the military losses in France. Also, he was charged with appeasement for having arranged the marriage of Henry VI to Margaret of Anjou, a French princess. In 1450 the commons impeached him and he was brutally murdered en route to France under sentence of banishment. That spring a rebellion broke out in Kent, led by one Jack Cade, directed mostly against Suffolk's followers, several of whom were murdered before the revolt was quelled. Suffolk's place in the favor of the king was soon taken by Edmund Beaufort, duke of Somerset, grandson of John of Gaunt, and therefore the late cardinal's nephew. Though much favored by Queen Margaret, a woman as forceful as her husband was weak, Somerset found a bitter rival in the person of Richard, duke of York. He too was of the blood royal. His paternal grandfather was Edmund of Langley, Edward III's fourth son; on his mother's side he was the great-great-grandson of Lionel, duke of Clarence, second son to Edward III. By the law of primogeniture alone, therefore, he had a better claim to the throne of England than did Henry VI who was descended only from the third son, John of Gaunt. (See genealogical chart of the houses of York and Lancaster.) When the king lost his senses, York succeeded in having himself declared protector and forthwith clapped his enemy Somerset in the Tower. There matters stood at court in the year the Hundred Years War drew to its final end.

In the country at large there was equal disarray. In the absence of an effective central government, lawlessness spread throughout the kingdom, and royal officials, sheriffs, and justices were either powerless to suppress it or too corrupt to try. The ends of justice were commonly defeated by bribery, by maintenance (armed intervention at court in behalf of a litigant), or by embracery (jury tampering), and though such acts were all forbidden by statute, few royal officials dared to enforce the law against the country magnates who chose to break it. These men, the baronage of England, held sway over their separate turfs like gangster chiefs, reinforced by paid bands of armed retainers wearing the private

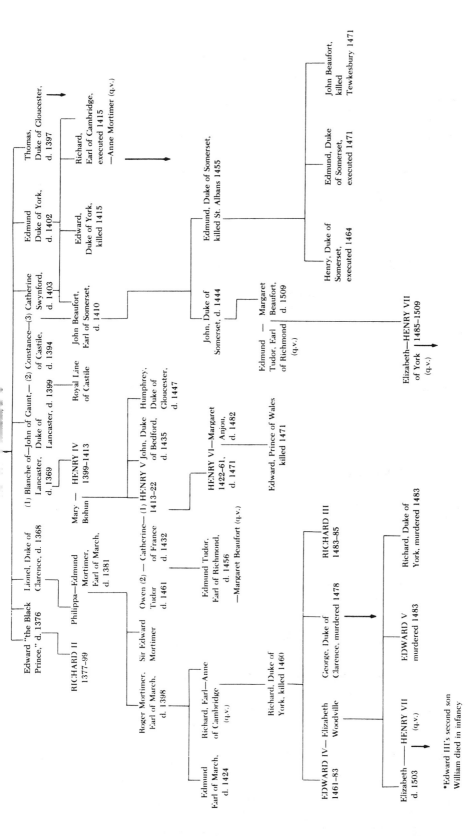

THE HOUSES OF YORK AND LANCASTER

uniforms, i.e., liveries of their employers. Sometimes their feuds with each other reached the proportion of civil war, as in the cases of the earl of Devon versus Lord Bonham and of Lord Cromwell versus the duke of Exeter. It was in the north, however, that the most serious of these vendettas took place: between the two long-powerful families of that region, the Percys and the Nevilles. After their discomfiture at the hands of Henry IV, the Percys had regained their estates under his conciliatory son. The Nevilles, meanwhile, had moved from strength to strength chiefly by marrying well. Ralph Neville, first earl of Westmoreland, had taken as his second wife Joan Beaufort, daughter of John of Gaunt. Their eldest son Richard became earl of Salisbury by marrying the heiress, Alice Montagu. Three of his brothers married the heiresses of the great families of Fauconberg, Latimer, and Abergavenny; their sister Cecily became wife to Richard, duke of York; and in the next generation Salisbury's eldest son Richard married the heiress of the wealthiest of England's earls, Richard Beauchamp, thereby becoming the earl of Warwick ("the king-maker"). In the violent climate of the late fourteenth century, that these two neighboring tribes should live at peace was unthinkable. And they did not. The long smoldering hostility between them erupted in July 1453 when the headstrong Thomas Percy, Lord Egremont, assembled a force of five thousand retainers at Heworth Moor near York for the sole purpose of harassing a party of Nevilles returning from a wedding. No bloodshed immediately followed, but by the end of the summer each family had armies of about ten thousand ready for the other's throat.

This then was the state of affairs when two events at the royal court brought the whole poisonous brew to a boil. In October 1453 Queen Margaret bore the king a son, thereby removing the duke of York as the next in succession to the throne. On Christmas Day 1454 the king recovered his senses, after which York was dismissed as protector and the duke of Somerset released from the Tower. In desperation, the duke of York prepared to do battle. He was joined by the Nevilles who had their own grievances against Somerset and against the queen who now controlled the court. Automatically, the Percys lined up with the court party. On 22 May 1455, under the shadow of the fifteenth century **Clock Tower** *(620)* in St. Albans, Hertfordshire, armies of the two factions met in combat. It was little more than a skirmish, but Somerset and the Percy earl of Northumberland were killed and the Yorkists captured the person of the king.

Thus began what history knows, though contemporaries did not, as the War of the Roses. The name probably derives from the famous scene in Shakespeare's *Henry VI, Part I*, Act II, scene iv, where in the Temple Garden in London the dukes of York and Somerset symbolize their implacable enmity by plucking each a rose, white for York and red for Lancaster. (Somerset represented the Beaufort line of the descendants of John of Gaunt.) And though Shakespeare's version is fiction, these respective blossoms were among the several badges displayed by the two rival factions. Yet the war between them was not originally a dynastic struggle, but rather a contest for dominance over a feeble king. Not until 1460 did Richard of York lay claim to the throne by right of superior descent from Lionel of Clarence, elder brother of John of Gaunt, the ancestor of Henry VI.

The battles that followed what is known as First St. Albans were mostly slugging matches fought on foot in open fields by dismounted knights, armed with swords, battle-axes, and flails. From their experience in France, the English had learned the folly of suicidal cavalry charges, so the longbow, which was effective chiefly against horses, ceased to be decisive. Battles usually commenced with barrages fired by bows and field cannon, but in the end neither weapon had much influence on the outcome, which was usually settled by hand-to-hand combat. Armor had undergone only slight changes since the days of Agincourt. More elaborate flutings and ridges are noticeable, designed to turn away the point of lance or sword. The chief novelty, however, is the appearance of a new headpiece, the *sallet,* a light helmet with a projecting brim at the back to protect the neck. A good example is the brass of Robert Staunton (1458) in **Castle Donington Church** *(658)*, Leicestershire. Another late fifteenth century innovation is the *tabard,* a short, sleeved surcoat, slit at the sides, reaching below the knees, and usually decorated with the wearer's heraldic arms. The brass of William Fynderne (1444) at **Childrey Church** *(637)*, near Wantage in Oxfordshire, offers a good illustration of the new fashion.

Of the individual battles themselves not much need be said nor is much to be seen on their sites today. After St. Albans, the Yorkists won another victory on 23 September 1459 at Blore Heath east of Market Drayton, Salop; were routed at Ludford Bridge soon afterwards; turned the tables in July of the following year at a battle fought near Northampton; but were in turn decisively beaten by a Lancastrian army in December 1460 just south of Wakefield, West Yorkshire. In that battle, fought near the duke of York's own **Sandal Castle** *(682)* (now a ruin), Richard and the Neville earl of Salisbury were both killed and decapitated, their heads sent to York to adorn the city walls, the duke's wearing a paper crown. Their places of leadership automatically fell to their sons, Edward, the earl of March, and Richard Neville, earl of Warwick. In early February 1461 Edward met and defeated a Lancastrian force at Mortimer's Cross, near **Croft Castle** *(648)* (originally a fifteenth century building), about six miles northwest of Leominster, Hereford, and Worcester. Here a new name appears on the scene, soon to take on far more significance than could then have been guessed at. Among the defeated was the Welshman Owen Tudor who had married the Dowager Queen Catherine, widow of Henry V, and, with his son Jasper, fought with the Lancastrians. Jasper escaped, but Owen was beheaded in the marketplace of Hereford, an unseemly end for the grandfather of a future king of England. The Yorkist victory, in any case, was short-lived. Later that month a Lancastrian army under Queen Margaret decisively defeated the forces of the earl of Warwick at the second battle of St. Albans. Notwithstanding, the earl of March proceeded to occupy London, laid claim to the throne by right of succession, and had himself crowned at Westminster as King Edward IV. A month later on Palm Sunday in a blinding snowstorm, he made good his claim at Towton, North Yorkshire, where he overwhelmed Queen Margaret's forces in the bloodiest battle of the entire war in which as many as twenty-five thousand Lancastrian supporters may have been slain. One of the casualties was Lord Dacre, whose tomb can still be seen on the north side of nearby **Saxton Church** *(688)*, where he was buried with his horse just after the battle.

EDWARD IV: 1461–1483

Towton secured the new king his throne, at least temporarily, as well as effective control over most of his kingdom. On the periphery, however, there was still trouble. The northern counties were Percy country with a long history of semi-autonomy and not easily subordinated to Westminster. Moreover, the doughty Queen Margaret, with her husband in tow, was just across the border in Scotland, ready to pounce again if the French and Scots would help her. The three great castles of **Alnwick** *(704)*, **Dunstanburgh** *(704)*, and **Bamburgh** *(704)* remained in Lancastrian hands. Not until 1464 were the king's forces able to reduce them all, and only then by bringing up the royal train of siege artillery. Bamburgh was the last to fall after the war's only siege in which heavy cannons were used. Even though its walls were battered, this massive castle sitting high above the sea had to be stormed by infantry before its garrison could finally be brought to surrender. Meanwhile, in two engagements in Northumberland, at Hedgely Moor and Hexham, the queen's forces were defeated again, thus ending Lancastrian resistance in the north. At the other end of the kingdom, however, the Yorkist cause suffered even greater difficulties. In 1461 a French force, acting on behalf of Queen Margaret, seized the island of Jersey, and occupied **Gorey Castle**, renamed **Mont Orgueil** *(744)*. Not until 1468 was it recaptured by Sir Richard Harliston who built the large tower commanding its entrance now bearing his name. In Wales, however, Jasper Tudor, having escaped the Yorkist slaughter at Mortimer's Cross, was still at large. After losing all his own Welsh castles, Jasper, with a garrison of fifty men, held out in the royal castle of **Harlech** *(740)* until the summer of 1468 when it too fell to a siege. (These are the "Men of Harlech" celebrated in the famous marching song of that name.) Jasper himself again escaped, this time to Brittany.

As a man, the new King Edward IV was everything his predecessor was not. He was young, tall, handsome, virile, audacious, extravagant, greedy, and lecherous—everything a medieval king should be. He was not yet, however, master in his own house. The earl of Warwick, by his own lights at least, had put his young cousin on the throne, and he expected from him deference, if not submission. He was affronted, then, when the king impetuously married an attractive young widow, Elizabeth Woodville, who was endowed with no wealth but with a large family of sons, brothers, and sisters all intent on capitalizing on their connection with the new queen. The quickest way to wealth in fifteenth century England was by advantageous marriage, and the Woodvilles, with the king's connivance, more or less monopolized that market for a while, incidentally thereby spoiling the chances of Warwick's own two eligible daughters. The earl was further offended when Edward on his own initiative betrothed his sister Margaret to the duke of Burgundy, thereby scotching Warwick's well-laid plans for a diplomatic marriage between the royal houses of England and France. In the time-honored tradition of English nobles disgruntled with their king, Warwick rebelled—first taking the precaution to suborn Edward's foolish youngest brother George, the duke of Clarence, to whom the earl married one of his daughters. For a while the rebels were successful, forcing the king to flee to the Netherlands and replacing on the throne poor King Henry who had wandered away from the battlefield of Hexham to be picked up later and clapped in the Tower.

It was a brief interlude. In March 1471, Edward IV returned, landing, as Bolingbroke had done, at Ravenspur in Humberside. Clarence redefected to his brother; Henry VI was seized; and at Barnet, a few miles north of London, Warwick's army of nine thousand men was routed and the earl himself was killed. A month later (4 May 1471) in the Bloody Meadow about a half mile south of Tewkesbury, Gloucestershire, the king's forces met and destroyed an expedition brought over from France by Queen Margaret. In **Tewkesbury Museum** *(642)*, on Barton Street, can be seen an interesting three-dimensional model of the battlefield. Among the many Lancastrians killed was Prince Edward, only son of Henry VI and Margaret of Anjou. In the church of **Tewkesbury Abbey** *(641)*, under the central tower, is a brass plate marking the site of his grave. Above it can be seen vaulting-bosses displaying the Sun in Splendor, the favorite Yorkist emblem (not the white rose) since the battle of Mortimer's Cross where the future King Edward IV had witnessed a meteorological phenomenon which looked to him like "three suns in the firmament shining full clear." After the battle of Tewkesbury, there were no more Lancastrian intrusions, except for the brief occupation by John de Vere, earl of Oxford, of **St. Michael's Mount** *(743)*, a tiny islet off the coast of Cornwall, where there is now a fourteenth century church incorporated into a later mansion owned by the St. Aubyn family. From this time on until his premature death in 1483, Edward IV was at last king in his own country. King Henry VI died in the Tower, undoubtedly murdered by royal orders. He was to be followed shortly by the new king's youngest brother, aptly dubbed by Shakespeare, "false, fleeting, perjured Clarence." This turncoat, once forgiven by the king, conspired again against him, was tried, imprisoned in the Tower, and secretly put to death, probably by drowning in a butt of Malmsey wine. His bones are on display in a glass case in the ambulatory of **Tewkesbury Abbey** *(641)*.

Once established, Edward IV proved to be a successful king. Unlike his Lancastrian predecessors, he summoned parliament infrequently and then only after stacking it with his own placemen. That he was mostly able to dispense with parliament he owed to his financial independence. This he achieved by confiscating the estates of the defeated and attainted Lancastrians, by collecting customs duties without authority, by engaging privately and profitably in the expanding overseas trade in woolens, and by blackmailing the French King Louis XI into paying him an annual subsidy of ten thousand pounds in return for breaking off the Anglo-Burgundian alliance. The first English king since Edward III with money to spare, he lavished much of it on building. His major surviving work is the great hall of **Eltham Palace** *(535)*, London, with its splendid hammer-beam roof and Perpendicular windows. At **Windsor Castle** *(565)*, he began the construction of St. George's Chapel, of which the present choir (except for the roof) was completed in his day. There he is buried, not far from the tomb of his most distinguished victim, King Henry VI.

Also in Edward's reign, and with his encouragement and financial assistance, was begun the great tower of **Dartmouth Castle** *(586)* on the west bank of the River Dart in Devon. Intended to guard this vulnerable coast against the possibility of an invasion from France by Henry Tudor (who, from his mother Margaret Beaufort, had a tenuous claim to the British throne) the castle was designed to house long-range artillery set almost at the waterline to sweep the harbor and sink enemy ships. Another castle of the period, though a private one, is **Baconsthorpe Castle** *(605)* southwest of Cromer in Norfolk. Started about 1460 by John Heydon and mostly completed between 1481 and 1486 by his son Sir Henry, who had been steward to the king's mother, this was a conventional late medieval quadrilateral courtyard castle with gatehouse and corner towers. Today it is a fairly imposing ruin. At about the same time, King Edward's chamberlain, William, Lord Hastings, was adding the great new tower, now ruined, at **Ashby de la Zouche Castle** *(657)* in Leicestershire on the site of an earlier establishment belonging to a Lancastrian supporter beheaded after the battle of Towton. Not far away, just west of Leicester, Hastings also began construction on **Kirby Muxloe** *(658)*, intended to be a great courtyard castle of brick with a gatehouse on the northern face, square towers at each corner, and rectangular towers on the other three faces. Only the gatehouse and west tower (both now in ruins) were completed when Hastings died in June 1483 two months after the death of his master, the king. Edward IV died probably of overeating and overdrinking; Hastings was beheaded at the instance of the successor king.

RICHARD III: 1483–1485

The legitimate heir to the throne was the late king's eldest son, who should have been crowned King Edward V. Before that could take place, however, this twelve-year-old boy was seized by his uncle, Richard of Gloucester, and clapped in the Tower, there soon to be joined by Richard of York, the late king's second son. The two little princes were seen no more. Presumably they were done in by their uncle who had them declared bastards and himself crowned king. Today, at the top of the Bloody Tower in the **Tower of London** *(513)* can be seen the room where it is supposed they were lodged and smothered to death. The evidence against King Richard as the instigator of their murder is circumstantial but strong. Certainly it was widely believed at the time, and the new king had only to produce their persons alive to dispel the ugly rumors. This he did not—in all probability because he could not.

That Richard III was not the deformed, hunchbacked monster imagined by Shakespeare is now seldom doubted. To the succeeding dynasty, the Tudors, it was expedient that he be painted in the blackest colors, and the Bard, for political as well as dramatic reasons, found it easy to comply. Unlike the duke of Clarence, Gloucester had remained loyal to his brother Edward even when the late king's hold on the throne was at its most tenuous. He had reason to believe, however, that unless he captured the government after his brother's death, he himself might be done in by the Woodvilles, the queen's ambitious relatives. Infanticide, however, was beyond the pale, even in the fifteenth century, and widespread revulsion against the suspected deed clearly sapped King Richard's support when another contender for the throne appeared on the scene.

This was Henry Tudor, duke of Richmond. He was the grandson of Owen Tudor, executed after Mortimer's Cross, and nephew of Jasper Tudor, earl of Pembroke, who had secreted the young man out of the kingdom and across the Channel to Brittany when the Lancastrian cause seemed lost for good. More importantly, his mother was Lady Margaret Beaufort, widow of Edmund Tudor and now wife to the powerful Thomas Stanley, lord of Man soon to be earl of Derby. She was, moreover, the great-granddaughter of John of Gaunt, which gave some color of legitimacy to Richmond's claim to the throne usurped from its last Lancastrian occupant, King Henry VI. To strengthen his position, he contracted to marry Elizabeth of York, Edward IV's oldest daughter, thereby intending, in Shakespeare's words, "to unite the white rose and the red" and bring an end to the fratricidal strife between the Houses of York and Lancaster.

In early August 1485 Richmond sailed from the mouth of the Seine with a motley expeditionary force of about two thousand men, landing at Milford Haven, Dyfed. Before the end of the month he was in Leicestershire, his army now doubled in size by Welsh reinforcements provided by Sir Rhys ap Thomas. There, in an open field about two miles south of Market Bosworth, near the spot now marked by an exhibition hall called **Battlefield Centre** *(658)*, he encountered King Richard with an army about twice the size of his own. What happened on the battlefield is obscure, but what is known is that, by switching sides at the last moment, Henry's stepfather Lord Stanley and the latter's brother, Sir William Stanley, swung the battle in Richmond's favor. Richard III died fighting. According to tradition, Lord Stanley found the dead monarch's gold circlet caught in a hawthorn bush and with it there and then crowned Henry Tudor, King of England. Thus ended the War of the Roses.

It is easy to exaggerate its significance, and until recently, historians, perhaps under the influence of Shakespeare, have tended to do so. The fact is that even among the ancient nobility of England who were the major participants, there was less bloodletting then one might suppose. The chief casualty of the war was the royal house of Plantagenet. As to the old baronage of England, the first two Tudor kings were to do more to exterminate them than did the civil war of the fifteenth century. On the remainder of the English population these thirty years of baronial and dynastic strife had little impact. Except on one occasion, after the battle of Wakefield, when Queen Margaret allowed her troops to pillage the towns of Grantham and Stamford, the country was mostly spared the wholesale arson and looting so commonplace in France and even on the Scottish borders. The military strategies pursued by both parties were not directed at conquest or territorial occupation. Armies, such as they were, aimed for each other. In the entire three decades of intermittent warfare, only about a dozen weeks were spent in active campaigning. Life went on. In the countryside, as we have seen, rich men continued to build their great houses with more thought to comfort than to defense. In the towns it was much the same. None of them attempted to withstand a siege. Nor could they have if they had tried. The urban centers of England, unlike those of France, were not fortified islands in an unfriendly feudal sea. They were primarily focal points of a flourishing interregional and international trade on which the War of the Roses inflicted only minor damage.

THE MEDIEVAL TOWN

Unlike ancient Greece or Renaissance Italy, medieval England was never intensively urbanized. Even as late as 1500 probably no more than ten percent of its total population lived in anything that could be called a town, and the average agglomeration of people so designated probably numbered no more than five or six hundred. In modern sociological terms, this was a preindustrial society, its wealth coming mostly from agriculture or sheep raising, its population mostly engaged in gaining a meager subsistence from the soil. Yet, even in primitive societies, some small scale industry usually takes place, and some buying and selling of surplus goods. And England, at least after its recovery from the shock of the Anglo-Saxon invasions, could not be classified as a primitive society by any accepted anthropological measurement.

The fact is that well before the Norman Conquest there were towns in England. Indeed Domesday Book lists over a hundred places as *burgi* or *civitates* and these could not have sprung up suddenly in the twenty years after 1066. Although some of them, like Canterbury, probably originated as communities serving great religious establishments, and others, like London and Southampton, because of their geographic suitability for trade, most of the Anglo-Saxon boroughs were created as fortified places during the Danish invasions and then attracted merchants and others seeking safety. Though the arrival of the Normans probably did little immediately to speed the process of urbanization, the establishment of a relatively strong central government under the descendants of William the Conqueror undoubtedly did. Royal castles at places like Newcastle and Rochester, great cathedrals, such as those built at Lincoln and York, or abbeys as at St. Albans or Bury St. Edmunds, inevitably served as nuclei for population growth. International commerce unquestionably received encouragement from the continental connections of these Norman and Angevin monarchs and from the wars they constantly were waging across the Channel. But the most important contribution of the English Crown to urban growth was the establishment of the King's peace throughout most of the realm. Kings and towns grew together. The business of towns was trade. The business of kings was to extract income from their kingdom so as to wage war, build castles, overawe their own feudal tenants, and live well. By various means the profits of trade could be taxed, and towns moreover would pay well for royal charters granting their merchants certain liberties, including monopolies over local trade and manufacture, fiscal autonomy, and the personal freedom of their citizens or burgesses from servitude to manorial lords. Almost all the early medieval English kings were liberal in their grants or confirmations of town charters, and by the end of the thirteenth century there were few population centers of any significant size that did not own one. By that time London had about thirty thousand to forty thousand inhabitants, while Bristol, York, Newcastle-upon-Tyne, Boston, Great Yarmouth, Lincoln, Norwich, Oxford, Shrewsbury, Lynn (King's Lynn), Salisbury, and Coventry ranged, in about that order, from approximately twelve thousand down to perhaps five thousand.

One of the rights that kings could grant to chartered towns was the right of *murage,* i.e., permission to build an encircling wall out of the proceeds of a toll on goods coming into town. Sometimes these were built largely for defensive purposes. As we have seen in the case of the walls of the North Welsh towns of Conway, Caernarvon, and Rhuddlan, King

Edward himself initiated the building in association with his newly constructed castles. Later, in the Hundred Years War, threats of invasion
from France produced the defensive circuits of Canterbury, Rye, and
Southampton of which portions can still be seen. In southern Wales, too,
there are a number of remaining walls which were clearly built as fortifications around the medieval boroughs that grew up at the foot of great
private castles. **Chepstow Town Wall** *(715)* in Gwent is fairly complete,
and a remnant of its western gate still spans the main street. The **Tenby
Town Wall** *(728)* in Dyfed was also built in the thirteenth century, then
rebuilt in the fifteenth, and partly restored in the sixteenth. Though the
once powerful town-castle has all but disappeared, the wall still stands in
places twenty feet high, is still buttressed externally by cylindrical stone
towers, and retains a single gate on the south side with a semicircular
barbican. **Pembroke Town Wall** *(727)*, also in Dyfed, on the other hand,
is fragmentary and far less impressive than the neighboring castle. On
the English side of the Welsh border, the most impressive **Chester City
Walls** *(673)*, a two-mile rectangular circuit enclosing the ancient city, are
chiefly medieval, though partly built on Roman foundations and, of
course, patched up and altered in more modern times. The existing
structure is high and wide and can be walked along for most of its length.

Chester was, of course, a bastion against the Welsh and the main
English forward base for armed expeditions into northern Wales. The
military function of its walls is therefore undeniable. In other parts of
England it is less clear just what purpose these enclosing circuits did
serve. As we have seen, none of the country's walled towns felt strong
enough to attempt resistance against the armies fielded by either side
in the War of the Roses. Probably their walls were not meant to be
military obstacles in the first place. Compared to the Continent, medieval England was a peaceful country, normally (except in the far north)
untroubled by the tramp of hostile soldiers. The towns were peopled
by merchants and craftsmen, and it was for commercial reasons chiefly
that these burgesses built their walls and the gates that pierced them.
Only thus could they effectively enjoy their local monopolies, keep out
interlopers, channel incoming traffic for purposes of toll collection, and
preserve the peace against strangers of ill intent. Despite their fashionable military gimmickry (arrow slits, bartizans, and the like) most of the
town walls of England are more mercantile than martial in their
origins.

Of those that still survive, the most impressive (except for Chester)
are the **York City Walls** *(690)* whose original circuit was three miles in
length, the north and west sides following the line of the old Roman
wall. Again large portions can, and should be, walked along. They date
mostly from the mid-fourteenth century. Along the northern stretch of
the circuit are two surviving gates: (from east to west) **Monk Bar** *(690)*
and **Bootham Bar** *(690)*; along the southern are **Walmgate Bar** *(690)*
with a fourteenth century barbican and **Micklegate Bar** *(690)* where

Richard of York's head was fixed, wearing a paper crown. In London the remnants of the city's medieval walls are much more fragmentary and mostly form the top courses of the older Roman walls, already described. All that is left of the **Norwich City Wall** *(608)*, Norfolk, is a short section on either side of King Street in the southeastern part of town near the remaining bastion called the Black Tower. Portions of the **Great Yarmouth Town Walls** *(606)* can be seen in the churchyard of St. Nicholas Church, while one of its surviving gates is still visible on North Quay and another in Blackfriar Road near the end of South Quay. A small section of the thirteenth century **Oxford City Wall** *(635)* now forms the north and east sides of the garden wall of New College and can best be seen along Longwall Street, or from inside the garden itself. The restored thirteenth century **Newcastle City Walls** *(700)*, Newcastle-upon-Tyne, Northumberland, run from St. Andrew's Church south along Bath Lane to Westgate Road. Otherwise, most of the 108 known town walls of medieval England have disappeared. Many were probably never finished in the first place. Others were allowed to deteriorate for lack of funds or lack of interest long before the pressures of modern industry and vehicular traffic overwhelmed them. The fact is that by and large English towns had less need for protective fortifications than did their Continental equivalents and their walls in consequence were less sophisticated, less sturdy, and more liable to neglect and decay.

Unfortunately for today's traveller, most of the secular buildings enclosed by these medieval walls have also disappeared. Much of what is touted by travel brochures as "medieval" in towns like York and Chester actually dates from the sixteenth century or later. Here and there, however, can be found genuine relics of the later Middle Ages, the most interesting of which are guild halls.

The earliest medieval guilds appear to have been fraternities organized around the parish churches for social and religious purposes, among them being the celebration of their patron saints' days with pageants and other festive activities, providing for their members' burial and for the singing of masses for their souls, etc. Very early in their history they assumed a commercial cast, though seldom losing entirely their initial religious coloration. A common feature of the town charters granted by English kings in the twelfth and thirteenth centuries was the concession of a merchant guild. These were associations whose primary purpose was the regulation of trade and commerce; and since the medieval borough was above all else a trading community, membership in the merchant guild or market guild was usually identical with membership in the borough. Its function, in any case, was monopolistic and regulatory. It was directed against outsiders who were subject to heavy tolls if they wished to trade within the town precincts, and, like a modern trade association, it tried to assure each of its members a reasonable share of the market by prohibiting what in modern times would be called unfair trade practices. As trade became specialized, separate associations of grocers, haberdashers, etc., were formed for the same purposes. With the appearance of industry, craft guilds put in their appearance. They were called mysteries (from the French word *metier* meaning "craft"), and the plays they put on during feast days were to comprise the earliest form of English drama. Craft guilds regulated prices, quality of product, conditions of labor, and above all restricted entry into the field by means of strict rules governing apprenticeship and tough examinations for mastership. In time, some guilds, especially in London, restricted their membership still further, excluding the less fortunate members of their crafts by imposing exorbitant entrance fees and requiring members to buy expensive uniforms or liveries. These were the so-called livery companies still to be found in London engaged in sundry social and ceremonial activities.

As guilds grew prosperous they often built great halls, which sometimes doubled as town halls, i.e., the headquarters of the local government. The best known of these today is the **London Guild Hall** *(511)*. Badly burned in the Great Fire of 1666 and again on the night of 29 December 1940 by German incendiary bombs, it survived, Phoenix-like, both disasters and is today an impressive medieval site, though much restored, nestled in the midst of a jungle of very modern architecture. The remaining fifteenth century portions of the building include most of the interior of the porch, the crypt, and much of the walls and columns of the hall, as well as some of the windows. The restored portions are meant to approximate the original. As to the halls belonging to the London livery companies, those that escaped the Great Fire of 1666 or were rebuilt after it, were almost all severely damaged or destroyed by German bombing raids in World War II. One that survived both disasters (though severely damaged in 1940) is the **Merchant Taylors Hall** *(511)*, on Threadneedle Street. Though much restored, its fourteenth century crypt survives, as does the great kitchen which has been continuously used since 1425.

The **York Guildhall** *(692)* received like damage in 1942 but has been mostly rebuilt along its original fifteenth century lines. In the same city are the fourteenth century **Merchant Adventurers' Hall** *(690)* and the much rebuilt **Merchant Taylors' Hall** *(690),* with a well-restored fourteenth century roof. In Coventry the bombs that destroyed St. Michael's Cathedral spared **St. Mary's Hall** *(665)* to the south of it. This was built in 1394 for the consolidated guilds of the city and much of it is original. The **Norwich Guildhall** *(608)* dates from the early fifteenth century, and though rebuilt in the sixteenth, retains some original glass in the council chamber. In nearby King's Lynn stands the **Guildhall** *(607),* built in 1421 in checkered flint and stone. In Bury St. Edmunds, Suffolk, stands the town **Guildhall** *(601)* with a porch dating to about 1480. In the Market Place of Lavenham, Suffolk, is the picturesque and well-preserved **Guildhall** *(603)* which, though dating from the early sixteenth century, is probably the most representative surviving example in England of a civic building in the late medieval style.

Lavenham was a wool town. Wool was the lifeblood of English trade throughout the Middle Ages. In the twelfth and thirteenth centuries raw wool was by all odds the leading export from England to the Continent. The north Italian city-states took some of it, but by far the major portion went across the North Sea to Flanders, thanks to the early development there of a flourishing textile industry. In the fourteenth century, however, and on into the fifteenth, native cloth-making received a number of stimuli. One was the mechanization of fulling, the process by which new-woven cloth was pounded under water into greater durability. Water-powered fulling mills, introduced in the thirteenth century and widespread by the middle of the fourteenth, greatly enhanced both the quality and the quantity of English cloth. Another stimulus was the imposition by King Edward III of a high export duty on raw wool, which of course, worked to the advantage of domestic manufacturers. Finally the spread of urban revolution in the Low Countries during the opening phases of the Hundred Years War seriously disrupted the Flemish textile industry, curtailed the export market, and drove many Flemish weavers to take up residence in England. The net result was a precipitous decline in the export of raw wool and a commensurate expansion of both overseas and domestic markets for English manufactured textiles.

Although cloth manufacture during the later Middle Ages was widespread, it came to be concentrated in three main areas: the West Country (Devon, Somerset, Gloucestershire, and Wiltshire), the West Riding (West Yorkshire), and East Anglia (Norfolk, Suffolk, and Essex). Lavenham was one of the Suffolk towns that grew rich in the fabrication of textiles. Although boasting a population of less than a thousand, it was rated, by the end of the fifteenth century, among the twenty most prosperous towns in England. It also provides today's traveller with the best surviving example in the country of a late medieval townscape. Not only the Guildhall mentioned above, but **Little Hall** (603) in the Market Place, the shop at 11 Lady Street, the houses at 87–90 Bear Lane, and the block of Flemish weavers' cottages at 23–26 Water Street date from the fifteenth century or before. No other sight in England or Wales approximates the authentic medieval look of the view of Lavenham from the juncture of Church Street and Bear Lane. Countless other towns must once have looked much the same.

For the most part, however, the secular buildings of urban Britain in the Middle Ages are gone—the victims of five centuries of intervening history. In contrast, an enormous number of ecclesiastical buildings in both town and country have survived. It is to the churches, then, that the traveller must look to find the true glories of medieval architecture.

CHAPTER VI

MEDIEVAL RELIGION, ART, AND LEARNING:
1066–1485

MEDIEVAL RELIGION

To place the medieval church in its proper historical perspective, the intelligent traveller could do no better than to begin with the city of York. Within the confines of this rather small provincial capital stand the great cathedral church of **York Minster** *(692)*, the ruined **Abbey of St. Mary's** *(692)*, and sixteen parish churches, all of medieval origin. Of the parish churches, seven—**All Saints, North Street** *(690)*, **Holy Trinity** *(690)*, **St. Martin-Le-Grand** *(692)*, **St. Michael-Le-Belfrey** *(692)*, **St. Denys** *(691)*, and **St. Michael Spurriergate** *(692)*—contain some of the most interesting medieval stained glass in the country. Twenty-five miles to the northwest lies **Ripon Cathedral** *(686)*; thirty miles to the southeast is the magnificent collegiate church of **Beverley Minster** *(676)*; and within a thirty-five mile radius lie the ruins of the great Cistercian **Abbeys of Fountains** *(686)*, **Jervaulx** *(686)*, **Rievaulx** *(689)*, and **Byland** *(688)*, and of the Carthusian **Priory of Mount Grace** *(684)*. Yet even this concentration of ecclesiastical buildings does scarce justice to the pervasive religiosity of the Middle Ages. In the mid-fourteenth century, York, with a population of no more than ten thousand, had forty-one parish churches; while the like-sized towns of Lincoln and Norwich had forty-nine and fifty respectively. London, with barely forty thousand inhabitants, had more than a hundred. In the country at large there was perhaps one church for every two hundred people; and even today there remain more than nine thousand parish churches of medieval foundation.

That the Middle Ages was the Age of Faith goes without saying; but faith alone does not explain the dominant role played by the church in the lives of every medieval man, woman, and child. For the church was not only a religious institution—at least not in the modern restrictive sense of the term. It was a political body of international scope and authority, a mammoth bureaucracy with a virtual monopoly of the intellectual skills essential to the functioning of organized society, a system of justice with a wide network of ecclesiastical courts of far-reaching jurisdiction, a great landholder whose vast domains were never diminished by division among heirs, a mammoth business enterprise controlling much of the fluid capital of western Europe, the employer of thousands of priests, clerks, monks, nuns, canons, friars, etc., to say nothing of the innumerable laymen engaged in various forms of service, an enormous building industry, the leading patron of the arts and repository of art objects, the sole institution of learning at all levels of instruction, the administrator of all health services and social welfare, and the center of almost all community life and activity. The church not only ministered to the spiritual and aesthetic needs of its communicants; it fed and clothed them when necessary, provided many of them an avenue of upward social and economic mobility, gave structure and meaning to their lives, and above all, offered hope of an afterlife where faith, charity, and obedience would ultimately be rewarded.

This promise was rooted in the belief that Jesus of Nazareth was the Christ, the only begotten Son of God, who, though crucified, had risen from the dead so that they who believed in Him might win forgiveness and everlasting life. It was rooted further in the dogma that Jesus had named His disciple Peter to be His earthly deputy and had endowed him with the keys to the kingdom of heaven; that Peter had founded the Church of Rome whose subsequent popes succeeded to his authority; and that the Roman Catholic church enjoyed therefore the exclusive right to establish the terms by which sinful man might win eternal salvation. Under this license the church had developed over the centuries a set of rites whose observance was believed to constitute an outward sign of man's submission to God's will and the necessary means to achieve His grace. Chief among these was the Mass—the celebration of the Eucharist or Holy Communion. This was a liturgical reenactment of Christ's sacrifice on the cross, first instituted at the Last Supper where Jesus Himself had offered His body and blood to His disciples in the form of bread and wine to be eaten and drunk in commemoration of Him. In the Catholic church, this act of worship was performed only by the ordained clergy, though its propitiary effects were believed to flow to all the faithful, both living and dead, thus placing the clergy in an intermediary role between sinful man and his Creator.

This brief excursion into Christian theology and church dogma has been thought necessary in order to explain the major purpose served by churches in the Middle Ages. The church, no matter what its size, was a building in which the clergy peformed their triple function of worship, intercession, and the administration of sacraments. The locus of this performance was in front of the high altar. So the church was, first and foremost, an altar house. This point must be kept in mind if the basic architecture of medieval churches is to be understood.

The high altar, upon which Mass was celebrated and before which psalms of praise were sung, was located at the eastern terminus of the chancel or choir which itself was at or near the eastern end of the church. This orientation guaranteed that worshipers would face in that direction during the service. The practice may have had its origins in pagan sun-worship, though the explanation could just as well lie in the symbolic connection between the rising sun and Christ's birth and resurrection. In any case almost all British and western European churches in the Middle Ages were laid out on an east-west axis with the altar set crosswise near the eastern end of the building. The altar itself was generally a long broad slab of stone, known as the *mensa,* resting on massive masonry supports and backed by a high altar screen of carved wood or stone, known as the *reredos* or *retable.* To the right of the altar, in the south wall of the chancel, was the *piscina,* a shallow basin used by the priests to wash their hands and rinse the chalice emptied of the consecrated wine consumed at Mass. On the same side, and built into the chancel wall, might be the *sedilia,* a range of seats occupied by the celebrant of the Mass and his assistants.

Back of the high altar in larger churches was a space reserved for a shrine containing the holy relics of a saint, or a lady chapel dedicated to the Virgin Mary, or both. On the Continent this easternmost end of the church is called the apse and, in shape, is usually rounded or polygonal (i.e., apsidal). In England it is normally square sided and is called the retrochoir.

Forward of the altar is a space known as the presbytery, clear of any other furnishings so as to allow the celebrants room to maneuver during the ceremony of the Mass. West of the presbytery, in all but the smaller parish churches, are the choir stalls, canopied benches facing each other toward north and south. On the underside of the hinged seats of the choir stalls were misericords—projecting brackets to provide a modicum of rest to members of the choir. This consisted of priests, canons, or monks, or their substitutes (vicars, choral, or choir boys) trained to chant the liturgy in Latin plainsong, after the practice set down by Pope Gregory the Great in the sixth century. Seven times a day, at least in cathedrals or monastic churches, they sang the special services prescribed by St. Benedict as the *Opus Dei,* God's work: matins/lauds, prime, tierce, sext, nones, vespers, and compline. All this was in addition to daily High Mass and in between other masses at altars distributed throughout the body of the church.

Immediately to the west of the choir stalls, the chancel terminated in a rood screen or *pulpitum* topped by a crucifix flanked by figures of St. John and the Virgin Mary. These were high screens of wood or stone, usually richly carved and pierced by doors into the chancel. A number of these chancel screens have survived from the Middle Ages. No other feature of ecclesiastical architecture, however, better demonstrates the centrality in medieval Christian worship of the high altar, the chancel which housed it, and of the clergy who performed the ordained rites before it. The screen did not allow an uninterrupted view of the services taking place behind it. The Mass could be heard by the laity, but not clearly seen—except perhaps for occasional glimpses through "squint holes" sometimes perforating the wall between chancel and nave.

At the line where the chancel ends, the nave begins. Also at or near the center of that line is the crossing, which marks the point where the east-west axis of the church is intersected by the line between the transepts, extensions projecting north and south on either side of nave and chancel, thus establishing the cruciform ground plan of almost all larger medieval churches. The obvious symbolic connection between this form and the cross on which Christ died may have influenced medieval builders in choosing it, but the more likely reasons for its adoption are structural and liturgical. The massive central tower above the crossing demanded strong abutment at the four corners where it joined the roof. The four transept walls running at right angles to the church's axis helped to exert the necessary counterpressure to the tower's outward thrust. Moreover, custom required the worshiper to face east, so transepts were liturgically useful in that they provided room for additional altars along their eastern walls. It was no doubt this consideration that induced church builders on occasion to construct double transepts, i.e., a pair of north-south projections on either side of nave and chancel, giving the ground plan the appearance of a cross of Lorraine. In smaller churches, where there are no transepts and therefore no crossing, the tower is usually, but not always, at the west end.

The nave is the great hall of a medieval church stretching to considerable length westward of the chancel screen. It is the church's largest single compartment and the one by which today's visitor normally first enters. Its size, however, is no measure of its original importance. The heart of the medieval church was the smaller chancel where High Mass was offered. The nave might hold large numbers of laity—in a cathedral, perhaps a town's entire population—but there were no pews or other places for them to sit, except possibly for a few stone benches along the walls or around the upright piers. In any case their role in church services was passive, and in some instances their presence was even discouraged. Cathedrals and monastic churches did contain altars in the nave where the Mass could be celebrated within full view of the laity, but bishops and abbots often preferred them to go where they could worship in smaller groups—which accounts for the large number of parish churches in the immediate vicinity of cathedrals and some abbeys.

It is true that the laity at times were treated to sermons delivered from pulpits of stone or wood, usually built into the rood screen or attached to a nearby pier. But with all the milling about in the nave to which the laity were consigned, it seems doubtful that there were many listeners. A number of extant pulpits date from the fifteenth century, but most of those in British churches today are of a later period. Preaching, to be sure, became more common as the Middle Ages approached their end, but, except in the case of friars' churches, it was not really until the Protestant Reformation that it assumed a central place in religious worship.

On either side of the nave are aisles, normally with relatively low ceilings and separated from the nave by arches resting on cylindrical columns or clustered piers. Above these is a second row of arches, opening into the space between the aisle ceiling and the sloping outer roof, which is called the triforium. Above this is the clerestory or clearstory—that portion on the nave's walls containing its upper side-windows.

Nave and aisles together normally form more than half the total area of a medieval church—which is surprising considering their relative unimportance to the central function of the building. The explanation is twofold. In the first place a large nave provided space for the multitude of altars which laymen were encouraged to endow for the good of their souls. Altars might be erected in front of the rood screen, against the walls flanking the chancel arch, in the transepts, in the aisles, between piers—indeed almost any place where there was available room. Sometimes they were open, sometimes fenced by screens to form separate chapels. Almost the only restriction on their number and location was the requirement that space be left for processions—which is the second reason for the large naves. In each church there was a Sunday procession, inside and often outside. Additional great processions were held on Palm Sunday, the Feast of Corpus Christi, Rogation days, and Candlemas. In large churches a special porch, called the Galilee, was sometimes added to the west end of the nave to provide a processional entry way.

Colorful these occasions were—but no more so than the interiors of the churches in which they took place. Almost every inch of space, whether on walls, ceilings, piers, or screens, was covered with paint. Bright blue, red, and gold were the preferred colors. Windows sparkled with stained and painted glass. Rich vestments and jewels adorned both priests and furnishings. Vessels and ornaments of gold and silver glistened. And against this kaleidoscope of color flickered the fires of countless tapers. It was a rich and vivid scene—far removed from the cool, gray dignity that greets today's visitor as he enters these ancient buildings.

Medieval churches varied greatly in size, though seldom in shape. True, in the early Middle Ages a few were built in the round, in imitation of the Church of the Holy Sepulcher in Jerusalem; and later, as preaching became more popular, especially among the various orders of friars, rectangular churches were sometimes built. But the normal ground plan was cruciform. Aboveground, however, medieval churches display a great variety of architectural styles. Today's visitor to these venerable sites should, above all, be able to recognize these styles and to distinguish one from another.

MEDIEVAL ARCHITECTURE

By long standing convention, art historians classify the styles of English medieval architecture into four main periods: (a) Norman (ca. 1066–1190); (b) Early English, (ca. 1140–1260); (c) Decorated (ca. 1250–1360);

and (d) Perpendicular (ca. 1340–1485). It will be noted that this chronological classification allows some overlap between periods to take into
account the transition from one style to another. One of these intervals,
i.e., the half century of change (ca. 1140–1190) between Norman and
Early English, witnessed such a radical change that it is uniquely labeled
Transitional and under that title is sometimes considered to be a fifth and
separate stylistic period.

NORMAN: 1066–1190

Roughly coinciding with the eleventh and twelfth centuries, Norman
or Romanesque architecture is chiefly characterized by massiveness
and roundness. Walls are inordinately thick. They may measure as
much as twenty-four feet at the base, though often not solidly made but
filled with rubble between two skins of stonework. Because the walls
are so heavy, there is little need for exterior buttresses. These, when
present at all, are mere shallow vertical projections, more decorative
than functional. Windows are small and almost always round headed.
As in Anglo-Saxon churches, they are sometimes twin openings divided
by a baluster. Doorways also are round headed, though sometimes the
top semicircle is a solid stone tympanum filled with carving. The more
important doorways are normally built up in two, three, or more diminishing and receding arches each resting on its own ornamented column. Interior columns or piers are huge and usually cylindrical, though
sometimes composite, i.e., semicircular sections built around a square.
All arches are semicircular. Though the interior roofing of most Norman churches was of wood, stone vaulting was occasionally used to
cover narrower spans such as those over aisles. These ceilings were almost always barrel or tunnel vaults, semicylindrical in form. Occasionally, two barrel vaults might intersect each other at right angles, the
result being a groined vault. Exterior towers were square and low, superimposed over the crossing or flanking the western facade or sometimes the transepts. They were normally topped by low pyramidal
spires of wood.

TRANSITIONAL: 1140–1190

This is the period when the semicircular arch was going out and the
pointed arch was coming in, both sometimes appearing side by side. The
Norman arch has two important structural limitations. In the first place,
its lateral thrust is so powerful that, even when resting on massive walls
or columns, it is unsafe for spanning wide passages such as church naves.
This accounts for the early wooden roofs of Norman naves, and these, of

course, were dangerously combustible. In the second place, the height of a semicircular arch is, by geometrical definition, exactly half its span. This means that if passages within a church varied in width, the vaulted roofs or arches above them would necessarily have to vary in height. Geometric necessity then imposed unwelcome constraints on church builders. If a uniform height was to be obtained, all the component parts (nave, aisles, chancel, transepts) would have to be the same width. Since this was obviously undesirable, the alternative was a building with ceilings of different heights, and this was awkward. In short, the semicircular arch was unsatisfactory on two counts: It was unsafe, and it imposed unwanted rigidities on church design. The answer to both problems was the same: the pointed arch, or, as its French inventors called it, the *arc brisé* (broken arch). The thrust of a pointed arch is more downward than outward, so that walls and columns supporting it do not have to be of extraordinary thickness. Wide areas can therefore be spanned without putting unbearable stress on the arch's supporting members. At the same time, uniform heights can be maintained no matter what the width of the area spanned, simply by varying the angle of the arch's apex. Safety and flexibility are thus equally served.

A second innovation of the Transitional period was the ribbed vault coupled with the flying buttress. On its underside a ribbed vault has the appearance of an umbrella of four or six ribs seen from below. The stone ribs rest on columns or walls or stone wall-brackets called corbels, and project diagonally across the nave or other opening, crossing each other at the ridge line. The weight of the vault's stone paneling is carried by the ribs. The ribs in turn can be reinforced at their terminal points by flying buttresses. A flying buttress is simply a half arch of stone placed in such a way as to provide a counterthrust to the lateral pressure of ribs against the columns and walls from which they spring. In France, and later in Britain, flying buttresses were often built against the exterior walls of churches, but in twelfth century England they were normally constructed on the inside where they are often concealed behind the triforium arcade above the side aisles.

These three characteristics: the pointed arch, the ribbed vault, and the flying buttress together comprise the elements of what came to be called Gothic architecture. Classical purists of the seventeenth and eighteenth centuries coined the phrase to describe all post-Norman architecture of the Middle Ages, which they considered un-Roman and therefore barbaric. Later generations, though preserving the word, dropped its pejorative connotations; and the term Gothic now proudly stands for all post-Romanesque styles of medieval architecture. In the Transitional period, pointed arches, round arches, ribbed vaults, heavy cylindrical columns, flying buttresses, and massively thick walls were all intermixed. By the late twelfth century, the purely Gothic features emerged alone in a distinctly new style.

EARLY ENGLISH: 1140–1260

All arches were now pointed and all vaults ribbed. This imparts a new vertical emphasis in contrast to the horizontal theme of both classical and Romanesque design. The impression left on the beholder is one of loftiness. Vaults are high, and uniformly high. They are supported by tall and slender piers consisting of shafts grouped in clusters. Flying buttresses began to appear outside the church—arched stone props against exterior walls. Slender towers with pointed spires replaced the square squat Norman structures with their pyramidal tops. Walls became thinner, and in them window openings were larger and more numerous. Indeed it is easier to identify the date and style of a Gothic church by its windows than by any other single feature. Early English windows are typically lancets, i.e., narrow pointed arched openings, called lights, arranged singly or in groups. Sometimes these groups are of uneven height, the tallest being at the center. Sometimes they are aligned under an arch, the space between window and arch (the spandrel) being pierced by quatrefoil- or trefoil-shaped openings. This is called plate tracery and is distinguished from later bar tracery by the solidity of the stone, i.e., the high ratio of stone to glass. Simplicity of decoration and purity of line are the hallmarks of the Early English. It is the noblest of all Gothic forms.

DECORATED: 1250–1360

Here again the most noticeable feature is the window. The openings are much larger and wider, though still leading up to a pointed arch. They are divided vertically by narrow stone bars, called mullions, forming five, seven, or even nine lights. Bar tracery of intricate design fills the space under the arch. At first these designs are generally geometric: circles, trefoils, and quatrefoils. Later they become curvilinear as window heads fill up with flowing, flamboyant shapes. The distinction is so marked that some art historians draw a sharp line at about the year 1300 between the Geometric period and the Curvilinear period. Reticulated tracery also appears, fine networks of stone bars in the shape of diamonds or interlocking S-shaped curves called ogees. The designs are often incorporated into great circular windows called rose windows. The ogee theme is repeated elsewhere, in arches of two double reverse curves (convex plus concave) joined at the top in a sort of onion-shaped design. These appear in wall arcades, in hoods placed over doorways, in canopied wall niches made to house the sculptured images of saints and martyrs. Piers are still clustered, often built on a diamond-shaped plan with a central shaft surrounded by others more slender. Vaults become more complex. Intermediate ribs, called tiercerons, now spring from pier or corbel to ridge-line, breaking the vault into series of pie-shaped slivers. Where ribs cross each other or cross the ridge-line, elaborate carved bosses of stone or wood cover the point of intersection. Later, cross-ribs, called liernes, are added. They serve no structural purpose, being purely decorative, crossing from one rib to another and making star patterns against the vault. An element of fussiness has crept into the Gothic style. Variety there is aplenty, and marvelous workmanship. But the scene has become riotous, not to say gaudy.

PERPENDICULAR: 1340–1485

Unlike other Gothic styles, the Perpendicular is peculiar to Britain— and to southern Britain at that, since it is almost unknown in Scotland. Again, the key to its identification is the shape and size of its windows. Underneath a very flattened four-centered arch, the Perpendicular window becomes a high rectangle, divided into panels by vertical stone mullions and horizontal stone transoms. The same rectangular motif is repeated in wall paneling. So dominant indeed is this theme that some art historians prefer the word *rectilinear* to describe this new phase of Gothic architecture with its increased emphasis on the horizontal line. Internal doorways become wider, topped also by obtuse four-centered arches, so flattened that they seem almost horizontal. With the arch of the central vault likewise flattened, exterior walls inevitably climb higher. At the same time the ratio of glass to stone within the walls increases. This makes the exterior flying buttress a necessity. Exterior walls of English churches now come to be surrounded by a jungle of graceful pinnacled semi-arches whose functional purpose is simply to shore up the more fragile sides of the building. As if to match this external embellishment, Perpendicular towers are heavily ornamented with pinnacles and fancy stonework. Inside, however, the decor tends to be plain, symmetrical, and even monotonous. Perpendicular interiors lack the variety of earlier Gothic styles, and the eye seems able to cover everything almost at a single glance. The exception is the vaulting. Lierne vaults become extraordinarily intricate in design. Even more ingenious are the fan vaults spanning smaller openings such as chapels, cloisters, porches, and retrochoirs. These are shaped like half-cones, with curving ribs radiating in every direction, thus producing an effect like a convex open fan. They represent the ultimate in Gothic rib design. Their widespread use was probably made possible by the growing centralization of the stonecutting industry which took place in the late fourteenth and early fifteenth centuries. This in turn may have been brought about by labor shortages created by the Black Death. The Perpendicular style originated before that terrible plague hit Britain and the pace of church building does not seem to have been interrupted by it. However, the standardization of architectural design so noticeable in the last century and a half of the Middle Ages and well into the Tudor period may be among the Black Death's many far-reaching consequences.

MEDIEVAL ART

With few exceptions all artistic effort in the Middle Ages was inspired by religious faith and had as its object the enrichment of that faith and the adornment of the ecclesiastical buildings where it was proclaimed and practiced. The medieval church was, of course, itself the supreme expression of the artistic spirit of its times. It was, moreover, a sort of studio for the execution of major and minor works of graphic and plastic art. It became, therefore, the chief repository of the products of this varied artistry. And, except for those objects of art that have found their way into the museums of Britain, it still is.

Queen of the ecclesiastical arts was sculpture. From the beginning the Normans carved the walls, pillars, and arches of their great stone churches with a wide variety of simple and repetitive designs. Their favorites were the chevron, the rhombus, the raised rectangle, the key, and the cable. On their baptismal fonts and the tympana over the doorways they tended to lavish greater care, sometimes carving grotesque birdlike faces in low relief, sometimes primitive figures of the Apostles or of Christ, Himself. Such efforts became more and more elaborate through the twelfth century, and by the thirteenth, stone sculpture was to achieve a high degree of sophistication. Sculpture in the round became as common as bas-relief. Life-size figures of Biblical characters, bishops, kings, nobles, etc., adorn the west fronts of cathedrals and stand in niches sunk in church walls inside and out. Stone angels in an infinite variety of poses become a common sight.

In the mid-thirteenth century Purbeck marble came into general use, as the quarries of Dorset were opened up and craftsmen in London and elsewhere began to fabricate and market shafts, bosses, and other fittings all over the country. Strictly speaking this is not marble at all, but an exceptionally hard dark shell limestone which takes a high polish. It became especially popular in the carving of recumbent effigies for tombs. In the thirteenth century it was fashionable for bishops to order for their cathedrals a series of tombs for their episcopal predecessors. Knightly effigies soon followed, convention dictating that the legs be crossed beneath the knees and the right hand cross the body to grasp the hilt of a sword, as though in the act of unsheathing it. By the fourteenth century Purbeck marble has gone out of fashion, replaced by softer freestone or by alabaster, a semitranslucent variety of gypsum. Though less durable than Purbeck, both materials held color better and were easier to work. After the Black Death, alabaster carving was among the first church-related industries to reach a commercial level of organization and production. Not far behind was the freestone carving of gargoyles for church exteriors and of intricate bosses to cover the junctions and crossing places of the lierne ribs that became so popular in this century. Architectural sculpture of the fifteenth century mostly follows the traditions of the fourteenth. Gargoyles became even more fashionable, especially as adornments to the exterior flying buttresses of Perpendicular churches. Carved baptismal fonts, which, for some reason, had gone out of style after the twelfth century again came back into fashion. Bronze began to be used in effigies. Woodcarving reached new heights in the work executed on misericords, those projections attached to the bottom of hinged choir seats for the support of weary singers. Here secular motifs often prevailed: scenes of sowing, plowing, and harvesting; pigs burrowing for acorns; a henpecked husband pushing his nagging wife in a wheelbarrow to the ducking stool, etc., etc.

No such mundane matters, however, intruded themselves into wall paintings, which were the most common form of medieval pictorial art. The perennial damp climate of Britain plus the combined destructiveness of iconoclastic Puritans and renovative church wardens has obliterated most of these, but a fair number do survive. They were intended to spread familiarity with the New Testament and the lives of the saints among an illiterate laity. Scenes from the Passion (i.e., sufferings) of Jesus and of the Resurrection were among the most popular. So were episodes from the life of Mary, especially from the thirteenth century onwards when the cult of the Virgin took hold throughout western Europe. Of the saints, the most popular in Britain were St. Christopher and St. George, although, of course, St. Thomas of Canterbury remained the favorite national martyr. Of all the surviving church wall paintings, however, by far the most numerous are those of the Doom, picturing in horrifying detail the Last Judgment with saints and unrepentant sinners being sent on their respective paths to eternal bliss or fiery torture. Lest their implicit warning be overlooked, Doom paintings in parish churches normally filled the entire wall space over the chancel arches. Akin to them were depictions of the Dance of Death and of the well-known fable of the Three Living and Three Dead where reminders of the mortality of man were reinforced by disgusting details of slugs, beetles, and worms at work on rotting human flesh. The art of the macabre, both in painting and funereal sculpture, reached its high-water mark during and after the incursions of the Black Death which no doubt served as its chief inspiration.

Surprisingly, very little of this fascination with the gruesome aspects of death and corruption is reflected in the brass memorial plates with which English churches are so plentifully endowed. These were precisely and beautifully incised with the figures of the persons commemorated, then set flush in stone matrices which were in turn sunk into church floors. The metal used was an alloy of copper and zinc, called latten. The main centers of production were in the south of England (London, the Home Counties, East Anglia, and the West Country), and it is in these regions where the majority of the four thousand surviving brasses are to be found. As already mentioned they are today among the chief sources of information on the details of armorial dress and medieval weaponry. They are equally illustrative of the history of civilian costume and of ecclesiastical vestments. Aesthetically, moreover, they are among the most delightful of all medieval art forms, and it is not surprising that their reproduction by the process known as brass-rubbing is today such a popular folk art in Britain.

Another important medieval art form (though it originated in the Dark Ages) is that of manuscript illumination. It flourished chiefly in the scriptoria attached to the cathedrals of Durham, Exeter, Canterbury, and Winchester and the Benedictine abbeys of St. Albans and Bury St. Edmunds. Bibles and psalters provided the primary materials for illumination. In the twelfth century the favorite form of manuscript decoration was the historiated initial, with elaborate narrative and decorative detail woven into and around the first letter of the first word of the first chapter of each book of the Bible. The letter *I*, for example, begins the first chapter of Genesis ("In the beginning [*In Principio*] God created the Heaven and the Earth."). Around this single vertical shaft extending from top to bottom of the opening page, medieval illuminators would weave all manner of leafy scrolls inhabited by men and beasts, and on it they would superimpose medallions filled with illustrations of Biblical stories and Christian allegories. Even greater license could be taken with the letter "B" beginning the first chapter of the Book of Psalms ("Blessed [*Beatus*] is the man that walketh not in the counsel of the ungodly."). Within the two semicircular loops of this initial an infinite variety of forms and figures could be worked. The larger the Bible, of course, the greater the freedom of the illustrator. By the mid-thirteenth century the great folio Bibles of the twelfth century began to go out of fashion to be replaced by much smaller volumes better designed to serve the needs of scholars engaged in the intensive Biblical studies pursued at the universities. The historiated initial thus shrank in size and lost much of the luxuriance of its illustration. By way of compensation, the increasing use of psalters by laymen in the late thirteenth and fourteenth centuries opened a new field for the illuminators. Now secular themes begin to intrude. Peacocks, monkeys, and other exotic birds and animals decorate the margins and play around the texts. Dragons, griffins, unicorns, and other representatives of the fabulous medieval bestiary take their place among the more specifically religious figures and symbols. All this, of course, is in glorious color: reds, greens, blues, and, above all, gold leaf.

Of all artistic inventions of the Middle Ages, none has had a more lasting appeal than that of colored church window glass. It was at first made by painting metallic oxides onto glass panels and then fusing the colors with the glass under high temperatures in a kiln. Iron oxide produced greens and yellows; cobalt, blue; manganese, purple; and copper, a deep red known as "ruby." These are the colors most common in the earliest surviving glass, that of the twelfth and early thirteenth centuries. Late in the thirteenth century a new type called grisaille, was introduced. It was greenish gray in color, though windows in which this type predominates usually incorporate small pieces of more brilliant hue to break the monotony. Another process discovered in the fourteenth century produced brilliant yellows. This was the silver-stain technique produced by applying silver chloride to plain glass under intense heat. Medieval church windows resemble modern jigsaw puzzles. Small pieces of glass of various colors were fitted inside of frames, mullions, transoms, and tracery according to prearranged patterns, then joined together with lead. As in the case of wall paintings, the themes were mostly religious in character, though a great variety of purely decorative elements abound, and in the fifteenth century heraldic devices became commonplace.

RELIGIOUS ESTABLISHMENTS

As already indicated, all medieval churches performed essentially the same function, which was to provide shelter for prescribed religious services, especially the Mass. There were, however, distinctions among the different types of Chrisitian communities, both clerical and lay, served by these churches. There were basically five different categories of religious establishments, which together account for the great bulk of ecclesiastical sites of interest to today's traveller to Britain. They are (a) cathedrals, (b) parish churches, (c) monasteries, (d) friaries, and (e) collegiate foundations.

CATHEDRALS

By definition a cathedral is a church that houses a bishop's throne, his *cathedra*. Other churches may be as large or larger, but the presence of the throne gives the cathedral the special distinction of being the mother church of the diocese, i.e., the ecclesiastical district presided over by a bishop. Architecturally, cathedral churches do tend to bigness, their east ends especially being more elongated than normal. This was to make room behind the high altar for a saint's shrine to attract pilgrims and incidentally, revenue. Also at the far east end, which in England was usually square in shape, was often placed a chapel dedicated to the Virgin

Mary, the Holy Trinity, or, in at least one instance, to Jesus, Himself. When all this space is added to the chancel or choir, the east end of a cathedral church (i.e., the end east of the crossing) tends to be as long as, or even longer than, the west end, or nave. This elongation in some instances made possible the addition of an extra set of transepts, giving the cruciform the shape of a cross of Lorraine.

A large choir was essential to the proper functioning of a cathedral, because, in addition to being the seat of the bishop, it was the scene of the constant round of services known as the *Opus Dei* performed by its attendant clergy, organized as a chapter. The chapter might consist either of regular or secular clergy, i.e., monks or canons. In medieval England there were ten monastic cathedrals and nine secular; in Wales, all four were secular. In monastic cathedrals the abbot of the monastery was also the bishop, but, owing to his frequent absence, management of affairs usually fell to his chief subordinate, the prior. In secular cathedrals it was the dean who, under the bishop, was in charge of the church and of the canons who served it. Bishops were always important feudal magnates and frequently in attendance on the king. Though they were usually assigned sumptuous living quarters close to their cathedrals, they more frequently than not occupied equally magnificent palaces outside of the cities in which British (especially English) cathedrals normally lay. In any case their actual presence in their cathedrals was infrequent, and as time passed more and more responsibility and power fell to priors and deans and to the chapters of monks and canons serving them. The monks, mostly Benedictines, lived in buildings arranged around a cloister as in any other monastery. Canons, not being under monastic vows, could live where they chose, but they tended to take up residence in private houses grouped around the cathedral church in a precinct known as the close. Most secular cathedrals, it is true, had cloisters attached, but these were more decorative than functional. Both secular and monastic cathedrals had chapter houses for the conduct of business; both had rooms for storing the church treasures; both had libraries for the copying of manuscripts and their storage; both had grammar schools and song schools for the instruction of boy choristers.

Once more it needs to be stressed that the cathedral church was not designed primarily to serve the spiritual needs of the laity, and the proximity of parish churches to most British cathedrals attests to that fact. Services in the cathedral were essentially those conducted by the community of resident monks or canons and their assistants, the principal one being daily High Mass. This is not to say, however, that laymen did not join the flocks of pilgrims regularly paying homage to the shrines of saints, or that they did not serve as spectators to the elaborate processions marking holy days and feast days in every cathedral church. Moreover, it must be remembered that it was mostly laymen—usually rich laymen—who endowed the innumerable chantry chapels which, in the later Middle Ages, came to fill up almost every available space in nave, aisles, and transepts, leaving only enough room for processions to take place without hindrance. A chantry is an endowment to maintain one or more priests to say daily masses for the souls of its founder, kinsmen, and friends either in perpetuity or for a fixed term of years. Chantries might be founded at church altars but from the thirteenth century onward the tendency was to build miniature chapels within the church's main structure, each enclosing an altar and an effigy of the dead person whose soul was to be the object of the chantry priest's prayers. And since cathedral churches normally had more space than parish churches and tended to be more centrally located than monasteries, they also tended to attract the most chantry chapels.

All the above needs to be kept in mind as the traveller enters a British cathedral. What he sees today is not what he would have seen five hundred years ago. The choir with its high altar and retable, its bishop's throne, its sedilia and piscina, its facing stalls may not look too different. Neither may the chapels in the far east end or in the transepts. But today's nave is another matter. All those rows of cane-seated chairs with cushions for kneeling and prayerbooks for responding are latter-day developments. So is the setting of pulpit and lectern. So are the bare stone walls and columns devoid of color. Gone with the Protestant Reformation is the great hall emblazoned with paint in the most vivid hues, chopped up into a myriad of compartments housing chantry tombs and altars, with no seating arrangements, and no clear view of the services being sung behind the great chancel screen.

Yet the structure of the building is the same, and these stones, stripped of their ancient paint, speak more clearly than ever of the architectural genius of the master masons who set them into place. It must be remembered that most of these great cathedrals took several centuries to build; and few of them therefore represent a single style of architecture. They are patchwork quilts of architectural history; but the intelligent traveller who has familiarized himself with the salient characteristics of each style should have no trouble distinguishing one period of construction from another.

Of the twenty-six English cathedral churches described in this chapter, sixteen were cathedrals at the end of the Middle Ages and still are (Canterbury, Carlisle, Chichester, Durham, Ely, Exeter, Hereford, Lichfield, Lincoln, Norwich, Rochester, Salisbury, Wells, Winchester, Worcester, and York); six were monastic churches during the Middle Ages but were converted to cathedral status at the time of Henry VIII's dissolution of the monasteries or since (Bristol, Chester, Gloucester, Peterborough, St. Albans, and Southwark); two were medieval collegiate churches of secular canons awarded cathedral status in the nineteenth and twentieth centuries (Ripon and Southwell); one was a cathedral during the Middle Ages but was not reestablished as such after the Reformation (Bath); and one was a Benedictine abbey during the Middle Ages and enjoyed cathedral status for only a decade after the Dissolution

(Westminster Abbey). All four of the Welsh cathedrals mentioned here were cathedrals during the Middle Ages and still are (Bangor, Llandaff, St. Asaph's, and St. David's). St. German's on the Isle of Man is a rarity: a cathedral fallen into ruin. Within each of these national categories, each cathedral will be briefly described in the chronological order of its oldest visible parts (not counting foundations and crypts). Again the reader is reminded that with rare exception all these churches were several centuries in the building and each therefore represents a composite of architectural styles.

ENGLAND

The impact of the Norman Conquest was as revolutionary for organized religion as for most other aspects of English life. For the loosely knit organization of the English church was substituted a centralized hierarchical structure under the watchful eye of Archbishop Lanfranc, the new Primate, at Canterbury. A council held at Windsor in 1072 required bishops to remove their sees (seats of authority) from rural areas to towns. Within ten years of the Conquest, all English bishoprics save one were held by Normans. By the end of the Conqueror's reign a beginning had been made on the construction of at least three new cathedrals in the Norman style, and within the lifetime of his two royal sons, William Rufus and Henry I, ten more were going up.

St. Albans Cathedral *(621)* in Hertfordshire, originally a Benedictine abbey church, was begun and finished by Abbot Paul of Caen between 1077 and 1088. Built almost entirely of Roman brick from the ancient settlement of *Verulamium*, St. Albans boasts the longest medieval nave in existence. Of the original Norman structure, the transepts, crossing, central tower, most of the north side of the nave, and the easternmost portion of its south side survive. The westernmost bays of the nave are Early English (1214–1235), and five bays on the south side are Decorated (1324–1327). The breaks between these three styles are abrupt and somewhat jarring to the eye, but St. Albans' nave does provide an excellent study in architectural contrasts. Most of the choir and the entire retrochoir (with St. Alban's shrine) are in the Decorated style, as is the lady chapel at the easternmost end. Among the chantries flanking the choir is the canopied tomb of Humphrey, duke of Gloucester, brother to King Henry V, murdered in 1447 possibly at the instance of his nephew, Henry VI. Of art works, the cathedral boasts a magnificent fourteenth century brass to Abbot Thomas de la Mare, thirteenth century wall paintings on some of the Norman piers in the nave, and a sixteenth century panel depicting the martyrdom of St. Alban in the aisle south of the choir. A rather ugly building from the outside, once entered, St. Albans offers the visitor a veritable kaleidoscope of art history.

Hereford Cathedral *(646)* in Hereford and Worcester was begun in 1079 but is such a jungle of medieval architectural styles mixed with nineteenth century restorations that only an expert eye could possibly disentangle them all. The Norman portions of the church include the piers and arches of the nave, the lower courses of the aisles, the southwest transept, and much of the choir, though its clerestory windows are Early English. Also Early English is the lady chapel with its beautiful lancet windows. The northwest transept is in the Decorated style with a window displaying one of the largest examples of geometrical tracery in the country. The eastern transepts are also Decorated. In the north choir is a *Mappa Mundi,* a fourteenth century map of the world with Jerusalem at the center. The library has a splendid collection of medieval books and art objects. Although a secular cathedral, Hereford boasts the substantial remains of two Perpendicular cloisters on the south side of the nave; also a fifteenth century college of vicars choral, a fourteenth century cathedral school, and a bishop's palace with the original Norman hall. For purity of style these buildings in the cathedral close rate higher than the church itself.

Begun also in 1079, **Winchester Cathedral** *(563)* in Hampshire is today the longest medieval church in Europe and certainly one of the leading tourist attractions of southern England. Of the great Norman church built by Bishop Walkelin, only the massive transepts survive above ground, though most of the crypt is of the same date. The retrochoir, which housed the shrine of St. Swithin, is Early English (1202–1235); the lady chapel is Perpendicular; and in the windows of the former are panels of thirteenth century grisaille glass. The choir is mostly Decorated and its richly carved fourteenth century stalls are the oldest in England. The enormous nave was mostly rebuilt in the fourteenth century by Bishop William of Wykeham whose chantry chapel in the same style dates from the early fifteenth. Winchester boasts other superbly designed chantry chapels: Edington's Chantry (1366), Prior Silkstede's Chapel (1524), Bishop Waynflete's Chapel (1486), Cardinal Beaufort's Chapel (1447), Bishop Fox's Chapel (1528), and Bishop Gardiner's Chapel (1525). A great reredos of the fifteenth century (restored) stands behind the high altar. The library boasts a large collection of books and illuminated manuscripts, including the famous Winchester Bible of the twelfth century. In the close are situated the Deanery, the fourteenth century Pilgrim's Hall and the seventeenth century Pilgrim's School for boy choristers. Not far from the cathedral are the ruins of the bishop's palace, called **Wolvesey Castle** *(563)*, built by Henry of Blois in the twelfth century. A dozen miles to the south at Bishop's Waltham, Hampshire, lie the tall ruins of another **Bishop's Palace** *(558)* built at about the same time by the same bishop, who was incidentally the younger brother of King Stephen and greatly instrumental in his capture of the throne in 1135. For a bishop to occupy two palaces simultaneously (one in the cathedral city and one nearby in the country) was customary among these princely ecclesiastics.

Not far away, in West Sussex, lies **Chichester Cathedral** *(551)*, a church of more modest size than Winchester, begun about 1088, a year after the

Conqueror's death. Choir and nave retain their predominantly Norman character, while the retrochoir, built in the final decade of the twelfth century, is Transitional. In the early fourteenth century the south transept was remodeled in the Geometric Decorated style as was the lady chapel. To roughly the same period belong the chapels lining the nave aisles. A well-preserved Perpendicular chancel screen separates nave from choir. Within the latter are fourteenth century stalls with well-carved misericords. The cloisters survive in part, as does the fourteenth century gateway to the thirteenth to eighteenth century bishop's palace, part of which has been converted into a theological college.

Begun about the same time as Chichester, **Gloucester Cathedral** *(640)*, Gloucestershire, originally belonged to a Benedictine abbey and became a secular cathedral church as a result of the Dissolution. Both architecturally and historically it is one of the most significant cathedrals in Britain. The nave and crypt retain their original Norman features, but in the late fourteenth century the choir and transepts were remodeled with delicate tracery laid over the original stonework while the piers were whittled down to finer proportions. The resulting combination of tall clerestory windows, the magnificent east (Crecy) window with its rectilinear tracery, and the lovely lierne vaulting above the high altar establishes Gloucester's claim to be the prototype of the Perpendicular style of church architecture. In the same vein are the central tower, the narrow, square-ended lady chapel, and the cloisters with fan vaulting unsurpassed in intricacy and charm. Among the cathedral's many funeral monuments are two of great historical distinction: (1) the tomb and effigy of Robert Curthose, eldest son of the Conquerer, from whom his youngest son Henry I wrested the dukedom of Normandy and who died a prisoner of war in Cardiff Castle; and (2) the richly canopied tomb and alabaster effigy of the unfortunate King Edward II murdered in nearby Berkeley Castle. In 1327 Edward III had his father's violated body brought to Gloucester to be buried in pomp. Soon thereafter public opinion made of the late much-hated king a martyr, and pilgrims to his tomb so swelled the coffers of the abbey church as to enable the monks to remodel it it in the new architectural style described above.

The construction of **Ely Cathedral** *(617)* in Cambridgeshire began about 1090 though it was not completed in its first phase until the end of the twelfth century. The oldest parts of the present church are the Norman nave and transepts. The Galilee porch at the church's western end is Early English, as is the eastern part of the choir. The western part is Decorated, as is the most unusual feature of the church, the great octagonal central tower which was built in the fourteenth century after the original Norman structure had collapsed. The startling effect of this unique late medieval tower with its wooden lantern tends to overshadow the predominantly Norman character of the rest of the cathedral. Also in the Decorated manner is the lady chapel, built out from the north transept in the fourteenth century. Ely was a monastic (Benedictine) cathedral, and remains of its cloisters and conventual buildings are still to be seen south of the church.

Of about the same date of original construction as Ely, though much smaller and less interesting architecturally, is **Chester Cathedral** *(673)*, Cheshire. Its architectural styles are almost as hard to disentangle as at Hereford. Within the existing church, only the small north transept and the northwest tower retain their original Norman characteristics. The lady chapel and the choir date from the late thirteenth and early fourteenth centuries and are a mix of Early English and Decorated styles. The nave is Decorated and Perpendicular, as is the south transept. Within the choir, the fourteenth century stalls with their spired canopies and carved bench ends and misericords, constitute perhaps the most interesting feature of the church. North of the church, however, the monastic remains of this Benedictine monastic cathedral merit close examination. The rectangular chapter house of the thirteenth century is a fine example of Early English workmanship; so is the refectory at the far north end of the cloisters, though the latter are Perpendicular in style. On the west side of the claustral square are the interesting remains of the Norman undercroft of what was originally the abbot's lodgings. The cathedral is built of red sandstone, and is not especially attractive, either outside or within.

Among the smallest of British cathedrals is **Carlisle Cathedral** *(709)*, Cumbria, reduced to its present size by the depredations of an invading Scottish army during the Civil Wars of the seventeenth century. (Though coreligionists, Scots and English alike were notoriously lacking in respect for each other's ecclesiastical property.) The church was begun in 1093 for a priory of Augustinian regular canons and not converted to cathedral status until 1123. The only Norman features left are the much foreshortened nave and the small south transept. The north transept and choir were constructed in the fourteenth century in both late Decorated and Perpendicular styles. The pride of the church is its magnificent Decorated east window whose curvilinear tracery is perhaps the loveliest in Britain. Southwest of the church are some remains of the conventual buildings including the Decorated chapter house and the refectory, now the cathedral library.

Probably the grandest example of Romanesque architecture in Britain, **Durham Cathedral** *(699)* stands high on its promontory above the River Wear, a perfect illustration of the medieval Church Militant. Begun in 1093 as a Benedictine monastic cathedral to house the sacred relics of St. Cuthbert, it was the seat of the bishop of Durham who also served as count palatine with extraordinary judicial and military powers to guard the northern marches of England against the barbarous Scots. Nave, transepts, and choir are Norman in construction, the nave's alternating circular columns and clustered piers being especially interesting. The vaults, however, are transverse pointed arches, perhaps the earliest in Britain, and therefore the prototype of the Transitional style. Also Transitional is the Galilee porch on the west end of the church. At the far eastern end is the thirteenth century Early English Chapel of Nine Altars which lies perpendicular to the church's main axis like a second set of transepts. The great central tower was rebuilt in the fifteenth century. Most interesting among the church's special features are the sixteenth century tomb of the Venerable Bede in the Galilee; thirteenth century wall paintings, also in the Galilee; the bishop's throne in the choir; the site of the shrine of St. Cuthbert behind the high altar; and the magnificent fourteenth century reredos. Outside, the remains of the abbey's claustral buildings are unusually complete and mostly still in use. They include a restored Norman chapter house, the priory (now the deanery), the refectory and kitchen, and the monks' dorter which now serves as the library, housing, among other things, some of the most famous of medieval illuminated manuscripts, including Bishop Puiset's Bible and St. Carilef's Bible. Adjacent to the cloister is **Durham Castle** *(699)* once the bishop's palace and now incorporated into the University of Durham.

Second only to Durham for the purity of its Romanesque lines is **Norwich Cathedral** *(608)*, Norfolk. Another Benedictine monastic cathedral, it was begun in 1096 and even today nave, aisles, transepts, choir, and central tower remain basically Norman in character. The fifteenth century lierne vaulting, however, is Perpendicular and is especially notable for its bosses. The choir clerestory was rebuilt in the late fourteenth century in a style midway between Decorated and Perpendicular. The east end is unusual for an English church, being apsidal in shape, but an Early English lady chapel has disappeared and been replaced by St. Saviour's Chapel, a twentieth century addition. Notable interior features are the Perpendicular Bishop Nykke's chantry; the bishop's throne; the Early English Bauchan Chapel; and the fifteenth century chantry of Sir Thomas Erpingham, wartime companion of King Henry V. Outside, the unique two-storied cloisters were rebuilt in the fourteenth and fifteenth centuries in a mix of Decorated and Perpendicular styles.

Coming into the twelfth century, **Southwell Cathedral** *(660)*, Nottinghamshire, was first constructed as a collegiate church of secular canons, beginning in 1108, and did not achieve cathedral status until 1844. The two west towers, nave, and transepts are Norman, though the great western window is a Perpendicular insertion of the fifteenth century. The choir, built in the second quarter of the thirteenth century, is Early English with an east window consisting of two rows of four lancets. The great stone rood screen between choir and nave was erected in the fourteenth century in the Decorated style. Outside, the octagonal chapter house is a superb example of late thirteenth century Geometric Decorated. South of the church are the remains of a bishop's palace, once belonging to the archbishop of York to whose see this collegiate church was attached.

Rochester Cathedral *(544)*, Kent, was rebuilt in the early twelfth century on top of a still earlier Benedictine monastic cathedral constructed by Bishop Gundulf, the builder of the White Tower in London and nearby Rochester Castle. Of Gundulf's church only the crypt remains. Of the second Norman church, begun in 1115, most of the nave survives as does the west front with its typically Romanesque recessed doorway. The west window, however, is Perpendicular, as are those of the nave clerestory and the lady chapel, oddly located south of the nave. Rochester is also unusual in having double transepts. The northwestern transept is Early English; its southwestern counterpart Geometric Decorated. The eastern end which includes both choir and smaller transepts is Early English. Most notable among the church's furnishings are the thirteenth century choir stalls, perhaps the oldest of their kind in England, though much restored. Outside is the ruined Early English chapter house.

Among the finest of England's Norman buildings is **Peterborough Cathedral** *(618)* in Cambridgeshire. Begun in 1117, the nave, transepts, and choir were completed in the Norman style before the end of the twelfth century. The west front, however, is Early English while the Galilee porch by which the nave today is entered is Perpendicular, as are the central tower and the fan-vaulted retrochoir built at the end of the fifteenth century. The church is famous for its painted ceilings and for being the burial place of Henry VIII's first wife, Catherine of Aragon, as well as of Mary Queen of Scots (whose remains were later removed to Westminster Abbey). On the south side of the church are the ruins of the cloister.

Of the earliest Norman building of the double-transepted **Worcester Cathedral** *(649)*, Hereford and Worcester, nothing remains but the apsidal crypt which is, however, one of the most interesting in England. Of the rebuilding which began about 1175 in the period known as Transitional, only the two western bays of the nave remain. The rest of the nave is a mix of Early English and Perpendicular; the western transepts combine Norman and Perpendicular work with bad nineteenth century restorations; while the splendid central tower, completed in 1374 is Perpendicular. East of the crossing, however, is almost pure Early English, among the best examples of that style in the country. In the choir lies the tomb and Purbeck marble effigy of King John. Adjacent is the Chantry of Prince Arthur, erected in 1504, two years after the death of this older brother of Henry VIII. In the lady chapel are some outstanding episcopal tombs of the thirteenth century. In the chapter library over the south aisle of the nave are some four thousand volumes including many priceless medieval manuscripts. Outside, the Perpendicular cloisters are notable for their bosses. The circular chapter house (rebuilt about 1400) has splendid vaults springing from a central shaft. The cathedral close borders on the River Severn and is one of the prettiest in England.

Not counting the western bays of Worcester, the Transitional period between Norman and Early English Gothic architecture really opens with the reconstruction of **Canterbury Cathedral** *(538)*, Kent, following a great fire which destroyed most of the eastern end of the original

Norman building in 1174. The disaster, coming so soon after the murder of Thomas Becket, offered the Benedictine monks of Canterbury a unique opportunity to erect a suitable shrine to the martyred saint which would be paid for many times over by the pilgrims who flocked there for the next 350 years until Henry VIII retroactively declared Becket a traitor, closed down the shrine, robbed it of its rich fittings, and dissolved the oldest monastery in England. In 1184, however, when the work of two master masons, William of Sens and William the Englishman, had been completed, the apsidal eastern end of Canterbury Cathedral was the masterpiece of Transitional and Early English architecture that it remains today. Here heavy circular columns alternate with octagonal piers surmounted by broken arches, while the vaults above are divided into quadrapartite sections by diagonal ribs. The choir is the longest in England. East of it, behind the raised high altar, lies Trinity Chapel, built to house the shrine of St. Thomas. East of that lies the Corona which houses St. Augustine's Chair, used for the enthronement of archbishops. Other special features of this part of the church are the splendid tombs of Archbishops Bourchier and Chichele; the tomb and lifelike effigies of King Henry IV and Queen Joan of Navarre; the magnificent effigy-tomb in copper gilt of Edward the Black Prince in full armor, with reproductions of his "achievements" (gauntlets, helmet, shield, and scabbard) hanging nearby; the late twelfth century glass in the circular window of the Transitional northeastern transept; the thirteenth century windows of the Trinity Chapel depicting the miracles of St. Thomas; the thirteenth century glass in the windows of the Corona; and the twelfth century wall painting of St. Paul in St. Anselm's Chapel. The choir is separated from the nave by a marvelously contrived fifteenth century pulpitum with six crowned figures representing English kings. West of it lie the western transepts and the great nave built by Henry Yevele between 1391 and 1405 in the new Perpendicular style. In the northwest transept lies a small slab of stone believed to mark the spot where Becket was killed. In the southwest transept is the tomb of Archbishop Stephen Langton who engineered the signing of the Magna Carta. Also in this transept are to be found perhaps the finest twelfth century glass windows in the country—three panels representing Lamech, Noah, and Terah, originally in the clerestory of the choir. From this point in the church, visitors may enter the crypt with its superb Norman capitals, its twelfth century wall paintings, and the beautiful Chapel of Our Lady Undercroft. Outside the church, the most notable features are: (1) the great cloister with its Perpendicular fan vaulting, (2) the early fifteenth century chapter house, and (3) the infirmary cloister. Also from the outside can best be observed the great central tower, called Bell Harry, perhaps the most magnificent Perpendicular church tower in the country.

Begun about the same time as Canterbury, **Wells Cathedral** *(585)*, Somerset, is perhaps the most graceful of England's cathedrals. The oldest parts are the nave, the western transepts, and the three western bays of the choir, all in the Transitional style. Over the crossing is the Decorated central tower supported by a unique pair of double arches shaped more or less like huge stone scissors. The eastern end of the church, starting at about mid-point in the choir, is in the Geometric Decorated style. This includes the retrochoir, the lady chapel, and the two eastern transepts. The octagonal chapter house, reached by a much worn stone staircase of surpassing beauty, is also Decorated, the finest of its kind in the country. Other features of note are the chapter library, with over three thousand volumes; the hexagonal Perpendicular chantry of Bishop Bubwith on the north side of the nave; the seven bishops' tombs in the choir aisles; and the fourteenth century clock in the north-west transept. From the outside, Wells Cathedral's outstanding feature is the spectacular Early English west front with its honeycomb of niches containing over three hundred life-size statues, sculpted in the mid-thirteenth century in the Early English style. Another exterior feature of note is the north porch, built in 1213. The cathedral close is, if anything, more rewarding than the church itself. Of special note are the Perpendicular cloisters, the fifteenth century deanery, the houses in the vicars' close, and, above all, the bishop's palace built in the thirteenth century, with walls and moat added in the fourteenth. It is here that the cathedral's famous swans can sometimes be caught in the act of ringing a bell for their noon meal. Beyond the castellated fourteenth century gatehouse are the ruins of the great hall built by Bishop Burnell at the end of the thirteenth century, with its superb Decorated chapel. The rural counterpart to this once magnificent dwelling was **Bishop Burnell's Palace** *(671)*, now a ruin, situated in Acton Burnell, south of Shrewsbury, Salop. Here Robert Burnell, chancellor to Edward I as well as bishop of Bath and Wells, built a great palace of red sandstone, half castle and half country house, a forerunner of the fortified residences which in the fourteenth century began to replace the strictly military castles of the thirteenth.

Like Canterbury and Wells, **Ripon Cathedral** *(686)* in North Yorkshire is basically Transitional in style, although later rebuildings and restorations have somewhat concealed the fact. First constructed in the late twelfth century as a collegiate church for secular canons, the nave and transepts still retain their basic Transitional look, although the two aisles on either side of the nave were added in the early sixteenth century and are therefore Perpendicular in style. Also Perpendicular is the west end of the choir, but the east end with its lovely window tracery is pure geometric Decorated. The central tower is curiously half Early English and half Perpendicular. Perhaps the most interesting internal feature of the church is the Anglo-Saxon crypt beneath it.

With **Lincoln Cathedral** *(651)*, Lincolnshire, we leave the Transitional period of church architecture and come at last to the Early English Gothic in its full flower. Except for the partly Norman west front, and the Decorated and Perpendicular central tower, and for the Decorated

Angel Choir at the extreme east end, the cathedral, rebuilt after an earthquake by Bishop Hugh (St. Hugh) of Avalon (1186–1200), is almost entirely Early English in structure and design. It vies therefore with Salisbury for purity of style. The great western window, however, is Decorated, as is the beautiful round window in the southwest transept, known as the Bishop's Eye—a splendid example of curvilinear tracery. The other great round window in the opposite northwest transept—the Dean's Eye—is Early English, as are the more typical and numerous lancet windows throughout the church. The Decorated Angel Choir with its great east window of geometric tracery, was built (1256–1280) as a retrochoir to hold the shrine of St. Hugh. It derives its name from the thirty carved stone angels, cherubim, seraphim, etc., that appear in the spandrels between the arches of the triforium. Field glasses are recommended for their proper observation. Other features of note within the church are the Perpendicular choir stalls with well carved bench ends and misericords, the Decorated stone rood screen between choir and nave, the Perpendicular chantry chapels, and the monument to Katherine Swynford, mistress and third wife to John of Gaunt, sister-in-law of Geoffrey Chaucer, and progenitress of the turbulent Beaufort clan from whom the Tudors were descended. Outside the church, the Early English polygonal chapter house with its vault ribs springing from a central shaft is an outstanding feature. Above the cloister is the chapter library which holds an original copy of Magna Carta. The cathedral close is full of medieval buildings, mostly not open to the public. Entrance from the town of Lincoln into the cathedral precincts and the western front of the church is by way of a great fourteenth century gatehouse, known as the Exchequer Gate. Since the cathedral, like the castle, stands on top of a steep hill, its view of the city and the surrounding Witham River valley is majestic.

Probably the earliest Gothic architecture seen in London was the choir and retrochoir of **Southwark Cathedral** *(534)*, a medieval Augustinian priory reduced to parochial status at the time of the Reformation and only in this century elevated to cathedral rank. The eastern end is Early English; transepts Perpendicular; and the nave Modern (nineteenth century). The central tower is in the Perpendicular style of the fifteenth century. This is perhaps the least distinguished architecturally of all English cathedrals of medieval origin.

Lichfield Cathedral *(667)* in Staffordshire, built of red sandstone, is one of England's smaller cathedrals. The oldest parts of the existing church are the western part of the choir and the two transepts, built in the Early English style toward the beginning of the thirteenth century. The nave was constructed later and is mostly early Decorated. The apsidal lady chapel at the eastern end is a good example of the Decorated style at the height of its elegance (1320–1340). The decagonal chapter house, completed in 1249, is Early English. The west front rivals Wells in its tiers of statuary, though all but a handful of these are modern reproductions.

This is the only church in England with three spires, of which the central and northeastern ones date from about 1320 while the northwest spire was rebuilt in the sixteenth century. Lichfield's chapter library owns a copy of a priceless seventh century manuscript, the Gospel of St. Chad.

The interior of **Salisbury Cathedral** *(574)*, Wiltshire, was completed in the course of a mere thirty-eight years (1220–1258), which makes it the only cathedral in Britain with a uniform design. The style is Early English in nave, choir, transepts, and lady chapel. A large part of the original building was constructed of stones from the cathedral at nearby **Old Sarum** *(585)*, a Norman structure of great size now reduced to its bare foundations. Salisbury's interior is exceptionally uncluttered. Of its furnishings, the most notable are the numerous episcopal and knightly tombs that line the nave aisles, especially those of the two William Longespees, Lord Hungerford, and Sir John de Montacute; the original choir screen now situated in the Morning Chapel; and, above all, the beautiful Purbeck marble shafts that enclose the columns of the nave. The ornate west front of the church dates from the mid-thirteenth century, while the famous central tower and spire, painted so often by Constable, were added in the fourteenth. Cloisters and chapter house date from the late thirteenth century and were built in the Decorated style. The chapter library has an unusually fine collection of books and manuscripts, including a copy of Magna Carta. The close is well studded with medieval, Tudor, and Stuart houses, including the exquisite **Mompesson House** *(574)* built in the first year of the eighteenth century. Inside and out, there is nothing that quite matches Salisbury. In purity of line and nobility of style, this is the most perfect of English cathedrals.

Equally magnificent (some would say more so), though of very mixed architectural styles, is **York Minster** *(692)*, a secular cathedral, seat of the archbishop of York, the second ranking churchman of England. Except for the Norman crypt at the eastern end, the oldest parts of the present church are the two transepts built in the thirteenth century in Early English style. That on the south has a handsome circular rose window, but the windows called the Five Sisters in the end wall of the northern transept are the best lancets in England and moreover are still filled with the typically gray-green grisaille glass of the thirteenth century. York Minster contains more original medieval stained glass than any church in the country. Next in order of construction are the west front and the nave, both done in the Decorated style of the late thirteenth and early fourteenth centuries. The west window is a fine example of Curvilinear Decorated tracery, though the glass is modern. The clerestory windows contain some glass of the twelfth and thirteenth centuries, and in the north nave aisle is a panel of perhaps the oldest glass in England (ca. 1150). Behind the elaborate fifteenth century rood screen, the choir and lady chapel date from the late fourteenth century and are Perpendicular in style. The glass in the great east window dates from the early fifteenth century and forms the largest single sheet of medieval stained glass in

Britain. The central tower dates also from the early fifteenth century. Standing under it at the crossing and facing north, the visitor has within the range of his vision a complete panorama of the three great periods of Gothic architecture. Straight ahead are the Five Sisters, the purest expression in Britain of the Early English style; to the left is the great wide Decorated nave with its curvilinear western window; to the right behind the rood screen is the Perpendicular choir with its typical lierne vaulting. From the north transept a vestibule leads into the octagonal chapter house, another masterpiece of Decorated architecture. There are no monastic buildings, of course, and not even any cloisters. Beneath the nave is a newly constructed undercroft containing the Cathedral Museum which houses extensive remains of both Roman and medieval York.

Westminster Abbey *(523)*, London, stands on the site of a Benedictine monastery dating at least to the year 740. Here stood the great Norman church and conventual buildings raised by Edward the Confessor in the last years of his life. Here in 1245 King Henry III commenced the construction of a new edifice in honor of his sainted predecessor Edward— a project that was not to be completed for a century and a half. Henry's motives were mixed. His piety was renowned and genuine. So was his admiration for the Confessor, after whom he named his eldest son (later Edward I). He also probably wished to detract from the popularity of Canterbury whose enshrined saint had earned martyrdom by flouting the king's own grandfather. Moreover, he was no doubt influenced by the example of his brother-in-law, King Louis IX of France, who had rebuilt the cathedral at Rheims and had begun construction on the elegant Sainte Chapelle within his palace. This emulation of the French king undoubtedly accounts for Westminster's architectural style; it stands at point of transition between Early English and Decorated, but resembles more than anything else the High Gothic style of the cathedrals of Rheims and Amiens. Of course, it was not a cathedral (except briefly from 1540 to 1550) but an abbey church until Queen Elizabeth I made it a collegiate church under an independent dean and chapter—which it remains today.

Except for the Chapel of Henry VII added in the early sixteenth century, the church is remarkably uniform in style—Early English with Decorated tierceron vaulting and French Gothic tracery—though the actual construction lasted well into the fifteenth century. Unfortunately the floor space of both nave and transepts is so crowded with heroic statuary of the eighteenth and nineteenth centuries that the building's quintessential thirteenth century character is easily lost sight of. It looks less like a church than a sculptor's atelier filled with unclaimed monumental statues, most of them bad. (The sixteenth century tomb of the poet Geoffrey Chaucer [d. 1400] in the Poets' Corner in the south transept has, however, some artistic merit.) Only in the apsidal east end is the full glory of King Henry's medieval vision made manifest to today's visitor. Behind the high altar in the choir is the heart of the church: the Chapel of St. Edward. Here stands the shrine dedicated to Edward the Confessor; in front of it is the royal coronation chair enclosing the Stone of Scone stolen from the Scots by Edward I; on either side are the royal tombs (some with effigies) of Henry III, Edward I, and his queen, Eleanor of Castile, Edward III and Queen Philippa of Hainault, and Richard II and his first wife, Anne of Bohemia. On either side of the Chapel of St. Edward, which is in effect a retrochoir, are four other semicircular chapels dedicated respectively to St. John the Baptist, St. Paul, St. Nicholas, and St. Edmund, each containing the expected number of noble tombs. Immediately to the east of the Confessor's shrine, on a bridge over the south ambulatory, is the Chantry of King Henry V adorned with beautifully contrived sculpture work of the fifteenth century. Beneath it is the king's defaced effigy and the grave of his queen. East of this is the lady chapel, called the Chapel of Henry VII. It is certainly among the best examples of Perpendicular architecture in the country and its fan vaulting categorically *is* the best. In addition to the tomb of Henry VII and his wife Elizabeth of York (done in Renaissance style by the Italian sculptor Torrigiano), the chapel houses the canopied tomb of Queen Elizabeth I with her sister Queen Mary Tudor buried beneath her in the same grave; the sarcophagus of the boy-king Edward V and his brother, the two Little Princes murdered in the Tower; the grave of Edward VI; and the tombs of Mary Queen of Scots; Margaret Beaufort, mother of Henry VII; King Charles II; Queen Mary II and her husband, William of Orange; and Queen Anne and her consort Prince George of Denmark. At the very eastern end, behind Henry VII's tomb, is the modern Chapel of the Royal Air Force with its splendid window commemorating the Battle of Britain of July–October 1940.

Outside the church itself the most notable features of Westminster Abbey are the thirteenth–fourteenth century cloisters and the octagonal chapter house, a masterpiece in the geometric Decorated style. This is where the House of Commons held its meetings from the reign of Edward III down to 1547 when it moved to nearby St. Stephen's Chapel. Mention has already been made of the Norman cloister and the Norman undercroft. In the latter can be found the abbey museum with its marvelous collection of lifelike effigies of English royalty and other historic notables.

If Westminster Abbey marks the transition between Early English and Decorated architecture, **Exeter Cathedral** *(587)*, Devon, is clearly in the new style. True, the massive transeptal towers were constructed in the twelfth century. But the main body of the church—nave, transepts, choir, and lady chapel, all built between 1270 and 1360, are uniformly Geometric Decorated. Most notable among Exeter's many interesting features are (a) the west front with its tiers of sculpted figures representing apostles, prophets, patriarchs, and the kings of Judah, (b) the fourteenth century "minstrels' gallery" with carved stone angels playing a variety of musical instruments, (c) the bishop's throne, (d) the Oldham and Sylke chantry chapels of the early sixteenth century, and (e) the lady chapel with its highly decorated episcopal tombs. Next to the south transept is an elegant chapter house done in both Early English and Perpendicular styles. Though secular, Exeter had a cloister in the usual southern position, once destroyed but rebuilt in the Decorated style. Also rebuilt is the nearby bishop's palace which now houses the cathedral library, containing numerous interesting manuscripts including the Exon Domesday Book.

Bristol Cathedral *(579)*, Avon, originally a foundation of Augustinian canons, presents a mix of medieval architectural styles, with the Decorated predominating. The choir and eastern lady chapel were built in the late thirteenth century, their best features being the former's lierne vaulting and the latter's geometric window. North of the choir is an Early English chapel (ca. 1220) called the Elder Lady Chapel to which Decorated vaulting and east window were added later. Transepts and central tower were rebuilt in the fifteenth century, the nave and western towers in the nineteenth—still in the Decorated style. Outside the church, the chapter house and the two gateways are in the Norman style of the twelfth century.

Bath Abbey *(578)*, Somerset, dates from the early sixteenth century and is therefore the last of the great pre-Reformation churches to be built in England. Its ecclesiastical history is complicated: founded as a Benedictine priory in 970, it replaced Wells as the cathedral of Somerset county in 1090, then became co-cathedral with Wells in 1192, and was dissolved by Henry VIII, though it is still linked with Wells in the bishop's title. If it is to be considered a cathedral, it is the only one in England built almost entirely along Perpendicular lines. Inside, tall rectilinear windows and rich fan vaulting reflect that style to perfection; outside, the west front with its carved ladders and multitude of angels are typically early Tudor, a style undistinguishable from Perpendicular.

WALES

Though Welsh churchmen might claim to be heirs to a Christian tradition more ancient than that of Canterbury, their subordination to the Primate of England was inevitable. In the reign of Henry I, the three existing Welsh cathedrals—at Llandaff, South Glamorgan; St. David's, Dyfed; and Bangor, Gwynedd—were put in the hands of Norman bishops subject to Canterbury. When St. Asaph's, Clwyd, received cathedral status in 1143, it too was promptly Normanized. A generation later, Henry II personally intervened to prevent the election to the see of St. David's of Gerald de Berri (Giraldus Cambrensis), a native Welshman born in **Manorbier Castle** *(727)*, Dyfed. Three times Gerald travelled to Rome in an effort to persuade Pope Innocent III to approve his installation. Each time he failed—which is fortunate for history, since in defeat, he retired to Lincoln to write the voluminous chronicles which constitute one of our chief sources of information about twelfth century Britain. In any case, there was no more serious talk of an independent Welsh church.

Of the four Welsh cathedrals, the oldest, wealthiest, and most prestigious is **St. David's** *(728)*, Dyfed, dedicated to Dewi, the country's patron saint. Begun in 1180, the Norman nave still stands, and though choir and transepts were rebuilt in the mid-thirteenth century, they are in the Norman and Transitional styles. The Chapel of St. Thomas, north of the choir, was constructed in the Decorated style in the early fourteenth century; Bishop Vaughan's Chapel in the retrochoir is a good example of late Perpendicular of the early sixteenth century; and the lady chapel at the east end is a modern restoration. Restored too is the church's exterior —and in a manner not especially pleasing to the eye. Inside, the most notable furnishings are the thirteenth century shrine of St. David; the tomb of a recumbent knight, thought to be the Welsh prince, Rhys ap Gruffydd (d. 1197); and the splendid fourteenth century rood screen separating the nave and choir. On the north side of the church lie the restored ruins of St. Mary's College founded in 1377 for a chapter of secular canons. West of the cathedral and far more elegant in design are the ruins of the **Bishop's Palace** *(728)*. To the late thirteenth century belong the chapel, bishop's hall, solar, and gatehouse. But the chief glories of this fine ruin are the great hall and the arcaded parapet which surmounts it and then continues around the walls of the chapel. These were the work of Bishop Gower in the second quarter of the fourteenth century. To the same prelate can be attributed the great hall of **Lamphey Palace** *(728)*, a rural retreat of the bishops of St. David's not far from Pembroke, Dyfed. Here the open parapets were no doubt copied from those that Gower added to his palace at St. David's. The remaining ruins at Lamphey, however, date mostly from the thirteenth century or from the sixteenth century when the confiscated palace was converted into a country house by Richard Devereux, grandfather of the earl of Essex who was Queen Elizabeth's favorite. Still a third bishop's palace belonging to the see of St. David's was **Llawhaden Castle** *(726)* near Narberth, Dyfed, whose moated ruins of the fourteenth century consist of a rectangular court with polygonal angle-towers and a high gateway with a flying arch.

Next in age to St. David's is **Llandaff Cathedral** *(718)* near Cardiff, South Glamorgan. Except for the Norman arch dividing the retrochoir from the lady chapel, the oldest parts of the church (oddly built without transepts) are the Early English west front, nave, and choir (west end) dating from the early thirteenth century. The lady chapel and east end of the choir are Geometric Decorated; the presbytery, Curvilinear Decorated; the chapter house, Early English. Much remodeling was done in the nineteenth century and there are some interesting Pre-Raphaelite additions to the nave, including the windows in the south aisle and the Rossetti Triptych. A German landmine hit the cathedral in 1941, and during the subsequent restoration the St. Euddogwy Memorial Chapel of the R.A.F. Auxiliary Squadron and the St. David's Welsh Regiment Memorial Chapel were added, as was a giant aluminum statue by Epstein on a concrete arch straddling the nave.

Much damaged throughout its history by English desecration, Owain Glyndwr's arson, and misguided restorations of the eighteenth and nineteenth centuries, **St. Asaph's Cathedral** *(732)*, Clwyd, is the smallest in Britain. Nave and transepts were rebuilt in the Decorated style after Edward I's troops destroyed an earlier church in 1282. The choir stalls date from a restoration following Glyndwr's fire. Most of the rest can be attributed to later restorations which were not very good.

Bangor Cathedral *(735)*, Gwynedd, suffered much the same sort of damage as did St. Asaph's—and from the same hands. Rebuilt in the fourteenth century and again in the fifteenth and sixteenth, it was almost completely restored in the nineteenth by G. G. Scott, the great master of Victorian neo-Gothic. The Perpendicular nave and western tower date from the early sixteenth century; the rest of the church is mostly Scott's restoration.

ISLE OF MAN

Not under the jurisdiction of Canterbury was **St. German's Cathedral** *(742)* on the Isle of Man. The see was founded in 1226 by Simon of Argyll who, under the Norse King Olaf, was Bishop of Sodor (the southern isles). Now a red sandstone ruin on St. Patrick's Isle overlooking the Irish Sea, the oldest part of the cathedral is the Early English east end with three fine lancet windows, while the tower and most of the transepts were rebuilt in the fourteenth century in the Decorated style.

PARISH CHURCHES

The parochial system goes back to before the Conquest and probably has its origins in the churches set up by Saxon thanes to accommodate their tenants and household servants. The system was perpetuated by the Normans, but in time the absolute control once exercised by the lord of the local manor over the parish church was surrendered to the bishop of the diocese in which it lay. Absentee control was further accelerated by the growing practice of endowing cathedral chapters and monasteries with the livings of parish churches, i.e., the rectorships and the fixed revenues that went to their support. It soon became commonplace for the appropriating monastery or chapter to keep the bulk of this income and assign a poorly paid vicar (from the Latin *vicarius*, meaning "substitute") to minister to the spiritual needs of the parishioners. By the time of the Reformation, then, most parish priests were poorly educated and poorly remunerated vicars, their meager livings only slightly enhanced by whatever produce they could wrest from the small strips of glebe land assigned to their churches' support.

The poverty of parish priests, however, was not necessarily reflected in the physical appearance of their churches, which were mostly soundly built of stone and often richly adorned. By the end of the thirteenth century there were approximately four thousand parish churches in England alone; by the end of the fifteenth, close to eleven thousand. Obviously only a tiny fraction of these (or of the less numerous churches of Wales) can be described here. Those mentioned below are arbitrarily selected, mostly on the basis of the purity of their architectural style. More than cathedrals which are usually conglomerates of many styles, parish churches tend to retain the essential characteristics of their original construction. Being smaller, they could be finished within a shorter time, before styles changed. They are therefore of special interest as prime examples of Norman, Early English, Decorated, or Perpendicular styles.

NORMAN AND TRANSITIONAL

For the first forty or fifty years after the Battle of Hastings, Norman building activity was confined mostly to castles, cathedrals, and abbeys. Only in the twelfth century did the conquerors begin the construction or reconstruction of parish churches. In general the small square Saxon chancel gave way to a choir of greater length terminating in a square or apsidal east end, while the three-celled rectangular buildings were gradually replaced or remodeled along cruciform lines. Among the many examples in England of twelfth century Norman parish churches are the following: **Barfreston** *(541)* near Dover in Kent, notable especially for its ornate carvings; **Stewkley** *(622)* near Wing, Buckinghamshire, a good example of a three-celled Norman church with axial tower; **Iffley** *(635)*, just south of Oxford, with a typical Norman square tower and a heavily ornamented recessed doorway; **Kilpeck** *(647)*, Hereford and Worcester, unusually well preserved and with an apsidal east end; **Haddiscoe** *(607)* near Great Yarmouth, Norfolk, with a round tower; **Castor** *(619)* near Peterborough, Cambridgeshire, with a richly decorated central tower; **Melbourne** *(663)*, Derbyshire, much restored in the nineteenth century; and **St. John's** *(674)*, Chester, whose interior is mostly Norman and Transitional. Other English Transitional churches of interest are **Abbey Dore** *(724)* near Kilpeck, Hereford and Worcester, a former Cistercian abbey-church; and the partly ruined **Malmsbury Abbey Church** *(573)*, Wiltshire.

Also dating to the Norman period are a number of round churches copied from the Church of the Holy Sepulcher in Jerusalem with which the Crusaders had become familiar. They are the **Temple Church** *(515)* on Inner Temple Lane, London, built about 1185 in late Norman or Transitional style, now restored after serious bomb damage in World War II; the **Church of the Holy Sepulchre** *(617)*, Cambridge, Cambridgeshire, dating mostly from about 1120; **St. Sepulchre's Church** *(655)*,

Northampton, Northamptonshire, from about 1100 and probably built by the first earl of Northampton, an ardent Crusader; and the Round Chapel of **Ludlow Castle** *(670)*, Salop, dating to about 1120. (A fifth round church at Little Maplestead, near Halstead, Essex, is an anachronism, having been built in the fourteenth century.)

In Wales, the two best examples of Norman parish church architecture are **Penmon Priory** *(735)*, Anglesey, Gwynedd, especially notable for its wall arcading and the tympanum of its south nave doorway, and the rebuilt parish church of **Llanbadarn Fawr** *(724)*, Dyfed, famous too for its tympanum.

EARLY ENGLISH

Parish churches built or rebuilt in the thirteenth century are distinguished by their pointed arches, their lancet windows, and by their square-ended choirs, made much longer than their Norman predecessors so as to accommodate the growing ritualism of the church offices. **Stone Church** *(540)*, overlooking the Thames just east of Dartford in Kent, was built probably by the masons used by Henry III at Westminster Abbey and in the same style. So is the church at **Uffington** *(638)*, Oxfordshire, and **Eaton Bray** *(624)* near Dunstable, Bedfordshire, with its fine arcades and capitals. **West Walton Church** *(607)* near King's Lynn, Norfolk, bears some resemblance to the choir at Lincoln Cathedral and may have been modeled on it. The choir and transepts of **St. Andrew's, Hexham** *(707)*, Northumberland, have been labeled a textbook of Early English architecture, though the nave is modern and the church furnishings range from Roman times to the present. In Wales, **Cheriton Church** *(720)* west of Swansea, West Glamorgan, is a fine example of Early English, somewhat surprising to find in this remote corner of the Gower Peninsula. **St. Mary's, Haverfordwest** *(726)*, Dyfed, is thought by some to be the handsomest church in South Wales. Though remodeled somewhat in the fifteenth century, it is predominantly Early English with especially interesting plate-tracery work in the east window. In northern Wales, **Beddgelert Church** *(736)*, Gwynedd, founded by Llywelyn the Great, has good thirteenth century lancet windows and other contemporary features.

DECORATED

Starting with the rebuilding of Exeter Cathedral toward the end of the thirteenth century, the Decorated style dominated new church construction down to the Black Death, after which time it slowly lost popularity. Lincolnshire is especially rich in Decorated churches. **St. Wulfram's, Grantham** *(650)* represents the Geometric phase; while **St. Denys, Sleaford** *(652)* and nearby **St. Andrew's, Heckington** *(652)* are typical of the later Curvilinear or flamboyant Decorated. So is **St.**

Botolph's, Boston *(649)*, one of England's largest parish churches, famous alike for the flowing tracery of its windows and its high Perpendicular tower, the Boston Stump, visible for miles around. Another large parish church in the Decorated style was **St. Nicholas** *(701)*, Newcastle-upon-Tyne, Tyne and Wear, converted to cathedral status in the late nineteenth century. This church is the most famous for its tower, an open crown spire which probably served as the model for that of St. Giles, Edinburgh. In Humberside, **Holy Trinity, Hull** *(677)* and **Patrington Church** *(678)* are Curvilinear Decorated. In Leicestershire, **Stoke Golding Church** *(658)* near Hinckley, is early Geometric Decorated. In Wales, the best examples of the Decorated style are the churches at **Coity** *(719)* and **Coychurch** *(719)*, both near Bridgend, Mid-Glamorgan.

PERPENDICULAR

This final phase of medieval architecture, uniquely British, lasted from the mid-fourteenth century to the end of the Middle Ages, and, if the Tudor style is considered a mere extension of the Perpendicular, well into the sixteenth century. It is possible that the labor shortage caused by the Black Death may have persuaded church builders to dispense with the convoluted elegancies of Curvilinear Decorated in favor of the more easily executed panels and rectilinear windows of the Perpendicular. It is certain that the huge profits enjoyed by the cloth trade resulted directly in a great building boom of "wool" churches in the fifteenth century—especially in East Anglia and the West Country. Of all the surviving churches of medieval origin in England, between a third and a half date from the Perpendicular period. The following sampling therefore represents a very small fraction of the total. In Suffolk, **Long Melford** *(604)* and **Lavenham** *(603)*, only six miles apart, share the honors for the magnificence of their fifteenth century parish churches. **Southwold** *(603)*, Suffolk, on the North Sea coast is another notable wool church. So is **Salle** *(604)* near Aylsham, in Norfolk, reputedly the burial place of Anne Boleyn whose mercantile family was one of those responsible for the church's building. In the West Country first honors must go to **St. Mary Redcliffe** *(580)*, Bristol, once proclaimed by Queen Elizabeth I to be "the fairest, the goodliest, and most famous parish church in England." Her Majesty's judgment was sound, in this as in most other matters, and the church fathers showed their appreciation by setting up a fine wooden figure of Elizabeth under the central crossing. In Gloucestershire there are three Perpendicular churches of almost equal merit. First is **St. John the Baptist, Cirencester** *(639)* with its beautiful fan vaulting in St. Catherine's Chapel, its many fine brasses, and one of the few pre-Reformation pulpits in Britain. Next is **Northleach Church** *(639)*, also renowned for its brasses. Finally comes **St. James, Chipping Camden** *(638)* in the heart of the Cotswolds and one of the more sumptuous of the great wool churches of the fifteenth century. Dorset boasts one of the finest examples of Perpendicular fan vaulting in the country. This is at **Sherborne Abbey Church** *(568)*, built in the fifteenth century on Anglo-Saxon and Norman foundations and converted to parochial use after the Dissolution.

In northern Wales the two best Perpendicular specimens are the parish church of **Gresford** *(732)*, Clwyd, and nearby **St. Giles, Wrexham** *(732)* in whose churchyard Elihu Yale is buried. In the south, **St. John's, Cardiff** *(718)* is typically fifteenth century; so is **St. Mary's, Tenby** *(728)* in Dyfed.

MONASTERIES

Monastery is the generic word for an establishment housing a community of persons under religious vows and living according to a rule established by the founder of the monastic order to which the particular house is attached. Because the Latin word for "rule" is *regulum,* members of monastic orders are called *regular* clergy as distinct from all other clergymen who are called *secular.* Monasteries are inhabited by monks unless the establishment is female, in which case they are called *nunneries.* An abbey is a monastery ruled by an abbot or a nunnery ruled by an abbess. A priory is ruled by a prior or a prioress. The difference between an abbey and a priory is simply one of status. In some cases, but not all, priories are subordinate to a mother house which is always an abbey.

Monks and nuns alike spent up to six hours of their day in the churches attached to their monasteries in communal prayer that God be glorified and that their own sins and those of their foundations' benefactors might be forgiven. The rest of the time, when not eating or sleeping, they devoted to manual, intellectual, or artistic labors. Though there were differences among the orders as to the degree of isolation required of their members, all regular clergy stood apart from the world about them. What induced such large numbers of men and women to opt out of the mainstream of medieval life is a question not easily answered—certainly not from a distance of eight or nine centuries. This much, however, can be said: The monastic movement offers convincing testimony to the irresistible appeal of the Christian faith and calling to the medieval mind. In an age so torn by violence and strife, the simple certainties of the ordered life behind monastery walls had a compelling attraction to large numbers of people from every station of life.

In Britain, as on the Continent, the oldest medieval monastic order was that of the Benedictines, the Black Monks, founded at Monte Cassino in Italy in 529 by St. Benedict. It was his set of community regulations—the Rule—which, with some modifications, was to govern practically all subsequent monasteries in medieval Europe, including the one founded by St. Augustine in England in 598. As monasteries acquired wealth, either by donations or through their members' labor, they tended to become lax in their observance of the Rule and to lapse into easy living. Inevitably this tendency gave rise to reform movements, all aimed at restoring monastic life to its original austerity or at achieving even higher standards of asceticism. Among the earliest of these was the Cluniac order, founded at Cluny in Burgundy in 940, which developed a more elaborate liturgy than had previously obtained and enforced a high degree of centralized control over its daughter houses as they spread throughout France and England. At the end of the eleventh century at the abbey of Citeaux, also in Burgundy, another stringent reform took place resulting in the founding of the new order of Cistercians, or White Monks, which spread rapidly throughout France and Britain. Cistercian monasteries were set up chiefly in remote rural regions and admitted lay brothers to perform most of the manual labor involved in cultivating their vast estates or tending their huge flocks of sheep. In their emphasis on simplicity and hard work, the Cistercians resembled two other orders founded at about the same time: the Tironensian (Brown Monks) and the Savignac (Grey Monks), the latter of which they absorbed in 1147.

At the beginning, none of these orders of cloistered monks administered to the cure of souls or performed the priestly services of baptism, marriage, and burial. Not so the orders of Augustinian and Premonstratensian canons, respectively called Black Canons and White Canons after the color of their habits. Although cloistered like the Benedictines, Cluniacs, and Cistercians, these regular canons were not sequestered, and indeed were encouraged to perform their priestly duties among laymen. All of the older orders had their female branches residing in nunneries or double orders in which men and women were housed within the same precincts, though separated by walls and grills. Since none of these, however, has left substantial archaeological remains in Britain, they will not be given further consideration. Two unusual orders, small in Britain though of considerable fame in the twelfth century, were the military orders—half monks, half warriors—originating in Palestine in the period of consolidation following the First Crusade. These were the Order of the Temple and the Order of St. John of Jerusalem, known respectively as the Knights Templars and the Knights Hospitallers. Finally, and most ascetic of all, were the Carthusian and Valliscaulian Orders, originating respectively in the valley of the Grande Chartreuse and the Val des Choux in France. Both were extremely severe in their requirements of self-denial and solitude, and the monasteries they founded in Britain—the charterhouses in England and the Valliscaulian houses in Scotland—provided a separate cell for each monk in which he prayed, worked, ate, and slept alone. The architectural plan of these communal hermitages, especially of the English charterhouses, clearly reflects the peculiarities of their rule. The requirement of strict seclusion produced a design of three courtyards in tandem, around which the monastic buildings were erected. The outer courtyard, accessible through a gatehouse, contained guest houses, barns, stables, and workshops; in the middle one was the church and chapter house, while within the inner court was the great cloister around which the individual cells of the monks were placed, each with a workroom, bedroom, and oratory standing within a walled garden with its own garderobe (latrine).

This design was distinctly different from that of all other major monastic houses which comprise the great majority of those still standing—though mostly in a ruined condition. As is well known, all English and Welsh monasteries and friaries were dissolved in the reign of King Henry VIII (1509–1547) and their properties confiscated by the Crown.

In many cases, especially in England, monastic buildings were quickly converted to other ecclesiastical uses and were therefore preserved. They survive today, as we have seen, in cathedrals and parish churches still serving religious purposes, albeit of a different faith and for a different type of worshiper. In many instances monastic properties fell into private hands and were incorporated into the country homes of the new owners. In most cases, however, the monasteries were allowed to fall into decay and became quarries from which building stones, roof and window lead, and statuary were pilfered and scattered far and wide. Sad as the Dissolution was for the monks and nuns who were deprived of their homes and places of worship, the ruination of these establishments offers special opportunities to today's traveller. Many of their walls still stand —stark and ghostly. The skeletal remains of their churches—where monks once daily sang the seven services of the *Opus Dei* and prayed at length for the souls of their monasteries' benefactors, both living and dead—today survive as fascinating examples of medieval architecture. Students of art history will find these ruins even more instructive than finished churches in distinguishing one architectural style from another. Interesting too, though perhaps less aesthetically pleasing, are the lines of low walls and foundation stones adjacent to the churches. These are the remains of the claustral buildings where the resident monks lived, ate, slept, and worked. Glistening white against the uniquely vivid green of rain-soaked British turf, these stones well advertise to the tutored eye the structure and meaning of monastic life in medieval Britain.

The ground plan outlined in these foundations is essentially the same for all monastic establishments, except for those of the Carthusian and Vallisculian orders. The main buildings were all grouped around the cloister, which was usually on the south side of the church's nave so as to catch the sun, though northern cloisters were not uncommon. The cloister is simply a low-roofed alley running along four sides of a square inside of which is a grass-covered yard called the garth. The base of the square (normally its north side) rests against the nave of the cruciform church. The east side of the square is an extension of the south transept. It is often called the dorter range because here, upstairs on the first floor, the monks slept. At the far (southern) end of this dormitory was the reredorter, or latrine. At the north end, leading into the south transept, was usually located a night stair for easy access during early morning or late nocturnal services. Underneath the sleeping quarters, on the ground floor of the dorter range, was a set of rooms arranged in tandem—the library, the sacristy, the vestry, the parlor, and, most important and largest of all, the chapter house. Here the entire convent assembled each day after morning Mass for a reading of a chapter of the Rule and to attend to current business. In Cistercian monasteries the chapter house usually jutted eastward, perpendicular to the range's axis. Somewhere among these rooms was a passageway called a slype leading through the range to the cemetery east of the church. The south side of the square comprised the dining room, (frater, or refectory), kitchen, and sometimes a warming parlor with the only open fireplace available to the monks. In most monasteries the frater ran east and west, but in Cistercian houses the axis was normally north-south, i.e., perpendicular to the south claustral range. Sometimes the kitchen was a separate building set to the south of the range for purposes of fire prevention. In the cloister in front of the frater was the lavatorium—a water-filled stone trough where monks could wash before meals. On the west side of the cloister was the cellarium, a store house situated in the ground floor. Above it on the first floor might be a public parlor, private rooms for the head of the convent, and guest rooms. Cistercian abbeys were unique in reserving the first floor of the west range as a dorter for lay brothers, for whom a second night stair was provided into the western end of the church's nave where they attended the choral prayers and Mass. This completes the claustral circuit. Outside it might be other buildings; a courtyard to the west entered by a gatehouse and containing guest quarters, an almonry, stables, barns, and workshops; to the south the farmary (infirmary) with a separate chapel, kitchen, and special frater; to the east a separate, and often luxurious, house for the head of the convent, where travelling notables could be received without interrupting the routine of the members.

Keeping this basic ground plan in mind, though making allowance for exceptions, the intelligent traveller should be well prepared to make sense out of the odd-shaped walls and stones that comprise the ruined abbeys and priories of southern Britain. Since there are so many that are worth examining, it will be convenient to treat separately those of England and Wales and to discuss them more or less in the chronological order of their establishment.

ENGLAND

A long time admirer and beneficiary of the great feudalized Benedictine monasteries of his native Normandy, William the Conqueror was not slow to give encouragement to the establishment of new religious houses in England. In spite of his preoccupation with war and castle building, he allowed only a short time to elapse after his initial victory over Harold Godwineson before building **Battle Abbey** *(547)*, East Sussex, to commemorate the occasion. The southwest angle of the nave aisle, parts of the south wall of the abbey church, parts of the Early English dorter and frater, the restored abbot's house, and the fourteenth century gatehouse remain standing. About the same time **St. Augustine's Abbey** *(539)* in Canterbury was begun by Abbot Scotland as a Benedictine house on the site of the earlier Saxon Abbey of Saints Peter and Paul. Both have been carefully excavated and, of the Norman building, the chief remains are the north wall of the church's nave, portions of the transepts, and much of the crypt of the apsidal choir (chancel). The first house settled in England by monks from Cluny was **Lewes Priory** *(550)*, East Sussex, founded in 1075 by William de Warenne and now a very sparse ruin. Others of the same order soon followed. Of these the best preserved ruins are those of **Wenlock Priory** *(669)*, Salop, and **Castle Acre Priory** *(609)*, Norfolk. The former was built by Roger de Montgomery in the early part of the twelfth century on the site of an earlier Saxon church. Most of the standing parts of the present ruin date from a rebuilding of the thirteenth century (Early English) but the remains of the chapter house are Norman. Castle Acre is the first of the monastic houses yet to be mentioned where the remains are sufficiently well preserved to afford the visitor a good impression of the layout of a medieval monastery. Founded also by William de Warenne, the earliest portions still standing are the beautiful west front of the church and parts of its nave and transepts. Also Norman, though of a later date, the walls of the chapter house, dorter, and reredorter still stand high; while the west range, originally containing the prior's chapel and lodging, has been completely restored. Also in Norfolk lie the scanty remains of **Thetford Priory** *(609)*, another Cluniac house, founded in 1103 by Roger Bigod of Framlingham Castle. Also in the same county lies **Binham Priory** *(606)*, a Benedictine foundation of about the same date, part of the Norman nave of which is now used as the parish church, with other remains lying neatly about the courtyard. Similar use has been made of the Norman nave of **Waltham Abbey** *(601)*, Essex, built about 1100 on the site of Harold Godwineson's tomb, and later refounded as an Augustinian abbey by Henry II in expiation of the murder of Thomas Becket. Further north in Tyne and Wear lies **Tynemouth Priory** *(704)*. Though founded as a Benedictine house in 1090 by the earl of Northumberland, nothing remains of the Norman building except the outlines of the ground plan. The well preserved east end of the church dates from the early thirteenth century (Early English); the small adjacent Perpendicular Percy Chapel from the fifteenth; while the east range of the cloister with its reredorter was rebuilt in the thirteenth century on eleventh century foundations. Another Benedictine house of the late eleventh century is **Lindisfarne Priory** *(706)* on Holy Island off the Northumberland coast. The priory was founded in 1083 and the standing ruins of the church date from soon thereafter. The substantial remains of the claustral buildings derive, however, from the thirteenth and fourteenth centuries. Approachable only at low tide over a causeway from the mainland, the site is magnificently situated over-looking the North Sea.

The last years of the eleventh century also saw the first establishment of Augustinian Canons in England. They settled in Colchester, Essex, at the **Priory of St. Botolph's** *(598)* where they received a charter of protection from King William Rufus, not otherwise renowned for his piety. Fairly high standing ruins of the early twelfth century Norman nave still stand opposite a large midtown carpark. Another Augustinian foundation of the early twelfth century is **Kirkham Priory** *(693)*, North Yorkshire. Kirkham still displays a Norman doorway which led into the refectory, but the only other substantial remains are a claustral lavatory and a gatehouse, both dating from the late thirteenth century. Much more significant are the remains of the Benedictine **Abbey of Bury St. Edmunds** *(601)* in Suffolk. It was built in the early twelfth century on the site of an earlier church constructed to house the bones of the East Anglian King Edmund—he who had been launched into martyrdom and sainthood by a redundancy of Danish arrows. Soon after its founding Bury became one of the wealthiest Benedictine abbeys in England. Portions of the Norman nave and north transept of the abbey church still stand aboveground as do foundations of the claustral buildings, which here lie north of the nave rather than in the usual southerly position. Guarding the western entrances to the public park containing these ruins are two splendid and much better preserved gateways, each representative of a distinct architectural period. The high Norman tower, known as the Tower of St. James, dates from 1120–1248. To the north of it is the even more impressive Great Gatehouse, built soon after 1327 in the typical pseudo-military fashion of the mid-fourteenth century with a crenellated tower, arrow slits, and a portcullis.

Of all the impulses that drove men and women of the twelfth century to build and populate new monasteries, certainly none was stronger than that emanating from Citeaux. The first Cistercian house in England, founded in 1128, was **Waverley Abbey** *(555)* near Farnham, Surrey, whose present remains are slight. More commonly the White Monks set up their establishments in the north and west, far from the normal habitations of men, where vast and uncultivated lands awaited their diligent exploitation. In the remote regions of Yorkshire, on lands especially suitable to the grazing of large flocks of sheep tended by their lay brothers, the Cistercians constructed the finest of the English abbeys and left for future generations the most magnificent of monastic ruins. Their first was **Rievaulx Abbey** *(689)* near Helmsley, North Yorkshire, founded in 1131 and eventually acquiring a population of 140 monks and 500 lay brothers. Of the considerable remains, only the nave and parts of the transepts of the church date from the early twelfth century. The choir, the well-preserved frater, and the chapter house with its unusual apsidal end are Early English, dating from a mid-thirteenth century rebuilding. Unusual also is the monastery's compass orientation, with the nave running north and south and the cloister lying to the west of the church. Some twenty miles westward lies the second great Cistercian foundation of Yorkshire, and today the most complete of England's abbey ruins. This is **Fountains Abbey** *(686)* south of Ripon, North Yorkshire, founded in 1135. Only the nave and transepts of the church are in the Norman style. The extensive claustral remains (chapter house, dorter, warming house, frater, and cellarium above which was the lay brothers' dormitory) were constructed in the years 1150 to 1250 and are Transitional and Early English, as are the infirmaries and guest houses to the east and west of the cloister. The unusual Early English east end of the church, called the Chapel of Nine Altars, was added in the thirteenth century; new windows were inserted in the fifteenth; and the tower was put up in the early sixteenth century (late Perpendicular). The total ensemble is spectacular. So is **Roche Abbey** *(679)* near Maltby, South Yorkshire, founded for the Cistercians in 1147. Here only the east walls of the church's transepts (Transitional) stand to any height, although the claustral ground plan can be traced in the foundations and the fourteenth century gatehouse is quite good. A greater state of disrepair greets the visitor to **Jervaulx Abbey** *(686)*, a Cistercian house near Middleham, North Yorkshire, founded in 1156. Under the tangle of grass and flowers, however, can be discerned the foundations of the chapter house and dorter, while fragments of the church stand fairly high.

Almost indistinguishable from the Cistercians were the Savignacs, the Grey Monks, who were in fact absorbed into the former order in 1147. Before then, in 1135, they founded **Buildwas Abbey** *(669)* near Much Wenlock, Salop, which today retains most of the shell of the original Norman church as well as significant remains of the claustral buildings including a vaulted chapter house of later construction. A larger and more famous Savignac-turned-Cisterican monastery is **Furness Abbey** *(709)*, founded by King Stephen near Barrow-in-Furness, Cumbria, an isolated spot south of the Lake Country. This is today a fine sight. Though only a section of the south wall of the original Norman nave remains standing, the rest of the church dates mostly from the late twelfth century (Transitional). In the choir are beautiful sedilia and a piscina of the fifteenth century. Of the cloister, most of the south and west ranges are missing, but the doorway to the slype in the east range is still standing, most of the thirteenth century Early English chapter house retains its walls and windows, and the Transitional reredorter is in fair shape. South of the cloister is the complete infirmary chapel which contains a small site museum. An offshoot of Furness, though not established until 1177, was **Byland Abbey** *(688)* southwest of Helmsley, North Yorkshire. Of the Transitional church, most of the west front, north wall, and south transept remain standing, and in the latter is some excellent tilework. Parts of the claustral buildings stand to some height, the oldest portion being the well-preserved lay brothers' range (Norman) on the west. Two even better preserved Cistercian monasteries are **Croxden Abbey** *(668)*, north of Uttoxeter, Staffordshire, and **Cleeve Abbey** *(584)* south of Watchet, Somerset, on the Bristol Channel. The former was colonized by monks from Normandy in 1176, though the ruined west front and south transepts of the church and the chapter house and other claustral buildings date mostly from the thirteenth century (Early English). Cleeve Abbey, dating from 1190, has lost its church completely, but the claustral buildings are in a better state of repair than is to be found in any of Britain's Cistercian abbeys. The east and south ranges have been reroofed and restored so that the Early English sacristy, library, chapter house, and dorter look much as they did in the thirteenth century, while the frater is a fifteenth century substitution. Northwest of the destroyed west front of the church is a two-storied gatehouse built in the thirteenth century but much remodeled in the sixteenth.

The great fame and wealth of the Cistercian monasteries should not be allowed to obscure the fact that most of the religious houses of England were not of that order. These others continued to prosper and found new establishments throughout the twelfth and thirteenth centuries. **Thornton Abbey** *(676)* near Barrow-upon-Humber, Humberside, was founded as a house for Augustinian Canons in 1139. Nothing remains of the original buildings, but the high walls of the early fourteenth century chapter houses (Decorated) are exquisite. The outstanding sight here, however, is the great gatehouse of brick and stone, its entry way approached by an oblique barbican, its western face studded with statuary, its half-octagonal projecting towers perforated with arrow slits. Built in the Perpendicular style soon after 1382, there is perhaps no better example in England of the late-medieval marriage between military and ecclesiastical architecture. Beautifully situated on the River Warfe near Skipton, North Yorkshire, is **Bolton Priory** *(688)*, another Augustinian foundation (ca. 1120) whose Early English nave has been converted into the parish church of Bolton Abbey [*sic*], North Yorkshire, but whose choir transepts, and claustral buildings are preserved as ruins. The Perpendicular west front of the church dates from the sixteenth century. Two other Augustinian houses of the first half of the twelfth century are **Haughmond Abbey** *(671)* and **Lilleshall Abbey** *(672)*, both in Salop. Haughmond's Early English chapter house and refectory and fourteenth century infirmary are well-preserved ruins, while at Lilleshall, the mostly Norman remains of the church, sacristy, chapter house, and frater still stand. A more famous Augustinian foundation is **Lanercost Priory** *(710)* in Cumbria, where Edward I spent his last days before his death on the way to Scotland. Here, too, the Early English monastic nave is incorporated into the present parish church, while, of the claustral buildings, the east range is reduced to foundations only, the undercroft of the frater (south range) is preserved, and the west range is intact.

Of the older orders of regular monks, the late twelfth century saw the foundations of **Monk Bretton Priory** *(679)* near Barnsley, South Yorkshire, and **Finchale Priory** *(700)*, County Durham, and the rebuilding of

Glastonbury Abbey *(583)* in Somerset. Monk Bretton was a Cluniac foundation of 1154 and the present remains of its claustral buildings are in fair shape, especially the Early English west range and the late thirteenth century (Decorated) frater refectory. Finchale was Benedictine, founded in 1190, as a cell to Durham Abbey. Today the walls of both church and claustral buildings stand quite high, though they are all of thirteenth and fourteenth century construction (Early English and Decorated). The sparse remains of Glastonbury Abbey stand on the site of one of the oldest Benedictine foundations in England, which once laid claim to being the repository of the Holy Grail brought to Britain by Joseph of Arimethea. The whole abbey burned to the ground in 1184 and the present ruins date from the rebuilding which took more than a century to complete. It was during this time that the bones of King Arthur and Queen Guinivere were unearthed and later reinterred in front of the high altar in the presence of King Edward I. Of the once great church, the only remains are the two east piers of the crossing, a chapel in the north transept, and parts of the south wall of the nave and choir. Walls of the late Norman lady chapel with their intricate interlaced arcading also still stand, but the claustral buildings have all but disappeared. The fourteenth century abbot's kitchen houses a small museum.

To the late twelfth century also belongs the first foundation in Britain of a charterhouse, the English term for a priory of Carthusian monks. This was **Witham Priory** *(583)* (misnamed Witham Friary) in Somerset, south of Frome. It was founded by King Henry II in 1178–1179 in expiation of the murder of Thomas Becket and its prior was St. Hugh of Avalon, a monk from the mother house of Grand Chartreuse, who later became bishop of Lincoln and builder of the famous choir of the cathedral there. Today the parish church incorporates the original lay brothers' house of worship; but nothing else remains. Also from the reign of Henry II date two Premonstratensian houses in the north of England: **Easby Abbey** *(685)* near Richmond, North Yorkshire, and **Egglestone Abbey** *(698)* in County Durham. Easby is unusual in that the resident canons' dorter (Early English) is in the west (rather than the east) range of claustral buildings. Much of it survives, as does the attached guests' solar and the beautiful Decorated frater in the south range. At Egglestone the surviving walls and windows of the Decorated church built in the late thirteenth century are noteworthy.

The twelfth century was the great age of monastery building in England. In the thirteenth the pace slackened somewhat in contrast to the building boom in secular cathedrals. Nevertheless, new monastic foundations did appear. In the first year of the century the Premonstratensians established **Shap Abbey** *(713)*, Cumbria. Not much remains, however, except for the high-standing sixteenth century (Perpendicular) west front of the church and the lower courses of a few claustral buildings. Another foundation of the same order and approximate date was **Bayham Abbey** *(544)* near Royal Tunbridge Wells, Kent. Still another is

Titchfield Abbey *(558)* near Fareham, Hampshire, converted after the Dissolution into a country home by Thomas Wriothesley, second earl of Southampton, but now a ruin. Here portions of the thirteenth century (Decorated) nave stand fairly high as does the dorter range of the cloister and the early fourteenth century gatehouse. Although the great wave of Cistercian monastic foundation had crested by the end of the twelfth century, two ruined houses of that order date from the reign of Henry III. **Netley Abbey** *(562)* now on the outskirts of Southampton, Hampshire, was founded in 1239 by Peter des Roches. The ruins of the Early English church and chapter house are substantial. **Hailes Abbey** *(642)* near Winchcombe, Gloucestershire, was established in 1246 by the patronage of Henry III's brother, Richard, earl of Cornwall. Only traces of the claustral buildings remain, although the site museum contains interesting miscellanea, including tiles from the church and vaulting bosses from the chapter house.

By the fourteenth century the monastic movement was definitely on the wane. The Black Death hit the monasteries hard, and although they recouped in terms of total population, very few new foundations appeared after 1350. Indeed some old ones disappeared, especially those in the category of alien priories. These were daughter houses of French monasteries, and, after the Hundred Years War began in 1337, many were dissolved—a process culminating in an Act of Parliament of 1414 by which they were all suppressed. The decline in monastic life, however, was not complete, and one new foundation toward the end of the fourteenth century deserves special mention. This was **Mount Grace Priory** *(684)* near Northallerton, North Yorkshire, an establishment of Carthusian monks founded by the duke of Surrey in 1398. It is the only English charterhouse whose remains are extensive enough to illustrate the unique living arrangements of this extraordinary order whose monks lived isolated in little cells under vows of silence. There were altogether twenty-one of these tiny houses arranged around the inner courtyard. One has been reconstructed in its original form. In the middle court was the unpretentious church, whose ruins today stand fairly high, especially the Perpendicular church tower. This is surely one of Yorkshire's most interesting monastic sites—one out of many.

WALES

Like Yorkshire, Wales was a natural habitat for monks. Earliest of the extant ruins among their monasteries is **St. Dogmael's Abbey** *(725)*, a Tironian establishment of 1115 near Cardigan in Dyfed. Some of the walls of the church, chapter house, and frater still stand, while the recently excavated foundations of the other claustral buildings provide a clear picture of a typical monastic layout. Of a somewhat later date is the Benedictine house of **Ewenny Priory** *(719)* in Mid-Glamorgan near Ogmore Castle whose lords were its founders and patrons. Although nothing remains of the claustral buildings, there are good portions of the precinct walls and the present parish church incorporates many Norman and Early English features of the original priory church. This building is especially interesting for its fortification. In the thirteenth century its south transept and central tower were crenellated and pierced with arrow loops—a military/ecclesiastical combination common enough in southern France but rare in Britain. Also rare is the thirteenth century stone pulpitum dividing the nave and chancel.

It was the White Monks of the Cisterican order, however, who found the vast mountain pasture lands of Wales especially congenial to their particular calling. Sheep grazing was their forte and, with lay brothers to tend their enormous flocks, the Cistercian monasteries of Wales were probably the biggest wool producers in medieval Britain. There were, altogether, thirteen of them, of which seven have survived in a sufficient state of preservation to warrant being visited.

Of these the two earliest are **Neath Abbey** *(720)*, West Glamorgan, and **Basinwerk Abbey** *(730)* near Holywell, Clwyd, both founded in the 1130s as Savignac houses and received into the Cistercian order in 1147. Of the two, the former is the better preserved. Parts of the west front and nave walls of the thirteenth century church still stand, as do remains of the lay brothers' dorter and the monks' frater, both partly incorporated in a private mansion constructed in the seventeenth century. At Basinwerk, the remains are fragmentary, consisting of parts of the church, chapter house, dorter, and a good section of the refectory.

Of all the Welsh Cistercian houses, the most famous is certainly **Tintern Abbey** *(716)* north of Chepstow, Gwent. Celebrated in a lyrical ballad by William Wordsworth ("Lines Composed a Few Miles Above Tintern Abbey . . . July 13, 1798"), it has ever since been held by common consent to be among the most romantic of medieval abbey ruins in Britain. Though established on a typically remote site overlooking the River Wye in the early twelfth century, the ruins date mostly from rebuildings of the late thirteenth century by Roger Bigod, earl of Norfolk. The greatest attraction is the Decorated church, its walls standing mostly to their original full height and the exquisite stone tracery of its windows largely intact. In the north transept is the night stair leading to the monks' dorter. (The cloister here, as at Bury St. Edmunds, lies on the church's north side.) The claustral remains are much less impressive than those of the church, but are well enough preserved to demonstrate their adherence to the standard Cistercian ground plan. Typically Cistercian in location, is **Strata Florida Abbey** *(729)* on the River Teifi in the northeast corner of Dyfed north of Tregaron. Founded in 1164, it was refounded twenty years later by Prince Rhys ap Gruffydd and became, in a sense, both the religious and political center of South Wales in the twelfth and thirteenth centuries. Of the remains, only the west front of the Transitional church is of much architectural interest, but the ground plan of the cloister is easily traceable in the foundation stones. Less interesting are the present remnants of **Cymmer Abbey** *(738)* founded in 1199, near

Dolgellau, Gwynedd. Little besides the north arcade of the thirteenth century nave, part of the east end, and a ruined sedilia survives. The great Cistercian abbey of **Valle Crucis** *(731)* is another story. Situated in a lovely glen sloping toward the River Dee near Llangolen, Clwyd, it was founded in 1201 by Madoc ap Gruffydd Maelor, Prince of Powys. The walls of the Decorated west front of the church are well preserved, as is the Early English east end. Of even greater interest, however, is the Decorated east range of the cloister which has been restored and looks very much like the original. Sacristy, chapter house, slype, dorter, reredorter, and warming room all look much as they must have when built, though the roof, of course, is modern.

As elsewhere in Britain, the Cistercians in Wales, despite their wealth and prominence, held no monopoly of the cloistered life. **Talley Abbey** *(726)* near Llandeilo, Dyfed, was Premonstratensian, the only house of that order in Wales. Founded near the end of the twelfth century by Rhys ap Gruffydd, not much is left except the ruined east end of the church and part of the crossing. Much more survives of **Llanthony Priory** *(714)*, a house of Augustinian canons dating from about the same period and situated north of Abergevanny, Gwent, adjacent to the border of Hereford and Worcester. Here the church's Transitional west front with its twin towers stands to its full original height, and substantial portions of the nave, transepts, choir, and central tower remain. Not much is left, however, of the claustral buildings, though the nearby prior's house has been incorporated into a private hotel. Of special interest is the neighboring and contemporary parish church, which was probably the priory's infirmary.

FRIARIES

The obvious contrast between the poverty and unworldliness of Jesus of Nazareth and the enormous wealth and power of the medieval church inevitably produced a series of *crises de conscience* within the Christian community. Recurring waves of organized asceticism were the result. Each of these waves produced a new monastic order more puritanical in intent than the one before it, and each new order in time succumbed to the temptations forced upon it by the endowments of pious benefactors. The Cistercians and Premonstratensians of the twelfth century had sought to escape seduction by retreating into the wilderness and following a strict rule of prayer and hard work. But the lands they acquired yielded unexpected riches to their toil, and they too fell under the curse of success. And so, in the early years of the thirteenth century, emerged a new manifestation of the ascetic ideal: the mendicant friars.

Of these there were four main orders: the Dominicans or Friars Preacher or Black Friars; the Franciscans or Friars Minor or Grey Friars; the Austin Friars; and the Carmelites or White Friars. Of these the first two were the more numerous. Organized by Dominic Guzman of Castile to preach against the Albigensian heretics of southern France, the Dominicans received papal recognition in 1216 and within five years reached England and established themselves at Oxford where they were to have a significant impact on the burgeoning intellectual life of the community of scholars who had already settled there. By the end of Henry III's reign (1272) they had founded forty-five houses in England and had penetrated into Scotland as well. They were followed shortly by the Franciscans, members of a still more numerous order of friars, founded by St. Francis of Assisi in northern Italy. They too established a house in Oxford and numerous other towns, as later did the Austin Friars and Carmelites.

Two characteristics distinguished the friars from all previous orders of regular clergy, and to some extent from the secular priests as well. First, they concentrated more on preaching than on liturgy. Secondly, they settled mostly in towns, among whose growing populations they rightly believed their evangelical and charitable efforts were most welcome and most needed. At first they eschewed endowments of either goods or real estate, preferring (the Franciscans at least) to walk barefoot, to beg for their sustenance, to preach in open fields or borrowed churches, and to dwell in "huts of wood and mud" as St. Francis had exhorted. But in time the hostility of both regular and secular clergy and the favor they won from the general populace and city fathers alike induced them to build churches of their own and cloistered friaries for their living quarters. Indeed by the end of the thirteenth century the mendicant friars all over England and Scotland were enjoying a building boom. (Dominican friaries were sometimes designated priories, and the Franciscans called theirs monasteries, even though technically they were not monks. This confusion of nomenclature is best resolved by calling all their convents friaries.)

In plan, their churches reflected architecturally the distinctive features of their calling as they perceived it. These buildings were essentially vessels for preaching, with aisleless naves and chancels and fewer structural divisions separating laity from clergy than was normal among medieval churches. Unfortunately most of these churches, as well as their attached domestic quarters, have been destroyed or so fully converted to other uses as to be unrecognizable. Unlike so many rural monasteries after the Dissolution, the friaries suffered not from desertion and neglect but from being overwhelmed by urban growth.

Some remnants, however, do survive, and are worth inspection. In Chichester, West Sussex, stands the chancel of a Grey Friars' church, later used as an assize court and now the **Guildhall Museum** *(551)*. In Lincoln the Franciscan Friary now houses the **Lincoln City and County Museum** *(651)*. In Gloucester, behind the Church of St. Mary-de-Crypt, is a thirteenth century **Grey Friar's Church** *(640)*. In Canterbury on Best Lane a Christian Science church now occupies the refectory and undercroft of a **Black Friars'** *(538)* (Dominican) establishment. In Norwich, Norfolk, **St. Andrews Hall** *(608)*, including Black Friars' Hall, contains the nave and chancel of a fifteenth century Dominican church. At Aylesford, Kent, **The Friars** *(538)* incorporates an interesting Carmelite cloister of the thirteenth century now reoccupied by members of the same order. Elsewhere, in various towns throughout Britain, there are scattered remnants of this once fervent and widespread religious movement, but none of sufficient architectural interest to warrant further exploration. The chief legacy of the mendicant friars was not architectural but intellectual. From their ranks in Britain, as on the Continent, came many of the leading theologians of the thirteenth century; and mostly from their inspiration came the stimulus that first transformed a tiny community of scholars at Oxford into an established and renowned seat of higher learning.

CHANTRIES

The word *chantry* can be defined as an endowed memorial service for the soul of its founder or of anyone else designated by him. The endowment usually covered the livings of one or more chantry priests whose primary function was to pray for those named by the donor as well as the cost of erecting a special altar for that purpose within an existing church or even a special chapel. The practice was rooted in the belief that the sufferings of a soul in Purgatory could be shortened by the prayers of the living and especially by special masses sung in his or her behalf. In the early Middle Ages monasteries took on responsibility for an enormous number of these soul masses in the names of their benefactors or of the deceased members of their order. In the mid-thirteenth century, for example, the monks of Durham Cathedral were obliged to say more than seven thousand such masses per year. With the decline in monastic endowments, after the Statute of Mortmain (1279) had prohibited the alienation of land to the church without royal license, responsibility for these services tended to shift to secular cathedrals, friaries, and parish churches. In the fourteenth and fifteenth centuries the practice of endowing chantries, either in perpetuity or for a fixed term, became as common as life insurance is today. Indeed it *was* a form of insurance—not against the liabilities of bereavement but against the perils to be encountered by the deceased en route to the kingdom of heaven. Hence, all manner of folk—kings, nobles, gentry, merchants, civic corporations, and even guilds of artisans—joined the prudential throng of benefactors. As a result, by the end of the fifteenth century chantry priests outnumbered parish curates, and the land was filled with altars and chapels, many of consummate grace and beauty. Whether or not they served their intended purposes, they remain today among the chief artistic delights in store for the intelligent traveller in Britain.

Naturally enough, the most magnificent of these medieval chantries are to be found in the great cathedrals. Those of special merit have already been described in connection with the cathedral churches they adorn. As a reminder, however, they deserve brief mention again. They include the monument of Henry V's brother, Humphrey, duke of Gloucester (d. 1447) in the retrochoir of **St. Albans Cathedral** *(621)*, Hertfordshire; the chantries of Bishops Edington (d. 1366) and William of Wykeham (d. 1404) in the nave, and of Cardinal Beaufort in the retrochoir of **Winchester Cathedral** *(563)*, Hampshire; the chantries of Bishop Nykke (d. 1535) and of Henry V's companion-in-arms Sir Thomas Erpingham (d. 1428) in the aisles of **Norwich Cathedral** *(608)*, Norfolk; the chantry of Bishop Bubwith (d. 1424) in the nave of **Wells Cathedral** *(585)*, Somerset; and, most glorious of all, the chantry of King Henry V (d. 1422) on the bridge over the south ambulatory of **Westminster Abbey** *(523)*, London, and the Chapel of King Henry VII (d. 1509) at the east end of the same church.

In addition to the above, two parish churches deserve special mention for the magnificence of their chantry chapels. The first is **Tewkesbury Abbey Church** *(641)*, Gloucestershire, originally Benedictine, a huge building essentially Norman in style, though with many later additions. Here, clustered around the ambulatory, is a sequence of splendid chapels, including the Beauchamp Chantry (1422), the Fitzhamon Chantry (1397), and three chantries dedicated to members of the notorious Despenser family. The second is **St. Mary's, Warwick** *(645)*, Warwickshire, with its famous Beauchamp Chapel, dedicated to Richard Beauchamp, earl of Warwick (d. 1439) and containing the tomb of Queen Elizabeth's favorite, Robert Dudley, earl of Leicester (d. 1588). This little chapel, though an adjunct to an architecturally undistinguished church, is a superb example of the Perpendicular style—one of the best in all of Britain.

Another outgrowth of the chantry movement was the establishment of collegiate churches served by a society or college of chantry priests bound to offer masses in perpetuity for the souls of the founder, his family, or anyone else specified in the founder's will. Colleges of clerks attached to a single church and living a more or less sequestered life within its precincts were not unknown to the early Middle Ages—the most notable example being the collegiate church of St. John at Beverley, Humberside, now known as **Beverley Minster** *(676)*. Unusual for its double transepts, this church is the rival to many English cathedrals in both size and magnificence. Though retaining some of its original Norman features, the church is essentially a blend of Gothic styles: choir and transepts are Early English, the nave is mostly Decorated, the west front Perpendicular.

Of a later date (mainly fourteenth and fifteenth centuries) was the large number of parish churches converted to collegiate status by the installation of a small society of resident chantry priests. Noteworthy among these are **Cobham Parish Church** *(544)* near Rochester, Kent, which has the largest collection of memorial brasses in England; **Edington Parish Church** *(577)* near Westbury, Wiltshire, Decorated and Perpendicular; **Ottery St. Mary Church** *(588)*, Devon, a partly Decorated church of particular architectural interest since it was deliberately copied from nearby Exeter Cathedral; **Ewelme Church** *(637)* near Wallingford, Oxfordshire, with a school and almshouse attached, a not unusual feature of a collegiate foundation; **Battlefield Church** *(671)* north of Shrewsbury, Salop, erected in 1408 to commemorate the battle where King Henry IV saved his newly won crown by defeating Harry Hotspur, son of the earl of Northumberland; the large Perpendicular **Collegiate Church of Tattershall** *(653)*, Lincolnshire, next to Tattershall Castle; **Higham Ferrers Church** *(654)*, Northamptonshire, with an associated school and bede-house and the remains of the nearby college erected in the early fifteenth century by Archbishop Chichele, founder of All Souls College, Oxford; the contemporary **Collegiate Church of Fotheringhay** *(656)* near Oundle, Northamptonshire, adjacent to the now demolished castle where Mary Queen of Scots was executed; and the **Church of St. Peter, Howden** *(677)*, Humberside, a lovely Decorated building with an adjacent ruined chapter house for the college of chantry priests who once served it. Another collegiate church, though in a class by itself, is St. George's Chapel at **Windsor Castle** *(565)*, Berkshire. Founded by King Edward IV in 1472, the chapel was dedicated to the patron saint of the Order of the Garter and provided with a dean and chapter as its governing body. Construction of this almost perfect specimen of Perpendicular architecture was completed under Henry VII, the first of the Tudor kings. Here are displayed the banners of the Knights of the Garter, and here too are the tombs of Kings Henry VI, Edward IV, Henry VIII (buried with his third wife, Jane Seymour, who bore his only son), Charles I, George III, George IV, William IV, and George VI.

COLLEGIATE FOUNDATIONS

Another distinct form of medieval foundation was the college, originally of the chantry priest type, to which a condition of learning was attached. Groups of scholars, always in holy orders, might be endowed with a residence and chapel to further their pursuit of higher studies, sometimes on the condition that they celebrate masses on behalf of the founders. Would-be patrons of such establishments naturally looked to those communities where scholars were already clustered. In the thirteenth century, the most important of such communities was Oxford, where by the beginning of the century a guild of masters, called a *universitas*, was well established and engaged in teaching and granting degrees. The main course of study, the *Studium Generale,* embraced the seven liberal arts, the *Trivium* (grammar, rhetoric, logic) and the *Quadrivium* (arithmetic, geometry, astronomy, music) and there were also courses in theology, law, and medicine. Students, usually beginning at about sixteen years of age, could receive a Bachelor of Arts degree after four years of study, and, after an additional three years, a Master's Degree, which was in effect a license to teach. By the year 1213 Oxford University had its own charter and its own chancellor, who within a short time was to become independent of the bishop of Lincoln in whose diocese the town lay. Its reputation for scholarship was such that it attracted in 1221 the first settlement of Dominican Friars in England, to be followed three years later by a group of Franciscans from Italy. These two orders in turn gave a still greater stimulus to learning and produced between them those great masters of theology who for a while made England the leading intellectual center of Europe: Robert Bacon, his nephew Roger Bacon, Adam Marsh, William of Ockham, John Pecham, and Duns Scotus, among others. Students flocked to attend the lectures of such luminaries, and by the second decade of the thirteenth century, Oxford already was giving shelter to some thirteen hundred scholars. Those not housed in convents had to seek rented lodgings from townspeople or find rooms in one of the halls owned by university masters. Student housing was therefore both scarce and dear. Thus the need of students for quarters, and of wealthy patrons for worthy objects of charity, combined to produce the Oxford college system—not unnaturally in imitation of existing foundations of chantry priests. That the word *college* now has an exclusively academic connotation is largely due to the accident that, of all English medieval religious foundations, only the university colleges escaped dissolution during the Reformation.

The honor of being the first Oxford college is shared among—and disputed by—the three earliest: Merton, Balliol, and University. Though either of the last two might claim precedence on the basis of the dates of their endowment, architecturally speaking, **Merton College** *(631)* is the oldest. With a charter from King Henry III issued in 1264, Walter de Merton, former chancellor of England and later bishop of Rochester, established at Oxford the college that bears his name for the purpose of training scholars for the secular priesthood. Of the present structure, the medieval portions include the treasury or muniment room dating from 1274—the oldest collegiate building in Oxford; the Decorated chapel choir finished in 1294, with Perpendicular transepts added in the fourteenth and fifteenth centuries; the Mob Quad (origin of name unknown) dating from the first decade of the fourteenth century; the library (1371–1379) which is the oldest in England; and the crenellated gatehouse dating from 1418. **Balliol College** *(620)* owes its origin to a quarrel between the bishop of Durham and John Balliol, father of the luckless

King John of Scotland, puppet and victim of Edward I's ambition. The bishop won, and Balliol was compelled to submit to a public scourging at the door of Durham Cathedral and to endow a society of scholars at Oxford. On his death, his widow Dervorgilla (who also founded Sweetheart Abbey in her native Galloway) assumed responsibility for her late lord's penance and in 1282 issued a charter to the college which among other things required its scholars to celebrate masses for the founders, in the manner of chantry priests. Perhaps the most distinguished of all Oxford colleges for its graduates, it is among the least so for its architecture. All that remains of the medieval buildings are the fifteenth century dining hall, now the library (restored); the masters' dining room with a splendid oriel window, and the upper library with the rooms underneath. Most of the rest is nineteenth century fake Gothic or twentieth century nondescript. Contrary to a myth long cultivated by its authorities, **University College** *(634)* was *not* founded by Alfred the Great, but by a mid-thirteenth century endowment from Bishop William of Durham. The college moved to its present site on High Street in 1332, but none of the present buildings is older than the seventeenth century. Even these were not built along the classical lines of the English Renaissance, but in the less fortunate style of the "Gothic" reaction to it.

One other thirteenth century Oxford foundation deserves notice, though, strictly speaking, it was not initially a college. This is **St. Edmund Hall** *(634)*, the only one of the medieval halls to survive to the present. Originally owned by the Benedictine Abbey of Oseney, it was bought by Queen's College at the time of the Dissolution, but achieved independent collegiate status in 1937. Except for a large fifteenth century fireplace in the Junior Common Room, nothing is left of the medieval building; the small but charming quadrangle and its surrounding buildings date mostly from the seventeenth and eighteenth centuries.

The earliest of the fourteenth century Oxford colleges is **Exeter College** *(629)*, founded in 1314 by Walter of Stapledon, bishop of Exeter for scholars from Devon and Cornwall. Its earliest existing building is Palmer's Tower, the former gatehouse, dating from 1432. The rest is an unfelicitous mixture of Jacobean and Victorian Gothic, of which the only worthy component is the hall with its collar-beam roof and Jacobean screen. **Oriel College** *(632)* started life in 1326 as the House of the Blessed Mary at Oxford whose scholars were obliged to provide nearby St. Mary's Church with four chaplains. It received its charter from King Edward II and its name from its early acquisition of a building with an oriel window, i.e., an upper-floor bay window resting on corbels or stone brackets. Almost nothing visible remains of its medieval origins. Its gatehouse, chapel, hall, first and third quadrangles are seventeenth century Jacobean Gothic. The rest is a mixture of eighteenth, nineteenth, and twentieth century construction.

St. Mary's Church *(636)* whose chaplains were furnished by the scholars of Oriel and whose vicar to this day is appointed by that college, is the oldest habitation of the university as a corporate entity. It was here where the various faculties assembled together, that degrees were granted, and ceremonies held. In the adjoining Congregation House the university installed its first library. Its tower dates from the end of the thirteenth century and its lofty Decorated spire from the early fourteenth. This was the first of the many towers, pinnacles, and domes that to this day give Oxford its special charm and moved Matthew Arnold to describe it as "that sweet city with her dreaming spires that needs not June for beauty's heightening." Inside the church, the magnificent Perpendicular nave and choir were constructed in the late fifteenth century, though the chapel of Adam de Brome (founder of Oriel) dates from 1328.

Two other additions to the fourteenth century scene at Oxford were **Queen's College** *(633)* and **New College** *(631)*. Queen's was founded in 1341 by the chaplain to Edward III's Queen Philippa and has ever since enjoyed the patronage of the Queens Consort of England. It was established for the benefit of Cumbrian scholars and their disciples, the original Oxford undergraduates, who were to pursue theological studies, pray for the souls of others, and give alms to the poor, including a daily portion of pea soup at the college gate. Nothing of medieval Queen's remains, but the late seventeenth and early eighteenth century buildings (1692–1716) are elegant enough to have moved Daniel Defoe in 1726 to describe it as "without comparison the most Beautiful College in the University." Especially noteworthy are the library, chapel, north quadrangle, and the somewhat later front quadrangle completed in 1760 by a donation from Queen Caroline. New College was established in 1379 —the juxtaposition of name and date seeming more incongruous to Americans than to the English. Its founder was William of Wykeham, Bishop of Winchester, and its earliest scholars were all required to have attended the bishop's recently established college in that city. In addition to their studies they were obliged to say daily masses for the souls of the founder and other benefactors, though Wykeham's major objective seems to have been to help fill the ranks of the clergy and civil service recently decimated by the Black Death. Like Salisbury Cathedral, Wykeham's college (most of which still stands) is all of one piece, the architectural style, early Perpendicular. Here is to be found the earliest of Oxford's college quadrangles (completed 1386) which set the fashion for all subsequent college buildings there. Contemporary with it are the gatehouse, hall, and chapel with some rare samples of fourteenth century glass. The detached cloister and the bell tower date from 1400, but the charming garden quadrangle is an addition of the late seventeenth and early eighteenth centuries.

In the year that William of Wykeham founded his new college at Oxford, another great religious figure in the same city, John Wycliffe, began preaching a startling new heresy—that there was no scriptural foundation for the doctrine of transubstantiation, which held that in the celebration of the Mass the eucharistic bread and wine were miraculously transformed into the real body and blood of Christ. Here was a body blow at the fundamental underpinnings of the Roman Catholic church—a harbinger of the Protestant Revolt which in the sixteenth century would split Christendom apart. It was not the first attack on the established ecclesiastical order from this Yorkshireman who had been a fellow at Merton, a master of Balliol, and was now the most distinguished Doctor of Divinity at Oxford. He had already publicized his views that man's salvation was consummated by God's grace alone without the mediating offices of the priesthood; that popes and cardinals alike might err; that if church property were misused by the ecclesiastics who controlled it, it should be confiscated by the state; and that the true word of God was to be discovered not in the laws, dogmas, and traditions of the church, but in the Holy Bible which should be translated into the vernacular for all men to read and to learn the truth. Already sternly admonished in 1378 after a noisy trial in the archbishop of Canterbury's Lambeth Palace, Wycliffe was to be tried again four years later by a synod of eminent theologians and barred from further teaching and preaching at Oxford. He retired to the tiny Leicestershire village of Lutterworth, and there he died in peace. Not so the heresies that he had given voice to. In popularized form they were taken up by a mixed group of scholars, knights, craftsmen, unlicensed preachers, and humbler folk, known as the Lollards (probably from a Dutch word meaning "those who mumble their prayers"). In the end Lollardy succumbed to the rigorous persecutions of both church and state, but not before the Bible had been translated into English and not without blazing a trail for the Protestant Reformation a century later.

In Oxford, Lollardy had one unintended consequence, i.e., the founding of **Lincoln College** *(630)* in 1427 for the express purpose of training theologians to confute the heresies of Wycliffe. Its founder was Richard Fleming, Bishop of Lincoln, who later distinguished himself by personally digging up Wycliffe's bones, burning them, and throwing the ashes into the River Swift. Much of medieval Lincoln survives, most of it from the founder's own time: the kitchen, gatehouse tower, hall, and front quadrangle. Chapel and inner quadrangle were erected in the seventeenth century, the former a good specimen of Jacobean Gothic. Ironically for this bastion of Catholic orthodoxy, John Wesley, the founder of Methodism, was a fellow here in the eighteenth century, and his rooms can still be visited. In the same year that Lincoln was founded, Chancellor Thomas Chase of Balliol procured the site for the first building to belong to the university as distinct from the colleges. This was the **Divinity School** *(632)*, completed in 1490—a gem of Perpendicular architecture. In its upper chamber was deposited the university's first great collection of manuscripts, the gift of Humphrey, duke of Gloucester, brother of Henry V. During the reign of Edward VI, when the Protestant Reformation attained its high water mark, the library's contents were destroyed; but toward the end of Elizabeth's reign a second start was made when Sir Thomas Bodley endowed the university with a new collection and arranged that the Stationer's Company of London send it a free copy of every book printed in England. This was the germ of **Bodleian Library** *(632)*, today one of the world's greatest libraries, housing over two million books and some fifty thousand volumes of manuscripts. To the original Divinity School was added the present east wing or Arts End in 1612, the Old Schools Quadrangle (1613–1624), the west wing or Convocation House (1634–1637), and the nearby New Bodleian Library completed in the present century.

Two more colleges, **All Souls** *(627)* and **Magdalen** *(631)* (pronounced *maudlin*), complete the roster of fifteenth century collegiate foundations at Oxford. All Souls has been described as "the greatest of all war memorials." It was founded in 1437 by Henry Chichele (pronounced *Chitchely*), Archbishop of Canterbury with King Henry VI as cofounder, and its twenty original scholars were obliged to pray for both king and archbishop in life and death, for the souls of King Henry V, Thomas, duke of Clarence, of the dukes, earls, barons, knights, esquires, and others who fell in the wars with France (the Hundred Years War), and "for the souls of all the faithful dead." Here unmistakably was an academic community *cum* chantry. Today its resident fellows are devoted exclusively to postgraduate study, making it one of the few colleges in modern Oxford not to admit undergraduates. The original buildings, completed in 1442, include the gatehouse, the exquisite Perpendicular chapel, and the front quadrangle. The warden's lodging, the great triangle with its high twin towers, and the library all date from the eighteenth century. Magdalen's charter was issued in 1458, the gift of King Henry IV to the founder, William of Waynflete. Of the original fifteenth century buildings, there remain the lengthy college wall, the hall, cloister quadrangle, and chapel with its detached bell tower, the Founder's Tower, and the Muniment Tower; while within the grounds are the kitchen and other relics of the thirteenth century St. John's Hospital on the site of which Magdalen was built. The restored Grammar Hall dates from 1614, the New Building from 1733, St. Swithun's quadrangle from the 1880s. Of all the Oxford colleges, Magdalen is and always has been among the best endowed. It is thought by many to be the most beautiful—partly no doubt because of its extensive grounds (over one hundred acres) backing on the River Cherwell, a tributary of the upper Thames.

Although Cambridge men are loath to admit it, England's other great university was probably originally an offshoot of Oxford. In 1208 when a local woman was killed by an unknown student, the townspeople of Oxford retaliated by lynching two or three of the escaped murderer's fellow lodgers. This touched off a panic and the student body fled to other towns to continue their studies. Cambridge was one, and though there were schools already there, the arrival of the refugees from Oxford was probably responsible for the establishment of a uniform course of study, the *Studium Generale*. In 1231, following the temporary dispersal of the

University of Paris which sent many students to England, King Henry III dispatched letters to the local authorities of both Oxford and Cambridge laying down rules for the governance of university students and the proper ordering of town-gown relationships. By this time, obviously, both universities had become established institutions, though Cambridge's early history is obscure by virtue of the fact that most of its thirteenth century records were destroyed during the Peasant's Revolt of 1381.

The oldest college in Cambridge is **Peterhouse** *(614)* (St. Peter's College), founded in 1281 by Hugh of Balsham, Bishop of Ely within whose diocesan jurisdiction the university still lay. Of its present buildings, only the hall (ca. 1290) dates from the time of the college's founding, and it is much restored. The library dates from the late sixteenth and early seventeenth centuries, the Jacobean Gothic chapel from 1628–1632, the Fellows Building from the eighteenth century, the Gisborne Court from the nineteenth. Next in age at Cambridge is **Clare College** *(611)* founded as University Hall in 1326 and refounded twelve years later by Elizabeth de Burgh, countess of Clare, who had recently inherited the estate of her brother, the earl of Gloucester, killed at the Battle of Bannockburn. None of its present buildings, however, are of medieval origin. The college was built mostly in the years between 1638 and 1715; the chapel was added in 1763–1769. Almost as old in date of founding is **Pembroke College** *(614)*, established in 1347 by the widow of Aymer de Valence, earl of Pembroke, who had survived Bannockburn and was almost alone among the English barons to have conducted himself with moderation in the troubled reign of Edward II. Nothing is left of the medieval buildings except the Old Library which was originally the chapel and which was later (1690) embellished with its present lovely plaster ceiling. Architecturally, Pembroke's masterpiece is the Chapel designed by Sir Christopher Wren in 1663–1665, though lengthened by George Gilbert Scott, Jr., in the late nineteenth century. Ivy Court also belongs to the seventeenth century; the rest of the college is the product of nineteenth and twentieth century rebuilding. **Trinity Hall** *(616)* was founded in 1350 by William Bateman, Bishop of Norwich. Although still retaining its medieval foundations and walls, the major portion of Trinity's buildings were completely refaced in the mid-eighteenth century. The library, however, dates from late in the reign of Queen Elizabeth I. **Corpus Christi College** *(611)* is unique in owing its foundation not to the largesse of any individual but to the endowment in 1352 by the united guilds of Corpus Christi and of the Blessed Virgin. Both were religious fraternities whose *raison d'être* was to provide for prayers for the souls of their deceased members. Only the Old Court dates from the period of the founding, though it is much restored. It is, incidentally, the oldest college quadrangle in England, antedating New College, Oxford, by about thirty years. The first court, facing the street, dates from the early nineteenth century and is undistinguished.

To the fifteenth century, Cambridge owes its greatest architectural glories. **King's College** *(613)* was founded in 1441 for the graduates of Eton College by Henry VI, that pious but half-mad king, the last of the Lancastrians of whom Shakespeare wrote:

> But all his mind is bent to holiness,
> To number Ave-Maries on his beads:
> His champions are the Prophets and Apostles:
> His weapons holy saws of sacred writ:
> His study is his tilt-yard, and his loves
> Are brazen images o' canonized saints.

Posterity, at least, can be grateful for the king's piety. For although the present college buildings date mostly from the eighteenth and nineteenth centuries and, except for the Fellows Building, are of no great architectural merit, King's College Chapel is the noblest specimen in Britain of the Perpendicular Gothic style. Commenced in 1446 and finished in 1515 in the reign of Henry VIII, this high rectangular building (289 feet long, 80 high, and 44½ wide) is noted chiefly for its magnificent fan vaulting; its great mullioned windows filled mostly with sixteenth century glass; its wooden rood screen bearing the arms of Anne Boleyn; its intricately carved choir stalls; and the stone armorials in the antechapel, representing the arms of Henry VIII. Amidst all this splendor, Rubens' altarpiece, *The Adoration of the Magi*, seems anticlimactic. **Queens' College** *(614)* owes its origin to the patronage of Margaret of Anjou, Henry VI's indomitable queen, who was not to be outdone by her devout husband in conspicuous piety. Absorbing the recently established College of St. Barnard's, Queens' was officially founded in 1448 and refounded in 1465 by Elizabeth Woodville, Edward IV's queen, after the War of the Roses had unseated the Lancastrians and placed a Yorkist king on the throne of England. Queens' was an architectural novelty in its day in that its walls were built of brick not stone, and in design it is closer to a late medieval manor house than to an ecclesiastical establishment. The first court is original (though restored) and includes the hall, the old chapel, and the library. The west range of the cloister court also dates from the fifteenth century, the north from the sixteenth, the south from the eighteenth. The Walnut Tree Court is of eighteenth century provenance, the chapel, nineteenth. The turret at the southwest angle of the college is thought to have housed the study of the great Dutch philosopher Erasmus when he taught Greek at Queens' in the early sixteenth century. The quiet secular dignity of Queens' today reflects, one likes to think, the undogmatic common sense of this famous humanist. All in all, it is the prettiest of the Cambridge colleges and the one most worth visiting. Last of Cambridge's great fifteenth century architectural relics is the **Church of St. Mary's the Great** *(615)*. Like St. Mary's, Oxford, this was the medieval university's corporate assembly hall. Rebuilt on the site of an older church between 1478 and 1508, it is another good example of the Perpendicular style.

Finally, two other English collegiate foundations of the later Middle Ages deserve special attention. These are **Winchester College** *(563)* in Hampshire and **Eton College** *(566)* outside of Windsor, Berkshire. Both were grammar schools where Latin was the principal subject of study; both were founded as nurseries to feed their founders' university colleges at Oxford and Cambridge. William of Wykeham, Bishop of Winchester and Chancellor of England under Edward III, founded Winchester College in 1382, and to this day its students are known as "Wykehamists." In its own day it was by far the largest foundation of its kind, numbering ninety-six scholars, choristers, and commoners. It was intended that these boys at the age of about sixteen should pass on to Wykeham's New College at Oxford which was built exclusively for them. Today, the best surviving portion of the original college is the chapel with its lovely wooden fan tracery ceiling and some fourteenth century glass. Within Wykeham's cloisters is Fromond's Chantry, dating from the early fifteenth century; a detached building known simply as School dates from 1783. This is the first of England's "public schools." It served as the model for the second, and today perhaps the better known—Eton College, lying among its famous playing fields within the shadow of Windsor Castle. Founded in 1440 by King Henry VI, its charter provided for the maintenance of seventy scholars, all bound for King's College, Cambridge. Remarkably, its doors were open to all sons of freemen, save bastards, "to learn the same science (i.e., Latin) and the rudiments of grammar freely." Today, the lower school and college hall date from the time of founding, as does the splendid Perpendicular chapel. The Upper School dates from the late seventeenth century; and the college library from the eighteenth.

In the eighteenth century, Thomas Grey, an Etonian, would write of his alma mater:

> Ye distant spires, ye antique towers,
> That crown the wat'ry glade,
> Where grateful Science still adores
> Her Henry's holy Shade.

Grateful science must have been alone. Few others mourned the passing of that unbalanced and ineffectual monarch, King Henry VI. His only significant accomplishments were the building of Eton and its counterpart King's College, Cambridge. These, unlike the Lancastrian dynasty, were to survive and prosper into the sixteenth century and beyond.

CHAPTER VII

THE REIGN OF THE TUDORS

1485–1603

POLITICS, WAR, AND RELIGION

HENRY VII: 1485–1509

On 30 October 1485 in Westminster Abbey, Henry of Richmond, at the age of twenty-eight, was crowned King, by the grace of God, of England and of France, Prince of Wales, and lord of Ireland. By the grace of God it had to be, for only the presumption that the victory at Bosworth Field had been divinely ordained could legitimatize Henry VII's claim to the throne. For in the veins of this grandson of a stepped-up Welsh squire ran a mere trickle of English royal blood, and that by way of his mother, Lady Margaret Beaufort, great-granddaughter of John of Gaunt by his mistress Catherine Swynford. If the law of primogeniture alone were to govern succession to the throne vacated by the death of Richard III, at least a half dozen men and boys in England had better claims. Small wonder that the new king clapped into the Tower of London the foremost contender, the youthful earl of Warwick, son of that duke of Clarence who had been drowned in a butt of Malmsey wine. Small wonder too that he promptly married Warwick's cousin Elizabeth, eldest daughter of King Edward IV, the last but one of the Yorkist kings (not counting the murdered Little Prince, Edward V).

Today the portrait of the first of the Tudor kings hangs in the front landing of the **National Portrait Gallery** (518) in St. Martin's Place, off Trafalgar Square in London. It was painted on panel in 1505 by Master Michael Sittow. In the **Victoria and Albert Museum** (526) on Cromwell Road, Kensington, London, is the only other contemporary representation of King Henry VII—the beautiful colored bust by the Italian sculptor Pietro Torrigiano, done in 1508–1509. By the same artist, though of a later date, is the full-length effigy of King Henry which, along with that of Queen Elizabeth his wife, adorns their tomb in **Westminster Abbey** (523) in what is now known as the Henry VII Chapel.

What we see here, and especially in the painting, is not the image of a medieval warrior king, but of an efficient modern chief-executive. This is a no-nonsense face—canny, skeptical, prudent. Though no stranger to war, Henry VII was not martial-minded; though orthodox in religion, he was neither lavish in his gifts to the church nor more than conventionally pious; though jealous of his royal honor, he shunned extravagant ceremony and always preferred a full treasury to a brilliant court. He was above all a realist. His primary aim was to establish a dynasty secure at home and recognized abroad. To that end he bent every effort to achieve

270

domestic tranquillity, peace with the other ruling houses of Europe, and above all financial solvency.

Domestic tranquillity was no sure thing in 1485. Richard III was dead, but the Yorkist party was not, and there were pretenders aplenty to contest the outcome of Bosworth Field. The first of these was a nobody —a naive imposter named Lambert Simnel. Egged on by the dowager duchess of Burgundy, sister to the late Edward IV, Simnel sought to impersonate the earl of Warwick, though the latter was still alive and in prison. Improbable as it was, the conspiracy attracted the support of a number of Yorkist nobles, including Francis, Viscount Lovell. When the rebels invaded England in May of 1487 with an army of some two thousand German mercenaries, they were easily routed by King Henry at Stoke, about three miles south of Newark-on-Trent in Nottinghamshire. Lord Lovell disappeared—possibly drowned in the River Trent, but also possibly to take refuge in his family estate in Oxfordshire called **Minster Lovell** *(626)*. Here in this now ruined medieval manor house, a skeleton was found in the early eighteenth century, seated at a table in a walled-off hidden chamber. Legend has it that this was Francis Lovell, left to die in his all-too-secret hiding place. As for Lambert Simnel, he was contemptuously assigned a job as scullion in the royal household, and on this note of derision passed out of history.

Not so the Yorkist cause of which this benighted lad was only the figurehead. Four years after Stoke, a more dangerous imposter made his appearance on the streets of Cork, claiming to be Richard of York, the younger of the two Little Princes done in by their uncle, King Richard III. His real name was Perkin Warbeck and for eight years he was the centerpiece of a truly serious Yorkist conspiracy against the Tudor succession. Warbeck's fantastic career is a case study of courtly intrigue in the Renaissance manner. This low-born fraud was cultivated by the Holy Roman Emperor, the archduke of Austria, and the king of Scotland before at last he ended his career on the scaffold after launching an abortive rebellion in Cornwall. In the wake of his conspiracy, however, three genuinely noble heads were to fall to the executioner's ax. The first was the poor earl of Warwick, innocent of any crime beyond being a nephew of King Edward IV and therefore a threat to the Tudor succession. The second, and not so innocent, was Sir William Stanley who had saved the day for Henry of Richmond at Bosworth but had since turned against the king and joined the Warbeck plot. The third was Edmund de la Pole, earl of Suffolk, another of Edward IV's nephews, who fled to the Emperor Maximilian's court in Vienna, was returned, imprisoned in the Tower, and in the following reign beheaded. His brother, the earl of Lincoln, had already been killed at Stoke; another brother, William, suffered life imprisonment in the Tower; and still another, Richard, died in exile, fighting for the king of France at Pavia in 1525. The Yorkist tree was slowly but inexorably being pruned away.

In this atmosphere of perennial conspiracy, it is no surprise that King

Henry saw fit to hire a personal bodyguard. Emulating the king of France, he retained a body of about two hundred armed men to protect his person against treachery. These were the Yeomen of the Guard, garbed in brilliant red and sometimes called buffetiers because, among their duties, was that of keeping watch over the king's plate when on display in cupboards around the royal table. In the next reign they would be largely restricted to guarding the **Tower of London** *(513)*, and there their lineal descendants can be seen today—the famous Beefeaters— their nickname as well as their splendid scarlet uniforms of Tudor origin.

Among the original body of yeomen was one David Seisyllt, an obscure Welshman who had joined Henry of Richmond's band of adventurers on their way to Bosworth. He was rewarded with lands in Northampton- shire and changed his name to Cecil; his son became a page in Henry VIII's court; his grandson, William Cecil, chief advisor to Queen Eliza- beth, was made Lord Burghley; his great-grandson became the earl of Salisbury under James I. Out of such stuff did the Tudors manufacture a new aristocracy to replace the "overmighty subjects" who had bedev- iled their Lancastrian and Yorkist predecessors. Another of Henry's Welsh henchmen who helped swell the ranks of his invading army was Rhys ap Thomas. He was richly rewarded with offices and manors in South Wales and became a notorious landgrabber. Among his new possessions was the ancient thirteenth century **Carew Castle** *(727)* in Pembrokeshire (Dyfed), to which he added the great hall with a splendid entrance tower. Here on St. George's Day 1507, this parvenu aristocrat, to advertise his new-won riches, put on a famous five-day tournament for the entertainment of six hundred guests. The king was not among them, but each day before the company sat down to dinner, his meal was served before an empty canopied chair with fanfares of trumpets for each course. It was a display of conspicuous waste that would have delighted Thorstein Veblen. The castle where this much-talked-of event took place is now a ruin, situated halfway between the towns of Tenby and Pem- broke in Dyfed. Another of Henry Tudor's companions-in-arms was the Cornishman Sir Richard Edgecombe who had been a fellow-exile in France. He too was knighted after Bosworth and otherwise substantially rewarded with offices and lands, especially in his native county. There he built **Cotehele House** *(589)*, a fortified manor house of granite still stand- ing above the west bank of the Tamar. The battlemented gatehouse dates from Sir Richard's time; the hall range from that of his son, Sir Piers. Today it can be classified as a charming stately home, replete with lavish furnishings, though mostly of a later date.

Reinforced by a new aristocracy of his own making, his rivals and his rebellious subjects mostly suppressed, Henry VII succeeded in the fore- most duty of a king: he survived. He survived, moreover, to found a dynasty that would preside over England's metamorphosis into a mod- ern nation-state, unified under a central government strong enough to maintain domestic peace and a fair degree of safety from foreign dangers. By Elizabeth of York he had four children who lived to maturity. His first-born was Arthur, so named to identify the house of Tudor with the most ancient of British national traditions. Arthur, Henry married to Catherine of Aragon, daughter of Ferdinand and Isabella, themselves the founders of the great new Spanish empire. The event was commemorated in a glorious stained glass window which was eventually installed in the Perpendicular church of **St. Margaret's Westminster** *(522)*, next door to the Abbey. When Arthur died, the alliance was maintained by betrothing the widowed Catherine to King Henry's second son and namesake. Before this marriage of in-laws could take place, a special papal bull of dispensation had to be obtained from Rome. Meanwhile, King Henry had married his daughter Margaret to James IV of Scotland and had betrothed his other daughter Mary to Archduke Charles of Austria who was destined to become Holy Roman Emperor (Charles V), although in fact the marriage fell through and Mary became briefly queen of France instead.

Thus, by skillful diplomacy, Henry was able to link his dynasty to some of the leading royal houses of Europe. And though he kept alive his inherited claim to the throne of France and even led an expedition across the Channel to lay siege to Boulogne, he was careful not to push the matter too far and quickly settled for a money payment from the French king, Charles VIII. The fact is that Henry VII was too sensible to waste his assets by renewing the Hundred Years War. Realizing that his Lancastrian forebears had been weak because they were poor, he spent sparingly and at the same time more than tripled the royal revenues. Indeed by medieval standards he was a financial wizard and his fiscal prudence earned him a widely held reputation for miserliness.

Yet in fact he was not stingy. He added six ships to the royal navy, including the *Regent* and the *Sovereign* which were the first to carry breechloading cannons and to engage in artillery duels at sea. He built the first naval dry dock at Portsmouth, which thenceforward became England's major naval base. He patronized and supported the voyages of John and Sebastian Cabot to the New World. He recommenced the building of Henry VI's chapel at **King's College** *(613)* in Cambridge, and though it was not completed in his lifetime, the fan vaulted porches, the buttress pinnacles, and the magnificent west window of that lovely Perpendicular masterpiece are standing testimony to the munificence of the first Tudor king. He conceived and carried through almost to completion that other gem of late Perpendicular architecture, the Chapel of Henry VII at the east end of **Westminster Abbey** *(523)* where he is buried. When he died on 21 April 1509 at the age of fifty-two, England lost the first true statesman to occupy her throne for at least two centuries; she would not gain another until his granddaughter Elizabeth succeeded to it.

HENRY VIII: 1509–1547

The new king was not quite eighteen when he ascended to the throne. Though his body had not yet achieved the girth portrayed in Holbein's design for a tapestry now hanging in the **National Portrait Gallery** *(518)*, London, the grandiosity of style so brilliantly captured by the artist was already very much in evidence. The sketch in question also includes a representation of Henry VII in the background and provides an interesting contrast between father and son. The former, garbed in a conservative full-length fur-lined robe, looks like a wise and seasoned judge. The latter, short skirted, a sword at his belt, his hands bejeweled, his well-turned legs prominently displayed, is the personification of a sixteenth century dandy. In neither case are looks deceiving. Henry VIII was a Renaissance prince: a patron of the arts and learning, an able linguist, well-versed in theology, a capable musician, a superb horseman, jouster, wrestler, and tennis-player. He was also inordinately willful, arrogant, immoderate in his appetites, wantonly cruel, paranoid, treacherous, moody, and erratic. One is driven almost to doubt his sanity. And yet, for all the pyrotechnics and bloody melodrama that disfigured his reign, it must be said that at the end of it both England and the monarchy were stronger than at the beginning.

At first the young king fancied himself a reincarnation of Henry V and was determined to resurrect the Hundred Years War. Egged on by his new father-in-law, King Ferdinand of Spain, he led an army across the Channel in 1513 and laid siege to the little town of Thérouanne. There he easily routed a small French reconaissance-in-force in a minor engagement that was blown all out of proportion as the Battle of the Spurs. He then took Tournai and went home, by which time an English army under Thomas Howard, earl of Surrey, had virtually massacred an invading Scottish force at Flodden Field in Northumberland just below the border at Coldstream. Among the nearly ten thousand slain was King James IV himself, Henry's own brother-in-law and the sixth of the Stuart dynasty to occupy the Scottish throne. Scotland now, and for most of the rest of Henry's reign, ceased to be a menace.

Flodden was a significant victory. Henry's expedition to France was merely expensive. Already he had used up a fair portion of the treasure so carefully hoarded by his father. His ambitions for martial glory, however, remained unsated. At a time when gunpowder had already rendered armored cavalry obsolete, he founded an armorers' workshop on the royal manor of Greenwich and imported German experts to supply a nonexistent need. Some of the products of this enterprise can still be seen in the Tudor Room of the White Tower in the **Tower of London** *(513)*. The Greenwich armor here can be distinguished from the more sophisticated Milanese and German specimens by the extra heavy pauldrons or shoulder guards, the two-piece elbow guards, and the concave visored helmets. It is unclear whether this unwieldy equipment was designed for real war or for knightly tournaments—a sport at which the king excelled. Indeed his most celebrated international triumph was at the Field of the Cloth of Gold, an extravagant tourney held in 1520 near Calais, where Henry asserted his manliness jousting and wrestling with Francis I, the new king of France. (Francis bested him in wrestling.)

A year later the English king signed a short-lived and unproductive treaty of alliance against France with his wife's nephew, Charles V. This young scion of the house of Hapsburg had been elected Holy Roman Emperor two years previously. More importantly the combined inheritance from both sides of his family included Spain, the Low Countries, part of western Germany, northern Italy, Austria, Bohemia, and Hungary. His only rival for complete domination of western and central Europe was the French royal house of Valois whose incursions into northern Italy threatened the Hapsburg hegemony at a vital spot. In the ensuing contest, in which the emperor eventually prevailed, England remained mostly on the sidelines. Here was an opportunity for the island nation to assume the role of Europe's power balancer which in later centuries she was to play with such success. Unfortunately Henry VIII's perception of the national interest was clouded. On the one hand his fixation on the ancient hereditary Anglo-French feud precluded his joining Francis I against the emperor; on the other he so alienated Charles V by divorcing the latter's aunt that an Anglo-Imperial league against France was for years out of the question. He was, moreover, a clumsy diplomat—both heavy-handed and erratic. Though a contemporary of Niccolo Machiavelli, Henry was no machiavellian—at least not in international affairs.

In domestic affairs, however, he was at least consistent in the pursuit of two major goals: (1) to eliminate all homegrown opposition, real or imagined, to his rule and (2) to ensure a peaceful succession by begetting a male heir. In the first he was successful. To achieve the second, he divorced his first wife and beheaded the second, seceded from the Roman Catholic church, and engineered a social revolution in Britain. The end result was a single son who survived him by a mere six years and never really reigned.

Twice during his reign the king delegated almost plenary powers to his chief ministers, first to Thomas Wolsey and later to Thomas Cromwell. Wolsey, son of an Ipswich butcher, fought his way up the ladder of ecclesiastical and royal preferment to become Archbishop of York, Cardinal Legate of England, and in 1515 the king's chancellor. He was as arrogant as his master and even more avaricious. Above all he was efficient, especially in the matter of enforcing law and order. In the court of the star chamber he rigorously punished crimes of force and fraud, especially those perpetrated by overmighty subjects; in the court of requests he offered poor men legal recourse against the exactions of their betters; in the council of the marches of Wales and the council of the north he curbed the endemic lawlessness of those two traditionally unruly regions. None of these measures pleased the ancient aristocracy of England, nor did the manners of the base-born upstart. When, however, Edward Stafford, duke of Buckingham, took steps to bring the haughty cardinal down, he came a cropper. Indeed, he lost his head upon the block, though not so much for his contemptuous treatment of Wolsey as for being a direct descendant of Edward III and therefore a threat to the Tudor dynasty. At the time of his execution Buckingham had not yet finished work on his splendid private palace of **Thornbury Castle** *(581)* north of Bristol. Only one of the four great towers he planned had reached full height by the time of his execution, and the three truncated towers to the left of the present entrance way are eloquent testimony to the abruptness of his demise. Wolsey's own palace at **Hampton Court** *(532)*, overlooking the Thames west of London, was even more magnificent—so much so that before it was completed the king took it off his hands. Under later sovereigns (especially William and Mary) the palace was much renovated and enlarged, but most of the western half of this great sprawling building dates from the occupancy of either Wolsey or Henry VIII. This is the side from which the palace is now entered and the Tudor portions of it include the bridge across the moat, the Base Court, Anne Boleyn's Gateway, the Clock Court, the King's Kitchen and the Tudor Kitchen, the Horn Room, the Wine and Beer Cellars, the Great Hall, the Great Watching Chamber, the Haunted Gallery, the Chapel, and Wolsey's Closet. Also the Pond Garden is laid out according to the original Tudor design and the tapestries in the Great Hall were installed by Henry VIII.

Wolsey's second great building venture was at Oxford where in 1525 he founded Cardinal College, financed out of the proceeds of a number of monastic houses suppressed with papal and royal permission. One of these was Canterbury College, founded in 1361 for monks from Christ Church, Canterbury, and on the site of which Wolsey decided to erect his own foundation. In doing so he pulled down the three west bays of the nave of the monastic church to make room for his main quadrangle, today called Tom Quad, on the south side of which stands the Cardinal's hall with its lovely hammer-beam roof. Further building was interrupted when Wolsey fell from grace in 1532. Patronage of the college was briefly assumed by King Henry who renamed it after himself. Still later, in 1546, after the half-destroyed monastic church had been restored, it was given cathedral status and the college was renamed **Christ Church** *(629)*. **Oxford Cathedral** *(629)*, which serves as the college's chapel, is today among England's smallest. What is left of the nave and the lower stages of the tower are Norman in architecture; the spire, lady chapel, and adjoining chapter house are Early English; and Wolsey's choir is Perpendicular with exquisite fan vaulting. In the library can be seen Cardinal Wolsey's hat, while over the great gate to the main college quadrangle, Tom Quad, stands his statue executed in 1719.

Wolsey's fall (the subject of Shakespeare's *King Henry VIII*), was the result of the failure of this mighty churchman to extort from the Pope an annulment of Henry's marriage to Queen Catherine of Aragon. It will be remembered that the union between the king and his late brother Arthur's widow had been made possible only by a papal bull of dispensation. In twenty years together, Catherine had borne him seven children, but none had survived for more than a few weeks except a single daughter, the princess Mary. The king, moreover, was five years younger than his wife and had a roving eye. When that eye settled on the dashing young brunette, Anne Boleyn, and when Anne declined seduction without matrimony, it was not hard for Henry to convince himself that Catherine's failure to produce a male heir was God's vengeance on an incestuous marriage which ought therefore be dissolved. To Cardinal Wolsey fell the task of persuading the Pope to retract the previous dispensation and declare the union void. Unfortunately, Pope Clement was now completely under the domination of the Emperor Charles V who refused to allow his aunt to be degraded and disgraced. Frustrated by the impasse, the king first sacked Wolsey and then had him arrested for treason. He would no doubt have been beheaded but for the fact that he conveniently died beforehand. Shakespeare succinctly summarized the tragedy of his life:

> Had I but served my God with half the zeal
> I served my king, he would not in mine age
> Have left me naked to mine enemies.
> —*King Henry VIII*, Act II, scene ii

As for Anne Boleyn, the king married her secretly in January 1533 a little more than seven months before the birth of their child—not the expected male heir, but the unwanted Princess Elizabeth. The following May a new Archbishop of Canterbury, Thomas Cranmer, pronounced the marriage with Anne valid and in July the Pope prepared, though did not execute, a sentence of excommunication of the king. Meanwhile, to reinforce the king's determination to have his way against the Pope's recalcitrance, a parliament was summoned. This Reformation Parliament sat for seven years, and, under the ministrations of a new chief minister, Thomas Cromwell, legalized the complete separation from Rome of the Church of England with King Henry as its supreme head. Catherine of Aragon was, of course, exiled from the court and sent to **Kimbolton Castle** *(618)*, Cambridgeshire, where she died in January 1536 to be buried in nearby **Peterborough Cathedral** *(618)*, where her much restored tomb can still be seen. She was preceded to the grave by John Fisher, Bishop of Rochester, and by Sir Thomas More, who, after succeeding Wolsey to the chancellorship, had resigned his post rather than associate himself with the king's inevitable breach with Rome. Fisher had courageously, if unsuccessfully, defended Queen Catherine's case in the divorce proceedings. More was the leading English humanist of his day and author of the famous tract, *Utopia*. Both were sent to the Tower for refusing to take the oath of succession which, failing a future male heir, would put Anne Boleyn's daughter on the throne of England. Both were executed on charges of treason for their refusal to acknowledge Henry as supreme head of the Church of England. They were soon followed to the block by Anne Boleyn herself, against whom trumped-up charges of adultery were brought, but whose real crime was her failure to produce a son. Four hundred years after the event Fisher and More would be canonized by a successor of the Pope for whose supremacy they had been martyred. For Anne Boleyn the verdict of history has been only pity.

All three were beheaded on Tower Hill, Fisher and More outside, Queen Anne inside, the **Tower of London** *(513)*. All were buried in the tiny royal chapel of St. Peter-ad-Vincula within the Tower grounds. This ancient fortress, in the reign of Henry VIII, ceased to be a royal residence, the Renaissance king preferring more elegant quarters up the river—at Westminster Palace to which he summoned his parliaments; at Whitehall (formerly York Place) which he confiscated from Wolsey; at **St. James's Palace** *(522)*, which he built in what is now London's West End; at his father's favorite Richmond Palace where he was born; at **Hampton Court Palace** *(532)* which he extracted from its builder, Wolsey; and at Nonsuch Palace in Cheam, long since demolished. The Tower itself remained (and would remain until the nineteenth century) the site of the royal mint, the royal armories, and the royal menagerie of wild and exotic beasts. But its chief fame resides in the fact that it was the prison, and often the site of execution, of a host of declared enemies of the state, many of them of royal and noble blood. The custom was well established before Henry VIII's reign; it became habitual during it. Among others, he all but finished off those few remote descendants of Edward III not yet exterminated by his father. The list included, besides the duke of Buckingham already mentioned, Sir Edward Neville; Henry Courtenay, the earl of Devon; Margaret, countess of Salisbury; her son Henry Pole, Lord Montague; and Edmund de la Pole, earl of Suffolk. The bloodstream of the Plantagenets was running dry.

After doing away with Anne Boleyn, Henry married Jane Seymour, who at last bore him the long-awaited son—Prince Edward. Soon afterwards she died, and for so well performing her queenly duty was buried in St. George's Chapel, **Windsor Castle** *(565)* in the vault which would a few years later receive the body of her royal husband. His next wife was Anne of Cleves, sister to a petty German duke, whose friendship Thomas Cromwell thought it wise to win for an otherwise isolated England. The artist Holbein was sent to the ducal court to paint her picture, and though the full-scale portrait now hangs in the Louvre, a miniature executed at the same time is on display at the **Victoria and Albert Museum** *(526)*. Holbein apparently flattered his subject, for Henry found her much too homely for his tastes and promptly had the marriage annulled. He also sent Cromwell to the block for perpetrating the mismatch. Anne, however, was merely pensioned off and lived out her life in peaceful retirement, mostly at **Hever Castle** *(544)*, Kent, where the king, ironically, had first cast a lecherous eye on Anne Boleyn. Next in line came Catherine Howard, niece of Thomas Howard, the victor of Flodden and now duke of Norfolk. (Another of his nieces had been Anne Boleyn.) Licentious before her marriage, Catherine turned adulterous after it, was exposed, and sent to the block on Tower Hill. The last of Henry's queens was Catherine Parr, born in the now ruined **Kendal Castle** *(712)*, Cumbria, and already twice widowed. She outlived the king, married again, and died in her bed. She is buried in the chapel adjoining **Sudeley Castle** *(642)* in Gloucestershire, the now much restored residence of her fourth husband, Thomas Seymour, himself a brother to the late Queen Jane and therefore uncle to the future King Edward VI.

Catherine Parr had strong Protestant leanings and may have been responsible for her stepson Prince Edward's being educated by radically Protestant tutors. For by now the winds of the Reformation were beginning to blow on England from the Continent. On 31 October 1517 Martin Luther, an Augustinian monk and professor of theology, had nailed to the main door of the castle church in Wittenberg his famous ninety-five theses denouncing the current papal practice of selling indulgences, i.e., blanket exemptions from the customary penances for sins, so as to raise money to build the new basilica of St. Peter's in Rome. Within three years Luther moved, or was driven, from a peripheral attack on what was generally acknowledged to be a minor, though serious, ecclesiastical abuse to a major challenge to the Pope's spiritual authority over Christendom. By 1520 he was charging the "Bishop of Rome" with being the Anti-Christ and vehemently urging the German princes of the Holy Roman Empire to cast off the Roman yoke and establish reformed Christian churches within their separate jurisdictions. Luther was, of course, excommunicated, but this did not prevent a number of these princes from protesting the emperor's prohibiting the establishment of independent churches. Thus came into being the word *protestant*. Meanwhile in Switzerland, Ulrich Zwingli, vicar of the leading church of Zurich, led a similar revolt and induced the city fathers there to break with Rome. Somewhat later, in Geneva, a refugee French lawyer named John Calvin carried the revolution even further and established a stern theocratic government which enforced a Protestant conformity by executing or banishing all dissidents.

Although the reformers differed bitterly among each other on what today seem to be minor points of church doctrine, they were agreed on certain fundamentals. First among these was their denial of the central Catholic doctrine that the Pope derived from St. Peter ultimate authority over the keys to the kingdom of heaven and that the church which he headed was endowed with the sole right of intercession between sinful man and almighty God. Against Rome's doctrine that man could be saved from eternal damnation only through good works, including sharing in the sacraments of the church, the Protestants maintained the doctrine of justification by faith, i.e., that man was saved by God's grace alone, bestowed on those who, by their faith in Christ as their personal savior, would be made worthy to receive this gift. From this fundamental Protestant premise, it followed that the Catholic church's chief sacrament, the Mass, was not only unnecessary, but a presumptuous and unholy abrogation of clerical authority. The Roman doctrine of transubstantiation, i.e., that a priest could transmute the bread and wine into the real body and blood of Christ and offer these elements to God as a sacrifice, was anathema to Protestants. (Luther believed in "consubstantiation," i.e., the Real Presence of Christ in the sacramental elements, but only by His own will and power and only to the true believer—not through the medium of the priestly rite of consecration. The Swiss and eventually most English reformers, held that Christ was spiritually, not physically, present in the bread and wine, and that the sacrament of the Mass was properly to be conceived as a Communion of the faithful merely commemorative of the Last Supper, not a reenactment of Christ's sacrifice on the cross.) Equally anathema to all good Protestants were such other priestly functions as taking auricular confession, assigning penance, and granting absolution, as well as such Romish doctrines and practices as prayers for souls in Purgatory, the adoration of the Virgin Mary and of the saints, the veneration of holy objects and pilgrimages to enshrined holy relics, and even the wearing of ornate vestments by ordained priests. Finally the exclusive use of Latin in church services and religious writings was condemned. The Bible, Protestants maintained, was the only ultimate source of spiritual authority and should be translated into the vernacular for all to read. For, in the true Church there was no clear distinction between clergy and laity; it was a priesthood of all believers.

In England similar ideas had been voiced by John Wycliffe more than a century before Luther. But Wycliffe's followers, the Lollards, had been brutally suppressed with fire and sword, and by the sixteenth century only occasionally did this heresy crop up. Anticlericalism, however, was widespread throughout the country. Perhaps it was for that reason that Lutheranism took early root at Cambridge University and thence spread out among certain humanist circles and even penetrated the royal court itself. Anne Boleyn and her entourage were thought to have been tainted, but, more important, Thomas Cranmer, the Archbishop of Canterbury, was deeply infected with the new heresy. Not Henry VIII, however. From the Pope himself he had won the title of Defender of the Faith for writing an anti-Lutheran tract of some scholarly merit. Henry's quarrel with Rome was juridical, not doctrinal. The Reformation came to England as a constitutional, not a theological, revolution. Or, to put it more simply, the Church of England seceded from the Church of Rome because the king could see no other way to bring about a divorce from his first wife who was past the age for bearing him a male heir. Still, the dike of orthodoxy, once pierced, was bound to spring more leaks. The king's personal doctrinal conservatism notwithstanding, Protestant sympathizers in high office—especially Cromwell and Cranmer—commenced undermining the foundations of the ancient faith. Images were removed from churches as idolatrous; holy relics were exposed as frauds; shrines were closed down and their rich furnishings confiscated; Thomas Becket was retroactively declared a traitor and pilgrimages to Canterbury forbidden. Most importantly the Bible was translated into English, although an act of 1542 tried to restrict its reading to clergymen, noblemen, gentlemen, and substantial merchants. In short, the new religious dispensation under Henry VIII was something more than Catholicism without the Pope.

The king's most radical move against the church (after the breach with Rome) was his dissolution of the monasteries. Here he was motivated purely by fiscal considerations. By the 1530s Henry's wars and other extravagances had driven him to a state of near bankruptcy, and Parliament was proving stingy in the matter of voting new taxation. There were in England and Wales some eight hundred religious houses which together owned perhaps as much as a third of all land in the kingdom as well as an untold quantity of movable wealth. Here was a tempting prize indeed to a greedy king and his ruthless first minister. In 1536 Cromwell persuaded Parliament to pass a bill to dissolve and confiscate the smaller monasteries, i.e., those with an annual income of less than two hundred pounds. While the Dissolution was in progress, rebellion broke out in Lincolnshire and spread to Yorkshire and neighboring counties in the conservative north. This so-called Pilgrimage of Grace was a violent reaction to the king's attacks on the church and it was violently put down. In its wake a number of abbots and priors were hanged, and those remaining took fright and voluntarily surrendered their houses to the king. By 1540 it was over: All monastic establishments great and small were now the property of the Crown.

Of the nine thousand religious men and women evicted, some were pensioned off, some became secular priests, and most were treated humanely, though there is no way of calculating the personal damage done to their lives by this radical disruption. Buildings and their contents fared less well. Royal commissioners were sent out to all the monasteries not converted into secular cathedrals or parish churches with orders to strip everything salable. Out came the rich treasuries of plate and jewels, the wooden screens, the stone statuary, the metal crucifixes; down came the tapestries, the leaded stained-glass windows, the bells; off came the roof lead to be melted into pigs in furnaces set up on the spot. Thus exposed to the elements and to the later looting of their building material, these once great religious houses quickly degenerated into the stark and stately ruins that still dot the countryside of Wales and England. Whether their romantic beauty in the eye of today's beholder compensates for this wholesale sacrilege is, of course, an aesthetic and moral question without answer.

In some cases, overzealous royal commissioners even tore down the walls of monastic churches and claustral buildings, perhaps on the principle that if the nests were destroyed the birds would never build again. In most instances, however, the buildings were sold with the land to private purchasers. A few were eventually converted by their new owners into dwelling places. Among the most interesting of these today is **Buckland Abbey** *(589)* south of Tavistock, Devon. It was sold in 1541 to Sir Richard Grenville who commenced building the house completed by his grandson and namesake, the famous Elizabethan seadog who in turn sold it to his fellow Devonian and rival adventurer, Sir Francis Drake. The Grenvilles tore down most of the claustral buildings of this once prospering Cistercian abbey and converted the church into a dwelling place. The younger Sir Richard installed his great hall in the center of church right under the square tower, inserted two floors above it, and, in the angle between the choir and the south transept, built a new wing to house the kitchen and domestic quarters. Over the fireplace he inscribed the date of his reconstruction, 1576, along with four figures representing Justice, Temperance, Prudence, and Fortitude, all sound Elizabethan virtues. Over another fireplace in an upper room of the tower are inscribed the arms of Sir Francis Drake. Of even greater architectural interest is **Lacock Abbey** *(572)* south of Chippenham, Wiltshire. Building on the site of a confiscated Augustinian abbey, which he bought in 1540, Sir William Sharrington kept the canons' lierne-vaulted cloister, their chapter house and warming room, but added an Italianate gallery and a polygonal corner-tower more or less in keeping with the new Renaissance fashions. **Forde Abbey** *(582)*, Dorset, a few miles east of Chard in Somerset, was another Cistercian establishment, sold to Richard Pollard, brother to one of the king's commissioners, who in turn sold it to a Devonshire knight, Sir Amias Paulet. The last of the abbots had constructed a magnificent gatehouse and great hall, and these became the nucleus of the still existing private residence with alteration made in the seventeenth century by the Edmund Prideaux, father and son. **Titchfield Abbey** *(558)*, a Premonstratensian house located a few miles west of Fareham, Hampshire, fell to Sir Thomas Wriothesley, Cromwell's secretary who survived his master's downfall and became secretary of state and lord chancellor under Henry VIII and, in the next reign, earl of Southampton. (His grandson, the third earl, was to achieve immortality as Shakespeare's patron.) The new owner converted the nave of the church into a gatehouse by demolishing the tower and transepts, rebuilding the walls of the central portion of the nave to rise a story higher than the original building, and converting both the western and eastern ends into apartments. Directly across the claustral garth (here north of the nave), he converted the monks' refectory into the great hall of his new residence, while the east and west ranges were modified for domestic uses. All is now in ruins, but Wriothesley's great gatehouse with its four battlemented corner towers is almost complete.

Beaulieu Abbey *(560)*, a Cistercian house near Lyndhurst, Hampshire, founded by King John was another of Wriothesley's purchases. Here the gatehouse became the nucleus of a great mansion called **Palace House** *(560)*. Remodeled in the nineteenth century, this much visited stately home still reveals elements of its sixteenth century construction in the twin gables, reception hall, drawing room, and private dining room. Of the surviving claustral buildings, the monks' refectory is now the parish church; the lay brothers' dorter is the site of an excellent and informative museum; and on the grounds is located, incongruously but not offensively so, a new building housing the **National Motor Museum** *(560)*, the best collection of antique automobiles in England. Also in Hampshire, near Romsey, is **Mottisfont Abbey** *(562)*, a former Augustinian priory converted into a private house by Henry VIII's lord chamberlain, Sir William Sandys. Here, as at Buckland, the nave of the church became part of the new owner's residential quarters. A different sort of fate befell Waverley Abbey, the first of England's Cistercian houses. From here, where so little remains today *in situ*, the building stones were mostly carted away to form the structural basis of **Losely House** *(556)* near Guildford, Surrey. In Suffolk, near Bury St. Edmunds, **Ixworth Abbey** *(602)* is a stately home which owes its origins to an Augustinian priory whose dormitory undercroft, prior's lodging, and frater were all incorporated into the new building. In the Midlands, another Augustinian priory near Nottingham suffered the same fate. This was **Newstead Abbey** *(659)*, better known today for its brief occupancy by the poet Byron than for its medieval associations. Here the west front of the priory church has been preserved in a semiruined condition, while the claustral buildings were incorporated into the now much remodeled residence.

A final example of monastic conversion is **Fountains Hall** *(687)*, southwest of Ripon, North Yorkshire. On the dissolution of the huge Cistercian abbey of Fountains, the property first passed to the great London merchant family of Gresham by whom it was eventually sold to Sir Stephen Proctor, son of a Yorkshire ironmaster. It was he who built in 1611 the present handsome stone mansion with its typically Jacobean facade of perfect Renaissance symmetry, its stepped gables, and its ample windows. Fortunately for today's traveller, Sir Stephen spared the great abbey church whose ruins still stand high in the fields below his still stately home. He quarried his building stones from the lay brothers' infirmary, the abbot's lodging, and the monks' hospital, leaving undisturbed what is today the most impressive monastic ruin in northern England.

This short list of beneficiaries of the Dissolution is representative. Most of the property was sold by the court of augmentations set up especially to administer its disposition. The first purchasers fall into three main groups: country gentry like the Grenvilles, individual courtiers in high favor like Wriothesley, and London merchants like the Greshams. But with such a gigantic transfer of real estate and so many sales and resales, there was bound to be wider distribution of landholding than had previously obtained and an expansion of the total number of landholders. Thus the king created a widespread vested interest in his religious settlement which would stand firm against the forces of reaction. He also achieved his major objective, which was to save himself from financial disaster. Between 1536 and 1547 the average annual net receipt of the court of augmentations was more than twice the normal revenues of the previous years. As a financial expedient, the Dissolution was a success.

It came, moreover, not a moment too soon to meet England's urgent requirements of national defense. At Nice in June 1538 Charles V and Francis I signed a ten-year truce; six months later Pope Paul at last pronounced the bull of excommunication against the king of England and dispatched the refugee English prelate Reginald Pole to rally the Catholic powers of Europe against the royal heretic. In January 1539 Charles and Francis signed an anti-English pact at Toledo. The country was promptly seized with a war panic and the government diverted most of its newly gained revenue to the hasty construction of a string of more than twenty coastal fortresses stretching from the mouth of the Medway around the southeast corner of England and along the south coast as far west as Cornwall. The scheme was reminiscent of the ancient Roman fortifications of the Saxon Shore and anticipated the much more closely spaced Martello Towers of the Napoleonic wars. Though these buildings are called castles, the name is a misnomer. They were forts, not fortified residences, though naturally they contained living space for garrisons. They were probably mostly designed by Stefan von Haschenperg, a German military engineer employed by Henry between 1539 and 1543 and they appear to have been modeled on the defenses of Antwerp built according to plans drawn by Albrecht Dürer. The basic layout was a round central tower of two or three stories, surrounded by lower circular or semicircular bastions protected by an enclosing ditch and perhaps by an outer curtain wall. Long-range artillery was to be mounted on the reinforced roofs of both central tower and bastions, while smaller weapons could be fired through numerous gunports on the lower levels. Defenses of this type were already out of date in Italy. There, engineers were encasing their fortifications with triangular or arrowhead bastions which had the advantage of permitting enfilade fire along the straight walls of their buildings, thus guarding against a close approach by attacking troops. Military historians have therefore tended to scoff at Henry's "castles" for being already obsolete at the time of their construction. On the other hand, their rounded contours were well designed to deflect low-velocity cannon balls fired from attacking ships, and for this purpose they may have been more appropriate than the more angular fortifications of contemporary Italy. In the event, they were never put to the test because the invasion threat of 1539 evaporated.

The first, the largest, the most complex, and the best preserved of them all is **Deal Castle** *(285)*, Kent, one of three put up to guard the Downs— that stretch of water between the Kentish coast and the Goodwin Sands which contained the best anchorage on the English side of the Channel at its narrowest point. (It is not to be confused with that large section of southeastern England between the lower Thames and the south coast called the North and South Downs.) Deal consists of a round central tower, surrounded by six slightly lower semicircular bastions, in turn surrounded by a still lower curtain wall also with six semicircular bastions, in turn enclosed by a stone moat abut 250 feet wide and 16 feet deep. In addition to the three tiers of artillery platforms provided by the roofs and central tower and bastions, the walls of Deal were pierced by no less than 145 gunports for weapons of lesser caliber. **Walmer Castle** *(540)* a few miles south along the coast, was built on the same principle, though to a smaller scale. It is quatrefoil in plan, the single round central tower being surrounded by four bastions, in turn enclosed by a moat. Unlike Deal, the original building has been much renovated and enlarged so as to serve as the official residence of the lords warden of the Cinque Ports. The last of the trio was nearby Sandown Castle, but the sea has so encroached on the site that today there is little left to be seen.

At **Dover Castle** *(541)*, farther south, the only significant feature added by Henry VIII to the already powerful fortress was the so-called Tudor Bulwark at the southern extremity of the curtain wall. There is, however, near the present entrance another interesting relic of his reign—a twenty-four-foot bronze cannon given him by the Emperor Charles V during one of their brief periods of amity. Bypassing Sandgate Castle near Folkstone, now a private house, and Camber Castle, near Rye, East Sussex, which is in so ruined a condition as to be unsafe to visit, we come to the Solent and the mouth of Southampton Harbor, Hampshire, where **Calshot Castle** *(562)* stands guard. On the grounds of a coast guard station this circular blockhouse with a surrounding gun platform is in the process of restoration by the Department of the Environment. At the southwest entrance to the Solent, near Lymington, Hampshire, is the more elaborate **Hurst Castle** *(559)*, originally a twelve-sided central tower surrounded by three large semicircular bastions. Built in 1544, it served briefly as King Charles's prison during the Civil War, as a coastal artillery-station in World War I, and an antiaircraft battery in World War II.

Leapfrogging now to Cornwall the traveller arrives at the twin castles of **St. Mawes** *(591)* and **Pendennis** *(591)*, guarding, respectively, the east and west sides of the entrance to Carrick Roads at Falmouth. Begun in 1540, St. Mawes consists of a huge central circular tower surrounded by three semicircular bastions in a trefoil arrangement. Over the main entrance way is a carved panel of the royal arms, the leopards of England quartered by French lilies and supported by the Tudor lion and dragon with the motto *DIEU ET MON DROIT* below. At various places around the building are carved Latin inscriptions honoring Henry VIII and his only son, e.g., *SEMPER HONOS HENRICE TUUS LAUDESQUE MANEBUNT*, "Henry, thy honor and praises will remain forever," and *EDWARDUS FAMA REFERAT FACTISQUE PAREN-TEM*, "May Edward resemble his father in fame and deeds." Across the harbor stands Pendennis, its three hundred-foot circular tower surrounded by a curtain wall and over its gatehouse another bas-relief of the Tudor arms. To Queen Elizabeth's reign belongs the outer rectangular curtain with its then up-to-date angle bastions, and to a still later date (1611) the huge Italianate gatehouse.

Under Henry VIII, the Channel Islands, too, were reinforced against the ever present threat of French attack. The governor of **Castle Cornet** *(745)*, St. Peter Port, Guernsey, under orders to modernize his ancient stronghold, built the bastion and artillery emplacement called Mewtis Bulwark. At the same time **Gorey (Mont Orgueil) Castle** *(744)*, Jersey, was strengthened by the addition of Somerset Tower, named after the island's governor, Edward Seymour, later duke of Somerset.

The years 1539 and 1540 passed without an invasion after all, and 1541 saw the king of France and the emperor at war again with each other. Henry now felt free to turn his attention to Scotland, where King James V had died in November 1542, leaving the throne to his daughter Mary then less than a week old. Intent on getting custody of the infant queen and eventually marrying her to his son, the English king launched a series of brutal raids against his northern neighbor, known in Scottish tradition as the Rough Wooing. His efforts succeeded only in driving Scotland back into the arms of France, with a renewal of the "Auld Alliance." Henry meanwhile signed a new treaty with the emperor and in the summer of 1544 sailed for France with an expeditionary force which succeeded in capturing Boulogne. The emperor then backed out of the treaty, leaving England again isolated. Once again the country prepared for an invasion. Edward Seymour stood at the head of an army on the Scottish borders, and in the south three armies of over thirty thousand were drawn up. Near Portsmouth the new fortress of **Southsea Castle** *(560)* was hastily erected. Unlike the earlier coastal forts, this was a square keep within a diamond, with two large triangular salients for added protection—an angle bastion fort designed in the Italian manner. Its guns were soon to be put to use when a French fleet of two hundred ships sailed into the Solent in the summer of 1545. An enemy landing party succeeded in getting ashore on the Isle of Wight, withdrew after twenty-four hours, landed again at Seaford in East Sussex, and withdrew again to sail for home.

Freed from the most serious threat that England had known for generations or would know again until the arrival of the Spanish Armada, Henry could now devote all his military efforts to subduing Scotland. The

Rough Wooing continued, but to no avail beyond leaving a long-lasting legacy of hatred for the Sassenach. The match between Mary Stuart and Prince Edward never took place.

Henry had better luck with Wales, the land of his Tudor forebears. By the so-called Acts of Union of 1536 and 1543 and subsequent enabling legislation, Wales was at last fully incorporated into England. The act dissolved the marcher lordships, annexed some of them to existing Welsh and English counties and created five new counties. Wales was now entitled to send twenty-four members to the House of Commons. English courts and English organs of local government were transplanted *in toto* into Wales. The official language was to be English, although in fact the ancient native tongue persisted, its survival guaranteed by the translation of the Bible into Welsh by a Denbighshire vicar and future bishop, William Morgan. (His birthplace, a remote farmhouse called **Ty Mawr** [736] just south of Betws-y-Coed, Gwynned, is today a minor Welsh national shrine.) Welsh nationalists in the twentieth century might deplore the settlement and strive mightily to undo it, but the fact is that the Acts of Union brought to Wales a degree of domestic peace it had never known.

By and large the same was true of England. After the brutal suppression of the Pilgrimage of Grace, there were no more serious civil disturbances in Henry's reign. Under Wolsey and Cromwell the power and reach of the central government achieved a new high-water mark. In the counties the justices of the peace—appointees of the Crown—brought new rigor to the enforcement of law and order. The once fractious nobility were permanently curbed and those who escaped the ax were mostly tamed into mere courtiers. Bishops and abbots could no longer challenge or evade royal authority. And all this the king accomplished with the cooperation and encouragement of Parliament, and especially of the House of Commons, which in his reign acquired full status as partner of the Crown.

King Henry VIII died on 28 January 1547 in the fifty-sixth year of his life and the thirty-eighth of his reign. By now his once athletic body had become obese, his legs were painfully ulcerated, and he was subject to frequent bouts of fever. Shortly after his death Requiem Mass was offered in every church in the land for the dead king's soul. The dying king himself had so arranged it. Soon, however, there would be no masses offered anywhere in England.

EDWARD VI: 1547–1553 AND MARY TUDOR: 1553–1558

English historians tend to look upon the brief reigns of Edward VI and his elder sister Mary as an embarrassing interlude between the high drama of Henry VIII and the triumphant glory of Queen Elizabeth I. In this short period England won a war but lost a peace in Scotland, surrendered all her remaining possessions in France, and for a while became virtually a satellite of Spain. More deplorably still, the country was wracked with religious dissension; abstract ideologies displaced common sense; and doctrinal orthodoxy took precedence over both domestic tranquillity and national security. These were years dominated by a most un-English approach to the affairs of state.

Edward VI was only nine years old at the time of his father's death, and, thanks to the radical Protestant tutors into whose hands the old king had inexplicably placed his education, was already a religious bigot. His uncle, Edward Seymour, earl of Hertford and duke of Somerset, was named lord protector. In keeping with the policies of the previous reign, he invaded Scotland, routed the Scots at the Battle of Pinkie, and occupied their capital, only to drive that unconquerable nation back into the arms of France. The young heiress to the Scottish throne, Mary Stuart, escaped across the Channel and married the Dauphin—who was to become King Francis II. A French army then occupied the port of Leith, and the English evacuated Edinburgh and their other Scottish outposts. Within a short time they were also compelled to surrender Boulogne. In the wake of all these misfortunes, Somerset fell victim to a palace coup and was replaced as protector by John Dudley, earl of Warwick and duke of Northumberland.

Under both protectors, and with the active encouragement of the boy-king, England moved steadily toward Protestantism. Influenced by immigrant reformers inspired chiefly by Zwingli and Calvin, the Archbishop of Canterbury, Thomas Cranmer, engineered a complete doctrinal break with Rome. The enduring monument to his endeavors is to be found today in the pew-racks of any Anglican church in England or Wales and, until recently, in those of the Protestant Episcopal church of the United States. This is the great *Book of Common Prayer.* In spite of revisions made in 1559, 1662, and 1928, it remains essentially as Cranmer wrote it. Only Shakespeare could match the splendid sonority of the archbishop's magnificent prose:

> Almighty and most merciful Father; We have erred, and strayed from thy ways like lost sheep. We have followed too much the devices and desires of our own hearts. We have offended against thy holy laws. We have left undone those things which we ought to have done; And we have done those things which we ought not to have done; And there is no health in us. . . .

Americans of the Episcopalian persuasion, deprived of Cranmer's moving lines by the substitution in their own church of a diluted version, may now go to England for services in the traditional style. They had best be quick about it, however, as the Church of England has recently issued an Alternative Service Book which promises to lead that venerable institution down the slippery American path to banality.

Theologically, the Church of England became, in Edward VI's reign, unmistakably Protestant. The Forty-Two Articles of Religion passed by Parliament in 1552 expressly declared the Church of Rome to be in error; rejected "the Romish doctrine concerning Purgatory"; outlawed services in any "tongue not understanded of the people" (i.e., Latin); condemned adoration of images and relics and invocation of the saints as "a fond thing, vainly invented"; denounced sacrifices of the Mass "as blasphemous fables"; denied the doctrine of transubstantiation; and removed all restrictions on the right of the clergy to marry. The Articles proclaimed the sufficiency of Holy Scriptures as containing "all things necessary for salvation"; established the doctrine of justification by faith alone irrespective of good works; and affirmed the doctrine of predestination. This was the belief, espoused by Calvin though not by Luther, that salvation was accorded only to those elected by God "before the foundations of the world were laid" to receive His grace. Although slightly modified in Elizabeth's reign by the Thirty-Nine Articles of 1559, the Act of 1552 clearly established the Church of England as Protestant. In doctrine, at least, this was not a *via media* between Rome and Geneva as Anglicans sometimes claim. It was the work of radical reformers, followers of Zwingli and Calvin, and, as such, was completely antithetical to the fundamental principles of Roman Catholicism.

Radical as these changes were, however, their impact on the structure and internal arrangements of the churches themselves is hard to discern today. Almost no new churches were built during the Tudor period. Medieval churches, of which there were more than enough, were instead converted to the new Anglican order of worship. First to be demolished or removed were the stone altars, those monuments to the Catholic doctrine of the Mass as sacrifice. In their place Communion tables, "the Lord's boards," were set up, usually in an east-west, i.e., lengthwise, direction near the front of the chancel or in the nave itself. There the laity could foregather to partake of the Communion in both kinds, i.e., both bread and wine, as an act commemorating Christ's sacrifice. Next were the chantries, their altars and parclose screens torn down to signify an end to the doctrine of Purgatory and to soul masses said there for the dead. In the empty spaces thus created, pews were installed—high-sided boxlike furnishings very unlike our modern low-backed bench pews. If a medieval church were without a pulpit, it now received one. Here the priest-turned-minister read the morning and evening services ordained by Cranmer's prayerbook and here he delivered sermons and homilies derived from Holy Scripture, now the sole source of spiritual authority. Down came the rood, the crucifix flanked by images of the Virgin Mary and St. John; down also, the rood loft and the tympanum behind it with its painting of the Doom or Last Judgment. The chancel screen under it, however, for a while remained, though the laity were no longer excluded from the chancel itself for purposes of taking Communion. Off went the wall paintings—whitewashed over as unwanted relics of popish superstition. Out came the stone statues of saints and of the Virgin Mary, though funereal statuary was mostly left untouched and still is much in evidence. Finally to be removed or destroyed were many of the stained-glass windows, though most of the damage done to these priceless and beautiful objects of medieval art was committed later by Puritans in the reign of Charles I. The net result of the Edwardian Reformation then was to rob the church interiors of England and Wales of most of their color and much of their statuary art, both good and bad. It did not, however, convert them into their present appearance. That was mostly the work of Victorian restoration—more bad than good. Neither did the reformers much alter the basic architecture of the church buildings themselves; here the medieval heritage was mostly left untouched.

The Reformation itself came to a temporary halt with the death of the king who had made it possible. Edward VI, always sickly, died in July 1553 at the age of fifteen. Just before his demise, Northumberland had persuaded the royal youth to will his crown to his cousin Lady Jane Grey, granddaughter to Henry VIII's youngest sister and, more significantly, daughter-in-law of the lord protector himself. Northumberland's purposes were clear: to protect his own ascendancy and to prevent a return to Catholicism under the legitimate heir, Henry VIII's eldest daughter Mary, who had remained firm in her allegiance to the old faith. In any event, the plot failed. Mary escaped to **Framlingham Castle** *(602)* in Suffolk, and thence made a triumphal entry into London where she was enthusiastically crowned queen. At this stage the English were more loyal to the principle of legitimacy than to the doctrines of the Reformation. The new queen herself would bring about a reversal of their attitudes.

Two months after her accession to the throne, Mary Tudor announced her intention to marry the Emperor Charles V's son and heir who would soon become King Philip II of Spain. This touched off a xenophobic revolt, led by one Sir Thomas Wyatt, which accomplished nothing beyond sending Lady Jane Grey to the executioner's block at the age of seventeen—an innocent victim of her father-in-law's ambitions and her fellow countrymen's fear of the proposed Spanish marriage. In any case, Mary and Philip were married in **Winchester Cathedral** *(563)* in July 1554, and the following November Cardinal Reginald Pole arrived as the papal legate to receive England back into the Roman communion. Parliament cooperated. All the antipapal and antichurch legislation passed since 1529 was repealed; the old heresy laws were reenacted; the Reformation was dead. But Parliament also made clear that nothing in these acts was to be construed to authorize the return of any significant amount of confiscated church property, which had by now been widely distributed among the nobility, gentry, and merchants of England—all well represented at Westminster. Salvation was not to be bought at the expense of property rights.

The new queen—now thirty-seven years of age—was passionately devoted to the Catholic faith and to her Spanish husband. In both respects she was at odds with the predominantly secular and nationalistic temper of her father and of her sister Elizabeth who would succeed her. Her first duty as she saw it, was to restore England to the bosom of Rome. To accomplish this required the forceful elimination of heresy and this in turn required the death of all discoverable heretics—preferably in the approved medieval manner of public burning at the stake. With impeccable logic, reinforced by the urgings of Pole and her Spanish confessors, she proceeded first against the high churchmen who had led the country down the path to perdition. Hugh Latimer, Bishop of Gloucester, and Nicholas Ridley, Bishop of London, were burned in a ditch outside the walls of Oxford, the occasion made forever memorable in Protestant annals by Latimer's dying words: "We shall this day light such a candle, by God's grace, in England as shall never be put out." Archbishop Cranmer was tried at **St. Mary's Church** (636), Oxford, and there he was returned, after two abject recantations, before the final *auto da fé*. To the assembled crowd he surprisingly apologized for his earlier timidity and promised that the hand that had penned the recantations would be the first to feel the fire. Not far away today stands the **Martyrs' Memorial** (636) in front of Balliol College near the spot where Cranmer, hand and all, was committed to the flames.

Altogether, almost three hundred Protestants were burned. The greatest number were from London and the Home Counties—laymen mostly who met their death at Smithfield. About sixty were women, and a fair number were teenagers. Most were people of low degree, a fact which was especially disturbing to contemporary Englishmen who might enjoy the occasional public execution of a great nobleman but were filled with fear when a similar fate was meted out to humble folk just like themselves. In any case, the Marian persecutions were in the long run counterproductive. The fires of Smithfield and such places served chiefly to ignite a bitter and bigoted anti-Catholicism which pervaded English society for at least two hundred years. This sentiment was kept alive by the publication in 1563 of John Foxe's *Book of Martyrs* (the *Acts and Monuments*), a Protestant hagiography that was to be a best seller in England and New England until well into the nineteenth century. Mary Tudor's name went down in history as Bloody Mary—a sad fate for a sincere and kindly woman whose major sin was her undeviating consistency.

The queen died in November 1558, full of sorrow and disappointment. She had failed to produce an heir to the English throne; she had sent an army to France to support her husband's war against the Valois king and for her pains had succeeded only in losing Calais to the French; her adored husband had deserted her to look after his own affairs on the Continent; her treasury was empty; her subjects restive. "When I die," she is reported to have said, "the name Calais will be found graven on my heart." Actually the loss of that last English outpost on the Continent was probably the only enduring benefit Queen Mary conferred on her kingdom. The ghost of the Hundred Years War could now be laid. England need no longer be saddled with this ancient liability. Her insularity was now assured, and in it she would find her greatest strength.

ELIZABETH I: 1558–1603

When they brought her the news of her elder sister's death, the princess Elizabeth was staying at the old **Palace** *(620)* on the grounds of the present **Hatfield House** *(620)* in Hertfordshire. This red-brick building had been erected in the late fifteenth century by the bishop of Ely and at the time of the dissolution of the religious houses given to Henry VIII. Most of the palace was later to be torn down by Robert Cecil, first earl of Salisbury, to build his sumptuous country house at Hatfield, but the still-standing great hall with its lofty open timber roof is a worthy relic of the quarters occupied by Elizabeth. Although legally bastardized by the annulment of the marriage between Henry VIII and Anne Boleyn, Elizabeth, as a child and adolescent, had lived in state at Hatfield and other royal palaces where she had received the best possible education at the hands of Cambridge tutors famous for their humanistic learning. She spoke French and Italian fluently, read Latin with ease and Greek moderately well. Unlike her brother, Edward, however, she was no pedant, nor was she a religious fanatic, in spite of having been exposed to the same radical Protestantism then fashionable at Cambridge University. This is just as well, since during her sister's reign, she had been briefly imprisoned in the Tower on suspicion of complicity with Wyatt's rebellion, and had escaped execution probably as a result of her success in feigning conversion to Catholicism.

She was twenty-five when she ascended to the throne in November 1558—a moderately tall woman, her hair golden with touches of red, her carriage erect, her mind quick, her dominant characteristics: prudence, skepticism, courage, and singleness of purpose. Given her detachment from the raging doctrinal controversies of the day and her predominantly secular views on religious matters, it is not surprising that the Elizabethan church settlement should have been a compromise. The Act of Uniformity of 1559 retained Cranmer's prayerbook, though with enough changes to satisfy the consciences of those traditionalists who resented the complete doctrinal break with Catholicism. The earlier explicit denial of the Real Presence in the eucharistic bread and wine was removed, and the substituted words were sufficiently ambiguous to permit a wide variety of beliefs on the exact nature of the Communion rite, short of transubstantiation. But altars were still taboo, Communion tables were ordered to be placed so as to allow convenient access to the laity, the work of destruction of "superstitious" images within the churches was continued, and the new Thirty-Nine Articles of Religion (which remain the approved doctrine of the Church of England and of the Protestant Episcopal church of the United States) retained most of the forty-two articles ordained in the reign of Edward VI. On the other hand the pre-1552 clerical vestments were reinstated, and, superficially at least, Anglican services retained some of the liturgical ceremony and ritual commonly associated with the Church of Rome. Certainly the Elizabethan settlement did not satisfy the radical wing of the Protestant party which became more and more vociferous throughout her reign, especially in the House of Commons, and which assumed increasing cohesiveness under the banner of Puritanism, i.e., the movement to purify the Church of England of all residual papist elements. On the other hand, devout Catholics were equally or more offended, and in time took to boycotting Church of England services altogether—from which practice they earned the name recusants (from the Latin *recusare*, meaning "to refuse"). Clearly the recusants had a greater grievance than did the Puritans, for doctrinally, the Elizabethan church was un-mistakably Protestant with a strong Calvinist coloration, and the Pope was doing no more than his duty when, in 1570, he excommunicated the queen who, by Parliamentary decree, was its "supreme governor."

Not religion, however, but reasons of state guided Elizabeth's policy both in domestic and foreign affairs. Like her principal secretary and mainstay Sir William Cecil (later Lord Burghley), she was above all things a realist. Her single objective was to establish and maintain her throne and her kingdom against her and England's many foes, domestic and foreign. In pursuit of that end she was tricky, devious, and on occasion ruthless—in short a model Renaissance prince in the approved Ma-chiavellian style. Unlike her father she allowed neither personal vanity nor lust to warp her single-minded concern for national security. Once, early in her reign, she fell in love with Robert Dudley, earl of Leicester; but when Dudley's wife, Amy Robsart, died in circumstances suggesting political murder, the queen, to protect her own reputation, set aside the thought of marriage. It was probably at this time that she decided never to marry, though throughout her reign she cleverly played the game of marital diplomacy, dangling the royal hand first before one foreign suitor, and then another, always with a view to promoting England's interest in the treacherous game of international politics. To the end she remained the Virgin Queen, aware that marriage to an English noble-man would precipitate factional strife at home while giving herself to a foreign prince would subordinate England's interests to those of another nation.

On her accession to the throne, the country's foreign policy was in disarray, its treasury empty, its credit gone, its military establishment disorganized. The most immediate threat to England's security came from France and Scotland. In 1559 Mary Stuart, Queen of Scotland, and next in succession to the English throne by virtue of being the sole surviving grandchild of Margaret Tudor, became queen of France on the accession to the throne of her husband Francis II. Her mother, Mary of Guise, was regent of Scotland, and French troops still occupied the port of Leith. The dangers of a joint Franco-Scottish attack on England were growing acute when there suddenly erupted in Scotland a Protestant revolution, spurred on by the provocative preaching of the radical Calvinist, John Knox. Elizabeth and Cecil acted quickly. Troops and ships were sent to besiege the French at Leith; Mary of Guise died; Cecil arrived to negotiate the Treaty of Edinburgh by which the French troops were expelled; and the government of Scotland passed into the hands of a group of Protestant lords. Meanwhile, Sir Richard Lee, England's leading military architect, was dispatched to Berwick-on-Tweed to strengthen its fortifications against the possibility of invasion from the north. There he began building the still extant **Berwick Ramparts** *(705)* to cover the eastern and northern sides of this important border city. Unlike Henry VIII's circular coastal forts, Lee's defenses were up to date in the manner of the most advanced engineering techniques developed in Italy over the previous half century. The main feature of the new style was the angle bastion, a massive triangular or arrowhead projection of earth and stone, placed at the corners and midway along the walls of fortifications so as to permit enfilade (flanking) fire along the axis of the walls and thus protect them from assault. At Berwick five of these bastions were put up, three at the corners and two along the sides. They remain today the most impressive and best preserved artillery fortifications in Britain. They proved, however, unnecessary. Mary Stuart's folly was to prove a far better safeguard to England's security than the best gun emplacements money could buy.

In December King Francis II of France died at the age of seventeen; less than a year later his widow returned to her native Scotland to claim her patrimony, the throne. Not quite nineteen years of age, Mary Queen of Scots was tall, dark of eye and hair, vivacious, clever, well-schooled in music, dancing, and horsemanship, though not so well in book learning. She was a bold, decisive woman, highly sexed, self-willed, impatient, and above all impetuous. On her arrival, however, she behaved with circumspection, promised liberty of worship for all, and, though herself a devout Catholic, seemed to accept ungrudgingly the domination of the Protestant lords and even personally submitted to the impudence of the evangelist John Knox who had labeled her mother's regime monstrous. Prudence, however, was foreign to her nature. In 1565 she married her cousin Henry Stuart, Lord Darnley, a vain and reckless youth of whom she quickly tired. Stung by her indifference, Darnley joined a group of Protestant lords in the butchery of the queen's new favorite, David Riccio, an Italian musician in her court. The murder took place in Holyrood Palace in the queen's presence under circumstances suggesting the assassins' intention to cause her to miscarry Darnley's unborn child. That part of the plot failed and in June, Prince James was born in Edinburgh Castle. Eight months later Darnley was strangled at Kirk O'Field in

Edinburgh and the house where he had been convalescing from a bout of syphilis was blown up with gunpowder. Whether the queen herself was a party to the murder plot is extremely doubtful, but inevitably the finger of suspicion pointed in her direction when she promptly eloped and married one of the murderers, James Hepburn, earl of Bothwell, a truculent Scottish baron of ill repute. Accused of being both an adulteress and a murderer, Mary was seized by a cabal of Protestant lords, forced to abdicate in favor of her infant son who was crowned James VI, and imprisoned in the island castle of Loch Leven in Fife. Escaping from this stronghold in May 1565, the Queen of Scots made her way into the southwest of Scotland, but there, at Langside, saw her meager army routed. Her cause in ruins, the royal fugitive barely managed to elude her enemies, and, not daring to wait for passage to France, sailed across the Solway Firth to throw herself on the mercy of her cousin, the queen of England.

With Scotland now in the hands of a Protestant regency and its half-French Catholic queen safely incarcerated in **Carlisle Castle** *(709)*, England had no more to fear from its traditional northern enemy. But like all political solutions, this one too generated problems of equal if not greater complexity. What to do? Obviously the English could not force an unwanted queen upon the Scots and anyway had no interest in trying to. If allowed transit to France, Mary might well become the spearhead of a French attack on both Scotland and England. Left alone in England, with her inherited claim to succession to the throne, she would inevitably be the focal point of plots to assassinate Elizabeth, unleash civil war, and forcibly return the country to the sway of Rome. The very real fear of such developments was reinforced by the outbreak of a Catholic rebellion in the northern counties in the summer of 1569, by the publication in 1570 of a papal bull excommunicating Elizabeth and releasing her Catholic subjects from allegiance to her, by the bloody massacre of French Huguenots (Protestants) on St. Bartholomew's Eve 23 August 1572, by the assassination of the Dutch Protestant leader, William of Orange, ten years later, and by the successful infiltration of scores of Catholic missionaries from the English seminary in Douai and from the Jesuit seminary in Rome. Death to the royal fugitive or imprisonment for life seemed to loyal Protestant Englishmen the only possible solutions, and since Elizabeth was loath to execute a fellow queen and kinswoman, Mary Queen of Scots was to live out the remaining nineteen years of her life in durance vile. And for nineteen years Queen Elizabeth lived in the shadow of her prisoner.

From Carlisle, Mary was moved to **Bolton Castle** *(685)* in North Yorkshire, less dangerously close to the Scottish border, then a hundred miles still farther south to **Tutbury Castle** *(666)* in Staffordshire. In these ancient, decrepit, and drafty quarters, which Mary loathed above all her prisons, she made the acquaintance of her jailor for the next fifteen years —the earl of Shrewsbury and his harridan wife, Bess of Hardwick, who entertained the Queen of Scots with malicious gossip about the English court while the two worked jointly on the embroideries still to be seen at **Hardwick Hall** *(622)* in Derbyshire and **Oxburgh Hall** *(609)* in Norfolk. All castles required periodic cleansing—washing down the stone walls and sweeping out the vermin-infested rushes that served in lieu of carpets. During periods of housecleaning, Mary was removed to Shrewsbury's now ruined **Wingfield Manor** *(664)* in Derbyshire or to Bess of Hardwick's Derbyshire manor of Chatsworth, since replaced by the vast baroque mansion of **Chatsworth** *(662)*. During the Northern rebellion of 1569, she was hustled off for a while to Coventry, then returned to Chatsworth, where she was in residence when a fantastic plot to liberate her came to light. Orchestrated by a Florentine banker named Ridolfi, the scheme contemplated a Spanish invasion from the Netherlands, a Catholic uprising in England, the marriage of Mary to Thomas Howard, duke of Norfolk, and their joint seizure of the English throne. The upshot was that Norfolk (the last remaining duke in England) was beheaded in the Tower and Mary moved again, this time to Sheffield. While she was there, another plot materialized, headed by a Francis Throckmorton, a young Catholic relative of one of Elizabeth's most trusted courtiers. Uncovered by Sir Francis Walsingham, Elizabeth's secretary of state and her most diligent intelligence agent, the Throckmorton plot led to the dismissal of the too cooperative Spanish ambassador Mendoza and to Mary's removal again to Tutbury but this time under the more rigid supervision of a new jailor—an unbending and incorruptible Puritan named Sir Amyas Paulet. Thence she was moved again, now to the moated manor house of Chartley, near Uttoxeter, Staffordshire. Here the trap which Walsingham had long been preparing for the Queen of Scots was sprung—triggered by her own connivance in another foolish plot to assassinate Elizabeth. This one was hatched by a young Derbyshire squire named Anthony Babington. His letters to and from the royal prisoner, concealed in casks of beer delivered by an agent of Walsingham, were, of course, intercepted and the plot laid bare. Mary was moved again, this time to her final prison in the since destroyed castle at Fotheringhay, Northamptonshire. There she was tried by a commission of thirty-six English peers, privy councillors, and judges. Conviction was inevitable, not only because the evidence against her was irrefutable, but because of the serious threat of an imminent Spanish invasion—King Philip II's long planned Enterprise of England, designed to put the Catholic Queen of Scots on the throne of a conquered and forcibly converted nation. Elizabeth, whose forbearance up to now had become intolerable to the Puritan party in the House of Commons and throughout the realm, yielded at last to political necessity and signed the writ of execution. At Fotheringhay Castle on the morning of 8 February 1587, Mary Stuart, aged forty-four, now corpulent and wearing an auburn wig over her thinning gray hair, laid her head upon the block, repeating *"In manus tuas, Domine, confide spiritum meum,"* while the axe fell and the dean of nearby Peterborough Cathedral called out, "So perish all the queen's enemies." It was the beginning of a romantic legend—the stuff of countless plays, novels, sentimental biographies, and a fine opera by Donizetti. It was the end, however, to the most immediate danger to the English throne: a Catholic uprising and a bloody civil war such as France was still enduring.

It was not the end, however, to the threat of a Spanish invasion, and indeed, as much as anything, precipitated the attempt. Anglo-Spanish relations had been deteriorating rapidly since 1568 when Elizabeth had confiscated a large shipment of bullion en route to the duke of Alva who was engaged in putting down Protestant dissension in the Spanish Netherlands. In 1572 open revolt flared up when four Dutch provinces declared for independence under the leadership of Prince William of Orange. For more than a decade Elizabeth undertook a delicate balancing act of lending assistance to the Dutch while at the same time blocking French expansion into the Netherlands at the expense of Spain. In 1584, however, William of Orange was assassinated; Antwerp fell to Spanish troops under the prince of Parma; and England was inexorably driven toward outright hostility to Spain. In May of the following year the king of Spain ordered the seizure of all English ships in Spanish harbors. In August, Elizabeth concluded a treaty of alliance with the Dutch States General and sent the earl of Leicester with an army of seventy-six hundred to assist them. War with Spain, though undeclared, had arrived. Meanwhile the queen had ordered that doughty Devon seaman, Sir Francis Drake, to intercept the Spanish bullion fleet en route from America to Spain. Drake, with a fleet of thirty vessels, missed the bullion ships but plundered the West Indies to his and the queen's enormous profit. During the spring of 1586 Drake put to sea again and collected booty worth half a million pounds. In April 1587 he sailed into Cadiz harbor, destroyed over thirty ships, and then repaired to Sagres on Cape St. Vincent, seized large quantities of Spanish naval stores, and virtually brought all Spanish coastal shipping to a halt.

Drake's glorious victories did not, however, deflect King Philip II from his intention to invade England and topple its heretic queen—his former sister-in-law—from her throne. Though the Pope himself was skeptical, Philip saw the Enterprise of England as a holy mission and himself as God's instrument for striking down the English Jezebel and extirpating forever the hated Protestant heresy. The execution of Mary Queen of Scots removed his final inhibition: The English could no longer threaten to kill this precious hostage in retaliation for an invasion; instead, her "martyrdom" invited revenge.

Elizabeth meanwhile was not idle. Under the leadership of Sir John Hawkins, treasurer of the Navy since 1578, a new navy had been built —twenty-five ships in all and eighteen ocean-going pinnaces. These vessels were longer and leaner than the heavy Spanish galleons and, most importantly, were heavily armed with culverins which could fire at longer ranges than any other contemporary shipboard artillery. In the queen's mind these ships were to be employed chiefly for home defense. Though her admirals and seadogs favored a "blue-water strategy," i.e., sending the fleet to blockade the Spanish coast and engaging her ships on the high seas, Elizabeth and Burghley insisted on a defensive strategic posture. And so it was that when the great Spanish Armada was sighted on 19 July 1588 off the Lizard (the southwesternmost point on the English coast), the English fleet, under command of Charles, Lord Howard of Effingham, was in Plymouth harbor ready to come out fighting.

The Armada of 130 ships, commanded by the duke of Medina Sidonia, was under orders not to attempt a landing on the south coast of England but to work its way eastward to the Kentish coast near Margate, seize a landing point there, and escort a flotilla of light-draught transports carrying Parma's army across the Channel from their bases in the Netherlands. From Plymouth to Calais is 240 nautical miles, and it took the ponderous Spanish galleons seven days to make the voyage—their passage constantly harassed and impeded by the faster-sailing and better-gunned English vessels, though their tight formations were never broken up. Lord Howard's main accomplishment during these seven days was to force the Armada to expend so much shot and powder that Medina Sidonia was compelled to anchor in the Calais Roads to take on more supplies. This was a fatal error. Under cover of darkness, the English launched six fire ships amongst the anchored Spanish vessels; the Spaniards panicked, cut their cables, and drifted out to sea. Next morning they were mostly scattered, and in a sea battle off Gravelines, so badly battered that those not sunk took off in flight to round the northern tip of Scotland before returning home. Foul weather completed the destruction, and in the end only half of King Philip's Glorious Armada returned to Spain. Ten days after the battle of Gravelines but before the totality of the Spanish defeat could have been appreciated, Queen Elizabeth went down to Tilbury in Essex to review the homeguard that the earl of Leicester had mustered there to defend the left bank of the Thames against invasion. There she declared her resolve "to live or die amongst you all, to lay down for my God, and for my kingdom, and for my people, my honour and my blood, even in the dust." Then she continued:

> I know I have the body of a weak and feeble woman, but I have the heart and stomach of a king, and a king of England, too, and think foul scorn that Parma or Spain, or any prince of Europe, should dare to invade the borders of my realm. . . .

It was Elizabeth's finest hour.

It was not the end, however, of the Spanish threat. The war with Spain dragged on for another sixteen years. In 1589 a joint stock expedition under Drake sailed off for Spain with the mission of destroying the Spanish fleet in Lisbon and overrunning Portugal. It was a total failure and most of the expeditionary force died of disease. In 1591 the queen sent troops to Brittany and Normandy to rescue the young Protestant king of France, Henry IV, from a Spanish invading force. In 1595 a small Spanish expedition landed briefly on Cornwall, to burn Penzance, Mousehole, and Newlyn. That same year Drake and Hawkins set sail again for the Spanish Main where both died of disease before accomplishing their mission of seizing the treasure fleet and plundering the Isthmus of Panama. Later that year an English expedition launched an attack on Cadiz which was a complete success and greatly enhanced the reputation of its leader, the queen's new favorite, Robert Devereux, earl of Essex. Six years later the Spanish retaliated with an invasion of Ireland which succeeded in capturing the port of Kinsale on the southern coast before being ousted by the English under Charles Blount, Lord Mountjoy.

It was against this background of ever present danger that Elizabeth continued and improved upon the coastal fortification policy commenced by her father. In the Channel Islands, **Castle Cornet** *(745)* at St. Peter Port in Guernsey, was reinforced with a series of protective bastions in the Italian style; and in the harbor of St. Helier, Jersey, the queen's engineer, Paul Ivy, began the fortification of the rocky islet that in the sixth century had given shelter to the sainted hermit after whom it was named and in the twelfth had been the site of a Benedictine abbey. The fort was first named Isabella Bellissima in honor of the queen by Sir Walter Raleigh, one of its early governors and one-time royal favorite. Later it assumed its present name, **Elizabeth Castle** *(743)*. Approachable today over a causeway at low tide or by boat from West Park, St. Helier, during high water, only the upper ward dates to Elizabeth's time. It is entered through a handsome stone gate above which, in low relief, is carved the queen's coat of arms. Across the Channel on the Isle of Wight, **Carisbrooke Castle** *(558)* received about this time its outer ramparts and the gatehouse through which the visitor today enters the castle grounds. Still farther west along the coast at Falmouth, Cornwall, Henry VIII's great fortress of **Pendennis Castle** *(591)* was furnished with its present thick curtain wall with arrowheaded bastions at four corners, projecting buttresses in the two long sides, and a triangular projection on the end facing the sea. This is, next to the ramparts at Berwick-on-Tweed, the best example in England of Italian-style sixteenth century military architecture. Finally on St. Mary's Island in the Isles of Scilly, Cornwall, the queen's engineer, Robert Adams, constructed **Star Castle** *(592)*, its keep shaped like an eight-pointed star surrounded by ramparts in the same pattern. Today it is a hotel, but the Elizabethan style is still observable.

The last years of her reign were sad ones for the aging queen. Leicester died in 1588, Walsingham in 1590, Burghley, the wisest and most loyal counsellor of them all, in 1598. Burghley's son, the hunchbacked Sir Robert Cecil, stepped into his father's shoes but could not take his place in the affections of the queen. For a while she thought she had found a replacement for the dashing Leicester in the person of his stepson, the arrogant and headstrong Robert Devereux, earl of Essex. But Essex proved a fool. Dispatched to Ireland in 1599 to put down a rebellion led by the earl of Tyrone, he failed utterly in his mission, signed a premature truce with Tyrone, discharged his troops, and fled back to England without authorization. Clapped in the Tower for insubordination and neglect of duty, and later put under house arrest in his own mansion on the Strand in London, this utterly self-deluded young man now attempted a coup d'etat, telegraphing his punch by suborning Shakespeare's company at the Globe Theatre to put on a performance of *Richard II*, presumably to incite its audience to support another dethronement by a latter-day Bolingbroke. The coup failed and Essex was again imprisoned in the Tower, this time headed for the block. The romantic stories about his sexual involvement with the queen are pure fiction. Ireland, incidentally, which he had lost, was soon reconquered by his sister's lover, the earl of Mountjoy.

With Essex out of the way, his rival at court, Sir Robert Cecil, began negotiating with Mary Stuart's son, James VI of Scotland, to assure his peaceful succession to the throne. It was his by right of primogeniture, and though Elizabeth in the end would obliquely indicate her approval, she did not intend just yet to be cast in the shadows by the rising sun. She was still in command, not only of her kingdom, but of her subjects' hearts. Her last address to the House of Commons in November 1601 was her *liebeslied* to the nation over which she had reigned for forty-three years.

> Though God has raised me high, yet this I count the glory of my crown, that I have reigned with your loves. . . . It is not my desire to live or reign longer than my life and reign shall be for your good. And though you have had and may have, many mightier and wiser princes sitting in this seat, yet you never had, nor shall have, any that will love you better. . . .

An unwonted modesty had led the queen into error. England was never to have again a mightier or a wiser prince. She died at Richmond Palace on 24 March 1603 at the age of sixty-nine years and six months.

DOMESTIC ARCHITECTURE

It was in the sixteenth century that the Englishman's home ceased to be his castle, except in the figurative and legal sense. The King's Peace, which in the Middle Ages had been honored as much in the breach as in the observance, now, in most parts of the country, became a fact. The court of star chamber, the court of requests, the councils of Wales and of the north, and most of all the omnipresent justices of the peace in every county kept steady watch over the land. No more did armed bands wearing the liveries of their wealthy patrons roam the countryside; no more could great magnates engage in private vendettas or forcibly warp the processes of royal justice to their own ends. Violence there was aplenty to be sure; murder, highway robbery, rioting, and rebellion did not disappear. But Tudor despotism, deplorable as it was in the eyes of later civil libertarians, did work. England, and even Wales, were to enjoy the blessings of law and order to a degree hitherto unknown. In consequence there was no further need for houses to be fortified. Domestic architecture, which in the fifteenth century was already losing many of its military attributes, would, in the sixteenth, at last become completely domestic.

The trend was accelerated by the greatest building boom that England would experience until the nineteenth century. It was brought about partly by the sudden transfer of vast quantities of church lands into private hands; partly by the doubling or even tripling of prices consequent upon the immense import of bullion from the American mines into western Europe and the enormous opportunities thus created for businessmen, speculators, and profiteers; partly by the great expansion of overseas trade and the resulting enrichment of both legitimate merchants and privateers like Drake and Hawkins; partly by improved methods of farming and estate management which multiplied rents and other profits from the soil; and partly by the expansion of government itself which opened special avenues of self-advancement particularly to courtiers and lawyers at Westminster.

This was a period, too, of rapid upward social mobility. Opportunities abounded for the ambitious, the bright, and the lucky. And out of all this ferment, one class of men and women, especially, grew in number and moved from strength to strength. This was the landed gentry—a term loosely used to define that large body of upwardly mobile people—merchants, lawyers, courtiers, soldiers, seamen, younger sons of the older aristocracy, and even yeomen—who capitalized on Tudor prosperity, invested heavily in real estate, and became landed gentlemen. To confirm their newly elevated status they applied for, and were liberally granted, coats of arms by the College of Arms, many of them now on display in the Heralds' Museum in the **Tower of London** *(513)*. The College of Arms, founded by Richard III to provide an orderly process to the granting of patents of arms, did a land-office business under the Tudors, and many of the proudest families in Britain today owe their pedigrees to this sixteenth century boom in status-seeking. "Gentility," Lord Burghley advised his son (the future earl of Salisbury), "is nothing else but ancient riches." And not too ancient at that, as none knew better than this grandson of an obscure Welsh man-at-arms whose name was Anglicized from Seissylit to Cecil.

Better as a status symbol than a coat of arms, however, was a country estate. Nothing served so well the need these parvenus felt to display conspicuously their newfound wealth and status. The sixteenth century then marks the beginning—and some would say the high-water mark— of that distinctly British phenomenon: the stately country home. Fortunately for today's traveller, their original owners built so well that a considerable number survive. Fortunately also (for the traveller) British death duties (inheritance taxes) are so outrageously high that the best of these houses have been turned over to the National Trust for public display or have been kept in private ownership only by virtue of their present occupants' selling tickets of admission—usually at a stiff price.

Tudor domestic architecture is so eclectic, so multiform, so variegated, and so wondrously busy as to defy easy generalization. These houses do display, however, certain typical, though by no means uniform, features, of which the intelligent traveller needs to be aware if he is to view them with an informed eye. First as to their interiors: Being built for comfort rather than defense, the main emphasis was on privacy. The great hall, with its raised dais at one end; its tall screen at the other to separate it from the kitchen, pantry, and buttery; its central hearth; its high open-timbered roof with a louvered opening in the center, had been the main internal feature of the medieval castle and had served as a combination dining room, reception room, court room, and even sleeping quarters for the lord's retainers. Even before the beginning of the fifteenth century, however, the desire for greater privacy on the part of the lord and his family had evidenced itself in the building of parlors and solars off the great hall itself and in the construction of guest lodgings extending out and around the inner courtyard. The tendency accelerated in the sixteenth century, and although the hall was still retained, its importance diminished, both structurally and functionally. Elaborately decorated wall fireplaces replaced the central hearth; flat ceilings of delicate plasterwork were inserted beneath the rafters of the roof; and on occasion the axis of the room was changed from lateral to longitudinal thus anticipating its later reduction to a mere entrance vestibule, as in the typical modern house. The place of honor vacated by the great hall was now assumed by the great chamber or drawing room, usually on the first floor above the ground floor. This was now the pivot of the house and could be used either as a dining room or reception room. Adjoining it were smaller withdrawing rooms, sitting rooms, or parlors, and bedchambers, the latter term itself first coming into general use in the sixteenth century to indicate the disappearance of the medieval bed-sitting room. Bedchambers, however, were still arranged in tandem with no common corridor to provide individual access to them. Another novelty was the long gallery, usually on the same upper story as the great chamber. Galleries originated as covered walkways for exercise in bad weather or as playrooms for the children. Soon, hangings and pictures began to appear on the walls, and as the fashion for collecting family portraits grew, the gallery tended to become the showpiece of the house. Finally, the lowering of the ceiling in the great hall and the installation of the gallery, great chamber, and most of the bedchambers on the first story above it, produced the Elizabethan staircase, usually of wood, though sometimes of stone, built around a central well or in a doglegged form with landings between every flight of steps.

It is in its external features, however, that the Tudor architectural style is most distinctive. Stone and brick were the common building materials, sometimes embellished with terra-cotta moldings of unglazed baked clay. Occasionally a substantial country dwelling might be built with timber sills, lintels, struts, ties, and braces, the interstices filled with plastered brick or lathing, although these half-timbered black-and-white buildings were mostly to be found in town. Most country houses, in spite of the occasional retention of ornamental battlements and magnificent residential gatehouses, were clearly not built for defense. True, at the beginning of the century, in emulation of late medieval models the great houses of the rich tended to be inward-looking courtyard castles—four wings hugging a central quadrilateral courtyard. Soon, however, though not altogether, these gave way to outward-looking buildings, U-shaped in ground plan, their side wings stretching forward as if to welcome, not repel, the approaching visitor. Sometimes the U became an E, the short stroke of which was represented by a projecting central entrance porch, or frontispiece. Later in the century, H-shaped ground plans became fashionable, the side wings projecting both fore and aft to half enclose both entry court and garden.

To the sixteenth century eye, accustomed as it still was to the sight of massive castle walls usually pierced by arrow slits or narrow lancet windows, the most impressive feature of these new buildings must have been the great expanse of window glass. To the modern visitor, more accustomed to extensive fenestration, the most notable aspect of a Tudor country house is likely to be its skyline. Chimney stacks abound, some ornamented, some plain, some disguised as classical columns, some single, some clustered into groups, some regimented into lines and crested with horizontal slabs to prevent down drafts, some sharing the crowded rooftops with cupolas and turrets. Gables also add to the variety of the silhouette. Some are triangles, the apex pointed skyward, some ogival in shape, some stepped, some "curly" in the Flemish manner. Finally, and perhaps the stateliest feature of these "stately homes," is the typically Tudor facade of contrasting masses, achieved by the advancing and receding lines of projecting wings, corner turrets at the inner angles of the wings and central block, bay windows, and above all the noble frontispieces, the central entrance porches. The total effect of these jagged and much indented exteriors is to provide a play of contrasting light and shadow more pleasing to the eye than the smooth, symmetrical facades of later classical fashions and far more so than the dull monotony of twentieth century functional designs.

Perhaps the most typical early Tudor country house is Compton Wynyates in Warwickshire. Unhappily it has recently been closed to the public, so perhaps the best place for the intelligent traveller to begin a survey of these early sixteenth century mansions is at **Barrington Court** *(584)*, a few miles northeast of Ilminster, Somerset. It was built in 1514–1520 by Henry, Lord d'Aubenay, chamberlain to Henry VII and present at the Field of the Cloth of Gold with Henry VIII who created him earl of Bridgewater. This stone house has an E-shaped ground plan, much more symmetrical than Compton Wynyates. Its most noticeable features are the three-storied, gabled central entrance porch and the gabled staircase turrets in the angles between the central block and either wing, giving the front facade a typically Tudor indented look. Twisted chimneys with ornamented tops, called finials, clutter the rooftops to form a fascinating skyline. Of about the same date as Barrington Court is **Layer Marney Hall** *(599)*, a few miles southwest of Colchester, Essex. It was begun by Henry, Lord Marney, treasurer to Henry VIII and companion-in-arms to his brother-in-law Charles Brandon, duke of Suffolk. Marney died in the French campaign of 1523, and his son two years later. By that time they had completed only the south side of his projected mansion and the enormous gatehouse of brick and terra-cotta consisting of a central block, three stories high, flanked by two semioctagonal turrets on the south side and two square ones on the north, each divided into eight stories. It is an impressive sight, especially so because of the large number and great size of its windows. Another of Henry VIII's courtiers was William Sandys who helped organize the Field of the Cloth of Gold and later became lord chamberlain. Between 1518 and 1527 he built **The Vyne** *(557)*, north of Basingstoke, Hampshire. Later owners (the Chutes) in the seventeenth century attached a portico with Corinthian pillars to the north front. This was designed by John Webb, Inigo Jones's nephew-in-law. Still later, in the eighteenth century, an elegant Palladian staircase was inserted into the original hall by John Chute. These additions only serve to enhance the beauty of this really splendid mansion. The rose-colored brick of the exterior walls, with purple diamond diapering, is pure Tudor, the Oak Gallery with its linenfold paneling is one of the best sixteenth century long galleries in the country, and the chapel is excellent late Perpendicular. Entirely different in appearance is **Coughton Court** *(645)*, west of Stratford-upon-Avon, Warwickshire. Tudor construction here is represented by the great three-storied gatehouse with mullioned oriel windows and octagonal battlemented turrets; the flanking wings were added in the eighteenth century. The gatehouse was built by the scion of an ancient Warwickshire family, Sir George Throckmorton, who, unlike the aforementioned, was not in favor at the court and indeed at one time so offended Thomas Cromwell that he was imprisoned in the Tower. Released, he later became high sheriff of Warwickshire and Leicestershire and, because of a family connection with Queen Catherine Parr, was exempted from further royal displeasure. On a much lower level of magnificence than any of the above is **Sulgrave Manor** *(626)*, in Northamptonshire, eight miles northeast of Banbury, Oxfordshire. Architecturally, it is of interest as a typical small manor house built in the sixteenth century, in this case by a prosperous wool merchant who had bought from the Crown the property confiscated from the Priory of St. Andrew. Of the present building, the gabled entrance porch, great hall, and great chamber date from the sixteenth century; the remainder from the later seventeenth and early eighteenth. Historically, Sulgrave's attraction stems from the fact that its builder, the Tudor merchant-turned-gentleman, was Lawrence Washington, the great-great-great-great-great-grandfather of the first President of the United States. Appropriately the American flag flies in the front garden, but inside the house is delightfully furnished in authentic Tudor style with Queen Anne furniture in the seventeenth century wing. The Stars and Stripes fly also on occasion above another English house associated with the Washingtons, **Washington Old Hall** *(703)* near Sunderland, Tyne and Wear, where the family originated. This is a small manor house built mostly in the seventeenth century after the Washingtons had sold the property, and, though the connection is remote, the National Trust has restored it, presumably as a gesture of Anglo-American amity.

Early Tudor domestic architecture was the product of evolution, not conscious subordination to aesthetic theory. The houses described above had their roots in the Middle Ages; they were mostly adaptations of the gatehouse or the courtyard castle—looking outward now that defense was no longer a requirement, full of windows, bristling with chimneys, their ground plans and exteriors primarily a function of the proliferation of interior rooms arranged for the greater comfort and privacy of their builders. They are essentially amateurish, and therefore quintessentially English. In the middle of the century, however, England suffered briefly from an attack of Renaissance classicism, though the infection was not serious. Classical architecture differs from the medieval Gothic chiefly in its emphasis on symmetry and on the simple structural form of horizontal beams (entablatures) supported by vertical cylindrical shafts (columns). Variations in the design of columns and entablatures were classified by Renaissance architects as the five orders: Ionic, Doric, Corinthian, Tuscan (unfluted), and Composite (Ionic and Corinthian). With the rediscovery of Roman and Greek civilizations by scholars and artists in the fourteenth century, classical fashions in architecture spread northward into western Europe in the fifteenth. England, however, was only slightly touched by this movement (as at Hampton Court) until the reign of Edward VI. Then a group of the boy-king's chief advisors—including Edward Seymour, duke of Somerset, his brother Thomas, lord high admiral, and his successor as lord protector, John Dudley, duke of Northumberland—suddenly became enraptured with Roman architecture, which seems ironical in view of their strong Protestant proclivities. Northumberland indeed dispatched a member of his household, one John Shute, to Italy in 1550 to study classical and Renaissance designs. On his return, Shute put out the first architectural book ever published in England, *The First and Chiefe Groundes of Architecture,* dealing with the five orders. Another member of the circle was Sir William Sharington who worked on two houses considered to be landmarks in English architectural history. One was **Sudeley Castle** *(642)* near Winchcombe, Gloucestershire, where Thomas Seymour lived with his third wife, Catherine Parr, but which was so much refurbished in the nineteenth century that Sharington's work has been all but obliterated. The second and best example of Sharington's work is **Lacock Abbey** *(572)*, south of Chippenham, Wiltshire, already mentioned as a monastic house converted to domestic use. This was Sharington's own residence, though he almost lost it when, as vice-treasurer of the Bristol Mint, he was caught cheating. Here to the remodeled medieval claustral buildings he attached an Italianate wing, joining the two parts together in a surprisingly harmonious manner, with a high octagonal tower topped by a classical balustrade.

The masterpiece of what is sometimes called Sharington school, was built, however, not by Sharington but by Sir John Thynne, a member of the duke of Somerset's entourage. Knighted for valor at the Battle of Pinkie, he went to the Tower along with his master, but was released after the lord protector's execution and spent the rest of his life building **Longleat House** *(577)* in Wiltshire just west of Warminster. Sir John Summerson, the dean of English architectural historians, has dubbed this masterpiece the "Momentary High Renaissance of our Architecture." Momentary because it inspired no imitations. Longleat is the unique example in sixteenth century England of an Italianate *palazzo* serving as a country house. It is a four-sided outward-looking building constructed around two small courtyards lying in a lovely bucolic park landscaped in the mid-eighteenth century by Lancelot (Capability) Brown. Its only typically Tudor features are the vast expanse of mullioned and transomed windows on the four facades and the busy skyline of pepperpot domes, heraldic finial beasts, and exotic chimneys. The rest is self-consciously classical, with its central doorway topped by a broken pediment and flanked by Doric columns, its thirteen shallow bays symmetrically placed around the four facades, each window flanked on the ground, first, and second stories by Doric, Ionic, and Corinthian pilasters respectively, the roofline guarded by a balustrade. The interior too is strongly Italian in flavor, but that was the work of a nineteenth century restoration.

One of the master craftsmen at Longleat was a young man named Robert Smythson, whose next architectural achievement was **Wollaton Hall** *(659)* built in 1580–1588 on the western outskirts of Nottingham for Sir Francis Willoughby, the high sheriff of Nottinghamshire who wanted quarters fit for the queen. Entertaining Her Majesty on her summer progresses was a prime motive in the building of what Summerson has labeled prodigy houses. Wollaton is one of them. It is completely outward looking with no courtyard at all and such a display of window glass as to make the whole enormous pile of stone fairly glitter. Wollaton offers a good illustration of Summerson's dictum that classical architecture made its way into England as a mode of decorative design. Superimposed on what was meant to resemble a medieval keep are Doric friezes and pilasters, balustrades, and classical niches, presumably to house appropriate statuary. At either corner of the central "keep" rise bartizans capped with pepperpot domes and the flanking square towers are topped with Flemish curly gables. Wollaton is a vulgar monstrosity, typically *nouveau riche*, but, in its way, magnificent. Today it houses the City of Nottingham's Natural History Museum. In much the same style of mixed Gothic and classical, and even more magnificent, is **Hardwick Hall** *(662)* in Derbyshire, about seven miles southeast of Chesterfield. Its builder was Mary Stuart's former unwanted duenna, the formidable Bess of Hardwick, who celebrated the death of her fourth husband, the earl of Shrewsbury, by raising, with his money, what some believe to be the supreme triumph of Elizabethan architecture. For her site she chose the grounds of her father's now ruined seat, called **Hardwick Old Hall** *(663)* which she had earlier rebuilt only to abandon it in favor of her new and much more ambitious project. Here too, Robert Smythson was probably the architect. Hardwick has to be seen to be believed. Here, as at Wollaton only more so, the expanse of window glass is overwhelming. The ground plan is a modified H, although from the outside it appears to be a huge three-storied rectangular house surrounded by projecting four-story towers symmetrically disposed around the exterior. Aside from the symmetry, the only other classical features are the Tuscan colonnades across both front and back and the roofline parapets, above which rise, in very unclassical manner, the huge initials *ES* (Elizabeth Shrewsbury) carved in stone. Inside, the central hall is laid out perpendicular to the axis of the central block, an innovation which in time would be widely copied as the great hall was gradually reduced in status to that of a mere entrance corridor. The two best rooms at Hardwick are the tapestry-hung high great chamber and the long gallery, both on the first floor and reached by an unusually grand stone staircase. Another house attributed to Smythson is **Burton Agnes Hall** *(677)*, six miles southwest of Bridlington, Humberside, a splendid red-brick courtyard house, built for Sir Henry Griffiths. It is typically Tudor/Jacobean with its facades interrupted with frequent projecting bays, its splendid frontispiece, and its rooftop alive with soaring chimney stacks. Still another Smythson house is **Doddington Hall** *(652)* near Lincoln, a splendid E-shaped mansion built in the last years of Elizabeth's reign.

Back to Elizabethan prodigy houses, we come next to **Kirby Hall** *(654)* near Corby, Northamptonshire. Here, at a traditional courtyard manor house built for Sir Humphrey Stafford of Blatherwycke in the 1570s, Ionic pilasters have been substituted for buttresses in a typically late sixteenth century melange of medieval and Renaissance styles. Altered in the seventeenth century, the house later became derelict, and though now partly restored, is mostly a very attractive shell. **Montacute House** *(585)* just west of Yeovil, Somerset, is another Elizabethan prodigy house combining native English and Mediterranean features. Here Sir Edward Phelips, speaker of the House of Commons, built an E-shaped house of honey-colored local stone whose original (eastern) front sported a classical balustrade with obelisks at roof level, and below the balustrade between the windows of the top story placed statues of the Nine Worthies all dressed as Roman soldiers. Other pseudo-classical features were a matching courtyard balustrade supporting obelisks and terminating in domed pavilions at each end. The multitude of paired chimneys are shaped like Roman columns, while the gables are Flemish curly. To the western (now the entrance) front was grafted, in the eighteenth century, a porch taken from another Tudor house in nearby Dorset. The interior remains mostly unaltered from its original condition and is extraordinarily handsome. In the windows are forty-seven separate coats of arms, perhaps the best collection of heraldic stained glass in the country. But Montacute, for all its elegance, pales before the most prodigious of all the prodigy houses, built by the greatest of Queen Elizabeth's statesmen, William Cecil, Lord Burghley. This is **Burghley House** *(653)* in Cambridgeshire just across the county line from Stamford, Lincolnshire. It was built at enormous expense, partly so that the lord high treasurer could suitably entertain the queen, who in fact did visit here at least a dozen times at the cost of two to three thousand pounds to the owner on each occasion. Burghley House is a monument to Tudor architectural eclecticism. Set in a huge deer park later landscaped by Capability Brown, in ground plan it is a throwback to the four-sided courtyard castle. The great five-story gatehouse, the four projecting square corner towers, the ample fenestration, and the busy rooftops alive with pepperpot domes and clustered chimneys—are all traditional Tudor English. But the frontispiece is adorned with the Italianate columns, and in the courtyard is a three-story tower displaying the three original classical orders (Doric, Ionic, and Corinthian) on the different stories, topped with a huge pyramid-shaped obelisk to remind the observer that he is looking at a Renaissance production. Unfortunately, the interior, though sumptuous to a fault, was so altered in the seventeenth century that, except for the hammer-beam roof in the great hall and the splendid stone staircase, there is little to remind one that this was a Tudor residence. Today it is so stuffed with great masters—paintings by Cranach, Veronese, Correggio, Andrea del Sarto, *et al;* and wall paintings by Verrio—that the visitor is likely to be stupefied, especially after undergoing the regimented and somewhat tedious guided tour which omits most of the Tudor portions of the house.

After Burghley House, all other Elizabethan mansions might seem anticlimactical, except that in so many cases charm is a more than adequate substitute for splendor. A case in point is **Broughton Castle** *(626)* just south of Banbury, Oxfordshire. This is a fourteenth century moated manor house converted into a Tudor mansion by the Richard Fiennes, father and son, the sixth and seventh Lords Saye and Sele. Though partially remodeled in the eighteenth and nineteenth centuries, the house remains essentially medieval and Tudor in spirit, the most noteworthy sixteenth century features being the two beautiful chimneypieces, the plaster ceiling in the White Room, and the west wing. The exterior is even more typically Tudor, replete with bay windows, protruding wings, ornamental battlements, large windows (some with Ionic or Corinthian columns for mullions), and lots of chimney stacks. A visit here is sheer delight. More typically Tudor, however, is **Melford Hall** *(604)* in Long Melford, about three miles north of Sudbury in Suffolk. Originally a four-sided courtyard house of brick, it is now U-shaped with the usual sixteenth century array of turrets and double chimneys, though the interior was much remodeled in the eighteenth century, when it belonged to the Parker family of nautical fame. The builder was William Cordell, another speaker of the House of Commons, who entertained Queen Elizabeth here in 1578. In the same village Sir Thomas Clopton built **Kentwell Hall** *(603)* in the mid-sixteenth century, though it cannot be said to rival Melford Hall in either grandeur or beauty. **Deene Park** *(654)*, northeast of Kirby, Northamptonshire, was the sixteenth century home of the Brudenall family who were responsible for its most interesting feature, i.e., the eastern bay, a two-layered window with Ionic columns serving as mullions and separated by a paneled frieze. **Sherborne Castle** *(569)*, about a mile east of Sherborne, Dorset, was built in part by Sir Walter Raleigh, the well-known Elizabethan courtier and seadog, and much enlarged by the earls of Bristol whose family seat (set in a park by Capability Brown) it became in the seventeenth century. In Wiltshire, near Chippenham, is **Corsham Court** *(572)* built in 1582 by Thomas Smythe, a London haberdasher and customs collector. Though much enlarged in the eighteenth century under the direction of Capability Brown and John Nash, at first glance the E-shaped building appears typically Elizabethan. Today it houses one of the best private collections of paintings in the country. **Cadhay** *(588)*, near Ottery St. Mary, Devon, is a rather plain quadrangular courtyard house built by John Haydon before 1587 and is distinguished mostly by effigies of Henry VIII and his three children standing respectively in niches in each of the four sides of the Court of the Kings. Also in Devon, near Torquay, is **Compton Castle** *(590)* a fourteenth century manor house updated by one of Queen Elizabeth's trusted seadogs, Sir John Gilbert, brother to the more famous Humphrey Gilbert, explorer of Newfoundland, and half brother to Sir Walter Raleigh who spent his boyhood and youth here. Another West Country Tudor house is **Trerice** *(593)* just east of Newquay, Cornwall. It is an E-plan gray limestone house with highly decorative Flemish gables, a traditional great hall with minstrel gallery, and a fireplace dated 1572. Sir Francis Knollys, cousin to Queen Elizabeth and one of her most faithful and trusted counsellors, was the builder of **Grey's Court** *(627)* near Henley, Oxfordshire. This is a fourteenth century fortified manor converted into an Elizabethan gabled house of brick and stone. **Hoghton Tower** *(696)*, located between Preston and Blackburn in Lancashire, is a four-sided courtyard house built in the 1560s. With exception of four pilasters on the north side of the house and the sculptured panel over the entrance way, there is no trace of Renaissance influence in this lonely back-country mansion. There are two courtyards here separated by a range of buildings. The builder, Thomas Hoghton, was a Catholic recusant who fled to the Continent rather than conform to the new religion. Another recusant, converted in 1580 by one of the missionaries from Douai, was Sir Thomas Tresham who built the curious **Rushton Triangular Lodge** *(655)* about three miles northwest of Kettering, Northamptonshire. The three-sided ground plan was meant to symbolize the Holy Trinity, and, to underline the message, each of the three sides is surmounted by three triangular gables, a triangular chimney shaft rises from the roof, and all the windows are trefoils. Tresham spent a good portion of the last twenty-five years of his life in prison.

Different in structure and design from any of the above and yet so unmistakably Tudor as to be sometimes erroneously considered the only pure examples of the style are the half-timbered black-and-white houses to be found everywhere in England but especially in the Midlands. As already mentioned, they owe their picturesque appearance to the intricate geometric patterns of dark, weathered timber struts, ties, lintels, etc., against the near-white of plaster interfillings. Two country houses of this description are especially noteworthy. The first is **Little Moreton Hall** *(675)*, a few miles southwest of Congleton in Cheshire. This moated quadrangular courtyard manor with its matching gatehouse looks like a stage set for Verdi's opera, *Falstaff*. Its black timber frame is cut into intricate patterns of squares, triangles, quatrefoils, and cusped lozenges against a gleaming background of white plaster. Its hexagonal bays jut out into a cobbled courtyard, its upper stories overhang, and its gatehouse is even more fantastically designed. **Speke Hall** *(696)* in Merseyside about eight miles southeast of Liverpool is much the same—a half-timbered spacious courtyard house of the sixteenth century, its interior now embellished with a good collection of arms and armor and tapestries, and containing a crafts museum.

An underdeveloped country in the sixteenth century, Wales produced little of the surplus wealth required to nourish and sustain a leisure class dedicated to conspicuous display in the form of great new country houses. **St. Fagan's Castle** *(718)*, just west of Cardiff, South Glamorgan, is, however, a fair-sized E-plan Tudor building, built between 1560 and 1580 within the curtain walls of an existing castle. The chief attraction of the site, however, is the **Welsh Folk Museum** *(718)*, a superb open-air museum containing a woolen mill, a tannery, a tollgate, a chapel, and numerous cottages moved to this location from various parts of Wales.

Another Welsh medieval castle converted into a country house is **Powis Castle** *(723)* in Welshpool, Powys, where the long gallery with its decorated plaster ceiling was added in the 1590s. New Tudor-style windows are inserted into the ancient walls. The most noteworthy feature of the site, however, is not the building but the splendid terraced garden lying below the castle and begun by the earl of Rochford in the 1790s. Considered by many to be the finest Italian baroque garden in Britain, it boasts great box hedges and enormous domes of yew trees that vie with the stone urns, balustrades, and ornamental figures for the viewer's delighted attention.

In spite of its comparative economic backwardness, Wales did enjoy, thanks to the Acts of Union and the "Tudor peace," a fair degree of commercial prosperity in the sixteenth century. A standing testimony to this development is **Plas Mawr** *(738)* in Conwy, Gwynedd, perhaps the best surviving example in Britain of an Elizabethan merchant's house. Built by Robert Wynn between 1576 and 1580, it is an H-plan house with a courtyard in the rear and a terraced lower courtyard between the side of the house and the gatehouse. Plaster ceilings and Italianate fireplaces decorate the interior, while on the outside the mullioned windows are topped with classical pediments. Of slightly older vintage, is the **Tudor Merchant's House** *(729)* in Tenby, Dyfed, now restored and appropriately furnished by the National Trust.

In England, surviving Tudor town houses, though not unknown, are sparse compared to the large number of contemporary country residences. Yet sixteenth century towns enjoyed the same building boom as did the countryside and for the same reasons. Because of limitations of space, town houses were normally narrow fronted, with a shop and kitchen at ground level, two or three floors above and a garret room under the gable fronting the street. To provide extra space the upper stories might be cantilevered out toward the street, thus giving the building a top-heavy appearance. A substantial merchant, desiring greater grandeur than the single-gabled unit house, could simply multiply the unit by two, three, or even four, thus ending up with a multi-gabled mansion of considerable size fronting the street. Not many, unfortunately, are left, owing of course to the rapidly changing requirements of urban life. Two good East Anglian examples are **Paycocke's** *(598)* in Coggeshall, Essex, and **South Quay** *(606)* in Great Yarmouth, Norfolk. Two others in Shrewsbury, Salop are **Ireland's Mansion** *(670)* and **Owen's Mansion** *(670)* both dating from the reign of Queen Elizabeth. In Chester, Cheshire, **Leche House** *(673)* is Elizabethan as is **Stanley Palace** *(674)* now serving as headquarters of the English-Speaking Union. In the same city the **Rows** *(674)*, a series of joined shops behind an arcade supporting a public walk date to the sixteenth century and before. The **Rows** *(606)* of Great Yarmouth, Norfolk, are of the same vintage, though much damaged by German bombs in World War II. A similar cluster of shops in York, called **The Shambles** *(692)*, dates partly from the sixteenth century, although precise attribution is difficult. Other examples of Tudor houses in cities, towns, and villages could be cited, but they are few. Except in the countryside and in the university towns, the face of Tudor England has mostly disappeared.

ART AND LEARNING

PAINTING

The sum of English painting in the Tudor period was portraiture. Not still-lifes, nor landscapes, nor the imagined features of the Holy Family, nor the agonies of saintly martyrdom filled the canvases of the handful of artists who worked in London, but the portraits of living men and women. The essence of Renaissance humanism was the celebration of mankind, and nowhere is the spirit of the new philosophy better reflected than in these painted representations of contemporary figures as they really were.

The greatest of all artists to work in England was Hans Holbein, the younger. Born in Augsburg, he came to London in 1526 with a letter of introduction from Erasmus to Sir Thomas More, and there he spent some thirteen years in all before his death in 1543. He became court painter to Henry VIII who sent him abroad in 1538 and 1539 to put on canvas the likenesses of the king's prospective wives. One of these was Christina of Denmark, duchess of Milan, whose full-scale portrait now hangs in the **National Gallery** *(518)*, London; another was the miniature of Anne of Cleves in the **Victoria and Albert Museum** *(526)*, London.

Miniature painting, or limning as it was called, reached its high-water mark in the Tudor period. The word itself comes from *minium* or red lead, used extensively in medieval manuscript illumination from which the art derived. (The fact that most of these paintings were very small imparted the connotation of minuteness to the word *miniature,* not *vice versa.*) Holbein was highly skilled in this as in large-scale painting, and another sample of his delicate brushwork is the tiny portrait of Mrs. Pemberton, also in the Victoria and Albert Museum. But one of his pupils was the greatest miniaturist of all. This was Nicholas Hilliard, Devon-born court painter to Queen Elizabeth, whose touch is so frail and delicate that his works are frequently likened to the more lyrical sonnets of Shakespeare. The Victoria and Albert Museum houses a sizeable collection of his surviving works, the best and most famous being the *Young Man Leaning Against a Tree.* Others in the same group are: *Unknown Man Against a Background of Flames, Sir Christopher Stratton, Mrs. Holland, Self-Portrait,* and three of Queen Elizabeth, all in Room 55 on the upper ground floor. In the same place are several miniatures of

Isaac Oliver who studied under Hilliard but never quite captured his refinement. Of the full-scale portraitists whose work dates from Elizabeth's reign, the best are George Gower, a native Englishman, and Hans Eworth of Antwerp. Gower's portraits of Sir Thomas Kitson and Lady Kitson hang in the **Tate Gallery** *(523)*, Millbank, London, SW 1. Eworth's best known work is his portrait of Sir John Luttrell now in the **Courtauld Institute Galleries** *(516)*, Woburn Square, London, WC 1. Both Gower and Eworth painted the queen herself, as did Hilliard (in full as well as miniature) and numerous lesser known artists. In the **National Portrait Gallery** *(518)*, London, hang the Cobham Portrait, the Ditchley Portrait, and another of Elizabeth holding a rose; the **Walker Art Gallery** *(695)*, Liverpool, has the Pelican Portrait; **Woburn Abbey** *(625)*, ten miles northwest of Luton, Bedfordshire, the Armada Portrait by Gower; **Hatfield House** *(620)* in Hertfordshire, the Ermine Portrait; and **Hardwick Hall** *(662)*, Derbyshire, displays the likenesses of both Mary Queen of Scots and her nemesis, the queen of England. Indeed, by the end of Elizabeth's reign she was in effect a cult figure, and it was an ill-furnished long gallery in England that did not display a portrait of Her Majesty decked in pearls and stiff brocades and usually wearing a bright red wig.

THE UNIVERSITIES

On being urged to follow up the dissolution of the monasteries with the confiscation of the properties and endowments of the colleges of Oxford and Cambridge, Henry VIII drew back from what would have been a logical and profitable step. "I judge no land in England better bestowed," he announced, "than that which is given to our Universities. For by their maintenance our Realm shall be well governed when we are dead and rotten." This was a sound Renaissance position, and any of the Tudor monarchs might just as easily have proclaimed it. Enthusiasm for the new learning spread to England early in the sixteenth century, and the two universities were inevitably affected. Erasmus himself spent the summer of 1499 at Oxford, and six years later he was at Cambridge, lecturing in Greek and living, probably, in rooms at **Queens' College** *(614)*. In the 1540s Henry VIII established at each university five regius professorships: in Greek, Hebrew, theology, medicine, and civil law. The dissolution of the monasteries, though temporarily disruptive, brought long-term benefits to both universities, as the colleges took over lands and buildings formerly occupied by monks and friars. Henry's secession from Rome opened the dikes to a flood of new religious doctrines originating on the Continent and finding a natural outlet in those centers of learning where the study of Greek and Hebrew had already led to a critical analysis of Biblical texts and a consequent undermining of the authoritarian claims of the papacy. The Reformation exercised a powerful influence over the universities, especially Cambridge, which became the leading center in England, first of Lutheranism and later of the teachings of the still more radical Swiss reformers, Calvin and Zwingli. From there the new doctrines spread to the royal court with devastating consequences for orthodoxy. Edward VI was educated entirely by tutors from Cambridge. More importantly, so was Elizabeth I. It was from this university too that the Elizabethan Puritans drew their major inspiration, and it is no surprise that the Puritan emigration to New England in the following reign was led by Cambridge men—John Cotton, Thomas Hooker, John Winthrop, and John Harvard, among others.

Materially also, the universities fared well in the sixteenth century, and especially the colleges. Before then most scholars had lived in hostels or lodgings; after 1500 they were organized more and more into colleges, until in Elizabeth's reign ordinances were passed requiring every university resident to belong to one college or another. By that time the university population had become predominantly undergraduate. The usual age of admission was from thirteen to sixteen, and the normal length of the course was seven years. By Elizabeth's reign it had become increasingly fashionable for the sons of the gentry and even of noblemen to acquire a university education. Between the 1550s and the 1570s the number of admissions increased by more than fifty percent, and by 1585 total enrollment at both universities came to about three thousand, with Oxford still slightly in the lead in respect of numbers. Evidence of this expansion is still visible in the college buildings erected in the sixteenth century to house the inflow. The great Tudor building boom left a more indelible mark on Oxford and Cambridge, and especially the latter, than on any other town in England.

The first of the Tudor colleges was **Jesus College** *(612)*, lying north of Jesus Lane, Cambridge, founded in 1496 by John Alcock, Bishop of Ely, who was also Henry VII's comptroller of works. He built his college over and around the existing buildings of a suppressed nunnery, so that the oldest parts of it today (the chapel and the buildings surrounding the cloister) date from as early as the twelfth century. The chapel has Early English features as well as Norman, but most of its stained-glass windows belong to the nineteenth century. Of the claustral buildings, the west front of the chapter house retains its thirteenth century appearance, but the beautiful ceilings and doorcases of this cloister court are the work of Alcock. His most notable legacy, however, is the great red-brick gatehouse (except for the top story added in the eighteenth century) and the south range of the outer court which lies to the west of it. The north range of this open court was added in the seventeenth century, while the much less attractive buildings to the east and north are products of the nineteenth and twentieth. Also dating to the reign of King Henry VII, and owing their foundation to the munificence of his mother, Lady Margaret Beaufort, are **Christ's College** *(611)* on St. Andrew's Street and **St. John's College** *(615)*, St. John's Street, both in Cambridge. Christ's was in fact a refoundation, dating 1505, of an older college called

Godshouse. Of Lady Margaret's building, the most striking survival is the enormous Beaufort coat of arms over the gatehouse leading from St. Andrew's Street. Inside the front court, the Tudor buildings were mostly ashlared over in the eighteenth century, though the oriel window in the Master's Lodge is original. Another Tudor relic in the chapel is the beautiful brass eagle lectern embellished with four greyhounds, a Beaufort emblem. The impressively classical Fellows Building was added to the college in the seventeenth century, and the rest of the additions, scattered over unusually spacious grounds, date from the nineteenth and twentieth centuries. Lady Margaret's second great project, chartered six years after Christ's, was St. John's College, whose great gatehouse also displays the Beaufort Arms, here brightly repainted. (The mythical beasts are *yales*, part goat, part antelope, part elephant.) This is today the second largest college in Cambridge, and its architectural history is easy to follow since the successive periods of construction are fairly well differentiated. Inside the gatehouse, the first court is early Tudor on every side except the north (right from the entry). Here the original wing was torn down to make way for a neo-Gothic apsidal-ended chapel by Sir George Gilbert Scott in the 1860s. Moving west from the first court, the second court is late Tudor, dating from 1598–1602, and was built with funds supplied by the countess of Shrewsbury, whose posthumous statue (1671) can be seen over the gateway. Next comes the library, constructed in 1623–1624, to which was adjoined in the later seventeenth century the west and south ranges of the third court. This brought the college to the river bank, and in the early nineteenth century, the new court was built on the other side, connected with the third court by the famous neo-Gothic Bridge of Sighs. The remainder of the college buildings on either side of the river belong to the twentieth century.

At Oxford, meanwhile, William Smith, Bishop of Lincoln, had founded in 1509 a new college curiously called **Brasenose** *(628)*, the name deriving from the form of doorknocker of the hall which had previously occupied the college's site on the west side of what is now called Radcliffe Square. The splendid gatehouse, the charming hall, and the old quadrangle date from about the time of the founding. The chapel and library, both an odd mixture of neo-Gothic and classical styles, were built in the late seventeenth century; the third quadrangle toward High Street was finished in 1909. The oldest part of the college, interestingly, predates its founding. This is the fifteenth-century kitchen which belonged to the original hall taken over by the bishop of Lincoln for his new foundation. The next college to go up in Oxford was **Corpus Christi College** *(629)* on the south side of Merton Street, founded in 1517 by Bishop Richard Foxe, who served as lord privy seal to both Henry VII and Henry VIII. Here the architecture is more predominantly Tudor than in most of Oxford's sixteenth century colleges. The gatehouse, chapel, hall, library, and first quadrangle all date from about the time of founding, and the sundial in the middle of the quadrangle was put up in 1518. The Fellows' Building and the Gentlemen-Commoners' Building belong to the eighteenth century and the President's Lodging to the nineteenth. **Christ Church** *(629)*, on the east side of St. Aldgate's, the largest of Oxford's colleges, has already been described. It was first known as Cardinal College in honor of its founder, Cardinal Wolsey; then as King Henry VIII's college when it was rechartered in 1532, and finally received its present name in 1546 when the king united it with the newly founded **Oxford Cathedral** *(629)*, whose church became the collegiate chapel. Nine years later (1555) two more Oxford colleges were founded on former monastic property: **St. John's** *(634)* and **Trinity** *(634)*, both architecturally distinguished for buildings added in the 17th century.

At Cambridge, King Henry's dissolution of the monasteries led directly to the founding of **Magdalene College** *(613)* (pronounced *maudlin*), Magdalene Street, in 1542 by Sir Thomas Audley, who had succeeded Thomas More as chancellor of England and had made a fortune in monastic spoils. For his new college he simply took over the premises of a hostel built in the late fifteenth century for Benedictine monks from Croyland Abbey. Hence, much of the first court of the present college is pre-Tudor in date, although the gatehouse is Elizabethan and the Hall is from the early sixteenth century. In the second court is the Pepysian Library, built in the late seventeenth century and, since 1724, the repository of Samuel Pepys' library, his desk, and bookcases, as well as the original manuscript of the great *Diary* which is on display. Four years after Magdalene's foundation, King Henry VIII himself founded **Trinity College** *(616)* on the west side of Trinity Street, Cambridge, incorporating some of the existing buildings of King's Hall and Michael House, both foundations of the early fourteenth century. Today Trinity has the largest enrollment of any college in either of the two medieval universities. Architecturally, it is an amalgam of seven successive period styles from the fourteenth through the twentieth centuries, and they are difficult to disentangle. The great gateway, by which one enters from Trinity Street, was built in the early sixteenth century, but the range of buildings on either side of it belong to the earlier King's Hall and date from the late fifteenth. Proceeding into the great court, to the right in the north range lies the chapel, built in the Perpendicular style by order of Queen Mary in the mid-sixteenth century. In the same range, west of the chapel, are situated the fifteenth century Michael House Hall and the fourteenth century King Edward's Tower, the latter reerected on its present site in the late sixteenth century. The remainder of the buildings surrounding the great court are the work of Thomas Neville, a favorite of Queen Elizabeth, and master of Trinity from 1597 to 1615, although the south half of the master's lodge dates from the 1550s. West of the great court is Neville's Court, the western range of which consists of the magnificent library built by Sir Christopher Wren between 1676 and 1695, inside of which are charming woodcarvings by Grinling Gibbons, a number of interesting busts by the eighteenth century sculptor Robiliac, and a statue of

Lord Byron which was refused admission into Westminster Abbey because of the subject's notoriously immoral behavior. South of Neville's Court is a smaller quadrangle called New Court in the neo-Gothic style of the early nineteenth century, and east of this another late seventeenth century building, called Bishop's Hostel. Across Trinity Street from the great gateway are two fairly attractive nineteenth century quadrangles, and on the college side of the street, to the south of the great gateway, stand two less attractive buildings of the nineteenth and twentieth centuries. Just south of Trinity College, across Trinity Lane, lies **Caius** (pronounced *keys*) **College** *(610)*, officially Gonville and Caius. It was founded by Edmund Gonville in 1348 and refounded in 1557 by Dr. John Kaye, or Caius, court physician to Edward VI, Mary, and Elizabeth whose lucrative practice enabled him to restore and enlarge his old school and indulge in a number of architectural fancies picked up during his travels on the Continent. Of the medieval buildings of the original college in what is now called Gonville Court, nothing remains in evidence, since they were all refaced in the eighteenth century with ashlar. To the south of them lies Caius Court, the south end of which is open and the east and west ranges built in the sixteenth century by the new founder. Here the most interesting features are two gateways designed by Dr. Caius himself in what was thought to be the classical manner. The Gate of Virtue is a three-bay, three-story composition with pilasters representing three orders, the central bay crowned by a pediment. The Gate of Honour, which leads into the Senate House Passage on the south side of the college, is even more ambitious, though smaller in size. It is a bizarre concoction of Ionic columns, Corinthian pilasters, classical niches, roundels, and obelisks, all crowned by an unclassical octagonal turret and a stone dome. A third gate, though meant to be the first in the series through which students symbolically passed, was the Gate of Humility since removed from the main entrance of the college to the master's garden. This is a simpler structure, composed of fluted pilasters flanking an arched gateway and topped by a scrolled entablature. The rest of the college buildings, including Tree Court through which the grounds are entered off Trinity Street, belong mostly to the nineteenth century, with a few twentieth century additions on the other side of the street.

While Dr. Caius, a crypto-Catholic, was building his fanciful pseudo-classical oddities, another Elizabethan, Hugh Price, treasurer of St. David's Cathedral in Wales, received a charter (in 1571) to found at Oxford a college dedicated to the pursuit of "the true religion," i.e., the Anglican version of the Protestant faith. This was **Jesus College** *(630)*, located on the west side of Turl Street between Market and Ship. Of the sixteenth century buildings only the east front facing Turl Street survives and this was mostly rebuilt in the Perpendicular style in the mid-nineteenth century, as was also the chapel and the Market Street front. The rest of the front quadrangle is good Jacobean Gothic, and the second quadrangle was built between 1639 and 1713. The Ship Street range belongs to the early years of this century, while the third quadrangle dates from 1971. Until World War I, the college enrollment was about half Welsh, and even now close to twenty percent of the students come from Welsh schools. More self-consciously Protestant even than Jesus College, Oxford, was **Emmanuel College** *(612)*, Cambridge, founded in 1584 by Sir Walter Mildmay, chancellor of the exchequer under Queen Elizabeth. His strong Puritan leanings were a source of worry to the queen, and before she granted the charter she asked for reassurance that the new foundation would not be a hotbed of religious radicalism. Mildmay was evasive, but events proved the queen's suspicions justified, for Emmanuel in fact did become the nerve center of English Puritanism both in her reign and the next. The college was established on the site of a thirteenth century Dominican friary at the corner of St. Andrews and Emmanuel Streets, Cambridge, but only fragments of their buildings survive in the sixteenth century hall which divides the front court from the new court and in the old library which constitutes the east range of the latter. The rest of the front court, including the main entry way to the college, dates from the eighteenth century, though a wing abutting from its southeast corner, called the Brick Building was built in the seventeenth. The north and west ranges enclosing the new court were built in the nineteenth and twentieth centuries respectively, and there are additional twentieth century structures to the north and south of the original college grounds. Emmanuel's greatest attraction, however, is its chapel lying immediately eastward of the front court which is open in that direction. It is basically Italian in design and is one of Sir Christopher Wren's earlier works (1677). American visitors will want to take note of the memorial window to John Harvard, one of Emmanuel's many important Puritan graduates, who is commemorated in the Harvard room in the Brick Building facing the chapel. It was no accident that America's greatest university was established in a town in Massachusetts called Cambridge. The last of the colleges chartered by Queen Elizabeth (and the last in Cambridge until the end of the eighteenth century) was **Sidney Sussex College** *(316)*, founded by Lady Frances Sidney of Penshurst, dowager countess of Sussex, in 1594 and located on the site of a medieval Franciscan friary on the east side of Sidney Street between Jesus Lane and Sussex Street. Architecturally this is the least interesting of all the old colleges, though it has a very pretty garden. The Hall Court, facing Sidney Street, was completed in 1598, but was almost completely Gothicized by the nineteenth century architect, Sir Jeffrey Wyatville. In the second court the chapel is partly eighteenth century, partly twentieth, while the court's south range dates from 1628. The rest of the buildings are of nineteenth and twentieth century provenance. Sidney Sussex's most famous former student is Oliver Cromwell whose portrait hangs in the hall and whose severed head is said to be buried on the premises.

England's third great university, although not designated as such, was in London and consisted of the four Inns of Court and the nine smaller Inns of Chancery. Here long before the sixteenth century (although how far back no one really knows), the sons of the gentry and nobility had gathered to study the laws of England, to practice argument and disputation, and to observe the pleadings in the nearby courts of Westminster. As a member of one of the inns of chancery, the novice learned the rudiments of the legal profession, then passed to one of the inns of court where, after seven or eight years in residence, he might become an "utter barrister," and after eight more might be selected as a sergeant-at-law to plead in the Court of Common Pleas in Westminster, and later still might be called to the bench as one of the royal justices. Or, if he were the son of a nobleman or a gentleman landholder or a prosperous merchant, he might merely spend enough time at the inns to pick up a smattering of legal learning sufficient to satisfy the requirements of estate management or commercial enterprise. The sixteenth century was a period of great and increasing expansion of the legal profession. The dispersal of the monastic lands caused exceptional activity in the property market; the acceleration of trade and commerce multiplied the number of legal transactions; the rise of importance of the House of Commons opened new political opportunities to ambitious lawyers; and the Tudor monarchs' reliance on justices of the peace created new requirements for legal training among the country gentry. Enrollment at the Inns in London mounted accordingly, and by the time of Elizabeth's reign there were probably as many as a thousand in residence there at any given time.

Like the university colleges, the Inns of Court and Chancery were essentially residential halls. The oldest of them was **Lincoln's Inn** *(518)*, whose grounds today are bounded on the north and south by High Holborn and Carey Streets and on the east and west by Chancery Lane and the huge square called Lincoln's Inn Fields. All the buildings here date from the Tudor period or later. Old Hall, a splendid red-brick edifice, was built in 1492, its south bay added in the 1620s. The gatehouse, by which the grounds are entered from Chancery Lane, was built in 1518. North of it is the chapel, dating to 1623; north of the chapel are the Stone Buildings constructed in the 1770s; and on the west, overlooking Lincoln's Inn Fields is the New Hall and Library built in the mid-nineteenth century in the Tudor style. North of High Holborn on the west side of Gray's Inn Road is **Gray's Inn** *(516)*. Badly damaged during the German bombings of World War II, the Elizabethan hall has been rebuilt, though some of its stained glass and woodwork is original; the ruined chapel and library have been completely replaced. The Verulan Buildings (1811) and the Raymond Buildings (1825) escaped destruction. In the lovely Gardens is a statue of the essayist Sir Francis Bacon, treasurer of the inn from 1577 to 1626. South of Lincoln's Inn, on the opposite side of the Strand, lies **Middle Temple Hall** *(514)*, between Middle Temple Lane and Milford Lane just north of Victoria Embankment. This too was badly damaged in World War II, but the lovely Elizabethan chamber has been rebuilt and restored, though the library of sixty-five thousand volumes was completely lost. West of Middle Temple Lane and just south of Fleet Street lies **Temple Church** *(515)* which the residents of Middle Temple shared with those of **Inner Temple** *(514)*, the fourth great Inn of Court whose hall is situated between Temple Church and Victoria Embankment. Here German bombs completely destroyed a nineteenth century structure which has been replaced by the present building, though underneath it are the remains of the crypt dating to the fourteenth century. World War II also saw the demise of the one remaining Inn of Chancery out of the nine that flourished in Elizabeth's day. This is **Staple Inn** *(517)*, on the south side of High Holborn across from the entry to Gray's Inn Road. The picturesque Tudor-style hall on this site is a reconstruction (using some of the old material) of the fine sixteenth century hall that was burned out in 1944.

It will not do to think of the Inns of Court and Chancery as just another law school. In Elizabethan days they were far more than that. They were, to resort to modern slang, where the action was. These precincts were to London what the Left Bank has traditionally been to Paris. Here was the center of England's literary *avant garde*. Bacon's *Essays* were written in his chamber at Gray's Inn; Sir Walter Raleigh penned his earliest verses while a resident of Middle Temple; the soldier/poet Sir Philip Sidney was a member of Gray's Inn; and on 2 February 1602 the hall of the Middle Temple was the scene of a performance of *Twelfth Night* by that most popular of Elizabethan playwrights, William Shakespeare of Stratford-upon-Avon.

WILLIAM SHAKESPEARE

No words can do justice to the genius of this greatest of English poets and dramatists and none will be attempted. He was born in April 1564 in the house on Henley Street, Stratford-upon-Avon, Warwickshire, now on exhibit as **Shakespeare's Birthplace** *(644)*. This is a double house owned by his father, John Shakespeare, a glover and wool merchant who became an alderman of Stratford. Tradition ascribes to the western half of the building the natal site, which allegedly took place in an upstairs room whose windows now bear the scratched signatures of a number of literary greats including Sir Walter Scott and Thomas Carlyle. The eastern half of the house, which was probably John Shakespeare's shop, is now a museum. The playwright's mother was Mary Arden who was born at Wilmcote about four miles northwest of Stratford in **Mary Arden's House** *(645)*, a half-timbered farmstead now open to view. On Church Street, Stratford, stands the fifteenth century **Guildhall** *(644)*, which housed the grammar school attended by the young William in the 1570s.

In November 1582, at the age of eighteen, he married Anne Hathaway, eight years his senior, the nuptials having been arranged in haste. She was born at Shottery, a mile west of Stratford, in a thatched black-and-white farmhouse now called **Anne Hathaway's Cottage** *(644)*. In May 1583 the couple's first child was born and christened Susanna. (She later married a local physician, John Hall, and lived with him in **Hall's Croft** *[644]* on the street called Old Town in Stratford.) A set of twins was then born to the Shakespeares in 1585; the boy, Hamnet, dying in 1596, but the girl, Judith, surviving to marry a vintner named Thomas Quiney and to live with him in a house at the corner of Bridge and High Streets, Stratford, now called **Quiney House** *(644)* in which is situated the local Information Center. Shakespeare probably left Stratford in 1585, the year of the twins' birth. Tradition has it that he took off abruptly after having been caught poaching deer at **Charlecote Park** *(644)* about five miles east of Stratford. Here can still be seen, though much restored, the house erected in 1558 by Sir Thomas Lucy, the magistrate whose stiff penalties allegedly induced Shakespeare to abandon Warwickshire and seek his fortune in London, and who perhaps was the prototype for the bumbling Justice Shallow of *Henry IV, Part II*, and *The Merry Wives of Windsor*. In any case, in London Shakespeare became an actor and then a successful playwright, producing *Love's Labour Lost* in 1591 followed in short order by *The Two Gentlemen of Verona* and *The Comedy of Errors*.

In 1597 he returned to Stratford, a local boy who had made good in the city, and purchased the best house in town, called New Place, originally built by Sir Hugh Clopton who, a hundred years previously, had also gone down to London to become its lord mayor. New Place was wantonly destroyed by a subsequent owner in the eighteenth century, but the site, now known as **New Place Estate** *(664)* on Chapel Street, has been converted into a lovely Elizabethan knot garden, an authentic reproduction of a typically sixteenth century arrangement of beds filled with intricate geometrical designs carried out in closely clipped shrubs. Shakespeare visited New Place yearly until 1610 when he settled there permanently. He died in 1616 and is buried in **Holy Trinity Church** *(644)* near the end of Church Street, Stratford. Here, on the north side of the chancel is his grave, covered by a slab on which is carved an epithet believed to have been written by the great playwright himself:

> Good friend for Jesus sake forbeare
> To digg the dust enclosed heare;
> Blest be ye man yt spares thes stones
> And curst be he yt moves my bones.

This was the greatest of the Elizabethans, after the queen herself. Yet, it will have been noted, he belongs also to the Jacobean age, for he survived Elizabeth by more than a decade—during which time he produced some of his greatest plays, including *Othello, Macbeth,* and *King Lear.* In one of his last, and perhaps unfinished dramas, *King Henry VIII,* he apotheosized Her Majesty in prophetic lines given to Archbishop Cranmer:

> She shall be loved and fear'd: her own shall
> bless her:
> Her foes shake like a field of beaten corn,
> And hang their heads with sorrow. Good grows
> with her:
> In her days every man shall eat in safety,
> Under his own vine, what he plants, and sing
> The merry songs of peace to all his neighbours.

Not forgetting, however, that Elizabeth was dead, and that a new ruler now occupied the throne, the playwright tactfully appended a few deferential lines in honor of James I:

> Wherever the bright sun of heaven shall shine,
> His honour and the greatness of his name
> Shall be, and make new nations; he shall flourish,
> And, like a mountain cedar, reach his branches
> To all the plains about him. Our children's
> children
> Shall see this, and bless Heaven.
> —*King Henry VIII,* Act V, scene v

In the event, these noble words proved more grandiloquent than prophetic.

CHAPTER VIII

THE REIGN OF THE STUARTS:

1603–1714

THE EARLY STUARTS

A short walk down Whitehall from Trafalgar Square will bring the visitor to London to the **Banqueting House** *(519)*—all that survives of the Royal Palace of Whitehall, otherwise destroyed by fire in 1698. It was built by England's first post-medieval architect of distinction, Inigo Jones, for England's first Stuart king, James I. In the following reign the ceiling was decorated by Peter Paul Rubens with a splendid baroque painting depicting James's apotheosis—a suitable tribute to a king who claimed to rule by divine right. The work was commissioned by Charles I, who, fifteen years later, would walk through a window of this same building onto the scaffold set up for his execution. Inigo Jones's masterpiece is in a sense then, a monument both to the grandiosity of the early Stuart monarchs and to their fatal alienation from their English subjects. It is a good place for the intelligent traveller to begin his exploration of seventeenth century Britain.

JAMES I: 1603–1625

James I was no stranger to kingship when he was crowned at Westminster Abbey on 25 July 1603. Thirty-six years before, at the age of one-and-a-half years, he had been proclaimed King James VI of Scotland on the heels of the forced abdication of his mother, Mary Queen of Scots. He had spent his childhood and adolescence more or less in bondage to one or another of the several feuding Scottish aristocratic factions. In time he had learned the principle of divide and rule and for the most part had succeeded in asserting the royal prerogative against the conflicting claims of a turbulent and lawless nobility. Historians have judged him to be the most competent king that Scotland ever had; and if his later exposition of the theory of the divine right of kings seemed presumptuous to English lawyers and parliamentarians, it was an appropriate response to the aristocratic anarchy that had been the curse of Scotland from its very foundation. Equally understandable was James's aversion to presbyterianism as a form of church government. When John Knox and other Scottish Protestants in the sixteenth century had established a national church independent of Rome, they had modeled their new organization on the presbyterian formula developed by John Calvin in Geneva. Scottish Presbyterianism was a system of ecclesiastical polity in which ultimate authority was vested in a general assembly elected by regional synods, in turn elected by local presbyteries, in turn chosen by the ruling elders of individual churches. Although laymen were eligible to sit on these various representative committees and in the general assembly, for the most part it was the clergy who dominated their deliberations. Thus the Church of Scotland approached, though it never quite achieved, the theocratic ideal of Calvin's Geneva. And, though far from democratic, church government in Scotland rested in principle upon the consent of the governed—a situation intolerable to a monarch who believed, as did James, that kings were "God's lieutenants upon earth and sit upon God's throne . . . [exercising] a manner or resemblance of divine power upon earth." James had no quarrel with the fundamental theology of the Scottish reformed clergy. He was himself a thorough Calvinist, believing that sinful man was to be saved from perdition not by works nor by priestly intercessory rites, but by the grace of God alone, predestined from before the foundations of time. His quarrel pertained only to church government and to church-state relationships. The king, he maintained, was the spiritual, as well as the temporal, leader of his subjects, and the king could best exercise his spiritual powers through bishops chosen by himself. Ecclesiastical authority should proceed downward from the throne, not upward from the ranks. And, for a while, James made good his point. By the time he left for England, the Scottish church was still run by presbyteries, synods, and general assemblies, but the king's appointed bishops sat as moderators over the last two of these bodies and, for the most part, had their way.

None of this Scottish background seemed worrisome to Robert Cecil and the English Privy Council as they prepared to welcome this new king from across the border. His assets were manifold in their eyes. A direct descendant on both sides from Henry VII, his hereditary claim to the throne vacated by the Virgin Queen was indisputable. He was a devout Protestant whose Calvinist theology conformed to that prescribed by the Thirty-nine Articles of the Church of England. His dual kingship over England and Scotland would mitigate the ancient danger of the northern country's being used as a launching pad for an invasion from the Continent. Best of all, he already had two sons, the Princes Henry and Charles, so that a peaceful succession seemed guaranteed. And, if rumors of James Stuart's suspected homosexuality reached English ears, they could be discounted by the certain knowledge that his wife, Queen Anne of Denmark, had already born him four children in addition to the two surviving princes and their sister Elizabeth. That he was somewhat loutish in appearance, boorish in manner, and afflicted with a heavy brogue was regrettable. But what more could be expected of a Scot?

Hardly had James crossed the Tweed into England, however, than he met with his first major, and as time would show, insoluble problem. It appeared in the form of the Millenary Petition, so called because its authors claimed to represent the views of a thousand clergymen, all of the Puritan persuasion. The petitioners' specific requests were moderate enough: to purify worship in the Church of England by abolishing certain residual popish practices such as making the sign of the cross at baptism and by making others optional, such as the wearing of cap and vestments by the clergy. But they were symptomatic of the Puritans' growing discontent with the failure of the Elizabethan church to break completely with its Roman Catholic origins. The new king, Protestant himself to the core, proved amenable at first, and called a conference of English divines to Hampton Court to discuss the matters raised by the petition. There, however, when some of the malcontents hinted at a presbyterian solution to the problem of church polity, James reacted fiercely. "No bishop, no king!" he declared and promised to harry nonconformists out of the land. It was a bad beginning, made worse by the king's subsequent appointment of an extreme anti-Puritan Richard Bancroft, to the see of Canterbury. The seeds of enmity between the Crown and a growing Puritan party had been sown.

Still, the Hampton Court Conference produced one happy result: the king's agreement to a new translation of the Holy Bible. It emerged seven years later as the King James (or Authorized) Version, a faithful if not always literal rendition of the original, and a masterpiece of English prose style matched only by Shakespeare and Cranmer's *Book of Common Prayer.* Here the awful majesty of the Protestant God at last found adequate expression in the majestic cadences of the English language at its high-water mark:

> Then the Lord answered Job out of the whirlwind, and said,
> Who is this that darkeneth counsel by words without knowledge?
> Gird up now thy loins like a man; for I will demand of thee, and
>   answer thou me.
> Where wast thou when I laid the foundations of the earth? Declare
>   if thou hast understanding.
> Who hath laid the measures thereof, if thou knowest? Or who hath
>   stretched the line upon it?
> Whereupon are the foundations thereof fastened? Or who laid the
>   cornerstone thereof:
> When the morning stars sang together, and all the sons of God
>   shouted for joy?
> —*Holy Bible,* Authorized Version, Job 38:1–7

Fast disappearing from pew racks in the Protestant churches of America, and even in England an endangered species threatened by graceless modernizers, the Authorized Version remains the greatest surviving monument to the Jacobean age.

A year after the Hampton Court Conference adjourned, King James and his government faced a more serious, or at least a more immediate, threat than the discontent of even a thousand Puritan preachers and their followers. It came from the opposite side of the religious spectrum.

Catholics in early seventeenth century England probably numbered no more than twenty-five thousand, mostly living in the backward regions of the north and west. Yet in a nation where Foxe's *Book of Martyrs* was to be found in almost every literate household and among a people only a generation removed from the Massacre of St. Bartholomew's Eve, fear of Rome and the counter-Reformation still stayed at a level approaching paranoia. In the first year of his reign James ordered renewed vigilance in the collection of fines from recusants (i.e., Catholics refusing to attend Church of England services) and in the apprehension and punishment of Jesuit missionaries. Repression produced a reaction in the form of a conspiracy of Catholics, directed by Robert Catesby of Warwickshire, to blow up both houses of Parliament as it opened its session on 5 November 1605, a day when the king was bound to be present. The conspirators bungled, and word of the plot reached Robert Cecil, whom James had wisely retained from the preceding regime as first minister. So it was that on the eve of the dread day, a search party discovered an ex-soldier named Guy Fawkes alone in a Westminster cellar ready to apply the torch to the barrels of gunpowder that could have blown to kingdom come the effective government of England. Fawkes was clapped in the Tower; the plot's details were extracted from him under torture; his fellow conspirators were mostly hunted down and killed. Henry Garnet, the Superior of the English Jesuits, was executed; and for 250 years the fifth of November was celebrated throughout Britain as a day of thanksgiving and is still the occasion for fireworks and the repetition of a well-known nursery rhyme:

> Remember, remember the Fifth of November,
> Gunpowder, Treason, and Plot!

The immediate upshot was the passage by Parliament of severe penal laws against Catholics. They do not appear, however, to have been rigorously enforced, and Catholicism continued to spread slowly so that by 1640 the number of communicants rose to an estimated sixty thousand. Under the protection of a significant body of landed gentry too powerful to be proceeded against by county magistrates, Jesuit and Benedictine missionaries diligently pursued the business of conversion with at least modest success. As any visitor to the stately homes of Britain knows, these brave zealots were sometimes concealed behind fireplaces and beneath staircases in what are known as priest holes, although the number of hideouts so advertised today greatly exceeds the number actually so used.

Between James I and his parliaments, no love was lost; but, on the other hand, no conflict of wills was allowed to escalate into serious controversy. Not legally obliged to convene a parliament at stated intervals, the king chose not to do so except when financial stringency required it. By bringing an end to the long-lasting war with Spain in 1604, he put a stop to the chief drain on the royal exchequer, and by letting the royal navy starve and rot he put the country at risk but did save money. Extravagant to a fault, however, especially in the matter of gifts to royal favorites, he usually required more funds than Parliament was willing to supply, and these he sought to obtain by extraparliamentary devices such as deficit borrowing, selling of Crown lands and monopolies, extracting benevolences or free gifts of money from his subjects, etc. Also James was the first English king to exploit his position as the fount of honor for purely fiscal purposes. First to be huckstered (or simply given away in grandiose gestures of generosity) were knighthoods. In the first four months of his reign James I dubbed 906 new knights, and by the end of 1604 England could boast three times as many as had enjoyed the honor in the last year of Elizabeth's reign. Then the king proclaimed that all Englishmen with incomes of at least forty pounds per year must be knighted or fined, which of course brought still larger numbers into the fold. In 1611 the Crown began to market the new hereditary dignity of baronet, in return for which the recipient was asked to pay the cost of maintaining thirty soldiers for three years in Ireland to defend the king's new plantations of Protestant settlers from Scotland and England in Ulster. The initial price was £1,095, though, by flooding the market, the king and his chief minister, the duke of Buckingham, brought the value of baronetcies down to £200. Peerages were the next to be put out for sale. By 1615 James had already increased the number of peers by forty percent, and from that year until 1628 the number of English peerages rose from 81 to 126 while Irish peerages increased by an even higher rate.

One consequence of this prodigal inflation of honors was to stimulate conspicuous consumption, especially in the form of setting up new and costly country seats. "Men with titles," as the historian Lawrence Stone points out, "felt themselves obliged to maintain a way of life commensurate with their degree." Hence the great number of "prodigy houses," many of which "still lie heavily about the English countryside like the fossilized bones of the giant reptiles of the Carboniferous Age."

Architecturally, there is little difference between Elizabethan and Jacobean designs except that in the seventeenth century the U-plan or E-plan house began to give way to an H-plan which endowed both front and back of the central block with a grander and more elegant appearance. It also allowed more interior rooms; and parlors, chambers, and saloons tended to multiply, while the great hall grew in size, often occupying either the whole length of the central block or the whole length of one of the sides of the H.

In point of time the first great Jacobean house is **Knole** (545) in the southern outskirts of Sevenoaks, Kent. This is really a hybrid because the original house here was built by Thomas Bourchier, Archbishop of Canterbury, in the late fifteenth century, and later enlarged by his successors before being seized by Henry VIII to be used as a royal palace until his daughter Elizabeth gave it to her cousin, Thomas Sackville, first earl of

Dorset. Between 1603 and 1608 Sackville rebuilt the house into essentially the shape and appearance it has today. On the outside he added curly Dutch gables and a Tuscan colonnade. Inside he lowered the ceiling of the hall, installed a Jacobean screen, built a timber staircase, installed new ceilings and fireplaces in most of the rooms, and added five long galleries, of which the most splendid are the Brown Gallery and the Leicester Gallery which contain the best collection of early seventeenth century furniture in England.

Perhaps the greatest of the Jacobean prodigy houses was built, appropriately enough, by Robert Cecil, son of Lord Burghley who had created the grandest of the Elizabethan private palaces. Cecil had been in no small way responsible for James Stuart's unobstructed accession to the throne of England, and the grateful king had wisely kept him on as first secretary and in 1605 made him earl of Salisbury, an elevation in rank more deserved than most. But James's gratitude did not prevent his coveting Cecil's fine mansion at Theobalds in Hertfordshire, so, like Henry VIII in the case of Wolsey's Hampton Court, the king prevailed on the first secretary to surrender it in exchange for the nearby royal estate of **Hatfield Palace** *(620)* where Queen Elizabeth had spent much of her early life. Salisbury pulled down three sides of the old brick palace and used the material, as well as stones taken from St. Augustine's Abbey in Canterbury, to build his magnificent **Hatfield House** *(620)*, completed in 1612. The ground plan is essentially H-shaped, though the central bar is pushed so far down as to make it look more like a U. The two wings of the garden front are wide enough to hold two or three rooms across; ogee-capped towers rise at each corner of the wings; the central frontispiece is a three-storied porch; and behind it rises a splendid clock tower, possibly designed by the famous architect Inigo Jones who is known to have visited Hatfield while building was in progress. Inside, the long gallery is exceptionally long and narrow; the great hall, untypically for the seventeenth century, runs in medieval fashion parallel to the front of the house; and the grand staircase with balustrades of carved oak is a masterpiece of Jacobean woodwork. The master carpenter was Robert Lyminge, though its major architect was the owner himself, who died in 1612, the year it was completed.

Five years after the completion of Hatfield, Sir Henry Hobart, lord chief justice and among the first baronets created by James I, began the construction of **Blickling Hall** *(604)* near Aylsham, Norfolk. Its similarities to Hatfield House can probably be attributed to Robert Lyminge's having been its chief architect and are observable chiefly on the south front with its ogee-capped corner towers, three-story frontispiece, and bay windows topped by curved gables. Unlike Hatfield, however, the house was designed not on a modified H-plan but as a rectangle built around two inner courtyards. Inside, except for the Jacobean staircase and the ceiling in the long gallery, the house was mostly redone in the eighteenth century in the Georgian manner. In the same county as

Blickling, though not so grand, is **Felbrigg Hall** *(605)* near Cromer, Norfolk. Only the south wing of this L-shaped house is Jacobean, built about 1620 by Thomas Windham. Its rustic exterior is made of brick, stone, and flint, its facade interrupted by a three-story frontispiece with Tuscan columns flanking the doorway, protruding bays symmetrically placed on either side, and the whole surmounted by a parapet pierced with stone letters spelling out the words *Gloria Deo In Excelsis.* Fifty-odd years later the west wing of the L was added, built in red brick in the typical classical style of the Restoration Period. Like Blickling, **Audley End** *(600)* near Saffron Waldon, Essex, was originally designed as a rectangle enclosing two square courtyards. It was begun in 1603 by the lord treasurer, Thomas Howard, earl of Suffolk. It was one of the grandest of all Jacobean prodigy houses, so much so that even James I is said to have remarked that it was too large for a king, though it might do for a lord treasurer. In the early eighteenth century, however, on the advice of the then fashionable architect Vanbrugh, half of it was torn down, so that what the visitor sees today, though impressive enough, is only the inner court. So many changes were made during Audley End's eighteenth century renovation that it is difficult today for the visitor to distinguish the original Jacobean construction from the later remodeling. The confusion is even greater inside where current restoration of the ground floor aims at duplicating the Georgian handiwork of Robert Adam, while the first floor is predominantly Victorian, complete with an enormous collection of stuffed birds.

Also dating to the reign of James I, though completely departing from the prevailing Jacobean fashion, is **Bolsover Castle** *(662)* near Chesterfield, Derbyshire. It was initially designed by the noted Elizabethan master builder Robert Smythson for Sir Charles Cavendish, son of Bess of Hardwick whose own great palace of Hardwick Hall is visible from Bolsover across the Derbyshire hills. Cavendish died in 1617 and his son, who later became the earl and first duke of Newcastle, completed the buildings, now in ruins. Though almost as grand in conception as Hatfield and Audley End, Bolsover is a sham castle of medieval design with fanciful Italianate ornamentation. It consists of a long, low residential block, now called the terrace range; a high castellated keep originally surrounded by ogee-capped towers; and an inside riding range which is today the best preserved part of the establishment. Less self-consciously medieval, but still sporting crenellated towers among its Flemish gables, Chipping Norton, is **Chastleton House** *(626)* near Chipping Norton, Oxfordshire. Built in the early seventeenth century by a wool merchant from nearby Witney, this smallish courtyard house has no great architectural merit but is distinguished on the inside by its well-preserved Jacobean paneling and plasterwork and the unusually large number of surviving pieces of contemporary furniture.

Of another order entirely is **Castle Ashby** *(656)* just east of the city of Northampton. This was a prodigy house begun in 1574 by the first Lord

Compton and was carried to completion during the first three decades of the seventeenth century by his son who married the heiress of a lord mayor of London and was made earl of Northampton by James I. Although the house today is noted chiefly for the richness of its furnishings and the excellence of its paintings, its most interesting architectural feature is the stone screen thrown across the open side of the original U-shaped building to form a new entrance front. This elegant two-story structure, embellished with pillars of the Doric and Ionic orders and a central Venetian window, may be the work of the first of England's great architects since the Middle Ages, Inigo Jones.

Inigo Jones was London born, took up drawing sometime in his youth, and became proficient enough to attract the attention of Queen Anne of Denmark who hired him as a designer of costumes and sets for her court masques—elaborate allegorical pageants that were in the height of fashion during the reign of her husband, James I. For a number of years he collaborated in these endeavors with Ben Jonson who had succeeded Shakespeare as London's most eminent dramatist and whose gravestone, inscribed "O Rare Ben Jonson" is still to be seen in the north aisle of the nave of **Westminster Abbey** *(523)*. Eventually the team split up after a quarrel over author's credits, and Jones joined the entourage of the heir apparent, Prince Henry, the leading art patron and connoisseur of the day. After the prince came to an untimely death in 1612, Jones left England for the Continent in the company of Thomas Howard, fourteenth earl of Arundel, a noted collector of art objects, chiefly statuary. With the peripatetic earl, Jones visited Rome and northern Italy, where he came across the writings of the sixteenth century Italian architect, Andrea Palladio, whose exposition and detailed drawings of the ruined villas and public buildings of ancient Rome became the major inspiration for Jones's own subsequent architectural endeavors. On his return home he received from James I the appointment as surveyor of the King's works, and to that lucky turn of events England owes some of its most exquisite gems of architecture.

The first of these was the villa he built for Queen Anne, overlooking the Thames in Greenwich. Its contemporary name was the Queen's House and it is now the home of the **National Maritime Museum** *(536)*. Here, on either side of the Deptford-Woolwich road, he laid out two identical rectangular buildings connected by a bridge which has since disappeared and the gap closed. Inspired by villas he had seen near Florence, Jones followed the Palladian principle of forcing the dimensions of his rooms into a precise mathematical ratio. Thus, in the north wing, the great two-story hall is a forty-foot cube, while the lateral dimensions of the adjacent rooms on the first (mezzanine) floor are in an exact ratio to each other of 1:1 or 1:2. Visitors to this place, naturally intent on viewing the fine collection of naval portraits and paintings and marine artifacts and memorabilia, should not overlook the splendid architectural setting in which these interesting objects are placed. Inigo

Jones's next endeavor, actually undertaken before the Queen's House was finished, was the **Banqueting House** *(519)* in Whitehall, already mentioned at the opening of this chapter. Here, behind a classical facade featuring regularly spaced Ionic columns and pilasters on the first floor, repeated on the second with those of the Corinthian order, Jones installed a double-cubed hall measuring 110 feet long by 55 feet broad and high, the room divided into two levels by a balustraded balcony with wall pilasters, again Ionic below and Corinthian above. It was not until the next reign that the great Flemish painter, Peter Paul Rubens, was commissioned to decorate the ceiling with his busy allegorical painting of the apotheosis of the late James I. The central oval of this lush work depicts the king being crowned with a laurel wreath in the midst of a crowd of angels and cherubs while the panels to the side and the end show the manifest benefits of government under the first king to rule both England and Scotland and the triumph of royal generosity over avarice and of reason over intemperate discord. Nothing could be more baroque. But the Banqueting House itself is not. It is distinctly Palladian: mathematically proportioned, serene, cool, and classical. So is Inigo Jones's final work for James I. This is the **Queen's Chapel** *(522)* opposite St. James's Palace, London. Commissioned in 1623 and finished four years later, it is today open to the public only during Sunday services in the summertime. The exterior is severe in the manner of a *cella* of a Roman temple. But the interior is splendid, in a restrained sort of way. Light pours into the east end, designed in the Venetian fashion with a high round-arched window flanked by two rectangles of glass. Below the central window is a richly paneled reredos and above it is a carving of the royal arms in high relief. The barrel-shaped ceiling is coffered and gilded. There is nothing here at all of the traditional ecclesiastical Gothic. As it was going up, even the king who commissioned it was shocked at its Romish appearance. "We are building," James I declared, "a temple to the devil."

The fact is the Queen's Chapel was intended to be a place of Roman Catholic worship for the Infanta of Spain to whom James hoped to marry the Prince of Wales, soon to become Charles I. The marriage portion from such a match promised to be substantial, and anyway the duke of Buckingham was for it. This resplendent courtier, born George Villiers, the second son of an impoverished Leicestershire squire, was the last of the king's favorites on whom he showered affection, wealth, and power. James's fatal fascination for handsome, ambitious, and amoral young men was notorious. Villiers had replaced an earlier protégé, a young Scotsman, Robert Carr, whom the king had promoted to the earldom of Somerset and whose subsequent involvement in a notorious murder case brought disgrace upon the court. James's public demonstrations of affection, first for Carr, and then for Villiers, were so blatantly immodest as to raise legitimate questions as to what went on behind closed doors. Nor could the king's frequent drunkenness fail to diminish respect for the throne among a large and important body of his subjects. His successor would inherit a tarnished crown.

Meanwhile James's foolish infatuation for Buckingham allowed him to be persuaded to endorse a hare-brained scheme for the duke and Prince Charles to take ship to Spain and there in person press the suit for the Infanta's hand. The mission failed; Buckingham was outraged over perceived personal slights from the Spanish court; and on his return to England persuaded the king to call a Parliament with a view to declaring war on Spain and giving armed support to James's son-in-law, the Elector Palatine, whose land had been invaded by an imperial army in what proved to be the beginning of the so-called Thirty Years War. And so the reign ended with England on the brink of an unnecessary if popular war —the avoidance of which for more than two decades had been James I's greatest achievement and greatest pride. Meanwhile, Inigo Jones's "temple to the devil" was nearing completion; in fact it would be completed in time for the arrival of another Roman Catholic princess who was to be the next queen of England—Henrietta Maria, sister of King Louis XIII of France.

CHARLES I: 1625–1649

"King Charles," wrote the diarist Lucy Hutchinson, "was temperate, chaste and serious." He was also shy, deficient in speech, a poor judge of character, stubborn, and devious. He was totally devoid of that political sense that had been the source of Queen Elizabeth's greatness or of the native canniness that enabled James I, for all his failings, to survive in a hostile environment. It was a tragedy, both personal and national, that Charles inherited the throne meant for his far abler elder brother Prince Henry who had prematurely died of typhoid fever in 1612.

Yet, from his brother the new king had acquired at least one talent: a sophisticated and discriminating taste for works of art. He was (with the possible exception of George III) the greatest patron of the arts ever to occupy the throne of England. During his abortive expedition to Spain to woo the reluctant Infanta, he had the opportunity to view perhaps the greatest single collection of paintings in the world and there to acquire a taste for the works of the Venetian painters of the High Renaissance, especially Titian. Later he was able to purchase for himself an almost equally notable collection from the impoverished duke of Mantua. All of these noble works of art, however, were eventually lost to England—sold to pay off the debts of the Commonwealth after the king's execution. Only a few have been repurchased, among them the great Raphael cartoons now on display in Room 48 of the **Victoria and Albert Museum** *(526)*, London.

Charles was also diligent in his search for a court painter who might raise the standards of English art to those already achieved on the Continent. First he tried out Daniel Mytens, a Dutchman who had served as artist in residence to King James and had painted the portrait of his patron now hanging in the **National Portrait Gallery** *(518)* in London.

Other Mytens works include portraits of Thomas Howard and his wife in **Arundel Castle** *(550)*, West Sussex; Sir Henry Hobart at **Blickling Hall** *(604)*, Norfolk; King James's favorite, the first duke of Buckingham, at **Euston Hall** *(609)*, Suffolk; the first Lord Baltimore, to whom Charles I gave the proprietorship of Maryland, in **Gorhambury House** *(620)*, Hertfordshire; and portraits of King Charles himself in **Hatfield House** *(620)*, Hertfordshire, **Parham Park** *(554)*, West Sussex, and, again the **National Portrait Gallery** *(518)*. Mytens lacked the elegance, however, that the king was apparently seeking, and in the Flemish painter, Sir Anthony Van Dyck (knighted by Charles) he found an artist equal to the great Rubens whom an English knighthood had not persuaded to establish permanent residence in London, and who had even gone home to execute the panels for his spectacular ceiling for the **Banqueting House** *(519)* in Whitehall. Van Dyck was everything a patron of the king's sensibilities could ask for. His brush was delicate, his style resembled Titian's but with baroque overtones not unlike Rubens, and best of all he flattered his subjects, especially the royal family. It is as much due to Van Dyck as to the facts of his life and death that Charles I has come down through history as a romantic and tragic figure. And of course Van Dyck's permanent fame was guaranteed when his name became synonomous with the peculiar facial hair style affected by so many of his male sitters. He was such a prolific painter, and his canvases are still scattered so widely among the galleries, palaces, and stately homes of Britain that it would be too much to try to name the present locations of all of them. The most interesting historically are the portraits he executed of the royal family: King Charles himself, Queen Henrietta Maria, and some or all of their older children. The best of these are to be found in the **National Gallery** *(518)* in London; **Euston Hall** *(609)*, Suffolk; **Goodwood House** *(552)*, West Sussex; **Lamport Hall** *(656)*, Northamptonshire; **Warwick Castle** *(646)*, Warwickshire; and in the famous double-cube room at **Wilton House** *(575)* in Wiltshire. Most interesting of all perhaps is his portrait, now hanging in **Windsor Castle** *(565)*, Berkshire, of *Charles I in Three Positions,* painted for the famous Roman sculptor Bernini to assist in his modeling of the king's bust.

Van Dyck died in 1641, the year before the Civil War broke out and the king and his court moved to Oxford. For the next four years his shoes were filled by a new court painter, this time a native Englishman named William Dobson. Not as prolific as Van Dyck, his portraits are more clearly in the mainstream of baroque art, with classical and allegorical figures commonly included in their backgrounds. He was, par excellence, the portraitist of the king's cause in the Civil War. Among his better works are the painting of three cavaliers now at **Alnwick Castle** *(704)*, Northumberland; the head of a cavalier at **Corsham Court** *(572)*, Wiltshire; the group portrait of King Charles's nephew, Prince Rupert, with two companions at **Ashdown House** *(576)*, Oxfordshire; and especially the three-quarter length study of Endymion Porter in the **Tate Gallery** *(523)* in London.

For architecture the king's enthusiasm was less pronounced than for portraiture. True, Inigo Jones stayed on as surveyor, but the buildings he put up at the king's request were of relative insignificance, and none has survived. He did prepare plans for a gorgeous new palace at Whitehall, but the Civil War aborted their realization. Jones was, however, busy at work for other patrons. He restored St. Paul's Cathedral in London and tacked a new classical front onto the west end of the Romanesque and Gothic church, all destroyed in the Great Fire of 1666. His only other ecclesiastical effort has survived, however, though much restored after another fire in 1795. This is **St. Paul, Covent Garden** *(578)*, also in London. Built in 1631 in the Tuscan style as interpreted by Palladio, it was the first entirely new Protestant church to be built in London since the Reformation. Equally classical, but far more elegant in style, was Jones's renovation after a fire of **Wilton House** *(575)* near Salisbury, Wiltshire, for the fourth earl of Pembroke. Here the center of the east front dates from the original Tudor construction, but the rest of the house appears to have been designed by Jones, although the building itself was probably done by Isaac de Caus and the interior restoration was finished by Jones's nephew-in-law, John Webb. Considered by some art historians to be the most splendid suite of rooms in England, the great double-cube and single-cube rooms of Wilton follow the precise mathematical ratios which Jones had learned from Palladio. The double-cube is particularly grand—sixty feet long by thirty feet wide and high, with a great double door topped by a broken pediment, a coved and painted ceiling, the walls adorned with gilded ornaments in high relief, between which hang Van Dyck's great paintings of the royal family and the magnificent group portrait of the Herbert family.

The end of Jones's life was full of woe. Although an old man, he joined the king's forces during the Civil War, was captured by Cromwell's soldiers during the siege of Basing House, stripped, and carried off half-naked on a blanket, possibly to prison in London where he was heavily fined before being pardoned. He died in 1652. His influence survived, however, in the person of John Webb who continued to build great houses, the most distinguished survivor being **Lamport Hall** *(656)*, Northamptonshire. This was commissioned in 1654 by Sir Justinian Isham, and though greatly modified in the eighteenth century, still retains Webb's five-bay facade, which looks somewhat like a miniature version of the Banqueting House in Whitehall.

The Civil War—between king and Parliament and their respective followers—was more than fifteen years in brewing. When Charles I became king in 1625 the egregious duke of Buckingham retained his dominant influence at court, though not for the same reasons as had accounted for his rise to power in the previous reign. War was declared against Spain; an English expedition to Cadiz ended in a drunken spree; Parliament was called, only to be dissolved after an effort to impeach Buckingham; Spain and France signed a treaty of alliance; Buckingham persuaded the king to go to war against France and himself led an unsuccessful expedition to relieve a band of French Protestants (Huguenots) besieged by King Louis XIII's forces in La Rochelle; Parliament was again summoned and prorogued for another threat to impeach Buckingham; the duke was finally assassinated by a mad naval officer whose promotion he had foiled; Parliament rejoiced in the killing but refused to grant the king's requests for additional revenues and voted its own adjournment in March of 1629. It would not meet again for eleven years. During this long period of personal rule, Charles kept solvent by resorting to a number of fiscal expedients considered extortionate by the merchants and landed gentry whose representatives in Parliament had caused him so much trouble. But these exactions, annoying as they were, might have been grudgingly tolerated in the country at large had it not been for the king's attempt to revolutionize the Church of England.

That the church should be uniform in theology and form of worship and that church membership should be universal and compulsory were propositions unanimously agreed upon in the early seventeenth century —except by a handful of radical separatists such as the Pilgrims who founded Plymouth colony in New England in 1620. Nor was there much argument about the right of the established church to collect tithes of money and kind from the entire laity. Only in the context of this prevailing ecclesiastical totalitarianism can the bitter religious controversies of the seventeenth century be understood. Ever since the Elizabethan Settlement, the Church of England had been Calvinist in doctrine and Protestant in practice, at least to the extent that preaching was emphasized over liturgy and Communion had replaced the Mass. Puritans might object that church worship had not been cleansed enough of the taint of Rome, but they were only slightly ahead of the mass of English clergy and laity in their anti-Catholicism. Then came Charles I and William Laud, a high-minded and energetic prelate whom the king raised from the bishopric of London to the archepiscopal see of Canterbury in 1633. Both were Arminians; that is they were followers of the Dutch theologian, Jacobus Arminius, who had rejected Calvin's predestinarian teachings in favor of the doctrines of free will and salvation by works. This struck at the heart of English Protestantism, especially when Arminians carried their theology to its logical conclusion by reemphasizing the sacramental and liturgical aspects of church worship (i.e., works) at the expense of preaching and Bible reading which Calvinists believed were the principal channels through which God's grace sought out and informed the elect. Indeed, Arminianism appeared to most Protestants as a thinly disguised form of popery.

No doubt the argument might have remained at a high level of abstract disputation had not Laud tried to impose a visible rearrangement of church furnishings and to reintroduce certain ceremonies long since forgotten in the reformed Church of England. Specifically, he ordered the removal of the Communion table from the nave to the extreme east end of the church where it was to be surrounded by a low railing in front of which communicants should kneel to receive the bread and wine from the officiating priest. This struck many a Protestant observer as the first step toward a revival of the Mass. The bitterness which this single act of the archbishop engendered was profound and widespread, and, when armed rebellion against the king eventually did break out, Laud's altar rails were the first victims of a wholesale desecration of the churches which included stained-glass windows and statuary as well.

Laud's name is also usually identified with a distinctive mid-seventeenth century trend in church and collegiate architecture, although admittedly the connection is somewhat tenuous. At Oxford, two colleges had been founded in the reign of James I. **Wadham College** *(635)*, established in 1610, can best be described as Jacobean Gothic, with traceried Perpendicular windows in the chapel; and a Renaissance-style frontispiece between antechapel and hall. **Pembroke College** *(633)*, sited against a portion of the old city wall, was founded in 1624 on the grounds of a number of medieval halls, including Broadgates, whose refectory still serves as the senior common room. There was some new construction here in the seventeenth century, but it has been so much renovated that it is difficult to discern. The most interesting Jacobean contribution to Oxford's architectural scene is the gatehouse entering into the **Old Schools Quadrangle** *(632)*: an elaborate tower featuring the five classic orders (Doric, Ionic, Corinthian, Tuscan, and Composite) with a statue of James I under a stone canopy and the Stuart arms at the top.

When Laud became chancellor in 1631 the university witnessed a flurry of building in the mixed Gothic and classical fashion that he favored—some historians say because the former reflected his reactionary theological opinions and the latter his leanings toward Rome. This hybrid style, commonly labeled Laudian, is to be seen best at **St. John's College** *(634)* where the Canterbury quadrangle has an Italianate loggia at either end, with medieval facades and battlemented parapets above, while superimposed columns adorn the centerpieces, and above the entrances are niches housing bronze statues of Charles I and his queen, Henrietta Maria. Another Laud-inspired addition to Oxford was the chapel of **Lincoln College** *(634)* which couples traceried Gothic windows with figures in stained glass wearing Van Dyck beards. At Cambridge, Laud's protégé, Matthew Wren (uncle to Sir Christopher), while master of **Peterhouse** *(614)*, built a new chapel in which Perpendicular windows are combined with a classical east end crowned with a pediment.

The only parish church actually consecrated by Laud was **St. Katherine Cree** *(512)* on Leadenhall Street, London, which has a Gothic vaulted ceiling springing from classical columns, classical arcades, and an eastern rose window. **St. John the Evangelist** *(651)* in Leeds, West Yorkshire, built about the same time, is in all respects a perfect copy of a medieval Perpendicular church, except that its fittings, including the splendid screen stretching across the full width of the nave, are pure seventeenth century. A similar combination obtained at **St. Mary's, Leighton**

Bromswold *(618)* near Huntingdon, Cambridgeshire, where a medieval church was rebuilt in Gothic style, but the interior was furnished with seventeenth century choir stalls and chancel screen and matching reading pew and canopied pulpit so that equal weight would be given to praying and preaching (a nice Laudian touch). Finally, the parish church (now a chapel under the care of the National Trust) at **Staunton Harold** *(657)*, near Ashby-de-la-Zouche in Leicestershire, is perhaps the supreme example of church architecture as an expression of conservative religious and political views. It was built by the royalist Sir Robert Shirley in the midst of the Civil War as an act of defiance to Parliament and the enemies of the king. Self-consciously late medieval (i.e., Perpendicular) in style, the church reflects the sentiment inscribed over its west door: "When all things Sacred were throughout ye nation Either demolisht or profaned Sir Robert Shirley, Baronet, Founded this church." Having thus called attention to himself, Sir Robert was required by the revolutionary government in London to raise a regiment to fight the king. He refused, of course, and was clapped in the Tower where he died at the age of 27. A decade before, Archbishop Laud, at the age of 72, had been beheaded in the same place by order of a vengeful Parliament. A devout and earnest man, his strenuous, and on occasion brutal, efforts to turn back the tide of English Puritanism had contributed, more than any other single factor, to the undoing of the king he tried to serve.

But for Laud's doctrinaire Arminianism, Charles I might have gone on indefinitely without summoning a Parliament. Peace was concluded with Spain and France, and the king agreed to abandon the cause of his sister's husband, the Protestant Elector Palatine, so that England stayed out of the Thirty Years War on the Continent. Freed of foreign entanglements and unencumbered by the host of venal favorites who had drained his father's purse, Charles could almost balance his budget. Increased customs revenues from England's expanding foreign trade, plus turning the screw on the taxpayers in imaginative, if arbitrary, ways, was keeping the government solvent. Then, Laud precipitated a war with Scotland.

In this heartland of Presbyterian Calvinism the archbishop promulgated a new Arminian prayerbook and tried to force its use on the Scottish church. In July 1637 a prearranged riot broke out in St. Giles Church, Edinburgh; petitions against the new dispensation began to circulate all over the country; the petitioners elected a representative body which drew up the National Covenant rejecting Laud's new liturgy and later abolishing the Scottish episcopacy altogether. The Scots then prepared for war, and Charles was forced to call a Parliament to Westminster. It met, refused to vote the king supply without first receiving satisfaction for its grievances, and was dissolved. A Scottish army crossed the Tweed, routed the king's forces, occupied Newcastle-upon-Tyne, and announced its determination to hold hostage the entire counties of Northumberland and Durham until the English paid a ransom calculated at £850 for each day of occupation. Once more the king summoned a Parliament.

This was the so-called Long Parliament which convened on 3 November 1640. The House of Commons was dominated by lawyers, merchants, and landed gentry, on whom the burden of the king's irregular fiscal exactions had most heavily fallen, and by Puritans who hated Laud, though these were not mutually exclusive groups. They attainted and then executed the king's chief minister, Lord Strafford, who was suspected of a design to bring an Irish army over to subdue Parliament; imprisoned Laud; abolished a number of royal prerogative courts; legislated against the king's recent tax innovations; and declared that the Communion table should be removed from the east end of the nation's churches and that Laud's rails be destroyed. Fear gripped the members when a Catholic rebellion broke out in Ireland resulting in a massacre of Protestants. The king was suspected of trying to raise an army ostensibly against the Irish rebels but in fact to be used against Parliament. Then on 3 January 1642 Charles personally invaded the House of Commons with an armed guard intent on seizing five of its members who had been his most vocal opponents. The coup failed but it was a virtual declaration of war. In April the king tried unsuccessfully to seize the important military supply depot at Hull. On 22 August he raised the royal standard at Nottingham and summoned all loyal Englishmen to his support. The Civil War had begun.

The first battle of the first phase of the war was fought on 23 October 1642 at Edgehill in Warwickshire between armies of about thirteen thousand each, led respectively by the king himself and the Puritan earl of Essex, one of several members of the nobility who had espoused the cause of Parliament. The battle ended in a draw, and both armies made for London, the king's to seize it from parliamentary control and Essex's to prevent its capture. Essex got there first and, with the help of the city militia, turned back the royalist forces at Turnham Green without a shot being fired on either side. Charles retreated to Oxford, which became his headquarters for the balance of the war.

The following summer, after the royalists had won significant victories in Yorkshire and the southwest, the king planned a three-pronged attack on London. The scheme failed when his northern and western armies declined to cooperate. He himself proved unable to capture Gloucester and open a line of communications with Wales which for most of the war remained loyal to the king. Thereafter his strategy disintegrated. Henrietta Maria was on the Continent trying to buy men and arms with the money realized from pawning the crown jewels (which is why none of the gems now in the Jewel Tower of the **Tower of London** *(513)* dates from before the reign of Charles II). She did succeed in landing at Bridlington with a shipload of arms which eventually got to the king's headquarters at Oxford. But it was not enough. Charles's other hope for help from across the sea rested in Ireland. The best he could get from that quarter, however, was a loan of thirty thousand pounds—but no soldiers. The fact is that the king could expect little help from abroad because the navy, which he himself had restored to viability after his father's long neglect, had declared for Parliament.

With both the fleet and the city of London in their hands, the king's enemies had a tremendous advantage, both military and financial. Yet they were long in capitalizing on it, and not until the Scots agreed to enter the war on Parliament's side, on the promise that a Presbyterian church would be established in England, did the tide turn in Parliament's favor. A Scottish army under Alexander Leslie, the earl of Leven, crossed the border in January 1644; the royalist leader in the north, the earl of Newcastle, retreated into York; parliamentary troops under Thomas Fairfax and their Scottish allies laid siege to that city; royalist troops under the king's nephew, Prince Rupert, marched north to rescue York, and at Marston Moor just west of the city suffered a decisive defeat with the loss of three to four thousand men. Today, a roadside monument on the B 1224 about seven miles west of York commemorates the battle, but there is not much to see among the open fields to the north where it was fought. A better idea of what took place can be gleaned from the three-dimensional model on view in the **Yorkshire Museum** *(693)* in Museum Gardens, York.

Although the Scots bore the brunt of the battle, credit for victory among the English went to the commander of a well-disciplined cavalry regiment from East Anglia whose third charge against Rupert's right flank proved to be the coup de grâce to the already faltering royalist lines. This was Oliver Cromwell, nicknamed Ironside by Prince Rupert in grudging admiration. Though soon to become the most powerful man in Britain, he was up to this point known only to be an able, though unremarkable Puritan country squire, who had served as a member of Parliament for Huntingdon and Cambridge and had recruited and trained a troop and then a regiment of horse (cavalry) which had played a significant part in securing East Anglia and Lincolnshire for Parliament. The seat of the Cromwell family was **Hinchingbrooke House** *(618)* just west of Huntingdon, Cambridgeshire. In this town young Oliver had attended grammar school in the building on Market Square that now houses the **Cromwell Museum** *(618)*. Hinchingbrooke was later sold to the Montague family and after the Restoration was the seat of Edward Montague, earl of Sandwich, admiral of the fleet and ambassador to Spain. When his protégé, the diarist Samuel Pepys, visited Hinchingbrooke in 1667 he found it more impressive than Audley End. From grammar school Cromwell went on to **Sidney Sussex College** *(616)*, Cambridge, where his posthumously decapitated head still lies buried in an unmarked spot within the college grounds. In 1628, at the age of twenty-nine, he was elected member of Parliament from Huntingdon, and, eleven years later, was chosen to represent the town of Cambridge in the first session of the Long Parliament. He was of medium height and stocky build, his red, weatherbeaten face slightly disfigured by warts or moles in the left eye socket, beneath the lower lip, and above the left eyebrow. After he became lord protector and sat frequently for portraits, he allegedly told the artist Peter Lely not to flatter him at all, but "remark all these roughnesses, pimples, warts, and everything." "Otherwise," he added, "I never will pay a farthing for it." This is the painting, presumably, that now hangs in the **Birmingham Art Gallery and Museum** *(664)*. Others, by Robert Walker, are in the **National Portrait Gallery** *(518)* in London; at **Althorp** *(655)*, Northamptonshire; and at **Sidney Sussex College** *(616)*, Cambridge.

The opposing armies of the Civil War were popularly referred to as Roundhead (after the short haircuts affected by many Puritans in protest against the shoulder-length hairstyles fashionable at court) and Cavalier (chosen by its English bearers as a badge of their alleged social superiority over their opponents). Roundhead or Cavalier, the two armies were organized and equipped alike and fought in the same manner. The infantry, called "foot," consisted of pikemen armed with iron-pointed pikes, eighteen to twenty feet in length; and musketeers carrying smoothbore muskets, called matchlocks because they were fired by the ignition of gunpowder by means of a lighted match, i.e., a cord impregnated with saltpeter. Field artillery consisted of heavy muzzleloading smoothbore guns, mounted on wooden carts or wheeled carriages and useful more for the noise they made than for the deadliness of their fire. The queen of battle was the cavalry, called simply "horse." Cavalrymen carried swords or rapiers and pistols or sometimes carbines, whose firing mechanism was the wheel lock, a device for igniting the gunpowder by sparks caused by the friction of a serrated wheel against a piece of iron pyrite. Some troops carried snaphances, the prototype of the eighteenth century flintlock which fired by sparks caused by friction of flint against metal.

Body armor was ubiquitous and varied. Pikemen normally wore breast and back plates, often with a metal collar or gorget, and tassets, which were metal thigh guards. Their helmet, called a pot, was a metal cap with a wide brim and a coxcomb ridge on top. Musketeers seldom wore any body armor at all, except for a large gorget extending down to the breastbone. Dragoons, who rode into battle on horseback and then dismounted to fight as infantrymen, usually wore no armor either, though they might wear a conical helmet with a small brim or simply a steel cap underneath a broad-brimmed hat. Both infantry and dragoons wore buff-colored coats of stout hide, but by 1645 parliamentary troops had mostly changed the color of their coats to red, thereby introducing a custom which was retained in the British army until the nineteenth century. A trooper of horse normally wore a breast and back plate over a buff coat and on his head a combed helmet with a canted neckguard on the rear shaped something like a lobster tail. A few units of horse wore the full armor of a continental cuirassier—that is, a complete suit of plate extending to the knee, a pair of large pauldrons (shoulder armor) buckled to the gorget, vambraces to protect the arms, laminated gauntlets covering the hands, knee-length laminated tassets to cover their legs, and sometimes an old-fashioned closed helmet with either visor or barred faceguard.

Fine examples of this cuirassier armor, much of it beautifully etched and embossed, are to be seen today in the Royal Armouries of the **Tower of London** *(513)*; in the **Wallace Collection** *(527)* also in London; and at **Warwick Castle** *(646)*, Warwickshire. Buff coats, red coats, and the more ordinary types of armored gear, as well as pikes, muskets, swords, etc., are on display all over England, especially in stately homes, where they lend an air of martial seriousness to the refined elegance of Adam ceilings, Chippendale consoles, and Sevres porcelain. The best collection of seventeenth century military equipment is at **Littlecote House** *(564)* near Hungerford, Berkshire; but there are others worth noting at **Bamburgh Castle** *(704)*, Northumberland; **Chirk Castle** *(729)*, Clwyd; **Cotehele House** *(589)* in Cornwall; **Hardwick Hall** *(662)* in Derbyshire; and **Levens Hall** *(712)* in Cumbria. Perhaps the best place, however, to see what a Civil War foot soldier looked like in action is at the splendid exhibits at the **National Army Museum** *(525)* near Chelsea Hospital in London. Contemporary artillery pieces can be observed at the **Museum of Artillery** *(536)* in Woolwich Arsenal south of the Thames in London.

In battle the cavalry was normally placed on the wings, their function being first to destroy or drive off the enemy horse and then move in on his infantry and scatter their formations. In the early part of the war, cavalry would normally advance in a solid block of about six ranks deep; then stop and fire pistols, one rank at a time; then close on the enemy at a fast trot, sword in hand. Prince Rupert, who had served on the Continent with the Swedish king, Gustavus Adolphus, introduced a new cavalry tactic soon adopted by both sides. This consisted of an open-order charge in three ranks, the fast trot quickening to a gallop, and pistol fire withheld until an enemy trooper presented himself at pointblank range. In the infantry attack, pikemen and musketeers moved in together, the latter firing in volleys with lengthy intervals in between, owing to the fact that muzzle-loading muskets took such a long time to recharge. As the opposing ranks closed, pike pushed against pike, while musketeers joined the fray using their weapons as clubs. Dragoons were supposed to cover the approaches of the infantry and cavalry and guard their flanks, usually by lining the hedges and ditches bordering the chosen battlefield.

Pitched battles of this sort, however, were not as frequent as siege operations. After war came, most towns and some castles threw up encircling girdles of earthworks, usually in the approved Continental style, with arrowheaded or triangular bastions placed at intervals along the embankments so as to provide protecting enfilade fire. These, of course, have mostly disappeared, but at **Donnington Castle** *(564)* northwest of Newbury, Berkshire, much of the elaborate breastwork, shaped more or less like a four-pointed star, has survived almost to its original height. The parliamentary siege of Donnington, which lasted from July 1644 to April 1646, offers a good case study of seventeenth century siege warfare. First, a summons to surrender was issued to Colonel John Boys, its royalist castellan; on his refusal, the Roundheads opened fire with cannon and knocked down three towers and part of the wall; another summons was delivered to the defenders and again refused; the attackers then dug saps (trenches) under cover of fire, and, though temporarily frustrated by a sally from the castle garrison, succeeded in setting up a battery close to the castle walls; with the approach of the king's army to relieve the castle, parliamentary troops intervened, and an inconclusive battle was fought nearby (the second Battle of Newbury); a third summons was issued and, on its rejection, the castle water supply was poisoned; the defenders then dug a new well; the king returned to relieve Donnington and succeeded in provisioning the castle; parliamentary troops withdrew but returned in force, dug more saps, fought off a sally, and succeeded in emplacing a heavy mortar which knocked down more of the castle walls but failed to make a dent in the enclosing earthworks; finally Colonel Boys agreed to surrender and was allowed to march out with bag and baggage, muskets charged and primed, drums beating, and colors flying. Had he resisted until the castle was stormed, custom would have allowed the attackers to put the entire garrison to the sword. This was rarely done in England, however, though in Ireland, Cromwell's troops had no compunctions about massacring stubborn Catholics. After a successful siege, however, it was customary for the victors to slight (i.e., partially blow up) whatever was left of the besieged fortifications. Although not all of today's ruined English castles owe their present state of dilapidation to such action, a large number do—so many that to list them here would be both tedious and redundant. A few examples should suffice. Typical samples of the destructive thoroughness of the victorious parliamentary armies are to be seen at **Corfe Castle** *(569)*, Dorset; **Pontefract Castle** *(681)*, West Yorkshire; **Knaresborough Castle** *(683)*, North Yorkshire, and **Monmouth Castle** *(716)*, Gwent.

It is easy enough for the historian to reconstruct the battle or siege tactics of the Civil War. Strategy is another matter. In essence there was none, if by *strategy* is meant the rational planning for, and conduct of, military operations to achieve clear-cut political objectives. After the king's failure to capture London in 1642, his military direction of the war makes little sense. Nor does Parliament's. Towns and castles were besieged at random for no apparent reason other than that they were in enemy hands. Battles were fought, more often than not, to prevent or accomplish the raising of a siege, or merely because the opposing armies met by chance. Advantages gained through tactical victories were dissipated by subsequent inaction. Isolated and local operations commonly took precedence over major campaigns.

Time, however, and a vast superiority of money and material resources eventually favored Parliament. As second in command to General Thomas Fairfax, Cromwell organized a new model army of ten regiments of horse and twelve of foot, about twenty-two thousand men in all. It was well disciplined and regularly paid; its officers were chosen on the basis of merit and not for reasons of social status or for precise adherence to the religious tenets of the increasingly doctrinaire Puritan majority in the House of Commons who had been won over to Presbyterian views on church polity. "I had rather," said Cromwell, "have a plain russet-coated captain that knows what he fights for, and loves what he knows, than that which you call a gentleman and nothing else." At the same time he was becoming more tolerant of, and even sympathetic with, those of his soldiers whom orthodox Puritans were labeling sectaries. These were the self-styled independents—Anabaptists and others who rejected the prevalent notion that the state had the right to enforce conformity to a single established church with a single form of worship. Writing of one of his officers charged with being an Anabaptist, Cromwell declared: "Admit that he be, shall that render him incapable to serve the public —Sir, the State, in choosing men to serve them, takes no notice of their opinions . . . . I [advise] you . . . to bear with men of different minds from yourself . . ." This last was but a foreshadow of his more famous statement, made later to a Scottish Presbyterian: "I beseech you, in the bowels of Christ, think it possible you may be mistaken." His spirit of tolerance, of course, did not extend to Roman Catholics.

Given the confusion that attended Parliament's management of the war after Marston Moor, the end came with surprising speed. At Naseby, five miles southwest of Market Harborough, Northamptonshire, the new model army met up with the king's main force, and on 14 June 1645 routed them completely, major credit for the victory going to Cromwell's cavalry charges. On the site today is the **Naseby Battle and Farm Museum** *(656)* which contains a miniature layout of the battlefield with commentary and memorabilia of the fight. Naseby was the beginning of the end. Fairfax went on to defeat the king's southwestern army at Langport in Somerset, and Prince Rupert surrendered Bristol, the royalists' only important seaport. The king sought refuge in Chester, only to see his dwindling forces routed again at Rowton Heath, a few miles to the southeast. Tradition has it that Charles watched the battle from Chester's **City Walls** *(673)*, though it is doubtful that he could have seen much except the closing stages when his troops fell back toward the city. In any case the bastion of the wall called Phoenix Tower or King Charles's Tower is now a museum commemorating the event, with displays of contemporary armor and weapons and a model of the battle in the upper room. From Chester the king rode to Newark and then to Oxford. His eldest son, the Prince of Wales, escaped to the Scilly Isles and thence to loyal Jersey, where he was made welcome by the governor and took up residence in **Elizabeth Castle** *(743)* before moving on to join his mother in France. One by one the king's few remaining strongholds fell and his army disappeared. Hoping to make a deal with the Scots, he escaped from Oxford and made his way to the Scottish army headquarters near Southwell and in May 1646 gave himself up. It was the end of the first phase of the Civil War.

THE INTERREGNUM:
1649–1660

For the better part of nine months the Scots tried to prevail upon Charles to agree to establishing a Presbyterian church in both his kingdoms as the price of their support. This he declined to do, so his captors turned him over to Parliament and agreed to return home on the payment of four hundred thousand pounds. The king was taken to Holmby House in Northamptonshire where his hopes were renewed by news of a falling-out between Parliament and the army over the issues of arrears of pay and the soldiers' demands for religious toleration for independents. In the event, Charles was to be disappointed. The army mutinied, took possession of the king, and occupied London. Charles then escaped to the Isle of Wight, hoping to make his way to France, but was instead imprisoned in **Carisbrooke Castle** (558). There he finally agreed to the Scots' demands that Presbyterianism be established in England for three years. In return a Scottish army invaded England only to be overwhelmed by Cromwell in the first battle of the second phase of the Civil War near Preston, Lancashire. It was now that Cromwell decided "to call Charles Stuart, that Man of Blood, to an account for the blood that he had shed and mischief he had done to his utmost against the Lord's cause and people." Parliament was purged of its anti-Cromwellian Presbyterians, leaving only a Rump of fifty-odd members dominated by the army. The king was removed from the Isle of Wight and lodged in a gloomy cell in **Hurst Castle** (559) overlooking the Solent, built a century before by Henry VIII. From there he was brought to Windsor and thence to **Westminster Hall** (524) to be tried for treason and other crimes by an *ad hoc* court dominated by Cromwell. He was of course convicted and sentenced to be "put to death by the severing of his head from his body." At two o'clock in the afternoon of 30 January 1649, King Charles I stepped through a window of the **Banqueting House** (519) onto a scaffold built for the occasion and shortly was beheaded. From the assembled crowd in Whitehall went up a deep groan, "A groan," said an eyewitness, "as I never heard before and desire I may never hear again."

Soon after the execution, the monarchy and the House of Lords were abolished by the Rump and England declared a commonwealth with an executive body consisting of a council of state of forty-one members. Cromwell, as commander-in-chief, was dispatched to Ireland to put down, a native Catholic rebellion there, which he did with such ferocity that, in that country, his name is still synonymous with merciless brutality. Meanwhile the Prince of Wales, in negotiations at Breda with a commission of Scottish covenanters, agreed to establish the Presbyterian form of church worship in exchange for the crown of Scotland, to which country he then repaired from his exile on the Continent. On his return from Ireland, Cromwell promptly marched into Scotland with an army of sixteen thousand men, met and defeated David Leslie's larger force at Dunbar, and then moved east to occupy Edinburgh and Perth. The royal heir, crowned King Charles II at Scone, now fell into a trap devised by Cromwell, and, seeing the road to England open, headed across the border with an army of about thirteen thousand. He got as far as Worcester when Cromwell caught up with him. On 3 September 1651 the two armies met in combat outside the city and the Scottish royalist forces lost the day. Charles himself escaped with a small party of henchmen and by dawn reached a house called **White Ladies** *(669)* north of the present village of Albrighton, Salop. The house belonged to a well-known Shropshire Catholic family and had been constructed after the Dissolution on the site of an Augustinian nunnery. Nothing now remains of the building where the fugitives holed-up, but a portion of the ruined priory church still stands. Parting company from most of his entourage, the would-be king spent the next night in a barn and on the morning of 5 September reached **Boscobel House** *(669)* just northeast of White Ladies and owned by the same family. Here the house still stands, though much changed from its seventeenth century appearance. Nearby, surrounded by an iron paling, is the so-called Royal Oak, possibly a descendant of the tree where Charles and a servant hid out during the day to avoid detection. Next he went on to **Moseley Old Hall** *(666)* about five miles west, now on the outskirts of the industrial city of Wolverhampton, West Midlands. This was the home of another Catholic, and here Charles was joined by the priest, Father Huddleston, who, thirty-four years later would receive him into the Church of Rome. Though the house today is much altered, its interior is authentic seventeenth century, and the garden and orchard have been restored to a design of 1640. From there Charles Stuart, to use the only name by which he was officially known in England, wound his furtive way through the southwest and southern counties, finally to take ship for France from Shoreham in West Sussex. He had been on the run for six weeks. It would be another eight years and more before he would see England again.

Meanwhile the government at Westminster was busy consolidating its rule and asserting itself on the international scene. Between 1649 and 1651 the navy received an addition of forty-one new ships, and, under the able leadership of William Penn and Robert Blake, succeeded in driving a fleet raised by Prince Rupert off the seas. In 1651, Blake captured the Scilly Isles which had been a nest of royalist privateers, and on Tresco the government put up a fort, now called **Cromwell's Castle** *(592)*, a tall, round tower with six gunports. Before the war, Blake had been a Bridgwater merchant, and during it had served in the parliamentary army. In 1649 he was commissioned by Parliament a General-at-Sea. Two years later Parliament passed the first Navigation Act which was designed to injure Dutch carrying trade and to provoke a commercial war with the United Netherlands, which it did. As fleet commander, Blake won several major naval battles against the Dutch, and in 1654 the United Netherlands agreed to the English terms for peace. The following year saw England at war with Spain. Penn captured Jamaica, but Blake scored what at the time was considered a more notable victory by destroying the Spanish treasure fleet in Santa Cruz harbor in the Canary Islands. He was the first authentic English naval hero since Drake, and even the great Lord Nelson is reported to have said, "I do not reckon myself equal to Blake." His birthplace in Bridgwater, Somerset, is now the **Blake Museum** *(582)*, though it contains little of interest beyond a diorama of the Battle of Santa Cruz.

Back in London the affairs of state were not going smoothly. Cromwell quarreled with the Rump and finally dissolved it, saying: "The Lord has done with you." He set up a council of state and chose another Parliament (the Barebones Parliament) from the names submitted by church congregations from Scotland and Ireland as well as England—the first United Kingdom Parliament in history. This body dissolved itself, and in 1653 the council of officers named Cromwell as lord protector with greater powers than Charles I or his father had ever wielded.

Under the Protectorate, England for the first and only time received a written constitution, the Instrument of Government. One of its clauses stated that no one, except for Roman Catholics, was to be compelled to conform to the newly established and puritanized Church of England, and that Christian sects which dissented from the established church were to be protected in the exercise of their religion. This was the high watermark of religious toleration in England, not to be reached again until 1689. It was the climax of a dozen years of public controversy unleashed by the Civil War but spawned originally by the Protestant Reformation itself. In Luther's argument for a "priesthood of all believers" lay the seeds of religious anarchy. For once the Bible and not the Church was accepted as the repository of the word of God, there was no limit to the number of doctrines that could be deduced from that ambiguous compendium of history, theology, ethical precepts, and revelations. And in the camps of Cromwell's army, in pulpit, field, and marketplace, a thousand unlicensed preachers rose to give voice to as many different interpretations of the Holy Word. There were the Anabaptists who believed that only adult baptism was valid; Ranters who held that since God was in every creature no man could logically sin; Levellers and Diggers with advanced ideas on political and economic equality allegedly derived from the New Testament; Fifth Monarchy Men who believed in the imminence of the Second Coming of Jesus; Seekers who rejected all existing churches and were awaiting a direct revelation from God Himself; and finally Quakers who claimed to have had such direct revelation and to be guided by the Inner Light present in all mankind and not just those whom Calvin had designated the elect.

The leader of the Quakers (so called because they trembled at the word of God) was a Leicestershire shoemaker named George Fox who proved to be the greatest religious leader the Civil War produced. He and his followers were especially obnoxious to upholders of law and order because of their refusal, on Biblical grounds, to take the legally required oaths, and because of an aggressive egalitarianism which compelled them to address their betters with the familiar *thee* and *thou* and to refuse to doff their hats in the presence of authority, including magistrates and judges. Most Englishmen in the 1650s would have concurred with the diarist John Evelyn's view of the Quakers as "a new phanatic sect of dangerous Principles, they shew no respect for any man, magistrate or other & seems a Melancholy proud sort of people, & exceedingly ignorant . . . ." This might too have been the verdict of history, but for the persistence and good fortune of George Fox. In 1652 Fox's missionary wanderings brought him to **Swarthmoor Hall** *(713)* near Ulverston, Cumbria, where he converted the lady of the house, Margaret Fell, who in turn persuaded her husband, Judge Thomas Fell, to give the Quakers protection and to turn their residence into a sort of missionary headquarters for this unpopular sect who now called themselves the Society of Friends. Swarthmoor Hall (after which Swarthmore College, Pennsylvania, is named) is today a well-restored and charming manor house, furnished with authentic seventeenth century pieces, and open to the public by courtesy of the London Quarterly Meeting of the Society of Friends. For almost half a century it was the nerve center of the Quaker movement which spread through England, Scotland, Ireland, Wales, the Isle of Man, and across the seas to Europe and North America. The Friends seemed to thrive on persecution, of which they received more than a fair portion. Fox himself, though on good terms with Cromwell, was, in 1656, thrown into the filthy Doomsdale prison of **Launceston Castle** *(593)*, Cornwall, for refusing to remove his hat in the presence of the chief justice of the Court of Assizes. This was only one of many incarcerations he was to suffer, the longest being in **Lancaster Castle** *(696)* where Margaret Fell (who later married Fox) was also confined for twenty months.

Cromwell himself was tolerant toward the Quakers and even toward the Jews whom he permitted to return legally to England for the first time since their expulsion in 1290. He did draw the line, however, at the Levellers, who encouraged mutiny in the army and promoted a brand of social and political democracy he found subversive. Their most vocal spokesman, John Lilbourne, was sent to the Tower and later exiled to Jersey. In all matters save liberty of conscience, however, Cromwell was conservative and autocratic. Parliaments he called, only to dismiss them as they grew fractious. He declined the kingship, but tried to establish a dynasty by naming his eldest son Richard to be his successor. To preserve good order throughout the land, he divided England into districts, each to be governed by a major general. It was this attempted militarization of the country, more than anything else, that brought an end to the Protectorate, and incidentally implanted in the British psyche a permanent dread of standing armies.

After Cromwell's death in 1658, his son lasted in office for only eight months. Then followed a period of intense jockeying for power among the army officers who hoped to inherit the protector's mantle. Finally, one of them, George Monck, put an end to the confusion by bringing his army down from Scotland, taking control of London, and calling a Convention Parliament to invite Charles Stuart back to England to reclaim his father's crown.

THE LATER STUARTS

CHARLES II: 1660–1685

On 25 May 1660 the royal exile disembarked at Dover to be received on bended knee by General Monck. Four days later, on his thirtieth birthday, Charles II entered London. He was almost six feet in height and saturnine in appearance; swarthy of complexion, black haired with unusually thick eyebrows, clean shaven, and long nosed. He was not the "merrie monarch" of legend and had no reason to be. Since boyhood his life had been studded with danger, tragedy, and deprivation. He was, nevertheless, debonair, witty, and extroverted, though his easy manners hid a deepseated and persistent cynicism. His only guiding principle was to stay on the throne. He was an insatiable womanizer and by the end of his life had sired at least fourteen bastards to prove it. Of his many mistresses, the most notorious were Barbara Villiers, countess of Castlemaine and duchess of Cleveland; Louise de Querouaille (Kéroualle), duchess of Portsmouth; and the actress Nell Gwynn, the self-styled "Protestant whore." Their forms and visages, and those of dozens of other Restoration beauties, are familiar to connoisseurs of the art of Sir Peter Lely, a Dutchman who had emigrated to England during the Civil War, had prospered under Cromwell, but had quickly ingratiated himself with the restored court to become in effect Van Dyck's successor. He was a skillful and prolific portraitist, though hardly a great artist. His work is easily recognizable: His women are heavy-lidded and languorous; his men, sensual and arrogant. So stereotyped, indeed, was his style that almost all his sitters look like brothers and sisters. Typical Lely collections are to be found at **Hampton Court Palace** *(532)* (the Windsor Beauties), outside London; **Althorp** *(655)*, Northamptonshire; **Broadlands** *(561)*, Hampshire; and **Petworth House** *(553)* in West Sussex.

The first few years of Charles's reign were punctuated with disaster. The Convention Parliament in 1660 passed a second navigation act even more pointedly aimed than the first against the Dutch carrying trade; Charles aggravated the worsening relations between the two countries by granting to his brother James, the duke of York, the Dutch colony at the mouth of the Hudson River (now New York). War at sea erupted, and went badly for the English in spite of one notable victory off Lowestoft, commemorated in a series of fine Lely portraits of naval flag officers now hanging in the **National Maritime Museum** *(536)* in Greenwich. In the spring of 1665 the bubonic plague struck again, the worst of such epidemics since the Black Death. London alone suffered as many as seventy thousand fatalities. The king and his court left for Hampton Court and a large number of the citizenry evacuated, among them the Puritan poet, John Milton, who had gone blind in Cromwell's service as his Latin secretary in charge of diplomatic correspondence. He found a small house in Chalfont St. Giles in nearby Buckinghamshire. Now designated **Milton's Cottage** *(623)*, it houses an interesting collection of the poet's first editions and personal memorabilia. Here it was that he completed *Paradise Lost,* the first and greatest of his three epic poems and one of English literature's major classics. It is the story of Satan's rebellion against Almighty God; of his being "Hurled headlong flaming from the ethereal sky/With hideous ruin and combustion, down/To bottomless perdition; there to dwell/ In adamantine chains and penal fire"; of his successful mission to earth to tempt Adam and Eve to eat of the forbidden fruit of the Tree of the Knowledge of Good and Evil; and of their being expelled from Eden, though not without God's promise that from their seed would one day spring the Redeemer whose sacrificial death would annul their sin and doom. And so, the long poem ends on a note of ineffable sadness mingled with hope, as the mother and father of mankind are thrust out of their earthly paradise:

> Some natural tears they dropped, but wiped them soon;
> The world was all before them, where to choose
> Their place of rest, and providence their guide.
> They hand in hand with wandering steps and slow,
> Through Eden took their solitary way.

Milton's imaginary reconstruction of the fires of hell was soon to be almost matched by reality. In the first week of September 1666 an easterly wind converted a small fire on Pudding Lane near London Bridge into a five-day conflagration that consumed most of the ancient city of London, destroying 13,200 houses, 89 churches, and goods valued at

£3,500,000. Some sense of the horror of it all can still be gleaned from the diary of an eyewitness:

> So near the fire as we could for smoke; and all over the Thames, with one's face in the wind you were almost burned with a shower of fire-drops . . . When we could endure no more upon the water, we to a little alehouse on the Bankside . . . and there stayed till it was dark almost and saw the fire grow; and as it grew darker, appeared more and more, and in corners and upon steeples and between churches and houses, as far as we could see up the hill of the City, in a most horrid malicious bloody flame, not like the fine flame of an ordinary fire. We stayed till, it being darkish, we saw the fire as only one entire arch of fire from this to the other side of the bridge, and in a bow up the hill, for an arch of about a mile long. It made me weep to see it. The churches, houses, and all on fire and flaming at once, and a horrid noise the flames made, and the cracking of houses at their ruins. So home with a sad heart.

The diarist of course was Samuel Pepys, a successful bureaucrat in the duke of York's Admiralty office, who recorded in shorthand his astute observations of life in London between 1660 and 1669. *Pepys' Diary* was willed to **Magdalene College** *(613)*, Cambridge, along with his library of three thousand books, and can be seen there today in what is known as the Pepysian Library. It was not deciphered and published until 1825, and the jottings of this busy, inquisitive, lecherous, and altogether engaging young man still constitute the most delightful literary legacy of seventeenth century England. On Fleet Street, London, opposite the foot of Chancery Lane, in what is claimed to be the oldest house in the city, **Prince Henry's Room** *(514)* (so named for no good reason after James I's oldest son) is a good small collection of Pepys' memorabilia open to view.

Pepys also recorded, with dismay, the great naval catastrophe of the summer of 1667 when the Dutch fleet sailed up the River Medway, broke the boom guarding Chatham harbor, burned four ships of the line, and towed away the pride of the English navy, the *Royal Charles*. The raid exposed the utter inadequacy of England's coastal fortification. The guns fired from the riverside **Upnor Castle** *(539)*, an Elizabethan fort built in 1559–1567, were completely ineffectual. Not long afterwards, Charles II put his chief engineer, a Dutchman named Bernard de Gomme, to work rebuilding **Tilbury Fort** *(600)* on the north side of the Thames across from Gravesend. De Gomme's work still survives in part, the most notable being his splendid Water Gate with its Corinthian columns and segmental pediment topped by an *achievement* of the Stuart arms in high relief.

Meanwhile, the City of London was rising from its ashes. The fluted Doric column, 202 feet high, at the top of Fish Street Hill and known simply as the **Monument** *(512)* marks the spot near which the Great Fire started. It is the work of Sir Christopher Wren and his assistant Robert

Hooke. Wren was the nephew of the Laudian bishop of Ely who had caused Peterhouse Chapel, Cambridge, to be built. He had, himself, held the chair of Savilian professor of astronomy at Oxford, and, in the manner of Renaissance men, had also shown a bent for architecture. In 1633 the chapel at **Pembroke College** *(614)*, Cambridge was built to his design: completely classical in character with one large arched window in front, a simple arched niche on either side, the three bays separated by four Corinthian pilasters supporting a pediment. Exactly contemporary was the **Sheldonian Theatre** *(632)* at Oxford, also designed by Wren. This high D-shaped building was modeled on the Theater of Marcellus in Rome, although, instead of being open to the sky like the original, was roofed over in a manner that was considered in its day an engineering *tour de force.* Wren's next collegiate building was again in Cambridge, where in 1668 he designed the chapel at **Emmanuel College** *(612)*, another classical building, with round arches separated by Corinthian pilasters supporting a pediment through which rises a clock surmounted by a cupola.

Given his experience, his reputation, and his connections, it is not surprising that Wren was appointed by the king to be one of three commissioners for rebuilding the city of London, a project to be financed by a new tax on imported coal. Wren submitted an ambitious scheme for restructuring all the city's thoroughfares along Parisian lines with diagonal avenues superimposed on a gridiron—not unlike Major l'Enfant's later design for Washington, D.C. The plan was approved by king and Parliament, but private citizens got the jump on the government and rebuilt their shops and houses according to their own desires, so that the part of London known as the City (the square mile extending roughly east of Temple Bar to Aldgate and north of the river to City Road) is today almost as scrambled as it was in the seventeenth century.

Nevertheless, Wren did receive a royal commission to rebuild fifty-one of the eighty-nine city churches destroyed by the Great Fire, plus three others to the west. Many of these were badly damaged during the bombings of World War II, but most have been restored. The would-be visitor should be warned, however, that not all are open to the public on weekdays and that in most instances the only sure guarantee of gaining admission is to attend Sunday services. Even so, the exteriors alone are of sufficient interest and beauty as to warrant a diligent search for these masterpieces among London's tangled streets and alleys. Five general points need to be made about Wren's churches. First, they are mostly classical in design, although the architect was driven to many variations on this theme partly by choice and partly by the restrictions imposed by the space allotted between other buildings that had already gone up before the money for churches became available. Secondly, the severe and horizontal lines of the classical canon are offset by towering spires and cupolas, which are indeed their crowning glory. Thirdly, these are functional buildings designed specifically for Protestant services according to the rubric of the Church of England. Wren himself observed that a church should be "a convenient auditory in which everyone should hear the preacher." It was for this reason that he installed galleries in many of them, dispensed with transepts, and erected high pulpits with sounding boards so that the Sunday sermons could be clearly heard by the entire congregation. Railed altars, it is true, were located at the east end (a posthumous Laudian victory), but the altar in Wren's churches was not the focal point of the design, as was the case in contemporary Catholic churches on the Continent, and was not hidden from the full view of the laity behind a chancel screen. Fourthly, Wren's interiors are mostly painted plain white and were originally illumined only by daylight pouring through clear glass windows (the stained glass found in some Wren churches today is an abomination perpetrated by Victorian and modern restorers). Fifthly, the exquisiteness of Wren's designs is usually matched by the ornamental woodcarving of pews, pulpits, altarpieces, etc. It is presumed, though not proved, that most of this was the work of the Dutch craftsman, Grinling Gibbons, who was essentially a sculptor in wood (though sometimes he worked in stone). His beautifully carved garlands of flowers, foliage, fruits, etc., were in much demand in the late seventeenth century and grace the saloons of a score or more of the stateliest of England's homes, as well as churches and public buildings. The inspiration for his remarkable genius came probably from the popular flower and still-life paintings of his native land.

Of the more than two dozen Wren churches still standing, the following are especially recommended as worthy of inspection. **St. Bride, Fleet Street** *(514)*: Here the best feature is the elegant wedding-cake steeple of diminishing octagons. The interior was gutted by fire in 1940, and in the restoration Wren's seating arrangements were unfortunately modified and a stained-glass window inserted in the east end. **St. James Garlickhythe** *(514)*, Upper Thames Street: Beautifully restored after being blitzed in the Second World War, the church is interesting as an example of how Wren could on occasion meld medieval and classical themes. **St. Magnus the Martyr** *(513)*, Lower Thames Street: The splendid Portland stone tower and steeple are especially noteworthy. Inside, two baroque restorations have somewhat marred Wren's original classical design. **St. Mary Abchurch** *(514)*, Cannon Street: This is a square building of pale-red brick with stone dressings, tower, and lead steeple. The interior is one of the most beautiful in the city, with a painted domed ceiling, circular and round-arched windows of clear glass, and a fine Grinling Gibbons altarpiece. **St. Mary at Hill** *(513)*, Lovat Lane: Thought by some to be the least spoiled and most beautiful of Wren's interiors, it is designed in the shape of a Greek cross with a shallow dome over the crossing; the woodwork is especially good; and Wren's high pews have not been cut down as has been the case in many of his churches. **St. Mary Le Bow** *(512)*, Cheapside: This would not be worth mentioning except for its legendary tower and steeple and the bells within whose range of sound all true Cockneys must be born. The body of the church, which was probably not by Wren anyway, was badly gutted in 1941 and the interior restoration is too grandiose for a Wren church. **St. Stephen Walbrook** *(515)*, Walbrook: An architectural *tour de force*, Wren superimposed a circular dome on a rectangular nave by a clever use of interior arches supported by Corinthian columns. At the date of writing (1980) the church is under repair and it can be hoped that the ugly Victorian mosaics and the inappropriate post-war stained glass will have been removed by the time it is reopened. **St. Vedast** *(512)*, Foster Lane: Here is the simplest and most delicate of Wren's towers and steeples. The church interior was gutted in 1940 but has been restored with a charming simplicity. In spite of London's prevalent vandalism, the doors of St. Vedast are never closed during the daytime—a feature unusual for a Wren church. Finally, comes **St. James, Piccadilly** *(527)* in the borough of Westminster: Within the old brick building topped by tower and steeple is a lovely restored rectangular aisled nave, with galleries on two sides and rear, Corinthian columns, and a splendid font by Grinling Gibbons. Like St. Vedast, it is open at all times and offers the additional advantage to the busy traveller of being located on the main thoroughfare of London's West End.

Wren's most spectacular achievement was, of course, the new **St. Paul's Cathedral** *(515)* to replace the medieval church so totally demolished by the Fire that the only remnant left to see is the shrouded funereal monument of its one-time dean, the poet John Donne, author of the famous lines: "Any man's death diminishes me, because I am involved in Mankind; And therefore never send to know for whom the bell tolls; It tolls for thee." This was the first cathedral to be built in England since the Reformation, therefore the first to be totally fashioned to meet the liturgical requirements of the Anglican church. Wren would have preferred a ground plan in the shape of a Greek cross, but the dean and chapter insisted on something more traditional, so the final design was a compromise: an orthodox Latin-cross plan with a long nave, but surmounted by a high exterior dome instead of a tall spire of the medieval type. In designing the dome, set on a great colonnaded drum—a remarkable engineering feat for its time—Wren was strongly influenced by Michelangelo. St. Paul's western facade is strongly classical, with two stages of Corinthian columns and a central pediment, but flanked, in an unclassical way, by two stone towers which are more baroque than anything else. Inside, Grinling Gibbons carved the ornaments of the choir stalls, organ case, and bishop's throne. Outside, much of the ornamental stonework is also the product of Gibbons's hand, though some of it is the work of another popular carver, a Dane named Caius Gabriel Cibber. The ironwork, notably the great wrought-iron gates, are the work of Jean Tijou who had fled from France to England after King Louis XIV revoked the Edict of Nantes guaranteeing freedom of worship to the Protestant Huguenots. Almost the final touch was applied by the English baroque painter Sir James Thornhill, who covered the inside of the cupola with eight huge paintings illustrating the life of St. Paul. This, like many of the cathedral's other interior features, can best be seen by day. But only during evening services do its glistening surfaces come alive. Only then, in the glitter of a host of flickering candles, does the great church light up with fire and gold.

The building of St. Paul's by no means occupied all of Christopher Wren's attention during his prime, which coincided roughly with the reign of Charles II. Among other things, he was one of the founders of the Royal Society, chartered by the king in 1662 as a permanent institution for the promotion of experiments in physics and mathematics. Though the society had its roots in the informal meetings of scientists and other intellectuals held during the 1640s at Gresham College, London, and in the 1650s at **Wadham College, Oxford** *(635)* it was not until November 1660, following a lecture by Wren at Gresham College, that it really got started. Its members, besides Wren, included John Wilkins, Cromwell's brother-in-law who, as master of Wadham, had been among the first to appreciate the advantage of scientific consultation; Robert Boyle, the father of modern chemistry and the propounder of Boyle's Law; and, most important of all, Isaac Newton, Lucasion professor of mathematics at Cambridge. Poetic license did not lead the poet Alexander Pope into error in writing his famous epitaph to Newton:

> Nature and Nature's Laws lay hid in Night,
> God said, Let Newton be! And all was Light.

He discovered the law of gravity, established the binomial theorem, developed the theory of equations, explained the operation of tides, advanced the science of optics, contributed to the invention of infinitesimal calculus, and created hydrodynamics. He was born in 1642 at **Woolsthorpe Hall** *(650)* in Lincolnshire, and while on a visit there in 1665 to escape the plague, hit upon the idea that later matured into the law of gravity. Newton's birthplace is still there, and so is the site of the famous apple tree whose dropping fruit, according to a later account by the French *philosophe* Voltaire, first inspired Newton to his great discovery.

Newton was a genius, but his instant fame is probably less attributable to that fact than to the favorable climate of opinion into which he was born. Science had become popular—at least among the educated and the well born. One notable architectural legacy of this new fashion is the **Old Ashmolean Museum** *(632)* on Broad Street, Oxford, next to the Sheldonian Theatre. Finished in 1683 and opened by James, duke of York, the king's brother, this splendid building, designed by an unknown architect in the best classical manner, was intended to house a collection of "natural curiosities" inherited by Elias Ashmole from John Tradescant and his father. Though a new and larger Ashmolean Museum was later built on Beaumont Street, the old building now appropriately serves as the Museum of the History of Science and contains a splendid collection of astrolabes and early mathematical instruments.

One of the many projects sponsored by the Royal Society was to discover a practical means by which to measure the earth's longitude. King Charles, himself something of a scientific dilettante, shared this interest and was responsible for the appointment of the first astronomer royal, John Flamsteed, and for the building of the **Greenwich Observatory** *(635)* "in order to the finding out of the longitude of places and for perfecting navigation and astronomy." Sir Christopher Wren designed the building, now known as Flamsteed House "for the observator's habitation and a little for pompe." Its main octagonal room is one of Wren's few surviving interiors (not having been hit by German bombs) and within it, and in the Meridian Building next door, are now exhibited a number of fascinating early astonomical instruments. Flamsteed did not discover the means to measure longitude, but he did significantly advance man's knowledge of the solar system and, at a more immediately practical level, began in 1683 the annual publication of tide tables for the port of London.

Wren received other architectural commissions, both from the Crown and from the universities. One of his finest works is the library of **Trinity College** *(616)*, Cambridge, which he began in 1676. This is a long rectangular building in the Roman style with a cloister below and the library above, with two stages of Tuscan columns between the round arched doors and windows, with four classical statues by Cibber on the balustrade facing Nevile's Court. Five years later, with customary versatility, Wren reverted to a pseudo-Gothic style in raising above the gatehouse of **Christ Church** *(629)*, Oxford, the fine octagon surmounted by an ogival dome that is known as Tom's Tower. Next he (probably) designed a new library for **Queen's College** *(633)*, Oxford, though it was not constructed until more than a decade later. Here the open loggia, high attic, and steep pediment are typically Wren. Also in 1682 he began **Chelsea Hospital** *(524)* in London, still in use as a retirement home for British army pensioners, whose blue or scarlet uniforms (depending on the occasion) add an incongruous note of pageantry to the stark classicism of the setting. Here the Doric order is the dominant theme, expressed in the columns of the central portico and the pilasters of the two barracks wings of the front court. Finally, the gracious cupola rising from the roof of the central block identifies the building as unmistakably Wren.

By the time King Charles laid the cornerstone of Chelsea Hospital, England had weathered two Dutch wars and would be at peace for the rest of his reign. The naval disaster in the Medway had been quickly followed by a treaty by which England kept New York, New Jersey, and Delaware but surrendered Surinam to the Dutch, thereby giving up the contest for control of the West Indies. Not long thereafter the king negotiated a secret treaty at Dover with representatives of Louis XIV of France by which the English monarch was to receive an annual pension of £225,000 in return for supporting a French war of aggression against the United Netherlands, and the additional sum of £150,000 "to reconcile himself with the Church of Rome as soon as his country's affairs permit." Two years later Charles declared war against the Dutch, the first target of Louis XIV's continental ambitions. The war went badly for the English, and in 1674 Charles was compelled to make a peace based on the *status quo ante.* Searching for scapegoats, Parliament had already lashed out at the king's closest advisers, his *cabal,* an acronym made up out of the first letters of the names of the five men wrongly blamed for Charles's unsuccessful foreign ventures.

The five members of the cabal were Lord Thoms Clifford; the earl of Arlington; the second duke of Buckingham; Lord Ashley; and the duke of Lauderdale. Parliament resolved that Lauderdale and Buckingham be removed from the king's council and brought articles of impeachment against the latter. Whatever their misdeeds in the eyes of their contemporaries, however, posterity can be grateful to both for leaving two splendid monuments of Restoration England. **Ham House** *(537)* near London on the south bank of the Thames, is a palatial red-brick mansion converted from a simpler H-plan Jacobean house by the duke and duchess of Lauderdale in the 1670s. Its sumptuous interior especially is reflective of the extravagance of its new owners, whose joint portrait by Lely hangs in the Round Gallery and reveals more of their callous arrogance than that usually sycophantic artist probably intended. The rich contents of the house today are mostly those accumulated by this avaricious pair and constitute perhaps the best collection in England of late seventeenth century furnishings. Arlington's country house called **Euston Hall** *(609)* near Thetford, Norfolk, though grand enough, is not nearly so palatial. Today its chief attraction is the series of seventeenth century portraits, unexcelled in any country house. Here is Lord Arlington himself, by Lely, proudly wearing a black patch over his nose to cover the scar of the wound he received during the Civil War while fighting for King Charles I. Here also is the first duke of Buckingham by Mytens; Charles I, Henrietta Maria, and their children by Van Dyck; Charles II by Lely, as well as two of his mistresses, the duchess of Cleveland and Nell Gwynn; and one of his bastards, the duke of Grafton. Contemporary with both the above is **Ashdown House** *(576)* in Oxfordshire just across the county line from Swindon, Wiltshire, possibly designed by William Winde, a Dutch soldier and amateur architect who came to England after the Restoration in the entourage of that romantic exile, Elizabeth, the Winter Queen of Bohemia, daughter of James I and King Charles's aunt. The widow of the Elector Palatine, who had touched off the Thirty Years War, she was so greatly admired by the first earl of Craven, that he built this house for her, though she died before it was ready for occupancy. It is in a style that is loosely called Dutch Palladian. Taller and slimmer than most country houses, Ashdown is nevertheless representative of the new style in its perfect symmetry, its sash windows, architraves, projecting cornice, and steep hipped-roof surmounted by a balustraded platform carrying an octagonal cupola. On a far grander scale is **Badminton** *(581)*, built by the immensely wealthy third marquess of Worcester, later first duke of Beaufort, not far from Bristol. Much modified in the eighteenth and nineteenth centuries, the chief Restoration survival here is the dining room with its superb set of Grinling Gibbons carvings of lobster, fruit, and game.

Residential building in Restoration England was not confined to the grandees of Charles II's court. Sir John Brownlow who built **Belton House** *(650)* near Grantham, Lincolnshire, was high sheriff of that county, but a man of no great national stature. Possibly designed by William Winde, this is considered by the art historian Sir John Summerson to be "much the finest example of a type of seventeenth century house" of a mixed Dutch, French, and English classical style. Inside some splendid work of Grinling Gibbons is displayed throughout. Roughly contemporary is **Honington Hall** *(643)* near Shipston-on-Stour, Warwickshire, built by a rich London merchant, Sir Henry Parker, of brick dressed with stone, with busts of Roman emperors standing on the window heads. Grinling Gibbons again did much of the interior woodcarving at **Sudbury Hall** *(669)* in Derbyshire east of Uttoxeter, Staffordshire. Here is a lavish Restoration house, the creation of Sir George Vernon, its high symmetrical facade of diapered brickwork topped by a balustraded roof with cupola above and bisected by a two-story frontispiece flanked by Doric columns. Even more distinctly classical is **Weston Park** *(666)* near Cannock, Staffordshire. Though nothing inside survives from the seventeenth century, the serene red-brick and stone exterior was designed by its owner, Lady Elizabeth Wilbraham, who appears to have copied the plan from one or more of Palladio's sketches.

It is a far cry from the elegance of these sumptuous private palaces to the stark simplicity of the **Swarthmoor Quaker Meeting House** *(713)* near Ulverston, Cumbria, which George Fox converted out of a barn in the late 1680s. The Society of Friends was coming to the end of its long ordeal. Between 1660 and 1685 more than fifteen thousand Quakers had been fined, imprisoned, or transported for their stubborn refusal to bow to the dictates of church and state. The wave of reaction that had brought Charles Stuart back to the throne carried with it the triumph of an intolerant Anglicanism that would have delighted the late Archbishop Laud. In spite of Charles's promise of "liberty to tender consciences," Parliament in 1662 passed a series of laws, known as the Clarendon Code, requiring strict conformity to the rubrics of the reestablished state church not only by all clergymen but by all teachers, university professors and tutors, members of Parliament, and municipal officials. All assemblies, or "conventicles" not held in accordance to the Book of Common Prayer were prohibited; all nonconforming preachers and teachers were forbidden to come within five miles of any town or city. A large number of Puritan clergy who had remained within the Church of England during the Civil War lost their jobs; transgressors were severely punished with fines and imprisonment, while many more of the radical Protestant persuasion saved themselves by occasional conformity (i.e., token church attendance and partaking of the Anglican sacraments) while secretly meeting with other nonconformists to worship in their own illegal fashion. Though the law singled out Quakers for especially severe treatment, other defiant sectaries also suffered persecution. Among them was the itinerant preacher John Bunyan, son of a tinsmith, who spent twelve years in the Bedford county jail, where he turned the tables on his pursuers by converting hundreds of fellow prisoners and writing dissenting tracts. His best known work is *The Pilgrim's Progress,* published in 1678–1684. Within Bunyan's own lifetime it sold one hundred thousand copies, and for more than two centuries thereafter it was a literary staple in the homes of Protestants all over the world. It is a simple and inelegant allegory in which the hero, Christian, flees the City of Destruction and, passing through the Slough of Despond, the Valley of Humiliation, the Valley of the Shadow of Death, Vanity Fair, the Delectable Mountains, and the River of Death, at length achieves Zion, the City of God. "So he passed over," concludes the author, "and all the trumpets sounded for him on the other side." Today, on Mill Street in Bedford, is the **Bunyan Museum** *(624)* on the site of a barn where he used to preach; it contains all of his surviving personal relics and editions of *The Pilgrim's Progress* in 165 languages.

Popular hostility to what might be called left-wing Protestantism, hard as it was on dissenters like Fox and Bunyan, was insignificant compared to the pervasive hatred and fear of Catholicism that held England in grip well into the eighteenth century. King Charles discovered this to his chagrin when, after his secret agreement with the French at Dover, he issued the declaration of indulgence allowing private worship to Roman Catholics as well as licenses to Protestant dissenters to hold public worship. Parliament and the public reacted so strongly that the king was forced to withdraw the indulgence and to assent to a Test Act barring all non-Anglicans from public office, including his own brother, the duke of York—a confessed Catholic. Then in 1678 came the Popish Plot—a totally fictitious conspiracy to kill the king, allegedly masterminded by English Jesuits. It was concocted in the warped minds of two shady characters named Titus Oates and Israel Tonge. Fictitious or not, the resultant wave of mass hysteria did not subside before thirty-five innocent Catholic priests and laymen had been executed. Strenuous efforts were made to exclude the duke of York from succeeding to the throne —a move frustrated only by the king's dissolving Parliament. The duke of York was next in line of succession because Charles, for all his sexual prowess, had not sired a legitimate child. Parliament's efforts to exclude the duke brought about the formation of political factions which attacked each other with the epithets of "whig" and "tory," the former for exclusion, the latter against it. (The name *whig* derived from the whiggamores, a group of rebellious Calvinist extremists in Scotland; *tories* were Irish papist bandits.) The labels would stick to the first two bona fide political parties in England formed long after the exclusion issue was dead. Meanwhile Charles II himself died on 6 February 1685, after having been received by Father Huddleston into the Roman Catholic faith and adjuring his brother "not to let poor Nelly [Gwynn] starve."

JAMES II: 1685–1688

James II's accession to the throne was at first unopposed. He had shown himself extraordinarily able as the head of the Royal Navy and, with the assistance of Samuel Pepys, had raised English seapower to a level never before attained. Though married twice—first to the Protestant–born Anne Hyde and, after her death, to the Catholic Mary of Modena—he had been almost as profligate sexually as his brother. (Charles, however, scorned the duke of York's choice of mistresses, allegedly saying they had been imposed upon him by his priests as penances.) The new king's only major defect however, from the viewpoint of the vast majority of his subjects, was that he was Roman Catholic to the core. Hoping to exploit this weakness, and encouraged by extreme Whigs, the duke of Monmouth, one of Charles II's bastard sons, raised the standard of revolt. Monmouth landed at Lyme Regis, Dorset, in June 1685 with a small band of followers, hoping to attract enough armed supporters in southern England to enable him to seize the throne. The rebellion fizzled after a brief skirmish at Sedgemoor near Bridgwater, Somerset, but the king used it as an excuse for keeping the army at full strength and, worse yet, for promoting Catholics to commanding positions in it—the Test Act notwithstanding. Nor did his efforts to extend religious toleration to Protestant dissenters assuage the growing, though no doubt unjustified fear, that he intended to re-Catholicize the country. Twice he issued declarations of indulgence in favor of both Catholics and dissenting Protestants; moreover, he befriended the converted Quaker William Penn (son of Admiral Penn, naval leader in the Dutch Wars) and confirmed Charles II's grant to him of Pennsylvania as a refuge for the persecuted Friends. Such gestures did little to rally to his support the mass of dissenting Protestants whose fear of renewed popery was aggravated by the influx of numbers of French Huguenots fleeing the persecutions of King Louis XIV following upon his revocation of the Edict of Nantes which had granted toleration to Protestants in France. King James's greatest political error, however, was to produce a son by Mary of Modena. His own reign might have been tolerated so long as his Protestant subjects could expect him to be succeeded soon by his daughter Mary, the issue of his first marriage to Anne Hyde and herself a Protestant, married to the Protestant William of Orange, Stadtholder of Holland. The birth of Prince James (later known as James III, the Old Pretender) at first produced desperate rumors that the baby was an impostor, smuggled into the queen's lying-in chamber in a warming pan. More importantly, it induced both Whig and Tory leaders to make contact with William of Orange, pledging their support for his invasion of England to seize for himself and his wife the throne of his father-in-law. William was compliant, chiefly because he needed English resources to resist King Louis XIV's invasion of the Lowlands. William landed at Torbay, Devon, on 5 November 1688, the anniversary of the Gunpowder Plot, and quickly gathered support as he moved eastward toward London. On 22 December James escaped to the Continent. He was the last male of the Stuart line to wear the English crown, though his departure would give birth to a lingering yearning among English romantics for a return of the King over the Water. Today, the student of lost causes can satisfy his curiosity at **Chiddingstone Castle** *(542)*, Kent, which houses a large and miscellaneous collection of memorabilia pertaining to the Stuart dynasty, beginning with Mary Queen of Scots and ending with Cardinal York, the younger brother of Bonnie Prince Charlie and the last of the direct line.

WILLIAM AND MARY: 1689–1702

Constitutionally the Glorious Revolution which set William and Mary upon the throne as equal sovereigns, established firmly the place of Parliament as coequal to the Crown in all important matters pertaining to the country's governance. The Declaration of Rights (later enacted in Parliament as the Bill of Rights) denied the monarch's right to suspend the operation of parliamentary laws, to maintain a standing army within the kingdom in time of peace or to levy customs or raise taxes without parliamentary consent, and to interfere with freedom of elections to Parliament or with freedom of speech in Parliament. The Triennial Act of 1694 required that Parliament meet at least once every three years and not last longer than three years, thus guaranteeing frequent elections. Somewhat later Parliament even established its authority over the right of succession to the throne by passing an act of settlement which declared that, after the death of William (Mary by this time had already died without issue) and of Mary's sister Anne and of any lawful children either of them might have, the throne should pass to the Protestant heirs of James I's daughter Elizabeth and her husband the Elector Palatine. This in effect settled the succession on Elizabeth's daughter Sophia, electress of Hanover, and her heirs, providing they "join in Communion with the Church of England." (See Stuart family tree.)

In the matter of religion, the Toleration Act of 1689 brought no relief to Roman Catholics or to Unitarians who denied the Christian concept of a Trinitarian God, but it did remove many of the disabilities that had plagued Protestant dissenters and nonconformists since the first years of Charles II's Restoration. They could now obtain licenses to hold their

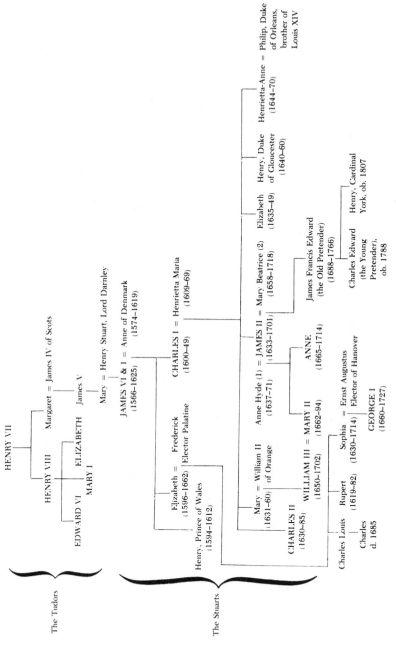

THE STUART FAMILY TREE

The Tudors

HENRY VII

HENRY VIII Margaret = James IV of Scots

EDWARD VI ELIZABETH James V

MARY I

Mary = Henry Stuart, Lord Darnley

JAMES VI & I = Anne of Denmark
(1566–1625) (1574–1619)

CHARLES I = Henrietta Maria
(1600–49) (1609–69)

Elizabeth = Frederick
(1596–1662) Elector Palatine

Mary = William II
(1631–60) of Orange

Anne Hyde (1) = JAMES II = Mary Beatrice (2)
(1637–71) (1633–1701) (1658–1718)

Elizabeth
(1635–49)

Henry, Duke
of Gloucester
(1640–60)

Henrietta-Anne = Philip, Duke
(1644–70) of Orleans,
brother of
Louis XIV

CHARLES II
(1630–85)

WILLIAM III = MARY II
(1650–1702) (1662–94)

ANNE
(1665–1714)

James Francis Edward
(the Old Pretender)
(1688–1766)

Sophia = Ernst Augustus
(1630–1714) Elector of Hanover

GEORGE I
(1660–1727)

Charles Louis Rupert
(1619–82)

Charles
d. 1685

Henry, Prince of Wales
(1594–1612)

Charles Edward
(the Young
Pretender),
ob. 1788

Henry, Cardinal
York, ob. 1807

The Stuarts

own meetings, and their ministers were excused from the requirement
to subscribe to all Thirty-nine Articles of the Church of England. Moreover, Baptist clergymen were specifically excused from subscription to
the Article on infant baptism, and Quakers were allowed to substitute
affirmations for oath taking in legal proceedings. Still the Test Act was
not repealed, so both Catholics and Protestant dissenters were barred
from holding public office and from the universities, although by 1719
"occasional conformity" was legalized so as to allow moderate dissenters
in under the tent.

With the Toleration Act begins the deep cleavage in English social and
political life between church and chapel. From 1689 until the end of the
eighteenth century, 2,418 buildings were registered for public worship
by Presbyterians, Independents, and Baptists, besides those for Quaker
meetinghouses. Many of them still stand, their defection from the
Church of England clearly registered in the arrangement of the pulpit
against one of the long walls so that the minister would be closer to his
flock, and the location of the Communion table in a central position.
Typical are the **Old Meeting House** *(608)* in Norwich (1693); the **Octagon Chapel** *(608)* in the same city (1755) built as a Presbyterian house
of worship and later converted to Unitarian use; the **Friar Street Chapel**
(602) in Ipswich, Suffolk (1700), also Presbyterian turned Unitarian; the
Unitarian Chapel *(661)* in Chesterfield, Derbyshire (1694), at first jointly
Independent and Presbyterian; and the **Jordans Quaker Meeting House**
(623) near Chalfont St. Giles, Buckinghamshire, where the younger William Penn lies buried. With their whitewashed walls, polished dark-
brown pews, and clear window glass, these meetinghouses, in the words
of the church historian Horton Davies, "were the perfect architectural
expression of the faith of the people who worshiped there."

William III, an ugly hunchbacked man who stood a full head shorter
than his wife, was above all else a soldier. Dedicated to the frustration
of King Louis XIV's plans for French hegemony of western Europe, his
assumption of royal power in England effected a revolution in that country's foreign policy that was to set it at odds with France for more than
a century. The so-called Second Hundred Years War, which ended only
with Napoleon's defeat at Waterloo in 1815, was in effect sired by William of Orange and was his major legacy to the country of his adoption.
In February 1689 the Dutch formally declared war on France and were
shortly joined in the League of Augsburg by the emperor, Spain, Savoy,
a number of German states, and England. William's first military operations were in Ireland, where the exiled James II, under French protection, was busy stirring up an Irish Catholic revolution. With the help of
Ulster Protestants (Orangemen) he beat the rebels decisively at the Battle of the Boyne on 1 July 1690, and Ireland again was reduced to colonial
subservience, to be exploited for more than two centuries by a small
landed class of Anglo-Irish aristocracy supported by an established
church to which few Irishmen belonged—not even the Ulsterites

who, as Presbyterians, became second-class citizens. At sea and on the Continent the war went less favorably for the English. Off Beachy Head an Anglo-Dutch fleet of fifty-eight ships was dispersed by the French navy, though two years later the tables were turned on the French at a battle off La Hogue. In the land battles in Flanders, the French were victorious more often than not, but when King William's War (as it was called in America) ended with the Peace of Ryswick in 1697, he won from Louis XIV the recognition of his claim to the throne of England, as well as the territorial independence of Holland.

The Royal Navy, moreover, got a hospital, meant to be the naval counterpart of Chelsea. The site was Greenwich and the architect again was Wren, assisted by his clerk, Nicholas Hawksmoor, and later by Sir John Vanbrugh—two architects about whom more will be heard later. Wren's first building on the premises of the Greenwich Hospital —now more often called the **Royal Naval College** *(535)* after its present occupant—was designed to match the existing wing of an unfinished palace designed by John Webb for Charles II. The two separate blocks of buildings, colonnaded, pedimented, and domed are, in fact, almost twins. Under one of the adjacent cupolas now sits Wren's Painted Hall with its busy baroque ceiling by Sir James Thornhill; under the other is the Chapel, rebuilt after a fire in the late eighteenth century.

Wren's best work for William and Mary was the mammoth eastern block of buildings which he added to **Hampton Court Palace** *(532)* almost, though not quite, overwhelming the original quarters built by Cardinal Wolsey and Henry VIII. On the south side of Wren's Fountain Court is the king's suite; on the north the queen's; each with its own grand staircase, guard chamber, presence chamber, audience chamber, bedchambers and drawing rooms. With its wall paintings by Antonio Verrio, Sir James Thornhill, and William Kent, its carvings by Grinling Gibbons, its paintings by Lely, Kneller, Mytens, et al., its elaborate tapestries, its intricate wrought-iron gate by the Huguenot Jean Tijou, and its charming restored seventeenth century gardens, to say nothing of its earlier Tudor handiwork, Hampton Court Palace is a museum of English art and artisanship unsurpassed in Britain.

Private building on a grand scale continued as before. Now a new architect of note put in his appearance. This was William Talman, son of a Wiltshire gentleman, about whose life or training little is known until he suddenly came into prominence as the architect employed by the third earl (later first duke) of Devonshire to rebuild **Chatsworth** *(662)*. This was the family seat of the Cavendishes in Derbyshire. Of the existing building, Talman was responsible for the east and south fronts, the other two sides of the house having been finished later under different hands, including the architect, Thomas Archer. Talman's east front, very Italianate with its heavy keystones, overhanging cornice, flat roof and balustrade, is considered by some art historians to be among the early examples of English baroque style. Even more baroque are Talman's interior designs: the chapel painted by the decidedly baroque artists Verrio and Laguerre; the great hall, also painted by Laguerre; the stone staircase decorated by Verrio; the great chamber; the second staircase with its painting by Sir James Thornhill who also covered the entire walls and ceiling of one room with a grandiose representation of the *Rape of the Sabine Women*. So grand is the total effect that the sculpted works by Cibber and the wrought-iron masterpieces by Jean Tijou seem almost supererogatory.

The word *baroque* is impossible to define, and there is some debate among art historians as to whether the term can properly be applied to English architecture at all. The adjectives most often used in connection with it are grandiose, monumental, majestic, gargantuan, palatial, animated, restless, elaborate, extravagant, dramatic, and ornate. These are too imprecise to be useful since they apply with equal appositeness to buildings of periods other than the late seventeenth and early eighteenth centuries, which constituted the floruit of the baroque style. Nor does it help much to know that the word is thought to have been derived from the Portugese *barocco*, meaning "misshapen pearl." About the closest one can come to describing baroque architecture is to say, with the art historian Doreen Yarwood, that "one of the predominant characteristics of the baroque is a free use of curves, within a classical framework of orders and ornament, the curves advancing from convex to concave giving the effect of movement." If this is so, then Talman's exteriors at Chatsworth are not baroque, but his interior designs are.

Even less baroque is his plan for **Uppark** *(552)* north of Chichester, West Sussex, built about 1690 for the earl of Tankerville. This is basically a Dutch-style house of the sort commonly associated with the reign of William and Mary. It was made of red brick, two stories high, with a steep hipped-roof intersected with dormer windows, the front doorway flanked by Corinthian columns and topped by a broken pediment above which, at the roofline, is a triangular pediment. Another Talman masterpiece is **Dyrham Park** *(579)* not far from Bath. Here he added the eastern front to the already existing mansion of William Blathwayt, secretary of war to William III. It is Italianate in design, the facade of Bath stone surmounted by a richly carved cornice and balustrade enclosing a flat roof. Inside the decor is predominantly Dutch—not surprising in view of its builder's close association with King William.

Holland and Italy were not the only continental countries to influence English architectural styles in the late seventeenth century. The period is known, after all, as the Age of Louis XIV, and it is not surprising that French fashions worked their way across the Channel. **Boughton House** *(654)* near Kettering, Northamptonshire, has indeed been described as a Louis XIV château, transplanted to English soil. The explanation no doubt is that its builder was the duke of Montagu who had served as ambassador to the French court. His French architect designed the principal facade as an open court with an arcaded loggia, two stories high under a mansard roof lined with dormer windows. Also in the French style is **Petworth House** *(553)* near Midhurst, West Sussex. Its builder was the sixth duke of Somerset, whose architectural preferences may have been shaped by Montagu, whose step-daughter he had married. It was she who inherited the house from her Percy ancestors—as well as the money to rebuild it in the seventeenth century. Laguerre was hired to decorate the grand staircase, and Grinling Gibbons to do the woodcarvings in the saloon—perhaps his finest. The Swedish painter Michael Dahl and the Dutch painter Godfrey Kneller were responsible for the fine series of female portraits, known as the Petworth Beauties. These, along with a sizeable collection of the works of Van Dyck and Lely formed the nucleus of what was to become perhaps the greatest private collection of paintings in England. Petworth today is more of an art museum than a typical stately home.

With these two notable exceptions, plus Montagu's London house on the site of the present British Museum, French influence on English architecture in the reign of William and Mary was insignificant when compared to that of the Dutch. Typical was **Stanford Hall** *(659)* near Rugby, Leicestershire. Begun in 1697, its high plain facade with hipped roof and high sash windows above ornamental balustrades date it unmistakably to the reign of William and Mary. **Hanbury Hall** *(646)* near Droitwich, Hereford and Worcester, was built in 1701 by Thomas Vernon. It is red brick, again with a hipped roof, broken by a central pediment and topped by a cupola, its front entrance flanked by voluted Corinthian columns. **Fenton House** *(530)* in Hampstead in northern London is a smaller version of the same model. Its builder and his architect are unknown, but the style is typically Dutch-English, with its simple classical doorway flanked by Doric pilasters carrying a pediment, its hipped roof intersected in front by another pediment, and its Flemish bond brickwork throughout. **Mompesson House** *(574)* in the Cathedral Close of Salisbury, Wiltshire, is another. Here the doorway is more ornately classical and the hipped roof is broken by dormer windows, but the effect is the same as at Fenton House. The date inscribed on the rainwater heads is 1701.

QUEEN ANNE: 1702–1714

Dutch William died the following year. He was succeeded by his deceased wife's sister Anne—the last of the royal Stuarts. She was thirty-seven years of age when she came to the throne and by her sottish husband, Prince George of Denmark, had born six children, all of whom had died. Her annual pregnancies, of which twelve had ended in miscarriages, had prematurely aged her. She was fat, gouty, and victim to various other circulatory complaints. She was given to passionate, though probably chaste, friendships with ladies of the court, the most notable being with Sarah, duchess of Marlborough, whose husband, the great duke, owed much of his powerful position to this connection. Eventually, the association ended in a bitter quarrel, dramatized by the queen's curt dismissal of the duchess from **Kensington Palace** *(528)*. This was Anne's favorite residence in London. Designed originally by Christopher Wren for William and Mary, it had been improved by Wren's assistant, Nicholas Hawksmoor, who added the orangery under the queen's personal direction. Situated at the western edge of Kensington Gardens, it is today a charming place, though without great architectural distinction.

Hawksmoor was also the architect for six new churches in the London area. Above all else Queen Anne was deeply religious, and it was partly through her interest that Parliament in 1711 passed an act providing for the building of fifty new churches—the first large-scale church building scheme since Wren's great project after the Fire. Although somewhat in the Wren tradition, all of Hawksmoor's churches are fussy enough in style to be called baroque. In the ancient City itself, at King and Lombard Streets, **St. Mary Woolnoth** *(513)* is a veritable jungle of fluted Corinthian columns, inside and out. The altarpiece has twisted pillars and a canopy of wood with imitation tassels. **St. Alphege** *(536)*, Greenwich (restored after World War II), is predominantly Doric in motif with an eastern portico sporting a broken pediment. **St. Anne's, Limehouse** *(530)*, though predominantly classical in design, has a columniated tower looking vaguely medieval. So does **St. George-in-the-East** *(529)* on Cannon Street Road, though its interior was much changed by restoration after being gutted by German bombs. At **St. George's Bloomsbury** *(517)*, Hawksmoor attached a giant Corinthian portico to a Greek-cross ground plan and put a tower on the side, rising to a steeple that supports a statue of Queen Anne's successor, King George I. At **Christ Church, Spitalfields** *(529)*, his heavy Doric porch sits below a wide classical tower which ascends to a single steeple like those ordinarily found on medieval parish churches. Hawksmoor's most visible work, however, though the attribution is often overlooked, is the west end of **Westminster Abbey** *(523)*, whose high flanking towers (not of course in the baroque style) he added in 1739.

Another London church, built in response to the Fifty New Churches Act of 1711, is **St. George, Hanover Square** *(527)*, designed by a little-known architect named John James. It is distinguished by its massive Corinthian portico and was to become one of London's favorite sites for fashionable weddings—including those of Benjamin Disraeli, Henry Herbert Asquith, and Theodore Roosevelt. Even more distinctly baroque in style is **St. Paul's, Deptford** *(535)*, designed by Thomas Archer. Unlike most of his English contemporaries, Archer had actually studied at Rome and had been much impressed by the works of Giovanni Lorenzo Bernini and Francesco Borromini. On his return, he was hired by the duke of Devonshire to complete the north front of **Chatsworth** *(662)* to which he gave a curved Corinthian-pilastered facade. His church at Deptford, derived from S. Agnese, Rome, is a splendid baroque composition in the Corinthian order, with three porticoes in Portland stone. Equally baroque is his St. Philip's, now the **Birmingham Cathedral** *(664)*, with its tower of four concave faces, its belfry openings flanked by Corinthian pillars, and its graceful cupola on top.

Oxford University was also the scene of considerable building activity in the first years of the eighteenth century. Dean Henry Aldrich laid out Peckwater Quad at his own **Christ Church** *(629)* and designed the Fellows Building at **Corpus Christi** *(629)*. His friend and colleague, George Clarke, fellow of All Souls, in collaboration with Nicholas Hawksmoor, designed a set of buildings for the newly founded **Worcester College** *(635)* though it was a long time before they were completed. The new college took over the lands and buildings of a medieval foundation called Gloucester College, which was itself a congeries of residential halls maintained by a number of Benedictine abbeys. Some of the initial work by Clarke and Hawksmoor can be seen in the classical north range, although the chapel, hall, and provost's lodgings were not completed until late in the eighteenth century. The south range of monastic cottages, the Pump Quad, and the Senior Common Room all belong to the fifteenth century. The combination of architectural styles, incidentally, is charming, as are Worcester's garden and expansive grounds. Hawksmoor was also responsible for a new great quadrangle at **All Souls** *(627)*, and he designed Codrington Library that abuts it. The style is neo-Gothic. His greatest work at Oxford, however, was his design for a new front quadrangle at **Queen's College** *(633)*. Facing the "High," these lovely classical buildings lend a distinct air of elegance to Oxford's main thoroughfare. One is inclined to agree with Daniel Defoe's description of Queen's as "without comparison the most Beautiful College in the University." The new quadrangle was not finished, however, until the reign of George II with a substantial gift from Queen Caroline. It is her statue, not Queen Anne's, that stands under the cupola of the gatehouse. Finally Hawksmoor is responsible for the **Clarendon Building** *(632)* on Broad Street, Oxford, next door to the Sheldonian Theatre. It was named after Edward Hyde, the first earl of Clarendon, Charles II's chief minister until 1667 when his impeachment by the House of Commons persuaded him to flee to France where he wrote his famous *History of the Great Rebellion* out of the profits of which this building was partly financed. Sir James Thornhill designed the leaden Muses which decorate the rooftop, though two of them have recently been replaced by fiberglass replicas.

Despite her many disappointments, Queen Anne did preside over two major English accomplishments in the field of foreign affairs. The first was the union of England and Scotland in 1707. The first Stuart monarch had desperately tried to bring about a unification of his two kingdoms; he failed and remained to the end James VI in Scotland and James I in England, Wales, and Ireland. A century later, the exigencies of war with France and the threat of a return of the Stuart pretenders to England by way of Scotland at last persuaded the English government to pursue the matter in earnest. Threatening the Scots with punitive economic measures if they refused, Anne's ministers at last prevailed upon the Scottish parliament to abolish itself and agree to a complete political union with England. Thus Great Britain came into being.

The deed it must be said was accomplished against the opposition of most English Tories. By Queen Anne's reign, the two parties, Tory and Whig, embryonic only in the late seventeenth century, were now fully formed and organized. Tories were generally unyielding supporters of the established Church of England, isolationist in foreign policy, indifferent or opposed to Britain's commercial and overseas expansion, lukewarm or antagonistic to the prospects of the succession to the throne by the House of Hanover, and therefore not unsympathetic with the pretensions of the exiled Stuart dynasty. The Whigs, on the contrary, tended to be tolerant toward religious dissent, supported the war against France, were closely linked with London's commercial and banking interests, and, most importantly, strongly favored the Hanoverian succession. At the summit of their political organization was a London drinking society known as the Kit-Cat Club. Forty-two of its members have their portraits hanging still in the **National Portrait Gallery** *(518)* in London. The painter was Sir Godfrey Kneller, a Hollander who came to England as early as 1675 but hit his stride only after the Glorious Revolution. Kneller was to the court and fashionable society of the reigns of William and Mary and Queen Anne what Van Dyck and Lely had been in the days of Charles I and Charles II respectively. His work at its best was better than either of his predecessor's—more incisive, more realistic, less stereotyped, and more intended to portray than to flatter. Aside from the Kit-Cat series, the best examples of his abundant *oeuvre* are the Hampton Court Beauties at **Hampton Court Palace** *(532)*; his Admirals series at the **National Maritime Museum** *(536)* in Greenwich; his portraits of Queen Anne, her son the duke of Gloucester, and Peter the Great at **Kensington Palace** *(528)*, London; portraits of Queen Anne, Prince George of Denmark, and George I at **Melbourne Hall** *(663)* in Derbyshire; Queen Anne again and some of the ladies of her court at **Petworth House** *(553)*, West Sussex; and finally the magnificent portraits of the duke of Marlborough and of his duchess Sarah at **Blenheim Palace** *(636)*, Oxfordshire.

John Churchill, a courtier to James II and personally responsible for the easy rout of the duke of Monmouth's rabble army at the Battle of Sedgmoor in 1685, had three years later joined the conspiracy which brought the Prince of Orange to the throne of England. Created earl of Marlborough for his efforts in behalf of the new king, he had cemented his power at court largely through his wife's influence over the queen's sister, the Princess Anne. Seasoned by campaigns in Ireland and the Low Countries, Churchill was well equipped to take over leadership of the British army after King William's death—less than a year after the outbreak of the War of the Spanish Succession, precipitated by Louis XIV's attempt to seize the throne of Spain for his grandson and his successful invasion of the Spanish Netherlands and of northern Italy. Queen Anne inherited the war. The British fought on land and sea for the preservation of the balance of power in Europe, for commercial and naval advantages in the Mediterranean, for trading privileges in Spanish America, and for the security of the Protestant succession to the throne of England against the claims of James II's son, the Old Pretender, now a puppet of Louis XIV. In command of allied army operations in Europe, Marlborough won a series of decisive victories—at Blenheim (1704) in Austria and at Ramillies (1706) and Oudenarde (1708) in the Low Countries. Allied military successes in Italy under Prince Eugene of Savoy and British naval conquests of Gibraltar, Minorca, and Sardinia combined with Marlborough's gains to persuade Louis XIV at last to concede partial defeat, in spite of French victory at the bloody battle of Malplaquet (1709) in which Marlborough's forces lost twenty thousand men against fifteen thousand for the French. The Treaty of Utrecht (1713) ending the war gave Britain unchallenged possession of Gibraltar and Minorca in the Mediterranean, St. Kitts in the Caribbean, and Nova Scotia, Newfoundland, and Hudson Bay in North America; allowed the British important trading rights in Spain and Spanish America; guaranteed French recognition of the Protestant, i.e., Hanoverian, succession to the British throne; awarded the emperor most of the Spanish Netherlands and northern Italy; and gave Sicily to the duke of Savoy. With Utrecht the British Empire and the Royal Navy came of age. "Before that war," wrote Alfred Thayer Mahan, "England was one of the sea powers. After it, she was *the* sea power, without any second." By that time, however, the duke of Marlborough had been dismissed from the Queen's service and was living in self-imposed exile in Holland and Germany. Not until the next reign would he return to England to take up residence in his splendid Oxfordshire palace, the gift of a once grateful Queen Anne.

When Marlborough, not long after his victory at Blenheim, was endowed with the royal manor of Woodstock, he chose as supervisor over the construction of his new country seat the most innovative architect in England. This was Sir John Vanbrugh, ex-soldier, playwright, and London socialite, an active member of the fashionable Whig Kit-Cat Club. Vanbrugh in turn chose Wren's assistant Nicholas Hawksmoor to be his collaborator, Grinling Gibbons to do the fancy stonework, and Louis Laguerre and Sir James Thornhill to decorate the interior walls and ceilings. These two painters, along with Antonio Verrio, had by now acquired reputations in England as great decorative artists in the style of Rubens, though it must be said that they were all men of modest talent, comparable to the great master only in their grandiosity.

Marlborough's great house, to be named in honor of his victory at Blenheim, was to be the second of Vanbrugh's architectural triumphs. The first was **Castle Howard** *(684)*, North Yorkshire, which he had recently completed, with Hawksmoor's assistance, for the third earl of Carlisle. The result of their collaboration is one of the noblest buildings in Britain; immense without being overpowering, ornate without being fussy, stately but not dull. In ground plan it is a long rectangle with two projecting wings on the north front, only the eastern one of which was finished by Vanbrugh before his patron ran out of money. The north or entrance front is faced with Doric pilasters; the south with those of the Corinthian order. The rooftops are studded with statuary, turrets, lanterns, and chimneys, while over all rises the splendid central drum and dome. On the grounds lie Vanbrugh's charming Temple of the Winds, a domed building with four Ionic porticoes, and Hawksmoor's magnificent and costly mausoleum, with its circle of Ionic columns supporting a flat dome. The interior furnishings of the house match its exterior splendor. Among the many notable works of art exhibited are two rare Holbeins (Henry VIII and the third duke of Norfolk) and a good collection of Lely portraits.

Blenheim Palace *(636)*, Oxfordshire, was all but completed by 1717 when Vanbrugh, no longer able to put up with Marlborough's shrewish duchess, resigned. He left behind a sprawling giant of a house; Voltaire would later describe it as *une grosse masse de pierre, sans agrément et sans goût*, "a great mass of stone, unattractive and tasteless." The exterior lines are too angular to be truly baroque in the continental manner, though the interior could hardly be more so. The entrance court is dominated by a huge Corinthian portico; Tuscan colonnades adorn the pavilions on either side of the central block; the balustraded roof is alive with statuary, the towers with high stone finials. In the great hall the ceiling is covered with Thornhill's painting of Marlborough pointing to a map of the Battle of Blenheim while a grateful Britannia bestows the victor's laurel wreath; in the saloon Laguerre depicts the great duke's apotheosis. Blenheim is frankly overdone. It stuns the viewer without inspiring in him a sense of awe. As Nigel Nicholson puts it, "It is like a declaration of war."

The last of Vanbrugh's stately homes was **Seaton Delaval** *(706)*, close to the Northumberland coast southeast of Blyth. It is a curious building, defying architectural classification. A pair of three massive Doric columns frame the central doorway; octagonal turrets guard the two front corners and taller square towers protrude from the sides; the central block ascends to a classic pediment. In 1822 a fire gutted the interior, and though the windows have been reglazed, the house is still a hollow shell.

Not so the multitude of stately homes that dot the countryside of Britain. They are, among other things, museums stuffed with antique furniture, much of it splendid, most of it good, some of it dating to the period under consideration. Like the Royal Navy, English furniture making came of age in the late seventeenth and early eighteenth centuries. Jacobean tables, chairs, chests, etc., are typically heavy, built of oak, deeply but simply carved or turned, more utilitarian than ornamental.

Straight chairs are common, with open arms and high panel backs, some with heavy baluster legs. So are settles, i.e., wooden benches with closed arms and solid backs. These were often placed close to the fire in poorer abodes, such as **Townend** *(709)* in Troutbeck near Ambleside, Cumbria, a yeoman's house built in 1626 and preserved by the National Trust. The homes of the rich might feature upholstered chairs, such as the rare surviving examples at **Knole** *(545)* in Kent. Jacobean beds tended to be enormous with massive bulbous footposts resting on square pediments at each corner, tapering upward to support a tester, or canopy, from which hung heavy curtains to keep out drafts. Draw-leaf tables replaced the trestle; table and chair legs might be bobbin turned giving the appearance of a number of balls joined together in a straight line.

With the Restoration of Charles II came an abrupt change as the exiled king and court returned from their camping-out expedition in the luxurious palaces of France and Holland. From 1660 to the death of Queen Anne was the first great period of English furniture design, and the best place to observe the change is at **Ham House** *(537)*. Oak gave way to walnut which could be shaped more elegantly and would take a higher polish. Fashionable too were veneers, thin sheets of fine wood glued onto flat surfaces of lesser quality. One variety of veneer was marquetry, small, thin pieces of different-colored woods, cut to various shapes and glued onto the surface of a piece of furniture according to a prepared design. Another was inlay, countersinking pieces of veneer or bone or ivory into solid wood. Lacquered chests and tables came in from the Orient in the holds of East India Company ships, soon to be copied by native English cabinetmakers in a process known as japanning. Gilt began to be liberally applied, often on a prepared base called gesso, a chalky paste that could be carved when hardened. Cane replaced solid wood in the backs and seats of chairs and settees. This in turn gave way to splat-backs with vaselike profiles, while chair legs now were curved outward in a form called cabriole. Heavily upholstered wing chairs came into fashion, also with cabriole legs. The emphasis in the early eighteenth century was on both comfort and grace—a combination that is still known as the Queen Anne style and is copied widely by cabinetmakers all over the English-speaking world. With it came many types of furniture: card tables, tea tables, gateleg tables, slant-top desks or escritoires, kneehole desks, chests of drawers, tall pier-glass mirrors to be hung between windows, etc., etc. The ground was being laid for the appearance of the first real genius of English cabinetmaking, Thomas Chippendale, who was born only four years after the death of Queen Anne.

The same trend toward variety and elegance affected the planting of private gardens in the late seventeenth and early eighteenth centuries. Ornamental arrangements of growing flowers and shrubs were of course not unknown in England when the first Stuart king came to the throne. The Tudor knot garden is famous, although none has survived and only in a few places has an attempt been made to reproduce it, notably on the grounds of **Hampton Court Palace** *(532)* and at **New Place Estate** *(644)* on the site of Shakespeare's house in Stratford-upon-Avon. The knot garden consisted of rectangular beds filled with intricate designs in box or other shrubs closely clipped into a low hedge and planted so as to give the appearance of being interwoven. The fashion appears to have endured well into the seventeenth century.

With the return of Charles II from his enforced travels, new styles in gardening were introduced in England to match the greater elegance in architecture and household furnishings. As in these cases, the three major sources of inspiration were France, Italy, and Holland, the influence of the latter becoming slightly more dominant after the accession of William and Mary. From France came the great formal garden of rectangular sections, called parterres, filled with close-cut shrubs, flowers, and sometimes colored earths or gravels. The most distinguished French practitioner of this style of gardening was André Le Nôtre, designer of the magnificent garden at Versailles which Louis XIV himself had praised as *"le miracle que fait M. Le Nôtre."* In England the two best known, and busiest, professional gardeners in the French style were George London and Henry Wise, who, in 1681, founded the Brompton Park Nurseries on the site now occupied by the Museum of Natural History in South Kensington, London. Another idea copied from the French was the allée, a straight walk through closely planted trees and shrubs known as boskage, usually intersecting other such walks in a geometric plan. From Holland came the art of topiary, i.e., training and clipping trees and shrubs into a great variety of shapes—cubes, spheres, cones, animals, birds, even people. Also from Holland came the idea of the water garden—great pools and long canals more or less in emulation of the Dutch countryside. From Italy came the terraced garden, where terrain permitted it, and also the practice of dotting the landscape with statuary.

Perhaps the greatest of English seventeenth century gardens in the French style (though with Dutch elements as well) is, appropriately, at **Hampton Court Palace** *(532)* where the formal parterres, radiating avenues, clipped trees and shrubs, etc., still bear the signature of the nurserymen, London and Wise, whom William III commissioned to embellish the grounds east of Wren's new buildings. The Long Water, a straight canal stretching still farther eastward from the palace, is reminiscent of the king's own homeland. The topiary maze was added by Queen Anne, but most of the flower borders and the rose garden are modern additions. At **Melbourne Hall** *(663)*, a renovated Jacobean country house not far from Derby, another garden by London and Wise is a small-scale version of Le Nôtre's spectacular productions at Versailles and other French palaces. Here are the usual parterres, allées, geometrically shaped pools, and a grand basin. The local craftsman, Robert Bakewell of Derby, did the splendid wrought-iron arbor, gaily painted in vermillion, blue, and gold. Statues adorn the intersections of the allées, and on the terrace stand four fascinating groups of Castor and Pollux fighting with each other and then making up. At **Bramham Park** *(682)* near Wetherby, West Yorkshire, the early eighteenth century Italianate villa (much restored after a fire) is not so interesting as the Le Nôtre–style garden, though it too suffered serious damage from a freak windstorm in 1962 that felled four hundred beech trees. The architectural features, however—pools, urns, statuary, stone pavilion, etc.—remain, and the replanted garden today looks like it must have appeared when first laid out. At **Penshurst Place** *(546)* in Kent most of the present landscaping was done in the nineteenth century, but the parterres of box are trimmed into slabs of shrubbery very much in the seventeenth century fashion. At **Blenheim Palace** *(636)*, Oxfordshire, the seventeenth century gardens of London and Wise were destroyed in the eighteenth by Capability Brown, but have been in part restored in the immediate vicinity of the palace. London and Wise were also responsible for the original layout at **Chatsworth** *(662)*, Derbyshire, but most of it has disappeared, except for the artificial water staircase behind the house and the canal pool to the south of it. (The 290-foot water-jet is a nineteenth century addition.) Capability Brown, who destroyed most of the Brompton Nursery's work at Blenheim and Chatsworth, left untouched the French-style garden laid out in Queen Anne's time at **Wrest Park** *(625)*, Bedfordshire. Its main feature is a long canal pool leading to a domed pavilion designed by Thomas Archer, with the boskage on either side cut through by a complex pattern of allées with the usual statues, urns, and other ornaments. Even more attractive today is the late seventeenth century Dutch-style canal garden at **Westbury Court Gardens** *(640)* in Gloucestershire, recently restored by the National Trust.

Among England's many topiary gardens, certainly the most interesting is at **Packwood House** *(645)* in Warwickshire, planted probably about 1650 by the Puritan John Fetherston and allegedly meant to represent the New Testament story of the Sermon on the Mount. It consists of a huge cone of yew (Christ) facing twelve more yews (the disciples) with many more (the multitude) scattered over the grounds. A second garden closer to the house is surrounded by a brick wall at each corner of which is a gazebo, the oldest dating to about 1680. The topiary at **Levens Hall** *(712)* near Kendal, Cumbria, is even more varied in shape and more fantastic in form and size. These yews and boxes were originally installed within the framework of a formal seventeenth century garden laid out by Guillaume Beaumont who had been trained by Le Nôtre himself and then employed by James II before coming to Levens. Contemporary with it are the great box hedges and domes of clipped yew at **Powis Castle** *(723)* near Welshpool, Powys. Here the steeply sloping terraced garden is more Italian than either French or Dutch, with stone balustrades, lots of urns, and many lead figures of shepherds and shepherdesses.

Finally, we come back to London and to the charming little Queen's

Garden behind **Kew Palace** *(537)* on the grounds of the **Royal Botanic Gardens** *(537)* on the south side of the Thames in Kew. It is a reproduction (laid out in 1960) in miniature of a formal seventeenth century garden in the French manner, with a parterre, a mount with a wrought-iron pavilion on top, and a gazebo copied from the one at Packwood House. Here is a good place for the traveller to look around and observe the passing of the Stuart age and the arrival of the Hanoverian. The palace itself is nothing more than a substantial brick house built in the Dutch style by a London merchant in the reign of Charles I. Not until the reign of George III did it become a royal palace, and its present furnishings are more in the Georgian than in the Stuart style. All about are the Royal Botanic Gardens, begun by Augusta, Dowager Princess of Wales and widow of Prince Frederick, the eldest son of George II. Most of the original buildings on these spacious grounds date to her time: the Temple of Aeolus, the Temple of Bellona, the Temple of Arethusa, the Ruined Arch, the Pagoda, and the Orangery, all designed by Sir William Chambers. We have clearly left the baroque world presided over by the later Stuarts and have entered into the age of Georgian neoclassicism.

CHAPTER IX

THE GEORGIAN PERIOD:
1714–1830

"I am no saint, no Spartan, no reformer," said Sir Robert Walpole, speaking of his long career as first lord of the treasury and prime minister to the first two Hanoverian kings of England. Indeed he was not, and the standing proof of his disclaimer is **Houghton Hall** *(606)*, the great rural palace that Walpole raised in his home county of Norfolk. It was built, furnished, and maintained out of his enormous profits garnered from two decades of influence peddling at a time when venality was the salient characteristic of British politics. Its owner owed his power to his ability to control the House of Commons at a time when the center of political gravity in the national government was inexorably shifting in the direction of that body. Houghton is a country seat, the residence of a great landowner at a time when agriculture was still the major source of Britain's wealth. It is designed in the prevailing Palladian fashion of the mid-eighteenth century with three of England's most stylish architects having had a hand in its construction and/or interior decoration. Houghton Hall is, in short, symbolic of the dominant political, economic, and aesthetic trends of the early Georgian period. It is a good starting point for the study of the era, which some historians have dubbed the Age of Walpole.

GEORGE I: 1714–1727 AND GEORGE II: 1727–1760

George Lewis, elector of Hanover, came to the throne of Great Britain not by virtue of a superior hereditary claim, but by the decree of Parliament. When put into operation, the Act of Settlement of 1701 bypassed more than fifty direct descendants of James I simply because they were Catholics—including of course James III, the Old Pretender whose birth had touched off the Glorious Revolution of 1688. George Lewis, the eldest son of Sophia, Electress of Hanover, was the senior Protestant in the line of succession. (See Stuart family tree, p. 362.) He had few other qualifications for kingship. Fifty-four years of age on his accession to the British throne, he was dull of wit and heavy of hand. As Lady Mary Wortley Montague remarked: "He could speak no English and was past the age of learning it. Our customs and laws were all mysteries to him, which he neither tried to understand nor was capable of understanding if he had endeavoured it." His wife had been divorced twenty years previously for an alleged affair with a Swedish count, for which indiscretion she was to spend the last thirty-two years of her life in prison. His *maîtresse en titre* was the Baroness von Schulenberg, a skinny hawk-faced woman of no apparent charm whom the king made duchess of Kendal. Equally unattractive was the corpulent Baroness Kielmansegge, countess of Darlington, the king's half sister with whom he spent so much time that people assumed she too was his mistress. On the credit side of the ledger, he also brought with him from Hanover his Kapellmeister, George Frederick Handel, who became a naturalized citizen and therefore one of the very few composers worth mentioning in the history of Britain, a country curiously wanting in original musical talent. His lovely Water Music was composed for a river fete organized by George I in 1717. It is one of the few bright spots in his reign. Of Handel's sponsor, the most charitable verdict is that pronounced by Lord Chesterfield: "If he had nothing great as a King, he had nothing bad as a man; and if he does not adorn, at least he will not stain the annals of this country."

The king's deficiencies, however, were seized as opportunities by Whig politicians who quickly established a near monopoly of power in the central government. The Tory party, which had mostly dominated the House of Commons in the reign of Queen Anne, virtually ceased to exist as a viable political grouping. Its demise was hastened by the flight of its two leaders, Lord Bolingbroke and the duke of Ormonde, to the "court" of the Old Pretender at St. Germain. Its fate was sealed when James III landed in Scotland in December of 1715 to assume the leadership of a rebellion that was already falling apart after a drawn battle between Scottish clansmen and royal troops at Sheriffmuir the previous month. After this abortive uprising, known as the Fifteen, the Tory party became so stigmatized as Jacobite (pro-Stuart) as to lose all credibility with the Hanoverian regime or with the bulk of the politically enfranchised English population, committed above all else to the Protestant succession. Thereafter, at least until 1760, Britain was, to all intents and purposes, a one-party state.

True, the Tory label did not cease to exist; it simply ceased to have any real meaning, as the claim of the Stuarts to be legitimate heirs to the throne became irrelevant. Nor can it be said that the now dominant Whigs were animated by any identifiable set of party principles. Indeed, the rage of party which had characterized the reign of Queen Anne now gave way to the strife of shifting factions composed of leading personalities in the national government and their "connexions"; of special economic interests such as the East India Company; or simply of ins and outs, i.e., those who enjoyed the favor of the central government, the court party, and those who did not, the country party. The aim of politics on the national level, and to some extent on the local, was, by and large, the pursuit of office. Because of the War of the Spanish Succession, the number of "places" at the disposal of the Crown had vastly multiplied with the expansion of the army and navy and of the customs and excise services under the jurisdiction of the treasury. The Crown became not so much the "fount of honor" as a fountain from which flowed all manner of monetary benefits in the form of military commissions, ecclesiastical preferments, sinecures, and government offices, great and small. The main arena in which the resultant scramble for these rewards took place was the House of Commons. The king was dependent on the Commons for the supply of funds necessary to maintain the army and navy and the civil establishment. The members were dependent on the king for the many financial favors which only the Crown could provide. Between the two, in the position of not-so-honest brokers, stood the king's ministers or cabinet, among whom the most influential was the first lord of the treasury, who had more places at his disposal than anyone else. The man who held that office from 1721 to 1742 was Sir Robert Walpole.

At **Houghton Hall** (606) there hangs a full-length portrait by John Wootton of Sir Robert—a short, square, thick-set figure, heavy of limb and double chinned. (He weighed more than 250 pounds.) Here he is represented in hunting costume surrounded by his dogs—a typical country squire. It was a pose that Walpole liked to affect. In the House of Commons he made a show of munching tiny red apples from his estate in Norfolk and bragged that he always read the weekly reports from his gamekeeper before scanning the diplomatic dispatches from abroad. The Commons was his real bailiwick, however, and it was because of his skill at manipulating its members, mostly by the systematic distribution of royal patronage, that he made himself indispensable to George I. In doing so he automatically incurred the enmity of the Prince of Wales, who hated his father with a passion that was returned in kind—a family trait among the Hanoverians that was to be repeated among succeeding generations of the dynasty. When the old king died in 1727 Walpole would probably have been sent packing back to Norfolk, except for the fact that he had prudently cultivated the good will of the new king's intelligent and influential wife, Queen Caroline. He had, in his own words, "caught the right sow by the ear," and the uxorious George II kept him on as "the king's minister in the House of Commons." He might have remained in that position until his death in 1745 but for the fact that, contrary to his advice, Britain became involved in a lengthy and expensive war with Spain and France.

The War of the Austrian Succession dragged on inconclusively. The great Whig landowners became restive as the burden of taxation mounted. In Scotland mobs rioted in the streets of Edinburgh when the government tried to enforce an excise tax. Gradually Walpole's managed majorities in the House of Commons dwindled to nothingness. His usefulness to the king thus diminished, he resigned to accept the earldom of Orford and a seat in the House of Lords. His chief rival in the Whig party, Henry Pelham, became prime minister.

The war continued. George II, a brave man and a good soldier (though not much brighter than his father) won a notable military victory at Dettingen in Germany—the last occasion when a British monarch led troops in battle. In 1745 Prince Charles Edward Stuart, the Young Pretender, took over the leadership of another uprising in Scotland—the Forty-Five. With the same blindness to political reality that had afflicted most of his forebears, Bonnie Prince Charlie foolishly believed he could reinstate his father on the throne "usurped" by the Hanoverians. Though he made a good showing in Scotland, his invasion of England aborted, and eventually his clansmen were cut to pieces by the king's son, the duke of Cumberland, at Culloden Moor in April 1746. Two and a half years later a peace was signed at Aix-la-Chapelle, which did little more than restore the *status quo ante* between Britain and her continental rivals. Pelham died and was succeeded by his brother-in-law, the duke of Newcastle, a master of corruption even more adroit than Walpole. The Whig oligarchy was still in command.

It was an oligarchy based mostly on the ownership of land. From twenty to twenty-five percent of the cultivated land of England and Wales was owned by as few as four hundred families. Most of it was let out to tenants, and the great landlords' average annual income of ten thousand pounds was chiefly derived from rents. About half of them were noblemen, the hereditary peers who sat in the House of Lords along with the bishops of the Church of England. The rest were members of the upper gentry, many of whom could be found in the House of Commons. The term gentry is a loose one. It includes the hereditary baronets, knights, esquires, and mere "gentlemen." Most of these people were armigerous, but that distinction had grown meaningless as the College of Arms had become more and more lax in dispensing coats of arms. What really distinguished the gentry from the bulk of the population was that they lived on unearned income from rents, mortgages, and other investments, supplemented perhaps by the profits of office. Excluding the great landowners among them, who fall in the same category of wealth as the hereditary peers, the gentry owned altogether about fifty or sixty percent of the cultivated land of England and Wales and enjoyed an average family income of from three hundred to five thousand pounds per annum. During the eighteenth century (and for most of the nineteenth as well) roughly half the land of Britain was owned by no more than four thousand persons. These were the country's ruling elite—the top of a pyramid where power and prestige gravitated, contrary to the law of nature, toward the apex. These were the people who populated both houses of Parliament, held most of the commissions in the army and navy, supplied the majority of the clergy, and, as justices of the peace, ruled the countryside. It was this landed class too—the aristocracy and gentry—who were responsible for the great eighteenth century building boom in country houses, made possible by the rising price of grain and other foodstuffs which became especially pronounced after mid-century and reached an unprecedented peak during the wars of the French Revolution and Napoleon (1793–1815).

Agriculture during these years was undergoing a radical change amounting, in the eyes of many economic historians, to a revolution. New methods of crop rotation both improved the soil and permitted more constant tillage. Turnips and seed grasses (hay) provided winter food for livestock which would otherwise have had to be slaughtered for salt meat each autumn. Jethro Tull's new seed drill permitted planting grain in straight lines far enough apart to allow deep cultivation by a horse-drawn hoe. The Rotherham triangular plow patented in 1730 made possible a rapid turning of the soil by means of a two-horse, one-man team instead of the traditional six or eight oxen accompanied by a driver and plowman. Acts of Parliament, mounting in number from 67 in the years 1721 to 1740 to 1,043 between 1761 and 1780, authorized the enclosure by ditch and hedgerow of large areas of open fields, common holdings, and wasteland so that arable lands could be consolidated into larger holdings with a consequent rise in their productivity. And the chief beneficiary of all these changes was the substantial landlord, whether squire or noble, with his ever-expanding acreage, his private deer park, and his great house on the hill.

The country house, the family seat of the great noble or his counterpart in the House of Commons, or of the retired admiral, the rich merchant turned landlord, or even the merely well-off county squire, was the cynosure of the genteel world of the eighteenth century. It was not a significant economic unit because most of the surrounding acres were normally farmed out to tenants. In addition to being a residence, a place of business, and a center of hospitality, it was the symbol, par excellence, of the gentleman's status, his prestige, his wealth, and his power. As such it required a lavish expenditure of his time, thought, and money. To assist this exercise in conspicuous display, he could, fortunately, call on the services of the most distinguished body of professional architects, interior decorators, landscape gardeners, and cabinetmakers that Britain has ever produced.

Within this galaxy, a few stars are especially distinguishable for their brilliance. Among them were the Scot, Colen Campbell, and the Italian, Giacomo Leoni, both of whom in 1715 published books that were to have a profound impact on architectural fashions for the rest of the century. Another was the third earl of Burlington who returned from Italy in 1719 full of zeal for the classical styles he had observed there and possessed of more than adequate funds to pursue his enthusiasm. Still another was Burlington's protégé, William Kent, a young Yorkshireman he had picked up in Italy. Kent was more than an architect. He was a notable interior decorator; he designed a magnificent barge for the Prince of Wales (on display in the **National Maritime Museum** [*536*], Greenwich), and he initiated a new fashion in gardens which departed radically from the rigid formalities of Le Nôtre. Other architects among his contemporaries were Henry Flitcroft, Sanderson Miller, John Carr, and James Gibbs, the latter better known for his churches and university buildings than for house design.

All of the above, with the exception of Gibbs, were Palladians. Like Inigo Jones before them they were conscious imitators of the Roman architect Vitruvius as interpreted in the sixteenth century by Andrea Palladio, who, in his *I Quattro Libri dell'Architettura*, postulated precise mathematical ratios of harmonic proportions for both buildings and individual rooms within them and was profuse in his employment of certain stereotyped classical motifs, among them the temple-front portico of columns (Ionic, Doric, Corinthian, Tuscan, or Composite) supporting a huge triangular pediment; heavy pediments over doors and windows; and the Venetian window, consisting of a central arched light flanked by two smaller rectangular lights, often recessed in the wall under an overriding Roman arch.

In their interior arrangements and decorations the mid-eighteenth century Palladians tended to be more eclectic and pragmatic, and therefore less doctrinaire, than in their structural designs. Though classical motifs abounded—columns, pilasters, pediments, coffered ceilings, etc. —the strict Palladian ratios for the dimension of rooms were often abandoned in favor of a melange of extended sculpture galleries, saloons, libraries, reception rooms, etc., all arranged in enfilade and opening out of each other so as to afford vistas along the whole length of the *piano-nobile,* the high-ceilinged story above the ground floor.

As buildings became more severely classical, however, the landscaping around them became less so. Here, Kent introduced enduring fashions, modeled not on the great French gardens of Versailles and Fontainebleau, but on the romantic Arcadian landscapes of the painters Claude Lorrain, Gaspard Poussin, and Salvator Rosa. Garden walls were knocked down and in their place were sunk ditches called *ha-ha's* whose aesthetic purpose was to merge the semiformal garden near the house with the wilder growth beyond. Kent also abolished the angular regularities of the formal garden in favor of glades, groves, winding paths, and artificially channeled serpentine streams. Still, the classical ideal was not abandoned altogether as evidenced by the proliferation of obelisks, tiny temples to the gods, and toga-draped busts and statues to remind the visitor of the glories that were ancient Rome's.

Burlington's first architectural effort was the remodeling of his own London mansion, that is, **Burlington House** *(526)* in Piccadilly, now occupied by the Royal Academy of Arts. Working from a Palladian design republished by Giacomo Leoni and executed by both Colen Campbell and William Kent, the original mansion, built in 1665, was completely redone in the new fashion. Unfortunately the Palladian work has been all but obscured by Victorian restoration so that all that is left from the eighteenth century are the lower part of the north facade of the present quadrangle and the first-floor rooms within. Of far greater architectural significance is Burlington's villa at **Chiswick** *(531)* on the western outskirts of London, modeled on Palladio's Villa Rotonda near Vicenza. Here can be seen most of the elements of English Palladianism. The entrance front, approached by a double flight of stairs, displays a splendid portico of Corinthian columns topped by a plain triangular pediment flanked on either side by simple rectangular pedimented windows. Above the center of the square-built house is an octagonal dome. On the garden front another double flight of stairs joins in front of a Venetian window with a round-arched central light flanked by rectangular side lights framed by columns. Inside, broken pediments surmount the doorways, stuccoed masks and garlands ornament the fireplaces, gilded scrolls and swags adorn the overmantels, and decorated ribs divide the ceilings into rectangles. Unfortunately, except for the Ionic temple and a few pieces of classical statuary, little is left of Kent's garden, one of the first to be laid out in the new informal style but now mostly overlaid with subsequent additions and much reduced by suburban encroachments.

Kent's great masterpiece is **Holkham Hall** *(610)* near the north coast of Norfolk. It was built for Thomas Coke, first earl of Leicester. Having travelled extensively in Italy and accumulated a superior collection of antique classical statuary, Leicester was naturally inclined to the Palladian style in designing an appropriate setting for his treasures. Kent, Burlington, and Leicester himself all contributed to the plan. Unfortunately a local yellow brick was selected for the building—a material that has weathered into the color of wet sand. The house is modeled on Palladio's Villa Mocenago. In the center of the original entrance (south front) stands the usual noble portico with Corinthian columns supporting a plain pediment; each of the corner turrets of the main block is pierced by a Venetian window; and on either side the wings stretch out in almost too perfect symmetry. Inside, the sense of severity vanishes. In the rich marble hall stand Ionic columns of variegated alabaster between which mounts a splendid flight of steps leading to the saloon. Here are displayed Kent's superb furniture, twin fireplaces of Sicilian pink and white marble, and a bust of Pallas Athene rising through the broken pediment above the central door. East of this lies the sculpture gallery, no doubt the owner's pride and joy where visitors could be brought to admire the booty of his Grand Tour, including a bust of Thucydides and the head of Aphrodite from the Parthenon. The great park at Holkham was also designed by Kent around an eighty foot obelisk, with avenues stretching in eight directions, the one to the north leading to the house, that to the southwest to a tiny domed temple, while the southern avenue terminates in a grand triumphal arch. It is by this road that today's visitor now leaves the grounds of Holkham. He would be well advised to stop here and look backwards up the glorious vista to the house itself. Thus he can view it as it was meant to be viewed by anyone approaching the estate, not as it is in fact first seen today from the entrance route that terminates in the rather unattractive north front.

At **Rousham Park** *(637)* near Oxford, remodeled by Kent in 1738, the Palladian motifs are less in evidence than at Holkham. Here Kent was asked to transform both house and garden, the former an "old-fashioned" Jacobean mansion with gables and three-story porches rising on both fronts. Kent "modernized" the building by lowering and straightening the roofline, adding wings of a slightly classical flavor, and creating two entirely new rooms inside, the painted parlor of strictly Palladian style and the great parlor in which the architect toyed with Gothic motifs. It is Kent's garden, however, that is the distinguishing feature of Rousham and one that has survived almost intact. Here, as one commentator has put it, "he set the English garden free"; that is, he broke completely from the seventeenth century traditions of Le Nôtre and created a landscape fashioned on the romantic paintings of Claude, Gaspard Poussin, and Rosa. Beyond the *ha-ha* which surrounds the house he planted woodlands with two cascades feeding a pool, a serpentine brook with a stone-lined basin, statues of Venus, Hercules, and satyrs, temples, and a colonnade of pedimented arches. At **Stowe Gardens** *(622)* in Buckinghamshire, Kent installed an even grander garden for Lord Cobham, whose house now serves as a school. Building on earlier beginnings by Charles Bridgeman (inventor of the *ha-ha*), Kent created a version of the Elysian Fields through which flows an artificial river spanned by a shell bridge and a Grecian Valley overlooked by a temple dedicated to Concord and Victory; he dug an artificial lake shaped like an octagon and over one end built a Palladian bridge; and he added to the statuary which Vanbrugh had already placed around the grounds. Vanbrugh and Bridgeman also began the landscaping of **Claremont Landscape Garden** *(555)*, Surrey, for that master Whig politician, the duke of Newcastle. Again Kent enlarged on the work by expanding a small pond into a lake, planting groves of trees, laying out serpentine paths, and scattering about a number of small classical buildings, most of which have since disappeared.

Much in the manner of Kent, and contemporary with his work, are two great English gardens created to take advantage of the romantic attraction offered by the proximity of ruined Cistercian abbeys. The first is **Rievaulx Terrace** *(689)* near Helmsley, North Yorkshire, which has an Ionic temple at one end, a Doric temple at the other, and in between dramatic glimpses of the abbey through the trees. Very similar in theme is **Studley Royal** *(687)*, also in North Yorkshire near Ripon, designed by its owner John Aislabie to allow the visitor spectacular views of nearby Fountains Abbey. From the little river flowing through his property Aislabie created a series of canals and pools, one of them shaped like a crescent. Along the bank he built a lovely little Doric temple, gleaming white. His architect was Colen Campbell, William Kent's distinguished competitor for Palladian honors.

Even before Kent started on Chiswick House, Campbell had secured a commission from the great Sir Robert Walpole himself to put up **Houghton Hall** *(606)* near King's Lynn in Norfolk. The building itself, constructed out of Yorkshire stone, is essentially Palladian, though James Gibbs later introduced a slightly baroque note by substituting domes for Campbell's pediments on the four corner towers. Otherwise, the symmetry, the large central pediment, the Venetian windows, the pedimented rectangular windows, the Tuscan colonnades leading to flanking pavilions, all betray the guiding spirit of Palladio. So do the interior rooms, designed and decorated by William Kent. The great stone hall is a perfect cube and the other rooms are lavishly painted, hung, and furnished in Kent's best manner. It is a fitting monument to the greatest man in England. Only the overscrupulous will remember that it was financed mostly by profits from the sale of offices and commissions. Another Campbell creation was **Stourhead** *(574)* in Wiltshire, designed in 1721–1724 for a rich banker, Henry Hoare, but much expanded and modified since. Here the house is overshadowed by the garden—the work of Henry Hoare II and another fashionable architect and protégé of Lord Burlington, Henry Flitcroft. Hoare dammed the river to create a three-pronged lake, and around its shores Flitcroft built a Tuscan Temple of Flora, a Pantheon, a Temple of Apollo, and a grotto with a leaden nymph and an incised quatrain by Alexander Pope. Piling Pelian on Ossa, Hoare then indulged his Gothic nostalgia, always dormant in the English psyche, by importing a genuine fourteenth century market cross from Bristol, and building a not-so-genuine rustic cottage with Gothic overtones, as well as a thatched-roof convent occasionally inhabited by a female servant dressed as a prioress.

It was Flitcroft too who is responsible for the eighteenth century facelift of **Woburn Abbey** *(625)*, Bedfordshire. The house dates back to the thirteenth century when it served as a monastery of the Cistercian order. Confiscated by Henry VIII, it was sold to John, Lord Russell, who was to become the first earl of Bedford. The family flourished throughout the sixteenth and seventeenth centuries and the fifth earl became the first duke of Bedford under William III. An extremely profitable marriage combined with astute landgrabbing brought the Russells enormous wealth along with a position of unexcelled eminence among the ruling Whig aristocracy of the mid-eighteenth century. It was the fourth duke who was responsible for the complete remodeling of the family seat at Woburn. His architect, Henry Flitcroft, raised a great Ionic centerpiece on the west front of the main block and made whatever other changes were necessary to squeeze the ancient abbey and its seventeenth century additions into a new Palladian dress. Flitcroft, known as Burlington Harry because of his association with the great pioneer of English Palladianism, also designed the staterooms at Woburn and the two stable blocks to the east of the main house, whose domes appear to have been copied from Chiswick. The fifth duke made further additions with the help of Henry Holland who belongs to the next generation of fashionable architects. The twelfth duke tore down the east wing of the four-sided courtyard mansion, thus reducing it to the shape of a U. The thirteenth duke, who inherited in 1953, with a practical acumen his Whig ancestors would surely have applauded, resolved the problem of punitive taxation by opening the family seat to the public (for a price) and importing a veritable arkful of wild animals to populate a safari park as an added attraction. As one commentator has written, Bedford virtually invented the stately-homes business, and to him the intelligent traveller owes a tremendous debt. Woburn, with its splendid furnishings and priceless works of art (some already, others to be, mentioned separately) deserves its high reputation as a tourist attraction. Nowhere in Britain are the needs and concerns of the paying customers treated with more courteous consideration.

Another Whig family of distinction, though not nearly so grand as the Russells, were the Onslows of Surrey. To remodel the family seat at **Clandon Park** *(555)*, Thomas, second Lord Onslow, commissioned the Venetian architect Giacomo Leoni as architect. The resultant square red-brick house with stone dressings is predominantly baroque on the outside, but the interior is definitely Palladian, especially the great two-story marble hall, with plasterwork by the Italian stuccoers Artari and Bagutti, and the so-called Palladio room still covered with its French wallpaper of about 1780. Another Leoni creation is **Lyme Park** *(695)* in Cheshire. Though the gateway, incorporating four of the classic orders, dates to the sixteenth century, the house itself, with its vast Ionic portico resting on a ground floor of rusticated arches, its noble pediment surmounted by lead figures of Neptune, Venus, and Pan, its high pilasters reaching to the cornice, is magnificently Palladian. Inside, Leoni's handiwork can still be seen in the entrance hall, the grand staircase, and the saloon.

Another mid-eighteenth century architect of some distinction, though an amateur, was the Warwickshire squire, Sanderson Miller. At **Lacock Abbey** *(572)*, Wiltshire, he added the pseudo-Gothic (or Gothick) entrance hall and great hall to the pre-existing building, but at **Hagley Hall** *(666)* near Stourbridge, West Midlands, rebuilt for the first Lord Lyttelton, he copied the Palladian lines of Holkham Hall in a rose-pink sandstone that has weathered far better than the unattractive brick of the original. In the garden Miller built a decorative Gothick castle to take its incongruous place alongside a Palladian rotunda and a later Doric Temple of Theseus designed by the master of the Greek Revival, James "Athenian" Stuart, of whom more will be said below. An even more distinguished amateur architect was Henry Herbert, ninth earl of Pembroke, who worked in tandem with Roger Morris, master carpenter to the Office of Ordnance (not to be confused with his kinsman Robert Morris whose book *Select Architecture* was the major source of Thomas Jefferson's design for Monticello near Charlottesville, Virginia). Pembroke and Morris designed the incomparable Palladian bridge on the former's estate at Wilton, and, on a larger scale, they built for George II's mistress, the countess of Suffolk, the splendid Palladian villa of **Marble Hill House** *(533)* at Twickenham in the western outskirts of London.

That the appeal of Palladianism was nationwide is evidenced in the career of John Carr, known as Carr of York, who was for more than half a century the leading architect north of the Trent. Typical of his work is **Constable Burton** *(685)* near Richmond, North Yorkshire. Here is the familiar double stairway leading to a pedimented entrance way graced by Ionic columns with rectangular pedimented windows on either side. **Cannon Hall** *(678)*, overlooking the village of Cawthorne near Barnsley, West Yorkshire, was built by Carr in the 1760s. It is typical of the hundreds of handsome but unpalatial country houses owned by members of the lesser gentry. Today it is the site of a country-house museum managed by the Barnsley Metropolitan Borough Council as well as the Museum of the Thirteenth/Eighteenth Royal Hussars (Queen Mary's Own). Somewhat far afield for Carr is the house he built for Sir Francis Sykes in Berkshire called **Basildon Park** *(564)*, a fine and typical Palladian mansion in a beautiful setting overlooking the Thames valley. Carr was also responsible for the original construction of **Harewood House** *(681)* near Leeds, West Yorkshire, but his work was so much modified by Charles Barry in the nineteenth century that it is hardly recognizable except in the Venetian windows in each corner tower and the many pedimented windows elsewhere. Anyway, Harewood is today chiefly distinguished for the interiors by Robert Adam which will be treated below. The same applies to **Kedleston Hall** *(633)* in Derbyshire, begun by the London architect, James Paine, in 1757 but finished by Adam. Paine's best surviving work is at **Wardour Castle** *(575)*, Wiltshire, now occupied by the Cranborne Chase School, but open in the summertime to the public. It too is firmly in the Palladian tradition.

Not so are the works of James Gibbs, a contemporary of Burlington, Kent, Campbell, et al., but more conservative in his tastes than they and closer to Wren than to Inigo Jones in his classicism. Best known for his churches and university buildings—to be considered below—Gibbs left at least three residential monuments to his memory. The first is **Ditchley Park** *(627)* in Oxfordshire with interior decorations by Kent and Flitcroft and now serving as an Anglo-American Conference Center. The second, in Twickenham, is called **Orleans House** *(533)* on account of its occupancy in the nineteenth century by duc d'Orleans, later King Louis Philippe of France. Most of the house was subsequently torn down, but Gibbs's fine Octagon Room remains, now used as an art gallery. The third is **Wimpole Hall** *(617)* near Cambridge, owned by Edward, Lord Harley, first earl of Oxford. Here Gibbs added a wing on either side of the central block of the original mid-seventeenth century house and later a library to contain the original Harleian collection of books and pamphlets subsequently transferred to the British Museum. Later, Henry Flitcroft remodeled the saloon and added a gallery for a new owner, the first earl of Hardwicke, and later still (in the 1790s) Sir John Soane designed the "yellow drawing room" and added another book room to Gibbs's library. Interior decorations here include work by the plasterers Giovanni Bagutti and Guiseppe Artari and the muralist Sir James Thornhill. Charles Bridgeman, Humphrey Repton, and Capability Brown all left their imprint on the park. The National Trust considers Wimpole to be "the most spectacular mansion in Cambridgeshire." Not done by Gibbs, but somewhat in his manner, is **Antony House** *(588)* in Cornwall just west of Plymouth. Here the classical exterior is spoiled by a nineteenth century *port-cochère* but otherwise the Roman severity is intact. This is a charming house, outside and in, set in a "natural" landscape designed by Humphrey Repton.

Though the professional architects of the eighteenth century found their widest (and best-paying) field of opportunity in the design and construction of country houses, it is not to be assumed that urban building was neglected altogether. On the High Street of Hull, for example, is **Maister House** *(677)*, a severe brick building with a fine pedimented central doorway and staircase-hall, all very much in the manner of Lord Burlington who may have personally suggested the design. Contemporary with it is **Peckover House** *(619)* in Wisbech, Cambridgeshire, again a plain town house with a brick cornice and parapet, brick pilasters, and brick panels beneath the windows. William Kent designed the famous **Horse Guards** *(521)* in Whitehall, London, more or less in the manner of Holkham Hall, with its Venetian windows and symmetrically disposed component parts. While waiting for the changing of the guard at 11:00 A.M., visitors should note the Palladian setting for this colorful scene. Another Palladian building is the **Mansion House** *(511)*, official residence of the lord mayor of London. George Dance the Elder designed it, and the pediment was sculptured by Sir Robert Taylor. But it was at Bath in Avon that the new fashion was to receive its most felicitous urban treatment.

Though famous in Roman times for its health-giving mineral waters, Bath at the beginning of the eighteenth century was a mere provincial backwash, the center of a decaying woolen textile industry. A visit by the ailing Queen Anne to take the waters encouraged others to do likewise, and by the third decade of this fashion-hungry century, Bath was a thriving spa with a highly-styled social life dominated by Richard "Beau" Nash (not to be confused with the Regency architect, John Nash). Nash was able to impose a rigid courtly etiquette upon his popular cotillions and assemblies and teach city manners to country squires whose wives and daughters found the new resort's attractions irresistible. In 1727 the architect John Wood moved to Bath and began the building program which, when completed by his son (another John), was to give the city one of the most attractive townscapes in Britain—a distinction that it still enjoys. Wood's first effort was **Queen's Square** *(578)* whose north facade is a model of Palladian severity. Next came the **Circus** *(578)*, a crescent-shaped row of town houses begun by the elder Wood and completed by his son after his father's death in 1754. John Wood, Jr. then proceeded to erect the **Royal Crescent** *(579)*, elliptical in shape, six hundred feet in length, a truly noble facade of Ionic columns raised on a high base. The younger Wood is also responsible for the **Assembly Rooms** *(578)*, now restored after a fire in 1942. Other eighteenth century architects followed in the wake of the Woods. **Lansdowne Crescent** *(578)* was built by

John Palmer in 1789–1793, **Somerset Place** *(579)* and the **Grand Pump Room** *(578)* by Thomas Baldwin and John Palmer in 1792–1796, by which time the ancient Roman Baths next door had been rediscovered by excavation.

Not all mid-eighteenth century architecture, however, was in the Roman mode. Among a people notorious for its dedication to eccentricity, there was bound to be a reaction to the strict rules of Palladio, and it came in the form of the "Gothick" revival. The leader in this rebellion was, perhaps surprisingly, Sir Horace Walpole, son of the great prime minister. In 1743 he bought **Strawberry Hill** *(533)*, a conventional Georgian house in Twickenham, which in thirty years time he converted into a Gothick fantasy with towers and cloisters and, inside, a melange of chimneypieces in the form of tombs, gilded fan vaults of plaster, and other oddities meant to invoke memories of the fifteenth century. The house is now a Catholic training college and admission can only be obtained by prior application. For the time being, at least, Walpole's innovations attracted few imitators in spite of being widely publicized, especially after he became the author of *The Castle of Otranto,* the first of a never-ending series of English Gothic novels. Independently of Walpole, however, Sanderson Miller, who had already added a Gothick hall to Lacock Abbey, began for Sir Roger Newdigate the reconstruction of his Elizabethan house called **Arbury Hall** *(643)* in Warwickshire in the same late Perpendicular fashion. Using the Henry VII Chapel at Westminster Abbey as a model, Miller and later architects simulated Gothic fan vaults, piers, window openings, etc., with plaster moldings of astonishing delicacy and grace. Not until the nineteenth century, however, would the taste for pseudo-Gothic fashions really come into its own.

GEORGE III: 1760–1810

George III, who succeeded to his grandfather's throne at the age of twenty-three, inherited a ministry he loathed and a war he found irksome and unacceptably expensive. The ministry was headed by that veteran Whig master-politician, the duke of Newcastle, with William Pitt the Elder (later Lord Chatham) its most aggressive member. The war was the so-called Seven Years War in which France and Britain with their respective allies had been engaged by land and sea on four continents and surrounding waters since 1756. By the time of the new king's accession, the war was going well for Britain. The French had been all but driven out of India; they had lost their important West African post at Goree; Guadeloupe in the French West Indies had been seized; a French fleet had been badly mauled by Admiral Hawke at Quiberon Bay; and Quebec and Montreal had fallen to James Wolfe and Lord Jeffrey Amherst, respectively, though the former had suffered death on the Plains of Abraham. Only on the Continent was Britain's ally Frederick the Great of Prussia not faring so well.

The new king, so much maligned by Whig historians and of course by their American counterparts, was a young and earnest idealist with little understanding of the realities of politics, a hatred of the Whig oligarchy that had dominated Parliament since the days of Walpole, and an exaggerated view of the wisdom of his Scottish tutor, John Stuart, the third earl of Bute, whom he hoped to elevate to a position of dominance within a new ministry. The king did succeed in forcing the resignations of Newcastle and Pitt, but before long was compelled to dispense with Bute, return Pitt to the ministry, and be content with the framework of politics as he had found it. There was no constitutional revolution, no usurpation by the Tory party, no monarchical tyranny imposed on Parliament and the country by the king's friends as was once believed. Nor is there any evidence that such had been George III's intention. True, he tended to meddle more in politics than had either of his predecessors. Also the king shared with his ministers, and especially Lord North, responsibility for the inept handling of the series of crises that culminated in the American Revolution.

The causes of the secession of the thirteen British colonies on the Atlantic coast of North America are too complex to be dealt with here in detail. Perhaps revolt was inevitable once France had yielded Canada and the Ohio Valley by the terms of the Peace of Paris which ended the Seven Years War in 1763. This eliminated the colonists' chief grounds for dependence on the mother country and at the same time gave the British government the opportunity to prohibit migration westward across the Appalachians, a restriction considered outrageous by land-hungry Americans. British insistence that the colonists share the financial costs of the late war clashed with colonial claims to autonomy nurtured by long years of very lax imperial controls coupled with somewhat grandiose American ideas about their natural rights derived chiefly from a biased reading of John Locke's *First Treatise on Civil Government.* In the event, war came. Inexperience and confusion among the rebelling colonists were more than matched by the bungling of Lord North's government, divided counsels, widespread domestic opposition in Britain to the war, faulty intelligence concerning American affairs, and the sheer magnitude of the task of pacifying so large a country. Though historical analogies are always suspect, one cannot help but be struck by the similarities between the insoluble problems facing the British in 1776–1781 and those of the United States government vis-à-vis Vietnam in the 1960s. In the final analysis, however, it was French intervention on the side of the colonists that proved decisive. For the one and only time during the "Second Hundred Years War" between France and Britain, the former nation was completely free of continental threats and commitments and therefore able to devote all her resources to engaging Great Britain. One result was that, of the 140,000 British regulars, German mercenaries, and American loyalists under arms, only 40,000 could be spared for service in North America, the remainder being assigned to home defense and the protection of other parts of the empire. Another was that the French navy could concentrate its forces so as seriously to threaten an invasion of England and at the same time disrupt the English line of communications with the main theater of operations. In the end it was the naval victory of a French fleet over that of Admiral Sir Robert Graves at the mouth of the Chesapeake Bay on 5 September 1781 that proved to be the coup de grâce. Graves's failure to bring relief to the beleaguered forces of Lord Cornwallis, pinned down on the Yorktown peninsula, compelled the latter to surrender to Generals Washington and Rochambeau, thus bringing an end to the war and independence to the United States of America.

A dozen years later, in 1793, Britain was again at war with France, a war that was to last intermittently for more than twenty years. The Revolution in France, beginning with the fall of the Bastille on 14 July 1789, had within the course of two years become a major threat to the stability of Europe. In April 1792 the new French Republic declared war on Austria; in November its government was offering assistance to all the peoples of Europe who would revolt against their own anciens régimes; in the same month General Dumouriez occupied the Austrian Nether-lands (Belgium) and announced the opening of the River Scheldt in an effort to reestablish Antwerp as a commercial rival to London; and in February 1793 France declared war on England and Holland. British strategy for the next fifteen years, mostly set by its great wartime leader, William Pitt the Younger, rested on two main principles: (1) subsidizing continental allies to engage the mass armies of Republican France and, after 1799, of Napoleon as First Consul and Emperor; and (2) attempting to drive the navies of France and her allies off the high seas, destroy their maritime commerce, and occupy their overseas possessions. This latter task was naturally entrusted to the Royal Navy.

British seapower, clearly superior to that of any other European na-tion by the end of the War of the Spanish Succession (1713), was, with the exception of a brief interlude during the American Revolution, to go from strength to strength throughout the balance of the century. The core of the fleet during these years was the ship of the line, a square-rigged sailing vessel up to two hundred feet in length, carrying from 74 to 120 guns emplaced in two or three gun decks and firing through rows of portholes pierced into the ship's hull on either side. Naval tactics were dictated by the fact that these muzzle-loading can-non, with a maximum range of twenty-five hundred yards, could fire only broadside, i.e., in a direction perpendicular to the axis of the ship. This is because, with their heavy wooden-wheeled carriages and their muzzles protruding through the narrow confines of a porthole, they lacked lateral train or traverse, i.e., the capability of changing aim from side to side. Thus, steering the ship and aiming its guns were one and the same maneuver, a tricky business in a square-rigged vessel that could head no closer to the wind than fifty degrees and could make no more than seven knots running before it. Given the cannon's low degree of accuracy, only mass fire could be effective, and this could best be achieved by bunching ships together in a linear formation, each ship except the first in line following the one ahead (a column formation in modern naval nomenclature). For all these reasons, the Admiralty in 1703 issued a *Book of Fighting Instructions* requiring British ships, while engaged with the enemy, always to maintain station on the ship ahead and never to break out of line without specific orders from the flagship. Although not unreasonable, given the limitations described above, the Fighting Instructions tended to discourage individual ship captains from breaking out of line, when the occasion warranted, to engage single ships, or to capture stragglers, or to pursue the enemy in retreat, or even to avoid ramming the ship ahead in line. Hence, to allow greater individual initiative, modifications in the regulations were made from time to time, the most important being the Additional Instructions issued by Admiral George Anson who was to become first lord of the Admiralty in 1754.

Anson was one of several remarkable sailors to rise to the top of the Royal Navy in the eighteenth century. In the 1740s he had circumnavigated the globe to return home safely in spite of serious errors in navigation that would no doubt have been avoided had he waited until after 1759 when the Royal Greenwich Observatory successfully tested John Harrison's fourth marine timekeeper or sea clock—a chronometer which for the first time permitted the accurate calculation of longitude at sea. Harrison's instruments are on view in the west wing of the **National Maritime Museum** *(536)* in Greenwich. In another room are mementos of Captain James Cook, also commemorated in the **Captain Cook Birthplace Museum** *(697)* at Stewart Park near Middlesbrough, Cleveland. An extraordinary and self-taught navigator, Cook, too, lacked a chronometer during his first Royal Society–sponsored voyage to the Pacific in 1762 when he charted the coast of New Zealand and the eastern shoreline of Australia. There his explorations are memorialized on the map in such place-names as New South Wales, Botany Bay, and Endeavour Straits, the latter named after his famous ship. On his second and third trips to the area, however, his expeditions went equipped with Harrison's sea clock.

Also at Greenwich are numerous eighteenth century ship models and paintings of sea battles to enrich the intelligent traveller's understanding of the nature of sea warfare in the age of sail. Another repository with a good collection of ship models is the **Buckler's Hard Maritime Museum** *(559)*, Hampshire, on the site of a thriving eighteenth century shipbuilding center on the Beaulieu River. In Portsmouth the **Royal Marines Museum** *(560)* has a nice model of an eighteenth century two-decker ship and of course many exhibits and mementos relating to the history of these soldiers of the sea whose services as marksmen, amphibious troops, and shipboard disciplinarians played a significant role in the ultimate triumph of the Royal Navy. As to Anson—he returned in 1774 from his trip around the world, rich enough in captured Spanish spoils to finance the rebuilding of the family's country seat at **Shugborough** *(667)*, Staffordshire, where the county council now maintains a museum of his relics.

Anson and other naval luminaries of the mid-eighteenth century, such as Edward Hawke, Edward Boscawen, and Samuel Hood, are remembered today mostly as forerunners of Britain's greatest naval personage, Horatio, Lord Nelson, whose high **Monument** *(518)* presides over London's Trafalgar Square, named after his last and most famous victory at sea. Born in a modest vicarage in Norfolk, he went to sea at the age of twelve and, before he was twenty-one, was given command of a frigate in West Indian waters, in spite of chronic seasickness and various other ailments that would have beached a less ambitious youth. At the outbreak of the war with France in 1793 he took command of the *Agamemnon*, a sixty-four-gun ship of the line, built at Buckler's Hard. While on duty in the Mediterranean, he first met the beautiful Lady Hamilton, formerly Emma Lyon Hart, who had already been mistress to two English aristocrats before marrying Sir William Hamilton, British minister to the Two Sicilies. The torrid love affair between Nelson and Emma would later be the talk of Europe and, of course, a source of acute embarrassment to Nelson's wife, though not apparently to Sir William. During a landing expedition on Corsica in 1794 Nelson lost his right eye. By 1796 he was in command of the *Captain*, a ship of seventy-four guns. While serving under Sir John Jervis in a battle off Cape St. Vincent in February 1797 he distinguished himself by breaking out of the battleline without orders to board and capture two Spanish ships, though his own had been almost completely disabled. Here was a spectacular demonstration of what soon came to be known in the fleet as the Nelson touch—his readiness to take bold initiatives, his fine sense of timing, and his utter fearlessness. His favored tactics were the complete opposite of those prescribed in the old *Fighting Instructions* and adhered to by most eighteenth century captains and admirals, sometimes, as in the case of Robert Graves at the Battle of the Chesapeake, with disastrous results. In Nelson's case, successful flouting of the rules brought rich rewards. He was made a rear admiral and knight of the Bath. In 1798 he led a foolhardy landing expedition on Teneriffe in the Canary Islands and lost his right arm. His next ship was the seventy-four-gun *Vanguard*. With her as flagship, he destroyed a French fleet at anchor in Aboukir Bay thus leaving Napoleon's expeditionary force to Egypt stranded. It was a spectacular victory, won by a most daring feat of seamanship, and its perpetrator was made Baron Nelson of the Nile. In 1801 he was second in command to Sir Hyde Parker in an attack on the Danish fleet in Copenhagen harbor. Here, on being apprised of Parker's flag-hoist ordering the engagement to be discontinued, he put his telescope to his blind eye, remarking, "I really do not see the signal," then proceeded to finish the destruction of the Danish flotilla. In May 1803 he hoisted his vice-admiral's flag aboard the *Victory* at Portsmouth. For the next two years he was busy maintaining a blockade of Toulon, and, when the French admiral, Villeneuve, escaped, Nelson chased him across the Atlantic to the West Indies and back again to Cadiz where Villeneuve took shelter. Coming out of Cadiz, the combined French and Spanish fleet sailed into the waiting arms of Horatio, Lord Nelson off Cape Trafalgar on 21 October 1805. Having already advised his subordinates (his "band of brothers") that "no Captain can do very wrong if he places his ship alongside that of an Enemy," Nelson raised on *Victory*'s yardarm the flag-hoist, "England expects that every man will do his duty," and then, as the battle began, "Engage the enemy more closely." By the end of perhaps the fiercest naval melee in history, Villeneuve had lost most of his fleet and Nelson his life. "Never did any man's death cause so universal a sorrow as Lord Nelson's," declared Admiral Cuthbert Collingwood, his long-time companion in arms. His body was carried by barge up the Thames to Greenwich where it lay in state for three days in the Painted Hall of what was the Royal Naval Hospital and is now the Royal Naval College; thence to the Admiralty where it rested for another night; thence slowly by carriage through the streets of London, preceded by 10,000 regular troops, and followed by the royal family, thirty admirals, and a hundred naval captains to **St. Paul's Cathedral** *(515)* where, beneath the center of the dome, still stands the consummate hero's enormous sarcophagus in black and white marble. A more significant monument to Nelson is **H.M.S. Victory** *(561)*, itself now in a permanent berth in Her Majesty's Dockyard in Portsmouth. Gaily painted in yellow and black, the colors used most commonly in the Mediterranean squadron, here is a noble first-rate one hundred–gun ship of the line, the emblem of Britain's mastery of the seas, one of "those distant, storm-beaten ships," in the words of Alfred Thayer Mahan, "upon which [Napoleon's] Grand Army never looked, [but which] stood between it and the dominion of the world." Here also can be seen the admiral's cabin, his cot, table, and armchair, though most of the furniture used by Nelson, along with other relics and a fine tabletop model of the battle of Trafalgar are in the Dockyard's **Victory Museum** *(561)*. The **National Maritime Museum** *(536)*, Greenwich, contains a large collection of Nelson busts, paintings, and miscellaneous memorabilia, including the vice-admiral's uniform coat he was wearing when shot by a French marine at Trafalgar. **Buckler's Hard Maritime Museum** *(559)*, Hampshire, has some of the hero's baby clothes and a ring he gave to Lady Hamilton. Poor Emma died a broken alcoholic in Paris in 1815. Their daughter, Horatia, survived to marry a clergyman and settle into obscure respectability.

Trafalgar unfortunately did not end the war, nor was it responsible for the failure of Napoleon's great scheme to launch a full-scale invasion of England. "Let us be masters of the Straits [i.e., the English Channel] for two hours," he declared, "and we shall be masters of the world." Hoping to distract the Royal Navy in distant waters, he prepared a flotilla of small craft capable of lifting 167,000 men and transporting them from Boulogne to the shores of Kent which the emperor expected to assault. This was no feint, no idle threat, and the British knew it. Nor were they content to place exclusive reliance on their traditional wall of ships, no matter how mighty the Royal Navy had become. Beginning in 1804 they began to construct along the Kentish and Sussex coasts a chain of martello towers so named after a French coastal fortification at Mortella Point in Corsica. These were round towers, each carrying a twenty-four-pound gun and two stubby cannons called carronades on the roof, all mounted on traversing platforms to fire over a circular parapet. The towers were about twenty-six feet in diameter, constructed of brick, three stories in height, and spaced all along the threatened coast at intervals of five to six hundred yards. Similar forts were built along the shores of the Channel Islands.

On 26 August, almost two months before Trafalgar, in response to Austria's joining the third coalition of Britain and the major continental powers against France, Napoleon decamped his invading army from Boulogne and began the march across the Rhine that was to culminate in his glorious victories at Ulm and Austerlitz. The immediate invasion threat was thus removed, but the fear of its renewal remained, and work on the martello towers continued. Altogether seventy-four were built, twenty-seven in Kent and forty-seven in Sussex. Jersey and Guernsey too received a substantial number of these installations. Of those still standing in England, at least two are worth a visit. These are the **Martello Tower** *(542)* on the beach at Dymchurch, Kent (No. 24 in the chain), and the **Wish Tower** *(548)* which was No. 73, on King's Parade in Eastbourne, East Sussex. Also in Eastbourne is the so-called **Great Redoubt** *(548)*, one of three blockhouses put up to supply and control the system of martello towers and now containing the museum of the Royal Sussex Regiment as well as a fine, though incongruously situated, aquarium. In addition to these coastal fortifications, the government then dug the nineteen-mile **Royal Military Canal** *(542)* backed by a rampart across the entire rear of the Romney Marsh in Kent. It can best be seen today in Hythe or where it intersects the B 2070 about five miles south of Ashford. On Guernsey's rugged north coast is a well-preserved martello tower called **Fort Grey** *(746)*. It stands within a circular curtain wall and houses a fascinating maritime museum devoted mostly to the history of ship-wrecks off this treacherous shore.

The war went on—in Europe, on the high seas, even in North America against the United States—but at home in Britain, once the threat of invasion had subsided, all seemed tranquil. Readers of the novels of Jane Austen, written during these years *(Sense and Sensibility, Pride and Prejudice, Mansfield Park,* and *Emma)*, will find little evidence that the lives of the country gentry whom she mildly satirized were much affected by the war. Yet she lived and worked at **Chawton Cottage** *(557)*, Hampshire (now a museum), no more than thirty miles from the busy naval base at Portsmouth.

For one thing, Britain was prosperous. The prices of grain and other farm products rose steadily throughout the war, bringing higher profits to farmers and higher rentals to landlords. One result was a renewed enthusiasm for building new homes or remodeling old ones. Once again supply rose to meet demand as a new generation of architects, decorators, and landscape gardeners came forth to help the rich, both new and old, spend their money.

The reign of the third George began with the Palladian style still in the ascendant. It was to be continued, though with a difference, by Robert Adam and his three brothers whose architectural firm in London set new fashions in classicism that were to dominate the building and decorating industries for most of the last half of the eighteenth century. Robert Adam, second son of a successful Scottish architect, studied in Italy for four years; viewed the newly excavated ruins of Herculaneum and Pompeii; became enamored of the Renaissance masters, especially Michelangelo and Raphael; crossed the Adriatic to inspect the ruins of Diocletian's palace in Dalmatia; and wrote books about much of what he had learned of art, architecture, and archaeology. Though no dissenter from the holy canon of Palladio as interpreted by Burlington, Kent, Campbell, et al., Adam's style was more cosmopolitan, more eclectic, and more experimental, as was that of most of his late eighteenth century contemporaries.

The new fashion can best be described as neoclassical. It was in marked contrast to contemporary developments in landscape gardening which carried Kent's stress on informality to its logical conclusion. The leader in this movement was Lancelot Brown, called Capability because of his habit of speaking of the capabilities inherent in any landscape he was commissioned to improve. He carried the cult of nature to a point where only the most discerning eye today can distinguish Brown's calculated arrangements from the natural growth one would expect to see surrounding any house in the country. His signature, however, can normally be seen in sweeping lawns running up to the edge of the house, irregular sheets of water at a distance, and circular clumps of trees strategically placed for their picturesque effect. Mention has already been made of his work at **Alnwick Castle** *(704)*, **Burleigh House** *(653)*, **Longleat** *(577)*, and **Blenheim Palace** *(636)*. Others will be indicated below. He was followed by Humphrey Repton who worked in the same tradition, though his parks tend to have more trees than Brown's, as at **Woburn Abbey** *(625)*, and he reintroduced terraces in the immediate vicinity of the house.

Robert Adam's earliest work in England was carried out in his capacity as interior decorator, not architect. His first commission was at **Hatchlands** *(556)*, an unpretentious red-brick Georgian house east of Guildford, Surrey, built by Admiral Edward Boscawen. Surviving features of Adam's work are the marble chimneypieces in the library and drawing room and the plaster ceilings appropriately incorporating nautical motifs. His next production, and some would say his best, was at **Kedleston Hall** *(633)* in Derbyshire where Adam took over an unfinished Palladian house being built for Nathaniel Curzon, Baron Scarsdale. To the south front he affixed what looks like a Roman triumphal arch approached by a curving double staircase. Inside, he created a marble hall intended to resemble a Roman *atrium,* with twenty fluted columns of green and pink alabaster; plaster statues in arched recesses; and twin fireplaces with classical female figures, also of plaster, supporting a circular painting. The saloon is circular with high coffered dome, and the other rooms are variegated in shape—squares, ovals, rectangles, etc.— indicating Adam's un-Palladian preference for variety and movement. **Harewood House** *(681)*, West Yorkshire, already mentioned as the creation of John Carr of York, was turned over to Adam to decorate, while Capability Brown was commissioned to redo the park. Here Adam is at his most typical, with his varicolored and multishaped rooms, fluted Ionic columns, classical fireplaces, and above all the delicately molded plaster ceilings. Thomas Chippendale, the most fashionable of London's cabinet-makers (to be discussed more fully below) was commissioned to make the furniture—splendid pieces in a classical mode unusual for Chippendale and therefore attributed to Adam's personal design. Of Brown's improvements to the grounds, the most noticeable survivor is the artificial lake, the terraces near the house being a nineteenth century addition. At one time the largest house in Devon, **Saltram** *(588)* near Plymouth, is basically of Tudor provenance with Restoration additions. Its charm, however, derives mostly from Adam's eighteenth century decorations of the saloon and dining room and from the Chippendale furniture, some in the classic, some in a Chinese, style. The saloon is a double cube with a coved ceiling of intricate geometric designs painted by Antonio Zucchi who often collaborated with Adam. The dining room, where Adam designed the furniture, is among his better works. The rest of the rooms are sumptuous though of no particular style. Capability Brown's garden, with a handsome orangery added later, has mostly resisted the encroachments of suburban Plymouth, though the present view can hardly be called picturesque. At **Newby Hall** *(682)* near Ripon, North Yorkshire, Adam added two new wings to an existing house of the seventeenth century, one of which was a domed sculpture-gallery whose contents have survived almost *in toto,* a good example of the kind of booty eighteenth century dilettantes (in this case William Weddell) normally brought back from the Grand Tour. The other rooms display the usual Adam signature: delicate plasterwork, ceiling paintings by Zucchi, and again chairs by Thomas Chippendale. Most of the mansion at **Bowood** *(572)* near Calne in Wiltshire has been torn down, but Adam's particular contribution to it remains in the Diocletian wing, vaguely resembling the Roman emperor's palace in Dalmatia which the architect had visited and written about. Bowood is mostly distinguished, however, for being the site of

Joseph Priestly's discovery of oxygen and for perhaps the best preserved of Capability Brown's landscapes, where he dammed the valley below the house to form a lake and planted clumps of trees in the foreground to channel the views. **Nostell Priory** *(682)* near Wakefield, West Yorkshire, is a Palladian house, begun in 1733, and enlarged later by Adam who designed the north wing. Wall and ceiling paintings by Zucchi and his wife Angelica Kauffmann, plasterwork executed by another frequent collaborator, Joseph Rose, and furniture crafted by Chippendale all reflect the taste and organizing ability of the architect. At **Syon House** *(533)* on the western outskirts of London, Adam undertook for the duke of Northumberland the interior reconstruction of a Tudor mansion which traced its origins to a nunnery confiscated by Henry VIII. The great hall here, furnished like an *atrium,* is certainly one of Adam's more spectacular works with a black-and-white checkered floor, fluted pilasters, and copies of the *Dying Gladiator* and the *Apollo Belvedere,* the latter, according to Olive Cook, "so well married to its setting that after a visit to Syon the sight of the original in the Vatican comes as a sad disappointment." In the anteroom stand twelve freestanding columns dragged up from the Tiber River, each supporting a gilded classical figure; the red drawing room has a fine ceiling painting by Angelica Kauffmann; the long gallery a full set of furniture designed by Adam himself. The garden here was done by Capability Brown but only the long lake on the northwest survives, the rest of the grounds having been relandscaped later. Another Tudor house near London, remodeled by Adam, is **Osterley Park** *(533)*. The entire interior was redecorated. Hall, library, dining room, and drawing room are pure neoclassical. The Etruscan room is modeled on Adam's recollection of Pompeii where the Greek vases were thought mistakenly to have originated in the pre-Roman culture of central Italy. Again the furniture is Adam's. Of all his creations this is perhaps the most typical, and its convenience to London gives it a special attraction to the average visitor to Britain. Even closer to central London is **Kenwood House** *(530)* in Hampstead, though its location no doubt accounts for the large crowds that can accumulate there on weekends, sometimes so flustering the custodial staff that they close off most of the rooms without warning. Adam was commissioned in 1769 to remodel what is now the central block, the two wings being of later construction. His employer was a fellow Scot, William Murray, Lord Mansfield, chief justice of England, and one of the most distinguished jurists in English history. Perhaps his most famous judgment was in the case of a black slave whom he freed on the grounds that "the state of slavery is . . . so odious that nothing can be suffered to support it but positive law," of which there was none on record in England. *Fiat justitia, ruat coelum,* "Let Justice be done, though the heavens fall," he decreed, and slavery was abolished in the British Isles though not in the empire. The stucco house that Adam completed for Lord Mansfield's use has a noble entrance portico of high Composite columns (part Ionic, part Corinthian) supporting a heavy classic pediment. Inside, Adam's work can best be seen in the library with its plasterwork by Joseph Rose and painted panels by Zucchi; the breakfast room with an Adam frieze, dado rail, and white marble mantelpiece; and the dressing room with an identical mantelpiece. Housed here also is the Iveagh Bequest, a collection of paintings by great masters, including Reynolds and Gainsborough.

While Robert Adam and his brothers worked for the rich and mighty subjects of the king, William Chambers, in the tradition of Inigo Jones and Wren, held commissions from the king himself and from his family. Son of a Scottish merchant, he had sailed on ships of the Swedish East India Company and had acquired enough firsthand knowledge of the Orient to free him from the single-minded classicism of most of his contemporary architects. As a protégé of Lord Bute, he was architectural tutor to Frederick, Prince of Wales, then architect to Augusta, the Princess Dowager after the death of Frederick, and finally comptroller of the works and surveyor general or, in effect, chief architect to King George III. Commissioned by the Princess Dowager to beautify the **Royal Botanic Gardens, Kew** *(537)*, he designed, as already mentioned at the end of the last chapter, a number of neoclassical decorative monuments —the Temple of Aeolus, the Temple of Bellona, the Temple of Arethusa, a simulated ruined Roman arch, and the orangery, and, no doubt influenced by his voyages to Asia, the 136-foot high pagoda, still the most prominent building on the grounds. Shortly thereafter he constructed for King George the **Kew Observatory** *(537)* south of the gardens in an area called Old Deer Park. Chambers's masterpiece is **Somerset House** *(523)*, the great long leviathan of a building overlooking the Thames just downstream from Waterloo Bridge and stretching back to the Strand. It was built to house government offices, and still does, though there is talk of transferring here the marvelous collection of paintings now housed at the **Courtauld Institute Galleries** *(516)* on Woburn Square. Chambers is responsible only for the central block, the two wings having been added in the nineteenth century. On the Strand front, Corinthian half columns rise above a multi-arched rusticated ground floor—a conventional neoclassic facade; behind it is an open quadrangle with Corinthian features on all four sides; while Chambers's construction on the river front (completed after his death, but to his design) takes the form of three separate blocks resting on rusticated arches which served as watergates before the river was narrowed here by landfill to create the Victoria Embankment.

When Chambers died in 1796 his position as surveyor general was taken by James Wyatt who filled it until his own death in 1813. The most eclectic of Georgian architects, his buildings run from Palladian to Gothic. Though some of his most interesting designs, as we shall see below, were made for university buildings, his major oeuvre consisted of country houses, where he was Adam's chief rival. **Heaton Hall** *(694)* near Manchester, and now owned by the city, is one of Wyatt's early works—a neoclassic building with a bowed front, Venetian windows, and octagonal pavilions connected with the central block by colonnaded wings. At **Ragley Hall** *(643)* near Alcester, Warwickshire, there is a Brown landscape with the inevitable artificial lake, clumps of trees, etc., surrounding a house built in the seventeenth century by Wren's colleague, Robert Hooke. It was later reworked by both James Gibbs and James Wyatt, the former being responsible for the splendid hall with plasterwork by Guiseppe Artari, the latter for the Adam-like neoclassical dining room, saloon, and staterooms. **Goodwood House** *(552)* near Chichester, West Sussex, is perhaps better known for its racetrack than for its architecture. The grandiose neoclassical house (an enlargement of an earlier building) was designed by Wyatt for the third duke of Richmond, though the original plan for a hollow octagon with eight round towers at the angles was never completed. Wyatt's interiors have been mostly redone. He also designed the kennels—now a golf club. The severely classical stable block was done by William Chambers. Wyatt also refaced the west front of the seventeenth century mansion at **Erddig** *(732)* just south of Wrexham, Clwyd, and decorated the entrance hall and drawing room. Acquired by the National Trust as recently as 1977, the most interesting feature of this great sprawling estate today is its large collection of portraits, daguerreotypes, and photographs of domestic servants from the eighteenth to the twentieth centuries. This fascinating display serves as a needed reminder that these great country houses, splendid though they may be as works of art, were run on a system of low-paid labor. Fashionable architects like James Wyatt and Robert Adam were well compensated for their services; upstairs' maids and stable boys came cheap. The sober respectability revealed in these rows of honest British faces lining the walls of Errdig tends to belie the fact that people like these were mostly underpaid and underprivileged.

Mention has already been made of the Gothic element in Wyatt's repertory. He, more than Horace Walpole at Strawberry Hill, was the father of the neo-Gothic revival, usually referred to by the eighteenth century spelling, Gothick. At **Sheffield Park** *(550)* near Uckfield, East Sussex, he transformed an existing house with battlements, blind Gothic arches, hood-molds over the windows, turrets, and stepped gables. The interior is a mix of classic and Gothic motifs. The garden here, though later much modified, was the work of Capability Brown who is responsible for one of the two lakes now on the premises. At **Plas Newydd** *(735)* on Anglesey, overlooking the Menai Strait, Wyatt and a mason named John Cooper completed the Gothicization of an established house, adding battlements, octagonal towers, turrets, etc. Inside, the Gothick hall has a fine plasterwork fan vault; a minstrels' gallery adorns the music room whose chimneypiece has two medieval knights on either side; but the rest of the rooms are mostly neoclassical, some of them adorned with fine wall paintings by Rex Whistler executed in this century. The Cavalry Museum, with its interesting relics of the Battle of Waterloo, will be returned to below; the stables are pure Gothick; the grounds were designed by Humphrey Repton. Even more distinctly medieval in appearance is Wyatt's **Norris Castle** *(558)* on the Isle of Wight overlooking the Solent. Everything here is castellated, though the arches and window openings are round headed, harking back to Norman, as distinct from Gothic, architecture. Here too are bedrooms used by Queen Victoria as a girl and a bath and shower installed for her grandson, the German emperor William II. For **Ashridge House** *(619)* near Berkhamstead, Hertfordshire, Wyatt leaped over four centuries of medieval architectural style from the Romanesque to late Perpendicular. This is a turreted house with oriels, bays, and towers built for the seventh earl of Bridgewater, commemorated in the grounds designed by Repton with a high (172 steps to the top) fluted classic column surmounted by an urn. Wyatt's last house before his death in a coach accident in 1813 was a reversion to the classical mode. This is **Dodington** *(579)* in Avon north of Bath. This has been judged his most mature classical work, not Palladian but Roman in style, with a deep columniated, pedimented portico, an entrance hall fashioned in the manner of an *atrium,* bronze vestal virgins holding urns, and a host of other features to remind the viewer of the Imperial City. The park was done by Capability Brown with two lakes and an aqueduct *cum* cascade between them.

Henry Holland was Brown's assistant, then son-in-law, though he turned his talents to architecture rather than landscaping. As designer of Brooks's Club in St. James Street he was introduced to the cream of Whig society and was rewarded in 1783 with the commission to build a London residence for the Prince of Wales—Carlton House, later torn down. For the banker Thomas Harley, former lord mayor of London, he designed **Berrington Hall** *(647)* near Leominster, Hereford and Worcester—an early example of the neo-Grecian, as distinct from Roman, fashion that would reach the height of its popularity after the turn of the century. It is a rather plain rectangular house with a pedimented Ionic portico for an entrance front and a superbly chaste entrance hall meant to reflect the pure classicism of Athens before it was coarsened by the Romans. The huge park was laid out by Capability Brown who probably also advised Harley on the choice of his housesite so as to assure a panoramic view of the distant mountains of Wales. At **Althorp** *(655)* near Northampton, Holland remodeled the Tudor/Jacobean family seat of the second Lord Spencer, giving the brick walls a new tile face and introducing Ionic motifs in the interior. Althorp is famous for its fine collection of English paintings, including portraits by Van Dyck, Lely, Gainsborough, and Reynolds, and a unique collection of hunting scenes by John Wootton. It has recently become famous too, as any follower of the royal family knows, as the childhood home of the Princess of Wales, nee Lady Diana Spencer. Also much in the news, as the honeymoon site of Prince Charles and his bride, is **Broadlands** *(561)* near Romsey, Hampshire, once too the home of the third Viscount Palmerston, Queen Victoria's prime minister, and, until his murder by the I.R.A., of Earl Mountbatten of Burma. On this estate the hands of Kent, Capability Brown, Henry Holland, Angelica Kauffmann, and possibly Robert Adam are all in evidence. Kent landscaped it in the 1730s; Capability Brown further developed the grounds in the 1760s and began the transformation of the Tudor manor house along more acceptably neoclassical lines; the job was completed by his son-in-law Henry Holland who added the east front portico and sculpture hall and redecorated most of the staterooms with the assistance of Angelica Kauffmann, possibly under the direction of Robert Adam. The priceless contents of this stately home are as impressive as its historic associations, and include paintings by Lely, Reynolds, and Lawrence (a fine portrait of Emma, Lady Hamilton), a superb collection of Wedgwood ceramics, and the Garter Star worn by the duke of Wellington at the Battle of Waterloo.

The Greek revival, already mentioned, was touched off in England in 1762 by the publication of *The Antiquities of Athens,* a four-volume study by James Stuart, known as Athenian Stuart, and his colleague Nicholas Revett. The burden of their argument was that pure classicism was to be discovered in ancient Greece rather than among the conquering Romans who had copied and corrupted the styles of their more refined neighbors to the east. In effect this was a plea for the elimination of two of the five orders (Tuscan and Composite), for greater simplicity of line, and less ponderosity. In practice only the most discerning and professional eye can tell the difference. Among Stuart's early efforts in this direction were the three monuments he raised in the park of Admiral Anson's lovely house called **Shugborough** *(667)* near Stafford, already mentioned as the repository of the circumnavigator's naval relics. Here the doyen of Greek revivalists put up three fine monuments to the glory that was Greece: a triumphal arch modeled precisely on the Arch of Hadrian in Athens; the Tower of the Winds, copied from the Tower of Andronicus Cyrrhestes; and the Lanthorn of Demosthenes, based on the fourth century Choragic Monument of Lysicrates. (The incongruous Chinese House nearby was the invention of one of Anson's officers.) The house at Shugborough, built originally in the seventeenth century, was remodeled in the late eighteenth by Samuel Wyatt, brother to the better known James. He added an Ionic portico to the east front and dressed up the interior, with the result that this is one of the prettiest neoclassical country houses in Britain. Not to be confused with James Stuart is George Stuart, another neoclassical architect who built **Attingham Park** *(671)* near Shrewsbury, Salop. To the existing house he added a plain Corinthian pedimented portico in front of a new central block attached on either side to pavilions linked by colonnades, the entire facade stretching to nearly four hundred feet. Humphrey Repton landscaped the park. James Stuart's partner, Nicholas Revett, added an Ionic portico to the west front of **West Wycombe Park** *(623)* in Buckinghamshire and installed a Temple of Music on an islet in the artificial lake to keep company with a Temple of Apollo and a Temple of the Winds already gracing the park designed by Capability Brown's student Thomas Cook and later modified by Repton. The house here is an unusual medley of neoclassical styles. Revett's Ionic west portico (today's entrance) is joined on the north face of the building by more Ionic columns, on the east by a Tuscan portico, and on the south by the Corinthian order superimposed on the Tuscan. The interior rooms are equally eclectic, though mostly within the neoclassical canon. Most of the planning seems to have been the work of the owner himself, Sir Francis Dashwood, with the assistance of an obscure architect named John Donowell. Dashwood, a founder of the Dilettanti Society of young aristocrats returned from the Grand Tour, he served disastrously as chancellor of the exchequer, and opened his house to a strange organization whose official title was the Knights of St. Francis but whose members were commonly known as the Mad Monks of Medmenham, dedicated it would seem to the profanation of religion and holding cock fights in the Temple of Apollo.

Not attributable to any of the fashionable architects mentioned above, but nevertheless deserving attention as representative of Georgian styles, is a handful of houses that have little architectural relationship to each other beyond being contemporaneous. The first is **Gorhambury House** *(620)* situated next to the Roman theater in St. Albans, Hertfordshire, a large Palladian mansion built between 1777 and 1784 designed by Sir Robert Taylor on the site of a Tudor house owned by Queen Elizabeth's councillor Sir Nicholas Bacon, father to the essayist Sir Francis. Good seventeenth century portraits (also a fine Reynolds) adorn the walls, and many of Francis Bacon's books still grace the shelves of the library. **Ickworth** *(601)* near Bury St. Edmunds, Suffolk, was started in the 1790s by Frederick Augustus Hervey, the fourth earl of Bristol and bishop of Derry—a central rotunda modeled on the Pantheon in Rome, flanked by rectangular pavilions joined to it by elliptical wings. Rich in great masters, English furniture, and silverware, the monumental grandeur of the building itself is more oppressive than inspiring. At **Claydon House** *(624)* in Buckinghamshire, within the Palladian shell the interior decoration is mostly rococo with Chinese themes predominating. In one room an immense alcove in the shape of a pagoda houses a sculpted family of four, indubitably Chinese, in the act of taking their tea. It is English eighteenth century *chinoiserie* at its peak. The fashion, as we shall see, was more commonly reserved for furniture.

EIGHTEENTH-CENTURY FURNITURE

The most important single event in the history of English furniture design in the eighteenth century was the passage in 1721 of an act of Parliament abolishing the heavy duties hitherto imposed on timber imported from British North America and the West Indies. Although the purpose of the act was to help the shipbuilding industry, badly hit by a rapid depletion of English forests for the production of charcoal for iron smelting, an important side effect was to encourage cabinetmakers to switch from walnut to imported mahogany. Jamaica was the first major source of supply, then Cuba and Santo Domingo, Spanish colonies from which the wood was easily smuggled, and finally Honduras, another Spanish colony. West Indian mahogany was dark, developed a beautiful patina with age, and most importantly had an almost metallic resiliency suitable to delicate and slender furniture parts (especially chair backs) that would stand up to wear and tear. The Honduran product was lighter in weight and color, but also tough.

The Palladian cult, however, presented a problem to those among its devotees who were interior decorators and cabinetmakers. Neither Vitruvius nor Palladio had anything to say about furniture, nor had archaeology much information to offer concerning what the Greeks and Romans slept on, sat on, wrote on, and ate from. The solution, already suggested by Inigo Jones, was to transfer classical architectural forms to the design of furniture and interior decoration. Cabinetmaking became architectonic. The pioneer in this direction was William Kent, the first English architect to try to integrate furniture with the interior and exterior design of his houses. Pedimented interior doorways and chimneypieces were framed by voluted pillars or pilasters; classical ornaments such as scallop shells, floral swags and pendants, caryatids, and human masks adorned the walls and ceilings, the same themes being repeated in cabinets, bookcases, and tables. Good examples of Kent's furniture survive at **Chatsworth** *(662)*, Derbyshire; **Holkham Hall** *(610)* and **Houghton Hall** *(606)* both in Norfolk; and **Wilton House** *(575)*, Wiltshire.

The second most important event in the history of English furniture making in the eighteenth century was the publication in 1754 by Thomas Chippendale, cabinetmaker of London, of *The Gentlemen and Cabinet Maker's Directory,* a book of design that circulated so widely throughout Britain that the author's name became attached to a wide range of mid-eighteenth century furniture patterns, many times copied ever since. Chippendale and his successors, Hepplewhite and Sheraton (to be discussed below), are significant not just because of the specific pieces they designed or made, but because they imparted a degree of standardization to a craft that had hitherto been almost completely individualistic. Any good cabinetmaker could copy a design from Chippendale's book, and many did—which accounts for the difficulty of distinguishing authentic pieces made in his shop in St. Martin's Lane from those made elsewhere and by other hands. Chippendale's style, varied as it was, was distinct from that of Kent in being organic rather than tectonic, i.e., in abandoning the straight and functional lines of vertical columns and horizontal entablatures for a welter of curves, spirals, and serpentine lines conforming more to nature than to classical architecture. The artist William Hogarth wrote in 1753 that "the waving line . . . is the line of beauty," and a little known predecessor of Chippendale, Matthew Lock, had adopted the same precept in a book of patterns he published in 1740. The style is called rococo, an outgrowth of the baroque, only lighter, daintier, and more self-consciously decorative. Chippendale was its major popularizer in Britain. In his hands the exuberant elegance of the rococo was expanded to include both Oriental and Gothic motifs which had nothing in common except that both departed from the strict canon of Renaissance classicism. Of these two forms the first was the more popular not only in England, but in France, where the word *chinoiserie* was coined to describe almost any art form that was vaguely related to the Far East. In England, Chippendale's name is so intimately associated with Orientalism, at least in furniture, that Chinese Chippendale is more of a generic name than a trade name.

In the **Victoria and Albert Museum** *(526)*, South Kensington, London, is a splendid example of the style—a pagoda-topped bed from Badminton House that may have been built in Chippendale's London shop. Elsewhere, throughout the stately homes of Britain, Chippendale furniture abounds. Among the houses with the best collections of his rococo pieces are **Arbury Hall** *(643)*, Warwickshire; **Chatsworth** *(662)*, Derbyshire; **Hardwick Hall** *(662)*, Derbyshire; and **Lyme Park** *(695)*, Cheshire (chairs covered with pieces of cloak worn by Charles I at his execution). Good examples of his Chinese style are at **Audley End** *(600)*, Essex; **Charlcote Park** *(644)*, Warwickshire (mirrors); **Clandon Park** *(555)*, Surrey (the best); **Felbrigg Hall** *(605)*, Norfolk; **Shugborough** *(667)*, Staffordshire; and **Woburn Abbey** *(625)*, Bedfordshire. In his Gothic style are pieces at **Althorp** *(655)*, Northamptonshire; and **St. Michael's Mount** *(743)*, Cornwall.

At **Harewood House** *(681)*, West Yorkshire, **Newby Hall** *(682)*, North Yorkshire, and **Nostell Priory** *(682)*, West Yorkshire, are sets of furniture made by Chippendale in a style not normally associated with his name. They were commissioned and designed by Robert Adam, a reminder that Chippendale was a a cabinetmaker as well as a style setter. Two points need to be made about Adam as a designer of furniture. First he favored the light-yellow satinwood which, in the latter part of the century, was beginning to come into England from both the East and the West Indies, as well as rosewood, a dark glossy material from Brazil. The second is that, to maintain harmony with his chaste and classical interiors, he abandoned completely the rococo flowing curves and returned to the tectonic form of straight vertical and horizontal lines. This angularity was relieved by curves on the horizontal plane, e.g., oval tabletops, bowed chest fronts, etc., and by inlaid or carved decorative features of a classical provenance—ram's heads, festoons of husks, Grecian amphora, acanthus leaves, medallions, etc. All his pieces have an elegant grace and lightness of touch hard to match. In addition to the three houses mentioned, the following contain good examples of Adam's work: **Corsham Court** *(572)*, Wiltshire; **Kedleston Hall** *(633)*, Derbyshire; **Osterley Park** *(533)*,

London; **Saltram House** *(588)*, Devon; and **Syon House** *(533)*, London.

Adam can be considered the forerunner and mentor of George Hepplewhite, who did a thriving business at his shop in Cripplegate, London, and whose three hundred illustrations of furniture were included in a book entitled *Cabinet Maker and Upholsterer's Guide* published in 1788 two years after his death. Hepplewhite is known chiefly for his heart- and shield-back chairs; chair backs in the shape of the Prince of Wales emblem, the three feathers; S-shaped chair arms; and chair- and table-legs of slender square sections tapering slightly to plinth feet. His products are widely distributed throughout Britain, though more commonly in the homes of the lesser gentry than in the great country palaces of the very rich. Jane Austen, for example, cherished her clergyman father's Hepplewhite bureau-bookcase and chairs, now still to be seen at **Chawton Cottage** *(557)*, Hampshire. There is a good collection of Hepplewhite pieces at **Cannon Hall** *(678)* near Barnsley, West Yorkshire, where the Country House Museum has a fine display of period furniture including as well the works of Chippendale and Thomas Sheraton.

Sheraton's popularity as a furniture designer straddles the eighteenth and nineteenth centuries and began with his publication of *The Cabinet Maker and Upholsterer's Drawing Book* between 1791 and 1794. His style was more severe than either Adam's or Hepplewhite's, though certainly in the same tectonic (as distinct from Chippendale's rococo) tradition. Square tapering legs, square and rectangular chair backs with little adornment are his most distinguishing marks, though he did experiment with curved, elliptical, and even serpentine forms in tables, sofas, and chair seats. There are good examples of Sheraton furniture at **Althorp** *(655)*, Northamptonshire; **Berkeley Castle** *(641)*, Gloucestershire; and **Ragley Hall** *(643)*, Warwickshire. Both Hepplewhite's and Sheraton's designs were, incidentally, very popular in America, where the Revolution did little to rupture Britain's cultural hegemony over her former colonies. Furniture from London was still imported after independence as before, and when not imported, often copied. Much of the best of what can be legitimately called antique in the United States is in the style of either Hepplewhite or Sheraton.

EIGHTEENTH CENTURY PAINTING

It is ironic that in the Age of Aristocracy, the first great English artist (and it could be argued the greatest ever) was the least aristocratic in style and subject matter of any of the painters who preceded him or those that immediately followed. This was William Hogarth, who lived for fifteen years in Chiswick just outside of London in **Hogarth's House** *(531)*, now a museum displaying copies of the artist's paintings, drawings, and other relics. He was married to Sir James Thornhill's daughter, but in no way does his work resemble that of his preceptor and father-in-law. He first appeared to the public as the painter of a scene from the stage performance of John Gay's *Beggar's Opera,* a satire on English society in the age of Walpole with thinly disguised digs at the great prime minister himself. The painting now hangs in **Hever Castle** *(544),* Kent, and was an appropriate beginning for an artist whose greatness lies as much in the social criticism implicit in much of his work as in its undoubted technical excellence. He was in business to make money, of course, and therefore much of his work was portraiture, including his *Mrs. Salter* in the **National Gallery** *(518),* the *Graham Children* in the **Tate Gallery** *(523),* and the *Holland House Group* at **Ickworth** *(601)* in Suffolk. But his best-known paintings are social satires, such as *A Rake's Progress* and the *Election* series in **Soane's Museum** *(518)* in Lincoln's Inn Fields, London, and *Marriage à la Mode* and *O the Roast Beef of Old England* in the **National Gallery** *(518),* London. For his own satisfaction presumably, or perhaps in silent protest against the portraitist's dependence on rich sitters, he executed a charming half-finished painting called *Hogarth's Servants* now hanging also in the **Tate Gallery** *(523),* London. And he was to strike a still more significant blow for artistic independence in sponsoring a bill passed by Parliament protecting the copyright of engraved reproductions—a process frequently used by Hogarth to assure mass circulation of his work.

In a different way Sir Joshua Reynolds too devoted a lifetime to raising the status of the artist in England—giving the lie to the prejudice against native practitioners exemplified in a statement by Lord Northcote: "You surely would not have me hang up a modern English picture in my house, unless it were a portrait?" Born in Devonshire, Reynolds visited Italy in the company of his friend Commodore August Keppel of the Royal Navy whose portrait, now hanging in the **National Maritime Museum** *(536),* Greenwich, received enough attention to attract other sitters. Reynolds then set up business in a studio in Leicester Square. His charges were initially £5 2s. per head but his popularity grew so fast that by 1764 he was asking, and getting, £30 pounds for a head, £70 for a half length, and £150 a full length, and when he died in 1792 his estate came to £80,000. Yet Reynolds was more than a mere fashionable and well-paid portraitist; he was a man with a mission. In 1768 King George III (for all his defects, perhaps the most cultured man ever to occupy the throne) sponsored the founding of the Royal Academy of Arts with Joshua Reynolds as its first president. Its purpose was to provide systematic instruction to art students, to hold annual exhibits of the work of British painters, and to give status to, and set standards for, a profession which had hitherto been noticeably lacking in both. Every year at the prize giving of the Royal Academy School, its president read a discourse, the sum of these coming to constitute a new artistic canon which was spoken of as the Grand Style. Reynolds's own brush was so prolific that it is hard to find a gallery or a stately home in Britain that does *not* boast at least one of his paintings, most commonly single or group portraits. In London, among his best are *Lady Cockburn and her Children* in the **National Portrait Gallery** *(518)*, *Lord Ligonier* at the **Tate** *(523)*, *Mrs. "Perdita" Robinson* in the **Wallace Collection** *(527)*, and, above all, his well-known rendering of Mrs. Siddons in the **Dulwich College Picture Gallery** *(536)*, a splendid small repository of paintings so remote from the center of town that visitors, unfortunately for themselves, are likely to miss it. Scattered throughout the country there are so many fine Reynolds portraits that only a fraction can be mentioned here. Among the most notable are *Georgiana, Countess Spencer and her Daughter* at **Althorp** *(655)*, Northamptonshire; *the Fourth Duchess of Marlborough and her Daughter* at **Blenheim Palace** *(636)*, Oxfordshire; *Georgiana, Duchess of Devonshire and her Daughter* at **Chatsworth** *(662)*, Derbyshire; *Lady Worsley* at **Harewood House** *(681)*, West Yorkshire; the Reynolds Room at **Knole** *(545)*, Kent, which includes portraits of Dr. Johnson, David Garrick, and Oliver Goldsmith, all intimate friends of the painter; portraits of Sir Joseph Banks, after his return from Captain Cook's first circumnavigation of the world, and Omai, the much lionized native Tahitian whom Cook brought back to England after his second expedition, both at **Parham Park** *(554)*, West Sussex; the roomful of portraits at **Saltram House** *(588)*, Devon; and those in the Reynolds room at **Woburn Abbey** *(625)*, Bedfordshire.

If Reynolds brought a new panache (and profit) to portrait painting, his contemporary Richard Wilson virtually founded British landscape painting. He was a Welshman from Penegoes in Powys who fell in love with the Roman Campagna in the 1750s and spent most of the rest of his life painting it. His *Lago di Agnano* in the **Ashmolean Museum** *(628)*, Oxford, and Hadrian's Villa in the **Manchester City Art Gallery** *(693)* are good examples of this preoccupation. No Welshman can completely forget his native land, however, and Wilson did justice to it in his painting of Snowdon in the **Walker Art Gallery** *(695)*, Liverpool, while his rendition of Roland Jones, the Welsh Bard, at **Chirk Castle** *(729)*, Clwyd, is one of the painter's rare essays in portraiture. He also turned a nice profit at portraying the country houses and grounds of the aristocracy, examples being his views of Chatsworth House and Croome Court, now in the **Birmingham Museum and Art Gallery** *(664)*, of Wilton House at **Wilton House** *(575)*, Wiltshire, of Houghton House at **Woburn Abbey** *(625)*, and at **Bamburgh Castle** *(704)*, Northumberland, a view of the castle ruins before restoration.

With a foot in both camps, Thomas Gainsborough was clearly superior to Wilson in landscape painting and a rival to Reynolds in the quality of his portraits, though he never equaled the latter in public esteem and proved himself something of a maverick by withdrawing from the Royal Academy. He hailed from Sudbury in Suffolk; his landscapes mostly dealt with simple rural scenes set in his home county; and today he is honored at Ipswich, the county town, by a small but excellent collection of his works at **Christchurch Mansion** *(602)*. His rendering, in

the predominantly red-brown tone which is his signature, of woodlands, streams, clouds, and English countrymen at their daily chores is
a far cry from Reynolds's Grand Style and clearly anticipates the still
greater work of John Constable in the same genre. Good examples are
The Gainsborough Forest in the **National Gallery** *(518)*; *Carthorses
Drinking at a Ford* in the **Tate Gallery** *(523)*; *Going to Market* at **Kenwood** *(530)*, London; and other landscapes and woodland scenes at **Belvoir Castle** *(650)*, Leicestershire; **Burton Agnes Hall** *(677)*, Humberside; and **Woburn Abbey** *(625)*, Bedfordshire. His portraits are remarkable for the fresh pink-and-white complexions of his female sitters and
above all for his superb handling of textiles, especially silk. Though examples abound, the following are representative: *Mr. and Mrs. Andrews* and *The Morning Walk* in the **National Gallery** *(518)*; *George III*
and *Queen Charlotte* at **Windsor Castle** *(565)*; *Mary, Countess Howe* at
Kenwood *(530)*, London; William Poyntz at **Althorp** *(655)*, Northamptonshire; and *Mrs. John Douglas* at **Waddesdon Manor** *(622)*, Buckinghamshire.

Other fashionable portraitists of the mid to late eighteenth century—
Alan Ramsey, George Romney, and John Hoppner—though competent, prolific, and popular—are today judged less than first-rate and
their work is so much in the Reynolds style that not much more than
that need be said about it. Anyone interested will have no trouble discovering their portraits on the walls of countless galleries and stately
homes. No such ubiquity can be ascribed to the works of the two exiled
Americans, Benjamin West and Thomas Singleton Copley, who are
chiefly responsible for the introduction of a new fashion among English
artists called history painting, though their best works in this genre
were in their own time contemporary. West's most famous painting of
course is his heroic representation of the death of General James Wolfe
on the Plains of Abraham during the Seven Years War, but the original
hangs in the National Gallery of Canada in Ottawa. Perhaps his second
best known work is his apotheosis of Nelson in the **National Maritime
Museum** *(536)* in Greenwich. Copley's major contribution to historical
painting is in the **Tate Gallery** *(523)*. *The Death of Major Pierson* is a
busy portrayal of an insignificant event in the annals of British military
history—a French raid on Jersey in the last year of the War of the
American Revolution.

Portraits of horses and dogs, with their masters usually astride or in the
background, are, if not great art, among the most typically English of all
artistic endeavors. Here the great names of the eighteenth century are
John Wootton and George Stubbs. Wootton's famous painting of Sir Robert Walpole (with horses and dogs) at **Houghton Hall** *(606)*, Norfolk, has
already been mentioned. In most of his oeuvre, less attention is paid to
the man and more to the animals. Fine hunting and racing scenes, as well
as individual portraits of favorite horses, can be seen at **Althorp** *(655)*,
Northamptonshire; **Antony House** *(588)*, Cornwall; **Castle Howard** *(684)*,

North Yorkshire; **Chirk Castle** *(729)*, Clwyd; **Goodwood House** *(552)*, West Sussex; **Parham Park** *(544)*, West Sussex; **Raby Castle** *(698)*, County Durham; **Ragley Hall** *(643)*, Warwickshire; and **Stourhead** *(574)*, Wiltshire. Stubbs, though a far better painter, is less in evidence. He was a lecturer in anatomy at York Hospital before becoming a painter, and his realistic renditions of a wide range of wild animals, as well as horses, show it. Indeed, in this somewhat specialized field, he has few peers and no superiors. In London the **National Gallery** *(518)* and the **Tate** *(523)* between them show Stubbs in his contrasting moods. At the former is a fine horsey painting of a well-turned-out couple in a horse-drawn phaeton; in the latter snarling and voracious lions, as well as mares and foals, and a gray hack with dog and groom. Other good examples of his work are *Mares and Foals by the River at Euston* in **Euston Hall** *(609)*, Suffolk; *The Duke of Richmond's Racehorses at Exercise* at **Goodwood House** *(698)*, West Sussex; a fine portrait of two horses at **Weston Park** *(666)*, Salop; and at **Parham Park** *(554)*, West Sussex, a fascinating study of a kangaroo and dingo dog painted from skins brought back in Captain Cook's flagship *Endeavour* from his first voyage to Australia. Unlike Wootton and Stubbs, Joseph Wright, commonly known as Wright of Derby, eschewed the great outdoors for indoor scenes of men at work, especially by hearthfire and candlelight. His total oeuvre is small. His best known painting is the *Experiment with the Air Pump* hanging in the **Tate Gallery** *(523)*, London, but the largest single collection of his work is in the **Derby Museum and Art Gallery** *(663)* in the artist's own home town.

LEARNING AND LITERATURE IN THE EIGHTEENTH CENTURY

The conventional historical judgment on the two English universities at Oxford and Cambridge in the eighteenth century is that by the end of it they had sunk to an all-time low as seats of learning. Hard-drinking, diehard Tory dons rubbed shoulders with spoiled and riotous sons of the rich while sycophantic and unscholarly would-be clergymen vied for future comfortable livings in a spiritual vacuum from which all religious zeal had been eliminated. This, at least, is the picture later drawn by Victorian reformers in their efforts to shake the universities out of their complacent lethargy. No doubt the judgment is too harsh. True, examinations were a farce, lectures ill attended or not delivered at all, curricula obsolete, and residency by undergraduates often so brief and fleeting as to negate any real learning. Yet it was during these years that Blackstone delivered his famous lectures on the common law at All Souls, that John Wesley formed the Holy Club at Oxford out of which sprang the Methodist movement, and that the young Samuel Johnson was absorbing the classics at Pembroke, to the eventual great benefit of English letters. It was also a period of architectural growth. The currents of Palladianism and later neoclassical styles left their distinctive marks on Oxford and Cambridge as elsewhere, to the considerable beautification of both cities.

First among the contributors was the maverick James Gibbs—Roman Catholic and Jacobite—as conservative in his architectural preferences as in his politics. Having himself studied in Rome, he remained unimpressed by the Palladian enthusiasm of Lord Burlington, et al., and developed a classical style of his own that lies somewhere between baroque and Italian mannerist. Between 1722 and 1730 he completed the **Senate House** *(615)* in Cambridge, a rather plain rectangular building faced with Corinthian pilasters, its central bays surmounted by a pediment and the roof balustraded and topped with decorative urns. For **King's College** *(613)* next door he designed the Fellows' Building in a somewhat more baroque manner, with a central archway flanked by a Doric porch, above which is a semicircular window surmounted by a pediment. Finally, in Oxford, where he built the **Radcliffe Camera** *(633)*, he gave full vent to his mannerist impulses in a decidedly Italianate building. It has a rusticated octagonal ground floor pierced by pedimented arches, surmounted by a drum faced with a circle of coupled Corinthian columns, on top of which rests a dome and cupola surrounded by stone urns.

Also at Oxford, James Wyatt built a soberly classical library for **Oriel College** *(632)* and, with Henry Keene, the lovely neo-Grecian **Radcliffe Observatory** *(630)* with its central octagonal tower modeled on the Tower of the Winds in Athens—the earliest example in Oxford of the Greek Revival. In Cambridge, in the first decade of the nineteenth century, William Wilkins designed for the newly chartered **Downing College** *(611)* what Summerson has called "for England, the first monument of the Greek Revival proper." Here the Ionic order prevails, and except for its sprawl and absence of marble, Downing College would not look out of place on the Acropolis. Two decades later Wilkins built for the new **University College** *(517)* on Gower Street, London, the first of its buildings, now the central block, with a Corinthian portico and dome—also neo-Grecian.

Neither an Oxonian nor a Cantabrigian was England's first great poet after Dryden's death in 1700. This was Alexander Pope. Born a Roman Catholic, he was naturally barred from either university, and his poor health might have prevented his attendance in any case. A hunchbacked dwarf (four-and-a-half feet tall) neither his appearance nor his chronic ailments impeded his rise to fame after the publication in 1711 of his *Essay on Criticism,* a long poem of rhymed couplets which has ever since served as a mine of clichés almost as rich as the works of Shakespeare ("A little learning is a dangerous thing"; "To err is human, to forgive divine"; "For fools rush in where angels fear to tread"; etc.). There followed *The Rape of the Lock,* rhymed translations of Homer's *Iliad* and *Odyssey, The Dunciad, The Essay on Man,* and the *Moral Essays.* By the time of his death in 1744 Pope was not only a much esteemed literary giant but, for a writer, rich. Two present sites in England have Pope associations. One is **Mapledurham** *(564)* in Oxfordshire, an attractive manor house, originally Elizabethan, where Pope often visited the Misses Teresa and Martha Blount, and where can still be seen his portrait by Kneller and two urns by William Kent from Pope's own villa at Twickenham, since disappeared. The other is **Stanton Harcourt** *(637)* also in Oxfordshire, a fourteenth-century manor, now partly ruined, where the poet completed the fifth volume of his version of the *Iliad*.

If the reign of George I can be defined in literary terms as the Age of Pope, the middle Georgian years deserve the title, the Age of Johnson. Samuel Johnson, son of a poor Lichfield bookseller and partly educated at Pembroke College, Oxford, owed his rise to stardom in the firmament of English letters by his publication in 1755 of *The Dictionary of the English Language*. This monumental work established standards of spelling and usage still followed today and at the same time provided its author ample opportunity to air his prejudices; e.g., "Patriotism: the last refuge of a scoundrel"; "Oats: a grain which in England is generally given to horses, but in Scotland supports the people." Though he published other works, it was the *Dictionary* that rightly established Johnson's reputation, just as it was his sardonic wit and brilliant conversation that made him leader of London's intelligentsia, or at least those who were members of the Literary Club which included, besides Johnson, the painter Sir Joshua Reynolds, the poet Oliver Goldsmith, the member of Parliament and political philosopher Edmund Burke, the actor David Garrick, the historian Edward Gibbon, the economist Adam Smith, and Johnson's own biographer, James Boswell. The **Samuel Johnson Birthplace** *(667)* in Market Street, Lichfield, Staffordshire, is now maintained as a museum housing sundry Johnson relics, and **Dr. Johnson's House** *(514)* in Gough Square, London, where the *Dictionary* was compiled, is a splendid repository of Johnsoniana and, in its own right, a charming eighteenth-century town house, beautifully maintained and managed for the edification of the interested traveller.

Johnson's death in 1784 marked the end of an era, his urbane, caustic, incisive pessimism soon to be inundated in the great wave of antirational, antiestablishment primitivism known as the Romantic movement. An early harbinger was Thomas Gray, whose grave in the yard of **Stoke Poges Church** *(623)* in Buckinghamshire, is a reminder of his famous *Elegy*, an exercise in sentimentality that would soon find many echoes in the works of a younger generation of prolific poets of the Romantic school. Nature was their God, human progress their goal, and the overthrow of tradition their purpose. "Bliss was it then to be alive/ But to be young was very heaven!" wrote William Wordsworth of the early days of the French Revolution when hopes ran high for a quantum leap in the fortunes of mankind out of the rubble of the fallen Bastille. Born in 1770 at Cockermouth in Cumbria in a house now maintained by the National Trust as the **Wordsworth House** *(710)*, educated at St. John's College,

Cambridge, Wordsworth's publication in 1798 (jointly with his friend Samuel Taylor Coleridge) of the *Lyrical Ballads* inaugurated the Romantic movement in English literature. Many years and many poems later, Wordsworth would lose his early faith in revolution and the perfectibility of man, but never his mystical belief in Nature as the primary source of Truth and Wisdom. Thus he wrote in "The Tables Turned" which appeared in the *Lyrical Ballads:*

> And hark! how blithe the throstle sings!
> He, too, is no mean preacher;
> Come forth into the light of things;
> Let Nature be your teacher . . .
>
> Enough of Science and of Art;
> Close up these barren leaves;
> Come forth, and bring with you a heart
> That watches and receives.

With his sister Dorothy, the poet moved in 1799 to **Dove Cottage** *(711)* near Grasmere on Rydal Water in the Lake District not many miles from his own birthplace. Not yet overrun with tourists, the neighborhood's scenic grandeur and rustic charm—more or less synonomous with the Nature celebrated by the Romantic poets—kept Wordsworth rooted there until his death in 1850. Tiny Dove Cottage, with its attached museum, is an enchanting place to visit, made more so by the courtesy of its present custodians and the exceptionally intelligent and well-informed guides who conduct visitors through the house on brief tours. Wordsworth and his menage (including wife and children as well as Dorothy) moved to more sumptuous quarters nearby in 1813. This was **Rydal Mount** *(711)*, two miles south of Grasmere, with a view of Lake Windermere in the distance. There he lived for thirty-seven years, prosperous and famous, an officeholder under the Crown, and, after 1843, poet laureate. "Just for a token of silver he left us," wrote the young Robert Browning, "Just for a riband to stick in his coat." Wordsworth's friendship with Coleridge had long since cooled. Together they had published *Lyrical Ballads* in which appeared Coleridge's *The Rime of the Ancient Mariner,* written at Nether Stowey, Somerset, in a little house now known as the **Coleridge Cottage** *(582)* preserved by the National Trust. In later years his muse deserted him and except for the unfinished "Kubla Khan" and "Christabel," no more rhymes of note flowed from his truly gifted hand—stilled perhaps by opium, a penchant for German metaphysics, and the withdrawal of Wordsworth's encouragement.

The second generation of distinguished Romantic poets all died young: George, Lord Byron of malaria near Missolonghi while fighting for Greek independence; Percy Bysshe Shelley of drowning in the Tyrrhenian Sea; John Keats of tuberculosis in Rome. Born with a club foot, his father a ne'er-do-well Scottish adventurer, Byron at the age of ten inherited a peerage and the estate that went with it at **Newstead Abbey** *(659)*, Nottinghamshire, now housing a museum to his memory. Most of his adult life he roamed the Continent, acting out the roles he had created for his heroes in such poems as *Childe Harold, The Corsair,* and *Don Juan.* Wild, lawless, romantic, and brave (farouche, in a word), he was in his own mind the consummate Byronic hero—"So young, so fair / Good without effort, great without a foe." When he died, so foul was the scandal surrounding his name that the dean of Westminster Abbey refused admission to his statue, which came at last to rest in Wren's library at **Trinity College** *(616)*, Cambridge, Lord Byron's alma mater.

His friend Shelley received like honors at **University College** *(634)*, Oxford, from which he had been sent down his first year there for publishing a tract on "The Necessity of Atheism." Long after his death the college made amends by building a mausoleum of sorts to house a marble statue of the drowned poet. Though celebrating Nature with unequaled lyricism ("O wild West Wind, thou breath of Autumn's being / Thou, from whose unseen presence the leaves dead / Are driven, like ghosts from an enchanter fleeing, / Yellow, and black, and pale, and hectic red . . ."), Shelley's most powerful poetry was politically inspired. Kings, priests, and other relics of the ancien régime were his targets, his ideal the demigod Prometheus, giver of fire and primal benefactor of Mankind. *Prometheus Unbound* was Shelley's *cri de coeur*, culminating in a noble passage where the great Jove himself is driven from his throne, the hero's shackles broken, and mankind freed at last. Obviously the poet had the French Revolution in mind when he wrote:

> The loathsome mask has fallen, the man remains
> Sceptreless, free, uncircumscribed, but man
> Exempt from awe, worship, degree, the king
> Over himself . . .

Yet for all his political preoccupation, Shelley was capable of the most tender personal sentiments, as in the case of that loveliest of English elegies (possibly excepting Milton's *Lycidas*):

> I weep for Adonais—he is dead:
> O weep for Adonais! though our tears
> Thaw not the frost which binds so dear a head.

Adonais is Keats, dead at the age of thirty-one. Little concerned with politics, his credo was: " 'Beauty is Truth, truth beauty'—that is all / Ye know on earth, and all ye need to know." And though he might address odes "To a Nightingale" and "To Autumn," it was not Nature but a man-made Grecian urn that inspired his finest passages, while a first perusal of Homer in translation moved him to startled wonder, ". . . like stout Cortez when with eagle eyes / He star'd at the Pacific—and all his men / Look'd at each other with a wild surmise— / Silent, upon a peak in Darien." No matter that it was Balboa, not Cortez, who discovered the Pacific or that Keats could not read his Homer in the original. He was not a university man. Born in London over a stable, his only sustained exposure to the Nature so much vaunted by his fellow poets was at Hampstead Heath on the northern outskirts of the city. There, his temporary quarters, now called **Keats House** *(530)*, is maintained as a museum. Scorned for his "Cockney rhymes" by the leading critics of his day, Keats was nonetheless without superior—or perhaps without equal—among the Romantic poets of the late eighteenth and early nineteenth centuries.

RELIGION IN THE EIGHTEENTH CENTURY

After occupying the center of the British stage for almost two centuries, religion moved into the wings after 1688 with a speed that seems astonishing. Possibly the actor overplayed his role and simply lost his audience. In any case, the religious zeal that had driven Archbishop Laud to the scaffold, George Fox to countless prisons, and James II to exile in France, soon all but vanished. True, anti-Catholicism remained strong enough to scotch the Stuarts' chances of regaining a throne rightly theirs by the law of primogeniture. But even the latent threat of a Jacobite restoration failed to unleash a pogrom against Catholics in Britain, in spite of two pro-Stuart insurrections in Scotland and an invasion of England by the Young Pretender. Indeed, the number of Roman communicants grew slightly throughout the century, but Catholics were wise enough to lay low, especially during and after the Forty-Five. As to the Protestant dissenters, heirs of the great Puritan tradition, but now excluded from public office unless they "occasionally conformed," they were otherwise tolerated. Church and meeting house coexisted in a state of comparative amity nurtured by a growing indifference to theological issues which had, in the previous century, pitted Arminians against Predestinarians and Presbyterians against Independents in conflict that had seemed irreconcilable. By the mid-eighteenth century not many people were left who even understood the controversies, and fewer cared.

This is not to say that church attendance fell off, except in those newly populated areas where neither the Church of England nor the dissenting sects saw fit to provide adequate facilities to match the demographic curve. Otherwise pews appear to have been regularly filled and new churches regularly built, some by architects of note. Chief among these was James Gibbs, a Scottish Catholic Tory who raised in Whiggish London some of the Church of England's most attractive edifices. Gibbs, it will be remembered, was not a Palladian. At **St. Mary-Le-Strand** *(518)* in the Strand, his style is distinctly Roman in the Italian mannerist fashion of the sixteenth century. The two-storied church with a chancel deep enough for a Roman Mass has unfortunately been marred by the insertion of very ugly glass. At **St. Clement Dane** *(519)*, also in the Strand, Gibbs added the splendid steeple built in the Wren manner to match the church which Sir Christopher himself had designed—now much restored after having been gutted by fire in 1941. In 1721–1724 Gibbs built a chapel on the earl of Oxford's estate near Cavendish Square in London, now known as **St. Peter, Vere Street** *(517)*. A brick building with a Tuscan portico and an attractive interior, its altarpiece and stained-glass windows were later done by the pre-Raphaelite Burne-Jones. This chapel appears to have been a trial run for Gibbs's best known creation, **St. Martin-in-the Fields** *(518)* facing Trafalgar Square, perhaps the most prominently displayed church in London. Here the Corinthian order prevails both outside and in. The giant portico dominates the busy square and is strangely undwarfed by the much more massive National Gallery across St. Martin's Lane. Inside, Corinthian columns divide the spacious gallery and support a vaulted nave with exceptionally fine plasterwork. If St. Martin's looks familiar on first acquaintance, it is because it has been so widely copied in Anglican parishes throughout the English-speaking world.

Besides Gibbs, there were other architects, better known for their work on stately homes, who also accepted commissions to erect places of Anglican worship. Henry Flitcroft built **St. Giles-in-the-Fields** *(518)* on Endall Street, London, in 1731–1733, and in Hampstead, **St. John, Church Row** *(531)*, a red-brick building with a castellated steeple. James "Athenian" Stuart helped to design **All Saints, Nuneham Courtenay** *(636)*, a few miles southeast of Oxford, though oddly the style is more Roman than Greek. Undoubtedly the best example of eighteenth century neo-Grecian is **St. Lawrence New Church** *(622)* at Ayot St. Lawrence, west of Welwyn, Hertfordshire. Here the architect was Nicholas Revett who designed the fine Doric portico, which compares favorably with his Ionic west portico at West Wycombe Park. After 1818 so many churches started up in Britain that they defy enumeration. Shocked by the virulent irreligion of the French Revolution and freed at last from wartime expenditures, Parliament in that year passed the Million Act, appropriating a million pounds for the construction of new churches. Within a decade forty had been built, the majority in a neo-Gothic style that was to retain its popularity throughout the nineteenth century.

Church building and attendance notwithstanding, there is little doubt that throughout the eighteenth century both the Church of England and the dissenting clergy were losing their capacity to inspire their congregations with either zeal or devotion. This was the Age of Reason, and the prevailing climate of opinion was rational not mystical. Mathematical science was in the ascendant; its high priest was Isaac Newton, an Englishman. To reconcile established religion with the demonstrable truths of Newtonian physics became a major preoccupation of leading divines and university dons. Archdeacon William Paley defined God as a clockmaker, active only in the fashioning of the universe as a working mechanism, thereafter abjuring miraculous intervention in the functioning of His perfect creation according to the decrees of natural law. Dr. John Tillotson, Archbishop of Canterbury, was the chief proponent within the Church of England of the thesis that the laws of God were good *because* they were reasonable. Among Presbyterians, with their traditional emphasis on intellectualism, faith in miracles, including the Resurrection, became so attenuated that many congregations defected to Unitarianism—a belief not inconsistent with the mechanistic deism of Paley and contemporary French *philosophes.*

Enlightened and complacent, the traditional churches, both Anglican and dissenting, had little tolerance for religious enthusiasm which they equated with unseemly fanaticism. Christian ethics of course were admirable. As Pope put it in the *Essay on Man:*

> For modes of faith let graceless zealots fight,
> His can't be wrong whose life is in the right,
> In Faith and Hope the world will disagree
> But all mankind's concern is Charity.

Yet Charity could produce enthusiasts as well, even in the Church of England. Among them was the so-called Clapham Sect, a group of influential laymen which included William Wilberforce, a member of Parliament from Hull, who dedicated himself to the abolition of the trade in black slaves within the British Empire and finally succeeded in pushing a bill to that effect through Parliament in 1808. The **Wilberforce House** *(678)*, on High Street, Hull, is maintained as a memorial to his service to the cause of justice and as a museum housing slave manacles and other detritus of that unsavory business.

Yet magnanimity of the sort that animated the antislavery movement was a luxury enjoyed mostly by the rich. Charity might satisfy the spiritual needs of an enlightened and comfortable minority but could scarcely fill the requirements of the poor who had nothing to give. Often undernourished, ill-clothed, and poorly housed, they suffered as well emotional starvation that neither the decorous and complacent Church of England nor the inbred and increasingly prosperous dissenting sects were prepared to appease. A hundred years earlier Puritan preachers had captured the imaginations of a vast multitude of high and low degree with stirring (and lengthy) sermons on the immensity of God's wrath and mercy. Or a man might achieve a sense of mystical union with the Almighty in the silence of a Quaker meeting. But neither the eighteenth century fox-hunting parson reading a canned homily from the pulpit of the parish church, nor the Presbyterian divine delivering a reasoned discourse in the meeting house was likely to arouse the passions of his listeners; and the Quakers by this time had lost much of George Fox's proselytizing zeal and were busy with good works and making money.

Also, as already mentioned, the established denominations, both Anglican and dissenting, were failing to keep abreast of the movement of
population from the countryside to newly flourishing centers of
commerce and industry, leaving large numbers of people without any
convenient church or meeting house to attend even if they had wanted
to. Into the spiritual desert thus created stepped John and Charles Wesley and their fellow revivalists in England and Wales.

The Wesley brothers were born at Epworth, near Scunthorpe in
Humberside, on the site of the now restored **Old Rectory** *(678)* where
they lived as children after a fire had destroyed their birthplace. Their
father was the Tory rector of the **Epworth Parish Church** *(678)*, their
mother, Susanna, the devout daughter of a well-known dissenting
preacher who had lost his living in the Church of England after the
restoration of Charles II. Church and parsonage together now constitute
a sort of unofficial Mecca for Methodists the world over. Both John and
Charles were sent to study at Oxford, where John later became a fellow
at **Lincoln College** *(630)*; there his rooms are still to be seen, as well as
his portrait in the college hall and his pulpit in the chapel. The high Tory
atmosphere of Oxford and the roistering of its worldly undergraduates
drove the Wesleys and other earnest students to founding a Holy Club
of pious young men, the regularity of whose lives and study habits gave
birth to the term *methodist* which later became attached to the religious
movement the Wesleys sponsored. After ordination in the Church of
England, the brothers visited General Oglethorpe's new colony in
Georgia and on returning fell in with a group of German Moravians
whose spirituality impressed them favorably. It was at Moravian gatherings in London where they each experienced a religious conversion
during which, as John later wrote, "I felt I did trust in Christ, Christ alone
for salvation; and so an assurance was given me that He had taken away
my sins, even *mine*, and saved *me* from the law of sin and death." Thus
reborn, he set out to share his good fortune with the multitudes of men
and women still living in darkness, and before his ministry ended with
his death in 1791, John Wesley had travelled 250,000 miles on horseback,
preached forty thousand sermons, and published numerous religious
tracts. He never left the Church of England and it was not until after his
death that the Methodist movement became a separate denomination,
largely because the Anglican hierarchy refused to ordain evangelizing
ministers of the new persuasion for Ireland and America. Though his
sermons were highly charged emotionally, John Wesley was a scholarly man who habitually read the New Testament in Greek before
expounding its lessons from the pulpit. But though he wrote much, it
was his brother Charles's hymns, collected and published in 1780,
that constitute the finest literary heritage of Methodism. Set to tune-
ful music, these simple rhymes capture the spirit of the Wes-
leyan message and go a long way to explaining its persuasive power.
Methodist chapels might be plain and bleak, but at Sabbath services

they rang with joyful song. Few troubled spirits could resist the infectious optimism of such well-known Wesley hymns as

> Love divine, all love excelling,
> Joy of heaven to earth come down,
> Fix in us thy humble dwelling,
> All thy faithful mercies crown.
> Jesus thou art all compassion,
> Pure unbounded love thou art,
> Visit us with thy salvation,
> Enter every trembling heart.

Early in his travels John Wesley joined forces with a revivalist preacher even more persuasive than he. This was George Whitfield, a Gloucesterman with such a sonorous voice that, without shouting, he could be heard at the outer fringes of a great mass meeting in Philadelphia, computed by Benjamin Franklin to number thirty thousand. It was Whitfield who first persuaded Wesley to preach in the open—in fields, at market crosses, or in natural amphitheaters, wherever a crowd could gather. Later the two split over the issue of predestination (Whitfield) versus Arminian free will (Wesley), but the question had by now become so irrelevant to most of their followers that the Methodist movement remained unaffected. In Wales, meanwhile, another handful of preachers had independently inaugurated a revival movement of a like nature and impact. Its principal leaders were Daniel Rowland, a young curate from Llangeitho, Dyfed, and Howell Harris whose conversion experience took place at **Talgarth Parish Church** *(722)* in Powys where a memorial plaque can still be seen, inscribed in words typical of the Methodist version of the "good news" of salvation:

> . . . He was convinced of Sin, Had his Pardon Sealed, And felt the Power of Christ's Precious Blood At the Holy Communion. Having Tasted Grace, He resolved to declare to others What God had done for his Soul. He was the first Itinerant Preacher of Redemption In this Period of Revival in England and Wales. . . .

Not until the nineteenth century did the Methodists begin a widespread program of church building. Until then they built a few chapels, but mostly met in the open in large gatherings or assembled in small bands, societies, or classes in whatever buildings they could find. In Bristol, on Broad Meade, John Wesley himself erected a meeting place, the **New Room** *(580)* now restored and open to view. On City Road in London he also built the now much-restored **Wesley's Chapel** *(511)*. Next to it stands **Wesley's House** *(511)* where he lived and died—today a well-preserved memorial to his life and work.

The appeal of Wesley and his fellow revivalists was primitive, emotional, nonintellectual, and highly satisfying, especially to the masses of common laborers and their wives now beginning to congregate in the burgeoning cities and among the newly opened minefields that were the centers of Britain's developing industrial revolution. George Whitfield's description of the impact of his and Wesley's preaching tells the story:

> Having no righteousness of their own to renounce, they were glad to hear of a Jesus who was a friend to publicans, and came not to call the righteous, but sinners to repentance. The first discovery of their being affected was to see the white gutters made by their tears, which plentifully ran down their black cheeks, as they came out of their coal pits.

Marxist historians are quick to cite the Methodist movement as the supreme example of religion as the opiate of the people, claiming that it served as a prophylactic against revolution among Britain's new industrial proletariat and noting that Wesley himself preached that the existing social hierarchy was divinely ordained and that hard labor was the just portion of the poor. In the long run, however, Methodism proved to be a socially liberating force. It helped significantly to spread literacy among the displaced laboring class; encouraged sobriety as a prime requisite to self-respect; and, in its system of classes, set up a mechanism of group action that was subsequently adopted by British political reform clubs and trades unions. No doubt the mine and factory owners of the eighteenth century had reason to be grateful for the sober and punctual Methodists who were swelling the ranks of their labor force, but their successors had little cause to thank John Wesley for spawning, however unwittingly, a literate, proud, well-organized, and articulate leadership among Britain's deprived classes.

THE INDUSTRIAL REVOLUTION

Economic historians argue incessantly about the exact date when Britain began to experience what Peter Mathias has called the "rapid, cumulative, structural change" in economic life known as the Industrial Revolution. Some time around the middle of the century, the consensus seems to be, Britain reached the point of "take-off into self-sustained growth" based on radical changes in methods of production; this process accelerated rapidly after the end of the war of the American Revolution; and by the turn of the century the manufacture of goods for sale was fast becoming the major component of the country's national wealth. Statistics are tiresome (and not especially reliable anyway), so a few will suffice to tell the story. In 1760 there were less than 20 blast furnaces in England and Wales; by 1805, there were 177; by 1830, 372. Pig iron output increased from about 50,000 tons in 1750 to 250,000 in 1800, to 650,000 by 1830. Imports of raw cotton for manufacture into cloth went from 8 million tons in 1780 to 37.5 million in 1800, to 250 million in 1830. The number of cotton spindles used in the manufacture of yarn increased from less than 2 million in 1780 to about 15 million in 1830. And so on. Clearly by the final date of the period under consideration, Britain had taken off toward becoming the first fully developed modern industrial state.

Certain antecedent (and concomitant) conditions were necessary for this to have happened. Among them were (1) an increase of population large enough to provide a surplus of labor for employment in manufacturing; (2) an increase in the domestic production of foodstuffs sufficient to supply a labor force no longer able to feed itself; (3) comparatively easy access to overseas markets to absorb "surplus" production; (4) a prior accumulation of capital for investment in industry and the existence of a banking system to facilitate the transfer of capital to industrial development; (5) a system of internal transportation capable of moving raw materials from their point of origin to their place of manufacture, and of finished goods thence to their markets; (6) an adequate supply of basic raw materials for fabrication and of sources of energy beyond human and animal power; and (7) a cultural environment of a sort to encourage and reward the development of the technological and managerial skills necessary to put all this together. Britain was fortunate (except perhaps in the eyes of today's doctrinaire environmentalists) to have enjoyed in the late eighteenth century a concurrence of all these factors.

A sharp reduction in the death rate after 1740 and a rise in the birthrate after 1750 brought about a population growth of from seven to ten percent by the end of the century. Agricultural production rose commensurately with the expansion of the amount of land under cultivation as a result of enclosures, the introduction of new soil-conserving crops, and improved techniques in farming. England's prosperous world trade produced excess profits for investment, while the founding of the Bank of England in 1694 and the subsequent establishment of a network of provincial banks rendered the transfer of capital from commerce to industry relatively easy. Colonies provided both a guaranteed market and a source of supply of vital raw materials, while British sea power kept the sea lanes open to commerce even in times of war. All these factors are important, but since we are concerned here only with the visible remains of Britain's past, attention will be focused on the last three listed above: internal transportation; raw material and energy resources; and technological and managerial skills; i.e., new inventions and their adaptation to industrial revolution.

At the beginning of the eighteenth century, English roads had the reputation of being the worst in Europe, except for those in Wales and Scotland, which were even more deplorable. Since 1555 responsibility for the upkeep of roads and highways had devolved on the authorities of the more than ten thousand individual parishes—a system guaranteed to produce chaos. After 1700, turnpike trusts began to take over from parish officials the task of road repair and maintenance. These were groups of justices of the peace or other local citizens who were authorized by acts of Parliament to charge tolls on the stretches of road under their jurisdiction in return for a guarantee of repair and upkeep. Though never universal, this new system was vastly superior to the old, especially when many of the trusts proved amenable to the introduction of new road-building techniques perfected chiefly by three men: "Blind Jack" Metcalf, John Loudon Macadam, and Thomas Telford; the first a Yorkshireman, the other two Scots. As a result of these improvements, travel time was perhaps cut in half for stagecoaches. Heavy goods, however, still moved slowly—at about five miles an hour for example on the London-Birmingham highway and at even lower speed in the rough country of the north and west.

Not much is left of these turnpikes themselves, but some of the bridges over which they crossed do survive. Thomas Telford was the great bridge builder. His first major work was **Montford Bridge** *(672)* across the Severn west of Shrewsbury, constructed of stone in 1792. After that he turned to iron. In 1815, at Betws-y-Coed, Gwynedd, he built the graceful arch of **Waterloo Bridge** *(737)* with the legend, *This arch was constructed in the same year the Battle of Waterloo was fought,* running across its full length. **Galton Bridge** *(665)* in Smethwick on the western outskirts of Birmingham, **Mythe Bridge** *(641)* across the Severn north of Tewksbury, Gloucestershire, and **Holt Fleet Bridge** *(649)* across the Severn on the present A 4133 about seven miles north of Worcester, though less spectacular, are worthy products of Telford's engineering skill. His two best-known iron bridges, however, were erected in 1826. First is the tiny **Conwy Suspension Bridge** *(738)* at the foot of the famous castle of the same name in Gwynedd, where Telford's towers are castellated in the medieval manner. To the west, across the water dividing mainland Wales from Anglesey is Telford's masterpiece (not counting his Scottish creations), the **Menai Suspension Bridge** *(736)* just west of Bangor. This is a glorious structure, 579 feet between piers, and rising 100 feet above the high watermark of the straits below—a precaution insisted upon by the Admiralty. No pains were spared to make it safe and permanent; the stones of the towers are doweled together with iron pegs and the supporting chains run back deep into tunnels blasted in the rock.

Notwithstanding the new roads and the replacement of fords and ferries with bridges, commercial traffic in most parts of Britain remained agonizingly slow. In the mid-eighteenth century it took twenty-four hours for stage wagons to cover the forty-five miles from Manchester to Leeds and a full forty hours over a like distance between Sheffield and Manchester. Time was money, and British industrial growth would no doubt have been seriously hampered had it had to depend entirely on turnpikes for internal transportation. A more viable alternative was the canal. The first real canal in England was dug by a Derbyshire millwright, James Brindley, the father of English canals, to connect the duke of Bridgewater's colliery at Worsley with the growing town of Manchester. After it was completed in 1761, the price of coal in Manchester dropped by half, and the canal age was launched.

Within thirty years England and parts of eastern Wales were criss-crossed with a canal system linking all the major rivers with each other and providing reasonably rapid and relatively cheap transportation for heavy goods moving in any direction. Today, most of the major links in the system survive, some still in use commercially, others very popular for pleasure boating. In the latter category are the **Grand Union Canal** *(531)* between the Thames at Brentford and Birmingham; the **Oxford Canal** *(636)* from Oxford to the Coventry Canal at Hawkesbury, Warwickshire, just northeast of Coventry; the **Kennet and Avon Canal** *(578)* from Reading to Bristol (only partially open); the **Staffordshire and Worcester Canal** *(649)* which connects the Severn River at Stourport, Hereford and Worcester, with the Trent and Mersey Canal at Great Haywood, east of Stafford; the **Trent and Mersey Canal** *(675)* running from the River Trent at Derwent Mouth, Derbyshire, through Middlewich, Cheshire, to the Bridgewater Canal at Preston Brook, Cheshire; the **Shropshire Union Canal** *(675)* from the Staffordshire and Worcester-shire Canal at Authersley, through Nantwich, Cheshire, to the Manchester Ship Canal at Ellesmere Port, Cheshire; the **Llangollen Canal** *(731)*, a branch of the Shropshire Union going west from Hurleston, Salop, through Llangollen, Clywd, to Llantysilio; the **Leeds and Liverpool Canal** *(680)* connecting those two cities; and the **Lancaster Canal** *(627)* which runs forty-six miles north from Preston through Lancaster and beyond. Certainly the best way for the traveller to acquaint himself with Britain's canals is to travel on them by boat. Except in foul weather this is easily one of the pleasantest ways of all to see Britain, or at least a small part of it. Arrangements are not hard to make and information can be obtained by writing either the British Waterways Board, Chester Road, Nantwich, Cheshire, or Boat Enquiries Ltd., 7 Walton Well Road, Oxford, Oxfordshire. Not much skill is required to navigate through a canal and working the locks is fun. Strangers to Britain should be warned, however, that most of the western Midlands canals (which include the majority of those mentioned above) pass through some very uncharming industrial areas. To serve industry, after all, is why they were dug in the first place.

A number of museums feature eighteenth–nineteenth century canal boats and other paraphernalia associated with this once thriving commerce. At Llangollen, Dyfed, there is a small **Canal Museum** *(731)* on the Wharf, featuring material connected with the history of the Shropshire Union Canal. The **Canal Boat Museum** *(675)* at Ellesmere Port, Cheshire, the northern terminus of the Shropshire Union Canal, has the largest collection of inland-waterway craft in Europe. The **Stoke Bruerne**

Waterways Museum *(656)*, about eight miles south of Northampton, is housed in a warehouse overlooking the Grand Union Canal and is the best of its kind in Britain. At **Stourport** *(649)*, Hereford and Worcester, the whole town is in a sense a museum. Here, where the Staffordshire and Worcester Canal joins the Severn River, Brindley built a warehouse to be joined by merchants' homes and workmen's cottages when this now quiet pleasure-boat center was a busy entrepot.

The law of gravity being what it is, canals cannot run uphill. Normally they follow the course of river valleys, but where hills or rivers must be crossed, tunnels or aqueducts are necessary. Of the latter, there are a number of interesting survivors from the great canal age. Two by John Rennie, Telford's chief rival as an engineer, are worth noting. They are the **Dundas Aqueduct** *(579)*, a single arch span carrying the Kennet and Avon Canal across the River Avon southeast of Bath, and the **Lune Aqueduct** *(697)* by which the Lancaster Canal crosses the River Lune about two miles north of Lancaster. Here, as in other feats of civil engineering, however, the palm must go again to Telford. His **Chirk Aqueduct** *(729)* in Clwyd about a mile east of Chirk Castle, carrying the Llangollen Canal across the River Ceiriog, is a handsome structure of ten arches; while the more famous and grander **Pont Cysyllte** *(731)* rises to 120 feet, its nineteen arches supporting a cast-iron trough bearing the same canal across the River Dee just east of Llangollen, Clwyd.

Roads and bridges, canals and aqueducts are significant, however, only insofar as they served the major actor in the industrial revolution which of course was industry itself. Here cotton textiles take precedence as the prime mover of change. This industry was in the words of Walter Rostow, "the original sector in the first take-off" of Britain toward industrialization. The manufacture of cotton cloth (or any other cloth made from natural fibers) involves two processes: first, spinning; second, weaving. Spinning twists the fibers around each other and locks them together in a yarn suitable for weaving. Weaving is the process by which strands of yarn on a horizontal plane (the woof) are threaded through alternate vertical strands (the warp) so as to produce an interlaced fabric or cloth. For at least five hundred years in Britain, spinning (mostly woolen fibers) had been carried out on spinning wheels which produced a strong, tight yarn wound around a bobbin or spindle. For about the same amount of time weaving was accomplished by hand looms—mechanical devices for shifting alternate strands of warp back and forth so that the woof could be shuttled between them. Spinning wheels and hand looms were common household fixtures, and textile manufacturing was a cottage industry with men mostly doing the weaving, their wives the spinning, and their children preparing the raw fibers by carding and combing. The two processes—spinning and weaving—were normally in equilibrium until the eighteenth century when a series of novel inventions produced radical imbalances between them and eventually drove spinners and weavers alike out of their homes and into the factories where the new textile machinery came to be housed. These events constitute the real beginning of the Industrial Revolution.

The first invention was John Kay's flying shuttle, a simple device, attachable to a hand loom, by which the process of shuttling the woof through the warp could be speeded up. The date of Kay's discovery was 1733 and within a decade it was being widely used. Numerous hand looms with and without flying shuttles may be seen at the **Bankfield Museum and Art Gallery** *(680)*, Halifax, West Yorkshire, and the **Lewis Museum of Textile Machinery** *(696)*, Blackburn, Lancashire. Soon weaving outran spinning. The imbalance was overcorrected, however, when in 1765 James Hargreaves, a Lancashire weaver, invented the spinning jenny, a hand-driven machine for spinning cotton on multiple spindles, first eight and later sixteen. A reproduction of Hargreaves's jenny can be seen at the **Higher Mill Museum** *(696)*, Helmshore, Lancashire, southeast of Accrington. Now, the weaver could not keep up with the spinner, though the jenny produced a thread too weak for the weaver's woof, so the imbalance was manageable. Then in 1769 Richard Arkwright, a Derbyshire textile worker of both mechanical and business acumen, invented a roller-spinning device that came to be called a water-frame because he installed it in a mill in Cromford, Derbyshire, which was driven by water power.

The water-frame was the most significant invention of them all because, for the first time in the textile industry, spinning was taken out of the cottage. Arkwright, like others after him, first found shelter for his machinery in a mill which, by definition, had originally been constructed to grind grain. The term *mill*, therefore, came to be applied to almost any building where workers were brought to their machinery rather than vice versa. This then was the beginning of the factory system. The **Old Mill** *(664)* at Cromford near Matlock still stands. A water-frame taken from it and dated about 1775 can be seen at the **North Western Museum of Science and Industry** *(694)*, Manchester. Another is located in the **Science Museum** *(526)*, South Kensington, London. Good collections of textile machinery are to be found in the **Tonge Moor Textile Museum** *(693)*, Bolton, Greater Manchester; and at the **Bradford Industrial Museum** *(680)*, Broadford, West Yorkshire (mostly for worsteds). Good examples of cotton factories with surviving eighteenth century components are **North Mill** *(661)*, Belper, Derbyshire, founded in 1776 by Arkwright and his partner William Strutt; and the **Masson Mills** *(664)* at Matlock Bath, Derbyshire, also originally owned by Arkwright. He was, incidentally, one of the few inventors to get rich from his ingenuity, though it is safe to assume that it was his managerial skill, not his technical genius, that made the difference. He died *Sir* Richard Arkwright.

Two other inventions need mention to round out the picture. In 1779 came Samuel Crompton's spinning mule which, in effect, combined features of the jenny and the water-frame to spin strong yarn for both warp and woof on spindles numbering 30 at first, then 130, and finally 1,000. Models can be seen in most of the textile machinery museums mentioned above. In 1784 came a breakthrough that at last was to right the imbalance between spinning and weaving. This was the invention by Edmund Cartwright, a Leicestershire parson, of a power loom which took weaving out of the cottage and into the factory.

The impact of the gradual destruction of cottage textile industry was staggering. Factory discipline meant loss of independence for the workers; employers discovered that women and children were often more adept than men at running power-driven machines—and could be paid less; families were uprooted as factory owners pursued cheap power and workers had to follow; villages where mills were opened became towns, and towns, cities, Manchester the largest.

But the process was not as rapid as the term *revolution* might imply. Weaving remained predominantly a cottage industry until well into the nineteenth century, and as long as mills were powered by running water, rural sites might be more advantageous to their owners than urban. The restored cotton mill (spinning *and* weaving) at **Styal Country Park** *(676)* just north of Wilmslow, Cheshire, is a case in point. Founded in 1784 by Samuel Greg, this was a planned company village, with nearby workers' houses, a dormitory for pauper apprentices, and a Methodist chapel converted from a barn. Newly opened as a museum, with live demonstrations of spinning and weaving, this place offers the intelligent traveller a splendid introduction to the history of the early Industrial Revolution. Also in regular operation is the water-powered Estair Moel Mill reerected at the **Welsh Folk Museum** *(718)* in St. Fagan's, west of Cardiff, South Glamorgan.

Both these mills are useful reminders of the importance of water power to the early industrialization of Britain. So much emphasis is normally put on the steam engine as *the* great technological breakthrough of the early machine age, that it is easy to forget the waterwheel. Both before and long after steam was successfully harnessed, running water was a prime source of energy for Britain's factories and mines. The **Finch Foundry** *(588)* at Sticklepath just east of Okehampton, Devon, is typical. Here in 1814 a water-powered corn and fulling mill was converted to make edged farm implements (hoes, sickles, etc.)—a business lasting until 1960. The waterwheel here is of the overshot variety, meaning that the flow of water, when coming from the right (facing the wheel) would strike its peripheral blades, or buckets, at the eleven o'clock position. The turning of the wheel of course imparted a rotary motion to its axle or shaft, at the other end of which would be a circular gear, which, when engaged with other gears, was capable of transmitting an almost infinite variety of motions. Also run by water power is **Cheddleton Mill** *(668)* northeast of Stoke-on-Trent, Staffordshire, for grinding flint into powder to be used in the nearby potteries. Here the two wheels are breastshot, with the water striking at the three o'clock position. At the **Abbeydale Industrial Hamlet** *(680)* outside of Sheffield can be seen another overshot wheel driving the blowing machine, while the tilt hammers are powered by a backshot wheel where the water strikes at the one o'clock position. As late as 1854 the **Laxey Waterwheel** *(742)* was installed on the Isle of Man to pump water from a deep lead and zinc mine. This is the largest ever built in Britain and is also of the backshot type. All these are variations on the simple and more primitive undershot wheel where the water strikes the blades near the six o'clock position.

No doubt the greatest single technological innovation of the early Industrial Revolution was the steam engine. It was first used for draining mines. Here is a good example of how industrial progress was driven by the reciprocal and mutually dependent action of two or more factors. Without the steam engine, it would have been impossible to mine sufficient coal to heat the boilers to make the steam to run the factories that in turn produced more steam engines. Thomas Savery, a Cornish engineer, patented, as early as 1698, a machine "to raise water by the impellant force of fire," but it proved impractical. In 1712 Thomas Newcomen, an ironmonger of Dartmouth, Devon, at last produced an engine that actually worked and was in fact put to use pumping water out of the Coneygree Coal Works at Tipton, near Dudley Castle, West Midlands. The **Newcomen Memorial Engine** *(587)* reerected in the Royal Avenue Gardens in Dartmouth dates from 1720 and was employed to pump water into the Hawkesbury Canal near Coventry from 1821 until 1913. It is the oldest steam engine in the world. This is called a beam engine, and it works like a child's seesaw or teeter-totter. From one end of the beam a vertical rod connects to a pump inside a shaft from which water is drawn up from below. At the other end, another rod is attached to a flat circular piston which moves up and down inside a cylinder, thus imparting the motion necessary to raise and lower the pump. The upward movement of the piston is caused by steam, heated in a boiler below, being admitted into the bottom of the cylinder; the piston's downward movement comes about after the steam has been condensed by the injection of a jet of cold water which creates a partial vacuum and allows the normal atmospheric pressure on the top of the piston to drive it down. After Newcomen, of course, many refinements were introduced, but, essentially, all beam engines operate on the same principle. They are to be seen today in many parts of Britain, notably in the **Science Museum** *(526)*, South Kensington, London; in the **Leicestershire Museum of Technology** *(658)* at the Abbey Pumping Station in Leicester; and in Cornwall where several engines are preserved by the Cornish Engines Preservation Society and are now under the care of the National Trust. These last are representative of the so-called Cornish pump—a very efficient beam engine developed by Richard Trevithick for use in the tin and copper mines of his native county where they continued in use as late as the 1930s. On view are the Harvey water-pumping engine at **East Pool Mine**

(591) in Pool just east of Camborne; the rotative beam engine at **Agar Mine** *(591)* just across the road; and the engines on display at **Holman's Engineering Museum** *(591)* in Camborne.

Useful as it was, the Newcomen engine was inefficient owing to the great thermal losses resulting from the cylinder's having to be reheated each time cold water was injected to condense the steam. James Watt, an instrument maker at Glasgow University, solved the problem. His solution was a separate condenser, patented in 1769, which allowed the working cylinder, in which the piston went up and down, to remain permanently hot inside a steam jacket. Moreover, in Watt's engine the downward pressure on the piston was exerted by steam introduced at the top of the cylinder instead of by atmospheric pressure. In 1773 Watt entered into partnership with a Birmingham businessman named Matthew Boulton and their products were an instant success. Watt's third innovation was to develop a steam engine that could convert the reciprocating movements of the beam-engine to rotary motion and thus drive machinery. This was accomplished by running a connecting rod between the free end of the beam to a flywheel, at first equipped with an elliptical sun-and-planet gear and later with a common crank. In either case, as the beam moved up and down it set the flywheel turning, the flywheel's axle rotating, and other connected gears in motion. With the advent of steam-generated rotary power, industry was freed from the waterwheel. Considerations other than the presence of running water now began to determine the siting of factories—proximity to coal fields, cheap water transportation, labor supply, etc. Hence the growth of the new industrial cities—Birmingham, Manchester, Leeds, etc.

In the **Science Museum** *(526)*, South Kensington, London, is a reconstructed Boulton and Watt rotative beam engine built in 1788. By 1800 when Watt's partnership with Boulton ended, 308 such engines had been constructed. Production on this scale would have been impossible but for the prior and concurrent modernization of the iron industry. Most of the iron in Britain occurred in carboniferous ores containing only about thirty percent of pure metal. The principle of ironmaking, then, involves separating the metal from the ore by applying enough heat to a mixture of carbon and ore so that the former will combine with the oxides of the latter and escape in the form of carbon monoxide or carbon dioxide gas. Traditionally charcoal was used to supply the carbon for this process, but charcoal is a wood derivative, and the forests of Britain were fast disappearing by the beginning of the eighteenth century. The alternative was coke, produced by burning coal in airless ovens to drive off the volatile elements, leaving lumps of almost pure carbon. Not all coal is useable for the production of coke, but in Salop there were veins of clod coal, almost eighty percent carbon with a very low sulfur content, which was ideal. The first big breakthrough, then, in the mass production of iron occurred in 1709 when Abraham Darby, a Quaker ironmaster and entrepreneur, succeeded in smelting iron with Salop coke at his blast furnace at

Coalbrookdale. Darby's furnace has recently been restored and is part of the **Ironbridge Gorge Museum** *(672)*, the most important industrial archaeological site in Britain. Darby's plant produced cast-iron products of an immense variety, many of which are on display in the Coalbrookdale Museum. The most famous single item in the foundry's output was the Iron Bridge downriver from the furnace itself. This was built in 1779 to Thomas Telford's design—a hundred-foot span with cast-iron ribs—the first of its kind ever constructed.

Darby's first ironworks depended on a waterwheel to generate the power to operate the bellows to create the blast required to raise the temperature of the burning mass of ore and coke inside the furnace to high enough temperatures to reduce the ore to molten iron. This liquid metal was then run off either into pigs or into a cup-shaped hole from which it could be ladled into molds to make castings. After 1775 steam engines were introduced to power the bellows. John Wilkinson, an eccentric ironmaster and entrepreneur from Staffordshire, was one of the first to order one of Watt's new devices. This was appropriate since the cylinders used by Watt and Boulton at their Soho works in Birmingham had been bored by Wilkinson who, for the manufacture of cannon, had succeeded in perfecting a process for constructing hollow cylinders with almost flawless interior surfaces—an essential requirement for an efficient steam engine. Wilkinson was an iron fanatic; he made cast-iron barges that miraculously stayed afloat, and he insisted on being buried in an iron coffin. His boring mill was, in the opinion of the industrial archaeologist Neil Cossons, "at least as important in the development of the steam engine as any of Watt's specific improvements." Another notable pioneer was Henry Cort, who in 1783 patented the puddling process in which wrought iron could be produced from pig iron by burning common coal in a separate chamber, called a reverberatory furnace, so that the sulfur fumes did not come into contact with the iron but were drained off as sulfuric acid, while the other impurities in the molten pig were removed by the stirring action of the so-called puddlers. Cort's plant has disappeared, but, at the Blists Open Air Museum just east of Coalbrookdale and part of the **Ironbridge Gorge Museum** *(672)* complex, can be seen a resmelting reverberatory furnace similar to Cort's, as well as two giant beam engines erected in 1851 to blow air into the blast furnaces.

Meanwhile Benjamin Huntsman, a Doncaster clockmaker, had developed a method for making steel in crucibles fired by coke. He was persuaded to settle in Sheffield, thus assuring that city a continuation of its dominance in the steel industry. At the **Abbeydale Industrial Hamlet** *(680)* on the southern outskirts of Sheffield, the visitor today can see a self-sufficient steel-producing unit, from the pot room where the clay crucibles were made to the furnace where the metal was melted before being poured into molds to form ingots, to the tilt forge where steel scythes were hammered out, to the blowing machine, to the water wheels that powered the operation. Next to the Ironbridge Gorge Museum, this is the most interesting industrial archaeological site in Britain, and the management's handling of visitors is exemplary.

No account of the early Industrial Revolution would be complete without mention of machine tools, i.e., machines that produced other machines. Wilkinson's boring mill, already described, falls in this category. So does Henry Maudslay's screw-cutting lathe, invented in 1800 and capable of manufacturing screws with a wide range of threads. Maudslay made forty-four machines to the designs of Marc Isambard Brunel for manufacturing pulley blocks for the Portsmouth Navy Yard—an exercise in mass production that contributed significantly to British naval strength during the vital years of the Napoleonic Wars. At the **Science Museum** *(526)*, South Kensington, London, can be seen Maudslay's original screw-cutting lathe and eight of his block-making machines.

Coal was of course the essential ingredient to the manufacture of iron and steel and the ultimate basis of steam power. Of this commodity Britain is blessed with an abundant supply. Coal occurred in three types of geological situations: (1) as outcrops where it could be picked up easily off the ground, (2) in hillside drifts where it could be fairly easily reached by driving horizontal tunnels into the shallow seams, and (3) in deep underground seams accessible only by vertical shafts from the bottom of which galleries had to be driven, their ceilings held up by pillars of unmined coal or shored by heavy wooden beams. A reconstructed drift mine can be seen at the Blists Hill site of the **Ironbridge Gorge Museum** *(672)* in Salop. At the **Chatterly Whitfield Mining Museum** *(667)* just north of Tunstall, Staffordshire, the visitor can descend seven hundred feet into the galleries of a now defunct mining operation which, in 1880, was producing more than 240,000 tons of coal per annum. Coal was being mined here at least as early as 1750, though the existing works all date from the nineteenth and twentieth centuries. A visit takes about an hour and a half, but it does offer the traveller a chance to acquire some appreciation for life in the mines, especially since the tour guides are former miners. A quicker and cleaner introduction to the mysteries of coal mining is provided by the **National Museum of Wales** *(717)* in Cardiff, where the mining gallery in the Department of Industry has a simulated coal mine complete with pit bottom, galleries, roof supports, ventilation devices, etc. At the Beamish Colliery, part of the **Beamish North of England Open Air Museum** *(699)* near Chester-le-Street, County Durham, the surface appearance of a coal mine is well demonstrated in the tall stone engine house, built in 1855, inside of which is a vertical winding steam engine used for raising and lowering both miners and coal. Nearby is a row of pitmen's cottages moved here from their original location—cramped living quarters bravely decked out with the few amenities these ill-paid workmen could afford. In the museum here too is a good collection of miners' tools. Among the most indispensable of these was the safety lamp devised by Humphrey Davy in 1815.

Firedamp, a highly flammable mixture of methane and air, was the chief cause of the many lethal mine explosions that plagued the early days of the coal-mining industry and continued to do so well into the nineteenth century. Davy's invention consisted simply of installing around the flame a wire-mesh screen which served as a preventive to igniting the gas, though not a foolproof one as proved by the occurrence of 643 explosions in northeastern England alone between 1835 and 1850. There is a good collection of safety lamps to be seen at the **Salford Science Museum** *(694)* in Buile Hill Park, Eccles Old Road, Greater Manchester, and another in the **National Museum of Wales** *(717)* in Cardiff.

Tin and copper mining, mostly confined to Cornwall, presented some of the same problems that plagued the coal industry. Drainage was the biggest one, and it is significant that both Savery's and Newcomen's steam engines were invented with the needs of the Cornish tin and copper mines in mind. Of the two metals, tin was more valued from ancient times down through the Middle Ages, and Cornwall and Devon had been known to be rich in the metal from at least the time when Phoenician merchants began to push beyond the straits of Gibraltar out into the Atlantic Ocean. In the eighteenth century copper eclipsed tin in importance, largely because it is one of the two metals used in the making of brass, an alloy of tremendous importance in the manufacture of tools, instruments, fittings, clocks, steam engines, and machinery of all kinds. Cornwall then stood unchallenged as the world's major supplier, a dominance that continued until the mid-nineteenth century when new fields in Australia, North America, and Chile virtually destroyed the industry there.

Ironically, the long-neglected tin deposits came partially to Cornwall's rescue, especially when it was discovered that lodes of tin were frequently to be found beneath the galleries dug to extract copper, so that the organization and machinery already in place could be easily converted to its extraction. The boom in Cornish tin, however, was short. Depression hit about 1875 when new Australian mines were open, and again in the 1890s when the Malayan fields increased their output, and still again after World War I when the postwar slump virtually wiped out an already failing industry. At present there are only two tin mines working in Cornwall, but one of them, the **Geevor Tin Mine** *(596)* just north of St. Just, has opened to the public an instructive Tin Mining Museum as well as a tour of the modern works above the mines (which in fact now run out under the ocean) where visitors can see how the ore is crushed and separated. Unlike iron, tin is extracted from its ore by crushing the latter into a fine sand, then subjecting it to repeated sifting, washing, and shaking (called vanning) until it is reduced to a fine powder called black tin which is then smelted. The crushers, when mechanically operated, were called Cornish stamps. There are several of these on view at the **Tolgus Tin Streaming Mill** *(595)* near Redruth. Here the production of tin by the process known as streaming was practiced for almost two hundred years before the plant closed down in 1928. In this case the ore came not from mines underneath the surface but from tin-laden sands captured from the nearby river. Tolgus is still operational, and visitors are welcome to a highly educational short tour. At the **Poldark Mine and Museum** *(592)*, associated with Wendron Forge north of Helston, visitors (wearing miners' hats) are escorted through the galleries themselves, some as old as the seventeenth century. On the grounds are a number of associated engines, none older than 1850; miscellaneous household and farm machinery, mostly nineteenth century; and a large overshot waterwheel, dating to 1904. Perhaps the best reminders of Cornwall's lost tin-mining industry, however, are the hundreds of derelict stone pumping-engine houses dotting the Cornish landscape. Romantic in appearance—in the manner of ruined medieval castles—these tumbling, ivy-covered structures, with their characteristic tapering chimneys, once housed the pumping engines that kept dry the mines below when Cornish tin and copper ruled the markets of the world.

What Cornwall was to tin and copper, North Wales was to slate. One of the effects of industrialization was to create an enormous demand for building materials for new housing—a demand which could not be met by lumber owing to the rapid depletion of Britain's forests by the end of the eighteenth century. Welsh slates proved to be the answer, especially for roofing. They were cheap to quarry and dress, thin, light, and easy to cut to uniform dimensions. With the development of England's network of canals, they were also easily transportable to almost any industrial town where new houses were going up for workers' occupation.

There were two basic techniques for extracting slate. First was quarrying by the open terrace method. It is these quarries, now almost altogether abandoned, that give parts of North Wales a vaguely lunar landscape reminiscent of etchings of Dante's *Inferno*. The sight of a Welsh slate quarry in the rain, its naked terraces and giant slag heaps gray and glistening, is the ultimate in bleakness. A good example is the Dinorwic Quarry near Llanberis, Gwynedd, on the site of which the Department of the Environment maintains the **North Wales Quarrying Museum** *(739)*. The first quarrying operation to open here began in 1782, followed by a second in 1809, and by the end of the nineteenth century three thousand people were employed and the slate terraces had reached a height of two thousand feet above sea level. Today the museum consists of various workshops connected with the operation: a carpentry shop, a foundry, smithies, repair shops, offices, storerooms, and a huge waterwheel to turn the machinery, though not so huge as the earlier one it replaced. Films are shown illustrating the history of the industry, and from time to time there are fascinating live demonstrations of slate cutting by skilled workmen whose facility at this arcane art is amazing to behold. The second method of extracting slate was to mine it by digging tunnels into the hillsides and going in after it. This process is illustrated at the **Gloddfa Ganol Ffestiniog Mountain Tourist Centre**

(738) near Ffestiniog, Gwynedd. Opened in 1818 and not closed until after the second world war, the industry here both quarried and mined for slate, and at least two of the tunnels which miners used to penetrate the mountain can still be entered by the adventurous. The museum includes the usual array of machinery, live slate-cutting demonstrations, and a nice gift shop featuring surprisingly attractive and useful slate artifacts.

Pottery-making in Britain was not quite so localized as were tin and copper mining or slate quarrying, but there were more potteries in Staffordshire than any place else, especially in the Five Towns centered on Stoke-on-Trent, which the writer Arnold Bennett was later to immortalize in his famous trilogy *(Clayhanger, Hilda Lesseays,* and *These Twain)*. The word *pottery* includes all kinds of ceramic wares—porcelain, earthenware, terra-cotta, and fireclay products. All are produced by firing clay in a kiln until vitrification occurs, and the differences among these categories is attributable to the temperature of firing, the quality of the clay, and the nature and amount of additional ingredients, including those used for glazing. The glaze is a vitrified glassy outer layer which renders baked clay impermeable. The most common Staffordshire earthenware, at least until the 1780s, was called stoneware which was glazed by common salt thrown into the kiln and allowed to vitrify on the articles being fired. Later, other glazing materials came into use to produce different consistencies, colors, and degrees of hardness. By the end of the eighteenth century the most common kiln was the so-called bottle oven, hundreds of which once dotted the landscape of the Five Towns filling the air with smoke and begriming the countryside with coal dust. Today, four of these are on view within the **Gladstone Pottery Museum** *(668)* in Longton on the southern outskirts of Stoke-on-Trent. The works here date from the nineteenth century, and a visit is almost mandatory for anyone wanting to gain a comprehension of the mechanics of pottery-making. It is altogether a splendid and splendidly managed industrial museum.

Porcelain is a delicate, translucent form of pottery, originating in China, and made by the fusion of kaolin (china clay) and petuntse (china stone) at very high temperatures. Chinese porcelain in the Middle Ages was so rare in Europe that it was often set in silver mounts like precious stones. In the seventeenth century it began to enter the West in increasing quantities and before long the French were producing at St. Cloud a mock porcelain so close to the original as to be almost indistinguishable from it. In 1709 a German potter, named Johann Friederick Bottger, working at Meissen in Saxony, discovered the secret of making true porcelain, and thereafter Meissenware preempted the European market. No such discovery was forthcoming in Britain, and though the English made an artificial porcelain, which they called *china*, its outer glaze was softer than either its Oriental or German counterparts. Early on, English factories at Bow (Devon), Chelsea (London), and Bristol began to add the ashes of calcined bones to their mix, thus creating a peculiarly English variety—bone china. By 1784 the Chelsea factory had closed down and its molds and workmen moved to Derby, which had also absorbed the works at Bow. By the end of the century, Derby, Worcester, and for a brief period Lowestoft in Suffolk, became the chief centers for porcelain manufacture. The **Victoria and Albert Museum** *(526)*, London, has a good representative display of porcelain tableware and figurines from all these factories. Good Derbyware, including samples of nineteenth century Royal Crown Derby, are on view at the **Museum and Art Gallery** *(663)* in Derby. Fine collections of English china are on display throughout the country in stately homes too numerous to mention. Late in the century china manufacture began to move into Staffordshire, already the leading center for earthenware goods. Thomas Minton and Josiah Spode set up china potteries in Stoke-on-Trent which are still in business. A smaller establishment was at Coalport, Salop, where the Coalport China Works Museum is now included in the **Ironbridge Gorge Museum** *(672)* complex and should definitely be included in a visit to that great industrial site. Eventually the Coalport Works were bought up by Josiah Wedgwood, the greatest of all the eighteenth century pottery manufacturers and the man who did more than anyone else to make the name of Staffordshire synonymous with high-quality ceramics throughout the world.

Wedgwood is the prototypical entrepreneur of the eighteenth century Industrial Revolution—craft-wise, individualistic, imaginative, and industrious. Unschooled beyond the age of fourteen when he was apprenticed to his brother's pottery in Burslem, he taught himself several languages, studied Greek and Roman antiquities, was an elected fellow in the Royal Society, associated on equal terms with the likes of Joshua Reynolds and Robert Adam, and did frequent business with royalty in England and elsewhere. He was also a man of remarkably enlightened political and social views—a sympathizer with revolutionaries in America and France and active in the antislavery movement, though admittedly an autocratic employer who at least once met a request from his workers for a wage increase with a threat to fire the lot of them. He first set up business for himself at Burslem, north of Stoke, in 1759, making the inexpensive but attractive cream-colored earthenware for table use which was to be the foundation of his great success. In 1765 Queen Charlotte, consort of George III, ordered a tea service from the Wedgwood pottery and was so pleased with the results that she named him Her Majesty's potter and allowed his product to be called Queensware. After moving to new quarters, which he called Etruria in response to the current rage for the misnamed "Etruscan" pottery found at Pompeii and Herculaneum, Wedgwood received a spectacular commission from the Empress Catherine the Great of Russia for a table and dessert service of 952 items of ware intended for use in her palace of La Grenouillere and therefore labeled the "frog service." The same year (1773) he began the manufacture of the jasperware which is today the product most commonly associated with the Wedgwood name. This was an unglazed but impermeable stoneware colored blue, green, lavender, yellow, or black, to which delicately modeled classical ornaments, busts, etc., were applied, usually in white. Other Wedgwood types were variegated wares looking like marble or agate and black basalt, an unglazed black stoneware. His final masterpiece was the black-and-white reproduction in jasper of the so-called Portland Vase, a beautiful third century Roman two-handled urn owned by the duke of Portland who loaned it to Wedgwood to copy. He did so well that, when the original in the British Museum was later smashed to pieces by a madman, it was restored with the aid of this copy. Samples of all the above, including the Portland Vase, a plate from the Empress Catherine's service, and several trial pieces run for the same collection, are on view in the magnificent new Wedgwood Museum at the **Wedgwood Visitor Centre** *(668)* in Barlaston, Staffordshire, a few miles south of Stoke. Here supreme elegance, utility, and economy are conjoined in the eighteenth century miracle known as the Industrial Revolution. Through mass production Josiah Wedgwood was able to democratize the classical ideal of beauty which up to his time had been mostly reserved for the enjoyment of the rich. Well before John Keats immortalized the Grecian urn in poetry, Wedgwood had made it available to the masses in jasper reproduction.

GEORGE IV, REGENT AND KING: 1811–1830

It is little short of embarrassing to turn from the productive career of Josiah Wedgwood to the sorry degeneracy of the royal family in the penultimate years of the Hanoverian dynasty. At the close of the year 1810 King George III went mad. It had happened before, notably in 1788, but then the monarch had recovered. This time it was for keeps. Though his physicians diagnosed the problem as the "flying gout" which had settled in his head, modern medical historians are mostly agreed that the king was a victim of porphyria, a hereditary sickness with symptoms indistinguishable from insanity. In any case George III was *non compos mentis* for the remainder of his life. He died in 1820 to be succeeded by his eldest son, George IV, who had already served for a decade as prince regent. The eldest of nine brothers, he was first among equals in extravagance and dissipation. Married illegally to Mrs. Fitzherbert, a twice widowed Roman Catholic six years older than himself, the prince had left her in 1795 to wed himself to the Princess Caroline of Brunswick whose dowry he needed to pay off his debts but whose conduct and demeanor were so offensive that he shortly parted company from her. After George III died, Caroline returned to England from a scandal-ridden sojourn on the Continent to claim her rights as queen; the new king sued for divorce in the House of Lords; the indictment had to be withdrawn for want of support; and the London mob, who hated the king, went wild with drunken enthusiasm. Nor was the conduct of the other royal princes more edifying. Small wonder that the poet Shelley characterized the period of the Regency thus:

> An old, mad, blind, despised and dying king,—
> Princes, the dregs of their dull race, who flow
> Through public scorn,—mud from a muddy spring,—
> Rulers who neither see, nor feel, nor know,
> But leech-like to their fainting country cling,
> Till they drop, blind in blood, without a blow.

Shelley was wrong of course in describing the last of the Hanoverians as rulers. After 1810 the monarch ceased to play a significant role in national politics, and George IV, both as regent and king, was too indolent to assert the few prerogatives he had inherited from his father. The government was in the hands of ministers whom their enemies labeled Tories, though they preferred to call themselves the friends of Mr. Pitt, i.e., William Pitt the Younger who, until his death in 1806, had been the chief architect of Europe's coalition against Napoleon. For most of the period of the Regency and reign of George IV, Lord Liverpool was prime minister. Under his aegis, the war was brought to a successful end, while the foreign secretary, Lord Castelreagh, in association with the Austrian foreign minister, Prince Metternich, arranged an international settlement which, with minor interruptions, kept Europe at peace for another hundred years. Nor was the government's handling of troubled postwar problems in Britain itself without some measure of success. The Test and Corporation Acts against Protestant dissenters were finally repealed; an emancipation act admitted Roman Catholics to full political rights; the creaky legal system was much reformed; and Sir Robert Peel founded the modern police force, still called "Bobbies" in his memory.

In none of these matters did George IV play any significant part. Yet, for all his folly, he was an enthusiastic patron of the arts and it is not inappropriate that in architecture, decoration, furniture design, and even painting, the period is known as Regency. Yet there is no such thing as a Regency style. For most of the eighteenth century, despite Chippendale's rococo or Horace Walpole's Gothick fancies, the dominant aesthetic ideal had been derived from classical antiquity. Now, in the second two decades of the nineteenth, there was no dominant ideal at all. Classicism in the Adam manner, Greek revival, Gothic revival, Chinese, Indian, and even Egyptian fashions vied with each other to produce a kaleidoscope of styles.

The best known of all the Regency architects was John Nash. The son of a Lambeth millwright, he became a speculative builder in London at about the age of thirty, went bankrupt, retired to Wales to recoup his fortunes by constructing and remodeling country houses, and about 1795 joined in a partnership with the gardener Humphrey Repton, who "improved" estates while Nash added such decorative features as cottages, dairies, etc., in the fashionable Picturesque manner. The cult of the Picturesque in landscape gardening and architecture was of a piece with the Romantic poetry of Wordsworth and Shelley in its glorification of pastoral simplicity and rustic charm. It was this tradition that informed Nash's creation of a rustic hamlet of thatched cottages on the grounds of **Blaise Castle House** *(657)* north of Bristol. Meanwhile, Repton, now in partnership with Thomas Daniell, was off on a different tack at **Sezincote Garden** *(640)* near Moreton-in-Marsh, Gloucestershire, where both house and grounds were designed in a manner meant to be reminiscent of India. Possibly borrowing from this example, another architect, William Porden, built for the prince regent, who had established a residence at Brighton, an Indian stable, now used as a concert hall and called the **Dome** *(548)*. A few years later the prince regent turned to Nash to enlarge the **Royal Pavilion** *(548)*, initially constructed some years earlier in a classical style by Henry Holland. The prince had previously consulted Repton who had recommended the Indian style already attempted in the Dome. Nash chose instead a peculiar mix of Gothic and Chinese which converted the regent's seaside palace into the most glorious architectural absurdity in England. He added the Music Room and the Banqueting Room and crowned them with inverted funnels meant to imitate the folds of an imaginary Crusader's tent. The onion-shaped domes, which were supposed to be Indian but in fact somewhat resemble those of the Kremlin in Moscow, were added later. The interior rooms are equally fantastic. In extravagance and eccentricity the Royal Pavilion is a perfect expression of the lifestyle of its owner.

While in London, however, the regent needed something more formal. Buckingham House at the west end of St. James's Park had come into the possession of the Crown in 1762 and it was here that the Prince of Wales had spent his boyhood. In 1825 he commissioned Nash to remodel it, and **Buckingham Palace** *(520)* is the result. George IV's death in 1830 prevented the architect from finishing the job, and indeed it was still incomplete on the death of George's brother, King William IV, so that Queen Victoria was the first of the British sovereigns to occupy it. The east front, which is all the public sees today, was not built until 1913 to the design of Sir Aston Webb. Nearby, however, is the **Royal Mews** *(522)* which Nash designed and where the coaches, carriage horses, and royal motor cars are on public view. Nash was also responsible for landscaping **St. James's Park** *(522)*, for designing **Carlton House Terrace** *(520)*, a row of stuccoed mansions facing the Mall, and for designing the **Marble Arch** *(527)*, originally situated in front of Buckingham Palace, but later moved to Hyde Park.

Nash's greatest opportunity in London, however, came in 1811 when he received the commission to supervise the gigantic program of public works called the Metropolitan Improvements. The plan called for the beautification of the whole area from Marylebone Park to the Mall, and before he was finished Nash had laid out **Regent's Park** *(529)*; had built the splendid **Park Crescent** *(529)* with its coupled Ionic columns, as well as the numerous other similar terraces and villas on the east and south sides of the park; and had laid out the nobly sweeping curves of Regent Street, now unhappily denuded of his buildings. Although his work was sometimes slipshod, Nash left his native city far more attractive than he found it. Regent's Park, with its adjacent buildings of light stucco and classic columns, is certainly one of the prettiest areas of London—an island of airy grace unexcelled in a city famous for its parks.

One final contribution of King George IV to the pleasure of today's sightseer is his remodeling of **Windsor Castle** *(565)*. A comfortless and semiruined place when he inherited the throne, Windsor was to achieve under his sponsorship the romantic castellated silhouette it now enjoys. The architect was James Wyatt's nephew, Jeffrey Wyatt, who changed his patronymic to Wyatville on commencing work at Windsor and in 1828 was knighted for his efforts. He raised the Round Tower by thirty-three feet, added numerous lesser towers, built a broad corridor of two stories around the inner side of the Quadrangle, and gave St. George's Hall its present character. Windsor Castle as it appears today is in no small measure the invention of King George IV, not surprisingly an avid reader of the novels of Sir Walter Scott.

Two other buildings of special interest to the intelligent traveller in London owe their being, in part at least, to George IV's interest in the arts. The first is the **National Gallery** *(518)* facing Trafalgar Square. It was designed by William Wilkins, architect for Downing College and University College, London, and like them in the neo-Grecian style which reached its apex in the first decades of the nineteenth century. The prominent classical portico came from Henry Holland's Carlton House, built for the Prince of Wales, but torn down after he became regent. The original gallery was constructed to house the thirty-eight paintings belonging to the estate of John Julius Angerstein which the government, urged on by the king himself, bought in 1824 for fifty-seven thousand pounds. It was completed and first opened to the public in 1838, and within the first seven months twenty-four thousand visitors had seen the paintings—a number that has since swollen to about two million annually. The critic William Hazlitt rejoiced that this exposure of the general public to some of the finest works of art in the world would "cure . . . low thoughted cares and uneasy passions," and Sir Robert Peel anticipated that the National Gallery would contribute "to the cementing of the bonds of union between the richer and poorer orders." Similar expectations attended the construction of the new **British Museum** *(516)* on Great Russell Street just west of Bloomsbury Square in London. The contents of an earlier museum were outgrowing the capacity of Montagu House on the same site, and, with the donation by George IV of his father's splendid library, it was decided to tear down the old quarters and raise an altogether new building. The architect was Sir Robert Smirke and the style again was neo-Grecian, with a splendid Ionic portico and columns of the same order extending around the whole facade. The glory that was Greece was given even greater homage when, in 1816, the Elgin marbles were installed in Montagu House, the predecessor of the British Museum. These great sculpted masterpieces of the Periclean Age which once graced the Parthenon of Athens were saved from probable destruction at the hand of the Turks by Thomas Bruce, seventh earl of Elgin, and British ambassador to the Porte. They reached England after a hazardous voyage and were bought by public subscription for thirty-five thousand pounds, less than half the sum Lord Elgin had spent for their rescue and transportation. Beautifully displayed today, they are a tribute not only to the workshop of the great Athenian sculptor Phidias, but to the efficacy of Lord Elgin's classical education.

Another architect in the neo-Grecian manner was Sir John Soane, though with a difference. In the **Dulwich College Picture Gallery** *(536)*, south of the Thames in London, he dispensed altogether with columns in favor of decorative grooved strips and produced a sort of primitivist classical building that was unique. Destroyed in 1944 by a flying bomb, today's building is almost a complete replica, housing one of the richest small galleries of paintings in Britain—not to be missed by art lovers. Soane's second noted architectural endeavor was his own residence at 13 Lincoln's Inn Fields, now **Soane's Museum** *(518)*, bequeathed to the nation along with its fine collection of Hogarths, Turners, etc. Here, in the interior rooms, the architect gave full play to his unconventional concepts of space and light: domes, vaults, lantern lights, clerestories, arched openings between rooms, and reflecting glass friezes combine to create a series of interesting vistas, making the house seem much more spacious than it actually is.

Soane was responsible too for the remodeling of **Chillington Hall** *(666)*, a country house near Wolverhampton, Staffordshire, where his use of interior arches and overhead natural lighting anticipates the later work on his own house. He also redesigned the interior of **Wotton House** *(622)* in Buckinghamshire, again with a liberal use of arched doorways, rounded corners, and other effects designed to give the illusion of lightness. Also, as mentioned above, he added two fine new rooms to **Wimpole Hall** *(617)*, Cambridgeshire. More distinctly in the neo-Grecian style is **Arlington Court** *(586)* near Barnstaple, Devon, by Thomas Lee, a local architect who had worked briefly in Soane's office. Here a semicircular Doric porch provides the only break in the plain facades of this severely classical building. An even more extreme statement of the Greek Revival is the **Philipps House** *(575)* at Dinton west of Salisbury, Wiltshire. Its architect surprisingly was Jeffrey Wyatt, better known for his neo-Gothic work at Windsor Castle under the name of Sir Jeffrey Wyatville. An Ionic portico graces the front facade and the interior is chastely classical throughout.

The leap from neo-Grecian to neo-Gothic was a mighty one, but easily accomplished by the eclectic genius of Regency architects. One of the best examples in the latter style is **Belvoir Castle** *(650)*, Leicestershire, a few miles west of Grantham, Lincolnshire, rebuilt for the fifth duke of Rutland by Wyatville's more famous uncle, James Wyatt, in 1801–1813. In his hands, and those of his successor Sir John Thoroton, a seventeenth century country house was converted into a great melange of castellated towers, turrets, bastions, bartizans, etc., not at all dissimilar in appearance to George IV's reconstruction of Windsor Castle. Another Gothic extravaganza is **Eastnor Castle** *(647)* near Ledbury, Hereford and Worcester. Here the architect was Robert Smirke, whose preference for the neo-Grecian, as evidenced in his design for the British Museum, did not prevent his raising for the first earl of Somers a great pseudo-feudal stronghold, still further Gothicized later by the interior decorations of Augustus Pugin. The greatest of Regency castles (Windsor only excepted) harks back to a still earlier medieval tradition. This is **Penrhyn Castle** *(736)* just east of Bangor, Gwynedd, perched high on a hilltop overlooking Beaumaris Bay. The architect was Thomas Hopper and the owner G. H. Dawkins Pennant who had made a fortune out of the nearby Penrhyn slate quarries. The style is pseudo-Norman with a square keep looking vaguely like Rochester Castle and a round machicolated tower not unlike Windsor's. Inside, the great hall was modeled on Durham Cathedral, though the floor is polished slate as are many of the other interior furnishings.

Heterogeneity is certainly the guiding principle of Regency architecture, yet there is one architectural type that is unmistakably associated with this period. This is the Regency terrace—long rows or blocks of town houses, often decorated with pillars or pilasters of the classical orders, usually faced with cream-colored stucco, and ornamented with ironwork balconies and trellises. The general effect is one of gaiety and lightness. Nash's terraces south and east of Regent's Park are typical. Other examples in London are George Basevi's **Belgrave Square** *(520)* and **Pelham Crescent** *(525)*; and in Hove near Brighton, **Brunswick Square** *(550)* and **Brunswick Terrace** *(550)* by C. A. Busby and **Adelaide Crescent** *(549)* by Decimus Burton.

Just as no single model dominated the architectural fashions of the second two decades of the nineteenth century, so in furniture design there is no one Regency style, but rather a miscellany of types, all more or less derivative from ancient Greece, Rome, and even Egypt—with a strong admixture of French Directoire and Empire fashions. The leading name in furniture design is Thomas Hope whose book of designs called *Household Furniture and Interior Decoration* was published in 1807. Hope was an admirer of Grecian "severity," deduced mostly from what could be observed of classical Greek household effects on recently excavated vases, urns, amphora, and the like. A typical Hope piece was the Grecian chair, much copied by his contemporaries and still a standard item. It can be recognized by the fact that the rear legs and back form a continuous curve balanced by a forward curve of the front legs. Another typical Regency piece is the Grecian couch with a boldly curved headpiece, a similarly scrolled end, and a short armrest on only one side. Still another is the convex circular mirror with a gilded frame decorated by evenly spaced little gilded balls. Gilt and black lacquer are indeed lavishly applied to all types of furniture. Woodcarving and wood inlays mostly disappear. Instead there is an abundance of brass inlay, brass colonnettes to support galleries and shelves, wire trellis in doors or sides of cabinets, lion feet on tables, castors on chairs and tables, and lion-mask handles on drawers. These last are meant to be in the Egyptian mode which became especially popular after Lord Nelson's famous victory at the Battle of the Nile. Other Egyptian motifs were the lotus leaf, the sphinx head, and even crocodiles and serpents. Hope, among others, was intrigued by the exotic splendor of the land of the pharaohs. But the cult of the exotic was easily carried to bizarre extremes, as Hope himself recognized when he warned that "extravagant caricatures, such as of late have begun to start up in every corner of the capital, seem calculated for the sole purpose of bringing this new style into disrepute." He was alert also to the new threat to good taste inherent in the appearance of furniture-making machinery and called attention to the danger of debasement "through the entire substitution of machinery to manual labor." The fact is that the era of the cabinetmaker was drawing to a close. In the near future, furniture factories geared to mass production, to quantity rather than quality, would take the place of such skilled craftsmen as Hope, Adam, Chippendale, et al.

In painting, too, there is no such thing as a Regency style, though it is customary to place England's two greatest artists, John Constable and J. M. W. Turner, in the Romantic school, akin to such contemporary poets as Wordsworth, Shelley, and Byron. Of the two, the most self-consciously Romantic, and also the most peculiarly English, was Constable. Born in Suffolk in 1776, he is the interpreter par excellence of the English landscape, not only of those parts of his native Stour valley now known as the Constable country, but also of Dorset, Brighton, Salisbury, and Hampstead Heath. No verbal description can do justice to his achievement. He is the greatest of all English exponents of the chiaroscuro, the pictorial representation of gradations of light and shade. No traveller through the countryside can fail to notice how exactly Constable captured the peculiar dappled beauty of English skies, fields, forests, houses, mills, castles, churches, lakes, streams, and shorelines. To look at a Constable painting is to see England. Fortunately, there are three major repositories where his works can be observed en masse: the **Tate Gallery** *(523)*, the **Victoria and Albert Museum** *(526)*, and the **National Gallery** *(518)*, all in London.

Turner, born in 1775, lived until 1851, so much of his mature work belongs to the Victorian, not the Georgian, era. Nevertheless he was already a full member of the Royal Academy in 1802, and his visit to

Venice, which was to have such a profound effect on his later painting, took place in 1819. Adept in watercolors as well as oils, Turner had a great preoccupation, especially in the last thirty years of his career, with light. No other British painter can approach him in his rendition of pure luminescence. Again the best collection of his works is to be seen in the **Tate** *(523)*, the **Victoria and Albert** *(526)*, and the **National Gallery** *(518)*, though there are some fine examples too at **Petworth House** *(553)*, West Sussex, which he frequently visited.

The **Tate Gallery** *(523)* also houses the best extant collection of the works of the poet/artist William Blake, though other of his works can be seen in the **Victoria and Albert Museum** *(526)*, the **Corporation Art Gallery and Museum** *(664)* in Birmingham, and in the Prints and Drawings Department of the **British Museum** *(516)* in London. More highly esteemed today than in his own lifetime (1757–1827), Blake stands apart from any identifiable artistic school or cultural movement. Eschewing oils, he painted in watercolor or in a gum medium he called tempera, but his true genius is revealed in the engraved linear drawings published as book illustrations and sometimes painted-in by the artist himself. He is closer to the medieval tradition of manuscript illumination and to certain twentieth century schools of design than to any artistic fashion in between.

Of portraiture one name dominates the Regency period: Sir Thomas Lawrence. His real career began in 1814 when he received a commission to paint the victorious allied kings, princes, and ministers gathered in London to celebrate the defeat of Napoleon. The work continued for four more years and its fruits are to be seen today in the Waterloo Chamber of **Windsor Castle** *(565)* designed by Wyatville specifically to house them. Lawrence's portraits are distinguished by the slightly flushed look he gives his sitters and by a dash and liveliness not to be found in the more sedate Reynolds. There is a good representation of his work at the **National Portrait Gallery** *(518)*, London, and in stately homes too numerous to mention. Best known probably of all his works are his portraits of George IV and of Arthur Wellesley, the first duke of Wellington.

Mention of the Iron Duke brings us to the British army he commanded and to a consideration of that era in military history which had its glorious and bloody finale in the Battle of Waterloo on 18 June 1815. The key to an understanding of land warfare in the eighteenth century is to be found in its basic infantry weapon—the smoothbore, flintlock musket, of which there are countless still in existence to be seen in almost any military museum in Britain. In 1702 pikemen finally disappeared from the British army and all units were eventually equipped with bayoneted muskets. The British regulation musket of 1768 weighed 10 pounds, 11 ounces and fired a .75 caliber lead bullet inserted into the barrel at the muzzle and driven down into the breech with a ramrod. The weapon was fired when the trigger released a spring causing a piece of flint to hit the gun's metal battery, thus striking a spark to ignite the loose powder in a shallow pan, which in turn produced a flash that penetrated the breech of the barrel through a touchhole and ignited the charge that fired the bullet. A skilled musketeer would take from twenty to thirty seconds to load his gun and fire a single shot. Since his piece was smoothbored, it was necessarily inaccurate, so there was no point in taking aim. The musket was effective, then, only when fired en masse, that is, in volleys by many men bunched close together. To bring the greatest volume of fire to bear against an enemy, infantrymen were normally lined up elbow to elbow and three ranks deep. Tactics consisted simply of deploying troops from marching order into linear formation, marching them against the enemy line, and opening fire when range was closed to about one hundred yards, the maximum effective distance a musket could be fired. Heavy artillery might be used in preparation for a battle and light fieldpieces during it, but by and large artillery was of secondary importance. So was the cavalry, normally stationed in the wings. Throughout most of the eighteenth century, all Western armies, including the American Continental Army, employed identical linear tactics in battle.

The British army was organized into regiments of one or two battalions, nine to thirteen companies to a battalion. Their officers came from the landed class—aristocrats and gentry. All commissions were bought, initially from the Crown and thereafter from the officer in possession when he retired or moved up in rank. Enlistment in the ranks was "voluntary," that is conscription was rarely resorted to, though other coercive means were used to persuade men to sign up, usually for life, in a profession that was ill-paid, demeaning, and dangerous. Partly because desertion was a perennial problem, bright and gaudy uniforms were issued to the soldier so that he could be quickly recognized if intent on escape. Also, given the nature of linear tactics, there was no good reason for camouflaged uniforms. In Britain the standard uniform for both enlisted men and officers was a long red coat, worn over a waistcoat, and a three-cornered hat; that is, until the Napoleonic wars when officers took to wearing a two-cornered hat, the ends pointing sidewise in the manner made familiar in portraits of the emperor himself. Grenadiers were always the exception; they wore tall miter-shaped hats which were originally adopted so that the musket could be easily slung to free the hands for arming and throwing grenades. By the end of the Napoleonic wars both infantry officers and men were normally wearing the shako, a conical cap with a flat top and beak and sometimes with a high false front. Uniforms of the sorts described above, and with many variations thereof, are to be seen in abundance in Britain's many regimental museums, some of which will be identified below. The great fund of lore and knowledge concerning military battle dress is such an arcane science that only the most dedicated buff can hope to master it, but to those interested, these museums constitute a sort of living encyclopedia.

The French Revolution and Napoleon as its heir radically changed battle tactics, though during those long years of international warfare there was little significant revision in weaponry. Napoleon's great successes on the battlefield can be attributed to his brilliant and flexible use of the mass conscript armies which the Revolutionary governments had raised; his effective employment of artillery in the field; and his skill in rapidly deploying large armies over great distances, supplying themselves off the countryside and therefore not tied down by the logistical constraints that had immobilized the armies of the old regime. Not until the British moved into the Iberian Peninsula in 1808 to support nationalist uprisings among the Spanish and Portuguese against Napoleonic rule did the imperial armies of France suffer any serious setback. In command of both British and Portuguese troops in the Peninsular Campaign was Arthur Wellesley, later first duke of Wellington.

Wellington's chief contribution to the art of warfare stemmed from his appreciation of terrain. Instead of following the traditional practice of lining his troops up in a standing position to meet head-on the advancing French columns and lines of infantry, he normally kept his thin (only two-ranks deep) red line of soldiers concealed behind a reverse slope to surprise and discombobulate the enemy as they marched over the crest not yet ready to do battle. In any case, with the significant assistance of Portuguese regulars and Spanish guerrillas, the British at last succeeded in driving the French beyond the Pyrenees and then themselves crossed the River Bidassoa into France in October 1813. By that time Napoleon had already suffered his disastrous setback in the winter campaign in Russia, and almost on the date the French were retreating before Wellington's advancing troops, Napoleon incurred a major defeat in a three-day battle at Leipzig. Five months later he abdicated and was exiled to the little island of Elba in the Mediterranean while the triumphant allies entered Paris. In another five months he was back again to lead his troops once more, this time to the final denouement at Waterloo in Belgium on 15 October 1815. Here bad luck, faulty leadership, lack of aggressiveness on the part of his subordinates, and the tactical genius of Wellington drove the mighty emperor off the field and eventually into permanent exile on the distant Atlantic islet of St. Helena.

There are many monuments to Wellington scattered throughout Britain, including his elaborate tomb in **St. Paul's Cathedral** *(515)*, London. Also in London can be seen a fine collection of his trophies (including some splendid paintings picked up in Spain) in **Apsley House** *(526)* at the west end of Piccadilly. Initially built by Robert Adam in 1771–1778, this house was acquired by Marquess Wellesley in 1805, sold by him to his younger brother Arthur in 1817, and is now a Wellington museum. Of the officers and men who fought under him, the weapons they used, and the uniforms they wore, there are instructive reminders at the **National Army Museum** *(525)* London, and in the Rotunda of the **Royal Artillery Museum** *(536)* across the river in Woolwich. In the Cavalry Museum at **Plas Newydd** *(735)*, Anglesey, Gwynedd, are some interesting campaign relics of the first Marquess of Anglesey, including an artificial leg to replace the real one he lost at Waterloo. ("By God! I've lost my leg," remarked the then Lord Uxbridge to Wellington during the battle. "Have you, by God," said the Iron Duke, before summoning aid and galloping away.) At the Essex Regimental Museum in the **Chelmsford and Essex Museum** *(597)*, Chelmsford, Essex, is the Salamanca Eagle captured in Spain in 1812. Regimental museums like this abound throughout the country and almost all of them contain interesting relics of the eighteenth century and Napoleonic wars. The following are recommended: the **Cheshire Military Museum** *(673)* in Chester; the **Dorset Military Museum** *(568)*, Dorchester; the **Green Howards' Museum** *(685)*, Richmond, North Yorkshire; the **Household Cavalry Museum** *(565)*, Combermere Barracks, Windsor; the **King's Shropshire Light Infantry Museum** *(670)*, Sir John Moore Barracks, Capthorne, Shrewsbury, Salop; the Museum of the Border Regiment and King's Own Royal Border Regiment in the **Castle** *(709)*, Carlisle, Cumbria; the Museum of the Queen's Royal Surrey Regiment in **Clandon Park** *(556)*; the Museum of the Royal Welch Fusiliers in **Caernarvon Castle** *(737)*, Caernarvon, Gwynedd; the Pembroke Yeomanry Museum in the **Pembrokeshire Museum** *(725)*, Haverfordwest, Dyfed; the **First Queen's Dragoon Guards Regimental Museum** *(670)* in Shrewsbury; the Queen's Own Royal West Kent Regimental Museum in the **Maidstone Museum** *(543)*, Maidstone, Kent; the Royal Fusiliers Museum in the **Tower of London** *(513)*; the **Museum of the South Wales Borderers** *(721)*, Brecon, Powys; the Welch Regimental Museum in **Cardiff Castle** *(717)*, Cardiff, South Glamorgan; and the Museum of the Royal Manx Fencibles in the **Manx Museum** *(741)*, Douglas, Isle of Man.

Finally there is the beautifully arranged Wellington Museum adjoining **Stratfield Saye** *(565)*, the lovely seventeenth century country house near Reading with which a grateful Parliament endowed the duke after his return from Waterloo. Here he lived while serving as prime minister during the last two years of George IV's reign and for more than two decades after. His famous horse Copenhagen is buried in the park, which the writer Anthony Powell suspects must have appealed to the Iron Duke because it resembles a conventional battlefield (with reverse slopes and everything). He died at the age of eighty-three in **Walmer Castle** *(540)*, Kent, in a room still preserved as his memorial. The year was 1852. Queen Victoria had already been on the throne for fifteen years and railway tracks were crisscrossing England. The old duke by then was a relic of what seemed a distant age and of a civilization long since passed away.

CHAPTER X

THE NINETEENTH AND TWENTIETH CENTURIES: 1830–1945

WILLIAM IV: 1830–1837

Of the long line of English and British sovereigns from 1066 to the present, the name of William IV is easily the most forgettable. As duke of Clarence, he had spent much of his early life at sea with the Royal Navy and there had picked up enough salty mannerisms of speech to acquire a reputation for refreshing candor. He had lived with an actress named Mrs. Jordan long enough for her to have produced ten little Fitzclarences. Then, the death of George IV's daughter Charlotte put this younger brother to the king in the direct line of succession, so he promptly married the Princess Adelaide in the vain hope of begetting a legitimate heir. When in fact he did succeed to the throne in 1830 he proved to be an amiable though somewhat stupid sovereign who accepted, if ungraciously, the reduced role of the monarch in the governance of Britain. Though his reign was brief, it did coincide with three events of some significance as harbingers of things to come. In the long succeeding reign of his niece Victoria, the face of Britain would be visibly changed by the coming of the railroad and by the Gothic Revival in architecture; its politics, by the democratization of the franchise. All three developments had their beginnings in the 1830s when William IV was king.

Although experiments in steam-powered locomotion over parallel sets of iron tracks had already been undertaken throughout the previous decade, the railway age was seriously launched with the ceremonial opening of the Liverpool and Manchester line on 15 September 1830. Eight steam engines pulling trains of passenger coaches slowly made their way over the thirty-five miles from Liverpool to Manchester—and back again the same day. In recognition of the historic significance of the occasion, the coaches were gaily decked in red and crimson. Aboard one of them rode the old duke of Wellington himself. Four hundred thousand spectators lined the route. One was William Huskisson, member of Parliament from Liverpool and recent president of the Board of Trade, who inadvertently stepped into the path of an oncoming locomotive and was killed. The accident caused a six-hour delay in the cavalcade's return to Liverpool, but there had been no mechanical failures. It was an engineering triumph. It was also the death knell for England's canals.

Two years later the country took another lurch into the future with the passage by a Whig government under Earl (Charles) Grey of the Reform Bill of 1832. The measure curtailed somewhat the traditional aristocratic monopoly of the House of Commons by disfranchising a number of underpopulated pocket boroughs hitherto controlled by a small coterie of great landlords; by redistributing representation in favor of such industrial cities as Birmingham and Manchester as well as northern England and Scotland; and by extending the right to vote to certain segments of the population previously disfranchised. In general the act served to increase middle-class representation in the national legislature and partially to correct the disproportionate influence of the southern English counties as compared with the rest of Britain. The duke of Wellington announced that the House of Commons would no longer be a fit place for a gentleman, and that conservative convert, William Wordsworth, threatened to emigrate to Austria where law and order were still safe under the rule of Prince Metternich. Both were needlessly alarmed. Although the electorate was increased from five hundred thousand to over eight hundred thousand, no more than one man in seven was entitled to vote for members in the reformed House of Commons. That ancient bastion of privilege remained an aristocratic body. The Great Reform Bill of 1832 was, however, a beginning, though it would take more than another fifty years for Wellington's fears to be borne out in fact.

The reformed Parliament was not to assemble much longer at its traditional meeting place in the Palace of Westminster. The Middle Ages had their revenge on 16 October 1834 when a conflagration of old exchequer tally-sticks set fire to the House of Lords. Within hours the ancient palace, with the exception of Westminster Hall and the Jewel Tower, was a smoking ruin. Parliament was homeless. But not for long. The architectural community was invited at once to submit plans for a new building, to be designed in the late Gothic style of Henry VII's chapel in the neighboring Westminster Abbey. The winner was Charles Barry, assisted by Augustus Welby Northmore Pugin. Barry's design was too symmetrical, especially along the facade facing the Thames, to be purely Gothic, but there is no doubt about the medieval provenance of Pugin's decorative details—Gothic down to the inkwells. This was to be expected of the leading spokesman of the Gothic Revival—a Roman Catholic who considered all classical forms to be pagan and Renaissance architecture corrupt. In any case, though Barry was a reluctant Gothicist, his great clock tower housing the bell called Big Ben, the Victoria Tower at the other end, the central spire between them, and the numerous pinnacles and turrets all combine to give the **Houses of Parliament** *(521)* an unmistakably medieval appearance. It comes as a surprise to American visitors to London to learn that this building is of later construction than either the Capitol or the White House in Washington—also reconstructed after fires of British origin. The foundations were begun in 1837, the last year of William IV's reign; the first stone was laid in 1840; the clock tower completed in 1848; the Victoria Tower, in 1860. By then of course Queen Victoria was the reigning monarch.

QUEEN VICTORIA: 1837–1901

Only eighteen years of age on the death of her uncle, whom she considered as wicked as his brothers, Victoria succeeded to the throne as the sole heir of the duke of Kent, fourth son of George III. Though less than five feet in height, she was regal in bearing, imperious in manner, an expert horsewoman, and strong as a peasant—as indicated by her successful delivery of nine healthy children in twenty-one years of married life. She promptly made clear her deep aversion to the raffish ways of her royal uncles and instituted at court the regime of strict decorum that has made her name synonymous with straitlaced prudery. She even succeeded in persuading her first prime minister, Lord Melbourne, to mend his manners, sit straight in his chair, and refrain from the earthy language common among county Whig aristocrats of which he was prototypical. Melbourne succeeded nevertheless in shaping the young queen's mind and preparing her to play the ambiguous role of a constitutional monarch. His influence was paramount until her marriage in 1840 to Prince Albert of Saxe-Coburg-Gotha, an earnest German who understood the British constitution somewhat better than the queen herself. His friendship with Sir Robert Peel, head of the Tory party, made it easy for Victoria to forget her initial attachment to the Whigs and thereby helped to establish the important constitutional principle of royal impartiality between the two dominant political parties.

By the end of Victoria's reign most of the peculiar and lasting features of the British constitution were in place: cabinet government managed by a prime minister representing the majority party in the House of Commons; the calling of general elections when a prime minister lost control of the Commons; and the replacement of the government in office by one representing the opposing party if the electorate so decided at the polls. Gradually the size of the electorate itself was expanded to include almost all adult males. The second Reform Act of 1867 gave the franchise to all borough householders, which meant virtually all of the male urban working class. The third, passed in 1884, extended the same privilege to the counties, and in effect enfranchised the rural laboring man. Only the residual powers of the House of Lords to obstruct legislation remained to be abolished and the vote extended to women to complete the political democratization of Britain.

The happy and fruitful marriage of Victoria and Albert was symbolically sealed by the construction, in 1845–1848, of **Osborne House** *(559)* on the Isle of Wight. The prince himself designed the central block with help from Thomas Cubitt who had built Belgravia Square in London. Because he thought the nearby waters of the Solent resembled the Bay of Naples, Albert chose to emulate the style of the typical Italian villa, with two tall towers or campaniles and a first floor balcony or loggia. And because he was a practical German with a taste for modern engineering, he converted one of the campaniles into a water tank and the other into a clock tower. He also insisted on fireproof construction, though he was not so advanced as to require central heating. The house was meant to be a family residence remote from the formal rigors of Windsor Castle and Buckingham Palace. To cap the domestic scene he imported from Switzerland a cottage with miniature furniture for the enjoyment of the children and behind it installed a miniature fortress for juvenile games of war. Here at Osborne, as well as at their Scottish retreat at Balmoral, the queen and Prince Consort spent their happiest hours.

Albert died of typhoid fever in 1861, and Victoria was disconsolate. For six years she wore heavy mourning, retreated to Osborne and Balmoral whenever possible, and avoided public appearances—so much so that her ministers feared that the prestige of the monarchy might be permanently damaged. One of her few consolations in this dark period of her life was to oversee the construction of the **Albert Memorial** (525) in Kensington Gardens, London. Here is a monument without equal to High Victorian taste. Sir George Gilbert Scott, the foremost Gothic Revival architect of the mid-nineteenth century, was chosen to design it. Beneath a spired and pinnacled Gothic tabernacle sits a colossal bronze statue of the Prince Consort surrounded by works of sculpture illustrating the arts and sciences which he fostered. At the four corners of the monument are other sculptural groups representing Asia, Europe, Africa, and America; steps lead up to a podium decorated with a frieze of 169 noted poets, composers, artists, and architects (including Scott); at each corner of the podium are figures symbolizing Agriculture, Manufacture, Commerce, and Engineering; and rising from it are columns of red and gray granite enriched with cabochons of colored marble. The queen was pleased with the results, and later generations can be thankful to Sir George for having so nicely distilled the essence of the Victorian aesthetic.

The middle years of nineteenth century Britain were enriched, or at least enlivened, by the figure of Viscount Palmerston who served in six different governments as either foreign minister, home secretary, or prime minister. He was, in the words of the historian Asa Briggs, "the personification of England both at home and abroad." He was also the personification of self-confident Whiggery. Contentedly surveying the green Hampshire acres of his family estate at **Broadlands** (561), Palmerston no doubt believed he spoke for England when he proclaimed: "We have shown the example of a nation in which every class of society accepts with cheerfulness the lot which Providence has assigned to it." In his dealings with Europe he helped Belgium to achieve independence from Holland, and Garibaldi and Cavour to unite most of the Italian peninsula into one kingdom against Austrian opposition. In general he supported liberal causes on the Continent, though never to the detriment of English national interests, maintaining always that "we have no eternal allies and no permanent enemies," only permanent interests which "it is our duty to follow." Above all he warmed the hearts of his countrymen when he asserted: "As the Roman, in days of old, held himself free from indignity, when he could say *Civis Romanus sum*, so also a British subject, in whatever land he may be, shall feel confident that the watchful eye and strong arm of England will protect him against injustice and wrong." Such talk fed the patriotic xenophobia of many an ordinary Englishman who in his heart, as Charles Dickens put it, "considered other countries a mistake."

By the time of Palmerston's death in 1865 the old labels, Whig and Tory, were giving way to the more dignified party appellations of Liberal and Conservative. "Every boy and every girl/That's born into the world alive," ran a song in Gilbert and Sullivan's *Iolanthe*, "Is either a little Liberal/Or else a little Conservative." The differences between the two, however, are not so easy to define as the ditty implies. In general the Liberals supported the demands of Nonconformists (Dissenters) for the complete secularization of the state and were somewhat isolationist, anti-imperialist, and parsimonious toward the army and navy; while the Conservatives defended the few remaining special privileges of the Church of England, were shameless imperialists, and supported the armed forces. In actuality, however, both were coalition parties and vied with each other in promoting progressive legislation to extend the political franchise, modernize the British government, and ameliorate some of the worst evils spawned by the country's rapid industrialization and urbanization. Their respective leaders for most of the two decades following Palmerston's death in 1865 were William Ewart Gladstone and Benjamin Disraeli. Both were extraordinarily complex in their make-ups—Gladstone a High Church Anglican who allied himself politically with Nonconformists; a natural conservative who attacked such citadels of privilege as the army and the civil service; a wealthy landowner (his country estate was Hawarden Castle, Clwyd) who sought to extend the franchise to the working class; a cheerless puritan who could hold large audiences spellbound with his matchless oratory; Disraeli a born Jew who gloried in the Church of England; a man of middle-class origins who advocated Tory democracy (i.e., an alliance between aristocracy and proletariat against the bourgeoisie); a grotesque figure who captivated women of high degree including the queen; a successful novelist *(Vivian Grey, Coningsby, Sybil,* and *Tancred)* who was an astute practical politician; a social climber whose company was sought by titled lords and ladies. The better to play the role of landed aristocrat appropriate to a leader of the Conservative party, he purchased **Hughenden Manor** *(623)* near High Wycombe, Buckinghamshire. This was an undistinguished country house which he and his wife transformed into a fashionably Gothic mansion and which now houses a museum of Disraeli mementos. After his death in 1881, Queen Victoria paid a special visit to Hughenden and closeted herself for a time in the study to mourn the passing of this dear friend who had bestowed on her the title of Empress of India.

Her affection for Disraeli was matched by her intense dislike of Gladstone whom she once described as "an old, wild, and incomprehensible man." But by this time the monarch's personal likes and dislikes had long since ceased to have much bearing on the course of British politics.

During the last two decades of Victoria's reign, the central political issue, whose solution escaped both parties, was the question of Irish home rule. At the beginning of the century the Act of Union had joined Ireland to Great Britain to form the United Kingdom, thereby admitting a hundred Irish members to the House of Commons and twenty-eight Irish peers and four bishops to the House of Lords. After the Catholic Emancipation Act of 1829, representatives of Ireland's dominant religion were eligible at last to sit in both houses. They were, however, easily outvoted, and by the mid-1870s the Irish bloc, under the leadership of Charles Parnell, began agitating for an independent parliament and civil service in Dublin under the British Crown but otherwise free of control by Westminster except in matters relating to foreign affairs. Parnell fell into public disgrace in 1890 as the result of being named correspondent in a much publicized divorce case. By this time Gladstone had taken up the cause of home rule in Parliament and in 1886 had split the Liberal party, causing the defection of a sizeable bloc of so-called Liberal Unionists. Four years later he succeeded in getting a modified home rule bill through the Commons only to be defeated in the House of Lords. There the matter stood when the old queen died in 1901. She had occupied the throne for sixty-four years, the longest reign in British history. Four years before her death the nation had celebrated her Diamond Jubilee—a great outpouring of patriotic affection for this strong-minded serious woman whose tastes, beliefs, and prejudices so accurately mirrored those of the British bourgeoisie. When he had learned the queen's opinion on any subject, remarked the Conservative prime minister, Lord Salisbury, he "knew pretty certainly what view her subjects would take, and especially the middle class of her subjects." Her death marked not only the end of a reign but of an era of progress, prosperity, and power which Britain would never see again. Statues representing her likeness are to be seen in public parks and in front of public buildings all over Britain. Perhaps the most conspicuous is the **Queen Victoria Memorial** *(520)* in front of Buckingham Palace, London. Designed by Sir Aston Webb, this monument of white marble consists of a seated figure of the great queen crowned by a gilded bronze figure of Victory and surrounded by statues of marble and bronze representing Truth, Motherhood, Justice, Peace and Progress, Science and Art, Manufacture and Agriculture, and Naval and Military Power. Now—on any weekday around eleven in the morning—it is likely to be overrun with disrespectful tourists, intent only on the spectacle afforded by the changing of the palace guard.

THE EDWARDIAN ERA: 1901–1914

In the light of what took place after 1914, the years before the first world war in retrospect seem carefree, colorful, and affluent. This was the Edwardian Era, though the aging King Edward VII held the scepter for only nine years, to be succeeded on his death in 1910 by his second son, George V, whose popular reign then lasted until 1936. Both as Prince of Wales and sovereign, Edward's imposing, portly figure impressed itself on the public imagination. His ebullient personality and raffish ways, his womanizing, gambling, and sporty extravagance set British manners and morals on a new course from which there was to be no return to the repressive respectability of Victoria's reign. Beatrice Webb referred to him as "this utterly commonplace person." She deplored "the new vulgarians, those loud, extremely rich men for whom the prince had an abiding taste." The judgment—not unexpected from a Victorian blue-stocking and Socialist to boot—is no doubt unduly harsh. He was a gregarious man of huge appetites, deprived of any serious responsibilities for the first sixty years of his life by his mother's refusal to delegate any of her regal responsibilities and easily seduced by the calculated generosity of the *nouveaux riches.*

On the heir apparent's coming of age in 1861 his parents had presented him with a country estate in Norfolk to which he soon brought his Danish bride, the Princess Alexandra. This was **Sandringham House** *(607)*, still among the favorite residences of the royal family, though now open to the public in summertime. It is a large though unpretentious mansion, built in 1870 in a neo-Jacobean style, set among magnificent parks and gardens. Here Edward as Prince of Wales and king could entertain his rich friends royally, especially during shooting season when the kill was gargantuan thanks to the recently invented quick-firing, breech-loading gun. In one year alone at Sandringham, 30,000 birds were shot. Queen Victoria visited here but twice; she found it "handsome."

In 1905 the Liberal party returned to power under the leadership of Sir Henry Campbell-Bannerman, who died in 1908 to be replaced by Herbert Henry Asquith who remained prime minister until 1916. But the real star in the Liberal galaxy was a Welshman of humble (though by no means impoverished) background named David Lloyd George. He grew up in the village of Llanystumdwy, Gwynedd, where the **Lloyd George Memorial Museum** *(740)* now houses an interesting collection of his relics. Though he would later emerge as Britain's wartime leader, in Asquith's government of 1908 he served as chancellor of the exchequer. It was in that capacity that he introduced his famous People's Budget. The revenue measures he proposed, though moderate by present standards, were deemed confiscatory by Britain's upper classes: a super tax on incomes, excise taxes on certain luxury goods, and stiff taxes on unearned increment from land. The fact that some of the moneys thus extracted were to go toward financing old-age pensions and social insurance for the poor seemed proof positive that this was a socialistic attack on the rights of property, and the House of Lords rejected the budget after it was passed in the Commons. The ensuing general election was defined by the Liberals as a test of "Peers versus people." The Peers lost. The Lords then bowed to necessity and passed the budget only to be faced with a new measure to deprive the upper house of all authority over money bills and reduce its veto power over other legislation to a mere delaying action of two years. As in 1832 the threat of swamping the House of Lords, by the creation of as many new Peers as necessary, was sufficient to bring a majority around to reason, and the Parliament Act of 1911 was passed.

The battle of the budget was only one indication that the social fabric of Britain, apparently so tightly woven at the end of Victoria's reign, was rapidly coming apart. Labor unions were becoming restive, and in 1913 railway men, transport workers, and miners threatened a general strike. Aggressive feminists, led by Mrs. Emmeline Pankhurst and her daughter Christobel, opened up a campaign of arson and vandalism to persuade Parliament to legalize women's suffrage. When the Liberal government finally passed a bill authorizing home rule for Ireland, civil war was threatened in Ulster where militant Protestants declined the honor of being incorporated into a semi-independent state ruled from Catholic Dublin. In March 1914, fifty-eight British army officers stationed at Curragh resigned their commissions rather than participate in the expected "coercion" of Ulster. Whether this was technically mutiny, as it was labeled at the time, is doubtful, but there is no doubt that the long-simmering Irish problem was rapidly coming to a boil. The politics of consensus, by which Britain had been governed since 1832, was no longer working. Only the outbreak of the Great War in August 1914 saved the country from a series of confrontations on a wide range of issues for which there were no easy solutions. Liberal England was approaching its demise.

THE BRITISH ECONOMY: 1830–1914

For the first fifty years of the nineteenth century industry expanded at an accelerating rate and Britain easily maintained her lead over other nations still in the infant-industry stage. By 1850 British mines were producing fifty million tons of coal per year; pig-iron output of over two million tons represented half the world's production; one thousand eight hundred cotton factories employed 328,000 workers and were powered by steam-engines with seventy-one thousand total horsepower. More statistics would be redundant. Britain had become, in the words of Disraeli, the "workshop of the world."

To celebrate this triumph of inventiveness, diligence, good management and good luck, Lord Palmerston's government, with strong encouragement from the Prince Consort, sponsored the Great Exhibition of the Works of Industry of All Nations which opened its gates on 1 May 1851 and closed on 11 October after having welcomed more than six million visitors. More than thirteen thousand exhibitors displayed an astonishing variety of factory-made products ranging in usefulness from square carriage wheels to the last word in coal scuttles. And the greatest of all the exhibits was the building itself in Hyde Park, London, where this fabulous collection of ingenious artifacts was housed. This was the great Crystal Palace designed by the duke of Devonshire's head gardener, Joseph Paxton. Built of glass and iron, its three tiers of shining, flat-roofed terraces, with a high central transept, covered eighteen acres of ground, enclosed two ancient elm trees, proved strong enough to withstand a gale, and was cleverly ventilated to prevent condensation. It was a miracle of engineering and a noble experiment in functional design, unfortunately mostly overlooked by professional architects for the remainder of the century and beyond. When the Exhibition closed down, the Crystal Palace was dismantled and reerected across the river in Sydenham where it was destroyed by fire in 1936.

The greatest of Britain's nineteenth century industrial accomplishments, however, could not be housed in the Crystal Palace. These were the railways with their vast network of tracks, tunnels, bridges, viaducts, stations, locomotives, cars, signal towers, and miscellaneous other equipment. The first railways were merely short stretches of track usually associated with collieries or canals over which horse-pulled cars could travel with relative ease. Stationary steam engines were occasionally installed to haul the cars up steep gradients. In 1802 Richard Trevithick designed a locomotive, i.e., a steam engine on wheels, which was put to use at the Coalbrookdale Ironworks in Salop. Trevithick's engine has not survived, but a similar model, called Puffing Billy and designed by William Hedley, is on view at the **Science Museum** *(526)* in South Kensington, London. In 1814 George Stephenson, usually considered the father of steam locomotion, designed a locomotive for use at Killingworth near Newcastle; it is now on view at the **Science Museum** *(701)* in Newcastle-upon-Tyne. By the late 1820s locomotives were being built with pistons connected directly to their wheels by connecting rods. Two of these—Locomotion and Derwent—can be seen at the **Darlington North Road Station Railway Museum** *(699)* in Darlington, County Durham. They were employed on the Stockton and Darlington railway which opened for business in 1825 and operated at first on the principle that the toll-paying customers would furnish their own cars and carriages, either to be pulled by horse or by locomotives hired out by the company. Then in 1829 the recently chartered Liverpool and Manchester Railway, whose directors were still undecided as to the relative merits of stationary engines and locomotives, offered a prize for the locomotive that performed best at a series of trials at Rainhill near Liverpool. George Stephenson entered two—Rocket and Sans Pareil, both now to be seen at the **Science Museum** *(526)* in London. Rocket won the day because of the superiority of Stephenson's boiler design. The next year occurred the grand opening of the Liverpool and Manchester, already described at the beginning of this chapter. This was the first line to carry passengers and the first to be completely worked by steam from the beginning. Its immediate commercial success set the pattern for all future railway development.

Within six years of the grand opening, nearly two thousand miles of railway had been sanctioned by acts of Parliament, including most of the major trunk routes terminating in London. In 1848 alone more than twelve hundred miles of track were opened. By 1852, with the completion of the Great Northern main line from London to York, nearly all the major routes in England had been developed, though more were still to be built in Scotland and Wales. By the end of the century the United Kingdom boasted a network of more than twenty thousand miles of train tracks.

Standard gauge for the distance between the two parallel tracks was four feet, eight and a half inches, the traditional width between the wheels of coal wagons first adopted by the Stockton and Darlington. Only one of the large companies used a wider gauge of seven feet, one quarter inch. This was the Great Western. Some of its unusual locomotives, as well as a great variety of other equipment, are on display at the **Great Western Railway Museum** *(576)* in Swindon, Wiltshire. This town built by the company itself—the first major railway town—was located approximately midway between London and Bristol and at a place where locomotives suitable for the heavy gradients to the west could be changed. Visitors to this excellent museum should pause to examine terraces of workers' houses, the institute, and the church—all built by the company, perhaps to the design of Isambard Kingdom Brunel, the Great Western's engineering genius. Only in Wales were narrow gauge railways retained in any significant number, mostly intended to haul slate to the west coast for transshipment. A number of these have recently been restored to operation for the benefit of tourists who can now enjoy the splendid mountain scenery of Wales in the comfort of renovated railway coaches pulled by tiny puffing steam locomotives. The **Talyllyn Railway** *(741)* can be picked up at either Tywyn or Abergwynolwyn in Gwynedd and covers the six and a half miles between them. The **Festiniog Railway** *(740)* runs for nine and a half miles between Porthmadog and Dduault in Gwynedd; the **Vale of Rheidol Railway** *(724)* from Aberysthwyth, Dyfed, twelve miles inland to the Devil's Bridge; the **Welshpool and Llanfair Railway** *(718)*, from Llanfair Caereinion six and a half miles west to Sylfaen, both near Welshpool, Powys; and the **Snowdon Mountain Railway** *(739)* climbs this spectacular mountain to its summit from Llanberis, Gwynedd.

But of all the relics of the railway age in Britain, nothing is quite so exciting to view as the great steam locomotives, of which there are almost nine hundred still in existence. The best single collection is on view at the **National Railway Museum** *(690)* in York. Here are thirty-two steam locomotives, four which ran by electric power, and three diesel engines. Americans who remember only the sooty black steam engines of their childhood will be astonished at the beautiful array of colors in which these powerful locomotives are garbed. The museum also houses a great variety of passenger and freight cars, stationary cable-winding engines, station equipment of all kinds, and the iron bridge that spanned the River Gaunless on the original route of the Stockton and Darlington.

Railway bridges *in situ* of course abound throughout the country. Brick and stone were commonly used in the early days of building, but gradually iron took over, and later steel and concrete. Of the extant wrought-iron bridges, three especially are worth noting. The first is the **Conwy Railway Bridge** *(738)* in Gwynedd, which crosses the broad Conwy estuary just upstream from Telford's castellated suspension bridge. As designed by George Stephenson's son Robert, it consisted of a pair of parallel iron tubes, each containing a single track. To avoid underwater engineering, the tubes were built on shore and floated into position, raised by hydraulic rams, then riveted end to end to form a pair of continuous beams. The same procedure was later used on the much longer **Britannia Bridge** *(734)* built by the Chester and Holyhead Railway across the Menai Strait parallel to, and southwest of, Telford's famous suspension bridge across which today's motorist still travels. Again Robert Stephenson was the engineer, and he himself drove the last rivet in March 1850. Unfortunately, a fire in 1970 required rebuilding the bridge in steel, so that much of Stephenson's work is no longer visible. Nine years after the opening of the Britannia Bridge an even more remarkable feat was accomplished by Isambard K. Brunel. This was the **Royal Albert Bridge** *(597)* at Saltash, Cornwall, built for the Cornwall Railway across the River Tamar west of Plymouth and opened to traffic in May 1859 by the Prince Consort himself. At Menai, Stephenson could raise a central pier on a rocky island midway across the strait. Here water covered the entire area to be spanned, so that Brunel had to create an artificial island by lowering a three-hundred-ton cylinder, seventeen feet in diameter, to rest on the bedrock of the estuary floor beneath the mud. It was the first occasion of the use of a pressurized caisson for underwater work, and an engineering milestone.

The daring ingenuity of men like Brunel and the two Stephensons deserves more credit than it normally gets and more attention than is usually accorded it by today's travellers, accustomed as they are to the more grandiose feats of twentieth century engineering. It must be remembered that these men, and others like them, were truly pioneers. They were working in fields where no precedents existed, no systematic body of knowledge, no textbooks, no formal university training, no well-endowed research foundations. They were improvisers *par excellence*.

Another good example of pragmatic innovation is the nineteenth century railway station. Large numbers of people arriving and departing simultaneously had to be accommodated; trains turned around or switched from track to track; tickets sold; freight loaded and discharged —all under one roof or at least in one central location, usually in a crowded city center. Also, inbound and outbound passengers required overnight accommodations close to the point of debarkation and embarkation. To meet these novel challenges, engineers and architects joined forces to create that most typical of Victorian architectural accomplishments—the railway station *cum* hotel.

King's Cross Station *(528)*, London, built in 1851–1852 to the design of Lewis Cubitt, best illustrates the purely engineering approach to the logistical challenge inherent in railway operation. This was the London terminus of the Great Northern Railway. Though hardly a thing of beauty, it is a unique example of nineteenth century functional design unadorned with the decorative frills common to later buildings of the same type. What Cubitt did here was simply to lay two huge semicylindrical sheds side by side—one for arrivals, the other for departures, the two joined together by crosswalks and faced with a rather simple brick facade with a colonnade for carriages underneath and a clock tower in the middle. Simple, however, is not the word to describe **St. Pancras Station** *(529)* across the street from King's Cross. Begun in 1865 and completed in 1868 to the design of the engineer William Henry Barlow, this London terminus of the Midland Railway had a single span of cast-iron arch braces stretching for 240 feet across the train shed—for a century the largest station roof in the world without internal supports. St. Pancras is notable today, however, not for its station but for the Midland Grand Hotel which fronts it. This was designed by Sir George Gilbert Scott, the foremost Gothic Revival architect of the Victorian era, and opened for business in 1873, the first hotel in London to have elevators (lifts) operated by hydraulic power—then called ascending rooms. This red-brick monster, now used for railway offices, was in its day considered a Gothic masterpiece. **Paddington Station** *(528)* was built in the 1850s for the Great Western Railway by I. K. Brunel. Here there is no visible exterior because the sheds were inserted into a cutting in a hillside which was roofed over. Inside, Brunel set cast-iron columns to support a gigantic triple roof of glass and wrought iron and hired the architect Digby Wyatt to design the ironwork in a style that has been variously described as Elizabethan, Moorish, and Renaissance. The adjacent **Great Western Royal Hotel** *(528)* was built to the plan of P. C. Hardwick in a style meant to resemble that of the French Renaissance; it was equipped not only with electric clocks and bells but with hot-water pipes as linen-racks—a luxury still to be found in some British hotels, to the great delight of their American guests unaccustomed to such sybaritic delights as hot towels. **Victoria Station** *(523)*, London, built in the 1860s as the combined terminal of the London, Chatham, and Dover and the London, Brighton, and South Coast railways has been so badly cut up and modernized by British Rail that it is barely recognizable today as a Victorian building. Next door, however, the **Grosvenor Hotel** *(521)* built in 1860–1861 to a design by J. T. Knowles is a splendid example of High Victorian French Renaissance, made doubly attractive by a recent recleaning. **Charing Cross Station and Hotel** *(517)* were constructed between 1859 and 1864 to designs by Sir John Hawkshaw and Edward Middleton Barry, the younger son of Sir Charles Barry, architect of the Houses of Parliament. Originally the London terminus of the South-Eastern Railway, the station has been modified beyond recognition, but the hotel, in spite of reconstruction of the upper stories following bomb damage in 1941, still reveals its Victorian Renaissance origins; and its interior, especially the dining room, has retained the nineteenth century splendor so typical of these early railway hotels. The most noticeable feature of the Charing Cross complex, however, is Barry's cast-iron Eleanor Cross meant to be a replica of the stone version erected in the thirteenth century near this site in honor of Edward I's recently deceased queen. **Liverpool Street Station** *(511)*, still serving the City of London, was opened in 1875 for the Great Eastern Railway. The original building, ecclesiastical Gothic in character, comprises the western part of the present station; the eastern end was added twenty years later. Up the hill is the **Great Eastern Hotel** *(511)* built in 1884 by Sir Charles Barry and enlarged in 1901–1906 by Robert Edis. The style is Anglo-French-Renaissance; the interior public rooms are grand; and it is the only hotel in the City.

Before leaving London, mention should be made of the origins of its justly famous underground. Under an act of Parliament passed in 1854 the Metropolitan Railway opened the first underground railway in the world on 10 January 1863. It ran from Paddington Station to King's Cross and on to Farringdon Street, and originally used broad-gauged locomotives and coaches supplied by the Great Western Railway. Later came the District Railway which ran along the Victoria Embankment on the north side of the river; in time the two companies together created the underground belt around central London, now called the Inner Circle. At the recently opened **London Transport Museum** *(518)*, situated in the old flower market of Covent Garden, can be seen a Metropolitan Railway Class-A locomotive, built in 1866 and designed specifically for use in the underground system with provision for capturing and reusing steam emissions so as to reduce the discharge of steam and smoke in the tunnels. Also to be seen here are underground coaches, an early lift from the Hampstead Station, a working model of an escalator, and various other pieces of equipment associated with this remarkable system which made London, of all the great cities in the world, the easiest to get around quickly, safely, and cheaply.

Provincial railway stations, some with adjacent hotels, are, in many respects, more attractive today than those in London. Smaller, usually cleaner, and less crowded than their metropolitan counterparts, many of them are well worth inspecting as monuments to Victorian industry and culture. One of the best is **Temple Meads Station** *(580)* in Bristol, Brunel's western terminus for the Great Western Railway. Its exterior is mock Tudor; its interior iron arches are flattened in the Perpendicular manner; and the roof is supported by hammer beams more or less copied from Westminster Hall. Later in the nineteenth century a second shed was added, with Gothic-type iron arches, not unlike those at St. Pancras. **York Railway Station** *(693)* was built in 1873–1877 to a design by Thomas Prosser. A plaque placed on the wall in 1977 describes it as one of the great buildings of Victorian England, which is perhaps hyperbolic, but not extravagantly so. On a hill overlooking the station is the lovely **Royal Station Hotel** *(690)* set in a colorful garden and still retaining its original aura of Victorian grandeur. **Newcastle Central Station** *(700)* in Newcastle-upon-Tyne also had Thomas Prosser as one of its builders, and, as at York, the train shed here has a pronounced curve which somehow emphasizes the feeling of spaciousness produced by the absence of intermediate supports for the curved ribs forming the framework of the roof. Manchester's station is now derelict and serves as a car park, but the nearby **Midland Hotel** *(694)* is a good example of *fin-de-siècle* Victorian baroque with a Frenchified interior. The **Railway Station** *(668)* at Stoke-on-Trent, Staffordshire, originally serving the North Staffordshire Railway and built in 1850, has a charming Jacobean appearance, a style also carried out in the **North Stafford Hotel** *(668)* just across the square. **Huddersfield Station** *(680)*, Huddersfield, West Yorkshire, is a splendid neoclassical structure with a pedimented portico supported by Corinthian columns and a fine symmetrical facade broken by Corinthian pilasters. It was opened in 1847. **Monkwearmouth Station** *(703)*, Sunderland, Tyne-and-Wear, opened the following year, sports an Ionic portico with Doric features at the corners and now serves as a railway museum. **Brighton Station's** *(547)* curving glass train shed with its tall and slender iron columns is a delightfully airy place; while **Riverside Station** *(565)*, Windsor, just across the bridge from Eton College, is a charming "Gothic" structure of red brick with mullioned Tudor windows and a waiting room reserved for the queen and Prince Consort with the initials *VR* and *PA* inlaid in the wall in black brick.

Railway building continued throughout the nineteenth century and into the twentieth, but by 1870 had reached its peak, and indeed in terms of total mileage Britain by that time had ceased to be the world's leading railway nation. It remained, however, the world's predominant maritime power. Of the total volume of world trade in 1885, Britain's share was roughly twenty percent, while that of Germany, France, and the United States together came to only twenty-seven percent. In shipbuilding Britain's leadership was even more pronounced. By the end of the century her shipyards were responsible for sixty percent of all ships launched, and this figure remained approximately the same up until the first world war. Iron ships driven by screw propellers powered by steam took the lead in maritime traffic after Isambard Kingdom Brunel designed the **S.S. Great Britain** *(580)* which became the prototype for a whole generation of oceangoing vessels. She was launched at Bristol by Prince Albert on 19 July 1843, served briefly on the Atlantic run to New York, made over thirty voyages to Melbourne, Australia, and ended her days as a storage hulk in the Falkland Islands after suffering such severe damage rounding Cape Horn in 1886 as to render her un- seaworthy. In 1970, however, she was towed back to Bristol and in- stalled in Wapping Dock where she had been built. Partially restored to her original appearance, "the most important ship ever built" is now open to view. Another Brunel-designed vessel, though on a much more modest scale is the dredger *Bertha* on display at the **Exeter Maritime Museum** *(587)*, Exeter, Devon. She was built in 1844 to clear mud from the docksides at Bridgewater. At the **Windermere Steamship Museum** *(714)* in Bowness, Cumbria, is a fascinating collection of lake steamers, including the steam launch *Dolly*, advertised as the oldest mechani- cally powered boat in the world.

Despite the obvious advantages of steam for inland-water sailing or for scheduled runs at sea where time was too precious to depend on the vagaries of wind and current, the day of the sailing ship was far from ended with the advent of marine engines fired by coal. In the decade of the 1860s, shipping tonnage registered in the United Kingdom showed only 724,000 tons for steamships as against 4,590,000 for sailing ships; and even as late as the first decade of the twentieth century, more than one sixth of British tonnage was still under sail. Though the opening of the Suez Canal in 1860 gave a distinct advantage to steamships in the trade to India and the Far East, sail was still the most economical means of power on many round-the-world routes, in the wool trade from Australia, and the grain trade from the west coast of America. Typical of the ships engaged in this commerce was the **Cutty Sark** *(535)*, now moored at King William's Walk in Greenwich. A clipper ship, built in Scotland in 1869 of iron frames with wooden planking, she was for a few years engaged in the China trade but after that employed mainly on the London-Aus- tralia run carrying general cargoes to Sydney and Melbourne and return- ing with bales of wool. Thanks mostly to the intervention of Prince Philip she has been restored and opened to the public since 1957. Another sailing ship open to view—and one of an unusual type—is the **Discovery** *(517)*, moored alongside the Victoria Embankment, London. She is a barque rigged vessel with an auxiliary steam engine, built in 1901 and commanded by Captain R. F. Scott on his expeditions to the Antarctic, including his last voyage there in 1904 when he met his death near the South Pole. Her hull, surprisingly, was built of wood.

Britain's headstart in the development of steam power was matched in the late nineteenth and early twentieth centuries by a remark- able tardiness in getting into the production of the gasoline (petrol)- powered internal combustion engine for use in the horseless carriage or automobile. In 1885–1886 a German, Gottfried Daimler, patented the high-speed internal combustion engine, and in 1894 the Frenchman Levassor in effect invented the modern automobile with an engine in front under a hood (bonnet) and hand- and foot-operated controls more or less as they still are. That British capital and industry played no part in these developments, nor in any of the early improvements in what came to be called the motor car, is partly attributable to restrictive legislation passed in 1865 which made it illegal to drive a powered vehicle along a public road at a speed of more than four miles an hour and furthermore required the driver to be accompanied by a helper walking in front with a red flag. In 1896 the Locomotives on Highways Act eliminated the helper and raised the speed limit to 14 miles an hour. To celebrate the occasion the London to Brighton Run was organized, though only ten of the thirty-three starters finished the course. It is still run, with antique cars, once a year. In 1904 a partnership was formed between a British engineer, F. H. Royce, and an importer of foreign cars, C. S. Rolls, and an automobile factory set up near Derby. The first model of the Rolls-Royce car was produced that year and is now on display at the **Science Museum** *(526)*, South Kensington, London. It is a two-cylinder, ten horsepower machine and registered one hundred thousand miles before it was retired. It cost, however, a thousand pounds, which of course confined its sale to the very rich. Automobile driving indeed was primarily a rich man's sport in Britain until after the first world war. No car was produced that could compare in cheapness to the mass-produced Model T with which Henry Ford was flooding the American market. It is not surprising then that the best displays of pre–World War I cars in Britain today are associated with the country homes of the wealthy. The most complete exhibit is at the **National Motor Museum** *(560)* on the grounds of Lord Montagu's **Palace House (Beaulieu Abbey)** *(560)* near Lyndhurst, Hampshire. This is a truly magnificent collection which includes such early models as Panhard's own seven horsepower car of 1902, a 1903 Daimler, and the Silver Ghost Rolls-Royce, manufactured in 1907. There is another, though less ambitious, antique car museum at **Caister Castle** *(606)* near Great Yarmouth, Norfolk. At **Sandringham House** *(607)*, Norfolk, can be seen a number of splendid Daimlers owned by members of the royal family, including the 1900 Daimler Tonneau driven by King Edward VII, the first motor car ever to be bought by a British sovereign. Also the **Museum of Science and Industry** *(665)*, Birmingham, has a nice collection of veteran cars as does the **Herbert Art Gallery and Museum** *(665)* in Coventry, West Midlands.

The lassitude of British engineers and entrepreneurs in respect to the infant automobile industry was a dangerous symptom, though few recognized it as such at the time. The fact is that by the turn of the century Britain was beginning to lose her industrial lead. In 1886 American steel output passed that of the United Kingdom, and beginning in 1893 so did Germany's. In the chemical industry, Germany, and even France, were far outstripping Britain. On the outbreak of World War I, the Germans were supplying the British market with eighty percent of its artificial dyes, and, astonishingly, the khaki used for the army's uniforms came from Stuttgart. Even in the cotton textile industry, the birthplace of the Industrial Revolution, American mills were beginning to outproduce those of Lancashire which clung to the outmoded spinning mule while their competitors were converting to ring spinning, a far more efficient process. American mines were installing coal-cutting machinery, while those in Wales and northeastern England still clung to the tried-and-true methods of pick and dynamite.

The fault lay not, however, in obsolescent machinery. Worn-out machines could have been replaced had there been a disposition to do so. What was more dangerously wearing out was British initiative, imagination, inventiveness, and diligence. Many industrial firms were now owned by the third and fourth generations of the families that had founded them. Nepotism bred indifferent management. The long weekend—an Edwardian invention—became a way of life. Businessmen bought country estates and seats in the House of Lords, while genuine peers accepted company directorships for which they had no experience and little talent. English higher education, dominated by the two medieval universities, though strong in classics (Oxford) and mathematics (Cambridge), was feeble in applied science and technology. Compulsory secondary education for the masses was slow in coming. While American companies were undertaking time-work studies and introducing efficient, if cold-blooded, systems of management, British factory and office discipline remained lax. Industrial output per man hour was standing still. Real wages, which had risen steadily since about 1850, leveled off after 1905. Capital that might have been invested in industrial modernization at home was instead going abroad or to the colonies. Imports were exceeding exports—the balance of payments kept favorable only by interest payments, insurance premiums, and shipping charges. Stagnation was setting in.

LITERATURE, EDUCATION, AND RELIGION: 1830–1914

Perhaps the dry rot afflicting British industry was no more than the inevitable decay of the capitalist system, occurring earlier in Britain than elsewhere because that was where it had reached its most advanced state of development. Such, certainly, would have been the explanation of Karl Marx, the German refugee who had spent long hours of study in the reading room of the British Museum to produce his great seminal work, *Das Kapital,* the first volume of which was published in 1867. He died in London and is buried, along with many other notables, in **Highgate Cemetery** *(530)* where his grave today is marked by an enormous bust. Few people in nineteenth century Britain, however, read Marx's turgid tome, if for no other reason than that the first English translation did not appear until 1887. Anyway, Britain was producing its own crop of highly readable social critics to challenge a system which seemed to sacrifice humane values to the pursuit of profit and to replace God with Mammon.

Foremost among them was Thomas Carlyle, a native of southern Scotland who moved to London in 1834. His place of residence until his death in 1881 was in Cheyne Row, Chelsea, and is now called **Carlyle's House** *(524)*, a fine museum run by the National Trust. In *Sartor Resartus* (first published in Boston in 1836) he attacked the hedonistic materialism of contemporary utilitarian philosophers (Jeremy Bentham, et al.) who had pronounced happiness, defined as the satisfaction of material wants, to be the prime objective of human existence. Not happiness, but union with God, said Carlyle, was the highest aim of life, and this was to be achieved by renunciation and hard work. In a later book, *Past and Present,* he specifically blamed industrialization, with its exaltation of "the cash nexus of man with man" as the cause of the nation's spiritual decline, and urged a return to the ideals of medieval monasticism.

Among Victorian England's many successful novelists, the most popular was Charles Dickens, whose pages teem with the pitiful victims of nineteenth century industrialism and the legal system which undergirded it. The specific evils he attacked included: debtors prisons in *David Copperfield* and *Little Dorritt,* the Poor Laws in *Oliver Twist,* the English schools in *Nicholas Nickleby,* niggardly employers in *A Christmas Carol,* business ethics in *Martin Chuzzlewit,* and chronic industrial unemployment in *Hard Times.* Today, there are several museums of Dickens's mementos. The best is the **Dickens House** *(516)*, 48 Doughty Street in the Bloomsbury section of London. Here the author lived while writing *Oliver Twist* and *Nicholas Nickleby.* The house contains a large library of Dickens's manuscripts and books as well as a museum of personal relics. On the grounds of **Eastgate House** *(543)*, Rochester, Kent, is the Swiss chalet which Dickens used as a study. His birthplace, now another **Dickens Museum** *(560)*, is on Commercial Road, Portsmouth, Hampshire.

Of the later nineteenth century novelist, Thomas Hardy, it could not be said that he was so much a social critic as a deeply pessimistic realist whose philosophy denied the comfortable Victorian assumption, so succinctly expressed by the poet Robert Browning that "God's in His heaven/All's right with the world." Born in Dorset, Hardy's best novels *(Far from the Madding Crowd, The Return of the Native, The Mayor of Casterbridge, Tess of the D'Urbervilles)* are laid in that and neighboring counties, and if his views of human behavior were jaundiced, his celebration of the natural beauties of the English countryside was almost as lyrical as Wordsworth's. His birthplace, **Hardy's Cottage** *(568)*, can still be seen (though not entered except by appointment) in Higher Bockhampton, northeast of Dorchester; while within Dorchester itself (Hardy's Casterbridge) on High West Street the **Dorset Museum** *(567)* contains a reconstruction of the author's study as it was about 1900, as well as other Hardy relics.

More incisive and devastating in his attacks on prevailing English mores than either Dickens or Hardy was the Irish-born George Bernard Shaw whose highly successful plays straddle the nineteenth and twentieth centuries. He was a socialist, pacificist, and iconoclast. The best of his dramas (except for *Saint Joan*) were written before the outbreak of the first world war, including *Arms and the Man, Candida, Major Barbara, Androcles and the Lion,* and *Pygmalion.* His house at Ayot St. Lawrence, Hertfordshire, called **Shaw's Corner** *(622)*, is maintained by the National Trust as a museum, full of Shaw memorabilia.

Two other novelists of note, whose home has been preserved, deserve mention here, though neither fits into the category of social critic. These are Charlotte and Emily Brontë, who grew up in their father's parsonage in Haworth, West Yorkshire, now preserved as the **Brontë Parsonage Museum** *(680)*. Here Charlotte wrote *Jane Eyre* and *Shirley*, and Emily, *Wuthering Heights,* all replete with vivid descriptions of the dark, wild Yorkshire moors surrounding their home—still dark and wild to the delectation of the many Brontë enthusiasts who visit this place. In another part of England, and commemorating an entirely different sort of novelist, is the **Lamb House** *(550)* on West Street, Rye, East Sussex. An attractive eighteenth century domicile, it was bought in 1899 by the American, Henry James, who lived most of the last years of his life here and wrote *The Awkward Age, The Ambassadors,* and *The Golden Bowl.* His refined, urbane, and subtly-drawn characters have nothing in common with those of any other nineteenth century English novelist, and their success is an indication of the abrupt shift away from Victorian literary tastes after 1900.

Few Victorian poets can be categorized in any sense as social critics. The two best known, Alfred, Lord Tennyson, and Robert Browning were optimists to the core. Algernon Charles Swinburne was a consummate lyricist who lapsed occasionally into melancholy ("We thank with brief thanksgiving/Whatever gods may be/That no man lives forever/That dead men rise up never/That even the weariest river/Winds somewhere safe to sea."). Matthew Arnold was more happily disposed toward life, though troubled by religious doubts, as indicated in his best-known poem, "Dover Beach." In any case, none of the above has been honored with a museum or any other sort of shrine, so they are of no concern, as such, to the traveller. Curiously perhaps, the Victorian poet most scorned by succeeding generations is the only one whose home has been preserved as a museum. This is Rudyard Kipling, panegyrist (with reservations) of British imperialism ("Take up the White Man's burden/Send forth the best ye breed/Go, bind your sons in exile/To serve your captives' need"). His home in Burwash, East Sussex, called **Batemans** *(549)*, where he lived from 1902 to 1936, is preserved by the National Trust which has maintained the author's study precisely as he left it.

Of Oxford, where he had attended Balliol College in the 1840s, Matthew Arnold wrote: "Beautiful city! so venerable, so lovely, so unravaged by the fierce intellectual life of our century, so serene! . . . Home of lost causes, and forsaken beliefs, and unpopular names, and impossible loyalties!" Historians of English education in the nineteenth century have mostly entertained a less roseate view of Arnold's alma mater. As indicated in the previous chapter, both of the medieval universities were seriously declining in intellectual vigor in the eighteenth century, and there was no significant improvement in the nineteenth at least until after the mid-century mark. Curricula were narrow and archaic, instruction was minimal, residency requirements lax, examinations, if taken at all, a farce. In the words of H. C. Barnard, "instead of being places of learning they had degenerated to a large extent into a preserve for the idle and the rich." A preserve also for communicants of the Church of England only. At Oxford, it was impossible to matriculate without subscribing to the Thirty-nine Articles; at Cambridge, nonconformists could attend the university, but not receive scholarships, fellowships, or university degrees. This discrimination explains in part why university enrollments in England were proportionately lower than in the leading universities of Europe or of Scotland.

In 1854 came the first significant break with the past when Parliament removed religious tests for candidates for the bachelor's degree at Oxford, and two years later at Cambridge. Not until 1871, however, were nonconformists admitted to full university privileges at either place. Whether the resultant infusion of new blood raised academic standards is impossible to say, but it may be more than coincidental that during these same years the curricula at both universities were expanded to include law, Oriental and modern languages, and even natural science. It was partly to check this tide of modernism that **Keble College** *(630)*, Oxford, and **Selwyn College** *(615)*, Cambridge, both with strong ties to the Church of England, were founded in 1870 and 1882 respectively.

The advent of women to the male bastions of Oxford and Cambridge was an even more startling development than the admission of nonconformists. Naturally it was a gradual process. In 1869 Miss Emily Davies opened a hall for young women at Hitchin in Hertfordshire and persuaded the university authorities at Cambridge to allow her students to do work equivalent to that required for an honors degree. Four years later the girls and their mistress relocated in Girton, a village only two miles outside of Cambridge, where the well-known architect, Alfred Waterhouse, built the first court of **Girton College** *(612)* in his favorite imitation red-brick Tudor style. Meanwhile, in 1871, **Newnham College** *(613)* had been set up within the very precincts of the town of Cambridge itself—though admittedly at a distance from most of the all-male foundations. The principal was Miss A. J. Clough, sister of the poet Arthur Hugh Clough, and the first buildings, by Basil Champneys (1875) were in the Dutch red-brick style then fashionable among intellectuals. Not until 1881 did the Cambridge University Senate formally admit female students from these two colleges to take examinations and receive certificates of completion, though not university degrees. Much the same pattern was followed at Oxford. **Somerville College** *(634)* and **Lady Margaret Hall** *(631)* were opened as residences for women scholars in 1879, the former nondenominational, the latter associated with the Church of England. Access to full academic privileges was denied to Oxford women until 1920, when they were admitted to full university membership, including the right to receive degrees. At Cambridge women received degrees after 1923 but not full university membership until 1948. Meanwhile, at Oxford came an equally radical departure from tradition with the foundation in 1899 of **Ruskin College** *(633)* not as a part of the university, but as a place where working men could come up to study for a year. One of its founders was the well-known American historian, Charles A. Beard. Americans—along with Canadians, Australians, New Zealanders, South Africans, and even Germans—began to appear at Oxford in significant numbers after 1902 with the establishment of a substantial scholarship endowment by Cecil Rhodes, an Oriel man who had made a fortune in South African gold and diamond mines.

Outside of Oxford and Cambridge, the progress of higher education was fairly rapid. In 1836 **University College** *(517)* on Gower Street, London, was linked with a new Anglican institution called King's College to form the University of London. At first the sole business of the new university was to give examinations and grant degrees on their satisfactory completion. That changed in 1896 when the University of London's constituent colleges were converted into teaching institutions. At Durham, meanwhile, the dean and chapter of the cathedral had endowed a university for the benefit of students from the northern counties and installed it in **Durham Castle** *(699)* where it is still housed. In the 1870s and early 1880s, privately endowed colleges were opened in Manchester, Liverpool, and Leeds and combined in 1884–1887 to form Victoria University, a degree-granting institution. This federal university broke up in 1904 when the **Universities of Manchester** *(694)*, **Liverpool** *(695)*, and **Leeds** *(681)* received independent charters. For Manchester, the architect Alfred Waterhouse designed a huge Gothic building in stone; at the other two he worked in brick. His choice of building material at Liverpool and Leeds accounts for the epithet "red-brick universities"—in Britain still a term of reproach synonymous with "upstart." **Birmingham University** *(664)*, founded in 1900, evolved from a college begun by a local industrialist in 1880 with the stipulation that it should foster scientific training "to the exclusion of mere literary education and . . . of all teaching in theology." Here indeed was a departure from the accepted canon of higher learning in Britain. The university's main buildings were designed by Sir Aston Webb—already mentioned as the sculptor of Queen Victoria's statue in front of Buckingham Palace. **Sheffield University** *(679)* received its charter in 1905, and **Bristol University** *(580)*, in 1909. **University College, Aberystwyth** *(724)* was opened in

1872 and first housed in a splendid Gothic pile originally intended for use as a hotel. It subsequently became the senior constituent college of the University of Wales, the others being located at Cardiff, Bangor, Swansea, and Lampeter. Starting in 1880 the government at Westminster began to pay annual grants to the universities, which mounted from an initial £5,000 to £170,000 by 1914. Total attendance, though large by mid-Victorian standards and growing, was hardly phenomenal. In 1908–1909 the number of full-time students in English universities was 12,778; by 1935–1936 it had reached 40,465—roughly the present size of a single large state university in the United States.

While higher education was becoming more secularized, the Church of England was becoming more religious. The beginning of what is called the Oxford Movement dates from a sermon on national apostasy delivered by John Keble at the Church of St. Mary the Virgin, Oxford, on 14 July 1833. Keble was a fellow of Oriel College and a university professor of poetry. Inspired by his emphasis on the sacraments and by his reassertion, in Anglican garb, of the Roman Catholic doctrine of apostolic succession, other members of Oriel joined in forming an Association of Friends of the Church and began publishing a number of Tracts for the Times which quickly won a sympathetic audience, especially among Anglican clergy. The Tractarians, of whom the best known came to be John Henry Newman, sought to revitalize the Church of England by reemphasizing the central role of the Eucharist and elevating the position of the priests who were its celebrants. The Oxford Movement unhappily served to rekindle the long-smoldering antagonism between High Church and Low Church elements within the Anglican communion. To the latter, the Tractarians' emphasis on ritual and their advocacy of incense, candles, genuflection, vestments, altar frontals in changing liturgical colors, etc., smacked too much of Catholicism; and when Newman pursued the logic of his convictions to the point of converting to Rome, many Anglicans were convinced that the Oxford Movement had been from the beginning little more than another popish plot. In the end, the Church of England was probably not much revitalized, though the Tractarians clearly left their mark on Sunday services which thereafter became, in most places of worship, decidedly more formal than before. Meanwhile, another group of High Church enthusiasts, centered at Cambridge, founded the Camden Society (later called the Ecclesiological Society) and began the publication of *The Ecclesiologist*, a periodical dedicated to the architectural reform of English churches along more strictly medieval—and therefore Catholic—lines. Specifically these people advocated more elaborate altars, the elevation of the floor of the chancel several steps above that of the nave, a reemphasis of the distinct functions of different parts of the church (nave, chancel, sacristy, etc.) by distinct ornamentation and different roof levels for each, substituting stained-glass windows for clear, removal of galleries, etc. All this of course was grist to the mill of the mid-nineteenth century school of architects known as Gothic Revival-ists, of whom more will be said later. Thanks in part to the Tractarians and the Camden Society, the Victorians by and large rejected the legacy of Sir Christopher Wren in favor of a bastard Gothicism which, some felt, sacrificed grace and proportion to the demands of dogma.

Disagreements between churchmen of High and Low persuasion, though bitter and divisive, do not appear, however, to have been a serious threat to organized religion, and of course were irrelevant to the fortune of the nonconformist sects who at mid-century could boast almost as many regular churchgoers as the Church of England. A far more serious threat to Christian orthodoxy of all denominations was the encroachment of scientific learning. In 1833, the year that Keble preached his famous sermon, Sir Charles Lyell published the third and last volume of his *Principles of Geology* which convincingly disproved the chronology of the book of Genesis, destroyed Bishop Ussher's widely accepted theses that the world was created in 4004 B.C., and reduced the literal interpretation of the Old Testament to absurdity. This was followed in 1859 by the publication of Charles Darwin's *Origin of the Species*, which offered more plausible explanations for the origin and evolution of the human species than those laid out in Holy Writ. Darwin's theories, given wide publicity by T. H. Huxley and oth-ers, were so fundamentally at odds with conventional Christian dogma as to shake the very foundations of organized religion. Yet fulminations from a thousand pulpits would not make Science go away, and, at least upon the educated classes, agnosticism and even atheism began for the first time in history to have a serious and lasting impact. Reflecting on the ebbing tide at Dover Beach, the poet Matthew Arnold sadly noted:

> The Sea of Faith
> Was once, too, at the full, and round earth's shore
> Lay like the folds of a bright girdle furl'd.
> But now I only hear
> Its melancholy, long, withdrawing roar,
> Retreating, to the breath
> Of the night-wind, down the vast edges drear
> And naked shingles of the world.

Yet neither poets nor scientists necessarily speak for the generality of mankind, and, Arnold and Darwin notwithstanding, church membership and church attendance in Victorian Britain did not slack off. Indeed it grew. A religious census taken on Easter Day 1851 showed a total of 875,000 Church of England communicants; another, taken thirty years later, indicated that the number had grown to 1,225,000. In the same period Methodist membership in England rose from 471,930 to 603,575.

Even more impressive are the figures for church construction. Between 1840 and 1876 the Anglicans alone built 1,727 new churches in England and Wales and rebuilt or restored 7,144. Here was plenty of work for architects and builders, and the supply rose to meet the demand.

ARCHITECTURE: 1830–1914

Like Victorian morality, Victorian architecture has come in for more than its fair share of ridicule, and indeed it is easy enough to dismiss the first as hypocritical and the second as grotesquely ugly. Historical revisionism, however, is a never-ending process, and recent years have witnessed a more sympathetic reassessment of both the ethical and aesthetic standards of the nineteenth century. No doubt the wide-spread lawlessness and civic irresponsibility of the second half of the twentieth century inevitably invoke nostalgia for Victorian rectitude. By the same token, the ostentatious gimcrackery of a hundred years ago seems rich and variegated when compared to the unrelieved monotony of much of what today passes for functionalism in architecture.

In any case the Victorians were what they were, and their buildings reflect not only the tastes of the times but the economic, political, and social conditions under which they lived. Among those conditions was the rapid mechanization of industry which made possible the mass production of cheap building materials, especially brick, iron (later steel), plate glass, terra-cotta, and encaustic tiles. Another was the mid-century outburst in Britain of national and civic pride which demanded expression in grandiose and monumental public buildings, and encouraged competitive ostentatiousness among architects. A third was ideological— an idealistic rejection of the materialistic values of an industrial and capitalistic society in favor of what was thought to be the more humane and "spiritual" ethic of the Middle Ages.

No British architect was more conscientiously medieval in his approach to design than Augustus Welby Northmore Pugin. Converted to Roman Catholicism in 1835, he published the following year a volume entitled *Contrasts: or a Parallel Between the Noble Edifices of the Middle Ages and the Corresponding Buildings of the Present Day; Showing the Present Decay of Taste,* an influential book whose readers needed go no further than the title to discover its message. Medieval was Catholic, Christian, and True; classical architecture was Pagan, Utilitarian, and Decadent. Five years later in his *True Principles of Pointed or Christian Architecture,* Pugin narrowed his preferences still further by elevating the Decorated Gothic (which he called Middle Pointed) above all other styles. Early English was too primitive; Perpendicular too close to the Renaissance and to the Tudors who had brought the Protestant Reformation to Britain. He was responsible, as we have seen, for most of the decorative details of the **Houses of Parliament** *(521)* and for their overall Gothic appearance. But he deplored Sir Charles Barry's regular fenestration and other symmetrical effects and dismissed the building as "All Grecian, Sir; Tudor details on a classic body." Pugin was a True Believer. Even Newman, himself a Catholic convert and later a cardinal, thought him too extreme in his Gothicism. "Mr. Pugin," he wrote in 1848, "is a genius . . . but he is intolerant, and if I might use a strong word, a bigot."

Pugin's most important church commission was **St. Chad's Cathedral** *(665)*, Birmingham, the first Roman Catholic cathedral to be built in Britain since the Middle Ages. It is a red-brick edifice, modeled on fourteenth century Gothic, but curiously more German than English in its style. He also designed the **Roman Catholic Cathedral** *(701)* in Newcastle-upon-Tyne (more clearly within the English Decorated tradition), as well as other Roman Catholic churches and cathedrals. None of these buildings has much architectural merit. The truth is that Catholic resources in England were still slender and the Church's communicants mostly poor Irish immigrants; and Pugin, for all his noble intentions, was usually constrained by lack of funds.

More widely read than Pugin's works were those of John Ruskin, who was to become professor of fine art at Oxford and whose books *The Seven Lamps of Architecture* (1849) and *The Stones of Venice* (1851–1853) were no less doctrinaire in their advocacy of a Gothic revival. Ruskin deplored the inhumanity of an industrial system that sacrificed the craftsman on the altar of mass production, and he saw the Middle Ages as a time when artisans were allowed free rein to their spiritual impulses and were therefore able to produce such splendid monuments of imaginative style as the Gothic church. Moreover, having fallen in love with Venice, he developed an affection for what he called constructional polychromy, i.e., variegated surfaces obtained by mixing building materials of different colors according to set patterns. He had little opportunity to work out these ideas in the house he bought for himself high above Coniston Water in Cumbria, called **Brantwood** *(710)*, now open to the public as a Ruskin museum. But Oxford was another matter. Here he inspired the architects of the **Oxford University Museum** *(632)* to create a really charming building of stone and iron and glass which represents the Gothic Revival at its best. Each of the polished stone columns which support the wrought-iron pointed arches carrying the glass roof is of a different British rock; each carved capital represents a different native plant; and each arched internal doorway and window is bonded in bricks of alternating colors. **Keble College** *(630)*, Oxford, is an even grander exercise in polychromy. It was built to honor the father of the Oxford Movement, and the architect was William Butterfield, a much respected Gothicist who had contributed to *The Ecclesiologist* and had already built a new chapel for **Balliol College** *(620)* and, under the auspices of the Camden Society, designed **All Saints, Margaret Street** *(526)* with walls of polychromatic brick. At Keble he again used brick—for the first time ever at an Oxford college. The exterior is of red brick with stone dressings and patterns of blue and yellow bricks inserted; the domineering chapel of almost cathedral size is distinguished for its colored mosaics. (Later the famous painting *The Light of the World* by the Pre-Raphaelite William Holman Hunt would be installed in the side chapel.) Another Butterfield innovation was to provide access to the students' rooms from long corridors, rather than by the usual arrangement of separate staircases. This novelty would provoke disfavor among university traditionalists almost as much as the red brick.

Another Ruskin disciple was George Edmund Street, who himself published an influential book entitled *Brick and Marble in the Middle Ages*. Typical of his work is the church of **St. James the Less** *(522)* at Thorndike Street and Vauxhall Bridge Road, London. It is a good example of constructional polychromy, built of red brick interlarded with other colors inside and out. Street's most noted accomplishment, however, was his design for the **Royal Courts of Justice (Law Courts)** *(519)* in the Strand, London. Completed after the architect's death in 1881, this has been called the last great national monument to be built in the Gothic style in Britain. Inside this sprawling, many-turreted pile of Portland stone lies a warren of vaulted halls, courtrooms, corridors, and staircases. Though egregiously inconvenient for those who have to work in it, the exterior has a fairy-castle look that is undeniably attractive and eminently photogenic. Among the most prolific of Victorian Gothicists was Alfred Waterhouse, whose work at the provincial universities and Girton College, Cambridge, has already been mentioned. His masterpiece was the **Town Hall** *(694)* in Manchester built in 1868–1877. Recently cleaned, its entrance front graced with a fine statue of the Prince Consort by Thomas Worthington, this is an altogether splendid public building. On Deansgate, Manchester, is the handiwork of another Victorian architect, Basil Champneys—the **John Rylands Library** *(694)*, a somewhat whimsical exercise in Late Gothic. Another leading figure of the Gothic Revival was John Pearson. His church of **St. Augustine, Kilburn** *(531)* in Paddington, London, is a gigantic building in red brick. Here the architect departed from Pugin's canon of Middle Pointed or Decorated style and used instead an Early English model with lancet windows, etc. He did the same, and more successfully, at **Truro Cathedral** *(597)*, Cornwall, one of the latest exercises in Victorian Gothic, not completed until 1910.

Of all the nineteenth century Gothicists, none was more highly regarded and therefore more financially successful than Sir George Gilbert Scott (not to be confused with his architect son, George Gilbert, Jr., or grandson, Sir Giles Gilbert Scott). His designs for the **Albert Memorial** *(525)* and the Midland Grand Hotel, **St. Pancras Station** *(529)*, have already been mentioned. He is also responsible for the **Martyrs' Memorial** *(636)*, Oxford, executed in the form of an Eleanor's Cross and commemorating Latimer, Ridley, et al., who were burned for their Protestant convictions in the reign of Bloody Mary. In 1873 he finished the **Foreign Office** *(521)* overlooking St. James's Park, London. The style is Italian Renaissance, but only because Lord Palmerston insisted on it, and indeed hinted strongly he would hire another architect if Scott refused to comply. Otherwise, almost all his *oeuvre* is Gothic of one sort or another. And it is prodigious in quantity: 39 cathedrals or minsters built or restored; 476 churches, 25 schools, 23 parsonages, 43 mansions, 26 public buildings, 48 monuments, and 25 colleges or college chapels. This listing does not include the 50-odd orphanages and workhouses he completed before 1847 when he was still relatively unknown.

With such an embarrassment of riches (so to speak), it is difficult to be selective. In the London area, **St. Giles, Camberwell** *(534)* is typical—a stately building in the Middle Pointed style. In Oxford he designed a new chapel for **Exeter College** *(629)* and at Cambridge another for **St. John's College** *(615)*, the latter lying on the north side of the lovely Tudor first court and somewhat spoiling it. In Trefnant, Clwyd, the church of **St. Giles** *(730)* is another typical Middle Pointed specimen, while **All Souls, Haley Hill** *(680)* in Halifax, West Yorkshire, is, in Scott's own opinion, "on the whole, my best church." As a restorer of genuine medieval churches, Scott was even busier than as a builder of new copies. At **Lichfield Cathedral** *(667)*, Staffordshire, most of the window tracery is his. At **Bath Abbey** *(474)*, Avon, he removed some seventeenth century additions and installed new stone vaulting in the nave and new stalls in the choir. He restored the interior of **St. Mary and All Saints** *(661)*, Chesterfield, Derbyshire, the church with the famous crooked spire. His reconstruction of **St. Mary Abbots** *(528)*, High Street, Kensington, was a relatively modest "improvement" on the original; that of **St. Mary's** *(532)*, Harrow, a ruthless remodeling of the church to fit the Middle Pointed canon. Ruthlessness indeed was a salient characteristic of Scott and other Victorian "restorers" whose doctrinaire Gothicism at times drove them to ridiculous extremes and resulted in the destruction of innumerable priceless ecclesiastical furnishings and decorative features simply because they lacked Gothic purity in the eyes of these nineteenth century architects whose medieval scholarship was at best amateurish. It was this aspect of Scott's enthusiasm that finally produced a reaction in the formation in 1877 of the Society for the Protection of Ancient Buildings, specifically aimed at saving Tewksbury Abbey from his clutches. One of the society's founders, and perhaps its most vocal spokesman, was William Morris.

William Morris, son of a well-to-do businessman, was born in Walthamstow in a house which now serves as the **William Morris Gallery** *(534)* containing a library and museum devoted to his work. At Exeter College, Oxford, he fell under the influence of Ruskin, and, along with his friend Edward Burne-Jones, founded the Brotherhood, an undergraduate society dedicated to "a crusade and holy war against the age," meaning the entire philistine culture of the nineteenth century with all its mass-produced geegaws, fake Gothic and fake Renaissance architecture, materialistic values, and worship of Mammon. After college Morris met up with Dante Gabriel Rossetti, leader of the Pre-Raphaelite school of artists, of which more will be said below. He married the artist's model, Jane Borden, and the couple set up housekeeping at the **Red House** *(536)* in Bexleyheath, South London, designed and built in 1850 by Philip Webb. This has been called a milestone in the history of Western architecture—essentially the first house of the modern age. It is a Picturesque red-brick building with steep roofs and little exterior ornamentation, plainly finished interiors hung with tapestries, and windows in bright colored glass, designed by Burne-Jones whose specialty this was (as is attested by the hundreds of his windows in countless parish churches throughout Britain). Here, Morris, Rossetti, Burne-Jones, the artist Ford Madox Brown, and others set up the Firm dedicated to the design and fabrication of furniture, wallpaper, chintz, tapestry, carpets, tiles, and stained glass in bright and contrasting colors, thereby initiating a mini-revolution in interior decoration the consequences of which can still be observed in many middle-class English homes today. There are good examples of the Firm's work in the **Victoria and Albert Museum** *(526)*, but perhaps the best place today to observe the Morris touch is at **Wightwick Manor** *(666)*, a late Victorian mansion near Wolverhampton, West Midlands, where he did the wallpaper, tapestries, and carpets, and where hang a number of good Pre-Raphaelite paintings. Another Morris-furnished house is **Standen** *(553)*, West Sussex, also designed by Philip Webb, architect of the Red House. In 1871, Morris, Rossetti, and Jane Morris (by this time Rossetti's mistress) moved to **Kelmscott Manor** *(577)*, Oxfordshire, which today also features some good Morris artifacts. In his London house in Hammersmith he set up the Kelmscott Press, aimed at rejuvenating the ancient art of printing, and was successful in turning out a number of beautiful volumes, including a magnificent edition of Chaucer. By this time Morris was disgusted with his rich clients and with himself for serving them and decided to become a socialist. With Karl Marx's daughter Eleanor, he founded a new Socialist League which published the *Commonweal*, a periodical edited by Morris. He also threw himself into political activism, but, after three demonstrators at a mass meeting in Trafalgar Square were killed as a result of police action, Morris ceased to be an agitator. He died in 1896, five years before the end of the Victorian Age he so much deplored. He would not have found its Edwardian successor any more to his liking.

The Red House was meant to be a statement of its owner's revulsion against the tasteless architectural fashions of his day—not only, in his words, "the ridiculous travesties of Gothic buildings," but also "pedantic imitations of classical architecture." For neoclassicism had never been completely displaced by the Gothic Revival, and in the end survived it. The earliest Victorian example is the **Fitzwilliam Museum** *(612)* in Cambridge, built to house, among other things, a fine collection of pictures owned by the university, and begun in 1837 to a design by George

Basevi. Its heavy central portico of Corinthian columns is flanked by colonnades terminating in classical pavilions. The interior decor, however, is more baroque than classical. In Oxford the **Ashmolean Museum** *(628)* was built 1841–1845 to house the university's collection of antiquities and accommodate the Taylor Institute for instruction in foreign languages. Designed by C. R. Cockerell (also co-architect for the Fitzwilliam), it is neo-Grecian with Ionic columns, modeled more or less on the Temple of Apollo at Bassae. Neoclassical architecture received an unexpected boost with the passage of the Municipal Corporations Act of 1835 which, in effect, established home rule and representative government for England's provincial towns and cities and unleashed a tidal wave of municipal building for which the great public monuments of ancient Greece and Rome provided the most appropriate models. Birmingham provides perhaps the best examples. Its **Town Hall** *(665)* by Joseph Hansom, inventor of the famous cab, is completely surrounded by Corinthian columns and was modeled on the Temple of Castor and Pollux, still to be seen (in ruins) within the Roman Forum. It was joined, to the north, by the **Council House** *(664)*, also in the Corinthian order. Next to it is the **Corporation Museum and Art Gallery** *(695)*, also classical, though in the Renaissance manner, and at the far corner of the group is Big Brum, a Renaissance version of Big Ben. In Liverpool, **St. George's Hall** *(695)* has been described as the summing up of neoclassicism in Britain. Built to house the municipal assembly room, law courts, and concert hall, its main entrance is a huge portico of sixteen Corinthian columns, while square Corinthian pillars continue the motif along the front of the building, and inside the theme is repeated in a series of red granite Corinthian columns supporting a coffered vault inspired by the Baths of Caracalla in Rome.

The **Town Hall** *(681)* of Leeds, West Yorkshire, is more Renaissance than purely classical, though as in Liverpool, the Corinthian order predominates. The English Renaissance of the Elizabethan period was the inspiration for the **Examination Schools** *(629)* built on the High in Oxford in 1882. **New Scotland Yard** *(521)*, Victoria Embankment, London, designed by Norman Shaw in 1889, is modeled on the French châteaux of the early Renaissance with a touch of Rhenish castle added. In South Kensington, on land purchased from the profits of the Great Exhibition of 1851, sprang up a group of buildings, which though vaguely sixteenth century Italian in appearance, can perhaps best be described as Victorian eclectic, a term which itself defies definition. The **Royal Albert Hall** *(525)* across Kensington Gore from the Albert Memorial is a great amphitheater seating eight thousand people, with a red-brick exterior embellished by buff terra-cotta and a continuous frieze depicting the triumph of the Arts and Letters. The **Victoria and Albert Museum** *(526)*, that fascinating repository of art and artifacts already frequently alluded to in this book, more or less follows North Italian Renaissance models, again in brick and terra-cotta. Across Exhibition Road is the

Natural History Museum *(525)* by Alfred Waterhouse, with its yellow walls and bands of bluish gray enlivened by figures of animals—a fine example of constructional polychromy.

In the late 1890s fashion took another turn—this time back to the baroque of Vanbrugh and Hawksmoor. One of the best examples is the **Town Hall** *(599)* in Colchester, Essex, designed by John Belcher as a two-level *piano nobile* with three pairs of Corinthian columns extending from the wall, and alternating round and pointed baroque pediments above, all topped by a fine baroque tower surmounted by a somewhat Wren-like steeple. Even grander in scope, and thoroughly baroque in the Victorian manner, is the **City Hall** *(717)* in Cardiff, its dome surmounted by a splendid Welsh dragon in Portland stone. More authentically baroque in the Roman manner is the **Brompton Oratory** *(524)*, London, opened in 1884 for the secular priests of the Institute of St. Philip Neri introduced into England by Cardinal Newman. Fortunately for Augustus Welby Northmore Pugin, he did not live to see this important center of the Roman Catholic revival in England housed in a building so blatantly non-Gothic as this. No doubt he would have been even more discomfited to see rise the great Roman Catholic **Westminster Cathedral** *(524)*, the most important church of that persuasion in England, built in 1895–1903 to a design by J. F. Bentley. The style is more Byzantine than anything else, with a long nave covered by a series of broad domes of bare brick over square bays and topped by a towering campanile—all in alternate bands of red brick and gray stone. Here is a monumental exercise in constructional polychromy which would have pleased Ruskin, if not Pugin.

FURNITURE AND PAINTING: 1830–1914

Pugin's zeal for the Gothic was not confined to architecture alone. In 1835 he published *Gothic Furniture,* full of suggestions for chairs, tables, mirrors, chests, etc., bristling with pinnacles, crotchets, finials, and pointed arcading. Pugin was among the few Victorian architects to concern himself with furniture design, but his own products do not appear to have attracted many buyers. A few of his pieces are on display in the **Victoria and Albert Museum** *(526)*; in the drawing room of **Eastnor Castle** *(647)*, Hereford and Worcester; and at **Lotherton Hall** *(681)* near Leeds. The extent of his influence on other furniture makers is impossible to trace. The term *Gothic* was often used to describe pieces that are in fact more Elizabethan or Jacobean in appearance than medieval—as in the Victorian-Gothic drawing room in the **Bowes Museum** *(698)*, Barnard Castle, County Durham, which contains one of the best collections of period furniture in the country.

Gothic designs were, in fact, too angular to satisfy Victorian requirements for comfort. One of the great contributions of the nineteenth century to the welfare of mankind was the introduction of the mass-produced coiled spring for settees, sofas, chairs, and bedding—a product mostly of Birmingham. Related to it was the improvement in cheap furniture-coverings produced by the worsted mills of Yorkshire after they went over to the power loom. Both innovations resulted in a flood of overstuffed chairs, sofas, ottomans, etc., which, though no doubt grace-less, were much easier on the anatomy than the elegant Hepplewhite or Regency settees. The bulging curves and ponderosity of these new pieces came to be reflected in the contours of all household furniture. By mid-century wooden legs and chair backs became visible again, but the curves remained. From about 1850 onward the typical drawing room chair had a lightly upholstered seat and an oval back, the latter framed with wood, while sofas and settees were often backed with a set of two or three oval frames. Later still, visible chair legs went into concealment as they and even the legs of tables, pianofortes, chimneypieces, and shelves were covered with heavy materials, often adorned with deep fringes.

Oak returned as a favored basic material, though never entirely replac-ing mahogany, walnut, satinwood, rosewood, etc. New materials too came into fashion. Italian marble tabletops abounded. Brass became popular, especially in the manufacture of beds. Cast-iron chairs and ta-bles were introduced into gardens, conservatories, and hallways. Papier-mâché was used for trays, small tables, and a host of other pieces. Plate-glass mirrors with beveled edges appeared on doors, sideboards, chiffoniers, and hall-stands—the latter a new invention combining the functions of coatrack, umbrella holder, settee, and looking-glass.

With the exception of such examples of intricate woodcarving as the enormous sideboard created for **Charlecote Park** *(644)* by James Morris Willcox of Warwick and the monstrous Kenilworth Buffet at **Warwick Castle** *(646)*, Victorian furniture was mostly mass produced. As Thomas Hope had predicted early in the century, the factory, with its steam-powered lathes and woodcarving machinery, would replace the skilled craftsman and the small shop. This of course was the burden of William Morris's complaint and the reason for his setting up the Firm for the production of hand-wrought household furnishings. The chief defect of mass production, however, was not ugliness but profusion. Except for occasional lapses into grotesquerie (by no means confined to the nine-teenth century), individual Victorian pieces are not so unattractive, and indeed today seem often charming—if given enough breathing room. The trouble was there was too much of everything: too many bulging pieces covered with antimacassars and edged with bobble-fringes, too many clocks and vases, too many mantels, tables, and what-nots loaded with wax fruits, stuffed birds under glass-domes, feather and wool flowers, ships in bottles, dead insects enclosed in glass paperweights, etc., etc. Charles Dickens said it all in *Our Mutual Friend* in describing the home of his character Mr. Pidsnap: "Everything was made to look as heavy as it could, and to take up as much room as possible . . ."

Superfluity as a characteristic of Victorian culture was not, however, confined to household furnishings. Painters were wont to crowd their huge canvases to overflowing. Few could match George Hayter in this regard. His *Trial of Queen Caroline* contained 186 identifiable portraits, and *The House of Commons,* done in 1833, had 375. Both now hang in the **National Portrait Gallery** *(518),* as does Hayter's really fine state portrait of the queen, seated, crowned, and holding the royal scepter. He was for a while the favorite portraitist at court but in the 1840s fell from favor after a quarrel with the Prince Consort. Eventually he was replaced in royal favor by Sir Edwin Landseer who pleased Victoria more than any of his contemporaries. When he died from alcoholism in 1873, the queen had in her possession thirty-nine of his oil paintings, sixteen chalk drawings, two frescoes, and many sketches. Although prolific in his output of portraits, scenes of the Scottish highlands and of the hunt, Landseer is most noted for his animals, especially dogs. Here he managed, with unique skill, to impart human expressions to his canine sitters—an art that brought him great acclaim among his contemporaries. His work, prodigious in quantity, is to be seen today at the **Tate Gallery** *(523)* and the **Victoria and Albert Museum** *(526)* in London; the **Ashmolean Museum** *(628),* Oxford; the **Walker Art Gallery** *(695),* Liverpool; the **Lady Lever Art Gallery** *(695)* in Port Sunlight, south of Birkenhead, Merseyside; and the **Corporation Art Gallery and Museum** *(664),* Birmingham.

Landseer was also much taken with monkeys, and some of his most esteemed oils portray these humanoid creatures in a variety of poses—usually up to no good. It was this infatuation, above everything else, this "monkeyana," that drew the fire of a group of rebellious contemporary artists who called themselves Pre-Raphaelites. The name originates in the Brotherhood formed in April 1848 by William Holman Hunt and John Everett Millais and soon joined by Dante Gabriel Rossetti and others. Their stated objective was to liberate painting from the stilted artificialities of the Royal Academicians (including Landseer), to be true to nature, and to emulate the sincerity of early Italian art before it was corrupted by Raphael. Specifically, they chose to render natural objects in the most precise and minute detail and strong color. Their preference for a representational literalness often clashed with their favorite subjects. Most of their paintings, and those of two men not in the Brotherhood but associated with it—Edward Burne-Jones and Ford Madox Brown—dealt with mythical figures of antiquity or of the Arthurian legend, Biblical personae, characters from Shakespeare, Keats, and Tennyson, and anthropomorphic renditions of symbolic virtues like Industry and Hope. The **Corporation Art Gallery and Museum** *(664)* in Birmingham has the best collection of their works. Others are to be seen at the **Tate** *(523)* and the **Victoria and Albert** *(526)* in London; the **City Art Gallery** *(693),* Manchester; the **Lady Lever Art Gallery** *(695),* Port Sunlight, Merseyside; **Buscot Park** *(576)* near Faringdon, Oxfordshire; the

Fitzwilliam Museum *(612)*, Cambridge; and the Ashmolean Museum *(628)*, Oxford. Probably the most famous Pre-Raphaelite painting of all is William Holman Hunt's *Light of the World*, a full-length representation of Christ, the original of which hangs in the chapel of Keble College *(630)*, Oxford.

It is hard to believe that the Pre-Raphaelites were contemporaries of Claude Monet and Auguste Renoir. French Impressionism, so unliteral and deliberately imprecise, finally came to Britain through the person of an American artist, James Abbott McNeill Whistler, who had studied in Paris, and whose *Nocturnes*, now in the Tate Gallery *(523)*, caused an uproar in London art circles when shown in 1877. More solidly within the Impressionist school is William Sickert, a *fin-de-siècle* English artist whose works can best be seen at the Tate *(523)* or in the Walker Art Gallery *(695)*, Liverpool. Sickert for a while was a student of another Anglicized American, John Singer Sargent. The first portraitist in England of any merit since Lawrence, his works grace the walls of, among others, Blenheim Palace *(636)*, Oxfordshire; Chatsworth *(662)*, Derbyshire; Holkham Hall *(610)*, Norfolk; and Longleat *(577)*, Wiltshire. Like all successful portraitists, Sargent depended upon the rich.

THE ARISTOCRACY, 1830–1914;
COUNTRY HOMES AND GARDENS

"Our Queen," wrote Disraeli in his novel *Sybil*, published in 1845, "reigns over . . . two nations; between whom there is no intercourse and no sympathy; who are as ignorant of each other's habits, thoughts and feelings, as if they were dwellers in different zones, or inhabitants of different planets; are formed by a different breeding, are fed by a different food, are ordered by different manners, and are not governed by the same laws . . . 'THE RICH AND THE POOR.'" The young author, to be sure, overlooked the growing middle class, as he was later inclined to do when he became prime minister. But he was not far off the mark in his indictment of British society near the mid-century mark as a rigid caste system, a hierarchy of social orders based on gross disparities of wealth.

With the passing of the Reform Act of 1832, the duke of Wellington and others had predicted the imminent collapse of the aristocracy. When, in 1846, Sir Robert Peel engineered the repeal of the Corn Laws so that foreign grain could be admitted duty free into the United Kingdom, alarmists spoke of the event as the death knell of the landed interest. Yet nothing happened—at least not right away. Landed families continued to provide a majority of the House of Commons until 1885 when, for the first time, the number of commercial men and industrialists exceeded that of landowners. A more ominous sign appeared in 1874 when two coal miners were elected to the Commons, but even so the heavens did not fall. Members of the landed aristocracy and gentry filled a majority of the positions in every cabinet until Campbell-Bannerman's in 1906. As to the landed interest, income and rents from agriculture stayed high until the 1870s when American and Australian wheat, wool, and refrigerated meat began to invade the unprotected market, but even then, it was the lesser gentry, and not the great landlords, who suffered seriously from what was called the great agricultural depression. As of 1873, large landowners, with estates of 10,000 acres or more, owned 25 percent of the soil of England; gentry with estates of 1,000 to 9,999 acres another 29.5 percent. Thus, 4,217 persons owned over half the acreage of England, and the comparative statistics for Scotland and Wales could not have been much different.

This is not to say that the composition of the still ruling class remained completely unchanged. The British aristocracy had never been a rigidly exclusive club and had always conceded (to paraphrase Tennyson) that wealth was more than coronets and ample coin than Norman blood. The new rich, with fortunes made from railways, shipping, banking, brewing, armaments, etc., found entry into the ranks of the privileged no more difficult than had their predecessors, the London merchants of the sixteenth century or the Indian nabobs of the eighteenth. Not even the House of Lords was immune. Of the two hundred new peers created between 1886 and 1914, approximately seventy had become rich through business enterprises. Edwardian "Society," with its extravagant London season followed by a week of yachting at Cowes, then grouse shooting in Scotland, and finally weekends of partridge shooting at country house parties, was a melting pot of old titles and new fortunes. And the country house remained, both for established families and *arrivistes*, the classic symbol of prestige and status. Indeed, almost as many new ones were erected in the nineteenth century as in the three previous centuries combined.

The Victorian and Edwardian country house, however, was significantly different in plan and function from its predecessors. For one thing, the coming of the railroad had made weekend entertaining on a large scale feasible. For another, the easy informality of master-servant relationships which had characterized the semifeudal agrarian society of an earlier age tended to disappear with the arrival on the scene of a new class of business-oriented landlords. These and other considerations complicated problems of domestic management and had a serious impact on architectural planning both for new building and the remodeling of old mansions.

Stated simply, the country house began to assume the attributes of a resort hotel, with separate quarters for the management (in this case the family); ample provision for the amusement of guests; and isolation of the domestic staff so as to create the illusion of effortless efficiency. Self-sufficient family wings came into fashion. So did billiard rooms and smoking rooms for the male guests down for the shooting. The dictates of

Victorian prudery required separate wings for unmarried men and women. Large guest lists required large houses which in turn required large staffs of servants which in turn required still larger houses. The problem was aggravated by the paucity of laborsaving devices—slow to be adopted in Britain even after they had become technologically feasible. Central heating, ample plumbing, and electric lighting would have saved thousands of man-hours (or woman-hours) spent in tending grates, drawing water, and cleaning lamps. But labor was cheap and the hand of custom heavy. So servants multiplied. Yet the dictates of nineteenth century snobbery required that they should be neither seen nor heard except when absolutely necessary. Domestics' quarters, with separate sets of back stairs for males and females, separate dormitories and dining rooms, separate rooms for different domestic functions, had to be so isolated that neither guest nor family member was likely to encounter accidentally a servant about his business. To quote W. R. Lethaby, a late Victorian designer, "it was the affectation of the time that work was done by magic; it was vulgar to recognize its existence or even see anybody doing it." It was not unknown for a domestic caught sweeping down the master's quarters at an unscheduled time to be fired on the spot. Ronald Blythe reports, in his penetrating study of village life in Suffolk, *Akenfield*, that in one of the county's greatest houses it was required of maidservants, on meeting her ladyship indoors, to scurry promptly aside and face the wall so as to avoid eye contact.

All these considerations of hospitality, propriety, and class consciousness imposed special requirements of design and account for the intricate and complex floor plans of Victorian and Edwardian country houses. But an even more important prerequisite was that these great mansions conform architecturally to one or another of the princely or baronial styles conventionally associated with the landed aristocracy. There was a wide spectrum to choose from, and in general throughout the Victorian and Edwardian years the trend of fashion moved from Italian Renaissance to Elizabethan and Jacobean, to Gothic to Picturesque, to French Renaissance, and finally back to the starkly feudal.

Cliveden *(623)*, near Taplow, Buckinghamshire, was rebuilt in 1850–1851 for the duke of Sutherland by Sir Charles Barry, designer of the Houses of Parliament, in the Renaissance manner which that architect preferred to the quasi-Gothic style required of him at Westminster. It is a huge balustraded *palazzo*, 150 feet long, its two upper stories with Ionic pilasters, its central block flanked by matching wings. **Mentmore Towers** *(625)*, near Leighton Buzzard, Bedfordshire, was built in 1850–1855 for Baron Amschel de Rothschild of the great banking family to a design of Joseph Paxton, architect of the Crystal Palace. It was meant to be Elizabethan in character and indeed was modeled on Wollaton Hall in Nottingham. **Somerleyton Hall** *(603)* near Lowestoft, Suffolk, was built by John Thomas in 1844–1851 for Samuel Morton Peto, a self-made building and railway contractor who later went bankrupt and lost his mansion to an even wealthier plutocrat, Sir Frank Crossley of Crossley Carpets, Halifax. The predominant style is Jacobean, with two advancing wings and a three-story central entrance porch with oriel windows; but an Italianate tower containing a water tank rises from one end of the house, while the stable block on the other is surmounted by a Wrenlike cupola. Also in the Elizabethan-Jacobean manner is **Thoresby Hall** *(660)* near Ollerton, Nottinghamshire, built by Anthony Salvin in 1864–1871 for the third earl of Manvers. It is an enormous pile, with a frontispiece surmounted by a clock tower and lantern and dormers and chimneys perhaps modeled on Burghley House. More Victorian furniture is to be seen here than in most of England's stately homes where later owners have discarded it.

Salvin's preferred style was Gothic, and in this he was in tune with the trend of Victorian taste after about mid-century. At **Muncaster Castle** *(711)* on the Cumbrian coast, he remodeled and expanded a fourteenth century pele tower for the fourth Lord Muncaster in what Mark Girouard calls "a soberly castellated style." At **Dunster Castle** *(584)* near Minehead, Somerset, he Gothicized the Luttrells' Jacobean house which had been originally a thirteenth century castle, adding two battlemented towers, a new main entrance, and great hall and remodeling the interior to suit Victorian requirements for a gun room, billiard room, new servants quarters, and workrooms. **Carlton Towers** *(688)* near Selby, North Yorkshire, was originally Jacobean and partly Gothicized in the 1840s by the eighth Lord Beaumont, but owes its present massively medieval features mostly to Edward Welby Pugin (son of the better known Augustus) and to John Francis Bentley who later designed Westminster Cathedral. Pugin added three castellated towers and innumerable turrets; Bentley redecorated the interior. There is a no more aggressively Gothic Victorian house in the country. **Knebworth House** *(621)* near Stevenage, Hertfordshire, remodeled twenty years earlier, presents an interesting contrast. Working over a family mansion of early Tudor provenance, the novelist Edward Bulwer-Lytton fashioned a delightfully graceful exterior of towers, pinnacles, gargoyles, traceried windows, etc., as fanciful as the owner's once popular historical fiction. But of all the nineteenth century Gothic architects, none was so worshipful of the Middle Ages as William Burges. In the 1860s he built for John Heathcot-Amery, a rich lace-manufacturer, the thoroughly Gothic **Knightshayes Court** *(589)* near Tiverton, Devon—half castle and half church in appearance, all vaguely thirteenth or fourteenth century. It was, however, the third marquess of Bute who was responsible for Burges's most grandiose creations. Heir to the family fortune derived from the development of Cardiff's port facilities, this young man became a medieval antiquarian and Catholic convert in the 1860s and soon joined forces with the like-minded Burges to create two of the most spectacular Gothic creations of the nineteenth century. The first of these was the southwest portion of the genuinely medieval **Cardiff Castle** *(717)*. Here Burges, working on earlier restorations by Henry Holland, added the machicolated clock tower containing two smoking rooms and a bachelor's bedroom decorated with "medieval" murals and installed the sumptuously decorated Arab Room, chapel, banqueting hall, dining room, roof garden, and library. At **Castell Coch** *(718)*, six miles north of Cardiff, he began the restoration of Bute's thirteenth century castle, superimposing towers of gray limestone on the original red sandstone base, topping them with conical roofs, and embellishing the interior with all manner of Gothic fancies.

Cragside *(708)* near Rothbury, Northumberland, has the sprawling asymmetrical look so dear to the hearts of Gothicists, but otherwise appears more Elizabethan than medieval. Its architect, Norman Shaw, called it Old English; some architectural historians have labeled it Picturesque, others Vernacular; and another still has characterized it as the quintessence of Victorian romanticism. It was built in the 1870s for the millionaire Newcastle industrialist, Sir William (later Lord) Armstrong, manufacturer of hydraulic pumps and lifts, inventor of the Armstrong breech-loading gun, and owner of one of the biggest armaments factories in the world. He was also to buy and restore **Bamburgh Castle** *(704)* on the Northumberland coast. Cragside was used primarily as a holiday retreat set in seventeen hundred acres of Northumberland moors which Armstrong planted with over a million trees, mostly conifers. This was the first private house in England to be supplied throughout with electric light fixtures; hydraulic engines operated a passenger lift, turned the kitchen spit, and provided central heating; telephone communications ran from room to room; and servants were summoned by electric gongs. The house itself is enormous—a curious combination of half-timbered gable ends, twisted chimneys, battlements, and pointed arches. The interior rooms are a melange of Gothic motifs and William Morris stained glass and other decorations. This is an altogether fascinating place. Another production of Norman Shaw's is **Adcote** *(671)*, near Shrewsbury, Salop, built about 1876 for Mrs. Rebecca Darby, widow of a grandson of the founder of Coalbrookdale and herself the heiress of a fortune made in the manufacture of hats. Here Shaw's intention was to duplicate an old English manor house built over several centuries of time. The great hall, with its screen and minstrels' gallery, is meant to simulate that of a medieval baron; the high chimneys, gables, and half timbering are supposed to be Elizabethan. **Holker Hall** *(714)* in Cumbria, built in 1871 for the seventh duke of Devonshire by the architects Paley and Austin, is also more or less Tudor with a great profusion of gables, finials, octagonal chimneys, and mullioned windows in assorted sizes. **Ascott** *(624)*, near Wing, Buckinghamshire, is a Victorian Tudor black-and-white house, more distinguished for its paintings and its garden than for its architecture. It was the property of Leopold de Rothschild.

Another Rothschild house (Baron Ferdinand de Rothschild) in the same county, near Aylesbury, is **Waddesdon Manor** *(622)* also well-stocked with paintings and a treasury of fine French furniture. It was built between 1874 and 1889 to the design of Gabriel-Hippolyte Destailleur on the model of the sixteenth century châteaux that fill the Loire valley. Another imitation French building, though designed in the manner of a Second Empire *hôtel de ville*, is **Bowes Museum** *(698)*, Barnard Castle, County Durham. It was designed by a French architect in 1869 and, though intended to be a residence as well as a private museum, was never used for the former purpose. Its owner was John Bowes, illegitimate son of the tenth earl of Strathmore and very rich in coal mines left to him by his father. The museum today is mostly dedicated to the decorative arts and includes a splendid series of rooms done up in English period styles from the sixteenth to the late nineteenth centuries. **Luton Hoo** *(625)*, near Luton, Bedfordshire, is also of French provenance. Its exterior was remodeled in 1903 in the Beaux Arts style then fashionable in Paris, but not much emulated in Britain except by the architect C. F. Mewes who also designed the Ritz Hotel on Piccadilly. The owner was Sir Julius Wernher, a South African diamond millionaire who filled the house with priceless *objets d'art* and paintings, though few by British artists.

With the turn of the century the era of country-house building in the grand manner was drawing to its close. Two others, though, deserve mention, both designed by Edwin Lutyens, the leading English architect of the early twentieth century. Both were reversions to the thirteenth century baronial castle—a fitting swan song for the final heyday of the rich. The first was **Lindisfarne Castle** *(706)* on Holy Island off the Northumberland coast, an abandoned Elizabethan block house bought by Edward Hudson, owner of the journal *Country Life* and imaginatively restored by Lutyens to look more medieval than it ever was. The other is **Castle Drogo** *(587)* near Moretonhampstead, Devon, begun in 1910 for a rich retail merchant, Julius Drewe. It is massive, granite, and pseudo-Norman—a strange sight in a county that boasts few castles of this vintage.

There is no doubt that Victorian houses tended toward a graceless chunkiness that to the modern eye seems heavy-handed and even ugly. Victorian gardens, on the contrary, were almost uniformly glorious. Indeed, the incomparable beauty of today's typical English flower garden can trace its origins no farther back than the mid-nineteenth century. For it was the Victorians who reintroduced flowers and flowering shrubs into the terraces and parks from which they had been mostly banished by the dogmatic landscapers of the seventeenth and eighteenth centuries, with their emphasis on topiary, statuary, parterres, allées, artificial lakes, vistas, cascades, classical temples, and the like. Many factors contributed to this floral revolution: improvements in the construction of glass hothouses; growing familiarity with the tropical and subtropical parts of the British Empire and their exotic flora; advances in botanical knowledge spread by the Royal Horticultural Society and kindred organizations, including local garden clubs; and finally perhaps the Victorians' love affair with polychromy which was to have a happier issue in their gardens than in their homes and buildings.

The first noteworthy innovation of the nineteenth century was the herbaceous border, i.e., a straight or curving bed or island of flowers, mostly perennials, which is the hallmark of almost any present English garden, great or small. Fine examples, visitable today, are so numerous as to defy listing, but the following can be recommended: **Arley Hall** *(676)* near Northwich, Cheshire; **Burford House** *(648)* in Tenbury Wells northeast of Leominster, Hereford and Worcester; **Newby Hall** *(682)* near Boroughbridge, North Yorkshire; **Nymans** *(552)* at Handcross south of Crawley, West Sussex; the **Oxford Botanic Garden** *(636)*, High Street, Oxford; and **Wisley Garden** *(557)* near Woking, Surrey, the official garden of the Royal Horticultural Society which also displays a fine rock garden, a woodland garden, a heather garden, and a rose garden.

Roses that would bloom all summer long and into the autumn were among the Victorian Age's more felicitous inventions. It came about with the discovery that imported China and tea roses could be crossbred successfully with sturdy native stock to produce the Bourbon rose, the hybrid perpetual, the hybrid tea, the floribunda, and many more. Though roses can now be found in almost any bed or border, specialized rose gardens also abound. Among the most distinguished are **Queen Mary's Garden** *(529)*, Regent's Park, London; the **Royal National Rose Society Garden** *(621)* at Chiswell Green near St. Albans, Hertfordshire; the **Harlow Car Garden** *(683)* near Harrogate, North Yorkshire, owned by the Northern Horticultural Society and featuring many species of flowers besides roses; **Syon House** *(533)* in Brentford, London; **Luton Hoo** *(625)* near Luton, Bedfordshire, also distinguished for its rock garden and its park by Capability Brown; and **Polesden Lacey** *(556)* near Dorking, Surrey, noted too for its iris garden, lavender garden, and peony borders.

Another Victorian innovation was the woodland garden which came about with the discovery that the colorless parks of Capability Brown, Humphrey Repton, et al., could be enlivened with the addition of shade-loving imports like the rhododendron and the azalea and of herbaceous plants like lily of the valley, violets, primroses, foxgloves, etc. In this department the embarrassment of riches is profound, and only some of the best known woodland gardens can be listed here. They include: **Bodnant Garden** *(739)* south of Llandudno, Gwynedd; **Borde Hill** *(553)* near Haywards Heath, West Sussex; **Cliveden** *(623)* near Taplow, Buckinghamshire; **Clyne Castle** *(720)* near Swansea, West Glamorgan; **Howick Hall** *(705)* northeast of Alnwick, Northumberland; **Knightshayes Court** *(589)* near Tiverton, Devon; **Lanhydrock** *(590)* south of Bodmin, Cornwall; **Rudding Park** *(683)* near Harrogate, North Yorkshire; **Sheffield Park** *(550)* near Haywards Heath, West Sussex; **Trelissick** *(597)* south of Truro, Cornwall; **Trewithin** *(597)* east of Truro; and **Wakehurst Place** *(553)* north of Haywards Heath, West Sussex.

An exotic variant of the woodland garden is to be found at **Tresco Abbey** *(592)*, Isles of Scilly, where the proximity of the Gulf Stream has made it possible to grow all manner of subtropical plant species behind a shelter belt of California conifers. Another Victorian favorite was the rock garden, originally intended to bring alpine plants into Britain. Today there are notable rock gardens in the **Cambridge Botanic Garden** *(617)* just south of the city; the **Royal Botanic Garden, Kew** *(537)* in London, which of course has all manner of other horticultural and architectural attractions as well; the **Liverpool University Botanic Garden** *(695)* south of the city near Neston, Cheshire; and **Sizergh Castle** *(712)* near Kendal, Cumbria.

The development of glass hothouses in the nineteenth century, popularized in part by the spectacular success of the Crystal Palace in 1851, was responsible in no small measure for the polychromatic glory of the Victorian garden as distinct from its predecessors. Gardeners discovered that plants which might die if left outdoors all year could be nurtured under glass and only transferred to garden beds when conditions were favorable and when they were at the height of their blooming season. This process was known as bedding out, and its development made possible an almost infinite variety of color arrangements in Victorian gardens. Today, the growing flowers on display in almost any public park in Britain will normally have been raised to maturity in hothouses and then bedded out. Especially fine examples are seen in London at **Regent's Park** *(529)* and **St. James's Park** *(522)*; at **Hampton Court Palace** *(532)*, Richmond; and in the municipal parks of Brighton, Torquay, and Harrogate. Private gardens illustrating the principle of bedding out include: **Ascott** *(624)* near Wing, Buckinghamshire; **Chatsworth** *(662)* west of Chesterfield, Derbyshire, scene of Joseph Paxton's pre–Crystal Palace experiments with glass houses; **Holker Hall** *(714)*, Cumbria; **Tatton Park** *(675)* near Knutsford, Cheshire; **Trentham Gardens** *(668)* south of Stoke-on-Trent, Staffordshire; and **Waddesdon Manor** *(627)* near Aylesbury, Buckinghamshire.

The high point in the development of the Victorian garden came at the turn of the century in the work of Miss Gertrude Jekyll, a painter in watercolors, disciple of John Ruskin and William Morris, and, late in life, a friend and collaborator of the architect Edwin Lutyens. After failing eyesight made it impossible for her to continue as a painter, she devoted herself to gardening. Not surprisingly, the results can best be described as pictorial. Her most distinctive contribution to gardening design was her close attention to color harmonies. She planted flowers as any artist would use his palette. The effects created were consequently as pleasing to the eye as a Renoir painting. Very few of her original gardens survive, though **Barrington Court** *(584)* near Ilminster, Somerset, and **Hestercombe** *(584)* near Taunton in the same county are exceptions. Her influence, however, was pervasive and long lasting, and some of England's loveliest gardens today are derivative of Miss Jekyll's style.

Among the best are **Coates Manor** *(554)* at Fittlesworth west of Pulborough, West Sussex; **Great Dixter** *(549)* near Northiam north of Hastings, East Sussex; and **Hidcote Manor** *(645)* in Gloucestershire south of Stratford-upon-Avon. Hidcote Manor was perhaps the inspiration for what many would say is the prettiest garden in England. This is at **Sissinghurst Castle** *(540)* north of Cranbrook, Kent. Here the late Vita Sackville-West and her husband, Sir Harold Nicolson, created a composition of flowering "rooms," each walled off from the others by high hedges or closely planted trees. Some of these geometrically shaped sections specialize in flowers maturing at different seasons; others have predominant color schemes; still others are devoted to particular species such as roses or aromatic herbs. Here, in a garden that was derelict in 1930, the Nicolsons have achieved the ultimate in floral beauty. It is hard to believe that it will ever be surpassed.

The twentieth century, which saw the culmination of the Victorian ideal in gardening, witnessed too the liquidation of the landed interest and the all but total disappearance of the Victorian country house as a way of life. Death duties, first imposed in 1894, were raised by Lloyd George in 1909. Between 1910 and 1913 several hundred thousands of rural acres were sold off. Then came the first world war. Income taxes went up, and in 1919 so did death duties again—this time sharply. War reduced the supply of cheap labor. Young men and young women alike left the countryside never to return. Death duties cut especially deep when first-born heirs, and sometimes their younger brothers, were killed in the trenches, thus requiring multiple payments in quick succession. The 1920s were a period of almost unrelieved agricultural depression, driving rents down to a new low. Between 1918 and 1921 almost a quarter of the English countryside changed hands, much of it to be parceled up among former tenants. And the trend continued. After the second world war and still higher income taxes and death duties, many a duke and marquess found that the only way he could hold on to his property was to open it to the public for a price. Others transferred ownership to the National Trust while retaining tenancy privileges. Thus was born the stately homes business. *Sic transit gloria mundi.* The British aristocracy had survived far longer than many had expected when its political monopoly of the House of Commons was first breached in 1832. And it must be said that in the long twilight of its power, Britain thrived as it had never done before, survived the shock of industrialization without internal revolution, created a worldwide empire and began the process of dissolving it peacefully, developed a mechanism of responsible government which served as a model for much of the world, and by a gradual process of peaceful change evolved into a stable political democracy. Few ruling classes in the history of mankind have done so well, and none has surrendered its power so gracefully.

THE ARMY AND NAVY: 1830–1914

Nowhere—not even in the House of Lords—was the tradition of aristocracy more devoutly preserved than in the British Army of the nineteenth century. Waterloo had been won, after all, by red-coated rabble officered by gentlemen, and few in Britain dared challenge the authority of the aging duke of Wellington who saw no need to quarrel with success. For the better part of four decades after 1815 not much, therefore, changed. Enlisted men signed up for life until 1847, and after that for twenty-one years. Officers, many of them peers or younger sons of peers, still got their commissions by purchase. The red coats multiplied, partly because King William IV had an extraordinary affection for the color; he made the hussars and dragoons switch from blue to scarlet and even forced red facings on his beloved navy. Infantry weapons evolved slowly, and artillery even more so, though the state of the art and the progress of technology would have permitted a much more rapid development. For more than two decades after Waterloo, British troops still carried the smooth bore, flintlock musket—unreliable in bad weather, slow firing and inaccurate under any conditions. Not until 1839 did the army adopt the percussion musket—almost twenty years after it had been first used for shooting game. This was a minor change, involving only the substitution of a copper percussion cap containing fulminate of mercury for the century-old flintlock firing mechanism. All that was required to modify the flintlock was to drill a small hole in top of the barrel near the breech so that when the hammer struck an inserted percussion cap the charge inside would be ignited. No more would loose powder have to be slowly sprinkled onto a firing pan, but the bullet still had to be rammed home through the muzzle and the smooth bore precluded accuracy of fire.

Then in the 1840s muzzleloading rifled muskets were introduced. Rifling consisted simply of scratching a spiral groove into the barrel's interior so as to give the bullet a spinning motion when fired and thus impart much greater accuracy. It was not a new discovery: Kentucky rifles had been used on the American frontier as early as 1760 and Frederick the Great had employed Swiss rifle-bearing Jaegers in the Seven Years War. Then in the 1850s came a truly radical breakthrough with the invention by a French army captain, C. E. Minie, of what the English called the minny-ball. This was a cylindro-conoidal bullet the base of which expanded on firing and thus engaged the barrel's rifling. Its use speeded up the process of loading because the bullet's diameter was now enough smaller than the barrel's that it no longer had to be rammed all the way down from muzzle to breech. Rate of fire was thereby considerably increased. In 1854 the British Army adopted the principle and issued the Enfield Patent Rifle with an effective range of eight hundred yards, the first accurate and quick firing infantry weapon since the longbow.

The army's conservatism in these matters, to be sure, can be partly explained by the lack of any sense of urgency. For almost forty years after Waterloo, peace reigned on the Continent, except for minor revolutions not involving Britain. This is not to say that the army was idle. Its peace-time size rose to an unprecedented figure of over one hundred thousand, four-fifths of whom were employed in fighting colonial wars—in Africa, Afghanistan, New Zealand, China, Burma, Malaya, and above all India. Though until about 1880, no British government embarked on a deliber-ate policy of colonial expansion, the empire expanded anyway, chiefly through the agency of the army. Refractory native potentates constantly threatened the security of Britain's established colonies and trading posts; military action ensued; the British won; their rule was thereby further extended; and on the new borders yet another set of potentates appeared to resist the benign spread of Pax Britannica. Until 1858 there were two armies in India under British control: Her Majesty's troops and those of the East India Company which consisted of native soldiers (Sepoys) and Western mercenaries, mostly Irish. In 1857 the Sepoys mutinied and were put down after savage reprisals for equally savage atrocities. The next year the political authority of the company was abolished, and India was annexed to the Crown with a viceroy appointed at Westminster. Still the wars on the fringes of the subcontinent went on. Some idea of the nature of the fighting there and of the life of the British soldier can be gained from a visit to the **National Army Museum, Sand-hurst Departments** *(555)* on the grounds of the Royal Military Academy, Sandhurst, near Camberley, Surrey. Both the Indian Army Memorial Room and the Hastings Room contain fascinating collections of weapons, uniforms, medals, regimental plate, and paintings pertaining to this great colonial enterprise once considered so vital to Britain's power and well-being. Here today's visitor can recapture some of the mystique of India, which held the Victorians spellbound. "Ship me somewheres east of Suez" wrote the poet Kipling, and a host of British readers nodded in agreement.

The impact of India on British foreign policy was enormous, especially after the opening of the Suez Canal in 1869. But even before then, Britain's concern for safeguarding her life-line to India, "the brightest jewel in the Imperial crown," had involved her deeply in the Eastern Question, i.e., the disposal of the dying Ottoman Empire ruled from Constantinople. It was because of this concern that British troops, along with French, were dispatched to the Crimean Peninsula in 1854, ostensi-bly to save the Turks from being overrun by Imperial Russia. The Crimean War was far from being Great Britain's finest hour. Except for avoiding Napoleon's strategic blunder of trying to march to Moscow in the dead of winter, the Allies botched the campaign completely. Small wonder, when British troops under Wellington's son-in-law Lord Raglan employed the same linear tactics used forty years before in the Peninsu-lar Campaign. Only the superiority of the Enfield rifle over the Rus-sian smooth-bore muskets kept the thin red line of soldiers from total decimation at the battles of Alma and Inkermann. The famous charge of the light brigade of cavalry under Lord Cardigan at Balaclava was a travesty, misbegotten and pointless. "C'est magnifique," commented the French General Pierre Bosquet, "mais ce n'est pas la guerre." "Someone," wrote Lord Tennyson later, "had blundered." Sevastopol, the object of the campaign, was later evacuated and the war brought to a successful conclusion, but only because of Russian inanity. Almost the only redeeming feature of the entire campaign was the performance of a team of hospital nurses sent out to cope with the devastating attacks of cholera, dysentery, and malaria among the troops for which the army's miserable service of supply was mostly responsible. The most publicized of these intrepid women was Miss Florence Nightingale whose suite of rooms at **Claydon House** *(624)* near Winslow, Buckinghamshire, is today preserved as a memorial to her Crimean mission. Uniforms (still red), Enfield rifles, and other mementos of the Crimean fiasco can be observed at the **National Army Museum** *(525)* in Chelsea, London, and among many of the regimental museums cited in the previous chapter.

It took more than another decade, after the scandal of Crimea, for the British Army at last to undertake serious reform—and then only on the insistence of Gladstone's secretary of war, Edward Cardwell. Cardwell abolished the flogging of troops in peacetime; reduced terms of enlistment to twelve years, six on active duty and six in the reserves; forbade the purchase of officers' commissions; and reorganized the army into sixty-six regiments of infantry, each with a recruiting and training depot within the county with which it was to be affiliated. It is thanks to Cardwell and a later secretary of war, Hugh Childers, that British Army regiments, until reorganized again after the second world war, bore such splendid titles as the Queen's Royal Regiment (West Surrey), the Royal Welch Fusiliers, and the Pembroke Yeomanry—titles now commemorated in the many regimental museums already mentioned. Despite Cardwell's abolition of purchase, however, the officer corps was not democratized. Life for the officers in the peacetime army was a round of polo, hunting, racing, balls, and parties, and this required a private income sufficiently high to exclude all but the well-to-do. This satisfied the liberal conscience of late Victorian Britain. As the military historian Correlli Barnett puts it, "What cheaper or less troublesome way of running a great empire could there be than a professional army whose officers all had private incomes and whose rank and file were all paupers?"

By this time, however, significant changes had taken place in weaponry and military dress. In 1843 the Prussian army had adopted the needle gun, a breechloading rifle with a bolt action, invented by Johann von Dreyse. It had a rate of fire six times faster than the old muzzleloader and could be discharged by a man lying prone behind cover. By 1870 the French had greatly improved on the weapon in their *chassepot*. In 1888 the British Army adopted the breechloading Lee-Metford rifle, fitted with a magazine holding ten rounds and capable of sustained rapid fire at a killing range of two thousand yards. Meanwhile the French had perfected an automatic machine gun, the *mitrailleuse*, worked by the rotation of multiple barrels, a principle also adapted to the American Gatling gun which emerged out of the war between the North and South. In 1884 the American inventor Hiram Maxim produced the first single-barreled automatic machine gun; it could fire between 450 and 500 rounds a minute at ranges of one and a half miles. The British Army adopted it soon afterwards, and as the Vickers-Maxim it was used in the Boer War and both world wars.

Artillery also underwent radical changes during these years. Again the Germans took the lead with breechloading rifled artillery which helped them in their quick victory over the French in the Franco-Prussian War of 1870–1871. The great English weapons-manufacturer, Sir William Armstrong, had anticipated this development in 1855 with a built-up wrought-iron rifled breechloader, but the Royal Artillery in 1866 discarded it in favor of a muzzleloading rifled cannon. Not until the 1880s was British artillery converted to breechloading guns in time for use in the Boer War. Models from this period can be seen at the **Royal Artillery Museum** *(536)* at the Rotunda in Woolwich, London.

All these changes added up to a quantum leap in the range, accuracy, and rapidity of firepower. They opened up the battlefield, rendered obsolete the close-order infantry lines and squares of the Napoleonic and colonial wars, and converted every infantryman into a skirmisher. They also enhanced the vulnerability of the soldier and therefore the desirability of concealment. At last the British Army was compelled to dispense with the old familiar red tunic in favor of less dangerously visible battledress. As early as the 1850s troops serving in India had taken to dying their garments a drab color called *khaki* (based on a Persian or Urdu word meaning "dust"). When soldiers were sent from India for South African service in the 1880s, they wore khaki; by the time of the Boer War this color was standard issue, as it was to be for all troops heading for France in 1914.

The Boer War came about in the autumn of 1899 when the Dutch-descended colonists of the Transvaal, fearing British designs on their gold and diamond mines, attacked the Cape Colony and Natal. In spite of military bungling and considerable domestic opposition to the war in Britain, the Boers were beaten in the field within a year, though guerrilla operations dragged on until 1902 when the Transvaal and Orange Free State were absorbed into the British Empire with the promise of future self-government. In one sense the Boer War came in the nick of time. It sparked an irresistible movement for sweeping changes within the British military establishment. Henceforth strategic direction was to be placed in the hands of a Committee of Imperial Defense headed by the prime minister. With the creation of a general staff, the old and antiquated curriculum at the Staff College at Camberley was swept away.

New tactical manuals were issued in 1904–1905. Quick-firing field guns were bought from Germany until enough eighteen-pounders could be made at home. An improved quick-firing rifle, the Lee-Enfield, was issued to the infantry. For all the surprises and frustrations that World War I would bring, Britain in 1914 was better prepared for a continental war than she had ever been.

The Royal Navy, meanwhile, was slowly adapting itself to the revolution in technology which was to render obsolete all the old modes of war at sea. Within thirty years of Trafalgar, Lord Nelson's great fleet of storm-tossed ships had become archaic, though it took longer than that for the navies of the world, including Britain's, fully to accept the fact that steam had replaced sail as the only feasible means of propulsion for ships of war. At first paddle wheels were used; then came the screw propeller. In 1842 the Admiralty ordered the construction of the *Rattler*, a screw steamer of two hundred horsepower, and held a much publicized tug-of-war between this ship and a paddle sloop of equal power, the *Alecto*. The *Rattler* won, though side-wheelers were not abandoned immediately by the Royal Navy. In 1859 France produced the *Gloire*, the first sea-going ironclad warship. Britain responded promptly with the *Warrior*, her hull protected by an iron belt of armor, four and a half inches thick. Her hulk now (as of 1978) serves as a fueling jetty in the harbor of Milford Haven, Dyfed, and there is talk of her being restored and preserved as a historic monument. Meanwhile a model of the original can be seen in the **Science Museum** *(526)*, South Kensington, London. Three additional ironclads were laid down in 1867, but for most of the rest of the century Britain fell behind her rivals in naval innovation. After the famous victory of the Federal *Monitor* in the American Civil War, the Royal Navy gradually abandoned broadside firing for turret guns. Not until 1882 were the first heavy breechloaders mounted on British naval ships; not until 1886, with *Collingwood*, did the Navy have an all-steel ship. She also mounted four twelve-inch breechloading guns, and two years later the *Rodney* was equipped with thirteen-and-a-half-inch guns.

Then in 1898 the Royal Navy received a shock greater than any since the death of Nelson. This was the passage by the Imperial German Reichstag of the First Navy Law authorizing the construction of a fleet of nineteen battleships, soon to be doubled. Queen Victoria's grandson, Kaiser Wilhelm II, and his naval chief, Admiral von Tirpitz, had taken to heart the writings of the American Captain Alfred Thayer Mahan and had decided to create a "risk fleet" capable of threatening Britain's historic naval superiority. The great Anglo-German naval race was on. Britain, under the leadership of First Sea Lord Admiral "Jackie" Fisher, responded with the *Dreadnought*, the first all-big-gun ship, which made all other battleships obsolete with its speed and firepower. By the autumn of 1914 the Royal Navy's battle fleet came to thirty-one dreadnoughts with another sixteen building, and thirty-nine predreadnoughts —a naval force of unequaled size and strength. All have long since been scrapped. To review the history of British naval developments from 1814 to 1914, the interested traveller had best visit the **National Maritime Museum** *(536)* in Greenwich where two full rooms, No. 20 and No. 21, are devoted to this period.

WORLD WAR I: 1914–1918

On the morning of 4 August 1914 the first contingent of the army of His Imperial Majesty the Emperor of Germany, Wilhelm II, marched across the border into Belgium. The British government, true to its ancient tradition of safeguarding the Low Countries against domination by a continental power and in support of a standing treaty guaranteeing Belgian neutrality, responded with an ultimatum demanding German withdrawal. At midnight the ultimatum expired and Britain was at war —allied with France and Russia, and later Italy and others, against Germany and Austria, and later Turkey. The causes of the conflict and the events immediately leading to it are beyond the scope of this book. As to the decision of Sir Henry Herbert Asquith's Liberal government to issue the ultimatum, there was little real choice. Germany's mobilization against France and Russia and her invasion of Belgium constituted an intolerable threat to the European balance of power upon which Britain's safety depended; Germany's newly built navy was a deliberate challenge to Britain's traditional command of the sea. So came the first world war, the Great War, the War of 1914–1918. Looking out of his window at the Foreign Office on that fateful August evening, Sir Edward Grey uttered the poignant prophecy that has since become a truism: "The lamps are going out all over Europe; we shall not see them lit again in our lifetime."

In accordance with agreements already reached with the French army, a British expeditionary force was promptly shipped across the Channel to take up position at the extreme left of the French line which stretched from Lorraine to the Oise River. Four divisions of infantry were sent, plus a cavalry division, 5,592 horses, fifty-four eighteen-pounder field pieces, eighteen 4.5 inch howitzers, forty heavy guns, twenty-four machine guns, and sixty-three reconnaissance aircraft of the newly organized Royal Flying Corps. It was strictly a volunteer army that fought the Germans at Mons and Le Cateau in late August. In early September the French succeeded against terrible odds in stopping the initial German offensive at the First Battle of the Marne. In October and November the Germans tried unsuccessfully to break through the British position at Ypres. By this time the two opposing lines of soldiers stretched five hundred miles from the Swiss border northwest to the English Channel. This was the Western Front, where by the end of 1914 one half the British Expeditionary Force had already become casualties.

Along this jagged line on either side stretched trenches, six feet deep;

between lay no-man's land entangled with barbed wire; over the scene reigned the machine gun, the decisive weapon of the first world war which mowed men down like wheat and made offensive infantry action next to impossible. Stalemate ensued. From November 1914 to February 1917, when the Germans decided to withdraw to the Hindenburg Line, the Western Front did not move as much as ten miles in either direction. Terrible battles were fought between waves of bayonetted soldiers advancing over the top into no-man's land to suffer terrible casualties with little or nothing gained by the sacrifice. In the annals of the British Army, the names of Ypres, Loos, the Somme, Cambrai, and Passchendaele signify only bloody graveyards. The horrors of trench warfare have too often been described to require repetition here. The fear, hopelessness, monotony, and futility of it all defy description. The word *casualty* itself is a bloodless euphemism. Better the lines of Siegfried Sassoon:

> . . . . I died in hell
> (They called it Passchendaele) my wound was slight
> And I was hobbling back; and then a shell
> Burst slick upon the duck boards; so I fell
> Into the bottomless mud, and lost the light.

Eventually the deadlock broke and the Germans yielded—partly out of exhaustion both in the army and on the home front, partly because of the arrival of American troops in France in the summer of 1918 with the promise of many more to come, partly because of the failure of the submarine campaign against British and American shipping, partly in the hope that the American President, Woodrow Wilson, might be gulled into agreeing to the "peace without victory" he had previously advocated. In any case, peace came at last with the armistice of 11 November 1918.

Meanwhile the Allies had undertaken two innovative moves to break the stalemate—one strategic, the other technological. Both were initiated by the British, both in part inspired by the imaginative genius of one man, Winston Churchill, First Lord of the Admiralty. Both failed, though not without teaching significant lessons for future warfare. The first was intended to capture the Gallipoli Peninsula which guards the western approach to the Dardanelles Strait, thereby, it was hoped, forcing Turkey out of the war and opening up a line of communications between Russia and her Western allies. It began in March 1915 with a failed effort by British and French naval units to force a passage through the Dardanelles; continued in April with an amphibious landing at Gallipoli by British, French, Australian, and New Zealand troops; and ended in January 1916 with the final evacuation of the last of the Allied troops. Meanwhile Churchill lost his job.

The second scheme to break the deadlock on the Western front was the tank. The idea of mounting guns and armor on a tracked vehicle seems first to have occurred to a British colonel named Edward D. Swinton after he had observed the operation of a little American-made Holt caterpillar tractor in the otherwise impassable mud around British General Headquarters in France. He failed to persuade the Committee of Imperial Defense that an armed and armored tractor might be feasible as a weapon of war, but did persuade Churchill to get the navy to build an experimental model of a landship (called *tank* as a counterintelligence measure). After Churchill's fall, the army recaptured the initiative, and the result was Little Willie, the first prototype tank—now proudly on display at Bovington Camp, east of Dorchester at the **Tank Museum** *(569)* of the Royal Armoured Corps and Royal Tank Regiment. Later models (some of them now on view at Bovington) were sent into action in the Somme offensive of September 1916; at Cambrai in November 1918; and, with greater effect, at Amiens on 8 August 1918, which German General Ludendorff was to designate "the black day of the German Army in the history of the war." It was quite clear by then that the tank was capable of restoring mobility to warfare by penetrating fixed enemy defenses; all that remained was to develop doctrines of mass assault and of tank-infantry cooperation which would allow the breakthrough to be exploited. That would come after the war, though not without much foot-dragging by reactionary army officers.

Another significant innovation of World War I, though not in any sense decisive to its outcome, was the airplane. As already noted, sixty-three aircraft of the Royal Flying Corps accompanied the first contingent of expeditionary troops to France. Their mission was largely reconnaissance. These early planes had a maximum speed of 80 miles per hour, a rate of climb from ground level of between three hundred and four hundred feet a minute, and were equipped with engines of up to one hundred horse power. By the end of the war the newly organized Royal Air Force had over twenty-two thousand effective airplanes, including fighters and bombers. By that time the fastest British military plane could reach 140 miles per hour and had a rate of climb from the ground of two thousand feet per minute. Models of these now frail-looking craft are to be seen in the superb **Royal Air Force Museum of Aviation History** *(531)* in Hendon on the northern outskirts of London. Also at the **Imperial War Museum** *(534)* in London are three British aircraft of World War I: a BE2C, typical of the unarmed reconnaissance planes used at the start of the war; a Bristol fighter, introduced in 1917; and a Sopwith Camel, the best British fighter of the first world war.

As for the Royal Navy, the mighty prewar dreadnoughts, now under command of Admiral Sir John Jellicoe, spent most of the war riding at anchor at Scapa Flow in the Orkneys or patrolling the North Sea against the possibility of a sortie by the German High Seas Fleet out of Wilhelmshaven. On 31 May 1916 the possibility materialized and the great naval battle of Jutland took place. The inferior German fleet sank three British battle cruisers and three armored cruisers before turning back to port with the loss of one predreadnought battleship and one battle cruiser. Admiral von Scheer could congratulate himself on a tactical victory, but Britain still ruled the high seas; and Jellicoe could congratulate himself that he had not, as Churchill feared he might have, lost the war "in an afternoon." Thereafter both fleet commanders played it safe, and no replay of Trafalgar took place, to the grave disappointment of many a Royal Navy officer steeped in the doctrines of Alfred Thayer Mahan.

The British then tightened their naval blockade of Germany with results that are still being argued by historians. The Germans unleashed unrestricted submarine warfare against shipping bound to and from the United Kingdom. In the first three months of 1917, 1,300,000 tons of Allied and neutral shipping were sunk by German U-boats, and Jellicoe himself confessed that it would be "impossible for us to go on with the war if losses like this continue." In April 1917, however, the United States, in response to this campaign of underwater *shrechlichkeit*, declared war on Germany. Within a month began the Anglo-American naval convoy system which saved Britain from starvation and made possible the safe transit of an American expeditionary force to France. Except for the inconclusive battle of Jutland, the naval war that materialized was not the war for which both Britain and Germany had prepared. What Britain needed, in the event, was a large fleet of destroyers and submarine chasers; what her naval planners gave her was more all-big-gun battleships and cruisers than were necessary. Room 22 of the **National Maritime Museum** *(536)* in Greenwich tells the story in pictures and artifacts. On the lawn in front of the **Imperial War Museum** *(534)* in London, are two great 15-inch naval guns, cast in 1915 and 1916 to be mounted on the battleships *Ramillies* and *Resolution*. Inside is a 4-inch gun from H.M.S. *Lance* which is advertised as having fired the first British shot in the first world war; also a 5.5 inch gun from H.M.S. *Chester* which saw action at Jutland; and models of both British and German ships of both world wars.

In the same museum is a fascinating section devoted to depicting everyday life in the trenches; samples of British guns and howitzers used in World War I (also to be seen at the **Royal Artillery Museum** [*536*] in the Rotunda at Woolwich); and a model of the Mark V tank, the type that was used at Amiens. These are good reminders that for most of the men who fought it, the real war was played out to its grisly end in the rain-soaked trenches and muddy fields of France and Belgium. By the time the end came in November of 1918 more than 700,000 British soldiers had been killed in action (compared to about 144,000 in World War II). When the survivors returned for a "victory march" up Whitehall they passed by the new **Cenotaph** *(520)*, a simple, slim, white monument designed by Edwin Lutyens and executed in plaster, later to be rebuilt in stone. On the south side is inscribed the Roman numerals MCMXIV (1914) and the inscription *The Glorious Dead;* on the north is MCMXIX (1919) and again, *The Glorious Dead*. There is hardly a town or village square in Britain today that does not have its memorial monument listing the names of the local lads who died in France or at Gallipoli or in the Atlantic; hardly a public school or college without its plaque inscribed with the names of those of its students killed in the Great War. Perhaps the most heartbreaking of all is the **War Memorial Chapel** *(555)* at the Royal Military Academy in Sandhurst commemorating four thousand cadets who gave their lives for King and Country in the great holocaust of 1914–1918.

THE TWENTY-YEAR TRUCE: 1919–1939

When the leaders of the victorious Allied and Associated Powers gathered at Versailles to write the treaty that would redraw the map of Europe to Germany's great disadvantage, Britain was represented not by Henry Herbert Asquith but by David Lloyd George who in 1916 had maneuvered his chief out of office and thereby created a permanent rift within the Liberal party. As the result of an election held a month after the armistice, Lloyd George retained the office of prime minister, but as head of a coalition government in which the Conservative party was dominant. By this time women over thirty had at last been given the vote. (Those between twenty-one and thirty would not receive it until 1928.) Thus one pressing item of prewar unfinished business was erased from the agenda. The other was Ireland. Instead of taking their seats at Westminster, the Irish members elected in 1918 to set up an independent Irish parliament in Dublin which proclaimed the independence of the Irish Republic. Guerrilla warfare against British Army forces and police (the Black and Tans) at last induced Lloyd George's government to acknowledge the Irish Free State, though minus the six counties of Ulster which remained within the United Kingdom.

The coalition government lasted only until the autumn of 1922 to be replaced by an exclusively Conservative cabinet headed by Bonar Law. In this election the number of Labour party members returned to the House of Commons exceeded the Liberals, by now irreparably split into hostile factions. Gladstone's great creation was fast disintegrating. In 1924 the Labour party came briefly into office with Ramsay J. MacDonald as prime minister; thereafter the Liberals sank to the position of a third party with diminishing strength.

The modern British Labour party dates from the formation in 1900 of the Labour Representation Committee among the handful of working-class representatives returned to the House of Commons. Its roots, however, go well back into the nineteenth century—to the utopian mill owner, Robert Owen, who founded the abortive Grand National Consolidated Trade Union in 1834; to the Chartist movement of the 1840s, which agitated unsuccessfully for political democracy; to the foundation of the Trades Union Congress in 1868 and of the National Agricultural

Labourers Union in 1872; to the establishment of the Fabian Society of socialist gradualists in 1884; and to the formation of the Independent Labour party in 1893. Some of this record is graphically described in the **National Museum of Labour History** *(529)*, situated in the Limehouse Town Hall in London's shabby East End. This is a pathetic little museum and difficult to reach; today's powerful Labour party and Trades Union Congress are not to be commended for such careless treatment of their own heroic past.

The distinct improvement in labor's political position after 1919 was not matched, however, by a rise in the standard of living of the working class. The British economy, already suffering before the war from declining exports, timid business leadership, obsolescent machinery, and increasing international competition, went now into a precipitate decline. The war itself had dislocated the country's foreign trade with consequent severe damage to the shipbuilding industry. Coal exports declined from 82 million tons in 1907 to 70 million in 1930; cotton textiles from £105 million to £86 million. Chronic depression in these three vital sectors was the result, and British agriculture fared no better. Unemployment figures mounted, especially in Wales, Scotland, and the north of England. Throughout the 1920s there was hardly a year when less than a million workers were without jobs. Life for these unfortunates was made only barely tolerable by the dole, the tiny allotments of unemployment insurance parceled out by a parsimonious government. Industrial leaders sought to solve the problem of Britain's declining competitive position in the world market by lowering labor costs. As Stanley Baldwin, thrice Conservative prime minister (1923–1924, 1924–1929, 1935–1937), explained: "All the workers of the country have got to take reductions in wages in order to help put industry on its feet." The workers were not convinced. When mine owners in 1926 decreed a reduction in wages and a lengthening of the workday, the miners struck. The Trades Union Congress, in the face of government refusal to intervene in favor of the workers, ordered a general strike. It began on midnight, 3 May; it ended on 12 May—a total failure. In 1927 Parliament passed the Trade Disputes and Trade Union Act which declared sympathetic strikes or any strike designed to coerce the government illegal. One commentator noted: "A ruling class living on dividends, masses of the people on the dole, and a Government trying to maintain an uneasy status quo, is a picture that fills thinking people with despair." After the onset of worldwide depression in 1929, matters grew worse. Unemployment in Britain rose from about 1⅓ million in November 1929 to 2½ million in December 1930. In 1932 the second MacDonald government devalued the pound, and by 1937 Britain's share in the gradual recovery of world trade had slightly increased. Unemployment, however, remained chronic until the outbreak of the second world war.

Britain's declining economic fortunes were matched by the rapid reduction of her defense establishment. Hopes that the Treaty of Versailles and the newly established League of Nations would somehow insure permanent peace engendered a national apathy to international dangers and a general consensus against military expenditures. Under the terms of the Washington Treaty of 1922, the Royal Navy was restricted to parity with that of the United States. The Royal Naval Air Service, embryonic in the first world war, was retarded by amalgamation with the Royal Flying Corps into the Royal Air Force. By 1939 the keel of only one new aircraft carrier had been laid. Naval aviation suffered from an under-development of up-to-date aircraft and the failure to work out a doctrine for the effective deployment of carriers in combat. Both the United States and Japanese navies far outstripped the Royal Navy in this regard.

As to the army, Britain's early lead in mechanization was soon dissipated. Hampered by a shortage of funds, the Armoured Corps was further handicapped by quarrels between tank enthusiasts and conventional infantry diehards, eventually resulting in the resignations of Colonel J. F. C. Fuller and Captain Basil H. Liddell-Hart, both ardent propagandists for mechanized warfare and both, to some extent, prophets without honor in their own country. Conflicts in doctrine as to whether tanks should be light and maneuverable for use in independent mobile armored divisions, or slower moving and heavily armored for employment in an infantry-supporting role, remained unresolved. Both types were produced—the cruiser and the infantry tank—and models can be seen today in the **Tank Museum** *(569)* at Bovington Camp, Dorset. The outbreak of the war in 1939, however, found the British Army with no fully equipped armored formations.

As to the Royal Air Force, it too suffered birth pangs caused by inadequate funding and disagreements within the ranks as to its primary mission: aerial combat, troop support, or the strategic bombing of enemy production centers. Among these alternatives, there was no doubt in the mind of Hugh Trenchard, Chief of Air Staff from 1919 to 1929, that the war of the future would be won by fleets of bombers raining terror from the skies on factories, power plants, and population centers. Trenchard's doleful predictions did little to loosen the Treasury's purse strings before 1934, but did succeed in strengthening the convictions of an important segment of the population that war should be avoided at all costs.

These convictions, born out of the trauma of four years of trench warfare and nurtured by a generation of intellectuals, laid the groundwork for the general deterioration of Britain's national defenses over a period of fifteen years. Revulsion against the dreadful carnage of the first world war was natural enough, but the distorted interpretation of the recent past by disillusioned scholars, academics, journalists, and other molders of public opinion proved dangerously irresponsible. The tone was set with the publication in 1920 by a former Treasury official, John Maynard Keynes, of *The Economic Consequences of the Peace,* a persuasive but mischievous book which so stressed the "Carthaginian" aspects of the Treaty of Versailles as to make Germany seem an innocent victim rather than the bellicose aggressor she had in fact been in 1914. Other revisionist interpretations followed. These, coupled with such antiwar literature as Siegfried Sassoon's *Memoirs of a Fox-hunting Man* (1928), Robert Graves's *Goodbye to All That* (1929), and Vera Brittain's *Testament of Youth* (1933), created a climate of disillusionment, pro-German sympathy, and pacifism that all but emasculated the British will to resist when the German menace reappeared for the second time in a generation.

In January 1933 Adolf Hitler, as leader of the National Socialist Party, took office as Chancellor of Germany. Within a little more than three years, he constructed a new conscripted army, created a formidable air force, began the rebuilding of a fleet, and militarized the Rhineland, all in defiance of the Treaty of Versailles. The reaction of the British government to this unilateral reversal of the peace settlement of 1919 was a mixture of appeasement and rearmament, the former outrunning the latter until Hitler's intentions to dominate Europe by force of arms became unmistakably apparent. The appeasers within the Conservative party included the new prime minister, Neville Chamberlain. He had taken office on 28 May 1937 shortly after the coronation of King George VI, second son of the late George V and younger brother to Edward VIII who had abdicated the throne to marry an American divorcée, Mrs. Simpson. While the new king would grow in public esteem, the prime minister would soon be consigned to obloquy. Fear of the Soviet Union and the hope of turning Hitler against the Red menace may have blinded Chamberlain and his cohorts to the German führer's implacable hostility to France and Britain. This at least was the charge made against the inner circle of Conservative politicians who were wont to meet informally at **Cliveden** *(623)*, the Buckinghamshire home of Lord and Lady Astor.

The charge of crypto-Fascism brought frequently against the Cliveden set was no doubt exaggerated, but the dangers of appeasement were not. In March 1938 German troops occupied Austria. In September Chamberlain flew to Hitler's mountain retreat at Berchtesgaden to discuss the latter's well-advertised plan to dismember Czechoslovakia. Later that month the British prime minister and the French premier, Edouard Deladier, flew to Munich and agreed that the predominantly German-speaking territory of Czechoslovakia, the Sudetenland, should be incorporated into what was now called the Third Reich. Chamberlain returned to London, claiming to have achieved "peace with honour." In March 1939 Hitler's troops marched into Prague, the Czech capital, and proclaimed Bohemia-Moravia to be a German protectorate. In March and April the policy of appeasement was at last reversed with Britain's guarantee of military assistance to Poland in the event its independence was threatened. On 22 August the Soviet Union and Germany signed a nonaggression pact with secret clauses for the division of Poland and much of the rest of Eastern Europe between the two powers. On

1 September 1939, the German invasion of Poland began. On 3 September, Britain and France declared war against Germany.

Something had been gained by the seventeen-month postponement of hostilities since the Munich crisis. Plans for the enlargement and reequipment of the Royal Air Force, already underway since early 1936, were speeded up after April 1938. By the time war came the R.A.F. had twenty-six squadrons of Hurricanes and Spitfires and production was up to over six hundred a month. An army of five divisions had been fully equipped. Civil defenses against the expected bombing raids were put in order. Pacificism all but disappeared or went underground. The Labour party abandoned its opposition to rearmament. What was lost were thirty-six Czech divisions delivered to Hitler free of charge at Munich plus a greatly improved German position on her western front.

In any case, on 3 September, without any means to come to the military assistance of beleaguered Poland, Great Britain was again at war. The twenty-year truce was over. The two decades of uncertainty and drift that Robert Graves was to label "the long weekend" had at last expired. To Parliament the prime minister confessed: ". . . everything that I have worked for, everything that I have hoped for, everything that I have believed in during my public life, has crashed in ruins."

WORLD WAR II: 1939–1945

In September, a British expeditionary force of four divisions crossed the Channel and, as in 1914, took up positions on the French left, this time along the Franco-Belgian border not covered by the Maginot Line —that monstrous monument to regressive military thought. Thanks largely to the prodding of Winston Churchill, again First Lord of the Admiralty, British troops were sent to Norway in April, only to be evacuated in May. Confidence in Chamberlain's government plummeted, and on 10 May Churchill became prime minister. On the same day German troops invaded the Netherlands and Belgium. It was the end of what journalists had foolishly called the phony war. Three days later the new prime minister made his first speech to the House of Commons:

> I have nothing to offer but blood, toil, tears and sweat. You ask: "What is our policy?" I will say: "it is to wage war by sea, land, and air, with all our might and with all the strength that God can give us . . . You ask: "What is our aim?" I can answer in one word: "Victory."

Four days later the Germans broke through at Sedan; in another five days they were at Abbeville on the English Channel. The British Expeditionary Force had been cut off with no way to reestablish contact with the French. On 28 May began the evacuation of these stranded men from Dunkirk; altogether the Royal Navy, merchant ships, and small private craft succeeded in bringing back 338,000 troops to the United Kingdom, including 139,000 French. All guns, tanks, and heavy equipment were lost. In June Sir Alan Brooke brought another two divisions out of St. Valery, including 20,000 Poles. Late in the month the French general, Henri Pétain, signed an armistice with the invaders. On 1 July the Germans occupied the Channel Islands where they remained for the balance of the war. Today the relics of that occupation are well preserved in Jersey at the **German Occupation Museum** *(744)* and the **German Underground Hospital** *(744)* as well as the numerous German gunsites and fortifications scattered along the coastline; in Guernsey at the **Occupation Museum** *(746)* and the **German Military Underground Hospital and Ammunition Store** *(746)*. Travellers from English-speaking lands, historically untouched by foreign invasion, would be well advised to visit these places and see with their own eyes what life can be like under the rule of an enemy army.

Britain now stood alone. Churchill warned of the imminence of German landings: "Let us therefore brace ourselves to our duties, and so bear ourselves that, if the British Empire and its Commonwealth last for a thousand years, men will still say: 'This was their finest hour.' " As in the days of Bonaparte, the country expected an invasion. Children were evacuated, some sent overseas. To the suggestion that the two royal princesses, Elizabeth (later Queen Elizabeth II) and Margaret, be shipped to one of the Dominions, their mother, Queen Elizabeth replied: "The children can't go without me. I can't leave the King, and of course the King won't go." People were reminded of the first Elizabeth's famous address at Tilbury during the Armada scare. Hitler, in fact, intended to launch Operation Sealion in September—a ten-division amphibious assault against the southern coast from Ramsgate to Lyme Bay. To assure freedom from aerial attack during the crossing, the German Air Force in early August commenced a series of massive raids on southeastern England with fleets of bombers protected by fighter planes. Now began the fabled Battle of Britain. The R.A.F.'s fighter command, made up chiefly of Hurricanes and Spitfires produced in the two years since Munich and aided immeasurably by a recently installed chain of radar stations (a British invention), flew countless sorties to intercept the oncoming waves of attackers. It was touch and go, but the R.A.F. prevailed. By 18 August the Germans had lost 238 planes against 95 British. On 7 September the Germans turned aside from their attacks on fighter bases in Kent to drop their bombs on London—an implicit admission of defeat. Their last great effort came on 15 September. It too failed. On the seventeenth Hitler postponed Operation Sealion; on 12 October he canceled it. "Never in the field of human conflict," announced Churchill, "was so much owed by so many to so few." Today the battle is commemorated in the Battle of Britain Museum, a separate building of the **Royal Air Force Museum** *(531)* in Hendon. It is one of the most impressive and instructive military museums in the country. In the main building next door there are Spitfires and a Hurricane to be seen. There is also a Spitfire on view at the **Imperial War Museum** *(534)* in London, and two others at the **Imperial War Museum, Duxford** *(600)* near Saffron Walden, Essex. On a hilltop near Staines, Surrey, overlooking the Thames and the meadow where the Magna Carta was signed is the **Runnymede Memorial** *(566)*, a severely monastic-looking building dedicated to "airmen who have no known grave." In the center of the quiet cloister is a simple stone dedicated to the R.A.F. and Dominion air forces dead of World War II with the inscription, *Their Name Liveth Forevermore*.

Germany's air war now took a new turn with the regular night bombing of British cities, which came to be known as the Blitz. London was bombed every night from 7 September through 2 November. On one such occasion a fire officer on the river docks looked about him and reported: "The Pool below London Bridge was a lake of light . . . Half a mile or more of the Surrey shore is burning . . . The whole bloody world's on fire." His words recall those of Samuel Pepys writing in his diary on the night of 2 September 1666. As on that earlier occasion too, the city's many churches lay ruined, black, and smoking—including most of the marvelous creations of Pepys's contemporary, Sir Christopher Wren. In October the great provincial cities began to have their turn. There was a heavy raid on Birmingham on 25 October. At Coventry on the night of 14 November, thirty thousand incendiaries and five hundred tons of bombs and landmines were dropped. It was then that **Coventry Cathedral** *(665)* was reduced to ruins. Its broken body is dramatically visible today through the clear glass windows of a new and very modern cathedral consecrated in 1962. In the ruined sanctuary of the bombed-out church stands a cross of wood charred by the fire of 14 November 1940 and another one of nails. In the wall behind are inscribed the words, *Father Forgive*. As bad as the raid on Coventry was, however, no more than five hundred lives were lost, and factories were back in production within five days. Still, the nationwide damage from the Blitz was catastrophic: over 3.5 million homes damaged or destroyed, over thirty thousand people killed, more than half in London. That figure would be doubled before the end of the war, partly as a result of Hitler's nine-month campaign of terror in 1944–1945 in the form of buzz bombs and rockets (V1 and V2) launched from northern France and the Low Countries. Today some faint idea of the daily lives of ordinary citizens living under these dreadful conditions can be gained by a look at the small Home Front exhibit at the **Imperial War Museum** *(534)* in London. This is a fascinating display of the survival kits that became the common accouterments of daily life under the Blitz: gas masks for babies, helmets for everyday wear, Morrison shelters for the bedroom, Anderson shelters for the garden, fire extinguishers, sand buckets, first-aid gear, etc., etc.

Of course the British gave as well as received. Sir Arthur "Bomber" Harris, commander-in-chief of the R.A.F.'s Bomber Command, was a True Believer in strategic bombing, which in effect meant indiscriminate area bombing of population centers in Germany. Lancasters and Wellingtons were Bomber Command's favorite airplanes. Examples of both can be seen today at the **Royal Air Force Museum** *(531)* in Hendon. They were not equipped for precision bombing and, without adequate long-range fighter protection, were vulnerable to interception over Germany. This explains largely why Bomber Harris preferred night missions. After the United States entered the war, a division of responsibility was worked out whereby the Americans bombed during the day, the British at night. This was appropriate since American planes were equipped with Norden bombsights which made precision targeting feasible. American B-17s, however, were just as vulnerable as the R.A.F. to German fighters until improvements in their own fighters (P-51s) made long-range escorts possible. As to the efficacy of all these thousands of tons of explosives dropped on the enemy, there remains much doubt. Certainly the promises of "victory through airpower" and of a total destruction of the enemy's will to fight through strategic bombardment were never realized. Combat at sea and on the land continued to be as vital as before to the achievement of war's purposes.

The performance of the Royal Navy in the second world war was noticeably better than in the first. Again, German U-boats threatened Britain's lifeline to the outside world, especially to the United States which, under the provisions of the Lend-Lease Act, became her major source of supply. Again the answer was the destroyer and related types of submarine killers serving as escorts to convoys of merchant ships. This time the convoy system was not so long in being organized. U-boat sinkings, nonetheless, became alarming in the spring and early summer of 1941 during the Battle of the Atlantic. By autumn the crisis was over, partly owing to the garrisoning of Iceland by the United States and to President Franklin D. Roosevelt's orders to the United States Navy to extend its patrols eastward and "shoot on sight" any intercepted German U-boat. This was an undeclared act of war, but Hitler did not retaliate until the following December after the United States had declared war on his ally, Japan, following the surprise attack on Pearl Harbor. In spite of American entry into the war, U-boat sinkings mounted to an all-time high in March 1943, but thereafter fell precipitately as American ship production stepped up. Also, American aircraft carriers and British bombers, diverted to escort duties over the protests of Bomber Harris, joined the attack. Room 23 of the **National Maritime Museum** *(536)* in Greenwich is devoted to the Battle of the Atlantic. In the **Imperial War Museum** *(534)*, the navy of World War II is represented mostly by ship models. Tied up to Symons Wharf in Southwark, London, is **H.M.S. Belfast** *(534)*, the last of the Royal Navy's big-gun cruisers which served on convoy duty in the second world war and as a naval support ship during the invasion of Normandy in 1944. A more typical veteran of the Battle of the Atlantic is **H.M.S. Cavalier** *(562)*, a destroyer built in 1944, now moored off Mayflower Park in Southampton. As already mentioned,

Britain, after an early start, lagged behind in the production of aircraft carriers. With only six to start with, moreover, the Admiralty allowed these limited assets to be wasted in operations of dubious value in Norwegian waters, the South Atlantic, and the Mediterranean, where eventually the *Ark Royal* was sunk. Today the **Fleet Air Arm Museum** *(583)* at Yeovilton, near Ilchester, Somerset, maintains a good collection of carrier aircraft as well as the prototype model of the supersonic transport aircraft, *Concorde.*

As to the British Army, miraculously saved from destruction at Dunkirk, its subsequent employment prior to June 1944 has drawn considerable criticism from military analysts and historians. Churchill, himself, was responsible for Britain's commitment to what came to be known as a peripheral strategy, which amounted to an avoidance of a direct confrontation with the German army in France in favor of waging war against Hitler's vulnerable ally, Italy, and nibbling away at the fringes of Axis power in the Mediterranean and around its littoral. The attractions of this indirect approach were many and deep-rooted in history as interpreted by the prime minister: Britain's traditional avoidance of continental war, bitter memories of the 1914–1918 bloodletting, Churchill's desire to vindicate his 1915 adventure at Gallipoli, concern for the Suez and Britain's lifeline to India, and, above all, contempt for the warmaking capability of Italy. Also it must be said, there was nowhere else in 1940 for the British Army to fight to any effect, except in North Africa where the only enemy at first was Italy. Early successes were canceled out with the arrival of German reinforcements under General Rommel, and the Desert Campaign dragged on until early 1943, by which time Morocco and Algeria had been invaded from the sea by Anglo-American amphibious forces. The war in North Africa was primarily a duel between formations of tanks. At the **Tank Museum** *(569)* at Bovington Camp, Dorset, is a fine display of many of the models used in the desert, including American and German tanks as well as British.

North Africa was a sideshow, and so was Italy, invaded by Allied forces in 1943, mostly as a result of Churchill's urging. Insistence on a cross Channel attack by American strategists coupled with pressure from the Soviet premier, Joseph Stalin, whose troops had been bloodily engaged with the Germans since Hitler invaded Russia in June 1941, at last persuaded Churchill to agree to a massive Anglo-American amphibious assault against the coast of Normandy. D-Day was 6 June 1944. It was a well-planned, well-timed, and well-executed operation. Much of its success can be attributed to the special amphibious equipment evolved by Britain's Combined Operations Command: shallow-draft landing ships, motor-driven barges with bow ramps to permit rapid disembarkation of troops and tanks, artificial harbors (mulberries), etc. Some of this materiel can be seen at the **Warnham Museum** *(553)*, north of Horsham, West Sussex, a private collection of miscellany pertaining to the second world war.

For eleven months after D-Day, British and Commonwealth armies led by General Sir Bernard Montgomery under the overall command of General Dwight D. Eisenhower, drove a bloody path across northern France, Belgium, the Netherlands, and on to Germany. To their right moved their American counterparts led by Generals Bradley, Patton, et al. Facing them, away to the east, came the dogged legions of the Soviet Union. Thus, in Churchill's words, was the ring closed around Nazi Germany. Montgomery's troops went armed with an amazing panoply of weapons and equipment, much of it of American origin: field guns, howitzers, rockets, antiaircraft guns, antitank guns, self-propelled mounts, tanks, armored cars, jeeps, Lee-Enfield rifles, light machine guns, heavy machine guns, carbines, mortars, flamethrowers, antitank projectors, radios, bulldozers, pontoons, parachutes, etc., etc. Large quantities of this gear survived, and can be seen at the **National Army Museum** *(525)*, London; the **Tank Museum** *(569)* at Bovington Camp, Dorset; the **Royal Artillery Museum** *(536)* at Woolwich; the **Royal Signals Museum** *(567)* near Blandford Forum, Dorset; the **Royal Corps of Transport Museum** *(557)* in Aldershot, Hampshire; and the **Airborne Forces Exhibition** *(557)*, also in Aldershot.

The end of the European war came officially on 7 May 1945 with the ceremonial signing of Germany's unconditional surrender at General Eisenhower's headquarters in Reims. The next day Prime Minister Churchill solemnly announced the event in the House of Commons. Later, to the jubilant crowds in Whitehall, he proclaimed: "God bless you all. This is your victory! It is the victory of the cause of freedom in every land." It was also his personal victory. He had been among the first of Britain's leaders to recognize the threat that Hitler posed to the security of the West; he had steadfastly opposed appeasement, had never lost his nerve during even the darkest days of the war, had shipped essential supplies to Russia which Britain could ill afford, had cajoled vital aid from the United States when that country was still strongly isolationist, and had compromised many of his own most cherished strategic preferences for the sake of the alliance. Above all, he had captured the imagination of a much battered people and steeled their will to fight with words of such incomparable eloquence as to live forever in the annals of English letters. Today, his wartime command post, the **Churchill War Rooms** *(520)* under the Treasury Chambers on Great George Street, can be visited on application. Better still is a visit to **Chartwell** *(547)* the Churchills' charming country house overlooking the Weald in Kent, now maintained as a memorial museum. His starkly simple gravestone can be seen in the churchyard of **St. Martin's, Bladon** *(637)* northwest of Oxford near Woodstock.

The war in Europe was over. The war against Japan dragged on until 2 September 1945 when unconditional surrender documents were signed in Tokyo Bay aboard the U.S.S. *Missouri.* By then Churchill was out of office. A general election had returned a majority of Labour members to the House of Commons, and Clement Attlee was prime minister. In his first major speech as leader of His Majesty's loyal opposition, Churchill pronounced the epilogue to his country's most recent and most terrible ordeal:

> When we look back on all the perils through which we have passed and at the mighty foes we have laid low and all the dark and deadly designs we have frustrated, why should we fear for our future? We have come safely through the worst.
>   "Home is the sailor, home from the sea,
>   And the hunter home from the hill."

If by *home,* the former prime minister (quoting Robert Louis Stevenson) meant Britain as it was before the war, he deceived himself. Another survivor, Anthony Powell, came closer to the mark. Of his departure from Paddington Station to join his regiment in Wales, he later wrote: "It was a long journey, one not only into a new life but entirely out of an old one, to which there was no return. Nothing was ever the same again."

For Britain, World War II was the end of an era. Nothing was ever the same again. Only the past remained unchanged—and unchangeable. Its traces still lay all about. Most of the damage done by German bombs and rockets could be repaired. What had escaped seemed doubly precious. To preserve it became a national obligation. Only the intelligent traveller in Britain appreciates how well that obligation has been met.

PART TWO

GAZETTEER

LONDON AND ENVIRONS

INNER LONDON, NORTH OF THAMES RIVER
EC 1

* **Wesley's House and Chapel** *(420)*, 47 City Road at Epworth Street

Here is the house where John Wesley lived and died, now converted into a museum housing a large collection of Wesley memorabilia. The chapel next door was built in 1778 but completely, and tastelessly, restored two hundred years later.

EC 2

Great Eastern Hotel *(460)*, Liverpool Street

Built in 1884 by Charles E. Barry and enlarged in 1901–1906 by Colonel Robert Edis to serve as the railway hotel for the nearby Liverpool Street Station. The design is a mixture of English and French Renaissance.

Liverpool Street Station *(460)*, Bishops Gate and Liverpool Street

This, the London terminus of the Great Eastern Railway, was built in 1875 to the design of Edward Wilson in a vaguely Gothic style. The interior ironwork is especially good.

* **London Guild Hall** *(208)*, off Basinghall Street

Much renovated in the nineteenth century and badly burned as a result of German bombing in 1940, a surprising amount of this fifteenth century building still survives: notably, the interior of the porch, the crypt, and much of the walls and windows. In the museum next door is a collection of seven hundred clocks and watches gathered together by the Clockmakers Company.

Mansion House *(389)*, Mansion House Street, e of Queen Victoria Street

The official residence of the lord mayor of London was built in the Palladian style by George Dance the Elder in 1739 to 1759 with a pediment sculpted by Sir Robert Taylor. No visitors except by special application.

* **Merchant Taylors' Hall** *(208)*, Threadneedle Street

The fourteenth century crypt and fifteenth century kitchen are original; the rest is rebuilt.

*** The Museum of London *(27, 32, 80, 81, 88, 89)*, London Wall

Chronologically arranged, the beautifully mounted exhibits here present the visual biography of the London area from about 250,000 B.C. to modern times. This is the largest and the best of Britain's many municipal museums of local history and archaeology.

Roman Wall *(80)*, St. Alphage Garden near corner of Wood Street and London Wall; Church of St. Giles Cripplegate, Noble Street

At both places a substantial portion of Roman work survives in the lower courses of the wall; the upper stones are of medieval provenance.

* St. Mary Le Bow *(353)*, Cheapside

Christopher Wren's fabulous tower and steeple survived the World War II bombing that almost destroyed the church, which has since been restored.

*** St. Vedast *(354)*, Foster Lane

One of Christopher Wren's most beautiful steeples rises above this church whose interior has been extremely well restored after German bombs set fire to the interior in 1940. To the traveller, the church has the additional advantage of always being open during the daytime. It lies almost in the shadow of St. Paul's Cathedral.

EC 3

*** The Monument *(351)*, Fish Street Hill

Designed by Christopher Wren and Robert Hooke to mark the spot near which began the Great Fire of 1666, this is a fluted Doric column, 202 feet high. The view from the top (311 steps up) is almost worth the climb.

Roman Wall *(80)*, Wardrobe Tower, Tower of London *(80)*: Trinity Square behind London Polytechnic School; Cooper's Row, Tower Hill, behind Midland House

At all these places the lower courses of Roman flat red bricks can be distinguished from the medieval stonework superimposed upon them.

* St. Katherine Cree *(337)*, Leadenall Street

Built in 1628, this is the only London church consecrated by William Laud (as bishop of London). It is mixed Gothic and classical in the manner preferred by that controversial prelate. The basic plan, vaulting, and window tracery are Gothic, while the west doorway and nave arcading are classical.

* **St. Magnus the Martyr** *(353)*, Lower Thames Street

The tower and steeple of this Christopher Wren church, built in 1671 to 1676, are especially beautiful. Inside, the church has twice been refurbished in a baroque style fussier than Wren's original.

* **St. Mary at Hill** *(353)*, St. Mary at Hill

Shaped like a Greek cross, the interior of this rather plain looking Wren church is magnificent. A central dome rises from four pendentives; plasterwork and woodcarving are unusually attractive.

St. Mary Woolnoth *(367)*, King and Lombard Streets

A baroque composition of 1716 to 1727 by Nicholas Hawksmoor, the dominant motif inside and out is expressed in its many Corinthian columns.

*** **Tower of London** *(80, 131, 150, 153, 156, 158, 182, 203, 272, 274, 278, 301, 339, 342, 446)*, Tower Hill

The White Tower was built about 1078 by William the Conqueror as a three-story rectangular stone keep. Although the exterior was altered in the seventeenth century by Sir Christopher Wren who enlarged the windows, the interior remains remarkably faithful to the original Norman architecture. Of special interest is St. John's Chapel on the second floor, the oldest church in London. In the Armouries is a collection of sixteenth and seventeenth century armor and weapons including crossbows. Associated with it is the recently installed Heralds' Museum containing a collection of documents from the College of Arms.

The Bell Tower was erected in the reign of Richard I or a little later.

The inner curtain walls, with their mural towers, were built by Henry III in the mid-thirteenth century, as was the Wakefield Tower.

The outer curtain wall and its surrounding moat (now dry), the Middle Tower, Lion's Tower, Beauchamp Tower, and Traitor's Gate were added in the reign of Edward I.

The Byward Tower and the Bloody Tower (scene of the murder of the Little Princes) was built by Richard II.

The Chapel Royal of St. Peter ad Vincula was rebuilt in the sixteenth century and is the burial place of Anne Boleyn, Catherine Howard, Lady Jane Grey, and others. Tower Green to the south was the site of many executions.

The Jewel House contains the Crown Jewels and the Royal Regalia of every English monarch since Charles II.

The Yeomen Warders (Beefeaters) were created by Henry VII and their present uniforms can be traced to the sixteenth century.

Here also is the Royal Fusiliers Museum with the usual array of regimental uniforms, weapons, etc.

EC 4

*** **Dr. Johnson's House** *(413)*, Gough Square, off Fleet Street via Johnson's Court, just e of Fetter Lane

A charming eighteenth century town house beautifully maintained as a Johnson museum. Here the great man lived between 1749 and 1759 and compiled his *Dictionary of the English Language.*

* **Inner Temple Hall** *(320)*, n of Victoria Embankment, w of Middle Temple Lane

Of this main building of one of the four Inns of Court, only the fourteenth century crypt survived the German World War II bombing, and the present structure is a contemporary replacement.

* **Middle Temple Hall** *(319)*, n of Victoria Embankment, between Middle Temple Lane and Milford Lane

One of the four Inns of Court, it was badly damaged by German bombing in World War II, but the Elizabethan chamber has been restored.

* **Prince Henry's Room** *(351)*, Fleet Street, opposite foot of Chancery Lane

A well-appointed room with Jacobean paneling and furnishings in what is thought to be the oldest domestic lodging in London. It serves as a museum of mementos of the diarist Samuel Pepys who lived not far away.

* **St. Bride, Fleet Street** *(353)*, Fleet Street

Built by Sir Christopher Wren in 1671 to 1678, the elegant wedding-cake steeple was added in 1701 to 1703. Reconstruction of the interior, destroyed by German bombs in 1940, unfortunately failed to copy the original, so, with no gallery and with stained-glass windows, this does not look much like the inside of a Wren church.

* **St. James Garlickhythe** *(353)*, Garlick Hill

An interesting example of Sir Christopher Wren's skill in adapting classical motifs to a medieval church plan, the church was badly blitzed during World War II but has been beautifully restored. Open only during services.

*** **St. Mary Abchurch** *(353)*, Abchurch Lane

The plain brick exterior of this Wren church, built in 1681 to 1686, masks a richly decorated interior with a domed roof and excellent woodwork by Grinling Gibbons.

*** **St. Paul's Cathedral** *(354, 395, 445)*, St. Paul's Churchyard

Sir Christopher Wren's great masterpiece was built between 1675 and 1710, the first cathedral in England after the Reformation. The great dome over the nave consists of three parts: an inner masonry dome with an oculus; an intermediary masonry cone to support the lantern; and an outer "cladding" of wood and lead for external effect. Grinling Gibbons carved the twenty-six delicate stone panels beneath the great round-headed windows and did the woodwork on the choir stalls, organ loft, and screen. The ironwork is by Jean Tijou. The carved keystones of the dome arches are by Caius Gabriel Cibber. The ceiling paintings of the life of St. Paul are by Sir James Thornhill. The facade of the west end consists of a colonnade of Corinthian columns topped by another colonnade of the composite order. It is flanked by two towers reflecting baroque tendencies unusual for Wren. The southwest tower contains the great seventeen-ton bell which sets off a deafening racket every afternoon at one o'clock and before services. Funerary monuments inside include those dedicated to John Donne (shrouded), the great duke of Wellington, and Lord Nelson. Wren himself is buried here, and on his tombstone is written the inscription: *Si monumentum requiris, circumspice* ("If you need to see his monument, look around"). The Jesus Chapel is dedicated to the Americans who lost their lives in World War II operations based in Britain (twenty-eight thousand names are listed on the honor roll).

*** **St. Stephen Walbrook** *(354)*, Walbrook

One of the most beautiful, and certainly the most interesting architecturally of Sir Christopher Wren's City churches, it has a coffered dome supported by Corinthian columns arranged in a square at one end of a short rectangular nave. The effect is admirable. Currently (1980) undergoing restoration, it can only be hoped that Wren's original arrangements will be preserved.

** **Temple Church** *(151, 155, 242, 319)*, Inner Temple Lane

The best of England's twelfth century "round churches," the west end of the existing structure was consecrated in 1185 to be the seat of the Order of Knights Templar in England. This round part of the church is Norman Transitional in style. The rectangular chancel was added in 1240 and is Early English. The church was badly bombed in 1941 and has been much restored.

Special features: the nine recumbent marble figures of twelfth and thirteenth century "associates of the Temple" (including both William Marshals, father and son), though much damaged, constitute the best collection of knightly effigies in the country; the reredos behind the altar was designed in the seventeenth century by Sir Christopher Wren.

* **Walbrook Mithraeum** *(81, 89)*, Queen Victoria Street, Temple Court near Bucklersbury House

Here are the foundations of a temple to Mithras, a very popular god in mercantile and military circles in fourth century Roman *Londinium*.

WC 1

*** **The British Museum** *(15, 26, 32, 51, 57, 58, 61, 62, 68, 80, 86, 88, 90, 101, 103, 104, 105, 119, 121, 148, 439, 443)*, Great Russell Street

This great neo-Grecian building was designed by Sir Robert Smirke and built mostly between 1823 and 1852. Among its many famous antiquities, the Elgin Marbles from the Periclean Parthenon are perhaps the most distinguished.

The following rooms are especially germane to British history and prehistory:

ROOM 35: Prehistory and Roman Britain
ROOM 36: Man before Metals
ROOMS 37, 38, 39: Later Prehistory of Europe
ROOM 40: Roman Britain
ROOM 41: Early Medieval Art
ROOM 42: Medieval Art
ROOM 43: Medieval Tiles and Pottery
ROOM 45: Waddesdon Bequest
ROOMS 46, 47: Renaissance and Later

*** **Courtauld Institute Galleries** *(313, 400)*, Woburn Square

A small but extremely well-arranged art gallery containing important paintings from the fourteenth through the nineteenth centuries, including samples of the work of a few British artists (Eworth, Lely, Romney, Gainsborough).

*** **Dickens House** *(465)*, 48 Doughty Street, n of Gray's Inn Gardens

Once the London residence of the novelist Charles Dickens, this is a good museum of his personal mementos, books, and manuscripts.

* **Gray's Inn** *(319)*, Gray's Inn Road, n of High Holborn

One of the four Inns of Court, it was badly damaged by German bombing in World War II. The Elizabethan Hall has been rebuilt with some of the original materials; the chapel and library had to be completely replaced; only the nineteenth century Verulam and Raymond buildings escaped destruction. In the garden is a statue of Sir Francis Bacon, treasurer of the Inn from 1577 to 1626.

* **St. George's, Bloomsbury** *(367)*, Bloomsbury Way

One of Nicholas Hawksmoor's grander productions in the baroque manner, the church is built on a Greek cross plan to which a Corinthian portico was attached. A statue of George I stands on the steeple rising from the tower curiously situated on the side of the church.

* **Staple Inn** *(320)*, s side of High Holborn across from the entry to Gray's Inn Road

The only survivor of the nine ancient Inns of Chancery, the Tudor-style building here is a reconstruction of a sixteenth century hall burned out in 1944 as a result of German air raids.

University College *(412, 468)*, Gower Street between University Street and Grafton Way

Founded in 1826 and opened in 1838, the college was incorporated with the University of London in 1907. The central building with its Corinthian portico and dome was designed by William Wilkins.

WC 2

Charing Cross Hotel *(460)*, The Strand

This fine Victorian French-Renaissance-style building was built in 1865 to serve as the railway hotel for the London terminus of the South-Eastern Railway next door. It was reroofed following bomb damage in World War II, but the interior retains some of its Victorian splendor.

Charing Cross Station *(460)*, The Strand

The original station here, since much modified, was built in 1859 to 1864 to the designs of Sir John Hawkshaw and Edward Middleton Barry for the London terminus of the South-Eastern Railway. The most interesting feature is Barry's cast-iron "Eleanor Cross" in front of the station. This was meant to be a replica of the original cross erected near here by Edward I in honor of his deceased queen, Eleanor of Castile.

* **H.M.S. Discovery** *(462)*, Victoria Embankment

Built in 1901 as an exploration vessel and commanded by Captain R. F. Scott on his expeditions to the Antarctic, this is a wooden-hulled, barque-rigged, screw-propeller, steam- and sailing-ship. She saw service in World War II as a minesweeper.

* Lincoln's Inn *(319)*, w of Chancery Lane between High Holborn and Carey Street

This is the best preserved of the four Inns of Court. Old Hall, red brick, dates from 1490 with a south bay added in the 1620s; the gatehouse was built in 1518; the chapel in 1623; the stone buildings in the 1770s; and the new hall and library in the mid-nineteenth century in a style meant to be Tudor. Lincoln's Inn Fields to the west of the buildings is the largest square in central London. Visitors should call at the Porter's Lodge in New Square off Carey Street for admission into the buildings.

*** London Transport Museum *(460)*, Covent Garden

Here is a fine collection of discarded London motor buses, trolley buses, trams, etc., as well as locomotives, coaches, and other equipment pertaining to London's famous Underground system. A new establishment, located in the old Covent Garden flower market, this is a good example of Britain's current high level of museumship.

*** The National Gallery *(182, 312, 334, 408, 410, 411, 439, 442, 443)*, n side of Trafalgar Square

Built in the 1820s to the design of William Wilkins to house a collection of thirty-eight paintings bought by the government from the estate of John Julius Angerstein, it is now one of the greatest art galleries in the world. The front portico by Henry Holland was moved here when the Prince Regent's Carlton House was demolished. Rooms 14 and 16 are repositories of English paintings. The Wilton Diptych is in Room 2.

*** The National Portrait Gallery *(270, 274, 313, 333, 341, 369, 409, 443, 479)*, St. Martin's Place (behind the National Gallery)

A collection of nearly ten thousand portraits of men and women of some significance in British history. Some of the paintings are intrinsically valuable as works of art.

*** Nelson Monument *(394)*, Trafalgar Square

This tall column, 145 feet high, was designed in 1843 by William Railton. The gigantic statue of Lord Nelson on top is the work of E. H. Bailey. The lions are by Sir Edwin Landseer.

** Public Records Office Museum *(133, 151)*, Chancery Lane

An excellent museum containing a variety of documents touching on numerous aspects of British history. Among the more important are Domesday Book (two volumes), Henry III's Confirmation of Magna Carta, Exchequer Tallies from the twelfth to the nineteenth century, Shakespeare's will, and the log of H.M.S. *Victory* kept during the Battle of Trafalgar.

*** **Royal Courts of Justice (Law Courts)** *(473)*, The Strand

Designed by George Edmund Street and completed in 1881, this is a masterpiece of Victorian Gothic in Portland stone.

* **St. Clement Danes** *(417)*, The Strand

Much restored after World War II bombing, the church was designed in 1680 to 1682 by Sir Christopher Wren, the steeple, in the Wren style, by James Gibbs in 1719.

* **St. Giles-in-the-Fields** *(417)*, Endell Street, off St. Giles High Street

A nice Georgian church, built in 1731–1733 by Henry Flitcroft.

*** **St. Martin-in-the-Fields** *(417)*, e side of Trafalgar Square

James Gibbs's masterpiece, built in 1722 to 1726, is today the most prominently displayed church in England because of its location on busy Trafalgar Square. The Corinthian order prevails outside and in, the interior plasterwork is exquisite, and the galleries well placed and well proportioned. It is widely copied throughout the world wherever Church of England services are held.

* **St. Mary-le-Strand** *(416)*, The Strand

Built in 1714 to 1717 to the design of James Gibbs, the church's Italianate exterior and deep chancel perhaps reflect the architect's own Roman Catholic affiliation.

*** **St. Paul, Covent Garden** *(335)*, w side of Covent Garden Market

Built in the Tuscan style by Inigo Jones in 1631, it was restored by Thomas Hardwick, Jr., in 1795 after a fire. Jones called it "the handsomest barn in England."

** **Soane's Museum** *(408, 440)*, No. 13, Lincoln's Inn Fields

An interesting house uniquely designed by its owner, Sir John Soane, in the early nineteenth century, it contains, among other things, a good collection of Hogarth and Turner paintings.

SW 1

*** **Banqueting House** *(324, 332, 334, 345)*, Whitehall; AM

Designed by Inigo Jones for James I and built between 1619 and 1622, this is a masterpiece of seventeenth century Palladian architecture. Outside, the symmetrical facade is faced with Ionic pillars and pilasters below and those of the Corinthian order above. The same juxtaposition is used on the interior, which, following Palladio's rule, is a double cube measuring 110 feet by 55 feet by 55 feet. The baroque ceiling was painted by Peter Paul Rubens and installed in 1635. It depicts the apotheosis of James I surrounded by allegorical scenes of the union of England and Scotland and the prosperity of the king's rule. This is the only really fine baroque painting that can be described as English, although the artist was Flemish and the panels were actually painted abroad and shipped to London. The room is hallowed in the eyes of some by the fact that from it the "martyred king," Charles I, stepped onto an adjoining scaffold to his execution on the block.

Belgrave Square *(441)*

Regency town houses by George Basevi.

* Buckingham Palace *(438)*, w end of The Mall

The chief London residence of the sovereign, it was built mostly by John Nash from 1825 to 1830 for George IV on the site of Buckingham House owned by George III. The east front toward the Mall was rebuilt in the twentieth century to the plan of Sir Aston Webb.

No admission is granted to the public, except to the attached Queen's Gallery where exhibitions of paintings are regularly shown.

The well-known changing of the guard takes place daily at 11:30 A.M. and can best be seen on the steps of the **Queen Victoria Memorial Statue** *(453)*, also designed by Webb and built in 1911.

Carlton House Terrace *(438)*, n side of The Mall

A typically Regency row of houses designed by John Nash.

The Cenotaph *(498)*, Whitehall

The monument designed by Edwin Lutyens to commemorate all of Britain's World War I dead. Twenty-six years later another set of inscriptions was added in honor of those killed in World War II.

Churchill War Rooms *(507)*, Treasury Chambers, Great George Street

Here, underneath the Treasury Chambers, is Churchill's World War II command post and the headquarters of his war cabinet. It consists of a bedroom, office, and maproom, all furnished in the Spartan manner appropriate to the occasion.

Visits must be arranged in advance and there is usually a long waiting list. Two months prior notice is not too much. Write to the Curator, Churchill War Rooms, c/o 41 sub-E, Treasury Chamber, Parliament Street, London SW1P 3AG, or call 233-8904 before 9:30 A.M.

Foreign Office *(474)*, King Charles Street

Built in 1874 to the design of Sir George Gilbert Scott, the style of the Foreign Office is Italian Renaissance because of the insistence of Lord Palmerston who rejected Scott's initial plans for a Gothic building.

* **Grosvenor Hotel** *(460)*, Buckingham Palace Road

This railway hotel built in 1861 by J. T. Knowles to serve the London terminus of the London, Brighton and South Coast Railway, is now part of Victoria Station. Recently cleaned, this is a fine Victorian Italianate building with French mansard roofs.

*** **Horse Guards** *(389)*, Whitehall

This building, in front of which the colorful daily changing of the Queen's Life Guards takes place, was designed in the Palladian style by William Kent, more or less in the manner of Holkham Hall in Norfolk.

*** **Houses of Parliament** *(157, 449, 472)*, Parliament Square

Also known as the New Palace of Westminster, this well-known landmark was built in 1840 to 1850 after a fire had destroyed most of the old palace. The architect was Sir Charles Barry, and Augustus W. N. Pugin is responsible for most of the decorative detail. The style is Victorian Gothic, though Barry inserted some Renaissance features, especially along the river facade. The crypt of St. Stephen's Chapel, also known as the Church of St. Mary Undercroft, survived the fire. It is underneath the site of the chapel where the House of Commons met from 1547 until 1834, the date of the fire. In the Clock Tower is "Big Ben," a thirteen and one-half ton bell, well-known to listeners of the BBC. Outstanding interior features are the Royal Gallery, the Queen's Robing Room, the House of Lords, the Peers' Lobby, and the House of Commons, restored after German bombing in 1941.

* **Jewel Tower** *(180)*, Old Palace Yard, Westminster; AM

Except for Westminster Hall, this is all that is left aboveground of the medieval royal palace of Westminster, otherwise destroyed by fire in 1834. It was built by Edward III in 1366 as a royal treasure house, and today houses miscellaneous medieval artifacts.

New Scotland Yard *(476)*, New Scotland Yard

Built in 1887 to 1890 to the design of Norman Shaw for the Metropolitan Police, this building has features of the French Renaissance, German baronial, and English baroque.

*** Queen's Chapel *(332)*, Marlborough Road, s of Pall Mall

Built by Inigo Jones in the Palladian style, first for the Spanish Infanta whom Charles I, as Prince of Wales, wooed and lost, and then for the French Princess Henrietta Maria who became his queen. Though originally constructed for Roman Catholic uses, it is now an Anglican church holding Sunday morning services between Good Friday and the end of July. The interior is especially elegant: a gilded barrel-roof ceiling, a richly paneled reredos, and a Venetian window in the east end. The well-dressed congregation of Sunday worshipers is almost as splendid as the church itself.

* The Royal Mews *(438)*, Buckingham Palace Road

Designed by John Nash to house the royal carriages, etc., which can still be seen, though visiting hours are limited.

* St. James's Palace *(278)*, Stable Yard off Cleveland Row

Of Henry VIII's brick palace only the gatehouse and Chapel Royal remain; the rest is mostly an early nineteenth century restoration carried out by John Nash at the behest of King George IV. After Whitehall burned down in 1698, this became the official London residence of the sovereign, and the royal court is still officially known as the Court of St. James. Except during services in the Chapel Royal, only the exterior is visible to the public today but the site attracts attention mostly because of the presence of a colorful sentry in front of it.

*** St. James's Park *(438, 487)*, s of The Mall

Laid out for George IV by John Nash, this is one of the world's most famous parks, and deservedly so.

St. James-the-Less *(473)*, Thorndike Street and Vauxhall Bridge Road

Designed by George Edmund Street and built in 1858 to 1861, this is a polychromatic-brick exercise in Victorian Gothic.

* St. Margaret's, Westminster *(273)*, Parliament Square

A much restored Perpendicular church of the sixteenth century, the chief attraction here is the east window which was made to commemorate the betrothal of Catherine of Aragon and Prince Arthur, Henry VII's oldest son. It serves as a sort of chapel for the House of Commons and is the site of many fashionable weddings.

*** Somerset House *(400)*, Victoria Embankment/Lancaster Place/The Strand

This mammoth government office building, the central block of which was designed by Sir William Chambers in the late eighteenth century, is a masterpiece of neoclassicism, the dominant order being Corinthian. The arches on the southern facade were originally watergates before the installation of the landfill called the Victoria Embankment.

*** Tate Gallery *(313, 334, 408, 409, 410, 411, 442, 443, 479, 480)*, Millbank

This is *the* great national collection of British painting. With few exceptions, all distinguished British artists from the sixteenth to the twentieth centuries are represented here. Especially noteworthy are the works of John Constable (1776–1837), J. M. W. Turner (1775–1851), William Blake (1757–1827), and the nineteenth century Pre-Raphaelites: D. G. Rossetti, J. E. Millais, William Holman Hunt, et al.

Victoria Station *(459)*, Buckingham Palace Road

Of the confused conglomeration here, the oldest part is the brick and plaster classical-style building erected in 1860 for the London, Chatham and Dover Railway that now constitutes the continental part of the station. Next to it is the addition put up in the 1890s in a flashy Edwardian baroque of Portland stone. Beyond that is the more massive brick Edwardian Renaissance building which served as a station for the London, Brighton and South Coast Railway. The Victoria Line Underground Station is modern.

*** Westminster Abbey *(123, 156, 163, 174, 180, 184, 188, 237, 259, 270, 273, 331, 367)*, Victoria Street

Originally a Benedictine abbey church, it enjoyed cathedral status only briefly (1540–1550) and was then converted into a collegiate church of secular canons. Because of its proximity to Westminster Palace around which grew up the permanent seat of the royal government, Westminster became, in fact if not in name, the state church of England.

Architectural styles: West front—seventeenth and eighteenth century "Gothic"; nave, transepts, choir, and retrochoir—Early English with Decorated features; Henry VII Chapel—Perpendicular; Royal Air Force Chapel—Modern; cloisters—Early English and Decorated; chapter house—Geometric Decorated; undercroft and adjacent cloister—Norman.

Special features: nave—portrait of Richard II; south transept—Poets Corner; retrochoir (St. Edward's chapel)—coronation chair and Stone of Scone, Henry V's chantry (on bridge over south ambulatory), tombs of

Henry III, Edward I and Queen Eleanor of Castile, Edward III and Queen Philippa, Richard II and Queen Anne of Bohemia, retrochoir chapels; Henry VII's chapel—tombs of Henry VII, Queen Elizabeth I, Queen Mary I, Edward V, Edward VI, Mary Queen of Scots, Margaret Beaufort, Charles II, William and Mary; undercroft—abbey museum with royal and other effigies.

* Westminster Cathedral *(447)*, Victoria Street

Seat of the cardinal archbishop of Westminster, this is the primary Roman Catholic church in Britain. Designed by J. F. Bentley and built in 1895 to 1903 it consists of a long nave covered by a series of broad domes over square bays topped by a campanile. The exterior construction is in alternate bands of red brick and gray stone. The style is vaguely Byzantine, chosen allegedly to mark the building off from nearby Westminster Abbey. In this respect the choice of architectural design was notably successful.

*** Westminster Hall *(134, 164, 182, 345)*, Parliament Square

Constructed by William II in about 1097 as part of Westminster Palace, it was given its splendid hammer-beam roof by Richard II in 1194 to 1402. Home of the first English law courts, it was the earliest seat of a stationary royal bureaucracy separate from the itinerant court. It is the site of a number of famous trials, including those of William Wallace, Sir Thomas More, and Charles I—all of whom were condemned to death.

SW 3

*** Brompton Oratory *(477)*, Brompton Square

More precisely the Oratory of St. Philip Neri, this was built in 1853 at the insistance of Cardinal Newman, who introduced the order into England. This is a charming baroque building, more Roman in appearance than most English essays in this direction.

*** Carlyle's House *(465)*, 24 Cheyne Row, Chelsea; NT

The writer Thomas Carlyle lived here from 1834 to 1881. It is among the best preserved and most interesting of all English literary homes, not only because of its association with the author, whose many memorabilia it houses, but because of its authentic air of Victorian middle-class respectability.

** Chelsea Hospital *(356)*, Royal Hospital Road, Chelsea

Built by Sir Christopher Wren, beginning in 1682, to house British Army pensioners, the great central portico is faced with Doric columns, and

Doric pilasters grace the two barracks wings on either side. The great hall, chapel, and council chamber are open to the public, the latter hung with portraits of Stuart royalty by Lely and Kneller. Blue- or scarlet-garbed pensioners act as guides.

*** **National Army Museum** *(342, 445, 491, 507)*, Royal Hospital Road, Chelsea

An outstanding museum depicting the history of the British Army from 1485 through the second world war. Exhibits are arranged chronologically so as to give the viewer a good understanding of the historical evolution of weapons, uniforms, and accouterments. The picture gallery includes portraits by Reynolds, Gainsborough, and Lawrence and some lively battle scenes.

SW 7

*** **Albert Memorial** *(451, 474)*, Kensington Gore

Designed by Sir George Gilbert Scott in 1872 to commemorate the late Prince Consort, Albert of Saxe-Coburg-Gotha, husband of Queen Victoria, this is a splendid monument to High Victorian taste as well as to the prince. Within a Gothic tabernacle Albert's seated bronze statue is surrounded by a variety of allegorical figures representing Asia, Africa, America, and Europe, as well as Agriculture, Manufacture, Commerce, and Engineering. The frieze depicts 169 noted poets, composers, artists, and architects (including G. G. Scott himself). Long ridiculed for its Victorian fussiness, this monument is at last coming to be esteemed as a splendid symbol of nineteenth century taste and accomplishments.

** **British Museum of Natural History** *(4, 9, 477)*, Cromwell Road, South Kensington

Among the many exhibits dealing with ecology, biology, mineralogy, ornithology, ichthyology, etc., one section pertains to Paleolithic man. Here is the oldest human fossil in Britain: the skull of Swanscombe Man.

Pelham Crescent *(441)*

Regency town houses by George Basevi.

Royal Albert Hall *(477)*, Kensington Gore

This great concert hall with a capacity of eight thousand was built in 1867 to 1871 on grounds bought from the profits of the Great Exhibition of 1851. Its red-brick and terra-cotta exterior is broken by a huge frieze provided by the Minton potteries of Staffordshire. The architectural style is vaguely North Italian Renaissance.

*** **Science Museum** *(426, 428, 429, 431, 456, 457, 463, 493)*, Exhibition Road

The best museum in the country for the study of Britain's industrial history. Of special interest are the exhibits of machine tools, textile machines (including Arkwright's originals), navigational instruments, ship models, steam engines, locomotives, and motor cars. Everything is beautifully arranged with ample instructional material and viewing aids. There is so much to see, however, that first visitors are advised to buy the museum's guidebook, *Fifty Things to See*, before undertaking an exploration on their own.

*** **Victoria and Albert Museum** *(126, 270, 278, 312, 333, 406, 435, 442, 443, 475, 477, 479, 480)*, Cromwell Road, South Kensington

Built in stages between 1856 and 1909, the building is vaguely Tuscan in appearance in a fashion known as the "Kensington style" of late Victorian England. It houses a vast and miscellaneous collection of paintings, statuary, ceramics, tapestries, and other *objets d'art*. Of special interest to the student of English history are (a) the photocopy of the Bayeux Tapestry, (b) the Syon Cope, (c) the Torrigiano bust of Henry VII, (d) the Great Bed of Ware, (e) the sixteenth and seventeenth century English miniatures, (f) the eighteenth century rooms and furniture by Robert Adam, Chippendale, et al., (g) paintings by English artists, especially Landseer and Constable, and (h) the Pre-Raphaelite Angeli Laudantes tapestry.

W 1

* **All Saints, Margaret Street** *(473)*, Margaret Street, off Cavendish Square

Built by William Butterfield in 1850 to 1859 under the auspices of the Camden Society, this is the pioneer church of the Victorian Gothic Revival. It is constructed in polychromatic brick.

** **Apsley House** *(445)*, Piccadilly

Designed by Robert Adam in 1771 to 1778 and acquired by the first duke of Wellington in 1817, this lovely neoclassical town house is now a museum commemorating the Iron Duke and his victory over Napoleon.

Burlington House *(526)*, n side of Piccadilly

Now occupied by the Royal Academy. The original house here was built in 1665, and most of the quadrangle was designed by R. R. Banks and Charles Barry in 1869 to 1873. On the north side stands Old Burlington

House designed by the third earl of Burlington in the early eighteenth century with the help of James Gibbs, Colen Campbell, and, especially, his lordship's protégé, William Kent. Though remodeled by Sidney Smirke in the nineteenth century, this was one of the earliest experiments in eighteenth century Palladianism and exercised considerable influence on architectural styles throughout England.

* **Marble Arch** *(438)*, Park Lane and Oxford Street, ne corner of Hyde Park

Erected in 1828 in front of Buckingham Palace and moved to its present location in 1850, this well-known monument was designed by John Nash more or less in emulation of the Arch of Constantine in Rome. Nearby is the site of Tyburn, London's favorite place of execution outside of Tower Hill and the scene of countless hangings, drawings, quarterings, etc., from the twelfth to close to the end of the eighteenth century.

* **St. George, Hanover Square** *(367)*, Hanover Square

Built by John James about 1712 to 1724, this is a minor baroque masterpiece, distinguished chiefly by its massive Corinthian portico.

*** **St. James, Piccadilly** *(354)*, Piccadilly

Perhaps the loveliest and certainly the most accessible of Sir Christopher Wren's post-Fire churches, it was built in 1682 to 1684 and restored after World War II damage. The exterior is plain brick with tower and steeple; inside, the galleried nave is spacious and well lighted, with a marble font by Grinling Gibbons and fine woodcarvings. The only jarring note is the stained glass in the east windows. The church is open at all times during the daylight hours, and contributions to its upkeep are welcomed and deserved.

* **St. Peter, Vere Street** *(417)*, Vere Street, off Oxford Street

This small brick church with a Tuscan portico and nice plasterwork inside was built by James Gibbs in 1724 in a style he later copied in his more famous work at St. Martin's-in-the-Fields. Good stained glass and altarpiece by Burne-Jones.

*** **The Wallace Collection** *(342, 409)*, Manchester Square

Among the splendid miscellany here of paintings, sculptures, and objects of art, students of British history and culture will be especially interested in the collection of sixteenth and seventeenth century armor (most of it continental and Oriental, however); and the paintings by Eworth,

Holbein, Van Dyck, Reynolds, Romney, and Lawrence. Admirers of the writer Anthony Powell will want to inspect the Poussin painting which inspired the title of his *Dance to the Music of Time.*

W 2

Great Western Royal Hotel *(459)*, Praed Street

A railway hotel opened in 1854 and designed by P. G. Hardwick in a Victorian baroque style, it served passengers to and from nearby Paddington Station, the London terminus of the Great Western Railway. The Victorian ambience of the interior has been lost in redecoration.

** Kensington Palace *(367, 369)*, Kensington Gardens

The original modest house here was bought by William III and enlarged with the help of Sir Christopher Wren. Wren's assistant, Nicholas Hawksmoor, designed the orangery for Queen Anne. George I added the state rooms which were decorated by William Kent. Noteworthy among the portraits here are Kneller's Peter the Great and Lely's Anne Hyde.

Paddington Station *(459)*, Bishops Bridge Road and Eastbourne Terrace

Designed and built in the 1850s for the Great Western Railway by Isambard Kingdom Brunel. The interior is an interesting example of fine nineteenth century engineering embellished by decorative ironwork by Matthew Digby Wyatt.

W 8

St. Mary Abbots *(474)*, Kensington High Street and Kensington Church Street

Rebuilt by Sir George Gilbert Scott in 1869 to 1872 in his usual Middle Pointed (Decorated) style.

N 1

King's Cross Station *(459)*, York Way

The first railway station to be built in central London (1851–1852), this very functional building of twin semicylindrical train sheds connected by crosswalks and fronted with a simple brick facade was the work of Lewis Cubitt. A grimy unprepossessing structure today, it is nevertheless admired by architectural historians as a rare example of functionalism in Victorian building design.

NW 1

*** Regent's Park *(439, 487)*, bounded by Park Road, Albany Street, Marylebone Road, and Prince Albert Road

A splendid park of 472 acres laid out after 1812 for the Prince Regent by John Nash. Nash also designed most of the terraces and villas on the east and south sides of the park, the handsomest being in **Park Crescent** *(439)*. In the center of the park, at the west end of Chester Road, is ***** Queen Mary's Garden** *(486)*, probably the finest rose garden in Britain. It was started in 1932 and is a must for rose lovers.

* St. Pancras Station *(459, 474)*, Euston Road and Pancras Road

Completed in 1868 to the design of William Henry Barlow, this was the London terminus of the great Midland Railway. Its most noticeable feature is the huge red-brick Victorian Gothic building in front of the station proper. This was designed by Sir George Gilbert Scott for the Midland Grand Hotel, opened in 1873. Today it is used as office space for British Rail. As a whole, the building is frankly ugly by almost any standard, but the architectural detail is worth close examination.

OUTER LONDON, NORTH OF THAMES RIVER
E 1

Christ Church, Spitalfields *(367)*, Brushfield Street, Spitalfields

A massive church by Nicholas Hawksmoor, built in 1723 to 1729; its heavy Doric porch underneath a wide tower is especially noteworthy. Inside, the pillars are Corinthian.

National Museum of Labour History *(499)*, Limehouse Town Hall, Commercial Road, Whitechapel

This small museum, hard to reach from central London, houses a display of drawings, photographs, documents, and artifacts pertaining to the history of the British labor movement and British socialism from the late eighteenth century to 1945. Although this is admittedly not a subject that lends itself easily to museumship, something more ambitious than this effort might have been undertaken.

St. George in the East *(367)*, Cannon Street Road

Much restored after a World War II bombing, this Nicholas Hawksmoor church, built in 1715 to 1723, is a remarkable melange of the original baroque with the Tuscan motif dominating, plus Georgian and Victorian decorative elements, and modern additions.

E 14

St. Anne's, Limehouse *(367)*, Commercial Road and St. Anne's Passage, Limehouse

This baroque church, built in 1715 to 1723, by Nicholas Hawksmoor, has an interesting tower and an unusual semidomed apse at the west end.

N 6

Highgate Cemetery *(464)*, Swain's Lane

The older and more attractive part of the cemetery lies to the east of the lane. Here, among others, the scientist Michael Faraday is buried. To the west, in the newer cemetery, is the grave of Karl Marx, marked by a huge bust placed there in 1956 by admirers of the progenitor of modern Communism.

** Kenwood House *(399, 410)*, Hampstead Heath

Designed in 1769 by Robert Adam for Chief Justice Lord Mansfield, this is a masterpiece of neoclassical style, both inside and out. It has a beautiful location at the north end of the famous and once very fashionable Hampstead Heath, now a much used public park. In 1927 Lord Iveagh bequeathed to the nation his superb collection of paintings, now housed here, so that the establishment is sometimes known as the Iveagh Bequest. From the viewpoint of stately-home visitors this is a mixed blessing because the crowds that gather to view the paintings (especially on weekends) are at times too much for the custodial staff to handle. Visitors should not be surprised, therefore, if the Adam rooms are closed off without warning.

NW 3

** Fenton House *(366)*, Hampstead Grove, Hampstead; NT

A handsome Dutch-style house of red brick, built in the reign of William and Mary, it is noted chiefly for its collections of keyboard instruments, Regency furniture, and porcelain figurines.

*** Keats House *(416)*, Keats Grove, off South End Road, Hampstead

The Regency house where John Keats lived for a while, now a good museum of manuscripts, editions of his poems, and other memorabilia. In the garden is a plum tree replacing the one under which he wrote the "Ode to the Nightingale."

St. John, Church Row *(417)*, Church Row, Hampstead

This brick church with a castellated steeple was built by Henry Flitcroft in 1744 to 1747 and modified in the west end in the nineteenth century.

NW 6

St. Augustine, Kilburn *(473)*, Kilburn Park Road, Paddington

Built in 1870 to 1880 to the design of John Pearson, this is a red-brick Victorian Gothic church in the Early English style favored by this architect.

NW 9

*** Royal Air Force Museum of Aviation History *(496, 504, 505)*, Hendon; Aerodrome Road, w from A 41 (Watford Way)

A magnificent display of planes from the beginning of aviation history through World War II; also photographs, documents, bombs, guns, uniforms, and equipment of the R.A.F. Next door is a separate building devoted to the Battle of Britain with a good collection of the British and German aircraft that were engaged in that crucial contest.

W 4

* Hogarth House *(407)*, Hogarth Lane, n of Great West Road (A 4)

This was the painter William Hogarth's summer home from 1749 to 1764. Restored after bomb damage, it contains a good collection of the artist's prints, drawings, and other memorabilia.

BRENTFORD

* Grand Union Canal *(424)*, Ferry Lane, s of Brentford High Street

This is the southeastern terminus of the important eighteenth century canal which joins London with Birmingham.

CHISWICK

*** Chiswick House *(383)*, Burlington Lane, off Great West Road (A 4)

Designed by William Kent and his patron, Lord Burlington, this villa is a pure example of early eighteenth century English Palladianism. The Corinthian columns, octagonal dome, Venetian windows, and interior classical decor, though not exact copies of features of Palladio's Villa Rotonda near Vicenza, are modeled on them. Kent's garden unfortunately has mostly been modified and reduced by encroaching suburbia, though his Ionic temple and some classical statuary survive. Easy to reach from central London, this is an important architectural landmark, preserved by the Department of the Environment.

HAMPTON

*** Hampton Court Palace *(276, 278, 330, 364, 369, 373, 487)*, Hampton Court Road (A 308) w of Kingston Bridge

Begun in 1514 by Cardinal Wolsey, this greatest of surviving sixteenth century palaces was taken over by Henry VIII who completed the building of what is now the western portion of this massive, sprawling complex. Sir Christopher Wren was the architect for the east and south wings built in the late seventeenth century for King William III. The Tudor portions include the great gatehouse, Anne Boleyn's gateway, all the rooms to the south (right from entry) of the Clock court (King's staircase, King's guard room, King's presence chamber, and Wolsey Room); and the entire north range of rooms (King's kitchen, Tudor kitchen, Horn room, cellars, great hall, great watching chamber, round kitchen court, haunted gallery, royal pew, chapel royal). The Fountain Court and all the buildings surrounding it, as well as the entire south and east ranges of the palace are the work of Sir Christopher Wren. Since the visitor normally enters through the great gatehouse on the west and moves counterclockwise, he will begin and end with the sixteenth century portions of the building, but the greatest number of rooms belong to the seventeenth and eighteenth centuries.

Special features: King Henry VIII's arms on great gatehouse; ceilings in great hall and chapel royal; weapons and armor in King's guard chamber; Verrio paintings in King's bedroom, King's staircase, and in the Queen's drawing room; tapestries in great hall; Sir Peter Lely paintings in the communication gallery; William III's state chamber; Grinling Gibbons woodcarvings in the Queen's gallery; sundry great masters throughout. Outside: wrought-iron gates by Jean Tijou in privy garden; Elizabethan knot garden; Henry VIII's sunken garden; William III's banqueting house; Bushy Park and Bushy House (seventeenth and eighteenth centuries) north of Lime Avenue.

HARROW

St. Mary's *(474)*, Harrow-on-the-Hill

A parish church dating from the twelfth through the fifteenth centuries, it was ruthlessly "restored" in the nineteenth century by Sir George Gilbert Scott in his preferred Middle Pointed (i.e., Decorated) style.

ISLEWORTH

*** Osterley Park House *(399, 407)*, Osterley Park, n of Great West Road (A 4) at Thornbury Road; NT

The original house here was built about 1577 by Sir Thomas Gresham, founder of the London Royal Exchange and promulgator of Gresham's Law warning of the inevitable triumph of bad money over good. Between 1761 and 1780 it was completely remodeled by Robert Adam, whose interiors here are among his best neoclassical efforts. Hall, library, dining room, drawing room, and Etruscan room are pure Adam. So is the furniture, designed personally by him. The house is administered by the Victoria and Albert Museum, a guarantee of authenticity.

*** Syon House *(399, 407, 486)*, in Syon Park, Park Road and London Road (A 315)

The original house here was a nunnery on the site of which a Tudor house was first built in the sixteenth century. Robert Adam radically reconstructed the interior and the results are breathtaking—perhaps his greatest single masterpiece, and certainly, close as it is to London, the most accessible to the ordinary traveller. The great hall, the anteroom, the red drawing room, and the long gallery are fine examples of Adam at his most sumptuous. Capability Brown did the landscaping, but only his elongated lake survives. The six-acre rose garden here is one of the best in the country.

TWICKENHAM

*** Marble Hill House *(387)*, Marble Hill Park, s of Richmond Road (A 305)

A splendid Palladian villa overlooking the Thames, built for George II's mistress, Henrietta Howard, countess of Suffolk, by the ninth earl of Pembroke and Roger Morris. Paintings by Richard Wilson, Hogarth, and Reynolds. Lovely view.

Orleans House *(388)*, Orleans Road, Riverside, s of Richmond Road (A 305)

Of James Gibbs's villa built in 1720, only the octagon room remains, attached to a modern art gallery. The duc d'Orleans, later King Louis Philippe of France, lived here in exile.

Strawberry Hill *(553)*, Strawberry Vale, s of Waldergate Road (A 309)

This is a famous architectural landmark, though it had little immediate influence on eighteenth century styles in spite of the publicity given it by Sir Horace Walpole. The style, outside and in, is Gothick, i.e., a fanciful reinterpretation of medieval building techniques by the author of the original Gothic novel, *The Castle of Otranto.* Now in the hands of St. Mary's Training College, admission can be obtained only by application to the principal.

WALTHAMSTOW

* William Morris Gallery *(475)*, Forest Road

Birthplace of the famous nineteenth century artist and decorator, here is a good museum of his designs and products.

INNER LONDON, SOUTH OF THAMES RIVER
SE 1

* H.M.S. Belfast *(506)*, Symons Wharf, Vine Lane off Tooley Street, Southwark; access by ferry from Tower of London landing stage across the river

The last of the Royal Navy's big-gun cruisers, she saw considerable action in World War II and is now open to the public. Well worth a visit.

*** Imperial War Museum *(497, 504, 505, 506)*, Lambeth Road

Devoted primarily to the history of World Wars I and II, here is a great miscellany of guns, small arms, aircraft, uniforms, military equipment, posters, photographs, ship and tank models, etc. In a somewhat obscure corner is the excellent exhibit of life on the home front during World War II, a poignant reminder of the impact of airpower on the lives of ordinary citizens.

Southwark Cathedral *(235)*, Southwark Street

Founded in 1106 as an Augustinian priory, the church was made parochial at the time of the Reformation and only achieved cathedral status in 1905. Whatever architectural distinction it might once have had is today obscured by the grimy industrial setting.

Architectural styles: west front—nineteenth century; nave—nineteenth century; central tower—Perpendicular; transepts—Perpendicular; choir—Early English; retrochoir—Early English.

Special features: restored Harvard Chapel in north transept; sixteenth century altar screen.

SE 5

*** St. Giles, Camberwell *(474)*, Camberwell Church Street

Built in 1844 to a design by Sir George Gilbert Scott, this is a typical Victorian Gothic church in the Middle Pointed, i.e., Decorated, style.

OUTER LONDON, SOUTH OF THAMES RIVER
SE 8

* **St. Paul's, Deptford** *(367)*, High Street, Deptford

A splendid baroque church of the Corinthian order built in 1712 to 1720 by Thomas Archer on the model of S. Agnese, Rome.

SE 9

* **Eltham Palace** *(202)*, King John's Walk, s of Eltham High Street, w of Court Road; nearest underground station: Well Hall, Mottingham; AM

Here are the remains of a royal palace whose building covered a span of three hundred years from the thirteenth to the sixteenth centuries. Of chief interest is the great hall with its fine hammer-beam roof erected by Edward IV in 1480. This is the third largest hammer-beam roof in England, after Westminster Hall and Christ Church College, Oxford. Current excavations are unearthing a chapel built by Henry VIII. Hours of admission are restricted.

SE 10

** **Cutty Sark** *(462)*, King William Walk, Greenwich

Built in 1869, this clipper ship, now restored and open to view, is typical of the many sailing vessels which plied the seas long after the introduction of steam propulsion.

** **Greenwich Hospital (Royal Naval College)** *(364)*, King William's Walk and Romney Road, Greenwich

The earliest building here (King Charles Block) was designed by John Webb for a palace for Charles II that was never completed. Sir Christopher Wren, with the assistance of Nicholas Hawksmoor, enlarged considerably on these beginnings to build the hospital for naval pensioners (1696–1715), pretty much as it now stands, though the chapel was completed as late as 1745. The ceiling in the Painted Hall was done by Sir James Thornhill. It depicts the victory of William and Mary over tyranny; the triumph of the Glorious Revolution; and the age of peace and prosperity under Queen Anne and her husband Prince George of Denmark. This is now the dining hall of the Royal Naval College which has occupied it since 1873.

** **Greenwich Observatory** *(356)*, Greenwich Park

Flamsteed House, with its beautiful octagon room, was built by Sir Christopher Wren in 1675 to house the first Astronomer Royal, John Flamsteed. Next to it is the Meridian Building, raised in the eighteenth century, which contains a fascinating collection of early astronomical instruments.

*** **National Maritime Museum** *(331, 350, 369, 382, 393, 395, 408, 410, 494, 497, 506)*, Greenwich Park

The central block consists of the slightly modified and restored Queen's House, built in 1616 to 1635 by Inigo Jones in his best Palladian style. The great hall is a typically Palladian cube and the other rooms conform to strict mathematical ratios. The contents of this building and the adjoining wings, of later construction connected by loggias, represent a vast array of art and artifacts pertaining to the maritime history of Britain. Noteworthy are the admirals' portraits by Lely and Kneller; the Nelson collection of paintings, busts, and memorabilia; the Barge House with its ornate barges and wherries that once transported royalty up and down the Thames; and, best of all, the Navigation Room with its really splendid collection of globes, charts, nautical instruments, and chronometers, including the original sea clock devised by John Harrison in the mid-eighteenth century.

St. Alphege *(367)*, Church Street, Greenwich

Built by Nicholas Hawksmoor, in 1711 to 1714, in the baroque style with the Doric order predominating, it was much restored after a World War II bombing.

SE 18

*** **Royal Artillery Museum** *(342, 445, 492, 497, 507)*, The Rotunda, Woolwich

A fine museum with a representative selection of guns, howitzers, etc., from a fifteenth century bombard through the antitank guns of World War II. Machine guns and small arms are also on display.

SE 21

*** **Dulwich College Picture Gallery** *(409, 440)*, Dulwich Village

Built originally by Sir John Soane in 1814 and rebuilt after bomb damage in 1944, this gallery has one of the finest small collections of paintings in Britain. British art is not emphasized, but there are good examples here of Reynolds, Gainsborough, Van Dyck, and Lawrence, among others.

BEXLEYHEATH

Red House *(475)*, Red House Lane

A Picturesque red-brick house designed by Philip Webb in 1859 for William Morris and considered to be the forerunner of one modern school of suburban domestic building. Admission by written appointment only from the owners, Mr. and Mrs. Hollamby.

KEW

** **Kew Palace** *(375)*, Kew Gardens; Department of the Environment

This attractive merchant's house was built in 1631 in the Dutch style, and was called the Dutch House until it was acquired by George III for use as a royal palace. The interior furnishings belong mostly to the late eighteenth century. Behind the house is a small formal garden, laid out in this century, called the Queen's Garden. Here is a fine representation in miniature of a typical French-style formal garden of the seventeenth century.

*** **Royal Botanic Gardens, Kew** *(375, 400, 487)*, Kew Gardens

Begun in 1759 by Augusta, Dowager Princess of Wales, mother of King George III, this splendid parkland of 300 acres now contains perhaps the greatest variety of cultivated plant life in Britain. Also, interspersed here and there are a number of architectural monuments of significance, especially those designed in the 1760s by Sir William Chambers: the Pagoda, the Temple of Belonna, the Temple of Arethusa, the Ruined Arch, and the Orangery. The Campanile to the north of Victoria Gate was built in the 1840s; the General Museum is housed in a building designed in the 1850s by Decimus Burton; the Wood Museum contains specimens of lumber from all over the British Commonwealth.

RICHMOND

*** **Ham House** *(357, 372)*, ¼ m. w of A 307 from Petersham; NT

First built in 1610 on an H-plan, the house was enlarged in 1673 by filling in the uprights of the *H* on the south front. Except for some minor changes in the 18th century, it belongs to the Restoration period when the duke and duchess of Lauderdale lived here in great splendor. Extravagant to a fault, they filled it to overflowing with the richest furniture, hangings, plasterwork, etc., they could obtain, and most of their purchases survive in what is a veritable museum of Restoration taste. There are lots of portraits by Kneller and Lely, the most interesting being the latter's painting of the duke and duchess—a study in self-satisfied opulence. The view of the Thames to the north is lovely.

Kew Observatory *(400)*, Old Deer Park, n of Twickenham Road

An attractive building designed by Sir William Chambers for King George III.

SOUTHEAST ENGLAND

KENT
AYLESFORD

** The Friars *(258)*, ½ m. w

Some of the buildings of the 13th century Carmelite friary situated on the north bank of the River Medway were, in the sixteenth century after the Dissolution, incorporated into a private house which in turn has been absorbed by the modern Carmelite priory and retreat. In this peaceful setting the great attraction of the religious vocation in the Middle Ages is not hard to imagine.

Kits Coty *(20)*, 2 m. n, w of A 229 (188 TQ 745 608) AM

A dolmen consisting of three uprights and a capstone is the sole surviving element of the rectangular burial chamber of a neolithic chambered tomb.

CANTERBURY

Black Friars *(257)*

A Christian Science church incorporates the thirteenth to fourteenth century undercroft and refectory of a Dominican priory.

*** Canterbury Cathedral *(144, 174, 188, 232)*, town center

Seat of the Primate of England, this Benedictine monastery-cathedral was begun in its present form in 1175. Scene of the murder of Thomas Becket in 1170, it became England's most popular shrine. It was secularized in 1541.

Architectural styles: west front (including towers)—Perpendicular; nave—Perpendicular; western transepts—Perpendicular; central tower (Bell Harry)—Perpendicular; choir—Transitional and Early English; eastern transepts—Transitional; Trinity Chapel (retrochoir)—Transitional and Early English; Corona (east end)—Transitional and Early English; crypt—Norman (western) and Early English (eastern); cloister—Perpendicular; chapter house—Perpendicular.

Special features: St. Augustine's chair (Corona); tombs of Archbishops Bourchier and Chichele, King Henry IV, Edward, the Black Prince (choir and retrochoir); Perpendicular pulpitum; site of Becket's murder (northwest transept); tomb of Archbishop Stephen Langton (southwest transept); medieval glass in west window and northeastern transept window; Trinity Chapel; Corona; southwest transept; wall paintings in St. Anselm's Chapel and crypt; Bell Harry Tower.

Roman Pavement *(81)*, Butchery Lane

In a shop basement entered from the street, this is a remnant of a Roman town house now converted into a museum, with a good segment of hypocaust and a well-preserved mosaic floor of geometric design.

* **Royal Museum** *(81)*, High Street

A good museum of local history and archaeology, especially rich in Roman finds.

* **St. Augustine's Abbey** *(116, 249)*, Monastery Gardens; AM

Sparse remains exist of the Benedictine abbey begun by Abbot Scotland in 1073, embedded in which are traces of the Church of Sts. Peter and Paul founded by St. Augustine himself in the late sixth century. Roman bricks in the foundations testify to the church's antiquity. To the east are the remains of St. Pancras' Chapel built in the seventh century. These walls, which survive in places to some height, are built entirely of Roman bricks.

Town Wall *(176)*, Broad Street and Lower Bridge Street

On either side of the Burrgate stretches a good section of the eastern portions of the medieval town wall.

* **Westgate** *(176)*, St. Peter's Street

The only remaining gate of seven built in the mid-fourteenth century to guard the walls of Canterbury, presumably against the danger of French invasion. In the guard chamber is an interesting museum containing armor and other military equipment.

* **Chartham Church** *(155)*, 3 m. sw, on A 28

A cruciform church, mainly fourteenth century, famous for its brasses, especially that of Sir Robert de Septvans (d. 1306).

Herne Church *(189)*, 6 m. n on A 291 and A 299

A large church, built mostly in the thirteenth and fourteenth centuries, though heavily restored; here is a fine fifteenth century memorial brass to P. Halle.

CHATHAM

* **Upnor Castle** *(351)*, 1½ m. n; AM (178 TQ 758 706)

Built in 1559 to 1567 to guard the Medway against the Spanish, the fort was only once put to use—in 1667 when its guns failed to stop the Dutch from breaking the boom across the river and setting fire to the Royal Navy ships anchored upstream, one of which, *The Royal Charles,* was towed away. The main building and water bastion date from the initial Tudor construction; the gatehouse and the north and south towers were added in 1599 to 1601. The barracks were built in 1718.

CRANBROOK

*** Sissinghurst Castle *(488)*, 4 m. ne, n of A 262

One of the most famous gardens in England was laid out here by the late Vita Sackville-West and her husband Sir Harold Nicholson not long before World War II. It is a sectionalized garden with separate "rooms" divided by hedgerows, each devoted to a distinct species or color. Thus there is a white garden, a yellow and orange garden, a rose garden, a lime walk, an herb garden, and an orchard filled with daffodils or roses depending on the season. Not to be missed.

DARTFORD

*** Stone Church *(243)*, 2 m. e, n of A 226

A splendid Early English church built in the thirteenth century probably by the same masons that worked on Westminster Abbey. Noteworthy are the plate tracery in the windows and the thirteenth century mural paintings.

DEAL

*** Deal Castle *(285)*, (179 TR 378 521) AM

This is the largest and best preserved of Henry VIII's coastal fortifications, built in 1539 and the years following. Structurally it consists of a tall cylindrical tower surrounded by six slightly lower semicircular bastions, in turn enclosed by a still lower curtain wall also with six semicircular bastions and encased by a wide dry moat. The flat roofs of the bastions were artillery platforms, while gun ports in the walls of the tower and bastions permitted handguns to command the area in the immediate vicinity.

*** Walmer Castle *(285, 446)*, 1 m. s on A 258 (177 TR 378 501) AM

One of Henry VIII's coastal fortifications built to guard the Downs against invasion from the Continent during the war scare of 1539 and after. Smaller than the castle at Deal, a mile to the north, it was built on a quatrefoil plan with a central tower surrounded by four bastions enclosed in a moat. The castle has been the long-time seat of the lord warden of the Cinque Ports and is closed to the public while he is in residence. The lord warden's sumptuously furnished apartment is at all other times open to the public and includes, among other things, a fine collection of Wellington memorabilia from the time the Iron Duke held the office. Here, for example, are the original Wellington boots as well as the wing chair where he died.

DOVER

*** **Dover Castle** *(139, 285)*, Castle Hill (179 TR 325 418) AM

The high rectangular keep with its immensely thick walls was the work of Henry II. Under King John and Henry III, residential quarters were added, as were both inner and outer curtain walls, making the establishment a concentric fort like its contemporary Tower of London. At the same time various towers and gatehouses were constructed. Under Henry VIII the Tudor bulwark was added to the southern end of the precincts, and the long mounted gun, which today greets the visitor as he drives into the grounds, was the gift to Henry VIII by the Emperor Charles V.

* **Pharos** *(74, 148)*, Dover Castle

The only surviving Roman lighthouse in Britain, the lower two-thirds of this sixty-two-foot-high ruin are of Roman construction, the top medieval.

*** **Roman Painted House** *(74)*, corner of Cannon and New Streets

The recently excavated remains of a second century Roman house, possibly the home of the commandant of the headquarters of the Channel fleet *(Classis Britannica)* at *Dubris.* With its painted walls and hypocaust, this is the best surviving Roman town house in Britain. It was partially destroyed in the late third century when the Roman army built a new wall across its premises. The foundations of this structure, as well as one of the bastions added to it in the fourth century, can still be observed. Roofed over for protection and blessed with one of the best Roman site museums in Britain, this is an archaeological *tour de force.*

*** **Barfreston Church** *(242)*, 6 m. n, w of A 256

A two-celled Norman church probably built in 1170 to 1180 with an intricately carved recessed south doorway and tympanum, blind arcading at the east end, and circular window above. Though badly signposted and hard to find, this is certainly one of the most attractive Norman churches in England.

DYMCHURCH

* **Martello Tower** *(396)*, town center

This was No. 24 of the seventy-four fortifications built from 1805 to 1810 to guard the southeast coast of England against an amphibious landing by Napoleon.

EDENBRIDGE

** **Chiddingstone Castle** *(361)*, 5 m. e, s of B 2027

A red-brick seventeenth century house unfortunately "Gothicized" in the nineteenth, its contents, not its architecture, lend it distinction. In addition to a remarkable display of Egyptian antiquities and Japanese *objets d'art,* Chiddingstone houses a fascinating collection of mementos and memorabilia pertaining to the royal house of Stuart. Included are: a nude painting of Nell Gwynn by Lely; miniatures of Charles I, Charles II, and James II (by Samuel Cooper); a silk-velvet bag containing part of the heart of James II; letters inscribed by Mary Queen of Scots, James I, Charles I, Charles II, James II, and both Old and Young Pretenders; locks of hair of Mary Queen of Scots, Charles I, James II, Bonnie Prince Charlie; etc., etc.

EYNSFORD

*** **Lullingstone Roman Villa** *(86)*, 1 m. sw, w of A 225 (177 TQ 529 651) AM

Dating from the fourth century this is one of the best preserved Roman villas in England. Enclosed in a large, well-illuminated shed, the outstanding features here are the two large mosaics, one of Jupiter as a white bull swimming with Europa on his back; the other of Bellerophon astride the winged horse Pegasus spearing the Chimaera. A Christian wall painting of six persons at prayer and two busts of Roman worthies, perhaps owners of the villa, are in the British Museum.

HYTHE

Royal Military Canal *(396)*, town center

The eastern end of the nineteen-mile canal built as a second line of defense against the possibility of a landing of Napoleonic troops. The idea was to keep the French bottled up in the Romney Marsh in case they succeeded in getting ashore.

* **Saltwood Castle** *(144)*, 2 m. n

The earliest part of this small and much restored castle dates from the reign of Henry II. It was here that the four assassins of Thomas Becket,

Archbishop of Canterbury, met on their way to murder him in December 1170. The gatehouse, which is now the inhabited part of the establishment, was built in the thirteenth century and restored in the nineteenth. Hours of admission are very restricted.

MAIDSTONE

* **Museum and Art Gallery** *(27, 446)*, St. Faith's Street

Housed in a Tudor manor this miscellaneous collection includes local prehistoric finds (e.g., grave goods from the nearby Coldrum chambered tomb), William Hazlitt relics, and uniforms and memorabilia of the Queen's Own Royal West Kent Regiment.

** **Leeds Castle** *(167)*, 6 m. se, on B 2163, ½ m. n of Leeds village

With some hyperbole this has been called the loveliest castle in the whole world. Unusually picturesque in its setting on two islands within a lake, the castle is approached by a ruined barbican and a gatehouse built in the reign of Edward I. Under Edward II it became the Queen's Castle, which it remained until the time of Henry V's queen, Catherine de Valois. It was the attempted exclusion of Queen Isabella from her rightful domain in 1321 that served as the pretext for Edward II's raising an army which he later used to overthrow Thomas of Lancaster and the Lords Ordainer. Henry VIII turned the castle into a palace, adding an upper story to the keep as well as the Maiden's Tower. It was converted into a stately home in this century, is now employed as a conference center, and boasts some good French Impressionist paintings in the conference room. Irrelevantly, there is a dog-collar museum on the grounds. The walk from the car park is long, but transportation is provided for handicapped persons and senior citizens, in England called Old Age Pensioners (OAPs).

ROCHESTER

Eastgate House *(465)*, High Street

Mementos of Charles Dickens can be seen in the Swiss chalet which was his study and is now part of the grounds of this museum.

*** **Rochester Castle** *(135, 149)*, town center; AM

The huge square keep, rising about 110 feet high, was built about 1127 to 1135, and, though a ruin, is, after the Tower of London, the best example of a Norman keep in England. It has four stories with a great forebuilding enclosing the entrance stairs. The cylindrical southeast corner was built after King John had mined that angle of the castle in 1216 during his war with rebellious barons who stood out for seven weeks before surrender.

** Rochester Cathedral *(231)*, High Street

Begun by Bishop Gundulf in 1082 as a Benedictine cathedral, it was refashioned in the years following 1115 and became secularized in 1541.

Architectural styles: west front—Norman with Perpendicular west window; nave—Norman; northwest transept—Early English; southwest transept—Geometric Decorated; eastern transepts—Early English; choir—Early English; lady chapel—Perpendicular; crypt—Norman; chapter house—Early English (ruined).

Special features: recessed Norman west doorway; thirteenth century choir stalls.

** Cobham Church *(259)*, 3 m. w, on B 2009

A thirteenth century church with the largest collection of memorial brasses in England, ranging in date from 1329 to 1539. Especially noteworthy are those of the two Sir John Cobhams, father and son, each depicted wearing the full armor fashionable at the time of their respective deaths in 1354 and 1365. This is what English knights in the first phase of the Hundred Years War looked like.

* Cooling Castle *(176)*, 5 m. n, e of B 2000

Only the gatehouse is left of this castle built by John de Cobham in the 1380s to defend the southern shore of the River Medway against French invasion. The ruination of the buildings began in 1554 when the rebel Wyatt captured the castle on his way to London to protest Queen Mary Tudor's Spanish marriage.

ROYAL TUNBRIDGE WELLS

* Bayham Abbey *(253)*, 5 m. e, s of A 21, in East Sussex (188 TQ 651 366) AM

Founded about 1210 as a Premonstratensian house from the union of two previously established foundations, the chief features of today's ruins are the church, with exquisite Decorated features; the east range of the cloister; and a fine gatehouse dating to the fourteenth and fifteenth centuries.

** Hever Castle *(176, 279, 408)*, 10 m. nw, e of B 2026, 2 m. e of Edenbridge

Though much restored by Viscount Astor in the twentieth century, the castle was originally a manor house fortified in 1384 by John de Cobham in the wake of French incursions against southeastern England. In the fifteenth and sixteenth centuries it was much altered by Sir Geoffrey Boleyn, lord mayor of London, and his grandson, Sir Thomas Boleyn, father of Henry VIII's second queen, Anne Boleyn. It was here that Henry and Anne allegedly met. Later, after Anne's execution and the death of Queen Jane Seymour, Henry gave it to his fourth wife, Anne of Cleves, as part of the divorce settlement. The garden, in the Italian Renaissance style, was designed and planted by Lord Astor. There is also a twentieth century Tudoresque maze and some interesting topiary. On the grounds is a mock Tudor village. Recently (1982) put up for sale.

** **Scotney Castle** *(176)*, 7 m. se on A 21 below Lamberhurst; NT

The remains of a medieval manor house fortified in the late fourteenth century as a result of French attacks on the southeast coast of England in the first phase of the Hundred Years War. Only one of four original towers survives, attached to a seventeenth century house. On the grounds is perhaps the best preserved of all early nineteenth century English landscape gardens of the pictorial type, laid out among the ruins by William Sawrey Gilpin in the 1830s.

SANDWICH

** **Richborough** *(Rutupiae) (56, 63, 74, 116)*, 1½ m. ne (179 TR 324 602) AM

Though now two or three miles inland, this was the site of the initial Roman landing in A.D. 43. Subsequently it became an important fort and supply depot. In the center of the present site are the cruciform foundations of a high four-way arch set up prematurely by Julius Agricola to commemorate the final conquest of Britain. Surrounding it on three sides are the earthen embankments and ditches of the third century fort, and outside these the stone walls of the fourth century Saxon Shore fort. The outlines of St. Augustine's Chapel have been picked out in the grass, but only fragments remain of this tiny church allegedly founded by Augustine in 597. The ditches dug for a temporary fort by the invading army are barely visible to the east. Across the road to the south is the site of an amphitheater.

SEVENOAKS

*** **Knole** *(328, 372, 409)*, end of town, off A 21; NT

Although here are portions of Archbishop Bouchier's fifteenth century building along with Henry VIII's additions, the house is essentially early seventeenth century as remodeled by Thomas Sackville, first earl of Dorset. Outside he tacked Dutch gables and a Tuscan colonnade onto the medieval surface; inside he completely remodeled the living quarters with lowered ceilings, new fireplaces, much plasterwork, and five long galleries, of which the best are the Brown Gallery and the Leicester Gallery. Except for the works of Sir Joshua Reynolds, many of the paintings here are copies, but much of the furniture is of early seventeenth century provenance.

* Ightham Mote *(192)*, 6 m. e, w of A 227

Here is a charming moated manor house of late medieval and Elizabethan provenance. The east wing was built in the fourteenth century; the other three wings surrounding the courtyard in the sixteenth. Some of the buildings are of stone, some half-timbered, thus offering a good contrast between medieval and Tudor architectural styles. Visiting hours very restricted.

SITTINGBOURNE

Minster Church *(173)*, 8 m. ne, on B 2008

A double church, part Saxon and part Early English, it boasts a fine memorial brass of Sir John de Northwood (d. 1333).

SNODLAND

* Coldrum *(20)*, 3 m. w, 1 m. ne of Trottiscliffe (188 TQ 654 607); NT

The most complete survival of the Medway group of Neolithic chambered tombs, this dolmen consists of the four sides of the stone burial chamber without the capstone that presumably once covered it.

TONBRIDGE

*** Penshurst Place *(193, 374)*, 5 m. w, off B 2176

This is one of the truly great country houses of southern England. The fourteenth century great hall and the adjacent solar were built by Sir John de Pulteney, mayor of London. Buckingham Hall was put up in the fifteenth century. The rest of this sprawling mansion was built mostly in the sixteenth and early seventeenth centuries by Sir Henry Sidney and his son Robert. (Another son, Sir Philip Sidney, was the famous Elizabethan poet, courtier, and soldier killed at Zutphen in 1586 during the earl of Leicester's mismanaged campaign in the Netherlands.) Here also is a splendid formal garden laid out in the nineteenth century but in the style of the seventeenth, with terraces, allées, and a parterre. Especially noteworthy are the beds of solid box, clipped low and level.

WESTERHAM

*** Chartwell *(508)*, 2 m. s, e of B 2026; NT

A nice house with a beautiful view and well furnished, this was the home of Winston and Clementine Churchill from 1922 until 1964 just before his death. Here is Churchill's library where he wrote his studies of Marlborough and of World War II, a number of his paintings, and a large collection of photographs and other mementos of the great events in which he participated. The brick work in the garden was laid by Sir Winston, though the flowers were the province of Lady Churchill. Everything here is in the best of taste, and, though architecturally undistinguished, the house and its arrangements would be a pleasure to see even without its important historical associations.

EAST SUSSEX

BATTLE

** Battle Abbey *(127, 248)*, High Street

Founded by William the Conqueror in gratitude for his great victory over Harold Godwineson on this site. (The high altar of the church is supposed to have been built over the spot where Harold was killed.) Of the eleventh century church, only a few fragments remain above ground. Of the claustral buildings erected in the thirteenth century, there are substantial remains of the rooms at the south end of the east range, the west wall of the frater, and the abbot's house on the west side of the cloister which is now used as a girls' school. Other buildings within the precincts include the well-preserved fourteenth century gatehouse, the undercroft of the guest house, and above it, two octagonal turrets which were part of a lodging begun for the Princess Elizabeth (later Queen Elizabeth I) but never used.

The battlefield lies mostly to the southeast of the abbey and can be viewed best from in front of the guesthouse. Here diagrammatic maps are posted which are helpful in understanding what took place. Inside the undercroft is a scale model of the battlefield peopled with toy soldiers.

BRIGHTON

Brighton Station *(461)*, Queen's Road

Built in 1882, this has a fine, curved train-shed of iron and glass—nineteenth century functional architecture at its best.

The Dome *(438)*, town center

Originally built as a royal stable for the Prince Regent by John Porden, the style was eventually to influence the architecture of the nearby Royal Pavilion.

*** Royal Pavilion *(438)*, town center

The original neoclassical house by Henry Holland was rebuilt in a quasi-Indian style by John Nash from 1815 to 1820 as a summer palace for the Prince Regent. The onion-shaped domes were added later, though the spires, looking like inverted funnels meant to resemble Crusaders' tents, are of Nash's design. Nash's music room and banqueting room are mixed Chinese and Gothic. Fine Regency furniture throughout. A spectacular, if bizarre, sight which should not be missed.

EASTBOURNE

* Great Redoubt *(396)*, town center

A blockhouse built at the same time as the string of Martello Towers was put up to guard the southeast coast of England against a Napoleonic invasion. It now contains an aquarium and the museum of the Sussex Combined Services.

* Wish Tower *(396)*, King's Parade

This was No. 73 of the Martello Towers, coastal fortifications built to guard England against an amphibious landing by Napoleon's armies.

*** Pevensey Castle *(75, 135)*, 4 m. ne, near juncture of A 27 and B 2191 (199 TQ 645 048) AM

Called Anderida when built in the mid-fourth century, this was the latest of the Saxon Shore forts. The exterior walls and bastions, some places twenty-eight feet in height, are Roman. The Norman keep was begun by Robert de Mortain, the Conqueror's half-brother, in the late eleventh century. The castle was once situated next to the coast, but, because of silting, now lies more than a mile inland.

HAILSHAM

*** Herstmonceux Castle *(191)*, 6 m. ne, s of A 271 from Herstmonceux village

Now the property and home of the Royal Greenwich Observatory, this great country house of Flemish brick was built in the 1140s by Sir Roger Fiennes, a veteran of Agincourt. With its twin-towered gatehouse, high curtain walls guarded at each corner by an octagonal tower and on each face by a semioctagonal tower, and a plethora of machicolations and arrow slits, it looks like a typical late medieval courtyard castle. The multitude of exterior windows, however, betrays its residential character. Inside is a museum partly devoted to the history of the castle and partly to that of the Royal Observatory. These are the only rooms open to the public. Outside is a dazzling walled garden purporting to be Elizabethan.

HASTINGS

*** **Bodiam Castle** *(177)*, 10 m. n, e of A 229; NT

This is considered by many to be the finest ruined castle in England. It was built in the late 1380s by Sir Edward Dalyngrigge from his profits out of the Hundred Years War, was partially ruined by parliamentarian troops under Sir William Waller in 1643, and partially restored by Lord Curzon in the twentieth century. It is a typical late-medieval moated courtyard castle: a rectangle of high curtain walls, with four cylindrical corner towers, gatehouses front and back, and rectangular towers positioned midway along each of the two sides. All are heavily crenellated and machicolated. Today's approach is by way of a causeway across the moat to the great gatehouse on the north side, which retains one of its three original portcullises. The interior court is in a greater state of ruin than the outside walls and towers. This was the residential part of the castle: great hall, kitchen, chapel, and living quarters for the castellan and his retainers. In one of these rooms a fifteen-minute cartoon film is regularly shown, depicting medieval castle life.

** **Great Dixter** *(488)*, 8 m. ne, off A 28, n of Northiam

A delightful garden planned by Edwin Lutyens and Gertrude Jekyll. Included are a sunken garden, a rose garden, and ample borders of shrubs, perennials, and bedding plants.

HEATHFIELD

*** **Bateman's** *(466)*, 8 m. e, ½ m. s of A 265 from Burwash; NT

A Jacobean house bought by the poet/novelist Rudyard Kipling in 1902. It is maintained as a Kipling museum pretty much in the condition in which it was left on his death in 1926.

HOVE

Adelaide Crescent *(441)*, town center

Regency town houses by Decimus Burton.

Brunswick Square; Brunswick Terrace *(441)*, town center

Regency town houses by C. A. Busby.

LEWES

Lewes Castle *(141)*, town center

Here are the rather sparse remains of a shell keep built in the late eleventh or early twelfth century, standing on one of the two mottes of the early castle. The fine gatehouse belongs to the fourteenth century.

Lewes Priory *(249)*, Mountfield Road

Very little is left aboveground of the monastery founded in 1075 by the first colony to arrive in England from the famous French abbey at Cluny. Its patron was William de Warenne, one of the Conqueror's most dependable Norman knights.

RYE

* Lamb House *(466)*, West Street

Built in the eighteenth century, bought by the American novelist Henry James in 1899, a rendezvous of Edwardian literati in the years before World War I, it is now a museum dedicated to James.

* Rye Landgate *(176)*, High Street

This twin-towered gatehouse with portcullis slots straddles the main road leading into the town center. It was built in the mid-fourteenth century in response to sackings of the town by French invaders.

UCKFIELD

** Sheffield Park *(401, 487)*, 5 m. w, e of A 275, 2 m. n of A 272; NT

A Tudor house altered in the eighteenth century by James Wyatt with a curious mixture of Gothic and classical motifs. The nearby gardens, under the care of the National Trust, were laid out by Capability Brown but have been much modified since, to include a fine woodland garden of azaleas, rhododendrons, etc.

WEST SUSSEX

ARUNDEL

*** Arundel Castle *(131, 334)*, High Street

The castle was first built in stone by Roger de Montgomery soon after the Norman Conquest. Of this original construction, only parts of the south wall, the shell keep on its high motte, and the inner gateway with portcullis survive. Today the castle is the ancestral home of the dukes of Norfolk who originally acquired it by the marriage in 1556 of Thomas Howard, fourth duke, to a daughter of the twelfth earl of Arundel. Much of the castle was destroyed by parliamentarians in 1645 and remained a ruin until the end of the eighteenth century. The present house is mostly a Victorian extravaganza built for the fifteenth duke between 1870 and 1910. It is a fine example of Victorian Gothic, sumptuously furnished. Its walls are covered with the customary plethora of portraits, of which the most interesting, from the point of view of English art history, are those of the fourth duke (beheaded in 1572 for plotting to marry Mary Queen of Scots) and his duchess by Hans Eworth and of the fourteenth earl of Arundel and his wife by Van Dyck. The Fitzalan Chapel is Roman Catholic as has been this branch of the Howard family since the late sixteenth century. Appropriately Arundel houses, among its many treasures, the rosary of Mary Queen of Scots and a fine portrait of Cardinal Newman by Sir John Millais.

*** **Bignor Roman Villa** *(86)*, 6½ m. n, 1½ m. w of A 29 from Bury (197 SU 988 147)

Here is the best collection in England of Roman mosaics *in situ*, preserved in a series of thatched cottages, one of which houses a fine site museum. The six mosaics include representations of Jupiter as an eagle kidnapping the boy Ganymede; Venus surrounded by Cupids dressed as gladiators; two Medusa heads; and two geometric panels.

CHICHESTER

** **Chichester Cathedral** *(228)*, West Street

A foundation of secular canons, the cathedral church was begun in 1088.
Architectural styles: west porch—Early English; nave—Norman with Early English additions; central tower—nineteenth century; south transept—Geometric Decorated; choir—Norman; retrochoir—Transitional; lady chapel—Geometric Decorated; cloister—Perpendicular; bishops' palace—13th-18th centuries; bell tower—Perpendicular.
Special features: Geometric Decorated aisle chapels; Perpendicular rood screen; 14th century choir stalls.

* **Guildhall Museum** *(257)*, Priory Park

This is a typical local museum, interesting chiefly for its Early English architecture which derives from the fact that the building was once the choir of the Grey Friars' (Franciscan) Church.

*** **Fishbourne** *(57)*, 1 m. w on A 27 (197 SU 841 047)

The most splendid Roman country house yet discovered in England, this was built about A.D. 75 probably by Cogidubnus, chief of the Atrebates and client king under the Emperor Claudius. The north wing has been excavated and is covered by a protective building which also houses the highly instructive site museum. The layout of the rooms is viewed from a catwalk inside the building. Especially noteworthy is the second century mosaic in the principal room. The palace boasted the first known formal garden (now replanted) in England.

** **Goodwood House** *(334, 401, 411)*, 3 m. ne, 1 m. ne of A 286 from East Lavant

James Wyatt's neoclassical enlargement of an earlier house owned by the third duke of Richmond was never carried to full completion here, but the results are nevertheless grand. Good paintings by Van Dyck, Lely, Stubbs, and Wootton. The kennels (now housing the golf club) are also by Wyatt; the stables are by Sir William Chambers. Visiting hours restricted.

The Trundle *(46)*, 4 m. n, near Goodwood Race Course (197 SU 877 111)

An Iron Age hill fort built on the site of a Neolithic causewayed camp. It is not easy to distinguish the earthworks of one from the other, except that the two concentric rings of interrupted ditches belong to the causewayed camp, and the octagonal embankment with two inturned entrances to the hill fort.

** **Uppark** *(365)*, 12 m. n, on B 2146 1 m. s of South Harting; NT

Very Dutch in appearance with its high elevation, steep hipped roof, and pronounced cornice, this country house was built for the earl of Tankerville by William Talman about 1690. Most of the interior was redecorated in the eighteenth century. Humphrey Repton added the north portico about 1810, at the insistance of the then owner, Sir Harry Fetherstonhaugh, who kept Emma Hart here as his mistress for a year before marrying his dairymaid. (Emma later became Lady Hamilton and Lord Nelson's mistress.) Uppark was offered gratis to the duke of Wellington, but he refused it because of the steep hill on which it was located. ("I have crossed the Alps once," he said.) H. G. Wells lived here with his mother who was housekeeper for thirteen years (for the long-widowed dairymaid).

CRAWLEY

*** **Nymans** *(486)*, 5 m. s, s of Handcross on B 2114; NT

A magnificent garden of herbaceous borders, woodland plantings of rhododendrons, magnolias, camellias, domesticated heather, eucryphias, fuchsias, hydrangeas, and daffodils in season.

* St. Nicholas', Worth *(122)*, 2 m. e on B 2036

A cruciform Saxon church with pilaster strips and long and short quoins on the outside; two-lighted windows with baluster shafts, beautiful round arches, especially the chancel arch which is the largest Saxon arch in England; and fine narrow Saxon doorways.

EAST GRINSTEAD

Lingfield Parish Church *(189)*, 4 m. n on B 2028 in Surrey

A Perpendicular church with a fourteenth century tower with a good brass memorializing J. Hadresham (1417).

* Standen *(475)*, 2 m. sw, off B 2110; NT

Built in 1894 to the design of Philip Webb, the house is particularly interesting for its furnishings by William Morris and the Firm.

HAYWARDS HEATH

* Borde Hill *(487)*, 2 m. n on road to Balcombe

A fine woodland garden, noted chiefly for its rhododendrons and azaleas.

*** Wakehurst Place *(487)*, 4 m. n, on B 2028 at Ardingly; NT

Herbaceous borders and island beds surround the house; beyond, among streams and pools, is a lovely woodland garden full of azaleas, rhododendrons, magnolias, heathers, and a pinetum.

HORSHAM

* Warnham War Museum *(507)*, 1 m. n, in Warnham, w of A 24

A private collection of World War II weapons, uniforms, equipment, tracked vehicles, and amphibious craft.

MIDHURST

*** Petworth House *(350, 366, 369, 443)*, 5½ m. e, at junction of A 272 and A 283; NT

Rebuilt in the French style in the late seventeenth century by the sixth duke of Somerset on the foundations of a fourteenth century manor house, Petworth is today more of an art museum than a stately home. Among the English paintings are a fine collection of Van Dycks, Lelys, and Turners, and the famous series known as the Petworth Beauties by

Michael Dahl and Godfrey Kneller. The Grinling Gibbons carvings are among his best. Laguerre decorated the staircase. Capability Brown landscaped the park.

PULBOROUGH

* **Coates Manor** *(488)*, 3 m. w on B 2138, s of Fittleworth

A charming small garden recently laid out in the manner of Gertrude Jekyll.

** **Parham Park** *(334, 409, 411)*, 4 m. se; w of A 283

An E-shaped manor house begun in 1577, Parham's Elizabethan features, both inside and out, have been less distorted by later renovations than have most contemporary residential buildings. The front door, it is true, belongs to the eighteenth century and the fenestration is mostly post-Tudor; otherwise, the exterior is typically sixteenth century. Inside, the hall, long gallery, parlor, and solar all date from the reign of Elizabeth. The most notable feature of the house, however, is its incomparable collection of Tudor and Stuart paintings, including a fine portrait of the queen herself, possibly by Zuccarro. Other Tudor portraits include likenesses of Edward VI, Lord Burghley, Leicester, Essex (by Gheeraerts), and Henry VIII. Here, also, is a Mytens portrait of Charles I as Prince of Wales and others of his sister, Elizabeth of Bohemia; her husband, the Elector Palatine; and Queen Henrietta Maria. From the reign of Charles II are the king himself; his wife Catherine of Braganza; his sister-in-law Anne Hyde, wife of the duke of York; and paintings by Lely of two of his mistresses, Barbara Villiers, countess of Castlemaine, and Louise de Quérouaille, duchess of Portsmouth.

Visiting hours, unfortunately, are restricted.

WORTHING

* **Cissbury Ring** *(46)*, 3 m. n, 1 m. se of Findon, e of A 24 (198 TQ 140 082); NT

An Iron Age univallate hill fort built on the site of Neolithic flint mines. Long climb from car park on east side of A 24. Fine view.

* **St. Mary's, Sompting** *(122)*, 2 m. ne, n of A 27

An interesting Anglo-Saxon church, in part rebuilt in the twelfth century. Noteworthy features are the pilaster strip, string courses, and windows in the west tower. The Rhenish helm spire looks Anglo-Saxon but is in fact an eighteenth century intrusion.

SURREY
CAMBERLEY

* **National Army Museum, Sandhurst Departments** *(490)*, Royal Military Academy, Sandhurst

Here are collections of weapons, uniforms, regimental plate, paintings, etc., associated with the East India Company and the Indian army. This is a good place to recapture the spirit of the British Empire at its nineteenth century zenith.

* **Sandhurst War Memorial Chapel** *(498)*, Royal Military Academy

Built in 1922 to commemorate the 4,000 Sandhurst cadets killed in action in the first world war.

ESHER

*** **Claremont Landscape Garden** *(385)*, 1 m. s, e of A 307; NT

A beautifully restored eighteenth century landscape garden, to which Sir John Vanbrugh, Charles Bridgeman, and William Kent all contributed. The belvedere was Vanbrugh's, the lake and its grotto Kent's.

FARNHAM

* **Farnham Castle Keep** *(141)*, town center; AM

The ruined twelfth century shell keep completely encases an earlier motte in the center of which was an earlier square keep whose foundations have recently been excavated. Adjacent is the palace of the Bishops of Winchester, restored in the seventeenth to nineteenth centuries.

Waverley Abbey *(250, 283)*, 2 m. se, on B 3001

Here are the scanty remains (fragments of the transepts and claustral buildings) of the first English Cistercian monastery, founded in 1128.

GUILDFORD

Guildford Castle *(136)*, Quarry Street

A ruined rectangular stone keep built probably during the contested reign of King Stephen (1135–1154).

** **Clandon Park** *(387, 406)*, 3 m. e, on A 247, n of A 246; NT

Built by Giacomo Leoni in the eighteenth century for the second Lord Onslow, the red-brick exterior is somewhat baroque, but the interior is in the Palladian style for which the architect was well known. Plasterwork is by Artari and Bagutti, two fashionable Italian stuccoists. The so-called Palladio room is a gem of classical decor. Fine collection of Chinese Chippendale furniture. Park by Capability Brown.

Here too is the Museum of the Queen's Royal Surrey Regiment, a typical regimental museum with the usual array of weapons, uniforms, regimental plate, etc.

* Hatchlands *(397)*, 5 m. e, n of A 246; NT

Built in the 1750s, by Admiral Edward Boscawen, the interiors were done by Robert Adam—his first commission. His work survives in the chimneypieces and plaster ceilings of the library and drawing room. Visiting hours are restricted.

* Loseley House *(283)*, 2½ m. sw off A 3100

An Elizabethan house built in part from stones taken from the nearby Waverley Abbey, this is the first Cistercian house in England. Some of the paneling may have come from Henry VIII's Nonsuch Palace. The interiors are still predominantly Elizabethan and Jacobean. In the hall are portraits of Edward VI, James I, and Queen Anne of Denmark. Mandatory guided tours of about forty-five minutes.

* Stoke d'Abernon Church *(155, 173)*, 11 m. ne, on A 245

An Early English rebuilding of a Saxon church, unfortunately remodeled in the nineteenth century, boasts the oldest surviving brass in England, i.e., that of Sir John d'Abernon (1277). Nearby is another memorial brass inscribed to the memory of his son, Sir John (1327).

LEATHERHEAD

* Polesden Lacey *(486)*, 3½ m. sw, 1½ m. s of Great Bookham (A 246); NT

A restored Regency house once owned by the playwright Richard B. Sheridan, today it contains a number of good English paintings, including those of Reynolds and Lawrence, but is notable chiefly for its rose garden, iris garden, lavender garden, and peony borders.

STAINES

Magna Carta Memorial *(148)*, 2½ m. w, s of A 308 (176 TQ 994 727)

A rotunda enclosing a small pillar, put up by the American Bar Association, marks the supposed spot in Runnymede Field where King John and his rebellious barons set their seals to the Articles of the Barons, later incorporated into the Great Charter of 1215.

WOKING

*** **Wisley Garden** *(486)*, 1½ m. ne, 1 m. nw of A 3

This is the official garden of the Royal Horticultural Society. It includes a woodland garden, a rock garden, heather gardens, herbaceous borders, and a pinetum.

SOUTHERN ENGLAND

HAMPSHIRE
ALDERSHOT

** **Airborne Forces Exhibition** *(507)*, Browning Barracks, Queen's Avenue

A good new museum featuring weapons, airborne vehicles, parachutes, dioramas, and other items pertaining to airborne operations, especially those in World War II.

* **Royal Corps of Transport Museum** *(507)*, Buller Barracks

Uniforms, equipment, and models of vehicles belonging to the Royal Corps of Transport and its predecessors from 1795 to date.

ALTON

*** **Chawton Cottage** *(396, 407)*, 1½ m. s in Chawton, s of A 31

The home of Jane Austen after 1809, now a museum of Austen memorabilia. Some good Hepplewhite furniture.

BASINGSTOKE

** **The Vyne** *(304)*, 4 m. n, off A 340; NT

Except for the fine seventeenth century portico by John Webb and the eighteenth century Palladian staircase, this is a splendid Tudor mansion built in the early sixteenth century by Sir William Sandys, lord chamberlain to Henry VIII. It is of rose-colored brick with purple diamond diapering. Inside, its most distinguished feature is the Oak Gallery with fine linden-paneling, one of the best examples in the country of this typically Tudor woodwork. The chapel is good late Perpendicular.

Bishop's Waltham

* **Bishop's Palace** *(228)*, town center (185 SU 552 173) AM

Built as a country house by Henry of Blois, Bishop of Winchester, in the twelfth century, it was much enlarged in the fifteenth. The ruins stand fairly high.

Fareham

* **Titchfield Abbey** *(253, 282)*, 2 m. w, on B 3334 s of A 27 (196 SU 541 067) AM

Also known as the Place House, here are the remains of a sixteenth century house built at the time of the Dissolution on the site of, and with materials from, a thirteenth century Premonstratensian abbey by Thomas Wriothesley, second earl of Southampton.

Fordingbridge

* **Rockbourne Roman Villa** *(87)*, 3 m. nw (184 SU 120 170)

A large fourth century structure with well-preserved hypocausts and baths. Mosaics are of geometric design and not extraordinary. Good site museum.

Isle of Wight: Newport

*** **Carisbrooke Castle** *(141, 299, 345)*, 1 m. w, on B 3401 (196 SZ 486 877) AM

The earliest part of the castle is the well-preserved shell keep of about 1150 on top of a still earlier Norman motte. This was the work of the earl Baldwin de Redvers, a supporter of the Empress Matilda during her war with King Stephen. Entrance is through a gateway built in the fourteenth century and up a long flight of steps. The curtain walls are mostly of twelfth century construction. The main gatehouse, the angle towers, ramparts, and domestic buildings are of Elizabethan date. The castle was Charles I's prison in 1647 to 1648 before he was taken to London for trial and execution. The site museum contains relics of this "martyred" king.

* **Norris Castle** *(402)*, 4 m. n, on A 3021, s of East Cowes

A pseudo-Norman castle built by James Wyatt for the first marquess of Hertford in the late eighteenth century. Queen Victoria stayed here often as a young girl, and it later served as a kind of guest house for nearby Osborne. The shower was built especially for her grandson, Kaiser Wilhelm II. Visiting hours are restricted.

*** Osborne House *(450)*, 4 m. n, e of A 3021, 1 m. se of East Cowes; Department of the Environment

This is the country retreat built for Queen Victoria in 1845 to 1848 by Thomas Cubitt to the design of Prince Albert, the Royal Consort. The style is more or less Italianate. Here the queen died in 1901, and most of the rooms have been preserved as she left them. The large number of Indian mementos reflect Victoria's pride in being named empress of India. The Swiss cottage and miniature fort were installed by Prince Albert for the amusement and edification of the royal children. An altogether fascinating relic of the Victorian Age set in lovely grounds.

ISLE OF WIGHT: SANDOWN

*** Brading Roman Villa *(80, 87)*, 2½ m. n, w of A 3055 from Brading (196 SZ 391 853)

Here is the west wing of an early fourth century villa, roofed over and equipped with a catwalk from which to get a good view of the mosaics. They include representations of Bacchus, maenads, a pair of gladiators, Orpheus surrounded by spellbound birds and beasts, Perseus and Andromeda, two Medusa heads, Lycurgus attacking Ambrosia, Ceres giving corn and a plowshare to Triptolemus, a satyr in pursuit of a maenad, and, most interesting of all, a curious Gnostic cult scene featuring the philosopher Abraxes, winged griffins, and a human body with a cock's head.

LYMINGTON

** Buckler's Hard Maritime Museum *(393, 395)*, 8 m. ne, on Beaulieu River

A well-organized museum in a charmingly restored village on a beautiful site on the riverbank. Here are models of Nelson's *Agamemnon,* H.M.S. *Illustrious,* and other vessels constructed here, plus a good collection of shipwright's tools, Nelson's baby clothes, and other miscellany connected with the maritime history of Britain especially in the eighteenth century when this was an important shipbuilding center.

* Hurst Castle *(285, 345)*, 4 m. s, off Milford-on-Sea at end of B 3058 (196 SZ 319 898) AM

Originally a twelve-sided tower surrounded by three large semicircular bastions, this was one of Henry VIII's coastal fortifications built in the 1540s. Charles I was imprisoned here briefly, and the castle was still in use for gun emplacements in both world wars. It can be reached by passenger ferry from Key Haven or by a mile-and-a-half trek along the beach from the car park in Milford-on-Sea. Beautiful location overlooking the sail-studded Solent.

*** Palace House (Beaulieu Abbey) *(283)*, 6 m. ne, on B 3055 and B 3056

At the time of the Dissolution, the Cistercian foundation of Beaulieu Abbey was sold to Thomas Wriothesley, later Henry VIII's lord chancellor and earl of Southampton, who first converted the abbey gatehouse into a private residence. Though greatly remodeled in the nineteenth century, the twin gables on the river side, the inner reception hall, drawing room, and private dining room are still basically Tudor. On the grounds is the parish church, originally the monastic refectory, and there is a fine site museum in the old lay brothers' dormitory in the west range of the cloister. Here also is ***** The National Motor Museum** *(463)*, the best collection of antique cars in Britain. Though this is among the more commercialized of England's stately homes, it is also among the most intelligently arranged for the pleasure and convenience of visitors.

LYNDHURST

* The New Forest *(133)*, surrounding area

This was the first of the royal forests set aside by William the Conqueror as a hunting preserve. Today the total acreage of Crown woodlands comes to 31,432. It is interlaced with good roads and paths, many of which converge on Lyndhurst. Wildlife abounds and the New Forest ponies are among the more attractive sights.

Rufus Stone *(134)*, 6 m. nw, n of A 31, 10 m. w of Southampton (184 SU 270 125)

A small inscribed stone commemorating the death of William II (Rufus) from an arrow wound while hunting here in the New Forest.

PORTSMOUTH

Dickens House *(465)*, 393 Commercial Road

The house where the novelist Charles Dickens was born in 1812 is now a museum.

* Royal Marines' Museum *(393)*, Eastney Esplanade

Uniforms, weapons, equipment, etc., relating to the history of the Royal Marines.

* Southsea Castle *(286)*, Castle Avenue and Esplanade, Southsea

One of Henry VIII's coastal fortifications, this is unique in being angular, rather than circular, in plan, and therefore more in keeping than the others with contemporary Italian styles of military architecture. It consists of a square keep within a hexagonal rampart with triangular bastions in the middle of each of the long sides. It was the only one of these fortifications actually to see action, when the French invaded the Isle of Wight across the Solent in 1545. Today it is situated in a fine public park overlooking the Solent. Good site museum.

*** H.M.S. Victory *(395)*, H.M. Dockyard

Though much restored, this is the very ship on which Lord Nelson carried his flag at the Battle of Trafalgar where he met his death. It is therefore something of a Royal Navy shrine and is beautifully maintained. Of special interest: the forecastle carronades; the brass plaque marking the spot where Nelson fell on 21 October 1805; Captain Thomas M. Hardy's quarters; Lord Nelson's quarters; the gundecks; the rigging, typical of an eighteenth century square-sailed ship of the line. Mandatory guided tour of about one-half hour by a Royal Marine, whose emphasis inevitably is on shipboard discipline. A must for naval persons of any nationality.

* The Victory Museum *(395)*, H.M. Dockyard

Here is a miscellany of materials relating to Lord Nelson and to British naval history in general: log books, ship models, nautical instruments, Nelson memorabilia, etc. Of great interest is the model of the Battle of Trafalgar. This place provides an instructive sequel to a visit aboard *Victory* tied up nearby.

*** Portchester Castle *(75, 135)*, 8 m. nw, ½ m. s of A 27 (196 SU 625 045) AM

The 18-foot-high exterior wall is mostly of Roman construction and originally enclosed the Saxon shore fort built here in the third century, probably by the usurper Carausius. In the northwest corner is a Norman keep put here about 1120 in the reign of Henry II. Under Richard II in the 1390s, a royal palace was built around the keep. In the opposite corner is a Norman church, originally belonging to the priory of Augustinian canons founded by Henry I. It is not open except for services.

ROMSEY

*** Broadlands *(350, 402, 451)*, ½ m. s, e of A 31

This is a splendid country house with many important historical, as well as architectural associations. The original Tudor house was remodeled in the eighteenth century by William Kent, Capability Brown, Henry Holland, Angelica Kauffmann, and possibly Robert Adam. The grounds were done by Capability Brown. This was the home of Queen Victoria's prime minister, Lord Palmerston, and, more recently, of Lord Mountbatten until his murder by Irish terrorists. Still more recently it was the much publicized honeymoon site of the newly wed Prince and Princess of Wales.

* Mottisfont Abbey *(283)*, 4½ m. nw, w of A 3057; NT

After the Dissolution, Henry VIII's lord chamberlain, William Sandys, converted the thirteenth century Augustinian priory into a private house incorporating the nave of the priory church and the undercroft of the cellarium. The house was much modified in the eighteenth century, and in the twentieth its saloon was decorated with an interesting *trompe l'oeil* by Rex Whistler.

SOUTHAMPTON

H.M.S. Cavalier *(506)*, Mayflower Park

Built in 1944, the last of the C-class World War II destroyers is now undergoing restoration (as of 1978) and is expected to be open to the public.

** Town Wall *(176)*, north of *** Westgate** *(176)*, West Quay Road

Here is about a half-mile of the mid-fourteenth century town wall which originally was one and one-quarter miles in length and encircled the town. This is the western segment of the wall, and the gate is one of seven that pierced the circuit. The northern entrance, called **Bargate** *(176)*, is at the juncture of High Street and Above Bar Street.

Calshot Castle *(285)*, 13 m. s at end of A 326

This is a small blockhouse with a round tower surrounded by a gun terrace, built by Henry VIII to guard the Solent against invasion. Today (1981) it is on the grounds of H.M. Coast Guard Station and is in the process of restoration by the Department of the Environment.

* Netley Abbey *(254)*, 3 m. se, off A 3025 (196 SU 453 089) AM

The substantial ruin of a late Cistercian foundation of 1229, established by the endowment of Peter des Roches, counselor to Henry III. The walls of the church (Early English with a Decorated window) and the Early English chapter house still stand high, largely owing to the fact that after the Dissolution, Sir William Paulet, later marquess of Winchester, converted the abbey into a country house. Poorly signposted and hard to find.

WINCHESTER

** Winchester Castle *(96, 153)*, Castle Hill

On the site of one of William the Conqueror's first castles, Henry III built the present Great Hall between 1222 and 1236. Considered by some experts to be "the finest medieval hall in England after Westminster," the room measures 110 by 55 feet and is 55 feet high. The stained glass dates from the nineteenth century. So does the huge bronze statue of Queen Victoria by Alfred Gilbert, sculptor of *Eros* in Piccadilly Circus. The wall painting at the eastern end records the names of all knights of the shire (Hampshire) returned to the House of Commons since 1295. On the west wall is the Round Table, constructed of oak, eighteen feet in diameter, and painted in the Tudor colors of green and white by order of Henry VIII. The table, though meant to evoke memories of King Arthur, probably dates from the mid-fourteenth century reign of Edward III.

*** Winchester Cathedral *(228, 259, 290)*, town center

Originally a Benedictine abbey church commenced in 1079, this, the longest medieval church in Europe, became secular in 1541.

Architectural styles: west front—Perpendicular; nave—Perpendicular; central tower—Norman; transepts—Norman; choir—Decorated; retrochoir—Early English; lady chapel—Perpendicular.

Special features: Chantry chapels to Bishop Edington (1366), Bishop Waynflete (1486), Prior Silkstede (1524), Bishop Gardiner (1525), Bishop Fox (1528), Bishop Wykeham (1404), and Cardinal Beaufort (1447); Norman crypt; Perpendicular reredos; effigy of Peter des Roches; Queen Mary Tudor chair in lady chapel; thirteenth century grisaille glass in retrochoir windows; library with ancient manuscripts including the Winchester Bible.

*** Winchester College *(268)*, College Street

This was a grammar school founded in 1382 by William of Wykeham, Bishop of Winchester and chancellor of England, to train boys for later matriculation at the founder's New College in Oxford. One of the most prestigious of England's public schools, its scholars are still known as Wykehamists. The gateway dates from 1394; the Perpendicular chapel from about the same time; the Warden's Lodgings in the outer court from the nineteenth century; Fromond's Chantry from 1425 to 1445; and a detached building known as School from the late eighteenth century. The chapel and the first two courts are open to the public; guided tours through the remainder of the college are once in the afternoon.

Wolvesey Castle *(228)*, College Street

Ruined palace of the Bishops of Winchester, begun by Henry of Blois, brother to King Stephen, in 1129. Undergoing restoration.

BERKSHIRE
HUNGERFORD

** Littlecote *(342)*, 4 m. w, in Wiltshire, n of A 4 from Froxfield

A red-brick early Tudor manor house (1490–1520), it is chiefly notable for its seventeenth century contents, including the Puritan chapel with its oak pulpit, the equestrian portrait of Colonel Alexander Popham in the uniform of the parliamentary army, and the best collection in the country of Civil War buff coats, armor, and weapons. The drawing room is furnished in the style of the eighteenth century. Mandatory guided tours.

NEWBURY

* Donnington Castle *(183, 342)*, 3 m. n (174 SU 461 694) AM

The castle was built in the 1380s by Richard de Adderbury, a veteran of the French wars and companion in arms of the Black Prince. The ruined twin-towered gatehouse is about all that remains of the original. Held by royalist forces during the Civil War, it withstood a siege of twenty-months duration before surrendering on 1 April 1646. The still visible, four-star breastwork with arrowhead bastions dates to this period and is a faint reflection of the highly sophisticated science of siegecraft developing at that time on the Continent.

READING

** The Museum and Art Gallery *(27, 81)*, Blagrave Street

A typical collection of prehistoric grave goods (including finds from Wayland's Smithy) plus a fine collection of Romano-British artifacts from nearby Silchester.

* Basildon Park *(388)*, 7 m. nw, w of A 329, 1 m. nw of Pangbourne; NT

A fine Palladian villa built 1776 to 1783 by John Carr (Carr of York) for Sir Francis Sykes, a nabob who had made his fortune in India. The interior is more in the style of Robert Adam. Beautiful octagon room. Nice garden.

* Mapledurham *(413)*, 3 m. nw in Oxfordshire, e of A 4074

A much restored Tudor house, known chiefly for its association with Alexander Pope. The poet was a frequent visitor here between 1707 and 1715, the guest of the sisters Martha and Theresa Blount. Visiting hours restricted.

* **Silchester** *(81, 90)*, in Hampshire 13 m. sw, 5 m. se of A 440 from Aldermaston (175 SU 640 625)

The remains of *Calleva*, the *civitas* set up for the *Atrebates*, consist of nothing more than the complete one and one-half mile circuit of high wall. To see the two surviving gates, permission must be obtained at Rye House and Manor Farm. After excavation, the town site was again plowed under, so nothing is to be seen inside the wall except a field. Near the rectory is a small site museum.

*** **Stratfield Saye** *(446)*, 8 m. s, in Hampshire, 1 m. w of A 33

A charming seventeenth century house bestowed by a grateful nation on the first duke of Wellington. The interior is furnished mostly as in his day, with numerous mementos from his campaigns against Napoleon's armies. Attached is a fine military museum devoted mostly to the Napoleonic wars. The duke's famous horse Copenhagen is buried on the grounds. Good Regency furniture.

WINDSOR

Household Cavalry Museum *(446)*, Combermere Barracks

Cavalry museums like this are less common than those devoted to the infantry. Here is a good place to note the difference, as to weapons, uniforms, etc.

Riverside Station *(461)*, Datchet Road

A red-brick Gothic structure built in 1850 to 1851, it contains the royal waiting room with the initials of Queen Victoria and the Prince Consort inlaid in black brick.

*** **Windsor Castle** *(140, 179, 202, 260, 278, 334, 410, 439, 443)*, town center

The shell keep (Round Tower) on an earlier Norman motte was built originally by Henry II, though heightened in the early nineteenth century. Henry III constructed the walls of the Lower Ward, including the west wall and its towers flanked by High Street, Windsor. Edward III undertook a radical reconstruction in the fourteenth century, rebuilding the Upper Ward and adding the misnamed Norman Gate. In the fifteenth century Edward IV commenced construction of St. George's Chapel in honor of the patron saint of the Order of the Garter, whose knights' banners still hang above the stalls reserved for their use. A splendid example of Perpendicular architectural style, the chapel was completed in the reign of Henry VII. It houses the tombs of Henry VI, Edward IV, Henry VIII and his third wife Jane Seymour, Charles I,

George III, George IV, William IV, and George VI, father of the present queen. Queen Elizabeth I added the castle gallery, which now forms part of the library, as well as the North Terrace. In the early nineteenth century George IV rebuilt most of the Upper Ward, added numerous towers here and there, and remodeled the State Apartments extensively. The Castle's present appearance is due mostly to his lavish "Gothic" reconstruction done under the guidance of the architect Sir Jeffrey Wyatville. The Prince Albert Memorial Chapel was added by Queen Victoria to commemorate her late beloved husband.

Among the many works of art now hanging in the State Apartments, are the portraits by Sir Thomas Lawrence in the Waterloo Chamber; the portraits by Kneller in the Garter Throne Room and St. George's Hall; the portraits by Van Dyck in the Queen's Drawing Room; a rare Holbein in the King's Dressing Room; and paintings by Rubens in the King's Drawing Room. Queen Mary's Dollhouse is also noteworthy and very popular with tourists.

*** Eton College *(268)*, ½ m. n in Buckinghamshire

Founded in 1440 by King Henry VI to train scholars for King's College, Cambridge, established the following year, Eton is perhaps the most famous of all of England's public schools. Its graduates include the elder and younger Pitt, George Canning, William E. Gladstone, and of course the duke of Wellington to whom is attributed the remark that "Waterloo was won on the playing fields of Eton." Of its present buildings, the chapel is the most noteworthy, being a fine specimen of Perpendicular architecture, though the fan-vaulted ceiling is not original. The fifteenth century wall paintings here are superb. Contemporary (or thereabouts) with the chapel are the lower school and the college hall. The upper school is a product of the late seventeenth century, the library of the eighteenth. Guided tours are informative but not mandatory.

* Runnymede Memorial *(504)*, 4 m. se, off Coopers Hill Lane in Egham, Surrey

On a beautiful bluff overlooking the Thames, here is a fine memorial to the airmen killed in World War II: R.A.F., British Commonwealth, and Empire, totalling more than 20,000. It is a dignified monasticlike monument, appropriate to the setting and to its purpose.

DORSET
BLANDFORD FORUM

Dorset Cursus *(22)*, 7 m. ne, s of A 354 on road to Gussage St. Michael (195 ST 972 122—184 SU 040 193)

Two parallel earthen banks of Neolithic construction, running southeast of, and parallel to, the A 354 and best observed from the crossroad that runs from Gussage St. Andrew to Gussage St. Michael. That they had some religious significance is more than likely, but just what significance is unknown.

Hambledon Hill *(47)*, 4½ m. nw, 1½ m. w of A 350 on road to Child Okeford (194 ST 845 126)

A multivallate Iron Age hill fort built on the site of a Neolithic causewayed camp, with entrances on north, southeast, and southwest. Hard to find.

* Hod Hill *(47, 60)*, 3½ m. nw, 1 m. nw of A 350 from Stourpaine (194 ST 856 106)

A rectangular Iron Age hill fort defended on three sides by two ramparts and attendant ditches. After the fort was slighted by Vespasian in A.D. 43, the Romans built a small fortress at the northwest corner, whose foundations can still be seen.

Pimperne Long Barrow *(15)*, 3½ m. ne, n of A 354 (195 ST 917 104)

One of the largest Neolithic long barrows in Dorset, measuring 350 by 90 feet.

* Royal Signals Museum *(507)*, 2 m. ne at Blandford Camp

A recently opened museum of uniforms, equipment, etc., associated with army signaling and communications.

Thickthorn Long Barrows *(15)*, 12½ m. ne, e of A 354 (195 ST 972 122)

Two Neolithic long barrows, each approximately seven-feet high, lying near the south end of the Dorset Cursus.

Wor Barrow *(15)*, 10 m. ne, w of A 354, ¾ m. e of Sixpenny Handley (134 SU 012 173)

A much excavated Neolithic long barrow, the mound has been flattened, but the surrounding ditch has been dug out to its original depth.

DORCHESTER

*** Dorset County Museum *(32, 60, 81, 89, 465)*, High West Street

Here is one of the finest archaeological museums in England. It contains a complete array of prehistoric pottery, a display of Bronze Age axes arranged in chronological sequence, and a large number of Iron Age implements. Finds from Dorset's many long barrows, round barrows, and hill forts are in abundance. Especially noteworthy are those from nearby

Maiden Castle, including a piece of human vertebrae pierced by a pointed iron bolt, a relic of Vespasian's successful siege of Maiden Castle during the Roman conquest of Britain. Here also is a replica of Thomas Hardy's study and a collection of Hardy manuscripts and memorabilia.

Dorset Military Museum *(446)*, The Keep, Bridgport Road

The county regimental museum with the usual array of weapons, uniforms, regimental plate, etc.

* **Maumbury Ring** *(81)*, south edge of town

The grassy remains of a Roman amphitheater built on the site of a Neolithic henge monument.

** **Cerne Abbas Giant** *(88)*, 7½ m. n, on e side of A 352 n of Cerne Abbas village (194 ST 666 016) NT

Viewed from the roadside, this hill figure looks like a chalk linear drawing of a naked man carrying a club in his right hand. The effect was gained by digging trenches into the soil to the level of the natural chalk underneath. The original figure was probably created in Roman times as a representation of Hercules, possibly in the reign of the Emperor Commodus (A.D. 180–193) who fancied himself a reincarnation of the demigod. It measures 180 feet from head to toe, and the club is 62 feet long. Easily observed from the A 352 just north of Cerne Abbas village.

Hardy's Cottage *(463)*, 3 m. ne in Higher Bockhampton, s of A 35; NT

Birthplace in 1840 of the novelist Thomas Hardy. Though owned by the National Trust, it can only be visited by appointment.

*** **Maiden Castle** *(47, 60, 89)*, 1 m. s, w of A 354 (194 SY 670 885) AM

The most famous, most visited, and best preserved of all Iron Age hill forts. Built in several stages over the site of a Neolithic causewayed camp, in its final version the fort consisted of forty-three acres enclosed by three high ramparts and their intervening ditches. The fort was stormed by Vespasian in A.D. 43. Three centuries later, the Romanized British built a temple at the east end whose foundations are still standing. Altogether a most impressive sight with a superb view.

SHERBORNE

*** **Sherborne Abbey Church** *(244)*, town center

Here the Perpendicular choir, magnificent nave, and central tower were built over a Norman infrastructure with a few residual Anglo-Saxon elements. The fan vaulting is unsurpassed. This was a Benedictine monastery church, converted to parochial use after the Dissolution. The claustral buildings have been incorporated into the adjacent school, but the monastic almshouse, built about 1440, is open to the public.

* Sherborne Castle *(309)*, 1 m. s, off A 30

A sixteenth century house built by Sir Walter Raleigh, much enlarged by the Digby earls of Bristol in the seventeenth century, with grounds landscaped by Capability Brown in the eighteenth. The house is replete with the usual fine furniture, porcelain and paintings.

* Sherborne Old Castle *(135)*, e edge of town (183 ST 647 167) AM

First built by Roger de Caen, Bishop of Old Sarum (predecessor of the see of Salisbury), the original buildings of the inner ward are badly ruined. The twelfth century gatehouse on the southwest, however, stands fairly high.

SWANAGE

* Corfe Castle *(147, 343)*, 4 m. nw, on A 351

A stark and romantic ruin, the curtain wall with its semicircular mural towers and the polygonal keep are the work of King John whose favorite castle this was. The outer bailey wall to the south was principally built in the reign of Henry III and the outer gatehouse in that of Edward I. It owes its present state of dilapidation to the savaging it received from Cromwell's troops during the Civil War.

WAREHAM

St. Martin's, Wareham *(122)*, n end of town on A 351

An unusual looking Anglo-Saxon church without tower or spire. Chancel and chancel arch are typically pre-Conquest. There is a fine modern recumbent statue of Lawrence of Arabia who lived in nearby Clouds Hill and is buried in Moreton, Dorset.

* Town Walls *(108)*, town boundary

Well-preserved remains of Anglo-Saxon fortifications. The embankment, with its footpath running along the top, measures more than one hundred feet across and as much as fifteen feet in height. The outer ditch is about ten feet deep.

*** The Tank Museum *(496, 500, 506, 507)*, 7 m. w, 1 m. n of A 352 at Bovington Camp

A representative collection of tanks, self-propelled guns, and armored cars, both British and foreign, from World War I through World War II and beyond. Among the most interesting items on display are Little Willie (1915), the Cromwell (1942), the Sherman (1944), the German Panzer and Tiger, and the Russian T34 from World War II.

WEYMOUTH

Jordan Hill *(89)*, 2½ m. ne, e of A 53 (194 SY 698 821) AM

Here are the foundations of a square Romano-British temple, probably dating from the end of the fourth century, and presumably dedicated to some Romanized Celtic deity.

WIMBORNE MINSTER

* **Badbury Rings** *(47)*, 3½ m. nw, n of B 3082 (195 ST 964 030)

The tree-covered hill is the site of a multivallate fort of three ramparts with intervening ditches with two entrances to the east and west. At the northwest end of the outer rampart runs a length of the Roman road called **Ackling Dyke** *(64)*, thirteen yards wide and elevated to a height of four to six feet.

WILTSHIRE
AMESBURY

Lake Round Barrows *(31)*, 3½ m. w, 1½ m. s of Stonehenge (184 SU 110 401)

Five Bronze Age round barrows.

Normanton Down Cemetery *(31)*, 3 m. w, s of A 303 (184 SU 115 413) NT

A group of about thirty-five Bronze Age round barrows just south of Stonehenge. No signposts.

*** **Stonehenge** *(23, 36)*, 2½ m. w on A 344 (184 SU 123 422) AM

The most famous and most visited prehistoric monument in Europe, now somewhat commercialized though not so much so as to warrant its removal from the intelligent traveller's must list. The monument today must be approached through a turnstile leading to an underground passage at the end of which it stands, roped off because of the heavy tourist traffic and the growing threat of vandalism. Even so, the visitor is allowed a fairly close view of its exterior, and the Department of the Environment has posted pictograms clearly demonstrating the monument's three stages of construction from Neolithic to Late Bronze Age. Looking from the outside toward the center, the following features should be noted: the circle of Neolithic Aubrey Holes now marked in the grass with chalk; the outer circle of sixteen (out of the original thirty) sarsen stones still standing, some capped by lintels, and ten in a prone position; the blue-stone circle of which only ten stubby stones remain; the horseshoe of sarsen trilithons of which three of the original five still stand; the horseshoe of blue stones, of which eight of the original nineteen remain; the altar stone now buried in the ground beneath one of the fallen sarsen trilithons. Outside the monument itself, in the direction of the road (northeast), is the heel stone, which was part of the original Neolithic henge.

Stonehenge Cursus *(22)*, 3 m. w, ½ m. n of Stonehenge (184 SU 124 430)

Two low parallel banks cut across the road north from Stonehenge to Larkhill. They undoubtedly had some religious significance in the New Stone Age, but exactly what purpose they served is unknown.

Stonehenge Cursus Round Barrows *(22)*, 3 m. e, ½ m. n of Stonehenge (184 SU 124 430)

Seven Bronze Age round barrows situated to the south of the west end of Stonehenge Cursus.

* **Winterbourne Stoke Round Barrow Group** *(31)*, 4 m. w, on e side of A 360 n of junction with A 303 (184 SU 101 417) NT

Two groups of mounds with examples of every type of Bronze Age round barrow: bowl, bell, disc, saucer, and pond. This is the best single display in Britain of these generally undistinguished-looking gravesites.

* **Woodhenge** *(23)*, 2 m. n, w of A 345 (184 SU 151 434) AM

A restored Neolithic henge monument, possibly a temple. The original concentric circles of wooden posts, which probably upheld a conical roof, have been replaced by small concrete pillars.

BRADFORD-ON-AVON

* **St. Laurence, Bradford-on-Avon** *(122)*, on A 363

A small eighth century church with a typical square-ended chancel and narrow chancel arch. There is only one porticus, the other having been destroyed.

CALNE

** Bowood *(398)*, 3 m. sw, s of A 4

One of the best preserved of Capability Brown's landscape gardens. Most of the eighteenth century house here has disappeared except for Robert Adam's Diocletian wing. This was the site of Joseph Priestly's experiments leading to the discovery of oxygen.

CHIPPENHAM

** Corsham Court *(309, 334, 406)*, 4 m. sw, s of A 4

The entrance side of the house was built in 1582 by Thomas Smythe, a successful haberdasher and Collector of the Customs for London. It is a typically Elizabethan E-shaped building with pedimented windows and pinnacled gables. The wings were rebuilt and the park side added in the 1760s by Paul Methuen who employed Lancelot (Capability) Brown as his architect. The house was later Gothicized by John Nash. Inside is a splendid collection of paintings, including Van Dyck's equestrian portrait of Charles I, and an equally impressive collection of furniture, including several pieces by Robert Adam.

*** Lacock Abbey *(282, 306, 387)*, 3 m. s, on A 150; NT

A thirteenth century Augustinian priory converted after the Dissolution into a private dwelling by Sir William Sharington, leader of the short-lived mid-sixteenth century movement to introduce Italian Renaissance motifs into Tudor architecture. This is, therefore, somewhat of a landmark in English architectural history, though it did not serve as a model for subsequent building. Sharington incorporated the medieval cloister, chapter house, and warming room into his dwelling, but added an Italianate gallery and joined the two wings together with a balustraded polygonal tower. The eighteenth century Gothick entrance hall is by Sanderson Miller.

DEVIZES

*** Devizes Museum *(27, 32)*, 31 Long Street

Maintained by the Wiltshire Archaeological and Natural History Society, this is one of the best museums in Britain specializing in archaeological finds. Its holdings extend from the New Stone Age through the period of Roman occupation. In addition to Neolithic implements, etc., recovered from West Kennet and other Wiltshire graves, the museum houses a priceless array of Bronze Age weapons, pottery, and ornaments; Iron Age brooches and other objects of La Tène art; Romano-British jewelry, glassware, sculpture, etc. Not to be missed.

Wansdyke *(98)*, 4 m. ne, e and w of A 361 (173 SU 024 670 120 649)

A long stretch on either side of the road of a single grass-covered rampart represents the remains of the eastern end of this linear earthwork, built probably by Anglo-Saxons in the late sixth century to mark the northern boundary of Wessex and keep out the native British.

MALMESBURY

* **Malmesbury Abbey Church** *(242)*, town center

A parochial church converted at the time of the Dissolution from a Benedictine abbey church built about 1160 to 1170. The style is predominantly Transitional, though the clerestory is fourteenth century. The south porch boasts some superior late Norman figure sculpture.

MARLBOROUGH

*** **Alexander Keiller Museum** *(27, 32)*, 6 m. w, in village of Avebury on A 361

A splendid collection of prehistoric pottery and implements from Windmill Hill, Avebury, and other Wiltshire sites, intelligently arranged with ample visual aids.

*** **Avebury** *(39)*, 6 m. w, in village of Avebury on A 361 (173 SU 103 700) AM NT

One of the great henge monuments of Neolithic Britain, it consists today of a great circle of thirty high sarsen stones out of an original one hundred. On the inside are two adjoining smaller circles of which only four stones remain of the original twenty-seven in the central circle, and five of the original twenty-nine in the south circle. There was possibly a third circle on the north, of which the only remains are two stones of a U-shaped cove. All of this is surrounded by a huge bank with an inside ditch, pierced with four entrances. To the south lies West Kennet Avenue consisting of one hundred pairs of standing stones approximately fifty feet apart, now lying along the B 4003. Avebury Circle today lies astraddle the village of the same name. This is a site absolutely not to be missed.

** **Silbury Hill** *(16)*, 6½ m. w, n of A 4 (173 SU 100 685) AM

A great mound 130 feet in height and 100 feet across the top, it rises dramatically above the Marlborough Downs. Though no evidence of burials has been found, this may have been begun as a Neolithic round barrow and completed later during the Bronze Age. It is clearly visible from the Neolithic causewayed camp at Windmill Hill and lies just across the A 4 from the Bronze Age chambered tomb of West Kennet.

*** West Kennet Chambered Tomb *(17)*, 6½ m. w, s of A 4 (173 SU 104 677) AM

Perhaps the most impressive of all English Neolithic chambered tombs, measuring 330 by 20 and standing 8 feet high at its eastern end. Inside, this Severn-Cotswold gallery grave has two pairs of side chambers leading off the gallery and a fifth at the end. It is lighted, well signposted, and roomy enough to permit comfortable examination by visitors.

Windmill Hill *(14)*, 7 m. nw, w of A 361, 1 m. n of Avebury (173 SU 087 714) NT

A much eroded early Neolithic causewayed camp on the crest of a hill overlooking the Wiltshire Downs. Faintly visible are three concentric ditches pierced by gaps. A Bronze Age barrow cemetery extends east from the camp.

MERE

*** Stourhead *(386, 411)*, 3 m. n, w of B 3092; NT

One of the finest eighteenth century gardens in England, designed by the banker Henry Hoare with the help of Henry Flitcroft. The contrived scenic views are marvelous, as are the classic decorative buildings put up by Flitcroft. Also note the fourteenth century market cross, imported here from Bristol, as well as the "Gothic" cottages.

SALISBURY

** Mompesson House *(236, 366)*, Cathedral Close; NT

A very handsome hipped-roof, Dutch-style town house built between 1680 and 1701. The interiors date mostly to the eighteenth century.

*** Salisbury Cathedral *(149, 155, 236)*, town center

A secular cathedral moved to Salisbury from Old Sarum in 1220, and, except for its tower and spire, built in its entirety within a fifty-year span of time—a unique accomplishment among medieval cathedrals.

Architectural styles: west front, nave, transepts, choir, and lady chapel —Early English; central tower and spire—Early English, though not built until 1320 to 1380; cloisters—Decorated; chapter house—Decorated; east window (Prisoners of Conscience)—20th century.

Special features: thirteenth century tombs of the two William Longspees; fourteenth century tomb of Sir John de Montacute; fifteenth century tomb of Walter, Lord Hungerford; library with copy of Magna Carta; multitude of stone carvings on corbels in chapter house.

** **Salisbury and South Wiltshire Museum** *(32, 37), town center*

Here is a good collection of prehistoric finds and fine models of Stonehenge.

* **Figsbury Ring** *(47)*, 4 m. ne, 1 m. e of A 338 from Winterbourne Dauntsey (184 SU 188 338) NT

A fifteen-acre univallate Iron Age hill fort. An unusual feature is the inner ditch without an attendant bank. Good view of Salisbury and the Wiltshire Downs.

** **Old Sarum** *(47, 98, 130, 236)*, 3 m. n, w of A 345 (184 SU 138 327) AM

A high Norman motte built on the site of an Iron Age hill fort. The foundations and some of the walling of the stone castle erected here in the late 11th century are visible. Adjacent to it are the foundations and other traces of the Norman cathedral which was mostly demolished to supply stone for the new cathedral at Salisbury in the early thirteenth century.

** **Old Wardour Castle** *(178)*, 14 m. w, 1 m. s of Tisbury (184 ST 939 263) AM

Modeled after a contemporary French château, this now-ruined castle was built in the 1390s by John, fifth Lord Lovel. It was a courtyard castle, hexagonal in shape, the great hall occupying the upper stories of the east facade flanked by two high towers. It was badly ruined as a result of two sieges during the Civil War, the first by a parliamentarian army, the second by royalists under the third Lord Arundell, its rightful owner. The entire rear face of the castle later collapsed.

Philips House *(440)*, 9 m. w in Dinton, n of B 3089; NT

A neo-Grecian house built about 1816 by Jeffrey Wyatt, later Sir Jeffrey Wyattville. Visiting hours very restricted.

* **Wardour Castle** *(388)*, 15 m. w, 2 m. s of Tisbury

A fine Palladian mansion designed by James Paine, now the property of the Cranbourne Chase School.

*** **Wilton House** *(334, 335, 405, 409)*, 2½ m. w, on A 30

Both in design and interior decoration and furnishings, this ranks at or near the top among England's stately homes. The building itself is the product of three distinct stages of construction. Of the original house, built on the grounds of a dissolved abbey by William Herbert, first earl of Pembroke (1507–1570), only the great tower in the center of the east front and the inner porch survive. The south front was probably designed by Inigo Jones but built by the French master, Isaac de Caux. Inside this wing is a set of seven staterooms, restored by Inigo Jones and his nephew-in-law, John Webb, after a fire. Among these, the double-cube room with its full set of Van Dyck portraits is thought by many to be the most beautiful single room in Britain. Its dimensions (60×30×30 feet) follow a ratio recommended by Palladio who was Jones's major source of inspiration. The single-cube room and the others *en suite* are almost as splendid. The final reconstruction was accomplished in the early nineteenth century by James Wyatt. He, unhappily, tore down the west and north fronts, including the original great hall, and added a two-tiered "Gothic" cloister around all four sides of the inner court. Finally, in 1737, the ninth earl put up the totally charming Palladian bridge across the little River Nadder in the grounds.

The splendor of Wilton's interior can only be seen to be appreciated. In this case the well-conducted guided tour enhances the appreciation.

Swindon

** Great Western Railway Museum *(457)*, Faringdon Road

A fine museum with a good collection of locomotives and other equipment belonging to the Great Western Railway which virtually built the original town here. The Iron Duke is a broad-gauge locomotive—a type peculiar to this one railway. The Brunel room is devoted to memorabilia of Isambard Kingdom Brunel, one of the nineteenth century's truly great engineers. Next door to the museum is a company house refurbished as it was in about 1900.

Ashdown House *(334, 357)*, 9 m. e, in Oxfordshire, w of B 4000, 2½ m. s of Ashbury; NT

A tall, hipped-roof building in the Dutch style, it was probably designed by William Winde, built by the first earl of Craven, and intended for the use of James I's daughter Elizabeth, the Winter Queen of Bohemia, mother of Prince Rupert, and widow of the Elector Palatine whose acceptance of the Crown of Bohemia touched off the Thirty Years War. Here is a fine portrait by Dobson of Prince Rupert and two of his cavalier associates of the Civil War. Visiting hours very restricted. Mandatory guided tours.

** Buscot Park *(480)*, 12 m. ne in Oxfordshire on A 417, 2 m. e of Lechlade, Gloucestorshire; NT

An eighteenth century house, much enlarged and modified in the twentieth century, it contains the Faringdon Collection of works of art, including paintings by Reynolds, Gainsborough, Richard Wilson, Lawrence, Landseer, and the Pre-Raphaelites, as well as some fine Chippendale and Regency furniture.

Cricklade Anglo-Saxon Ramparts *(108)*, 6 m. nw on A 419

A rectangular earthen rampart with outer ditch, originally built to fortify this Anglo-Saxon *burh*.

Kelmscott Manor *(457)*, 12 m. ne in Kelmscott, Oxfordshire, 2 m. e of A 361 from Lechlade, Gloucestershire

Home of William Morris after 1871, now a museum featuring a number of his products. Visiting hours very restricted.

TROWBRIDGE

* **Farleigh Hungerford Castle** *(178)*, in Somerset 3 m. w, off A 366 (173 ST 801 577) AM

The now-ruined castle was built in the 1370s by Sir Thomas Hungerford, a veteran of the French wars. The chapel was added in the mid-fifteenth century. The castle was besieged and taken by parliamentarian troops in the Civil War, but the fact that Hungerfords played prominent roles locally on both sides of the quarrel between king and Parliament saved it from complete destruction. The chapel and two towers have survived. In the former is a display of seventeenth century armor.

Great Chalfield Manor *(194)*, 5 m. n, 3 m. n, 3 m. ne of Bradford-on-Avon off A 3053; NT

A stone-built fifteenth century manor house with beautiful oriel windows. Visiting hours very restricted. Mandatory guided tours.

WARMINSTER

*** **Longleat House** *(306, 397, 480)*, 4 m. w, s of A 362

Distinguished in architectural history for being the sole surviving Elizabethan example of a true Renaissance-style house, this four-sided building with two inner courtyards lies in a huge park landscaped in the eighteenth century by Capability Brown. Designed by its owner, Sir John Thynne, and built in part by the master craftsman Robert Smythson, the outside is noteworthy for its symmetrical bays, its profusion of classical pilasters, its roofline parapet, and the large number of domes and elaborate chimneys. The interior was redone in an Italianate style in the nineteenth century. The safari park boasts a large variety of wild animals; also available is a children's playground, a Paddington Bear exhibit, and a gorilla island.

WESTBURY

** **Edington Church** *(260)*, 3½ m. ne on B 3098

A late fourteenth century collegiate church with both Decorated and Perpendicular features, this is one of the loveliest churches in Wiltshire.

There is good fourteenth century glass in the east window of the north transept, and the oak pulpitum dates from the thirteenth century.

SOUTHWEST ENGLAND

AVON
BATH

* **Assembly Rooms** *(389)*, Alfred Street; NT

Designed by John Wood the younger in 1769, restored in the 1940s.

** **Bath Abbey** *(239, 474)*, Abbey Churchyard

An abbey church built for Benedictine monks at the beginning of the sixteenth century, this is the last of the great pre-Reformation churches of England.

Architectural styles: the entire church is Perpendicular, though the interior was much restored in the nineteenth century by Sir George Gilbert Scott.

Special features: The fan tracery is among the best in England.

The Circus *(389)*, town center

An arc of town houses begun by John Wood, and completed after 1754 by his son, John Wood the younger.

* **Grand Pump Room** *(389)*, town center

Next door to the Roman Baths. Built by Thomas Baldwin and John Palmer in 1793 to 1796. Visitors may sample the famous sulphurous water that was the source of Bath's initial attraction.

Kennet and Avon Canal *(424)*, Claverton Street

The eastern terminus of one section of the eighteenth century canal that runs from here uninterruptedly to Bristol. Another section is open from Reading to Sulhamstead, Berkshire, and still another (five miles only) in the area of Newbury, Berkshire.

Lansdowne Crescent *(389)*, town center

Built by John Palmer in 1789 to 1793.

Queen's Square *(389)*, town center

John Wood's first building in Bath, constructed in the Palladian style in the 1720s.

*** **Roman Bath** *(82, 88)*, entered from the Grand Pump Room on Bath Street or from Stall Street

The most-visited Roman ruin in England, this was the heart of the Roman spa of *Aquae Sulis*. The great bath, now open to the sky, measures 83 by 40 feet, and is surrounded by smaller baths. Within the establishment is one of the best Roman museums in Britain. Note especially the sculpted shield from the pediment of the temple to Sulis Minerva with the head of the Celtic water god Sul in low relief.

** Royal Crescent *(389)*, town center

This impressive semiellipse of town houses faced with Ionic columns raised on a high base is the work of John Wood the younger, completed in the 1760s. No. 1 in the block has been completely restored and is open to the public.

Somerset Place *(389)*, town center

Built by John Eveleigh in 1788 to 1790.

Dundas Aqueduct *(425)*, 3½ m. se, 1 m. e of Monckton Combe (172 ST 784 625)

An aqueduct designed by John Rennie to carry the Kennet and Avon Canal across the River Avon.

** Dodington *(402)*, 10 m. n, 1 m. sw of A 46 from Old Sodbury, 3 m. se of Chipping Sodbury

A magnificent neoclassical house designed by James Wyatt—his last before his death in 1813. Inside and out the general effect is one of Roman splendor. Capability Brown did the park, including the Gothic Cascade House.

** Dyrham Park *(365)*, 7 m. n, w of A 46; NT

A lovely reconstruction of an older Tudor house set in the valley of an enchanting deer park (by Repton). The east front was designed by William Talman for William III's Secretary of War, William Blathwayt, between 1700 and 1704. The attached orangery is of the same date. Most of the original paintings inside are Dutch, and the collection of Dutch Delftware is unexcelled anywhere in England.

BRISTOL

** Bristol Cathedral *(239)*, Deanery Road

Originally a foundation of Augustinian Regular Canons, it became a secular cathedral in 1542, which it has remained except for a short time in the nineteenth century.

Architectural styles: west front and nave—nineteenth century restoration (in Decorated style); central tower—Perpendicular; transepts—Perpendicular; choir and lady chapel—Decorated; Elder Lady Chapel—Early English; chapter house—Norman; abbey gateways—Norman.

Special features: lierne vaulting in choir; Decorated east window.

** City Museum and Art Gallery *(27, 32)*, Queen's Road

A fine municipal museum containing, among other things, a good collection of archaeological finds, including items from the Cheddar Caves, grave goods from Stoney Littleton, and a complete collection of representative Bronze Age and Iron Age artifacts.

New Room *(420)*, Broad Mead

Considered to be the earliest Methodist chapel in Britain, this simple meeting house was built by John Wesley in 1739.

*** St. Mary Redcliffe *(244)*, Redcliffe Way

Though Queen Elizabeth I's pronouncement that it was "the fairest, the goodliest, and most famous parish church in England" may have been hyperbolic, this is certainly one of the most magnificent of the country's Perpendicular churches and one of the most uniform in style. Built between 1325 and 1375 out of the munificence of the Canynges, a Bristol shipping family, high tower, spire, pinnacles, lierne vaulting, ornamental stone carving, and large windows are all consummately Perpendicular.

Special features: the octagonal north porch with its star (lierne) vaulting; wooden statue of Elizabeth I (ca. 1574) in the northwest chapel; monuments to the Canynges in the south transept; in the crossing, the tomb slab of Admiral Sir William Penn (d. 1670), who captured Jamaica from the Dutch and fathered the founder of Pennsylvania.

* S.S. Great Britain *(462)*, Great Western Dock, Cumberland Road

A ship of great historical significance, this restored vessel was designed by I. K. Brunel with screw propulsion for the transatlantic run and launched by Prince Albert in 1843. Restoration has been in progress since 1970.

* Temple Meads Station *(461)*, Victoria Street

Opened in 1841 and designed by I. K. Brunel as the western terminus of the Great Western Railway, the exterior is a nice example of Victorian Tudor architecture; the interior is late Gothic with Perpendicular-style flattened iron arches and mock hammer beams.

University of Bristol *(469)*, Queen's Road

Founded in 1909, the university's buildings are undistinguished, but its grounds on a high hill overlooking the central city are charming.

* Badminton House *(338)*, 15 m. ne, 5 m. e of Chipping Sodbury

Built in the late seventeenth century by the third earl of Worcester, altered about 1740 by William Kent, and again in 1811 by Wyatville, the house is noted chiefly for Kent's great entrance hall (where the game of badminton was evolved) and for the original seventeenth century dining room with its fine woodcarvings by Grinling Gibbons. Capability Brown is responsible for the landscaping. Visiting hours very restricted.

* Blaise Castle House *(438)*, 4 m. nw, off B 4018 in Henbury

An eighteenth century house, now a folk museum. In the grounds are picturesque rustic cottages by John Nash.

** Stanton Drew *(40)*, 7 m. s, off B 3130 1 m. w of A 37 (173 ST 603 630)

An extensive Bronze Age monument consisting of an outer circle of twenty-seven stones (three standing) out of an original thirty; two inner circles of eight stones (half standing) and eleven stones (all recumbent). Avenues of stones lead from the outer circle and from the northeastern circle toward the River Chew. To the west, behind the Druid's Arms Inn, lies a "cove" consisting of two uprights and one fallen stone between them. On the other side of the river stands Hautville's Quoit, a single stone which doubtless was associated with the circles.

CLEVEDON

* Clevedon Court *(192)*, 1 m. e, off M 5; NT

A well-restored fourteenth century manor house with Elizabethan modifications.

RADSTOCK

** Stoney Littleton Chambered Tomb *(17)*, 3 m. ne, ¾ m. sw of Wellow (172 ST 735 572)

A well-restored chambered tomb of the Severn-Cotswold gallery grave variety, 107 by 54 feet. Inside three pairs of side chambers lead off the main gallery which also has an end chamber. The roof is corbelled dry-stone.

THORNBURY

* Thornbury Castle *(276)*, w of A 38

Now housing a very good restaurant, this was the unfinished fortified manor house of Edward Stafford, duke of Buckingham, executed by Henry VIII because of the enmity of Cardinal Wolsey and because, as a direct descendant of Edward III, he could have pressed a claim to the throne. Only one of the four great towers planned to guard the entrance front was finished before Stafford went to the block; the others remain truncated.

SOMERSET
BRIDGWATER

Blake Museum *(347)*, Blake Street

The birthplace of Robert Blake, the great Puritan naval hero of the Civil War. The contents of the museum, however, are disappointing, and almost the only display pertaining to Blake himself is a mockup of his victory over the Spanish fleet at Santa Cruz Harbor, Canary Islands.

* **Coleridge Cottage** *(414)*, in Nether Stowey, 8 m. w, on A 39; NT

Occupied by the poet Samuel Taylor Coleridge and now maintained as a museum in his memory. Here he was visited by Wordsworth, and here he wrote *The Rime of the Ancient Mariner.*

CHARD

** **Forde Abbey** *(282)*, 4 m. e in Dorset, 1 m. s of B 3162

The gatehouse, cloister, and hall of this mansion are sixteenth century additions to the medieval Cistercian monastery which fell into private hands at the time of the Dissolution. The facade was much altered in the seventeenth century by Oliver Cromwell's attorney general, Edmund Prideaux. On display is a fine set of Mortlake tapestries after a cartoon by Raphael. Visiting hours restricted.

CHEDDAR

*** **Cheddar Caves Museum** *(12, 27)*, The Cliffs

Perhaps the best place in Britain for the layman to learn about the Stone Age. The museum is divided into two parts: (a) the North Room displays archaeological finds from the Cheddar Caves and the surrounding neighborhood in chronological order from early Upper Paleolithic to medieval times. Included are the skeletal remains of Cheddar Man, probably a late Paleolithic or early Mesolithic hunter of about 8000 B.C.; two *batons de commandement* from Gough's Cave; and numerous other prehistoric objects; (b) the South Room contains an exhibit called Men on Mendip which offers a pictorial and dioramic description of Cheddar Man from early Upper Paleolithic to Victorian times.

FROME

** **Nunney Castle** *(178)*, 3 m. sw, ½ m. n of A 361 (183 ST 737 457) AM

Possibly modeled on the Bastille of Paris, this ruined castle was built in the 1370s by Sir John de la Mare, a veteran of the French wars. It was a rectangular courtyard castle with cylindrical towers at each corner, those on the shorter sides in close proximity to each other. The north face has collapsed, probably as a result of the castle's being besieged and captured during the Civil War by parliamentarian troops under Sir Thomas Fairfax.

Witham Priory *(144, 253)*, in Witham Friary, 5 m. s

This was the lay brothers' church of the first Carthusian monastery (Charterhouse) in Britain. It was founded in 1178 to 1179 by Henry II in expiation for the murder of Thomas Becket and now serves as a parish church. Key available at the general store across the road.

GLASTONBURY

** **Glastonbury Abbey** *(95, 97, 252)*

The traditional site of King Arthur's burial place, the present sparse remains date mostly from a late twelfth century rebuilding following a fire in 1184 that destroyed the Anglo-Saxon Benedictine abbey, one of the oldest in England. Visible above ground are portions of the transepts, south nave aisle, west doorway, and lady chapel. Below ground is a fifteenth century crypt. The location of the claustral buildings is marked. A fifteenth century abbot's kitchen houses the site museum. The thorn tree grew from a cutting of the Glastonbury Thorn, which tradition holds took root from the staff of Joseph of Arimathea, who brought the Holy Grail to England.

** **Glastonbury Tribunal** *(50)*, High Street

In this fifteenth century building where once the abbots of Glastonbury held court are now housed a large number of finds from the nearby Iron Age lake village long since sunk into the bog.

ILCHESTER

* **Fleet Air Arm Museum** *(506)*, 2½ m. ne on B 3151 at the Royal Naval Air Station, Yeovilton

Here is a collection of more than forty historic aircraft associated with British naval aviation; also other memorabilia of the Royal Naval Air Service and its successor, the Fleet Air Arm. Here too is the prototype model of the supersonic Concorde 002.

ILMINSTER

** **Barrington Court** *(304, 488)*, 3 m. ne, on B 3168; NT

Built in the sixteenth century and restored in the twentieth, this E-shaped house of golden Ham Hill stone is distinguished for its three-story gabled porch, the gabled staircase towers in the angles between the central block and both wings, its twisting chimneys, and the finials rising from the apex of every gable. Mandatory guided tour, somewhat rushed.

The lovely formal iris garden, mixed borders, walled garden, and moat garden were designed in the early twentieth century by the famous gardener Gertrude Jekyll.

MINEHEAD

* **Dunster Castle** *(483)*, 2 m. se, on A 396; NT

A thirteenth century castle, modified in the seventeenth, and radically restored in a neo-Gothic manner by Anthony Salvin in the nineteenth. The interior design is typically Victorian, especially with respect to the many rooms for exclusively male use—gun room, billiard room, smoking room, etc.

TAUNTON

** **Somerset County Museum** *(32, 50)*, Taunton Castle

A well-organized museum of local archaeology and history. Noteworthy are finds from the Iron Age lake villages of Glastonbury and Meare, and from the hill forts at Ham Hill and South Cadbury.

** **Hestercombe** *(488)*, 1½ m. n, off A 361 at Cheddon Fitzpaine

A fine garden laid out in 1910 by Gertrude Jekyll and Edwin Lutyens.

WATCHET

*** **Cleeve Abbey** *(251)*, 2 m. s, in Washford on A 39 (181 ST 047 407) AM

A Cistercian monastery founded about 1190. The east and south ranges of the cloister are completely restored and offer perhaps the best view in Britain of what monastic buildings looked like before they fell to ruin or were put to other uses. The east range is mid-thirteenth century with an eighteenth century roof; it includes (from north to south) the sacristy, library, chapter house, parlor, slype, and warming room. The south range was rebuilt in the fifteenth century and houses the refectory. The west range has been incorporated into a farmhouse. The church has been robbed of all its building stone down to the foundations. West of the church stands a fine sixteenth century gatehouse.

WELLS

*** Wells Cathedral *(233, 259)*, town center

A foundation of secular canons, the present cathedral church was begun about 1175, and since 1218 has been the see of the bishops of Bath and Wells.

Architectural styles: west front (with over three hundred sculpted figures)—Early English; west towers—Perpendicular; north porch—Early English; nave—Transitional; central tower—Decorated; transepts—Transitional; choir—Transitional (western end) and Geometric Decorated (eastern end); retrochoir—Geometric Decorated; lady chapel—Geometric Decorated; chapter house—Geometric Decorated; cloisters—Perpendicular; deanery—Perpendicular; bishop's palace—Early English; Bishop Burnell's chapel—Decorated.

Special features: double arch ("scissors" arch) under central tower; Perpendicular chantry of Bishop Bubwith; bishops' tombs; fourteenth century clock; vaulting of retrochoir and chapter house; external statuary; cathedral close.

** Wookey Hole *(11)*, 3 m. w, n of (182 ST 533 478)

A somewhat commercialized but spectacular lighted cavern. Mandatory guided tours of about half-hour length and frequent. The cavern itself shows no sign of human habitation until the Iron Age, but on the grounds is the Hyena Den once occupied by Upper Paleolithic hunters. The small site museum displays finds recovered from this small cave.

YEOVIL

* Lytes Cary *(194)*, 7 m. n, 2½ m. ne of Ilchester off A 303; NT

The great hall here dates from the fifteenth century; the rest of the well-preserved manor from the sixteenth to the eighteenth.

*** Montacute *(308)*, 4 m. w, on A 3088; NT

An Elizabethan prodigy house built after 1588 by Sir Edward Phelips, speaker of the House of Commons, it was altered in the eighteenth century with the addition to the western front of a new porch taken from another Tudor house in Dorset. The eastern front of this H-shaped house of honey-colored Ham Hill stone displays a great variety of Renaissance motifs (friezes, balustrades, obelisks, pedimented windows, classical entablatures, and statues in Roman costume) as well as Flemish gables and a multitude of chimneys. Inside, the house has a splendid collection of heraldic stained glass, excellent sixteenth century paneling, and a long gallery full of Tudor and Jacobean portraits from the National Portrait Gallery. The dignified formal garden laid out in the nineteenth century was embellished by herbaceous borders, shrubs, and rose bushes installed by Vita Sackville-West, creator of the more famous garden at Sissinghurst Castle in Kent.

South Cadbury *(96)*, 9 m. ne, 2½ m. e of A 359 from Queen Camel (183 ST 628 252)

An isolated hill about five hundred feet high, this was one of the Iron Age hill forts assaulted by Vespasian in A.D. 43. Abandoned by the Romans, it was reoccupied in the late fifth century and was apparently the headquarters of a powerful Somerset chieftain who some say was the legendary King Arthur. Approached by way of a steep footpath leading from the post office in the village of South Cadbury, the only visible remains are a low circle of grass-covered ramparts.

DEVON
BARNSTAPLE

* **Arlington Court** *(440)*, 7 m. ne, e of A 39

Built about 1830 by Thomas Lee, a follower of Sir John Soane, in the then popular neo-Grecian style. Nice Victorian garden. Good Regency and Victorian furniture.

DARTMOUTH

** **Dartmouth Castle** *(202)*, town harbor; AM

Built on the site of a fourteenth century fortification, the castle was begun in 1481 in the reign of Edward IV. It was the first in England to have gunports. Ten years later the now much ruined Kingswear Castle was erected as a companion fort across the River Dart. During the Civil War, Dartmouth was captured from the royalists by the parliamentarian army of Sir Thomas Fairfax, but was not slighted, and indeed was reinforced during the Restoration against the threat of a naval incursion by the Dutch. Today the castle's substantial ruins consist chiefly of a three-story round tower joined by a shorter square tower. The most interesting feature is the series of seven gunports in the basement. They face the sea, are rectangular, and are splayed internally to permit traverse (i.e., lateral range) for the cannon, which were installed on flat wooden beds.

* Newcomen Memorial Engine *(428)*, Royal Avenue Gardens

Here is the oldest steam engine in existence, designed by Thomas Newcomen, and transferred here from the Hawkesbury Canal near Coventry. This is a beam engine, still in working condition, though electrically powered. A friendly custodian will explain its operation.

EXETER

*** Exeter Cathedral *(133, 238)*, town center

A secular cathedral since 1050, the oldest part of the church dates from the eleventh century.

Architectural styles: west front with statuary—Decorated; nave, transepts, choir, lady chapel—Geometric Decorated; transeptal towers—Norman; chapter house—Early English and Perpendicular; bishop's palace (library)—rebuilt Decorated.

Special features: west front sculptured figures; minstrels' gallery with carved stone angels; bishop's throne; Perpendicular Oldham and Slyke chantry chapels; library with Exon Domesday Book.

* Exeter Maritime Museum *(462)*, The Quay

This is advertised as the world's biggest collection of working boats, with more than eighty craft afloat, ashore, and under cover; including tugs, dredgers, cutters, and miscellaneous boats of foreign design. I.K. Brunel's *Bertha* is among those on display—a dredger built in 1844 to clear mud from Bridgwater harbor.

* Rougemont House Museum *(32)*, Castle Street

An eighteenth century town house with a good museum of Devon prehistoric and Roman artifacts.

MORETONHAMPSTEAD

* Castle Drogo *(485)*, 5 m. n, at Drewsteignton, 1 m. ne of A 382; NT

The last gasp of the Gothic (or more precisely Norman) Revival, this massive pseudo-medieval keep was built by Edwin Lutyens in 1910.

** Grimspound Village *(30)*, 5½ m. sw, 1¼ m. s of B 3212 on Widecombe Road (191 SX 701 809)

A rare example of a Bronze Age village, the site consists of a circular stone wall within which are the foundations of twenty-four circular huts. No signposts and no car park. At point indicated above, park car in lay-by and proceed up well-beaten footpath to brow of first hill. Here is a splendid view of desolate Dartmoor.

NEWTON ABBOT

* Bradley Manor *(194)*, ½ m. w, off A 381; NT

Here is a charming stone manor house with beautiful fenestration; most of the building dates from the fifteenth century. Mandatory guided tour.

OKEHAMPTON

Finch Foundry *(427)*, 3½ m. e in Sticklepath on A 30

The overshot waterwheel here powered this farm implement factory from 1814 to 1960.

OTTERY ST. MARY

** Ottery St. Mary Church *(260)*, town center

Originally a parish church, this was made collegiate in 1335 and rebuilt by Bishop Grandisson of Exeter. Though it retains some Early English features in the nave (including the west window), the chancel and lady chapel are mostly Decorated, copied no doubt from nearby Exeter Cathedral.

* Cadhay *(309)*, 1 m. n (s of Fairmile)

A four-sided courtyard house built by John Haydon in the late sixteenth century, it is distinguished by the effigies of Henry VIII and his three children in the Court of Kings. Visiting hours restricted.

PLYMOUTH

* Antony House *(388, 411)*, 5 m. w, in Cornwall on A 374, 2 m. w of Torpoint; NT

Finished in 1721 in the style of James Gibbs, the pure classical features of the entrance facade are spoiled somewhat by a nineteenth century *porte-cochère*. The interior rooms are finished in Dutch oak, unusual for a house of this period. The garden is by Humphrey Repton. Mandatory guided tours of about forty minutes.

** Saltram House *(398,407,409)*, 3½ m. e; 2 m. w of Plympton,s of A 38; NT

A Tudor house rebuilt in Georgian style about 1750. Saloon and dining room are by Robert Adam, with the assistance of Joseph Rose and

Antonio Zucchi. Fine Chinese Chippendale furniture. Good collection of Reynolds's paintings. Park by Capability Brown.

TAVISTOCK

*** **Buckland Abbey** *(282)*, 6 m. s, 3 m. w of A 386 from Yelverton; NT

A Cistercian abbey converted into a private home after the Dissolution by Sir Richard Grenville and his grandson of the same name, who sold it in 1581 to Sir Francis Drake. The great hall occupies the site of the crossing of the monastic church; the fireplace in the gallery displays the Grenville arms; Drake's coat of arms is on the fireplace in the "naval gallery"; and one of the drawing rooms is furnished elegantly in the Georgian style. There is a fine fourteenth century tithe barn on the premises and a charming small garden.

*** **Cotehele House** *(272, 342)*, 8 m. sw, in Cornwall; 2½ m. e of A 388, 1½ m. s of Callington; NT

Overlooking the River Tamar, this is a well-preserved double-courtyard house of granite built in the late fifteenth and early sixteenth centuries by Sir Richard Edgecumbe and his son Piers. The former was a companion-of-arms of Henry of Richmond, later Henry VII. The furniture is mostly seventeenth century. On the riverside the quay has a good small maritime museum, and tied alongside is a restored river boat. There is also an old mill on the premises. A fine site beautifully displayed and efficiently managed.

TIVERTON

** **Knightshayes Court** *(483, 487)*, 2 m. n, e of A 396; NT

Built in the 1860s for John Heathcoat-Amery to the design of William Burges. The exterior is ecclesiastical Gothic mixed with elements appropriate to a medieval castle. An attractive feature here is the garden, or rather gardens, mostly planted since World War II. Both the formal parterres near the house and the woodland garden beyond are splendid creations.

TORQUAY

** **Kent's Cavern** *(9, 11)*, Ilsham Road, ¼ m. e of Baddacombe Road (B 3199)

A natural cave consisting of two parallel main corridors with radiating galleries, inhabited by Old Stone Age hunters between 100,000 and 8000 B.C. Electric lighting illuminates the colorful stalactites and stalagmites and a few fossilized imprints in the stone. Mandatory conducted tours of about one-half hour are informative and frequent.

* Torquay Museum of Natural History *(27)*, Baddacombe Road

Here are finds from Kent's Cavern, including the skull of a young woman from about 14,000 B.C.

* Compton Castle *(309)*, 4 m. w, off A 381; 1 m. n of Marldon; NT

A much restored fourteenth century fortified manor house, it was owned in the sixteenth century by John Gilbert, who was vice admiral of the Western Coast during the final decades of the reign of Elizabeth I, whose brother, Humphrey, was one of the great Elizabethan seadogs and explorer of Newfoundland; and whose half-brother was Sir Walter Raleigh. In spite of these important Elizabethan associations, the house itself is typically late medieval.

TOTNES

** Totnes Castle *(141)*, town center; AM

This well-preserved ruin of a shell keep built by the Nonants in the twelfth century surrounds a Norman motte. The interior of the shell is empty. The castle was restored in the fourteenth century by the de la Zouche family.

CORNWALL
BODMIN

*** Lanhydrock *(487)*, 2½ m. s, on B 3268; NT

Formal terraces dating from the mid-nineteenth century plus a splendid woodland garden featuring rhododendrons, azaleas, magnolias, camellias, hydrangeas, Japanese maples, etc. The house is Victorian.

BUDE

*** Tintagel Castle *(97, 115, 153)*, 15½ m. s; ½ m. w of B 3263, 3½ m. s of Boscastle (200 SX 258 714) AM

On one of the most thrilling scenic spots in England, with a view of the Cornish coast from Hartland Point to Trevose Head, this badly ruined thirteenth century castle is the legendary birthplace of King Arthur. A railed path leads seaward to the remains of a small thirteenth century chapel on the site of, and perhaps incorporating portions of, a fifth century Celtic Christian monastery or hermitage.

CAMBORNE

Holman's Engineering Museum *(429)*, town center

A museum devoted mostly to steam engines used in the Cornish mines.

Agar Mine *(428)*, 1 m. e in Pool on A 30; NT

Here is an early rotative beam engine.

East Pool Mine *(428)*, 1 m. e in Pool on A 30; NT

A Harvey water-pumping engine is displayed here.

FALMOUTH

*** Pendennis Castle *(285, 299)*, (204 SW 824 318) AM

Built by Henry VIII to guard the western coast of Carrick Roads (opposite St. Mawes), this is a thick circular tower with a surrounding gun platform, displaying the royal arms over the gateway. In the reign of Elizabeth, the outer curtain wall and angle bastions were added, and in 1611, a huge Italianate gatehouse. During the Civil War, the castle resisted a siege by Colonel Fairfax's parliamentarian army for five months, thanks mostly to the effectiveness of the Elizabethan ramparts.

*** St. Mawes Castle *(285)*, 2 m. e by ferry across Carrick Roads (204 SW 842 328) AM

Begun by Henry VIII in 1540 this well-preserved coastal fortification consists of a huge circular tower surrounded by three semicircular bastions. Note the royal arms over the main entrance and the Latin inscriptions honoring Henry and Prince Edward.

FOWEY

* Castle Dore *(97, 111)*, 3 m. n, e of B 3269 (200 SX 103 548)

A small but well-preserved Iron Age hill fort with circular banks as high as seven feet. During the fifth century it was the headquarters of a Cornish chieftain who may have been the King Mark of the Arthurian legend, whose betrothed Iseult became the lover of Tristan. Two miles to the south where the B 3269 touches the A 3082 (200 SX 109 524) stands the **Tristan Stone** *(97)*, dedicated to Tristan, son of Cunomorus (King Mark). True believers in the Arthurian story make much of this connection.

HELSTON

*** Poldark Mine and Museum *(433)*, e of B 3297 at Wendron

Here is one of the most complete open-air industrial museums in England. A half-hour guided tour takes the visitor through the well-lighted galleries of a tin mine with underground museums. On the grounds is a great variety of machinery, including a Cornish beam engine for pumping water out of the mines and a huge overshot waterwheel.

ISLES OF SCILLY: ST. MARY'S ISLAND

* Bant's Carn *(18)*, nw coast, 1½ m. n of Hughtown (203 SV 911 124) AM

A small Neolithic entrance-grave chambered tomb covered by a mound. Marvelous coastal view.

* Innisidgen Chambered Tomb *(18)*, ne coast, 2 m. ne of Hughtown (203 SV 921 127) AM

A partially covered Neolithic chambered tomb of the entrance-grave type.

* Porth Hellick Down *(18)*, e coast, 1½ m. e of Hughtown (203 SV 929 108) AM

A small Neolithic entrance grave, partially covered.

Star Castle *(299)*

This is an Elizabethan fortification built to defend the southwest coast of England against the return of the Spanish after the defeat of the great Armada in 1588. Designed by the court engineer, Robert Adams, it was built in 1593 in the shape of an eight-pointed star surrounded by a thick curtain wall. Today it is a hotel.

ISLES OF SCILLY: TRESCO

Cromwell's Castle *(346)*, (203 SV 882 159) AM

This tall round tower represents the remains of the fort built by Robert Blake in 1651 to 1652 to guard the west coast of England against royalist privateers and landing parties.

*** Tresco Abbey *(487)*, by ferry from Hughtown, St. Mary's

A fascinating and lush subtropical garden with a great variety of exotic plants from Africa and such places grown here because of the proximity of the Gulf Stream.

LAUNCESTON

** **Launceston Castle** *(141, 348)*, town center; AM

A unique double-shell keep, the outer ring was built in the late twelfth or early thirteenth century, while the inner and much higher shell was raised in the mid-thirteenth century by Richard, earl of Cornwall, brother to Henry III. This is a very well-preserved ruin. On the grounds is the Domesdale Prison, the ruined gatehouse in which the seventeenth century Quaker George Fox was imprisoned for eighteen months for refusing to remove his hat before a county judge.

LISKEARD

* **The Hurlers** *(40)*, 5 m. n, 1½ m. w of B 3254 from Upton Cross, ¼ m. nw of Minions (201 SX 258 714) AM

A Bronze Age monument consisting today of three stone circles in a line, with thirteen, seventeen, and nine stones still standing out of an original number of twenty-five to thirty-five stones in each circle.

* **Trethevy Stone** *(20)*, 3 m. n, w of B 3254 (201 SX 259 688) AM

Originally a Neolithic entrance grave, this portal dolmen consists of six standing stones supporting a capstone; one stone has fallen.

LOSTWITHIEL

*** **Restormel Castle** *(141)*, 1½ m. n (200 SX 104 614) AM

In many respects this is the most complete ruined shell keep in England. The outer wall was built by Robert de Cardinan late in the twelfth century; the interior buildings by Richard, earl of Cornwall, and his son Edmund in the mid- to late thirteenth century.

NEWQUAY

** **Trerice** *(309)*, 3 m. se, w of A 3058; NT

Built about 1572 (the date inscribed on one of the fireplaces) by Sir John Arundell, this is a typically E-shaped Tudor mansion of gray limestone with Flemish gables and lots of chimneys. Inside, the great hall follows the medieval pattern with a screen passage entered from the porch and a minstrels' gallery.

** **Trevelgue Head** *(48)*, 1 m. n, w of B 3276 (200 SX 827 630)

An Iron Age promontory fort on the Cornish coast, with three pairs of banks and ditches guarding the landward approach, and two more banks and a sea-channel protecting it from the sea. Both banks and ditches are steep. The coastline on either side offers a spectacular view.

PENZANCE

* **Boscawen-Un Stone Circle** *(40)*, 5 m. w, ½ m. s of A 30, w of Boscawen-noon (203 SW 413 274)

A famous circle and scene of Cornish folk festivals, this is really an ellipse of nineteen standing stones with a leaning, off-center monolith.

* **Carn Euny** *(50)*, 5 m. sw, 1 m. w of Sancreed (203 SW 402 289) AM

A cluster of foundations of Iron Age huts surrounding a *fougou*.

** **Chun Castle** *(48,111)*, 5 m. nw, 1 m. w of Penzance-Madron-Morvah Road (203 SW 405 339)

Up a steep footpath from Trehyllis Farm, past a whitewashed boulder, on the crest of the hill overlooking the rocky Cornish coast is this Iron Age hill fort with two concentric stone walls having staggered entrances. Signposted and not too hard to find despite its remoteness from main and secondary roads. Less than a hundred yards away is **Chun Quoit** *(20)*, a fine dolmen consisting of a square of large uprights supporting a huge capstone. The view of the Cornish coast from here is magnificent.

* **Lanyon Quoit** *(20)*, 3½ m. nw, on e side of Penzance-Madron-Morvah Road (203 SW 430 337) NT

Rebuilt after a collapse in 1815 the dolmen, representing the remains of a Neolithic entrance grave, today consists of three upright stones about six feet in height topped by a seventeen-foot capstone.

* **The Merry Maidens** *(40)*, 5 m. sw, s of B 3315 (203 SW 432 245)

A well-preserved Bronze Age stone circle of nineteen stones about four feet in height, with another pair of large stones, thirteen and one-half and fifteen feet high (the Pipers) about one quarter mile to the northeast, and another single upright (the Fiddler) to the west.

** **St. Michael's Mount** *(201,406)*, 4 m. e, ½ m. s of Marazion in Mount's Bay; accessible by causeway at low tide, by boat from Marazion at high tide; NT

The most attractive feature of this sea-girt rock is its silhouette as viewed from the mainland. Site of a Benedictine abbey in the early Middle Ages, in the fifteenth century the tiny island became the home of a Bridgettine convent as well as a fortress guarding the extreme southwestern tip of England. It was briefly seized by the earl of Oxford in a last futile effort to unseat Edward IV in 1471; it also served for a while as the base of operations for Perkin Warbeck, the colorful pretender to Henry VII's throne. The oldest building left on the island is the late fourteenth century church which has been incorporated into the mostly nineteenth century house owned and occupied by the St. Aubyn family to whom the property went in 1657. Guided tours only through the mansion. Sunday services in the chapel are open to the public.

REDRUTH

* Carn Brea *(47)*, 1½ m. sw (203 SW 685 407)

A hillside Iron Age fort of thirty-six acres with ramparts to north and south. Inside are the foundations of a number of Iron Age huts; also the remains of guard chambers.

** Tolgus Tin Streaming Mill *(432)*, 1 m. n, w of B 3300

Here is a mill which, until its closure in 1928, was devoted to separating tin from ore mostly taken from the wastes deposited by other larger mills upriver. Most of the machinery dates to the nineteenth century, though the operation itself began here in the eighteenth. The half-hour tour, conducted by an exceptionally able guide, provides an excellent introduction to the technological history of the Cornish tin industry. Small museum attached.

ST. IVES

** Chysauster *(50)*, 7 m. sw, 2 m. nw of B 3311 from Badger's Cross (203 SW 473 350) AM

An Iron Age village consisting today of the substantial foundations of four pairs of circular houses with inner courtyards, set on either side of what appears to have been a street. A short distance away are the ruins of a *fougou*. Well signposted and well tended by the Department of the Environment.

Men Scryfa *(111)*, 6 m. ne (203 SW 427 353)

Up the lane past the curious Bronze Age (?) holed-stone called Men-an-Tol, in an open field to the left, is this solitary standing stone with a nearly illegible inscription memorializing a Dark Age Cornish chieftain and his father *(Rialobran Cunoval Fil)*.

* Zennor Quoit *(20)*, 5 m. se, s of B 3306, ¼ m. n of Zennor (203 SW 469 380)

Approached by footpath from the B 3306 just north of Zennor village, the remains of this Neolithic entrance grave consist of five uprights constituting the sides of the burial chamber and two additional slabs forming the antechamber. The capstone, eighteen feet by nine and one-half feet, has partially slid off the uprights originally supporting it.

St. Just

* Geevor Tin Mining Museum *(432)*, 2½ m. n, w of B 3306

A modern working tin mine, founded in 1911, with an ore-crushing and separating plant above ground and a museum illustrating the history of the Cornish industry. The half-hour tour through the plant is enlightening in spite of the fact that the noise of the machinery renders the guide's voice almost inaudible. No admittance to the mines below, which in this instance project westward underneath the ocean bed.

Brane Chambered Tomb *(18)*, 2½ m. se, n of A 30 (203 SW 401 282)

A small Neolithic chambered tomb of the entrance grave variety covered by a round barrow twenty feet across and six and one-half feet high.

Pennance Chambered Tomb *(18)*, 8 m. ne; ¾ m. sw of Zennor, s of B 3306 (203 SW 448 376)

Otherwise known as the Giant's House, a small Neolithic entrance grave chambered tomb measuring twenty-five feet in diameter and six feet in height.

The Nine Maidens *(40)*, 5 m. ne; ½ m. n of Lanyon Farm on Madron-Morvah Road, 1½ m. se of Morvah; near Ding Dong Mine (203 SW 434 353)

Also known as Boskednan, the site is unusually hard to find, even for Cornwall. It lies just to the north of an almost impassable road which connects the abandoned Ding Dong Mine with the Madron-Morvah Road and can be reached by an almost invisible footpath leading from the area of the mine itself. The circle has eleven stones remaining out of an original nineteen, of which seven are standing, the tallest slightly over six feet.

* Tregeseal Stone Circles *(40)*, 1½ m. ne (203 SW 387 324)

Originally there were three circles in this Bronze Age monument, but only two remain, one with sixteen stones surviving and one with only two. Fine view.

SALTASH

* Royal Albert Bridge *(458)*, e of town center across Tamar River, s of highway bridge (A 38)

Built by Isambard Kingdom Brunel and opened in 1859 by Prince Albert, the bridge carried the Cornwall Railway across the Tamar from Plymouth. Its most novel engineering feature is the three-hundred-ton cylinder which Brunel sank in the river bed to support the central pier.

* Trematon Castle *(141)*, 1½ m. s

A ruined shell keep built by Reginald de Valletort in the late twelfth century. The attached curtain wall surrounding the bailey and the gatehouse were probably added later.

TRURO

* Cornwall County Museum and Art Gallery *(27,32)*, River Street

A good small archaeological collection, including grave goods from Zennor Quoit and some beautiful Bronze Age personal ornaments (gold *lunulae*, bracelets, and necklace).

* Truro Cathedral *(473)*, town center

Built in 1880 to 1910 to the design of John Pearson, this is a very late example of Victorian Gothic, though in the Early English style rather than the more usual Decorated.

*** Trelissick *(487)*, 2 m. s, on B 3289; NT

A fine Cornish woodland garden with splendid displays of camellias, rhododendrons, etc., in season.

** Trewithin *(487)*, 6 m. e, on A 390

A fine woodland garden featuring azaleas, rhododendrons, camellias, etc.

EAST ANGLIA

ESSEX
CHELMSFORD

Chelmsford and Essex Museum *(446)*, Oaklands Park, Moulsham Street

Here is the Essex Regimental Museum with the Salamanca Eagle captured in Spain and the usual array of weapons, uniforms, and regimental plate.

Pleshey Castle Mound *(129)*, 5 m. ne, 1 m. se of A 130 from Ford End

On this motte, now fifty feet high, Geoffrey de Mandeville built a castle in the early twelfth century, since disappeared. Also observable are the earthworks of the Norman bailey which still enclose most of the village.

*** St. Andrew's, Greensted *(122)*, 10 m. w; w of A 113, 1 m. sw of Chipping Ongar

This charming little church is the only one of wooden construction to have survived from Anglo-Saxon times. The ninth century nave is constructed of split-oak logs. The chancel is early sixteenth century, but the chancel arch is Norman. The aperture in the north wall, called a leper's squint, is in all probability the opening to a niche for holy water installed in the thirteenth century.

COGGESHALL

* Paycocke's *(311)*, West Street; NT

Built about 1500 by a rich Essex clothier, Thomas Paycocke, this is a typical early Tudor half-timbered town house.

COLCHESTER

*** Colchester Castle (Colchester and Essex Museum) (58,82,88), High Street

This Norman keep was built about 1080, partly out of bricks from Roman *Camulodunum* on the site of the first century temple to Claudius, remains of which are to be seen in the undercroft. The museum contains an excellent collection of Roman antiquities.

* Holy Trinity *(122)*, Trinity Street

The west wall of the nave dates from the Anglo-Saxon period as does the west tower, with its triangular-headed doorway faced with Roman brick, pilaster strips, string courses, and double-splayed windows (blocked).

* Roman Wall and **Balkerne Gate** *(82)*, near Hole in the Wall Inn

This is the best section of the Roman wall which enclosed the *civitas* of *Camulodunum*.

* St. Botolph's Priory *(250)*, Priory Street; AM

This was the first priory of Augustinian canons founded in England. Established by King William Rufus sometime before the year 1100, its present ruins consist mostly of the arcaded west front of the church and portions of its nave and aisles. It was built mostly of bricks, presumably from the Roman settlement of *Camulodunum*.

*** **Town Hall** *(477)*, High Street

One of the best examples in the country of late Victorian baroque, the architect was John Belcher and the dates of construction 1898 to 1902. Three pairs of Corinthian columns support baroque pediments topped by a baroque tower surmounted by a steeple reminiscent of Wren.

* **Layer Marney Hall** *(304)*, 7 m. sw, 1 m. s of B 1022 from Smyth's Green

Built of brick and terra-cotta in the early sixteenth century, by Henry, Lord Marney, treasurer to Henry VIII, the present structure represents only the gatehouse and south side of a mansion unfinished at the time of the builder's death. The gatehouse rises to three stories and is flanked by semioctagonal turrets on the south and square turrets on the north, each is eight stories in height. The fenestration is spectacular. Visiting hours restricted.

ENFIELD

Eleanor Cross *(157)*, 2 m. n on A 1010 in Waltham Cross, 2 m. w of Waltham Abbey (166 TL 356 005)

The most heavily restored of the three surviving Eleanor Crosses, this is hexagonal in plan with three statues of Queen Eleanor of Castile enclosed in graduated buttresses rising from the angles of the bases.

EPPING

Chipping Ongar Castle Mound *(129)*, 8 m. e; on A 128, ½ m. s of A 122

A well-preserved motte of probable Norman date.

Epping Forest *(133)*, 4 m. s on A 11

A tiny remnant of the great royal forest of early medieval times that once covered most of the county of Essex.

MALDON

Othana Roman Fort *(74,116)*, 13 m. e, 1½ m. ne of Bradwell-on-Sea (168 TM 031 082), near Bradwell Power Station.

The partial ruin of a Saxon Shore fort built in the third century to guard the Essex coast south of Colchester. In one corner are the remains of an early Christian church called **St. Peter-on-the-Wall** *(74,116)*, founded in the mid-seventh century by St. Cedd. Hard to reach, but the site offers a splendid view of the North Sea.

SAFFRON WALDEN

** **Audley End** *(330,406)*, 1 m. w, on A 11; Department of the Environment

Originally a huge double-courtyard house built for Thomas Howard, first earl of Suffolk between 1603 and 1616, this still-large mansion was reduced by two-thirds in the following century on the advice of Sir John Vanbrugh. The great hall has a marvelously intricate carved-oak Jacobean screen at one end, facing a severely classical stone screen at the other, possibly designed by Vanbrugh. Current restoration of the ground-floor rooms, decorated by Robert Adam in the eighteenth century, promises to make this the most attractive feature of the house.

* **Imperial War Museum, Duxford** *(504)*, 10 m. ne, on A 505, 2 m. w of Duxford

A large collection of aircraft housed in the open or under hangars; a few are of World War II vintage (e.g., a Spitfire, a B-17 Flying Fortress, and a P-51 Mustang), but most date from after the war.

SOUTHEND-ON-SEA

* **Hadleigh Castle** *(153)*, 4 m. w, s of A 13 (178 TQ 810 860) AM

Painted by Constable, this is probably Essex's most famous medieval castle ruin, though indeed not much remains of the original *enciente* built by Hubert de Burgh in the thirteenth century. The remaining mural towers and part of the curtain wall are mostly the product of a rebuilding by Edward III in the fourteenth century to guard the nearby Thames estuary against invasion by the French in the first phase of the Hundred Years War.

TILBURY

* **Avely Church** *(174)*, 6 m. nw on B 1335

A twelfth to thirteenth century church with a brass memorializing Sir Ralph de Knevyngton (ca. 1370).

* **Tilbury Fort** *(351)*, ½ m. s, at river terminus of A 126, behind World's End public house

Built 1670 to 1683 in response to De Ruyter's invasion of the Medway during the Second Dutch War, the major seventeenth century survival is Sir Bernard de Gomme's baroque Water Gate. The guardroom with the chapel above may have been built as early as 1700; the officers' barracks were added in the mid-eighteenth century and expanded in the nineteenth. This was not the location of Tilbury camp where Queen

Elizabeth I made her famous speech in 1588 at the time of the threatened invasion by the Spanish Armada. Fine view of the Thames.

WALTHAM HOLY CROSS

** **Waltham Abbey** *(157,249)*, Waltham Abbey district; AM

The present parish church incorporates the nave of a great church in the
Norman style begun by Harold Godwineson. Here the Anglo-Saxon
claimant to the throne was buried after the fatal arrow pierced his eye
at Hastings. A century later, King Henry II, in expiation of the murder
of Thomas Becket, refounded the establishment as an Augustinian abbey,
but his additions were mostly torn down at the time of the Dissolution.
The existing church has a sixteenth century wall painting of the Last
Judgment, and nineteenth century windows by Burne-Jones in the east
end. The gatehouse is of fourteenth century date.

SUFFOLK
BURY ST. EDMUNDS

** **Bury St. Edmund's Abbey** *(250)*, town center; AM

One of the greatest Benedictine abbeys in England was established here
in the eleventh century in honor of the martyred East Anglian king, St.
Edmund. Fragmentary portions of the abbey church's nave and north
transept still stand fairly high in the town's well-groomed public park,
and the outline of the cloister can be traced in the stones lying to the
north of the nave. Far better preserved are the two gatehouses on the
west side of the abbey precincts: the Norman Tower of St. James, dating
from the twelfth century, and the Great Gatehouse (1330–1380), a splendid example of ecclesiastical/military architecture in its decadent phase.

Guildhall *(208)*, Guildhall Street

The porch here dates to about 1480.

* **Moyse's Hall Museum** *(32,146)*, Cornhill

A rare twelfth century town house, believed to have been built by a
Jewish moneylender, now housing a good museum of Suffolk history and
archaeology. Noteworthy here is the Isleham hoard of Bronze Age implements and scrap metal, which the museum claims to be the largest of its
kind found in Europe.

** **Ickworth** *(404,408)*, 3 m. sw, w of A 143; NT

An almost oppressively neoclassical mansion begun in the 1790s by the
fourth earl of Bristol and bishop of Derry and modeled on the Pantheon
in Rome. Magnificent furniture and paintings.

* Ixworth Abbey *(283)*, 6 m. ne on A 143

An Augustinian priory converted into a private house after the Dissolution, the twelfth century dormitory undercroft, the prior's lodging, and the frater were all incorporated into the new building. The entrance hall was added about 1690. Visiting hours are restricted.

FRAMLINGHAM

*** Framlingham Castle *(149,290)*, town center; AM

A very well-preserved ruin, its towers and walls rising almost to their original height, this was in the early Middle Ages the most important castle in Suffolk. After being destroyed by Henry II, it was rebuilt by Roger Bigod between 1190 and 1210 as a castle of *enceinte*—a very early example of the principle of perimeter defense by which mural towers replaced a central keep. In the sixteenth century the castle belonged to the Howard dukes of Norfolk who made a number of alterations in brick that are still observable. In 1553 Mary Tudor took refuge here during the plot to unseat her in favor of Lady Jane Grey, and it was here that Queen Mary began her successful march to London to capture the throne.

* Wingfield Castle *(178)*, 10 m. n, 1½ m. w of B 1116 from Fressingfield

This is a manor house converted into a castle in the 1380s by Michael de la Pole, earl of Suffolk. Not much is left of the original building except the brick south front and gatehouse.

IPSWICH

* Christchurch Mansion *(410)*, Christchurch Park

A small gallery containing a good collection of Gainsborough paintings, many of scenes of the surrounding county.

Friar Street Chapel *(363)*, Friar Street

A Presbyterian meeting house, built in 1700, since converted to Unitarian use.

* Ipswich Museum *(27)*, High Street

A good small museum of local history and archaeology containing a representative collection of prehistoric artifacts, including finds from Grimes Graves. Also Roman and medieval objects of interest.

LOWESTOFT

* **Somerleyton Hall** *(483)*, 5 m. nw off B 1074

A neo-Jacobean mansion built in 1844 to 1851 by John Thomas for Samuel Morton Peto, a railway magnate. Good Victorian garden.

*** **Southwold Church** *(244)*, 11 m. s, on A 1095

Built in the mid-fifteenth century (1430–1460), this fine wool church is especially famous for its great expanse of window glass. Viewed from inside or out, here is a textbook illustration of typical Perpendicular window construction.

SUDBURY

* **Acton Church** *(155)*, 2 m. n

The superb brass of Robert de Bures (1302) lies in the north aisle, with smaller brasses of the fifteenth and sixteenth centuries nearby. A replica of the Bures brass lies on a nearby table for the use of brass rubbers.

*** **Lavenham Church** *(244)*, 6 m. ne, on A 1141

A wool church built (1480–1530) from funds supplied by John de Vere, fourteenth earl of Oxford, and Thomas Spring, a wealthy clothier, this is an almost perfect example of the Perpendicular style. The high tower at the west end is especially fine, as is the south porch. Inside, the misericords are worthy of note, as are the chantries dedicated to the two chief donors and their families.

** **Lavenham Market Place** *(208,209)*, 6 m. ne, on A 1141

This ancient wool town retains the most authentic medieval townscape in Britain. In Market Place are the fifteenth century **Little Hall** and the slightly later **Guildhall** (NT), probably the best of its genre in the country. Nearby, the shop at 11 Lady Street, the houses at 87 to 90 Bear Lane, and the block of Flemish weavers' cottages at 23-26 Water Street are all late medieval, and though there are many shops and houses of later provenance intermingled among them, the town preserves much of the medieval silhouette of the period when it was among the most prosperous in England.

Kentwell Hall *(309)*, 4 m. n on A 134, in Long Melford

A mid-sixteenth century brick house built by Sir Thomas Clopton, restored in the nineteenth century by Thomas Hooper, and re-restored recently. Visiting hours restricted.

*** Long Melford Church *(244)*, 3 m. n, on A 134

A splendid Perpendicular wool church, it is particularly noteworthy for the fifteenth century stained glass in the aisles, the Clapton chantry, the lady chapel, and the fine alabaster carving of the Adoration of the Magi in the north aisle.

** Melford Hall *(309)*, 4 m. n on A 134 in Long Melford; NT

Originally a four-sided courtyard house, which has since lost its back range, this red-brick mansion built in the 1570s by Sir William Cordell, a speaker of the House of Commons, displays the usual indented facade, clustered chimneys, and manifold turrets of the high-Tudor style. It was remodeled in the eighteenth century and occupied by Sir Harry Parker, brother of the admiral whose commands Nelson so blithely disregarded at the Battle of Copenhagen. Good porcelain, furniture, and paintings.

WOODBRIDGE

*** Orford Castle *(139)*, 12 m. e, at end of B 1084 (169 TM 419 499) AM

Built by Henry II in 1165 to maintain guard over East Anglia, the keep is polygonal (eighteen sides) with three large square projections serving as buttresses running the entire height of the building from ground to roof. It has been reroofed and is well preserved both inside and out. Good view of the Suffolk coast from the battlements. This was Henry II's favorite castle.

NORFOLK
AYLSHAM

** Blickling Hall *(329,334)*, 2 m. nw, on B 1354; NT

Designed by Robert Lyminge and built for Sir Henry Hobart, lord chief justice, between 1616 and 1627, this great red-brick courtyard house has a classical central doorway, curly Flemish gables, and ogee-capped towers—all typical Jacobean embellishments. The interior was redesigned in the eighteenth century, but the long gallery still has its Jacobean plasterwork, and there are a few good seventeenth century portraits by Mytens and Dahl. The garden on the east side dates from the early eighteenth century.

** Salle Church *(244)*, 6 m. w, off B 1145

A fine Perpendicular wool church built by the mercantile families of Brigge, Fontayne, and Boleyn, and possibly the burial place of Henry VIII's second queen, Anne Boleyn. Especially noteworthy are the lierne vaulting, the chancel bosses, and the woodcarving on stalls, misericords, and pulpit.

CROMER

* Baconsthorpe Castle *(202)*, 8 m. sw, 4 m. s of A 148 (133 TG 122 382) AM

Built in the late fifteenth century by John and Henry Heydon, this was a standard late medieval moated courtyard castle, except that it was less symmetrical than some. Today's remains consist chiefly of the gatehouse and the south and west curtain walls, with mural towers. The so-called outer gatehouse is a late sixteenth century intrusion. Mary Queen of Scots was taken here briefly after the Northern Rising in 1569. The castle was captured by parliamentarians in the Civil War and later slighted.

* Felbrig Church *(189)*, 2 m. sw, w of B 1436

On the grounds of **Felbrigg Hall,** this undistinguished church houses a famous collection of brasses, including a memorial to Sir Simon Felbrygge (1416).

** Felbrigg Hall *(330,406)*, 3 m. sw, w of B 1436; NT

This L-shaped house has two parts: the south wing which is Jacobean with a typical frontispiece featuring Tuscan columns flanked by protruding bays; and the still more classical west wing added in the 1680s. The interior decoration and furnishings are mostly eighteenth century.

EAST DEREHAM

** Elsing Church *(173)*, 5 m. ne, of B 1147

A handsome small parish church in curvilinear Decorated style with some fourteenth century glass in the south window of the chancel and a lovely Decorated font-canopy. The church is famous for the Hastings Brass, a memorial to Sir Hugh Hastyngs (ca. 1347) with his figure surrounded by panels depicting King Edward III and five of his great captains. The brass itself is under cover in the chancel, but a replica has been set up in the west end of the nave for the convenience of brass rubbers.

* North Elmham Cathedral *(122)*, 6 m. n, on B 1110 (132 TF 988 216)

Here are the sparse ruins of an Anglo-Saxon cathedral built in the late tenth or early eleventh century. As the foundations show, it was only 130 feet in length and was constructed with a tower at the west end, one in front of each transept, and an apsidal east end. Key at Nelson House across the road.

FAKENHAM

* Binham Priority *(249)*, 10 m. ne, off B 1388 (132 TF 982 399) AM

The mostly Norman nave of this Benedictine house founded early in the twelfth century is still used as a parish church. Remains of the claustral buildings are in the churchyard.

** Houghton Hall *(378,380,385,405,410)*, 8 m. w, 1 m. n of A 148

A splendid Palladian palace designed by Colen Campbell, with additions by James Gibbs, for Sir Robert Walpole, first minister to George I and George II. The interior was decorated by William Kent, protégé of the Palladian pioneer, Lord Burlington. The house was built, decorated, and furnished between 1722 and 1735. Most of the original furnishings remain intact. Fine paintings, including John Wootton's portrait of Sir Robert. Visiting hours are restricted.

GREAT YARMOUTH

* The Rows *(311)*, between Hally Quay and Market Place

Though badly damaged by German bombing in World War II, a few of these narrow lanes and their abutting buildings of the sixteenth and seventeenth centuries survive, providing a rare example of a Tudor-Stuart townscape.

* South Quay *(311)*, South Quay; NT

A typical late Elizabethan town house, refaced in the nineteenth century. Good oak paneling and plastered ceilings.

Town Walls *(207)*

Short sections of the medieval wall lie in St. Nicholas churchyard; North Quay has a surviving gate; there is a second gate near South Quay in Blackfriars Road.

*** Burgh Castle *(74)*, 5 m. sw, on unnumbered road 4 m. w of junction of A 12 and A 43 (134 TG 475 046) AM

The quite substantial ruin of the Saxon shore fort, *Gariannonum*, built in the third and fourth centuries. The walls rise in places to their original height of fifteen feet. Noteworthy are the semicircular bastions with concave platforms for *ballistae*.

*** Caister Castle *(194,463)*, 4 m. n, off A 1064

Built of brick in the mid-fifteenth century by Sir John Fastolf out of his profits from the French wars, this ruined castle's well-preserved great tower rises ninety feet high above the River Bure to which it originally was linked by a canal. Next to it is the great hall which now incongruously houses an antique car museum. When constructed, these buildings were part of a huge fortified complex consisting of a moated courtyard castle surrounded by high curtain walls with towers at each corner and a second moated court in front. After Sir John's death, the castle passed to the Paston family, highly esteemed by historians because of the survival of a collection of their letters which are a major source of information about fifteenth century England. One of the Pastons, with only thirty retainers, unsuccessfully defended the castle against a force of three thousand led by the Duke of Norfolk in 1469. The family eventually regained possession, however, and kept it until 1660.

* **Haddiscoe Church** *(242)*, 8 m. sw, on A 143

An early Norman church, probably constructed over a still earlier Saxon foundation, it is chiefly distinguished by its tall cylindrical tower no doubt built for defensive, as much as for religious purposes.

KING'S LYNN

* **Guildhall** *(208)*, Saturday Market Place

A mid-fifteenth century building of checkered flint and stone.

*** **Castle Rising** *(135,169)*, 5½ m. ne, w of A 149 (132 TF 666 246) AM

A ruined rectangular keep, fifty feet high, built by William d'Albini who married the widow of Henry I. It stands in the midst of huge earthenworks which presumably once supported the curtain wall of the bailey. The Norman gatehouse still stands. Noteworthy is the first floor chapel with two Early English lancet windows. This was where Queen Isabella was exiled by her son Edward III after the execution of her paramour Mortimer.

** **Sandringham House** *(454)*, 8 m. ne, e of A 149

A neo-Jacobean house built in 1870 for the Prince of Wales, later Edward VII, it has recently been opened to public inspection during the summer months, though not when the royal family is in residence. Good china, furnishings, etc., and interesting paintings of the royal family since 1845. Long wait possible as only a limited number of visitors are admitted at any one time. Long walk from car park. Grounds magnificent.

* **West Walton Church** *(243)*, 9 m. w, n of A 47

Except for the Perpendicular west window, this is a fairly pure specimen of thirteenth century Early English architecture.

NORWICH

City Wall (207), King Street to Carrow Hill

A short section of surviving medieval wall lies on either side of King Street and runs west along Carrow Hill; also a mural tower called Black Tower.

** Norwich Castle Museum (28,32,63,100,135), Castle Meadow

Housed in the restored Norman castle keep, the museum has an excellent collection of archaeological finds, well displayed. Among other things on exhibit are artifacts from Grimes Graves, a rare Mesolithic harpoon, gold jewelry from the Bronze Age, the Snettisham hoard of Iron Age metalwork (shared with the British Museum), a Roman cavalry helmet, and an early medieval sword hilt. There are also five dioramas representing local scenes from Paleolithic times to the Iron Age, and a reconstruction of a Grimes Graves flint mine. The museum has fine collections of eighteenth century Lowestoft porcelain, English silver, and paintings of the Norfolk school.

*** Norwich Cathedral (231,251,259), town center

Begun in 1096 as a foundation of Benedictine monks, the church enjoyed cathedral status from the beginning.

Architectural styles: west front—Norman with Perpendicular windows; nave, central tower, transepts, and apsidal choir—Norman with Perpendicular lierne vaulting; lady chapel—Modern; claustral buildings—Decorated and Perpendicular.

Special features: Perpendicular chantries to Bishop Nykke and Sir Thomas Erpingham; Early English Bauchan chapel; eighth century bishop's throne.

* Norwich Guildhall (208), near City Hall

A fifteenth century building rebuilt in the sixteenth.

* Octagon Chapel (363), Colegate

Originally Presbyterian, now Unitarian, this very attractive dissenting meetinghouse was built in 1755.

Old Meeting House (363), Colegate

A Congregationalist meetinghouse built in 1693.

St. Andrews Hall (257), Elm Hill and Princes Streets

This building with good Decorated and Perpendicular windows incorporates Blackfriars Hall which was the church of the Dominican friary.

* **Reepham Church** *(174)*, 12 m. nw, 3 m. n of A 1067

Of the two churches in the same yard, St. Mary's is the more important because of the splendid effigy of Sir Roger de Kerdiston (1337).

SWAFFHAM

*** **Castle Acre Priory** *(249)*, 4 m. n, w of A 1065 (132 TF 814 148)

A Cluniac house founded in 1090 by the Conqueror's powerful hench-man, William de Warenne (see also Lewes Priory), this is a substantial ruin, mostly dating from the Norman period. The heavily arcaded west front of the church is a thing of beauty. Nave and transepts date from the late eleventh and early twelfth centuries, the choir from the fourteenth. From the mid-twelfth century comes the east range (chapter house, dorter, and reredorter) and the south range (frater). The west range (cellarium on ground floor, prior's chapel and lodging on the first) has been restored and reroofed.

*** **Oxburgh Hall** *(194,296)*, 7 m. sw, on Stoke Ferry Road; NT

Built of brick by Sir Edmund Bedingfield in the 1480s, this splendid fortified residence is distinguished chiefly by its brave front, a moated twin-towered gatehouse with battlemented turrets. Actually the house was built for enjoyment and not for defense; the machicolations are sealed, the exterior windows spacious. The back range of the enclosed courtyard was torn down so as to provide an open vista to the rear. The two back-corner turrets are Victorian restorations. The lovely garden was modeled on an eighteenth century French design.

THETFORD

Castle Hill *(129)*, e end of town

An exceptionally high and massive Norman motte located in the city's public park. The long-gone castle that surmounted it was built by William de Warenne.

* **Thetford Priory** *(249)*, town center; AM

An insubstantial ruin, this Cluniac priory was founded in 1103 by Roger Bigod of Framlingham Castle, one of Henry I's powerful Anglo-Norman barons. The walls of church and claustral buildings are high enough to reveal the general ground plan of the establishment, but not much more. The gatehouse, lying outside the priory precincts on private property, is of a later vintage and is almost complete.

* **Euston Hall** *(334,357,411)*, 4 m. se (in Suffolk), e of A 1088

Built originally in 1670 by the first earl of Arlington (one of Charles II's cabal), and since then considerably reduced in size and reworked, the house today is remarkable chiefly for its portraits of important seventeenth century historic personages. Van Somer's James I, Anne of Denmark, and the duke of Buckingham; Van Dyck's Charles I and Henrietta Maria; and Lely's Charles II, the duchess of Cleveland, Nell Gwynn, and the duke of Grafton are the most noteworthy. Park by William Kent modified by Capability Brown. Visiting hours very restricted.

** **Grimes Graves** *(24)*, 5 m. nw, 2 m. w of A 134 (144 TL 818 898) AM

The well-maintained site of the best-known Neolithic flint-mining center. One of the mines can be descended by ladder, and the visitor can observe at close quarters the manner in which stone-age miners dug galleries off the main shaft, much in the manner of modern coal miners. On occasion the custodian will demonstrate the art of flint-knapping.

WELLS-NEXT-THE-SEA

*** **Holkham Hall** *(384,405,480)*, 2 m. w, s of A 149

The magnificent and mammoth Palladian mansion of Thomas Coke, first earl of Leicester, designed by William Kent with the help of the owner and Kent's patron, Lord Burlington. The approach from the north to what was originally the rear of the house is somewhat disappointing, especially because the yellow-brick facade has weathered badly. The south front by which today's visitor leaves the grounds is more impressive, especially when viewed from Kent's triumphal arch, now the exit from the park. Inside, all is splendor with fine statuary, paintings by Van Dyck, Lely, Kneller, and numerous continental artists, and furniture designed by Kent himself.

CAMBRIDGESHIRE
CAMBRIDGE, COLLEGES AND UNIVERSITY BUILDINGS

** **Caius College** (pronounced *keys*) *(317)*, Trinity Street

The full title of the college is Gonville and Caius. It was reestablished in 1557 on the site of Edmund Gonville's fourteenth century foundation by Dr. John Kaye (or Caius), court physician. Almost nothing remains of the original fourteenth century buildings. The entry way off Trinity Street and the first court, called tree court, were rebuilt in the nineteenth century. To the west of this are two quadrangles divided by the chapel. North of the chapel lies Gonville court and, like it, completely refaced in the eighteenth century. South of it are the remains of Dr. Caius's work: a court open to the south to the Senate House passage. Here are two strange architectural fantasies meant to represent the latest in sixteenth century Renaissance fashion: the Gate of Virtue and the Gate of Honour, both bizarre melanges of classical columns, pilasters, niches, roundels, obelisks, and pediments, both inventions of the founder. A third and simpler gate, the Gate of Humility, has been removed from its original position to the Master's garden.

** Christ's College *(611)*, St. Andrews Street

Founded in 1505 by Lady Margaret Beaufort, countess of Richmond and mother to Henry VII, on the site of a fifteenth century college called God's House, the Tudor gateway on St. Andrews Street is surmounted by an enormous coat of arms of the foundress. The street front and the first court, however, were covered with dressed stone (ashlar) in the eighteenth century; the hall was rebuilt by G. G. Scott, Jr. in the mid-nineteenth century; the chapel is partly medieval, partly sixteenth century with an early eighteenth century interior; the Fellows Building in the second court was built in the classical style in 1640 to 1643; the third court is twentieth century. In the chapel is a rare fifteenth century brass eagle lectern supported by four metal greyhounds—a Beaufort badge. Good gardens on the extensive grounds.

* Clare College *(266)*, Trinity Lane

Founded in 1326 and refounded by Elizabeth de Burgh, countess of Clare in 1338, none of the college's original buildings remains. The four ranges of the quadrangle date from 1638 to 1715, giving Clare a greater uniformity of style than is enjoyed by most Cambridge colleges. The bridge across the River Cam at the rear of the college was built at the same time. This is a good place from which to view the famous Cambridge backs. The chapel was added in 1763 to 1769.

* Corpus Christi College *(266)*, Bene't and Trumpington Streets

Unique among colleges at either Oxford or Cambridge, this was founded (1352) by two town guilds, Corpus Christi and St. Mary's. Today the Old Court, lying south of Bene't Street and partly concealed by St. Bene't's Church is the oldest English academic quadrangle in existence antedating even Merton's Mob Quad and New College's quadrangle in Oxford. In this case, however, antiquity lends little charm, because the fourteenth century building material (called clunch) has weathered badly, and the walls are streaked with the stains of time. The short passageway between St. Bene't's Church and Old Court dates from the sixteenth century. The other buildings facing Trumpington Street and Free School Lane are not very good Victorian Gothic.

* Downing College *(412)*, Regent Street

Designed by William Wilkins about 1807, the east and west ranges are fine examples of Greek Revival architecture. The buildings to the north were raised in the twentieth century. Note that the college has a single open court, unlike its medieval predecessors, but similar to Thomas Jeffersons's plan for the University of Virginia which was put into effect ten years later.

** Emmanuel College *(318,352)*, corner of St. Andrews and Emmanuel Streets

Founded in 1584 by Sir Walter Mildmay as a center for radical Protestantism, the college turned out a fair number of seventeenth century Puritan leaders, including several who settled Massachusetts Bay. Built on the site of a Dominican friary, only fragments of whose buildings survive, the present entry way is the product of an eighteenth century remodeling, as is the south (right) range of the front court, though the brick building attached to it at right angles belongs to the seventeenth century. Facing the entry way to the open front court is the Italianate chapel designed in 1677 by Sir Christopher Wren. To the north (left) of the entry way is the sixteenth century hall which divides this court from the second court whose buildings date from the sixteenth, nineteenth, and twentieth centuries.

*** Fitzwilliam Museum *(476,480)*, Trumpington Street

A classical building in the Corinthian order, designed by George Basevi in 1837 to house a fine collection of pictures bequeathed to the University by the seventh Viscount Fitzwilliam. Among the many fine English paintings now on display are those by Eworth, Hogarth, Reynolds, Wright of Derby, Lawrence, Constable, Turner, Richard Wilson, and the Pre-Raphaelites. Also a good collection of English miniatures.

* Girton College *(487)*, 2 m. n in Girton

Moved here from Hitchin in 1873, this is the earliest college for women at either Cambridge or Oxford. Most of the buildings were designed by Alfred Waterhouse in his usual imitation Tudor style of red brick and terra-cotta. Rooms are accessible through corridors instead of separate staircases, an innovation also carried out at Newnham College, Cambridge, and Keble College, Oxford.

** Jesus College *(314)*, north of Jesus Lane

The college was founded in 1496 by John Alcock, Bishop of Ely and comptroller of works to Henry VII, on the site of a suppressed nunnery some of whose buildings were incorporated. The great red-brick gatehouse was built by Alcock, except for the top story added in the eighteenth century. The outer court, which is open on the west (left), is partly sixteenth and partly seventeenth century work; to the east (right) is Alcock's cloister court, on the south side of which is the conventual church converted into the college chapel. It is part Norman, but mostly Early English, with interesting Pre-Raphaelite windows and a ceiling painted by William Morris.

*** **King's College** *(267,273,412)*, King's Parade

The most noticeable of all of Cambridge's colleges, King's was founded in 1441 by King Henry VI as an educational capstone for the students at his recently established college at Eton. Behind its nineteenth century stone screen by William Wilkins and spacious lawn, the classical Fellows' Building by James Gibbs dates from the eighteenth century, and to its south is the nineteenth century hall, also by Wilkins. The most imposing of this college's buildings, however, lies on the north side of the great court. This is King's College Chapel, thought by many to be the most perfect specimen of Perpendicular architecture in Britain. It was begun by Henry VI and completed by Henry VIII. Outside, this high rectangular building fairly bristles with delicate stone pinnacles. Inside the nave and choir, their lofty fan-vaulted ceilings and typically Perpendicular stained-glass windows are breathtaking in their splendor. Of special interest are the Tudor armorials in the antechapel, the carved wooden rood screen between nave and choir with the arms of Anne Boleyn, the choir stalls, and the altarpiece by Peter Paul Rubens *(The Adoration of the Magi)*. Choral services are held here regularly and the Christmas performance called the *Festival of Lessons and Carols* is an outstanding attraction.

** **Magdalene College** (pronounced *maudlen*) *(316,351)*, Magdalene Street

Founded in 1542 by Lord Thomas Audley on the site of a hostel built in the late fifteenth century for Benedictine monks from Croyland Abbey, called Buckingham College, the college retains portions of the earlier medieval buildings. The gatehouse dates from 1585; parts of the first court (especially on the southeast side) are late fifteenth century; the chapel dates from the fifteenth century though much altered; the hall is early sixteenth century. In the second court is the late seventeenth century Pepysian Library in which are deposited the library of Samuel Pepys and the original manuscript of his *Diary* in shorthand.

* **Newnham College** *(467)*, Newnham Way and Sidgwick Avenue

The second Cambridge college for women, Newnham was founded in 1875 under the leadership of Miss A. J. Clough, sister of the poet Arthur Hugh Clough ("Say not the struggle naught availeth. . . ."). The architect was Basil Champneys, and the style is vaguely Dutch, red brick with white woodwork—rather pretty. Rooms are entered from corridors rather than separate staircases, as had been the practice at Oxford and Cambridge colleges up until the late nineteenth century.

*** Pembroke College *(266,352)*, Trumpington Street

Founded in 1347 by the widow of Aymer de Valence, earl of Pembroke, the college retains only a small portion of its original fourteenth century buildings. This consists of that part of the north range of buildings along Pembroke Street containing the Old Library which was originally the college chapel and which in 1690 received a fine plaster ceiling. The present chapel facing Trumpington Street was designed and built by Sir Christopher Wren in 1659 to 1665. Along with the Sheldonian Theatre at Oxford, it was his first architectural effort and therefore the prototype of his many parish churches in London and elsewhere. In 1880 the chapel was lengthened eastward by George Gilbert Scott the Younger. To the east of the Old Court is Ivy Court, a construction of the early seventeenth century. Farther east along Pembroke Street are buildings of the nineteenth and twentieth centuries.

** Peterhouse *(266,337)*, Trumpington Street

Founded by Hugh de Balsham, Bishop of Ely, in 1280, this is the oldest of Cambridge University's colleges. Fronting on Trumpington Street is the First Court, at the center of which is a magnificent chapel built in 1628 to 1632 by Matthew Wren (uncle to Sir Christopher) in the mixture of neoclassical and Gothic styles favored by Archbishop Laud. The chapel is flanked by the early eighteenth century Fellows Building and the sixteenth and seventeenth century library. Extending westward from the library is the hall, parts of which date from the thirteenth century, but which was heavily restored in the nineteenth century by the younger George Gilbert Scott. It contains interesting Pre-Raphaelite stained glass by Ford Madox Brown, Burne-Jones, and William Morris, and a charming fireplace by the latter. This hall forms the south range of the four-sided Principal Court, most of which dates from the fifteenth century. Behind it lies Gisborne Court, built in the nineteenth century.

*** Queen's College *(267,313)*, Queen's Lane

Founded in 1448 on the site of St. Bernard's College by Margaret of Anjou, consort to King Henry VI, "to laud and honneure of sexe feminine," the college was refounded in 1465 by Elizabeth Woodville, Edward IV's queen.

The gatehouse and first court were built in the mid-fifteenth century. The former is brick; the latter brick and half-timber. In the southwest tower facing Silver Street are rooms thought to have been occupied by the Dutch philosopher Erasmus in the early sixteenth century. Back of the front court is the cloister court, its western range also dating from the fifteenth century, north and south ranges from the sixteenth and eighteenth respectively. To the north of the front court along Queen's Lane, runs a seventeenth century red-brick building, back of which lies Walnut

Tree Court on the north side of which is the nineteenth century chapel. Beyond, lies the Erasmus Building, a twentieth century brick edifice built on stilts, which curiously does not jar with the older architecture. The Hall is covered with decorations by William Morris.

Queen's is the prettiest of the Cambridge colleges, and more of it is open to public view than in most instances. It should not be missed.

*** St. John's College *(314,474)*, St. John's Street

Founded in 1511 by Lady Margaret Beaufort, countess of Richmond and mother to Henry VII, the college is entered from St. John's Street through the splendid sixteenth century three-storied brick gateway surmounted by the now brightly painted Beaufort *yales* (part goat, part antelope, part elephant), supporting the Tudor rose and portcullis. Above it is a seventeenth century statue of St. John. In the first court, the south (left) side was refaced in the eighteenth century, and the north side consists of the nineteenth century chapel by Sir George Gilbert Scott. The hall in the facing west range, however, is mostly sixteenth century with its original hammer-beam roof. The second court was built in the late sixteenth century with money provided by the countess of Shrewsbury, whose seventeenth century statue stands above the gateway. In the seventeenth century third court is the splendid library built in 1623 to 1624. The early nineteenth century New Court across the river is reached by the lovely arched Bridge of Sighs, built in 1831.

** Church of St. Mary the Great *(267)*, Trinity Street

A parish church which also serves the university. It was mainly built between 1478 and 1508 in the Perpendicular style. The front portal, designed by Sir George Gilbert Scott, was installed in 1851; the vestry dates from 1522; the south porch from 1888.

Selwyn College *(467)*, Grange Road and Sidgwick Avenue

Founded in 1882 for Church of England students "willing to live economically," the red-brick Tudor-style buildings were designed by Sir Arthur Blomfield.

Senate House *(412)*, King's Parade

Designed by James Gibbs about 1722. No admission to the public.

* Sidney Sussex College *(318,340,341)*, Sidney Street between Sussex and Jesus Lane

Architecturally the least distinguished of all the older Cambridge colleges, it was founded in 1594 by Lady Frances Sidney, dowager countess of Sussex. Separated from Sidney Street only by a wall, the U-shaped hall court is surrounded on three sides by the original sixteenth century buildings, although the front of the hall was defaced in the nineteenth century by a Gothicized porch of Sir Jeffrey Wyatville. To the south (right) is the second court, dating mostly from the seventeenth and eighteenth centuries. The college's most famous student was Oliver Cromwell whose head lies buried on the premises, and whose portrait hangs in the hall. Chapel closed to public.

*** Trinity College *(316,356,415)*, Trinity Street

The largest of Cambridge University's colleges, Trinity was founded by King Henry VIII in 1546 incorporating two medieval foundations, King's Hall and Michaelhouse. The gatehouse, over which, on the street side, is a statue of the royal founder, dates from about 1518, but the range of buildings on either side belongs to the fifteenth century. In the great court, the chapel on the right is sixteenth century Perpendicular; beyond it lies the fourteenth century King Edward's Tower re-erected on this site, while the remainder of the buildings here date from the late sixteenth and early seventeenth centuries. West (left from the entry) of the great court lies Neville's court, the far range of which consists of the splendid library built by Sir Christopher Wren in the late seventeenth century. Inside it are woodcarvings by Grinling Gibbons, busts by Roubiliac, and a statue of Lord Byron barred from Westminster Abbey because of its subject's scandalous behavior. South of Neville's court (left from the entry through Neville's gate) is New Court in nineteenth century neo-Gothic, and east of that, another late seventeenth century building called Bishop's Hostel. Across the street are two attractive nineteenth century quadrangles belonging to the college.

* Trinity Hall *(266)*, Trinity Lane

Founded in 1350 by Bishop William Bateman of Norwich for students of canon and civil law, the principal court retains its original fourteenth century buildings, though they have all been refaced. Only in the north court facing Garret Hostel Lane can a number of original medieval windows be observed. The library extends westward from the principal court and was built of red brick in the sixteenth century.

The rest of the buildings belong to the nineteenth and twentieth centuries.

* The University Museum of Archaeology and Anthropology *(26,32, 105)*, Downing Street

Contains a large collection of prehistoric and medieval British miscellany not very well exhibited. As of 1980 undergoing reorganization.

OTHER CAMBRIDGE SITES

Cambridge Botanic Garden *(487)*, Bateman Street off Trumpington Road

Managed by the University Department of Botany, this is primarily a teaching garden. It is noted especially for its rock garden.

** Church of the Holy Sepulchre *(242)*, Bridge Street

Though much restored, the round part of the church, founded by the Order of Knights Templar, dates from about 1130 and is Norman in style. The chancel was added in the fifteenth century, the vestry and south aisle in the nineteenth.

* St. Bene't's Church *(122)*, Bene't Street

The west tower with its double windows and the upper parts of the nave walls are part of the original construction, possibly sixth or seventh century.

* Trumpington Church *(155)*, 2 m. s, w of A 10

This much restored early fourteenth century church boasts the second oldest knightly brass in England. It lies in the chancel under glass and commemorates Sir Roger de Trumpington (d. 1289). There are some fragments of thirteenth century glass in the northwest window of the chancel.

** Wimpole Hall *(388,440)*, 8 m. sw, off A 603 from New Wimpole; NT

The central block was built in the mid-seventeenth century. James Gibbs, in the early 18th, added the two wings and the library for the first earl of Oxford. In one wing is the chapel with wall paintings by Sir James Thornhill. After the house was bought by the lord chancellor, Philip Yorke, first earl of Hardwicke, a new gallery was added and the saloon remodeled by Henry Flitcroft. Late in the eighteenth century Sir John Soane designed the "yellow drawing room" and added a delightfully airy book room to the library. Some of the plasterwork is by Bagutti and Artari. The park was worked on by Bridgeman, Repton, and Capability Brown. The house was recently acquired by the National Trust from Rudyard Kipling's youngest daughter, Mrs. George Bambridge.

ELY

*** Ely Cathedral *(229)*, town center

A foundation of Benedictine monks, the church was begun about 1090 and became a cathedral in 1109.

Architectural styles: west front and southwest transept—Transitional; Galilee porch—Early English; nave—Norman; choir—Decorated (west end) and Early English (east end); lady chapel—Decorated.

Special features: Bishop Alcock chantry (1501); Bishop West chantry (1534); fourteenth century choir stalls; claustral remains south of church. (Of course, *the* special feature of Ely is the great central octagonal tower with its wooden lantern, visible for miles around the low-lying East Anglia countryside.) Also in the north triforium is a unique museum of stained glass with over two hundred panels, mostly of Victorian provenance, including some fine examples of the work of Edward Burne-Jones.

HUNTINGDON

* Cromwell Museum *(340)*, Market Square

The building that once housed the grammar school attended by Oliver Cromwell now contains a museum of his memorabilia.

Hinchingbrooke House *(340)*, ½ m. w, on A 604

The home successively of the Cromwell family and of the Montagu earls of Sandwich, the house now belongs to the Hinchingbrooke School. Open to the public only on Sunday afternoons.

* Kimbolton Castle *(277)*, 11 m. w, on A 45

A handsome Tudor house remodeled in the seventeenth century and again in the eighteenth by Vanbrugh with mural paintings by Pellegrini and a gatehouse by Robert Adam. It was the home of Catherine of Aragon after her enforced divorce from Henry VIII. Today a private school, the staterooms and grounds are open to the public, though on a very restricted basis.

* St. Mary's, Leighton Bromswold *(337)*, 8 m. w, n of A 604

A medieval parish church restored in the 1630s to give its interior a Jacobean Gothic appearance. Noteworthy is the splendid seventeenth century woodwork on choir stalls, chancel screen, and the pulpit and lectern.

PETERBOROUGH

*** Peterborough Cathedral *(232,277)*, town center

Begun as an abbey church in 1117, it became a secular cathedral in 1541.

Architectural styles: west front—Early English; Galilee porch—Perpendicular; nave—Norman; central tower—Perpendicular; transepts—Norman; choir—Norman; retrochoir—Perpendicular.

Special features: thirteenth century painted ceiling; sites of graves of Catherine of Aragon and Mary Queen of Scots (later transferred to Westminster Abbey).

* Castor Church *(242)*, 4 m. w, on A 47

A cruciform Norman church built in 1124 and noted chiefly for its central tower pierced by richly carved, arcaded, and round-headed double windows and one recessed triple window. The parapet and spire are fourteenth century additions.

** Longthorpe Tower *(192)*, 2 m. w, off A 47 (142 TL 163 983) AM

This crenellated tower was built by Robert Thorpe about 1300, presumably as protection for a preexisting manor house. The famous wall paintings were commissioned somewhat later either by this Robert or by his son of the same name. Bibilical and allegorical in subject matter, they are the most complete surviving set of medieval mural paintings in England.

WISBECH

* Peckover House *(389)*, town center; NT

A lovely Georgian town house built in 1722, appropriately furnished with especially fine Sheraton pieces. Nice Victorian garden. Elegant plasterwork.

NORTHERN HOME COUNTIES

HERTFORDSHIRE
BERKHAMSTEAD

Ashridge House *(402)*, 3½ m. n, w of Berkhamstead-Little Gaddesden Road

A Gothick house built in the early nineteenth century by James Wyatt for the seventh earl of Bridgewater. The grounds are by Humphrey Repton. Visiting hours very restricted.

** Berkhamstead Castle *(140)*, (165 SP 996 083) AM

A ruined shell keep, probably built by Thomas Becket when he was chancellor to Henry II. It stands on the summit of an earlier Norman motte at the corner of a bailey enclosed by a ruined stone curtain wall built over earthworks. Both motte and bailey are enclosed by moats. Presumably the stone castle replaced timber palisades of the Norman motte-and-bailey castle, built on or near the place where William the Conqueror received the surrender of the city of London.

HATFIELD

*** Hatfield House *(292,313,329,334)*, east end of town

A Jacobean prodigy house built by Robert Cecil in the reign of James I who named him earl of Salisbury. The ground plan is H-shaped, though the bar of the H is pushed down so far that it looks more like a U. The three-story central frontispiece in the forecourt and the ogee-capped towers identify this as being vintage Jacobean. The interior is magnificent, its most notable features being the great hall, the oak staircase, and the long gallery. Here are a number of fine paintings, including two famous portraits of Queen Elizabeth I (the Ermine Portrait by Nicholas Hilliard and the Rainbow Portrait by Zuccarro).

On the grounds is the much truncated *Hatfield Palace *(292,329)*, once the property of the bishops of Ely and later confiscated by Henry VIII. This was one of the homes of Elizabeth I before her accession to the throne. Most of it was torn down by Cecil for building material for his new house.

ST. ALBANS

* Clock Tower *(198)*, High Street

An early fourteenth century building in the neighborhood of which was fought the first battle of St. Albans which marked the outbreak of the War of the Roses in 1455. The Yorkists won this round.

Gorhambury House *(334,404)*, 2 m. nw, s of A 5

A large Palladian house designed by Sir Robert Taylor, with good seventeenth century paintings and a fine Reynolds; also parts of Sir Francis Bacon's library. Visiting hours are very restricted.

Roman House *(82)*, in public playing field outside Verulamium Museum

A small bungalow housing a well-preserved mosaic floor of geometric pattern.

* Roman Theatre *(82)*, on southern leg of ring road (A 414)

The only authenticated surviving Roman theater in Britain, the foundations and lower walls are substantial.

Roman Wall *(82)*, in public park on sw edge of town, across River Ver

A substantial segment of the south wall of the Roman city of *Verulamium.*

* **Royal National Rose Society's Garden** *(486)*, 2 m. e, near M 1, Exit 6

An experimental garden with a fine display section with a pool, pergolas, etc.

*** **St. Albans Cathedral** *(227,259)*, town center

Originally a Benedictine abbey church built by Abbot Paul of Caen between 1077 and 1088, it became parochial at the time of the Reformation and achieved cathedral status only in 1877.

Architectural styles: west front—Norman; nave—Early English (west end), Decorated (five middle bays on south side), and Norman (middle bays on north side and entire east end); central tower—Norman; transepts—Norman; choir—Norman (east end) and Decorated (west end); retrochoir—Decorated; lady chapel—Decorated.

Special features: Chantry of Duke Humphrey of Gloucester; fourteenth century brass to Abbot Thomas de la Mare; thirteenth century pier paintings in northeast section of nave; sixteenth century painting of martyrdom of St. Alban in south choir aisle.

*** **Verulamium Museum** *(82)*, near St. Michael's Church

A fine museum specializing in finds from Roman *Verulamium,* including an excellent collection of geometric mosaics. On display also is a model of the Roman city built to scale.

STEVENAGE

* **Knebworth House** *(483)*, 1 m. s, ½ m. e of M 1

A Tudor mansion Gothicized in the 1840s by the novelist Edward Bulwer-Lytton, it presents a delightful display of castellated towers, turrets, pinnacles, gargoyles, tracery, etc. The Edwardian architect, Edwin Lutyens, later married into the family and redid some of the rooms. Nice grounds.

Walkern Church *(155)*, 4 m. e on B 1037

Noteworthy only for its thirteenth century cross-legged knightly effigy of Purbeck marble.

WELWYN GARDEN CITY

* Ayot St. Lawrence Church *(417)*, 2 m. nw, e of B 651

A neo-Grecian masterpiece designed by Nicholas Revett in 1778 to 1779. The interior is more Palladian than Greek with a fine coffered ceiling and coffered apse.

* Shaw's Corner *(466)*, 4 m. nw, in Ayot St. Lawrence, w of M 1

The home of George Bernard Shaw between 1906 and 1950, it is full of the playwright's memorabilia and of Edwardian furnishings, surprisingly conventional for such a committed maverick and iconoclast.

BUCKINGHAMSHIRE
AYLESBURY

* Stewkley Church *(242)*, 9 m. n, on B 4032

A fine three-celled Norman church with an axial tower and a typical eleventh to twelfth century west front.

* Waddesdon Manor *(410,485,487)*, 6 m. nw, on A 41; NT

Built in 1874 to 1879 in the style of a sixteenth century French château by Gabriel-Hippolyte Destailleur for Baron Ferdinand de Rothschild, this is a museum of fabulously expensive French furnishings. The formal terraces around the house were designed for bedding out. There is a great deal of statuary scattered about the grounds and an unusual aviary.

Wotton House *(440)*, 10 m. w, 2 m. s of A 41

The house, built in 1704, probably resembles Buckingham House in London which formed the core of Nash's Buckingham Palace. The interiors here were done by Sir John Soane in the 1820s. Park landscaped by Capability Brown. Visiting hours are very restricted.

BUCKINGHAM

*** Stowe Gardens *(385)*, 3 m. nw, on road to Silverstone; NT

This is the finest of the eighteenth century landscape gardens designed by William Kent, though with later modifications by Capability Brown, Robert Adam, and the estate's owners, Lord Cobham and Earl Temple. Kent's imprint can be seen in the Elysian Fields, the Grecian Fields, the Shell Bridge, the Temple of Concord and Victory, the octagonal lake, and the Palladian bridge. This very natural looking series of vistas is all contrived.

CHALFONT ST. GILES

*** **Milton's Cottage** *(350)*, town center

The residence of John Milton in 1665 when the Great Plague hit London. Here he finished *Paradise Lost.* The house contains important relics of the poet and early editions of his works, intelligently arranged and displayed.

* **Jordans Quaker Meeting House** *(363)*, 1½ m. s

Built in 1688; burial ground of William Penn, founder of Pennsylvania.

HIGH WYCOMBE

*** **Hughenden Manor** *(623)*, 1½ m. n, on A 4128; NT

More distinguished for its historical associations than its architecture, this was the home of Benjamin Disraeli, novelist and prime minister under Queen Victoria. The library, the Disraeli room, the Politician's Room, and the Berlin Congress room are full of mementos of his distinguished political career.

*** **West Wycombe Park** *(403)*, 2½ m. w, on A 40; NT

A neoclassical mansion belonging to Sir Francis Dashwood and the product of fifty years of remodeling (1730–1780). Nicholas Revett built the west portico; the others are by an obscure architect named John Donowell. The west portico was done in the Ionic order; the south in Corinthian superimposed on Tuscan, the east in Tuscan, the north, Ionic. The park with its many neo-Grecian monuments, was laid out by Thomas Cook, a pupil of Capability Brown, and later modified by Humphrey Repton. This was the scene of the meetings of the Knights of St. Francis of Wycombe, also known as the Mad Monks of Medmenham, a drinking club dedicated to irreligion and cockfighting.

SLOUGH

Stoke Poges Church *(413)*, 1½ m. n, e of A 355 from Farnham Royal

Here is the churchyard about which Thomas Gray in 1750 wrote his famous *Elegy:* "The curfew tolls the knell of parting day—" The poet's own tomb is also here.

TAPLOW

* **Cliveden** *(482,487,501)*, 2 m. n, off B 476; NT

Rebuilt in the 1850s by Sir Charles Barry (architect for the Houses of Parliament) in the neo-Renaissance style of an Italian *palazzo*. The woodland gardens extending down to the Thames are magnificent. This was the meeting place of the Cliveden Set in the 1930s with the American-born Lady Astor as their hostess—an inner circle of the Conservative Party much criticized for their appeasement of Hitler and Mussolini. Today the building houses a study center run by Stanford University. Visiting hours restricted.

WING

* All Saints *(122)*, on A 418

An unusually large Anglo-Saxon church with an aisled nave and a polygonal apse.

* Ascott *(485,487)*, ½ m. e, s of A 418; NT

A Victorian Tudor black-and-white house acquired by Leopold de Rothschild in 1874, it is notable chiefly for its fine paintings, including those by Reynolds, Gainsborough, Turner, and Stubbs, and for its garden. Parts of the garden, laid out by the Chelsea nursery of James Veitch and Son, are formal and intended for bedding out; others more natural in a style favored by the Victorian landscaper William Robinson. Here also is an arboretum and a topiary garden.

WINSLOW

** Claydon House *(404,491)*, 3½ m. sw on Mid-Claydon Road; NT

A Palladian house distinguished for its rococo interiors, especially the fascinating chinoiserie. Here also is Florence Nightingale's bedroom and an adjoining room devoted to relics of her mission to the Crimea. She lived here with her sister Parthenope Verney, mistress of the house after 1858.

BEDFORDSHIRE
BEDFORD

* Bunyan Museum *(359)*, Mill Street

Built on the site of a barn where John Bunyan preached (when he was not languishing in the nearby Bedford county gaol). The museum contains interesting mementos of his life and career, and editions of *The Pilgrim's Progress* in 165 languages.

DUNSTABLE

** Eaton Bray Church *(243)*, 3 m. w, off A 4146

Behind its Perpendicular facade, this is one of the most perfect Early English parish churches in existence. Built around 1230 out of an unusual local ochre yellow stone, its deeply splayed lancets, sexpartite vault, and capitals carved in luxuriant foliage, all loudly proclaim the beginnings of the Gothic Age in architecture.

LEIGHTON BUZZARD

* **Mentmore Towers** *(483)*, 5 m. se in Buckinghamshire

Built by Joseph Paxton in 1850 to 1855 for Baron Amschel de Rothschild in the Elizabethan style of Wollaton, Nottinghamshire, this is now the center of The World Government of the Age of Enlightenment, an organization given to transcendental meditation and the like. Mandatory guided tours of one hour or more.

*** **Woburn Abbey** *(313,386,397,406,409)*, 6 m. n, e of A 418

Originally constructed on the site of a dissolved Cistercian abbey, the present house owes its appearance chiefly to the work of the eighteenth century Palladian architect, Henry Flitcroft, under commission from the fourth duke of Bedford, with further modifications by Henry Holland for the fifth duke. This is one of England's great stately homes with an abundance of priceless contents including Chinese Chippendale furniture, fine English porcelain, the Armada Portrait of Queen Elizabeth I, and an outstanding collection of the works of Sir Joshua Reynolds. On the grounds is a safari park with an interesting collection of wild animals. The estate is efficiently managed with every consideration for the concerns of its large body of visitors.

LUTON

* **Luton Hoo** *(485,486)*, 1½ m. s, w of A 6129

Rebuilt in 1903 to 1907 by C. F. Mewes for Sir Julius Wernher, a South African diamond magnate, the house is unusual for having been designed in the Beaux Arts manner currently fashionable in France, but rare in Britain except for a few public buildings and hotels (e.g., the Ritz in London, also built by Mewes). The purity of style, however, is somewhat marred by the retention from an earlier remodeling of Sir Robert Smirke's neo-Grecian portico resembling the front of the British Museum, done by the same architect. The park was landscaped by Capability Brown and the lovely rose garden is of Edwardian provenance. It is considered by some horticulturists to be the best rose garden in Britain.

* **Wrest Park** *(374)*, 10 m. n, w of A 6 at Silsoe

Only the gardens are open here, and those only on weekends and bank holidays. This is one of the few surviving examples in England of a seventeenth century Dutch canal garden.

COTSWOLD AND MALVERN HILLS

OXFORDSHIRE
BANBURY

*** **Broughton Castle** *(308)*, 2 m. sw on B 4035

This is a fourteenth century red-brick moated manor house "modernized" in the sixteenth century by the Lords Saye and Sele. The multitude of chimneys, indented facades, ample fenestration, and numerous gables all proclaim the Tudor character of this altogether charming country house. Inside, the rooms vary in style from the fourteenth century chapel to the late eighteenth century "Gothic" long gallery. In the reign of Charles I, the upstairs council chamber was a much frequented meeting place for Puritan leaders engaged in antiroyalist activity. Visitors are sometimes welcomed into this delightful home by the present Lady Saye and Sele.

** **Sulgrave Manor** *(304)*, 8 m. ne, in Northamptonshire, ½ m. s of B 4525

This is a modest manor house built in the sixteenth century (with later seventeenth and eighteenth century additions) by Lawrence Washington, a wool merchant and, more importantly, a direct ancestor of George Washington. The porch bears the family coat of arms, stars and stripes surmounted by an eagle. Appropriately the American flag flies in front of it. Aside from its historical connections, this is a charming house, beautifully and appropriately furnished where visitors are treated with a quiet informality that puts many of the great stately homes to shame.

BURFORD

** **Minster Lovell Hall** *(271)*, 5 m. e, n of A 40 (164 SP 324 114) AM

A ruined manor house built mostly in the early fifteenth century, this was the home of Francis Viscount Lovell who took part in Lambert Simnel's rebellion against Henry VII and disappeared after the Battle of Stoke in June 1487. Tradition, supported by some circumstantial evidence, has it that he fled to this place and hid in a secret cellar room where his skeleton was discovered 350 years later, the presumption being that he was locked into his hideout and deserted to die of starvation.

CHIPPING NORTON

** **Chastleton House** *(330)*, 4 m. nw, n of A 436

Built for Walter Jones, a Whitney wool merchant, about 1603, this is a courtyard house with anachronistic battlements combined with Dutch gables and other typically Jacobean features. The interior has good carved woodwork and some fine seventeenth century plastering, as well as a good collection of Jacobean furniture. The builder's son, Arthur Jones, allegedly hid here in a secret chamber while escaping from Cromwellian soldiers. The great hall has some good Civil War armor, and the garden some fine topiary. Mandatory guided tour, lasting about a half-hour.

* **Ditchley Park** *(388)*, 8 m. se, w of A 34

A splendid classical mansion built by James Gibbs with interior decorations by William Kent and Henry Flitcroft, masters of the Palladian style of the mid-eighteenth century. Outstanding plasterwork. Now a conference center. Visiting hours very restricted.

** **The Rollright Stones** *(40)*, 3½ m. n, ½ m. w of A 34 on Little Compton road (151 SP 296 302)

A large Bronze Age circle with fifty-three or fifty-four stones standing. Across the road, in Warwickshire, is the King Stone, a monolith eight feet in height. Well-tended and beautifully situated in the heart of the lovely Cotswold hills.

* **Whispering Knights** *(20,41)*, 2½ m. n, w of A 34 (151 SP 299 308)

A portal dolmen surviving from a Neolithic chambered tomb, consisting of four uprights and a capstone resting at an angle. Situated across the road from the Rollright Stones.

HENLEY

** **Grey's Court** *(309)*, 3 m. nw, near Rotherfield Greys; NT

A fourteenth century fortified manor converted into a typically Elizabethan gabled house of brick and stone by Sir Francis Knollys, the queen's cousin and lord treasurer of her household.

OXFORD, COLLEGES AND UNIVERSITY BUILDINGS

** **All Souls' College** *(265,368)*, High Street

Founded in 1437 by Henry Chichele, Archbishop of Canterbury, and King Henry VI, as a memorial to the English veterans of the Hundred Years War, it is today exclusively a graduate college. The gatehouse on High Street, the chapel, and front quadrangle all date from the time of founding. The chapel is a particularly fine specimen of Perpendicular architecture, with a good reredos. The second quadrangle (with Codrington Library) was built in Gothic style by Nicholas Hawksmoor in 1715 to

1740; the library in 1756; and the charming Wardens' Lodgings in 1704 to 1706.

*** Ashmolean Museum *(26,32,104,105,409,476,479,480)*, Beaumont Street

Built in 1841 to 1845, to the design of C. R. Cockerell, to house the university's collection of antiquities as well as the Taylor Institute of foreign languages, the building is neo-Grecian in the Ionic order, more or less copied from the Temple of Apollo at Bassae.

To students of the British past, the most interesting rooms are (a) the John Evans Room which has a superb collection of British Bronze Age and Iron Age artifacts; (b) the Leeds Room with an equally fine array of Romano-British objects as well as items from the post-Roman Dark Ages; (c) the Medieval Gallery containing the Alfred Jewel and a number of other Late Saxon pieces; (d) the Tradescant Collection which houses, among other things, Guy Fawkes's lantern; and (e) the Chambers Hall Gallery containing eighteenth and nineteenth century British paintings, furniture, sculpture, etc.

* Balliol College *(261,473)*, St. Giles Street

Founded about 1264 by John Balliol of Bernard Castle as a penance imposed by the bishop of Durham and refounded in 1282 by his widow Devorgilla, Balliol has produced more distinguished graduates than perhaps any Oxford college. The list includes the economist Adam Smith; the poets, Matthew Arnold, A. H. Clough, and Algernon Swinburne; the churchmen, John Wycliffe, Cardinal Manning, and Archbishop C. G. Lang; the historians, Arnold Toynbee, R. H. Tawney, and Gordon A. Craig; and the statesmen, Henry Herbert Asquith, Viscount Grey of Falloden, Lord Curzon of Kedleston, Prime Minister Harold Macmillan, Prime Minister Edward Heath, and Governor-General Vincent Massey of Canada.

Unfortunately its original buildings were mostly effaced by nineteenth century restorations, and what is left is predominantly Victorian Gothic. The facade and gatehouse are Scottish baronial put up by Alfred Waterhouse in 1867 to 1868; the chapel was finished in 1857; the west and part of the north ranges of the front quadrangle are medieval; including the fifteenth century dining hall, now the library; the hall and masters' lodging date from 1867; Salvin's tower from 1853; and the rest are of mixed provenance—from the eighteenth to the twentieth centuries.

** Brasenose College *(315)*, Radcliffe Square

Founded by William Smith, Bishop of Lincoln, in 1509, the college takes its name from the brass door knocker in the original medieval hall occupying the site. The gatehouse, front quadrangle, and hall date from the time of the founder; the chapel and library were built in the third quarter of the seventeenth century; the third quadrangle in the late nineteenth and early twentieth centuries. The fifteenth century kitchen is the oldest part of the college and was inherited from the earlier hall situated here.

*** Christ Church College and Oxford Cathedral *(276,316,356,368)*, St. Aldgate's Street

Founded in 1525 by Cardinal Wolsey on the site of the suppressed monastic establishment of Canterbury College, it was first named Cardinal's College; then King Henry VIII College when, after Wolsey's fall, the monarch refounded it in 1532; and finally Christ Church in 1546 when the former monastic church, which did double duty as the college chapel, was given cathedral status which it still enjoys. The sixteenth century gatehouse was rebuilt in the seventeenth century and is surmounted by a great tower designed by Sir Christopher Wren; three sides (south, east, and west) of the great quadrangle, Tom Quad, were started in 1529, the north side in the mid-seventeenth century; Wolsey's great hall with its splendid carved roof is approached by a staircase leading off the southwest corner of Tom Quad; Peckwater Quadrangle, built in the early eighteenth century lies off the northeast corner and contains the library (1761); next to it is Canterbury Quadrangle built in 1773 to 1783 by James Wyatt; Oxford Cathedral, situated off the east side of Tom Quad, is restored Norman with a thirteenth century spire and lady chapel and a fifteenth century roof in the choir; adjacent to the cathedral is the Perpendicular cloister leading to the Early English chapter house with a Norman doorway.

*** Corpus Christi College *(315,368)*, Merton Street

Founded in 1517 by Bishop Richard Fox, this is the most uniformly Tudor in style of all Oxford colleges. The gatehouse, first quadrangle, chapel, hall, and library all date from the time of the founder. In the cloister court is the handsome Fellows Building built in 1706 to 1712 and the Gentlemen-Commoners' Building of 1737. The sundial in the middle of the front quadrangle, surmounted by a pelican, was installed in 1581, and the perpetual clock was added to its pillar in 1606.

The Examination Schools *(476)*, High Street

An essay in neo-English Renaissance style built in 1876 to 1882 to the design of Sir T. G. Jackson.

* Exeter College *(262,474)*, Turl Street

Founded in 1314 by Walter de Stapledon, Bishop of Exeter for scholars from Devon and Cornwall, this is one of the largest of Oxford's colleges. The gatehouse on Turl Street is a nineteenth century renovation of a much more attractive seventeenth century Palladian structure; in the

1850s Sir George Gilbert Scott rebuilt the chapel and library in imitation French Gothic; the lovely hall dates from 1618; the first quadrangle from the seventeenth and eighteenth centuries; the second quadrangle from the twentieth. Of the medieval college, the only relic is Palmer's Tower built in 1432 as the original gatehouse.

** Jesus College *(317)*, Turl Street between Market and Ship

Founded in 1571 by Hugh Price, Bishop of St. David's, this is the first post-Reformation college at Oxford, and for a long while remained predominantly Welsh in character. The Elizabethan gatehouse survives, but was radically remodeled in the nineteenth century. Remodeled also was the seventeenth century chapel, but the rest of the front quadrangle escaped and is a good example of Jacobean Gothic style. The second quadrangle, with the library, dates from the late seventeenth and early eighteenth centuries. The Ship Street range dates to the early twentieth century, while the third quadrangle is of very recent vintage but has been much better integrated with the older buildings than most contemporary additions to Oxford colleges. On St. David's day, chapel services are in Welsh.

*** Keble College *(467,473,480)*, Parks Road and Keble Road

Opened in 1870 as a memorial to John Keble, one of the founders of the Oxford Movement, and designed by William Butterfield, this is the first Oxford college to have been built in brick. It is also the first to have had its rooms made accessible from corridors rather than separate staircases. The red brick is dressed with stone and inlaid with patterns of yellow and blue bricks, in keeping with mid-Victorian preferences for polychromy as preached especially by John Ruskin. The huge chapel is noted for its colored mosaics and for William Holman Hunt's famous Pre-Raphaelite painting, *The Light of the World*.

** Lincoln College *(264,337,419)*, Turl Street

Founded in 1427 by Richard Fleming, Bishop of Lincoln to stem the tide of Lollardy, the college today retains much of its original medieval flavor. The front quadrangle dates from the time of the founding (with late eighteenth century revisions to the hall), as does the kitchen; the chapel and second quadrangle from the early seventeenth century (the chapel is a Laudian mixture of neoclassical and Gothic); the Grove Building from the late nineteenth. Next door to Lincoln is All Saints' Church, constructed in 1706 to 1709 and since converted into the college library. John Wesley, the founder of Methodism, was a Fellow at Lincoln in the eighteenth century; his portrait hangs in the hall, his pulpit is preserved in the chapel, and his supposed rooms are situated over the passage between the two quadrangles.

Lady Margaret Hall *(468)*, Norham Gardens

Along with Somerville College, this is the first of the Oxford women's colleges, founded in 1879. The early buildings were designed by Basil Champneys, to be followed by Sir Reginald Blomfield who built Talbot and Toynbee Halls in the French Renaissance manner which was his specialty.

*** **Magdalen College** *(265)*, High Street

Magdalen (pronounced *maudlen*) was founded in 1457 by William of Waynflete on the site of St. John's Hospital. Its extensive grounds lead to the River Cherwell. The gatehouse dates only from 1884, but the wall enclosing the college grounds was built soon after the founding. To the right of the gatehouse are the adapted thirteenth and fourteenth century buildings of St. John's Hospital. In the front quadrangle are the chapel (1475), the Founder's Tower (1485 to 1488), the Muniment Tower (1487 to 1488), and the Bell Tower (1492 to 1509). Beyond, the new buildings date from 1733, West's building from 1783, and the rest from the nineteenth and twentieth centuries.

* **Merton College** *(261)*, Merton Street

Founded in 1284 by Walter de Merton to train scholars for the secular priesthood, this is, architecturally speaking, the oldest college of Oxford University. The gate tower dates from 1418; the medieval hall was rebuilt and restored in the eighteenth and nineteenth centuries by James Wyatt and George Gilbert Scott; the treasury, dating from 1274 is the oldest collegiate building in Oxford; the so-called Mob Quad, dating from about 1309, is Oxford's oldest quadrangle; the library was built in the 1370s and is the oldest in England; the Decorated chapel choir was completed in 1294, the Perpendicular transepts in 1367 (south) and 1424 (north). This completes the medieval portions of the buildings. The Fellow's quadrangle was built in 1608 to 1610 in a style known as Jacobean Gothic; the remainder of the buildings went up in the twentieth century. Unfortunately, all the above is closed to the public except for the quadrangles.

*** **New College** *(263)*, New College Lane

Founded in 1379 by William of Wykeham, Bishop of Winchester and twice chancellor of England, for graduates of his recently established Winchester College, this is the most completely medieval of all of Oxford's colleges. The style is predominantly Perpendicular, though there are of course additions of a later date. The gatehouse, chapel, hall, library, and first quadrangle date from the initial building (1380–1386); cloisters and detached belltower from 1400; the Garden quadrangle from 1782 to 1791 except for a stretch of thirteenth to fourteenth century town wall taken over by the college; the Holywell Buildings were begun by George Gilbert Scott in 1872. Notable features include Epstein's modern statue of Lazarus in the antechapel and El Greco's painting of St. James in the choir. Of all Oxford's colleges, this is the one most worth visiting and the most hospitable to visitors.

*** Old Schools Quadrangle *(337)*, Catte Street and Broad Street

Here is a cluster of important university buildings dating from the fifteenth through the eighteenth century. Entry from Catte Street on the east is through the gate tower (1613 to 1619), the west side of which is adorned with columns of the five classical orders superimposed on one another, and a statue of James I overlooking the quadrangle. Ahead is the old **Bodleian Library** *(196, 265)*, founded in 1602 by a gift from Sir Thomas Bodley who also arranged with the Stationer's Company of London to send it a free copy of every book published in England. Today it is among the world's largest libraries, and has spread across Broad Street where the New Bodleian was built in 1935. Behind (west of) Old Bodleian, is a wing of the same building housing the ** **Divinity School** *(264)*, built in the late fifteenth century in the Perpendicular style. This beautiful room with a magnificent pendant ceiling is open to the public, but not Duke Humphrey's Room above, where once was housed his munificent gift of manuscripts, destroyed during the Reformation. Immediately north of the Divinity School and fronting on Broad Street is Christopher Wren's masterpiece, the *** **Sheldonian Theatre** *(352)*, a D-shaped building modeled after the Theater of Marcellus in Rome. On its right (east) is the **Clarendon Building** *(368)*, designed by Nicholas Hawksmoor (1713); and to the left (west) is the Museum of the History of Science housed in the **Old Ashmolean Museum** *(355)*, built in the late seventeenth century.

* Oriel College *(262, 412)*, Oriel Square

Founded in 1326, the college received its name from one of its original buildings which had a prominent oriel window, i.e., an upper-floor bay window supported on corbels projecting from the wall. Nothing is left of its medieval architecture, the predominant style being Jacobean Gothic. The gatehouse dates from 1620; chapel, hall, and first quadrangle (with statues of Edward II and Charles I) from 1620 to 1648; library and second quadrangle from the eighteenth century; and third quadrangle and chapel from 1640. None of the above is open to the public except the quadrangles.

** Oxford University Museum *(11, 26, 472)*, Parks Road

The building was erected in 1855 to 1860 in the style called Victorian Gothic, with miscellaneous polychromatic effects inspired by John Ruskin. Aside from the building itself, with its splendid glass roof, cast-iron ornamented capitals, and banded brickwork in the arcades, the major item of interest here is the ochred skeleton of the Red Lady of Paviland, an Upper Paleolithic human fossil mistakenly identified by the nineteenth century geologist, William Buckland, as the remains of a Romano-British female.

Pembroke College *(337)*, St. Aldgate's Street

Founded in 1624 on the site of Broadgates and other medieval halls, the remains of both the original buildings and the seventeenth century additions have been so overlaid with nineteenth century restorations as to be almost indistinguishable. The early eighteenth century chapel has good workmanship in the classical style.

* Pitt Rivers Museum *(26, 32)*, Parks Road (entrance through Oxford University Museum)

One of the oldest archaeological museums in Britain, it is presently overcrowded, and the large collection of prehistoric finds (especially Stone Age and Bronze Age implements) is badly exhibited from the point of view of the layman.

*** Queen's College *(263, 356, 368)*, High Street

Founded in 1341 by the court chaplain to Queen Philippa for scholars from Cumbria, the college has ever since been under the patronage of the Queens Consort of England. Nothing remains of the medieval buildings, but the classical elegance of Queen's makes it one of Oxford's handsomest colleges. The entrance on High Street, chapel, and hall date from the early eighteenth century; the library from the 1690s; the first quadrangle (designed by Hawksmoor) from 1709 to 1760; and the second from 1607 to 1707. A statue of Queen Caroline graces the entranceway.

** Radcliffe Camera *(412)*, Catte Street

A lovely Italianate building faced with coupled Corinthian columns and topped by a dome and cupola, designed by James Gibbs about 1737.

* Radcliffe Observatory *(412)*, Observatory Street

Designed by James Wyatt and Henry Keene, 1772 to 1775, and modeled on the Tower of the Winds in Athens, this the first example in Oxford of the Greek Revival.

Ruskin College *(468)*, Walton Street

Undistinguished architecturally, but historically interesting as the lineal descendant of Ruskin Hall, founded in 1899 as a place where workingmen could come up to Oxford and study for a year.

* **St. Edmund Hall** *(262)*, Queen's Lane

The only surviving medieval hall (as distinct from college) in Oxford, it belonged originally to Oseney Abbey, was bought by neighboring Queen's College after the Dissolution, and achieved collegiate status within the university only in 1937. The only medieval relic left is the fifteenth century fireplace in the Junior Common Room. Hall, chapel, and library date from the late seventeenth century; the east half of the north range from the late sixteenth century, the west half from the mid-eighteenth.

** **St. John's College** *(316, 337)*, St. Giles Street

The college was founded in 1555 by Thomas White, Lord Mayor of London, on the site of the former Cistercian college of St. Bernard. In the early 17th century, under the chancellorship of William Laud, the buildings were extended and given a face-lifting in the hybrid Gothic / Classical style known as "Laudian."

Architectural styles: front, east, and west sides of first quadrangle— 16th century; chapel—originally 16th century, but much altered in the 17th and 19th; hall—18th century; south side of 2d (Canterbury) quadrangle—16th century; remainder of Canterbury quadrangle and colonnade—"Laudian"; south and north quadrangles—19th and 20th centuries. The exquisite garden (Oxford's best) was originally laid out by Capability Brown. The bronze statues of Charles I and Queen Henrietta Maria are by Le Sueur.

* **Somerville College** *(468)*, Little Clarendon Street and Woodstock Road

The first of Oxford's women's colleges (along with Lady Margaret Hall), Somerville was founded in 1879, though not incorporated until 1926. The first quadrangle is modern (1933); in the second is Walton House, a fine Queen Anne mansion; most of the other red-brick buildings are in the Queen Anne style.

** **Trinity College** *(316)*, Broad Street

Founded in 1555 on the site of Medieval Durham College, Trinity lies between St. Johns and Balliol but is entered by a lane leading from Broad Street. In the front quadrangle lies the 17th-century Hall (Jacobean Gothic), the 19th-century President's House, and the superb chapel (1691–1694) with a screen and altarpiece by Grinling Gibbons. The north side of the Garden quadrangle was designed by Sir Christopher Wren. The gardens were laid out in the 18th century.

** **University College** *(262, 415)*, High Street

University's claim to be the oldest college in Oxford rises from a decision in the Court of King's Bench in 1727 confirming the college's spurious assertion that it had been founded by Alfred the Great, whose bust in low relief is carved over the fireplace in the hall. In fact the college originated from an endowment by Bishop William of Durham in 1249, though it did not acquire its present site until 1332. Nothing remains of the medieval college, the present buildings being predominantly seventeenth century. The gatehouse on High Street dates from 1638; the hall and first triangle from the mid-seventeenth century; the chapel is a George Gilbert Scott restoration of the seventeenth century original; the library is pure Scott; the first quadrangle dates from 1634 to 1675; the second from the early eighteenth century; the Master's Lodging from the nineteenth. Near the entrance there are statues to James II and Queen Anne; in the first quadrangle one to Queen Mary II. Here also is a recumbent more-than-life-size statue of the poet Percy Bysshe Shelley who was for a short time a student here until he was sent down for publishing a pamphlet defending atheism. Here he is represented in the nude, just washed up from the Italian sea where he was drowned.

* **Wadham College** *(337, 355)*, Parks Road

Founded in 1610, the first quadrangle and library were built shortly thereafter in the Jacobean Gothic style. Good features are the Perpendicular-type chapel with a fine stained-glass east window; and the hall with a hammer-beam roof and Jacobean screen. Under the wardenship of John Wilkins, Cromwell's brother-in-law, Wadham was an important center of the mid–seventeenth century scientific revolution that flowered after the Restoration with the chartering of the Royal Society.

** **Worcester College** *(368)*, Worcester Street at foot of Beaumont Street

Founded in 1714 on the site of Gloucester College, the north range of buildings was designed in classical style by George Clarke and Nicholas Hawksmoor, although the hall (by James Wyatt) and chapel were not completed until the end of the eighteenth century. Except for some contemporary buildings, most of the rest of the college buildings date from the fifteenth century, including the Pump Quad, the monastic cottages, and the Senior Common Room. There is a delightfully pastoral quality to the extensive grounds.

OTHER OXFORD SITES

City Wall *(207)*, Longwall Street

The north and east sides of the garden wall of New College are formed by remnants of the medieval city wall.

** **Iffley Church** *(242)*, Iffley Road

A Norman church built about 1170 with an axial tower, it is noted especially for the beakhead and chevron motifs in the recessed doorway and windows of the west front. The rose window and the blind window in the gable are Victorian insertions.

Martyrs' Memorial *(291, 474)*, St. Giles Street

A monument erected in 1841 in the style of an Eleanor Cross to the memory of the Protestant martyrs Latimer, Ridley, and Cranmer burned in Broad Street by order of Queen Mary Tudor in 1555 to 1556. The architect was Sir George Gilbert Scott.

*** Oxford Botanic Garden *(486)*, High Street

One of the oldest botanical gardens in Britain; here are herbaceous borders, a rose garden, and a rock garden, along with the expected botanical specimens still grown in traditional rectangular beds.

* Oxford Canal *(424)*, Hythebridge Street, w of Worcester Street

This is the southern terminus of the canal joining the upper Thames (here called the Isis) with the Coventry Canal northeast of Coventry.

** St. Mary's Church *(262, 291)*, High Street

Originally the assembly hall for Oxford University, the church is a mélange of Decorated and Perpendicular architecture, but the west front is a 17th-century restoration by William Laud in his favorite Gothic / Classical style.

OXFORD ENVIRONS

All Saints, Nuneham Courtenay *(417)*, 5 m. se, on A 423

A small church designed by James "Athenian" Stuart, though in a style more Roman than his usual neo-Grecian.

** Blenheim Palace *(369, 371, 374, 347, 409, 480)*, 8 m. n, w of A 34 on southern edge of Woodstock

The gift of a grateful Queen Anne to John Churchill, first duke of Marlborough, this massive palace was designed by John Vanbrugh and mostly completed before his departure from the job in 1716 after a series of quarrels with the duchess Sarah. The most striking features are the great Corinthian portico enclosing the main entrance; the Tuscan colonnades on either wing; the busy roof line filled with statuary, towers, and high stone finials. Inside, the same heroic mode prevails, the decor being distinctly baroque. Wall and ceiling paintings are by Thornhill and Laguerre; Hawksmoor designed some of the rooms. At the end of the west corridor is the room where Sir Winston Churchill was born in 1874, with appropriate mementos on exhibit. Outside, Vanbrugh's original parterres were destroyed by Capability Brown who installed a large lake and planted picturesque clumps of trees. In the twentieth century, the ninth duke reinstalled a parterre on the east front and a water parterre on the west. Mandatory guided tours, but frequent and brief.

** Ewelme Church *(260)*, 13 m. se, e of A 423

A parish church converted to collegiate status in the mid-fifteenth century by the duke of Suffolk, it is joined by a school and almshouse which were, typically, included in the collegiate foundation. The style is late Perpendicular and the church contains the lovely tomb of the founder's duchess (d. 1475) who was the poet Chaucer's reputed granddaughter.

** Rousham Park *(384)*, 12 m. n, e of A 423

A seventeenth century country house, remodeled in 1738 with Palladian touches by William Kent. Kent also is responsible for some of the furniture and for creating the garden, one of the earliest eighteenth century landscapes to survive. Note the "ha-ha," the serpentine stream, the cascades and ponds, the classical statuary, the Gothic "ruins," and the Praeneste, a pedimented colonnade of mixed classical and Romanesque design.

* St. Martin's, Bladon *(508)*, 8 m. nw, in Bladon on A 4095

This nineteenth century parish church of no architectural distinction is the site of the Churchill family burial plot which includes the simple grave marker of Winston Leonard Spencer Churchill (1874–1965).

Stanton Harcourt *(413)*, 6 m. sw, w of A 420

A partially ruined fifteenth century manor house where Alexander Pope stayed in 1717 to 1718 and where he finished his translation of the fifth volume of *The Iliad*.

WALLINGFORD

Anglo-Saxon Ramparts *(108)*, town boundary

The earthen embankment, dating from the ninth or tenth century, surrounds the town on three sides, the eastern side being the Thames River. It is about ten feet in height with an outer ditch five feet deep.

WANTAGE

Childrey Church *(199)*, 2 m. w on B 4001

A large cruciform church, mainly Decorated and Perpendicular, with a good brass memorializing William Fynderne (1444).

** Uffington Castle and White Horse *(48)*, 6½ m. w, ½ m. s of B 4507 (174 SU 300 863—301 866) AM

An eight-acre Iron Age hill fort enclosed by a single bank and ditch, plus a counterscarp bank. Just to the northwest and over the brow of the hill from the castle is the famous White Horse, the earliest chalk-cut hill figure in Britain, probably first designed as a tribal emblem by Iron Age Celts. The figure should be viewed at a distance from the bottom of the hill as well as close at hand from the top.

* **Uffington Church** *(243)*, 5 m. w, on B 4507

Except for the octagon tower and a single Decorated window, this is an almost perfect specimen of thirteenth century Early English architectural style.

*** **Wayland's Smithy Chambered Tomb** *(18)*, 9 m. w; n of B 4507, 1 m. e of Ashbury (174 SU 281 854) AM

A large Neolithic Severn-Cotswold gallery grave covered by a mound 180 by 48 feet and 4 feet high. It is transepted by a single pair of side chambers, making it cruciform in shape, and is roofed by a huge capstone. A long walk uphill leads to a charming copse beneath whose trees the chambered tomb lies.

WITNEY

* **North Leigh Roman Villa** *(87)*, 4 m. ne, 1 m. n of A 4095 (164 SP 397 154) AM

Here are the remains of a large courtyard villa with a well-preserved bath house with handsome blue and coral geometric mosaics.

GLOUCESTERSHIRE
CHIPPING CAMDEN

*** **St. James's Church** *(244)*, town center

Set in the midst of the serene Cotswold Hills, this typically late fifteenth century Perpendicular church was built mostly from funds donated by William Grevel whose tomb bears the inscription, *Flos Mercatorum Tocius Anglie* ("The Flower of the Wool Merchants of all England"). The church is especially noteworthy for its handsome tower, its brasses, and its elaborate tomb carvings.

CIRENCESTER

*** **Corinium Museum** *(58, 82, 88, 89)*, Park Street

All in all, this is the finest museum of Roman antiquities in England. Especially noteworthy are the Hare mosaic, the Hunting Dogs mosaic, and the Orpheus mosaic; the collection of Samian pottery; the *Genialis* tombstone; the Christian acrostic; and the replicas of a Roman kitchen and a Roman dining room.

Roman Amphitheater *(82)*, western edge of town (163 SP 020 014) AM

The grassy remains of *Corinium's* amphitheater.

Roman Wall *(82)*, London Road

A short section of the ruined wall that once surrounded the Roman *civitas* of *Corinium.*

*** St. John the Baptist *(244)*, town center

A West Country "wool church" rebuilt in the fifteenth century on a Norman foundation, this great Perpendicular masterpiece is one of the largest parish churches in England. The high stone-paneled tower is especially typical, though the elaborately carved three-story north porch is unusual.

Special features: fan vaulting in St. Catherine's chapel; rare pre-Reformation pulpit (1515); profusion of brasses throughout the nave and Trinity Chapel. (This is one of the most popular haunts of amateur brass rubbers in the country.)

*** Chedworth Roman Villa *(87)*, 8 m. n, 1 m. nw of A 429 (163 SP 053 135) NT

A well-preserved Roman villa with fine mosaics of Bacchus, three of the Four Seasons, and a Chi Rho monogram, indicating the likelihood of Christian owners. Here is the best surviving private Roman bath suite in Britain, with five rooms and a hypocaust.

* Northleach Church *(244)*, 10 m. ne, on A 429

A fifteenth century wool church, typically Perpendicular in style, it is noted chiefly for its fine brasses and the intricately carved two-story south porch.

CHELTENHAM

* Art Gallery and Museum *(32)*, Clarence Street

A somewhat old-fashioned museum of local history and archaeology containing a representative collection of prehistoric finds of all periods, rather unimaginatively displayed.

* St. Mary's, Deerhurst *(122)*, 7 m. nw, w of A 38

An Anglo-Saxon church with Early English and Perpendicular windows; the tall tower with its double triangular-headed window, was probably rebuilt in the tenth century after the Viking invasions. The baptismal font dates from the ninth century. Nearby is Odda's Chapel dedicated in 1056.

GLOUCESTER

** City Museum and Art Gallery *(32, 51, 83)*, Brunswick Road

A fine modernized museum of local history and archaeology, with representative items from all prehistoric ages, and from the period of Roman occupation, intelligently arranged and displayed. Noteworthy are the Bronze Age Birdlip Mirror and Iron Age currency bars.

*** Gloucester Cathedral *(168, 229)*, town center

Originally a Benedictine abbey church begun in 1089, it became a secular cathedral in 1541.

Architectural styles: west front—Perpendicular; nave—Norman; central tower—Perpendicular; transepts—Perpendicular; choir—Perpendicular; lady chapel—late Perpendicular.

Special features: fourteenth century choir stalls and misericords; tomb of Robert Curthose, eldest son of William the Conqueror; tomb and alabaster effigy of Edward II; Perpendicular east (Crecy) window; Perpendicular fan-vaulted cloister; Norman crypt.

Greyfriars' Church *(257)*, behind the Church of St. Mary-le-Crypt, Southgate Street

Built in the 13th century, this was originally a Franciscan friary church.

* Great Witcombe Roman Villa *(87)*, 6 m. se, 1 m. s of A 417 from ½ m. e of Brockworth (163 SO 899 142)

The roofed-over remains of a courtyard villa with good geometric mosaics and representations of dolphins, fish, eels, and other aquatic animals.

* Westbury Court Garden *(374)*, 9 m sw, on A 48; NT

A Dutch-style late seventeenth century canal garden, recently replanted and restored by the National Trust.

MORETON-IN-MARSH

* Sezincote Gardens *(438)*, 1 m. w, s of A 44

To match the onion-shaped dome of the house (not open to the public), Humphrey Repton installed numerous Indian features in the garden, including a stone bridge ornamented with crouching bulls, a temple to the goddess Souriya, and a climbing bronze serpent in the middle of a pool. Visiting hours are very restricted.

STROUD

*** **Berkeley Castle** *(141, 168, 407)*, 10 m. sw; 1 m. w of A 38, 16 m. s of Gloucester

The oldest part of this splendid castle and stately home is the shell keep built by Robert fitz Harding in the reign of Henry II, ca. 1160. Somewhere inside it occurred the grisly murder of Edward II in 1307. Most of the buildings around the inner courtyard were products of the fourteenth century, including the Great Hall. The furnishings are exquisite, and there are some good paintings, including portraits of the lords Berkeley and their families by Kneller, Reynolds, and Hoppner. No stately home in England is better arranged for the convenience and pleasure of the public.

*** **Hetty Pegler's Tump** *(18)*, 5½ m. sw, w of B 4066, 1 m. n of Uley (162 SO 789 001); key at nearest roadside farmhouse

A Neolithic Severn-Cotswold covered tomb (partially restored), 123 feet by 85 feet and 10 feet in height. Originally the gallery was double-transepted, but the two north chambers have been sealed off, leaving the two on the south and the one on the end open for inspection. The gallery can be entered only on hands and knees, and though there is standing room inside the chambers, there is no visibility. Flashlight recommended.

TEWKESBURY

Mythe Bridge *(423)*, 1 m. n, on A 438 across Severn (150 SO 888 337)

A minor Thomas Telford bridge.

*** **Tewkesbury Abbey Church** *(201)*, town center

Now the second largest parish church in England, it originally belonged to the great Benedictine Abbey of the Blessed Virgin Mary and was saved from destruction at the time of the Dissolution by the intervention of the local citizenry. Though it contains a number of fine architectural features, both Norman and Decorated, the church is noteworthy chiefly for its fourteenth and fifteenth century chantry chapels, especially the Despenser Chantry (Trinity Chantry) which contains perhaps the earliest example of Perpendicular fan vaulting in England.

Architectural styles: west front—Norman with Perpendicular window; nave—Norman with Decorated vaulting; central tower—Norman; transepts—Norman with Decorated windows; choir—Norman (arches) and Decorated (vaulting and windows); ambulatory chapels—Decorated and Perpendicular (Despenser Chapel).

Special features: Beauchamp Chantry (1422); Fitzhamon Chantry (1397); Despenser Monument (1349); Despenser Chantry (1378); fourteenth century glass in east windows; Raphael's Madonna del Passeggio in lady chapel; tomb of George, duke of Clarence, whom Shakespeare describes as "false, fleeting, perjured Clarence," executed in 1478 by order of his brother King Edward IV, reputedly by being drowned in a butt of Malmsey wine.

* Tewkesbury Museum *(201)*, town center

A typical local museum of archaeological and historical artifacts. Of chief interest is the model of the battlefield about a half-mile south of town where the Lancastrian forces of Margaret of Anjou were routed on 4 May 1471, thus securing the throne for the Yorkist claimant, Edward IV.

WINCHCOMBE

*** Belas Knap Chambered Tomb *(18)*, 1¾ m. s, 1 m. nw of Charlton Abbots (163 SP 021 254) AM

A partially restored Severn-Cotswold gallery grave, with a false entrance facing a horned court and small burial chambers inserted into the ends and sides. No entry. A steep climb from the nearest road and a glorious view at the end of it.

* Hailes Abbey *(254)*, 2 m. ne, e of A 46 (150 SP 050 300) AM

Noteworthy as the last Cistercian house to be founded in England, it was established in 1246 by King Henry III's brother, Richard, earl of Cornwall. It later became a popular pilgrimage center owing to its possession of a phial of the Blood of Christ guaranteed to be authentic by Pope Urban IV (see Chaucer's "Pardoner's Tale"). Little remains of the abbey church except the foundations. Only the cloister walls reach any considerable height; the rest of the buildings have disappeared.

*** Sudeley Castle *(197, 279, 306)*, 1 m. se, off A 46

Originally a mid-fourteenth century fortified manor house built in part from the spoils of the French wars, the castle was forfeited to the Crown in 1469, and Richard III is responsible for the magnificent great hall which is the most attractive portion of the medieval ruins still to be seen on the grounds. In the sixteenth century, Sudeley became the property of the Dowager Queen Catherine Parr's fourth husband, Sir Thomas Seymour. Her tomb can be seen inside the Victorianized fourteenth century chapel. Much wasted during the Civil War, the major buildings were restored in the nineteenth century under the direction of the great Victorian architect, Sir George Gilbert Scott. The Queen's Garden, though of modern vintage, is laid out in an authentic Tudor style. The comfortably furnished rooms are graced with a number of fine English paintings, including a portrait of Elizabeth I by Zuccarro, a famous group portrait, *The Tudor Succession* by Hans Eworth, and works of Rubens, Van Dyck, Turner, and Constable.

WARWICKSHIRE
ALCESTER

** **Ragley Hall** *(401, 407, 411)*, 2 m. sw, w of A 435

A seventeenth century house built by Robert Hooke, at one time assistant to Sir Christopher Wren, it was remodeled in the eighteenth century by James Gibbs and James Wyatt. Notable are Gibbs's hall with its fine plasterwork by Artari, and Wyatt's dining room, saloon, and staterooms in the neoclassic manner. The park was created by Capability Brown.

KENILWORTH

*** **Kenilworth Castle** *(152, 168, 179)*, town center

This magnificent ruin, one of the most visited castles in England, dates from many periods. The rectangular keep was probably built by Henry de Clinton in the twelfth century. King John, in the early thirteenth century laid out the curtain walls and dammed the surrounding lake, now drained. Simon de Montfort erected the mural towers, called Lunn's Tower, the Water Tower, and Mortimer's Tower. In the fourteenth century John of Gaunt, duke of Lancaster, built the Great Hall and the Strong Tower. In the sixteenth, Robert Dudley, earl of Leicester, added Leicester's Stable, Leicester's Building, and Leicester's Gatehouse. Extravagant like all Elizabethan courtiers, his lavishness in entertaining the queen during her visit here in 1575 became legendary for conspicuous waste.

NUNEATON

* **Arbury Hall** *(390, 406)*, 2 m. sw of B 4102

A Gothic Revival house built by Sanderson Miller in the 1750s on an earlier foundation and consciously modeled on Henry VII's chapel in Westminster Abbey. Good Chippendale furniture in the Gothic style. Mandatory guided tours last about a half-hour.

SHIPSTON-ON-STOUR

* **Honington Hall** *(358)*, 1 m. n, e of A 34

Built by Sir Henry Parker in the 1680s, it is a fine late seventeenth century red-brick country house in the classical style, distinguished on the outside by the busts of Roman emperors standing on the window heads. Inside, the most attractive feature is the eighteenth century plasterwork. Visiting hours are restricted.

STRATFORD-UPON-AVON

* Guildhall *(320)*, Church Street

A fifteenth century building which housed the grammar school attended by Shakespeare.

* Hall's Croft *(321)*, Old Town

Home of Shakespeare's daughter Susanna and her husband, John Hall.

** Holy Trinity Church *(321)*, Church Street

An Early English and Decorated cruciform church, with the tomb of William Shakespeare on the north side of the chancel.

*** New Place Estate *(321, 373)*, Chapel Street

On the site of the house bought by Shakespeare in 1597 and since destroyed is an authentic reproduction of an Elizabethan knot garden, the best of its kind in England.

* Quiney House *(321)*, corner of Bridge and High Streets

Home of Shakespeare's daughter Judith and her husband, Thomas Quiney. Now the town Information Centre.

*** Shakespeare's Birthplace *(320)*, Henley Street

William Shakespeare was born here in 1565, probably in the western side of this double house owned by his father, a glover and wool merchant. Note the names of literary greats scratched in the windows of the birthroom. In the other half of the house is a Shakespeare museum.

** Anne Hathaway's Cottage *(320)*, 1 m. w at Shottery

A thatched black-and-white half-timbered farmhouse where Shakespeare's wife was born. Very picturesque.

** Charlecote Park *(321, 406, 478)*, 5 m. e, n of B 4086; NT

A country house built in 1558 by Sir Thomas Lucy who is said to have sentenced Shakespeare for poaching on his property and may have thereby driven him to seek his fortune in London. Much altered in the nineteenth century. Interesting Victorian furniture.

** **Coughton Court** *(304)*, 9 m. w, on A 435, 2 m. n of Alcester; NT

Built by Sir George Throckmorton soon after 1518, the present house consists of a magnificent Tudor gatehouse to which were added flanking Gothick wings in the eighteenth century. The Throckmortons were well-known recusants and the house is full of hiding places for priests and displays a number of relics of Catholic persecution. In the early seventeenth century the Throckmortons were deeply implicated in the Gunpowder Plot and the house gave shelter to numerous relatives of the conspirators.

*** **Hidcote Manor** *(488)*, 10 m. sw, in Gloucestershire, s of A 46 from Mickleton; NT

One of the great twentieth century gardens of Britain, it was among the first to be sectionalized with different "rooms" separated by hedges devoted to separate species, combinations of species, or colors. Thus, there is a room planted in pink, blue, and white; another in red and orange; still another in fuchsias, and so on. Not to be missed.

* **Mary Arden's House** *(320)*, 4 m. nw, at Wilmcote

A half-timbered house where Shakespeare's mother was born.

*** **Packwood House** *(374)*, 14 m. n, 2 m. e of A 34 from Hockley Heath; NT

This pleasant Tudor house with seventeenth century additions is noted chiefly for its topiary garden, first planted in the mid-seventeenth century. The arrangement of the now towering yews is thought by some to represent the Sermon on the Mount, with the huge conical yew on top of a mount representing Christ and the others his disciples and the multitude. The inner garden is enclosed by brick walls with a gazebo at each corner, the oldest dating to about 1680.

WARWICK

*** **St. Mary's Church** *(188, 259)*, Church Street

The church, rebuilt after a fire in 1694, is essentially pseudo-Gothic and of no great distinction. In the choir is the tomb with the recumbent effigies of Thomas Beauchamp, earl of Warwick (d. 1369) and his countess. The best feature of the church, however, is the Beauchamp Chapel which is a separate room south of the choir. It is one of the best specimens of Perpendicular architecture in Britain, with perhaps the most elaborate fan vaulting anywhere. In it are the tombs of Richard Beauchamp, earl of Warwick (d. 1439) and Robert Dudley, earl of Leicester (d. 1588). The former was the husband of Isabella Despenser and father-in-law of

Richard Neville, who inherited the title and was known as the King-maker. The latter was Queen Elizabeth's perennial favorite. He is buried here with his second wife, Lettice, the mother by a former marriage of Robert Devereux, earl of Essex, another favorite of Elizabeth, though eventually beheaded by her order.

*** Warwick Castle *(182, 334, 342, 478)*, Castle Hill

The present well-preserved castle was built mostly by two successive Thomas Beauchamps, earls of Warwick in the fourteenth century. The second earl was responsible for Guy's Tower and Caesar's Tower which cover the angles of the castle's eastern curtain and flank the gatehouse with its barbican. The former tower is 128 feet high, the latter, 147. Though besieged by a royalist army in the Civil War, the castle was not badly damaged. In the seventeeth and eighteenth centuries it was converted into the stately mansion that it is today. Well stocked with paintings, the castle also boasts an excellent collection of armor, mostly Italian from the sixteenth century and later. Park by Capability Brown.

HEREFORD AND WORCESTER
Droitwich

** Hanbury Hall *(366)*, 2½ m. e, 1 m. n of B 4090; NT

A typical William and Mary red-brick house with hipped roof and a front porch flanked by Corinthian columns. Good eighteenth century furniture and porcelain and a fascinating ceiling painting by Sir James Thornhill of Dr. Sacheverell, the controversial High Church Tory rector of Queen Anne's reign, being readied for destruction by the Furies while an approving crowd of Olympian deities looks on.

Hereford

* Hereford Cathedral *(227)*, town center

Founded as a cathedral of secular canons, the church began building in 1079 and has since undergone so many rebuildings and restorations as to make it even more of an architectural patchwork than most English cathedrals.

Architectural styles: west front—twentieth century restoration; nave —Norman (piers, arches, and lower parts) and eighteenth century (upper parts); central tower—Decorated; northwest transept—Decorated; southwest transept—Norman and Perpendicular; choir—Norman and Early English; eastern transepts—Decorated; lady chapel—Early English; cloisters—Perpendicular; college of vicars choral—Perpendicular; bishop's palace—Norman.

Special features: fourteenth century *mappa mundi;* chained library.

* **Abbey Dore Church** *(242)*, 9 m. sw, on B 4347

The present church consists of the Early English and Transitional choir and transepts of a Cistercian abbey church built in the late twelfth and early thirteenth centuries and converted to parochial use after the Dissolution. The church has a rare altar rail and screen dating from the reign of Charles I when Archbishop Laud tried unsuccessfully to de-Puritanize the Church of England.

** **Kilpeck Church** *(242)*, 8 m. sw, e of A 465

A three-celled Norman church with an especially well-done carving of a Tree of Life in the tympanum of the south door and fine chevron carving on the arch separating nave and choir.

* **Longtown Castle** *(140)*, 20 m. sw, 4 m. n of A 465 from Pandy (161 SO 321 296)

A well-preserved ruin, the circular keep, two stories high, stands on an early Norman motte. It was built by the de Lacy family in the late twelfth or early thirteenth century.

* **Offa's Dyke** *(102)*, 7 m. nw, 1½ m. n of A 438 from Bridge Sollers (149 SO 405 436)

A good section of the ninth century rampart between Mercia and Wales.

LEDBURY

* **Eastnor Castle** *(441, 447)*, 2 m. e on A 438

A neo-Gothic house built by Sir Robert Smirke about 1820, the drawing room was redecorated by August W. N. Pugin in the mid-nineteenth century in an aggressively pseudo-medieval manner typical of this prophet of Victorian Gothic. Visiting hours are restricted.

Herefordshire Beacon *(48)*, 4 m. e; s of A 449, ½ m. s of juncture with A 4104 (150 SO 760 399)

A large (32-acre) Iron Age hill fort enclosed by a single bank, ditch, and counterscarp. Inside are the remains of a Norman motte. Steep climb.

LEOMINSTER

** **Berrington Hall** *(402)*, 3 m. n, w of A 49; NT

Built by Henry Holland in 1781 for the banker Thomas Harley out of his profits made from equipping British troops in the American War, this is a fine early example of the neo-Grecian style that was to reach fruition after the turn of the century. Capability Brown was responsible for the extensive park.

Burford House *(468)*, 8 m. ne in Salop near Tenbury Wells (A 4112)

Only the garden here is of interest. Though recently laid out, its island beds and herbaceous borders are in the Victorian style.

** Croft Castle *(199)*, 5 m. nw, n of B 4362; NT

The basic structure with its corner drum towers, is fourteenth and fifteenth century from the time the castle was owned by Sir Richard Croft, a veteran of the Yorkist victory at nearby Mortimer's Cross in February 1481. His altar tomb can be seen in the church lying across the lawn. In the eighteenth century the castle was restored by Richard Knight, a Shropshire iron-master, in the Gothic style, and the interiors still reflect that fashion. The grounds escaped the heavy hand of Capability Brown in the eighteenth century and therefore still boast some of the oldest oaks in the country.

* Lower Brockhampton Hall *(194)*, 12 m. w, n of A 44, 2 m. e of Bromyard; NT

This is an interesting specimen of black-and-white half-timbered construction. The hall dates from the early fifteenth century, the unusual gatehouse in the same style from the late fifteenth or early sixteenth.

PERSHORE

* Pershore Abbey Church *(155)*, town center

Originally belonging to a Benedictine abbey and now serving as the parish church, it displays Norman (crossing and south transept), Early English (apsidal choir), and Decorated (tower) features. Best known, however, is its freestone knightly effigy dating from the thirteenth century.

Bredon Hill *(48)*, 4 m. s, 2½ m. se of B 4080 from Eckington (150 SO 958 402)

An inland promontory hill fort with two lines of ramparts cutting across one of the northern spurs of Bredon Hill; scene of a bloody battle between Belgaic invaders and native Celts. Access is difficult.

ROSS-ON-WYE

* Goodrich Castle *(139)*, 4 m. sw, on B 4229 (162 SO 579 199) AM

A small but imposing ruin of red sandstone built by the Talbot family in the reign of Henry II. The barbican, gateway, and curtain walls date from the thirteenth century occupancy of William de Valence, earl of Pembroke and half-brother to Henry III.

STOURPORT

* Staffordshire and Worcester Canal *(425)*, town center

Here is the southern terminus of this important eighteenth century canal connecting the Severn River with the Trent and Mersey Canal at Great Haywood, Staffordshire. The town itself displays many interesting relics of the days when this was an important inland port lying at the head of the locks leading down to the river from the canal.

WORCESTER

** Worcester Cathedral *(149, 232)*, town center

Begun in 1084 as a Benedictine abbey church, it became a secular cathedral in 1541.

Architectural styles: west front—Modern; nave—Transitional (western bays), Decorated (most of northern bays), and Perpendicular (most of southern bays); central tower—Perpendicular; west transepts—Norman and Perpendicular; choir—Early English; east transepts—Early English; lady chapel—Early English; crypt—Norman; cloisters—Perpendicular; chapter house—Norman and Perpendicular.

Special features: tomb of King John; chantry of Prince Arthur; tombs in lady chapel; library manuscripts.

Holt Fleet Bridge *(423)*, 7 m. n, on A 4133, across Severn (150 SO 824 634)

A small bridge built by Thomas Telford.

EAST MIDLANDS

LINCOLNSHIRE
BOSTON

*** St. Botolph's Church *(243)*, town center

Most famous for its high Perpendicular tower, the Boston Stump, the remainder of the church is almost pure Curvilinear Decorated. Still one of the largest parish churches in England, it was built in the reign of Edward III (1327 to 1377) when Boston was a thriving coastal port rivaling London in the wool export trade and one of the country's chief importers of wine.

GRANTHAM

* St. Wulfram's Church *(243)*, town center

Built mostly in the thirteenth century in the period of transition between Early English and Decorated architectural styles, the interior displays features of both. The 280-feet high fourteenth century spire, however, falls clearly in the Decorated period.

*** Belton House *(358)*, 2 m. ne, on A 607

Built in 1685 to 1688 by Sir John Brownlow, possibly to a design by William Winde, this is one of the best examples in the country of late seventeenth century architecture and interior furnishings. Classic in design, with balustrade and cupola, it was modeled after Roger Pratt's Clarendon House in Piccadilly, long since destroyed. James Wyatt then remodeled it in the 1770s. Portraits by Lely, Reynolds, Romney, and Hoppner; beautiful plaster ceilings; and fine seventeenth and eighteenth century furniture enrich the interior rooms. Belton's best feature, however, is the wealth of Grinling Gibbons's woodcarvings in the marble hall, saloon, and chapel gallery. Extra attractions include a miniature steam railway, a museum dedicated to the horse, and a woodland playground for children.

* Belvoir Castle *(410, 441)*, 7 m. w, in Leicestershire, 3 m. s of A 52 from Bottesford

A fine example of Regency Gothic architecture, the house was rebuilt after 1801 by James Wyatt.

* Irnham Church *(174)*, 9 m. se, n of A 151

A fine thirteenth to fourteenth century church with a brass memorializing Sir Andrew Luttrell (1390).

* Woolsthorpe Manor *(355)*, 7 m. s, w of A 1 from Colsterworth

A small Jacobean farmhouse, birthplace of Isaac Newton. Legend attributes the discovery of the law of gravity to his having observed the fall of an apple while sojourning here during the plague of 1665.

LINCOLN

East Gate *(83)*, East Gate Hotel grounds

The excavated base of the eastern gate to Roman *Lindum.*

The Jew's House *(146)*, Steep Hill

A rare example of an urban house surviving from the early Middle Ages, this stone structure was probably built for a local Jewish merchant and money lender.

* Lincoln Castle *(131)*, Castle Hill

The original Norman stone castle was built by William the Conqueror on two mottes with a bailey. The Norman remains today consist of the base of the Observatory Tower on the southeastern motte and the western gateway. The second motte supports Lucy's Tower, the remains of a twelfth century shell keep. The castle grounds also contain the present Assize Court and County Court.

*** Lincoln Cathedral *(149, 234)*, Castle Hill

Construction of the present church for secular canons began in 1084 when the episcopal see was moved to Lincoln. It was rebuilt 1192 to 1250 after an earthquake, chiefly by Bishop, St. Hugh of Avalon who was entombed there.

Architectural features: west front—Norman and Early English (with Decorated west window); western towers—Norman and Perpendicular; Galilee porch—Early English; nave—Early English; central tower— Decorated and Perpendicular; west transepts—Early English (with Decorated circular window in southwest transept); choir—Early English; east transepts—Early English; retrochoir (Angel Choir)—Geometric Decorated; chapter house—Early English; cloister—Early English.

Special features: round windows in the west transepts (Early English Dean's Eye in north, Curvilinear Decorated Bishop's Eye in south); carved stone angels in spandrels of Angel Choir; Decorated rood screen; fifteenth century choir stalls and misericords; Perpendicular chantry chapels; monument to Catherine Swynford; Norman baptismal font; treasury with copy of Magna Carta; Bishop's Palace ruins.

** Lincoln City and Country Museum *(32, 257)*, Broadgate

Housed in a thirteenth century Franciscan (Grey Friars) Friary, the museum is small but contains a number of noteworthy prehistoric items including a bronze ax-mold and a Late Bronze Age dugout canoe. Near the entrance of the building is a good collection of sixteenth to eighteenth century ceremonial armor.

* Newport Arch *(83)*, Bailgate, near w end of East Bight

This was the northern gate to the Roman city of *Lindum*.

Roman Wall *(83)*, south of Bishop's Palace near Temple Gardens

A short segment of the ruined wall on the east side of Roman *Lindum.*

West Gate *(83)*, off Orchard Street between West Parade and Newland

This was the western gate to the lower city of Roman *Lindum.*

* **Doddington Hall** *(307)*, 5 m. w on B 1190

A splendid E-shaped mansion, designed probably by Robert Smythson, and built in the last years of the reign of Elizabeth I (1600–1603). The interior decor belongs mostly to the eighteenth century.

LOUTH

Ash Hill Long Barrow *(15)*, 10 m. nw; w of Swinhope, off B 1203 (113 TF 209 962)

The best preserved of the Lincolnshire Neolithic long barrows, measuring 128 by 53 feet and 7 feet in height.

SKEGNESS

Deadman's Graves *(15)*, 10 m. nw, 3½ m. ne of Partney (122 TF 444 720)

Two Neolithic long barrows, measuring 164 by 54 feet and 173 by 60 feet, each 6 feet in height.

Giants Hill Long Barrows *(15)*, 9 m. nw, 2 m. ne of Partney (122 TF 429 712)

A five-foot high Neolithic long barrow 210 feet in length. A second barrow nearby is barely visible.

SLEAFORD

* **St. Denys Church** *(243)*, town center

Decorated and Perpendicular in style, the church is noted chiefly for its Curvilinear window tracery and ornamentation.

* **St. Andrew's Heckington** *(243)*, 5 m. e, on A 17

A fine specimen of late fourteenth century Curvilinear Decorated style, it is noteworthy for its east window, Easter sepulcher, and canopied sedilia.

*** **Tattershall Castle** *(191)*, 13 m. ne, on A 153; NT

This most impressive brick tower was built about 1440 by Ralph, Lord Cromwell, who fought with Henry V at Agincourt and later served Henry VI as treasurer. He was reputedly one of the richest men in fifteenth century England and imported Flemish workmen to build this five-story rectangular tower which, with its corner octagonal turrets, rises to a height of 120 feet. Although the castle is machicolated and crenellated in the approved medieval military manner, the spacious exterior windows betray the essentially residential character of the building. It was partially restored in the twentieth century by Lord Curzon.

* **Tattershall Collegiate Church** *(260)*, 12 m. ne, on A 153

An unusually large collegiate church, it was founded by the Cromwell family of nearby Tattershall Castle in the late fifteenth century. The style is Perpendicular and the church is noted for the splendid glass in the east window. Here also are a number of good brasses of the fifteenth and sixteenth centuries.

SPALDING

* **Holbeach Church** *(174)*, 7 m. e on A 151

A late Decorated church, this has a fine memorial brass to an unnamed knight of the Hundred Years War.

STAMFORD

* **Burghley House** *(308, 397)*, ½ m. e, s of B 1443 in Cambridgeshire

This, the most prodigious of Elizabethan prodigy houses, was built by William Cecil, Lord Burghley for the express purpose of entertaining the queen as well as displaying his own greatness as the first of her ministers. Set in a huge park, landscaped in the eighteenth century by Capability Brown, this is a four-sided courtyard palace of stone, extensively fenestrated, the huge rounded frontispiece adorned with classical columns, the roof-tops filled with pepper-pot domes and clustered chimneys. Within the court (not open to the public) is a high pyramidal obelisk. Except for the stone staircase and the hammer-beam roof, the interior was completely altered in the seventeenth century. Famous for its wall paintings by Verrio and its enormous collection of great masters, including Lely, Kneller, Gainesborough, and Lawrence, this is more of a museum than most Tudor country houses. Mandatory guided tours. Long delays possible.

*** St. John the Baptist, Barnack *(122)*, 3 m. e, in Cambridgeshire on B 1448

Though much remodeled, this is a fundamentally Anglo-Saxon church, especially the west tower with long-and-short quoins, pilaster strips, and both rounded-headed and triangular-headed windows.

NORTHAMPTONSHIRE
CORBY

Deene Park *(309)*, 6 m. ne, w of A 43

A sixteenth century country house built by the Brudenall family, with an interesting Renaissance bay window of Ionic columns serving as mullions. In the nineteenth century the house was occupied by the earl of Cadigan, leader of the Charge of the Light Brigade at Balaclava in the Crimean War. Visiting hours very restricted.

* Kirby Hall *(307)*, 4 m. ne, 2 m. n of A 427 from Weldon (141 SP 926 927) AM

A partly ruined Elizabethan prodigy house built for Sir Humphrey Stafford of Blatherwycke, this had a four-sided courtyard plan with a lofty projecting porch, ample fenestration, and Renaissance motifs in the form of giant classical pilasters with Ionic capitals. It was altered in the mid-seventeenth century by John Thorpe for the Lord Chancellor, Sir Christopher Hatton, and again later in the century.

DAVENTRY

Dodford Church *(155)*, 3 m. e, on A 45

The church houses a Purbeck marble effigy of a thirteenth century knight in full armor.

HIGHAM FERRERS

* Higham Ferrers Church *(260)*, town center

This is an Early English and Decorated collegiate church to which was added in 1424 a schoolhouse, Bede house, and college (remains 1¼ m. north), under the patronage of Archbishop Chichele, founder also of All Souls College, Oxford.

KETTERING

** Boughton House *(365)*, 3 m. n, e of A 43 from Geddington

Built mostly by the duke of Montagu, ambassador to France under Charles II, this was meant to resemble a French château. The Huguenot

Louis Cheron decorated the ceilings. Most of the furniture and porcelain is French, in the styles of Louis XIV and XV. There are some good English paintings by Gheeraerts (*Queen Elizabeth*), Lely, Kneller, and Gainsborough, and a set of sketches by Van Dyck.

* **Eleanor Cross** *(157)*, 3½ m. n, e of A 43 in Geddington village (141 SP 896 831) AM

The smallest, though best preserved, of the three surviving Eleanor Crosses, with a triangular base and three gabled canopies over three statues representing King Edward I's much mourned queen.

** **Rushton Triangular Lodge** *(310)*, 4 m. nw, 1 m. w of A 6003 (141 SP 830 831) AM

A Catholic convert, Sir Thomas Tresham built this lodge on his estate in a triangular form and covered it with three-sided symbols in commemoration of the Holy Trinity. Each face of the building is surmounted by a triangular gable; a triangular chimney shaft emerges from the roof; all the windows are trefoils. Above the door is the inscription *TRES TESTIMONIUM DANT.*

NORTHAMPTON

* **St. Sepulchre's Church** *(242)*, Sheep Street

Possibly built by the Crusader Simon de Senlis in imitation of the Church of the Holy Sepulchre at Jerusalem, the round part of the present church retains its Norman piers (ca. 1110) topped by fourteenth century arches. The present nave dates from the thirteenth and fourteenth centuries, the choir from the nineteenth. Church closed except for services.

*** **All Saints, Brixworth** *(118)*, 7 m. n on A 508

Most of the present church dates from the seventh century when it was founded as a daughter house of the Benedictine abbey at Peterborough, though there was some rebuilding in the tenth century to repair the damage done by Danish raiders.

*** **Althorp** *(341, 350, 402, 406, 407, 409, 410)*, 6 m. nw, s of A 428

An early Tudor house extensively rebuilt and remodeled in 1790 by Henry Holland in a somewhat classical style. Long famous for its collection of paintings (including some by Van Dyck, Lely, Reynolds, Wootton, and Gainsborough), it has achieved recent publicity as the girlhood home of Diana (Spencer), Princess of Wales. Hour-long mandatory guided tours by very well-informed guides.

** Castle Ashby *(330)*, 6 m. e, n of A 428

A great courtyard prodigy house commenced about 1574 and expanded in the early seventeenth century by the first earl of Northampton. The most interesting feature of the exterior is the stone screen on the south side of the house, attributed to Inigo Jones, with the inscription *DOMINUS CUSTODIAT INTROITUM TUUM* on the outside and *DOMINUS CUSTODIAT EXITUM TUUM* on the inside. ("The Lord guard your coming in," and "The Lord guard your going out.") The fine collection of paintings includes portraits by Dobson, Kneller, Reynolds, Ramsay, Lawrence, West, Copley, and Hoppner, and a representation of Queen Mary Tudor by Antonio Moro. The future disposition of this collection is somewhat in doubt owing to the marquess of Northampton's leaving Castle Ashby to take up residence at Compton Wynyates. Mandatory guided tour of about a half-hour's duration.

* Eleanor Cross *(157)*, 1½ m, s on A 508 in Hardingstone village

The oldest of the three surviving Eleanor Crosses (1291), the stepped base and arcaded pedestal are hexagonal; three statues representing the queen are contained in canopied niches with ogival arches.

* Lamport Hall *(334, 335)*, 8 m. n, e of A 508

The original Italianate *palazzo* built by John Webb in the 1650s survives in the central portion of the house, expanded after 1732. The main entrance front has a nice Palladian look reminiscent of the works of Webb's uncle-in-law, Inigo Jones. Inside is a Van Dyck equestrian portrait of Charles I and a rare portrait of James I's wife, Queen Anne of Denmark, by Van Somer. Visiting hours restricted.

Naseby Battle and Farm Museum *(344)*, 15 m. nw, 1 m. n of B 4036 from Naseby village

A small handicraft museum with a miniature model of the Civil War Battle of 14 June 1645.

* Stoke Bruerne Waterways Museum *(425)*, 8 m. s, w of A 508

Located in a warehouse overlooking the Grand Union Canal, this is a fine museum of artifacts and memorabilia connected with the canal-boating industry.

OUNDLE

* Collegiate Church of Fotheringhay *(260)*, 5 m. n, w of A 605

Nearby the now nonexistent Castle of Fotheringhay where Mary Queen of Scots was tried and executed, this collegiate church was built in the early fifteenth century. All that survives are the nave and aisles, the chancel having been pulled down at the time of the Dissolution. The octagonal west tower is noteworthy.

TOWCESTER

Blakesley Church *(189)*, 4 m. e

A small parish church distinguished chiefly by the memorial brass to Sir Mathew Swetenham (1416).

WELLINGBOROUGH

*** All Saints, Earls Barton *(122)*, 4 m. sw, on B 573

An outstanding Anglo-Saxon tower with pilaster strips, double windows, and triangular-headed windows. The rest of the church is Norman and later.

LEICESTERSHIRE
ASHBY-DE-LA-ZOUCHE

** Ashby-de-la-Zouche Castle *(202)*, AM

The now ruined "Hastings Tower" was raised by William, Lord Hastings in the 1470s as an addition to the manor house on the site which he had received as a reward from King Edward IV whom he served as lord chamberlain. The previous owner had been the Lancastrian earl of Ormond who was beheaded after his capture at the battle of Towton in 1461. The tower, ninety feet in height, was clearly built for defensive purposes and is therefore somewhat archaic for the late fifteenth century.

St. Mary's and St. Hardulph's, Breedon-on-the-Hill *(119)*, 5 m. ne on A 453

In this otherwise undistinguished church there are some fine eighth century carved stones situated in the south aisle and inside the tower.

* Staunton Harold Chapel *(338)*, 4 m. nw, w of A 453; NT

A small seventeenth century Gothic church built in 1653 by Sir Robert Shirley as an act of defiance against Cromwell and the Puritan establishment. Shirley's effrontery, coupled with his refusal to raise a regiment for Parliament, sent him to the Tower, where he died.

CASTLE DONINGTON

* Castle Donington Church *(199)*

Here is a good brass of Robert Staunton (1458) wearing a sallet, a light helmet with a rim on the back, worn by men-at-arms in the War of the Roses.

HINCKLEY

* Stoke Golding Church *(244)*, 4 m. nw, off A 5

One of the best examples in the Midlands of Geometric Decorated architecture.

LEICESTER

** Jewry Wall Museum *(32, 83)*, off St. Nicholas Circle

A fine museum of local history and archaeology, especially strong in Roman finds, including some good mosaics. Outside the front door is a Roman column, presumably from one of the public buildings of Roman *Ratae*. Between the museum and St. Nicholas church next door is a stretch of Roman wall, and the church itself is built partly of stones and brick from the Roman city.

Leicestershire Museum of Technology *(428)*, Abbey Lane Pumping Station, Corporation Road

The county museum of industry and transport, containing, among other things, several beam engines.

* Bosworth Battlefield Centre *(204)*, 12 m. w, 2 m. s of B 585 from Market Bosworth

Here is a phenomenon rare in England: a well-marked battlefield with an exhibition and diorama to describe the battle. Unfortunately historians disagree as to what actually happened so the explanations may not be as accurate as might be wished.

** Kirby Muxloe Castle *(202)*, 4 m. w, off A 47; AM

Like Ashby-de-la-Zouche, the property here escheated to King Edward IV after the execution of the earl of Ormond following the Battle of Towton in 1461. The king gave it to his chamberlain, William, Lord Hastings, who had commenced to build a great courtyard castle of brick when he too was executed by his benefactor's brother, King Richard III. He was able to complete only the gatehouse and west tower (one of four corner towers intended), and these today, though ruined, still stand high.

* **Stanford Hall** *(366)*, 16 m. s, s of B 5414

Built in 1697 this is typical of the William and Mary style of architecture with a classical facade and hipped roof. The house contains numerous portraits of the exiled Stuart pretenders and relics of the Battle of Naseby fought nearby. There is an Aviation Museum dedicated to Percy Pilcher, an English pioneer of manned flight who was killed here in 1899. Visiting hours are restricted.

NOTTINGHAMSHIRE
NOTTINGHAM

* **Nottingham Castle** *(168)*, Standard Hill Street

The original thirteenth century castle was demolished after the Civil War and replaced in the seventeenth century with an Italianate mansion built by the duke of Newcastle. This in turn was burned during the Reform Bill Riots of 1831 and restored to its present form in the nineteenth century. Mortimer's hole, the only relic of the medieval castle, is the subterranean passage through which the young King Edward III made his entry in October 1330 to capture his mother's paramour, Roger de Mortimer, whom he dispatched to London for execution. Mandatory guided tours.

** **Wollaton Hall** *(306)*, Wollaton Park, 3 m. w, off A 609

Now housing the city of Nottingham's natural history museum, this was originally a great Elizabethan prodigy house, built in 1580 to 1588 by Sir Francis Willoughby, high sheriff of Nottinghamshire. It is an enormous high rectangular building of stone, flanked by gabled towers, profusely fenestrated, and decorated with a variety of classical friezes, pilasters, and balustrades. In the adjoining stable is a museum of Nottinghamshire industrial history.

*** **Newstead Abbey** *(283, 415)*, 12 m. n, w of A 60

The thirteenth to fifteenth century buildings of the priory of Augustinian canons were converted into a private dwelling after the Dissolution by Sir John Byron of Colwick. His descendant, the fourth Lord Byron made major improvements in the late seventeenth century. The sixth lord was George Gordon Byron, the most romantic of England's nineteenth century Romantic poets, who lived here only briefly before selling the estate for £ 94,000. The new owners were chiefly responsible for the extensive restorations that brought this very run-down mansion to its present state of magnificence. Remnants of the original priory are to be seen in the undercroft of the great hall, the chapel, bedrooms, and saloon. Of particular architectural merit is the ruined west front of the priory church which the Byrons kept as a sort of decorative appendage to the house. The Byron Museum here includes the Roe collection of the poet's manuscripts, a number of portraits, and an interesting collection of memorabilia, including the shoe lasts he used unsuccessfully to correct his club foot. The magnificent garden is Victorian.

OLLERTON

Sherwood Forest Visitors' Centre *(113, 146)*, 3 m. w; w of B 6034, ½ m. n of B 6075 from Edwinstowe (120 SK 628 676)

The center, featuring souvenirs and literature concerning Robin Hood, lies within an area of about 150 acres of woodland surviving from the early medieval royal forest which once covered most of Nottinghamshire. Within easy distance of the center is the Major Oak, a tree of tremendous girth. Other tracts of forest can be seen at Thoresby Park and Clumber Park, east of the A 614, north of Ollerton.

* Thoresby Hall *(483)*, 3 m. n on A 614

A neo-Jacobean mansion built by Anthony Salvin in 1865 to 1871 for the third Earl Manvers. Fine Victorian furniture. Visiting hours are very restricted.

SOUTHWELL

** Southwell Cathedral *(231)*, town center

Begun as a collegiate church of secular canons in 1108, it did not achieve cathedral status until 1884.

Architectural styles: west front (including two western towers)—Norman with Perpendicular west window; nave—Norman; central tower—Norman; transepts—Norman; choir—Early English; chapter house—Geometric Decorated.

Special features: Early English east window (eight lancets); Decorated rood screen.

WORKSOP

* Creswell Crags *(10, 11)*, 4½–5 m. sw, in Derbyshire on both sides of B 6042 e of Creswell village (120 SK 527 744). Take footpath leading from municipal waterworks on s side of road.

The caves, whose openings are visible on either side of the road, were occupied by Neanderthal Man and later by *Homo sapiens* during the final glaciation of the Ice Age. Entry is barred by iron grills, but the cave mouths can be closely inspected from a footpath running along the south side of the road.

DERBYSHIRE

BELPER

North Mill *(426)*, Belper Bridge

Built in 1803 to 1804, this is one of the earliest extant cotton spinning mills in Britain. It was established by Richard Arkwright and William Strutt.

BAKEWELL

All Saints, Bakewell *(119)*, 12 m. se on A 6

In the churchyard are two good Anglo-Saxon carved cross shafts, and in the south porch a number of Anglo-Saxon and Norman carved stones.

*** **Arbor Low** *(41)*, 5 m. sw, 2½ m. w of Youlgreave (119 SK 161 636) AM

An unusual Bronze Age henge monument consisting of nearly fifty fallen stones belonging to a circle and a central U-shaped "cove," all lying within a circular bank with an interior ditch. The site is approached through a farmyard and across two stiles, and if the visitor is lucky he may be escorted by a farm dog trained to chase the cattle off the monument. The view of the surrounding Derbyshire Peaks is breathtaking.

BUXTON

* **Peveril Castle** *(139)*, 12 m. ne, s of A 625 from Castleton (110 SK 150 827) AM

The smallest of Henry II's rectangular keeps, this ruin measures only thirty-five feet square. It is situated on the summit of a limestone crag offering splendid views of the surrounding Derbyshire Peaks.

CHESTERFIELD

* **St. Mary and All Saints** *(474)*, town center

A fine fourteenth century parish church with a curious twisted tower. The interior was restored by Sir Gilbert Scott in 1843.

Unitarian Chapel *(363)*, Elder Yard

Built in 1694 for the joint use of Presbyterians and Independents, this meetinghouse was later converted to Unitarian use.

** Bolsover Castle *(330)*, 7 m. e, on A 632 (120 SK 471 707) AM

A now-ruined sham castle built by John Smythson for Sir Charles Cavendish about 1612 and two decades later rather fancifully "classicized" by his son, the first duke of Newcastle. The least ruined part of the establishment is the duke's riding range. The view from here of the surrounding Derbyshire hills is magnificent.

*** Chatsworth *(296, 364)*, 9 m. w, on B 6012

On the site of a demolished manor house which occasionally served as a temporary prison for Mary Queen of Scots, the fourth earl and first duke of Devonshire began the reconstruction of this palatial estate in 1686. Between that date and 1697, William Talman finished the south and east fronts in a rather severe classical style. Talman is also responsible for most of the heavily baroque interiors. The west front may have been designed by the duke himself, while the north front is the work of Thomas Archer in 1704. Interior wall and ceiling paintings are by Laguerre, Verrio, and Thornhill (all very baroque); portraits by Van Dyck, Lely, Reynolds, Kneller, Hayter, and Sargent; some of the sculpture is by Caius Gabriel Cibber; the ironwork by Jean Tijou. The first duke installed the long stepped canal; Archer designed the distinctly baroque Cascade House; the Emperor Fountain, with its 290-foot water jet, was constructed in the nineteenth century for a prospective visit of Czar Nicholas I, which never materialized. Capability Brown designed the park. The view of the Derbyshire peaks is spectacular.

*** Haddon Hall *(193)*, 13 m. w; on A 6, 2 m. s of Bakewell

This is one English country house that should not be missed. Begun in the twelfth century, it was greatly expanded in the fourteenth and fifteenth by the Vernons, and still further elaborated in the sixteenth by Sir John Manners who built the Long Gallery. It is the scene of a romantic legend concerning the elopement of Dorothy Vernon and Sir John. The house, which is mostly medieval, is set among the gorgeous Derbyshire Peaks. The lovely informal terraced garden is modern.

*** Hardwick Hall *(296, 307, 313, 342, 406)*, 9 m. se, 2 m. s of A 617 from Glapwell; NT

Built in 1587 by Robert Smythson for Bess of Hardwick, countess of Shrewsbury, this is an enormous three-storied prodigy house of stone, surrounded by projecting four-story rectangular towers, the entire facade pierced by an expansive display of window glass. Tuscan colonnades decorate both front and back, and above the roofline parapet rises the huge initials, *ES*, of the builder, Elizabeth Shrewsbury. The interior is lavishly decorated with tapestries and paintings, and displays some of the embroideries executed by Bess and Mary Queen of Scots while the latter was in the custody of the former's husband. The formal gardens are attractive, though mostly of modern vintage.

A hundred yards away, Bess of Hardwick rebuilt her father's manor house on a lavish scale rising to six stories in height. Now called **Hardwick Old Hall** *(307)*, this ruined house stands in interesting contrast to the neighboring mansion built a few years later. Unfortunately, at the time of writing and for the indefinite future, it is closed for repairs.

DERBY

* Museum and Art Gallery *(411, 435)*, The Strand (or The Wardwick)

A small provincial museum containing good collections of paintings by Wright of Derby and of Derby porcelain from the eighteenth and nineteenth centuries.

* Kedleston Hall *(388, 398, 407)*, 4 m. nw, w of Derby-Holland Road

Begun by James Paine and mostly completed by Robert Adam, this is one of England's finest Georgian houses, though its very restricted visiting hours render it inaccessible to most time-pressed visitors to Britain. Adam's interiors are dazzling—especially the great marble hall, the saloon, and the dining room. There are good paintings by Van Dyck, Lely, and Reynolds. The park has a pretty bridge, also designed by Adam. Visiting hours very restricted.

*** Melbourne Church *(242)*, 8 m. s, on B 587

An unusually ambitious Norman parish church, it is cruciform in plan with an apsidal east end, a central tower, and two western towers. The chevron motif dominates the carvings of the arches. The church was restored by G. G. Scott in the nineteenth century.

*** Melbourne Hall *(369, 373)*, 7 m. s, on A 514

The house here is a much enlarged and remodeled seventeenth century parsonage of no great architectural distinction, though some of the paintings and furnishings are good. Melbourne's chief claim to fame is its garden, designed in the first decade of the eighteenth century by London and Wise of the Brompton Nursery in London in the style made fashionable at Versailles by Le Nôtre. This is a formal garden of parterres, intersecting allées, pools, statuary, etc. Robert Bakewell of Derby is responsible for the charming and gaily painted wrought-iron arbor.

* St. Wystan's, Repton *(118)*, 7½ m. s, 3 m. s of A 5132 on B 5008 through Willington

The crypt dates from the seventh century and was used as the final resting place of the saint to whom the church was dedicated, as well as a number of members of the Mercian royal family. The chancel is also partly Anglo-Saxon, though of a later date (tenth century).

MATLOCK

Masson Mills *(426)*, 1 m. s in Matlock Bath

Originally owned by Richard Arkwright, this six-story red-brick cotton textile mill is one of Britain's finest early factories.

Old Mill, Cromford *(426)*, 3 m. s on A 6

Arkwright's original mill which housed his water-frame, the single invention most responsible for the spread of the factory system in the textile industry.

* **Wingfield Manor** *(296)*, 5 m. se, in South Wingfield, B 5035

The much ruined remains of a late fifteenth century manor house which, under the ownership of the earl of Shrewsbury, served occasionally as a temporary prison for Mary Queen of Scots.

WESTERN MIDLANDS

WEST MIDLANDS
BIRMINGHAM

* **Birmingham Cathedral** *(368)*, St. Philip's Churchyard

Originally the Church of St. Philip, it was designed about 1715 by Thomas Archer. Noteworthy are the fine baroque tower and the nineteenth century Burne-Jones stained-glass windows.

Birmingham University *(468)*, 3 m. sw in Selly Oak

Founded in 1900 as a technical college, it received university status in 1909. The main buildings are by Sir Aston Webb.

*** **City Museum and Art Gallery** *(341, 409, 443, 476, 479, 480)*, Congreve Street

Adjoining the Council House, it was designed by Yeoville Thomason in the 1880s, using the Corinthian order. British archaeological finds date from the prehistoric, Anglo-Saxon, Roman, and medieval periods. British paintings include those by Reynolds, Gainsborough, Lely, Hogarth, Constable, Landseer, and the Pre-Raphaelites.

Council House *(476)*, Victoria Square

Designed in 1874 by Yeoville Thomason, this is a classical building in the Corinthian Order, expressed in pilasters as well as columns.

Galton Bridge *(423)*, in Smethwick, w of city center on A 4030 (139 SP 015 894)

A small bridge built by Thomas Telford.

*** Museum of Science and Industry *(463)*, Newhall Street

A fine museum of technology and industry, with a locomotive hall, a transport section containing veteran cars, and an aircraft section with a Spitfire and a Hurricane from World War II.

St. Chad's Cathedral *(472)*, St. Chad's Circus

The first Roman Catholic cathedral built in Britain since the Reformation, it was constructed in 1830 to 1841, to the design of Augustus W. N. Pugin, in a fourteenth century Gothic style, more or less of German provenance.

Town Hall *(476)*, Victoria Square

Designed by Joseph Hansom (inventor of the hansom cab) in 1832, the building is surrounded by forty Corinthian columns and was modeled on the Temple of Castor and Pollux in the Roman Forum.

COVENTRY

*** Coventry Cathedral *(504)*, town center

Adjoining each other are the ruined fourteenth century cathedral, bombed out by German raiders on the night of 14 November 1940, and a very modern building consecrated in 1962. Of the former, the most interesting feature is the sanctuary with its crosses of charred wood and of nails from the ruins. Major points of interest in the new cathedral are the statue of St. Michael by Sir Jacob Epstein, the nave windows, the baptistry windows, the tapestry behind the high altar, the Chapel of Christ, and the Chapel of Unity.

* Herbert Art Gallery and Museum *(463)*, Jordan Well

A good museum of local history and archaeology with a representative collection of industrial products including early motor cars.

St. Mary's Hall *(208)*, near cathedral

A late fourteenth century guildhall, much of it original.

** The Lunt *(59)*, 3 m. s, in Baginton (140 SP 345 752)

A reconstructed Roman fort of the first century A.D., with earthen ramparts topped by a palisade fence, timber gateway and tower, barracks block, and granary. The site museum and interpretive center is excellent.

STOURBRIDGE

* **Hagley Hall** *(387)*, 2 m. s, on A 456

Rebuilt by Sanderson Miller for Lord Lyttelton in 1760 in the current Palladian fashion. Fine plasterwork by Francisco Vassali. In the park Miller placed a Gothick castle alongside a Palladian rotunda, and James "Athenian" Stuart later added the Doric Temple of Theseus.

WOLVERHAMPTON

Chillington Hall *(460)*, 8 m. nw, in Staffordshire, 2 m. sw of Brewood

The earlier Georgian house was rebuilt about 1785 by Sir John Soane. Grounds by Capability Brown. Visiting hours are very restricted.

* **Moseley Old Hall** *(346)*, 4 m. n, e of A 449; NT

A late Elizabethan manor house, bricked over in the nineteenth century, it is notable chiefly as one of the hideouts of Prince Charles (later Charles II) on his flight from the Battle of Worcester on 3 September 1651. Here he met Father Huddleston who, 34 years later on the king's deathbed, received him into the Roman Catholic church. The interior retains some of its seventeenth century furnishings and paneling, and the priest hole here is probably authentic. Mandatory guided tours of about forty minutes.

** **Weston Park** *(358, 411)*, 9 m. nw (in Staffordshire), s of A 5

The stately exterior, designed by its seventeenth century owner, Lady Elizabeth Wilbraham, is Dutch Palladian. The interior is restored nineteenth century Victorian. There is a rare Holbein here (Sir George Carew) and several Van Dycks. The park was landscaped by Capability Brown.

** **Wightwick Manor** *(475)*, 3 m. w, s of A 454

A late Victorian mansion decorated by William Morris whose work here includes wallpaper, tapestries, and carpets. There are also good paintings by a number of the Pre-Raphaelites and stained glass by Burne-Jones. Good topiary garden. Visiting hours restricted.

STAFFORDSHIRE
BURTON-UPON-TRENT

* **Tutbury Castle** *(295)*, 4 m. nw, on A 50

A much ruined fourteenth century castle built by John of Gaunt, this was one of the English prisons of Mary Queen of Scots, where she lived under the surveillance of the earl of Shrewsbury and his wife, Bess of Hardwick.

LICHFIELD

*** **Lichfield Cathedral** *(119, 235, 474)*, town center

A secular cathedral associated with Coventry since 1148, the present red sandstone church was begun in the last years of the twelfth century. It is one of England's smaller cathedrals, mostly renowned for its unique arrangement of three spires.

Architectural features: west front—Modern restored Decorated with facade of 113 statues; west spires—Decorated (northwest spire rebuilt in sixteenth century); nave—Early English and Decorated; central tower—Decorated; transepts—Early English with Perpendicular roofs; choir—Early English (western end); lady chapel—Decorated; sacristy—Early English; chapter house—Early English.

Special features: statuary on west front; seventh century Gospel of St. Chad in library.

Interior restored by Sir George Gilbert Scott in the mid-nineteenth century.

Samuel Johnson Birthplace *(413)*, Market Street

A small museum of memorabilia pertaining to Dr. Johnson in the house where he was born in 1709.

* **Wall** *(83)*, 1½ m. sw; n of A 5, 1 m. e of Muckley Corner (139 SK 099 067) AM NT

The substantial remains of a bathhouse, including well-preserved hypocausts, of the Roman posting station of *Letocetum*.

NEWCASTLE-UNDER-LYME

* **Chatterley Whitfield Mining Museum** *(431)*, 6 m. ne, e of A 527
A defunct coal mine offering a one and one-half hour guided tour through extensive galleries 700 feet below ground. Tour guides are former miners. Not for the claustrophobic.

STAFFORD

** **Shugborough** *(394, 403, 406)*, 5½ m. se, n of A 513
The family home of Admiral Lord Anson and maintained as a museum commemorating his naval career by the Staffordshire County Council. The grounds were decorated by James "Athenian" Stuart with a liberal sprinkling of neo-Grecian "temples," and the Chinese pavilion was designed by one of Anson's ship captains. Sailors, architects, and gardeners equally will find this place appealing.

STOKE-ON-TRENT

North Stafford Hotel *(461)*, Station Road

A railway hotel built in the 1840s in a Jacobean style to match the station across the square.

* Railway Station *(461)*, Station Road

Opened in 1850, this is a charming red-brick building with stone dressings designed by H. A. Hunt in the style of a Jacobean country house, with Flemish gables, finials, etc.

Cheddleton Mill *(427)*, 8 m. ne, in Cheddleton on A 520

An eighteenth century flint mill powered by two breastshot waterwheels.

*** Gladstone Pottery Museum *(434)*, 2½ m. se, n of Uttoxeter Road (A 50) in Longton

Here are fine exhibits illustrating the development of pottery since prehistoric times, with an emphasis on the Staffordshire potteries of the eighteenth and nineteenth centuries. In the yard are four bottle kilns and a complete set of shops pertaining to the manufacture of earthenware. This should not be missed by anyone interested in the history of the Industrial Revolution.

* Trentham Gardens *(487)*, 3½ m. s, on A 34

A Capability Brown landscape redone by Sir Charles Barry with terraces for bedding out.

*** Wedgwood Visitor Centre *(436)*, 7 m. s, 1 m. e of A 34 in Barlaston

Here is a truly spectacular display of historic examples of Wedgwood ware, including the famous Queensware, items from Catherine the Great's "frog service," black basalt ware, jasperware, and a copy of the Portland Vase. An eighteen-minute color film explains the development of the industry. The display of modern Wedgwood in the gift shop is irresistible.

UTTOXETER

** Croxden Abbey *(251)*, 7 m. n, w of B 5030 (128 SK 065 397) AM

A ruined Cistercian abbey colonized by monks from Normandy in 1176, its substantial remains consist chiefly of the high west front and south transept of the church, the chapter house, and adjacent buildings in the east range of the cloister—all in thirteenth century Early English style.

** **Sudbury Hall** *(358)*, 6 m. e (in Derbyshire) on A 50; NT

A splendid Restoration house built by George Vernon in the 1660s and 1670s, the symmetrical front with hipped roof and cupola above are typical of the period. In the drawing room are lovely woodcarvings by Grinling Gibbons and on the staircase others by Edward Pearce. The staircase hall and saloon were decorated by Laguerre. There is a Museum of Childhood in the east wing.

SALOP
ALBRIGHTON

* **White Ladies Priory; Boscobel House** *(346)*, 3 m. n (127 SJ 826 076) AM

A much ruined nunnery and a seventeenth century manor house, both of them significant only as hideouts for the Prince of Wales (later Charles II) on his flight from Worcester where the decisive defeat by Cromwell of his invading army from Scotland brought an end to the Civil War. On the property is an oak tree, possibly descended from the Royal Oak where the fugitive hid during the daytime.

BRIDGNORTH

** **Buildwas Abbey** *(251)*, 12 m. n, on B 4378 (127 SJ 642 044) AM

A Savignac monastery founded in 1135 and later converted to Cistercian, the high-standing church walls date to the twelfth century; the remains of the vaulted chapter house to the thirteenth or fourteenth.

*** **Wenlock Priory** *(249)*, 8 m. nw, in Much Wenlock (127 SJ 625 001) AM

Founded by Roger de Montgomery early in the twelfth century as a Cluniac abbey on the site of an earlier religious house established by Leofric, earl of Mercia, and his wife, Lady Godiva, the only Norman part of the ruins is the chapter house with intricate interlaced blind arcading. Walls of the thirteenth century Early English church still stand quite high.

CLUN

Clun Castle *(137)*, town center

A ruined rectangular keep standing on a motte with three associated baileys, probably built during the civil war between Stephen and Matilda.

LUDLOW

*** Ludlow Castle *(132, 243)*, Castle Square

One of the major castles guarding the Welsh marches, this ruin contains remnants of construction undertaken in every century from the eleventh through the sixteenth. The Norman parts include the 110-foot-high keep, presumably built by Roger de Lacy about 1086, and remains of the chapel which was built in the round in the twelfth century according to a brief architectural fashion produced by the Crusades. Mortimer's Tower belongs to the thirteenth century, the two gateways to the fourteenth, and most of the remaining buildings to the fourteenth, fifteenth, and sixteenth centuries.

*** Stokesay Castle *(192)*, 8 m. nw, off A 49

Thought to be the most complete and most representative of the surviving medieval fortified manor houses in England, it was built in the last decade of the thirteenth century by Lawrence of Ludlow, a prosperous wool merchant. Especially noteworthy are the great hall, the adjoining solar, and the two towers. Not seriously damaged during the Civil War, the original features of the house and grounds have been very well preserved, though it is not presently inhabited.

OSWESTRY

Old Oswestry *(49)*, 1 m. n (126 SJ 295 310) AM

A large Iron Age hill fort with three ramparts and attendant ditches, an earthen barbican, and an unusual long bank running perpendicular to the enclosing embankments toward the center.

SHREWSBURY

The First Queen's Dragoon Guards Regimental Museum *(446)*, Clive House, College Hill

A regimental museum with the usual array of uniforms, weapons, regimental plate, etc.

Ireland's Mansion *(311)*, High Street

A half-timbered Tudor town house, built about 1580.

The King's Shropshire Light Infantry Museum *(446)*, Sir John Moore Barracks, Copthorne

A regimental museum with the usual array of weapons, uniforms, plate, etc.

Owen's Mansion *(311)*, High Street

A half-timbered Tudor town house, built about 1592.

* **Rowley's House Museum** *(84)*, High Street

A good museum of local history and archaeology, especially noted for its Roman collection, including finds from nearby Wroxeter.

* **Adcote** *(484)*, 7 m. w, off A 5

Built about 1876 for Mrs. Rebecca Darby to the design of Norman Shaw. It is part pseudo-Gothic, part pseudo-Elizabethan, the architect's intention having been to simulate the normal evolution of a medieval manor house. Now a school; mandatory guided tours.

** **Attingham Park** *(403)*, 4 m. se, n of A 5; NT

Rebuilt in the 1780s by George Stewart and subsequently altered by John Nash, who added the picture gallery. The park was landscaped by Humphrey Repton.

Battlefield Church *(186, 260)*, 7 m. n, off A 49

Originally a chantry founded by Henry IV to pray for the souls of those slain in the battle of Shrewsbury, the style is Decorated and Perpendicular with an ugly Victorian interior.

** **Bishop Burnell's Palace (Acton Burnell Castle)** *(234)*, 8 m. s (126 SJ 534 019) AM

A ruined fortified residence of red sandstone, it was built by Edward I's chancellor, Robert Burnell, Bishop of Bath and Wells, in the ninth decade of the thirteenth century. A good specimen of military/ecclesiastical architecture more typical of France than England and of the fourteenth century than the thirteenth.

* **Haughmond Abbey** *(252)*, 3 m. ne, off B 5062 near Uffington (126 SJ 542 152) AM

Of this Augustinian establishment founded in 1135, almost nothing is left of the church, but the ruins of the twelfth century chapter house and fourteenth century infirmary are substantial.

Hemford Stone Circle *(41)*, 15 m. s; 6½ m. n of Lydham; ½ m. nw of A 488, n of Blackmarsh (137 SO 324 999)

A Bronze Age circle of stubby stones with a single stone in the center. Hard to find. Fine view.

Mitchell's Fold *(41)*, 16 m. s; 6 m. n of Lydham; 1 m. w of A 488, w of Whitegrit (137 SO 305 984)

A Bronze Age circle with fourteen surviving stones, the highest six feet. Difficult to find, but with spectacular views of the Welsh mountains to the west.

Montford Bridge *(423)*, 4½ m. w, on A 5 (126 SJ 433 153)

A stone bridge across the Severn, built by Thomas Telford in 1792.

*** Wroxeter *(84)*, 5 m. se, on B 5380 (126 SJ 568 088) AM

The site of *Virconium, civitas* of the *Cornovi,* this is the best preserved of all Roman *civitates* owing to its having been deserted in Anglo-Saxon times and never reoccupied. The most impressive of the ruined buildings is the great public bathhouse. The site museum is one of the best of its kind in Britain.

TELFORD

*** Ironbridge Gorge Museum *(430, 431, 435)*, 6 m. s, in Coalport (B 4373)

This is the finest of Britain's many fine museums of industrial archaeology. Stretching along the River Severn, it includes the Coalbrookdale Museum and Andrew Darby's Blast Furnace, the first iron bridge ever made (designed by Thomas Telford), the Coalbrookdale Institute built in 1859, the Bedlam Furnaces, the Blists Hill Open Air Museum, and the Coalport China Works Museum. There is a visitors' center at the north end of the Iron Bridge. A full day should be allowed to do justice to this important site.

* Lillieshall Abbey *(252)*, 3 m. n, e of A 518 (127 SJ 738 142) AM

An Augustinian house founded about 1145, the ruins, though not extensive, are excellent examples of Norman ecclesiastical style. Especially noteworthy are the west front of the church, the east processional door, the east range (book locker, slype, and chapter house), and the south range (day room and frater).

The Wrekin *(49)*, 4 m. se, 2 m. s of Wellington (127 SJ 630 083)

A much eroded Iron Age hill fort situated at the summit of a very high solitary hill overlooking miles of countryside in all directions. Steep climb by footpath opposite Forest Glen Hotel.

CHESHIRE
CHESTER

Cheshire Military Museum *(446)*, The Castle

A good regimental museum with the usual array of weapons, uniforms, regimental plate, etc.

* Chester Cathedral *(230)*, town center

Founded as a Benedictine abbey in 1093, the church achieved cathedral status in 1541.

Architectural styles: west front—Perpendicular; nave—Decorated and Perpendicular; south transept—Early English and Decorated; north transept—Norman; choir—Early English and Decorated; lady chapel—Early English and Decorated; chapter house—Early English; cloisters—Perpendicular; refectory—Early English; abbot's house (undercroft)—Norman.

Special features: late fourteenth century choir stalls and misericords.

** City Walls *(66, 206, 344)*, town center

Here is one of the best sets of medieval town walls in England. More than two miles of it have survived, rising in places to as much as forty feet in height. The northern and eastern sides followed the line of the old Roman Wall and at **Newgate** *(66)*, the lower courses of brick, are of Roman provenance. Most of the present structure is medieval, though much restored. **Phoenix Tower** *(344)*, at the northeast corner is the place from which King Charles I watched his troops suffer defeat at the hands of parliamentarians on Rowton Moor three miles to the southeast. Here is a small museum with contour maps of the battle. Most of the circuit can and should be walked.

*** Grosvenor Museum *(58, 61)*, Grosvenor Street

Contains one of the finest collections of Roman remains in England, particularly pertaining to the Roman army. Noteworthy are the life-size model of a Roman legionary in full uniform and the replicas of the Roman fortress of *Deva*. Note also the large collection of Roman tombstones and other inscribed sculpted stones.

Leche House *(311)*, 17 Watergate

A Tudor town house.

* Roman Amphitheatre *(66)*, e of Eastgate

The remains of less than half of what was probably the largest amphitheater in Britain, capable of holding a crowd of over 8,000 spectators.

* Roman Gardens *(67)*, s of Eastgate

In this lovely public park abutting Chester's city wall is a fine reconstructed hypocaust and some classical columns that were found near the site of the headquarters building of the twentieth legion and relocated here.

* The Rows *(311)*, town center

Here are galleries or arcades running along the first floor above the ground level in front of numerous houses and shops which are probably of medieval origin with extensive Tudor reconstruction. What we have here is essentially a sixteenth century townscape, though dressed up in the nineteenth.

** St. John's Church *(242)*, St. John Street

The present church is a much reduced remnant of the original early Norman (1075) collegiate church. Pillars and arches of the nave are Norman, the triforium is Transitional (ca. 1200) and the clerestory Early English. The west and east windows are Victorian insertions. A fourteenth century wall painting of John the Baptist adorns the easternmost pillar on the north side of the nave. A visit to this church is more rewarding than to the nearby Chester Cathedral.

Stanley Palace *(311)*, Watergate

An exceptionally fine Tudor town house, once the property of the earls of Derby, now headquarters of the English Speaking Union.

** Beeston Castle *(153)*, 12 m. sw, w of A 49 (117 SJ 537 593) AM

Once an immense fortress built on a high sandstone crag by the earl of Chester to guard the Welsh borders, the remaining ruins consist mostly of the inner curtain wall with three strong cylindrical mural towers and an immense twin-towered gatehouse.

Eddisbury Hill Fort *(108)*, 11 m. e, 1 m. n of A 556, ½ m. w of B 5152 from n end of Delamere village (117 SJ 552 693)

An unmarked monument difficult to locate, this is an Iron Age hill fort reinforced in the ninth century by the Queen of Mercia to protect her country from the Irish-Norse who had settled in the neighboring Wirral Peninsula. Some of the earthen embankments are faced with stone. Private property; permission to view should be obtained from farmhouse across road from site.

CONGLETON

*** Little Moreton Hall *(310)*, 4 m. sw, on A 34; NT

This is an unusually picturesque black-and-white half-timbered manor house with overhanging upper stories, cobbled courtyard, mullioned windows, a long gallery, and an adjacent gatehouse of the same construction. It was built by William Moreton and his son in the sixteenth century, though the earliest parts of the house are probably late medieval. Little Moreton is easily one of the best examples of Tudor half-timbered construction in the country.

CREWE

Sandbach Crosses *(119)*, 6 m. ne, on A 534 and A 533

In the marketplace stand this pair of Anglo-Saxon carved crosses, thought to date from the ninth century.

ELLESMERE PORT

Canal Boat Museum *(424)*, town center

Here at the northern terminus of the Shropshire Union Canal is the largest collection of inland-waterways craft in Europe.

KNUTSFORD

* Tatton Park *(487)*, 2 m. ne, e of A 5034; NT

A fine Victorian-style garden with an orangery, a fern house, and terraces, said to have been designed for bedding out by Joseph Paxton. The house was begun in 1780 to a design by Samuel Wyatt.

MIDDLEWICH

Trent and Mersey Canal *(424)*, town center

An intermediate point on this important eighteenth century canal.

NANTWICH

* Shropshire Union Canal *(424)*, town center

A favorite among pleasure-boat cruisers, because of the prevalence of open countryside along the entire length of the canal built in the eighteenth and nineteenth centuries.

NORTHWICH

* Arley Hall *(486)*, 2 m. ne of A 559

Only the garden here is of interest. The herbaceous borders and curving island beds are typically mid-Victorian.

WILMSLOW

*** Styal Country Park *(427)*, 2 m. n, w of B 5166

Here is a splendid new industrial museum containing a restored cotton textile mill, workers' houses, a dormitory for apprentices, a Methodist chapel, etc. This is one of Britain's best memorials to the Industrial Revolution.

YORKSHIRE AND LANCASHIRE

HUMBERSIDE
BARROW-UPON-HUMBER

** Thornton Abbey *(252)*, 4 m. se, 1 m. e of A 1077 from Thornton Curtis (113 TA 115 190) AM

An Augustinian foundation of 1139, nothing remains of the original buildings, although the fourteenth century Decorated chapter house is a substantial ruin. The site's main feature, however, is the Perpendicular gatehouse built in 1382. It is among the country's best examples of fourteenth century decadent military architectural style, i.e., the employment of defensive building devices (crenellation arrow slits, etc.) for decorative purposes.

BEVERLEY

*** Beverley Minster *(212, 259)*, town center

There was a collegiate church on this site as early as the tenth century, founded by Alfred the Great's grandson, King Athelstan. Following a fire in the late twelfth century, the early Norman church was rebuilt along Gothic lines, and, though it lacked a ruling bishop, in size, magnificence, and prestige, it approached cathedral status.

Architectural styles: west front—Perpendicular; nave—Decorated (except for two Early English east bays and the Perpendicular west bay); central tower—Early English; central transepts—Early English; choir—Early English; eastern transepts—Early English; lady chapel—Early English with Perpendicular east window.

Special features: choir stalls and misericords; fourteenth century Percy tomb on north side of altar; sixteenth century Perpendicular Percy Chapel off northeast transept.

BRIDLINGTON

** **Burton Agnes Hall** *(307, 410)*, 6 m. sw, on A 166

A lovely three-story gabled brick prodigy house built about 1600 for Sir Henry Griffiths by Robert Smythson. The ceilings and overmantels here are outstanding, and the house has an unusually fine collection of furniture, china, and tapestries, as well as a number of distinguished paintings by British artists and French impressionists.

* **Rudstone** *(41)*, 5½ m. w in Rudston churchyard s of B 1253 (101 TA 097 677)

The largest monolith in England, this huge standing stone is more than twenty-five feet in height. It is a Bronze Age monument and the stone was quarried near Cayton more than ten miles away.

Skipsea Castle *(129)*, 8 m. s, on B 1242 and B 1249 (107 TA 163 551) AM

An unusually large Norman motte minus the castle that once surmounted it.

Willy Howe Round Barrow *(16)*, 9 m. nw, 1 m. w of Burton Fleming (101 TA 063 724)

A large Neolithic round barrow, 24 feet high and 130 feet in diameter.

HOWDEN

* **Church of St. Peter** *(260)*, town center

The ruined early Perpendicular chapter house attests to the collegiate status of this foundation of 1297. The extant church is mostly fourteenth century Decorated, though the fifteenth century tower is Perpendicular. The chancel is also ruined, the present church consisting entirely of the original nave and crossing.

HULL (KINGSTON-UPON-HULL)

* **Holy Trinity Church** *(244)*, Trinity House Lane

The predominant style of this unusually long parish church is Curvilinear Decorated, though the nave was not built until the end of the fourteenth century.

* **Maister House** *(389)*, 160 High Street; NT

An unusual Palladian town house with a fine hall and staircase.

* **Wilberforce House** *(418)*, 25 High Street

Birthplace of William Wilberforce whose efforts were chiefly responsible for bringing an end to the slave trade within the British Empire in the early nineteenth century. This is a Wilberforce museum and research library, with a good collection of slave-trade relics.

* **St. Peter's, Barton-on-Humber** *(123)*, 6 m. sw, on A 1077

The west tower is Anglo-Saxon with typical long and short quoins, pilaster strips, and double windows; the north arcade is Norman, the south arcade Early English; and the clerestory is Perpendicular.

SCUNTHORPE

Epworth Parish Church *(419)*, 11 m. sw, in Epworth on A 161

Architecturally undistinguished with a mixture of Early English, Decorated, and Perpendicular styles, the church is noteworthy only because its pastor from 1696 to 1735 was Samuel Wesley, father of the Methodist leaders John and Charles who were confirmed here in the Church of England which they never abandoned, in spite of their significant deviation from main-line Anglicanism.

* **Epworth Old Rectory** *(419)*, 11 m. sw, in Epworth on A 161

Childhood home of John and Charles Wesley, furnished with good but simple seventeenth and eighteenth century pieces.

WITHERNSEA

*** **Patrington Church** *(244)*, 4 m. sw, on A 1033

Though its great spire (189 feet) dates from the fifteenth century, the rest of the church is a splendid example of fourteenth century Curvilinear Decorated style. Especially noteworthy are the flowing tracery of its windows, the vaulted lady chapel, the carvings of its capitals, and, outside, its pinnacled buttresses.

SOUTH YORKSHIRE
BARNSLEY

** **Cannon Hall** *(388, 407)*, 5 m. w, in Cawthorne on A 635

An eighteenth century house designed by John Carr (Carr of York) now a "country house museum" maintained by the Barnsley Metropolitan Borough Council. Here also is the museum of the 13th/18th Royal

Hussars (Queen Mary's Own). The house contains an excellent and representative collection of eighteenth century furniture.

* **Monk Bretton Priory** *(252)*, 2 m. ne, on A 628 (111 SE 373 065) AM

A Cluniac foundation of 1154, the remains of the twelfth century church are slight as are those of the east range of the claustral buildings. In the south range is the lovely outline of two Decorated windows looking into the ruined refectory. The west range, which contained the prior's lodging, is the best preserved of all, having been used as a house in the sixteenth century.

DONCASTER

** **Conisbrough Castle** *(140)*, 5 m. sw, on A 630 (111 SE 515 989) AM

Built by Hamelin, half brother of Henry II, this well-preserved round keep with six massive buttresses rises to a height of eighty-six feet. The inner bailey curtain is of a later date. Situated in a heavily industrialized area.

ROTHERHAM

*** **Roche Abbey** *(251)*, 11 m. e; 1½ m. se of Maltby, s of A 634 (111 SK 544 898) AM

A Cistercian monastery founded in 1147, the ruins today consist of the eastern walls of the transepts (Transitional) and the foundation stones of the rest of the church and the claustral ranges. There is also a well-preserved fourteenth century gatehouse and interesting remains of the reredorter straddling a running stream, a typical example of medieval hygiene. The ruins are nestled against a high cliff and are very romantic in appearance.

SHEFFIELD

** **Sheffield City Museum** *(32, 104, 105)*, Weston Park

The Antiquities section contains a representative collection of local finds from the Bronze Age through the Saxon period. Even better are the Applied Arts galleries with a unique display of Sheffield cutlery, old Sheffield plate, ceramics, etc.

Sheffield University *(469)*, Western Bank

An outgrowth of Firth College, founded in 1879, and the Sheffield School of Medicine, founded in 1828, the university received its charter in 1905.

*** **Abbeydale Industrial Hamlet** *(428, 430)*, 5 m. sw on A 621 in Abbeydale

One of the best industrial museums in Britain containing, among other things, the complete layout of an early nineteenth century steel foundry, from the pot room where clay crucibles were made to the water-powered tilt forge where scythes were hammered out.

WEST YORKSHIRE
BRADFORD

* **Bradford Industrial Museum** *(426)*, in Eccleshill on Moorside Road, e from A 658

Housed in an old mill, the museum is devoted mostly to machinery connected with the worsted industry.

HALIFAX

*** **All Souls, Haley Hill** *(474)*, New Bank (A 58)

Built in 1856 to 1859 to the design of Sir George Gilbert Scott in his usual Victorian Gothic style, it was regarded by the architect as "on the whole, my best church."

* **Bankfield Museum and Art Gallery** *(426)*, Akroyd Park

A good museum of local industry, especially textiles. Here is a collection of hand looms with and without flying shuttles.

HUDDERSFIELD

* **Huddersfield Station** *(461)*, New North Road

Opened in 1847, this is a splendid small railway station designed as a Roman public building with a Corinthian facade.

KEIGHLEY

*** **Brontë Parsonage Museum** *(466)*, 2 m. sw in Haworth, w of A 6033

The home of Charlotte, Emily, Anne, and Branwell Brontë where Charlotte wrote *Jane Eyre* and *Shirley*, and Emily, *Wuthering Heights*. Now a well-kept museum featuring Brontë memorabilia. Close by are the dark and windswept Yorkshire moors that inspired much of their writing.

LEEDS

Leeds and Liverpool Canal *(424)*, Neville Street

The eastern end of this important canal connecting the River Aire with the Mersey.

*** St. John the Evangelist *(337)*, New Briggate

A Laudian-style church built in 1634, this has a double nave in the late Perpendicular style with an interior that is essentially Jacobean, its most striking feature being the great screen extending across the entire width of the nave.

Town Hall *(476)*, The Headrow

A nineteenth century neoclassical building of the Corinthian order with mixed Renaissance features.

University of Leeds *(468)*, Woodhouse Lane

Originating as the Leeds School of Medicine and the Yorkshire College of Science, it became a constituent college of Victoria University in 1881 and received its separate charter in 1904. The original building of the Yorkshire College of Science (1877) was designed by Alfred Waterhouse in his usual Victorian Gothic style and built of red brick and terra-cotta.

*** Harewood House *(388, 398, 406, 409)*, 8 m. n, w of A 61

The house itself was built by Carr of York in the 1760s and altered in the nineteenth century by Charles Barry. The glorious interior is among the finer works of Robert Adam. With the assistance of the muralists, Antonio Zucchi and his wife Angelica Kauffmann, and the plasterer Joseph Rose, Adam succeeded in making this one of the most exquisite set of rooms in Britain. Much of the furniture was made by Thomas Chippendale to Adam's own designs. Paintings include portraits by Reynolds, Gainsborough, and Lawrence. The landscape garden is by Capability Brown.

* Lotherton Hall *(477)*, 12 m. ne, on B 1217 at Aberford

Inside this much enlarged eighteenth century house is a fine collection of nineteenth century china (Derby, Worcester, and Coalbrookdale) and of Victorian furniture including Gothic pieces by Augustus W. N. Pugin and William Burges.

PONTEFRACT

* Pontefract Castle *(167, 184, 343)*, Micklegate

Built in the twelfth century, the castle belonged to Thomas, earl of Lancaster in the reign of Edward II, and here the earl was beheaded by order of the king. At the end of the fourteenth century Richard II was imprisoned here following his forced abdication in favor of Henry IV, and here he died—probably murdered. In the Civil War the castle was twice taken from its royalist defenders by parliamentarian forces, the second time in 1648, whereupon it was slighted. All that remains are portions of the keep and Piper's Tower, maintained in the town park.

WAKEFIELD

*** Nostell Priory *(399, 406)*, 6 m. se, n of A 638; NT

This is a fine Palladian mansion of about 1735, later enlarged and decorated by Robert Adam. Plasterwork is by Joseph Rose, wall and ceiling paintings are by Antonio Zucchi and his wife Angelica Kauffmann. Much of the superb furniture was done by Thomas Chippendale to designs of Adam. Among other priceless Chippendale pieces is a splendid writing desk. Attributed to Chippendale is the famous dollhouse. Antique furniture lovers should not miss this display.

* Sandal Castle *(199)*, 1 m. s at Sandal Magna

This much ruined fourteenth century castle is close to the site of the battle of Wakefield where its owner, Richard, duke of York was killed in December 1460. The victorious Lancastrians then had the duke's severed head put on display on the town wall of York. The castle, however, survived until the Civil War when it was slighted by parliamentarian troops after surrendering in 1645.

WETHERBY

*** Bramham Park *(374)*, 5 m. s, w of A 1

This fine Italianate house was built by Robert Benson, Lord Bingley, chancellor of the Exchequer under Queen Anne. Here are some good family paintings by Kneller, Hoppner, Benjamin West, et al., and a splendid portrait by Reynolds of the victor of Culloden, the duke of Cumberland. It is the garden, however, that is Bramham's chief attraction—a formal affair in the style of Le Nôtre, with boskage framing the intersecting allées, pools, statuary, urns, etc. A windstorm in 1962 destroyed most of the trees, but the boskage has been replanted, and the garden is beginning to take shape again.

NORTH YORKSHIRE
BOROUGHBRIDGE

** Newby Hall *(398, 406)*, 3 m. nw, at Skelton on Ripon Road

A late seventeenth century house decorated by Robert Adam with ceiling paintings by Antonio Zucchi. Sculpture gallery outstanding. Superb chairs by Thomas Chippendale. Good Victorian-style garden.

* **Aldborough** *(84)*, 1 m. se, n of B 6265 (99 SE 405 667)

Here was *Isurium,* the *civitas* of the *Brigantes* who were settled here by the Romans long after their great hill fort at Stanwick had been overrun. A small portion of the town wall remains, as well as two good mosaics. The site museum is too small to be distinguished.

* **The Devil's Arrows** *(41)*, sw end of town (99 SE 391 666)

Three undressed stones in a line, 200 and 370 feet apart, with heights of eighteen and twenty-two and one-half feet, quarried at Knaresborough six miles away. This is a Bronze Age sacred site.

HARROGATE

** **Harlow Car Garden** *(486)*, 1 m. sw, off A 59

This is the official garden of the Northern Horticultural Society; it includes rock gardens, a rose garden, herbaceous borders, and an extensive woodland garden.

* **Rudding Park** *(487)*, 1½ m. e, s of A 661

A fine woodland garden with rhododendrons, candelabra primulas, lilies, hydrangeas, etc. The park may have originally been laid out by Hugh Repton.

* **Spofforth Castle** *(184)*, 4 m. se on A 661 (104 SE 360 511) AM

Original seat of the Percy family and birthplace of Harry Hotspur, all that remains are the ruined fourteenth century hall of an earlier fortified manor house.

KNARESBOROUGH

Knaresborough Castle *(179, 343)*, town center

The present remains, standing in a public park, consist chiefly of the ruined rectangular keep, dating from the late fourteenth century when the castle was owned by John of Gaunt. It was captured by a parliamentarian army in the Civil War and slighted.

LEYBURN

* **Middleham Castle** *(139, 186)*, 2 m. s, on A 6108 (99 SE 128 875) AM

Here are the ruins of an exceptionally large rectangular keep built by Ralph fitz Ranulph in the reign of Henry II. In the fifteenth century it was the home of Richard Neville, earl of Warwick (the Kingmaker) and the favorite residence of Richard III.

MALTON

*** Castle Howard *(371, 411)*, 6 m. se, off A 64

Begun in 1700 for the third earl of Carlisle and designed by Sir John Vanbrugh with the assistance of Nicholas Hawksmoor, this great private palace is the closest thing to a masterpiece in the baroque style that England has to offer. The north front, flanked by projecting wings (only the eastern one of which was completed by Vanbrugh) is faced with majestic Doric pilasters; the south with Corinthian. Over the center of a roof studded with chimneys, lanterns, domelets, urns, and statuary, rises the splendid dome-capped drum. Outstanding among the house's contents are Holbein portraits of Henry VIII and the third duke of Norfolk; and Howard family portraits by Van Dyck, Lely, Kneller, Hoppner, and Lawrence. Wall and ceiling paintings are by Laguerre and Pellegrini (restored after a fire in 1940). Statuary and fine furniture abound. On the grounds are Vanbrugh's Temple of the Winds and Hawksmoor's mausoleum where the third earl is buried. Facilities for handling visitors are especially well organized, including transportation from the car park to the house on a tractor-drawn carriage. Well-informed staff members are posted at convenient positions throughout the house to answer questions. From the visitor's point of view, Castle Howard is perhaps the best-run stately home in Britain.

Duggleby Howe Round Barrow *(16)*, 6 m. se, e side of B1253 from Duggleby (101 SE 881 669)

A large Neolithic round barrow, 20 feet high and 120 feet in diameter.

NORTHALLERTON

*** Mount Grace Priory *(212, 254)*, 8 m. ne, 1 m. n of juncture of A 19 and A 684 (99 SE 453 982) AM

The only surviving Charterhouse in England of any architectural significance, it was settled by Carthusian monks in 1398. Following the strict rule of the order, the monastery was laid out as a large cloister surrounded by tiny cells in which the monks lived more or less like hermits, a modest church, a small refectory, and no dormitory. Of chief interest today are the ruined church, with a well-preserved Perpendicular tower, and a reconstructed monk's cell with the usual garden walls attached.

PICKERING

* **Pickering Castle** *(141)*, town center; AM

The much ruined shell keep standing on an unusually high Norman motte was built in the late twelfth century by the Marmion family. By the thirteenth century, the castle was owned by the dukes of Lancaster, and Richard II was imprisoned here briefly after his abdication to Henry of Bolingbroke, founder of the Lancastrian dynasty. Except for the keep, most of the construction belongs to the fourteenth century.

RICHMOND

*** **Richmond Castle** *(132, 186)*, (92 NZ 174 006) AM

A magnificent ruin standing high above the River Swale, this is one of the best examples in England of an early medieval stone castle. The main hall (Scolland's Hall) and the castle wall date from the Conqueror's time and were built by Alan Rufus, first earl of Richmond. The keep is mostly of a twelfth century date from the reign of Henry II.

Green Howards' Museum *(446)*, Trinity Church Square

A well-organized regimental museum with the usual array of weapons, uniforms, regimental plate, etc.

** **Bolton Castle** *(178, 295)*, 10 m. se, 4 m. s of B 6270 from High Fremington

Built by Richard, Baron Scrope, in the last two decades of the fourteenth century from profits from the French wars, this was in its day one of the largest and most costly castles in England. Here Mary Queen of Scots was held prisoner for six months after her escape from Scotland and before being consigned to Tutbury. It was taken by parliamentarian troops in the Civil War and slighted. Today's remains are well preserved and the great hall houses an interesting folk museum of local artifacts.

* **Constable Burton** *(387)*, 6 m. s, n of 684

A Palladian villa designed by John Carr (Carr of York) in the 1760s. Handsome portico with double stairway. Nice garden. Visiting hours restricted.

** **Easby Abbey** *(253)*, ½ m. e, on B 6271 (92 NZ 185 003) AM

This was a Premonstratensian establishment founded in 1155. Not much of the church remains, but the ruins of the claustral buildings are unusually fine, though the ground plan is somewhat unusual with the canons' dorter occupying the west range rather than the east. Especially noteworthy are the Early English sacristy, chapter house, and slype, and the Decorated frater with much of the window tracery still in place. Also Early English is the dorter and its attached guests' solar.

Jervaulx Abbey *(212, 251)*, 14 m. s, n of A 6108, 4 m. se of Middleham

This is a very sparse ruin of a Cistercian monastery founded about 1156. The highest-standing portions belong to the church; the low lying foundations to the chapter house and dorter. The property is in private hands and upkeep of the grounds is minimal.

St. Agatha's, Easby *(119)*, 1 m. se on B 6271

Noteworthy for the "Easby Cross," a fine example of Anglo-Saxon stone carving. Here is a replica only, the original now being housed in the Victoria and Albert Museum in London.

Stanwick *(62)*, 7 m. n, e of B 6274 between Forcett and Aldbrough (92 NZ 180–190 115) AM

The largest Iron Age hill fort in England, built by the *Brigantes*, garrisoned by Cartimandua and overrun by Roman soldiers of the Ninth Legion in A.D. 71 to 74. Although the earthen embankments and their accompanying ditches were high and deep, enclosing 750 acres, they are today badly eroded or plowed under. Near the village of Forcett, a little east of the B 6374 there is a small rampart faced with stone, partially restored by the Department of the Environment. On the unnumbered road between Forcett and Aldbrough, it is possible to get an occasional glimpse of the eroded ramparts to the south. Another view can be obtained from the Stanwick parish churchyard just to the south of this same road.

RIPON

*** Ripon Cathedral *(118, 212, 234)*, town center

Founded as a collegiate church for secular canons, the present building, begun about 1180, stands on the site of an earlier Anglo-Saxon church whose crypt has survived. It achieved cathedral status in 1836.

    Architectural styles: west front and tower—Early English; nave—Transitional (with Perpendicular aisles); central tower—Early English and Perpendicular; transepts—Transitional; choir—Perpendicular (west end) and Geometric Decorated (east end); crypt—Anglo-Saxon.

    Special features: fifteenth century rood screen; fifteenth century choir stalls.

*** Fountains Abbey *(212, 251)*, 4 m. se, 1 m. s of B 6265 (99 SE 274 683) AM

This is one of the most complete, and perhaps the most spectacular, monastic ruins in Britain. Established by the Cistercians in 1135 it soon became enormously wealthy—in land, sheep, and tangible wealth, all of which is reflected in the magnificence of the monastic buildings. Of the high-standing church walls and columns, only those of the nave and transepts are twelfth century Norman. The east end of the church, with the Chapel of Nine Altars, is a thirteenth century Early English rebuilding. The graceful Perpendicular central tower was added in the sixteenth century on the very eve of the Dissolution.

The claustral buildings lying south of the nave, mostly Transitional and Early English in style, are among the best preserved in Britain. They are best viewed in the following sequence: go south from the south transept to the chapter house and then to the undercroft of the monks' dorter; west (right) through the warming house, refectory, and kitchen; north (right) through the cellarium above which was the lay brothers' dorter, then back into the western end of the nave. To the southeast of the nave lies another block of buildings clustered around the monks' infirmary; to the southwest was the lay brothers' infirmary; and west of that are the remains of two guest houses.

* Fountains Hall (283), 5 m. sw, 1 m. s of B 6265

A handsome Jacobean mansion built in 1611 on the grounds of, and using materials from, the great Cistercian abbey of Fountains whose ruins the house now overlooks. Good sixteenth and seventeenth century furniture.

** Studley Royal (383), 3 m. w, s of B 6265

A fine eighteenth century landscape garden designed by John Aislabie to overlook the ruins of Fountains Abbey across the River Skell. The little Doric temple is probably the handiwork of the great Palladian architect Colen Campbell.

SCARBOROUGH

Roman Signal Station (76), Scarborough Castle (101 TA 050 893) AM

This ruined tower is the best surviving signal station built by Count Theodosius in the late fourth century as a defensive measure against raiding Saxons.

Rotunda Museum (28), Vernon Road

A typical small museum of local history and archaeology, distinguished only by its holdings of microliths and other Mesolithic artifacts from nearby Star Carr.

** Scarborough Castle (139, 167), north end of town; AM

The keep of this splendid ruin overlooking the North Sea was built ca. 1157 to 1169 by Henry II. King John is responsible for the outer curtain wall. Here in 1312 Piers Gaveston was besieged and captured when the castle surrendered to the earl of Pembroke. Splendid views up and down the North Yorkshire coast.

SELBY

*** **Carlton Towers** *(483)*, 6 m. s, 6 m. w of Goole on A 1041, 1½ m. n of Snaith

This is an immense Victorian Gothic country house. The earliest portions were built in 1614; stable and chapel were added in the 1770s; and the house was first Gothicized in the 1840s by the eighth Lord Beaumont. In the 1870s E. W. Pugin (son of Augustus W. N. Pugin) remodeled the exterior, and John Francis Bentley (architect for Westminster Cathedral) redid the interior in the High Victorian taste it still displays.

Wressle Castle *(184)*, 7 m. e in Humberside, 1 m. n of A 63

This much ruined and badly cared for late fourteenth century castle of the Percys overlooks the River Derwent. The oriel window is interesting and the building is unusual in these parts for having been built of dressed stone. It was damaged during the Civil War, and again by fire in 1796.

SKIPTON

* **Bolton Priory** *(252)*, 5 m. e, n of A 59

The Early English nave of this Augustinian priory, founded about 1120, is incorporated into the parish church of Bolton Abbey which has a Perpendicular west front. The rest of the priory church and the claustral buildings are ruins.

TADCASTER

Saxton Church *(200)*, 4 m. s, w of A 162

A small church with a Norman chancel arch. In the churchyard is the altar tomb of Lord Dacre, killed at the Battle of Towton fought nearby in 1461, along with the unmarked graves of other Lancastrians killed in action.

THIRSK

*** **Byland Abbey** *(212, 251)*, 11 m. e, 1 m. s of A 170 (100 SE 549 789) AM

A ruined Cistercian monastery founded in 1177 as a colony of Furness Abbey in Cumbria, its best features are the high west front of the church, including the lower arc of a great rose window, and the exquisite tile mosaic in the south transept. The style is Transitional. Of the claustral buildings, which are well preserved, the most interesting remains are those of the twelfth century (Norman) lay brothers' dorter in the west range.

* **Helmsley Castle** *(153)*, 12 m. e, on A 170 (100 SE 611 836) AM

Built mostly in the thirteenth century by the de Roos family, this huge ruin is a good example of the castle of *enceinte*. Stone barbicans guard either end of a ring of outer earthworks, inside of which stands a high rectangular curtain wall with mural towers, gatehouses at either end, and a D-shaped tower keep on the northeast face. The chapel is sixteenth century.

*** **Rievaulx Abbey** *(212, 250)*, 11 m. e; w of B 1257, 3 m. ne of Helmsley (100 SE 577 849) AM

This is the first of the Cistercian monasteries to have been established in Yorkshire, and its ruins are extensive. The nave and the transepts (except for their southern walls) are of twelfth century Norman construction; the south end of the church is thirteenth century Early English. The cloister lies to the west of the church rather than in the usual southern position. Of the claustral ruins the most interesting are the low standing walls of the apsidal chapter house and the more substantial refectory, both built in the thirteenth century. Note that this latter building was laid out on an east-west axis at right angles to the cloister walk and to the axis of the church nave, which atypically runs north and south.

** **Rievaulx Terrace** *(285)*, 11 m. e, s of B 1257; NT

A lovely landscape garden in the eighteenth century style, designed to provide a romantic view of the Rievaulx Abbey ruins through the trees. Two temples, Ionic and Doric respectively, grace the sylvan scene.

WHITBY

** **Whitby Abbey** *(117)*, ½ m. e (94 NZ 904 115) AM

The present splendid ruins standing high on a cliff above the town date to a thirteenth century rebuilding of the Norman church which replaced the Anglian abbey founded by St. Hilda in the seventh century. The chancel and north transept of the thirteenth century church stand quite high and are good examples of the Early English architectural style. (Note especially the splendid lancet window openings.) North of the church are traces of the seventh century monastery.

Wade's Causeway *(64)*, 10½ m. sw; 4 m. sw of village of Goathland, itself 2½ m. sw of A 169 (94 SE 793 93–SE 812 988)

About a mile-and-a-half stretch of Roman pavement, sixteen feet in width, running across the Wheeldale Moor. Second only to Blackstone Edge in the state of its preservation, it is extremely difficult to find. (Follow the unfinished road south from the village of Goathland for about three and one-half miles to Wheeldale Lodge; then proceed by footpath about another half-mile southwest.) The view of the moors alone may justify the effort.

YORK

** All Saints Church *(212)*, North Street

This has the best collection of medieval glass of any church in the city, mostly fifteenth century though some fourteenth. The two best examples are the "Prick of Conscience" window, depicting the last fifteen days before Judgment Day, and the fifteenth century window of St. Anne teaching the Child Virgin to read.

** City Walls *(206)*, town center

Here are substantial stretches of the medieval wall, dating probably from the fourteenth century. Four of the city gates have survived: Monk Bar and Bootham Bar on the north side of the wall; Walmgate Bar and Micklegate Bar on the south. A footpath extends along most of the surviving top of the wall and provides good views of the city.

** Clifford's Tower *(146, 153)*, Tower Street

A shell keep of unusual quatrefoil design standing on top of a high Norman motte, the castle was built in stone from 1245 to 1271 by order of Henry III. The walls still stand mostly to their original height, though the interior has been gutted. On this site stood an earlier wooden castle which was burned in 1190 along with 150 Jews of the city of York who had taken refuge there during that year's anti-Semitic riots.

* Holy Trinity Church *(212)*, Goodramgate

The church is noteworthy chiefly for its fifteenth century glass in the east window and the fourteenth century heraldic glass in the south aisle.

* Merchant Adventurers' Hall *(208)*, Fossgate

A fourteenth century building, much rebuilt.

* **Merchant Tailors' Hall** *(208)*, Aldwark

Rebuilt medieval building with a well-restored fourteenth century roof.

* **Multiangular Tower** *(67, 75)*, Museum Gardens, off Museum Street

The substantial remains of a corner bastion added in the fourth century to the second century wall of *Eboracum*, the great fortress of the ninth Roman legion.

*** **National Railway Museum** *(458)*, Leeman Road

A superb museum illustrating the history of British railway engineering and the tremendous impact of the railways on British life in the nineteenth century. Among other items are twenty-five locomotives, a variety of other rolling stock, miscellaneous railway equipment, a winding engine, the Gaunless railway bridge, and other railway-associated gear too numerous to list. This is a branch of the Science Museum in London and is organized with equal concern for the convenience and edification of the visitors.

* **Roman Bathhouse** *(67)*, Roman Bath Inn, St. Sampson's Square

The owners of this well-appointed pub have cleverly installed a segment of glass floor through which can be observed the hypocaust and foundations of a bathhouse presumably belonging to the ninth Roman legionary headquarters at *Eboracum.*

Roman East Bastion *(67)*, off Aldwarck Street behind Merchant Taylor's Hall

Incorporated in the medieval city wall is this easily distinguished bastion of Roman construction raised in the fourth century.

Royal Station Hotel *(461)*, Station Road

A nineteenth century railway hotel which has retained some of its Victorian ambience.

* **St. Denys Church** *(212)*, Walmgate

In the central light of one window in the north aisle is the oldest parish church glass in the city—two colored medallions on a background of grisaille, dating from the late twelfth or early thirteenth century. Seven other windows, including the east window of the north aisle and the central east window above the choir, contain excellent examples of fourteenth and fifteenth century glass painting.

* St. Martin-le-Grand *(212)*, Coney Street

The most important sight here is the former great west window, thirty-one feet high and dating from 1437, which was removed for safekeeping at the outbreak of World War II and reinserted later in the north wall. It is of fifteenth century provenance. The church itself was almost entirely destroyed in an air raid and has been rebuilt.

St. Mary's Abbey *(212)*, Museum Gardens

This was a Benedictine abbey founded in 1089. Not much is left besides the foundations and lower walls of the ambulatory and lady chapel east of the choir.

* St. Michael Spurriergate *(212)*, Spurriergate

The east window of the south aisle contains an excellent fifteenth century representation of the Woman Clothed with the Sun.

* St. Michael-le-Belfrey *(212)*, Petergate

A Perpendicular church, it has some excellent and rare sixteenth century windows—from a period in which the art of glass painting was declining.

* The Shambles *(311)*, south of King's Square

A busy shopping district with crowded half-timbered and brick buildings, some of which date from the Tudor period or before.

* York Guildhall *(208)*, off St. Helen's Square

Rebuilt along fifteenth century lines after being almost destroyed by German bombing in 1942.

*** York Minster *(67, 212, 236)*, town center

A secular cathedral begun in the twelfth century, this has always been the seat of the archbishop of York, second ranking ecclesiastic in England. York has more medieval glass than any church in Britain.

Architectural styles: west front—Decorated; western towers—Perpendicular; nave—Decorated; central tower—Perpendicular; transepts—Early English; choir—Perpendicular; retrochoir—Perpendicular; crypt—Norman; chapter house—Decorated.

Special features: Curvilinear Decorated west window; Early English Five Sisters lancets in north transept; rose window in south transept; Perpendicular east window; Perpendicular rood screen; undercroft museum.

* York Railway Station *(461)*, Station Road

A fine Victorian station built in 1873–1877 to the design of Thomas Prosser.

*** Yorkshire Museum *(62, 67, 75, 88, 340)*, Museum Gardens

A splendid museum of local history and archaeology, especially strong in Roman finds. Noteworthy items include a larger-than-life bust of the Emperor Constantine, who was born in York; a Roman sword and scabbard from Stanwick hill fort; and an inscription from the southeastern gate to the fortress of *Eboracum* (York).

* Kirkham Priory *(250)*, 12 m. ne, e of A 64 (100 SE 735 657) AM

Of the Augustinian priory founded in 1122, almost nothing of the original building remains, except possibly the Norman doorway to the refectory. The thirteenth century gatehouse with St. George and the dragon and David and Goliath carved in high relief, and the Decorated lavatorium in the south range of the cloister are the items of greatest interest here.

* St. Helen's, Skipwith *(123)*, 10 m. se, 2 m. e of A 19

The lower part of the western tower is Anglo-Saxon; the chancel fourteenth century.

Sheriff Hutton Castle *(186)*, 10 m. n, 4 m. nw of A 64 from Flaxton

This once great Neville castle is a sparse and tumbled ruin now standing in a private farmyard. Permission to view obtainable from farmhouse for a contribution to the local fund for seamen's relief.

GREATER MANCHESTER
BOLTON

* Tonge Moor Textile Museum *(426)*, 1 m. n on Tonge Moor Road (A 676)

Here is the only surviving Crompton mule as well as several replicas of spinning jennies, the originals of which are in the Science Museum in South Kensington. The museum is located in a room of the public library.

MANCHESTER

*** City Art Gallery *(409, 480)*, Mosely Street

This is a splendid provincial gallery with, among other things, a fine collection of British paintings, including those of Gainsborough, Stubbs, Turner, and the Pre-Raphaelites.

John Rylands Library *(473)*, Deansgate

Completed in 1900 to the design of Basil Champneys, this is a fine example of Victorian Gothic in its final phase.

Midland Hotel *(461)*, Peter Street

Built in 1898 as a railway hotel to the design of Charles Trubshaw, this is a fine example of Edwardian baroque.

* North Western Museum of Science and Industry *(426)*, 97 Grosvenor Street

A well-stocked museum of machinery of all kinds, including an Arkwright water-frame, machine tools, steam engines, etc.

*** Town Hall *(473)*, Albert Square

A splendid example of Victorian Gothic by Alfred Waterhouse, it was built in 1867 to 1876. Inside is a mock hammer-beam roof and good murals by Ford Madox Brown who was associated with the Pre-Raphaelite Brotherhood.

* University of Manchester *(468)*, Oxford Road

Founded as Owens College in 1851, and incorporated as a constituent college of Victoria University in 1880, it received a separate charter in 1904. The main building dates from 1873 and was designed by Alfred Waterhouse. It is a classic of the Victorian Gothic style, though in stone instead of the architect's customary red brick and terra-cotta.

PRESTWICH

* Heaton Hall *(400)*, Heaton Park, off A 576

Designed by James Wyatt in 1722 for the earl of Wilton, this is a fine neoclassical mansion with a good collection of English porcelain and other valuable furnishings, maintained by the Manchester City Art Galleries.

SALFORD

Salford Science Museum *(432)*, Buile Hill Park, Eccles Old Road

Here, among other items of industrial interest, is a good collection of miners' safety lamps.

STOCKPORT

* **Lyme Park** *(387, 406)*, 6½ m. se, in Cheshire, 1 m. e of A 523 from Poynton; NT

A Tudor house radically remodeled in the eighteenth century Palladian style by Giacomo Leoni. The Ionic portico with its pediment surmounted by lead figures of classical deities is an outstanding Palladian accomplishment. Good Chippendale furniture.

MERSEYSIDE
BERKENHEAD

*** **Lady Lever Art Gallery** *(479, 480)*, 4 m. s in Port Sunlight (A 41)

A fine art gallery with a good selection of British paintings including those of Reynolds, Turner, Gainsborough, Landseer, and the Pre-Raphaelites.

LIVERPOOL

** **Merseyside County Museums** *(51, 105)*, William Brown Street

Of special interest to the student of English prehistory is the Joseph Mayer collection with its superb collection of Iron Age artifacts, including a La Tène mirror, and its equally fine collection of Anglo-Saxon jewelry. In the basement is a good transport museum and in another gallery a collection of ship models associated with the thriving port of Liverpool.

*** **St. George's Hall** *(476)*, Lime Street

A splendid essay in neoclassicism in the Corinthian order, this is a combination town hall, law court, and concert hall.

University of Liverpool *(468)*, Brownlow Hill

Founded in 1881 as a constituent college of Victoria University, it received its separate charter in 1904. The Victoria Building (1890) of red brick and terra-cotta, is typical of the Gothic style of its architect, Alfred Waterhouse. This, along with the University of Leeds, is the first of the English red-brick universities. The **Botanic Garden** *(487)*, 1½ m. s of Neston, is noted for its rock garden.

*** **Walker Art Gallery** *(313, 409, 479, 480)*, William Brown Street

This is a splendid provincial gallery with a good collection of British paintings, including those of William Dobson, Lely, Hogarth, Reynolds,

Richard Wilson, Stubbs, Wright of Derby, Constable, Turner, Lawrence, and the Pre-Raphaelites.

*** **Speke Hall** *(310)*, ½ m. w of Liverpool Airport, off A 581; NT

A very well-preserved and well-appointed sixteenth century four-sided courtyard manor house of black-and-white half-timbered construction. Noteworthy interior features are the plastered ceilings and the Mortlake tapestries.

LANCASHIRE
ACCRINGTON

Higher Mill Museum *(426)*, 5 m. se, on Holcombe Road, Helmshore, s of A 680

Here among other things is a reproduction of Hargreaves's Jenny.

BLACKBURN

* **Lewis Museum of Textile Machinery** *(426)*, Exchange Street

Contains both looms and spinning machines.

** **Hoghton Tower** *(310)*, 5 m. w on A 675

Built in the 1560s by Sir Thomas Hoghton, a Catholic recusant, this is a four-sided house constructed around two courtyards with only a slight nod to contemporary Renaissance fashions in the form of four pilasters and an entablature on the north side. The builder's son, Sir Richard, almost bankrupted himself entertaining James I on his royal progress in 1617. Tradition holds that on this occasion the king knighted a round of beef (hence the word "sirloin").

LANCASTER

** **Lancaster Castle** *(132, 150, 348)*, town center

Still functioning as a prison and law court, much of the castle cannot be visited, but its most ancient parts are open to the public. These include the Norman keep, ca. 1090, and the so-called Hadrian's Tower, ca. 1200. The Shire Hall contains a beautiful collection of coats of arms. The dungeon cell where the Quakers George Fox and Margaret Fell were imprisoned is on view. Mandatory guided tours run frequently and are more instructive than most, though with undue emphasis on instruments of torture and the barbarities of the prenineteenth century prison code.

* **Lancaster Canal** *(424)*, town center

Near the north end of the canal running up from Preston. Popular among pleasure-boat cruisers because of the absence of locks.

Lune Aqueduct *(425)*, 1 m. n, w of A 683 (97 SD 484 639)

An aqueduct designed by John Rennie to carry the Lancaster Canal across the River Lune.

LITTLEBOROUGH

* **Blackstone Edge** *(64)*, 4–5 m.e, e and s of A 58 (109 SD 973 170—988 184)

The most interesting section of Roman road left in Britain, this long stretch of paving stones, sixteen feet in width, was part of a military road running from Manchester to Ilkley. The trough in the middle probably served to help brake wagons on the downgrade.

LONGRIDGE

* **Ribchester** *(Bremetennacum) (62)*, 4 m. se off B 6245 (103 SD 650 350) NT

Foundations of two granaries and a gateway of the Roman auxiliary fort established by Agricola about A.D. 80. Small site museum with Roman finds.

NORTHERN ENGLAND

CLEVELAND
MIDDLESBROUGH

* **Captain Cook Birthplace Museum** *(393)*, 2 m. s in Stewart Park, Marton

Housed in a lodge near the gates to Stewart Park is a large model of Cook's ship, *Endeavour*, and other mementoes of his life and work. His cottage has been removed from nearby Great Ayton to Melbourne, Australia.

COUNTY DURHAM
BARNARD CASTLE

** **Barnard Castle** *(139, 163)*, town center (92 NZ 049 165) AM

A fine ruin high above the River Tees consisting today of a round corner tower, and an exceptionally high curtain wall. It was owned by the Balliol family and the main construction appears to have taken place in the mid-twelfth century, though there was some building here earlier. One of its owners was John Balliol who was Edward I's puppet king of Scotland. The castle was badly slighted by parliamentarian troops during the Civil War.

** Bowes Museum *(478, 485)*, town center

An imitation Second Empire *hôtel de ville* built for John Bowes (illegitimate son of the earl of Strathmore) in 1869, it is now a museum devoted chiefly to the decorative arts. Students of British culture will be especially interested in the splendid series of rooms furnished authentically in the styles of different periods from the Tudor to the mid-nineteenth century.

* Bowes Castle *(139)*, 5 m. w on A 66 (92 NY 992 135) AM

This ruined rectangular keep standing high over the River Greta was built by Henry II ca. 1170. Of the curtain walls only the earthworks remain.

* Egglestone Abbey *(253)*, 1 m. s (92 NZ 062 151)

Founded in 1195 to 1198 as a Premonstratensian establishment, the most substantial remains today are those of the church built in the Decorated style in the late thirteenth century. Noteworthy especially are the south transept with a full set of windows and the east end of the choir with a magnificent window of five lights separated by narrow stone mullions. The claustral ruins are fragmentary.

BISHOP AUCKLAND

*** Escombe Parish Church *(118)*, 2 m. w, off B 6268

Except for the windows, this small rectangular church with a square chancel is pure early Anglo-Saxon, dating from the time of Bede. The key is kept on a hook in the porch of the house across the street.

*** Raby Castle *(185, 411)*, about 4 m. sw on A 688; 1 m. n of Staindrop

This is the least altered of the great northern fourteenth century castles still used as residences. It was the primary seat of the Neville family. Rectangular in shape, the castle courtyard is entered through two gatehouses, and contains a number of residential and service buildings. The oldest part is the twelfth century Bulmer's Tower, but most of the construction was done in the fourteenth century, including Clifford's Tower which is the major building on the grounds. The interior is sumptuous Victorian with some fine English sporting paintings of horses and hounds.

CHESTER-LE-STREET

** Beamish North of England Open Air Museum *(431)*, 5 m. w, n of A 693

Here is a wide variety of objects illustrating the industrial history of England in the nineteenth century: an engine house which once contained the steam beam-engine for raising and lowering men and coal from and to an underground mine; pit cottages once housing miners and their families; a coal car locomotive; a passenger train and railway station; and a tram, the last three in operation. At the "home farm" there is a good exhibition of farm machinery, livestock, and so on. Especially entertaining for children.

DARLINGTON

** Darlington North Road Station Railway Museum *(456)*, Station Road

Built in 1842, this restored railway station (probably the oldest in Britain) houses an excellent musem of locomotives and other rolling stock associated with the Stockton and Darlington railway, the first in the country to be opened for general use. Here is the original locomotive built by George Stephenson: the "Locomotive"; also the "Derwent," built in 1845.

DURHAM

* Durham Castle *(131, 231)*, Palace Green

The original Norman castle built here by William the Conqueror, ca. 1072, has been so altered over the years as to be unrecognizable, especially after its inclusion within the precincts of the University of Durham *(468)*. The oldest part of the building is the small chapel underneath the University Senate room. Other Norman remnants are the doorway between the gallery and the state rooms, and the Norman Gallery, once the castle constable's great hall. Most of the rest is nineteenth century Gothic.

*** Durham Cathedral *(92, 106, 119, 230)*, Palace Green

Founded in 1081 as a fortified Benedictine cathedral-monastery, the church building began in 1093.

Architectural styles: west front—Norman with Decorated window; Galilee porch—Transitional; nave—Norman and Transitional; central tower—Perpendicular; transepts—Norman with Decorated and Perpendicular windows; choir—Norman; lady chapel (Chapel of the Nine Altars) —Early English; claustral buildings—Norman and Early English.

Special features: tomb of the Venerable Bede (Galilee porch);

fourteenth century bishop's throne; fourteenth century reredos; relics of St. Cuthbert in Treasury; Bishop Puiset's Bible and St. Carilef's Bible in Library.

** Finchale Priory *(252)*, 4 m. n, e of A 167 (88 NZ 297 471)

The illegitimate son of Bishop Puiset of Durham founded this Benedictine house beside the River Wear in 1196 as a sort of hostel/retreat for the no-doubt overworked monks of nearby Durham Cathedral. The ruins are extensive, notably the Early English and Decorated church; the claustral east range, including the chapter house; the south range, especially the frater undercroft; and the prior's lodging east of the church, all dating from the thirteenth and fourteenth centuries.

TYNE AND WEAR
JARROW

* St. Paul's, Jarrow *(118)*, n of A 185; ½ m. e of south entrance to Tyne Tunnel

The church built in 681 for the monastery where the Venerable Bede spent most of his life and where he died, survives only in the chancel of the present edifice. The rest of the church is a nineteenth century building designed by Sir George Gilbert Scott. The original stone inscription, recording its dedication in 685, is inside the church. Sparse remains of the seventh century claustral buildings lie to the southeast. Across the street in Jarrow Hall is the *** Bede Monastery Museum *(118)*, a superb modern repository of site-finds as well as an outstanding center of information concerning the history of early British Christianity.

NEWCASTLE-UPON-TYNE

City Walls *(207)*, Bath Lane

Part of the thirteenth century town wall (restored) runs from St. Andrew's Church south along Bath Lane to Westgate Road.

** Newcastle *(139)*, St. Nicholas Street

Under the care of the County Council of Tyne and Wear, this restored rectangular keep of three stories and many mural chambers was built originally by Henry II in 1172 to 1177. Visitors can climb to the parapets.

Newcastle Central Station *(461)*, Neville Street

Built in 1848 to 1865 to designs by John Dobson and Thomas Prosser, its exterior is an especially fine example of Victorian classical design.

Roman Catholic Cathedral *(472)*, Neville Street

A late nineteenth century building in the Victorian Gothic style designed by Augustus W. N. Pugin.

* **St. Nicholas Cathedral** *(244)*, Mosley Street

Now a cathedral, it was once one of the largest parish churches in England. Built in 1333 to 1360, the interior is essentially Curvilinear Decorated, though the lierne vault of the tower is Perpendicular. Also built within the Perpendicular period (ca. 1442), though atypical, is the famous open crown spire atop the western tower. This was no doubt the model for the more famous spire of St. Giles, Edinburgh, built somewhat later.

*** **Science Museum** *(456)*, Exhibition Park, Great North Road

An excellent museum of science and industry with emphasis on the industrial development of northeastern England. Among the many historically important exhibits are a Stephenson locomotive, the first breech-loading gun built by Sir William Armstrong, and Armstrong's first hydraulic engine.

*** **The University Museum of Antiquities** *(32, 58, 69, 88, 89)*, The Quadrangle, University of Newcastle-upon-Tyne

An outstanding museum rich in artifacts from the Mesolithic Age through the Saxon period, with special emphasis on Roman items, mostly from Hadrian's Wall, displayed here in great abundance. Also of interest is the scale-model of Hadrian's Wall and the reproduction of a third century Mithraeum.

*** **Hadrian's Wall** *(68, 89)*, 2 to 42 m. w in Northumberland and Cumbria, in vicinity of A 69 and B 6318

Commenced by the Emperor Hadrian in A.D. 122, and rebuilt many times during the following three centuries, this line of forts, fortlets, and milecastles interconnected by a high stone wall marked the frontier between Roman Britain and barbarian Caledonia except for a brief period when the line of occupation was pushed forward to the Antonine Wall across the narrow waist of Scotland. Whether considered as an engineering feat, an archaeological site, or a vantage point for viewing some of England's most spectacular scenery, it is, of all Roman ruins in Britain, the most worthy of an extended visit. At least a full day should be devoted to exploring the wall and its associated military establishments, the most important of which are listed below. All but the last are in Northumberland.

*** **Corbridge** *(Corstopitium) (69, 88)*, 17 m. w, on A 68 (87 NY 982 648)

The present remains date mostly to the third century rebuilding by the Emperor Septimius Severus and include the foundations of two granaries, a water tank, a storehouse, three temples, and a subterranean chapel. Excellent site museum whose collection includes the famous Corbridge Lion, a stone statue of a lion attacking a stag. The west tower and porch of * **St. Andrew's Church** *(123)* are of Anglo-Saxon date, but built of Roman stones from *Corstopitium*. The rest of the church is mostly thirteenth century with good Early English lancet windows. The ** **Vicar's Pele** *(171)* was built in the fourteenth century, also from Roman stones.

*** **Chesters** *(Cilernum) (69, 88)*, 21½ m. w (87 NY 911 701) AM

Foundations and lower courses of a Roman cavalry fort, commandant's house, hypocaust, barracks block, headquarters building, and a subterranean chapel. Note especially how the fort projects north of the wall, where three gateways are located for easy exit on horseback. This is the chief architectural feature distinguishing cavalry from infantry forts. Outside the fort are the abutments of a Roman bridge across the River Tyne. Just downstream (east) is a ruined bathhouse, one of the best in Britain. Note especially the niches in the stone wall which served as lockers for bathers.

* **Carrawburgh** *(Brocolita) (70)*, 24 m. w (87 NY 869 713) AM

Just to the south of the B 6318 are the foundations of a Mithraic Temple. Otherwise very little remains of the fort here.

*** **Housesteads** *(Borcovicium) (70)*, 29½ m. w (87 NY 790 687) AM, NT

One of the chief tourist attractions along Hadrian's Wall, *Borcovicium* (sometimes spelled *Vercovicium*) housed a Roman cohort of infantry. Substantial remains can be seen of the four gates, the commandant's house, hospital, and granaries. Good site museum. Marvelous views of Hadrian's Wall and the Northumberland countryside. Long climb uphill from car park.

*** **Chesterholm** *(Vindolanda) (70)*, 32 m. w (87 NY 771 664) AM

Two gates and the headquarters building survive in part from the Roman military station behind Hadrian's Wall. The bathhouse and other buildings belong to the *vicus*, the civilian settlement that grew up around the military establishment. Recent excavations have unearthed an extraordinary number of Roman domestic articles, all beautifully displayed in the site museum. On the ground is a full scale replica of a wall turret.

* **Cawfields** *(71)*, 35½ m. w (87 NY 726 669) AM

A well-preserved wall milecastle. To the south lies a good view of the Vallum.

** **Birdoswald** *(Camboglanna)* *(71, 94)* Cumbria, 42 m. w (86 NY 615 663) AM

The westernmost surviving fort on Hadrian's Wall, there are remains of the walls, two gates, headquarters building, and commandant's house. This is also the traditional site of King Arthur's last battle in the early sixth century.

SOUTH SHIELDS

Roman Remains Park *(72)*, Baring Street

Mostly foundations of the granaries and other buildings of *Arbeia*, a Roman fort and supply station on the south shore of Tynemouth, from which the Emperor Severus sailed in his expedition against Scotland. Maintained by the county council of Tyne and Wear, the site lacks explanatory signposts, and the site museum has little or no instructional material. Located in a shabby industrial district, the site is extremely difficult to find.

SUNDERLAND

* **Monkwearmouth Station** *(461)*, Bridge Street

Opened in 1848 and designed by Thomas Moore, this is a charming Victorian neoclassical structure displaying both the Ionic and Doric orders. The station now houses a railway museum with a restored booking office and rolling stock in the grounds outside.

* **St. Peter's, Monkwearmouth** *(118)*, St. Peter's Way, off Dame Dorothy Street, ¼ m. e of North Bridge Street

Now situated in an area of urban blight, this is the much renovated church of the abbey founded by Benedict Biscop in 674 and is the scene of the Venerable Bede's novitiate. Of the original church, only the west wall and part of the tower remain. In the barrel-vaulted porch are carvings made by stonemasons imported by Benedict from France. Inside are showcases with several rare examples of Saxon stonework. In the modern chapter house is a good information center.

* **Washington Old Hall** *(305)*, 5 m. w; in Washington Village, Washington New Town, District 4; off A 1231; NT

The family home of the ancestors of George Washington from the twelfth century to the fifteenth, most of the present small manor house was built in the seventeenth century after the property had passed to the bishop of Durham. Restored by the National Trust, this is something of a shrine for American tourists, even though the connection with the first president of the United States is remote.

TYNEMOUTH

** Tynemouth Priory *(249)*, town center

Of the Benedictine abbey founded in 1090 by the earl of Northumberland, nothing survives. The high east end of the existing ruined church is Early English, dating from the early thirteenth century and the Percy chapel (Perpendicular) from the fifteenth. Very little remains of the claustral buildings except parts of the thirteenth century east range with its reredorter. The monastery gatehouse was rebuilt in the 1380s and again in the 1560s as a coastal defense station and has all the earmarks of a ruined castle. This is a very attractive ruin.

NORTHUMBERLAND
ALNWICK

*** Alnwick Castle *(185, 200, 334, 397)*, town center

Much restored and still occupied by the present duke of Northumberland, this was the major seat of the Percys in the fourteenth and fifteenth centuries. The gatehouse and barbican through which the castle is entered today, date from the mid-fifteenth century; the inner gatehouse and the towers along the curtain wall to an earlier construction in the twelfth. The main building was subjected to so much renovation and restoration in the eighteenth and nineteenth centuries that its original late medieval character has been all but submerged. It is now on display as a stately home with the usual multitude of prized possessions, including a Van Dyck portrait of Queen Henrietta Maria.

*** Bamburgh Castle *(99, 139, 185, 200, 342, 409, 484)*, 16 m. ne, on B 1340

On the site of the seventh century capital of the Anglian kings of Bernicia, Henry II built here a great Norman keep, part of which is incorporated in the present building. Much restored in the late nineteenth century by Sir William (later Lord) Armstrong, it is now displayed as a stately home. There is some good Victorian furniture here and a fine collection of seventeenth century armor. The view of the Northumberland coast from the basalt rock on which the castle sits is spectacular.

** Dunstanburgh Castle *(179, 200)*, 10 m. ne, 1 m. e of B 1339 from Engleton (75 NU 258 220) AM

This is one of the most picturesque coastal castles in England, though badly ruined. Built by Henry of Lancaster in the early fourteenth century, it was refortified by John of Gaunt in the 1370s, though most of the remains date from the earlier period of construction. These consist chiefly of the gatehouse and part of the curtain wall with three of its small towers. From the car park at Craster, the mile-and-a-half walk over the moor along the coast to the castle offers as spectacular a view as any in England.

* **Elingham Castle** *(170)*, 5 m. sw on B 6341

A ruined fourteenth century rectangular pele tower.

* **Howick Hall** *(487)*, 5 m. ne, on B 1339

A splendid woodland garden with rhododendrons, azaleas, magnolias, hydrangeas, meconopsis, primulas, and peonies.

*** **Warkworth Castle** *(185)*, 6 m. s on A 1068 (75 NU 247 057) AM

A Percy stronghold from the early fourteenth century, this marvelous ruin is one of the great castles of the north. It is entered today by way of the gatehouse built in the early thirteenth century; to the left are the remains of an early fourteenth century chapel, and beyond that is the great hall, the western wall of which dates to the twelfth century. An appendage to this building is the Lion Tower, constructed in the fifteenth century and bearing on its face the Percy crest carved in high relief. Beyond it, atop the castle's ancient motte, is the great keep erected in the early fifteenth century by the first and second earls of Northumberland. It is three stories in height, shaped somewhat like a Greek cross, and hollow within so as to permit ample light through its interior windows. On the outside, all stories but the ground floor also have spacious windows. This is a telltale sign of the shift from the purely military castle architecture of the early Middle Ages to the more residential forms of the fourteenth and fifteenth centuries.

BERWICK-UPON-TWEED

Berwick Castle *(163)*, town center; AM

Very fragmentary remains of what was in the late thirteenth century the strongest royal castle in the north. Best viewed from the river bank which is accessible by footpath through the public park next to the railway station.

** **Berwick Ramparts** *(294)*, surrounding northern and eastern sides of present city center; AM

Begun in 1555, these are the best preserved of all Tudor fortifications in England. They were designed by Sir Richard Lee to conform to the contemporary Italian standards of military architecture, i.e., with angle bastions to permit enfilade artillery fire along the axis of the adjoining walls. Not completed altogether until the eighteenth century, they were never put to the test of an attack by the Scots, against whom they were intended.

Lindisfarne Castle *(485)*, 12 m. se on Holy Island, 5 m. e of Beal; NT

An Edwardian curiosity: an Elizabethan fortress remodeled by Edwin Lutyens in a style more or less medieval. Nearby is the splendid ruin of *** **Lindisfarne Priory** *(106, 249)*, (75 NU 126 418) AM. Nothing except the site itself remains of St. Aidan's monastery, sacked by Vikings in 793 and again in 875. The present ruins are those of the red sandstone church of the Benedictine priory founded here in 1083. The substantial remains still standing are those of the twelfth century west front and tower, transepts, and portions of the nave. The outline of the thirteenth to fourteenth century claustral buildings can be easily traced in the ruins. Small site museum.

Holy Island can be reached by foot, bicycle, or car across a causeway from the village of Beal, but only at low tide. Information about tides can be obtained from the Tourist Information Centres at Berwick-upon-Tweed, Alnwick, or Seahouses. The island itself, though more populated than in St. Aidan's time, is still a desolate spot and scenically awe inspiring.

** **Norham Castle** *(139, 163)*, 8 m. sw, on A 6470 (75 NT 907 476) AM

This fine ruined rectangular keep stands on the River Tweed on the border between Northumberland and Scotland. Built in the reign of Henry II by Hugh de Puiset (Pudsey), Bishop of Durham, it was besieged or captured by the Scots ten times between the twelfth and sixteenth centuries. It was the scene of Edward I's recognition of John Balliol as king of Scotland in 1293 and of the latter's submission to the English king.

Blythe

* **Seaton Deleval** *(371)*, 5 m. se, on A 190

Only partially restored after having been gutted by fire in 1822, this great gaunt classicized castle was one of Vanbrugh's last architectural triumphs. Built between 1717 and 1723, the entrance front is flanked on either side by Doric columns extending to the roof line, in turn flanked by corner octagonal towers. The architectural style is more fantastic than properly baroque. Except for a few unburned rooms in the wings, the house is an empty shell.

Haltwhistle

* **Featherstone Castle** *(170)*, 3 m. sw

A thirteenth century pele tower on the banks of the South Tyne, it was further fortified with two watch towers in the fourteenth century.

HEXHAM

* Hexham Moot Hall *(171)*, town center

This is a fifteenth century pele tower which belonged to the archbishopric of York.

*** St. Andrew's, Hexham *(118, 120, 243)*, town center

A church of unusual longevity, even for England, the crypt dates from the initial building of the monastery here by St. Wilfred in 675 and contains still older building materials quarried from the nearby ruins of *Corstopitium.* The church itself is a mix of Norman and Early English styles. Noteworthy features are the Anglo-Saxon Acca Cross; the monument to a Roman cavalry standard bearer; the Saxon stool; the twelfth century monks' staircase; and the fifteenth century pulpit, chancel screen, and misericords. Good small church museum.

* Aydon Castle *(170)*, 5 m. e, 1 m. ne of Corbridge on B 6321

A well-preserved fourteenth century pele tower, it has an inner and outer bailey, a solar with a large fireplace, and an unusual chimney with lancets.

* Clocklaw Tower *(170)*, 4 m. n, ½ m. e of A 6079

A fifteenth century pele tower.

* Halton Tower *(170)*, 4 m. ne; 1 m. n of Corbridge, e of A 68

A fifteenth century pele tower with seventeenth century additions.

* Langley Castle *(170)*, 8 m. w, 1 m. s of Haydon Bridge on A 687

A well-restored pele tower of the mid-fourteenth century, it was built by Sir Thomas Lucy, a veteran of Crecy. A portcullis defends the entrance and four protruding towers guard the face of the castle.

MORPETH

* Belsay Castle *(170)*, 10 m. sw, w of A 696

The pele tower stands behind a nineteenth century house and is three stories high, L-shaped, and has four bartizans.

ROTHBURY

All Saints Church *(120)*

Noteworthy is the baptismal font, the shaft of which consists of an Anglo-Saxon carved cross.

*** Cragside *(484)*, ½ m. e, off B 6344; NT

The most spectacular of all late Victorian country houses, this was built in the 1870s for the great armaments manufacturer, Sir William (later Lord) Armstrong to the design of Norman Shaw. The style is a curious mixture of Tudor, medieval, and modern, best described as picturesque. In its day it was very advanced, being the first private house in England to have electric wiring. It also had a passenger lift (elevator) and central heating. The surrounding pine forest was planted by Lord Armstrong.

WOOLER

* Chillingham Castle Park *(170)*, 6 m. se, 1 m. s of Chatton

The present herd of about thirty-five white cattle are the lineal descendants of wild cattle kept here for at least seven hundred years, and are possibly descended from the original wild oxen (aurochs) of prehistoric Britain. That they were maintained throughout the Middle Ages and into modern times in their undomesticated state, may have been a deliberate precaution on the part of the Lords Tankerville to prevent their being stolen by Scottish raiders and driven back across the nearby border. Mandatory guided tours are conducted by the park warden. Long walk from car park to point where cattle can be observed. About two hours should be allowed for the visit.

* Etal Castle *(171)*, 10 m. nw, ½ m. n of Ford

A substantial portion of this ruined pele tower remains standing, as well as the adjacent gatehouse to which are attached portions of the original fourteenth-century barmkin wall.

CUMBRIA
AMBLESIDE

Hardknott Castle *(Mediobogdum)* *(67)*, 10½ m. w, on mountain pass between Ravenglass and A 593, 3 m. sw of Ambleside (90/96 NY 218 015)

This partly rebuilt Roman fort dating to the first century can be reached only by way of an extremely treacherous mountain road which is frequently fogged in. Not recommended except for the adventurous.

Pike of Stickel Axe Factory *(24)*, 9 m. w, 2 m. w of terminus of B 5343 (90 NY 270 072)

On this formidable hillside is the site of a Neolithic stone quarry where rough ax heads were shaped for shipment all over Britain. For mountain climbers only.

** **Townend** *(372)*, 3 m. se, in Troutbeck, w of A 592; NT

A uniquely well preserved home of a yeoman family, built in 1623, still equipped with much of its original heavy oak furniture of Jacobean vintage.

BARROW-IN-FURNESS

*** **Furness Abbey** *(257)*, 1 m. n, off A 590 (96 SD 218 717) AM

Founded in 1124 as a Savignac monastery by Stephen of Blois (later king), it was converted to the Cistercian order in 1147. It became one of the wealthier of the Cistercian establishments in England. Only the south wall of the nave is Norman; the rest of the church is late twelfth century Transitional with fifteenth century restorations. Of the claustral buildings, only the east range survives to any height; here the Early English chapter house, the slype doorway, and the Transitional reredorter are the best preserved. Of special interest are the Perpendicular sedilia and piscina located in the choir. This is a most impressive ruin to be found in such a remote corner of England.

CARLISLE

*** **Carlisle Castle** *(137, 295, 446)*, Castle Street; AM

Situated on the top of a typical high Norman motte, this formidable-looking castle of red sandstone was many centuries a-building. The first wooden castle on the site was erected by William Rufus; in the mid-twelfth century King David of Scotland built a strong castle here which probably is incorporated into the present rectangular stone keep; the outer bailey was built between the twelfth and fourteenth centuries; the inner bailey dates from the fourteenth century; gunports were first added in the reign of Queen Elizabeth I, during which time also Mary Queen of Scots was briefly imprisoned here; the barracks blocks were built in the nineteenth century. Here also is the Museum of the Border Regiment and King's Own Royal Border Regiment, a typical regimental collection of weapons, uniforms, plate, etc.

* **Carlisle Cathedral** *(230)*, Castle Street

Founded as a priory for Augustinian regular canons, the church was begun in 1093 and achieved cathedral status in 1123. In the seventeenth century most of the nave was destroyed by Scottish invaders.

Architectural styles: nave—Norman; south transept—Norman; north transept—Decorated and Perpendicular; choir—Decorated and Perpendicular; refectory (library)—Decorated.

Special features: Curvilinear Decorated east windows.

** Tullie House Museum and Art Gallery *(71, 89, 119)*, Castle Street

An excellent museum of local history and archaeology, especially rich in Roman finds from the western end of Hadrian's Wall. Here also is a full scale model of Bewcastle Cross.

** Bewcastle Cross *(119)*, 18 m. ne, 3 m. e of B 6318 (86 NY 565 745)

In one of the most isolated and unpopulated parts of England, this fourteen-and-one-half-foot-high cross shaft stands in the church yard neighboring a much ruined border tower-castle and the scant remains of a Roman fort. Except for Ruthwell Cross in Dumfries and Galloway, Scotland, this is the best surviving Anglian cross in Britain. The "inhabited vine" stone carving is magnificent, as is the figure of Christ on the west face. The monument dates from the seventh century.

** Lanercost Priory *(164, 252)*, 12 m. ne, 3 m. n of A 69 from Brampton (86 NY 556 637) AM

An Augustinian establishment of about 1166, the twelfth century nave is incorporated into the parish church. The choir of the abbey church is a ruin, as are the claustral buildings of red sandstone. Of the latter, the west range is complete, the east range is represented by foundations only, while the south range still has the undercroft of the canons' frater. The priory is beautifully sited on the banks of the Irthing River almost in the shadow of Hadrian's Wall. Here Edward I took shelter just before his death at nearby Burgh-on-Sands during his aborted final invasion of Scotland in July 1307.

* Newton Arlosh Tower *(171)*, 13 m. w on B 5307

Adjoining the parish church, this is an early fourteenth century pele tower built by the monks of Holmculgram Abbey. For security it was constructed without exterior entrances and is accessible only through the interior of the church.

COCKERMOUTH

* Wordsworth House *(414)*, High Street; NT

Built in 1745, this is the birthplace of William Wordsworth, born in 1770. His much beloved sister Dorothy was born here the following year. The house contains a number of memorabilia vaguely associated with the poet's life. Attractive, but not very exciting.

CONISTON

Brantwood *(472)*, 2 m. se, e of Coniston Water

The residence of John Ruskin after 1871, an undistinguished house with a marvelous view of Coniston Water.

DALTON-IN-FURNESS

* Dalton Tower *(171)*, town center; NT

A restored fourteenth century pele tower which later served as the court of the head of Furness Abbey and still later as a jail. Inside are some fairly good pieces of sixteenth and seventeenth century armor. Key at No. 18 Marketplace.

EGREMONT

* Gosforth Cross *(120)*, 6 m. s, e of Gosforth village

The best preserved Viking Cross on the British mainland (as distinct from the Isle of Man), this fourteen-and-one-half foot wheel-headed (mis-named Celtic) cross stands in the churchyard just east of the village. It probably dates from the ninth century. Its carvings are typical of that mix of Nordic and Christian Celtic styles called Hiberno-Norse. This is one of the few relics of the significant, but largely unrecorded, migration of Scandinavian settlers from Ireland into northwestern England in the ninth and tenth centuries.

* Muncaster Castle *(483)*, 16 m. s, on A 596 at Ravenglass

A neo-Gothic "castle" built around a fourteenth century pele tower in the 1860s by Anthony Salvin for the fourth Lord Muncaster. Good sixteenth and seventeenth century furniture and a fine woodland garden featuring azaleas and rhododendron. Near the Cumbrian coast.

GRASMERE

*** Dove Cottage *(414)*, south edge of town

This tiny and altogether charming cottage, along with the museum next door, is among the very best literary sites in Britain from the point of view of the visitor. The museum contains many Wordsworth manuscripts and editions. The house is furnished mostly with the poet's belongings, or at least with contemporary pieces. The short conducted tour (traffic would be otherwise unmanageable) is highly informative, sensitive, and witty. The management of this site is a model of graciousness combined with efficiency. Few stately homes, for all their large staffs and high entrance fees, do as well. One doesn't have to be an admirer of Words-worth's poetry to enjoy this place.

* Rydal Mount *(414)*, 2 m. s, e of A 591

William Wordsworth's home from 1813 until his death in 1850. The garden affords glimpses of Lake Windermere. Many memorabilia of the poet and his wife and sister.

KENDAL

Kendal Castle *(279)*, town center

This much ruined medieval castle was the birthplace of Catherine Parr, Henry VIII's sixth and final queen.

* Arnside Tower *(171)*, 10 m. s on B 5282

Overlooking Morecambe Bay, this is a badly ruined three-story pele tower on a beautiful site.

*** Levens Hall *(171, 342, 374)*, 5 m. s, w of A 6

Here is a splendid Elizabethan mansion attached to a fourteenth century pele tower. The interior rooms are distinguished by their sixteenth century Spanish tooled leather paneling, mullioned windows, and plasterwork. Their furniture is mostly from the late seventeenth century. The superb topiary garden dates from 1690 and was designed by Guillaume Beaumont, a disciple of the great French landscape architect, Le Nôtre who was responsible for the gardens at Versailles. For children young and old there is a collection of nineteenth century steam engines, including a steam calliope which lends an exotic carnival note to an otherwise very stately home.

** Sizergh Castle *(171, 487)*, 4 m. s, w of A 6; NT

Owned for seven hundred years by the Strickland family (connected by marriage to the Washingtons of County Durham), the present house consists of a mid-fourteenth century pele tower flanked by Elizabethan wings. The interior is noted for its fine sixteenth century carved oak paneling and its oak furniture of the sixteenth and seventeenth centuries. The terraces date from the eighteenth century, but the remarkable rock garden is modern. Visiting hours restricted.

KESWICK

** The Carles, Castlerigg *(41)*, 1½ m. e (90 NY 293 236) AM, NT

Situated with the hills of the Lake District as a backdrop, this Bronze Age flattened circle has thirty-eight surviving stones with an interior rectangle of ten. Beautiful view.

PENRITH

** Brougham Castle *(139)*, 2½ m. se, e of junction of A 66 and B 6262 (90 NY 537 290)

The massive four-story ruined red sandstone keep was built about 1170 probably by Hugh d'Albini. The gatehouse dates from the late thirteenth or fourteenth century. Most of the rest of these rather substantial ruins can be attributed to Lady Anne Clifford in the seventeenth century.

* Brough Castle *(139)*, 20 m. se, on A 66 (91 NY 791 141) AM

The surviving ruins consist of the keep and curtain walls of a castle built in the twelfth century and restored by Lady Anne Clifford in the seventeenth. Good view of the Pennines.

*** Long Meg and Her Daughters *(41)*, 8 m. ne, 2½ m. n of A 686 from Langwathby (91 NY 571 373)

A flattened Bronze Age circle with twenty-seven surviving stones all nearly ten feet high. These are the daughters. Long Meg is a single stone about twelve feet high lying about sixty feet to the southwest. On one of her faces is a series of cup-and-ring markings peculiar to this part of England, as well as to Scotland.

Shap Abbey *(253)*, 11 m. s, w of A 6 (90 NY 548 153) AM

Of this small Premonstratensian house founded in 1201, not much has survived except the sixteenth century west front with its high tower and the foundations and lower walls of the claustral buildings.

Yanwath Hall *(171)*, 2 m. s

A fine pele tower altered in Elizabethan times.

ULVERSTON

Gleaston Tower *(171)*, 6 m. s, ½ m. w of A 5087

A ruined fourteenth century pele tower.

** Swarthmoor Hall *(348)*, ¼ m. sw

A sixteenth century manor house, owned in the mid-seventeenth century by Judge Thomas Fell, whose wife Margaret turned it into a sort of headquarters for the Quaker missionary movement after George Fox's first visit here in 1652. Owned today by the London Quarterly Meeting of the Society of Friends, it is a well-preserved house containing much seventeenth century furniture, some of it belonging to the Fells or to Fox himself. Well-informed and gracious guides are provided. Swarthmore College in Pennsylvania was named after the house.

* Swarthmoor Quaker Meeting House *(358)*, ½ m. sw, near Swarthmoor Hall

This is a barn converted into a meetinghouse by George Fox himself in 1688. The benches are arranged in a square facing the center, and there is a gallery in the rear. A key to the front door can be obtained at a neighboring house.

WINDERMERE

* Holker Hall *(484, 487)*, 14 m. s, on B 5278

Built in 1871 by Paley and Austin for the seventh duke of Devonshire in a vaguely Tudor style, the house is notable chiefly for the fine collection of Victorian furnishings. Good garden in the Victorian manner.

* Windermere Steamboat Museum *(462)*, Bowness, Rayrigg Road

This is a unique collection of lake steamers and other boats, including some very early steam launches.

SOUTH AND CENTRAL WALES

GWENT
ABERGAVENNY

* Grosmont Castle *(151)*, 10 m. ne; on B 4347, e of A 465 (161 SO 405 244) AM

This is the most ruined of the Three Castles guarding the Monnow valley owned by Hubert de Burgh, justiciar of England during the minority of Henry III. The oldest part is the Great Hall, built about 1210 as a residence. The single ward has a typical early thirteenth century gatehouse flanked by cylindrical towers, one of which abuts the hall. Three additional mural towers defend the curtain wall. These and the gatehouse belong to the mid-thirteenth century rebuilding by Hubert de Burgh.

** Llanthony Priory *(256)*, 11 m. n, on B 4423 (171 SO 289 278) AM

Here is the substantial ruin of a twelfth century church built for the Augustinian canons who established a house here about 1100 under the patronage of Hugh de Lacy. The building is an excellent specimen of the Transitional style of architecture, especially noticeable in the west front and flanking towers, the central tower, and choir. The nearby hotel incorporates the prior's lodgings, and the parish church was probably the infirmary.

*** Raglan Castle *(191)*, 9 m. se, ¼ m. s of A 40 (161 SO 415 083) AM

The South Gate and ruined polygonal great tower, known as the yellow tower of Gwent from the color of its stone, were built in the early fifteenth century by William ap Thomas. His son, Sir William Herbert, is responsible for the adjacent Fountain Court. A later owner, the third earl of Worcester, added the Pitched Stone Court in Elizabethan times. In 1646 the castle was seized by a parliamentary army under Sir Thomas Fairfax and badly slighted. Substantial portions of the exterior walls remain, however, all well-equipped with arrow slits, gunports, and other defensive accouterments. Altogether, though built at a time when castles were losing their military *raison d'être*, this was the mighty fortress that it still appears to be.

* **Skenfrith Castle** *(151)*, 10 m. ne, on B 4521 (161 SO 457 202) AM, NT

The smallest of the Three Castles, it was built in the early thirteenth century, probably by Hubert de Burgh, the justiciar. The well-preserved ruin consists of a round keep, not unlike that at Pembroke Castle, surrounded by a rectangular curtain wall with a round tower at each corner.

** **White Castle** *(151)*, 4 m. ne, between B 4233 and B 4521 (161 SO 380 168) AM

One of the Three Castles granted to Hubert de Burgh, justiciar of England during the minority of Henry III, this well-preserved ruin is an early thirteenth century example of a castle of *enceinte*. The inner ward is hexagonal with cylindrical mural towers at each angle and two gateways, that on the north protected by a large outer ward surrounded by curtain walls. The westernmost of the two towers guarding the main gate can be climbed for a superb view.

CHEPSTOW

*** **Chepstow Castle** *(132, 151)*, town center (162 ST 533 941) AM

A splendid ruined castle overlooking the River Wye, constructed in several stages from the eleventh century through the thirteenth. The central rectangular stone keep, called the Great Tower, was built by William fitz Osbern, earl of Hereford, ca. 1088; William Marshal and his son added the eastern and western gatehouses and Marten's Tower in the early thirteenth century. The domestic buildings on the north side of the lower bailey were constructed in the reign of Edward I.

* **Chepstow Town Walls** *(132, 206)*, (162 ST 533 937) AM

Of thirteenth century construction, these have survived better than most medieval town walls.

** **Caerwent** *(84)*, 4 m. sw, s of A 48 (171 ST 470 905) AM

Substantial remains of *Venta Silurum*, the *civitas* of the *Silures*. The town walls and bastions of this frontier Roman city are especially impressive. Unfortunately there is no site museum and no signposts to help the visitor understand what he is seeing.

* Caldicot Castle *(140)*, 5 m. sw, on B 4245

This is a much restored castle with a round keep built probably by Humphrey de Bohun in the second half of the twelfth century.

* Offa's Dyke *(102)*, 5 m. n, ½ s of Brockweir (165 ST 543 005)

A small section of the southern end of the ninth century barrier rampart between Mercia and Wales, lying just across the River Wye from Tintern Abbey; reached by footpath from Brockweir village.

*** Tintern Abbey *(255)*, 4 m. n, on A 48 (162 SO 533 000) AM

Founded as a Cistercian monastery in 1113 by Walter de Clare of Chepstow Castle, the present ruins date mostly from a rebuilding by Roger Bigod, earl of Norfolk, in the last three decades of the thirteenth century. Owing to its location among the rocky cliffs of the River Wye and to the publicity given it by the poet William Wordsworth, Tintern is among the best known and most visited of medieval abbey ruins. Chief among its attractions is the high-walled Decorated church with most of its intricate window tracery still intact. Much less remains of the claustral buildings, which lie north of the church rather than in the customary southern location.

MONMOUTH

* Monmouth Castle *(188, 343)*, Castle Hill; AM

Once a great stronghold of marcher lords, all that remains of the twelfth century castle are the broken walls of the Norman keep (the Great Tower) and a portion of the great hall running at right angles to it. The residence at the Great Castle House is a handsome structure built in 1673 and now used as an officers' mess by the Royal Monmouthshire Engineer Militia. The old castle is renowned as the birthplace of Henry of Monmouth (b. 1387), Prince of Wales and later King Henry V. His statue (not a likeness) can be seen in Agincourt Square. Already in a decaying condition by the sixteenth century, the castle was slighted in 1647 by Cromwell's troops.

NEWPORT

*** Caerleon *(Isca)* *(58, 65)*, 2 m. n on B 4236 (171 ST 338 903) AM

The best-preserved of the three great Roman legionary forts, *Isca* was the headquarters of the 2nd Legion. Surviving portions include fragments of the wall; Prysg Field containing foundations and lower courses of a barracks block with its latrine; and the now grass-covered oval rampart where a fine amphitheater was situated. Next to the parish church at the head of the lane running into the fortress is a small but instructive site museum.

SOUTH GLAMORGAN
CARDIFF

*** Cardiff Castle *(141, 446, 484)*, Castle Street

The polygonal shell keep on top of a Norman motte was built in the late twelfth century, and enlarged in the late thirteenth by Gilbert de Clare, who also rebuilt the gatehouse towers and the great central wall linking the keep with the Black Tower and cutting the castle grounds into two wards. The southwest corner was rebuilt in the 1860s by the combined efforts of the third marquess of Bute and his architect, William Burges, both Catholic converts and ardent Gothic revivalists. The Arab Room, Banqueting Hall, Chapel, Chaucer Room, Dining Room, Roof Garden, and Library are all splendid examples of High Victorian taste at its most dazzling. The castle also houses the Welsh Regiment Museum with the usual array of uniforms, weapons, plate, etc.

*** City Hall *(477)*, Cathays Park

This is a fine example of Victorian baroque, designed by Lanchester and Rickards in 1904, with a dome surmounted by the Welsh dragon and an impressive clock tower.

*** The National Museum of Wales *(26, 32, 56, 61, 115, 119, 431, 432)*, Cathays Park

One of the truly great museums of Britain. The departments of special interest to students of British prehistory and history are:

Department of Archaeology: Good Welsh finds from all prehistoric periods; especially notable are the Bronze Age gold ornaments; the Iron Age firedogs; samples of La Tène ornamental metalwork; and especially the Llyn Cerrig-bach hoard from Anglesey. A special gallery contains early Christian crosses and other monuments, mostly original, but some casts.

Department of Art: Here are a few paintings by J.M.W. Turner, though pride of place goes to the Davies Collection of French Impressionists.

Department of Industry: One of the best industrial museums in Britain. Notable are the coal-mining gallery; model steam engines; a full-sized tilt hammer; and numerous ship models.

* St. John's Church *(245)*, Church Street

A fifteenth century church built on thirteenth century foundations, the style is essentially Perpendicular with the usual high tower at the west end. Noteworthy are the fifteenth century front, the clerestory windows, and the Herbert family monument.

*** Castell Coch *(484)*, 5 m. n, ¼ m. e of A 470 from Tongwynlais (171 ST 131 826) Department of the Environment

A thirteenth century castle restored and repaired in the mid-nineteenth century by William Burges for the third marquess of Bute in the High Victorian Gothic style to which both were devoted. Of special interest are the hall, drawing room, Lord Bute's bedroom, and Lady Bute's bedroom. This is a masterpiece of Gothic fancy.

Dinas Powys *(112)*, 5 m. sw, ½ m. n of A 4055 from Dinas Powis village (171 ST 150 718)

Excavations at this small Iron Age hill fort have revealed Dark Age occupation, probably by a Welsh chieftain who refortified the site in the sixth or seventh century. Not much to see.

* Llandaff Cathedral *(240)*, 2½ m. w

A secular cathedral since 1107, the earliest part of the present building dates from 1193. The cathedral was much damaged by a German landmine in 1941.

   Architectural styles: west front—Early English; southwest tower—Early English; northwest tower—Perpendicular; nave—Early English; choir—Early English (west end) and Curvilinear Decorated (east end); lady chapel—Geometric Decorated; chapter house—Early English; St. David's Welsh Regiment Memorial Chapel—Modern.

   Special features: Epstein aluminum *Majestas* in nave; Rossetti Triptych; Pre-Raphaelite windows in south aisle.

St. Lythan's Burial Chamber *(20)*, 8 m. sw, 2 m. s of A 48 from St. Nicolas (171 ST 101 723) AM

Originally a Severn-Cotswold Neolithic gallery grave, the present small cromlech consists of three uprights and a capstone.

* Tinkinswood Burial Chamber *(20)*, 7 m. sw, 1 m. s of A 48 from St. Nicholas (171 ST 092 733) AM

The remains of a Severn-Cotswold Neolithic gallery grave, the cromlech now consists of five uprights supporting a forty-ton capstone.

*** Welsh Folk Museum *(310, 427)*, 4½ m. w, at St. Fagan's

An outstanding open-air museum which includes a fine E-shaped Tudor mansion called **St. Fagan's Castle** *(310)*; the Estair Moel Woollen Mill, complete with a working water wheel; a chapel from the Vale of Teifi; a slate-quarryman's cottage; and miscellaneous other items of great interest to the student of Welsh national culture.

MID-GLAMORGAN
BRIDGEND

* Coity Castle *(136)*, ½ m. n, e of A 4061 (170 SS 923 816) AM

The ruined rectangular keep and part of the east curtain wall are all that remains of the castle built by the Turbervilles in the early twelfth century. The rectangular outer ward and the connecting gateway to the original inner ward date from the fourteenth century.

* Coity Church *(244)*, 3 m. n, e of A 4061

An unusually good example of Welsh Decorated architecture, this is a fourteenth century church with a fifteenth century spire.

* St. Crallo, Coychurch *(244)*, 1½ m. e, on A 48

A Welsh Decorated church, noteworthy chiefly for the geometric designs of the windows.

** Ewenny Priory *(254)*, 2 m. s, on B 4265 (170 SS 912 778) AM

This was a Benedictine monastery founded about 1120 by the lord of nearby Ogmore Castle. Though all the claustral buildings have disappeared, the twelfth century priory church is now parochial. It is one of the best examples of military/ecclesiastical architecture in the country and stands as silent testimony to the lawlessness of Wales and the role of the church in its suppression. Of special interest are the arrow slits and crenellation of the central tower and south transepts. The ruined but substantial precinct wall tells the same story.

* Ogmore Castle *(136)*, 3½ m. sw on B 4524 (170 SS 882 769) AM

Overlooking a ford in the Ewenny River, famous for its stepping stones, stands this ruined early twelfth century rectangular keep inside a curtain wall built in the thirteenth century.

CAERPHILLY

*** Caerphilly Castle *(158)*, in village center, 6½ m. n of Cardiff on A 469 (171 ST 155 871) AM

Begun by Gilbert de Clare, earl of Gloucester, in 1271, the grounds of this well-preserved castle ruin are larger than those of any other castle in Britain (thirty acres) except for Windsor. The castle consists of two concentric rectangles of curtain walls; the outer one is very low with no mural towers except for two pairs of twin towers at each gatehouse, east and west; the inner curtain is high, also with two twin-towered gatehouses as well as four huge cylindrical towers at the four angles of the wall. Inside the inner ward is the great hall built in the fourteenth century. The outer curtain was originally surrounded by a lake, now partly dry. To the west is a great stone horn-work. Directly opposite, to the east of the outer curtain, is the great barrage, a high crenellated wall stretching north and south for some 340 yards. This shelters a raised earthen platform which is, in turn, separated from the eastern gateway by a moat over which a drawbridge extended. Today's visitor enters the castle by way of a bridge across what remains of the lake, through the barrage gatehouse, over another bridge across the moat, and into the outer ward through its eastern gateway.

WEST GLAMORGAN

NEATH

* **Neath Abbey** *(255)*, 1 m. w, off A 465 (170 SS 738 974) AM

Originally a Savignac monastery founded about 1130, it was taken over by the Cistercians, probably in 1147. Though much begrimed by reason of its location in this heavily industrialized area of South Wales, a fair portion of the abbey remains standing: the church walls, much of the lay brothers' west range of claustral buildings, and the undercroft of the frater. The abbot's house to the east was incorporated into a seventeenth century mansion.

PORT TALBOT

* **Margam Stones Museum** *(115, 119)*, 3 m. se, e of M 4 (170 SS 801 864) AM

Good collection of early Christian crosses and memorial stones including some with Ogam incisions.

SWANSEA

* **Cheriton Church** *(243)*, 15 m. w, near nw point of Gower Peninsula

A small thirteenth century Early English church with an axial tower over the choir and a fine south doorway.

* **Clyne Castle** *(487)*, 3 m. sw, on A 4067

A fine woodland garden, noted especially for its rhododendrons.

* **Maen Ceti** *(21)*, 14 m. w, 1 m. ne of Reynoldstone (159 SS 491 905)

Otherwise known as Arthur's Stone, this unusual cromlech consists of a huge glacial boulder underpinned with nine uprights.

* **Parc Cwm Chambered Tomb** *(19)*, 10 m w, n of A 4118 from Parkhill (159 SS 537 898) AM

Also known as Parc le Breos, a classic Severn-Cotswold Neolithic gallery grave with a horned forecourt and a central gallery transepted by two pairs of side chambers.

POWYS
BRECON

* **Brecknock Museum** *(115)*, Captain's Walk

Good museum of local history and genealogy with a small collection of Ogam stones.

Museum of the South Wales Borderers *(446)*, The Barracks

A good regimental museum with the usual array of weapons, uniforms, plate, etc.

Brecon Gaer *(67)*, 1 m. w, 1 m. s of Battle (160 SO 003 296) AM

Difficult to find, here are the substantial remains of an auxiliary Roman fort, including foundations of two gates and the enclosing wall.

Cerrig Duon *(42)*, 12 m. w, 2 m. s of A 40 from Trecastle (160 SN 852 206)

A Bronze Age circle of twenty stones, situated on the west bank of the River Tawe near its source. Hard to find.

Mynydd-Bach Trecastell Circles *(42)*, 12 m. w, 2 m. sw of A 40 from Trecastle (160 SN 833 311)

Two Bronze Age circles, one with fifteen, the other with five remaining stones. Hard to find.

Nant Tarw *(42)*, 13 m. w, 3 m. sw of A 40 from Trecastle (160 SN 819 258)

Two small Bronze Age circles with about fifteen stones surviving, situated near the headwaters of the River Usk. Hard to find.

CRICKHOWELL

* **Tretower Castle and Court** *(153, 194)*, 4 m. n, on A 479 (161 SO 186 211) AM

This thirteenth century castle ruin is unusual in that it has a cylindrical keep built inside a shell keep. It is well preserved, as is the adjacent ruined manor house, Tretower Court, built in the fourteenth and fifteenth centuries by Sir Roger Vaughan and his son, Sir Thomas. The house lacked significant defenses, in contrast to the nearby castle. The court has been partly restored and reroofed.

LLANDRINDOD WELLS

* **Castell Collon** *(67)*, 1½ m. n (137 SO 055 628)

Fairly substantial remains of a Roman auxiliary fort, including foundations of walls, headquarters building, commandant's house, granary, and bathhouse.

MACHYNLLETH

Owain Glyndwr Institute *(186)*, Maengwyn Street

The probable site of a parliament convened by Owain Glyndwr in 1404 to declare Welsh autonomy and name him supreme Prince of Wales.

NEWTOWN

Dolforwyn Castle *(156)*, in Abermule, 4 m. ne, on A 483 (136 SO 152 850) AM

A much ruined castle, originally a stronghold of Llywelyn ap Gruffydd, the last and greatest of the independent Princes of Wales. Only fragments remain of the rectangular ward with a cylindrical keep partly recessed into the east curtain wall.

TALGARTH

Talgarth Parish Church *(420)*, town center

Noteworthy as the site of the conversion and burial place of Howel Harris (1714 to 1753), one of the founders of the Methodist movement in Wales.

Bronllys Castle *(140)*, 1 m. nw, on A 438 (161 SO 149 347) AM (exterior only)

A ruined round keep about eighty feet high, built on an early Norman motte. The keep dates from the late twelfth century.

* **Ty-Isaf Chambered Tomb** *(19)*, 4 m. s, e of A 479 (162 SO 182 290)

A Severn-Cotswold covered gallery grave with a false portal and burial chambers on the sides and at the end of the tomb.

WELSHPOOL

Breiddin Hill *(49)*, 6½ m. ne, 2½ m. n of A 458 from Trewern (126 SJ 297 143)

An Iron Age hill fort overlooking the Severn near Offa's Dyke, with two ramparts covering the southern and eastern approaches to this formidable mountain peak. Access is difficult.

Montgomery Castle *(130, 151)*, 7 m. s on B 4388, ½ m. n of Montgomery (137 SO 221 967) AM

The high motte called Hen Domen (the Old Mound) is the site of a motte-and-bailey castle built by Roger de Montgomery about 1072. The scanty stone ruins are those of the third castle built on the site in the late thirteenth century.

* **Offa's Dyke** *(102)*, 5 m. s, e of B 4388 just s of Kingswood (126 SJ 235 012)

A segment of the ninth century rampart between Mercia and Wales, easily observable from the road.

** **Powis Castle** *(311, 374)*, 1 m. sw; NT

A late medieval castle "modernized" in the sixteenth century, with the insertion of large Tudor windows, a long gallery, and plastered ceilings, it was further remodeled in the nineteenth century. The noteworthy feature here is not the house but the gardens. They were laid out in the 1790s by the earl of Rochford in the Italian manner with huge stone-buttressed terraces falling away in front of the house, ornamented with balustrades, urns, and lead figures of shepherds and shepherdesses. Of the beautiful plantings, the most noticeable are the huge yews and the great box hedges.

* **Welshpool and Llanfair Railway** *(457)*, 9 m. w on A 458 at Llanfair Caereinion

This is the eastern terminus of a short narrow-gauge railway built in 1903 from Llanfair to Sylfaen, eleven miles round trip. Excursion trains run daily from mid-July to early September.

DYFED
ABERYSTWYTH

* **Aberystwyth Castle** *(168, 186)*, Castle Grounds south of University College of Wales

Probably designed by Master James of St. George for Edward I, this much ruined castle was typically concentric, roughly diamond shaped. A fair length of the outer curtain wall survives, as does a massive cylindrical tower at the west corner. On the northwest face of the inner curtain there is a large semicylindrical tower pierced by a postern gate with steps descending from the inner ward to a second passage in the outer. Part of the castle's ruined condition can be attributed to the successful siege conducted in 1408 by Prince Henry (later Henry V) when the stronghold was briefly occupied by Owain Glyndwr.

University College of Wales *(469)*, King Street

Founded in 1872 and incorporated as the senior constituent college of the University of Wales in 1893, the university's main building was originally the Castle House Hotel, built in 1864, a splendid example of Victorian Gothic.

* **Vale of Rheidol Railway** *(457)*, British Rail, town center

A narrow gauge railway linking Aberystwyth with Devil's Bridge, twelve miles inland. Frequent excursions. Fine views.

* **Llandbadarn Fawr Church** *(243)*, 1½ m. e, on A 44

A restored Norman church noted chiefly for its south doorway with a well executed carved tympanum.

CARDIGAN

* **Cilgerran Castle** *(153)*, 4 m. e, s of A 484 (145 SN 195 431) AM, NT

A lovely ruin standing high on a rocky promontory overlooking the River Teifi, its two huge cylindrical towers in the inner ward resemble the great tower of Pembroke Castle and may indeed have been built by one of the latter's custodians, William Marshal's son William, who captured the castle from the Welsh in 1223.

** **Pentre Ifan** *(21)*, 11 m. sw, 1½ m. n of B 4329 from Brynberian (145 SN 099 370) AM

Though poorly signposted, this is one of Wales's more impressive cromlechs, with four high-pointed uprights supporting (apparently precariously) a seventeen-ton capstone. The view of the Nevern valley is splendid.

* St. Brynach's, Nevern *(115,120)*, 8 m. sw in Nevern on B 4582

Though otherwise undistinguished, this small church is the repository of several important early Christian stones, including the Ogam stone in the nave; an early Christian crucifixion stone in the window sill of the south transept; an Ogam stone with Latin inscriptions; and a tenth century cross, the last two in the churchyard.

* St. Dogmael's Abbey *(254)*, 1 m. w, off B 4546 (145 SN 163 458) AM

A much ruined monastery founded in 1115 for Tironian monks, the present remains consist mostly of portions of the church, chapter house, and frater.

* St. Dogmael's Church *(115)*, 1 m. w on B 4546

At the west end of the nave is the Segranus Stone in both Ogam and Latin, which first enabled scholars to decipher the Ogam script.

CARMARTHEN

* Carmarthen Museum *(85,112,115)*, ½ m. e in Abergwili on A 40

A good newly organized museum of local history and archaeology with emphasis on Roman finds from the nearby *civitas* of *Moridunum.*

Roman Amphitheatre *(85)*, northern edge of town

Insubstantial remains from *Moridunum, civitas* of the *Demetae.* More may be revealed as excavations continue.

* Llanstephan Castle *(159)*, 8½ m. s, on B 4312, ½ m. s of Llanstephan village (159 SN 351 101) AM

The substantial ruins of this late thirteenth century castle stand on a magnificent site overlooking the beaches of the Tywi estuary. Two sides of the rectangular inner ward are protected by steep cliffs falling down to the river; the other two by an outer curtain wall with mural towers and a great gatehouse. The remains consist mostly of the great gatehouse, the western outer curtain wall with its mural towers, and the smaller gatehouse into the inner ward.

HAVERFORDWEST

Pembrokeshire Museum *(446)*, The Castle

A museum of local history containing, among other things, the regimental relics of the Pembroke Yeomanry.

*** St. Mary's Church *(243)*, High Street

This is one of the best examples of Early English church architecture in Wales. The west window consists of three fine lancets; the east window displays lovely plate tracery. The north aisle, clerestories, and nave roof date from the fifteenth century.

KIDWELLY

** Kidwelly Castle *(159)*, town center (159 SN 409 071) AM

This well-preserved ruin is a late thirteenth century concentric castle consisting of a rectangle inside a semicircle, the straight wall of the outer curtain hugging the River Gwendraeth. The inner ward has cylindrical towers at each angle and contains fairly complete remains of the domestic buildings, the most interesting of which is the chapel built on a scarp projecting over the river. The semi-circular outer ward has two gatehouses; the larger on the south was reconstructed in the early fifteenth century and is the most elaborate part of the whole structure. This placing of the most heavily defended gatehouse in the outer, rather than the inner, curtain wall is unusual. This is the entrance by which today's visitor will approach the castle.

LLANDEILO

* Carreg Cennen Castle *(159)*, 4½ m. se on unmarked road through Ffairfach and Trapp (159 SN 668 191) AM

A much ruined castle consisting of a rectangular inner ward, two sides of which rest against the edges of a steep cliff, the other two sides covered by an outer curtain wall. The most interesting feature here is the long barbican passage with three sets of drawbridges protecting the main gatehouse to the inner ward.

* Talley Abbey *(256)*, 8 m. n, on B 4302 (146 SN 632 327) AM

Not much remains of this Premonstratensian house (unique in Wales) founded by Rhys ap Gruffydd in the 1180s. The claustral buildings have disappeared, but of the Transitional church, the crossing and east end stand fairly high in a plot of land surrounded by farm buildings.

NARBERTH

* Llawhaden Castle *(240)*, 4 m. nw (158 SN 073 175) AM

The substantial ruins of a remote country palace of the Bishops of St. David's, built in the fourteenth century, consist mostly of the court with its usual range of domestic buildings, protected at each corner by a polygonal tower, and approached by a high gateway with a flying arch.

PEMBROKE

*** Pembroke Castle *(151)*, town center

One of the greatest of the pre-Edwardian castles in Wales, Pembroke's great cylindrical keep, eighty feet in height, was probably built in the first years of the thirteenth century by William Marshal, earl of Pembroke and Striguil. The outer ward probably belongs to the later thirteenth century. Of particular interest are the main gatehouse with slots for three portcullises; the external barbican, which would have forced attackers to make an oblique approach to the main gate; and the five cylindrical mural towers.

Pembroke Town Wall *(206)*, town center

A fragmentary relic of the medieval town wall.

** Carew Castle *(272)*, 4 m. e, n of A 4075 (157 SN 047 037) AM

A well-preserved ruined castle, built mostly in the late thirteenth century, but enlarged in the late fifteenth with the addition of the great hall constructed by Sir Rhys ap Thomas whose armed aid to Henry of Richmond in 1485 was instrumental in his capturing the throne as Henry VII. This was the scene of a famous tourney in 1507, an extravaganza of a type rare in Wales.

** Lamphey Palace *(240)*, 3 m. w, n of A 4139 (158 SN 018 009) AM

A ruined rural palace of the Bishops of St. David's, the so-called camera dates from the thirteenth century and the great hall, with an open parapet like that of Bishop Gower's Palace at St. David's, from the fourteenth. There are also scanty remains of the country house into which the palace was converted after the Dissolution under Henry VIII. This was the residence of Richard Devereux and early home of his grandson Robert, earl of Essex, favorite of Queen Elizabeth I.

*** Manorbier Castle *(139,239)*, 8½ m. w on B 4585

The original rectangular keep, called the Square Tower, was built in the mid-twelfth century and was the birthplace of Gerald Barri (Giraldus Cambrensis) the noted Welsh chronicler. Most of the castle dates from the thirteenth century. It has been restored and is beautifully maintained, though some might find the costumed dummies of medieval personages scattered here and there to be somewhat contrived. In a room above the main gateway is an exhibit demonstrating how a portcullis was raised and lowered. Fine view of the Pembrokeshire coast.

St. David's

** St. David's Cathedral *(240)*, town center

Dedicated to the patron saint of Wales, it is the oldest cathedral in that country. Established in the early twelfth century as a foundation for secular canons, the church's earliest building date is 1180.

Architectural styles: west front—nineteenth century restoration (Sir George Gilbert Scott); nave—Norman but with Decorated windows; central tower—Decorated (middle stage); transepts—thirteenth century but in Norman and Transitional style; choir—thirteenth century but in Norman and Transitional style with Decorated windows; retrochoir (Bishop Vaughan's Chapel)—Perpendicular; lady chapel—twentieth century restoration; St. Thomas Chapel—Decorated.

Special features: fourteenth century rood screen; choir stalls and misericords; bishop's throne; thirteenth century shrine of St. David; recumbent effigy of Rhys ap Gruffydd (?); ruins of fourteenth century College of St. Mary north of nave.

** Bishop's Palace *(240)*, town center

This splendid red sandstone ruin outshines the nearby cathedral to which it belonged. Wall, hall, solar, chapel, and gatehouse were built in the late thirteenth century by Bishop Thomas Beck; great hall and arcaded parapet by Bishop Gower in the early fourteenth. An excellent illustration of the high style of episcopal living in the Middle Ages.

Tenby

*** St. Mary's Church *(245)*, St. George Street

An aisled church without transepts, it was built mostly in the fifteenth century on thirteenth century foundations. While the windows are typically Perpendicular, the ceiling, called a wagon roof, is unusual. The painted bosses in the nave and chancel are especially good. The monuments mostly commemorate merchants of this once prosperous seaport. In the north aisle is a typically fifteenth century *memento mori*, no doubt inspired by the Black Death—a stone skeleton enclosed in a pinnacled canopy.

* Tenby Town Wall *(206)*, South Parade

Here is a section of the twenty-feet-high wall built first in the thirteenth century and subsequently rebuilt and restored.

** **Tudor Merchant's House** *(311)*, Quay Hill; NT

A fine example of a Tudor town house with excellent furnishings.

TREGARON

*** **Strata Florida Abbey** *(255)*, 8 m. n, 1 m. e of Pontrhydfendigaid on B 4340 (135 SN 746 657) AM

A Cistercian monastery, typically located in a remote spot on the upper reaches of the River Teifi, it owes its present ruined buildings to a re-founding by Prince Rhys ap Gruffydd in 1134. The remains are sparse, consisting mostly of the west front of the Transitional church, the nave arcades, fourteenth century tiles in the transeptal chapels, and the thirteenth century Early English chapter house. This was the religious, and to some extent the political, center of South Wales in the twelfth and thirteenth centuries. Though much wasted, the site is in some ways the most typically Welsh of all monastic ruins.

NORTH WALES

CLWYD
CHIRK

* **Chirk Aqueduct** *(425)*, 1 m. sw, w of A 5 (126 SJ 287 372)

A fine aqueduct by Thomas Telford carrying the Shropshire Union Canal across the River Ceiriog.

** **Chirk Castle** *(159,342,409,411)*, 2 m. w, 1½ m. n of A 5 (126 SJ 281 377) AM, NT

The outside of the castle, though much restored, is typically late thirteenth century, consisting of a rectangular inner ward surrounded by a high curtain wall with cylindrical towers at each corner and a semicylindrical tower on each face. The interior has rooms dating from the seventeenth and eighteenth centuries and some Victorian Gothic work by A. W. N. Pugin.

DENBIGH

** **Denbigh Castle** *(159)*, south edge of town (116 SJ 052 658) AM

On a hill above the present town stand these ruins of a late thirteenth century castle and town walls built by Henry de Lacey, earl of Lincoln, and Thomas, earl of Lancaster. Parts of the old town walls, including three mural towers, can still be seen. The inner ward of the castle is pentagonal in shape, entered by a great gatehouse flanked by two octagonal towers between which is an archway surmounted by a mutilated statue, thought to be of Edward I. Just inside the gateway is another octagonal building backed by a still smaller octagon.

St. Giles, Trefnant *(474)*, 4 m. n on A 525

Built in 1861–1869 to the design of Sir George Gilbert Scott, the style is Early English instead of the architect's usual Middle Pointed (Decorated) style.

FLINT

* Flint Castle *(160)*, town center; AM

A much ruined castle, the first to be commenced by Edward I in his 1277 campaign in North Wales. It was built in the concentric style favored in the late thirteenth century. Most of the outer curtain wall has disappeared. Outside the southeast corner of the inner ward is a massive cylindrical tower with its separate moat. The other three corners of the rectangular inner ward have protecting mural towers.

HAWARDEN

Hawarden Old Castle *(160)*, ½ m. se, s of A 55

The scanty remains of a mid-thirteenth century castle captured by the Welsh in 1282, then recaptured by Edward I and rebuilt.

* Ewloe Castle *(156)*, ½ m. w, on A 55 (117 SJ 288 675) AM

The D-shaped tower in the upper ward of this ruined castle dates from about 1200; the lower ward and the west tower were probably built by Llywelyn ap Gruffydd (the Last) about 1257.

HOLYWELL

* Basingwerk Abbey *(255)*, ½ m. n, on B 5121 (116 SJ 196 774) AM

This is a Savignac monastery founded about 1131 and later turned Cistercian. The ruins are fragmentary and consist of parts of the south aisle and transept of the church plus portions of the dorter, chapter house, and frater.

Maen Achwynfan Cross *(120)*, 4 m. nw, 1¼ m. w of Whitford (116 SJ 129 788) AM

An exceptionally high (almost eleven feet) Anglo-Saxon cross standing on the roadside.

LLANGOLLEN

* **Llangollen Canal** *(424)*, town center

Here is the western branch of the Shropshire Union Canal which goes as far as Llantysilio and is considered by some to be Britain's most beautiful canal.

Canal Museum *(424)*, The Wharf

A nice small museum of displays, memorabilia, etc., associated with the Shropshire Union Canal of which the Llangollen Canal is the western branch.

Eliseg's Pillar *(120)*, 2 m. n; e of A 542, ¼ m. n of Valle Crucis Abbey (117 SJ 203 445) AM

In an open field to the east of the A 542 stands an 8-foot cross shaft put up in the ninth century in honor of the seventh century king of Powys who was one of Mercian King Offa's chief opponents in the continuous border warfare that led to the building of Offa's Dyke.

** **Pont Cysyllte** *(425)*, 4 m. e, s of A 539 (117 SJ 271 420)

This is the handsomest aqueduct in Britain—built by Thomas Telford to carry the Llangollen Canal across the River Dee.

*** **Valle Crucis Abbey** *(256)*, 1 m. n, on A 542 (117 SJ 205 442) AM

The remains of this Cistercian abbey, founded in 1201 by Madoc ap Gruffydd Maelor, prince of Powys, are considerable. The substantial ruins of the church include excellent specimens of both Early English (east end) and Decorated (west end) style. The east range of the claustral buildings built in the early fourteenth century in the Decorated style, has been restored and reroofed. Proceeding south from the south transept: sacristy, chapter house, slype, dorter, reredorter, and warming room can be seen in much the same condition as originally built.

RHUDDLAN

** **Rhuddlan Castle** *(160)*, town center; AM

A well-preserved ruin designed by Master James of St. George for Edward I to command the Clwyd River, this was a concentric castle consisting of a high-curtained square inside a low-curtained pentagon. So as to supply it directly from the sea, Edward I had the river diverted and canalized to run along one side of the outer curtain wall, the other sides being guarded by a moat. Not much is left of the outer curtain, though the southwest mural tower (Gillot's Tower) overlooking the river is in a fair state of preservation. The square-shaped high-walled inner ward has twin-towered gatehouses in diagonal juxtaposition at the east and west corners and massive single cylindrical towers at the north and south corners.

ST. ASAPH

* St. Asaph's Cathedral *(241)*, town center

Like the other Welsh cathedrals, this is a secular foundation, dating from 1115. Building began in 1180, but the present structure is the product of much rebuilding and restoration, chiefly because of damage done by rival Welsh and English armies.

Architectural styles: west front—nineteenth century restoration (G. G. Scott); nave—Curvilinear Decorated; central tower—eighteenth century; transepts—Curvilinear Decorated; choir—nineteenth century restoration (G. G. Scott).

Special features: Chapter Museum with early Protestant prayer books and Bibles.

WREXHAM

* Church of St. Giles *(245)*, town center

This fifteenth century Perpendicular church is noteworthy chiefly for its high (135 ft.) pinnacled and paneled tower, one of the so-called seven wonders of Wales. Alumni and other admirers of Yale University can see the tomb of the founder, Elihu Yale, in the churchyard (his birthplace was at Bryn Eglwys, 15 miles west on A 5104).

** Erdigg *(401)*, 1 m. s, off A 483; NT

A seventeenth century house, refaced by James Wyatt in the eighteenth century, the estate includes laundry, bakehouse, sawmill, and smithy, all still operable. The most interesting feature here is the series of portraits and photographs of domestic servants, covering a span of about two centuries.

* Gresford Church *(245)*, 4 m. n on A 483

An unusually good Welsh example of Perpendicular architecture, the fifteenth century church has a good contemporary font and beautifully carved choir stalls and misericords.

* **Offa's Dyke** *(102)*, 11 m. s (126 SJ 269 386—250 345)

A long section of the ninth century rampart, built by the Mercian king along the Welsh border. Here it runs south from the Chirk Castle grounds.

* **Offa's Dyke** *(102)*, 2½ m. sw, 1 m. w of A 483 from Bersham (117 SJ 297 486—296 500)

A good section of the ninth century rampart separating Wales from Mercia, running on either side of the unmarked road west of Bersham village.

GWYNEDD
ANGLESEY: HOLYHEAD

Caer Gybi *(76)*, harborside

The walls enclosing the medieval church of St. Gybi are originally of Roman construction, having been built in the fourth century, probably by Count Theodosius, to guard the northern coast of Anglesey against Irish raiders.

** **Barclodiad Y Gawres** *(19)*, 12 m. s on coastal side of A 4080, 2 m. n of Aberffraw (114 SH 329 707) AM

A high restored mound covering a Neolithic passage grave with a polygonal burial chamber from which three side chambers radiate. The interior cannot be entered but is visible from the entry way through an iron grill. On the premises are standing stones inscribed with chevrons, lozenges, and spirals. The view of Anglesey's west coast is splendid.

* **Caer Y Twr** *(49)*, 1½ m. w (114 SH 228 830) AM

A seventeen-acre Iron Age hill fort enclosed by a dry stone wall which still stands nine feet high in places.

* **Llangadwaladr Church** *(112)*, 14 m. se; n of A 4080, 1½ m. e of Aberffraw

Embedded in the north wall of the twelfth century nave of this pretty church is a stone inscribed with Latin characters, *Catamanus Rex Sapientisimus Opinatismus.* The dedication is to the Dark Age Welsh King Cadfan, father of King Cadwallon of Gwynedd. Key to church can be obtained from neighboring house.

* **Trefignath Burial Chamber** *(21)*, 2 m. s (114 SH 258 805) AM

A rare Neolithic segmented cist, forty-five feet in length, with two portal stones, seven feet in height.

Ty Mawr *(287)*, 2 m. w (114 SH 212 820)

An Iron Age village with the foundations of twenty of the original fifty huts still to be seen.

ANGLESEY: MENAI BRIDGE

*** **Beaumaris Castle** *(162)*, 4½ m. ne on A 545 (114 SH 607 762) AM

The well-preserved ruin of Edward I's final Welsh castle, commenced in 1295. The plan is concentric: a square within an octagon. The low outer curtain wall features twelve mural towers. The higher inner curtain has a great drum tower at each of the four corners and two D-shaped towers on the east and west faces. Twin-towered gatehouses intersect the north and south walls of the inner ward. Smaller gateways pierce those of the outer curtain at points set deliberately out of line with the inner gatehouses so as to require an oblique approach to the latter. Today's visitor enters the grounds over a wooden bridge which replaces the original drawbridge across the moat. This is called the Gate-next-the Sea. Two unusual features are the Gothic vaulted chapel in the inner ward and the stone extension from the south wall called the Gunners Walk. This contained the castle mill and still features a buttress shaped like a bent horseshoe to which boats coming in from the sea were tied.

* **Britannia Bridge** *(458)*, across Menai Strait southwest of Telford's highway bridge (A 5)

Built by Robert Stephenson and completed in 1850, this was an engineering miracle in its day: a tubular bridge with two parallel iron tubes each containing more than fifteen hundred feet of railway track, the tubes having been hoisted into position by means of hydraulic rams. The central pier is built on the mid-channel Britannia Rock. Unfortunately the original profile of the bridge was distorted in its rebuilding after a fire in 1970.

** **Bryn Celli Ddu** *(19)*, 5 m. sw, 1 m. n of A 4080 (114/115 SH 508 702) AM

A Neolithic passage grave with a restored covering mound, the sixteen-foot passageway terminates in a polygonal chamber eight feet in diameter and about six feet high. On the grounds is the cast of a rare Neolithic stone, inscribed with meandering linear decorations (original in the National Museum of Wales in Cardiff).

** **Din Lligwy** *(87)*, 12 m. n, 1½ m. w of Moelfre (114 SH 497 861) AM

A beautifully situated ruin consisting of a native circular stone house and three rectangular buildings surrounded by a stone wall. The site dates from the period of the Roman occupation of Anglesey, but presumably was occupied by Welsh farmers of a basically Iron Age culture.

* **Lligwy Burial Chamber** *(21)*, 11 m. n, 2 m. w of Moelfre (114 SH 501 860) AM

An unusual cromlech in that the uprights of the Neolithic burial chamber now rise only about two feet above ground, thus giving their huge capstone the appearance of a table top.

* **Penmon Priory Church** *(243)*, 9 m. ne (114 SH 630 807) AM

The claustral ruins of this Augustinian priory built in the twelfth century are sparse, but the priory church has been incorporated into the present parish church, whose nave and south transept are early Norman.

Special features: carvings in crossing arches; much weathered tympanum of south nave doorway; Norman piscina; ruins of refectory and warming house.

*** **Plas Newydd** *(401,445)*, 4 m. s, e of A 4080; NT

A delightful eighteenth century Gothick restoration by James Wyatt of an earlier house belonging to the first marquess of Anglesey, whose artificial leg is among the other mementos of the Napoleonic Wars to be found in the Cavalry Room. Beautiful location overlooking the Menai Strait. Nice Gothick features inside; also fine twentieth century murals by Rex Whistler. Unobtrusive but helpful guides stationed conveniently throughout the house to assist visitors.

Plas Newydd Cromlech *(21)*, 3 m. w (114 SH 519 697)

On the grounds of the marquess of Anglesey's country estate, this ruined Neolithic tomb consists of two adjacent stone chambers each with its own capstone.

BANGOR

* **Bangor Cathedral** *(241)*, High Street

Founded as a secular cathedral in 1092, first building began in 1075.

Architectural styles: although various portions of the church date from the fourteenth, fifteenth, and sixteenth centuries, G. G. Scott's nineteenth century restoration was so thorough as to conceal or disguise most of the original. Architecturally, the cathedral is far more Victorian than medieval.

** **Menai Suspension Bridge** *(423)*, 1 m. w, on A 5 across Menai Strait

Thomas Telford's iron masterpiece, 579 feet between piers and 100 feet above high water.

** **Penrhyn Castle** *(441)*, 1 m. e, at junction of A 5 and A 55; NT

A splendid fake-Norman castle built in the early nineteenth century for the slate baron, G. H. Dawkins Pennant. Fine Victorian garden.

BEDDGELERT

* **Beddgelert Church** *(243)*, 12 m. se on A 498

Basically Early English with three lancets in the east wall, the church was built in the thirteenth century for the use of a small Augustinian priory founded by Llywelyn the Great.

Dinas Emrys *(93,112)*, 1½ m. ne, n of A 498 (115 SH 606 492)

The site name means fort of Aurelianus, and is the traditional home of the sub-Roman Welsh king or chieftain named Ambrosius Aurelianus. A very steep climb leads to the scanty remains of what was probably a fifth century fortified dwelling, now consisting only of a few feet of dry-stone wall.

BETWS-Y-COED

* **Capel Garmon Chambered Tomb** *(19)*, 2 m. e; n of A 5, ½ m. s of Capel Garmon village (116 SH 818 544) AM

A Neolithic covered gallery grave of the Severn-Cotswold group, geographically well separated from the major concentration of this type in South Wales and Southwest England, with a false portal and a double chamber entered by a passage from one side.

* **Dolwyddelan Castle** *(143)*, 5½ m. sw, n of A 470 (115 SH 721 523) AM

This ruined rectangular keep, erected in the twelfth century, probably by Owain of Gwynedd, and later repaired by Edward I, is traditionally held to be the birthplace of Llywelyn the Great.

Ty Mawr *(49)*, 3 m. se, 1 m. s of A 470 from Cethin's Bridge

An interesting, though almost inaccessible, Welsh stone cottage, birthplace of Bishop William Morgan who in the sixteenth century translated the English Bible into Welsh, thus contributing greatly to the Protestantization of Wales.

* **Waterloo Bridge** *(423)*, 1 m. s, on A 5 (115 SH 799 558)

Built by Thomas Telford in 1815, the year of Waterloo, this is one of the most graceful bridges in Britain.

CAERNARVON

*** **Caernarvon Castle** *(161,446)*, town center; AM

Laid out longitudinally on an east-west axis, this ruined castle of Edward I was begun in 1283. The curtain walls and seven polygonal turreted towers stand almost to their original height. One, the Eagle Tower, has three turrets and an eagle carved on its face. The castle has no protecting barbicans. The eastern (outer) ward is hexagonal, and the western (inner) pentagonal. The original wall separating the two is gone, as are most of the other interior buildings. The present entry is by way of the massive King's Gate with a much eroded statue of Edward II standing above its archway. At the opposite (southeast) corner of the outer ward is another huge gateway called Queensgate.

Here also is the Museum of the Royal Welch Fusiliers with the usual display of uniforms, weapons, etc.

* **Caernarvon Town Wall** *(162)*, town center; AM

Projecting out from the castle, the town wall, also built by Edward I, stretches about a half mile in length and stands twenty-eight feet high between the towers which reach a height of about thirty-eight feet.

** **Segontium** *(67,89)*, se end of town n of A 4085; NT

Here are fairly substantial ruins of a first century Roman auxiliary fort, first built by Agricola to guard the Menai Strait and later converted to stone. Well preserved by the National Trust, this is a good place to observe the structural outlines of a typical small Roman fort. It is enclosed by a stone wall pierced with four gateways inside of which are the remaining foundations of the headquarters building, commandant's house, three granaries, barracks block, and an exterior bathhouse and Mithraic temple. The site museum is excellent.

CONWY

*** **Conwy Castle** *(161)*, town center; AM

Designed by Edward I's master mason, James of St. George, this beautifully preserved ruin overlooking the Menai Strait is laid out longitudinally on an east-west axis. The oblong outer ward guards the square inner ward, the two separated by a cross wall. The curtain walls of both are about fifteen feet thick and contain eight huge projecting drum towers, the four to the east defining the inner ward and each surmounted by a turret. Altogether, the castle had 142 arrow slits. Barbicans cover both eastern and western approaches, the former abutting on the sea, and now looking out on the charming *Conwy Suspension Bridge (NT) *(423)*, designed by the great nineteenth century Scottish engineer, Thomas Telford. Today's visitor enters the outer ward at the northwest corner by way of the western barbican. This ward contains ruins of the great hall and kitchen, as well as entrances to four of the eight towers. The inner ward contains the remains of the royal apartments, including a presence chamber and a chapel.

Conwy Railway Bridge *(458)*, across Conwy Estuary s of A 55

Built in the 1840s by Robert Stephenson, the railway tracks run over two parallel iron tubes which were floated into position and raised by hydraulic rams—an innovation in engineering that was later repeated at the much larger bridge over Menai Strait.

** **Conwy Town Wall** *(161)*, town center; AM

The town wall stretching north and northwest from the castle measures about 1,400 yards in length with three great gates and twenty-one half-round towers. The latter were open at the back so that an enemy which might have scaled the town wall would still be exposed to fire from the castle. Built by Edward I, this is the best preserved medieval town wall in Britain.

** **Plas Mawr** *(311)*, High Street

This is perhaps the best surviving example in Britain of an Elizabethan town house. Built by Robert Wynn of Gwydir, it is an H-plan house with mullioned windows with Renaissance pediments and crow-stepped gables. The well-preserved interior is noteworthy for its elaborate fireplaces and decorated plaster ceilings.

DOLGELLAU

Cymmer Abbey *(255)*, 1½ m. n, on A 470 (124 SH 721 195) AM

A much ruined Cistercian monastery founded in 1199. Not much is left except the sparse remains of the Early English church.

FFESTINIOG

** **Gloddfa Ganol Ffestiniog Mountain Tourist Centre** *(433)*, 2½ m. n, w of A 470 in Blaenau Ffestiniog

A defunct slate quarry and mine with a good display of machinery and a fascinating gift shop featuring numerous slate artifacts. Visits may be made into galleries where slate was mined. Live slate cutting demonstrations.

* **Tomen Y Mur** *(62)*, 4 m. s, 1 m. e of A 470 (124 SH 707 387)

The scanty remains of a fort built by the Roman general Agricola in about A.D. 78, and refortified in about the year 110. A Norman motte rises from one of the Roman ramparts. Immediately to the north is the site of an amphitheater. Magnificent view of surrounding Snowdonian mountains.

LLANBERIS

* **Dolbadarn Castle** *(152)*, se end of town (115 SH 586 598) AM

A well-preserved ruin, this round keep, 40 feet high, is dramatically situated between two lakes, though the view is marred somewhat by the nearby stone works. It was built in the early thirteenth century, possibly by Llywelyn the Great who is supposed to have kept his brother Owen a prisoner here for twenty years.

** **North Wales Quarrying Museum** *(433)*, 1 m. e, across Llyn Padarn Lake

Here are numerous workshops associated with the slate quarrying operation that began on this site in 1782. Regular film showings illustrate the history of the industry; also live demonstrations of slate cutting. Maintained by the Department of the Environment.

* **Snowdon Mountain Railway** *(457)*, town center

This is the terminus of a narrow-gauge railway running from here to the summit of Snowdon Mountain and back, a two-hour trip through unbelievably magnificent scenery.

LLANDUDNO

*** **Bodnant Garden** *(487)*, 8 m. s, on A 470 n of Tal-y-cafn

Splendid formal gardens plus a woodland garden and a rock garden. Famous for its rhododendrons, camellias, magnolias, embothriums, and euchryphias.

PENMAENMAWR

Craig Lwyd Axe Factory *(24)*, ½ m. s (115 SH 715 750)

On the eastern end of Penmaenmawr Mountain, this is the site of an important Neolithic stone quarry where rough axes were shaped for shipment to various parts of England and Wales. For mountain climbers only.

Druid's Circle, Cefn Coch *(42)*, 1½ m. s (115 HS 723 746)

Reached by a steep climb, this Bronze Age circle consists of ten stones, six feet high.

PORTHMADOG

* **Festiniog Railway** *(457)*, town center

This is the eastern terminus of the narrow-gauge railway, built in 1836 to carry slate from Blaenau Ffestiniog to the sea. Excursion trips now run from here nine-and-one-half miles west to Ddault. Trains can also be picked up at Minffordd and at Tan-y-bwich near Maentwrog. Fine views of the Vale of Ffestiniog.

*** **Harlech Castle** *(162,186,200)*, 10 m. s, on A 496 (124 SH 581 312) AM

This substantial ruin of Edward I's castle sits magnificently on a high rock above what used to be a river on the western coast of Wales. It was built by Master James of St. George on a concentric plan with the outer curtain walls unusually low and close to the inner curtain which rises to a tremendous height. A massive twin-towered gatehouse guards the eastern entrance which is taken by today's visitor. Great drum towers cover the four corners of this ward, where the castle's domestic buildings also are located: great hall, granary, bakehouse, and chapel. North of the outer curtain is a rocky shelf leading down to what once was water. This is girdled by a low wall and is reached from the castle proper by a postern gate. This was one of the castles seized by Owain Glyndwr in 1404 and not returned to English control until 1409. During the Wars of the Roses it was occupied by Jasper Tudor and a band of fifty Lancastrian soldiers who finally surrendered in 1468 after a long siege ordered by the Yorkist king, Edward IV. The defenders on this occasion were the Men of Harlech of the famous marching song.

PWLLHELLI

* **Criccieth Castle** *(152)*, 8 m. e, s of A 497 (123 SH 499 376)

The inner ward of this ruined castle, whose west curtain wall stands almost to its original height, dates from around 1230, i.e., the period of Llywelyn the Great's ascendancy in North Wales. The castle fell to the forces of Edward I in 1283, at which time the outer curtain wall and the powerful gatehouse flanked by semi-cylindrical towers were added. Marvelous view of Tremadoc Bay.

Lloyd George Memorial Museum *(454)*, 6 m. e on A 497 in Llanystumdwy

A small museum with a number of mementos, photographs, etc., of the Liberal prime minister who spent part of his childhood here and whose permanent residence was nearby.

* **Tre'r Ceiri** *(49)*, 7 m. n, 1 m. w of A 499 from Llanaelhearn (123 SH 373 446)

An Iron Age hill fort, it is guarded by two concentric ramparts, the larger of which still stands to a height of thirteen feet in places. Inside are the foundations of 150 round huts, making this one of the largest Iron Age villages to have been discovered in Britain. Access is difficult.

TYWYN

* **Talyllyn Railway** *(457)*, town center

Here is the eastern terminus of a narrow-gauge railway built in 1866 to carry slates from Abergynolwyn, six-and-one-half miles inland, to Cardigan Bay. The road has been restored and now carries round-trip passenger excursion trains. It can be boarded also at Dolgoch Falls and Abergynolwyn. Near the Tywyn station is a narrow-gauge railway museum.

CROWN DEPENDENCIES

ISLE OF MAN
CASTLETOWN

*** **Castle Rushen** *(169,187)*, town center

Although the lower courses of the keep date from the mid-twelfth century, most of the keep and curtain walls of this splendid castle were built in the fourteenth. Though much restored during the six centuries since, the building has an authentic medieval air, and few castles in Britain provide better illustration of the military functions served by these great fortified residences. Note especially the moats, the barbican with two sharp bends, the *meurtrières*, portcullises, and arrow slits. Mandatory guided tours are short, frequent, and informative.

DOUGLAS

*** **The Manx Museum, Library and Art Gallery** *(26,32,114,115,120)*, Crellin's Hill

An excellent small museum, the most interesting rooms are:

Archaeological galleries: notable holdings are the Neolithic grave goods from Cashtal yn Ard; early Christian inscribed stones, especially the famous Calf of Man Crucifixion; Viking jewelry; and casts of Manx Runic crosses.

Folk-Life galleries: notable features are the craft exhibits, ship models, Manx costume displays; uniforms and memorabilia of the Royal Manx Fencibles and Volunteers; and the model Manx farmhouse.

** Cashtal yn Ard *(21)*, 12 m. n, e of A 2 (95 SC 457 890)

A splendid Neolithic dolmen beautifully situated near the Isle of Man's east coast, it consists of a forecourt of ten uprights, two portal stones, and five burial chambers. Great view.

King Orry's Grave *(21)*, 8 m. n, on B 11 n of Minorca (95 SC 442 845)

A Neolithic dolmen of indeterminate shape owing to the site's being bisected by the modern road (B 11).

* Laxey Waterwheel *(428)*, 8 m. n, w of A 2

The largest waterwheel in Britain, installed in 1854 to pump water from the nearby lead and zinc mines. This is a backshot wheel.

** Maughold Parish Church *(115,120)*, 15 m. ne, on A 15

In the churchyard are the foundations of three early Christian keills, which served as monastic cells or oraries probably in the sixth or seventh century. Nearby, under shelter, is the best collection of Manx crosses on the island.

* Tynwald Hill *(114)*, 8 m. nw, n of A 1 in St. John's village

A rebuilt terraced mound, site of the ancient assembly of ninth century Norse settlers in Man.

PEEL

*** Peel Castle *(182,187)*, St. Patrick's Isle

A magnificent sandstone ruin, this mostly fourteenth century castle occupies a splendid site overlooking the Irish Sea. It was built mostly by William de Montacute and his successor William le Scrope in the fourteenth century, though the outer buildings belong to the fifteenth and sixteenth centuries and were erected by the Stanleys who became lords of Man under Henry IV and earls of Derby beginning with the reign of Henry VII.

*** St. German's Cathedral *(241)*, St. Patrick's Isle

Here are the ruins of the red sandstone cathedral begun in 1226 by Simon, Bishop of Sodor, in the archdiocese of Trondheim, Norway. The early parts of the church are in the Early English style. Much of it was rebuilt by William le Scrope in the fourteenth century in the Decorated style.

Special features: Early English lancet windows (three in the east end and five in each of the nave walls); the crypt which served as the bishop's prison; the Decorated central tower and north and south transepts.

Jurby Parish Church *(120)*, 12 m. ne; w of A 10, ½ m. n of Jurby village

Inside the church are eight slabs or fragments of Manx crosses. The site is beautifully located on a high bluff overlooking the Irish Sea.

St. Andreas Church *(120)*, 15 m. ne, on B 14

Inside the church are eleven Manx crosses, slabs, or fragments of crosses.

St. Michael, Kirkmichael *(120)*, 6 m. ne on A 3

In the northeast corner of the church are twelve carved Manx crosses and cross slabs.

St. Patrick's Chapel *(115)*, 8 m. ne, 1 m. s of A 3 from 1 m. s of Kirkmichael (95 SC 305 886)

A solitary early Christian keill or hermitage, reduced to bare foundations, situated in an isolated wooded dell, can be reached by footpath leading to Spooyt Vane waterfall. (Take fork to right after crossing wooden bridge and proceed about fifty yards beyond steps leading down to waterfall.) No signposts.

JERSEY
ST. HELIER

*** **Elizabeth Castle** *(299,344)*, town harbor

Built by Sir Paul Ivy for Queen Elizabeth I between 1594 and 1601 on the site of a Benedictine abbey and the ninth century hermitage of St. Helier, the castle was much enlarged in the seventeenth century (during which time it briefly withstood a siege by parliamentarian forces) and further fortified by German troops during their World War II occupation of Jersey.

From the causeway through the landward gate, a tour of the castle proceeds to Fort Charles (named in honor of Charles II, who, as Prince of Wales, lived at the castle in 1646 en route to exile in France); King William's Gate, bearing the arms of William III; from the lower ward to the Elizabethan upper ward through the gate above which are carved the queen's coat of arms and that of her governor, Sir Anthony Paulet; into the keep which includes the governor's house where Sir Walter Raleigh resided; and to the castle summit with a German fire control tower and antiaircraft emplacement.

The castle is approachable by boat at high tide or by causeway at low tide, both from West Park.

* **Hermitage Rock** *(115)*, Elizabeth Castle Island, St. Aubin's Bay

Site of a sixth century hermitage attributed to St. Helier, patron saint of Jersey. The present stone cell is restored medieval.

** Faldouet Dolmen *(21)*, 4½ m. ne, n of A 3 from Gorey

Also called La Poquelaye or Gorey Dolmen, this was a Neolithic passage grave, the remains of which consist of a stone-lined passageway leading to a narrow central area containing a number of low cists, which in turn opens onto a terminal burial chamber ten feet in width and roofed by a huge capstone. The ensemble has the bottle-shaped appearance of this type of tomb.

** German Occupation Museum *(503)*, 1½ m. ne, La Hogue Bie

A small but impressive museum depicting conditions on Jersey during the German occupation of World War II.

*** German Underground Hospital *(503)*, 3 m. w off B 89

An amazing engineering feat wrought by slave labor imported from the Ukraine by the German Army of Occupation during World War II. It was hewn out of solid rock and took two-and-one-half years to build and equip, but, before it could be put to much use as a safe haven for wounded German troops, the Allies had landed in France, occupied the adjacent coastline, and cut off the Germans in Jersey from communication with their home bases.

*** Gorey (Mont Orgueil) Castle *(147,175,200,286)*, 4 m. ne on A 3

Overlooking the rugged east coast of Jersey, this immense and complex structure was for centuries the island's main defense against incursions from nearby France. Though originally built in the early thirteenth century, most of the existing structure dates from the fifteenth, sixteenth, and seventeenth centuries. Which parts of the castle were built when is difficult to judge, and the official handbook is of little help toward an understanding of the castle's architectural history. The view toward France is magnificent.

*** The Jersey (La Hogue Bie) Museum *(26,32)*, 3 m. ne, n of B 28

Though situated on the site of La Hogue Bie Chambered Tomb, this is more than a mere site museum. It contains important prehistoric finds from Jersey's many caves and chambered tombs, beautifully arranged, and intelligently explained with visual aids.

*** La Hogue Bie Chambered Tomb *(19)*, 3 m. ne, n of B 28

A gigantic Neolithic passage grave, topped by a forty-foot mound crowned by a medieval chapel. The thirty-two-foot-long passage opens onto an oval chamber, thirty feet by twelve feet, off which lie three side cells. Well lighted and well displayed, this is one of Britain's best preserved Neolithic monuments.

** **Le Couperon** *(21)*, 8 m. n; ½ m. e of Rozel, e of B 38

Also known as Sae Dolmen, this is an unusual Neolithic segmented cist or *allée couverte,* forty-five feet long, three feet wide, and about three feet high; twenty uprights in all, roofed by seven capstones. Though poorly signposted and hard to find, the monument itself, as well as the breathtaking view of Rozel Bay, easily warrants the effort.

GUERNSEY
ST. PETER PORT

*** **Castle Cornet** *(147,175,286,299),* town center

This splendid castle overlooking the harbor of Guernsey's principal city, originated in the thirteenth century and has undergone extensive alterations since. Of the thirteenth century work, the only surviving parts are a portion of the northeast curtain wall running alongside what is now called the prisoners' walk, and the lowest courses of the doorway into the citadel. Much repair work was done in the fourteenth and fifteenth centuries, but the specifics are difficult to distinguish. In the mid-sixteenth century, Henry VIII, in keeping with his general policy of coastal fortification, added Mewtis Bulwark and Well Tower. Most of the present form of the castle, however, derives from Elizabethan rebuilding. The Town Bastion and Royal Battery, Hart Bulwark, and much of the curtain wall were built in the late sixteenth century, and the royal arms of Queen Elizabeth appear over the gate in the Town Bastion. A great powder explosion in 1672 destroyed most of the medieval castle and some of the Elizabethan. In the eighteenth century the troop barracks and guard rooms were added. During the German occupation in World War II, massive concrete gun emplacements were built on top of the earlier works, and some are still visible.

*** **Guernsey Museum and Art Gallery** *(26,32),* Candie Gardens

A new building beautifully situated in a charming public park overlooking both town and harbor. Prehistoric finds from Guernsey's chambered tombs are numerous and well displayed. Of particular interest is the Alderney hoard of Bronze Age spearheads, axes, etc. The museum theater offers a good audio-visual program. Altogether this is a model of modern museumship.

* **Catel Menhir** *(42),* 2 m. w, Catel Parish, Rohais de Haut

A shaped stone, six-and-one-half-feet high, faintly carved to represent the upper torso of a woman, probably in connection with a Bronze Age fertility cult.

** Fort Grey Maritime Museum *(396)*, 7½ m. w, on Route de la Lague (west coast)

A well restored Martello Tower built to guard the coast of Guernsey against a Napoleonic invasion, this is now a fascinating museum specializing in materials relating to shipwrecks and ship salvage. Very well organized and maintained.

* German Military Underground Hospital and Ammunition Store *(503)*, 2½ m. w in St. Andrew

Built by the World War II German Army of Occupation using slave labor imported from Eastern Europe, the hospital was used for only a short time before Guernsey was cut off from the Continent by the Allied landings in France and occupation of the adjacent coast. All that remains in this dank and dreary place are a few hospital beds and the central heating equipment.

*** German Occupation Museum *(503)*, 4 m. sw, in Forest, s of Airport

A small museum displaying the equipment used by German troops during the World War II occupation of the Channel Islands; posters, newspapers, currency, and other such documents; an occupation kitchen; a secret crystal set; Red Cross food parcels; and other mementos of life under military occupation.

* La Gran'mère du Chimiquière *(42)*, 1½ m. s, St. Martin's Church, Rue d'Eglise

A shaped stone, five-and-one-half feet high, incorporated into the gateway to the parish churchyard. The upper portion is carved in the shape of a woman's head and shoulders, probably in connection with a Bronze Age fertility cult.

** La Varde Dolmen *(22)*, 3½ m. n, at west end of golf course on l'Ancresse Common

A typical bottle-shaped Channel Islands Neolithic passage grave, this is the largest chambered tomb on Guernsey. The burial chamber measures thirty-three feet by twelve feet and consists of uprights supporting a roof of six capstones approached by a short, narrow alley marked by stones on either side.

* Le Creux des Faies *(19)*, 7 m. w, se of Fort Saumerez

A Neolithic passage grave, twenty-eight feet by ten feet and six feet high. Splendid view of the rocky northwest coast of Guernsey.

** **Le Dehus** *(22)*, 5 m. n, near juncture of La Rochelle Road and Grande Rue, n. of Bordeaux

A Neolithic passage grave, the bottle-shaped dolmen consists of a narrow alley of uprights, three feet across and eleven feet in length, terminating in a burial chamber eleven feet by twenty feet. The entire ensemble is roofed by seven capstones. A rare Neolithic drawing is incised on the underside of the second capstone.

Le Trepied *(22)*, 6 m. w; on La Roque Road, 1 m. n of l'Eree

A small dolmen with a chamber about eighteen feet by six feet with three capstones supported by four-foot uprights. The site overlooks Le Catiorac Point and offers a spectacular view.

THE BEST OF BRITAIN

THREE STAR SITES AND MUSEUMS

PREHISTORIC SITES

Arbor Low *(661)*, nr. Bakewell, Derbyshire
Avebury *(573)*, nr. Marlborough, Wiltshire
Belas Knap Chambered Tomb *(642)*, nr. Winchcombe, Gloucestershire
Hetty Pegler's Tump *(641)*, nr. Stroud, Gloucestershire
La Hogue Bie Chambered Tomb *(744)*, Jersey
Long Meg and Her Daughters *(713)*, nr. Penrith, Cumbria
Maiden Castle *(568)*, nr. Dorchester, Dorset
Stonehenge *(570)*, nr. Amesbury, Wiltshire
Wayland's Smithy Chambered Tomb *(638)*, nr. Wantage, Oxfordshire
West Kennet Chambered Tomb *(574)*, nr. Marlborough, Wiltshire

ROMAN SITES

Bignor *(551)*, nr. Arundel, West Sussex
Brading Roman Villa *(559)*, nr. Fordingham, Hampshire
Burgh Castle *(606)*, nr. Great Yarmouth, Norfolk
Caerleon *(716)*, nr. Newport, Gwent
Chedworth *(750)*, nr. Cirencester, Oxfordshire
Fishbourne *(551)*, nr. Chichester, West Sussex
Hadrian's Wall *(701)*, nr. Newcastle-upon-Tyne, Tyne and Wear
[(Corbridge *(702)*; Chesters *(702)*; Housesteads *(702)*; Ches-
terholm *(702)*]
Lullingstone *(542)*, nr. Eynsford, Kent
Pevensey Castle *(548)*, nr. Eastbourne, East Sussex
Portchester Castle *(561)*, nr. Portsmouth, Hampshire
Roman Bath *(578)*, Bath, Avon
Roman Painted House *(541)*, Dover, Kent
Wroxeter *(672)*, nr. Shrewsbury, Salop

RUINED CASTLES

Beaumaris Castle *(734)*, nr. Menai Bridge, Anglesey, Gwynedd
Bodiam Castle *(549)*, nr. Hastings, East Sussex
Caernarvon Castle *(737)*, Caernarvon, Gwynedd

Caerphilly Castle *(719)*, Caerphilly, Mid-Glamorgan
Caister Castle *(606)*, nr. Great Yarmouth, Norfolk
Carisbrooke Castle *(558)*, nr. Newport, Isle of Wight, Hampshire
Castle Rising *(607)*, nr. King's Lynn, Norfolk
Chepstow Castle *(715)*, Chepstow, Gwent
Conwy Castle *(737)*, Conwy, Gwynedd
Framlingham Castle *(602)*, Framlingham, Suffolk
Harlech Castle *(740)*, nr. Porthmadog, Gwynedd
Kenilworth Castle *(643)*, Kenilworth, Warwickshire
Ludlow Castle *(670)*, Ludlow, Salop
Orford Castle *(604)*, nr. Woodbridge, Suffolk
Peel Castle *(742)*, Isle of Man
Pembroke Castle *(727)*, Pembroke, Dyfed
Pevensey Castle *(548)*, nr. Eastbourne, East Sussex
Portchester Castle *(561)*, nr. Portsmouth, Hampshire
Raglan Castle *(714)*, nr. Abergavenny, Gwent
Restormel Castle *(593)*, nr. Lostwithiel, Cornwall
Richmond Castle *(685)*, North Yorkshire
Rochester Castle *(543)*, nr. Rochester, Kent
Tintagel Castle *(590)*, nr. Bude, Cornwall
Warkworth Castle *(705)*, nr. Alnwick, Northumberland

HABITABLE CASTLES

Alnwick Castle *(704)*, Alnwick, Northumberland
Arundel Castle *(550)*, Arundel, West Sussex
Bamburgh Castle *(704)*, nr. Alnwick, Northumberland
Berkeley Castle *(641)*, nr. Stroud, Gloucestershire
Cardiff Castle *(717)*, Cardiff, South Glamorgan
Carlisle Castle *(709)*, Carlisle, Cumbria
Castle Cornet *(745)*, St. Peter Port, Guernsey
Castle Rushen *(741)*, Isle of Man
Colchester Castle *(598)*, Colchester, Essex
Deal Castle *(540)*, Deal, Kent
Dover Castle *(541)*, Dover, Kent
Elizabeth Castle *(743)*, St. Helier, Jersey
Gory (Mont Orgueil) Castle *(744)*, Jersey
Herstmonceux Castle *(548)*, nr. Hailsham, East Sussex
Manorbier Castle *(727)*, nr. Pembroke, Dyfed
Pendennis Castle *(591)*, Falmouth, Cornwall
Raby Castle *(698)*, nr. Bishop Auckland, County Durham
St. Mawes Castle *(591)*, nr. Falmouth, Cornwall
Stokesay Castle *(670)*, nr. Ludlow, Salop
Sudeley Castle *(642)*, nr. Winchcombe, Gloucestershire

Tattershall Castle *(653)*, nr. Sleaford, Lincolnshire
Tower of London *(513)*, London
Walmer Castle *(540)*, nr. Deal, Kent
Warwick Castle *(646)*, Warwick, Warwickshire
Windsor Castle *(565)*, Windsor, Berkshire

CATHEDRALS

Canterbury Cathedral *(538)*, Canterbury, Kent
Coventry Cathedral *(665)*, Coventry, West Midlands
Durham Cathedral *(699)*, Durham, County Durham
Ely Cathedral *(617)*, Ely, Cambridgeshire
Exeter Cathedral *(587)*, Exeter, Devon
Gloucester Cathedral *(640)*, Gloucester, Gloucestershire
Lichfield Cathedral *(667)*, Lichfield, Staffordshire
Lincoln Cathedral *(651)*, Lincoln, Lincolnshire
Norwich Cathedral *(608)*, Norwich, Norfolk
Oxford Cathedral *(629)*, Oxford, Oxfordshire
Peterborough Cathedral *(618)*, Peterborough, Cambridgeshire
Ripon Cathedral *(686)*, Ripon, North Yorkshire
St. Alban's Cathedral *(621)*, St. Albans, Hertfordshire
St. German's Cathedral (Ruins) *(742)*, Isle of Man
St. Paul's Cathedral *(515)*, London
Salisbury Cathedral *(574)*, Salisbury, Wiltshire
Wells Cathedral *(585)*, Wells, Somerset
Westminster Abbey *(523)*, London
Winchester Cathedral *(563)*, Winchester, Hampshire
York Minster *(692)*, York, North Yorkshire

RUINED ABBEYS

Byland Abbey *(688)*, nr. Thirsk, North Yorkshire
Castle Acre Priory *(609)*, nr. Swaffham, Norfolk
Cleeve Abbey *(584)*, nr. Watchet, Somerset
Fountains Abbey *(686)*, nr. Ripon, North Yorkshire
Furness Abbey *(709)*, nr. Barrow-in-Furness, Cumbria
Lindisfarne Priory *(706)*, nr. Berwick-upon-Tweed, Northumberland
Mount Grace Priory *(684)*, nr. Northallerton, North Yorkshire
Rievaulx Abbey *(689)*, nr. Thirsk, North Yorkshire
Roche Abbey *(679)*, nr. Rotherham, South Yorkshire
Strata Florida Abbey *(729)*, nr. Tregaron, Dyfed
Tintern Abbey *(716)*, nr. Chepstow, Gwent
Valle Crucis Abbey *(731)*, nr. Llangollen, Clwyd
Wenlock Priory *(669)*, nr. Bridgenorth, Salop

PARISH CHURCHES: ANGLO-SAXON AND MEDIEVAL

All Saints, Brixworth *(655)*, nr. Northampton, Northamptonshire
All Saints, Earls Barton *(657)*, nr. Northampton, Northamptonshire
Barfreston Church *(541)*, nr. Dover, Kent
Beverley Minster *(676)*, Beverley, Humberside
Escombe Parish Church *(698)*, nr. Bishop Auckland, County Durham
Lavenham Church *(603)*, nr. Sudbury, Suffolk
Long Melford Church *(604)*, nr. Sudbury, Suffolk
Melbourne Church *(663)*, nr. Derby, Derbyshire
Patrington Church *(678)*, nr. Withernsea, Humberside
St. Andrew's Greensted *(598)*, nr. Chelmsford, Essex
St. Andrew's Hexham *(707)*, Northumberland
St. Botolph's *(649)*, Boston, Lincolnshire
St. James Chipping Camden *(638)*, nr. Moreton-in-Marsh, Oxfordshire
St. John the Baptist, Barnack *(654)*, nr. Stamford, Lincolnshire
St. John the Baptist *(639)*, Cirencester, Gloucestershire
St. Mary's *(726)*, Haverfordwest, Dyfed
St. Mary Redcliffe *(580)*, Bristol, Avon
St. Mary's *(728)*, Tenby, Dyfed
St. Mary's Warwick *(645)*, Warwick, Warwickshire
Sherborne Abbey Church *(568)*, Sherborne, Dorset
Southwold Church *(603)*, nr. Lowestoft, Suffolk
Stone Church *(540)*, nr. Dartford, Kent
Tewkesbury Abbey Church *(641)*, Tewkesbury, Gloucestershire

PARISH CHURCHES: SEVENTEENTH, EIGHTEENTH, AND NINETEENTH CENTURIES

All Souls, Haley Hill *(680)*, nr. Sheffield, South Yorkshire
Brompton Oratory *(524)*, London
Queen's Chapel *(522)*, London
St. Giles, Camberwell *(534)*, London
St. James, Piccadilly *(527)*, London
St. John the Evangelist *(681)*, Leeds, West Yorkshire
St. Martin-in-the-Fields *(518)*, London
St. Mary Abchurch *(514)*, London
St. Paul, Convent Garden *(578)*, London
St. Stephen Walbrook *(515)*, London
St. Vedast's *(512)*, London

COLLEGES AND UNIVERSITY BUILDINGS

Eton College *(566)*, nr. Windsor, Berkshire
Winchester College *(563)*, Winchester, Hampshire

CAMBRIDGE

King's College *(613)*
Pembroke College *(614)*
Queen's College *(614)*
St. John's College *(615)*
Trinity College *(616)*

OXFORD

Christ Church College *(629)*
Corpus Christi College *(629)*
Keble College *(630)*
Magdalen College *(631)*
New College *(631)*
Old Schools Quadrangle (Sheldonian Theatre) *(632)*
Queen's College *(633)*

STATELY HOMES: MEDIEVAL, TUDOR, STUART

Belton House *(650)*, nr. Grantham, Lincolnshire
Broughton Castle *(626)*, nr. Banbury, Oxfordshire
Buckland Abbey *(589)*, nr. Tavistock, Devon
Castle Howard *(684)*, nr. Malton, North Yorkshire
Chatsworth *(662)*, nr. Chesterfield, Derbyshire
Cotehele House *(589)*, nr. Tavistock, Devon
Haddon Hall *(662)*, nr. Chesterfield, Derbyshire
Ham House *(537)*, Greater London
Hampton Court Palace *(532)*, Greater London
Hardwick Hall *(662)*, nr. Chesterfield, Derbyshire
Hatfield House *(620)*, Hatfield, Hertfordshire
Knole *(545)*, Sevenoaks, Kent
Lacock Abbey *(572)*, nr. Chippenham, Wiltshire
Levens Hall *(712)*, nr. Kendal, Cumbria
Little Moreton Hall *(675)*, nr. Congleton, Cheshire
Longleat House *(577)*, nr. Warminster, Wiltshire
Montacute *(585)*, nr. Yeovil, Somerset
Oxburgh Hall *(609)*, nr. Swaffham, Norfolk
Palace House (Beaulieu Abbey) *(560)*, nr. Lyndhurst, Hampshire
Penshurst Place *(546)*, nr. Tonbridge, Kent
Petworth House *(553)*, nr. Midhurst, West Sussex
Speke Hall *(696)*, nr. Liverpool, Merseyside
Wilton House *(575)*, nr. Salisbury, Wiltshire

STATELY HOMES: GEORGIAN AND VICTORIAN

Althorp *(655)*, nr. Northampton, Northamptonshire
Broadlands *(561)*, nr. Southampton, Hampshire
Carlton Towers *(688)*, nr. Selby, North Yorkshire
Castell Coch *(718)*, nr. Cardiff, South Glamorgan
Chartwell *(547)*, nr. Westerham, Kent
Chiswick House *(531)*, Greater London
Cragside *(708)*, nr. Rothbury, Northumberland
Harewood House *(681)*, nr. Leeds, West Yorkshire
Holkham Hall *(610)*, nr. Wells-next-the-Sea, Norfolk
Hughenden Manor *(623)*, nr. High Wycombe, Buckinghamshire
Nostell Priory *(682)*, nr. Wakefield, West Yorkshire
Osborne House *(559)*, nr. Newport, Isle of Wight
Osterley Park House *(533)*, Greater London
Plas Newydd *(735)*, nr. Menai Bridge, Anglesey, Gwynedd
Royal Pavilion *(548)*, Brighton, East Sussex
Stratfield Saye House *(565)*, nr. Reading, Berkshire
Syon House *(533)*, Greater London
West Wycombe Park *(623)*, High Wycombe, Buckinghamshire
Woburn Abbey *(625)*, nr. Leighton Buzzard, Bedfordshire

PARKS AND GARDENS

Bodnant Garden *(739)*, nr. Llandudno, Gwynedd
Bramham Park *(682)*, nr. Wetherby, West Yorkshire
Claremont Landscape Garden *(555)*, nr. Esher, Surrey
Hampton Court Palace *(532)*, Greater London
Hidcote Manor *(645)*, nr. Stratford-upon-Avon, Warwickshire
Lanhydrock *(590)*, nr. Bodmin, Cornwall
Melbourne Hall *(663)*, nr. Derby, Derbyshire
New Place Estate *(644)*, Stratford-upon-Avon, Warwickshire
Nymans *(552)*, nr. Crawley, West Sussex
Oxford Botanic Garden *(636)*, Oxford, Oxfordshire
Packwood House *(645)*, nr. Stratford-upon-Avon, Warwickshire
Regent's Park and Queen Mary's Garden *(529)*, London
Royal Botanic Gardens, Kew *(537)*, London
St. James's Park *(522)*, London
Sissinghurst Castle *(540)*, nr. Cranbrook, Kent
Stourhead *(574)*, nr. Mere, Wiltshire
Stowe Gardens *(622)*, nr. Buckingham, Buckinghamshire
Trelissick *(597)*, nr. Truro, Cornwall
Tresco Abbey *(592)*, Isles of Scilly, Cornwall
Wakehurst Place *(553)*, nr. Haywards Heath, West Sussex
Wisley Gardens *(557)*, nr. Woking, Surrey

MONUMENTS AND PUBLIC BUILDINGS

Albert Memorial *(525)*, London
Banqueting House *(519)*, London
City Hall *(717)*, Cardiff, South Glamorgan
Colchester Town Hall *(599)*, Colchester, Essex
Horseguards *(521)*, London
Houses of Parliament *(521)*, London
Manchester Town Hall *(694)*, Manchester, Greater Manchester
The Monument *(512)*, London
Nelson Monument *(518)*, London
Royal Courts of Justice *(519)*, London
St. George's Hall *(695)*, Liverpool, Merseyside
Somerset House *(523)*, London
Westminster Hall *(524)*, London

MUSEUMS

GENERAL

British Museum *(516)*, London
Museum of London *(512)*, London
National Museum of Wales *(717)*, Cardiff, South Glamorgan
Victoria and Albert Museum *(526)*, London
Welsh Folk Museum *(310,427)*, Cardiff, South Glamorgan

ART GALLERIES

Ashmolean Museum of Art and Archaeology *(628)*, Oxford, Oxfordshire
City Art Gallery *(693)*, Manchester, Greater Manchester
Courtauld Institute Galleries *(516)*, London
Dulwich College Picture Gallery *(536)*, London
Fitzwilliam Museum *(612)*, Cambridge, Cambridgeshire
Lady Lever Art Gallery *(695)*, nr. Berkenhead, Merseyside
Museum and Art Gallery *(664)*, Birmingham, West Midlands
National Gallery *(518)*, London
National Portrait Gallery *(518)*, London
Tate Gallery *(523)*, London
Victoria and Albert Museum *(526)*, London
Walker Art Gallery *(695)*, Liverpool, Merseyside
Wallace Collection *(527)*, London

ARCHAEOLOGICAL

Alexander Keiller Museum *(573)*, Avebury, nr. Marlborough, Wiltshire
Ashmolean Museum of Art and Archaeology *(628)*, Oxford, Oxfordshire
Bede Monastery Museum *(700)*, nr. Newcastle-upon-Tyne, Tyne and Wear
Cheddar Caves Museum *(582)*, Cheddar, Somerset
Colchester and Essex Museum *(598)*, Colchester, Essex
Corinium Museum *(638)*, Cirencester, Oxfordshire
Dorset County Museum *(567)*, Dorchester, Dorset
Grosvenor Museum *(673)*, Chester, Cheshire
Guernsey Museum and Art Gallery *(745)*, St. Peter Port, Guernsey
Jersey (La Hogue Bie) Museum *(744)*, Jersey
Manx Museum, Library and Art Gallery *(741)*, Douglas, Isle of Man
Museum and Art Gallery *(664)*, Birmingham, West Midlands
University Museum of Antiquities *(701)*, Newcastle-upon-Tyne, Tyne and Wear
Verulamium Museum *(621)*, St. Albans, Hertfordshire
Yorkshire Museum *(693)*, York, North Yorkshire

INDUSTRY, SCIENCE, AND TECHNOLOGY

Abbeydale Industrial Hamlet *(680)*, nr. Sheffield, South Yorkshire
Gladstone Pottery Museum *(668)*, nr. Stoke-on-Trent, Staffordshire
Ironbridge Gorge Museum *(672)*, nr. Telford, Salop
London Transport Museum *(518)*, London
Museum of Science and Industry *(665)*, Birmingham, West Midlands
National Motor Museum *(560)*, nr. Lyndhurst, Hampshire
National Railway Museum *(690)*, York, North Yorkshire
Poldark Mine and Museum *(592)*, nr. Camborne, Cornwall
Science Museum *(526)*, London
Science Museum *(701)*, Newcastle-upon-Tyne, Tyne and Wear
Styal Country Park *(676)*, nr. Wilmslow, Cheshire
Wedgwood Visitor Centre *(668)*, nr. Stoke-on-Trent, Staffordshire

MILITARY

German Occupation Museum *(746)*, Guernsey
German Underground Hospital *(744)*, Jersey
H.M.S. Victory *(561)*, Portsmouth, Hampshire
Imperial War Museum *(534)*, London
National Army Museum *(525)*, London
National Maritime Museum *(536)*, London
Royal Airforce Museum of Aviation History *(531)*, Greater London

Royal Artillery Museum *(536)*, London
Tank Museum *(569)*, nr. Wareham, Dorset

LITERARY

Bateman's (Kipling) *(549)*, nr. Heathfield, East Sussex
Brontë Parsonage *(680)*, nr. Keighley, West Yorkshire
Carlyle's House *(524)*, London
Chawton Cottage (Austen) *(557)*, nr. Alton, Hampshire
Dickens House *(516)*, London
Dr. Johnson's House *(514)*, London
Dove Cottage (Wordsworth) *(711)*, nr. Grasmere, Cumbria
Keats House *(530)*, London
Milton's Cottage *(623)*, Chalfont St. Giles, Buckinghamshire
Newstead Abbey (Byron) *(659)*, nr. Nottingham, Nottinghamshire
Shakespeare's Birthplace *(644)*, Stratford-upon-Avon, Warwickshire

SELECTED READINGS

GUIDE BOOKS

ABC Historic Publications. *Museums and Galleries in Great Britain and Ireland.*
Dunstable, Bedfordshire: ABC Travel Guides, 1981 and annually.

————. *Historic Houses, Castles, and Gardens in Great Britain and Ireland.*
Dunstable, Bedfordshire: ABC Travel Guides, 1981 and annually.

Baedeker. *Great Britain.* Englewood Cliffs, N.J.: Prentice-Hall, 1980.

Betjeman, John, ed. *Collins Guide to Parish Churches of England and Wales.*
London: Collins, 1980.

Boumphrey, Geoffrey, ed. *The Shell Guide to Britain.* London: Ebury Press &
George Rainbird, 1975.

British Automobile Association. *Stately Homes, Museums, Castles, and Gardens in Britain.* Basingstoke, Hampshire: Publications Division, 1981 and
annually.

British Automobile Association. *Treasures of Britain.* New York: W. W. Norton
& Co., 1976.

Burne, Alfred H. *The Battlefields of England.* London: Methuen & Co.; New
York: Barnes & Noble, 1973.

Burton, Neil. *RAC Historic Houses Handbook.* London: Papermac, 1981.

Clifton-Taylor, Alec. *English Parish Churches as Works of Art.* London: B. T.
Batsford, 1974.

Discovering Series. Aylesbury, Bucks: Shire Publications, 1970–1979.
Discovering Heraldry and Military History. 6 vols.
Discovering Buildings and Places of Interest. 18 vols.
Discovering Local History and Research. 9 vols.
Discovering London. 6 vols.
Discovering the Steam Age. 11 vols.
Discovering Canals and Shipping. 5 vols.
Discovering Shire Archaeology. 13 vols.
Discovering Gardens and Natural History. 15 vols.
Discovering Famous Men. 26 vols.

Eagle, Dorothy, and Carnell, Hilary. *The Oxford Literary Guide to the British
Isles.* Oxford: Clarendon Press, 1977.

Fedden, Robin, and Joekes, Rosemary, eds. *The National Trust Guide to England, Wales, and Northern Ireland.* New York: Alfred A. Knopf, 1974.

Fedden, Robin, and Kenworthy-Browne, John. *The Country House Guide.* New
York: W. W. Norton & Co., 1979.

Fodor, Eugene, and Fisher, Robert C., eds. *Fodor's Great Britain, 1976.* New
York: David McKay Co., 1976.

Foss, Arthur. *Country House Treasures.* London: Weidenfeld & Nicolson, 1980.

George, William. *British Heritage in Colour.* Poole, Dorset: Blandford Press,
1976.

Gilyard-Beer, R. *Abbeys: An Illustrated Guide to the Abbeys of England and
Wales.* London: Her Majesty's Stationery Office, 1976.

Girouard, Mark. *Historic Houses of Britain.* New York: William Morrow & Co.,
1979.

760

Hammond, Reginald J. W., ed. *Red Guide to Britain.* London: Ward Lock & Co., 1969.

Hellyer, Arthur. *The Shell Guide to Gardens.* London: Heinemann, 1977.

Hudson, Kenneth. *Exploring Cathedrals.* London: Hodder & Stoughton, 1978.

————. *The Good Museum Guide.* London: Macmillan Press, 1980.

Johnston, Paul. *The National Trust Book of British Castles.* London: Weidenfeld & Nicolson, 1978.

Jones, Lawrence E. *The Observer's Book of Old English Churches.* London: Frederick Warne & Co., 1965.

Michelin (Green Guide Series). *London.* London: Michelin Tyre Co., 1977.

Morley, Frank. *Literary Britain: A Reader's Guide to its Writers and Landmarks.* New York: Harper & Row, 1980.

National Trust. *Properties of the National Trust.* London, 1978.

National Trust. *Properties Open.* London, 1981 and annually.

New, Anthony S. B. *The Observer's Book of Cathedrals.* London: Frederick Warne & Co., 1972.

Nicholson's Guide to Great Britain. London: Robert Nicholson Publications, 1976.

Nicholson's London Guide. London: Robert Nicholson Publications, 1976.

Nicolson, Nigel. *The National Trust Book of Great Houses of Britain.* London: Weidenfeld & Nicolson, 1978.

O'Neil, B. H. St. J. *Castles: An Introduction to the Castles of England and Wales.* London: Department of the Environment, Her Majesty's Stationery Office, 1973.

Pevsner, Nikolaus. *The Buildings of England.* 1 vol. per county. Harmondsworth, Middlesex: Penguin Books, 1951–77.

Reader's Digest Association. *Hand-Picked Tours in Britain.* London, 1975.

Rossiter, Stuart, ed. *Blue Guide to England.* London: Ernest Benn, 1972.

————, ed. *Blue Guide to London.* London: Ernest Benn, 1973.

————, ed. *Blue Guide to Wales.* London: Ernest Benn, 1969.

Rowse, A. L. *Heritage of Britain.* New York: G. P. Putnam's Sons, 1977.

Smith, Edwin; Cook, Olive; and Hutton, Graham. *English Parish Churches.* London: Thames & Hudson, 1976.

Sturdy, David and Sturdy, Fiona. *Historic Monuments of England and Wales.* London: J. M. Dent & Sons, 1977.

Thomas, Nicholas. *A Guide to Prehistoric England.* London: B. T. Batsford, 1976.

Thompson, A. Hamilton. *The Cathedral Churches of England.* New York and Toronto: Society for Promoting Christian Knowledge, 1925.

Wales Tourist Board. *Castles and Historic Places in Wales.* Cardiff, 1974.

Winks, Robin W. *An American's Guide to Britain.* New York: Charles Scribner's Sons, 1977.

Wood, Eric S. *Collins Field Guide to Archaeology in Britain.* London: Collins, 1975.

TOPICAL STUDIES

Brown, R. Allen. *English Castles.* rev. London: B. T. Batsford, 1976.

Carman, W. Y. *British Military Uniforms.* New York: Arco Publishing Co., 1957.

Clifton-Taylor, Alec. *The Cathedrals of England.* London: Thames & Hudson, 1967.

Cook, Olive. *The English Country House.* London: Thames & Hudson, 1974.

Corran, H. S. *The Isle of Man.* London: David & Charles, 1977.

Dampier, Sir William Cecil. *A History of Science.* 4th ed. Cambridge: At the University Press, 1968.

Darby, H. C. *A New Historical Geography of England.* 2 vols. Cambridge: At the University Press, 1976.

Dodd, A. H. *A Short History of Wales.* London: B. T. Batsford, 1972.

Forde-Johnston, J. *Castles and Fortifications of Britain and Ireland.* London, J. M. Dent & Sons, 1977.

Gaunt, William. *A Concise History of English Painting.* London: Thames & Hudson, 1976.

Girouard, Mark. *Life in the English Country House.* New Haven: Yale University Press, 1978.

Gloag, John. *English Furniture.* 6th ed. London: A. & C. Black, 1973.

Grebanier, Bernard D. N. *Essentials of English Literature.* 2 vols. Woodbury, N. Y.: Barron's Educational Series, 1959.

Harvey, John. *Cathedrals of England and Wales.* London: B. T. Batsford, 1974.

Hasell, Jock. *The British Army: A Concise History.* London: Thames & Hudson, 1975.

Hilling, John B. *The Historic Architecture of Wales.* Cardiff: University of Wales Press, 1976.

Hughes, Quentin. *Military Architecture.* New York: St. Martin's Press, 1974.

Kelly, Francis M., and Schwabe, Randolph. *A Short History of Costume and Armour.* 2 vols. New York: Arco Publishing Co., 1973.

Kennedy, Paul M. *The Rise and Fall of British Naval Mastery.* New York: Charles Scribner's Sons, 1976.

Knightly, Charles. *Strongholds of the Realm: Defences in Britain from Prehistory to the Twentieth Century.* London: Thames & Hudson, 1979.

Laver, J. *British Military Uniforms.* London: Penguin Books, 1948.

Lempriere, Raoul. *History of the Channel Islands.* London: Robert Hale & Co., 1974.

Montgomery of Alamein, Field-Marshal Viscount. *A History of Warfare.* Cleveland: World Publishing Company, 1968.

Summerson, John. *Architecture in Britain, 1530–1830.* 6th rev. ed. Pelican History of Art. Harmondsworth, Middlesex: Penguin Books, 1977.

Ward, A. W., and Waller, A. R., eds. *Cambridge History of English Literature.* 15 vols. Cambridge: At the University Press, 1933.

Waterhouse, Ellis. *Painting in Britain 1530 to 1790.* Harmondsworth, Middlesex: Penguin Books, 1978.

Watkin, David. *English Architecture: A Concise History.* London: Thames & Hudson, 1979.

Yarwood, Doreen. *The Architecture of Britain.* London: B. T. Batsford, 1976.

PREHISTORIC AND ROMAN PERIODS
(CHAPTERS 1 AND 2)

Atkinson, R. J. C. *Stonehenge.* Harmondsworth, Middlesex: Penguin Books, Pelican, 1960.

Balfour, Michael. *Stonehenge and its Mysteries.* New York: Charles Scribner's Sons, 1980.

Birley, Anthony. *Life in Roman Britain.* London: B. T. Batsford, 1964.

Burl, Aubrey. *Prehistoric Avebury.* New Haven: Yale University Press, 1979.

Clark, J. Graham D. *Prehistoric England.* London: B. T. Batsford, 1940.

Clayton, Peter. *Archaeological Sites of Britain.* London: Weidenfeld & Nicolson, 1976.

Collingwood, R. G., and Myres, J. N. L. *Roman Britain and the English Settlements.* Oxford History of England, vol. 1. Oxford: Clarendon Press, 1936.

Collingwood, R. G., and Richmond, Ian. *The Archaeology of Roman Britain.* London: Methuen & Co., 1971.

Dudley, D. R., and Webster, G. *The Roman Conquest of Britain, A.D. 43–57.* London: Dufour Editions, 1965.

Evans, John G. *The Environment of Early Man in the British Isles.* Berkeley and Los Angeles: University of California Press, 1975.

Forde-Johnston, J. *Prehistoric Britain and Ireland.* London: J. M. Dent & Sons, 1976.

Frere, Sheppard. *Britannia: A History of Roman Britain.* Cambridge, Mass.: Harvard University Press, 1967.

Hadingham, Evan. *Circles and Standing Stones: An Illustrated Exploration of Megalith Mysteries of Early Britain.* New York: Walker & Co., 1973.

Hawkes, Jacquetta. *The Bailiwick of Jersey.* The Archeology of the Channel Islands, vol. 2. Jersey, Channel Islands: Société Jersiaise, 1937.

———, and Hawkes, Christopher. *Prehistoric Britain.* Harmondsworth, Middlesex: Penguin Books, 1958.

Hawkins, Gerald S. *Stonehenge Decoded.* New York: Collins, Fontana, 1970.

Houlder, Christopher. *Wales: An Archaeological Guide.* London: Faber & Faber, 1974.

Kendrick, Thomas D. *The Bailiwick of Guernsey.* The Archaeology of the Channel Islands, vol. 1. London: Methuen & Co., 1928.

Laing, Jennifer. *Finding Roman Britain.* Newton Abbot, Devon: David & Charles, 1977.

Piggott, Stuart. *British Prehistory.* London: Oxford University Press, 1955.

Renfrew, Colin, ed. *British Prehistory: A New Outline.* London: Gerald Duckworth and Co., 1974.

Richmond, Ian A. *Roman Britain.* Pelican History of England, vol. 1. Harmondsworth, Middlesex: Penguin Books, 1963.

Rivet, A. L. F. *Town and Country in Roman Britain.* London: Hutchinson University Library, 1975.

———, ed. *The Roman Villa in Britain.* London: Routledge & Kegan Paul, 1969.

Thom, Alexander. *Megalithic Sites in Britain.* Oxford: Clarendon Press, 1967.

Wacher, John. *Roman Britain.* London: J. M. Dent & Sons, 1975.

———. *The Towns of Roman Britain.* Berkeley and Los Angeles: University of California Press, 1975.

ANGLO-SAXON AND MEDIEVAL PERIODS
CHAPTERS 3, 4, 5, AND 6

Alcock, Leslie. *Arthur's Britain: History and Archaeology, A.D. 367–634.* London: Penguin Press, 1971.

Ashe, Geoffrey, et al. *The Quest for Arthur's Britain.* New York: Frederick A. Praeger, 1968.

Barlow, Frank. *Edward the Confessor*. Berkeley and Los Angeles: University of California Press, 1970.

Barrow, G. W. S. *Feudal Britain*. London: Edward Arnold, 1971.

Blair, Peter Hunter. *An Introduction to Anglo-Saxon England*. 2d ed. Cambridge: At the University Press, 1977.

Boase, T. S. R., ed. *The Oxford History of English Art*. Vol. 3, 1100–1216. Oxford: Clarendon Press, 1953.

———, ed. *The Oxford History of English Art*. Vol. 4, 1216–1307. Oxford: Clarendon Press, 1957.

———, ed. *The Oxford History of English Art*. Vol. 5, 1307–1461. Oxford: Clarendon Press, 1949.

Clapham, A. W. *English Romanesque Architecture Before the Conquest*. Oxford: Clarendon Press, 1930.

———. *English Romanesque Architecture After the Conquest*. Oxford: Clarendon Press, 1934.

Douglas, David C. *William the Conqueror*. Berkeley and Los Angeles: University of California Press, 1964.

Fineberg, H. P. R. *The Formation of England, 550–1042*. St. Albans, Herts: Paladin, 1976.

Fisher, D. J. V. *The Anglo-Saxon Age, c. 400–1042*. London: Longman, 1973.

Fraser, David. *The Defenders*. Wales in History, Book 2, 1066–1485. Cardiff: University of Wales Press, 1975.

Gardner, John. *The Life and Times of Chaucer*. New York: Alfred A. Knopf, 1977.

Gillingham, John. *Richard the Lionheart*. New York: Times Books, 1978.

Hindley, Geoffrey. *Medieval Warfare*. London: Wayland Publishers, 1971.

———. *England in the Age of Caxton*. New York: St. Martin's Press, 1979.

Jacob, E. F. *The Fifteenth Century, 1399–1485*. Oxford History of England, vol. 6. Oxford: Clarendon Press, 1961.

Jones, Gwyn. *A History of the Vikings*. New York: Oxford University Press, 1968.

Keen, M. H. *England in the Later Middle Ages*. London: Methuen & Co., 1973.

Kendall, Paul M. *Richard the Third*. London: George Allen & Unwin, 1955.

Kirby, D. P. *The Making of Early England*. New York: Schocken Books, 1968.

Knowles, David, and Hadcock, R. Neveille. *Medieval Religious Houses: England and Wales*. New York: St. Martin's Press, 1971.

Labarge, Margaret Wade. *Henry V: The Cautious Conqueror*. New York: Stein & Day, 1976.

Lander, J. R. *The Wars of the Roses*. New York: G. P. Putnam's Sons, 1966.

Lyon, H. R. *Anglo-Saxon England and the Norman Conquest*. London: Longman, 1962.

McFarlane, K. B. *Lancastrian Kings and Lollard Knights*. Oxford: Clarendon Press, 1972.

McKisack, May. *The Fourteenth Century, 1307–1399*. Oxford History of England, vol. 5. Oxford: Clarendon Press, 1959.

Morris, John. *The Age of Arthur: A History of the British Isles from 350 to 650*. New York: Charles Scribner's Sons, 1973.

Myers, A. R. *England in the Late Middle Ages*. Harmondsworth, Middlesex: Penguin Books, 1974.

Painter, Sidney. *William Marshal*. Baltimore: Johns Hopkins University Press, 1933.

———. *The Reign of King John*. Baltimore, Johns Hopkins University Press, 1946.

Platt, Colin. *Medieval England*. New York: Charles Scribner's Sons, 1978.

———. *The English Medieval Town*. London: Secker & Warburg, 1976.

Poole, Austin Lane. *From Domesday Book to Magna Carta, 1087–1216*. 2d ed. Oxford History of England, vol. 3. Oxford: Clarendon Press, 1955.

Postan, M. M. *The Medieval Economy and Society: An Economic History of Britain, 1100–1500*. Berkeley and Los Angeles: University of California Press, 1972.

Powicke, Sir Maurice. *The Thirteenth Century*. The Oxford History of England, vol. 4. Oxford: Clarendon Press, 1962.

Ross, Charles. *Edward IV*. Berkeley and Los Angeles: University of California Press, 1974.

———. *The Wars of the Roses: A Concise History*. London: Thames & Hudson, 1976.

Saccio, Peter. *Shakespeare's English Kings*. New York: Oxford University Press, 1977.

Salter, H. E. *Medieval Oxford*. Oxford: Clarendon Press, 1936.

Salzman, L. F. *Edward I*. New York: Frederick A. Praeger, 1968.

Sellman, R. R. *Medieval English Warfare*. New York: Roy Publishers, 1960.

Seward, Desmond. *The Hundred Years War: The English in France, 1337–1453*. New York: Atheneum, 1978.

Steel, Anthony. *Richard II*. Cambridge: At the University Press, 1962.

Stenton, Dorothy Mary. *English Society in the Early Middle Ages, 1066–1307*. Pelican History of England, vol. 3. Harmondsworth, Middlesex: Penguin Books, 1965.

Stenton, F. M. *Anglo-Saxon England*. Oxford History of England, vol. 2. Oxford: Clarendon Press, 1947.

Storey, R. L. *The End of the House of Lancaster*. New York: Stein & Day, 1967.

Strayer, Joseph R. *Feudalism*. New York: D. Van Nostrand Co., 1965.

Thompson, A. Hamilton. *Military Architecture in Medieval England*. Totowa, N. J.: Rowman & Littlefield, 1975.

Taylor, H. M., and Taylor, Joan. *Anglo-Saxon Architecture*. 2 vols. Cambridge: At the University Press, 1965.

Thomas, Charles. *Britain and Ireland in Early Christian Times, A.D. 400–800*. London: Thames & Hudson, 1971.

———. *The Early Christian Archaeology of North Britain*. London: Oxford University Press, 1971.

Walker, David. *The Norman Conquerors*. New History of Wales Series. Swansea: Christopher Davies, 1977.

Warren, W. L. *King John*. Berkeley and Los Angeles: University of California Press, 1978.

———. *Henry II*. Berkeley and Los Angeles: University of California Press, 1973.

Whitelock, Dorothy. *The Beginnings of English Society*. Harmondsworth, Middlesex: Penguin Books, 1974.

Wilkinson, B. *The Later Middle Ages in England, 1216–1485*. London: Longman, 1977.

Williams, A. H. *An Introduction to the History of Wales*. Vol. I, *Prehistoric Times to 1063*. Cardiff: University of Wales Press, 1962.

Wilson, David M. *The Anglo-Saxons.* New York: Frederick A. Praeger, 1960.
——, ed. *The Archaeology of Anglo-Saxon England.* London: Methuen & Co., 1976.

TUDOR AND STUART PERIODS
CHAPTERS 7 AND 8

Ashley, Maurice. *England in the Seventeenth Century.* New York: Harper & Row, 1980.

Bindoff, S. T. *Tudor England.* Pelican History of England, vol. 5. Harmondsworth, Middlesex: Penguin Books, 1950.

Black, John B. *The Reign of Elizabeth, 1558–1603.* Oxford History of England, vol. 8. Oxford: Clarendon Press, 1959.

Chrimes, S. B. *Henry VII.* Berkeley and Los Angeles: University of California Press, 1972.

Clark, Francis. *Eucharistic Sacrifice and the Reformation.* Oxford: Basil Blackwell, 1967.

Clark, Sir George. *The Later Stuarts, 1660–1714.* 2d ed. Oxford History of England, vol. 10. Oxford: Clarendon Press, 1965.

Coward, Barry. *The Stuart Age: A History of England, 1603–1714.* London: Longman, 1980.

Davies, Godfrey. *The Early Stuarts, 1603–1660.* 2d ed. Oxford History of England, vol. 9. Oxford: Clarendon Press, 1959.

Davies, Horton. *Worship and Theology in England from Andrews to Baxter and Fox, 1603–1680.* Princeton, N. J.: Princeton University Press, 1975.

Dickens, A. G. *The English Reformation.* New York: Collins, Fontana, 1967.

Edwards, Ralph, and Ramsey, L. G. G., eds. *The Connoisseur Period Guides to the Houses, Decoration, Furnishing, and Chattels of the Classic Periods.* New York: Reynal and Company, 1979. Vol. 1, *The Tudor Period, 1500–1603.* Vol. 2, *The Stuart Period, 1603–1714.*

Elton, G. R. *England Under the Tudors.* London: Methuen & Co., 1977.

Fraser, Antonia. *Mary Queen of Scots.* New York: Delacorte Press, 1969.

——. *King James.* New York: Alfred A. Knopf, 1975.

——. *Cromwell, The Lord Protector.* New York: Alfred A. Knopf, 1973.

——. *Royal Charles: Charles II and the Restoration.* New York: Alfred A. Knopf, 1979.

Green, David. *Queen Anne.* New York: Charles Scribner's Sons, 1970.

Hibbert, Christopher. *Charles I.* New York: Harper & Row, 1968.

Hill, Christopher. *The Century of Revolution, 1603–1714.* New York: W. W. Norton & Co., 1961.

Jones, J. R. *Country and Court: England, 1658–1714.* Cambridge, Mass.: Harvard University Press, 1978.

Knowles, Dom David. *The Religious Orders in England.* Vol. 3, *The Tudor Age.* Cambridge: At the University Press, 1959.

Latham, Robert. *The Illustrated Pepys.* Berkeley and Los Angeles: University of California Press, 1978.

Mathew, David. *James I.* London: Eyre & Spottiswoode, 1967.

Mercer, Eric. *English Art, 1553–1625.* Oxford History of English Art, vol. 7. Oxford: Clarendon Press, 1962.

Neale, J. E. *Queen Elizabeth I.* Garden City, N. Y.: Doubleday & Co., 1957.

Ogg, David. *England in the Reigns of James II and William III.* Oxford: Clarendon Press, 1953.

———. *England in the Reign of Charles II.* Oxford: Clarendon Press, 1955.

———. *William III.* New York: Macmillan Co., 1958.

Ollard, Richard. *The War Without an Enemy: A History of the English Civil Wars.* New York: Atheneum, 1976.

Mackie, J. D. *The Early Tudors, 1485–1558.* Oxford History of England, vol. 7. Oxford: Clarendon Press, 1966.

Roots, Ivan. *The Great Rebellion: 1642–1660.* London: B. T. Batsford, 1966.

Rowse, A. L. *The England of Elizabeth.* New York: Collier Books, 1966.

Scarisbrick, J. J. *Henry VIII.* Berkeley and Los Angeles: University of California Press, 1968.

Stone, Lawrence. *The Causes of the English Revolution, 1529–1642.* New York: Harper & Row, 1972.

———. *Social Change and Revolution in England, 1540–1640.* London: Longman, 1965.

Trevelyan, G. M. *England under the Stuarts.* London: Methuen & Co., 1904.

Wedgwood, C. V. *The King's Peace, 1637–41.* New York: Macmillan Co., 1955.

———. *The King's War, 1641–47.* New York: Macmillan Co., 1958.

———. *A Coffin for King Charles: The Trial and Execution of Charles I.* New York: Macmillan Co., 1964.

———. *Oliver Cromwell.* London: Duckworth, 1973.

Whinney, Margaret, and Millar, Oliver. *English Art, 1625–1714.* Oxford History of English Art, vol. 8. Oxford: Clarendon Press, 1957.

Woolrych, Austin. *Battles of the English Civil War.* London: B. T. Batsford, 1961.

EIGHTEENTH, NINETEENTH, AND TWENTIETH CENTURIES
CHAPTERS 9 AND 10

Ashworth, W. *An Economic History of England, 1870–1939.* London: Methuen & Co., 1960.

Barnett, Correlli. *Britain and Her Army, 1509–1970.* New York: William Morrow & Co., 1970.

Beales, Derek. *From Castlereagh to Gladstone, 1815–1885.* New York: W. W. Norton & Co., 1969.

Binney, Marcus, and Pearce, David, eds. *Railway Architecture.* London: Orbis Publishing, 1979.

Blake, R. *Disraeli.* London: Oxford University Press, 1969.

Boase, T. S. R. *English Art, 1800–1870.* Oxford History of English Art, vol. 10. Oxford: Clarendon Press, 1959.

Briggs, Asa. *The Age of Improvement, 1783–1867.* London: Longman, 1959.

Brooke, John. *King George III.* London: Constable, 1972.

Cecil, Lord David. *Melbourne.* Indianapolis: Bobbs-Merrill Co., Charter Books, 1962.

Checkland, S. G. *The Rise of Industrial Society in England, 1815–1885.* London: Longman, 1964.

Churchill, Winston S. *The Second World War.* 6 vols. Boston: Houghton Mifflin Co., 1948–54.

Cossons, Neil. *The BP Book of Industrial Archaeology.* London: David & Charles, 1975.

Dangerfield, George. *The Strange Death of Liberal England, 1910–1914.* New York: Capricorn Books, 1935.

Davies, Horton. *Worship and Theology in England from Watts and Wesley to Maurice, 1690–1850.* Princeton, N. J.: Princeton University Press, 1961.

———. *Worship and Theology in England from Newman to Martineau, 1850–1900.* Princeton, N. J.: Princeton University Press, 1962.

Deane, Phyllis. *The First Industrial Revolution.* Cambridge: At the University Press, 1965.

Dixon, Roger, and Muthesius, Stefan. *Victorian Architecture.* London: Thames & Hudson, 1978.

Edwards, Ralph, and Ramsey, L. G. G. *The Connoisseur Period Guides to the Houses, Decoration, Furnishings, and Chattels of the Classic Periods.* New York: Reynal & Co., 1979. Vol. 3, *The Early Georgian Period, 1714–1760.* Vol. 4, *The Late Georgian Period, 1760–1810.* Vol. 5, *The Regency Period, 1819–1830.* Vol. 6, *The Early Victorian Period, 1830–1860.*

Ensor, R. C. K. *England, 1870–1914.* Oxford History of England, vol. 14. Oxford: Clarendon Press, 1936.

Falls, Cyril. *The Great War, 1914–1918.* New York: Capricorn Books, 1959.

Fraser, David. *The Adventurers.* Wales in History, book 3. Cardiff: University of Wales Press, 1976.

Gash, Norman. *Aristocracy and People: Britain, 1815–1865.* Cambridge, Mass.: Harvard University Press, 1979.

Girouard, Mark. *The Victorian Country House.* New Haven: Yale University Press, 1979.

Graves, Robert, and Hodge, Alan. *The Long Week-end: A Social History of Great Britain, 1918–1939.* New York: W. W. Norton & Co., 1963.

Grigg, J. *Lloyd George, The People's Champion.* Berkeley and Los Angeles: University of California Press, 1978.

James, Robert Rhodes. *The British Revolution: 1880–1939.* New York: Alfred A. Knopf, 1977.

Jenkins, Roy. *Asquith.* New York: Chilmark Press, 1964.

Liddell Hart, Sir Basil H. *The Real War, 1914–1918.* Boston: Little, Brown & Co., 1930.

———. *History of the Second World War.* New York: G. P. Putnam's Sons, 1971.

Longford, Elizabeth. *Wellington: The Years of the Sword.* New York: Harper & Row, 1969.

———. *Queen Victoria.* New York: Harper & Row, 1965.

Magnus, Philip. *King Edward VII.* London: John Murray, 1964.

Marshall, Dorothy. *Eighteenth Century England.* London: Longman, 1962.

Marwick, Arthur. *The Home Front: The British and the Second World War.* London: Thames & Hudson, 1976.

———. *Britain in the Century of Total War: War, Peace, and Social Change, 1900–1967.* Boston: Little, Brown & Co., 1968.

Mathias, P. *The First Industrial Nation: An Economic History of Britain, 1700–1914.* New York: Charles Scribner's Sons, 1969.

Medlicott, W. N. *Contemporary England, 1914–1964.* London: Longman, 1967.

Mingay, Gordon E. *The Gentry: The Rise and Fall of a Ruling Class.* London: Longman, 1976.

Mowat, Charles Loch. *Britain Between the Wars, 1918–1940.* Chicago: University of Chicago Press, 1955.

Nicolson, Harold. *King George V, His Life and Reign.* London: Constable, 1952.

Pelling, Henry. *Modern Britain, 1885–1955.* New York: W. W. Norton & Co., 1960.

———. *History of British Trade Unionism.* New York: St. Martin's Press, 1963.

———. *A Short History of the Labour Party.* New York: St. Martin's Press, 1968.

Plumb, J. H. *England in the Eighteenth Century, 1714–1815.* Harmondsworth, Middlesex: Penguin Books, 1950.

———. *The First Four Georges.* Boston: Little, Brown & Co., 1975.

Pollins, Harold. *Britain's Railways: An Industrial History.* Totowa, N. J.: Rowman & Littlefield, 1971.

Read, Donald. *England, 1868–1914.* London: Longman, 1979.

Ross, Steven. *From Flintlock to Rifle: Infantry Tactics, 1740–1866.* Rutherford, N. J.: Fairleigh Dickinson University Press, 1979.

Service, Alastair. *Edwardian Architecture.* London: Thames & Hudson, 1977.

Southgate, Donald. *The Most English Minister: The Policies and Politics of Palmerston.* London: Macmillan & Co., 1966.

Speck, W. A. *Stability and Strife: England, 1714–1760.* Cambridge, Mass.: Harvard University Press, 1979.

Stansky, Peter. *Gladstone: A Progress in Politics.* Boston: Little, Brown & Co., 1979.

Summerson, John. *The Architecture of Victorian London.* Charlottesville, Va.: University of Virginia Press, 1972.

Taylor, A. J. P. *English History: 1914–1945.* Oxford History of England, vol. 15. Oxford: Clarendon Press, 1965.

Thompson, Francis M. L. *English Landed Society in the Nineteenth Century.* London: Routledge & Kegan Paul, 1963.

Thomson, David. *England in the Nineteenth Century.* Harmondsworth, Middlesex: Penguin Books, 1950.

———. *England in the Twentieth Century.* Harmondsworth, Middlesex: Penguin Books, 1965.

Williams, David. *A History of Modern Wales.* 2d ed. London: John Murray, 1977.

Wilson, Charles. *England's Apprenticeship, 1603–1763.* London: Longman, 1965.

Wood, Alan, and Wood, Mary Seaton. *Islands in Danger.* London: Four Square Books, 1965.

Woodward, Sir Llewellyn *The Age of Reform: 1815–1870.* Oxford History of England, vol. 13. Oxford: Clarendon Press, 1962.

———. *Great Britain and the War of 1914–1918.* Boston: Beacon Press, 1967.

INDEX

Page numbers in **boldface** refer to the Gazetteer.